DICTIONARY OF
AMERICAN BIOGRAPHY

American Council of Learned Societies

American Philosophical Society, Philadelphia, Pennsylvania
American Academy of Arts and Sciences, Cambridge, Massachusetts
American Antiquarian Society, Worcester, Massachusetts
American Oriental Society, New Haven, Connecticut
American Numismatic Society, New York, New York
American Philological Association, Swarthmore, Pennsylvania
Archeological Institute of America, New York, New York
Society of Biblical Literature and Exegesis, Haverford, Pennsylvania
Modern Language Association of America, New York, New York
American Historical Association, Washington, District of Columbia
American Economic Association, Evanston, Illinois
American Philosophical Association, Middletown, Connecticut
American Anthropological Association, Chicago, Illinois
American Political Science Association, Evanston, Illinois
Bibliographical Society of America, Albany, New York
Association of American Geographers, Minneapolis, Minnesota
American Sociological Society, Washington, District of Columbia
American Society of International Law, Washington, District of Columbia
College Art Association of America, New York, New York
History of Science, South Hadley, Massachusetts
Linguistic Society of America, Washington, District of Columbia
Mediaeval Academy of America, Cambridge, Massachusetts
Population Association of America, Washington, District of Columbia

Dictionary of

American Biography

PUBLISHED UNDER THE AUSPICES OF

American Council of Learned Societies

EDITED BY

Dumas Malone

Robert — Seward

VOLUME XVI

NEW YORK

Charles Scribner's Sons

MCMXLIII

Prompted solely by a desire for public service the New York Times Company and its President, Mr. Adolph S. Ochs, have made possible the preparation of the manuscript of the Dictionary of American Biography through a subvention of more than $500,000 and with the understanding that the entire responsibility for the contents of the volumes rests with the American Council of Learned Societies.

The Dictionary of American Biography is published under the auspices of the American Council of Learned Societies and under the direction of a Committee of Management which consists of J. FRANKLIN JAMESON, *Chairman*, JOHN H. FINLEY, DUMAS MALONE, FREDERIC L. PAXSON, IPHIGENE OCHS SULZBERGER, CARL VAN DOREN, CHARLES WARREN.

The editorial staff consists of DUMAS MALONE, *Editor*; HARRIS E. STARR, *Associate Editor*; ELEANOR R. DOBSON, MILDRED B. PALMER, KATHARINE ELIZABETH CRANE, *Assistant Editors*.

The American Council of Learned Societies consists of the following societies:

American Philosophical Society
American Academy of Arts and Sciences
American Antiquarian Society
American Oriental Society
American Philological Association
Archaeological Institute of America
Society of Biblical Literature and Exegesis
Modern Language Association of America
American Historical Association

American Economic Association
American Philosophical Association
American Anthropological Association
American Political Science Association
Bibliographical Society of America
American Sociological Society
History of Science Society
Linguistic Society of America
Mediaeval Academy of America

CONTRIBUTORS TO VOLUME XVI

Wilbur Cortez Abbott	W. C. A.		Eliot Clark	E. C.
Thomas P. Abernethy	T. P. A.		Hubert Lyman Clark	H. L. C.
Adeline Adams	A. A.		Jane Clark	J. C.
James Truslow Adams	J. T. A.		Robert C. Clark	R. C. C.
Nelson F. Adkins	N. F. A.		Robert Glass Cleland	R. G. C.
Cyrus Adler	C. A.		Frederick W. Coburn	F. W. C.
Robert Greenhalgh Albion	R. G. A.		Joseph B. Code	J. B. C.
William F. Albright	W. F. A.		Fannie L. Gwinner Cole	F. L. G. C.
Carroll S. Alden	C. S. A.		Guy N. Collins	G. N. C.
Gardner W. Allen	G. W. A.		Royal Cortissoz	R. C.
Joseph Sweetman Ames	J. S. A.		E. Merton Coulter	E. M. C.
Gertrude L. Annan	G. L. A.		Isaac J. Cox	I. J. C.
John Archer	J. A.		Katharine Elizabeth Crane	K. E. C.
John Clark Archer	J. C. A.		Avery O. Craven	A. O. C.
Preston A. Barba	P. A. B.		Frederic R. Crownfield	F. R. C.
Thomas S. Barclay	T. S. B.		Merle E. Curti	M. E. C.
John H. Barnhart	J. H. B—t.		Carl C. Cutler	C. C. C.
Adriaan J. Barnouw	A. J. B.		Edward E. Dale	E. E. D.
Harold K. Barrows	H. K. B.		Norman H. Dawes	N. H. D.
George A. Barton	G. A. B.		Clive Day	C. D.
Ernest Sutherland Bates	E. S. B.		Richard E. Day	R. E. D.
G. Philip Bauer	G. P. B.		William H. S. Demarest	W. H. S. D.
Marcus Benjamin	M. B.		Herman J. Deutsch	H. J. D.
C. C. Benson	C. C. B.		Irving Dilliard	I. D.
Elbert J. Benton	E. J. B.		Charles Wright Dodge	C. W. D.
Theodore C. Blegen	T. C. B.		Elizabeth Donnan	E. D.
Willard Grosvenor Bleyer	W. G. B.		Randolph C. Downes	R. C. D.
Louise Pearson Blodget	L. P. B.		William Howe Downes	W. H. D.
Lansing B. Bloom	L. B. B.		Carl S. Driver	C. S. D.
George Verne Blue	G. V. B.		Stella M. Drumm	S. M. D.
Louis H. Bolander	L. H. B.		W. E. Burghardt Du Bois	W. E. B. D-B
Robert W. Bolwell	R. W. B.		Edward A. Duddy	E. A. D.
Sarah G. Bowerman	S. G. B.		Raymond S. Dugan	R. S. D.
Julian P. Boyd	J. P. B.		Edward Dwight Eaton	E. D. E.
Jessica Hill Bridenbaugh	J. H. B—h.		Edwin Francis Edgett	E. F. E.
John E. Briggs	J. E. B.		Everett E. Edwards	E. E. E.
Paul Brockett	P. B.		L. Ethan Ellis	L. E. E.
Margaret Louise Brown	M. L. B.		Milton Ellis	M. E.
Solon J. Buck	S. J. B.		William M. Emery	W. M. E.
George K. Burgess	G. K. B.		Carl Engel	C. E.
Huntington Cairns	H. C.		Charles R. Erdman, Jr.	C. R. E., Jr.
William B. Cairns	W. B. C.		Paul D. Evans	P. D. E.
Leon Campbell	L. C.		Walter G. Everett	W. G. E.
Samuel McCrea Cavert	S. M. C.		John O. Evjen	J. O. E.
F. Stanton Cawley	F. S. C.		Charles Fairman	C. F.
Zechariah Chafee, Jr.	Z. C., Jr.		John I. Falconer	J. I. F.
Wayland J. Chase	W. J. C.		Paul Patton Faris	P. P. F.
Samuel Harden Church	S. H. C.		Hallie Farmer	H. F—r.
Charles E. Clark	C. E. C.		James Waldo Fawcett	J. W. F.

Contributors to Volume XVI

Harriet Faxon	H. Fa—n.	Robert L. Jones	R. L. J.
Felix Fellner	F. F.	Rufus M. Jones	R. M. J.
Vergilius Ferm	V. F.	Philip D. Jordan	P. D. J.
John T. Flynn	J. T. F.	James R. Joy	J. R. J.
Arthur Foote	A. F.	Paul Kaufman	P. K.
Henry Thatcher Fowler	H. T. F.	Herbert Anthony Kellar	H. A. K.
John H. Frederick	J. H. F.	Katharine Amend Kellock	K. A. K.
Edna Tutt Frederikson	E. T. F.	Louise Phelps Kellogg	L. P. K.
Herbert Friedmann	H. Fr—n.	Remington Kellogg	R. K.
Charles B. Galbreath	C. B. G—h.	Rayner W. Kelsey	R. W. K.
Esson M. Gale	E. M. G.	Warnick J. Kernan	W. J. K.
William A. Ganoe	W. A. G.	John Kieran	J. K.
Hazel Shields Garrison	H. S. G.	Max J. Kohler	M. J. K.
Winfred Ernest Garrison	W. E. G.	John A. Kolmer	J. A. K—r.
Sylvester Gates	S. G—s.	John A. Krout	J. A. K—t.
Winfield R. Gaylord	W. R. G.	Ernest A. Kubler	E. A. K.
George Harvey Genzmer	G. H. G.	Leonard W. Labaree	L. W. L.
W. J. Ghent	W. J. G.	Arthur B. Lamb	A. B. L.
M. B. Giffen	M. B. G.	William G. Land	W. G. L.
Lawrence H. Gipson	L. H. G.	Winthrop D. Lane	W. D. L.
Colin B. Goodykoontz	C. B. G—z.	William Chauncy Langdon	W. C. L.
Armistead Churchill Gordon, Jr	A. C. G., Jr.	John H. Latané	J. H. L.
Dorothy Grafly	D. G—y.	Kenneth S. Latourette	K. S. L.
Charles Graves	C. G.	Henry Leffert	H. L.
Dorothy Greenwald	D. G—d.	Max Lerner	M. L.
Frederick Grill	F. G.	Charles Lee Lewis	C. L. L.
Sidney Gunn	S. G—n.	Anna Lane Lingelbach	A. L. L.
Edwin H. Hall	E. H. H.	John Stockton Littell II	J. S. L.
Thomas B. Hall	T. B. H.	Charles Sumner Lobingier	C. S. L.
J. G. deR. Hamilton	J. G. deR. H.	Mildred E. Lombard	M. E. L.
Talbot Faulkner Hamlin	T. F. H.	Ella Lonn	E. L.
J. W. Hammond	J. W. H.	Earnest W. Lundeen	E. W. L.
William A. Hammond	W. A. H.	William T. Lyle	W. T. L.
Lewis Hanke	L. H.	Charles H. Lyttle	C. H. L.
Elizabeth Deering Hanscom	E. D. H.	Alexander McAdie	A. M.
Joseph Mills Hanson	J. M. H.	Philip B. McDonald	P. B. M.
Edward Rochie Hardy, Jr.	E. R. H., Jr.	W. J. McGlothlin	W. J. M.
Alvin F. Harlow	A. F. H.	Seth Shepard McKay	S. S. M.
Margaret Harwood	M. H.	Katherine McNamara	K. M.
Einar I. Haugen	E. I. H.	T. F. McNeill	T. F. M.
Earl L. W. Heck	E. L. W. H.	James C. Malin	J. C. M.
Samuel J. Heidner	S. J. H.	Louis L. Mann	L. L. M.
Elizabeth Wiltbank Heilman	E. W. H.	William M. Manross	W. W. M.
Granville Hicks	G. H.	H. A. Marmer	H. A. M.
John Donald Hicks	J. D. H.	Frederick H. Martens	F. H. M.
William J. Hinke	W. J. H.	Daniel Gregory Mason	D. G. M.
William H. Hobbs	W. H. H.	William R. Maxon	W. R. M.
Oliver W. Holmes	O. W. H.	Robert Douthat Meade	R. D. M.
W. Stull Holt	W. S. H.	Donald H. Menzel	D. H. M.
Walter Hough	W. H.	Newton D. Mereness	N. D. M.
John Tasker Howard	J. T. H.	Robert L. Meriwether	R. L. M.
Leland Ossian Howard	L. O. H.	George P. Merrill	G. P. M.
M. A. DeWolfe Howe	M. A. DeW. H.	Frank J. Metcalf	F. J. M.
John G. Jack	J. G. J.	Herman H. B. Meyer	H. H. B. M.
Joseph Jackson	J. J.	George L. Meylan	G. L. M.
T. Cary Johnson, Jr.	T. C. J., Jr.	Broadus Mitchell	B. M.
Howard Mumford Jones	H. M. J.	Stewart Mitchell	S. M.
		Walter Mitchell, Jr.	W. M., Jr.

Contributors to Volume XVI

Carl W. Mitman . . . . . . C. W. M.
Conrad Henry Moehlman . . C. H. M.
Frank Monaghan . . . . . F. M.
Edward Caldwell Moore . . E. C. M—e.
Richard B. Morris . . . . . R. B. M.
Edmund C. Mower . . . . . E. C. M—r.
George Fulmer Mull . . . . G. F. M.
Carl Murchison . . . . . . C. M.
J. Florence Murray . . . J. F. M.
William Allan Neilson . . W. A. N.
Lowry Nelson . . . . L. N.
Lyman C. Newell . . . . . . L. C. N.
A. R. Newsome . . . . A. R. N.
Jeannette P. Nichols . . . J. P. N.
Robert Hastings Nichols . . R. H. N.
Herman C. Nixon . . . . . . H. C. N.
John Scholte Nollen . . . J. S. N.
Fillmore Norfleet . . . . . F. N.
George A. Orrok . . . . . . G. A. O.
Robert B. Osgood . . . . . R. B. O.
Francis R. Packard . . . . F. R. P.
Victor H. Paltsits . . . . . V. H. P.
Stanley M. Pargellis . . . S. M. P.
Henry Bamford Parkes . . H. B. P.
Clarence Paschall . . . . . C. P.
Charles O. Paullin . . . . C. O. P.
Frederic Logan Paxson . . F. L. P.
C. C. Pearson . . . . C. C. P.
John B. Peddle . . . . . . J. B. P.
James H. Peeling . . . . . J. H. P.
Dexter Perkins . . . . . . D. P.
Ralph Barton Perry . . . R. B. P.
Benjamin H. Pershing . . . B. H. P.
Frederick T. Persons . . . F. T. P.
James M. Phalen . . . . . J. M. P—n.
Paul Chrisler Phillips . . P. C. P.
Charles S. Plumb . . . . . C. S. P—b.
David deSola Pool . . . . D. deS. P.
John M. Poor . . . . J. M. P—r.
Dorothy B. Porter . . . . D. B. P.
Kenneth Wiggins Porter . K. W. P.
Charles Shirley Potts . . . C. S. P—s.
Alden L. Powell . . . . . A. L. P.
Richard J. Purcell . . . . R. J. P.
James Watt Raine . . . . J. W. R.
Belle Rankin . . . . B. R.
Albert G. Rau . . . . A. G. R.
P. O. Ray . . . . P. O. R.
Philip M. Rhinelander . . P. M. R.
Charles Dudley Rhodes . . C. D. R.
Leon B. Richardson . . . . L. B. R.
Burr Arthur Robinson . . B. A. R.
Henry Morton Robinson . . H. M. R.
William A. Robinson . . . W. A. R.
William M. Robinson, Jr. . W. M. R., Jr.
Octavia F. Rogan . . . . . O. F. R.
Allen Rogers . . . . A. R.
Lois K. M. Rosenberry . . L. K. M. R.

Marvin B. Rosenberry . . . M. B. R.
William Sener Rusk . . . . W. S. R.
William L. Russell . . . . W. L. R.
George H. Ryden . . . . . G. H. R.
Bernard Sachs . . . . . . B. S.
Lazare Saminsky . . . . . L. S.
Verne Lockwood Samson . . V. L. S.
David J. Saposs . . . . . . D. J. S.
Wallace S. Sayre . . . . . W. S. S.
Joseph Schafer . . . . . . J. S.
Israel Schapiro . . . . . . I. S.
Herbert W. Schneider . . . H. W. S.
Frank W. Scott . . . . . . F. W. S—t.
James Lee Sellers . . . . . J. L. S.
Robert Francis Seybolt . . R. F. S.
William Bristol Shaw . . . W. B. S.
Augustus H. Shearer . . . . A. H. S.
Richard H. Shryock . . . . R. H. S—k.
Eleanor M. Sickels . . . . E. M. S.
Wilbur H. Siebert . . . . . W. H. S—t.
Francis Butler Simkins . . . F. B. S—s.
Frederic W. Simonds . . . F. W. S—s.
Mary B. Slade . . . . M. B. S.
David Eugene Smith . . . . D. E. S.
Edward Conrad Smith . . . E. C. S.
Marion Parris Smith . . . M. P. S.
William E. Smith . . . . . W. E. S.
Herbert Solow . . . . . . H. S.
James P. C. Southall . . . J. P. C. S.
Charles L. Souvay . . . . . C. L. S.
E. Wilder Spaulding . . . . E. W. S.
Oliver L. Spaulding, Jr. . . O. L. S., Jr.
C. P. Stacey . . . . C. P. S.
Harris Elwood Starr . . . . H. E. S.
Bertha Monica Stearns . . B. M. S.
Francis Borgia Steck . . . F. B. S—k.
Wendell H. Stephenson . . W. H. S—n.
Helen R. Steward . . . . . H. R. S.
Tracy E. Strevey . . . . . T. E. S.
William Strunk, Jr. . . . . W. S., Jr.
R. H. Sudds . . . . R. H. S—s.
William W. Sweet . . . . . W. W. S.
William A. Taylor . . . . . W. A. T.
David Y. Thomas . . . . . D. Y. T.
Milton Halsey Thomas . . M. H. T.
C. Mildred Thompson . . . C. M. T.
Ernest Trice Thompson . . E. T. T.
Frederic L. Thompson . . . F. L. T.
Charles J. Tilden . . . . . C. J. T.
Edward Larocque Tinker . E. L. T.
James A. Tobey . . . . . . J. A. T.
Francis A. Tondorf . . . . F. A. T.
Charles C. Torrey . . . . . C. C. T.
Rexford G. Tugwell . . . . R. G. T.
George B. Utley . . . . . . G. B. U.
Clarence H. Vance . . . . . C. H. V.
Edward M. Van Cleve . . . E. M. V-C.
Henry R. Viets . . . . . . H. R. V.

Contributors to Volume XVI

DICTIONARY OF

AMERICAN BIOGRAPHY

Robert — Seward

ROBERT, CHRISTOPHER RHINE-LANDER (Mar. 23, 1802–Oct. 27, 1878), merchant and philanthropist, son of Daniel and Mary Tangier (Smith) Robert, was born near Brook Haven, Suffolk County, Long Island, on the estate of his father, a physician educated at Columbia College and at Edinburgh University. His great-grandfather, also Daniel Robert, was a Huguenot of La Rochelle who reached New York in 1686. Becoming a New York shipping clerk at the age of fifteen, Christopher five years later entered business on his own account, first in New Orleans and later in Galena, Ill. In 1830 he returned to New York and married Anna Maria, daughter of William Shaw of that city. Establishing in 1835 the firm of Robert & Williams, importers of sugar, cotton, and tea, he had made a considerable fortune by 1862, when the partnership was dissolved. Active in many other business enterprises, he was from 1858 to 1863 president of the Delaware, Lackawanna & Western Railroad Company. Always deeply religious, he served for nearly thirty years as superintendent of the Sunday school and elder of the Laight Street Presbyterian Church and supported financially a German congregation on Rivington Street. His appeal to the Home Missionary Society in 1828 led to the establishment in Galena of the first church in Northern Illinois. Henceforth Robert was closely connected with this society, a member of its executive committee after 1838, and treasurer from 1855 to 1870. To its work, to Beloit and Hamilton colleges, and to Auburn Theological Seminary he made substantial anonymous gifts. At the close of the Civil War he bought from the government its hospital buildings at Lookout Mountain, Tennessee, and established there in 1866 a college

for the "poor whites" of the South, but local opposition to its Yankee origin led him soon to abandon the experiment.

While visiting Constantinople during the Crimean War he became acquainted with the educational work which Cyrus Hamlin [q.v.] was doing under the American Board of Commissioners for Foreign Missions. After the war he became interested in the scheme of James H. and William B. Dwight for founding a purely secular college at Constantinople but he believed that little financial support could be obtained in the United States without a definitely Christian basis. When this plan fell through, he offered in 1859 the task of establishing an institution in accordance with his own ideas to Hamlin. The latter accepted the offer and on Sept. 16, 1863, opened at Bebek, a suburb of Constantinople, Robert College, adopting this name despite repeated objections from the founder. In the following year the state of New York granted a charter providing for an American board of trustees, whose dominating personality was Robert. Eventually Hamlin secured a magnificent site above Rumeli Hissar on the Bosphorus and supervised the construction of a building. In 1870 when the new quarters were occupied, Robert visited the college, which had over a hundred students. On this visit as on another in 1875 he investigated in detail every phase of the work, giving freely both advice and criticism, and obtained an intimate understanding of the situation. When campaigns for endowment by Hamlin and his successor, George Washburn [q.v.], proved unsuccessful, practically the whole burden of supporting the institution fell upon Robert, who covered the yearly deficit of $10,000 or more until his death in Paris while seeking to mend his broken health by European travel. One-fifth of his estate was left to the college, raising the amount of his gifts to at least $600,000. A cultured and unassuming gentleman of unusual ability and most decided character, Robert cherished such democratic austerity that he refused a decoration offered by the Ottoman government. The college which he founded has trained many of the builders of the Balkan and Near Eastern nations and remains one of the finest monuments of American philanthropy.

[See: Cuyler Reynolds, *Geneal. and Family Hist. of Southern N. Y. and the Hudson River Valley*, vol. I (1914); Geo. Washburn, *Fifty Years in Constantinople* (1911); Cyrus Hamlin, *My Life and Times* (1893); F. A. Virkus, *The Compendium of Am. Geneal.*, vol. IV (1930); *Home Missionary*, Dec. 1878; *N. Y. Herald*, Oct. 31, 1878; *N. Y. Observer*, Nov. 7, 1878; information as to certain facts supplied by Arthur Remington Robert, London, England.]   W. L. W., Jr.

ROBERTS, BENJAMIN STONE (Nov. 18, 1810–Jan. 29, 1875), soldier, engineer, inventor, was born at Manchester, Vt., of Welsh ancestry, the son of Gen. Martin and Betsey (Stone) Roberts. His grandfather was Gen. Christopher Roberts, of the colonial wars. After a common-school preparation, he was graduated from the United States Military Academy with the class of 1835, fifty-third in a class of fifty-five. He joined the 1st Dragoons as a lieutenant, and after frontier service in Iowa and Kansas, resigned in the year 1839 to become chief engineer of the Champlain & Ogdensburg Railroad. He became geologist of the state of New York in the year 1841, and the following year was an assistant to George Washington Whistler [*q.v.*] in the construction of a railway in Russia from St. Petersburg to Moscow. When he returned to the United States he studied law and began to practise in Des Moines, Iowa, in 1843. He served as lieutenant-colonel of the state militia from 1844 to 1846. At the outbreak of the Mexican War, he was reappointed a first lieutenant with the Mounted Rifles, and was promoted captain in February 1847. He participated in the battles of General Scott's campaign and was brevetted major on Sept. 13, 1847, for gallantry in leading a storming party at the taking of Chapultepec (Smith, *post*, p. 164). On Nov. 24, 1847, he was brevetted lieutenant-colonel for gallantry in action against Mexican guerrillas near Matamoras, and when he returned to the United States, he received a sword of honor from the state of Iowa.

During the following decade, he served at various parts of the frontier, and was promoted to the rank of major, 3rd Cavalry, on May 13, 1861, commanding the southern military district of New Mexico under General Canby, and partici-

pating in engagements at Fort Craig, Albuquerque, Valverde, and Peralta. For gallant and meritorious service at Valverde, he was brevetted colonel on Feb. 21, 1862. He was promoted brigadier-general of volunteers the following June, and as a member of General Pope's staff, was engaged in the battles of Cedar Mountain, Rappahannock Station, Sulphur Springs, and Second Manassas (Ropes, *post*, p. 20 ff.). For gallant services in this campaign he was brevetted brigadier-general and major-general on Mar. 13, 1865. In the fall of 1862, he was detached to lead an expedition against hostile Chippewa Indians in Minnesota, but was recalled to Washington in 1863 to command a unit in the defenses of that city. In the summer of 1864, he was placed in command of the 1st Division, XIX Corps, in Louisiana, and until January 1865, was chief of cavalry, Department of the Gulf. During the remainder of the year he commanded the district and the cavalry division of West Tennessee, and after discharge from the volunteer service on Jan. 15, 1866, was promoted to the rank of lieutenant-colonel, 3rd Cavalry. He served in New Mexico during 1867 and 1868, and was an instructor in military science at Yale College from 1868 to 1870.

He was retired from active service on Dec. 16, 1870, and entered upon the practice of law and the prosecution of claims before the government in Washington. While so engaged, he organized a stock company to finance the manufacture of a breech-loading rifle of his own invention, and although he succeeded in negotiating a European contract, the venture was not successful. He died of pleuro-pneumonia at Washington, D. C., in the sixty-fourth year of his age. He was survived by his wife, Elizabeth, daughter of Anson and Laura (Pierpont) Sperry, of Plattsburg, N. Y., to whom he was married on Sept. 18, 1835. They had three children. Among his writings are, *Description of Newly Patented Solid Shot and Shells for Use in Rifled Ordnance* (1864), and *Lieut.-General U. S. Grant* (1869), an address delivered at Yale College.

[R. B. Moffat, *Pierrepont Geneal.* (privately printed, 1913); F. B. Heitman, *Hist. Register and Dict. of the U. S. Army* (1903); J. H. Smith, *The War With Mexico* (1919) vol. II; *Battles and Leaders of the Civil War*, vol. II (1887); J. C. Ropes, *The Army Under Pope* (1881); *Annual Reunion, Asso. of Grads., U. S. Mil. Acad.*, 1875.]   C. D. R.

ROBERTS, BENJAMIN TITUS (July 25, 1823–Feb. 27, 1893), clergyman, one of the organizers of the Free Methodist Church, was born in Gowanda, Cattaraugus County, N. Y., the son of Titus and Sally (Ellis) Roberts. He was a descendant of William Roberts of East Hartford, Conn., whose father (Robards), husband of Catharine Leete, or Leeke, emigrated to New England about the middle of the seventeenth century. As a boy Benjamin showed more than ordinary mental alertness, won renown in the spelling matches of the countryside, and revealed a genius for mathematics. At the age of sixteen he was teaching school. In 1842 he entered a law office in Little Falls, N. Y., but returned to his home town two years later to continue his legal training in an office there. About this time he experienced conversion and a call to the ministry. After a few months' preparation in Lima Seminary, he entered the sophomore class of Wesleyan University, Middletown, Conn., in 1845, and graduated in 1848. That same year he was admitted to the Genesee Conference of the Methodist Episcopal Church on trial, and on May 3, 1849, he married Ellen Lois Stowe, by whom he had seven children. He was ordained deacon, Sept. 29, 1850; and elder, Sept. 12, 1852. Until the fall of 1858 he was pastor of various churches in Western New York.

Roberts was one of a group of preachers in the Genesee Conference who laid much stress on the doctrine of Christian perfection, or sanctification, and whose piety was fervid and aggressive. They felt that the Conference as a whole had flagrantly departed from the precepts and practices of early Methodism, and condemned especially violation of the Discipline rules regarding plain churches with free seats and the wearing of adornments; the compromising attitude of the Church toward slavery; and membership of Christians in secret societies. They also contended that the Conference was virtually controlled by a band of secret-society men. A conflict arose, carried on in part through pamphlets and religious periodicals, which resulted in disciplinary measures being taken by the Conference against some of the reformers. On specifications based on an article entitled "New School Methodism," published in the *Northern Independent* of Aurora, N. Y., in 1857, Roberts was charged with unchristian and unmoral conduct. At the annual meeting of the Conference, 1857, he was tried, found guilty, and reprimanded. At the Conference of the following year, because of the republishing and circulation of his article—with which he claimed to have had nothing to do—he was expelled. Against both decisions he appealed to the General Conference, but without avail.

A result of this disturbance was the organization at Pekin, N. Y., in August 1860, of the Free Methodist Church, of which Roberts was elected the first general superintendent, an office which he held until his death, thirty-three years later. During this period he served the interests of the growing denomination vigorously and in manifold ways. In January 1860 he established the *Earnest Christian,* which he published and edited for the remainder of his life; from 1886 to 1890 he was also editor of the *Free Methodist.* He took the leading part in the founding of Chili Seminary (A. M. Chesbrough Seminary) at North Chili, N. Y., in 1866, and served for a time as its principal. In the midst of his varied duties, which entailed much travel, he found time to write several books, among them: *Fishers of Men or, Practical Hints to Those Who Would Win Souls* (1878); *Why Another Sect* (1879); *First Lessons in Money* (1886), called forth by the prevailing discussion of the silver question; and *Ordaining Women* (1891), in which he advocated on Scriptural grounds the right of women to be admitted to the ministry. His death occurred at Cattaraugus, N. Y., in his seventieth year.

[*Alumni Records of Wesleyan Univ., Middletown, Conn.* (1911); B. H. Roberts, *Benjamin Titus Roberts* (1900); W. T. Hogue, *Hist. of the Free Meth. Ch. of North America* (2 vols., 1915); Elias Bowen, *Hist. of the Origin of the Free Meth. Ch.* (1871); F. W. Conable, *Hist. of the Genesee Ann. Conference of M. E. Ch.* (1876); *Buffalo Courier,* Mar. 1, 1893; information from a son, Benjamin T. Roberts.]   H. E. S.

ROBERTS, BRIGHAM HENRY (Mar. 13, 1857–Sept. 27, 1933), Mormon leader, was born in Warrington, Lancashire, England, the son of Benjamin Roberts, a blacksmith, and Ann Everington Roberts. Before his birth the family had joined the Mormon Church. To this new faith his mother was passionately devoted, and in 1862 she left her husband in England and made the trip to Utah, taking with her the two youngest children. Brigham Henry and an elder sister were left with fellow religionists until the mother could send for them. In 1866 the son joined his mother who was living in Bountiful, a few miles north of Salt Lake City. He worked on farms and in mines, and in his early teens attended school for the first time in his life, in Davis County. At seventeen he was apprenticed to a blacksmith. In 1877 he entered the University of Deseret (now the University of Utah) and completed his course in 1878 as valedictorian of his class. He then taught school and also worked at his trade. His talents as an orator and debater were early recognized by the Mormon Church authorities who, in 1880, called him on a mission to the Middle Western and Southern states. He returned in 1882 but went on a second mission in 1883, when he became mission president. In 1886 he was transferred to the British Mission where he remained for two years and was engaged primarily in the task of editing the *Millennial Star,* a church periodical. In 1888, upon his return from England, he was made one of the First Council of Seventy. He was president of the Eastern States Mission from April 1922 to April 1927. In politics he affiliated himself with the Democratic party in 1890 and was active in the campaigns of 1892 and 1894. In the latter year he was elected a member of the Utah constitutional convention which framed the organic law of the state. In 1898 he was elected to Congress, but the House of Representatives, by action taken on Jan. 25, 1900, refused him a seat on account of his being a polygamist. He was the father of fifteen children, seven by his first wife, Louisa Smith, whom he married in 1878, and eight by his second wife, Celia Dibble, whom he married about 1885. There were no children by his third wife, Margaret Shipp.

Roberts served as chaplain on the staff of Governor Bamberger in 1917 and later as chaplain of the 145th Field Artillery. He was at Camp Kearney in California and with the regiment in France from August 1918 to January 1919. After the war he was chairman of the Mormon Battalion Monument Committee which raised two hundred thousand dollars for the Monument which now adorns the grounds of the Utah State Capitol. His chief work was in the field of historical and ecclesiastical writing. When the conflict between his people and the outside world was at its height, he brought his power of oratory and writing to bear in behalf of his people, by whom he was loved and revered as the great "Defender of the Faith." Upwards of thirty volumes and numerous pamphlets came from his pen. From 1890 to 1896 he was with the *Salt Lake Tribune,* first as associate editor and later as editor-in-chief. The crowning effort of his life in the field of historical writing was the publication, in 1930, the centennial year of the Mormon Church, of *A Comprehensive History of the Church of Jesus Christ of Latter Day Saints, Century I,* in six volumes. It represents a revision of the series of articles which he published in the *Americana* from June 1909 to July 1915. Among his other publications are: *The Life of John Taylor* (1892); *Outlines of Ecclesiastical History* (1893); *New Witnesses for God* (3 vols., 1895); *The Missouri Persecutions* (1900); *The Rise and Fall of Nauvoo* (1900); *Mormonism: The Relation of the Church to Christian Sects* (1908); *The Seventy's Course in Theology* (5 vols., 1907–12); *The Mormon Battalion* (1919); *Why Mormonism* (1919); and *Rasha—the Jew* (1932). Roberts was a man of striking physical appearance, about six feet in height, with a well-proportioned frame, a somewhat massive head adorned in his later years by a shock of white hair. In spite of the fact that he was largely self-educated, he possessed perhaps the most sophisticated mind among his ecclesiastical contemporaries. This often resulted in his being in intellectual conflict with them. He was able to see the history of his people with the perspective of one viewing it in terms of the entire sweep of history.

[The sketch is based largely upon a manuscript autobiography of Roberts in the possession of Ben Roberts, Salt Lake City. For printed sources see: *Latter-Day Saint Biog. Encyc.,* vol. I (1901); *Cong. Record,* 56 Cong., 1 Sess., pp. 47–49, 1072–1104, 1123–49, 1175–1217, App. pp. 23, 25, 40; *Deseret News,* Sept. 28, 1933; *Salt Lake Tribune,* Sept. 28, 29, 1933.] L. N.

ROBERTS, EDMUND (June 29, 1784–June 12, 1836), merchant and special diplomatic agent of the United States in the Far East, was born at Portsmouth, N. H., to Captain Edmund and Sarah Griffiths Roberts. His father died when Edmund was a small child; his mother when he was sixteen, leaving him to the care of his bachelor uncle, Capt. Joshua Roberts, a merchant then at Buenos Aires. After eight years of commercial apprenticeship and travel, he succeeded upon his uncle's death to a substantial business. Returning to Portsmouth he was married in September 1808 to Catharine Langdon, daughter of a distinguished Portsmouth family. The Berlin and Milan decrees injured his mercantile business. French and Spanish privateers caused him heavy losses, and although he eventually recovered small amounts from the French government, he remained in straitened circumstances until his death. In 1823 he was appointed American consul at Demerara, British Guiana, but apparently did not serve. Four years later he borrowed money, chartered the brig *Mary Ann,* and sailed to Zanzibar. There he encountered costly delays and a vexatious government monopoly of trade. He protested vigorously to the ruler of Zanzibar, the Sultan of Muscat, formed an intimate acquaintance with that potentate, visited Bombay, and returned home to urge upon his kinsman through marriage, Senator Levi Woodbury of New Hampshire, a mission to the Far East to negotiate a number of commercial treaties. Roberts also urged that American naval vessels be sent occasionally to the Indian Ocean. John Shellaber, American consul at Batavia, was advocating a similar mission and hoping to receive the appointment. But through the influence of

Woodbury, who had become Jackson's secretary of the navy, Roberts was appointed on Jan. 26, 1832, special agent of the United States to negotiate treaties with Muscat, Siam, and Cochin China. On Oct. 28, 1832, he was authorized to negotiate also with Japan if practicable, and was instructed to investigate the operations of the British East India Company. His mission, however, was to be secret, and he was given as "ostensible employment" the position of clerk to the commander of the United States sloop *Peacock* at $1500 a year.

Roberts went first to Cochin China, but disagreeing with the authorities upon questions of etiquette, sailed for Bankok where on Mar. 20, 1833, he concluded a treaty of amity and commerce with Siam. The treaty freed American trade with Siam from governmental monopoly and from all export and import duties. The *Peacock* then sailed to Muscat where Roberts signed on Sept. 21, 1833, a treaty of amity and commerce with the Sultan. This treaty granted the American consul extraterritorial powers, fixed duties at five per cent., and contained a most-favored-nation clause. Although he had received further instructions to proceed to Japan, he thought it unwise and returned to Portsmouth, arriving in April 1834. In March of the following year Secretary of State Forsyth instructed him to proceed to Muscat and Siam to exchange the ratifications of the treaties he had negotiated and to attempt to negotiate commercial treaties with Cochin China and Japan. After successful visits to Muscat and Siam, he contracted a disease which caused his death at Macao on June 12, 1836. His treaties with Muscat and Siam were proclaimed June 24, 1837.

[The Edmund Roberts Papers at the Lib. of Cong. contain letters, journals, copies of diplomatic correspondence, and prepared biographical material. The archives of the Department of State contain numerous dispatches from and some instructions to Roberts. See W. M. Malloy, *Treaties, Conventions, International Acts, Protocols* (2 vols., 1910) or 8 *U. S. Statutes at Large* for the treaties of 1833 with Siam and Muscat. Edmund Roberts, *Embassy to the Eastern Courts of Cochin-China, Siam and Muscat; in the U. S. Sloop of war Peacock* (1837) suffered from official censorship. The story of the last voyage is contained in W. S. W. Ruschenberger, *A Voyage around the World: Including an Embassy to Muscat and Siam* (1838). See also: Tyler Dennett, *Americans in Eastern Asia* (1922) and H. M. Wriston, *Executive Agents in Am. Foreign Relations* (1929).]
E. W. S.

ROBERTS, ELIZABETH WENTWORTH (June 10, 1871–Mar. 12, 1927), painter, was born at Philadelphia, Pa., the daughter of well-to-do parents, G. Theodore and Sarah (Green) Roberts. They spent their summers in New Hampshire where Elizabeth, known to her friends as "Elsie," early revealed talent for out-door sketching. She was given the best masters —Elizabeth Bonsall and Henry R. Poore in Philadelphia, and Tony Robert-Fleury, Jules Lefebvre, and Luc-Olivier Merson in Paris— and in 1889 she was awarded the Mary Smith Prize of the Pennsylvania Academy of the Fine Arts. At the Paris Salon, 1892, she received honorable mention. From Paris her studies extended into Italy where she gave special attention to Botticelli and other masters of religious art. She returned to the United States after six years' study and for a short time she had a studio in New York. During a summer at the Emerson house, Concord, Mass., while she was engaged in making a series of paintings of the historic and literary landmarks of the neighborhood, she formed friendships and associations that induced her to establish an all-year residence at Concord. Her services to American art and her assistance to other artists were even more remarkable than her own professional achievement, highly creditable though the latter was. She devoted much of her large income to forwarding the exhibitions of the Concord Art Association which under her management were of metropolitan quality. Sedulously following the seasonal exhibitions of the principal cities, she secured for the annual summer show at Concord many of the finest paintings and sculptures, and she offered generous prizes and bought many works of art for the association's permanent collection. The catalogues of these exhibitions, which Miss Roberts wrote, were models of biographical completeness and accuracy. She served also as president of the Concord Antiquarian Society.

While engaged in these and other activities Miss Roberts painted proficiently and with fervor: at first religious paintings, some of them mural decorations for the Church of St. Asaph, Bala, Pa. (described by Downes, *post*); many sketchy seascapes, made at Cape Ann and elsewhere, exquisite in tone, refined in color; and occasionally a larger, more ambitious conversation piece, such as her full-size portrait of such veterans of the Civil War as survived at Concord after the World War. The last-named work, now owned by the town of Concord, was favorably criticized by John Singer Sargent (see Coburn, *post*). During the World War Miss Roberts organized in New York and Boston several exhibitions of her "Figures on the Sand" which were sold for the benefit of the war sufferers in France. "Painted in a thin, rapidly wrought medium, her pictures of the broad and shining expanse of sand beach showing the North Shore, with the agile, buoyant, active figures of children at play or wading or swimming or digging against the splendid background of the blue ocean, are brilliant and luminous in the extreme, and notable for their expression of atmospheric spaciousness. The bigness and freedom of these scenes lend them a joyous and stimulating charm which is unique." Physically frail, emotionally subject to periods of deep melancholy, Miss Roberts was following her useful and outwardly pleasant career when she shocked her many friends by taking her life at her Concord home. She left to the Concord Art Association its building which shortly after her death housed a memorial exhibition of her works.

[Sources include: W. H. Downes, "Miss Roberts's Religious Paintings," *New Eng. Mag.*, July 1901, and "Figures on the Sand," *Boston Transcript*, Mar. 25, 1919; F. W. Coburn, "Civil War Piece at Concord," *Sunday Herald* (Boston), July 6, 1924; "Sand Pictures by Elizabeth W. Roberts," *Am. Art News*, Mar. 9, 1918; *Boston Transcript*, Mar. 12, 1927; *Lowell Courier-Citizen*, Mar. 17, 1927; information from associates of Miss Roberts, and personal recollections.]

F. W. C.

ROBERTS, ELLIS HENRY (Sept. 30, 1827–Jan. 8, 1918), congressman, financier, was born in Utica, N. Y., then a village, his parents, Watkin and Gwen (Williams) Roberts, having emigrated from North Wales some ten years previously. His father died when Ellis was four years of age, and the boy was early thrown on his own resources. He learned the printer's trade, and with his own earnings pursued his education at Whitestown Seminary and Yale College, where he graduated in 1850. Returning to Utica, he became identified with the *Oneida Morning Herald,* a daily newspaper of which his brother was one of the owners. This journal, later known as the *Utica Morning Herald,* he continued to serve in an editorial capacity, save for an interim of a few months, until the year 1890.

In politics he was a Republican; in 1866 he was elected to the state legislature, where he served one term, and in 1870 he was elected to Congress; he was returned in 1872, but defeated in 1874 by Scott Lord in the Democrat landslide of that year. In his early political life he was a supporter of Roscoe Conkling [q.v.], taking an active part, when a member of the New York legislature, in Conkling's first election as United States senator, but very shortly thereafter there was a breach in their friendly relations which was never healed. Roberts became the leader of the local faction of the Republican party known as the "Half-Breeds," opposed to Conkling and his "Stalwart" supporters, and in 1884 the diminished Republican vote in Oneida County, where the two leaders had their residence, was sufficient to account for the small plurality

by which the electoral vote of New York was lost to the Republican presidential candidate.

In 1889 Roberts was appointed assistant treasurer of the United States by President Benjamin Harrison, in which office he served until 1893, when he became president of the Franklin National Bank of New York. In 1897, he was appointed treasurer of the United States by President McKinley, continuing in that office until 1905. After his retirement he returned to Utica, where he died in 1918 at the advanced age of ninety years.

Roberts early acquired distinction as a writer and speaker, and during his service in Congress gained recognition as one versed in questions of finance. He took a prominent part in the discussion and enactment of legislation for the resumption of specie payments, the refunding of the national debt, the redemption of bonds, and the reduction of war debts, as well as at all times advocating a policy of protection. In his first term he was accorded the unusual honor of an appointment upon the ways and means committee. He was also a member of a sub-committee which investigated the collection of customs, with a report which prompted several resignations and helped to bring about the repeal of the moiety laws. In 1884 he delivered a course of lectures at Cornell University which formed the basis of a volume entitled *Government Revenue: Especially the American System; an Argument against the Fallacies of Free Trade* (1884; 4th ed., 1888). He also wrote *New York: The Planting and the Growth of the Empire State* (2 vols., 1887), in the American Commonwealths Series. In June 1851 he married Elizabeth Morris, but they were without children.

[M. M. Bagg, *Memorial Hist. of Utica* (1892); H. J. Cookinham, *Hist. of Oneida County, N. Y.* (1912), vol. I, esp. pp. 289–92; D. E. Wager, *Our County and Its People . . . Oneida County, N. Y.* (1896); J. G. Blaine, *Twenty Years in Congress,* vol. II (1886); *Obit. Record Grads. Yale Univ.,* 1918 (1919); D. S. Alexander, *A Pol. Hist. of the State of N. Y.,* III (1909), 169–70, 388; *N. Y. Times,* Jan. 9, 1918; files of *Utica Daily Press* and *Utica Observer-Dispatch.*]

W. J. K.

ROBERTS, GEORGE BROOKE (Jan. 15, 1833–Jan. 30, 1897), railroad executive, was born on his father's farm, "Pencoed," near Bala, Montgomery County, Pa., the son of Isaac Warner and Rosalinda Evans (Brooke) Roberts. He received his early education in the schools near his home and then attended the Rensselaer Polytechnic Institute at Troy, N. Y., where he was graduated in 1849. Two years later he entered the service of the Pennsylvania Railroad as a rodman on the mountain division. In 1852, he became assistant engineer on the Sunbury &

Erie Railroad, forerunner of the Philadelphia & Erie, and for the next ten years he was in the employ of various railroad companies engaged in construction work. In 1862, he became assistant to the president of the Pennsylvania Railroad, J. Edgar Thomson [q.v.], being in full charge of the building of the company's lines. He served also as a director after May 3, 1869, and in that year was promoted to the fourth, soon afterward to the second, vice-presidency. In 1874, when Thomas A. Scott [q.v.] became president of the company, Roberts succeeded him in the position of first vice-president. He now assisted the president in all business pertaining to leased or controlled roads and had charge of all engineering matters relating to the construction, extension, and improvement of the company's lines, as well as a general supervision of its accounts. On June 1, 1880, he was elected president of the Pennsylvania Railroad Company to succeed Scott, and served in that capacity until his death. During his administration much additional trackage and a number of new feeder lines were constructed, equipment and terminals were improved, grades were reduced, and many grade crossings eliminated. A number of roads west of Pittsburgh were leased and reorganized as part of the Pennsylvania system; the Philadelphia, Wilmington & Baltimore Railroad was taken over to afford a connection with the South; and the company's financial position was improved until its credit standing was unequaled in the country at the time.

Roberts frequently served as chairman of the board of presidents of the Trunk Line Association, in which position he did much to solve the problems growing out of the incessant competition then existing between rival railway interests. He was always ready to aid any movement looking to the bettering of the condition of the company's employees and in this connection encouraged the formation and development of the railroad departments of the Young Men's Christian Association. He was a devout Episcopalian and a liberal giver to charitable and public objects, serving as a director of the Free Public Library of Philadelphia and vice-president of the Fairmount Park Art Association. He was twice married: in 1868 to Sarah Lapsley Brinton, and in 1874 to Miriam P. Williams. He died on his family's farm near Bala, Pa., survived by two daughters and four sons.

[Minute on the Death of George B. Roberts, Adopted by the Board of Directors of the Pa. R. R. Company (1897); official biog. of G. B. Roberts (MS.), in possession of the Pa. R. R. Company, Phila.; W. B. Wilson, Hist. of the Pa. R. R. Company (1899), vol. II, and Hist. of the Pa. R. R. Dept. of the Y. M. C. A. of Phila. (1911); H. W. Schotter, The Growth and Development of the Pa. R. R. Company (1927); A. K. McClure, Old Time Notes of Pa. (1905), vol. I; Railroad Gazette, Feb. 5, 1897; Pub. Ledger (Phila.), Feb. 1, 1897; name of mother from Roberts' sons, G. B. Roberts and T. W. Roberts.]   J. H. F.

ROBERTS, HOWARD (Apr. 9, 1843–Apr. 18, 1900), sculptor, the son of Edward Roberts, merchant, and Mary Elizabeth Reford, was born in Philadelphia, Pa., the last of a family of nine children. He was descended from ancestors who emigrated from North Wales and settled in Merion, Pa., in 1683. His grandfather, Algernon Roberts, was an officer in the Pennsylvania militia in the Revolution, while earlier members of the family were prominent in affairs of the provincial government. Howard Roberts attended the Classical Institute of the Rev. John W. Faires in Philadelphia and began to study art under J. A. Bailly at the Pennsylvania Academy of the Fine Arts. At the age of twenty-three he entered the École des Beaux-Arts in Paris, working under Dumont and Gumery. After completing his European studies he returned to America in 1871 and established a studio in Philadelphia where in the following year he modeled his first important work, a statuette of Hester and Pearl based upon Hawthorne's Scarlet Letter. Exhibited at the Pennsylvania Academy, it attracted considerable attention and won for its sculptor membership in the Academy itself. Roberts had joined the Sketch Club in 1861 and served that organization variously through succeeding years as treasurer, vice-president, and president.

In Paris again from 1873 to 1876 Roberts produced "La Première Pose" (now in the Philadelphia Museum of Art), which won him at the Philadelphia Centennial Exhibition of 1876 one of the three medals accorded work by American sculptors. His "Hypatia" (now at the Pennsylvania Academy) and "Lot's Wife" were considered bold compositions in their day. At the time of the Centennial, when his popularity was at its height, his work was said to have "technical qualities the highest, perhaps, of any among the American statuary" (Illustrated Catalogue of the Masterpieces of the International Exhibition, 1876). As the result of a competition for the life-size statue of Robert Fulton for the Rotunda of the National Capitol, Washington, D. C., Roberts won a national reputation, having been selected from among thirty leading sculptors. The statue was erected in 1883. Always active in art and intellectual circles, Roberts became a member of the Penn Club in which he was associated with men of art, science, and literature, and his name appears as a member of the Club's board of management when a charter was granted in 1889. In addition to statues and statuettes of literary or classical flavor, Roberts produced many portrait busts. An ideal head, "Eleanor," acquired by Henry C. Gibson for his collection, has passed through bequest to the Pennsylvania Academy of the Fine Arts. Roberts was married, on June 1, 1876, to Helen Pauline Lewis. In 1900, with his wife and son, he went to Paris expecting to remain three years, but his career was abruptly terminated by his sudden death.

[Sources include: C. J. Cohen, *The Penn Club* (1924); C. E. Clement and Laurence Hutton, *Artists of the Nineteenth Century* (1885); Lorado Taft, *The Hist. of Am. Sculpture* (1924); *Am. Art Annual,* 1900–01; *Who's Who in America,* 1899–1900; J. W. Jordan, *Colonial and Revolutionary Families of Pa.,* vol. I (1911); *Pub. Ledger* (Phila.), Apr. 19, 1900; Roberts family papers in the possession of the Pa. Hist. Soc.]
D. G—y.

ROBERTS, ISSACHAR JACOB (Feb. 17, 1802–Dec. 28, 1871), missionary to China, began his picturesque existence in Sumner County, Tenn. When he was about nineteen years old he was converted, and later pursued his studies at the Furman Theological Institution, South Carolina. On Apr. 27, 1827, he was ordained at Shelbyville, Tenn. Subsequently, he organized the Roberts Fund and China Mission Society on the basis of property which he owned in Mississippi, reputedly worth $30,000, and in 1836 sailed for China under this fund, arriving there the following year. He began his missionary labors at Macao, working as a saddler and preaching to a colony of lepers, which connection ostracized him from his fellow missionaries. Finding his income insufficient, in 1841 he joined the Baptist Mission and following the organization of the Southern Baptist Convention transferred to the latter (Jan. 1, 1846); in 1852 he finally reverted to a completely independent status. He helped open the Baptist Mission at Hong Kong in 1842, laboring first at the village of Chek-chu—partly among British troops (*Baptist Missionary Magazine,* June 1843)—and the next year at Victoria (Hong Kong). In 1844 he moved to Canton, where he leased a lot and built a chapel. The plundering of his house by a mob in 1847 formed the basis of a long-standing claim against the Chinese government (*Senate Executive Document No. 30,* 36 Cong., 1 Sess., pp. 105–06); subsequently, January 1849, an attack was made on his life, which resulted in an appeal to the American consul for "official interposition" and protection (China Despatches, MSS., Department of State, Jan. 27, 1849).

About 1847 Roberts gave instruction for two months to an inquirer named Hung, who afterward, as the Tien Wang ("Heavenly King"),

became leader of the pseudo-Christian Taiping Rebellion. In 1853 he addressed from his capital at Nanking a letter to Roberts asking him to come and instruct the people. The zealous missionary felt "constrained to go" and, disregarding the strong disapproval of the project on the part of the American Commissioner, he turned up in Shanghai with two rebel princes (L. S. Foster, *Fifty Years in China,* 1909, pp. 80–81) and made a futile attempt to reach Nanking. He contented himself for the time being with fulsome and egotistical writings on the revolution and on his own unique connection with its leader (see *Spirit of Missions,* May 1854; *Putnam's Magazine,* October 1856). On Oct. 13, 1860, he finally reached Nanking, where he was assistant to the chief minister of state, a former "convert" named Hung Jin and denoted the Kan Wang ("Shield King"). Roberts wore yellow robes and a crown, and became minister of foreign affairs. On Jan. 13, 1862, he accused the Kan Wang of murdering his servant and the dignified mandarin retaliated by dousing his astonished assistant with the dregs of a cup of tea. Roberts, fearing for his life, fled to Shanghai, where he published a letter giving his version of the incident and asserting furthermore that the Tien Wang was mad and his movement hopeless (*North China Herald,* Feb. 8, 1862, quoted in Henri Cordier, *Histoire des Relations de la Chine avec les Puissances Occidentales,* vol. I, 1901, p. 209). In 1866 Roberts returned to the United States, whither his wife and two children had preceded him in 1855. He had gone back to marry her in 1849, a former wife, to whom he was married Jan. 4, 1830, having died in 1831. Roberts died of leprosy at Upper Alton, Ill. He was strikingly uncouth and had marked eccentricities. On one occasion he ignored a dying missionary with the remark, "Let the dead bury their dead, but I must preach the gospel." His writings, however, reveal religious sincerity.

[G. W. Hervey, *The Story of Baptist Missions* (1884); K. S. Latourette, *The Hist. of Early Relations between the U. S. and China* (1917); Alexander Wylie, *Memorials of Protestant Missionaries to the Chinese* (1867); E. F. Merriam, *A Hist. of Am. Baptist Missions* (1900); W. A. P. Martin, *A Cycle of Cathay* (1896); Tyler Dennett, *Americans in Eastern Asia* (1922); Lindesay Brine, *The Taeping Rebellion in China* (1862); *The Missionary Jubilee* (1865).]
J. S. L.

ROBERTS, JOB (Mar. 23, 1756–Aug. 20, 1851), pioneer agriculturist, was born at "Woodlawn Farm," Whitpain, near Gwynedd, Pa. He was the third son and ninth child of John Roberts and Jane Hank, and a great-grandson of Robert Cadwalader who emigrated from Wales some time prior to 1698. Cadwalader's children adopted the surname Robert, which was later again changed to Roberts. According to tradition, the family joined the Society of Friends shortly after their arrival, for Roberts' grandfather married according to the order of the Friends in 1706, and for generations his descendants have been members of Gwynedd Meeting. Job Roberts married first Mary Naylor, on May 22, 1781, by whom he had two daughters. His second wife, to whom he was married on Oct. 12, 1820, was Sarah (Williams) Thomas, daughter of Joseph Williams. For his achievements in better farming, crop experiment, and improved farm machinery, "Squire Job Roberts" deserves to be remembered. His interest in scientific agriculture is said to have been inspired by the Philadelphia Society for Promoting Agriculture which was founded in 1785. He experimented with fertilizers, the use of lime, plaster, and various barnyard manures, and in the deep ploughing of land. In 1804 he published the results of experiments in *The Pennsylvania Farmer,* a practical book, simply written, full of interesting material, and still valuable. He records intensive methods of cultivation which resulted in bumper wheat crops of sixty bushels to the acre.

His experiments with plaster of Paris and with gypsum as fertilizers began in 1785. In 1792 he built an improved harrow and devised a new roller. In 1797 he attached a water-wheel to a dairy churn making it possible to produce with it 150 pounds of butter a week. In 1815 he invented a machine for planting corn at even distances in hills. By soaking the grains of Indian corn in water before planting, to bring about quick germination, he advanced the growing season, and it is recorded that he rarely produced less than eighty bushels to an acre. He introduced into Pennsylvania Merino sheep; and he was interested, as were the other scientific farmers of his age, in cultivating the mulberry for silk culture. He substituted green fodder for his cattle in place of grazing, and built a barn "which was enormously large, according to usual standards, but which he soon had full of crops." Despite the obvious utility of his experiments and activities, his neighbors and chroniclers seem to have been most impressed by the fact that in 1780 "he built himself a carriage, the first to be seen in the county, in which for the next twenty-five years, he drove himself to Gwynedd Meeting." In 1791 Governor Mifflin appointed Roberts justice of the peace. Beyond that he would accept no public office, though he devoted much of his time to public

trusts and to private charity, and he was "habitually consulted by his neighbors in matters of difficulty, whether in political, personal or rural affairs" (Tyson, *post*, p. 10).

[See: J. R. Tyson, *Address Delivered Before the Montgomery County Agric. Soc.* (1856); H. M. Jenkins, *Hist. Colls. Relating to Gwynedd* (1897); *Germantown Telegraph,* Dec. 17, 1856.]   M. P. S.

ROBERTS, JONATHAN (Aug. 16, 1771–July 21, 1854), congressman and senator from Pennsylvania, was born near Norristown, Pa., the son of Jonathan and Anna (Thomas) Roberts and the descendant of John Roberts, a Welsh Friend who emigrated to Pennsylvania in William Penn's time. On that portion of his original plantation known as "Swamp Vrass," in Upper Merion Township, Montgomery County, his great-grand-son passed his childhood. The boy received private tutoring, learned farming, and acquired a fondness for books under the guidance of his mother, who taught him to appreciate the ancient Stoics. After apprenticeship to a wheelwright, he returned to farming, and he and his brother reported, "in seven years we could command seven thousand dollars, and had greatly increased our stock and improved our land" (Auge, *post*, p. 73). Nurtured upon the excitements of the whiskey and house tax rebellions and breathing naturally the atmosphere of violent partisanship characteristic of that period, he equipped himself carefully for polemical politics and joined the Republicans in wresting control of Montgomery County from the Federalists. He helped to make up the majority of two in the lower house of the Assembly, 1799–1800, confronting the Senate Federalist majority of one. His next activity was in the state Senate, 1807–11, from which he was carried, along with other "war hawks," into the federal Congress, 1811 to 1814. There he confidently faced a war with the traditional enemy, "I repose safely in the maxim, 'Never to despair of the Republic.'" While the vote for war with Great Britain was pending, he prevented delay through indefinite adjournment by cannily proposing to suspend members' pay while adjourned, and at a crucial moment he called for the previous question (*Annals of Congress,* 12 Cong., 1 Sess., cols. 1337–38, 1340). This stand, perforce, severed his religious connections with the Friends; but political connections grew apace. His close relations with Madison were revealed in his controversial letters defending the administration in the *Aurora.* As a committeeman on ways and means he guarded the national pursestrings and took the rôle of floor defender of the secretary of the treasury, Albert

Gallatin, against Cheves, Calhoun, and Lowndes. At Gallatin's instance he visited Governor Snyder to urge veto of a Pennsylvania bank bill. Meanwhile, he had married in 1813 Eliza Hite Bushby of Washington. They had nine children. Soon, in February 1814, factional warfare deprived Michael Leib [q.v.] of his seat in the Senate, and the Pennsylvania legislature placed Roberts in it. There he marvelled at the peaceful years ensuing, "I never knew a time so politically tranquil. . . . There is nothing indicative of that acrimony we have long been accustomed to" (Roberts to Monroe, June 9, Aug. 22, 1818, in possession of Historical Society of Pennsylvania). But Roberts' existence speedily became normal, for from his cordial disapproval of Jackson's Florida foray sprang a lifelong antipathy between them. The Maine-Missouri question also brought conflict, for Roberts stoutly defended a plan of his own to prevent the introduction of any more slaves into Missouri (*Annals of Congress,* 16 Cong., 1 Sess., cols. 85–86, 116–17, 119–28, 335–46).

After leaving the Senate in 1821, he endeavored to diminish Jackson's presidential chances, being "very decided" (*Life of Gallatin, post,* p. 588) that the Democracy needed Gallatin as a candidate in 1824 and serving in the Pennsylvania House, 1823–26, to stem the tide of Jacksonianism. The economic advancement of his own state he also held dear, advocating internal improvements, serving on the canal commission, and attending pioneer tariff conventions. After membership upon Biddle's bank board in 1836 he naturally gravitated into the Whig camp, supporting Clay, and he nominated Tyler for vice-president at the Harrisburg convention in 1839. Characteristically, when made collector of the port of Philadelphia he balked over the spoils system, and the president removed him in 1842. With this bold engagement the active political warfare of this sturdy Roman was concluded. He died on his farm in Montgomery County.

[Manuscript memoirs willed to his grandson, Jonathan Roberts of Atlantic City; letters to Madison, Monroe, and Gallatin in Lib. of Hist. Soc. Pa., and Lib. of Cong.; Moses Auge, *Lives of the Eminent Dead* (1879); Henry Adams, *Hist. of the U. S.,* vol. VII (1891) and *The Life of Albert Gallatin* (1872); H. R. Mueller, *The Whig Party in Pa.* (1922); *Hist. Sketches. A Collection of Papers Prepared for the Hist. Soc. of Montgomery County, Pa.,* vol. III, IV (1905–10); *Letters and Other Writings of James Madison* (1865), vol. III.]   J. P. N.

ROBERTS, JOSEPH JENKINS (Mar. 15, 1809–Feb. 24, 1876), first president of Liberia, West Africa, was born of free, colored parents at Petersburg, Va., having seven-eighths or more of white blood. He married at an early age in Virginia but lost his wife, and in 1829 he migrated to Liberia with his widowed mother and younger brothers and there became a merchant. The governor of the colony at that time, Thomas H. Buchanan, a white appointee of the American Colonization Society, was having trouble with the natives, who were not reconciled to the invasion of the American freedmen. During the fighting with the Dey and Golah tribes, Roberts became one of Buchanan's most efficient leaders. Owing to his energetic work, most of the more threatening natives were reduced to submission. He then made every effort to make friends with the natives, and, after Buchanan died, he was appointed in January 1842 the first colored man to become governor of Liberia, at that time, however, comprising only the northern part of what is now its best territory. Although the colony of Maryland was not formally a part of Liberia until 1857, its governor, John Russwurm [q.v.], gave Roberts full coöperation. The necessity of organizing the country, pacifying the natives, and repelling the illicit slave traders, called for larger revenues than Roberts or Russwurm had. Accordingly, they decided to lay import duties on goods brought to Liberia. This precipitated grave international difficulties, for Liberia was not a sovereign country, nor was it, on the other hand, a recognized colony of the United States. The British approached the United States on the subject but received a non-committal answer. Since positive action seemed to be necessary, Roberts, after strengthening his treaties with the native tribes, visited the United States in 1844 in the hope of adjusting the matter. At such a difficult time, when the question of the annexation of Texas was forcing the slavery question to the front, the American government avoided taking any strong ground in defense of Liberia, and the American Colonization Society gave up all claims upon the colony.

He returned, continued his purchase of lands from the chiefs, and in 1847 called a conference at which the new republic of Liberia was proclaimed. He was elected as the first president, and, reëlected in 1849, 1851, and 1853, he served his country carefully and wisely. As soon as the new nation was proclaimed, he hurried to England. His unexpected success there was due largely to his own character and finesse. He was a man of intelligence and poise, slight and handsome, with olive skin and crisp hair. He was an excellent conversationalist and had the manners of a gentleman. His second wife, Jane (Waring) Roberts, to whom he was married in Monrovia in 1836, was a woman of education and spoke excellent French. In Europe he received unusual attention. He signed a commercial treaty in 1849 with Great Britain, which recognized Liberia as an independent nation and gave Englishmen freedom of domicile. Before he left England, ten thousand dollars was raised by his English friends and given to him to buy the territory between Liberia and Sierra Leone, where the slave trade was flourishing. Later he visited France and Belgium, where he was received by Leopold I, and also Holland and Prussia. In 1852 he again visited France, where he was received by the prince president, afterward Napoleon III. These visits were largely instrumental in obtaining speedy recognition of Liberia. After finishing his term he continued to be active in the interests of Liberia, even to the extent of taking the field against rebellious natives. In 1856 he was elected first president of the new College of Liberia and continued in that office until his death. He visited Europe again in 1854 and 1862, and on his return from the last trip he was appointed Belgian consul in Liberia. In 1869 he visited the United States, where he addressed the annual meeting of the African Colonization Society at Washington on *African Colonization* (1869). When there arose in Liberia the financial difficulties with regard to a British loan (see sketch of Edward James Roye) Liberia came near to revolution. At the age of 63 and already broken in health by his long service, he was again elected to the presidency in 1871. Reëlected, he served until January 1876 and died at Monrovia in February.

[H. H. Johnston, *Liberia* (1906), vol. I; B. G. Brawley, *A Social Hist. of the Am. Negro* (1921); "A Visit to Monrovia," *African Repository*, Jan. 1876; "Obituary," *Ibid.*, Apr. 1876; *Sixtieth Ann. Report of the Am. Colonization Soc.* (1877), p. 6; date of death from *African Repository* and *Report of the Am. Colonization Soc.*]
              W. E. B. D–B.

ROBERTS, MARSHALL OWEN (Mar. 22, 1814–Sept. 11, 1880), capitalist, was apparently the son of Owen Roberts, a Welsh physician who settled in New York City about 1800 and died when Marshall was a child. The latter is said to have worked for a grocer, a saddler, and a ship chandler. By 1834 he was a ship chandler himself. He engaged in Hudson River navigation and is said to have been among the original promoters of the Erie and the Lackawanna railroads: of the former he was a director. Although he was financially successful almost from the beginning of his independent career, a search of the records reveals no basis for the story that President Harrison appointed him naval agent in charge of contracts at New York and that

heavy naval contracts in the Mexican War were the basis of his fortune.

In 1847 Roberts came into prominence through connection with government subsidy of mail steamships. With George Law [*q.v.*] and others as joint trustees, he took over the contract just awarded to Albert G. Sloo. This contract granted $290,000 annually for ten years for fortnightly service from New York to New Orleans, touching at Havana, where a branch line was run to the Isthmus of Panama to connect with the Pacific Mail Steamship Company of William Henry Aspinwall [*q.v.*]. Their first ship sailed late in 1848, just at the start of the gold rush, an unforeseen piece of luck which tremendously increased business. In 1851, they started direct lines from New York and New Orleans to Aspinwall on the Isthmus, in addition to the stipulated Havana run, receiving no added subsidy. Meanwhile in 1850 Roberts and his associates organized the United States Mail Steamship Company (incorporated Apr. 6, 1850), to which they assigned their interests in the Sloo contract. In 1854 Roberts, who had been New York agent, succeeded Law as president and two years later, in a suit in equity brought by Sloo (3 *Blatchford, Circuit Court Reports,* 459) he in particular was charged with unscrupulous manipulation of "the business controlled by the trustees" in favor of the United States Mail Steamship Company. Sloo was granted an injunction which somewhat hampered Roberts' operations. By this time the gold rush had waned and the competition of Cornelius Vanderbilt [*q.v.*] had materially reduced profits; in 1858 when the contract expired, Roberts estimated that the company had lost two millions. He then made a brazen attempt to recover this loss from the government on the flimsy ground that there had been no added subsidy for the extra direct service to Aspinwall. Intensive lobbying finally produced an act of Congress referring Roberts' case to the Court of Claims, which rejected his claim (6 *Court of Claims Reports,* 84), but in 1875 Roberts and an associate received $1,031,000 through a Supreme Court decision (*Roberts* vs. *U. S., 92 U. S.,* 41, and 11 *Court of Claims,* 774).

Roberts' chartering and selling of steamships during the Civil War forms an interesting chapter in the history of profiteering. He made nearly three millions from a half dozen steamers picked up for a song. The $12,500 he received for sending the *Star of the West* to relieve Fort Sumter was a mere bagatelle. It is said that he sold the *Union* as a transport for $100,000 and she sank almost at once. He bought the *Empire City* at auction from his old company for

$12,000 and the army alone paid him at least $900,000 in addition to what he received from naval charters. The *Illinois* brought some $414,-000 in charters and then, early in 1865, was purchased at Lincoln's order for $400,000. This price was set by a board headed by Roberts' friend Moses Taylor, though army officers thought her worth only half that price. Congress investigated these dealings in 1866 and 1878 but nothing happened. Roberts made several generous gestures during the war with gifts and bond purchases, and, as his obituary remarked, "his patriotism stood him in good stead" (*New York Herald,* Sept. 12, 1880).

His political career may partially explain this success. He was rated with A. T. Stewart as one of the leading Republican contributors. An anti-Seward Whig and then a Republican, he was defeated for Congress in 1852 and was a delegate to the first Republican National Convention in 1856. In 1865, he lost the New York mayoralty to J. T. Hoffman [*q.v.*] by a narrow margin. In 1868, he was a presidential elector and helped finance the senatorial election of R. E. Fenton [*q.v.*], but Fenton's backing failed to secure for Roberts the nomination for governor in 1870. Just before the exposure of the "Tweed ring," Roberts, John Jacob Astor, Moses Taylor, and three others certified that its financial affairs were "administered in a correct and faithful manner" (Lynch, *post,* p. 347).

Roberts continued active in shipping, running a line to Havana, planning Nicaragua service, and keeping alive the Mexican charter for a Tehuantepec railroad. He was for many years president of the North River Bank. In 1854, he had been one of a group of five to finance Field's first cable venture. He had an art collection appraised at half a million in his mansion at 107 Fifth Avenue. He worshipped for years at the Broadway Tabernacle; finally at Calvary Church. The first of his three wives was a Miss C. D. Amerman of New York City; the second, Caroline D. Smith of Hartford, whom he married in 1847; she was an organizer of the Young Women's Christian Association, and died in 1874. His third wife was Susan Lawrence Endicott, daughter of John Endicott of New York City. Roberts died at Saratoga Springs at the age of sixty-six.

[Gustavus Myers, *Hist. of the Great Am. Fortunes* (1910); D. T. Lynch, *"Boss" Tweed* (1927); D. S. Alexander, *A Pol. Hist. of the State of N. Y.,* vol. III (1909); E. H. Mott, *Between the Ocean and the Lakes: The Story of Erie* (1899); for the U. S. Mail S. S. Company, *Sen. Report 440,* 34 Cong., 3 Sess., *Sen. Report 326,* 35 Cong., 1 Sess., *House Report 648,* 36 Cong., 1 Sess., pp. 797, 809, 823–29, *Sen. Report 292,* 36 Cong., 2 Sess., *House Report 49,* 37 Cong., 3 Sess., pp. 94–96; for Civil War charters and sales,

House Report 49, 37 Cong., 3 Sess., p. 95; *House Ex. Doc. 65,* 39 Cong., 2 Sess.; *House Ex. Doc. 337,* 40 Cong., 2 Sess.; *House Ex. Doc. 92,* 45 Cong., 2 Sess.; *Official Records of the Union and Confederate Navies,* 1 ser. IV, 245, VII, 158–64.]   R. G. A.

ROBERTS, NATHAN S. (July 28, 1776–Nov. 24, 1852), civil engineer, was born in Piles Grove, N. J., the son of Abraham Roberts, a native of New Hampshire whose Puritan forefathers, emigrating from England in 1640, had settled in Auburn, Mass. During his minority Nathan helped to support his parents and younger brothers. When he became of age he purchased a hundred acres of land in Vermont, where he began the cutting of timber, but he returned to New Jersey and taught school at Plainfield during the winter. In 1804, he moved to Oneida County, N. Y., where he acquired some land. He taught school at Oriskany until 1806, when he was appointed principal of the academy at Whitesboro. Here, on Nov. 4, 1816, he married Lavinia, daughter of Ansel White and grand-daughter of Judge Hugh White, pioneer settler of the region; in the same year he purchased a farm in Lenox, Madison County, which was his home during the remainder of his life.

In July 1816 he became an assistant to Benjamin Wright of Rome, engineer in charge of the building of the middle section of the Erie Canal, in making a survey of the route. From that time until 1822 he was engaged in exploratory surveys and location work on the section of the canal between Rome and Rochester, including the drafting of plans for locks between Clyde and Rochester. From 1822 until its completion in 1825, he was in charge of the construction of the western section of the canal, from Lockport to Buffalo. He drafted the plan which was adopted and superintended the construction of five pairs of locks at Lockport to overcome the barrier formed by a sixty-foot rocky ridge—a more elaborate scheme of locks than had ever been constructed in America.

Upon the completion of the Erie Canal, he became a consulting engineer for the Chesapeake & Delaware Canal and in 1826, for the state of New York, made a survey and reported on a route for a ship canal around Niagara Falls. Then followed service as chief engineer of the western end of the Pennsylvania State Canal, that part between Pittsburgh and Kiskimenetas. During a visit home he made an investigation and report for the New York State Canal Board on the practicability of supplying the summit level of the projected Chenango Canal with water. In association with James Geddes [*q.v.*] he reviewed the estimates of the line of the Chesapeake & Ohio Canal for the secretary of war and subsequently examined the country between Johnstown and Franktown for a possible route for a railroad or portage over the mountains to connect the eastern and western sections of the Pennsylvania State Canal. From December 1828, as a member of the board of engineers of the Chesapeake & Ohio Canal Company, he was engaged for some two years in the revision and location of extensions of that canal, building the section between Point of Rocks and Harpers Ferry, and during the same period was associated with Jonathan Knight [q.v.] in preliminary work in the same territory for the Baltimore & Ohio Railroad. Having made a reputation as a canal engineer, he was appointed by the federal government to take charge of surveys for a ship canal around Muscle Shoals in the Tennessee River, Alabama. In the spring of 1835, in association with John B. Jervis [q.v.] and Holmes Hutchinson, he made a series of examinations and surveys for the New York State Canal Board to estimate the expense of enlarging the Erie Canal, and in 1839, as chief engineer, began the enlargement of the canal between Rochester and Buffalo. In 1841, while still thus engaged and about to complete his last great task, the Rochester Aqueduct, he was removed from office for political reasons, by the new Whig administration. Since through his profession he had attained sufficient means to make him financially independent, he now retired to his farm in Madison County, where he spent his remaining years.

[Practically the only biography is that in C. B. Stuart, *Lives and Works of Civil and Military Engineers* (1871), although scattered references occur in material on the Erie Canal and the other works with which Roberts was connected. Since Roberts had a son named Nathan Smith Roberts, it seems probable that Smith was the father's middle name. See A. S. Kellogg, *White Geneal.* (1860).]

B. A. R.

ROBERTS, ORAN MILO (July 1815–May 19, 1898), lawyer, jurist, soldier, statesman, was born in Laurens District, S. C., the son of Obe Roberts, of Welsh ancestry, and Margaret Ewing. From South Carolina his father removed with his family to Ashville, in the mountain region of northern Alabama, where he died when Oran was but ten years of age. Soon thereafter the widow moved to a small farm on which her son labored until he was sixteen. At that age he announced that he was going to college, a resolve that he was enabled to carry into execution with the financial assistance of his brother-in-law, Robert Bourland, a blacksmith, and with the tutoring of Ralph P. Lowe [q.v.], afterward a member of the supreme court of Iowa, who prepared him to enter the university. In

1836, at the age of twenty-one, he graduated from the University of Alabama. He at once began the study of law with Judge Ptolemy Harris, whose children he tutored to defray his expenses. Later he read law in the office of William P. Chilton, who was subsequently a member of the supreme court of Alabama. He was admitted to the bar on Sept. 22, 1837, and for four years practised law, first in Talladega and later in Ashville, Ala. During this time he served one term in the legislature to which he was elected when but twenty-three years of age. In 1841 he answered the call of the new West and moved to Texas and took up the practice of law at San Augustine, near the eastern border of the infant republic. Although this little city then had one of the strongest bars in the country, young Roberts rose rapidly and was soon riding an extensive circuit of eastern Texas counties along with the district judge and the lawyers of established practice. On Feb. 6, 1844, a little more than two years after his arrival in Texas, President Houston appointed him district attorney. Two years later he was appointed district judge by J. Pinkney Henderson, the first governor of Texas. This position he held until 1851. On Feb. 1, 1857, he was elected associate justice of the supreme court of Texas to fill the vacancy caused by the death of Judge A. S. Lipscomb.

In spite of his position on the bench, he took an active part in the slavery controversy and was elected by acclamation president of the convention that met in Austin in January 1861 and submitted the secession ordinance to a vote of the people. Late in 1861 he resigned from the court and early in 1862 he raised a regiment, the 11th Texas Infantry, and became its colonel. For two years he served in the army with distinction, but upon the death of Chief Justice Royall T. Wheeler, Roberts, while still with his command in Louisiana, was elected chief justice in 1864. This office he held until the collapse of the Confederate cause in 1865. He was chairman of the judiciary committee in the constitutional convention of 1866. In August of that year he was elected to the United States Senate but was not allowed to take his seat. During the next eight years he practised his profession at Tyler, and at Gilmer, where for a time he conducted a law school.

After the Democratic party returned to power in Texas in 1873, Roberts in January 1874 was appointed chief justice of the supreme court. His opinions show a capacity for research and a power of analysis that mark him as one of the greatest judges the state of Texas has ever had. In *Hancock* vs. *Butler* (21 *Tex.*, 804) he introduced into the jurisprudence of Texas the rule in Shelley's Case and explained its intricacies; while in *Chambers* vs. *Fisk* (*22 Tex.*, 504) he discussed the action of trespass to try title to land and gave a comprehensive history of the land law of Texas from early Spanish days. In *McCoy* vs. *The State* (*25 Tex.*, 33) he gave an exhaustive treatment of "malice aforethought" in murder, while an equally thorough treatment of assault is to be found in *McKay* vs. *The State* (*44 Tex.*, 43). In *Houston Tap and Brazoria Railway Company* vs. *Randolph* (*24 Tex.*, 317) and in his dissenting opinion in *Kuechler* vs. *Wright* (*40 Tex.*, 600, 647) he strongly argued that, in a government divided into separate and coördinate departments, no court could have jurisdiction to issue a writ of *mandamus* to the head of any executive department to compel the performance of an official duty, but in this opinion the majority of the court refused to follow him, and their view was incorporated into the constitution of 1876.

In 1878, while still chief justice, Roberts was elected governor, and in 1880 he was reëlected. As governor he adopted as his motto "Pay as you go," and as a result the financial condition of the state was greatly improved. The outstanding achievement of his administration was the establishment of the University of Texas, which opened its doors in the fall of 1883. Upon his retirement from the governor's office, in 1883, he was elected professor of law in the University. He resigned this position in 1893 and died in Austin on May 19, 1898. In December 1837, shortly after having been admitted to the bar, he had married Frances W. Edwards, daughter of Maj. Peter Edwards, of Ashville, Ala. They lived together until her death in 1883 and reared a family of six children, a seventh having died in infancy. In December 1887 he was married at Tyler to Catherine E. Border, widow of one of his earliest friends in Texas, Col. John P. Border, who had fought in the battle of San Jacinto and had been a colonel in the Confederate army. In spite of his arduous duties as a public officer and a teacher of law, the "Old Alcalde," as Roberts was affectionately called, found time to do some literary work. In 1881, while serving as governor, he published *A Description of Texas, Its Advantages and Resources*, a booklet of 133 pages. In 1890 he published *The Elements of Texas Pleading*, and two years later *Our Federal Relations, from a Southern View of Them*. In 1898, there appeared from his pen the political history of Texas down to 1895, published as the first 325 pages of Volume II of D. G. Wooten's *Comprehensive History of*

Texas. He also contributed chapters on Texas to Clement A. Evans' *Confederate Military History* (vol. XI, 1899).

[See: L. E. Daniell, *Types of Successful Men of Tex.* (1890); J. D. Lynch, *The Bench and Bar of Tex.* (1885); D. G. Wooten, "The Life and Services of Oran Milo Roberts," *Quart. of the Tex. State Hist. Asso.*, July 1898; 92 *Tex. Reports*, v–xii; *Biog. Encyc. of Tex.* (1880); W. S. Speer and J. H. Brown, *The Encyc. of the New West* (1881); H. S. Thrall, *A Pictorial Hist. of Tex.* (1879); *Daily Express* (San Antonio, Tex.), May 20, 1898. Roberts' opinions are to be found in 19–27 and 40–49 *Tex. Reports*.]
C. S. P—s.

ROBERTS, ROBERT RICHFORD (Aug. 2, 1778–Mar. 26, 1843), bishop of the Methodist Episcopal Church for nearly twenty-seven years, was born in Frederick County, Md. His father, Robert Morgan Roberts, of Welsh descent, was a farmer of small means and a Revolutionary soldier; his mother, Mary, daughter of Thomas and Esther Richford, was probably of Irish ancestry. Robert was one of thirteen children and the third of that name, two others to whom it was given having died when young. He was taught the rudiments of reading, writing, and arithmetic and instructed in the catechism of the Church of England, of which his father was a stanch adherent. In 1785 the family moved to Ligonier Valley, Westmoreland County, Pa., undeveloped country where frontier conditions prevailed. Although he was but seven years old, Robert's schooling was now practically ended; his time was occupied in helping clear the land for cultivation. Methodist preachers entered the neighborhood, and yielding to their influence in spite of his father's Episcopalian prejudices, Robert was converted and joined a Methodist society. In the spring of 1796, with several companions, he made an exploratory expedition into the Shenango district, now Mercer County, Pa., and the following year with two of his brothers took up land there. For some five years he was a frontiersman, living in a log cabin, clearing land, planting crops, fishing, hunting, and selling furs. In January 1799 he married Elizabeth, daughter of Thomas and Hannah Oldham of York County, Pa.

From the time of his conversion he was regarded by his Methodist associates as suited for the ministry. Although without education, he had a good mind, was sincerely religious, and possessed the qualities of character that command confidence. The Shenango settlement grew and a Methodist society was formed there, Roberts becoming class leader. He was urged to become a preacher but natural diffidence and a feeling of unpreparedness held him back. In 1802, however, he applied for a license, which was granted, and the same year he was admitted on trial to the Baltimore Conference. On Apr. 28, 1804, he was ordained deacon by Bishop Asbury, and on Mar. 20, 1806, elder. The first years of his ministry were spent on long and hard circuits in Pennsylvania, Maryland, and Virginia. He received little salary, was very poor, and, unlike most of the itinerant preachers, was encumbered by a wife. In the hope of adding to his means of support he built a mill on land he owned in Erie County. This took him from his calling and caused some grumbling. One person, zealous for the interests of the kingdom of God, harshly declared that "it would be well for the people if his (Roberts') wife were dead and the mill swept down the river" (Elliott, *post*, p. 131). His Conference reproved him in 1808 for neglecting his appointments. That same year he started for the General Conference to be held in Baltimore with only a dollar in his pocket, and biscuits, cheese, and oats in his saddle-bags. During the session he preached to the Methodists of Baltimore with such acceptance that on their request Bishop Asbury stationed him there. Later he was appointed to Fell's Point (1810), Alexandria (1811), Georgetown (1812), and Philadelphia (1813–14). In 1815 he became presiding elder of the Schuylkill district. Owing to the death of Bishop Asbury and the illness of Bishop McKendree, it was necessary to elect a presiding officer at the Philadelphia Conference of 1816, and Roberts was chosen. He filled the chair with such dignity and displayed such well-balanced judgment that he became the nominee of the Northern Conferences for bishop. The Westerners were surprised and delighted to have one of their "fellow backwoodsmen" put forward, and at the General Conference of 1816 he was elected.

For more than a quarter of a century he performed the arduous duties of his office, involving thousands of miles of travel to all sections of the country. Of more than average height and of heavy frame, he was physically fitted for strenuous activity, and his frontier training stood him in good stead. During the last year of his life he visited six different states and four Indian territories, on horseback and in carriage, stage, and steamboat covering 5,484 miles. He was a simple, direct, and effective speaker, and a dignified, imperturbable, and judicious administrator. "It was his peculiar temperament," says a contemporary, "to pursue with steady and untiring perseverance whatever he undertook, without even the appearance of zeal, or any movement that would create the least noise, or attract the gaze of public attention to his course. He was

always silent, except when compelled to speak; he was in the rear and shade, except when thrust out into observation . . ." (Elliott, pp. 256–57). In some respects he remained a backwoodsman. His first episcopal residence was his old cabin in Shenango; in 1819 he moved to Lawrence County, Ind., where he had as a home another rough cabin, built in part by himself. Here he died, and his body was buried in a cornfield on his own farm. Soon, however, it was removed to the grounds of Indiana Asbury University (now De Pauw), Greencastle, Ind.

[Chas. Elliott, *The Life of the Rev. Robert R. Roberts* (1844); *Minutes of the Ann. Conferences of the M. E. Ch., for the Years 1842–1843* (1843); *Ladies' Repository*, Apr. 1844; T. L. Flood and J. W. Hamilton, *Lives of Meth. Bishops* (1882); Abel Stevens, *Hist. of the M. E. Ch. in the U. S. A.*, vol. IV (1867).]

H. E. S.

ROBERTS, SOLOMON WHITE (Aug. 3, 1811–Mar. 22, 1882), civil engineer, was born in Philadelphia, Pa., the son of Charles and Hannah (White) Roberts. His father taught in one of the Friends' schools of that city and there the boy received his early education. When about sixteen years old he left school and was employed by his uncle, Josiah White, manager of the Lehigh Coal & Navigation Company's works at Mauch Chunk, Pa., as an assistant in the building of the first tramway constructed in Pennsylvania, opened for use in the spring of 1827. Shortly afterward he became rodman with a party of engineers of this same company and was subsequently assistant engineer on a section of the Lehigh Canal being built near Mauch Chunk. Here he was associated with William Milnor Roberts [*q.v.*], who was later his colleague on the Allegheny Portage Railroad. Upon completion of the Lehigh Canal in the autumn of 1829, he entered the service of the state of Pennsylvania in connection with its canal construction on the Conemaugh River, and was stationed at Blairsville, Pa., as assistant to Sylvester Welch, the principal engineer, until the work was completed in the spring of 1831. He then became a principal assistant engineer on the Portage Railroad over the Alleghanies, another section of the Pennsylvania public works, and led the exploring and locating party upon the western half of the line. Later he designed and supervised the construction of a masonry viaduct to carry the railroad over the Conemaugh River at Horse Shoe Bend. After the completion of the Portage Railroad he remained as its resident engineer and superintendent of transportation until 1836, when he resigned and went to England to procure and superintend the manufacture of iron rails for the Philadelphia & Reading and other railroads. During the two years which he spent in this way he formed a friendship with George Crane, a Welshman who had obtained a patent from the British government for the application of the hot-blast to the smelting of iron ore with anthracite coal. It was through Roberts' explanation of Crane's process to his uncle, Josiah White, and to the Franklin Institute of Pennsylvania, that the first successful anthracite furnace in the Lehigh Valley was built, at Catasauqua, Pa., in 1839–40, by the Lehigh Crane Iron Company. From 1838 to 1841, Roberts was the chief engineer of the Catawissa Railroad. In 1842 he became president of the Philadelphia, Germantown & Norristown Railroad Company and in 1843, president of the Schuylkill Navigation Company, holding this office until 1845. In 1847 he took an active part in securing the charter of the Pennsylvania Railroad Company and that same year was elected to the state House of Representatives, where he served during the session of 1848. During this session much important railroad legislation was passed and his experience in railroad matters enabled him to take a leading part in shaping it. In 1848 he became the chief engineer of the Ohio & Pennsylvania Railroad then being constructed from Pittsburgh to the Ohio state line and was responsible for the location of the line as far as Crestline, Ohio; he selected both the sites and the names of the towns of Crestline and Alliance. He planned the railroad bridge across the Allegheny River at Pittsburgh, connecting the Ohio & Pennsylvania Railroad with the Pennsylvania Railroad. As the various sections of the Ohio & Pennsylvania were opened he became the general superintendent and remained in charge of the road until 1856, when he resigned and returned to Philadelphia to accept the position of chief engineer and general superintendent of the North Pennsylvania Railroad, which was completed to Bethlehem, Pa., in 1857. He retained this position until 1879, when he retired. He was a member of a number of learned societies and contributed several papers to the *Transactions* of the American Philosophical Society and to scientific journals. He also wrote "Reminiscences of the First Railroad Over the Allegheny Mountain" (*Pennsylvania Magazine of History and Biography,* vol. II, no. 4, 1878; separately printed, 1879) and a published address, *The Destiny of Pittsburgh and the Duty of Her Young Men* (1850). He was married to Anna Smith Rickey. He died while on a visit to Atlantic City, N. J.

[W. B. Wilson, *Hist. of the Pa. Railroad Company* (1899), vol. I; J. M. Swank, *Introduction to a Hist. of Ironmaking and Coal Mining in Pa.* (1878) and *Hist. of the Manufacture of Iron in All Ages* (1884); *Biog.*

Encyc. of Pa. (1874); *Railroad Gazette,* Mar. 31, 1882; *Public Ledger* (Phila.), Mar. 24, 1882.]   J. H. F.

ROBERTS, THEODORE (Oct. 8, 1861–Dec. 14, 1928), actor, was born in San Francisco, the son of Martin R. and Mary E. (Newlin) Roberts, and was educated in the public schools there and at the California Military Academy in Oakland. With the exception of two and a half years at sea, a part of the time as captain of a schooner trading along the Pacific coast, he was uninterruptedly on the stage, acting many rôles, especially those to which he was individually suited because of his large stature, his heavy voice, and his imperious manner. He made his first appearance at the Baldwin Theatre in San Francisco, May 1, 1880, as Baradas to James O'Neill's Richelieu; but he soon found, as he said later, that he was "too big to support an American tragedian," meaning that his size, even if not his acting, would be to the disadvantage of the star by turning the eyes of the audience too often in his own direction. One of his earliest traveling engagements was in *Our Bachelors,* in support of Stuart Robson and William H. Crane, with whom he made his first New York appearance in 1881. After his return to the stage following his sea adventure, he acted for several seasons in support of Fanny Davenport, playing leading parts in her repertory; later he was with Mrs. Leslie Carter as Colonel Fulton Thorpe in *The Heart of Maryland,* as Colonel Sapt in *Rupert of Hentzau,* and as Henry Canby in Augustus Thomas' *Arizona,* in which he gave an extremely realistic portraiture of a typical stage ranchman, a part he played in 1902 at the Adelphi Theatre in London. Other stars whom he supported were Lawrence Barrett, James K. Hackett, and Bertha Kalich. When he appeared in New York as Tabywana in *The Squaw Man,* he equipped himself for the accurate interpretation of the Indian manner and nature by engaging a Ute Indian as coach; this, however, was not his début as an Indian, for twelve years before he had acted Scar Brow in *The Girl I Left Behind Me.* For a number of years thereafter he acted many rôles in a varied assortment of plays, the last that of Buck Kamman, the sheriff in *Believe Me, Xantippe,* in 1913. His final years as an actor, after a brief experience on the vaudeville stage, were spent in California in the making of motion pictures, his attitude towards that modern development of his profession being expressed in his remark (*New York Herald Tribune, post*) that he "looked upon the industry as a retiring place for broken-down actors." He died in Los Angeles while he was in the midst of preparations for the making of a new film.

His stalwart and heavily built figure, his long, straight features, his ruddy complexion and dark blue eyes especially adapted him to the impersonation of Indians, frontiersmen, sheriffs, and other primitive and robustious types conspicuous in the characteristically American plays that have long been popular in the United States. His first wife was Clyde O'Brien, known on the stage as Clyde Harron, whom he married in San Francisco in 1890 and later divorced; his second wife, according to an interview in the *New York Herald Tribune* (*post*), was Florence Smythe.

[*Who's Who in America*, 1918–19; John Parker, *Who's Who in the Theatre*, 1925; *N. Y. Dramatic Mirror*, Jan. 11, 1911; *N. Y. Herald Tribune*, Jan. 3, 1926; obit. notice in *Boston Transcript*, Dec. 15, 1928.]

E. F. E.

ROBERTS, WILLIAM CHARLES (Sept. 23, 1832–Nov. 27, 1903), Presbyterian clergyman, educator, was born at Galltmai, near Aberystwyth, Wales, the son of Charles Cross and Magdalene (Evans) Roberts. His father was a well-educated farmer. During William's seventeenth year financial reverses brought the family to America while the cholera epidemic of 1849 was raging at New York. Within a week after landing both parents and two of the children died of the disease. Left the eldest of six orphans, William in a few months began work for a leather manufacturer at Elizabeth, N. J. The ambition to become a professional man which had led him to Evans Academy in Aberystwyth soon took him, however, to the school of the Rev. David H. Pierson, and in 1852 he entered the College of New Jersey as a sophomore. After graduation with honors in 1855, he read law and served as private tutor, but during the winters studied in Princeton Theological Seminary, from which he was graduated in 1858. On Oct. 13 of that year he was ordained by the Presbytery of Newcastle, and six days later was married to Mary Louise Fuller.

His initial pastorate was at the First Presbyterian Church, Wilmington, Del., where he remained until 1862. The next two years he served the First Church, Columbus, Ohio. In December 1864 he became the colleague of his former pastor, Dr. David Magie, at the Second Church, Elizabeth, N. J., and, on the latter's death the following May, his successor. When the city's growth required the organization of another church, Westminster was formed with one hundred members—all except seven from Second Church—with Roberts as pastor. The congregation grew rapidly, and in time erected one of the most costly edifices in New Jersey. He was sent to Great Britain in 1877 as a delegate to the Council of Presbyterian Churches, an honor

twice repeated in later years. In 1889 he was moderator of the General Assembly.

Although Roberts held these notable pastorates, his most marked contribution was to Christian education. While at Wilmington he served Lafayette College as a trustee (1859–62); during his pastorate at Columbus, he was a member of a committee that prepared the way for the founding of the College of Wooster; he was a trustee of the College of New Jersey (1866–86); and he declined the presidency of Rutgers College in 1882. In that year he became secretary of the denomination's Board of Home Missions, holding the position until 1886 and again from 1893 to 1898. During the intervening seven years he was president of Lake Forest College, Ill. Under his leadership, the faculty was augmented, new departments were created, and funds amounting to about $1,000,000 were raised. The number of students increased to more than 1,500. His last five years were spent as president of Centre College, Danville, Ky., during which period, in 1901, Centre College and Central University at Richmond, Ky., united to form the Central University of Kentucky. His death occurred at Danville two years after the union.

A versatile man, Roberts attained appreciable success in education, as a preacher and pastor, as an executive, and as a writer. He published numerous religious pamphlets in both English and Welsh, and several books, of which *Great Preachers of Wales* (1865) and *New Testament Conversions* attracted most attention.

[H. E. Dosker, *In Memoriam* (1908); *The Biog. Encyc. of N. J. of the Nineteenth Century* (1877); *Gen. Cat. of Princeton Univ.*, 1746–1906 (1908); *Princeton Theological Sem. Biog. Cat.* (1909); *Necrological Report . . . Alumni Asso. of Princeton Theological Seminary* (1904); *The Presbyterian*, Dec. 2, 1903; *Who's Who in America*, 1903–05; *Evening Post* (Louisville, Ky.), Nov. 28, 1903.]

P. P. F.

ROBERTS, WILLIAM HENRY (Jan. 31, 1844–June 26, 1920), clergyman, leader in the Presbyterian Church, was born at Holyhead, Wales, the son of the Rev. William Roberts and Catherine (Parry). His father came to the United States in 1855, and for thirty years was a famous preacher in the Welsh Presbyterian Church. From him, in New York City, William Henry received much of his schooling, and then entered New York Free Academy (now the College of the City of New York), graduating in 1863. After four years as a statistician in the Treasury Department at Washington, he was assistant librarian in the Library of Congress from 1867 to 1872. During the later part of this time he carried on study in Princeton Theological Seminary, where he graduated in 1873. He was ordained by the Presbytery of Elizabeth on Dec.

5, 1873, and until 1877 was pastor of the Presbyterian Church at Cranford, N. J. During the next nine years he was librarian of Princeton Seminary. He was elected permanent clerk of the General Assembly of the Presbyterian Church in 1880, and in 1884, its stated clerk. From 1886 to 1893 he was professor of practical theology in Lane Theological Seminary, also having charge for two years of the Second Presbyterian Church of Cincinnati. To devote himself to the office of stated clerk he removed in 1893 to Philadelphia, thenceforth his home. From 1894 to 1899 he preached in the Second Presbyterian Church of Trenton, N. J. Intensely occupied with administration, he kept his enthusiasm for preaching, especially for evangelism. In Philadelphia he was a leader in social reforms and charities.

As stated clerk of the General Assembly for thirty-six years Roberts displayed an encyclopedic knowledge of the history, doctrine, law, and work of the Presbyterian Church, and a convinced devotion to Presbyterianism which would allow superiority to no other Christian organization. He managed the general organization of the Church with the ardor which marked his preaching. To keep pace with its rapid growth, he introduced improvements in administrative methods and records. Through the contacts with all of the church's activities—missionary, educational and philanthropic—which his office gave him, he exerted a wide and strong influence. Especially learned in church law, he edited *Supplement to the Presbyterian Digest, 1898–1906* (1907) and a revision of the *Manual of Law and Usage* (1913), and wrote *Laws Relative to Religious Corporations* (1896). In sessions of the General Assembly he displayed unequaled grasp of details, accomplished parliamentary skill, and a dynamic personality. His services won him unanimous election as moderator in 1907.

He was an inveterate foe of everything narrow and provincial in church life, and a tireless worker for larger fellowships. For forty-two years he was American secretary of the Alliance of Reformed Churches Holding the Presbyterian System and was president of the Council of the Alliance at Glasgow in 1896. As chairman of the commission on church cooperation and union of the General Assembly he did much to bring his church closer to others. For unity among Presbyterians he strove especially, and the unions of the Cumberland Presbyterian Church and the Welsh Presbyterian Church with the Presbyterian Church in the United States of America were largely due to him. In his personal capacity and then as a representative of his church he presided over the long negotiations which issued in the formation of the Federal Council of the Churches of Christ in America in 1908; and he was always foremost in its leadership. He zealously promoted the work preparatory to the World Conference on Faith and Order (Lausanne) which was done before the World War and was a member of a deputation representing the American churches which in 1914 visited the non-Anglican churches of the British Isles to secure their participation in the Conference.

Besides his legal works, he published *A History of the Presbyterian Church* (1888), *The Presbyterian System* (1895), *A Concise History of the Presbyterian Church in the U. S. A.* (1917), and numerous articles and addresses. He also edited the *Minutes of the General Assembly* from 1884 to 1919. He was married on June 11, 1867, to Sarah Esther McLean, of Washington, and left two sons and two daughters.

[*Princeton Theol. Sem. Biog. Cat.* (1909); *Necrological Report . . . Alumni Asso. of Princeton Theol. Sem.* (1921); J. R. Stevenson, "Churchmanship of William Henry Roberts," *Princeton Theol. Rev.*, Oct. 1920; *Minutes Gen. Assembly, passim*; *Who's Who in America,* 1920–21; *Public Ledger* (Phila.), June 27, 1920.]

R. H. N.

ROBERTS, WILLIAM MILNOR (Feb. 12, 1810–July 14, 1881), civil engineer, was born in Philadelphia, Pa., the son of Thomas Pascal and Mary Louise (Baker) Roberts. He was of Welsh Quaker descent, his family having come to America with William Penn. Roberts was educated in a Friends' school in Philadelphia, then took a special course in mathematics for two terms, after which he studied architectural drafting under John Haviland [*q.v.*]. Completing his education at the age of fifteen, he joined the engineering corps under Sylvester Welch which was engaged in the construction of the Union Canal of Pennsylvania from the Schuylkill at Reading to the Susquehanna a little below Harrisburg. In 1826 he was a rodman in the preliminary survey for the construction of a macadam road across the Alleghany Mountains in Pennsylvania to connect the canal system on the eastern with that on the western slope, and in the following year he began work as an assistant in the survey and construction of the Lehigh Canal between Mauch Chunk and Philadelphia. He helped in the improvement of the inclined planes at Mauch Chunk and took part in the construction and operation of the coal railroad connected therewith. Four years later, in 1831, he was appointed senior assistant engineer under Welch for the survey of the proposed Alleghany Portage Railroad. William Milnor Roberts was in charge of the location of the eastern part of the line, from the headwaters of the

Conemaugh over the summit and down to Hollidaysburg, and subsequently superintended the construction of eight of the ten inclined planes. Upon the completion of this work in 1834 he served as general manager of the road until January 1835, when he became chief engineer of the Lancaster & Harrisburg Railroad.

Roberts was now only twenty-five years old, but he had had ten years' experience in canal and railway transportation, possessed much mechanical ability, and had developed a special aptitude for design. He remained with the Lancaster & Harrisburg from 1835 to 1837, assuming, in addition, the position of chief engineer of the Cumberland Valley, and completed the construction of both roads. One of his greatest engineering feats at this time was the construction at Harrisburg in 1837 of a two-level lattice-truss bridge across the Susquehanna River, carrying a double-track railroad above and a double carriage-way and footpaths below. Continuing in the capacity of consulting engineer for the railroads, he was given charge, 1838–40, of the extensions of the Pennsylvania state canals, particularly in the western part of the state. For the next eight years he was engaged chiefly in canal construction, enlarging the Welland Canal in Canada, directing the enlargement of the Erie Canal of Pennsylvania, and acting as chief engineer of the Sandy & Beaver Canal in Ohio. In 1849 he returned to railroad work, building the Bellefontaine & Indiana, the Allegheny Valley, the Atlantic & Mississippi, and the Iron Mountain railroads, and serving as chairman of a commission appointed by the legislature to consider the reconstruction of the Allegheny Portage Railroad. During this period the battle of railroad gauges was being waged, some railroads favoring a 6' and others a 4' 8½" width. Roberts strongly advocated the latter gauge and succeeded in bringing about its adoption as the standard. In 1855–57 he was engaged in the construction of a number of Middle-Western railroads, and late in the latter year went to Brazil, where he obtained the contract to build the Dom Pedro Segundo Railroad. This difficult undertaking involved considerable tunneling and required eight years' time to complete.

Roberts returned to the United States in 1866, was almost immediately appointed on the commission to propose improvements of the Mississippi River at Keokuk, Iowa, and was also made United States engineer in charge of the improvement of navigation of the Ohio River. Taking leave of absence in 1868 from this position, he served as associate chief engineer in the construction of the Eads Bridge across the Mississippi at St. Louis. Late in 1869 he was appointed chief engineer of the Northern Pacific Railroad and continued in that position for a decade, during which time he also served as a member of the Mississippi River Jetty Commission by appointment of President Grant. In 1879 he accepted the appointment of chief engineer of all public works in Brazil, and for the remaining two and a half years of his life was occupied with the examination of rivers, harbors, and waterworks there.

Roberts was vice-president (1873–78) and president (1878) of the American Society of Civil Engineers. His writings, published principally in its *Transactions*, were usually descriptions of actual observations and expressions of opinion as to the application of experience to new engineering problems. He rarely developed mathematical theories, for he was opposed to the too free use of theoretical formulae. He was married twice: in June 1837 to Annie Gibson of Pennsylvania, who died in 1857; and in November 1868 to Adeline Beelen of Pittsburgh, who with three children and six children of his first wife survived him. He died of typhus fever at Soledade, Brazil, and was buried in Philadelphia.

[John Bogart, "William Milnor Roberts," in *Trans. Am. Soc. Civil Engineers,* vol. XXXVI (1897); Frederick Fraley, obituary notice of Roberts, in *Proc. Am. Philosophical Soc.,* vol. XX (1883); S. W. Roberts, "Reminiscences . . .," *Pa. Mag. of Hist. and Biog.,* vol. II, no. 4 (1878); *N. Y. Tribune,* July 22, 1881.]

C. W. M.

ROBERTS, WILLIAM RANDALL (Feb. 6, 1830–Aug. 9, 1897), politician, Fenian leader, congressman, was born at Mitchelstown, County Cork, Ireland. His parents are said to have been Randall and Mary (Bishop) Roberts. After receiving a limited schooling, he emigrated to New York in 1849. He worked as a drygoods clerk until 1857, when he set up in the same business on his own account, only to be ruined in the panic of that year. He succeeded in reëstablishing himself, however, and his store on the Bowery later became so popular that in 1869 he was able to retire with the reputation of being a millionaire.

During the Civil War he became prominent in the Irish societies of New York. In 1865 he was president of the Knights of St. Patrick. In 1863 he joined the Fenian Brotherhood, becoming president of its senate when the latter was organized in October 1865. He was a leader in the agitation against the president of the Brotherhood, John O'Mahony [q.v.]; and when in December an open quarrel occurred, the senate deposed O'Mahony and elected Roberts in his stead. O'Mahony and his followers continued their attempts to foment revolution in Ireland, while Roberts, on the other hand, with Gen. T. W. Sweeny [*q.v.*] as his "secretary of war," set in motion plans for invading Canada. They hurried the project on because of their desire to appear the party of action, and in the first week of June 1866, concentrated several thousand men at various points along the border. Except for a temporary success obtained by John O'Neill [*q.v.*], however, the scheme was a complete fiasco. The United States government, which so far had offered no opposition to the Fenian plans, now interfered; President Johnson issued a proclamation, and on June 7 Roberts and other leaders were arrested on charges of breech of the neutrality laws. Roberts, refusing to give bail, was soon released, and the government chose to *nolle prosequi* the charges before the congressional elections that autumn. In June 1867, Roberts went to Paris to meet representatives of the Brotherhood in the British Isles, to arrange for cooperation between their organization and his own; but the agreement then made does not seem to have been effectively implemented. At the end of 1867 he resigned from the presidency of the Brotherhood, believing mistakenly that his resignation would be followed by a reunion of his group with that formerly headed by O'Mahony.

His Fenian record was a useful foundation for a political career in New York City; and in 1870 he was elected as a Democratic representative to the Forty-second Congress, and reëlected in 1872. He did not stand for reëlection in 1874. Among the causes which he particularly supported in the House were the protection of American citizens abroad (with special reference to the Fenians imprisoned in Canada) and opposition to repressive measures in the South. He made more than one vehement attack on British policy. In 1878 and 1879 he was a member of the New York board of aldermen, and president of the board in the former year. In the Democratic rout of 1879, running on the Tammany ticket, he failed of election for sheriff. Although he had been a faithful Tammany man, he was one of the group that seceded from Tammany Hall in 1881 to form the New York County Democracy. For supporting Grover Cleveland in his state and national campaigns, he was rewarded by appointment in 1885 as United States minister to Chile (1885–89). His tenure of the post was uneventful, and before its end he suffered a paralytic stroke, May 18, 1888. He was brought back to the United States in 1889, and lived eight years longer without recovering his mental and physical health. He died at Bellevue Hospital, New York, in greatly reduced circumstances, survived by his wife, from whom he had been separated for some years, and by one son. Though he had once been a popular figure in New York politics, his reputation does not seem to have outlived his good health, and his death attracted little attention.

[John Rutherford, *The Secret Hist. of the Fenian Conspiracy* (2 vols., 1877); M. P. Breen, *Thirty Years of New York Politics* (1899); C. P. Stacey, "Fenianism and the Rise of National Feeling in Canada" (*Canadian Hist. Rev.*, Sept. 1931); *Papers Relating to the Foreign Relations of the U. S., 1888* (1889), pt. 1; *Biog. Dir. Am. Cong.* (1928); *Trow's New York City Directory,* 1869–70, 1879–80; *Irish American* (N. Y.), Jan. 13, Mar. 31 (portrait), 1866; *N. Y. Herald,* June 7, 8, 1866, Apr. 1, 1885; *Indianapolis News,* Aug. 12, 1897; *N. Y. Times,* Aug. 13, 1897; *Irish World* (N. Y.), Aug. 21, 1897.]   C. P. S.

ROBERTSON, ALICE MARY (Jan. 2, 1854– July 1, 1931), representative in Congress from Oklahoma, educator and social worker, was born at Tullahassee Mission, Indian Territory, the daughter of William Schenck [*q.v.*] and Ann Eliza (Worcester) Robertson. Her mother was the daughter of the noted missionary to the Cherokees, the Rev. Samuel A. Worcester [*q.v.*], and both parents gave the greater part of their lives to missionary work among the Creeks. When the Civil War broke out the Robertsons left the Indian Territory. Alice attended school in Wisconsin and at Highland, Kan., but returned with her parents to Tullahassee in 1866. For the next five years she received no formal schooling but studied under the direction of her father. In 1871 she entered Elmira College, New York, where she remained until 1873. Compelled to leave before graduating in order to provide for the education of her sister, she received from the college the honorary degree of A. M. in 1886. From 1873 to 1880 she was clerk in the Office of Indian Affairs at Washington and for the following two years she was secretary to Captain Pratt of Carlisle Indian School, but the death of her father and the failing health of her mother caused her to return to Indian Territory in 1882. Here she taught in an Indian school at Okmulgee and collected funds to erect the Creek school called Nuyaka Mission. In 1885 she was placed in charge of a Presbyterian school for girls at Muskogee. This later became Henry Kendall College and was eventually removed to Tulsa and became the University of Tulsa.

For nearly fifteen years Miss Robertson held various positions in Henry Kendall College. Her services to soldiers during the Spanish-American War brought her honorary membership in the organization of the Spanish American War Veterans. In 1900 she was made superintendent of Creek schools in Indian Territory and in 1905 was appointed postmaster of Muskogee by President Roosevelt. She held this position until 1913. For the next seven years she lived at her country place near Muskogee and operated it as "Sawokla Dairy Farm," at the same time operating "Sawokla Cafeteria" in Muskogee. During the World War she provided food and hot coffee for the soldiers who passed through Muskogee. Others joined her in this work and she became head of the canteen service of the city which fed thousands of soldiers. At her cafeteria, where no soldier was permitted to pay for a meal, she fed hundreds more. Her work attracted so much attention that in 1920 she was elected to Congress on the Republican ticket from the second Oklahoma district. When her term expired in 1923 she entered the Veterans' Hospital at Muskogee and for two years served as a welfare worker. Later she went to Washington as correspondent for the Muskogee *News*. Returning to Oklahoma she was employed by the Oklahoma Historical Society for two or three years to do research work, but age and ill health at last forced her to retire from active employment. The University of Oklahoma has named one of its largest dormitories for women, Robertson Hall, in her honor.

[Most of Alice Robertson's papers are in the manuscript collections of the University of Tulsa. Others consisting mostly of personal letters are in the possession of her sister, Mrs. Augusta R. Moore of Haskell, Okla. For printed sources see especially Grant Foreman, "The Lady from Okla.," *Independent*, Mar. 26, 1921; *Who's Who in America*, 1930–31; *Biog. Dir. Am. Cong.* (1928); S. A. Worcester, *The Descendants of Rev. Wm. Worcester* (1914); *Muskogee Daily Phœnix*, Nov. 19, 1922; July 2, 1931.]　　E. E. D.

ROBERTSON, ARCHIBALD (May 8, 1765–Dec. 6, 1835), miniaturist, the eldest son of William Robertson and Jean Ross, was born at Monymusk, Scotland. The father was an architect who removed to Aberdeen when Archibald was a child. Here, at King's College, the latter received his education, although apparently he was not graduated. In 1782 he went to Edinburgh to study the art of painting, having as associates Henry Raeburn, Walter Weir, and George Watson. After a few years he returned to Aberdeen for the benefit of his health, and in 1786 went to London, where he sought introductions to Benjamin West [q.v.] and Sir Joshua Reynolds. The latter was then the president of the Royal Academy, and told Robertson the steps necessary to enter that school. After a period of study there, Robertson again returned to Aberdeen where he became a successful painter of portraits of all sizes, including miniatures,

and of devices for jewelry. He also conducted a drawing academy until 1791, when he was invited by Dr. John Kemp [q.v.] of Columbia College (through Dr. Gordon of King's College, Aberdeen) to come to America. The Earl of Buchan, upon hearing of his intended departure, commissioned him to paint a portrait of George Washington. This he did in Philadelphia, then the capital of the United States, a few months after his arrival. He was received with much cordiality by Washington and his family, and while with them painted miniatures of both the President and Mrs. Washington. In 1792 Robertson sent for his brother, Alexander, still abroad studying art, and together they opened the Columbian Academy of Painting at 89 William St., New York. Four years later they settled at 79 Liberty St., and here Archibald continued his painting until 1828. Alexander conducted a drawing academy at various addresses in the city. Another brother, Andrew, was a very successful artist in London. A collection of his paintings is in the South Kensington Museum, London.

In addition to his work in portraiture, Robertson executed a number of water-color views of New York City. He had drawings and miniatures in the first, and later, exhibitions of the American Academy of Fine Arts (from 1816 on), and is listed as an Academician in 1817 when his brother, Alexander, was secretary. In that year he exhibited in the Academy his well-known cabinet portrait of Washington, painted in water-color on marble, and now, together with a number of his family miniatures, in the possession of the New York Historical Society. From 1817 to 1833 he served as a director of the Academy, and, with another artist, recommended the establishment of schools in that institution, but this proposal was defeated by the president through his influence with the board of directors, and the Academy became merely a society for the exhibition of pictures. Robertson wrote a "Treatise on Miniature Painting" which he sent to his brother Andrew at Aberdeen. This valuable work is printed in the *Letters and Papers of Andrew Robertson, A.M., Born 1777, Died 1845,* edited by Emily Robertson and published in London in 1895. He also edited a treatise for the use of his pupils, published under the title, *Elements of the Graphic Arts* (1802). At the opening of the Erie Canal in 1825 Robertson was placed in charge of the department of the fine arts in connection with the celebration, designing the badge used and the medal struck upon that occasion. His report is printed in Cadwallader D. Colden's *Memoir . . . at the*

Celebration of the Completion of the New York Canals (1825).

Robertson was a gentleman and a scholar. His literary pursuits included the study of several languages; as an amateur architect he made several designs for buildings; and he also recorded that he had an acquaintance with the construction of ships. In 1794 he married Eliza Abramse, daughter of Jacob Abramse, Jr., and Rachel Walker, his wife; to them were born ten children, six sons and four daughters. Mrs. Robertson was also an artist, judging by her pen-and-ink sketches of Shakespearian subjects in the possession of the family. The latter years of Robertson's life, when he was nearly blind, were spent in retirement.

[William Dunlap, *A Hist. of the Rise and Progress of the Arts of Design in the U. S.* (1834; rev. ed., 3 vols., 1918, ed. by F. W. Bayley and C. E. Goodspeed); I. N. Phelps Stokes, *The Iconography of Manhattan Island* (6 vols., 1915–28), esp. vols. I, III, V, VI; *N. Y. Hist. Soc. Quart. Bull.*, Apr. 1929; New York City directories; catalogues of the American Academy of Fine Arts; article by Edith Robertson Cleveland, a great-grand-daughter, in *Century Mag.*, May 1890; *N. Y. Geneal. and Biog. Record*, Apr. 1920.]

A. J. W.

ROBERTSON, ASHLEY HERMAN (Dec. 14, 1867–July 13, 1930), naval officer, the son of Alsephus Turner Robertson and Rebecca (Mitchell) Robertson, was born at Ashmore, Ill. He was graduated from the United States Naval Academy in 1888, and commissioned ensign in 1890. During the Spanish-American War he served in the gunboat *Castine* of the North Atlantic Fleet. In 1905 he was made executive officer of the monitor *Terror,* and in 1906 engineer officer of the battle-ship *Tennessee.* Two years later he became executive officer of the same ship, and was transferred to the navy yard at Puget Sound in 1909, being raised to the grade of commander the same year. After completing his tour of duty here in 1913, he commanded successively the cruisers *Charleston* and *Denver.* He was raised to the grade of captain on July 1, 1914, and took command in the same year of the battle-ship *California.* In 1915 he was made commander of the battle-ship *Colorado* and was then assigned to the *San Diego,* retaining that command until July 1, 1916, when he was sent to the Naval War College at Newport, R. I.

When the United States entered the World War in 1917, he was chief of the first naval district with headquarters at Boston. In July of that year he was placed in command of the transport *Mount Vernon,* formerly the German liner *Kronprinzessin Cecilie,* which had been taken over by the United States for naval transport

service. After a short period of liaison work with the army in the spring of 1918, he was given command of the battle-ship *New Mexico,* the first electric-drive battle-ship in the American navy. The year following the war he was made chief-of-staff at the Naval War College. In 1918 he was commissioned rear admiral and, from 1920 to 1922, commanded the destroyer force in the Atlantic Fleet. He was made assistant to the chief of naval operations in 1922 and served in this position until May 1923. He was then ordered to duty as commandant of the eleventh naval district and naval operating base with headquarters at San Diego, Cal. In 1926 he was given command of the Scouting Fleet for two years, with the rank of vice admiral, and was then ordered back to his former duty at San Diego.

In his forty-two years of active service he became one of the most notable figures of the American sea force, having commanded some of the best fighting units in the service, as well as having risen to the highest rank in the power of the navy to bestow. At his death he was third in rank by reason of seniority in his grade. For his services during the war he was awarded the Navy Cross and the Distinguished Service Medal. In 1908 he married Mrs. Juliette Winston Graham Bixby, who survived him at his death in San Diego. He was buried at Arlington National Cemetery, Washington, D. C.

[*Who's Who in America*, 1930–31; W. H. Perrin, A. A. Graham, D. M. Blair, *The Hist. of Coles County, Ill.* (1879); U. S. Navy Dept. Registers; *U. S. Navy Dept., Record of Medals of Honor Issued to Officers and Men of U. S. Navy* (1924); H. R. Stringer, ed., *The Navy Book of Distinguished Service* (1921); *Army and Navy Jour.,* and *Army and Navy Register,* July 19, 1930; *N. Y. Times,* July 14, 1930.]

L. H. B.

ROBERTSON, GEORGE (Nov. 18, 1790–May 16, 1874), congressman from Kentucky, jurist, author, was born near Harrodsburg, in Mercer County, Ky., the son of Alexander and Margaret (Robinson) Robertson who had moved to the Kentucky region from old Virginia in 1779. He was the grandson of James Robertson who, with his father of the same name, emigrated from the north of Ireland about 1737 and settled in western Virginia. After receiving an elementary education in his community, the boy was sent to Joshua Fry's school five miles from Danville, where he was taught Latin, French, and geography. He then studied at Transylvania University for about a year before going to Lancaster to enter the Rev. Samuel Finley's classical school. In this school he studied for about four months and taught for the following six months. Deciding to study law, he went to Frankfort to begin under Martin D. Hardin [q.v.], but, changing his mind, he returned to Lancaster to complete his course. In September 1809 he received his license to practise, and the following Nov. 28, he married Eleanor Bainbridge and began housekeeping in the small two-room house in which John Boyle [q.v.], Samuel McKee, his brother-in-law, and later Robert P. Letcher [q.v.] also set up housekeeping and from which each was first elected to the federal Congress. Elected to the Fifteenth Congress and two years later returned to the Sixteenth he served from 1817 until his resignation in 1821. He declined a third term. In Congress he developed a reputation as an able debater and fearless leader, connecting his name with at least three important questions. He introduced and helped push through the bill organizing the territory of Arkansas, and in the debate that followed he opposed the restrictions the antislavery members attempted to fasten upon the region; he initiated the legislation, passed in 1820, changing the land system, whereby the minimum acreage that could be bought was reduced to eighty and the price to $1.25 an acre; and he took a prominent part in opposing the attempt made to force the president to recognize the revolted South American countries, in spite of the facts that Clay was strongly advocating it and that Robertson was a Whig and had never before supported an administration measure.

He returned to Kentucky to pursue his own desires, resolutely refusing to be enticed away by high position either at home or abroad. Among the honors he pushed aside were the attorney-generalship of Kentucky, the governorship of the Territory of Arkansas, and a ministership to each of the countries of Colombia and Peru. Instead he served in the lower house of the Kentucky legislature, from 1822 to 1826 for Garrard County and in 1848 and 1851 to 1853 for Fayette County, and during the years 1823, 1825, 1826, and 1851 to 1853 he was the speaker. He took especial interest in the development of a common-school system of education for the state, and in 1823, as chairman of a committee on education, he made a detailed report to the legislature. In 1828 he accepted the appointment by Gov. Thomas Metcalfe of the secretaryship of state, but he soon relinquished it for a more important and congenial position. Back in the early twenties, when attempts had been made to legislate people out of their property, he had been a leader in the anti-relief party organized to combat the money heresies. In the old-court and the new-court troubles that fol-

lowed, he introduced a powerful protest in the legislature against banishing the old court. By 1828 the contest had been largely settled, and he was appointed to the court of appeals. The next year he was elevated to the chief justiceship, where he remained until 1843, when he resigned from the court. In 1834 he agreed to become a lecturer in the law school of Transylvania University, and this position he held for twenty-three years. He opposed emancipation as a cure for slavery; but when the Civil War came, he supported the Union. With the passing of time, in common with many other loyal Kentuckians, he became increasingly impatient with the military régime that was settled down upon the state. By 1864 many Kentuckians, having reached the limits of their patience, sent out, on the day of the election of a judge to the court of appeals, the name of Robertson in opposition to the military candidate. He was elected. He held his judgeship until 1870 when he became again the chief justice. The next year he was stricken with paralysis, and he became almost totally blind. He resigned on Sept. 5, 1871. Three years later he died in Lexington, where he had long made his home. His reputation as a jurist was high; he was an able orator, and he was a writer of some note. The state created a new county to be named for him. Among his writings are, *Scrap Book on Law and Politics, Men and Times* (1855), made up of various addresses, lectures before his law classes, formal papers, and reports; *An Address Delivered at Camp Madison, on the Fourth of July, 1843* (1843), and *An Outline of the Life of George Robertson, Written by Himself, with an Introduction and Appendix by his Son* (1876).

[Autobiography, *ante*; Lewis and R. H. Collins, *Hist. of Ky.* (2 vols., 1874); *Annals of Cong.*, 15 Cong., 2 Sess., cols. 1235, 1272, 1273, 16 Cong., 1 Sess., col. 1866–87, 2 Sess., col. 1043–55; *Biog. Encyc. of Ky.* (1878); *Biog. Cyc. of the Commonwealth of Ky.* (1896); *Daily Lexington Press*, May 17, 19, 1874.]

E. M. C.

ROBERTSON, JAMES (b. 1740), Royalist, printer and journalist, learned the printing trade from his father in Edinburgh, Scotland, and came to Boston with some of his countrymen before 1766. He worked as a journeyman with Mein & Fleming, who like himself were Royalists. His younger brother, Alexander (1742–1784), also trained as a printer at home, joined James at New York in a partnership on Beaver Street near the residence of General Gage, where, on May 8, 1769, they began the *New-York Chronicle*, a small quarto newspaper, which did not last a year; but it printed a number of distinctive articles, with diagrams, by members of the King's College faculty, on the theory of comets and the transit of Venus. They removed to Albany, where, subsidized by Sir William Johnson, they began a printery, and on Nov. 25, 1771, issued the first newspaper printed in the province outside of New York City. This newspaper, the *Albany Gazette,* continued until after Aug. 3, 1772, the last issue traced. The firm continued to do public printing in Albany as late as June 1776. Thomas (*post,* I, p. 313) says their press and types were left with a friend, who buried them on his farm outside of Albany, and that they were used in 1782 by Albany's second printing house.

In the same period the Robertsons formed a partnership with John Trumbull of Norwich, Conn., as general printers and publishers of the *Norwich Packet and the Connecticut, Massachusetts, New-Hampshire, & Rhode-Island Weekly Advertiser,* established on Oct. 7, 1773. Partnership with Trumbull was dissolved the beginning of May 1776, when Trumbull announced his adherence to the Whig interests. On May 29 of this year James's wife, Amy, died at Norwich, which seems to prove that James was active there while Alexander carried on simultaneously joint interests at Albany. These brothers, both Royalists, removed to New York City after the British captured the city in September 1776. James began there, at Queen Street, on Jan. 16, 1777, the *Royal American Gazette.* From this time until the end of July 1783 the journal was published by him, or with his brother, or by Alexander alone, or, as from Jan. 1, 1782, until the partnership was dissolved on Aug. 5, 1783, by the Robertsons in partnership with Nathaniel Mills and John Hicks.

James Robertson had followed the British army to Philadelphia in February 1778 and opened a printing office on Front Street, between Chestnut and Walnut Streets, establishing the *Royal Pennsylvania Gazette,* a semi-weekly, on Mar. 3, which was suspended with Number 25, May 26, 1778. The two last issues printed descriptive accounts of the Meschianza entertainment given in honor of General Sir William Howe. James Robertson returned to New York when the British evacuated Philadelphia in June 1778 and opened a new business at 857 Hanover Square. With Donald Macdonald and Alexander Cameron, fellow countrymen whom he had known in Philadelphia, he went to Charleston, S. C., and began, at 20 Broad Street, in the spring of 1780, the *Royal South Carolina Gazette.* In time he became the sole proprietor, and carried on till the issue of Sept. 12, 1782,

and then suspended publication. After the British evacuation of New York the Robertsons removed to Shelburne, Nova Scotia, where, on King Street, they revived the *Royal American Gazette* for several years, continuing the volume and series numbering from New York. Alexander suffered illness, being "deprived of the use of his limbs, and incapacitated for labor," dying at Roseway, a point near Shelburne, in 1784. He was "intelligent, well educated, and possessed some abilities as a writer" (Thomas, *post,* I, p. 193). James continued the newspaper in Nova Scotia for some time thereafter and eventually returned to his native city of Edinburgh, engaging in the printing business until 1810, or later. According to Thomas he "was a worthy man and a very good printer."

[The major sources are the various newspapers printed by the Robertsons and their partners. These are very rare, and information of fragmentary files is given by C. S. Brigham in "Bibliog. of Am. Newspapers," in *Proc. Am. Antiquarian Soc.,* n.s. XXIII (1913), XXVII (1917), XXXII (1923), XXIV (1925). Contemporary and therefore useful secondary information is in Isaiah Thomas's *Hist. of Printing in America* (2nd ed., 1874), vols. I and II; also "Additions" of Wm. McCulloch, in *Proc. Am. Antiquarian Soc.,* n.s. XXXI (1922), p. 201; of less account, because full of errors, is C. R. Hildeburn's *Sketches of Printers and Printing in Colonial N. Y.* (1895), pp. 98–104.]

V. H. P.

ROBERTSON, JAMES (June 28, 1742–Sept. 1, 1814), pioneer, the eldest son of John and Mary (Gower) Robertson, was born in Brunswick County, Va. In his youth his parents removed to Wake County, N. C. There on Oct. 20, 1768, he married Charlotte Reeves, the daughter of George Reeves, who became the mother of his eleven children. In 1770 with a party of hunters he visited the lands on the Holston in search of a place for a home. He located a claim and planted a crop near other settlers on the Watauga. In the autumn he returned to Wake County and removed his family to the West in 1771. He became a member of the court created by the Watauga Association and one of the agents for the settlers in treating with the Indians for the lease under which their land was held before 1775. He participated in Lord Dunmore's War at the battle of Point Pleasant in 1774.

When in 1775 Richard Henderson [*q.v.*] made his purchase of Kentucky lands from the Indians, Robertson was present and probably exerted influence on the negotiations. He signed the petition of the Wataugans for incorporation into North Carolina in 1776. He acted as agent to the Cherokee for North Carolina and Virginia during these early years and for a time lived among them, but in 1777 he accompanied the Virginia troops on an expedition against them. He also conducted the defense of the Watauga fort in 1777, holding the rank of captain. In 1778 the North Carolina Assembly instructed him as agent to reside permanently among the Cherokee, but he resigned the following year. During the latter year he carried a warning to the Wataugans of a Chickamauga attack. In 1779 he headed an exploring party that contemplated a settlement at French Lick, a trading post on the Cumberland, on land purchased by the Transylvania Company. He returned to Watauga to lead a group of settlers who, on Jan. 1, 1780, arrived on the Cumberland at the present site of Nashville. They, with others who came in April, adopted the Cumberland Compact as a basis of government, and he served as presiding officer of the court set up. In 1781 he made an alliance with the Chickasaw Indians in order to avert danger of their further attacks. He was elected colonel of the militia for the region and exhibited a firm and wise leadership during the early, critical years on the Cumberland. He had received a meager education from his wife, and he took an interest in providing educational facilities in the settlement. When the North Carolina Assembly chartered Davidson Academy, later the University of Nashville, in 1785, he became a trustee. In 1785 he represented his county in the North Carolina Assembly. When difficulties in the western settlements led the frontiersmen to believe that the states were indifferent to their interests, he, with others, played an active though obscure part in the Spanish Conspiracy from 1786 to 1789 (see Whitaker, *post*). In 1787 he again sat in the North Carolina Assembly. During the same year, he led the Coldwater expedition against the Indians.

When William Blount organized the territorial government southwest of the Ohio, he nominated Robertson as one of the brigadier-generals, a position from which he resigned in 1794 after ordering the Nickajack campaign. He also aided Blount in negotiating the Holston treaty in 1791. He represented Davidson County in the constitutional convention of Tennessee in 1796. In 1798 he entered the Tennessee Senate in place of Thomas Hardeman, who had resigned. During that year Governor Sevier appointed him to represent Tennessee at the first treaty of Tellico between the United States and the Cherokee. In 1807 he acted with Return J. Meigs in negotiating another treaty with the Cherokee. During the later years of his life, he served as Indian agent to the Chickasaw and resided for some time at the agency

at Chickasaw Bluffs. There he died. In 1825 his remains were removed to Nashville and reinterred in the old city cemetery. He was one of the few really influential frontier leaders in Tennessee. Although he did not aspire to official position, he assumed county and state offices when urged by the settlers, who had confidence in his ability. His influence was personal rather than political, and men of all groups sought his counsel. His fairness, wisdom, and firmness brought him his greatest success as a mediator between the settlers and the Indians. Although he associated himself with land companies, he did not attempt speculation on an extensive scale. According to his grand-daughter's description, he was of medium height, heavy but not fat, and his manner quiet and business-like. As a typical pioneer, he remained the leader in the Cumberland settlements until his death.

[Correspondence of James Robertson, Lib. George Peabody College for Teachers, Nashville; MSS. and documents, Tenn. State Archives; MSS., Lib. of the State of Tenn.; MSS., Tenn. Hist. Soc.; Draper Coll. of MSS., Wis. Hist. Soc., Madison, Wis.; "Correspondence of Gen. James Robertson," *Am. Hist. Mag.* (Nashville), Jan. 1896–July 1900; L. R. H. Brown, "The Family of Gen. James Robertson," *Ibid.*, Jan. 1896; "Letters of James Robertson and Daniel Smith," ed. by A. P. Whitaker, *Miss. Valley Hist. Rev.*, Dec. 1925; *The State Records of N. C.*, vols. XII, XIII, XVIII, XX, XXIV (1895–1905); A. W. Putnam, *Hist. of Middle Tenn. or the Life and Times of Gen. James Robertson* (1859); John Haywood, *The Civil and Pol. Hist. of the State of Tenn.* (1823); J. G. M. Ramsey, *Annals of Tenn.*, with index by J. T. Fain (1926); Archibald Henderson, *The Conquest of the Old Southwest* (1920); T. E. Matthews, *General James Robertson* (1934).]

C. S. D.

ROBERTSON, JEROME BONAPARTE (Mar. 14, 1815–Jan. 7, 1891), physician, soldier, Texas official, the fourth and youngest son of Cornelius and Clarissa (Hill) Robertson, was born in Woodford County, Ky. His parents had moved to Kentucky from Maryland in 1808. In 1819 they lost their property and in the same year the father died, leaving his widow and five small children penniless. The boys were apprenticed to neighboring tradesmen, and at the age of twelve Jerome Bonaparte was serving a hatter of Union County. Upon the death of his master, three years later, he was transferred to a man in St. Louis with whom he remained till he was seventeen, when, through his industry and frugality, he was able to buy release from the last three years of his contract. During his apprenticeship he had only three months of schooling, but a physician of St. Louis, Dr. M. W. Harris, who was attracted by the lad's fine characteristics, gave him informal instruction in both literary subjects and medicine. In 1832 Dr. Harris moved to Owensboro, Ky., and young Robertson went with him as pupil and office assistant. In 1835 he graduated in medicine from Transylvania University. He returned to Owensboro to practise his profession, but he was interested in the reports of the Revolution in Texas and raised a company of volunteers. When they arrived in Texas in May 1836, the battle of San Jacinto had been fought, and Texan independence was already assured, but the company joined the Texan army and remained with it until it was mustered out in June 1837.

Robertson then began the practice of medicine at Washington on the Brazos. On May 4, 1838, he married Mary Elizabeth Cummins, a daughter of Moses Cummins. Three children were born of this marriage, and in 1845 the family moved to Independence for school advantages. There Robertson practised medicine for thirty-four years and was the beloved physician for a large part of Washington County. From 1838 to 1844 he participated in as many as two yearly campaigns against the Indians and won a reputation throughout Texas as an Indian fighter. He also took an active part in the campaigns against Vasquez and Wohl. Besides his military service he held many minor civil offices in Washington County, ranging from coroner to state senator. He was a member of the convention that passed the ordinance of secession in 1861, and was one of the first in Texas to raise a company for service in the Civil War. He entered the Confederate army as a captain in the 5th Texas Infantry, Hood's brigade, but was advanced step by step until he became, in 1862, a brigadier-general and succeeded General Hood in command. During the war, Robertson fought in more than forty battles and was severely wounded three times. After the war he returned to his practice at Independence, but upon the death of his wife in 1868 he gave up active practice, and in 1874 became superintendent of the state Bureau of Immigration. In 1879 he moved from Independence to Waco, and in that same year he married Mrs. Harriet (Hendly) Hook. During the last ten years of his life he was an active promoter of railroad building in West Texas, in which section he is still remembered as a benefactor.

[Sources include: C. A. Evans, *Confed. Mil. Hist.* (1899), vol. XI; Sid S. Johnson, *Texans Who Wore the Gray* (1907); H. S. Thrall, *A Pictorial Hist. of Tex.* (1879); *Biog. Encyc. of Tex.* (1880); W. S. Speer and J. H. Brown, *The Encyc. of the New West* (1881); Comptroller Military Service Records, Nos. 873, 1409, Tex. State Lib.; information as to certain facts from Robertson's grandson, Judge Felix D. Robertson, and from his grand-daughter, Mrs. Julia R. Cleveland.]　　　　　　　　　　A. W—s.

ROBERTSON, JOHN (Apr. 13, 1787–July 5, 1873), congressman, jurist, author, was born at "Belfield," below Petersburg, Va., of stock descended from the Princess Pocahontas, son of William and Elizabeth (Bolling) Robertson, and brother of Wyndham and Thomas Bolling Robertson [*qq.v.*]. After graduating from the College of William and Mary, he studied law, was admitted to the bar, and commenced practice in Richmond, whither his parents had removed about 1803. He married Anne, daughter of John A. Trent of Cumberland County. His personal charm combined with his industry, his ingenuity and ability of intellect, and his high sense of honor to win him rapid distinction; he served three terms, 1816–19, in the legislature; and in 1823 was made attorney-general of the state, filling this office conscientiously and well for eleven years. A "doctrinal Democrat of the Jefferson school," he was too independent to be a thrall to party and in 1834 was elected as a Whig to succeed Andrew Stevenson in Congress. Reëlected to the Twenty-fourth and Twenty-fifth congresses, he made himself known as a stinging and aggressive debater, a stickler for the Constitution, and an uncompromising critic of Jacksonian policy. His candor and veneration for truth gained him a reputation for eccentricity, for he is said never to have cloaked a thought. On Mar. 18, 1841, he was appointed judge of the twenty-first Virginia judicial circuit, to administer the chancery side of the superior court of law and chancery. Upon the reorganization of the judiciary ten years later, he became judge of the circuit court of Richmond and Henrico. Over both courts he presided with a dignity approaching severity, but with recognized impartiality and discernment. As the break between North and South threatened, Robertson, although a stern exponent of the inviolability of his state's domestic system, so earnestly deprecated violent measures that in January 1861 he was chosen commissioner from Virginia to urge forbearance upon the seceding states, pending the proposed peace convention. His overtures failing and Virginia having subsequently seceded, Governor Letcher commissioned him to invite Robert E. Lee, Joseph E. Johnston, and other Virginians holding federal military or naval appointments, to transfer to the service of their state. A similar interview with his former college-mate, Winfield Scott, proved unsuccessful. His public career ended with his duties in the Virginia Senate, 1861–62 and 1862–63, but he continued an active supporter of the Confederacy, giving his Richmond home as a soldiers' hospital, and dying an unreconstructed and "unrepentant rebel."

Besides occasional speeches, he published at widely separated intervals four volumes, three of them deriving largely from pride in and love for his family and his state, and too local, too definitely dated to have enduring appeal save to antiquarian or genealogist. These were a translation of Robert Bolling's memoirs of the Bolling family from the French (published in 1868 under the title: *A Memoir . . . of the Bolling Family in England and Virginia*); a metrical romance, *Virginia, or the Fatal Patent* (1825), dealing with the separation of the colony from the British crown; and, shortly before his death at Mount Athos in Campbell County, a miscellany, *Opuscula* (1870), which, while primarily concerned with Virginian affairs, looses numerous satirical barbs at New England intolerance and guile. More significant artistically was *Riego, or the Spanish Martyr* (1850), based on the revolution in Spain in 1820. A conventionally romantic five-act tragedy, in correct if undistinguished verse, it was superior to the average American play of its time and proved fairly popular in print, although Robertson was destined to be disappointed in his hope that Boucicault would produce it.

[Wyndham Robertson, *Pocahontas . . . and Her Descendants* (1887); E. G. Swem and J. W. Williams, *Reg. of Gen. Assembly of Va.* (1918); *Jour. of the Senate of the Commonwealth of Va. . . . Extra Sess.*, 1861; *Richmond Enquirer* and *Daily Dispatch* (Richmond), July 8, 1873.]   A. C. G., Jr.

ROBERTSON, MORGAN ANDREW (Sept. 30, 1861–Mar. 24, 1915), author, was born at Oswego, N. Y., the son of Andrew and Ruth Amelia (Glassford) Robertson. His father was a ship-captain on the Great Lakes. After a public-school education, Morgan went to sea in the merchant service, 1877–86, attaining the rank of first mate. He then gave up seafaring, and went to New York, where he studied the jeweler's trade at Cooper Union and opened a small shop, specializing in diamond setting. On May 27, 1894, he married Alice M. Doyle, daughter of William and Anna (Ross) Doyle of New York. Two years later, impaired eyesight forced him to give up his business and he was soon financially embarrassed. The reading of a sea story by Kipling now determined him to capitalize his own sea experiences and he spent a night writing an 8000-word story on the backs of circulars he had been hired to distribute. For this story, "The Destruction of the Unfit," finally accepted by a magazine, he received twenty-five dollars. The following year he wrote some twenty stories, the cream of his work, thus earning about a thousand dollars. The wolf was often just outside the door, and when his frail wife was ill, he did both the cooking and the washing. For one story an editor traded a bicycle, Rob-

ertson's choice of the merchandise advertised in the magazine. Writing steadily, however, he produced more than two hundred stories, which appeared in leading American magazines and in English periodicals.

After the publication of a collection of his stories in book form he was paid more for his work and in time enjoyed a fairly comfortable income, although he never earned as much as $5000 a year. He was never a spendthrift, he declared ("Gathering No Moss," *post*, p. 28), but he was improvident and a poor business man and was never entirely free from financial worries. His education being limited, he found writing painfully tedious, and eventually his ideas grew scarce. Threatened with a nervous breakdown and fearing insanity, he voluntarily entered the psychopathic ward of Bellevue Hospital. A psychologist whom he later consulted turned his mind to invention, and he undertook, after visiting a submarine, to solve the problem of the periscope; this he accomplished practically, but he could not patent his device because a fantastic description embodying the same principle had previously appeared in a French magazine. Returning to his writing, he found, as he said, that "my punch was gone" ("Gathering No Moss," p. 32); his work gradually declined in sales value, and he became practically penniless. A few months before his death, of heart disease, in an Atlantic City hotel, he was given financial relief by the publication of a special edition of his works, sponsored by friends. He had no children, but was survived by his wife, a brother, and a sister.

Robertson's published books include: *A Tale of a Halo* (1894), an unusual allegorical poem; *Spun-Yarn: Sea Stories* (1898), "*Where Angels Fear to Tread*" *and Other Tales of the Sea* (1899), *Shipmates* (1901), *Down to the Sea* (1905), and *Land-Ho!* (1905), all collections of short stories; *Futility* (1898), a short novel; *Masters of Men: A Romance of the New Navy* (1901); and *Sinful Peck* (1903), another full-length novel. His stories deal with sailing ships, steam vessels, and the long, steel men-of-war. They treat of mutiny and bloody fights, shipwreck and rescue, brutality, shanghaiing, courage and wild daring, telepathy, hypnotism, dual personality, and extraordinary inventions. "His stories are *bully*," wrote Booth Tarkington, "his sea is foamy, and his men have hair on their chests" (*McClure's Magazine*, October 1915, p. 90). He gave life and reality to his characters, the most famous being Finnegan, a sort of Mulvaney of the sea, but he was more concerned with the reality of adventurous action than the psychological aspects of the sailor like Conrad, who wrote to Robertson (*Ibid.*): "Indeed, my dear sir, you are a first rate seaman—one can see that with half-an-eye."

[Bibliography by Merle Johnson in *Publishers' Weekly*, Mar. 15, 1930; obituaries in *Truth Seeker*, Apr. 3, 1915, *Bookman*, May 1915, *N. Y. Times*, Mar. 25, 1915, and *Daily Press* (Atlantic City, N. J.), Mar. 26, 1915; "Gathering No Moss: An Autobiography," *Saturday Evening Post*, Mar. 28, 1914; *Morgan Robertson, the Man* (1915); *Who's Who in America*, 1914–15; James MacArthur, "Books and Bookmen," *Harper's Weekly*, Apr. 29, 1905; *Reedy's Mirror*, July 16, 1915.]   C. L. L.

ROBERTSON, THOMAS BOLLING (Feb. 27, 1779–Oct. 5, 1828), third governor of the state of Louisiana, was born near Petersburg, Va., the son of William and Elizabeth (Bolling) Robertson. He was an elder brother of John Robertson [*q.v.*], the Virginia jurist and congressman, and of Wyndham Robertson [*q.v.*], who was governor of Virginia. For a time he attended the College of William and Mary. In 1806 he was admitted to the bar and began the practice of law at Petersburg, but he soon removed to the territory of Orleans where he became territorial attorney-general. In 1807 President Jefferson appointed him secretary of the territory with the power of succession to the governorship in case of a vacancy. When the territory was admitted to the Union under the name of Louisiana in 1812, he was elected as the first representative to Congress from the new state, and he was three times reëlected. While visiting France during his congressional career he wrote a series of letters which appeared in the *Richmond Enquirer* (Sept. 30–Dec. 23, 1815) and were also published in book form as *Events in Paris* (Philadelphia, 1816).

Robertson resigned from Congress in April 1818, but ill health, of which he complained after his removal to Louisiana, did not long keep him out of politics. In 1820 he was elected governor of Louisiana, and he went about his new duties with somewhat fiery manifestations of republicanism, expressing sympathy in messages and pronouncements for the Greeks and Latin Americans in their struggles for independence and advocating the abolition of imprisonment for debt. He opposed the relinquishment by the United States of the claim to Texas in the treaty acquiring Florida, complained of the neglect of Louisiana coast defenses, and criticized the national land policy in Louisiana as interfering with land improvement and progress. His administration was marked by legislation for the benefit of parish schools and for highway improvement, especially on the Louisiana link of the road connecting New Orleans with Nash-

ville, Tenn. Licenses were granted to six gambling houses for payment of $5000 fees for the benefit of Charity Hospital, New Orleans, and the College of Orleans. In 1824 Robertson resigned the governorship to accept from President Monroe the appointment to the United States district judgeship for Louisiana, and he resigned the judgeship in 1828, a few months before his death at White Sulphur Springs, Va. He was married to Lelia Skipwith, daughter of a political friend, Fulwar Skipwith, governor of West Florida. According to descriptions, he was tall and handsome. He was capable of using strong denunciatory language, and his comparatively short life was crowded with public activity and office-holding, to which he applied himself with energy and conviction.

[References include: Alcée Fortier, *Louisiana*, vol. II (1909) and *Hist. of La.*, vol. III (1904), with a portrait; Catherine B. Dillon, manuscript on Robertson in Howard Memorial Lib., New Orleans (published in part in the *New Orleans States*, Mar. 1, 1931); Wyndham Robertson, *Pocahontas . . . and Her Descendants* (1887); Mrs. Eugene Soniat du Fossat, *Biog. Sketches of Louisiana's Governors* (1885). The date of Robertson's birth is variously given. The date in this sketch is that given in the *Biog. Dir. Am. Cong.* (1928).]   H. C. N.

ROBERTSON, WILLIAM HENRY (Oct. 10, 1823–Dec. 6, 1898), politician, son of Henry and Huldah (Fanton) Robertson, was born at Bedford, Westchester County, N. Y. He was educated in the district schools and the academy of his native town. At the age of seventeen he began his political career by making speeches for Harrison and Tyler in the campaign of 1840. His first public office was superintendent of schools of Bedford, followed by four terms as a supervisor of Westchester County. He spent his leisure in studying law and was admitted to the bar in 1847. His practice, though continued throughout the remainder of his life, was constantly interrupted by office-holding and by party activities. After two terms in the New York Assembly and a term in the Senate, he served as county judge of Westchester County, 1855–67. In addition to his duties on the bench he was county draft commissioner during the Civil War, county leader of the Republican party organization, and a frequent participant in political conventions, national, state, and local. He was sometimes credited with having made possible Andrew Johnson's nomination to the vice-presidency in 1864. In 1866 he was elected to Congress but after a single term he declined a renomination. In 1871 he was again elected to the state Senate and by reëlection served continuously for ten years.

In 1872 it was generally thought that Robertson would receive the Republican nomination for governor, but at the last minute the convention was stampeded into choosing another candidate. Robertson believed that Senator Conkling, the state Republican leader, was responsible for his disappointment, and his attitude toward the state organization, always rather independent, changed into open hostility. In 1876 and in 1879 he was a candidate for the gubernatorial nomination against men whom Conkling was known to favor. In 1880 he opposed the efforts of Conkling and other "Stalwarts" to obtain a third nomination for Grant and organized a strong minority group of delegates who announced that they would not obey the instructions of the state convention. The "Stalwarts" then planned to introduce the unit rule into the national convention and thus force the whole delegation to vote for Grant. But Robertson's group, reinforced by independent delegates from other states, prevented the adoption of the rule. After a prolonged deadlock Garfield was nominated. The new president in recognition of Robertson's part in making his nomination possible considered inviting him into his cabinet, but instead sent his nomination to the Senate for the collectorship of the port of New York. The nomination provoked the most noteworthy of all the controversies over the right of senators to dictate appointment from their states. Conkling and Platt, the senators from New York, did everything in their power to prevent its confirmation. When it became evident that a majority of the Senate would uphold the President, both resigned and sought reëlection as a vote of confidence from the legislature of New York. Robertson led the opposition to their candidacies and both were defeated. After the expiration of his term as collector in 1885 Robertson again returned to the state Senate in 1887. His last active participation in politics was in the state Republican convention of 1896. He died at Katonah, N. Y., survived by his wife, Mary (Ballard) Robertson, whom he had married in 1865.

[*Biog. Dir. of the State of N. Y.* (1900); *Biog. Dir. Am. Cong.* (1928); DeA. S. Alexander, *A Pol. Hist. of the State of N. Y.,* vol. III (1909); *The Autobiog. of Thos. Collier Platt* (1910); Royal Cortissoz, *The Life of Whitelaw Reid* (1921), vol. II; T. C. Smith, *The Life and Letters of Jas. A. Garfield* (1925), vol. II; *N. Y. Tribune,* Mar. 24, 25, 1881, Mar. 20, Dec. 7, 1898; *Sun* (N. Y.), Dec. 7, 1898.]   E. C. S.

ROBERTSON, WILLIAM JOSEPH (Dec. 30, 1817–May 27, 1898), lawyer, was born in Culpeper County, Va., the son of John and Sarah (Brand) Robertson. His father, an emigrant from Glasgow, Scotland, had settled in Albemarle County in 1791 and had opened there a school for boys which he subsequently removed to Culpeper County. He died in 1818, but his son was given the best education then available in the Virginia piedmont. At the age of nine the boy was sent to the school of John Lewis of Llangollen in Spotsylvania County and in 1834 he entered the academic schools of the University of Virginia. During the course of his third session there, he left the University, taught school for two years, and then returned for the study of law. He was graduated from the law school in 1842 and began practice at Louisa Court House, but in a short time he moved to Charlottesville where he resided for the remainder of his life. In 1852 he was elected attorney for the commonwealth for the county of Albemarle. It was while he held this office that he conducted the prosecution of John Singleton Mosby [*q.v.*], then a student at the University, in such a way as to secure both Mosby's conviction and his respect and lifelong friendship. From 1853 to 1859 he served on the board of visitors of the University. He also served as the attorney of the University and in 1854 finally forced the administrator of President Madison's estate to surrender books bequeathed to its library.

In 1859 he was elected by popular vote to the bench of the supreme court of appeals of Virginia. In 1865 Virginia became Military District No. 1, and the judges of its supreme court were removed by order of the major-general commanding. During the six years, 1859–65, that Robertson was on the bench there was not a great deal of litigation before the court and Robertson himself delivered the opinion of the court in only twelve cases. He had had an average of six months for the preparation of each opinion. It was as a practising attorney rather than as a judge that he made his mark. When the courts were reopened after the war he began anew the practice of law. His professional reputation and income grew steadily. He became the great "corporation lawyer" of post-bellum Virginia, and for his time and section a rich man. He was made general counsel of the Chesapeake & Ohio Railroad Company and also of the Norfolk & Western Railroad. The Samuel Miller Will Case (*27 Grattan,* 110) and that of *Gilbert* vs. *Railroad Company* (*33 Grattan,* 586) were two of his conspicuous successes in the Virginia courts. The Arlington cases (*United States* vs. *Lee* and *Kaufman* vs. *Lee,* 106 *U. S.,* 196) were perhaps his greatest victories before the United States Supreme Court. In July 1888 he was elected the first president of the Virginia State Bar Association. He died in Charlottesville, May 27, 1898. He was twice married: first, on

Aug. 16, 1842, to Hannah, daughter of Gen. William F. Gordon [*q.v.*] of Albemarle, who died in 1861, and on July 16, 1863, to Alice, daughter of Gen. Edward Watts and widow of Dr. G. W. Morris of South Carolina. He had nine children by his first marriage and five by his second marriage.

[See: C. M. Blackford, "Wm. J. Robertson," *Report of the . . . Va. State Bar Asso.*, 1898; A. C. Gordon, "Wm. Jos. Robertson," in *Great Am. Lawyers*, vol. VII (1909), ed. by W. D. Lewis, reprinted in Gordon's *Virginian Portraits* (1924); J. S. Patton, "Mosby the Ranger as a College Student," in the Baltimore *Sun*, Jan. 15, 1911; the *Times* (Richmond, Va.), May 28, 1898.]

T. C. J., Jr.

ROBERTSON, WILLIAM SCHENCK (Jan. 11, 1820–June 26, 1881), pioneer educator among the Indians, was born at Huntington, Long Island, the son of the Rev. Samuel and Dorcas (Platt) Robertson. He was graduated from Union College, Schenectady, N. Y., in 1842 and began the study of medicine but, after completing about two-thirds of the course, gave it up to become a teacher. He taught for a few years in various academies in the state of New York and after uniting with the Presbyterian Church at Northport, Long Island, offered his services to the Presbyterian board for foreign missions. Requesting to be assigned to work among the Indians, he was given the position of principal teacher at the new manual labor boarding school among the Creeks later known as Tullahassee Mission in Indian Territory. He reached Tullahassee in the summer of 1849 to find the building still unfinished. On Jan. 1, 1850, however, he opened a day school, and two months later thirty boarding students were received. This number was increased to the full quota of eighty, when school opened in the autumn. On Apr. 15, 1850, he was married to Ann Eliza Worcester, the eldest child of the Rev. Samuel A. Worcester [*q.v.*] who had for some years been in charge of the Cherokee mission at Park Hill. One of their daughters was Alice Mary Robertson [*q.v.*]. For more than ten years Robertson continued, without interruption, his work at Tullahassee. With the able help of his wife he published in the Creek language a first and a second reader, which were widely distributed. When the Civil War broke out the school was closed by the southern wing of the Creeks, who had obtained control of the tribal government. With his family he went north and spent the winter of 1861–62 at his father's home at Winneconne, Wis. For the next two years he taught in Illinois, the first year at Mattoon and the second at Centralia.

In 1864 the Presbyterian mission board placed him in charge of the orphan institute at Highland, Kan., where he remained for two years. He was ordained a minister by the presbytery of Highland early in November 1866 and was then sent by the mission board to reopen Tullahassee, since the Creeks had earnestly requested that he be returned to them. To stimulate interest in education he obtained a small printing press and with the aid of his son and daughter published and distributed for four years a small newspaper in the Creek language called *Our Monthly*. In 1876 he was for a month in charge of the Indian educational exhibit at the Philadelphia Centennial Exhibition. He was also for years interested in the work of the Indian international fair held annually at Muskogee. During the later years of his life he began the translation of the New Testament into the Creek language, based on the earlier work of Robert M. Loughbridge [*q.v.*], and issued in parts between 1875 and 1886. After his death the complete edition, *Pu Pucase Momet Pu Hesayecv Cesus Klist in Testement Mucvsat*, was finished by his wife and published in 1887.

[Letters in the Alice Robertson Papers, University of Tulsa, Okla., in files of Indian Office, Washington, D. C., and among the missionary letters in the Lib. of Andover Theological Seminary; MSS., including a brief sketch of his life written by his widow, in possession of Okla. Hist. Soc.; J. B. Thoburn and M. H. Wright, *Okla.* (1929), vol. I; A. H. Abel, *The Indian as Slaveholder and Secessionist* (1915); J. H. Beadle, *The Undeveloped West* (1873), pp. 380–86; J. D. Benedict, *Muskogee and Northeastern Okla.* (1922), vol. I.]

E. E. D.

ROBERTSON, WYNDHAM (Jan. 26, 1803–Feb. 11, 1888), twentieth governor of Virginia, was born near Richmond and lived during the greater part of his active life in that city. He was the brother of John and Thomas Bolling Robertson [*qq.v.*] and grandson of William Robertson who emigrated from Scotland in the early eighteenth century and settled in Bristol Parish near the present Petersburg, Va. His father, William Robertson, was a native of Bristol Parish and served it in the capacity of vestryman, warden, and deputy from 1779 to 1789. He was also a member of the Council of Virginia and its secretary for many years. He married Elizabeth Bolling, and Wyndham was their seventh child. The boy was educated in Richmond and at the College of William and Mary. He studied law for several years and was admitted to the Richmond bar in 1824. In 1830 and again in 1833 he was elected to the Executive Council of Virginia and during this period took an active part in the development of internal improvements within the state, especially in connection with the organization of the James River and Kanawha Company, the object of which was to connect Richmond and Lynchburg by canal. In 1836 he became senior member of the Council and as

such succeeded to the governorship, when Tazewell resigned the office in that year. Being a
Whig in politics, he was succeeded after one year
by David Campbell, a Democrat. From 1838 to
1841 he served as a member of the House of
Delegates. In the latter year on account of his
health he retired to the country, where he engaged in agricultural pursuits to the exclusion
of all public business. In 1858 he returned to
Richmond and from 1859 to 1865 served continuously in the House of Delegates. After John
Brown's raid he became captain of a company
of home guards organized in Richmond. During the crisis of 1861 he opposed secession and
was author of the resolution adopted by the legislature declaring against separation but warning the North that Virginia would join the South
in case coercion were attempted against those
states that had already seceded. During 1863
and 1864 he strenuously opposed in the legislature a movement designed to fix the prices of
food by law. After the war he removed to the
home of his wife, Mary T. (Smith) Robertson
of Abingdon, Va., and resided there until the
end of his life. During these latter years he took
no active part in public affairs but devoted his
time to literary pursuits, publishing in 1887 his
most important work, *Pocahontas, alias Matooka,
and her Descendants through her Marriage . . .
with John Rolfe.* This was his last effort, for he
died the next year.

[Wyndham Robertson MSS. in the Lawson McGhee
Library, Knoxville, Tenn.; R. A. Brock, *Virginia and
Virginians* (1888), Vol. I, pp. 171–75; M. V. Smith,
Virginia, . . . A History of the Executives (1893); W.
A. Christian, *Richmond* (1912), pp. 116, 119, 129; E.
G. Swem and J. W. Williams, *A Register of the Gen.
Assembly of Va.* (1918); *Richmond Whig*, Feb. 15,
1888.]
T. P. A.

ROBESON, GEORGE MAXWELL (Mar.
16, 1829–Sept. 27, 1897), attorney-general of
New Jersey, secretary of the navy, was born at
Oxford Furnace, Warren County, N. J., the son
of William Penn and Ann (Maxwell) Robeson.
He was descended from Andrew Robeson, of
Scotland, who emigrated to America in 1676.
His father was an iron manufacturer. Imme-
diately after graduating with honors from the
College of New Jersey (Princeton) in 1847,
Robeson began the study of the law in the offices
of Chief Justice Hornblower in Newark. He was
admitted to the bar in 1850, practised law in
Jersey City, and was licensed as a counselor in
1854. In 1859 he was appointed by Governor
Newell prosecutor of Camden County, a political
move which occasioned much criticism, because
Robeson was not at the time a resident of Camden. During the Civil War he was appointed a

brigadier-general by Governor Olden and took
an active part in the organization of the state
troops, commanding the camp of volunteers at
Woodbury, N. J. In January 1867 he was appointed attorney-general of New Jersey by Governor Ward. Following the resignation of A.
E. Borie as secretary of the navy, Robeson was
appointed by President Grant to fill the vacancy
in the cabinet. It was reported at the time that
the appointment was made on the recommendation of Borie (*Nation*, July 1, 1869). Robeson
held office from June 25, 1869, until Mar. 12,
1877. His administration of the Navy Department was so severely criticized by the newspapers, which charged him with extravagance and
favoritism, that a congressional investigation was
instituted (*House Miscellaneous Document 170,
44 Cong., 1 Sess., and House Reports 788 and
789, 44 Cong., 1 Sess.*), but no definite action resulted. In 1871 Robeson was instrumental in securing the federal appropriation for the ill-fated
North Polar Expedition of Capt. C. F. Hall,
who, before his death in northern Greenland,
named Robeson Channel in recognition of the
services of the Secretary of the Navy (C. F.
Hall, *Narrative of the North Polar Expedition,*
1876, ed. by C. H. Davis).

In January 1877 Robeson was the Republican
candidate for United States senator from New
Jersey, but he lost the election by one vote in the
legislature, where he was suspected of trying to
buy the vote of a Democratic member (Sackett,
post, p. 134). In March 1877 he retired from
the cabinet and returned to Camden, where he
resumed his law practice. In 1878 he was elected to Congress from the first New Jersey district, being reëlected in 1880. Although a new-
comer, he was one of the leaders in the House
and was said to be "as strong in parliamentary
debate as he was known to be in argument at the
bar" (J. G. Blaine, *Twenty Years of Congress,*
II, 1886, 638). He was again an unsuccessful
senatorial candidate in 1881 and following his
defeat in the congressional elections of 1882 devoted himself to the practice of law, at first in
Camden and later in Trenton where he died. His
striking personal traits and his size made him a
favorite with cartoonists. *Puck* had a cartoon
featuring him almost every week and it has been
said that he was the most caricatured man of his
day. In 1872 he married Mary Isabelle (Ogs-
ton) Aulick, a widow with a son, Richard Aulick.
They had one daughter.

[*Proc. N. J. Hist. Soc.*, 3 ser. II (1897), 195–96;
W. E. Sackett, *Modern Battles of Trenton*, vol. I
(1895); *A History of Trenton*, II, 620–21, pub. by
the Trenton Hist. Soc. (1929); Geo. R. Prowell, *The
Hist. of Camden County* (1886); S. S. Robeson and

C. F. Stroud, *An Hist. and Geneal. Account of Andrew Robeson* (1916); *Daily State Gazette* (Trenton), Sept. 28, 1897.]   C. R. E., Jr.

ROBIDOU, ANTOINE (Sept. 24, 1794–Aug. 29, 1860), trapper, trader, was born in St. Louis, Mo., the son of Joseph and Catherine (Rollet) Robidou and the brother of Joseph (1783–1868), François (1788–1856), Louis (1796–*c.* 1862), and Michel (b. 1798) Robidou, all of them noted frontiersmen. Signatures of both Joseph and François show that the name was spelled without the terminal *x* used by the present generation of the family. "The first fur trader out of old Taos," Antoine has been called, and unless a prior claim can be proved for Ewing Young or William Wolfskill the distinction stands; he may have reached Taos as early as 1822. On what was probably his second expedition he set out with a small party, Sept. 20, 1824, from Fort Atkinson, north of the present Omaha; and the *Missouri Intelligencer* (Franklin, Mo.) of Apr. 19, 1825, mentions him as having been encountered in the previous fall on the "Green River (probably the Colorado of the West)" at some point in the present Utah. In 1828 Robidou married Carmel Benavides, of a prominent New Mexican family, and established a home either in Taos or Santa Fé. It was probably in the same year that he built a trading post on the Gunnison in what is now Colorado; about 1832 he established another post, Fort Robidou or Fort Uinta, in the Uinta Valley, northeastern Utah, that became a famous rendezvous for trappers, and for the next ten or eleven years he seems to have spent most of his time between these two posts and his New Mexican home. He probably revisited the Missouri region in the winter of 1840–41, since there is general agreement that he was the "Roubideaux" who set in motion the first emigrant wagon train to the Pacific by telling John Bidwell [*q.v.*] wonderful stories about California. John Charles Frémont [*q.v.*], who was at the Uinta post on June 3–5, 1844, writes that it was attacked by Utes during Robidou's absence and that all its inmates were killed. Robidou may have returned to the mountains in 1841 or 1842; in 1845 he abandoned them and moved with his wife and adopted daughter to St. Joseph, Mo., laid out by his brother Joseph two years before, July 1843. But his western adventures were not yet over, for in the spring of 1846 he engaged with Gen. S. W. Kearny [*q.v.*] as interpreter for the New Mexican expedition, accompanied the detachment later sent to California, and was desperately wounded at the battle of San Pascual, Dec. 6, 1846. In 1847, partly recovered, he returned once more to St.

Joseph. He is said to have become blind in 1852, and on May 23 of that year Congress voted him a small pension. He died in St. Joseph. Robidou was of slight figure—"a thin man," writes Lieutenant Emory (*post*, p. 111)—and his portrait reveals a handsome, refined, and intelligent face. Well known over the whole frontier and highly regarded, he was one of the most energetic, daring, and adventurous of all the trader-trappers.

[See J. J. Hill, "Antoine Robidoux," *Touring Topics* (Los Angeles), Dec. 1928; W. H. Emory, *Notes of a Mil. Reconnaissance, from Fort Leavenworth in Mo. to San Diego in Cal.* (1848); J. C. Luttig, *Jour. of a Fur-Trading Expedition on the Upper Missouri, 1812–1813* (1920), ed. by S. M. Drumm; E. L. Sabin, *Kit Carson Days* (1914); H. M. Chittenden, *The Am. Fur Trade of the Far West*, vol. II (1902); C. L. Camp, ed., "The Chronicles of George C. Yount," *Cal. Hist. Soc. Quart.*, Apr. 1923. Voluminous data concerning the Robidou family, some of it unreliable, will be found in C. L. Rutt, *The Daily News' Hist. of Buchanan County and St. Joseph, Mo.* (n.d.), and O. M. Robidoux, *Memorial to the Robidoux Brothers* (1924).]   W. J. G.

ROBINS, HENRY EPHRAIM (Sept. 30, 1827–Apr. 23, 1917), Baptist clergyman, educator, son of Gurdon and Julia (Savage) Robins, was born at Hartford, Conn. Descended from old New England stock, he numbered among his ancestors Peter Bulkeley of Concord, Mass., and Charles Chauncy, second president of Harvard College. His grandfather, Ephraim Robins, broke with the Standing Order, becoming a Baptist lay-preacher. In Gurdon Robins' home, with Ephraim Robins as prime mover, there was drawn up a petition on behalf of the Baptists which was influential in securing the inclusion of an article upon religious freedom in the new constitution adopted by Connecticut in 1818. The father of Henry E. Robins abandoned a business career to become editor of the *Christian Secretary*, the organ of Connecticut Baptists; he was later a Baptist minister, and finally a publisher and retailer of books.

After attending Fairmount Theological Seminary and graduating from the Newton Theological Institution in 1861, Henry E. Robins was ordained a Baptist minister, at Hartford, Dec. 6, 1861. For twelve years he continued in the pastorate, efficiently serving the Central Baptist Church of Newport, R. I. (January 1862–May 1867), first as associate and then as full pastor, and the First Baptist Church of Rochester, N. Y. (1867–73). In Rochester an addition to the church building, costing in excess of $53,000, was erected to be used for educational and social purposes, and the Memorial Mission of the church was developed until it became in 1871 the Lake Avenue Baptist Church. From 1873 to 1882, Robins was president of Colby University (now Colby College), Waterville, Me. Finding it with fifty students, he left it with an enrollment of 157. During his administration, through the bequest of Gardner Colby [*q.v.*] and other gifts, over $120,000 was added to its resources. His arduous and intense labors for the college impaired his health to the extent of making a leave of absence and at last a reluctant resignation unavoidable. Returning to Rochester, he was appointed professor of Christian ethics in the Rochester Theological Seminary (now the Colgate-Rochester Divinity School). Although he delivered only a few lectures, he held this professorship nominally until 1903. During the next decade and a half, he engaged in literary work. His minor writings include *Qualifications for Baptism* (*circa* 1867); *Harmony of Ethics with Theology* (1891); *The Christian Idea of Education as Distinguished from the Secular Idea of Education* (1895); *Faith Rational* (no date). His one major work was a comprehensive survey, of nearly 500 pages, *The Ethics of the Christian Life* (1904).

Robins was a preacher of exceptional excellence, a minister of spiritual fervor, sympathetic with young people, lovable yet of great strength of will, mature in his convictions, familiar with the educational problems of his denomination. A firm believer in the theory that right thinking precedes right living, he was alert, energetic, magnetic, and possessed unusual business and executive ability. Recognized throughout the East as a Baptist leader, he held the office of president of the New York State Baptist Convention in 1873 and of the Maine State Baptist Convention in 1879 and 1880. He was married thrice: first, Aug. 11, 1864, to Martha J. Bird of Hartford, Conn., who died in 1867; second, Sept. 4, 1872, to Margaret Richardson of Rochester, N. Y., who died the following year; and third, Aug. 7, 1876, to Cornelia Ewell Nott of Boston, who died in 1888. He died at the home of a daughter in Greenfield, Mass., survived by her and by a son.

[*Who's Who in America*, 1916–17; H. S. Burrage, *Hist. of the Baptists in Me.* (1904); *Gen. Cat. Colgate-Rochester Divinity School* (1930); *The Newton Theol. Inst. Gen. Cat.* (1899); *N. Y. Baptist Union for Ministerial Educ., Ann. Report*, 1883, 1903; *Springfield Republican*, Apr. 24, 1917; records of Central Bapt. Ch., Newport, R. I., First Bapt. Ch., Rochester, N. Y., and Newport Hist. Soc.; unpub. hist. of the Robins family prepared by Henry E. Robins and genealogy traced by a nephew, Henry B. Robins.]   C. H. M.

ROBINSON, ALBERT ALONZO (Oct. 21, 1844–Nov. 7, 1918), civil engineer, railway builder and operator, younger brother of Stillman Williams Robinson [*q.v.*], was born in South Reading, Vt., the son of Ebenezer and Adeline (Williams) Robinson. He was descended from William Robinson, one of the early settlers of Newton, Mass. His father, a country school-teacher, farmer, and carpenter of unusual mechanical ability—a talent which later appeared in his son—died in 1848. In 1853 his mother married Albert Childs and the family moved to the West. After graduating from the academy at Milton, Wis., Albert entered the University of Michigan, from which he received the degrees of B.S. and C.E. in 1869 and that of M.S. in 1871. Outside of school hours he worked on a farm or as a clerk in stores, and while a student at the University of Michigan he spent about five months of each year as assistant engineer with the United States Lake Survey.

His active career in railroad construction and administration began in May 1869, when he joined the engineering corps of the St. Joseph & Denver City Railroad. He continued with this road in various positions from axeman to assistant engineer until Apr. 1, 1871, when he went to the Atchison, Topeka & Santa Fé as assistant engineer in charge of location and construction. He was with the Santa Fé road for twenty-two years, eventually becoming second vice-president and general manager. When he became connected with the road it was scarcely a hundred miles long; when he left, it had grown to a system of over 9,000 miles, more than half of which, as chief engineer, Robinson had built. He was personally in charge of the party which early in 1878 occupied Raton Pass a few hours ahead of the force sent out by the rival Denver & Rio Grande, thus capturing for the Santa Fé the only practicable gateway into northern New Mexico; and he designed and constructed the "switchback" by means of which, before the completion of the tunnel, the first Santa Fé locomotive crossed the summit of the Pass and entered that region. The tremendous expansion of the Santa Fé system during his term of service was due in no small measure to his engineering skill and keen judgment, particularly in the selection of men.

In 1893 he became president of the Mexico Central Railway Company, Ltd., with headquarters in Boston, Mass., which position he held until Dec. 1, 1906, when he retired because of age and ill health. He proved himself an able administrator as well as a great engineer. On Dec. 9, 1869, he was married to Julia Caroline Burdick of Edgerton, Wis., who died Aug. 3, 1881; on Sept. 3, 1885, he married Ellen Frances (Burdick) Williams, sister of his first wife, who with a daughter by his first marriage survived him.

[G. A. Davis, *Hist. of Reading, Windsor County, Vt.*, vol. II (1903); G. D. Bradley, *The Story of the Santa Fe* (1920), dedicated to Robinson; J. B. Robinson, *A Hist. Sketch of the Robinson Family of the Line of Ebenezer Robinson* (1903); J. M. Meade in *Trans., Am. Soc. of Civil Engineers*, vol. LXXXIII (1921); *Topeka State Jour.*, Nov. 7, 1918; *Who's Who in America*, 1916–17.]   B. A. R.

ROBINSON, BEVERLEY (Jan. 11, 1722 o.s.–Apr. 9, 1792), Loyalist, was born in Middlesex County, Va., from a family active in the life of the colony. He was the brother of John Robinson [*q.v.*] and the sixth son of Catherine (Beverley) and John Robinson who was president of the Council and, at the time of his death in 1749, acting governor. In 1746 Beverley Robinson raised a company for the expedition intended against Canada and was ordered with it to New York. There on July 7, 1748, he had the good fortune to marry the daughter of Frederick Philipse, Susanna, sister of Mary the wife of Roger Morris [*q.v.*]. Susanna was heiress to part of the vast estates on the Hudson. By trading ventures and capable management of the estate, he increased his wife's fortune until he was one of New York's wealthiest landowners. During the French and Indian War, he was one of the commissaries and paymasters of the New York troops and after its conclusion served the colony in various capacities.

Retirement on his estate in Dutchess County was interrupted by the Revolution. Although he objected to some of the measures of the British ministry, he tried "from the very earliest period of the Rebellion to stop its progress" (Robinson memorial, Dec. 11, 1783). He refused to take the oath of allegiance to the state on Feb. 20, 1777, and was obliged to fly to the British in New York City. Offering his services to the army, he raised the Loyal American Regiment, of which he was made colonel, and was later also colonel and director of the loyal Guides and Pioneers. According to Sir Henry Clinton, Robinson "distinguished himself upon several occasions, particularly at the storming of fort Montgomery," Oct. 6, 1777 (Robinson's memorial and "Evidence," Dec. 16, 1785, *post*). His chief services, however, were not in the field. He was constantly employed on various boards and committees. His inclination, though, was toward the secret service, for which his knowledge of the country, his wide acquaintance, and a certain shrewdness in his nature admirably fitted him. He furnished information as to the terrain, roads, and disposition of the people; he directed spies and messengers; and he was active in cases of defection from the American side. He was eager to have Vermont join the British and sent the first invitation to Ethan Allen [*q.v.*]. He also sounded out General Putnam. There is no sound basis for the supposition that it was he who urged Benedict Arnold to change colors. He knew of the treasonable correspondence, though, and offered himself to Sir Henry Clinton for the rôle afterwards played by Major André. He was conspicuous, too, in the attempts to arrange a meeting between the conspirators. He accompanied André up the Hudson to his fateful interview with Arnold and, when André was captured, wrote Washington, who had been his friend before the Revolution, urging the prisoner's release (*Sparks, post*, pp. 533–34).

With his wife and eldest son he was banished by New York state in October 1779, and their property was confiscated. At the conclusion of the war, however, when, in reduced circumstances, he was faced with the necessity of leaving his native land, he could still write: ". . . was it to do over again I should take the same part" (Robinson to Clinton, Aug. 8, 1782). He was recommended to the British government by every officer he had served under, especially by Sir Henry Clinton who wrote, "It is impossible to speak too highly of him" (Robinson's memorial and "Evidence," *post*), and Parliament voted him a partial compensation for his losses. He died in England, where he lived after the Revolution, and his body was buried in St. James' Church at Bath. His wife and seven children survived him, and all of his five sons, four of whom served the British during the Revolution, achieved in later life a measure of distinction.

[See Robinson's Revolutionary correspondence in Sir Henry Clinton Papers, William L. Clements Lib., Univ. of Mich.; the American Loyalists Transcripts, N. Y. Pub. Lib., contain autobiographical material, including memorials cited, and estimates ("Evidence") by Sir Henry Clinton and others, vol. 43, 203–282; *Mag. of Hist.*, July 1909, pp. 47–48; *The Writings of George Washington*, vol. VII (1835), app. vii, ed. by Jared Sparks; compare literary style, etc. of Robinson to Ethan Allen, Mar. 30, 1780, and Feb. 2, 1781, in John Pell, *Ethan Allen* (1929), with letter supposedly written by Robinson to Arnold, in Winthrop Sargent, *The Life and Career of Major André* (1861), pp. 447–49; see also *Parish Register of Christ Church, Middlesex Co., Va.*, 1653–1812 (1897); Great Britain, Hist. MSS. Commission, *Report on American MSS. in the Royal Institution* (4 vols. 1904–09); *Calendar of Hist. MSS. . . . in the Office of the Secy. of State, Albany* (2 vols. 1868); *Memorial History of the City of N. Y.* (1892), II, ed. by J. G. Wilson; *Gentleman's Mag.*, Oct. 1749, p. 476, May 1792, p. 479; inscriptions from tombstone, Bath, and memorial tablet, Thornbury, Bristol, England; of the secondary sources, all with inaccuracies, the best is Lorenzo Sabine, *Biog. Sketches of Loyalists of the Am. Rev.* (1864), vol. II.]   J. C.

ROBINSON, CHARLES (July 21, 1818–Aug. 17, 1894), pioneer, first governor of the state of Kansas, was born at Hardwick, Mass., the son of Jonathan and Huldah (Woodward) Robinson. He grew up in an abolition atmosphere, attended a private school in his native town, and was then sent to Hadley and Amherst academies. He entered Amherst College but was forced to withdraw after a year and a half because of weak eyes. Subsequently he studied medicine under Dr. Amos Twitchell at Keene, N. H., and attended medical lectures at Pittsfield, Mass., and Woodstock, Vt. In 1843 he was married to Sarah Adams of Brookfield, and in the same year he began to practise his profession at Belchertown, Mass. Two years later he and Josiah G. Holland [q.v.] opened a hospital at Springfield. After his wife's death in 1846 he joined a brother at Fitchburg and there continued the practice of medicine. In 1849 he accompanied a party of about forty Bostonians to California. After two weeks at mining on Bear Creek he formed a partnership and established a restaurant at Sacramento. In the contest between land speculators and settlers he was chosen president of the squatters' association. In an armed collision with town officials he received a wound thought to be fatal. He was arrested and placed on a prison ship, where he unexpectedly recovered. After miners and squatters had elected him to the legislature, he was admitted to bail and soon became co-editor of the *Settlers' and Miners' Tribune* at Sacramento. In the state Assembly he was antislavery and supported Frémont for the federal Senate. Eventually a *nolle prosequi* was entered on charges of assault, conspiracy, and murder. He returned to Massachusetts by way of Panama in 1851, and on Oct. 30 of that year he was married to Sara Tappan Doolittle Lawrence, a young woman of good birth and education, daughter of Myron Lawrence of Belchertown, Mass. She shared his interests and ambitions and was an important factor in helping him throughout his life. Her *Kansas: its Interior and Exterior Life* (1856) is a history of the Kansas struggle with a Free-State bias. For two years Robinson edited the *Fitchburg News* and practised medicine.

In 1854 Eli Thayer appointed him Kansas resident agent of the New England Emigrant Aid Company. He was well qualified for the position since his California adventure had given him a glimpse of Kansas and had introduced him to the contentious life of the frontier. In July 1854 the company sent him to the territory to arrange for its settlement. He had noted the beauty and fertility of the Kansas valley in 1849, so he explored the Missouri to Fort Leavenworth while a companion followed the Kansas to Fort Riley. He then went to St. Louis to meet the first body of New England emigrants and continued to conduct a second to the terri-

tory, which arrived at Kansas City in September. The two groups united at the present site of Lawrence and began the settlement of that town. In the spring of 1855 he conducted another party to the territory, which arrived in time to participate in the election of a legislature on Mar. 30. Although there was illegal voting on both sides, proslavery candidates won a large majority of the seats. Three days after the election he wrote to Thayer for the loan of 200 Sharps rifles and two field pieces. At the first Fourth of July celebration at Lawrence he breathed defiance as he recommended, "Let us repudiate all laws enacted by foreign legislative bodies" (*Kansas Conflict, post,* p. 152). During the summer and fall of 1855 he attended numerous conferences held to unite antislavery factions in the territory. At the Lawrence convention of Aug. 14, he was appointed chairman of a Free-State executive committee of twenty-three, but a month later it was superseded by a smaller body headed by James H. Lane [q.v.]. A Free-State party was organized at Big Springs in September, and a constitutional convention was called to meet at Topeka on Oct. 23. He was a delegate and led the radical wing of the party that opposed discrimination against free negroes, but without success. Largely through his influence, however, the convention refused to indorse the principle of popular sovereignty, urged by Lane and the administration faction.

When proslavery Missourians gathered on Wakarusa River in December and threatened to destroy Lawrence, he was appointed commander-in-chief. His cautious policy probably averted bloodshed for the belligerent Lane wished to take the offensive. The timely arrival of Gov. Wilson Shannon ended the controversy, and both sides disbanded their forces. Yet the Wakarusa War was significant for it gave Lane the leadership of the radicals. On Jan. 15, 1856, the Free-State party elected officers under the Topeka constitution, and Robinson was chosen governor. A legislature was organized at Topeka on Mar. 4, and he delivered an inaugural address. He was soon indicted by a proslavery grand jury for treason and usurpation of office. While on his way east in May to obtain aid for Kansas he was arrested near Lexington, Mo. After four months of imprisonment at Lecompton he was released on bail, but the charges remained until the following year. In the fall of 1856 he resigned the governorship and went east; but the Free-State legislature did not act upon his resignation, and he withdrew it when he returned. He and Lane advised participation in the October election of 1857 for members of a territorial legislature. That policy was adopted, the Free-State party captured control of the territorial government, and the Topeka movement came to an end. In 1859 the Republican party supplanted the Free-State organization, and a new constitution was framed at Wyandotte.

Robinson was nominated for governor and elected over the Democratic candidate, Samuel Medary, but of course he did not take office until the state was admitted in 1861. He was sworn in as governor on Feb. 9, and summoned the legislature to meet Mar. 26. His message to the Assembly was able and comprehensive, and he evinced sound statesmanship in inaugurating the forms and functions of a new state government. Nevertheless, his administration of two years was beset with difficulties. Before he had been in office a year an abortive attempt was made to displace him. An election was held, but the canvassing board refused to count the votes, and the state supreme court held it illegal. Early in 1862 articles of impeachment were preferred against the auditor, secretary of state, and the governor because of alleged irregularities in the sale of state bonds. The first two were found guilty and removed from office, but Robinson was acquitted almost unanimously. Nevertheless, the bond transactions hurt him politically. In raising and officering state troops for the Civil War he and Lane worked at cross purposes. Lane had the confidence of Lincoln and Stanton, controlled Kansas patronage, and even usurped a part of the governor's prerogative.

After the expiration of his term of office, he remained a great deal in retirement at his country home of "Oakridge" a few miles from Lawrence, although he engaged in politics sporadically. Always an independent, he joined the Liberal Republican movement. He was elected to the state Senate in 1874 and again in 1876. A decade later he was defeated for Congress on the Democratic ticket, and in 1890 he was an unsuccessful candidate for governor on a fusion ticket composed of Greenbackers, Populists, and Democrats. Throughout his Kansas career he was a promoter of education. As a member of the state Senate he obtained the passage of a comprehensive law regulating the public school system. From 1864 to 1874 and again from 1893 to 1894 he was a regent of the University of Kansas. As superintendent of Haskell Institute, 1887–89, he adopted a policy of industrialization, under which the school began to flourish. He was president of the Kansas State Historical Society from 1879 to 1880 and in 1892 published *The Kansas Conflict.* Cautious and calculative, logical and shrewd, judicious and argumentative, his greatest service to Kansas was that he gave the Topeka movement equilibrium and was the brake and balance wheel of the Free-State party. He was never very popular, but his common sense and business acumen gave great weight to his judgment, and his decisions were usually sound.

[*"Webb Scrap Book," 17 vols., a collection of newspaper clippings, 1854–56, 1859, in the Kan. State Hist. Lib.; The Kansas Conflict* and *Kansas: its . . . Life, ante;* F. W. Blackmar, *The Life of Charles Robinson* (1902), and "A Chapter in the Life of Charles Robinson, the First Governor of Kansas," *Am. Hist. Asso. Report . . . 1894* (1896); Eli Thayer, *A Hist. of the Kansas Crusade* (1889); *Kan. Hist. Colls.,* vol. XIII (1915); D. W. Wilder's *Annals of Kansas* (new ed., 1886).]   W. H. S—n.

ROBINSON, CHARLES MULFORD (Apr. 30, 1869–Dec. 30, 1917), city planner, author, and journalist, was born at Ramapo, Rockland County, N. Y., the son of Arthur and Jane Howell (Porter) Robinson, who soon moved to Rochester, N. Y. He attended school there and in 1891 received the degree of A.B. from the University of Rochester. After college and between trips abroad he became an associate editor of the Rochester *Post-Express,* 1891–1902; in 1904 he was employed in an editorial capacity by the *Public Ledger* (Philadelphia), and in 1907 by the *Municipal Journal* (New York). He was also a regular contributing editor to the *Survey,* the *Architectural Record,* the *National Municipal Review,* and the *Boston Transcript.* His career as a city planner began with a series of three articles on municipal improvement contributed to the *Atlantic Monthly* in 1899, which aroused such interest that *Harper's Magazine* asked for a similar series on civic improvement abroad. The abundant material gathered in preparation for the articles was used later in a book that, strangely enough in view of its later success, went begging for a publisher and was finally brought out at the author's expense under the title of *The Improvement of Towns and Cities; or The Practical Basis of Civic Æsthetics* (1901). This was followed in 1903 by *Modern Civic Art; or The City Made Beautiful,* and in 1908 by *The Call of the City,* a collection of essays and verse. In 1911, largely as the result of a year at Harvard as a guest of the University, he published *The Width and Arrangement of Streets; A Study in Town Planning,* which five years later he rewrote as *City Planning: With Special Reference to the Planning of Streets and Lots.*

His work was not limited to writing, however. Early in his career he served as acting secretary of the American Park and Outdoor Art Association, made up largely of landscape architects, park commissioners and superintendents, and a few public-spirited citizens; and in 1904 he was influential in forming the American Civic Association at St. Louis, a union of the American Park Association and a federation of civic improvement societies in the Middle West. For a while he acted as secretary but soon retired from the position in order to devote more time to his increasingly active practice.

His work as a consultant began when Buffalo, N. Y., through its recently formed Society for Beautifying Buffalo, asked him to make a report (published in 1902) upon local conditions. Later he was consulted by many other cities, among them Detroit, Denver, Omaha, Los Angeles, Oakland, Cal., Cedar Rapids, Iowa, and Columbus, Ohio; his recommendations for all of these and for many towns, large and small, have been embodied in published reports. In the Detroit project Robinson was associated with Frederick Law Olmsted, Jr.; in Omaha with George B. Ford and E. P. Goodrich; and in Columbus with Austin W. Lord, Albert Kelsey, Charles N. Lowrie, and H. A. McNeil. In 1915 he associated himself professionally with William Pitkin, Jr., a landscape architect of Rochester, N. Y. In 1913 he accepted and held until his death the Chair of Civic Design established at the University of Illinois, the first of its kind in any American university although the subject had been taught for years at Harvard. Robinson's approach to city planning was primarily an æsthetic one and his rôle—for he was virtually without technical training—that of publicist and teacher rather than technical designer. It was to the lasting advantage of the profession in which he so ably pioneered that its cause was sponsored by a man of such broad vision, rare initiative, and good judgment. He died after a brief illness on Sunday, Dec. 30, 1917, at Albany, N. Y., survived by his widow, Eliza Ten Eyck Pruyn of Albany, whom he had married in 1896. After his death appeared *The City Sleeps* (1920), a volume of his verse and essays compiled and edited by Mrs. Robinson. His professional library, comprising books, reports, periodicals and original studies, maps, and plans, was given by his widow to Harvard University as a memorial collection.

[*Who's Who in America*, 1916–17; *Landscape Architecture*, July 1919, reprint with portrait and bibliography from *Trans. Am. Soc. Landscape Architects,* 1909–21, pp. 93–99; *Revista Municipal* (Havana), Mar. 1908, bibliography and notes on life and work corrected by Robinson; *Nat. Municipal Rev.,* Mar. 1918; *Municipal Jour.* (N. Y.), Jan. 5, 1918; *Albany Evening Jour.,* Dec. 31, 1917.]   K. M.

ROBINSON, CHARLES SEYMOUR (Mar. 31, 1829–Feb. 1, 1899), Presbyterian clergyman, hymnologist, editor, was born in Bennington, Vt., son of Henry and Martha Prime (Haynes) Robinson. The family was related to John Robinson, pastor of the Pilgrims in Leyden, and included honored founders of Bennington and the state. Charles prepared for college at Union Academy, East Bennington, and graduated at Williams in 1849. After teaching for two years he spent a year at Union Seminary, New York, and graduated in 1855 at Princeton Seminary. He was ordained Apr. 19, 1855, as pastor of the Park Presbyterian Church, Troy, N. Y. Freshness of thought and personal charm gave marked attractiveness to his ministry. He was married in 1858 to Harriet Reed Church of Troy, who died in 1896. In 1860 he was called to the First Presbyterian Church of Brooklyn, N. Y.

From boyhood Robinson had been passionately fond of music; he played the flute and would walk miles to hear a good band; as pastor he was deeply interested in promoting a higher type of congregational singing. To this end, during his pastorate in Brooklyn he entered upon the studies in hymnology which were his absorbing avocation for thirty years and greatly extended his influence and usefulness. His first venture in the preparation of hymnals was *Hymns of the Church,* published in 1862. This was followed in 1865 by *Songs for the Sanctuary,* which met with wide acceptance especially in Presbyterian and Congregational churches; over half a million copies of it were issued.

In 1868 he resigned his charge at Brooklyn and became pastor of the American Chapel in Paris, which under his leadership united the work of several Christian bodies and became the "American Church in Paris." Obliged to leave that city when it was besieged by the German army in 1870, he returned to New York and was called to the pastorate of the Eleventh (later Madison Avenue) Presbyterian Church, where he gave devoted service for seventeen years. In 1875 he published *Psalms and Hymns,* which became the official hymnal of the Southern Presbyterian Church, and in 1878, *Selection of Spiritual Songs,* which showed the influence of the modern English hymn and tune writers. This influence was much more marked in *Laudes Domini* (1884), characterized in Julian's *Dictionary of Hymnology* (London, 1915) as "a book of great excellence," which came into extensive use; *New Laudes Domini* appeared in 1892. Regarding all this work in hymnology as his special contribution to the life of the churches, Robinson would not use his large royalties from his hymnals for himself or his family, but devoted them to the building fund of his church and other benefactions.

The breaking of his health under continuous overstrain led him to resign his pastorate, and he turned to literary work, still doing much preaching. He had edited the *Illustrated Christian Weekly* in 1876–77; he now conducted *Every Thursday,* a periodical of his own (March 1890–April 1891). Besides the hymnals already mentioned he had edited some fifteen minor collections and had written several volumes mainly of an expository character. He now published *Sabbath Evening Sermons* (1887), *The Pharaohs of the Bondage and the Exodus* (1887), *Simon Peter, His Early Life and Times* (1889), *Simon Peter, His Later Life and Labours* (1894), and *Annotations upon Popular Hymns* (1893). Notwithstanding his rapidly failing strength, he undertook a brief pastorate (1891) with the Thirteenth Street Presbyterian Church, and another (1892–98) with the New York Presbyterian Church on 128th Street. He died in New York and was buried in Bennington.

[Obituary and editorial, *N. Y. Evangelist,* Feb. 9, 1899; *N. Y. Tribune,* Feb. 2, 1899; John Julian, *A Dictionary of Hymnology* (1915); letters from Mary Robinson Gaylord.]   E. D. E.

ROBINSON, CHRISTOPHER (May 15, 1806–Oct. 3, 1889), lawyer, diplomatist, was born in Providence, R. I., the son of Benjamin Robinson and his wife, Ann (Pitts). He was sent to a private school and thence to Brown University, where he was graduated in 1825. His personal inclinations were toward a career in which success would depend upon powers of speech: in education, religion, or the law. He chose the last, retaining a practical interest in the other two throughout his life. After his graduation he engaged for a time in academy teaching, and then read law under Senator Albert C. Greene. He was admitted to the bar in 1833, and made his appearance in public life the same year as Fourth-of-July orator in Woonsocket, where he had settled. A Universalist, he preached for the Universalist society before the completion of their meeting-house in 1839. In 1847 he was prominent, though unsuccessful, in an effort to link Woonsocket to Boston by a railroad. He was thrice married: to Mary Tillinghast, by whom he had one child who died; to Mary Jencks, who had no issue; and to Louisa Aldrich, to whom four children were born. Robinson did not enter politics until after the

death of his third wife, in 1853. His political ambitions were rewarded when he was made attorney-general of Rhode Island, 1854–55. He was elected to the Thirty-sixth Congress (1859–61), where he voted for John Sherman for speaker and was a member of the Judiciary Committee and of the select committee of thirty-three on the "state of the Union." His sentiments were strongly anti-slavery and pro-Union. He was not returned in the election of 1860, but on June 8, 1861, was appointed minister to Peru by President Lincoln. This was an important, even critical, post, for diplomatic relations had been suspended in November 1860 by President Buchanan, and there were many partisans of the Confederacy in Lima. Robinson presented his credentials Jan. 11, 1862, and with patient persistence and unruffled temper urged upon dilatory and changing ministries the settlement of the claims of American citizens. He yielded to the Peruvian contention that the two most controversial cases should be submitted to arbitration (which was never effected, since the King of the Belgians declined to act as arbitrator), but he obtained the satisfactory settlement of the other claims by means of a mixed commission. He also won Peruvian sentiment over to the Federal government, turning to his advantage Peru's fears of European aggression, of which he offered Mexico as an example. When these fears were realized in 1864 by Spain's seizure of the Chincha Islands, he exerted himself to assure Peru of the active sympathy of the United States.

Robinson's mission was terminated in a peculiar manner. In July 1865 he received an instruction from the Department of State that his resignation had been accepted. He replied that any document purporting to be his resignation was a forgery, but that he was ready to retire. The investigation which followed involved the secretary of the legation, who was recalled. A new minister arrived in November, and Robinson's last important official act was to assemble the diplomatic corps at the legation (he was acting without instructions), where it was resolved to recognize a revolutionary government which had just overthrown the old. Robinson left Peru on Dec. 21, and returned to private life in Woonsocket, Jan. 16, 1866. He lived quietly and in comfortable circumstances there until his death at the age of eighty-three.

[E. Richardson, *Hist. of Woonsocket* (1876); Woonsocket and other Rhode Island newspapers, esp. obituary notice in *Providence Daily Journal,* Oct. 5, 1889, and note in Brown Univ. Necrology, *Ibid.,* June 18, 1890; Robinson's dispatches in the archives of the State Dept.; and Woonsocket tax records.]   G. V. B.

ROBINSON, CONWAY (Sept. 15, 1805–Jan. 30, 1884), lawyer and author, the son of John and Agnes Conway (Moncure) Robinson and brother of Moncure Robinson [q.v.], was born in Richmond, Va. He was descended from John Robinson who is recorded as owning land in New Charles Parish in 1653. He was not related to John Robinson, the colonial treasurer, nor to Christopher Robinson, the president of the council. His father put in a long life as a law clerk. From 1787 to 1812 he was assistant or principal clerk in one or more of the local courts, and from 1827 to his death in 1850 he was clerk to the state circuit court in Richmond. He was presumably well qualified for his task as compiler of *A Collection of . . . Forms . . . used in the . . . Courts of Law in Virginia* (1809). Conway Robinson attended the school of a Mr. Terrill until he was thirteen years old. At that age he began to follow in his father's footsteps. He became the assistant of Thomas C. Howard, clerk of two of Richmond's local courts, and after six years of the latter's teaching he became clerk of a local court. In 1827 he was admitted to the bar. In the following year he was made clerk of the general court. He had already (1826) issued a new edition of his father's *Forms.* Resigning his clerkship in July 1831 to engage in practice, he became a successful attorney and in January 1839 was admitted to the bar of the United States Supreme Court. In the conduct of his cases he made both reputation and money, but from the first he devoted a part of his time and energy to legal and historical scholarship. In 1831 he assisted in founding the Virginia Historical and Philosophical Society. He prepared for it several studies, some of which were published in *An Account of Discoveries in the West until 1519, and of Voyages to and along the Atlantic Coast of North America, from 1520 to 1573* (1848). In 1832 he published Volume I of his *Practice in the Courts of Law and Equity in Virginia,* followed by Volume II in 1835, and Volume III in 1839. This work is still spoken of with respect and affection by Virginia lawyers of the old school. It was as a "black letter lawyer" that Conway Robinson attained eminence, and his accurate, scrupulous scholarship and luminous style never appear to better advantage than in his "Old Practice."

In 1836 he became president of the struggling Richmond, Fredericksburg & Potomac Railroad Company. By November 1838 he had established it so firmly that in spite of the unanimous request of the stockholders that he continue at its head he felt free to resign. In 1842 he became official reporter of the court of appeals and issued two volumes of *Virginia Reports.* As a preface to the first of these volumes he inserted a sketch of the development of the judicial system of the state. In 1846 he and John Mercer Patton [q.v.] were chosen by the legislature to revise the civil code, and in 1847, the criminal code of Virginia. In 1852 he was elected to the legislature to assist in adapting these codes to the new constitution, adopted by the state in 1851. In 1854 he published the first volume of his *Practice in Courts of Justice in England and the United States,* the seventh and last volume of which appeared in 1874. Because of the superior libraries in the national capital, he moved his residence to the District of Columbia in 1858. At the time of his removal from Virginia he had appeared as counsel before the Virginia court of appeals in 137 cases, and before the United States Supreme Court in five of the fourteen cases brought before that court from Virginia since 1839. He disapproved of secession, but three of his sons served the Confederacy and two of them died for it. After 1866 he resumed his practice before the Virginia court of appeals and continued to practise before that court until 1878 and before the United States Supreme Court until his death. In 1882 he published the first volume of his *History of the High Court of Chancery and Other Institutions of England.* This volume was an exhaustive exposition of English constitutional development to the death of Henry VIII. Work on the second volume was cut short by Robinson's death at the home of his brother in Philadelphia on Jan. 30, 1884. He had married, on July 14, 1836, Mary Susan Selden Leigh, daughter of Benjamin Watkins Leigh [q.v.] of Virginia, who with five children survived him.

[John Selden, "Conway Robinson," *Va. Law Reg.,* Jan. 1896; A. H. Sands, "Conway Robinson," *Va. Law Jour.,* May 1884; H. E. Hayden, *Va. Geneals.* (1891); the *State* (Richmond), Feb. 1, 1884.]   T. C. J., Jr.

ROBINSON, EDWARD (Apr. 10, 1794–Jan. 27, 1863), philologist, geographer, and professor of Biblical literature, was the son of Rev. William Robinson by his fourth wife, Elisabeth (Norton). His earliest American ancestor was William Robinson who was in Dorchester, Mass., as early as 1637. Edward was born in Southington, Conn., where his father was pastor for forty-one years and also a shrewd and successful farmer. The boy attended the common schools of the vicinity and for a time was a student in the family of a neighboring pastor. At the age of sixteen he was apprenticed to a Southington merchant who put him in charge of the drug department of his store. Robinson was eager for further education, however, and in a couple of years was allowed to go to Hamilton College, Clinton, N. Y., where an uncle, Seth Norton, was a professor. After graduating in 1816, he studied law for a year in Hudson, N. Y., and the next year was tutor in mathematics and Greek at Hamilton. On Sept. 3, 1818, he married Eliza Kirkland, daughter of Samuel Kirkland [q.v.], missionary to the Oneidas. After her death, the following July, he remained on a farm she had owned, where he combined agricultural pursuits with study.

In 1821, he went to Andover, Mass., in order to see through the press certain portions of the *Iliad* which he had edited with a Latin introduction and notes—*Iliadis Libri Novem Priores Librique XVIII et XXII* (1822). At Andover he came under the influence of the distinguished Hebraist, Moses Stuart [q.v.], professor in the Theological Seminary, who persuaded him to devote himself to Hebrew studies. On Oct. 1, 1822, he was licensed to preach by the Hartford South Association and the following year he became instructor in Hebrew at the Seminary, continuing in this capacity until 1826. During this period he assisted Stuart in preparing *A Greek Grammar of the New Testament* (1825), a translation from the German of G. B. Winer, and himself made and published in 1825 a translation of Wahl's *Clavis Philologica Novi Testamenti*. The year 1826, in which he went to Germany to study, was a turning point in his career, since he then came into direct contact with German scholarship and methods at a time when scholarly research, in the modern sense of the term, was quite unknown in America. For four years he pursued studies at Göttingen, Halle, and Berlin, making a great impression by his ability, and becoming the personal friend of the philologists Gesenius and Rödiger, the theologian Tholuck, the historian Neander, and especially of the great geographer Ritter, whose influence on him was to be decisive. In 1828 he married Therese Albertine Louise, the brilliant daughter of Ludwig Heinrich von Jakob, professor of philosophy at Halle [see Therese A. L. von Jakob Robinson].

After his return to America, Robinson was appointed professor extraordinary of Biblical literature at Andover, a post which he combined with that of librarian. In 1831 he founded the *American Biblical Repository*, of which he was editor for four years and to which he contributed much of the material; later, 1843, he founded the *Bibliotheca Sacra*, which the next year was taken over by Edwards A. Park and Bela B. Edwards [qq.v.] of Andover. Subject to attacks of epilepsy, he was forced by ill health to resign his

professorship in 1833. Removing to Boston, he continued his work, however, publishing several books and numerous papers. The most important of these were *A Hebrew and English Lexicon of the Old Testament . . .* (1836), a translation of Gesenius' work with additions and alterations; and *A Greek and English Lexicon of the New Testament* (1836). In 1837 he was invited to the chair of Biblical literature at Union Theological Seminary, New York City, and at the same time given leave of absence in order to visit the Holy Land. From March to July 1838 he traveled in Sinai, Palestine, and southern Syria, with the aid of an American missionary, Eli Smith [q.v.]. Robinson himself emphasizes the invaluable assistance given him by Smith, whose command of Arabic and knowledge of the people formed a perfect complement to his own historical and philological training. It is difficult to overestimate the value of their joint achievement. For the first time a trained scholar, possessed of a sound critical method in historical and topographical research, explored Palestine, paying the most careful attention to cartography, to the correct Arabic form of place-names (*sine qua non*), and to the vestiges of antiquity. It is not surprising that the publication of his great work, *Biblical Researches in Palestine, Mount Sinai and Arabia Petraea* (3 vols., London, 1841), and the simultaneous appearance of a German translation, at once established his reputation as one of the foremost geographers and Biblical scholars of his time. The lapse of three generations has placed him even higher in the history of scholarship, for it is now recognized that his work marks an epoch in the development of historical geography and related fields. In 1852 he visited Palestine again, for a shorter period, and in 1856 brought out the results of this reconnaissance in a second edition of his work, with a supplementary volume, *Later Biblical Researches in Palestine and the Adjacent Regions*. Three years later he published a *Memoir of the Rev. William Robinson* (1859), with a genealogy of his family. Unhappily, his health began to interfere seriously with his activities, and he was at last stricken with an incurable disease of the eyes. He died in New York City after a short illness.

[H. B. Smith and R. D. Hitchcock, *The Life, Writings, and Character of Edward Robinson* (1863); Robinson's *Memoir of the Rev. William Robinson* (1859); H. R. Timlow, *Ecclesiastical and Other Sketches of Southington, Conn.* (1875); G. L. Prentiss, *The Union Theological Sem. in the City of N. Y.* (1889); *N. Y. Tribune*, Jan. 29, 1863.]   W. F. A.

ROBINSON, EDWARD (Nov. 1, 1858–Apr. 18, 1931), director of the Metropolitan Museum of Art, only son of Edwin Augustus and Ellen (Coburn) Robinson, was born in Boston, Mass. He attended the Boston Latin School and graduated from Harvard in 1879. In 1881 he married Elizabeth H. Gould, of Boston, and a son was born in 1882. After five years spent in study in Europe, including fifteen months in Greece and three semesters at the University of Berlin, he returned to Boston in 1885 and became curator of classical antiquities at the Museum of Fine Arts. He was elected its director in 1902, holding this position until 1905, when he went to New York as assistant director and curator of classical art at the Metropolitan Museum of Art. In 1910 he was elected director, remaining in office during his lifetime. He was the third to hold the chief administrative position, and the first of American parentage.

Robinson's administration was notable. His first care was the assembling of a scientific staff and the organizing of departments with a competent curator at the head of each. His own chosen field was classical archaeology, and he set the same high standard for the classical department of the Metropolitan Museum that had made the collection in the Boston Museum outstanding, but he was equally interested in the development of other departments, which all came under the influence of his sound judgment and unerring taste. Several new wings were built to house the rapidly growing collections, many of which, coming as gifts or bequests, presented special problems in their exhibition and care. At the same time the increased use of the Museum by the public made necessary constant cooperation in the way of publications, lectures, and temporary exhibitions. A new stage of Museum development was reached with the establishment, in 1925, of a branch museum, The Cloisters, and the series of symphony concerts given each winter after 1919. In spite of all these activities, which made so great a demand on the time of the Director, he found it possible to serve on the boards of several other institutions. He was a member of the Council of the Archaeological Institute of America and president of its New York society; a member of the managing committee of the American School of Classical Studies in Athens; a trustee of the American Academy in Rome; a member of the Executive Committee of the American Society for the Excavation of Sardis; a director of the American Federation of Arts; a trustee of the Museum of the City of New York, and a member of the Commission for the Excavation of the Agora of Athens. He was also a fellow of the American Academy of Arts and Sciences; a

member of the German Archaeological Institute; a corresponding member of the American Institute of Architects; a member of the Architectural League of New York; a member of the Commission des Musées royaux des Beaux Arts de Belgique, and of many other learned societies.

While in Boston Robinson served for eight years as secretary of the art commission of the city of Boston. He selected and arranged the collection of casts of classical and renaissance sculpture in the Slater Memorial Museum at Norwich, Conn., and also formed the collection of casts in the Metropolitan Museum. In 1893–94 and from 1898 to 1902 he was lecturer in classical archaeology at Harvard University. His catalogues of Greek and Roman casts and Greek, Etruscan, and Roman vases in the Boston Museum, as well as scholarly publications in the annual reports, were of value to scholars and students alike. After taking up work in New York, his administrative duties restricted his writing to short articles, appearing chiefly in the *Bulletin* of the Metropolitan Museum. In recognition of his long and varied service to the world of art numerous degrees and foreign orders were conferred upon him.

[See Harvard College, Class of 1879, *Ninth Report* (1929); *Who's Who in America*, 1930–31; and the *Bulletin* of the Metropolitan Museum of Art, May 1931. New York newspapers, as well as other papers and periodicals, published obituary articles and editorials at the time of Robinson's death.] H. Fa—n.

ROBINSON, EDWARD MOTT (Jan. 8, 1800–June 14, 1865), merchant, son of James and Mary (Attmore) Robinson, was born in Philadelphia, where his father had married and engaged in mercantile business. He was taken to South Kingstown, R. I., to which his ancestor, Rowland Robinson a Quaker, emigrated from England, late in the seventeenth century. He was the great-grandson of William Robinson, a large landed proprietor and deputy governor of Rhode Island in the middle of the eighteenth century. After his academic education had been completed, at the age of twenty-one he began business in Wakefield, South Kingstown, with his elder brother. They first engaged in cotton and woolen manufacturing, subsequently carrying on a commission business in sperm oil in Providence, R. I. Some time after 1830 he removed to New Bedford, Mass., where he soon entered the firm of Isaac Howland, Junior, & Company, whaling merchants. On Dec. 29, 1833, he was married in New Bedford to Abby Slocum Howland, the daughter of Gideon Howland and grand-daughter of Isaac Howland, his partners in the whaling firm. The young partner was forceful, energetic, and far-sighted, and through his shrewd management helped make the house of Howland one of the wealthiest and most prominent in the golden days of the whaling industry. For nearly thirty years he was a leading figure in New Bedford. His firm owned more than thirty vessels, administered successfully the details of equipment and personnel, and exerted a wide influence on the community and the industry. He served as president of the Bedford Commercial Bank. Entering politics, he was elected to the city government, though failing in an ambition to reach the mayor's chair. A man who had known him wrote in 1918 that "he was not personally popular" (Emery, *post*, p. iv), but an anonymous writer of 1851 characterized him as "affable and colloquial . . . with the soubriquet of 'Black Hawk,' to which he answers with good nature. In business matters he is strictly honorable, but he does not claim to be anything more" (*Rich Men, post*, p. 190).

After the death of his wife in 1860 and the outbreak of the Civil War with its adverse consequences to the whale fisheries, he removed to New York, where he joined the firm of William T. Coleman & Company, in which he became a large owner. They were proprietors of a line of California packets, at one time being in control of more than seventy vessels. He also added to his wealth by successful operations in Wall Street. Tall and distinguished, he was always well-dressed, though many stories were told of his personal economies. He once refused an imported cigar, remarking that he was satisfied with cheap ones and was fearful of a cultivated taste, which he could not afford. At his death in New York he left a fortune somewhat in excess of $5,000,000, the bulk of which, after a bequest of $10,000 to the town of South Kingstown and small legacies to friends, he bequeathed, mostly in trust, to his then unmarried daughter, who, as Hetty Howland (Robinson) Green [*q.v.*] subsequently became known as "the richest woman in the world." He refused to name her as his executor, believing women could not take care of money and little dreaming she would expand his wealth twenty-fold.

[W. M. Emery, *The Howland Heirs* (1919); Abner Forbes and J. W. Greene, *Rich Men of Massachusetts* (1851); T. R. Hazard, *Recollections of Olden Times* (1879); *Providence Daily Journal*, Apr. 7, 1873.]

W. M. E.

ROBINSON, EDWARD VAN DYKE (Dec. 20, 1867–Dec. 10, 1915), economist, was born at Bloomington, Ill., the son of Charles Stanley and Wilhelmina (von Schwanenflügel) Robinson. He graduated from the University of Michigan (A.B., 1890, A.M., 1891) and received his doctorate at Leipzig in 1895. Prior to study in

Europe he had been superintendent of schools at Schoolcraft, Mich., and on his return to America he reëntered secondary school work, becoming principal of high schools in Muskegon, Mich., Rock Island, Ill., and in St. Paul. During this period he was at different times special lecturer on economics and politics at Augustana College at Rock Island, and acting professor at Albion College, Albion, Mich. He had taught physiography and commercial geography in the summer school of the University of Minnesota, and in 1907 was appointed professor of economics in this institution. Two years later he revisited Europe, as delegate of his university to the Darwin Centennial Celebration, at Cambridge, England, and to the five hundredth anniversary celebration of the University of Leipzig. He was a student of wide interests—geography, economic history, taxation, transportation, governmental administration, education. His inquiries in remote fields and periods were matched by others of immediate importance to Minnesota. He worked closely with the Minnesota Tax Commission, as director of its department of research and statistics, and for its report, 1912, prepared the studies of the cost of the state's government, and of railroad taxation in Minnesota. The University published his elaborate account of *Early Economic Conditions and the Development of Agriculture in Minnesota* (1915). Scientific journals were carrying articles from his pen which showed his skill in less utilitarian investigations, such as into the division of governmental power in ancient Greece.

Robinson's high school teaching had yielded a textbook on commercial geography in 1910, which, many times reprinted, influenced the teaching of this subject. He was opposed to the rigidity which characterized the curriculum and system of promotion of pupils in the public schools and was among the earliest to advocate the junior high school as a means of reform. In 1915, following a year of study abroad, he was elected to a professorship in economics in Columbia University, his responsibility being chiefly for the undergraduate department. For this work he was fitted not only by his competent scholarship (particularly evident in his "War and Economics in History and in Theory," in the *Political Science Quarterly*, December 1900), but by his knowledge of pedagogy and his pronounced turn for educational administration. He had barely entered upon his new duties, however, when he died of an attack of heart disease. He was survived by his wife, Clare (Howard) Robinson, whom he had married at Muskegon, Mich., on June 30, 1897, and by a daughter.

Robinson was a man of fine presence, good judgment, sincerity, and much personal magnetism. He put students under obligation by his generous devotion of time to their individual problems. [*Minneapolis Morning Tribune*, Dec. 11, 1915; *Minn. Alumni Weekly*, Dec. 20, 1915; *Who's Who in America*, 1914–15; *N. Y. Times*, Dec. 11, 1915.]   B. M.

ROBINSON, EZEKIEL GILMAN (Mar. 23, 1815–June 13, 1894), Baptist clergyman, educator, for seventeen years president of Brown University, was born on the ancestral farm in South Attleboro, Mass., the youngest of the four children of Ezekiel and Cynthia (Slack) Robinson. His early boyhood was spent at his birthplace and in that portion of Pawtucket which was then in the state of Massachusetts. He attended various schools, which in general, he states, did him more harm than good, and was poorly prepared for college at two academies, one in New Hampton, N. H., and the other in Pawtucket. He graduated from Brown University in 1838, having, as he says, "drifted aimlessly into college and drifted aimlessly through it, waking up only during the last year to see what I might and ought to have done" (*An Autobiography, post*, p. 18). He seems also to have drifted into the ministry. Judging him to be a promising candidate, the Baptist Church in Pawtucket of which he was a member licensed him to preach before he had finished his college course. After his graduation, for six months or more he represented the American Tract Society among the churches of Hartford County, Conn., with notable success. He then did some graduate work at Brown, occasionally preaching with acceptance to his hearers and encouragement to himself. He was thus led to enter Newton Theological Institution, from which he graduated in 1842.

His first pastorate was at the Cumberland Street Baptist Church, Norfolk, Va., where he was ordained in November 1842. Here he remained until the autumn of 1845, serving on leave of absence (1843–44) as chaplain of the University of Virginia, where he preached each Sunday and lectured once a week. During this period he was married, Feb. 21, 1844, to Harriet Richards Parker, daughter of Caleb Parker of Roxbury, Mass. From October 1845 to September 1846 he was pastor of the Old Cambridge Baptist Church, Cambridge, Mass. Leaving here in the interest of his wife's health, he became professor of Biblical interpretation in the Western Baptist Theological Institute, recently established at Covington, Ky. With the virtual breaking up of that school in 1848 over the question of slavery, he accepted the pastorate of the

Ninth Street Baptist Church, Cincinnati. Early in 1853 he resigned to become professor of Biblical theology at the Rochester Theological Seminary, Rochester, N. Y.

In spite of the somewhat fortuitous character of his early career, Robinson later revealed a vigorous will, intense application, and a bold, keen, acquisitive intellect. Preëminently a thinker, and endowed with no little oratorical ability, he took high rank among preachers of the scholarly type. "Tall, erect, broad-shouldered, with an intellectual cast of countenance made venerable by the hoary locks which even in the prime of manhood were prematurely gray," he was a man whose "words gained weight from his physical stature and his dignified demeanor" (*Memorial Address, post*, p. 5). He had an unconquerable dislike for pastoral duties, however, and felt that teaching was his proper vocation. This feeling was justified by his success at Rochester. Fearlessly devoted to the truth, scornful of superficiality and sham, relentlessly logical, intensely virile, he captivated the students and inspired them with something of his own spirit. Theologically he was unchained, rationalistic, and in advance of his times. The substance of his lectures at Rochester is contained in his *Christian Theology* (1894). Among his other published works are a translation of Neander's *Planting and Training of the Christian Church* (1865); *Lectures on Preaching* (1883), delivered in 1882 at Yale; *Principles and Practice of Morality* (1888, 1891, 1896); *Christian Evidences* (1895); *Christian Character, Baccalaureate Sermons* (1896); and numerous articles, some of them in the *Christian Review* of which from 1859 to 1864 he was the editor.

From 1860 until 1872 he served as president of Rochester Theological Seminary, and in the latter year succeeded Alexis Caswell [*q.v.*] as president of Brown University. He at once perceived the defects and needs of the institution and with all the force of his inflexible will inaugurated improvements. A little lacking in patience and tact, and brusque in manners, he sometimes made his lot unnecessarily difficult. A certain sternness and a rigorous attitude in the matter of discipline prevented him from commanding the affection of the students. In spite of these defects, after seventeen years of leadership he left the college far richer in equipment and much further advanced in educational policy. Resigning in March 1889 at the age of seventy-four, he continued active for the remainder of his life, preaching, lecturing, and from the fall of 1892 serving as professor of ethics and apologetics at the University of Chicago. His death occurred in a Boston hospital and he was buried in Rochester.

[*Ezekiel Gilman Robinson, An Autobiog.* (1896), ed. by E. H. Johnson; T. D. Anderson, *Memorial Address on Ezekiel Gilman Robinson* (1895); W. C. Bronson, *The Hist. of Brown Univ.* (1914); *Providence Jour.*, June 14, 1894.]
H. E. S.

ROBINSON, FREDERICK BYRON (Apr. 11, 1855–Mar. 23, 1910), anatomist and surgeon, was born on a farm near Hollandale, Iowa County, Wis., where his parents, William and Mary Robinson, English immigrants, had settled in 1845. After elementary instruction in the log school house of Hollandale he attended Mineral Point Seminary and later worked his way through the University of Wisconsin, where he obtained the degree of B.S. in 1878. He taught school to finance his course through Rush Medical College, Chicago, receiving his medical degree in 1882. He practised medicine at Grand Rapids, Wis., for six years broken by study trips to Heidelberg, Berlin, Vienna, London, and Birmingham. A course under Lawson Tait at Birmingham had a lasting influence upon his career. In 1889 he moved to Toledo, Ohio, where he was made professor of anatomy and clinical surgery in the Toledo Medical College. Two years later he took up his residence in Chicago and was appointed professor of gynecology in the Chicago Post-Graduate Medical School. Later, he was professor of gynecology and abdominal surgery successively at the Illinois Medical School and the Chicago College of Medicine and Surgery. For many years he served on the staff of the Woman's Hospital and of the Mary Thompson Hospital. In 1894 he married Dr. Lucy Waite, head surgeon of the Mary Thompson Hospital, and they were thereafter associated in hospital and office work.

Though always a busy practitioner of surgery, his chief claim to distinction rests upon his researches and writings in the field of anatomy. For years he frequented the morgue of the Cook County Hospital, where he made a study of the material which came for autopsy. He confined his studies to the abdomen and pelvis and their contents. Most notable were his investigations upon the physiological anatomy of the peritoneum, but they included the anatomy and pathology of the ureters, the seminal vesicles, the biliary and pancreatic ducts, and the abdominal sympathetic nervous system. Of particular interest to the practising surgeon were his investigations upon the pathology of the psoas muscle and its relation to appendicitis. His untiring industry and enthusiasm brought to him an astonishing wealth of material. Equally no-

table is the quantity of his literary output. He is credited with having written over five hundred articles, in addition to several large volumes devoted to surgery and anatomy. His books include *Experimental Intestinal Surgery* (1889), *Practical Intestinal Surgery* (2 vols., 1891), *Landmarks in Gynecology* (2 vols., 1894), *The Peritoneum—Histology and Physiology* (1897), and *Abdominal and Pelvic Brain* (1906). Another of his important achievements was a life-size chart illustrating the sympathetic nervous system. Many of his articles are but slight variations of the same theme. As might be expected, their literary quality suffered much from this overproduction. His writings are marked by poor arrangement and faulty diction and are seriously marred by a bizarre technical terminology. That his investigations were in the main sound is evidenced by their frequent citation in the standard works on anatomy. His name is carried by several anatomical eponyms. Personally he was short and heavy-set, an intense person with tireless nervous energy, egotistical, and intolerant of criticism or of the opinions of others. He had developed highly the "gentle art of making enemies." The glaring faults of his literary style and his unattractive personality doubtless account in some measure for the fact that his books never had the backing of a leading publisher, that his articles seldom appeared in the more substantial journals, and that he never achieved the highest recognition as a teacher.

[Lucy Waite, *In Memoriam: Byron Robinson* (1910); *Am. Medic. Compend.* (Toledo), Jan. 1907; *Am. Jour. of Clinical Medicine,* July 1910, Apr. 1922; *Medic. Standard* (Chicago), Sept. 1910; *Who's Who in America,* 1908–09, where he is listed as Byron Robinson; H. A. Kelly and W. L. Burrage, *Am. Medic. Biogs.* (1920), where he is listed as Fred Byron Robinson.]
J. M. P—n.

ROBINSON, HARRIET JANE HANSON (Feb. 8, 1825–Dec. 22, 1911), woman's suffrage leader, was born in Boston, of old New England stock, the daughter of William and Harriet (Browne) Hanson. When about eight years old she moved with her widowed mother and three brothers to Lowell "where they lived for some years on one of the manufacturing 'corporations'" (*Loom and Spindle, post,* p. 160). Here she received her early education, and then became an operative in a Lowell mill. As one of Lowell's literary mill girls she wrote for *The Lowell Offering,* and was on intimate terms with its editors. She also contributed to the "annuals" and newspapers of the time, and it was through such contributions to the *Lowell Courier* that she met the journalist and reformer, William Stevens Robinson [*q.v.*] whom, on Nov.

30, 1848, she married; they had two daughters and two sons. Throughout his lifetime, she loyally and enthusiastically supported her husband's activities in the anti-slavery crusade and other reform movements.

Her own particular interest, however, was in the advancement of women, and, following Robinson's death in 1876, she wrote and spoke freely in their behalf. She was the first woman to appear before the Select Committee on Woman Suffrage in Congress, and she advocated the cause of suffrage before the legislature of Massachusetts. In 1888 she served as a member of the International Council of Women which met in Washington. She was keenly interested in the women's club movement, assisting in the formation of the General Federation of Women's Clubs in 1890, and serving as a member of its first advisory board. In association with Julia Ward Howe [*q.v.*] and others she helped to organize the New England Women's Club. She was also one of the first members of the Wintergreen Club of Boston.

Her earliest book was *"Warrington" Pen-Portraits* (1877), a memoir of her husband with selections from his writings. This was followed by *Massachusetts in the Woman Suffrage Movement: A General, Political, Legal and Legislative History from 1774 to 1881* (1881, 1883); *Captain Mary Miller* (1887), a suffrage drama; *The New Pandora* (1889), a classical drama and "the heart-and-brain product of one who grew up as a working-girl"; *Early Factory Labor in New England* (1883, 1889); and *Loom and Spindle, or Life Among the Early Mill Girls* (1898). The closing years of her life were spent in Malden, Mass., where she died in her eighty-seventh year.

[Lucy Larcom, in *Loom and Spindle* (1898); E. C. Stanton, S. B. Anthony, and M. J. Gage, *Hist. of Woman Suffrage* (4 vols., 1881–1902); *Who's Who in America*, 1910–11; *Boston Transcript*, Dec. 22, 1911.]
W. R. W.

ROBINSON, HENRY CORNELIUS (Aug. 28, 1832–Feb. 14, 1900), lawyer and legislator, was the son of David Franklin and Anne (Seymour) Robinson of Hartford and a descendant of Thomas Robinson who settled at Guilford, Conn., in 1664. After preparation at the Hartford Grammar School and at the Hartford Public High School, he was sent in 1849 to Yale where he achieved both social and scholastic success. After graduation in 1853 he studied law with his brother Lucius F. Robinson and with Judge William Lucius Storrs [*q.v.*], and on Aug. 17, 1855, he was admitted to the bar at Hartford. In 1858 he became his brother's partner, and from 1861 to 1888, when he was joined by his

eldest son, he continued the firm alone. On Aug. 28, 1862, he married Eliza Niles Trumbull, daughter of John F. Trumbull of Stonington, thus joining the heritage of two of Connecticut's oldest families. His legal practice became outstanding, for he not only secured a large private clientele, but as a corporation counsel he came to represent the largest interests in the state. He was an ardent supporter of the Republican party from its foundation and in 1866 was appointed by Governor Hawley as fish commissioner. Since his college days he had been interested in the fisheries problem, an important one on the Connecticut River, and with this opportunity to put his theories into practice he demonstrated that it was possible to hatch shad artificially. Unfortunately his proposals for conservation were soon brought to an end by a change in administration.

In 1872 Robinson was elected mayor of Hartford. His two-year term showed him to be an able and popular administrator, and in 1876 he was nominated by acclamation as candidate for governor, but he was defeated. In 1879 he was elected a member of the lower house of the legislature. As chairman of the judiciary committee he championed measures of judicial reform and in a strenuous campaign carried them through. Yet he was a liberal rather than a reformer, for he tempered his natural desire for progress with his conservative point of view. In 1880 he was a member of the Republican National Convention at Chicago and drafted a considerable portion of the platform. In 1888 he was active in securing Harrison's election and was offered the appointment as minister to Spain. He declined the honor, for he was at that time at the height of his professional career. He was counsel for many large enterprises, among them the Connecticut Fire Insurance Company and the firm of Pratt & Whitney. He was also a director of the New York, New Haven & Hartford Railroad, and as its counsel successfully opposed in 1889 the building of a parallel line between New Haven and New York by the Housatonic and "Air-Line" interests. Shortly afterward he was offered its presidency, but again felt that he could not leave his extensive legal practice. In the years 1891–93 he headed the counsel for the Republican party in the dispute which grew out of the contest for the governorship.

In addition to his work as lawyer and legislator Robinson was one of the leading laymen of the Congregational denomination. For fifty years he was a member of the South Church in Hartford, and active in the social and religious enterprises of the community. "In times of theological controversy he warmly espoused, but in a truly conservative spirit, the side of liberty and progress" (*Yale Class of 1853 Report*, 1903). At the height of the Andover religious disputes he set forward a legal argument for a liberal interpretation of creeds. Throughout his life he was in demand as an orator on public occasions. Two of his addresses were published. Other writings, on legal and religious subjects, appeared in the *Yale Law Journal* and the *New Englander and Yale Review*. Robinson suffered injuries in a fall which cut short a life of ceaseless activity, and for some time before his death he was confined to his home. He died in Hartford on Feb. 14, 1900, survived by three sons and two daughters.

[See especially the published reports of the Yale class of 1853: 1856, 1859, 1893, 1903, the last of which contains a list of Robinson's writings. Other sources include: Dwight Loomis and J. G. Calhoun, *The Judicial and Civil Hist. of Conn.* (1895); *Obit. Record of Grads. of Yale Univ. . . . June 1900*; *The Robinson Family Geneal. and Hist. Asso.* (1902); the *Hartford Courant*, Feb. 15, 1900.]   W. G. L.

ROBINSON, JOHN (Feb. 3, 1704–May 11, 1766), speaker of the House of Burgesses and treasurer of Virginia, was the grandson of Christopher Robinson who emigrated from England to Virginia in the seventeenth century, the son of John and Catherine (Beverley) Robinson, and the brother of Beverley Robinson [*q.v.*]. His father was a man of considerable consequence in the colony, having inherited the estate of an uncle, John Robinson, the Bishop of London, and having held, for a short time, the office of president of the Council. The son was educated at the College of William and Mary and in 1736 became a member of the House of Burgesses from the county of King and Queen. Two years later he became speaker of the House and treasurer of the colony, both of which offices he held until his death. His administration, however, ended in disaster to himself. In 1765 panic bore down upon Virginia, and the treasury found it difficult to redeem certain notes which it had previously issued and which now fell due. An investigation into the financial situation was ordered by the House of Burgesses under the leadership of Richard Henry Lee. The following year Robinson died, and a report showed that his accounts were short by more than one hundred thousand pounds. It appeared that he had been induced not to destroy notes the treasury had redeemed, as required by law, but to reissue them. For these treasury notes he had received the personal notes of the borrowers. The executors of his estate proposed that they make good the deficit out of his property, but the Revolu-

tion came on before the transaction was completed. In 1765 and 1767 efforts were made to establish a public loan office on the basis of capital to be borrowed in England, but both attempts were defeated by the Council (Eckenrode, *post,* pp. 15–17). It has been charged that the first of these attempts was an effort on the part of Robinson to transfer his loans to the public account, but there is no direct evidence to substantiate the accusation. While the treasurer was guilty of a breach of trust, it is not clear that he was guilty of a design to defraud the public. Proceedings were never instituted against the borrowers, whose notes Robinson had taken, nor were their names ever published. Some reform was accomplished, however, in that Robert Carter Nicholas, who had had a part in the exposure of the scandal, was now made treasurer, and Peyton Randolph became speaker of the House (Charles Campbell, *History of the Colony and Ancient Dominion of Virginia,* 1860, pp. 544–48).

John Robinson was typical of the colonial aristocracy of Virginia. He belonged to a distinguished family, was wealthy, suave, and popular. His home was at "Mount Pleasant" on the Mattapony in King and Queen County. He was married three times, first to Mary Storey, then to Lucy Moore, and last to Susanna Chiswell, the daughter of Col. John Chiswell of Williamsburg. For more than a quarter of a century he was, after the governor, the most powerful man in the province, but his fall ruined his house, and Virginia has made every effort to forget him.

[Fully documented account of Robinson's defalcation in *Jour. of the House of Burgesses of Virginia*, 1766–1769, ed. by J. P. Kennedy (1906), pp. x–xxvi; M. V. Smith, *Va., . . . a Hist. of the Executives* (1893); L. G. Tyler, *Encyc. of Va. Biog.* (1915), vol. I; *Va. Mag. of Hist. and Biog.*, Apr. 1897, Apr. 1902, Apr. 1908, Oct. 1909; H. J. Eckenrode, *The Revolution in Va.* (1916).]   T. P. A.

ROBINSON, JOHN CLEVELAND (Apr. 10, 1817–Feb. 18, 1897), soldier, born at Binghamton, N. Y., the son of Dr. Tracy and Sarah (Cleveland) Robinson, was a descendant of the Rev. John Robinson, pastor of the Pilgrims in Leyden. His early schooling was under tutors and at Oxford Academy, Oxford, N. Y. He entered the United States Military Academy in June 1835 and left in March 1838 to study law. The following year he became a second lieutenant of the 5th Infantry. During the Mexican War he was regimental and brigade quartermaster, and saw action at the battles of Palo Alto, Resaca de la Palma, and at the siege of Monterey. After the war he continued in the army, becoming captain in 1850. Between the two wars which were the high spots of his career, he was engaged in various services in the expanding West, with the exception of one period of campaigning against the Seminole Indians in Florida in 1856–57. Of his service in Utah in 1857–58, he wrote clearly and engagingly, expressing the opinion that the large expedition directed against the Mormons was a part of a plot to denude the eastern states of troops, so that "the dissolution of the Union" might be the easier (J. C. Robinson, "The Utah Expedition," *Magazine of American History,* April 1884, p. 340).

Robinson was in command of Fort McHenry when the 6th Massachusetts Infantry was attacked in the streets of Baltimore, Md., on Apr. 19, 1861. Although commanding only sixty men, threats and cajoling on the part of city officials failed to move him. He turned the guns towards the city, secretly revictualled the fort, and made such an excellent show of resistance that the rioters decided it was best not to attack at that time. He was elected colonel of the 1st Michigan Volunteers while on a recruiting trip in the West in September 1861. On Apr. 28, 1862, he was appointed brigadier-general of volunteers and assumed command of the 1st Brigade of Kearney's division of the III Corps, Army of the Potomac. He served with distinction throughout the Peninsular campaign, and later commanded the 2nd Division in the I and V Corps. His military career in the Civil War was full of honors. He was brevetted for actions at Gettysburg and for gallant conduct in the battle of the Wilderness. He served continuously with the Army of the Potomac until Spotsylvania, where he was wounded in the left knee while leading his command and suffered amputation of the leg. Upon his recovery, he was given command of military districts in New York. In June 1864 he was brevetted major-general, and in March 1865, by special appointment of the president, he became military commander and commissioner of the Bureau of Freedmen in North Carolina, with the rank of brigadier-general bestowed for bravery at Spotsylvania. He was commander of the Department of the South in 1867, and in 1868 was commander of the Department of the Lakes. He was retired with the rank of major-general on May 6, 1869.

After his retirement Robinson was lieutenant-governor of New York from 1872 to 1874, and thereafter was prominent in the activities of veterans' organizations. He was commander-in-chief of the G. A. R., 1877–78, and president of the Society of the Army of the Potomac in 1887. On the one-hundredth anniversary of his birth,

a statue was dedicated to him at Gettysburg, at the place where, with two brigades, he held at bay five brigades of the enemy for four hours and materially aided the Union victory. Three years before his death he was awarded the Congressional Medal of Honor for "most distinguished gallantry" at Laurel Hill, Va. He spent the latter years of his life in Binghamton, being totally blind from the year 1893 as a result of his old wound. On May 15, 1842, he married Sarah Maria Pease, in Green Bay, Wis. From this marriage, seven children were born.

[*N. Y. State Monuments Commission. In Memoriam, Abner Doubleday . . . and John Cleveland Robinson* (1918); E. J. and H. G. Cleveland, *The Geneal. of the Cleveland and Cleaveland Families* (1899), vol. II; C. E. Robinson, *Robinson Geneal.* (1926), vol. I; *Army and Navy Register,* Feb. 20, 27, 1897; *N. Y. Times,* Feb. 19, 1897.]
D. Y.

ROBINSON, JOHN MITCHELL (Dec. 6, 1827–Jan. 14, 1896), jurist, was a descendant of English Protestants who settled in Sussex County, Del., about 1700. His grandfather, Ralph, and his father, Peter, were Delaware farmers; his mother, Sarah Mitchell, was the daughter of John Mitchell, a merchant of Milford, Del. John Mitchell Robinson, the second son of this marriage, was born on his father's farm in Tuckahoe Neck, Caroline County, Md. His father died while John was very young and his mother moved to Denton, Md., where he was educated in the public schools. When he was sixteen years old he entered Dickinson College where he graduated in 1847. He at once began the study of law with William M. Meredith of the Philadelphia bar, but shortly afterward he returned to Centreville and continued his studies in the offices of Judge Richard B. Carmichael and of Madison Brown. He was admitted to the bar in November 1849 and immediately established himself in practice in Centreville.

In January 1851 Robinson was appointed deputy attorney-general for Queen Anne's and Kent counties. In November of that year a new constitution went into effect under the provisions of which he was elected state's attorney for Queen Anne's County. He held this office for four years (1851–55). While still in his thirties, Robinson had built up a lucrative trial practice which he hesitated to relinquish, but during the unsettled war days he was approached by a committee of citizens who persuaded him that his place was on the bench. His election in November 1864, as judge of a new circuit, which comprised Kent and Queen Anne's counties, was the turning point in his life and for the following twenty-nine years he was continuously on the bench. He was elected in 1867 to the court of appeals, the highest court in Maryland, and in 1882 he was reëlected. In 1884 he was a candidate for the Democratic nomination for the United States Senate; his defeat, which he always attributed to the activities of Senator Arthur Pue Gorman [*q.v.*], the party boss in Maryland, is one of the dramatic incidents in the political history of the state. Robinson was appointed chief judge of the court of appeals on May 1, 1893, and retained the office until his death. During his years on the bench he delivered over four hundred opinions which have had a considerable influence on the development of the jurisprudence of the state. It had been the custom for the judges in writing opinions to give the reasons for their conclusions at length but Robinson anticipated the modern style, emphasizing the conclusions and treating summarily the arguments and authorities. His most important decisions were concerned with the validity of a tax imposed upon the gross receipts of railroad companies, in which his views prevailed over those of Judge Richard Henry Alvey, one of the state's ablest judges (*The State of Maryland* vs. *The Northern Central Railway Company*, 44 *Md.*, 131, 1876; *The State of Maryland* vs. *The Philadelphia, Wilmington & Baltimore Railroad Company*, 45 *Md.*, 361, 1876; *State* vs. *Baltimore & Ohio Railroad Company*, 48 *Md.*, 49, 1878). Robinson had, on Nov. 19, 1857, married Marianna Stoughton Emory, daughter of Arthur Emory of "Poplar Grove," Queen Anne's County; they had five daughters and one son. He died suddenly in Annapolis and was buried at "Waverly," their country home on the Chester River.

[Sources include: *Report of the Seventeenth Ann. Meeting of the Md. State Bar Asso.* (1912); C. T. Bond, *The Court of Appeals of Md.: A Hist.* (1928); 82 *Md. Reports*, xix–xxvii; *Baltimore American,* Jan. 15, 1896; *Baltimore News,* Jan. 17, 1896; information as to certain facts from Ralph Robinson, Esq., Baltimore, Md. Robinson's opinions appear in 26–82 *Md. Reports.*]   H. C.

ROBINSON, MONCURE (Feb. 2, 1802–Nov. 10, 1891), civil engineer, was born at Richmond, Va., the eldest son of John Robinson, a merchant, and Agnes Conway (Moncure) Robinson, and a descendant of John Robinson who emigrated to Virginia from England and died in New Charles Parish in 1688. Conway Robinson [*q.v.*] was his younger brother. As a child Moncure attended Gerardine Academy where he received a grounding in the French language which later proved useful; in 1816–17 he was a student at the College of William and Mary. His father intended him to be a lawyer, but the boy's taste for adventure led him into another career.

In 1818 the Board of Public Works of Virginia authorized a topographic survey and connected line of levels from Richmond to the Ohio River, and young Robinson applied for a position on the corps of surveyors. This was refused on account of his youth, but he was permitted to accompany the party as a volunteer, without compensation. On this trip he made accurate notes of the coal deposits in the region that is now West Virginia. In 1819 he undertook a second trip of reconnaissance toward Pittsburgh for the purpose of locating and examining his father's wild lands. Two years later, having reached maturity, he was employed in the location of an extension of the James River Canal in Virginia. That same year he made a professional visit to the Erie Canal, then in process of construction. This inspection changed his opinion as to the relative advantages of canals and railroads, and from this time forward his interest was mainly in railroad building. For some three years, 1825–28, he was in Europe, attending lectures in mathematics and science in France, and studying public works in France, England, Wales, and the Low Countries.

After his return, he was called upon in 1828 by the canal commissioners of Pennsylvania to make surveys for the Pottsville and Danville railway in the interest of the development of the anthracite coal fields, and was also appointed to make surveys for the Allegheny Portage Railroad. During the next three years he was engaged in railroad construction in Virginia, building the Petersburg and Roanoke and the Richmond and Petersburg lines. For the latter railroad he constructed a bridge over the James River which attracted attention both at home and abroad (see Michel Chevalier, *Histoire et Description des Voies de Communication aux États-Unis et des Travaux d'Art qu'en Dépendent*, 1841, pp. 567, 571–76). This bridge was 2,844 feet long, with a grade line sixty feet above the water. There were nineteen spans of lengths varying from 140 to 153 feet. The superstructure was latticed.

In 1834 Robinson began his *chef-d'œuvre,* the Philadelphia & Reading Railroad, which involved the construction of a 1,932-foot tunnel at Phoenixville and a stone bridge of four spans, each seventy-two feet long. In connection with the building of this road he formulated three fundamental rules for determining grades and curvatures. In 1836 he went to England in its interest and succeeded in procuring large investments for its completion to Pottsville. The locomotive *Gowan and Marx* was built in Philadelphia from Robinson's plans and named for his English banker friends. So noteworthy were Robinson's achievements as an engineer of railroads that in 1840 the Czar of Russia made advances toward the procuring of his services as engineer in charge of the system of railroads which was then being planned for the Russian empire. Robinson gave valuable counsel to the Czar's emissaries, but declined to serve. In 1839 he made a reconnaissance for a railroad from Brunswick on the Georgia coast to the Gulf of Mexico. By appointment of the secretary of the navy in 1842 he served with Commodores Shubrick and David Conner [*q.v.*] on the commission which recommended Wallabout Bay as the site for the drydock to be constructed in New York Harbor.

He retired from professional activity in 1847, making his home in Philadelphia, and for more than forty years devoted his attention to his personal investments. He died in 1891. On Feb. 2, 1835, he had married Charlotte Randolph Taylor, daughter of Bennett Taylor, a member of the Richmond bar. They had five sons and five daughters, of whom all but two daughters survived their father. As an engineer Robinson belonged to the old school. As were the other engineers of his day, with the exception of those from West Point, he was untrained in the technique of the profession. These men worked out their technique in the school of experience, and for that reason their lives were characterized by a peculiar initiative and resourcefulness. By extensive travel and inspection Robinson equipped himself for those positions of responsibility which he occupied in rapid succession. He was elected to membership in the American Philosophical Society (1833) and by his professional brethren of a younger generation was awarded one of the highest honors within their power to bestow, that of honorary membership in the American Society of Civil Engineers.

[Robinson's reports of 1829 and 1831 in regard to the Allegheny Portage R. R. were printed, with an editorial note, in *Trans. Am. Soc. Civil Engineers*, vol. XV (1886). For biographical material see R. B. Osborne, *Professional Biog. of Moncure Robinson, Civil Engineer* (1889); *Proc. Am. Soc. Civil Engineers*, vol. XVIII (1892); *Proc. Engineers' Club of Phila.*, vol. X (1892); *Illustrated American*, Dec. 5, 1891; H. E. Hayden, *Va. Geneals.* (1891); *Phila. Press*, Nov. 11, 1891; *N. Y. Tribune*, Nov. 11, 1891.]   W. T. L.

ROBINSON, MOSES (Mar. 26, 1742–May 26, 1813), soldier, jurist, statesman, was a dominant figure in the early history of Vermont. He was born in Hardwick, Mass., the son of Samuel and Mercy (Lennard, or Leonard) Robinson and a descendant of William Robinson, an early settler in Newton. In 1761 his father helped

to found the town of Bennington, Vt., and in the next few years was prominent in the pioneer life of the future state. He died in 1767 while on a mission to England in behalf of the settlers on the New Hampshire Grants. Moses Robinson played a varied and distinguished rôle in the establishment of the republic, later the state, of Vermont. He was one of the outstanding leaders in the resistance interposed by the inhabitants of the New Hampshire Grants to the authority of New York. With the outbreak of the Revolutionary War he threw himself into the conflict, serving as a colonel of militia. He was a member of the Vermont Council of Safety and took part in the measures resorted to by that body, in 1777, to secure aid from Massachusetts, New Hampshire, and Connecticut against impending invasion by the British. In January 1777 he sat in the convention which declared the independence of Vermont, under the name of New Connecticut, and he was elected a member of the Governor's Council by the first General Assembly under the constitution adopted the same year. With Ethan Allen and three others he was chosen, in 1779, to appear before Congress as a representative of Vermont empowered to enter into articles of union and confederation with the United States; and later, in 1782, he served on a committee authorized to agree upon terms for the admission of Vermont into the Union. The main obstacle to such admission was the long-pending boundary dispute with New York, and he took a prominent part in its adjustment. He also served as a member of the third Council of Censors, charged with supervision over the state constitution, and over the legislative and executive departments of the state government.

Although Robinson was not a lawyer by profession he was elected the first chief justice of the supreme court of Vermont—at first called the superior court—in 1778, holding that office, except for one year when he failed of election, until 1789, when he was elected governor of Vermont by the General Assembly. Twice thereafter, in 1797 and 1798, he was a candidate for the same office. In January 1791 he was a member of the convention which ratified the Constitution of the United States, and later in the same month he was elected United States senator from Vermont, sharing with Stephen R. Bradley [*q.v.*] the honor of being the first senator from the newly admitted state. He served in the Senate until he resigned in 1796. His most conspicuous activity in that body was his determined opposition to the Jay treaty of 1794—an opposition he continued in his state after the ratification of the treaty, in support of the movement to defeat the appropriation by Congress of the funds necessary to carry it into effect. He performed his last public service in 1802 when he represented the town of Bennington in the General Assembly. Robinson was twice married. His first wife was Mary Fay, by whom he had six sons. His second wife was Susana Howe.

[See: A. M. Hemenway, ed., *The Vt. Hist. Gazetteer*, vol. I (1868); W. H. Crockett, *Vermont*, vol. II (1921) and vol. V (1923); J. G. Ullery, *Men of Vt.* (1894); J. B. Robinson, *A Hist. Sketch of the Robinson Family of the Line of Ebenezer Robinson* (1903); *The Robinson Family Geneal. and Hist. Asso.*, 1 ser. (1902), 2 ser. (1904); Manning Leonard, *Memorial: Geneal., Hist., and Biog., of Solomon Leonard* (1896); Leonard Deming, *Cat. of the Principal Officers of Vt.* (1851).]

E. C. M—r.

ROBINSON, ROWLAND EVANS (May 14, 1833–Oct. 15, 1900), author, was born in Ferrisburg, Addison County, Vt., on the farm cleared by his paternal grandfather in 1796. The youngest of the four children of Rowland Thomas and Rachael (Gilpin) Robinson and a descendant of Rowland Robinson, who settled at Narragansett, R. I., about 1675, he was of English stock and a birthright Quaker; in his boyhood the dress, speech, and manners of the primitive Friends were natural to him, and the ways of the "world's people" strange. He attended the country schools and the Ferrisburg Academy but was by his own account an unwilling pupil. He formed his literary taste by repeated readings of the poems and novels of Sir Walter Scott and became familiar with every aspect of the life of the fields and woods. Technically he was a farmer for the greater part of his life, but although he did not neglect his farm he was interested primarily in other things. From his mother he inherited a propensity for drawing, and the butter-tubs that he sent to market were often adorned with home-made political cartoons. On coming of age he went to New York, hoping to learn something of drawing while working in a draftsman's shop, but he soon returned home disappointed. In 1866 he went again to New York, made illustrations on wood of rural scenes for the periodicals of Orange Judd and Frank Leslie [*qq.v.*], did fashion-plate and catalogue work, and sold a cartoon occasionally to a comic paper, but working at night on rush orders injured his eyes, and in 1873 he returned once more to his native farm, this time to stay. Meanwhile, in 1870, he had married Anna Stevens of East Montpelier, who with their two daughters and son survived him.

His literary work began in 1877. At his wife's suggestion he wrote an article on "Fox-Hunting in New England" and sent it to *Scribner's Monthly*, which published it in January 1878 after inquiring about the identity and qualifications of the unknown author. He was on the staff of *Forest and Stream* for a number of years and was later a contributor to the *Atlantic Monthly* and other magazines. As an illustrator he was never distinguished, and when his sight began to fail in 1887 he turned altogether to literature. Even after he became totally blind in 1893 he was able to write by using a grooved board to guide his pencil. His wife revised his manuscripts and copied them on the typewriter. His publications were: *Forest and Stream Fables* (1886); *Uncle Lisha's Shop: Life in a Corner of Yankee-land* (1887; Centennial edition, Rutland, 1933); *Sam Lovel's Camps: Uncle Lisha's Friends under Bark and Canvas* (1889); *Vermont: A Study of Independence* (1892, American Commonwealths Series); *Danvis Folks* (1894); *In New England Fields and Woods* (1896); *Uncle Lisha's Outing* (1897); *A Hero of Ticonderoga* (1898); *In the Green Wood* (1899); *A Danvis Pioneer* (1900; republished with *Uncle Lisha's Shop*, 1933); *Sam Lovel's Boy* (1901); *Hunting without a Gun, and Other Papers* (1905); *Out of Bondage, and Other Stories* (1905); and *Silver Fields, and Other Sketches of a Farmer-Sportsman* (1921). His style is simple, graceful, and apparently effortless, and he wrote only on themes that he knew intimately and loved. His work is permeated by an old man's memories of his youth and by a blind man's memories of the beauty of the visible world. He was rather a humorist and essayist than a novelist; a master in depicting manners and easily recognized types of character, he shunned, or touched only lightly, the graver aspects of personality and experience. He recorded the dialect of rural Vermonters and of English-speaking French-Canadians with minute attention to detail. His best volumes are secure of their place as Vermont classics. For the last eighteen months of his life he was bedridden with an inoperable cancer, but he bore his afflictions serenely and cheerfully. He died in the room in which he had been born.

[H. L. Bailey, "The Chronicler of 'Danvis Folks,'" *New Eng. Mag.*, Dec. 1900; Mrs. M. F. Allen, "In Memoriam: Rowland E. Robinson," *Vermonter*, Dec. 1900; J. C. R. Dorr, "Rowland Robinson," *Atlantic Monthly*, Jan. 1901; Rowland E. Robinson, "Recollections of a Quaker Boy," *Ibid.*, July 1901; biog. preface to *Hunting without a Gun* (1905); Genevra Cook, sketch in *Vermonters* (1931), ed. by W. H. Crockett; T. R. Hazard, *Recollections of Olden Times: Rowland Robinson of Narragansett* (1879); *Burlington Free Press and Times*, Oct. 16, 1900.]

G. H. G.

ROBINSON, SOLON (Oct. 21, 1803–Nov. 3, 1880), pioneer, agriculturist, author, was born at Tolland, Conn., the fourth child of Jacob and Salinda (Ladd) Robinson and a descendant of the Rev. John Robinson, pastor of the Pilgrims at Leyden. An orphan at the age of ten, a carpenter's apprentice at fourteen, and a Yankee pedler at eighteen, he made his way alone in the world. In 1828 he had become a cashier for a theatre in Cincinnati, and in October of that year married Mariah Evans of Bucks County, Pa.

Two years later, at Madison, Ind., the young man was writing for the local press and interested in the promotion of an urban land site near North Vernon. In the fall of 1834, because of a dearth of buyers, he disposed of most of his land and traveled to northern Indiana. Here, in the wilderness, he opened a general store and soon built up a large trade with the Potawatomi Indians and incoming settlers. The Indians gave him the name of "Wyonett Tshmokeman," sometimes translated "Chief Big Knife." To preserve his own holdings and those of others, in the area then known as Robinson's Prairie, he formed a Squatters' Union in 1836 for protection against speculators and made it possible for some five hundred members to secure their land at government prices. Henceforth, by popular acclaim, he was known as the "King of the Squatters." After Lake County was organized in 1837, he served at various times as county clerk, justice of the peace, register of claims, and postmaster. At the county seat, Crown Point, on the first printing press in the region he published intermittently a small news sheet. Active in politics, he took a prominent part in the Log Cabin Convention at LaFayette in 1840. In 1847 he delivered a detailed address, later published under the title, *History of Lake County.*

As early as 1837 Robinson began to contribute articles on various aspects of the frontier to the Albany *Cultivator* and other agricultural periodicals. The simple, homely, and often humorous style of these essays, signed "Solon Robinson of Indiana," reflected the personality of the author, and they soon won a large following. His enthusiasm and spirit carried conviction. Before 1840, in company with James Mercer Garnett, Henry L. Ellsworth [*qq.v.*], and others, he advocated the formation of a national agricultural society (*Cultivator,* May 1838) and in 1841 presided at a preliminary meeting held for that purpose in Washington (*Ibid.,* October 1841). The society had hoped to establish a national agricultural school and journal, but failure to receive an anticipated bequest made by James Smithson to the United States defeated this plan and was largely responsible for the premature dissolution of the organization. How-

ever, these activities paved the way for the formation of the United States Agricultural Society in 1852 by Robinson and others. This in turn played an influential rôle in the establishment of the Department of Agriculture ten years later.

Robinson's descriptions of rural life observed on his journey to and from Washington in 1841 were the first of his discerning travel sketches. During the next decade he made a number of tours, covering practically every state in the Union, and regularly reported his observations in the *Cultivator, Prairie Farmer,* and *American Agriculturist,* from which they were reprinted in the *Southern Cultivator* and other periodicals. These travel sketches today form an invaluable historical record of rural society of that period (see especially *American Agriculturist,* 1849–51). In 1852 at New York City he published a periodical called *The Plow,* and the following year became agricultural editor of the *New York Tribune.* His editorial work, combined with visits to various parts of the country, was largely responsible for the widespread circulation of the weekly edition of the *Tribune* and the subsequent national influence of that publication. At Westchester, N. Y., Robinson conducted an experimental farm which provided the basis for many of his articles.

Illness in 1868—he suffered nearly all his life with tubercular tendencies—forced him to retire to Florida. Residing at Jacksonville, he published the *Florida Republican,* wrote for the *New York Tribune,* and carried on other literary work. He was the author of novels, short stories, and poetry, in addition to his travel sketches and agricultural articles. Among his books were *The Will; A Tale of the Lake of the Red Cedars and Shabbona* (1841); *Guano, a Treatise of Practical Information for Farmers* (1852); *Hot Corn: Life Scenes in New York, Tales of Slum Life* (1854), of which 50,000 copies were sold in six months; *Facts for Farmers: Also for the Family Circle* (1864, and subsequent editions); *Me-won-i-toc, A Tale of Frontier Life and Indian Character* (1867); and *How to Live; Saving and Wasting; or Domestic Economy Illustrated by the Life of Two Families of Opposite Character, including the Story of a Dime a Day* (1873). After the death of his first wife, by whom he had five children, he married, June 30, 1872, Mary Johnson of Barton, Vt. He died at Jacksonville in November 1880.

[Robinson's own writings, and files of the periodicals mentioned above; *Robinson Geneal.: Descendants of the Rev. John Robinson* (1926); *Counties of Porter and Lake, Ind.* (1882); J. C. Derby, *Fifty Years among Authors, Books, and Publishers* (1884); T. H. Ball,

Encyc. of Geneal. and Biog. of Lake County, Ind. (1904); G. S. Cottman, *Centennial Hist. and Handbook of Ind.* (1915); Susan B. Eppes, *Through Some Eventful Years* (1926); *N. Y. Tribune*, Nov. 5, 1880; *Lake County Star* (Crown Point, Ind.), Sept. 15, 1916; *Gary Evening Post* (Gary, Ind.), Aug. 27, 1918, Aug. 27, 1921; MSS. and other historical material relating to Solon Robinson in the possession of the writer.]

H. A. K.

ROBINSON, STILLMAN WILLIAMS (Mar. 6, 1838–Oct. 31, 1910), engineer, educator, inventor, author, son of Ebenezer and Adeline (Williams) Robinson, was born on his father's farm near South Reading, Vt. He was descended from William Robinson, one of the early settlers of Newton, Mass. After attending the district school of his native town, he was bound out to a farmer, but his desire for more education and his interest in mechanics and mathematics caused him to give up farm work in 1855 to learn a trade as a means of acquiring money for his education. He served a four-year apprenticeship as a machinist, studied in his spare time, and in January 1861 entered the University of Michigan. He paid his expenses by working at his trade, attaining considerable proficiency as an instrument maker and during his college course devising a machine for graduating thermometers.

For three years after his graduation (C.E.) in 1863 he was an assistant engineer in the federal survey of the Great Lakes, then returned to the University of Michigan (1866–70), first as assistant and then as assistant professor in the department of mining engineering and geodesy. Called to the Illinois Industrial University (now the University of Illinois) in 1870, he there established a department of mechanical engineering which was one of the first in the United States. Eight years later he was made dean of the college of engineering, but resigned almost at once to accept the professorship of physics and mechanical engineering at Ohio State University. Here he continued until his resignation and retirement from academic life in 1895. Robinson was a pioneer in the field of experimental instruction in engineering education, and as early as 1870 ideas now accepted as fundamental in this field had become settled convictions with him. He was instrumental in organizing in 1890 an association of teachers of mechanical engineering which in 1893 became the Society for the Promotion of Engineering Education. He retained until his death an interest in Ohio State University, establishing a fellowship in the department of mechanical engineering and contributing from time to time to its equipment.

In the course of his career Robinson secured over forty patents, all of which were based upon scientific research and mathematical investigation. A group of eight or ten were concerned with shoe manufacture, the most profitable being the flattened and threaded shoe-sole fastening (Patent No. 265,149, Sept. 26, 1882). The development through a number of years of this device and the many machines which he contrived to manufacture it and to drive the fastening rapidly and automatically through the sole illustrates Robinson's ability to utilize his profound knowledge of mechanics in the solution of difficult practical problems. The variety of his inventions was unusual and they were all profitable to him. Others which he patented were a clock escapement, a steam rock drill, valve gearing for steam engines, an improvement in the telephone, a metal piling and substructure, a gauge for measuring the flow of natural gas, an automatic air-brake mechanism, and a right-angled shaft coupling for transmitting power. Throughout his career he was called in as a consultant in a variety of industrial and professional undertakings. Thus he was inspector of railways and bridges for the railroad commission of Ohio (1880–84), consulting engineer for the Lick telescope and mountings (1887), and consulting engineer (1887–90) for the Atchison, Topeka & Santa Fé Railroad, of which his brother, Albert Alonzo Robinson [*q.v.*], was second vice-president and general manager. He was the author of a number of important technical books and contributed many papers to technical journals. His report as a result of his inspection of the railways and bridges of Ohio includes what is probably some of his best scientific work; it was published by D. Van Nostrand under the title *Railroad Economics* in 1882. His *Principles of Mechanism,* first published in 1896, is still widely used as a college textbook, and his *Practical Treatise on the Teeth of Wheels, with the Theory and the Use of Robinson's Odontograph* (1876) is still in wide circulation. Among his other publications were *Strength of Wrought-Iron Bridge Members* (1882), and *A Treatise on the Compound Engine* (1884) written in collaboration with John Turnbull. He was a member of numerous engineering societies and a fellow of the American Association for the Advancement of Science. Twice married—first on Dec. 29, 1863, to Mary Elizabeth Holden, and after her death, on Apr. 12, 1888, to Mary Haines of Ada, Ohio, he was survived by his second wife and three daughters by his first marriage. He died in Columbus, at the age of seventy-two.

[J. B. Robinson, *A Hist. Sketch of the Robinson Family of the Line of Ebenezer Robinson* (1903); *Stillman Williams Robinson: a Memorial* (Ohio State Univ., 1912); *Who's Who in America*, 1910–11; *Trans. Am.*

Soc. Mechanical Engineers, vol. XXXII (1911); *Ohio State Journal* (Columbus), Nov. 1, 1910.] C. W. M.

ROBINSON, STUART (Nov. 14, 1814–Oct. 5, 1881), Presbyterian clergyman, editor, was born in Strabane, County Tyrone, Ireland, the fourth son of James and Martha (Porter) Robinson, both of Scotch-Irish descent. The father, for a time successful as a linen merchant, lost his property and emigrated to America in 1816, settling first in New York City, and later in or near Martinsburg, then in the state of Virginia. His mother died when Stuart was about twelve years of age, and the boy was put out to work on the farm of some German Presbyterians, Troutman by name, who, seeing his promise, took him to the Rev. James M. Brown, their pastor. Brown trained and educated him as if he had been his own son; he attended the clergyman's private school and the academy at Romney, and then entered Amherst College. Graduating in 1836, he studied during the following year at Union Theological Seminary, Virginia. After teaching in an academy at Charleston (1838–39), he spent a year at Princeton Seminary.

He was licensed by Greenbrier Presbytery Apr. 10, 1841, and ordained Oct. 8, 1842. The same day he was installed pastor of the church at Kanawha-Salines (now Malden, W. Va.), from which he was released May 8, 1847. He served the Presbyterian Church at Frankfort, Ky., from June 18, 1847, to Sept. 2, 1852, and the Fayette Street Church (Independent) in Baltimore for nearly one year, at the end of which time he organized the Central Presbyterian Church of that city, continuing as its pastor until Oct. 27, 1856. In this year the General Assembly transferred him to Danville Theological Seminary, Kentucky, to fill the chair of church government and pastoral theology. On Apr. 27, 1858, he became pastor of the Second Presbyterian Church of Louisville, Ky., which position he retained until June 16, 1881. In addition to his pastoral work he did much teaching. While at Kanawha-Salines he conducted a school; at Frankfort he carried on a flourishing seminary for girls, and for a time in Louisville he taught a boy's school. In September 1841 he married Mary Elizabeth Brigham, eldest daughter of Col. William Brigham, a native of Massachusetts; they had eight children, five of whom died in early childhood.

Robinson also entered the field of religious journalism. In collaboration with Thomas E. Peck [*q.v.*] he published in Baltimore (January 1855–November 1856) the *Presbyterial Critic and Monthly Review,* a controversial journal which sought to maintain the pure traditions of Presbyterianism. In Louisville he bought the *Presbyterian Herald,* changed its name to *True Presbyterian,* and became its aggressive editor. He contended especially for the "spirituality of the church," insisting that the church should deal only with spiritual matters and take no stand on the political issues dividing the nation. His zeal brought him into sharp conflict with other Presbyterians in Kentucky, especially Dr. Robert J. Breckinridge [*q.v.*], a former colleague in Danville Seminary. During the Civil War he was suspected of disloyalty and, facing active persecution, in July 1862 sought refuge in Toronto, Canada. Here he preached, lectured, and wrote; aided Southern refugees; and refuted a slanderous charge of conspiracy to infect the Federal armies with yellow fever. His paper was suppressed by the military authorities in 1864. Returning to Louisville in April 1866, he resumed the editorial direction of the publication, which had been continued with the same policy under the title *Free Christian Commonwealth.*

He was a commissioner to the General Assembly of 1866 at St. Louis, which refused to seat him and his colleagues from Louisville Presbytery because of a "Declaration and Testimony" signed by members of this Presbytery protesting against the political deliverances of the Assembly since the beginning of the war. It was mainly through Robinson's efforts that the main part of the Synod of Kentucky, excluded finally from the Northern Assembly, was induced to unite with the General Assembly of the Southern Presbyterian Church in 1869. He was elected moderator of the Assembly that year by acclamation. Through his influence the Southern Church (Presbyterian Church in the United States) in 1875 became a constituent member of the Alliance of Presbyterian and Reformed Churches throughout the World. Among his publications were: *The Church of God, an Essential Element of the Gospel* (1858); *Slavery as Recognized in the Mosaic Civil Law* (1865); *Discourses of Redemption* (1868); *The Infamous Perjuries of the 'Bureau of Military Justice' Exposed* (1865), a letter to Hon. Mr. Emmons. He died of cancer of the stomach, having been active in religious and civic affairs almost to the end.

[Robinson's scrapbook, in Presbyterian Hist. Foundation, Montreat, N. C.; J. M. Saunders, *Memorial upon the Life of Rev. Stuart Robinson* (1883); T. E. Peck, in *Southern Presbyterian Rev.,* Apr. 1882, and in *Miscellanies,* vol. I (1895); H. A. White, *Southern Presbyterian Leaders* (1911); Alfred Nevin, *Encyc. of the Presbyterian Church in the U. S. of America* (1884); *Presbyterian Visitor,* May 1909; *Courier-Jour.* (Louisville), Oct. 6, 1881.] E. T. T.

ROBINSON, THEODORE (June 3, 1852–Apr. 2, 1896), artist, was born in Irasburg, Vt., the son of Elijah and Ellen (Brown) Robinson, both originally of Jamaica, Vt. In 1855 the father, a minister, moved west with his family, settling at Barry, Ill., and later at Milwaukee, Wis.; because of ill-health, he resigned from the ministry and started a clothing store at Evansville, Wis. Encouraged by his mother, at the age of eighteen Robinson went from the Evansville Seminary to Chicago to study art; then, having acquired a certain proficiency in making "likenesses," he returned to Evansville, and devoted himself to crayon portraits which he enlarged from photographs. At this period he seems also to have studied music and was for several years organist in the church at Evansville of which his father at one time had been pastor. Always of a frail constitution, from childhood he had suffered from asthma and was advised by the local doctor to go to Denver for his health. Strengthened by his western experience, he came to New York in 1874 to continue his studies at the school of the National Academy of Design. During the short interim in which the Academy schools were discontinued, Robinson and a number of his fellow students, as a means of continuing their instruction, organized the Art Students' League of New York, the name of which he suggested. Going to Paris in 1877 he studied first in the atelier of Carolus-Duran and later under Jean-Léon Gérôme. Here he not only acquired a thorough academic training but made many friends who were later to be famous—John Singer Sargent, Robert Louis Stevenson, Will Low, Carroll Beckwith, J. Alden Weir, and others. On returning to the United States, he was made a member in 1881 of the newly organized Society of American Artists, receiving the Webb Prize for landscape in 1890 and the Shaw Prize for figure in 1892. After a short term as art instructor in a private school, he became an assistant of John La Farge [q.v.] in carrying out the mural decorations for the Vanderbilt house in New York. The following year he accepted a position in the firm of Prentice Treadwell of Boston, where he remained three years, thus being enabled to save enough money to allow him to follow his more individual purposes. Accordingly he returned to Paris in 1884, a decisive period in his career, for he came under the influence of the French impressionists and went to Giverney, where Monet had established himself a few years before. From then on, until his final return to America in 1892, he divided his time between the two countries, and many of his most noteworthy canvases were painted at Giverney. After 1889 he moved from studio to studio in New York in search of one that suited his frugal habits and inclination, finally escaping from what he called "the tyranny of modern conveniences" to a studio in East Fourteenth Street formerly occupied by his friend J. Alden Weir. His health had been gradually declining and he was often compelled to lay aside his brush, but he was always uncomplaining. For a short time he was not seen by his intimates. He died alone, Apr. 2, 1896.

Robinson combined a determined will and an indefatigable energy with a frail body. Will Low, his devoted friend and artistic executor, gives a vivid description of him: "Frail, with a husky asthmatic voice and a laugh that shook his meagre sides, and yet hardly made itself heard, timid and reticent, saying little, yet blessed with as keen a sense of humor as any one I have ever known" (*post*, p. 66). Sociable and spirited in manner, Robinson nevertheless lived much alone and he never married. From an early age he had accustomed himself to the utmost frugality and by means of it maintained a true independence. Although he had had simply the elements of early education, his receptive interest enabled him to acquire a varied culture, and his sensitive nature made him an excellent critic. He contributed to the *Century*, September 1892, an essay on Claude Monet; a posthumous poem, "A Normandy Pastoral," published in *Scribner's* for June 1897, shows his literary interest.

Robinson's position in the impressionist movement in America was an important one, rather like that of William Morris Hunt in relation to the Barbizon school. He was both a pioneer of the new realism and an apostle, led by the principles of the impressionists to Monet and by Monet to nature itself. Painting directly from nature, avoiding any preconceived idea of what a picture ought to be, he saw his subject under the transient effects of light and in the surroundings of his everyday environment. In consequence, his pictures convey a sense of intimacy that comes only from first-hand observation. His mood is pensive and serene, or joyous; his pictures full of delicate neutral hues—violet, with cool greens and vivacious touches of gold—and beautiful, closely related harmonies of color. His technique is sensitive and reserved, yet direct and emphatic; and his style is characterized by integrity and sincerity, the true stamp of his own nature. Once considered radical, his pictures today seem highly refined and naturalistic. Robinson maintains, however, a definite and unique place in American painting and, with John Twachtman, J. Alden Weir, and Childe

Hassam, must be considered one of the outstanding painters of the impressionist movement in America.

[Eliot Clark in *Art in America,* Oct. 1918, and *Scribner's,* Dec. 1921; Birge Harrison, "With Stevenson at Grez," *Century,* Dec. 1916; W. H. Low, *A Chronicle of Friendships, 1873–1900* (1908); *N. Y. Times,* Apr. 4, 1896; F. F. Sherman, "Theodore Robinson" (in press, 1934).]

E.C.

ROBINSON, THERESE ALBERTINE LOUISE VON JAKOB (Jan. 26, 1797–Apr. 13, 1870), author, translator philologist, was born in Halle, Prussian Saxony, the daughter of Ludwig Heinrich von Jakob, professor of philosophy at the University of Halle. In 1807 the latter accepted a call by the University of Kharkov to help in the revision of the Russian code of criminal laws in St. Petersburg, and took his small daughter with him. Residence in a foreign land in the midst of the social and political changes wrought by the Napoleonic wars developed in the young girl a rich inner life which yearned for expression. She listened to the peasant songs in the markets and was moved to undertake serious study of the Slavic languages and history. In 1816 she returned to Halle with her father, and endeavored to master the classical languages as well as Anglo-Saxon, Scandinavian, English, French, and Spanish. She translated and published, in 1821, Walter Scott's *Old Mortality* and *The Black Dwarf,* under the name Ernst Berthold, for the pen-name, Talvj, which she coined from the initials of her full name, was not used before 1825. The works of Jacob Grimm directed her interest toward Serbian popular poetry, and in 1825–26 three editions of her *Volkslieder der Serben* were published. The preparation of this work brought her into intimate contact with Goethe, who expressed a deep appreciation for her work (J. P. Eckermann, *Gespräche Mit Goethe,* Jena, 1908, vol. I, p. 165).

On Aug. 7, 1828, at the beginning of a very promising literary career in Europe, she was married to Edward Robinson [*q.v.*], of Southington, Conn., and came to Andover, Mass., with him two years later. In 1833 they established their home in Boston, each exhibiting a keen interest in the work of the other. Therese Robinson, as she came to be known, began to study the customs and poetry of the Indians and early life in the American colonies. In 1834 she translated into German John Pickering's *Essay on . . . the Indian Languages of North America* (1820), and added very valuable philological notes, many of them original. Her first literary work in English, *Historical View of the Slavic Language,* published in 1834, appeared first in the *Biblical Repository* for April and July of that year. Several essays on the popular poetry of the Teutonic and Slavic nations were published in the *North American Review,* April, July, and October 1836; these appeared four years later together with other material as: *Versuch einer Geschichtlichen Charakteristik der Volkslieder germanischer Nationen,* and included a survey of the popular songs outside of Europe, largely the poetry of the Indians. The publication of this work was followed by *Die Unächtheit der Lieder Ossians und des Mcpherson'schen Ossians insbesondere* (Leipzig, 1840), a treatise which settled for many years the dispute among scholars about the genuineness of Mcpherson's *Ossian.*

In 1837 she went to Europe and moved in the literary circles of Hamburg, Leipzig, and Dresden. She returned to the United States in 1840, and opened her home in New York to such literary figures as George Bancroft, William Cullen Bryant, and James Bayard Taylor [*qq.v.*]. A visit by Friedrich von Raumer, the historian, led to the publication of *Aus der Geschichte der ersten Ansiedlungen in den Vereinigten Staaten (Captain John Smith)* in 1845, followed two years later by her *Geschichte der Colonisation von Neu-England.* Her training in the observation of cultural habits and traditions gave to this work a sociological emphasis which has made it a valuable source book for American history, although the heavy German style did not add to its popularity among her contemporaries. Many of her articles were accepted by leading European or American magazines, among them, *Putnam's Monthly Magazine,* the *North American Review,* the *Atlantic Monthly, Westermann's Monatshefte,* and Raumer's *Historisches Taschenbuch.* Her best known novels are *Heloise,* published in 1850, and *Die Auswanderer,* 1852. *Heloise* was published in America three times in one year and *Die Auswanderer* found its way to the American reader as *The Exiles* or *Woodhill* (1853). Although her novels lacked "a wide appeal, they possess a depth and truth in the portrayal of characters and situations which should insure for them a lasting existence in literature" (Voigt, *post,* p. 125). In her scientific work she followed the ideas of Herder, Goethe, and Grimm, emphasizing the cultural more than the philological aspect. In her esthetic work she was spurred by the idea of drawing closer together the nations to which she belonged, and was guided in all her undertakings by an impartial and scholarly attitude. After the death of her husband in 1863, she returned to Hamburg where she spent the rest of her life. She was survived by two children,

[Talvj's manuscripts and letters were destroyed by fire. The best source of information is J. C. Voigt, *The Life and Works of Mrs. Therese Robinson (Talvj)*, a doctoral thesis, University of Ill., 1913, and also published in the *Jahrb. der Deutsch-Amerikanischen Historischen Gesellschaft von Ill.*, vol. XIII (1914). See also, G. P. Körner, *Das Deutsche Element in den Vereinigten Staaten* (1884); H. R. Timlow, *Ecclesiastical and Other Sketches of Southington, Conn.* (1875); *Allgemeine Deutsche Biog.*]   E. A. K.

ROBINSON, WILLIAM (Nov. 22, 1840–Jan. 2, 1921), inventor, engineer, was born in Coal Island, County Tyrone, Ulster, Ireland, the son of Scotch-Irish and English parents. When he was four years old the family emigrated to the United States, settling in Brooklyn, N. Y. Here William received his early schooling and prepared for college. He graduated from Wesleyan University, Middletown, Conn., in 1865 and during the school term following was principal of the high school in Ansonia, Conn. Part of the year 1866 he spent in the Pennsylvania oil fields, but in 1867 resumed teaching, serving as principal of Spring Valley Academy, New York, for two years. In 1869 he returned to western Pennsylvania and for three years was engaged in the oil business, making his headquarters in St. Petersburg, Clarion County.

Meanwhile his attention had been given for some time to the development of an automatic signal system as a means of preventing accidents of various kinds on railroads. Choosing electricity as the active agent, he had devised what is now known as a "wire" or "open circuit" system of signalling, and in 1869 he constructed an elaborate model illustrating a road-crossing gong signal operated by trains approaching in either direction. He exhibited his model at the American Institute Fair in New York in 1870, and the same year installed a practical automatic block signal of this character on a section of the Philadelphia & Erie Railroad at Kinzua, Pa. It worked perfectly, but Robinson, dissatisfied with its inherent limitations, immediately undertook to correct them and after much study devised the closed track circuit system of automatic electric signalling which he patented both in the United States and France, his United States patent being No. 130,661, dated Aug. 20, 1872. This invention is conceded to be the basis of every block signalling system used on the railroads of the world today, and "perhaps no single invention in the history of the development of railway transportation has contributed more toward safety and dispatch in that field than the track circuit" (*Third Annual Report of the Block Signal and Train Control Board to the Interstate Commerce Commission, Nov. 22, 1910*, 1911, p. 177). After receiving his patents and exhibit-ing his signal at the State Fair in Erie, Pa., Robinson made his first installation of the system on the Philadelphia & Erie Railroad at Kinzua and Irvine, Pa. In 1873 he organized the Robinson Electric Railway Signal Company in St. Petersburg, Pa., and as president and general manager made a number of installations on railroads in Pennsylvania and Maryland. In 1875 he transferred his headquarters to Boston, Mass., and in the course of the next six years installed his signalling system on many railroads of New England. In 1878, having received by this time nine signal patents, he reorganized his company as the Union Electric Signal Company, but in 1881 sold his entire holdings to George Westinghouse [*q.v.*], who reorganized the concern as the Union Switch & Signal Company.

After two years of foreign travel, Robinson settled in Brooklyn, N. Y., where he resided for the balance of his life, practising electrical engineering and continuing to exercise his inventive talent. He devised the bond wire system of connecting adjacent rails electrically which has made modern electric railroading possible; he developed the use of fiber for insulated rail joints; he invented the wireless electric railway signal system; he patented the radial car truck now extensively used on electric railways, and made some important improvements in steam turbines. He also invented a bicycle coaster-brake and roller-bearing skates. He never married, but had nine nieces and nephews. In 1906 he published *History of Automatic Electric and Electrically Controlled Fluid Pressure Signal Systems for Railroads* and the following year, at the age of sixty-seven, completed a post-graduate course in electrical and mechanical engineering at Boston University and received the degree of Ph.D. He was a fellow of the American Institute of Electrical Engineers and an honorary member of the American Railway Association. He died in his eighty-first year and was buried in Brooklyn, N. Y.

[*Alumni Record of Wesleyan Univ.* (1911); *The Invention of the Track Circuit: The Hist. of Dr. Wm. Robinson's Invention* (1922), pub. by the Signal Section of the Am. Railway Asso.; *Brooklyn Daily Eagle*, Jan. 4, 1921; *N. Y. Times*, Jan. 5, 1921; *Railway Age*, Jan. 7, 1921; Patent Office records.]   C. W. M.

ROBINSON, WILLIAM CALLYHAN (July 26, 1834–Nov. 6, 1911), legal educator and author, was born at Norwich, Conn., the son of John A. and Mary (Callyhan) Robinson. He was educated in the public schools of his native town, at Wesleyan University, Middletown, Conn., and Dartmouth College, whence he graduated in 1854. Entering the General Theological Seminary in New York City, he prepared for the priesthood of the Episcopal Church to which he was ordained on Feb. 9, 1859 (*Protestant Episcopal Quarterly Review,* April 1859, p. 307). He had been reared in the Methodist Episcopal Church, and his adherence to Anglicanism proved but the half-way house in a profound change of religious conviction. That he was of a speculative turn is evident from his *Clavis Rerum* (printed anonymously at Norwich in 1883), which probably represented the results of a long period of reflection and internal conflict and in which he sought to reconcile the fundamentals of orthodoxy with the new ideas of science, then just becoming popularly known. Boldly, for that day, he declared therein that "the law of life is a law of evolution"; but he also asserted that he was "permanently committed to no theory or hypothesis." Whatever the process, it led him eventually to adopt the Roman Catholic viewpoint and, after a few years in the Episcopal ministry, as missionary at Pittston, Pa., and rector at Scranton, where he came into contact with some of the Paulist Fathers, he left that fold for the former. Undoubtedly he would have entered the Catholic priesthood but for the bar of marriage. That necessitated a complete change of vocation and he chose the law.

Entering upon the study of his new profession in 1862, he was admitted to the bar of Luzerne County, Pa., two years later and began practice at New Haven, Conn., in 1865. For a time he served on the city and common pleas courts of New Haven County, and in 1874 sat in the Connecticut House of Representatives. Meanwhile the Yale Law School had reached a crisis in its history and Robinson was one of three selected in 1869 to take charge of it. In 1872 he became a full professor there teaching elementary, criminal, and real property law, and pleading, to undergraduates, and patent and Canon law to graduate students. In 1875 he published *Notes on Elementary Law,* expanded into a book in 1882, with a larger edition in 1910. The work met a longfelt want by reason of the growing disuse of Blackstone's *Commentaries* and because the "case method" of instruction had not yet come into general use. From 1884 to 1886 he was chairman of the Connecticut Tax Commission, and its *Report,* signed by Robinson and eight others, was published in 1886. In 1890 he published a three-volume work, *The Law of Patents for Useful Inventions.* His *Forensic Oratory* followed in 1893.

Robinson remained at Yale for twenty-seven years; but the establishment of the Catholic University of Washington called for an eminent non-clerical jurist to head its Law Department. Robinson was chosen, accepted the position in 1896, and remained in it for the rest of his life. He not only gave direction to the new school but found ampler opportunity to continue his legal literary work. His *Elements of American Jurisprudence* appeared in 1900 and his edition of Andrew Horne's *Mirrour of Justices* in 1903, both representing a high order of workmanship and the latter affording a real contribution to the source books of early English law. Robinson died in 1911 in his seventy-eighth year. On July 2, 1857, Robinson married Anna E. Haviland of New York City. After her death he was married, on Mar. 31, 1891, to Ultima Marie Smith of New Haven. There were five children by the first marriage and four by the second.

[See: *Who's Who in America,* 1910–11; obituary notice in the *Yale Law Jour.,* Jan. 1912; Leonard M. Daggett, "The Yale Law School," *Green Bag,* June 1889; *Cath. World,* Dec. 1911; *Washington Post,* Nov. 7, 1911.]
C. S. L.

ROBINSON, WILLIAM ERIGENA (May 6, 1814–Jan. 23, 1892), journalist and politician, son of Thomas and Mary (Sloss) Robinson, was born at Unagh, County Tyrone, Ireland. He received his early education in the village schools of Tubermore and Lipan, entered the classical school, Cookstown, at the age of twelve, and the Royal Academical Institution in Belfast in 1832. Enfeebled by typhus fever, he retired to his father's farm; there he remained until he emigrated to the United States in 1836. Arriving in New York City in August of that year, he resumed his classical studies and entered Yale College in 1837. Poverty forced him to seek employment; while a junior in college he made over a hundred speeches in the successful presidential campaign of William H. Harrison. He also contributed poetry and prose to Horace Greeley's *Log Cabin.* He founded the *Yale Banner* and established a chapter of the Psi Upsilon Fraternity at Yale. During his college days he contributed much of the original matter in the *New Haven Daily Herald.* Following his graduation in 1841, he studied at the Yale Law School (1842–43).

In the political campaign of 1844 he spoke extensively for Henry Clay and became connected with the *New York Tribune.* To this paper he contributed, under the signature of "Richelieu," the Washington dispatches from 1844 until 1848, with the exception of a brief period in 1846 when he was editor of the *Buffalo Daily Express.* He was active in Irish circles during the famine of 1847 and was an ardent supporter of the Young Ireland Rebellion of

1848. He collaborated in the foundation of *The People* (1849), a short-lived publication devoted to European politics. From 1850 to 1853 he was editor of the *Newark Daily Mercury* and, until 1853, weigher in the New York custom house. When these occupations failed him he turned to the law and was admitted to the New York bar in 1854. He occasionally dabbled in politics, running for office independently and unsuccessfully. In 1859 he visited Ireland and toured the Continent. He was appointed in 1862 by President Lincoln as assessor of internal revenue for the Third District of New York (Brooklyn); he served in this capacity until 1867, resigning to take his seat in Congress, to which he had been elected on the Democratic ticket. As a member of Congress he was chiefly responsible for the bill establishing the right to expatriation (*Congressional Globe,* 40 Cong., 1 Sess., p. 791; 3 Sess., Appendix, p. 258). He was a member of the editorial board of the *Irish World* during 1871; during the following year he published the *Shamrock,* a Brooklyn weekly newspaper. He was returned to Congress in 1880 and 1882. His wife, the former Helen Augusta Dougherty, whom he had married in 1853, died in 1875; they had four daughters and two sons.

Robinson's tall, bent figure and his shaggy white hair were a familiar sight in New York City, where he enjoyed a reputation for his extensive acquaintance with men in public life and for his intense hatred of England. He was a political changeling: originally a Whig, he became a Republican and later a Democrat. When he could find no place on any regular ticket he ran independently. He was a prodigious egotist, a ready wit, and an animated and bombastic public speaker. His eloquence was chiefly effective before Irish patriotic societies, to which he presented many times during a half century a speech on Saint Patrick and the Irish that he had originally given at New Haven in 1842. The declining years of his life were spent in collecting materials for a treatise on the "Origin and Source of the American People," intended to demonstrate the superiority and preponderance of the Irish in American life.

[*Semi-centennial Hist. and Biog. Record of the Class of 1841 in Yale Univ.* (1892); *Obit. Record Grads. Yale Univ., 1890–1900* (1900); class records in Yale Univ. Library; *The Tenth Gen. Cat. of the Psi Upsilon Fraternity* (1888); *World* (N. Y.), Jan. 24, 1892; *N. Y. Tribune,* Jan. 24, 1892; *Irish World and Am. Industrial Liberator* (N. Y.), Jan. 30, 1892; *Brooklyn Eagle,* Jan. 24, 1892.]   F. M.

ROBINSON, WILLIAM STEVENS (Dec. 7, 1818–Mar. 11, 1876), journalist, was born in Concord, Mass., the sixth and last child of William and Martha (Cogswell) Robinson, and a descendant of Jonathan Robinson of Exeter, N. H., who died in 1675. After attending the town school, he learned the printer's trade and in 1837 joined his brother in the office of the *Norfolk Advertiser* of Dedham, a strong temperance paper. In 1839 he became editor of the *Yeoman's Gazette,* later *The Republican,* of Concord, a Whig paper, and as an ardent Whig he attended, as delegate, the Whig Convention in Baltimore in 1840. Two years later he became assistant editor of the *Lowell Courier and Journal,* acting for a time as its Washington correspondent. In 1845 he went to Manchester, N. H., to edit *The American,* but soon returned to the *Lowell Courier,* in which connection his strong anti-slavery views began to attract marked attention among the radicals of Massachusetts. His vigorous condemnation of slavery and caustic comments on Massachusetts politics and politicians finally cost him his position, and in 1848 he removed to Boston to succeed Charles Francis Adams [*q.v.*] as editor of the *Boston Daily Whig,* later the *Boston Daily Republican,* which he conducted through the presidential campaign of 1848. The same year he served as secretary of the Free-Soil Convention which met in Worcester. Again, however, his vigorous opinions on slavery and Massachusetts politics cost him his position, and he returned to Lowell to start the *Lowell American,* which he conducted for nearly four years, becoming recognized as one of the most radical of Massachusetts anti-slavery journalists. In 1852, and again in 1853, he was elected to the Massachusetts legislature, and in the latter year served as clerk of the constitutional convention. Following the failure of the *Lowell American* in 1854, he joined the editorial staffs of *The Commonwealth* and the *Boston Telegraph* and violently opposed the rising tide of Know-Nothingism in Massachusetts. In 1856 his "Warrington" letters on Massachusetts politics and politicians began to appear in the *Springfield Republican* and at once attracted state-wide attention because of their thorough knowledge of Massachusetts politics and their frank personal comment on the public men of the state. Similar letters over the pen name "Gilbert" were contributed to the *New York Tribune,* on which paper Robinson was offered an editorial berth in 1859 which, feeling that his best work could be done in Massachusetts, he refused.

The friend of Charles Sumner, John A. Andrew, Henry Wilson, John G. Whittier, and other Massachusetts radicals, he was early associated with the fortunes of the Republican party in the state, and in 1861, on the eve of the Civil War, he aided in editing *The Tocsin,* a campaign paper "published by an association of Republicans who are in earnest, and who will be heard" (*"Warrington" Pen-Portraits, post,* p. 94). In 1862 he was chosen as clerk of the Massachusetts House of Representatives, a position which he held for eleven years, during which he became known as the "Warwick" of Massachusetts politics. In 1863 he was made secretary of the Republican state committee, which important office he occupied until 1868, writing many of the addresses and memorials of the committee during these critical years of war and reconstruction. The strength of Robinson's political power in Massachusetts was most evident, perhaps, in 1871 and 1872 when he successfully led the opposition against Benjamin F. Butler [*q.v.*] in the latter's efforts to gain the governorship of Massachusetts. It was due to Butler's machinations, he believed, that he finally lost his clerkship in 1873. He then served for a short time on the staff of the *Boston Journal,* but in 1874 increasing ill health caused him to make a European trip, following which he returned to complete and publish *Warrington's Manual* (1875), a handbook of parliamentary law. He died the following year at his home in Malden, Mass.

Robinson is described as "a lymphatic, shut-in man, smiling only around the mouth, which is carefully covered with hair to hide the smile; short, thick-set, with his head ... set ... directly on his shoulders; high forehead; slightly bald; thin hair; ruddy of face; ... the keenest political writer in America, and the best political writer since 'Junius'" (quoted in *"Warrington" Pen-Portraits,* p. 128). On Nov. 30, 1848, he married Harriet Jane Hanson [see Harriet Jane Hanson Robinson], one of the literary mill girls of Lowell and for many years a leader in the woman suffrage movement in Massachusetts, a cause in which Robinson himself took much interest. They had four children, of whom three survived their father.

[*Memoir in "Warrington" Pen-Portraits* (1877), ed. by Harriet J. H. Robinson; *New England Hist. and Geneal. Reg.,* Oct. 1885, July 1890; *Springfield Republican,* Mar. 13, 1876.]

W. R. W.

ROBOT, ISIDORE (July 18, 1837–Feb. 15, 1887), Catholic missionary and prelate, was born at Tharoiseau in Burgundy, France, of a patriarchal family which maintained the traditions of faith and piety. He was threatened with consumption while in school and in the seminary, but at the age of twenty he entered the austere

Benedictine Preachers of the Monastery of Pierre-Qui-Vire, in the diocese of Sens, under the founder, the Venerable Mary John Baptist Muard (1808–54), whose life by Abbé Brullée he later translated and published (1882). Here he completed his theological studies and was ordained to the priesthood in December 1862. After several years in the monastery, he volunteered for the American missions on the invitation of Archbishop Napoleon Joseph Perché of New Orleans and arrived in New Orleans in 1871. Four years later he founded a monastery of the Benedictine Congregation Casinese of the Primitive Observance at Sacred Heart, Okla.

The Benedictines became the first resident priests in Indian Territory, and under the indomitable Robot, who lacked no courage for the arduous and dangerous labors on the frontier, they founded the first Catholic mission among the Potawatomi Indians. Stations were soon established for the Choctaws at Atoka, MacAlister, and Caddo, while the Jesuits were assigned to the Osages. In 1876 Indian Territory was made a prefecture-apostolic under Dom Isidore, and a year later his monastery was elevated to an abbey by Pius IX. As prefect apostolic, Robot labored ten years, laying the foundations of Catholicity in the region, building a college for boys at Sacred Heart, establishing Indian agricultural and missionary schools, founding an academy for girls, and conducting annual visitations on horseback to the isolated mission stations and scattered settlers. In 1884 he took a prominent part in the deliberations in the Third Plenary Council of Baltimore where he pleaded the cause of the Indian missions. A year later he was in Europe seeking recruits and further financial aid for the construction of stations and schools in the villages along the Missouri Pacific Railroad. In 1886 he resigned his duties to his successor, Ignatius Jean, O.S.B., and retired to Dallas, Tex., where he died. His remains were interred in the monastic cemetery at his Sacred Heart Abbey.

[*Cath. Encyc.,* XI (1911), 233; *Sadliers' Directory* (1888), p. 35; *N. Y. Freeman's Jour.,* Feb. 10, 1877, Nov. 16, 1878; materials from Robot's associates, Bernard Murphy, O.S.B., and Father Leo, O.S.B.]

R. J. P.

ROBSON, STUART (Mar. 4, 1836–Apr. 29, 1903), actor, was a comedian whose humorous appeal depended largely upon an odd voice and a quaint personality that underwent but little change during his many years of popularity. He was born in Annapolis, Md., the son of a lawyer named Charles Stuart, his own name being Henry Robson Stuart. When he was about twelve years of age, the family moved to Baltimore. After a brief schooling and employment as a page in the Capitol at Washington until he was about sixteen, he ventured on the stage, and with his name on the program as S. Robson acted the part of Horace Courtney in *Uncle Tom's Cabin as It Is,* a play written as a counterblast to *Uncle Tom's Cabin,* at the Baltimore Museum. Thereafter he was on the stage continuously for fifty-one years and acted over seven hundred characters, by far the greater number of them in the first half of that period. After some ten years with stock companies in Baltimore, Washington, Troy, Cincinnati, Richmond, St. Louis, and other cities, and in touring companies on the western circuit, he became a comedian at Laura Keene's Theatre in New York in the season of 1862–63, making his début there on Sept. 15, 1862, as Bob in *Old Heads and Young Hearts.* For three seasons following he was a member of Mrs. John Drew's stock company at the Arch Street Theatre in Philadelphia, and for three seasons more with the stock company at Selwyn's (afterwards the Globe) Theatre in Boston. His first appearance at the Union Square Theatre in New York was made on Oct. 1, 1873, as Simon Carmichel in *The Geneva Cross,* and his success there as Hector in Dion Boucicault's *Led Astray* led to his going with Charles R. Thorne, Jr., to London, to play the same part at the Gayety Theatre. He was Picard in *The Two Orphans* during its long run at the Union Square, Suter in *The Wicked World,* Gaston in *Camille,* Jean Ruse in *Love's Sacrifice,* and Moulinet in *Rose Michel.*

An attempt to star in 1876 in *Two Men of Sandy Bar,* for which he paid Bret Harte $6,000, was a failure. His association with William H. Crane [*q.v.*] which began early in 1877 at the Park Theatre in New York and continued for twelve years, is the most notable episode in his career, and indeed in the careers of both actors. After acting most successfully in *Our Boarding House* for a few months, they formed a congenial partnership, and on Sept. 3, 1877, began their first joint starring tour. A contemporary critic said of Robson acting in *Our Boarding House*: "He was Gillypod last night in the same sense that he was Colonel Starbottle a few months ago. In other words, he assumed the clothing and the wig of Gillypod and thus presented Mr. Robson in a new disguise. He was as funny as he has been before, and as he will be to the end of the chapter" (*Evening Post,* New York, Jan. 30, 1877). Their repertory through successive seasons ranged from such trivialities as *Our Bachelors, The Two Cherubs, Champagne and Oysters,* and *D. A. M.,* to *Twelfth*

Night, She Stoops to Conquer, A Comedy of Errors, with the stars as the two Dromios, and *The Merry Wives of Windsor,* which gave Crane, in his own words, " a fine chance as Falstaff, but . . . Robson as Slender no chance at all" (*Footprints and Echoes,* 1927, p. 113). Of this performance Crane writes: "Robson and I were totally unlike, both as to face and figure. It was necessary for him to use a good deal of padding and to increase his height, while I had the difficult task of imitating his voice, manner and peculiar laugh" (*Ibid.,* p. 103). After two seasons in *The Henrietta,* written especially for them by Bronson Howard and produced Sept. 26, 1887, they gave their last performance together at the Star Theatre in New York on May 11, 1889. Thereafter for a time Robson continued to play in *The Henrietta*; then he revived *She Stoops to Conquer, A Comedy of Errors,* and the more modern English comedy of *Married Life,* and produced a number of new plays, among them *An Arrant Knave, Mrs. Ponderbury's Past, The Jucklins, Oliver Goldsmith, The Meddler,* and *Is Marriage a Failure?* He died suddenly of heart disease in New York City, in the midst of a starring tour. His first wife, whom he married in 1858, was the daughter of the Rev. Henry Johnson of Baltimore; in 1891, a year after her death, he married May Waldron, a member of his company, who, with their son and a daughter by his first wife, survived him.

[L. C. Strang, *Famous Actors of the Day in America* (1900); C. M. Skinner in *Famous American Actors of Today* (1896); J. B. Clapp and E. F. Edgett, *Players of the Present,* Pt. III (1901); *N. Y. Clipper,* Mar. 15, 1884; *N. Y. Dramatic Mirror,* Feb. 1, 1896, July 16, 1898; interview in *N. Y. Times,* Aug. 25, 1901; obit. notices in *N. Y. Times, Boston Transcript,* Apr. 30, 1903, and *N. Y. Dramatic Mirror,* May 9, 1903.]

E. F. E.

ROCHAMBEAU, JEAN BAPTISTE DONATIEN DE VIMEUR, Comte de (July 1, 1725–May 10, 1807), the commander of the French army in America during the War of the Revolution, was born at Vendôme, France, of an ancient and honorable family, the third son of Joseph Charles de Vimeur, Comte de Rochambeau, and his wife, Marie Claire Thérèse Bégon. He was sent to the Collège de Vendôme in 1730, and received under Père Houbigant an excellent training in history, literature, mathematics, and the physical sciences. Being a puny lad and a younger son he was designated for the priesthood. The Bishop of Blois, a friend of the family, snatched the youth from the dangerous heresies of Jansenism at Vendôme and placed him in a Jesuit school at Blois. He was about to receive the tonsure when his elder brother died, and he returned to the Hôtel de Rochambeau to continue his studies. There, and at Paris, he came in contact with authors and scholars and so became acquainted with some of the advanced thought of the century. At the outbreak of the War of the Austrian Succession he secured a commission as junior officer of cavalry in the regiment of Saint-Simon. He was given command of a troop of horse in July 1743 and three years later became aide-de-camp to the Duc d'Orléans. Shortly afterwards he was employed in the siege of Namur under the Comte de Clermont. Rochambeau returned to the army in 1747 as colonel on Clermont's staff, was severely wounded at the battle of Lawfeld, and served gallantly in the battle of Maestricht in 1748.

He married Jeanne Thérèse Tellez d'Acosta, daughter of a wealthy merchant, in December 1749, and retired to Vendômois. He disliked the intrigue and pomp of Versailles and found the life of a provincial country gentleman most congenial. This leisurely existence was interrupted by garrison duties at Verdun, Metz, and Besançon. In 1756 he participated in the brilliant campaign against Minorca and in the capture of Port Mahon from the English. He distinguished himself at Crefeld in June 1758 and during the following March he was placed in command of a regiment of infantry of Auvergne. His skilful maneuvering and personal bravery saved the French from a surprise attack and a disaster at Clostercamp in October 1760. Early in 1761 he was made a brigadier-general and was called to the post of inspector of cavalry. In this latter position he introduced a number of tactical improvements and displayed his unusual solicitude for the welfare of the soldiers—and for discipline. He was appointed governor of Villefranche-en-Roussillon in 1776.

France allied herself with the American insurgents early in 1778. D'Estaing's attempts to cooperate with the Americans in that year had been futile and unfortunate, but the following year the French were persuaded, chiefly by Lafayette, that a military and naval force ought to be sent to the assistance of the Americans: the momentous decision was finally made in February 1780. Lafayette had hoped to secure the command of this expeditionary army, but he cheerfully acquiesced in the appointment of Rochambeau and embarked for America to inform Washington of the imminent aid from France. Elaborate preparations were made for the expedition. Rochambeau's administrative skill and his unceasing application did something to counteract the characteristic inefficiency of the French war department, but noth-

ing could prevail against the ineptitude of the naval department and the refusal of the Spanish to cooperate. In April 1780 some 7,600 soldiers had assembled at Brest ready to embark for America, but there were accommodations for only 5,500. After several tedious delays the fleet of ten ships of war and thirty convoys sailed from Brest on May 1. Admiral Ternay, with caution and ability, brought his fleet across the Atlantic and anchored off Rhode Island on July 11. The following day Rochambeau wrote to Washington that he had arrived full of "submission" and "zeal" and that the king's orders placed him and his army at the disposal of Washington (Washington Papers, Library of Congress). The admirable conduct of the French soldiers, together with the tact, courtesy, and charm of the officers, removed many old American prejudices against the French and prepared the way for effective cooperation and mutual good-will.

Rochambeau's position as commander of the French forces was complicated by the interference of Lafayette. In his impetuous zeal Lafayette, in August 1780, urged Rochambeau to cast off his lethargy and attack New York. But the French commander still awaited the remainder of his troops from France and was unwilling to attempt such a dangerous project unless the French had command of the sea. He rebuked Lafayette, but added a delicate touch: "it is always the old father Rochambeau who talks to his dear son whom he loves . . ." (Doniol, *post*, IV, 380). Washington felt that there might be difficulties in giving Lafayette too active a part in the dealings between himself and Rochambeau and accordingly arranged a conference with the French commander at Hartford on Sept. 21. Washington was inclined to favor an attack against New York, but when he observed that the opinion of the French generals was unfavorable he tactfully abandoned the project. However, Washington, Rochambeau, and Ternay joined in a request to the French government for more men and money; they declared that an attack against New York would be desirable only if the allies had a superiority at sea. Rochambeau and the French army then went into winter-quarters in Rhode Island.

Early in May 1781, the Comte de Barras arrived at Boston with the Vicomte de Rochambeau, who brought his father the unwelcome news that there was no second division of French troops to be expected. But he brought news that the French king had consented to a new subsidy of six million *livres tournois* and that the Comte de Grasse, in command of a powerful fleet, had sailed to the West Indies and would later cooperate with Washington and Rochambeau. A second conference between Washington and Rochambeau was held at Wethersfield, Conn., on May 21. Washington still favored the attempt against New York, but Rochambeau urged that operations against Cornwallis in Virginia be undertaken in conjunction with the fleet under De Grasse. This insistence upon the Virginia campaign was the work of La Luzerne, the French minister to the United States (Jusserand, *post*, pp. 61–63). It was agreed at Wethersfield that the movement against New York was perhaps the only practicable one, because of the great difficulties in transporting the troops to Virginia. The French fleet was to remain at Newport, but the army was to join the American forces on the Hudson. On June 10 the French broke camp at Newport and on July 5 the two armies were united at White Plains, N. Y. The combined Franco-American forces now numbered some 10,000. There were several skirmishes with the British, but Washington did not wish to hazard a general engagement. The strategy of the Franco-Americans was to depend upon the destination of De Grasse. On Aug. 14 news arrived that the French fleet was sailing for the Chesapeake. Washington, urged by Rochambeau, now prepared to march southward against Cornwallis who was being harassed by Lafayette in Virginia. If the British lost control of the sea and if Clinton at New York did not attempt to succor the British forces in Virginia, the fate of Cornwallis was sealed.

On Aug. 19 Washington and Rochambeau began their long march southward; William Heath [*q.v.*], with about 3,000 men, was left before New York to deceive the British. By Aug. 26 the rest of the army had gained the west side of the Hudson and they marched directly southward, still feinting an attack against New York. On the 29th they turned their backs on New York and marched rapidly towards Philadelphia. The American treasury was so bare that Rochambeau lent 20,000 hard dollars to enable Washington to pay his troops a month's salary. The speed with which both armies traveled and the skill with which two fleets and two armies formed a perfect union were both extraordinary. De Grasse anchored his fleet in the roadstead of Chesapeake Bay late in August and within several days disembarked 4,000 soldiers, who joined the army of Lafayette. The English fleet under Graves were repulsed in an attack against De Grasse on Sept. 5, and four days later the arrival of Barras with

the French fleet from Newport gave the French forces such an advantage that Graves withdrew to New York. Barras had been induced to assist De Grasse only after repeated urgings by Rochambeau and Washington. Lafayette resisted the temptation to attack Cornwallis and wrote Washington and Rochambeau to make all haste to Yorktown, where the British were now encamped.

On Sept. 14 Washington and Rochambeau joined Lafayette and Saint-Simon at Williamsburg, Va. After a conference with De Grasse plans for the siege were drawn up: preparations were expedited by the fear that De Grasse would soon withdraw his fleet to the West Indies. There were skirmishes and bombardments by the siege guns, but casualties were small on both sides. Seventeen days after the siege was formally begun Cornwallis sent a flag of truce to consider terms of surrender. Rochambeau and Barras signed the articles of capitulation for the French. On Oct. 19 the surrender took place. The British wished to surrender themselves to the French, but Rochambeau discreetly held to a strict observance of the proprieties.

Following the surrender of Cornwallis, De Grasse sailed for the West Indies, Washington returned to the Hudson and Rochambeau and the French army went into winter quarters near Williamsburg. The Virginians thought the war was over and did not look kindly upon the presence of an army. But the French soldiers were kept under extraordinarily good discipline by Rochambeau and his staff. The French commander had requested his recall in June 1781, because his health had long been poor, and there was not much glory to be gathered in America. Fortunately for his fame he did not receive the message granting him permission to return until Dec. 6, 1781. After making a short tour in Virginia he finally embarked for France on Jan. 11, 1783. In one of his several last conferences with Washington the American commander spoke enthusiastically of a Canadian expedition, but Rochambeau knew that Vergennes did not favor any such campaign and politely declined. Rochambeau was suitably fêted before his long-delayed departure for France.

Upon his return to France there was no great public celebration for him, since Lafayette monopolized the public attention, but the king declared that he owed the peace to Rochambeau. Early in 1784 he was made commander of an important military district, with headquarters at Calais. He was an active member of the Society of the Cincinnati. Rochambeau participated in the second Assembly of Notables. In 1789 he was made commander of the important district of Alsace; poor health caused his retirement in December of that year. In September 1790 he was placed in charge of the northern military department and was created a marshal of France in December 1791. During the Terror he was arrested, imprisoned, and was about to be guillotined when Robespierre's death stopped the wholesale carnage. Rochambeau was honored by Napoleon and made a member of the Legion of Honor before his death at his château in 1807. He is buried at Thoré.

[Comte de Rochambeau, *Mémoires militaires, historiques et politiques* (2 vols., Paris, 1809); *Memoirs* (extracts translated by M. W. E. Wright, Paris, 1838); J. E. Weelen, *Rochambeau* (Paris, 1934); D. R. Keim, *Rochambeau. A Commemoration by the Congress of the U. S. A. . . .* (Washington, 1907); J. J. Jusserand, *With Americans of Past and Present Days* (1916); J. B. Perkins, *France in the American Revolution* (1911); Henri Doniol, *Histoire de la participation de la France à l'établissement des États-Unis . . .* (5 vols., Paris, 1886–1899). Weelen has written the only satisfactory biography, but has failed to use the large collection of Rochambeau MSS. in the Lib. of Cong.; this collection was partly used by Jusserand. Doniol prints almost three hundred pages of Rochambeau documents from French archives. The materials listed in the bibliography of the Lafayette article should also be consulted for Rochambeau in America.] F. M.

ROCHE, JAMES JEFFREY (May 31, 1847–Apr. 3, 1908), journalist and poet, son of Edward and Mary Margaret (Doyle) Roche, was born at Mountmellick, Queen's County, Ireland, from which place his parents emigrated to Charlottetown, Prince Edward Island. Here his father taught mathematics, conducted a school, and became provincial librarian. James was educated by his father and at St. Dunstan's College. In 1866 he went to Boston, where he made friends easily in Irish circles and succeeded in a business way. In 1883, he became assistant editor of the Boston *Pilot,* which had long been the leading Irish Catholic journal in the United States. Seven years later he succeeded John Boyle O'Reilly [*q.v.*] as editor and as the idol of a Catholic intellectual group in Boston. A man of humor and generous social qualities, he became a leader in the St. Botolph and Papyrus Clubs, where the sons of old New England enjoyed his romances and cherished his friendship. While not a violent Irish partisan, he was, however, an intense nationalist, keenly concerned with the uplifting of the Irish in America. In 1904, he welcomed an appointment as consul at Genoa from the hands of President Theodore Roosevelt as a relief from business worries and from a severe climate which made his delicate health more precarious. His life was prolonged for four years but the end came at Berne in the Alps where he was then consul.

He was twice married: first, to Mary Halloran, who died in 1885; and second, in 1904, to Mrs. Elizabeth Vaughan Okie; the latter, a son and a daughter survived him. He was buried in Holyhood Cemetery, Brookline, Mass.

He contributed much to the *Pilot* and to other periodicals, including the *Atlantic, Century,* and *Harpers,* and was the author of a stirring novel of adventure, *The Story of the Filibusters* (1891), translated into Spanish (1908), and reissued as *By-Ways of War: the Story of the Filibusters* (1901), which Richard Harding Davis described as a classic. He published a *Life of John Boyle O'Reilly* (1891) and contributed an introduction to Henry B. Carpenter's *A Poet's Last Songs* (1891), and a biographical and critical introduction to *The Collected Writings of Samuel Lover* (10 vols., 1901–13). He edited Thackeray's *The Mahogany Tree* (1887), and with Justin McCarthy, Lady Gregory, Maurice Francis Egan, and Douglas Hyde, he collaborated in preparing *Irish Literature* (10 vols., 1904). In his *Songs and Satires* (1886), *Her Majesty the King; a Romance of the Harem* (1898), *Ballads of Blue Water and Other Poems* (1895), *The V-a-s-e and Other Bric-à-Brac* (1900), and *The Sorrows of Sap'ed* (1904), Roche displayed a delicate touch, sweetness of voice, humorous satire, and ringing patriotism as a balladist.

[*James Jeffrey Roche: A Memorial and Appreciation* (1908); *Jour. Am. Irish Hist. Soc.,* vol. VIII (1909); J. B. Cullen, *The Story of the Irish in Boston* (1889); *Who's Who in America,* 1908–09; C. McGuire, *Catholic Builders of the Nation,* IV (1923), 175; *Boston Transcript,* Apr. 3, May 3, 1908; *Boston Globe,* Apr. 4, 1908.] R. J. P.

ROCHESTER, NATHANIEL (Feb. 21, 1752–May 17, 1831), merchant and founder of Rochester, N. Y., was born in Westmoreland County, Va., the son of John and Hester (Thrift) Rochester and the grandson of Nicholas Rochester who emigrated from England to Westmoreland County at the end of the seventeenth century. His father died when the boy was only four years old, and his mother, marrying again, took the family to Granville County, N. C. The young Nathaniel must have received but a limited education, and there is no reference to schooling in his modest autobiography (*post,* pp. 305–14). At the age of sixteen he was employed in a country store in Hillsboro, N. C., and was taken into partnership in 1773. He was a member of the revolutionary committee of safety for Orange County in 1775 and of the two provincial conventions of 1775 and 1776. He saw brief active service as a major of militia, receiving the surrender of a part of the

British force defeated at Moore's Creek in February 1776. On Apr. 22, 1776, he was appointed lieutenant-colonel of the North Carolina troops. He also acted as deputy-commissary general of military stores and clothing. In 1777 he was appointed a commissioner to establish and superintend an arms manufactory at Hillsboro, and he served in the Assembly the same year. For reasons not entirely clear, perhaps from lack of health, he gave up the pursuit of arms, and in 1778 he went into business with Col. Thomas Hart, first at Hillsboro and a little later at Hagerstown, Md. The two partners rented a gristmill and established nail and rope factories. In 1792 the partnership was dissolved. While in Hagerstown, Rochester served one term in the legislature but refused reëlection because of disgust "with the intrigue and management among the members" (autobiography, *post*, p. 311). In 1807 he became president of the Hagerstown bank, a modest establishment housed for seven years in his own dwelling.

Associated with him in his bank were Charles Carroll and William Fitzhugh. Carroll and Fitzhugh's brother, Peregrine Fitzhugh, had visited western New York in 1799. It was through these men that Rochester became interested in western New York, which was then opening up to settlement. Visiting the Genesee country in 1800, he bought a small amount of land there, especially a tract at Dansville, covering the water-power sites along the Canaseraga. In 1803, with his friends, he purchased the one-hundred-acre tract at the so-called Upper Falls of the Genesee for the large price of $17.50 an acre. The tract was not laid out, however, till some time later, and sales of land did not begin till November 1811. In the meantime he decided to close out his business at Hagerstown and remove to the Genesee country. He settled first at Dansville with his wife, Sophia (Beatty) Rochester, whom he had married in 1788, and nine children, and there established three mills and a wool-carding shop. From Dansville he removed to Bloomfield and in 1818 to Rochester, a village of some 700 persons and called from 1817 to 1822 by the name of Rochesterville. In 1821 he took an active part in obtaining the creation of the county of Monroe, in which Rochester is situated, and became clerk of the county when it was set up. In 1824 he organized a bank at Rochester. He was then a man of over seventy years; yet he took an active interest in the campaign of 1828, strongly supporting the claims of John Quincy Adams to the presidency. He was steadily weakening, and his last years were not marked by any further participation in public affairs. In appearance he was tall, and rather spare, with distinctly attractive features. Notwithstanding the fact that his manners were somewhat austere, and his temper was strong, it is clear that he commanded a high degree of respect in the community in which he settled.

[*N. C. Colonial Records*, esp. vol. X (1890); *N. C. State Records*, esp. vols. XI, XII (1895); a number of accounts of his life in the *Rochester Hist. Soc. Publication Fund Series*, vol. III (1924), including autobiography, excerpts from correspondence, and a bibliography; Henry O'Reilly, *Sketches of Rochester* (1838), pp. 407–415.]   D. P.

ROCK, JOHN (Aug. 19, 1836–Aug. 9, 1904), nurseryman, was born in Lauter, Hesse-Darmstadt, Germany, the son of Heinrich and Elisabeth Roch. As a youth he left home secretly and emigrated to America, where he changed his name to Rock. He first resided in New York, employed as a florist and later as a nurseryman. At the outbreak of the Civil War he joined the Union forces, enlisting with the 5th New York Regiment, Duryée's Zouaves. He was in many engagements, was made a sergeant, and remained in the army until the end of the war. In 1866 he moved to California and was one of the pioneer nurserymen of that state. His first nursery was at Santa Clara. Later he opened the Rock Nurseries on the Milpitas Road and in 1884 established the California Nursery Company at Niles. This nursery, which became a great storehouse of horticultural material, played a most important part in California horticulture. It was here that he assembled the large collection of grape varieties from all parts of the world that provided the material from which phylloxera-resistant stocks were developed. He also introduced many fig varieties into California and was the first to call the attention of American investigators to the fig collection of the London Royal Horticulture Society. When in 1894 the United States Department of Agriculture imported this collection it was placed in Rock's hands for propagation and all of the sixty-six varieties were successfully established. Among the other plants that he introduced into California were the pistacia, black Spanish mulberry, rose-colored seedless Sultana grape, Moorpark apricot, Cork oak, Oriental plane tree, Cedar of Lebanon, Deodara cedar, Damson and Mirabelle plums, thin-shelled almonds, and Italian chestnut. In a tribute to Rock it has been said of him: "Intensely in love with his work, it is no wonder that he spent thousands of dollars in exploiting new and little known fruits and plants, many of which proved worthless; nor that, on the other hand, his untiring zeal in the development of California horticulture has been the direct means of introducing a larger number of varieties of fruits and plants into this State than any other one man" (Kruckeberg, *post*, p. 5). Personally Rock was modest and retiring, a man of few words. It would seem that his influence on California horticulture, generally recognized by his contemporaries and successors, was due as much to his personality as to his material contributions.

[Sources include: H. W. Kruckeberg, "John Rock, A Tribute," *Trans. and Proc. of the Second Ann. Meeting of the Cal. Asso. of Nurserymen* (1913); E. J. Wickson, "Cal. Nurserymen of Second and Third Decade," *Trans. and Proc. of the Seventh Annual Meeting of the Cal. Asso. of Nurserymen* (1917); L. H. Bailey, *The Standard Cyc. of Horticulture*, III (1915), 1593; *San Francisco Examiner*, Aug. 11, 1904. Information for this sketch was supplied by Dr. Gustavus Eisen, one of Rock's associates, W. V. Eberly, and by members of the family.]   G. N. C.

ROCKEFELLER, WILLIAM (May 31, 1841–June 24, 1922), industrialist and financier, born in Richford, Tioga County, N. Y., was the third child of William Avery and Eliza (Davison) Rockefeller and the younger brother of John D. Rockefeller. The family apparently originated in Germany, the original American ancestor, Johann Peter Rockefeller, and his son Peter, coming to America from Sagendorf, Germany, about 1722 and settling in Somerville, N. J. William's father departed from the long ancestral vocation of farming to become an itinerant peddler of patent medicines. He moved his family about a great deal, to Moravia in Cayuga County and, in 1850, to Owego, the county seat of Tioga, where, after some instruction in a small village school, William, with his more famous brother, John D., attended Owego Academy. In 1853 the roving father moved his family again to Strongsville, Ohio; then, in a year, to Parma, a neighboring district, and in 1857 to Cleveland, where the family settled definitely. There, after attending the public schools, William, when about sixteen years of age, began his business career as a bookkeeper for a small miller in Cleveland. After a year he went into the produce business in which his brother was already laying the first foundation stones of his vast fortunes and, when but twenty-one years of age, set up in business for himself under the firm name of Hughes and Rockefeller, commission merchants.

Meantime, petroleum had been found by Edwin L. Drake [*q.v.*] in Venango County, Pa., an event which changed the whole course of business in Cleveland. John D. Rockefeller became interested, like most Cleveland business men, and ventured into the refining industry with Samuel Andrews, as Rockefeller and An-

drews. This firm was the progenitor of the Standard Oil Company. When the oil industry, which then consisted largely of refining and selling kerosene for illuminating purposes, gave signs of becoming a great export business, John D. Rockefeller invited his younger brother to join his firm to take charge of its export selling functions in New York. A new firm, William Rockefeller & Company, was formed in 1867, which was in reality only a subsidiary of Rockefeller and Andrews. Its habitat was New York City to which place William went that year to remain throughout his life. He built up the great export business and this firm became in time the Standard Oil Company of New York, of which William Rockefeller was president until 1911. On May 25, 1864, he married Almira Geraldine Goodsell, to which union were born six children, four sons and two daughters.

With his brother he played a leading rôle in the troublous battles between the refiners' combinations and the crude oil producers in 1872 and the years following. He was active in bringing the Eastern refiners, who had opposed the young Standard Oil group—men like Henry H. Rogers, Charles Pratt, Alfred C. Bedford, and others—into the Standard Oil mergers which combined most of the able leaders of the industry against the horde of small refiners and producers. When the first trust agreement was made, William was a member of the trust until its dissolution in 1890 by the Ohio courts. Later he played an important rôle in that extensive series of combinations and absorptions in which the Standard Oil Company of New Jersey, acting as a holding company, gathered under its wing the vast organization of refineries, pipe lines, oil fields, ship lines, and related manufacturing industries which the Supreme Court of the United States dissolved as a violation of the Sherman Anti-Trust Law in 1911.

While John D. Rockefeller's supreme talent was for organization, William blossomed first as an able salesman and commercial diplomat and later as a financier and promoter of extraordinary ability. Unlike his famous brother, who disliked speculation and all sorts of adventures in securities, William formed one of the group made up chiefly of himself, Henry H. Rogers, and James Stillman [*qq.v.*] of the National City Bank, and which came to be known as the "Standard Oil Gang." They carried on numerous adventurous and audacious promotions in Wall Street, chief of which was the Amalgamated Copper deal which led Thomas W. Lawson to write his sensational denunciation under the title, *Frenzied Finance* (1905). The years

1898 to 1912 were the golden years of the promoters. William Rockefeller and Rogers went heavily into numerous corporate fields. Rockefeller became a director in countless corporations. They centered their attention finally on railroad and gas companies. Occupying strategic positions because of the Standard's control over artificial gas fields and petroleum, which was coming into use for making gas, they got control of the Consolidated Gas Company of New York and the United Gas Improvement Company in Philadelphia, which was a forerunner of the modern holding company form of organization applied to utilities.

After 1911 and the dissolution of the Standard Oil Trust, William, like his brother and other leaders of the great corporation, withdrew from an active part in the management of the industry. He devoted himself chiefly to his investments and those railroad properties, like the Chicago, Milwaukee & St. Paul Railroad, in which he held a dominant position. He differed in many characteristics from his brother. He was a jovial man who loved good living. He had but small piety, though he occasionally made contributions to the Baptist Church. He had little interest in philanthropy and such gifts as he made he was very secretive about. In his later years he retired to the beautiful estate, "Rockwood Hall," adjoining his brother's at Tarrytown, N. Y., and there died of pneumonia June 24, 1922, at the age of eighty-one. He left a fortune variously estimated at between $150,-000,000 and $200,000,000, a large part of it in Standard Oil securities, but many score mil-lions in widely diversified corporation bonds and shares. There were no charitable bequests, the whole fortune being left to his four surviving children.

[H. O. Rockefeller, ed., *The Transactions of the Rockefeller Family Asso.* . . . (3 vols., 1910, 1915, 1926); E. M. Avery, *A Hist. of Cleveland and Its Environs* (1918), vol. III; Ida M. Tarbell, *The Hist. of the Standard Oil Co.* (2 vols., 1904); J. T. Flynn, *God's Gold, The Story of Rockefeller and His Times* (1932); *Who's Who in America,* 1922–23; obituary in *N. Y. Times,* June 25, 1922.]   J. T. F.

ROCKHILL, WILLIAM WOODVILLE (April 1854–Dec. 8, 1914), Orientalist and diplomat, was born in Philadelphia, Pa., the son of Thomas Cadwallader and Dorothy Anna (Woodville) Rockhill. After graduating from the École Spéciale Militaire de St. Cyr, France, in 1873, he served three years as lieutenant in the French army in Algeria. Throughout a career of thirty years he combined a profound interest in Far-Eastern studies with the professional duties of a diplomat. His first assignments involved ap-pointments to Peking as second secretary of the American legation from Apr. 9, 1884, as secretary of the legation from July 1, 1885, and as chargé d'affaires at Seoul, from Dec. 11, 1886, to Apr. 3, 1887, at a time when China, Russia, and Japan were each centered on gaining control of Korea. While at Peking Rockhill had viewed his appointment as an opportunity to continue Tibetan studies commenced at Paris. He had already published (1884) a translation into French of the *Prâtimoksha Sutra* (*Le traité d'émancipation*) and *The Life of the Buddha* (1884). Upon his temporary withdrawal from the diplomatic service on July 5, 1888, he engaged himself to the Smithsonian Institution, under whose auspices he made two scientific expeditions to Mongolia and Tibet (1888–89 and 1891–92). His journeys, directed into eastern and southern Tibet, regions difficult to traverse but rich for geographical and ethnographical observations, produced a variety of valuable reports and works on the then secluded and little-known country. His researches in later years included the pre-modern relations of China with the Western world by the routes along the coasts of India and overland through Turkestan. While at St. Petersburg, he edited and translated with Professor Friedrich Hirth of Columbia University the *Chu-fan-Chï* (1912) of Chau Ju-kua, Imperial trade commissioner at Amoy, on Chinese and Arab trade in the twelfth and thirteenth centuries. His researches on the relations and trade of China with the Eastern Archipelago and the coasts of the Indian Ocean during the fourteenth and fifteenth centuries continued until his death. His interest in East Asiatic bibliography was expressed in gifts of over 6,000 volumes of rare Chinese works to the Chinese Division of the Library of Congress. The Library acquired from him also a 1733 edition of the Tibetan *Kanjur*.

Rockhill's public services still remain to be fully recognized. Secretary of State John Hay associated him with Henry White as one of the two best American diplomats of the time (W. R. Thayer, *Life and Letters of John Hay,* 1908, II, 244). He had returned to the service of the Department of State, Apr. 14, 1893, as chief clerk, and was made third assistant secretary of state a year later. Until 1899 he served in various capacities, as delegate to the International Congress of Geography, London, in 1895, as assist-ant secretary of state from Feb. 14, 1896, until May 10, 1897, as minister and consul-general to Greece, Roumania, and Servia from July 8, 1897, to May 19, 1899, when he resigned to accept an appointment as director of the International Bureau of the American Republics, a position said to have been secured for him in order that the Department of State might still have the benefit of his advice on diplomatic matters in Asia. His hand is clearly evident in the policy of John Hay throughout the Boxer insurrection in China, and the subsequent settlements. Just prior to the international cataclysm of 1900, Hay had announced his open-door doctrine as applicable to China, employing almost the precise words of a lengthy memorandum of Rockhill under date of Aug. 28, 1899. In July 1900, Hay dispatched Rockhill to China as special agent of the United States to perform, in the ensuing negotiations, his most notable diplomatic services. It was Rockhill's rôle to adhere to the formula, announced in Hay's circular note to the powers of July 3, 1900, of regarding the Boxer disturbance as a state of anarchy, not of war against the Chinese Empire. The American phase of the negotiations thus facilitated the mitigation of the penalties imposed upon the Chinese people in the protocol of Sept. 7, 1901. The eventual determination of the monetary indemnity ($333,-000,000) was doubtless less than it would have been but for the good offices of the United States. The subsequent proposal for the remission of one half of the unexpended balance of the American portion of the indemnity for the education of Chinese was a part of the general benevolent policy advocated by Rockhill for the strengthening of China.

Rockhill's subsequent public career included his resumption of duty as director of the International Bureau of American Republics on Oct. 24, 1901, his resignation on Mar. 7, 1905, enabling him to return to China as American minister, a congenial post which he held until appointed ambassador to Russia, May 17, 1909. His diplomatic career terminated as ambassador to Turkey (Apr. 24, 1911, until the autumn of 1913). In 1914 he revisited China, including a journey to Mongolia, under the auspices of the American Asiatic Association. In the same year he accepted an appointment as personal advisor to the President of China, Yuan Shih-k'ai, whose acquaintance as the representative of China he had first made in Korea in 1886. While returning to China for this purpose, Rockhill died at Honolulu. He had married twice. His first wife was Caroline Adams of Philadelphia, whom he had married on Dec. 14, 1876. In April 1900 he was married to Edith Howell Perkins of Litchfield, Conn. Two daughters survived him. His principal published works, aside from those already mentioned, comprised: "Tibet, . . . from Chinese Sources" *Journal of the Royal Asiatic*

Society, January, April 1891; *Udânavarga, the Northern Buddhist Version of Dhammapada* (1883); *The Land of the Lamas* (1891); *Diary of a Journey in Mongolia and Tibet in 1891 and 1892* (1894); *Notes on the Ethnology of Tibet* (1895); *The Journey of William of Rubruck* (1900); *Report of William W. Rockhill, late Commissioner to China* (1901); *China's Intercourse with Korea from the XVth Century to 1895* (1905), *Conventions and Treaties with or concerning China and Korea* (1904), supplemented by another volume in 1908; and monographs appearing in *T'oung Pao* (Paris) and other journals.

[Rockhill's papers, now in private hands, have not yet been published. The *Registers* of the Department of State contain data of his official career. Other sources include: Henri Cordier, tribute in *T'oung Pao*, Mar. 1915, supplemented by an article and bibliography of Rockhill's writings by Berthold Laufer, *Ibid.*, May 1915; A. E. Hippisley, memoir in *Jour. Royal Asiatic Soc.*, Apr. 1915; F. E. Hinckley, memoir in *Jour. North-China Branch Royal Asiatic Soc.*, vol. XLVI (1915); E. F. Egan, in *Jour. Am. Asiatic Asso.*, Jan. 1915; Tyler Dennett, *Americans in Eastern Asia* (1922); A. L. P. Dennis, *Adventures in Am. Diplomacy* (1928); *Who's Who in America*, 1912–13; *Papers Relating to the Foreign Relations of the U. S.*, 1901, App.; *N. Y. Times*, Dec. 9, 1914. Every Rockhill letter in the Hay papers has disappeared.]   E. M. G.

ROCKNE, KNUTE KENNETH (Mar. 4, 1888–Mar. 31, 1931), football coach, the son of Lars Knutson and Martha (Gjermo) Rockne, was born in Voss, Norway. He was the second child and the only son in a family of five children. His father, a stationary engineer with a taste for invention, came to the United States in October 1891 to prepare a carriage of his contrivance for exhibition at the Columbian Exposition in Chicago. The family followed eighteen months later and Knute grew up in Chicago where he attended Brentano Grammar School and the Northwest Division High School. Before he finished high school, however, he was dropped for cutting classes. He washed windows in Chicago, worked on a ferry-boat, harvested in Wisconsin, and was for four years a mail dispatcher in the Chicago Post Office. He saved enough money to begin a delayed college career and entered the University of Notre Dame, Ind., in 1910 and was graduated with the degree of B.S., with distinction, in 1914, having specialized in chemistry.

In college he was an all around athlete and a good scholar. He was editor of the college literary annual in his senior year and in 1913 was captain of the Notre Dame team which astonished the intercollegiate football world by defeating the strong Army team at West Point by brilliant use of the forward pass. Football critics agree that the work of Charles Dorais and Rockne in that game opened the eyes of the football coaches of the country to the possibilities of the "open game." After graduation, Rockne became a chemistry instructor at Notre Dame and assistant football coach. Upon the retirement of Jesse Harper in 1918 he became head football coach and from that year he developed football teams of remarkable excellence. During the thirteen years of his coaching, Notre Dame won 105 games, lost twelve, and tied five. He was an advocate of intersectional football and the Notre Dame team traveled all over the country, meeting strong opponents in the East, the West, and the South. Rockne's colorful and highly trained teams became favorites with the non-college public and attracted huge crowds. Over 110,000 spectators witnessed the game between Notre Dame and the University of Southern California on Nov. 16, 1929. Five of the Rockne-coached Notre Dame teams were undefeated and several were acclaimed unofficial national champions. The so-called "Rockne System" featured speed and deception and provided a place for the lighter and faster man on the football field. Though Rockne originated little in football strategy, he brought the forward pass, the shift, the spinner plays, and the flexing-end play to a high type of perfection. Through the success and popularity of his teams, he became a figure of national prominence and a powerful influence in the development of the game. His players went out in great numbers to be football coaches at colleges all over the country, carrying with them the splendid technique and infectious enthusiasm of their famous coach.

Medium in size, muscular, bronzed, and prematurely bald, he was a man of energy, with a keen mind, a ready tongue, and a rollicking sense of humor. He became noted as an after-dinner speaker, and met many demands for radio talks, moving pictures, and syndicated articles on football. He conducted summer schools for football coaches, managed a tour of Europe, and was for a brief time a partner in a brokerage firm in South Bend, Ind. His contact with the Studebaker Corporation as sales promotion manager began in May 1928 and continued until his death. Partly as a result of his many activities he suffered a serious breakdown in 1929 but was well on the road to complete recovery when, on Mar. 31, 1931, he met death in an airplane crash on the plains of southeastern Kansas. He is buried at Notre Dame, Ind. He was married on July 15, 1914, to Bonnie Gwendoline Skiles, who, with their four children, survived him. He became a Roman Catholic in 1925.

[Who's Who in America, 1930–31; Bonnie Skiles Rockne, ed., The Autobiog. of Knute K. Rockne (1931); Warren Brown, Rockne (1931); Robert Harron, Rockne, Idol of Am. Football (1931); McCready Huston, Salesman from the Sidelines, being the Business Career of Knute K. Rockne (1932); D. W. Lovelace, Rockne of Notre Dame (1931); Harry A. Stuhldreher, Knute Rockne (1931); N. Y. Times, Apr. 1, 1931.]
J. K.

ROCKWELL, ALPHONSO DAVID (May 18, 1840–Apr. 12, 1933), pioneer in electrotherapeutics, was born in New Canaan, Conn., the son of David S. and Betty (Comstock) Rockwell. He was educated at the New Canaan Seminary conducted by his father and at Kenyon College at Gambier, Ohio. His father had purchased a farm near Milan, Ohio, and here he returned after graduation to teach a rural school and begin the study of medicine with a local practitioner. In the spring of 1862 he served a three-months' enlistment in the 85th Ohio Infantry, guarding Confederate prisoners at Camp Chase at Columbus. He spent a year in the medical department of the University of Michigan and a second at the Bellevue Hospital Medical School in New York where he received his medical degree in 1864. He immediately took the examination for the army medical service, was appointed an assistant surgeon, and was assigned to the 6th Ohio Cavalry in Gregg's division of Sheridan's cavalry corps. Joining his regiment at Warrenton, Va., he participated in the campaign which began at the Wilderness and ended with the investment of Richmond, and was with Sheridan's cavalry when it blocked the Confederate retreat at Appomattox. In the meantime he had been promoted to the office of surgeon with the grade of major. Discharged with his regiment in August 1865, he settled in New York City for practice.

In 1866 Rockwell became associated with George M. Beard [q.v.] in the investigation of the therapeutic applications of electricity, an association which later developed into a business partnership. At this time electricity was not used to any extent by physicians in the United States, and very little elsewhere. They issued a series of articles in the Medical Record (1866–67, 1867–68), published in book form in 1867 under the title, The Medical Use of Electricity, which created wide interest. In these articles emphasis was placed upon general electrization with its constitutional tonic effects. In 1871 he published with Beard their larger work: A Practical Treatise on the Medical and Surgical Uses of Electricity, which went through eleven editions and was introduced into Germany by a translation by Professor Väter of the University of Prague. In this exhaustive work they described and illustrated in detail the modus operandi of general electrization which they had been the first to give systematic investigation, and directed attention to the growing importance of "central galvanization," especially galvanization of the sympathetic system. Numerous carefully prepared case reports gave added value to the book. Individually or in collaboration with Beard, Rockwell produced a flow of articles for the literature of neurology and electro-therapeutics. Their association was terminated in 1876 by an estrangement, which was later healed. In 1884 Rockwell edited a volume on *Sexual Neurasthenia* from the posthumous manuscript of Beard and in 1888 he brought out a second edition of Beard's *Practical Treatise on Nervous Exhaustion.* He edited an American edition of Sir William Atkin's *Complete Handbook of Treatment* (1887) and wrote the chapter on electrotherapeutics for H. A. Hare's *System of Practical Therapeutics* (1891). In 1920 he published *Rambling Recollections: An Autobiography.* He was appointed professor of electro-therapeutics at the New York Postgraduate Medical School in 1886, holding the position for four years. Owing to his admitted limitations as a public speaker, he was extremely modest concerning his success as an instructor. He was neurologist and electrotherapeutist to the Flushing Hospital and served on the medical staffs of the Woman's Hospital and Demilt Dispensary in New York. He was a member and one-time president of the American Electro-Therapeutic Association.

When the New York state law was enacted changing the method of legal execution from hanging to the electric chair, Rockwell was chosen by the commissioner of prisons as one of a committee of three to advise the state as to the best method of carrying out the provisions of the law. Not only did he advise upon the apparatus and its application, but he gave testimony for the state in defense of the new law and was a witness of some of the earliest electro-executions in the state. He retired from active professional work some years before his death. He was married on Oct. 7, 1868, in New York, to Susannah Landon of that city. It is to be said of Rockwell and his associate, Beard, that they wrested electro-therapeutics from the grasp of charlatanry, gave it respectability, and placed it upon a scientific basis.

[In addition to Rockwell's autobiography see: *New Eng. Medic. Monthly* (Sandy Hook, Conn.), Apr. 1884; *Jour. Am. Medic. Asso.,* May 20, 1933; R. F. Stone, *Eminent Am. Physicians and Surgeons* (1898); *Who's Who in Am. Medicine,* 1925; *N. Y. Times,* Apr. 13, 1933. By a curious error, an obituary notice of Rockwell appeared in the *Jour. Am. Medic. Asso.* at the time of his wife's death in 1925.]   J. M. P—n.

ROCKWELL, KIFFIN YATES (Sept. 20, 1892–Sept. 23, 1916), soldier and aviator in the World War, one of the original members of the Escadrille Lafayette, was born in Newport, Tenn., the son of James Chester and Loula (Ayres) Rockwell. He was a descendant of William Rockwell who in 1630 came to America and settled in Dorchester, Mass., later removing to Windsor, Conn.; his great-grandfather, Chester, born in Middletown, Conn., married a Southern girl and went to South Carolina, where he bought a plantation near Whiteville; both his grandfathers served in the Confederate army. His father died when Kiffin was barely a year old. The boy spent several months each year on the plantation of his maternal grandfather in South Carolina, where he early learned to hunt and fish, became an excellent horseman, and, stirred by stories of the chivalry displayed in the Civil War, made up his mind to be a soldier. When he was fourteen the family moved to Asheville, N. C., and after attending the high school there, in 1908 he entered the Virginia Military Institute. The following year, believing he was more likely to see action in the navy than in the army, he secured an appointment to the United States Naval Academy. Soon, however, persuaded that wartime service on either sea or land was but a remote possibility, he resigned the appointment and entered Washington and Lee University, where an older brother, Paul, was a student. The impulse to roam strong within him, in 1912 he journeyed to the Pacific Coast, and for a time ran an advertising agency in San Francisco. In January 1914 he joined his brother in Atlanta.

The outbreak of the World War that same year brought him his opportunity. On Aug. 3, in a letter to the French consul at New Orleans, he offered his services to France. Not waiting for a reply, he hastened to New York and with his brother Paul sailed for Europe and enlisted in the Foreign Legion. After a brief training he went to the front as a private in the Second Foreign Regiment. During the winter he saw hard and dangerous service in the trenches, the squad to which he belonged, composed of the tallest men in his battalion, being assigned the most exacting and unpleasant tasks. Rockwell proved himself a born soldier, doing more work and guard duty than any one else, and displaying exceptional physical stamina and morale. Transferred to the First Foreign Regiment in March 1915, he took part in the fierce battle of May 9, when the Legion stormed La Targette, and was shot through the thigh. After hospitalization and convalescence he returned to his regiment, but in September was permitted to transfer to aviation. Having received his training as a pilot, in April 1916 he became one of the Escadrille Lafayette.

Rockwell's letters, published after his death, reveal the motives that led him to enter the war. "You would not wish my life to be a failure in my own mind . . .," he wrote his mother. "If I should be killed in this war I will at least die as a man should and would not consider myself a complete failure" (*Letters, post*, p. 7). "I pay my part for Lafayette and Rochambeau," he said, and was happy in the consciousness that he was adventuring "for a greater cause than most people do—the cause of all humanity" (*Ibid.*, p. 57). As an aviator he showed great courage, endurance, and good judgment. Whenever possible he was in the air, and where he was no enemy passed. He was the first of the Escadrille, May 18, 1916, to bring down a plane. On May 24, he was wounded in the face by an explosive bullet that hit his windshield, but in a couple of days was active again. During July and August he fought more than seventy combats. On Sept. 23, flying at 12,000 feet, he attacked a German plane below him, and received an explosive bullet through his breast, his plane crashing to the ground near Thann, Alsace. He was buried, as he had requested in the event of his death, where he fell. The Médaille Militaire and the Croix de Guerre with four palms and one star had already been conferred upon him, and after his death he was awarded the Cross of Chevalier of the Legion of Honor. He had also been proposed for promotion from the grade of sergeant to that of second lieutenant.

[*War Letters of Kiffin Yates Rockwell* (1925), with memoir by P. A. Rockwell; *The Story of the Lafayette Escadrille* (1921), translated by Walter Duranty from the French of Georges Thenault; Laurence La Tourette Driggs, *Heroes of Aviation* (1918); P. A. Rockwell, *Am. Fighters in the Foreign Legion* (1930) and *Three Centuries of the Rockwell Family* (1930).]

H. E. S.

RODDEY, PHILIP DALE (1820–Aug. 1897), Confederate soldier, merchant, was born at Moulton, Ala., the son of Sarah Roddey. His parentage is obscure and his early schooling was fragmentary. After working several years in Moulton as a tailor, he served a term of three years as sheriff, and was subsequently engaged in steam-boating on the Tennessee River. He married Margaret A. McGaughey of Lawrence County, Ala., and from this union four children were born. At the outbreak of the Civil War he formed a troop of cavalry and was elected cap-

tain. Like Nathan Bedford Forrest [*q.v.*], with whom he was later associated, Roddey had an almost uncanny *flair* for cavalry command, considering the totally unmilitary nature of his training. His troop was used for mounted scouting and such was its reputation that it formed Bragg's personal escort at the battle of Shiloh. Roddey received high commendation from Bragg for actions during this battle, and was given a squadron and sent on semi-independent missions. In December 1862 he was commissioned colonel, and organized and commanded the 4th Alabama Cavalry. In this capacity he was destined to spend more than three years defending the banks of the Tennessee River. Usually dispatched on independent or semi-independent missions, his quick-riding, disappearing habits made the Confederate cavalry the despair of the North during the first two years of the war. In August, still operating under Bragg, he executed a successful raid towards Corinth, Miss., that drew high praise from his superiors and netted 123 prisoners. In the winter of 1862–63 he repulsed a Federal expedition from Corinth into northern Alabama.

As circumstances demanded, he acted under the command of Joseph Wheeler [*q.v.*] or Forrest, but never got very far away from northern Alabama. He was called "the Swamp Fox of the Tennessee Valley." In the early spring of 1863 he operated in Mississippi, and was so successful in actions at Tuscumbia, Ala., and Columbia, Tenn., that he was commissioned brigadier-general and given a composite brigade. He operated in close connection with Forrest, sometimes raiding for himself, and was often left along the Tennessee River to protect flanks and communications while Forrest's cavalry harried far into northern territory. He made a successful raid against Rosecrans, and prevented Dodge and his men from joining the Federal forces, while Forrest annihilated Streit's forces in a brilliant campaign. He was active both in the Atlanta campaign and in Hood's campaign in Tennessee, and the force under his command became a composite division which he maneuvered with particular distinction at the battle of Iuka. In Forrest's last desperate attempts to stem the Federal invasions in the spring of 1865, Roddey's command was indispensable. Here parrying, there withdrawing, continually fighting against greatly superior forces and resources, he was finally pushed back to Selma, Ala., where with Forrest, Armstrong, and Adams, he made a last stand on Apr. 1, 1865. Although his own lines were not penetrated, the situation was untenable and he escaped with

Forrest by swimming the river under cover of darkness. Following Forrest's decision to discontinue the struggle after General Johnston surrendered, he took the oath of allegiance and was paroled in May 1865. He engaged in the commission business in New York after the war, and died while on a business trip to London.

[M. J. Wright, *General Officers of the Confed. Army* (1911); *War of the Rebellion: Official Records (Army)*, see general index; *Confed. Mil. Hist.* (1899), vol. VII; T. M. Owen, *Hist. of Ala. and Dict. of Ala. Biog.* (1921), vol. IV; B. F. Riley, *Makers and Romance of Ala. Hist.* (1915); Willis Brewer, *Alabama: Her Hist., Resources, War Record, and Public Men* (1872); J. D. Cox, *The March to the Sea* (1882); E. W. Sheppard, *Bedford Forrest* (1930); J. W. DuBose, *Gen. Jos. Wheeler and the Army of Tenn.* (1912).]   D.Y.

RODENBOUGH, THEOPHILUS FRANCIS (Nov. 5, 1838–Dec. 19, 1912), soldier and author, was born at Easton, Pa., the son of Charles and Emily (Cauffman) Rodenbough. His family on both sides were of pioneer, pre-Revolutionary stock, his paternal ancestor, Heinrich Rodenbough, having come from the Palatinate to settle in Hunterdon County, N. J., in 1738. His early schooling was in private schools and under tutors and he attended Lafayette College in 1854. Upon the outbreak of the Civil War he was appointed by President Lincoln second lieutenant of the 2nd Dragoons, later the 2nd Cavalry. He served in staff capacities at the Cavalry School of Practice at Carlisle, Pa., in 1861 and 1862. In 1863 and 1864 he saw combat service with his regiment in all actions of the Army of the Potomac during that period. He was promoted to the rank of captain in July 1862, and was captured in the second Manassas campaign. He was soon exchanged, however, and took part in Stoneman's raid. At Beverly Ford, Va., in June 1863, he was slightly wounded and had two horses shot under him. He commanded his regiment in all the cavalry engagements of the Gettysburg campaign. His conduct was noticeable in the engagements before Richmond in 1864. He was severely wounded and lost his right arm while leading a charge at Winchester, Va., on Sept. 19, 1864. He was brevetted major for this action, lieutenant-colonel for gallant and meritorious conduct at Todd's Tavern, and brigadier-general for gallantry at Cold Harbor.

Following the war, he was commissioned colonel, United States Army, and by special direction of the president was given command of the 18th Pennsylvania Cavalry and District of Clarksburg, W. Va., with the rank of brigadier-general. He was mustered out of the Volunteer Service in October of that year and upon the reorganization of the army was appointed major

of the 42nd Infantry. He served at Fort Leavenworth, Kan., and Madison Barracks, N. Y., until he was retired with the rank of colonel on Dec. 15, 1870. After retirement, he was deputy governor of the Soldiers' Home in Washington, D. C., for two years. He was further distinguished by being awarded the Congressional Medal of Honor for gallantry at Trevilian Station, Va., in 1864. During the latter part of his life, Rodenbough wrote extensively. In 1873 he published: *From Everglade to Cañon with the Second Dragoons,* a full and interesting history of the 2nd Cavalry; *Afghanistan and the Anglo-Russian Dispute* (1885); *Uncle Sam's Medal of Honor* (1886); and a genealogical work, *Autumn Leaves from Family Trees* (1892). He also contributed articles to numerous periodicals. He acted for a time as general eastern agent for the Pullman Company after 1872, was associate editor of the *Army and Navy Journal,* 1876–77, corresponding secretary of the Society of the Army of the Potomac, 1878, secretary and editor for the *Army and Navy Journal,* 1878–90, secretary of the Military Service Institute from 1878 to 1891 and from 1902 until his death, and chief of the Bureau of Elections, New York City, from 1890 to 1901. His wife, Elinor Frances Foster, to whom he had been married on Sept. 1, 1868, survived him at his death in New York City.

[For genealogical material see Rodenbough's *Autumn Leaves from Family Trees,* and for verification of his military record, *From Everglade to Cañon.* See also, *Who's Who in America,* 1912–13; the *Army and Navy Jour.,* Dec. 21, 1912; and the *N. Y. Times,* Dec. 20, 1912.]   D.Y.

RODES, ROBERT EMMETT (Mar. 29, 1829–Sept. 19, 1864), Confederate soldier, was born at Lynchburg, Va., the son of Gen. David Rodes, Virginia State Militia, and Martha (Yancey) Rodes. His ancestors had been established in Virginia in the seventeenth century. He entered the Virginia Military Institute in 1845, was graduated with distinction in 1848, and was appointed an assistant professor. He aspired to a professorship in 1850, but Thomas Jonathan Jackson [*q.v.*] was chosen instead, and Rodes resigned in 1851 to adopt the profession of civil engineering in which he had acquired some experience. He became chief engineer of the N. E. and S. W. Alabama Railroad in 1858. Late in 1860 he was elected professor of civil engineering and applied mechanics in the Virginia Military Institute, but the Civil War began before he could assume his chair.

He volunteered at the first clash of arms, and in May 1861 became colonel of the 5th Alabama Infantry. In the Manassas campaign his military ability attracted notice, and he was commissioned brigadier-general the following October. He commanded a brigade with conspicuous gallantry at the battle of Fair Oaks, Va., in which he was badly wounded. He resumed his command to take part in the battle of Gaines's Mill before his wound was healed and a long illness followed. He rejoined his brigade in the fall of 1862 and distinguished himself by prolonged and stubborn resistance to McClellan's passage of South Mountain on Sept. 14. Three days later, at Antietam, he shared the desperate fighting at the "Bloody Lane." Upon the transfer of Daniel Harvey Hill [q.v.] to North Carolina in January 1863, Rodes was given command of Hill's division. On May 2, Rodes, with "Stonewall" Jackson riding at his side, led the van of the flank march at Chancellorsville, and with his division launched the surprise attack against the rear of the Union army which gave Lee the victory on that field. Jackson, mortally wounded, asked promotion for the man whose hopes he had thwarted twelve years before. Five days later Rodes was appointed major-general.

In June his division led the advance into Pennsylvania and at Gettysburg, on July 1, he delivered a decisive attack in a critical moment and drove the Union forces back through the town. General Lee complimented him on the battlefield for this action and on the retreat Rodes's division formed the rear-guard. In the battle of the Wilderness on May 5, 1864, Rodes made the counter-attack south of the Plank Road which stopped Warren's victorious advance. At Spotsylvania he directed the defense of the salient, and by his coolness and skill prevented penetration of Lee's position. His division was sent to the Shenandoah Valley in June as a part of Early's command, and participated in the battle of Monocacy and the raid on Washington. On July 18, Rodes defeated a Federal force at Castleman's Ferry, Va., and helped to defeat Crook at Kernstown six days later. Sheridan, taking advantage of a temporary dispersion of Early's army, attacked Winchester on Sept. 19, 1864. Rodes arrived as the Confederate line was breaking, and launched a charge before which Sheridan's attack recoiled. Rodes fell mortally wounded and died on the battlefield, but his timely action saved the army from annihilation. He was known as a fighting general and as a battle leader he had few superiors in either army. On Sept. 10, 1857, he was married to Virginia Hortense Woodruff, at Tuscaloosa, Ala. She and their two children survived him.

[S. R. Patterson, *A Short Hist. and Geneal. of the English Family Rodes* (1929); sketch by Maj. Green Peyton in C. D. Walker, *Memorial, Va. Mil. Institute* (1875); J. C. Wise, *The Mil. Hist. of the Va. Mil. Institute* (1915); J. B. Gordon, *Reminiscences of the Civil War* (1904); G. E. Pond, *The Shenandoah Valley in 1864* (1883); *Battles and Leaders of the Civil War* (4 vols., 1887–88); *War of the Rebellion: Official Records (Army)*, 1 ser., vols. II, V, X, XVII, and XXV, part 1.]   T. F. M.

RODGERS, CHRISTOPHER RAYMOND PERRY (Nov. 14, 1819–Jan. 8, 1892), naval officer, was born at Brooklyn, N. Y., the son of George Washington Rodgers, 1787–1832 [q.v.], and Ann Maria (Perry) Rodgers. On Oct. 5, 1833, he was appointed a midshipman from New London, Conn. After a brief period at the New York naval school he went to sea in the *Brandywine* of the Pacific Squadron. A brief term of duty at the New York navy yard, 1836–37, was followed by a cruise on the *Fairfield* of the Brazil Squadron. In the Seminole War, 1839–42, he served on board the *Flirt, Wave,* and *Phoenix,* commanding the last-named vessel. He was promoted passed midshipman from July 8, 1839, and lieutenant from Sept. 4, 1844. From 1842 to 1843 he was with the *Saratoga* of the African Squadron, and from 1843 to 1845 with the *Cumberland* of the Mediterranean Squadron, serving on both ships as acting master. After a year with the Coast Survey, he participated in the Mexican War and was present at the reduction of Vera Cruz and the capture of Tabasco and Túxpan. Returning to the Coast Survey, he remained there more than three years, then transferring to the *Congress* of the Brazil Squadron. In 1852–53 he was with the *Constitution,* flagship of the African Squadron; in 1856–58, with the Coast Survey; and in 1858–59, with the *Wabash* of the Mediterranean Squadron. His next duty was performed at the Naval Academy where he served as commandant of midshipmen from 1860 to 1861. He drew sharp distinctions between the four classes and made of the first or senior class a quasi-aristocracy. This action left a mark on the school that has never been effaced (Benjamin, *post,* p. 219). At the outbreak of the Civil War he took an active part in removing the Academy to Newport, R. I., and tried to arouse the disaffected midshipmen from the South to a loyalty to the Union.

On Sept. 19, 1861, he was detached from the Academy and ordered to take command of the *Wabash* of the fleet of Admiral Du Pont. In the battle of Port Royal his vessel served as the flagship. He was promoted to the rank of commander from Nov. 15. He was employed in reducing the coast towns of Georgia and Florida early in 1862 and received himself the surrender of St. Augustine. He cooperated with the army in the bombardment of Fort Pulaski, going into the trenches and participating in the surrender. In August he was made fleet captain of the South Atlantic Blockading Squadron, and served on board the flagship *New Ironsides* during the battle of Charleston, Apr. 7, 1863. In a report of the battle Du Pont referred to the "invaluable assistance" rendered by Rodgers and declared that for "over eighteen months in this war this officer has been afloat with me, and, in my opinion, no language could overstate his services to his country, to this fleet, and to myself as its commander in chief" (*Official Records, post,* XIV, 8). On July 6 he was relieved from duty with the squadron. In the following October he was ordered to the *Iroquois* and until the end of the war cruised in European, South American, and East Indian waters, searching for the *Shenandoah* and other Confederate privateers. At Saint-Nazaire and Bordeaux, he went ashore in civilian clothes and inspected some ships being built by the French for the Confederates.

Rodgers was promoted captain from July 25, 1866, commodore from Aug. 28, 1870, and rear admiral from June 14, 1874. After three years at the Norfolk navy yard, he commanded the *Franklin* of the European Squadron, 1863–70, being detached therefrom for special duty in Europe. From 1871 to 1874 he was chief of the Bureau of Yards and Docks, and for part of this period acting chief of the Bureau of Equipment. From 1874 to 1878 he served as superintendent of the Naval Academy, the first in that office to have had preliminary service there as an officer. He cherished high ideals, and attempted to institute reforms, but with only a measure of success. He established elective courses in advanced studies, enforced the rules against hazing, elaborated the punishment for misdemeanors, and prohibited smoking. His unfriendly critics accused him of trying to make a "galaxy of Sidneys and Bayards" out of a collection of school boys of divers origins (Benjamin, *post,* p. 302).

He performed his last active service as commander in chief of the Pacific Squadron from 1878 to 1880. After a few months as superintendent of the Academy he was retired from Nov. 14. In 1875–78 and 1882–83, he served as president of the United States Naval Institute, and in 1884 as president of the International Meridian Conference. He contributed an article entitled "Dupont's Attack at Charleston," to *Battles and Leaders of the Civil War* (1887–88). He died in Washington and was buried at Annapolis, beside his wife Jane (Slidell) Rodgers, to whom he had been married on July 7, 1845. Of the five children born to them, two entered the navy and rose to the rank of rear admiral. Rodgers was of distinguished appearance, and was devoutly religious, being a member of the Episcopalian church.

[Record of Officers, Bur. of Navigation, 1832–93; *Navy Register,* 1834–81; *War of the Rebellion: Official Records* (Navy), 1 ser., vols, III, XII–XIV; Park Benjamin, *The U. S. Naval Acad.* (1900); obit. in *Evening Star* (Wash., D. C.), Jan. 9, 1892.]   C. O. P.

RODGERS, GEORGE WASHINGTON (Feb. 22, 1787–May 21, 1832), naval officer, was born in Cecil County, Md., on the Susquehanna River, opposite Havre de Grace, the youngest of the eight children of John and Elizabeth (Reynolds) Rodgers. On Apr. 2, 1804, he entered the navy as a midshipman, a warrant having been procured for him by his brother, John Rodgers, 1773–1838 [*q.v.*]. In 1804–06 he cruised in the Mediterranean on board the *President.* Returning home in the *Essex,* he was again sent to the Mediterranean within a few months. In January 1809, he was ordered to the *Vixen* as sailing master and a month or two later to the *United States* as acting lieutenant. He was promoted lieutenant from Apr. 24, 1810. In the following year he joined the *Wasp* and was serving on board her at the outbreak of the War of 1812. He participated in the successful engagement of that vessel with the *Frolic,* and was commended by his commodore in the official account of the victory. When both vessels were captured later by a superior force, he was made prisoner, taken to Bermuda, and sent thence in a cartel to New York. Congress recognized his services in the engagement with the *Frolic* by voting him a silver medal; and his native state rewarded him by giving him a sword. From Dec. 20, 1812, to Apr. 25, 1814, he was attached to the *Macedonian,* kept in port at New London, Conn., because of the British blockade. When the war came to an end he was serving on board the *Mohawk* at Sacketts Harbor, N. Y.

On Mar. 10, 1815, Rodgers was ordered to command the *Fire Fly,* one of the smaller vessels assembled at New York by Commodore Stephen Decatur for service in the American war with Algiers. Soon after sailing she encountered a heavy gale, sprang her masts, and was compelled to return to port. She joined the Mediterranean Squadron at Cartagena, Spain, too late to take part in the war with Algiers.

Promoted master commandant from Apr. 27, 1816, Rodgers served as commander of the *Peacock* of the Mediterranean Squadron from 1816 until 1819. In the latter year he was ordered to the New York navy yard where he remained until 1825, part of the time acting as commandant. He was promoted captain from Mar. 3,

1825. For several years he was relatively inactive, waiting orders or serving on the Naval Board of Examiners. On Nov. 26, 1831, he was chosen to command the Brazil Squadron, with the *Warren* as his flagship. The seizure of American sealing vessels at the Falkland Islands and the political disturbances on the mainland made his duties somewhat arduous. Arriving at Rio de Janeiro on Mar. 13, 1832, he proceeded to Montevideo, and thence to Buenos Aires, where, after a brief illness, he died of visceral inflammation, endemic to South American ports. His full habit of body and close confinement on shipboard made him an easy prey to the disease. He was buried in the Protestant cemetery at Buenos Aires. In 1850 his remains were disinterred, conveyed to New York on board the U. S. S. *Lexington,* and reinterred at New London, Conn., where he had made his home. He had been married on July 5, 1815, to Ann Maria Perry, a daughter of Christopher Raymond Perry, and a sister of Oliver Hazard and Matthew Calbraith Perry [*qq.v.*]. Two of his sons, George Washington Rodgers, and Christopher Raymond Perry Rodgers [*qq.v.*], distinguished themselves in the navy. A third son, Alexander P. Rodgers, was killed in 1847 at the storming of Chapultepec, Mexico. Several of his grandsons reached the highest naval rank.

[Record of Officers, Bur. of Navigation, 1804–40; Navy Dept. Archives, Letters to Officers, Ships of War, 1831–34, Captains' Letters, Mar.–May 1832; *Navy Register,* 1815–32; C. O. Paullin, *Commodore John Rodgers* (1910); Niles' *Weekly Register,* Nov. 28, Dec. 5, 1812.]   C. O. P.

RODGERS, GEORGE WASHINGTON (Oct. 30, 1822–Aug. 17, 1863), naval officer, was born in Brooklyn, N. Y., the son of George Washington Rodgers [*q.v.*], and Ann Maria (Perry) Rodgers. He entered the navy as midshipman on Apr. 30, 1836, and saw his first sea service in the West Indies on board the *Boston* and *Constellation.* From 1839 to 1841 he served on the *Brandywine* in the Mediterranean. Soon after returning home he entered the Philadelphia naval school, and was promoted to the rank of passed midshipman from July 1, 1842. In 1844–45 he was with the *Saratoga* of the African Squadron. In the Mexican War he served in the Gulf of Mexico, first on board the *Colonel Harney* and later the *John Adams.* During 1848–50 he was with the Coast Survey, part of the time as acting master of the steamer *Bibb.* His first sea duty after his promotion to a lieutenancy on June 4, 1850, was with the *Germantown* of the Home and African Squadrons. After shore duty at the New York naval rendezvous from 1853 to 1856, he sought more active service, and

was ordered to the *Falmouth* of the Brazil Squadron. Detached from her in 1859, he was engaged in ordnance duties for more than a year at the New York navy yard. In September 1860 he took command of the *Constitution,* the school ship at the Naval Academy. Early in the war he conveyed the midshipmen to Newport, R. I., where the Academy had been moved and saved the *Constitution* from falling into the hands of some secessionists who had resolved that she should be the first captured ship of war to fly the Confederate flag. For a brief period at the Boston navy yard he instructed officers in ordnance duty and received the commendation of the commandant for his efficiency, zeal and ability.

On Sept. 22, 1861, he succeeded his brother, Christopher Raymond Perry Rodgers [*q.v.*], as commandant of midshipmen. Desiring more active duty, he was placed in command of the *Tioga* of the James River Flotilla on May 16, 1862. With the West India Squadron she was later engaged in searching for Confederate commerce destroyers. Rodgers was promoted commander from July 16, 1862. His first command in his new rank was the *Catskill,* one of the ships of the fleet of Admiral Du Pont off the South Atlantic coast. He arrived on the station on Mar. 5, 1863, in time to take part in the attack on Charleston a month later, and gave a good account of himself, approaching within six hundred yards of Fort Sumter. On July 19 Rear Admiral Dahlgren appointed him chief of staff. When Dahlgren attacked Charleston again on Aug. 17, Rodgers resumed command of the *Catskill,* since that station offered greater opportunity for service. He placed his vessel within a very short distance of the enemy, having resolved that no other commander should be nearer. At the beginning of hostilities a heavy shot struck the pilot house and Rodgers was killed instantly. Dahlgren described him as "brave, intelligent, and highly capable, devoted to his duty and to the flag under which he passed his life" (*Official Records, post,* XIV, 453). Unworldly and devoutly religious, Rodgers was a man of gentle manners and shy, retiring nature. On Aug. 21, 1842, he was married to Kate Margaret Lane. He left no children.

[Record of Officers, Bur. of Navigation, 1832–63; *Navy Register,* 1837–63; *War of the Rebellion: Official Records (Navy),* 1 ser., vols. I, VI, VII, XIII, XIV; C. B. Perry, *The Perrys of R. I.* (1913); *Portrait Monthly,* Nov. 1863; *Army and Navy Jour.,* Aug. 29, 1863; *Daily Natl. Intelligencer* (Wash., D. C.), Aug. 25, 1863.]   C. O. P.

RODGERS, JOHN (Aug. 5, 1727–May 7, 1811), Presbyterian clergyman, was born in Boston, Mass., the son of Thomas and Elizabeth (Baxter) Rodgers, who six years before had emigrated to that city from Londonderry, Ireland. In 1728 the family moved to Philadelphia. During George Whitefield's visit there in 1739, young Rodgers held a lantern for him as he spoke to a crowd of people from the courthouse steps. So absorbed in the speaker's words did the boy become that he dropped the lantern. Whitefield's effect on Rodgers was lasting and finally led to his entering the ministry and being a stanch supporter of New Side views. His education was received, first, under a Mr. Stevenson, an Irishman who had established a grammar school in Philadelphia; next, at the school in Neshaminy, Pa., conducted by Rev. John Roan; and finally, under Rev. Samuel Blair [q.v.], at Fagg's Manor, Chester County, with whom he began the study of theology. On Oct. 14, 1747, he was licensed by the Presbytery of New Castle.

His first assignment was to accompany Rev. Samuel Davies [q.v.] to Virginia and assist him in evangelistic work. When, however, he presented himself to the general court at Williamsburg to qualify for a license to preach in the dominion, the court refused to consider his credentials, and he crossed over to Somerset County, Md., where he labored during the summer of 1748. In the autumn he accepted a call to St. George's, New Castle County, Del., where on Mar. 16, 1749, he was ordained and installed. His sixteen years' service here was marked by extraordinary success. He was a zealous pastor and preached with moving effect. His church, though more than once enlarged, was invariably filled, including aisles, doors, and windows. In 1765 he was elected a trustee of the College of New Jersey, to the duties of which office he gave faithful attention for more than twenty years. His wife, Elizabeth, daughter of Peter Bayard of Cecil County, Md., whom he married Sept. 19, 1752, died in January 1763, having borne him four children, and on Aug. 15, 1764, he married Mary (Antrobus) Grant, widow of William Grant, a Philadelphia merchant; by this marriage he had one child.

His pastorate in St. George's was followed by one in New York, covering a period of forty-five years (1765–1810). Here his congregation so increased that it was soon necessary to build a second church, the congregation utilizing both, but remaining one ecclesiastical body. He was an active member of the convention created in 1766 by non-episcopal churches to oppose an American episcopate. Driven from New York during the Revolution, he resided chiefly in Connecticut towns and ministered to several churches. From April to November 1776, however, he was chaplain in General Heath's brigade, and in April 1777 was elected chaplain of the Convention of the State of New York, later serving the Council of Safety in the same capacity. After the war he gathered his congregation together and restored its places of worship, which had been partly destroyed by the British. When the first legislature of the state convened he was its chaplain. He was a member of the committee that revised the standards of the Presbyterian Church in 1788 and was moderator of the first General Assembly under the new arrangement, held in Philadelphia the following year. When the legislature in 1784 created the Board of Regents of the University of the State of New York, he was chosen vice-chancellor and served till his death.

Among the leaders of Presbyterianism during the late colonial period and the early days of the republic, Rodgers exerted a calm, wise influence. He was a friend of Gilbert Tennent, Samuel Finley, and Alexander MacWhorter [qq.v.], and also of John Witherspoon [q.v.], whose funeral sermon he preached. On the recommendation of Franklin, prompted by George Whitefield, the University of Edinburgh conferred upon him in 1768 the degree of D.D. His prudence and practical wisdom were widely recognized; Washington consulted him on several occasions during the Revolution. In him evangelistic zeal and tolerance were united in a rather rare degree. He refused to denounce the errors of others, saying, "let us out-preach them, out-pray them, and out-live them, and we need not fear" (Miller, *post*, p. 329). As he walked the streets, a middle-sized, thick-set person, grave and sedate, always punctiliously dressed, and wearing a large white wig, he was the personification of clerical solidity and dignity. Several of his sermons survive in published form. His death occurred in New York in his eighty-fourth year.

[*A Report of the Commissioners of the City of Boston Containing Boston Births, 1700–1800* (1894); Samuel Miller, *Memoirs of the Rev. John Rodgers, D.D.* (1813); W. B. Sprague, *Annals Am. Pulpit,* vol. III (1858); Richard Webster, *A Hist. of the Presbyt. Ch. in America* (1857); S. D. Alexander, *The Presbytery of N. Y., 1738 to 1888* (n.d.); *N. Y. Evening Post,* May 8, 10, 1811.]   H. E. S.

RODGERS, JOHN (1773–Aug. 1, 1838), naval officer, was born on a farm two miles from Lower Susquehanna Ferry (now Havre de Grace), Md., the son of Col. John and Elizabeth (Reynolds) Rodgers. The father, founder of one of the most noted of American naval families, was born in Scotland, and came to America from Glasgow and settled in Harford County, Md., about 1760. He was an officer of the Maryland militia during the Revolution. The mother was the daughter of a Presbyterian clergyman of Delaware. John was one of the first of eight children. He acquired the rudiments of an education at the village school and through his reading of books about the sea received an impress that determined his career. At an early age his father bound him out as an apprentice to a Baltimore shipmaster trading with French and West Indian ports. He was a first mate before he was eighteen, and, after two years of service in that grade was made master of the ship *Jane,* sailing out of Baltimore for European ports.

After spending eleven years in the merchant service, Rodgers found in the naval war with France an opportunity for a wider career. On Mar. 8, 1798, President Adams appointed him second lieutenant on board the *Constellation* under Thomas Truxtun [*q.v.*], then fitting for sea at Baltimore, and when the first lieutenant resigned soon afterwards Rodgers succeeded him, becoming executive officer of the ship. He participated in the capture of the frigate *Insurgente,* and received with the other officers of the *Constellation* the thanks of the secretary of the navy and the president. In further recognition of his services he was promoted captain on Mar. 5, 1799, the first lieutenant in the navy under the Constitution to be advanced to this rank. After a cruise in command of the *Insurgente,* he was transferred to the *Maryland* and again sailed in the West Indies, part of the time as the senior officer on the Surinam station. At the close of the war he had the honor to be selected to convey John Dawson, the bearer of the new French-American treaty, to France.

Under the peace establishment of 1801 it was for a time uncertain whether Rodgers should be retained in the navy. In the fall of that year he returned to the merchant service and sailed for Santo Domingo as master of the *Nelly,* with a cargo of American products. Since the islanders were at war with France the cruise was not without stirring incidents. On the night of the burning of Cape Français, Rodgers was on shore leading a band of friendly negroes in their work of rescue and succor. The American consul, Tobias Lear [*q.v.*], bore witness that the young captain saved many lives and much property from destruction. Later he was arrested and imprisoned by the French general, LeClerc, who confiscated his property and finally ordered him under penalty to leave the island. He took passage on the *Pomona* and arrived at Baltimore in May 1802.

He was recalled to the navy, and, with the exception of a brief visit to America, was in the Mediterranean from the fall of 1802 until the summer of 1806. He participated in the wars with the Barbary corsairs, playing a part exceeded in importance by that of no other naval officer. As senior officer under Commodores Morris and Barron he served as their chief of staff and as commander of the blockading fleet off Tripoli. Two of the largest cruisers of the Tripolitan navy and several smaller craft surrendered to him. President Jefferson in a message to Congress referred to his services in most complimentary terms. He was commander in chief of the squadron three times, the first time at the age of thirty, the office entitling him to the designation of "commodore." In the negotiations for a treaty with Morocco he shared the honors with Commodore Preble, during the peace negotiations with Tripoli he commanded the squadron, and in an expedition to Tunis, he was the most prominent figure and the commanding officer.

As a result of a war-scare growing out of the affair of the *Chesapeake* and *Leopard,* he was placed in command of the New York flotilla and naval station in July 1807. This was the most important office at the disposal of the navy department, and in the following year the duty of enforcing the Embargo in the waters between the Delaware and the Passamaquoddy Bay fell to him. When President Madison decided to follow a more active naval policy in 1810, Rodgers received orders to command the "northern division of ships for the protection of the American coast," with the frigate *President,* 44 guns, as his flagship (Paullin, *post,* p. 210). Cruising under these orders, on May 16, 1811, he engaged off Cape Henry the British naval sloop *Little Belt,* 20 guns, for some fifteen minutes and inflicted on her a loss of thirteen men killed and nineteen wounded. His conduct was cordially approved by the secretary of the navy and the president and he was hailed and toasted as a popular hero. His request for a court of inquiry was at first refused by the federal government but it was later granted when it appeared that there were discrepancies between his account of the fight and that of the British captain. The court considered the details of the fight at great length and made a report confirming Rodgers' account in every essential particular.

In the War of 1812 Rodgers was the ranking officer in active service. Three days after the declaration of war he went to sea with a fleet of five vessels and two days later sighted the British frigate *Belvidera.* A long chase ensued and in a running fight the *Belvidera* escaped after a small loss on both sides. A gun of the *President* burst, fracturing one leg of the commodore, who, supported by his men, continued to direct the fight. The cruise was extended as far eastward as the coast of Spain and ended at Boston after the capture of eight merchantmen. Rodgers made three additional cruises, and during one captured the British schooner *High Flyer*. While his services were not as brilliant as those of some of his juniors in rank who fought the famous sea duels of the war, they were with a few exceptions the more useful. He understood best the principles of naval strategy (A. T. Mahan, *From Sail to Steam*, 1906, 1907, pp. 5–6). In the spring of 1814 Rodgers was placed in command of the Delaware flotilla and the *Guerrière,* then under construction at Philadelphia. When the British made their expedition against Washington he was ordered to the capital with a detachment of sailors and marines, and arrived in time to harass the enemy's squadron in its retreat down the Potomac. When Baltimore was threatened later he came to its defense with his detachment, part of which manned a small fleet in the Patapsco River and the rest some land batteries on Hampstead Hill.

In February 1815, Rodgers was chosen by President Madison to head the newly created Board of Navy Commissioners, authorized by Congress to administer the naval material. The commissioners ranked next to the members of the cabinet in the administrative hierarchy of Washington, and were always chosen from the most distinguished officers of the navy. In 1821 Rodgers became the senior officer of the navy, and in 1823 he served for a time as secretary of the navy *ad interim*. His service in Washington was interrupted in 1825–27 by a tour of duty in the Mediterranean, where once again he commanded the American Squadron, this time with the 74-gun ship *North Carolina* as his flagship. This duty, which proved to be his last sea service, was marked by an interview with the Turkish minister of marine respecting a treaty with Turkey, by a visit to the capital of the Greek revolutionists, and by an improvement in the discipline of the squadron.

On May 1, 1837, Rodgers resigned his commissionership, owing to declining health, partly the result of an attack of cholera. He died at the Naval Asylum in Philadelphia and is buried in the Congressional Cemetery, Washington, D. C. On Oct. 21, 1806, he had been married to Minerva Denison at Sion Hill, Md. She was a descendant of Capt. George Denison, called the "Miles Standish of Connecticut." After 1815,

they made their home in Washington, D. C. Their last residence, an historic one in the annals of the capital, was built on the site of the present Belasco Theatre. They had eleven children, one of the sons, John Rodgers [*q.v.*], reaching the rank of rear admiral. Many of their descendants entered the army or the navy. A daughter, Louisa, married Montgomery Cunningham Meigs [*q.v.*]. Rodgers was of middle height, solid, compact, well-proportioned. He was grave in demeanor, rather bluff, independent and a stickler for the forms of his profession.

[This sketch has been prepared from C. O. Paullin, *Commodore John Rodgers* (1910), in which is a bibliography of sources, pp. 405–10. A naval order, announcing Rodgers' death, was published in *Poulson's Am. Daily Advertiser* (Phila., Pa.), Aug. 3, 1838.]

C. O. P.

RODGERS, JOHN (Aug. 8, 1812–May 5, 1882), naval officer, was born at Sion Hill near Havre de Grace, Md., the fourth child of John Rodgers [*q.v.*] and Minerva (Denison) Rodgers. On Apr. 18, 1828, he was appointed midshipman and saw his first active service on board the *Constellation* and the *Concord* in the Mediterranean. On his return he entered the Norfolk naval school preliminary to an examination for passed midshipman, to which he was promoted in 1834. After a year at the University of Virginia where he was engaged in general study, he was ordered to the Coast Survey and then to the *Dolphin* of the Brazil Squadron. At the end of three years of duty with that squadron, he was employed in surveying the coast of Florida and in cooperating with the army in the Seminole War, first as commander of the *Wave* and later of the *Jefferson*. He was promoted lieutenant from Jan. 28, 1840. From 1842 to 1844 he commanded the *Boxer* of the Home Squadron. In the latter year he was sent to Pittsburgh, Pa., to aid in the construction of the steamer *Alleghany*. He spent the next three years on the coast of Africa and in the Mediterranean. On his return in 1849 he was three years with the Coast Survey, part of the time in command of surveying vessels.

On Oct. 12, 1852, he was ordered to duty in connection with the North Pacific Exploring and Surveying Expedition, which lasted, with a few brief interruptions, until the Civil War. He was second in rank, commanding the *John Hancock,* but succeeded Cadwalader Ringgold [*q.v.*] in command of the expedition in the summer of 1854. At the Liu-Kiu Islands he landed a detachment and forced the natives to guarantee the performance of their obligations under their treaty with the United States. After surveying the Liu-Kius, Ladrones, and other islands, the coast of Japan, and the sea of Okhotsk, he sailed into the Arctic Ocean where he explored unknown regions and obtained information that corrected the Admiralty charts. He next surveyed the Hawaiian and Society islands. In 1856, he returned to the United States and was placed in charge of an office in Washington engaged in preparing for publication the results of the expedition. The reports, however, were never published. During his absence he had been promoted commander from Sept. 14, 1855.

On May 16, 1861, Rodgers was ordered to special duty under General McClellan at Cincinnati, Ohio, where he purchased and fitted out three small steamers, the nucleus of the Mississippi Flotilla. On Oct. 17 he was appointed to command the *Flag* of the squadron of Admiral Du Pont. At the battle of Port Royal he acted as aide to Du Pont, who showed his appreciation of his services by allowing him to hoist the "first American flag on the rebellious soil of South Carolina" (*Official Records, post,* XII, 265). Later he commanded a small fleet of gunboats on the Savannah River. On Apr. 21, 1862, he was ordered to command the *Galena,* the flagship of a small fleet operating on the James River. At Drewry's Bluff he encountered obstructions in the river and an action lasting three hours took place, the brunt of which was borne by the *Galena* at close range, with a loss of twenty-four men. He was promoted to the rank of captain from July 16 and in November was transferred from the *Galena* to the *Weehawken,* one of the new monitors. In the attack on Fort Sumter on Apr. 7, 1863, the *Weehawken* headed the line of ships and for two hours received the concentrated fire of the Confederate batteries, being struck fifty-three times. On June 17 in Wassaw Sound, Ga., she encountered the *Atlanta,* reputed to be the strongest of the Confederate ironclads, and received her surrender after an engagement of fifteen minutes. In recognition of Rodgers' services President Lincoln recommended to Congress that he be thanked for his exhibition of "eminent skill and gallantry" in the fight with the *Atlanta,* and for his "zeal, bravery, and general good conduct" shown on other occasions (*Official Records, post,* XIV, 184). Congress complied with the President's recommendation, promoting him to the rank of commodore from the date of the battle. In July he was ordered to command the *Canonicus* and in November was transferred to the *Dictator,* in which he saw his last active service in the war.

In September 1865, Rodgers was placed in command of a small fleet, with the *Vanderbilt* as his flagship, and proceeded with it to the Pacific.

On his arrival at Valparaiso early in the following year he found a Spanish squadron threatening to bombard the city. He proposed to join with the English, French, Prussians, and Italians in an armed intervention, but when they declined he refused to act alone. He did what he could, however, to protect peacefully American and neutral interests. He was commandant of the Boston navy yard from 1866 to 1869. He commanded the Asiatic Squadron as a rear admiral, 1870–72, his promotion to that rank being dated Dec. 31, 1869. In 1871 he conveyed to Korea, on board the flagship *Colorado,* Frederick Ferdinand Low [*q.v.*], the American minister to China, who was authorized to negotiate a treaty with the Koreans. After anchoring his fleet of five vessels in the Salée or Han River he sent up the river a surveying party, which was attacked by the Koreans and suffered a loss of two men wounded. Rodgers landed a detachment which destroyed five forts, killed two hundred and forty Koreans, and captured about 500 pieces of artillery, with a loss of three men killed and ten wounded. No treaty was concluded.

Rodgers was president of the Naval Examining and Retiring boards, 1872–73; commandant of the Mare Island navy yard, 1873–77; superintendent of the Naval Observatory, 1877–82; and chairman of the Light-House Board, 1878–82. He secured for the observatory its present site and made certain its reconstruction on more ample lines. In the last years of his life his eminence led to his selection as president of the United States Naval Institute, of the Transit of Venus Commission, of the First Naval Advisory Board, from which dates the new navy, and of the *Jeannette* Relief Board.

Until the approach of his last illness, Rodgers preserved a remarkable vigor of mind and body, never losing his faculty for initiative. Independent and straightforward, he was open to argument in preliminary discussion, but was persistent and tenacious in action. He was a charter member of the National Academy of Sciences. At the time of his death in Washington, D. C., he was the senior rear admiral on the active list. On Nov. 27, 1857, he was married to Ann Elizabeth Hodge of Washington, D. C., by whom he had three children.

[Record of Officers, Bur. of Navigation, 1825–88; *War of the Rebellion: Official Records (Navy),* 1 ser., vols. VII, VIII, XII, XIV, XXII; Asaph Hall, "Biog. Memoir of John Rodgers," *Nat. Acad. of Sci., Biog. Memoirs,* vol. VI (1909); J. R. Soley, "Rear-Admiral John Rodgers," *Proc. of the U. S. Naval Institute,* vol. VIII, no. 2, 1882; *Ann. Report of the Sec. of the Navy* (1871); Wilhelm Heine, *Die Expedition in die Seen von China, Japan und Ochotsk* (1858); *The Am. Ann. Encyc. and Register, 1866,* vol. VI (1867); *Evening Star* (Wash., D. C.), May 6, 1882.]   C. O. P.

RODGERS, JOHN (Jan. 15, 1881–Aug. 27, 1926), naval officer, aviator, son of Rear Admiral John Augustus and Elizabeth (Chambers) Rodgers, was born in Washington, D. C., although the Rodgers' home was at Havre de Grace, Md. He was of a family long distinguished in the annals of the United States Navy, being a great-grandson of John Rodgers [1773–1838, *q.v.*], who was one of the first of the name to attain renown as an American naval officer. Sarah (Perry) Rodgers, daughter of Matthew C. Perry [*q.v.*], was his grandmother. John attended the Lawrenceville School, Lawrenceville, N. J., served on the *Columbia* during the Spanish-American War, and in 1899 entered the Naval Academy, from which he graduated in 1903. During the ensuing years he was promoted through the various grades and was made commander, Nov. 4, 1920. Becoming interested in aviation, he attended the Wright Flying School, Dayton, Ohio, and was the second naval officer to be licensed as an aviator. During the World War he was in the submarine service and on North Sea mine barrage duty. Returning later to aviation, from 1922 to 1925 he was commander of the Naval Air Station, Pearl Harbor, Hawaii. In the latter part of 1925, the resourcefulness and heroism he displayed as commander of the San Francisco-Hawaiian flight brought him wide acclaim. On Aug. 31, two navy seaplanes took off from near San Francisco. One of these was forced down after covering about 300 miles. The second, which contained Commander Rodgers and four others, was obliged to descend on Sept. 1, when 400 miles from its destination, because of lack of fuel. For nine days it was tossed about on the deep, its occupants never losing courage. They subsisted on the scanty emergency rations which they had with them, and on sea water which Rodgers distilled in a still given him by his mother. From the fabric of a wing he also fashioned a sail. On Sept. 10 they sighted Kauai and were picked up by a submarine when about fifteen miles from that island. The following day Rodgers wrote a concise and vivid account of the adventure, which was published in United States papers. In recognition of his sterling qualities as an aviator and his ability as a seaman and navigator, he was appointed assistant chief of the Bureau of Naval Aeronautics. Office work at Washington was not suited to his taste or temperament, however, and on Aug. 16, 1926, he was placed in command of a new scouting seaplane squadron, created for experimental purposes, at San Diego, Cal. Eleven days later he started in a land plane from the Naval Air Station, Washington, for Philadelphia, where he was to inspect some new planes at the aircraft factory of the Navy Yard. When nearing the city, his plane fell from a comparatively low height into the shallow water of the Delaware, and Rodgers was pinioned in the cockpit. After an hour of intense suffering he was released and taken to the Naval Hospital, where he died. At the time of his death he was listed for promotion to captain. His wife, from whom he was divorced in 1924, was Ethel Greiner Rodgers.

[*N.Y.Times,* Sept. 11, 12, 1925, Aug. 28, 1926; *Washington Post* and *Evening Star* (Washington), Aug. 28, 1926; *Army and Navy Register,* Sept. 4, 1926.]   H.E.S.

RODMAN, ISAAC PEACE (Aug. 18, 1822–Sept. 30, 1862), legislator, Union soldier, was born at South Kingstown, R. I., the eldest of sixteen children of Samuel Rodman and his first wife, Mary Peckham, both of pre-Revolutionary ancestry. His father, a prosperous merchant, was a descendant of Thomas Rodman, a Quaker physician, who settled in Newport, R. I., in 1675. Rodman received a common-school education, and at an early age entered business as an associate of his father. For several years he was president of the town council of South Kingstown and director of the Wakefield Bank. He entered state politics, serving in both branches of the legislature. On June 17, 1847, he was married to Sally Lyman Arnold, the daughter of Gov. Lemuel N. Arnold. They had seven children.

When the Civil War was imminent, Rodman, true to his religious training, was strongly on the side of peace, but when war was declared, he was a member of the state Senate and strongly supported the government, giving proof of his loyalty by accepting a captaincy in the 2nd Rhode Island Infantry on June 6, 1861. For his gallantry at the first battle of Bull Run he was later commissioned lieutenant-colonel. He was assigned to command the 4th Rhode Island Volunteers and was commissioned colonel on Oct. 30. He spent the winter of 1861–62 at Alexandria, Va., training his regiment. In the early spring of 1862 Rodman joined Burnside in North Carolina, his regiment being in General Parke's 3rd Brigade, and took a distinguished part in the capture of Roanoke Island on Feb. 8, 1862. At this battle his troops being the only ones wearing blue overcoats, were mistaken by the enemy for regulars, and consequently received the heaviest fire. Rodman himself believed this to be his hottest engagement. At the battle of New Bern on Mar. 14, at his own suggestion, he was permitted to charge a weak point in the enemy trenches with the bayonet. His regiment pierced the defenses, captured cannon and colors, and turned the tide of battle. Burnside gave him full credit for his perspicacity and bravery, and for this and his gallantry at the capture of Fort Macon in April he was advanced to the rank of brigadier-general on Apr. 28, 1862.

Rodman's campaigning in the swamps of North Carolina undermined his health, and, ill with typhoid, he was sent home to South Kingstown to recuperate until August. Still weak from fever, he joined Reno's IX Corps for the Maryland Campaign at Frederick and was given the 4th Division. On the morning of Sept. 13 he was ordered to support Pleasanton's cavalry reconnaissance in the mountains, but missed the road and supported other forces. The following day he took active part in the battle of South Mountain and advanced across a ford against heavy hostile fire towards Sharpsburg. At the battle of Antietam on Sept. 17, he was wounded in the chest while leading his troops and died twelve days later. His body was moved to Providence, R. I., where it lay in state in the Old State House, and he was buried at South Kingstown.

[C. H. Jones, *Geneal. of the Rodman Family* (1886); W. W. Rodman, *Notes on Rodman Geneal.* (1887); *War of the Rebellion: Official Records (Army)*, 1 ser., vol. XIX; *Ann. Report of the Adj.-Gen. of the State of R. I.*, 1865, vol. I (1893); Frederick Phisterer, *Statistical Record of the Armies of the U. S.*, (1907), supp. vol. to *Campaigns of the Civil War*; J. R. Bartlett, *Memoirs of R. I. Officers* (1867); *Representative Men and Old Families of R. I.* (1908), vol. II; J. D. Cox, *Reminiscences of the Civil War* (1900), vol. I; *Boston Daily Advertiser*, Oct. 6, 1862.]   D. Y.

RODMAN, THOMAS JACKSON (July 30, 1815–June 7, 1871), soldier, inventor, was born on a farm near Salem, Ind. His father, James Rodman, was a descendant of Thomas Rodman, a Quaker physician, who came to Newport, R. I., from Barbados in 1675. His mother was Elizabeth (Burton) Rodman of Virginia. Although his early educational advantages were quite limited, he entered the United States Military Academy in 1837 and was graduated four years later, seventh in a class of fifty-two members. He was commissioned in the ordnance department, and was promoted through all grades to the rank of captain in 1855, and lieutenant-colonel in 1867. From the first, he demonstrated marked gifts as an inventor, with a decided bent towards mechanics and the details of practical shop construction—his earlier service having been spent with government arsenals at the Alleghany Arsenal, Pittsburgh, Pa., Richmond, Va., and Baton Rouge, La. During the Mexican War, he served as ordnance officer at Camargo and Point Isabel.

After studying closely the heavy ordnance devised by George Bomford [*q.v.*] and used by Americans in the War of 1812, and the improvements in manufacture developed by Henri Joseph Paixhans of the French army and Dahlgren of the American navy, Rodman conceived the original idea of casting guns upon a hollow core, cooling the inner surface by a flow of water so that each successive layer of metal was compressed by the shrinkage of outer layers. He received little or no encouragement from the ordnance department, which rejected the offer of his invention and refused him an opportunity to develop his ideas, so the manufacture of ordnance under Rodman's patented processes was begun by private enterprise. The results demonstrated a marked increase in strength and endurance for heavy ordnance and much greater resistance to gas erosion in the bore.

About the same time, his experiments resulted in the successful manufacture of so-called mammoth and perforated-cake or prismatic gunpowder, both types being used by him in the testing of his large-bore cannon. A detailed description of his work is contained in his admirable book, *Reports of Experiments on the Properties of Metals for Cannon, and the Qualities of Cannon Powder,* published in 1861. His inventions were finally approved and adopted by the government in 1859, about fourteen years after their conception, and his methods were promptly utilized by the governments of Russia, Great Britain, and Prussia. Rodman was placed in command of the arsenal at Watertown, Mass., and during the Civil War, supervised the casting of twelve-inch, fifteen-inch, and twenty-inch smooth-bores, and of twelve-inch rifled guns. He applied his methods to the casting of projectiles, and greatly increased the capacity of his plant for making field and sea-coast artillery carriages. His guns were mounted by Captain Ericsson in the newly constructed monitors of the navy and many military authorities of the period held that Rodman's inventions had a pronounced deterrent effect in staying foreign intervention during a critical period of the Civil War. His personal application and his interest in the success of his labors were so constant at this time that he suffered a severe illness as a result in the summer of 1864, recovering only with difficulty. In 1865, he was honored with the brevets of lieutenant-colonel, colonel, and brigadier-general, for faithful, meritorious, and distinguished services in the ordnance department.

At the close of the war he was transferred to the command of Rock Island Arsenal in Illinois, where, with characteristic energy, he perfected elaborate plans for the construction on a large scale of a combined armory and arsenal. Adequate Congressional appropriations were secured and the work was started when Rodman's health, already impaired, broke down under the strain of responsibility, and he died at his post after a prolonged illness. He was survived by his widow, Martha Ann (Black) Rodman, daughter of a Presbyterian clergyman of Pittsburgh, Pa., to whom he had been married in 1843, and by five sons and two daughters.

[Information from Mrs. Florence Rodman Butler, of Honolulu; W. W. Rodman, *Notes on the Rodman Family* (1887); G. W. Cullum, *Biog. Reg. . . . U. S. Mil. Acad.* (1891); *Army and Navy Jour.*, June 17, Aug. 5, 1871; *Orders from the Ordnance Office, War Dept., Series 1871*; *N. Y. Herald*, June 8, 1871.]   C. D. R.

RODNEY, CÆSAR (Oct. 7, 1728–June 26, 1784), statesman, was the eldest child of Cæsar Rodney, the son of William Rodeney [*sic*] who emigrated to America about 1681, and of Elizabeth (Crawford) Rodeney, daughter of the Rev. Thomas Crawford, the first missionary sent to Dover, Del., and its environs by the Society for the Propagation of the Gospel in Foreign Parts. Born on his father's farm near Dover, Cæsar Rodney was reared in a cultured home and probably secured most of his education from his parents. When his father died in 1745, he was placed under the guardianship of Nicholas Ridgely, prothonotary and clerk of the peace of Kent County. He entered public life in 1755 when he was commissioned as high sheriff of Kent County. Reappointed to this office the two following years, he subsequently served his county as register of wills, recorder of deeds, clerk of the orphans' court, clerk of the peace, and justice of the peace. In 1769, he was appointed co-trustee with John Vining of the Kent County Loan Office and sole trustee from 1775 until his death. Appointed third justice of the supreme court for the Three Lower Counties in 1769, he was commissioned second justice of the same court in 1773.

In 1758 Rodney was elected for the first time as delegate from Kent County to the colonial legislature at New Castle. From 1761 to 1776, with the exception of the assembly of 1771, he served continuously as a member of the legislature and was elected speaker in 1769, 1773, 1774, and 1775, holding that post until the end of the colonial régime in 1776. In 1765 he was elected by the House of Assembly as the representative of Kent County in the Stamp Act Congress and together with Thomas McKean [*q.v.*] took an active part in the work of that body. When the Assembly adopted several resolutions condemning the Townshend Act in October 1768, Rod-ney, McKean, and George Read [*q.v.*] were designated a committee of correspondence and instructed to draw up an address to the king. Following the passage by Parliament of the Boston Port Bill in the spring of 1774, Rodney, as speaker of the Assembly and upon express requests from mass meetings held in the three counties in June and July, took the extra-legal step of calling the Assembly for a special session (the prerogative of the proprietary governor) to meet in New Castle on Aug. 1, 1774. This body appointed Rodney, McKean, and Read to attend the First Continental Congress.

After meeting Rodney for the first time at the Congress, John Adams wrote in his diary for Sept. 3, "Cæsar Rodney is the oddest looking man in the world; he is tall, thin and slender as a reed, pale; his face is not bigger than a large apple, yet there is sense and fire, spirit, wit, and humor in his countenance" (*The Works of John Adams*, vol. II, 1850, p. 364). The colonial assembly, at a regular session held in March 1775, approved the acts of the irregular meeting of the previous August and the report prepared by the three delegates to the First Continental Congress, and reëlected them to the Second Continental Congress scheduled to meet in May. Meanwhile, Rodney was elected colonel of the so-called "Upper'" regiment of Kent County militia and in the following September, was elected brigadier-general of the militia of Kent County and of the western battalion of Sussex County. He presided as speaker over the regular session of the assembly in October 1775 and together with McKean and Read was again returned to Congress. In June 1776 he presided over the session of the colonial assembly at New Castle which passed a resolution supplanting the authority of the crown in the government of the Three Lower Counties and which issued new instructions to Rodney and his two colleagues from Delaware, authorizing them to cooperate with the other colonies.

On June 22 Rodney hurried to Sussex County to investigate a threatened Loyalist uprising there and had just returned to his home in Kent County when he received an "express" from his colleague, McKean, urging his immediate return to Philadelphia to vote on Richard Henry Lee's resolution for independence. He rode eighty miles on horseback, arriving in the late afternoon of July 2, 1776, in time to cast Delaware's vote for independence—his vote and McKean's overriding the negative vote of Read, the more conservative member of the delegation. He likewise voted with McKean for the adoption of the Declaration of Independence. On

July 22 he was back in New Castle presiding over the last session of the colonial assembly which he had summoned for the purpose of fixing a date for the assembling of a state constitutional convention and of arranging for the election of delegates. The conservatives of Kent County defeated him as delegate to the convention and, when the new state constitution went into effect, he also failed of election to the first state legislature and was not returned by that body in the autumn as a delegate to the Congress. This demonstration of ingratitude on the part of his contemporaries did not affect Rodney's patriotic fervor for he now turned to military affairs again, and in November 1776 was made chairman of the Kent County branch of the council of safety. When the American cause seemed at its lowest ebb in December, Rodney was busily engaged in recruiting men in his county and sending them forward to join the main army. In January 1777, after Washington had taken up his winter-quarters at Morristown, he was placed in command of the post at Trenton for a few weeks of active service. He was in command of the Delaware militia with the rank of brigadier-general when the British invaded the state in September, but only succeeded in harassing the enemy's outposts. A few days later the acting president of the state, Thomas McKean, commissioned Rodney as major-general of the Delaware militia.

Rodney's political star rose again in 1777. In the spring the legislature elected him as judge of the admiralty and in December as member to the Continental Congress. In the spring of 1778 it also elected him president of the state for a term of three years to succeed John McKinly [q.v.] who had been captured by the British when they temporarily occupied Wilmington. He served as Delaware's war executive seven months beyond the full term until November 1781. It fell to his lot during this critical period to furnish Delaware's quota of Continental troops, and to arm and clothe them as well as to raise Delaware's quota of provisions and money. For about ten years Rodney had suffered from a serious cancerous growth on his face and when he relinquished the duties of president, he immediately went to Philadelphia to obtain medical and surgical relief. The malady, however, had made too great an inroad upon his physical constitution and although he returned to Dover in a hopeful mood after several months of treatment, he constantly lost strength until his death. In the fall of 1783, he was elected once more to office, this time as member of the upper house of the legislature. This body honored him

with the speakership, but before the legislative year had expired Rodney was dead.

His main interests, aside from political affairs, had been those of a land owner. He died a comparatively wealthy man, and, since he never married, most of his real estate was bequeathed to his nephew, Cæsar Augustus, son of his brother, Thomas Rodney [qq.v.]. His remains lay buried on his farm, "Poplar Grove," for over a century when, in 1888, they were removed to the Christ Episcopal Churchyard in Dover. Although he did not enjoy the legal training of his three immediate collaborators, Thomas McKean, George Read, and John Dickinson [q.v.], Cæsar Rodney was a man of clear perception and understanding, of high courage, and of effective application.

[The principal primary material is to be found in the public archives of the State of Del. at Dover, Kent County Records at Dover, Hist. Soc. of Del. at Wilmington, Lib. of Cong., Geneal. Soc. of Pa., N. Y. Public Lib., and in the private collections of the Hon. Richard S. Rodney, New Castle, Del., Frank H. Stewart, Woodbury, N. J., John Stuart Groves, Wilmington, Del., and others. The principal printed material will be found in G. H. Ryden, ed., *Letters to and From Cæsar Rodney, 1756–1784* (1933); *Jour. of the Continental Cong., 1774–1789* (1904–); E. C. Burnett, ed., *Letters of Members of the Continental Cong.* (1921–); *Minutes of the Council of Del. State, 1776–1792* (1887); Hezekiah Niles, *Principles and Acts of the Revolution in America* (1822); *Del. Archives,* vols. I, II, III (1911, 1912, 1919); W. T. Read, *Life and Correspondence of George Read of Delaware* (1870); C. J. Stillé, *Life and Times of John Dickinson, Memoirs of the Hist. Soc. of Pa.,* vol. XIII (1891); Reprints of the *Votes and Proceed. of the House of Rep. of the Government of the Counties of New Castle, Kent, and Sussex,* 1762, reprinted 1930; 1765 to 1770 inclusive, reprinted 1931.]

G. H. R.

RODNEY, CÆSAR AUGUSTUS (Jan. 4, 1772–June 10, 1824), lawyer, statesman, and diplomat, was born in Dover, Del., the son of Thomas Rodney [q.v.] and Elizabeth (Fisher) Rodney. He was the nephew of Cæsar Rodney [q.v.], who, having never married, took a particular interest in the boy and not only assisted in his education but bequeathed to him most of his real estate. After living for two years in Philadelphia, and then again in Dover, the family settled in 1780 in Wilmington, Del., where for upwards of two years Thomas Rodney was engaged in the flour exporting business. In 1786 Cæsar Augustus matriculated at the University of Pennsylvania. Upon his graduation in 1789 he commenced the study of law under Joseph B. McKean [q.v.] in Philadelphia. He was admitted to the bar in 1793 and began practice in Wilmington and New Castle. In 1796 he entered the Delaware House of Representatives as a member from New Castle County and continued a member of that body until the year 1802. A stanch supporter of Jefferson, he was prevailed upon to run for Congress in that year against the Federalist candidate, James A. Bayard [q.v.]. With Jefferson's backing, he succeeded in defeating Bayard and served as a member of the House of Representatives for two years. During this term he proved himself a firm supporter of the administration relative to the Louisiana Purchase treaty and of the Twelfth Amendment to the Federal Constitution.

In January 1804 Rodney was chosen one of the House managers to conduct the impeachment proceedings against John Pickering, judge of the United States district court for New Hampshire, and in December of the same year he was appointed one of the House managers to conduct the impeachment proceedings against Justice Samuel Chase. On Jan. 20, 1807, he became Jefferson's attorney-general, continuing in this post in Madison's administration as well until he resigned on Dec. 5, 1811. In the War of 1812 he served actively in the defense of his state. Commissioned on Apr. 7, 1813, as captain of the 2nd Company of artillery attached to the 1st Brigade of the militia, he was promoted major of a battalion of artillery after the close of the war on Mar. 15, 1815. In the meantime, he had been elected a member of the state Senate and served in the sessions beginning Jan. 3, 1815, Jan. 2, 1816, and Nov. 11, 1816. In 1817 he was appointed by President Monroe a member of a special commission to South America for the purpose of ascertaining the political status of newly established republics in that continent. His fellow commissioners were Theodorick Bland and John Graham. Proceeding directly to Buenos Aires, the commission remained there from February 1818 until the last of April. Rodney and Graham then returned to the United States while Bland proceeded to Chile. Reports by the commissioners were transmitted to Congress on Nov. 17, 1818 (House Document 2, 15 Cong., 2 Sess.).

As a result of his vigorous stand in opposition to the extension of slavery into the territories, Rodney was elected to Congress in 1820. He took his seat in December 1821 but in the following January he was elected by the Delaware legislature to fill a vacancy in the Senate. He resigned from the House on Jan. 24, 1822, and qualified as a member of the Senate the same day. A year later he resigned to accept an appointment by Monroe as the first United States minister plenipotentiary to the Argentine Republic. He arrived in Buenos Aires on Nov. 14, 1823, a few days before the President promulgated the Monroe Doctrine. The appointment was very acceptable to the Argentinians but Rodney's ca-

reer as a minister proved to be a short one. Falling dangerously ill on Nov. 23, he recovered sufficiently to speak at a public dinner held in his honor on May 27, 1824, but died, following a relapse, on June 10. His remains were interred in the English churchyard in Buenos Aires. When not in the public service of the United States, Rodney maintained with his large family a lovely home in Wilmington, Del., named "Cool Spring." His wife was Susan Hunn, daughter of Captain John Hunn of Philadelphia. By her he had fifteen children, ten daughters and five sons.

[Sources include: W. T. Read, *Biog. Sketch of Cæsar Augustus Rodney* (1853); *Del. Archives*, vols. IV and V (1916); W. R. Manning, *Diplomatic Correspondence of the U. S. Concerning the Independence of the Latin-American Nations* (1925), vol. I, published by the Carnegie Endowment for International Peace; *Biog. Dir. Am. Cong.* (1928); J. B. Moore, *A Digest of Internat. Law* (1906), vol. I; *Letters to and from Cæsar Rodney, 1756–84* (1933), ed. by George H. Ryden; *Governors' Reg.: State of Del.*, vol. I (1926); J. T. Scharf, *Hist. of Del.* (1888), vol. I; J. M. McCarter and B. F. Jackson, *Hist. and Biog. Encyc. of Del.* (1882); Henry C. Conrad, *Hist. of the State of Del.*, vol. III (1908).]   G. H. R.

RODNEY, THOMAS (June 4, 1744–Jan. 2, 1811), farmer, soldier, and jurist, was the eighth and youngest child of Cæsar Rodney, the elder, and Elizabeth (Crawford) Rodney. He was born on his father's farm in St. Jones Neck, Kent County, Del. When Thomas was about a year old his father died and his mother married Thomas Wilson. The task of educating the son fell to her and she early inculcated in the boy a taste for reading. Three years before he attained his majority, Thomas left his childhood home to live with his brother, Cæsar Rodney [q.v.], in order to assist him in the management of his farms, and in 1764 removed with him to Dover to assist him there in his official duties as a county officer. With the exception of two years spent in Philadelphia (1772–74) as a shop-keeper and two years in Wilmington, Del. (1781–83) in a business partnership for the exporting of flour, he was engaged principally in farming, both as a manager of Cæsar's lands, when the latter was absent in Philadelphia on public business, and as a landowner himself. In 1770 he was appointed a justice of the peace in Kent County and in 1774 was reappointed to that position. Elected in 1775 as a member for Kent County of the colonial Assembly of the Government of the Three Lower Counties of New Castle, Kent, and Sussex, he participated in the legislative steps taken to transform the colonial government into the state government of Delaware in the summer of 1776.

In 1775, shortly after the Battle of Bunker Hill, Thomas Rodney organized a volunteer militia force and in the same year was elected a member of the Council of Safety and of the Committee of Observation for Kent County. When in the autumn and early winter of 1776 Washington's army was retreating across New Jersey, Rodney, in command as captain of a company of Kent County militia, joined the division of General Cadwalader at Bristol, Pa., at Christmas time, and led his men in the second battle of Trenton on Jan. 2 and in the battle of Princeton the following day. Later in the same year (1777), when General Howe's army invaded northern Delaware on its way from the Head of Elk to Philadelphia, Thomas Rodney acted as adjutant to his brother Cæsar who was then in command of the Delaware militia encamped near the British posts in New Castle County.

From 1778 to 1785 Thomas Rodney served his state as judge of the admiralty court, and between the years 1781 and 1788 he was elected by the General Assembly five times to membership in the Confederation Congress. Elected twice to membership in the lower house of the General Assembly (1786 and 1787), he was chosen speaker of that body in October 1787, but after serving for a few days he asked to be relieved. Appointed associate justice of the supreme court of Delaware in December 1802, he held this post until August 1803, when he resigned to accept an appointment by President Jefferson as United States judge for Mississippi Territory. He remained in this position until his death at Natchez in 1811. Rodney was married, Apr. 8, 1771, to Elizabeth Fisher, daughter of Jabez Maud Fisher of Philadelphia. Two of their children attained maturity, one of whom was Cæsar Augustus Rodney [q.v.].

[The principal public depositaries of Thomas Rodney manuscripts are the Delaware Public Archives, Hist. Soc. of Del.; the Geneal. Soc. of Pa., and the Lib. of Cong. For printed material see: "Diary of Capt. Thos. Rodney, 1776–77," Papers of the Hist. Soc. of Del., vol. VII (1888); Simon Gratz, "Thos. Rodney," Pa. Mag. of Hist. and Biog., Jan. 1919–Oct. 1920; Letters to and from Cæsar Rodney (1933), ed. by George H. Ryden; Letters of Members of the Continental Cong., vols. I–VII (1921–34), ed. by E. C. Burnett; Del. Archives, vols. II and III (1912–19).]
G. H. R.

ROE, EDWARD PAYSON (Mar. 7, 1838– July 19, 1888), author, was born in what is now New Windsor, Orange County, N. Y., fourth of the six children of Peter and Susan (Williams) Roe. His father was a New York merchant who, having saved a competence, retired to the country to spend the last forty years of his life; he was enough of an abolitionist to convoy at least one fugitive negro across the ice-bound Hudson

in mid-winter. Roe's mother, who died in 1859, was for as long as he could remember her an invalid; to her literary taste, nourished largely on the Bible and "Paradise Lost," her son attributed his own gift for writing. He attended Burr and Burton Seminary in Manchester, Vt., and entered Williams College with the class of 1863, but developed a dangerous case of eye strain and on the advice of President Mark Hopkins pursued a special two years' course. Then for another year he studied at the Auburn Theological Seminary. Having been ordained at Somers, N. Y., in the summer of 1862 by the North River Presbytery, he served as chaplain of the 2nd (Harris' Light) New York Cavalry and later of the hospital at Fortress Monroe, Va., until the close of the Civil War, and was pastor of the Highland Falls, N. Y., Presbyterian Church, 1866–74. During the war he was married, Nov. 24, 1863, to Anna Paulina Sands of New York City, who with five children survived him.

The Chicago fire of 1871 turned the country clergyman into the most popular American novelist of the period. Drawn by a curiosity so powerful that he could neither resist it nor approve it, he visited the city while the embers were still smoldering, wandered about the ruins for several days, and returned home with the germ of a novel in his head. His *Barriers Burned Away* was published as a magazine serial and also in book form in 1872, and became immediately and lastingly popular. With proper caution Roe composed a second novel, *Opening a Chestnut Burr* (1874), to determine whether the amazing sale of the first was an accident or the product of a dependable formula. Satisfied on that point, he resigned his charge in 1874, bought an estate at Cornwall on the Hudson, and devoted himself to authorship. His seventeen novels were all best-sellers and continued in demand long after their first publication. The great favorites, besides the first two, were: *Near to Nature's Heart* (1876); *A Knight of the Nineteenth Century* (1877); *Without a Home* (1881); *He Fell in Love with His Wife* (1886); and *The Earth Trembled* (1887). His income from his books and magazine work was about $15,000 a year. He worked methodically, took pains with his style, and, despite the unremitting efforts of Lyman Abbott, Julian Hawthorne, and other friends to flatter him into the illusion that he was the equal of Thackeray, always had a fairly accurate notion of his literary status. He was one of several clerical novelists who, combining entertainment with moral purpose, helped to dispel the lingering American prejudice against the novel. His work, however, did not rise above the popular level.

The adulation that was lavished on him as a writer he deserved as a man. In all the relations of life he was kindly, helpful, and decent. Characteristic of him was his behavior in 1882 when his brother, whose notes he had indorsed, defaulted. Roe was forced into bankruptcy and had to sell his copyrights at auction, but he accepted his responsibilities without complaint and ultimately paid his brother's creditors in full. His avocation was horticulture and the growing of small fruits. For a number of years he did a thriving business as a nurseryman. Five books —*Play and Profit in My Garden* (1873; new ed., 1886), *A Manual on the Culture of Small Fruits* (brochure, 1876), *Success with Small Fruits* (1880), *Nature's Serial Story* (1885), and *The Home Acre* (1889)—were his literary harvests from this field. He was fond of hospitality, using every means he could devise to keep his guest-room occupied. For several years he was host to the Authors' Club of New York on an annual junket to Cornwall. He died, practically without warning, of a heart attack, after reading aloud to his family from one of Hawthorne's novels.

[E. P. Roe, "My First Novel," *Cosmopolitan,* July 1887, and "'A Native Author Called Roe,'" *Lippincott's Mag.,* Oct. 1888; Roe's letters to Edgar Alexander Mearns, Div. of MSS., Lib. of Cong.; *Report of the Class of 1861 Williams College* (1887); Mary A. Roe, *E. P. Roe: Reminiscences of His Life* (1899); *Critic,* July 28, Aug. 4, 1888; *Publishers' Weekly,* July 28, 1888; E. D. Walker, "Edward P. Roe," *Cosmopolitan,* Sept. 1888; *N. Y. Daily Tribune,* July 21, 1888; names of parents from Prof. Wm. J. Hinke of Auburn Theol. Sem.; for a terse, exact description of Roe's novelistic formula see Carl Van Doren, *The Am. Novel* (1921), p. 122.]   G. H. G.

ROE, FRANCIS ASBURY (Oct. 4, 1823– Dec. 28, 1901), naval officer, was a descendant in the sixth generation of David Roe, who settled in Flushing, Long Island, in the latter part of the seventeenth century. His great-grandfather, Benjamin Roe, fought in the French and Indian War, his grandfather, John Roe, in the Revolution, and his father, Isaac Roe, in the War of 1812. His mother, Hannah Drake, was said to be a direct descendant of Sir Francis Drake. Born in Elmira, N. Y., he had his schooling in Elmira Academy. He was appointed an acting midshipman in 1841, cruised on the coast of Brazil and the southeast coast of Africa, and then joined in the suppression of the slave-trade on the west coast of Africa. He was later ordered to the *Boston* and was to have joined the squadron of Commodore O. H. Perry at Vera Cruz, but was prevented from taking an active part in the Mexican War by the ground-

ing and loss of that vessel. A year of instruction at the newly established Naval Academy followed. In October 1849, he was dismissed from the service by a sentence of court martial for the disobedience of an illegal order, but was reappointed a passed midshipman and given his former place on the navy list the following year. In 1854, as executive officer of the *Porpoise,* he had an engagement with thirteen pirate junks at Koulan Bay, China, destroying six and dispersing the others.

In the Civil War he was ordered as executive officer to the *Pensacola,* fitting out at Washington, and after the defeat of the Union army at Bull Run he occupied Fort Ellsworth near Alexandria, Va., with 500 seamen for the defense of Washington. Later he made a perilous run down the Potomac, past nine miles of Confederate batteries, on his way south to join Farragut's fleet. In the attack on New Orleans, the *Pensacola* steamed past the forts below the city, her position being in the van of the fleet, immediately after the gunboat *Cayuga,* which led the Union forces. For his capable handling of the ship, Roe was especially commended by Captain Morris in his report. Promoted to the rank of lieutenant commander, he was given command of the gunboat *Katahdin,* in the fleet that was to keep the Mississippi open from New Orleans to Port Hudson—a task that involved constant fighting. In September 1863, he took command of the double-ended paddle-wheel steamer *Sassacus,* and while engaged in the blockade of Wilmington, N. C., destroyed two blockade-runners, the *Wild Dayrell* and the *Nutfield.* On May 5, 1864, when the Union "paste-board fleet" in Albemarle Sound was ineffectually engaging the heavy Confederate ironclad *Albemarle,* the *Sassacus* captured the gunboat *Bombshell,* and then attacked the *Albemarle* and drove her bronze beak into the casemate of her enemy. In this courageous but unequal combat, the *Sassacus* was disabled by a shell that exploded her boiler. She fought on, however, until the *Albemarle* withdrew up the Roanoke River. For this action Roe received a letter of commendation from the secretary of the navy and was advanced five numbers in rank. In 1867 he was ordered to command the Mexican division of the Gulf Squadron. In the *Tacony* at Vera Cruz he rendered important service at the time when Maximilian was executed and the Mexican imperial government was changed to republican. For his skilful handling of affairs he was given a commendatory letter by the secretary of the navy and was presented to President Johnson at a cabinet meeting. Various assignments followed, the last being that of governor of the Naval Asylum for Retired Seamen at Philadelphia. In 1884 he was promoted to the rank of rear admiral, and in October of the next year was placed on the retired list. He was married in September 1849, to Eliza J. Snyder. In 1865 he wrote a book that received considerable recognition on *Naval Duties and Discipline.* After retirement he made his home in Washington, D. C., and took an active part in the patriotic societies of which he was a member. He occasionally wrote articles for magazines, the most important being a description of the actions of Farragut's fleet in the capture of New Orleans in *Self Culture,* January 1899.

[*Who's Who in America,* 1901–02; Marcus Benjamin, "Francis Asbury Roe," *Memorial Papers of the Soc. of Colonial Wars, District of Columbia, no. 4, 1903*; C. A. Torrey, *David Roe of Flushing, L. I., and Some of His Descendants* (1926); *War of the Rebellion: Official Records* (*Navy*), 1 ser., vols. III, IV, IX, X, XVIII, XIX, XXVI; personal papers and journals in the possession of a relative; *Washington* (D. C.) *Post,* Dec. 29, 1901.]   C. S. A.

ROE, GILBERT ERNSTEIN (Feb. 7, 1865–Dec. 22, 1929), lawyer, author, was born in the town of Oregon, Dane County, Wis., the son of John and Jane (McKeeby) Roe. Of English and Scotch descent, he was educated at the University of Wisconsin and graduated from the law school in 1890. He immediately entered the law firm of Robert M. LaFollette, with whom he was intimately associated for thirty-five years. It was in this association that Roe, as the trusted political and legal adviser of LaFollette, found the opportunity for his most significant activities in public affairs. Particularly in connection with direct primary, and with railroad and insurance legislation was his political and legal skill of value in effectuating the LaFollette program. He led the successful contest in the Republican State Convention of 1898 for a platform declaration favorable to the direct primary, and his advice was influential in the subsequent political and legislative development of the proposal. In the drafting of the railroad and insurance statutes he was equally valuable, returning several times from New York City, whence he had removed in 1899, to aid in the solution of some difficult problem.

After several years spent in establishing a law practice in New York City, from 1905 to 1910 in partnership with William F. McCombs, Roe became prominent in the movement to apply in New York state the major ideas of the Wisconsin plan. He was a member of the commission appointed by Gov. William Sulzer to draft a direct primary law; he was active in behalf of workmen's compensation legislation and,

when the New York court of appeals declared the original law unconstitutional in 1911, he drafted the new and improved law. His devotion to the liberal tenets of the Progressive movement led him to defend those who opposed the war activities of the government and who were prosecuted for violation of the espionage acts. He was *amicus curiae* in the appeal of the Debs case to the United States Supreme Court; he won all his jury cases which involved charges of disloyalty; he successfully contested exclusion of several anti-war newspapers from the mails; and he was counsel to the five Socialist New York assemblymen who were deprived of their seats for their war attitudes. As counsel to the Teachers' Union in New York he was influential in the repeal of the Lusk laws. In the unsuccessful proceedings to expel LaFollette from the Senate in December 1918 for alleged seditious activities, he was counsel to the Senator (*Senate Report 614,* 65 Cong., 3 Sess.).

During 1922–23, as counsel to the Senate committee on manufactures, of which LaFollette was chairman, Roe made an investigation of the oil industry which laid the basis for the Teapot Dome and other investigations of the Harding administration (*Senate Report 1263,* 67 Cong., 4 Sess.). He was throughout his life a critic of the judicial process. His *Selected Opinions of Luther S. Dixon and Edward G. Ryan, Late Chief Justices of the Supreme Court of Wisconsin* (1907) expressed his opposition to the conservative tendencies of the law. In *Our Judicial Oligarchy* (1912) he developed the thesis that the courts had usurped authority in their review of legislative acts, and elaborated, through a careful analysis of judicial decisions, his charge that judges were disposed to preserve property rights at an excessive cost to society. His pronounced ideas on this subject were the mainspring for LaFollette's proposal in 1912 and in 1924 that the courts be curbed in their power to nullify the decisions of the law-making agencies. Roe died in New York City in the winter of 1929. He had married, on Nov. 12, 1899, Gwyneth King, who with three children survived him.

[A considerable portion of the Roe papers are in the LaFollette collection, Wis. State Hist. Soc.; the remainder are in the possession of Mrs. Gilbert E. Roe, New York City. See also: A. O. Barton, *LaFollette's Winning of Wis.* (1922); R. M. LaFollette, *LaFollette's Autobiog.* (1913); *Who's Who in America,* 1928–29; *N. Y. Times,* Dec. 23, 1929.]   W. S. S.

ROEBLING, JOHN AUGUSTUS (June 12, 1806–July 22, 1869), engineer, bridge builder, and manufacturer, was born in Mühlhausen, Thuringia, Germany, the youngest son of Christoph Polycarpus Roebling and his wife, Friederike Dorothea (Mueller). The family traced its history in a direct line to Nicholaus Roebling, or Rebeling, who was born in Tennstedt in 1560. He appears to have been a man of substance and a city official. Christoph, the father of John Augustus, is noted in the records of Mühlhausen as a tobacco manufacturer.

For the time and place, John's education was unusually good. He attended the Mühlhausen public schools and the city Gymnasium, and was also tutored privately to qualify him for entrance to the Royal Polytechnic Institute in Berlin. For his opportunity to study there he was chiefly indebted to his mother, whose determined self-denial and thrift had made it possible, because the family circumstances were far from affluent. In the Institute his course included architecture and engineering, bridge construction, hydraulics, languages, and philosophy. He was a pupil of the great Hegel, and there is a tradition in the Roebling family that he was the philosopher's favorite disciple. At the age of twenty he was granted the degree of civil engineer, and for three years thereafter worked for the Prussian government on road building in Westphalia. His keenest interest was in bridge construction, especially that of suspension bridges. He made a special study of a chain suspension bridge at Bamberg, in Bavaria, and subsequently presented his observations of the structure as a thesis for his state examination.

Roebling showed already that originality and inventiveness which was later to carry him so far in the field of long-span bridge construction. He was eager to develop his ideas but found himself hampered by red tape and official inertia. It is not surprising therefore that his thoughts turned to America, whither so many of his countrymen were looking. With his brother he planned carefully the contemplated step and read as widely as he could on opportunities in the United States. He seems to have decided that the best field to enter would be agriculture, and it was with the intention of buying farm land in the new country that he left Germany. His strong feeling against slavery, considered by many essential to agricultural progress, turned him definitely against the South and in favor of the North. With his brother Karl he left Mühlhausen for Bremen in the spring of 1831 and a little later sailed for Philadelphia on the bark *August Eduard,* intending to find and purchase a tract of land for some of their countrymen. They reached Philadelphia on Aug. 6, and after a few weeks in that city, left for Pitts-

burgh, traveling mainly by the Pennsylvania Canal, and crossing the mountains by means of the inclined planes of the Allegheny Portage Railroad. Roebling kept a journal of the trip which was printed in 1832 and a century later, translated from the original German by Edward Underwood, was published under the title, *Diary of My Journey from Muehlhausen in Thuringia via Bremen to the United States of North America in the Year 1831, Written for My Friends* (1931). The brothers bought seven thousand acres of land in Butler County, about twenty-five miles from Pittsburgh, and settled it, in company with the little group of thrifty German colonists with whom they were associated. The small town or hamlet was first known as Germania and afterwards as Saxonburg. The colonists kept in touch with their friends and relatives in Germany, persuading a number of them also to emigrate and join the community in Butler County. Among these later emigrants was Ernst Herting, who came to Saxonburg from Mühlhausen in 1834. In May 1836 John Roebling married Johanna, Herting's eldest daughter.

Roebling was not a successful farmer. This cannot be charged, however, entirely to his lack of experience, for the colonists certainly chose anything but prime agricultural land when they settled on the western slope of the Alleghanies. It was not many years before he felt a yearning to get back to the professional work for which he had been so well trained. The year after his marriage (1837) he went to Harrisburg and applied for employment by the state as an engineer. In this year he became a naturalized citizen of the United States. He spent several months on the state canal projects, mainly in building dams and locks on Beaver River, then joined a surveying party which was laying out a railway over the mountains.

At this time the canal era was about at its height, and the Allegheny Portage Railroad was an important link between the eastern and western sections of the Pennsylvania Canal. Roebling was evidently impressed by the long reaches of steeply inclined railway, up and down which the canal boats were moved in specially constructed wheeled cradles, and by the clumsy and expensive cables used for hauling the cars up and down the slopes. These hawsers, generally about three inches in diameter, made of Kentucky hemp, were subjected to severe usage which necessitated frequent replacement. Roebling conceived the idea of substituting for these hempen cables ropes of twisted wire which would give far greater strength and longer life, with the added advantage of smaller diameter and consequently greater ease in handling. He made a number of experiments and had the usual difficulty of the pioneer in convincing the Pennsylvania board of public works that the idea was of value. These obstacles were finally overcome, however, and in 1841 he manufactured the first wire rope made in America in a small factory in Saxonburg equipped with machinery of his own design and fabrication. Additional uses for the new wire rope were found and although the demand for the product for canal use waned with the diminishing importance of the canals, rope for rigging vessels, for tow lines, and for dredges was increasingly demanded. Roebling wrote an article describing his product which was published in the *American Railroad Journal* of November 1843. In 1848 or 1849 he moved his factory to Trenton, N. J.

While becoming a manufacturer he also continued his interest in bridge building and designed a number of notable structures. In 1844–45 he built a wooden aqueduct for the Pennsylvania Canal, comprising seven spans of 162 feet each, carried on two continuous wire cables each seven inches in diameter. The design was without precedent in America although it made use of some of the principles of the chain suspension bridge at Bamberg, Bavaria, which Roebling had studied in his youth. In 1846 he completed his first suspension bridge, built to carry a highway over the Monongahela River at Pittsburgh. This bridge comprised eight spans of 188 feet each, supported by two 4½-inch cables which were constructed on the bank of the river and hoisted into place from flatboats. Roebling described it in an article in the *American Railroad Journal*, June 13, 1846. The structure was in use for thirty-five years. In the years 1848–50, Roebling constructed four suspension aqueducts for the Delaware & Hudson Canal.

In spite of his early interest in canals and canal operation, he readily foresaw that the faster and surer agency of the railway must absorb the greater part of the service heretofore given by the canals. In 1847 he read a paper before the Pittsburgh Board of Trade in which he strongly advocated a railroad through Pennsylvania. Early in 1850, four years before Cyrus W. Field [*q.v.*] became actively interested in such a project, Roebling wrote to the *Journal of Commerce,* expressing his conviction that a transatlantic telegraph was perfectly feasible. He gave detailed estimates of the cost, which he believed should not exceed $1,300,000.

The list of Roebling's works in the field of important bridge construction is a long one. In many ways the most striking structure was the pioneer railroad suspension bridge which he built at Niagara Falls in the years 1851–55. In addition to the natural obstacles to be overcome, there was a cholera epidemic at the bridge site in 1854. The bridge was opened in March 1855, and stood for many years, a monument to the ingenuity and resourcefulness of its builder. It was described by him in a memoir included in *Public Works of Recent Construction Both British and American* (London, 1856). In 1856 Roebling's plans for a bridge over the Ohio River, between Cincinnati and Covington, Ky., were accepted and work was begun, but the undertaking was interrupted by the Civil War and not completed until 1867. In 1858–60 the bridge over the Alleghany River at Pittsburgh was built, in which work Roebling and his son Washington A. Roebling [*q.v.*] were associated. Roebling's hatred of the institution of slavery had continued unabated and he vigorously supported the Union cause, encouraging his son Washington to offer his services to the Federal army.

In June 1857, Roebling had written a letter to Abram S. Hewitt [*q.v.*], of New York, suggesting the possibility of a bridge over the East River between lower Manhattan and Brooklyn which would not interfere with navigation, but it was ten years later before the project finally assumed shape and a charter for the construction of the work was granted. Roebling was appointed chief engineer, and plans for the bridge were perfected by him and received the approval of the commission early in 1869. The surveys had been made and work was about to begin when he suffered the accident—at first believed not to be serious—which cost his life. On June 28, 1869, he was making certain observations at the bridge site, from a point of vantage on a cluster of piles at the Fulton Ferry slip on the Brooklyn side. A ferry-boat entering the slip pushed back the piling on which he was standing, catching his foot and crushing several of his toes. He was taken at once to his son's home in Brooklyn, and the injured toes were amputated. Although he was in considerable pain, there was every expectation that with his vigorous physique he would soon be about again, but tetanus set in, and he died on Thursday, July 22, less than six weeks after his sixty-third birthday.

Roebling at his death was a rich man for his time. He had accumulated his wealth by means of mental and physical energy of a high order and relentless personal industry. In addition to his professional activity and the management of his factory he was a prolific writer for technical and scientific periodicals, and at the time of his death a book by him, *Long and Short Span Railway Bridges* (1869), was in press. His one recreation appears to have been music, and he usually found opportunity for practising the flute and the piano. He was jealous of his time, never wasted it himself, and would not allow others to do so. Punctual to the minute himself, if an associate was five minutes late in keeping an appointment, Roebling would postpone the conference. When he established the wire-rope factory in Saxonburg in 1841 and began the manufacture of a product up to that time unknown in America, he founded an industrial dynasty. The John A. Roebling's Sons Company of Trenton has developed without a break from the little ropewalk in Saxonburg, and at no time has it been out of the control of the Roebling family—sons, grandsons, and great-grandsons of the founder. John Augustus Roebling and his wife Johanna had nine children, of whom four sons and three daughters were living at the time of their father's death in 1869. The youngest daughter, Josephine, became the wife of the pianist Charles H. Jarvis [q.v.]. Johanna (Herting) Roebling died Nov. 22, 1864, and Roebling married, second, Lucia W. Cooper, whom he survived five years.

[Hamilton Schuyler, *The Roeblings—A Century of Engineers, Bridge-Builders and Industrialists* (1931), is a standard work, with many quotations from diaries, letters and other original sources. See also "John Augustus Roebling," *Trans. Am. Soc. of Civil Engineers*, vol. XCVIII (1933); C. B. Stuart, *Lives and Works of Civil and Military Engineers of America* (1871); *John A. Roebling: An Account of the Ceremonies at the Unveiling of a Monument to His Memory* (1908); J. K. Mumford, *Outspinning the Spider: The Story of Wire and Wire Rope* (1921); *N. Y. Daily Tribune*, July 23, 1869.]
                                        C. J. T.

ROEBLING, WASHINGTON AUGUSTUS (May 26, 1837–July 21, 1926), civil engineer, industrialist, was born in Saxonburg, Butler County, Pa., eldest of the nine children of John Augustus Roebling [q.v.] and Johanna (Herting) Roebling. His father was the leader of a group of German colonists who settled Saxonburg in 1831. Washington spent his boyhood in that town under stern paternal discipline, sharing the privations and limitations of pioneer life until his thirteenth year. At that time the family moved to Trenton, N. J., where John A. Roebling established a new factory for the production of wire rope.

Washington all his life used English and German with equal facility. As a little child he had a tutor; he now entered the Trenton Academy, and after four years of preparation, matriculated at Rensselaer Polytechnic Institute, Troy, N. Y.,

then the leading school of professional engineering in the country. The Rensselaer curriculum of the day he described as "that terrible treadmill of forcing an avalanche of figures and facts into young brains not qualified to assimilate them as yet" (Schuyler, *post*, p. 173); his class numbered sixty-five on entering but only twelve were graduated three years later. Immediately after receiving his degree as civil engineer, young Roebling started to work in his father's wire-rope mill, in which he had already had some experience, and apparently for considerable periods of time he was in charge during his father's prolonged absences. After a year in the mill he joined his father at Pittsburgh to assist in building the Alleghany River Bridge, and remained on that job until its completion in the summer of 1860, when he returned to Trenton. On Apr. 16, 1861, four days after the attack on Fort Sumter, he enlisted as a private in the National Guard of New Jersey, in June joined the 83rd New York Infantry, and in January 1862 became a second lieutenant in the 6th New York Battery, from which he was discharged in April 1864 to accept a commission as major of volunteers. On Dec. 2, 1864, he was brevetted lieutenant-colonel for gallant service before Richmond and on Mar. 13, 1865, he was brevetted colonel of volunteers, "for gallant and meritorious service during the War." His duties were mainly those of an engineer officer and included a considerable amount of bridge building, notably the construction of suspension bridges across the Rappahannock and Shenandoah rivers. He served on the staff of Gen. Irvin McDowell and later on that of Gen. John Pope [qq.v.]. He took part in the campaign which ended in the second battle of Bull Run and was also at Antietam and South Mountain. At one time, after Chancellorsville, it was his daily task to ascend in a captive balloon to observe and report on Confederate movements. He was on the staff of Gen. Gouverneur K. Warren [q.v.] at the battle of Gettysburg and throughout the fierce campaign around Richmond.

The war over, he returned to his profession of civil engineering. For two years (1865–67) he assisted his father in completing the bridge between Cincinnati and Covington, Ky. He then spent a year abroad conferring with the leading engineers in England, France, and Germany and studying especially the principles and practice of caisson foundations, with a view to helping his father in the newly projected Brooklyn Bridge, of which the elder Roebling had been appointed chief engineer. Immediately on his return from Europe, he entered his father's office as principal assistant and prepared the detailed plans and specifications for the great bridge. The elder Roebling died just as the field work was beginning and his son succeeded him as chief engineer.

For the next three years Roebling's work was continuous and unusually severe. The Brooklyn Bridge project was unprecedented in many ways and the details of procedure needed constant watching and direction. The foundations of the great towers were built by the caisson method, under compressed air, and the chief engineer spent long hours in the damp high-pressure of the caisson chambers. Caisson disease, the dreaded "bends," attacked the laborers; at that time little was known of methods of treatment and much had to be learned by costly experience. One afternoon in the spring of 1872, Roebling was taken almost unconscious from the caisson on the New York side, but in a few days he was back on the work. By the end of the year, however, his health had been seriously and permanently affected, and he did not visit the bridge site again. From that time until the bridge was finished in 1883, except for six months abroad in a vain attempt to regain his health, he directed the work from his house in Brooklyn, too sick to leave it. Such a record, a decade of exacting work, is a rare tribute to the man's mental alertness, minute knowledge of technical detail, and gift for effective organization. During much of this time he maintained an active part in conducting the business of the John A. Roebling's Sons Company, of which he became president upon its incorporation in 1876.

Shortly after the bridge was completed and opened to traffic, he moved with his wife to Troy, N. Y., where they lived from 1884 to 1888 while their son, John A. Roebling II, was a student at Rensselaer Polytechnic Institute. They then removed to Trenton and established a permanent home. Owing to his seriously impaired health, Roebling took no further active part in professional engineering work, although for a short time, at the age of eighty-three, after the death of his nephew, Karl G. Roebling, he resumed the presidency of the Roebling company, and during his brief administration took and filled the contract for the Bear Mountain Bridge over the Hudson. For the most part, however, he lived quietly in Trenton, read widely, and indulged his hobby of collecting rare minerals, of which he had some fifteen thousand specimens. His remarkable collection is now in the Smithsonian Institution in Washington. In 1924 he wrote a paper on the early history of Saxonburg for the Butler County Historical Society.

Washington Augustus Roebling was twice married. His first wife, whom he married Jan. 18, 1865, was Emily Warren, of Cold Spring, N. Y., daughter of Sylvanus Warren and sister of Major-General G. K. Warren on whose staff Roebling served during the Civil War. By her he had one son, born in Mühlhausen, Germany, the birthplace of his ancestors. Mrs. Roebling died Feb. 28, 1903, and five years later, Apr. 21, 1908, Roebling married Mrs. Cornelia Witsell Farrow, of Charleston, S. C. He died at his home in Trenton a few weeks after his eighty-ninth birthday.

[Hamilton Schuyler, *The Roeblings* (1931), the standard work, contains many additional references, including an extensive list of works relating to the Brooklyn Bridge. See also *Who's Who in America*, 1918–19; Wm. C. Conant and Montgomery Schuyler, *The Brooklyn Bridge . . . With an Account of the Opening Exercises* (1883), reprinting articles first pub. in *Harper's Mag.*, May 1883, and *Harper's Weekly*, May 26, 1883; E. F. Farrington, *Concise Description of the East River Bridge . . . Lectures Delivered at the Cooper Union* (1881); *N. Y. Times*, July 22, 1926.]   C. J. T.

ROEDING, GEORGE CHRISTIAN (Feb. 4, 1868–July 23, 1928), horticulturist and nurseryman, was born in San Francisco, Cal., of German parentage. His father, Frederick Christian Roeding (Dec. 31, 1824–July 18, 1910), was a native of Hamburg who went to Chile in 1846 and thence, in 1849, to California. He engaged briefly in mining but soon became a successful banker. In 1867 he married Marianna Lazarus, who had emigrated from Germany the year before. George Christian was the eldest of their five children. Shortly after his birth, his father, with some compatriots, bought 80,000 acres of land in the San Joaquin Valley; subsequently, some 1200 acres of this tract, given by the elder Roeding to the Southern Pacific Railroad, became a part of the city of Fresno. George's early years were spent mostly in San Francisco, where he graduated from the Boys' High School in 1885, but his summer vacations were passed on a farm in Contra Costa County. His interests in plants dated from childhood and is said to have been aroused by botanizing trips taken with Dr. H. H. Behr. In 1886 he began work with the three-year-old Fancher Creek Nurseries at that time owned by his father and Dr. Gustavus Eisen. He soon became manager and eventually owner of these nurseries, to which were added others in various parts of the state. In 1910 he was president of the Pacific Coast Association of Nurserymen and in 1911 organized the California Association of Nurserymen, of which he was an active member until his death. He was an ardent advocate of plant quarantine and of a protective tariff on agricultural products.

Roeding has been called the father of Smyrna-fig culture in California, and undoubtedly his greatest single contribution to American horticulture was the part he took in establishing that industry. Figs had been grown in ˙California since the time of the early missionaries but none of these early introductions were equal in quality to figs of the Smyrna type. In 1887 Roeding's father imported fig cuttings from Smyrna with the hope of producing a fig to compete with the imported fruit. These first plantings were augmented until the Roedings had some sixty acres planted to Smyrna figs. The trees prospered, but they matured no fruit. The father became discouraged and retired from the enterprise, but the son persisted, in the face of many disappointments and great expense, until the problem was solved.

The chief difficulty that had to be surmounted was caprification, or the fertilization of the female flowers through the agency of a small wasp. This age-old process was thought by most European botanists to be unnecessary, and the practice of hanging male capri figs containing the Blastophaga wasp in the fruit-bearing trees was considered a superstition, but when the Smyrna figs introduced into America failed to produce fruit, attention was directed to the absence of the fig insects. Roeding was captivated by the idea of the intricate cooperation of plant and insect whereby the wasp, mistaking the edible female figs for the capri figs in which she wishes to lay her eggs, is entrapped and dies without posterity, but not before she has distributed pollen to the female flowers of the fig, thus enabling them to develop for the use of man and providing for future generations of fig trees. Roeding was the first to demonstrate that when pollinated the Smyrna fig would mature. This he did by introducing pollen through the opening at the tip of the fig. He cooperated with the Department of Agriculture in introducing the Blastophaga wasp, and it was in his trees that the insects were liberated and became established. In 1901 he visited Smyrna to study the fig industry and in 1903 he published *The Smyrna Fig at Home and Abroad,* an account of his trip and description of Smyrna fig culture in California. He was the author also of *The Fruit Growers' Guide* (1919), a practical treatise on fruit growing. He married, Dec. 15, 1897, Elizabeth Evelyn Thorne, whose father was one of the pioneers of Fresno County. They had three daughters and one son. Roeding died by his own hand after about a year spent in a sanitarium following a nervous breakdown from overwork.

[In addition to Roeding's *The Smyrna Fig at Home and Abroad,* see H. W. Kruckeberg, *George Christian Roeding, a Tribute* (1930); *Trans. and Proc. of the Cal. Asso. of Nurserymen,* 1911–28; L. H. Bailey, *The Standard Cyc. of Horticulture,* III (1915), 1593; *Sacramento Union,* July 25, 1928.]   G. N. C.

ROEMER, KARL FERDINAND (Jan. 5, 1818–Dec. 14, 1891), German geologist, better known simply as Ferdinand Roemer, was born in Hildesheim, Hanover. His father, Friedrich Roemer, councilor of the high court of justice (*Obergerichtsrath*), was of Prussian descent, a native of Magdeburg; his mother, Charlotte Lüntzel, a daughter of the last of the independent burgomasters of Hildesheim. Roemer's early education was along classical lines, but during his Gymnasium days he became deeply interested in natural sciences, especially geology. Family influence, however, induced him to undertake the study of law at Göttingen (1836–39) where, on the side, he listened with much satisfaction to the lectures on geology by Dr. Hausmann. In 1840, having abandoned the law, he matriculated as a student of science at the University of Berlin. Here he attended the lectures of Heinrich and Gustav Rose, Weiss, von Dechen, and other celebrated professors. On May 10, 1842, he was awarded the doctor's degree and soon thereafter began his contributions to the *Neues Jahrbuch für Mineralogie, Geologie und Palæontologie* which were continued at frequent intervals for forty-five years.

In the spring of 1845, with funds provided by the Society for the Protection of German Emigrants in Texas and the Berlin Academy of Science, and with the approval of Alexander von Humboldt, Roemer sailed for America. His special mission was to study the condition of the colonists in Texas and to report upon the natural resources of the country. Of his many publications those resulting from this trip are of the greatest interest to Americans. Omitting letters and briefer articles, they are: *Texas-Mit besonderer Rücksicht auf deutsche Auswanderung und die physischen Verhältnisse des Landes nach eigener Beobachtung geschildert* (Bonn, 1849), *Die Kreidbildungen von Texas und ihre organischen Einschlüsse* (Bonn, 1852), and *Die silurische Fauna des westlichen Tennessee* (1860). The first work treats of a great variety of subjects, personal, descriptive, and scientific, and is accompanied with the first geological map of the state printed in color; the second, a quarto volume, deals with the physiography and geology of the state in general, but particularly with the Cretaceous formations, followed by a description of fossils illustrated by eleven beautifully executed plates. This work, still a useful reference, has given Roemer a permanent place among the geologists of Texas. Long after his return to Germany he prepared and published the third work—a monograph on the Silurian fossils of western Tennessee.

In 1848 Roemer became privat-docent in mineralogy and paleontology at Bonn. Later, in 1855, he accepted a call to Breslau where, in addition to his professorship in geology and paleontology, he undertook the directorship of the mineralogical cabinet which under his fostering care became one of the finest in Germany. His success as a teacher was notable and his reward ample, for under his guidance there were given to the scientific world many distinguished scholars. He traveled extensively. It has been said that he visited every country in Europe and some of them several times. The bibliography of his publications lists more than three-hundred and fifty titles. Important among his works is his *Geologie von Oberschlesien* (3 vols., with maps and plates, 1870). In recognition of his unusual ability as a researcher, he was the recipient of many honors from both the state and learned societies. In 1885 he was awarded the Murchison Medal by the Geological Society of London. Aside from his scientific attainments Roemer was well versed in the classics. He possessed great aptitude in acquiring foreign languages, a gift of no little importance in prosecuting his studies outside of Germany. In the spring of 1869 he married Katharina Schäfer with whom he lived happily for twenty-three years. He died, without issue, in Breslau.

[W. Dames, memoir and bibliography of Roemer's writings in *Neues Jahrbuch für Mineralogie, Geologie und Palæontologie,* vol. I (1892), Supp.; Carl Hintze, "Karl Ferdinand Roemer," *Allgemeine Deutsche Biographie,* LIII (1907), 451–58; Frederic W. Simonds, "Dr. Ferdinand von Roemer, the Father of the Geology of Tex.," with a bibliography, *Am. Geologist,* Mar. 1902, reprinted, without the bibliography, in the *Geol. Mag.* (London), Sept. 1902.]   F. W. S—s.

ROGERS, CLARA KATHLEEN BARNETT (Jan. 14, 1844–Mar. 8, 1931), singer, author, composer, was born in Cheltenham, England. Her father, John Barnett, a composer, was the son of Bernhard Beer, a Prussian watch-maker, who had settled in Bedford and had changed his name to Barnett. Clara Kathleen, growing up in a musical household, studied with her parents until 1856. She then went to the Leipzig Conservatory where she studied piano with Moscheles and Plaidy, theory with Papperitz and Richter, ensemble with David and Rietz, and singing with Goetze. After further study in Berlin, and with San Giovanni

and Bruni in Milan, she made her début in Turin in 1863 as Isabella in Meyerbeer's *Roberto il Diavolo* under her stage-name, "Clara Doria." Later she sang in Genoa, Leghorn, Florence, and Naples, in *Lucia di Lammermoor, Maria di Rohan,* in which she sang the title rôle, *Maria Padilla, La Sonnambula, La Vestale, Rigoletto.* Leaving Italy she went to London where she was prominent on the concert stage for five years. In 1871 she came to America with the Parepa-Rosa Opera Company, of which Tom Karl was the tenor. She made her début on Oct. 4, 1871, at the New York Academy of Music in *The Bohemian Girl,* and subsequently sang Donna Elvira in *Don Giovanni,* the Countess in *The Marriage of Figaro,* and other soprano rôles. She appeared in New York, Boston, and Philadelphia, and in 1872-73 sang with the Maretzek company.

Leaving the operatic stage, she went to Boston as the solo soprano of Trinity Church, and there, on Apr. 24, 1878, she was married to a Boston lawyer, Henry Munroe Rogers. She continued active as a concert singer, teacher, composer, and author, and in 1902 became professor of singing at the New England Conservatory of Music. Her compositions include a number of albums of songs, some piano pieces, and a sonata for violin and piano. She also wrote a number of educational books on her art: *The Philosophy of Singing* (1893), *Dreaming True* (1899), *My Voice and I* (1910), *English Diction, in Song and Speech* (1912), *Your Voice and You* (1925) and *Clearcut Speech in Song* (1927). As an opera singer Clara Kathleen Rogers seems to have fallen short of the first rank, and there is probably much truth in Carlo Rosa's remark to her: "If you only had two more notes in your voice you would be one of the great artists of the world" (*Memories, post,* p. 395). She died in Boston at the age of eighty-seven.

[The main sources of information are the autobiographical *Memories of a Musical Career* (1919), and *The Story of Two Lives: Home, Friends, and Travels. Sequence to "Memories of a Musical Career"* (1932). See also: *Who's Who in America,* 1930–31; *Musical America,* Mar. 25, 1931; *Boston Herald,* Mar. 9, 1931. There are biographies of John Barnett and Robert Lindley in the *Dict. Nat. Biog.*]   F. H. M.

ROGERS, EDWARD STANIFORD (June 28, 1826–Mar. 29, 1899), horticulturist, was born in the family homestead on Essex Street, in Salem, Mass., a descendant of Rev. John Rogers, who was president of Harvard College in 1682–84; his parents were Nathaniel Leverett Rogers, an old-time Salem merchant, and Harriet Wait, his wife. Edward was educated in Master Ira Cheever's school, made several sea voyages in his father's ships as clerk and super-cargo, and then entered the counting room of his father's firm, where he was employed until its dissolution. After his father's death in 1858, he continued to live in the family home with his brother and his mother. In the half-acre garden extending from the house on Essex Street to Federal Street he indulged his taste for horti-culture and conducted his experiments in grape hybridization. The garden was quite large for a city lot, although, according to the horticul-turist Marshall P. Wilder, it was "150 years old; a cold, matted soil, filled with old apple, and pear trees, currant bushes, flax, and everything mingled in together. It is in a close, hived up place in the city of Salem, and it is a wonder that he [Rogers] ever had a bunch of grapes to show" (*Proceedings of the Ninth Session of the American Pomological Society*, 1862, p. 148). The suggestion which incited his experi-ments in hybridizing came from an article by Dr. Lindley of the University of London, printed in the London *Horticulturist* and reprinted in Downing's *Horticulturist* for September 1847. This article, "Remarks on Hybridizing Plants," was a general discussion of the results of plant-breeding practices so far as they were then known. In the summer of 1851, Rogers crossed one of the native American grapes, *Vitis la-brusca*, by two representatives of *Vitis vinifera*, or European wine grape. The seeds obtained were sown, and from these came forty-five seed-lings which finally fruited. These, known as the Rogers Hybrids, were unique in that the stand-ard of quality was very high in each of them, and their weaknesses were also equally distrib-uted. Only one of them, Rogers' No. 15, which was named Agawam, is still in cultivation, but it remains one of the more popular home varie-ties of grapes. Rogers gained practically no profit from his grapes, since he gave them away freely, especially his better seedlings. His chief claim to remembrance lies not in the varieties which he produced but rather in the impetus his re-sults gave to grape growing in America; never before or since has grape growing in the United States received the attention given it during the decade following the introduction of the Rogers Hybrids.

By temperament, Edward Rogers was quiet and retiring. When he left the counting room, for fifteen years he withdrew almost wholly from the public eye and devoted himself to his garden. While he possessed some literary abil-ity and was an extensive reader, he could rarely be drawn into discussion except among those intimate friends who were wont to "drop in"

at his long, low greenhouse in the garden or at his office, extemporized in the old colonial barn at the rear of the house. After the death of their mother in 1882, the two brothers moved to an-other house in Salem, and some years later, after his brother died, Edward Rogers bought a place in Peabody, Mass., where he continued his grape-breeding experiments. None of his later seedlings ever showed promise equal to the original forty-five, however, and none was ever introduced. An accident which resulted in per-manent lameness kept him from much physical labor during his last years and probably in some measure hastened his death. He never married and was the last survivor of his family.

[G. B. Brackett, in L. H. Bailey, *The Standard Cyc. of Horticulture*, III (1915), 1593; U. P. Hedrick, *The Grapes of New York* (1908), containing a por-trait of Rogers as the frontispiece; obituary in *Salem Evening News*, Mar. 30, 1899, which contains several errors; *Boston Transcript*, Mar. 30, 1899; *Gardening and Am. Gardening*, both Apr. 15, 1899; *New-Eng. Hist. and Geneal. Reg.*, Jan. 1859; abundant refer-ences in the horticultural literature of the day.]
R. H. S—s.

ROGERS, HARRIET BURBANK (Apr. 12, 1834–Dec. 12, 1919), pioneer oral teacher of the deaf, was born in North Billerica, Mass., the daughter of Calvin and Ann (Faulkner) Rogers. An older sister was a teacher of Laura Bridgman [*q.v.*]. Harriet was educated in the public schools of Billerica and for six years in the academy at Westford, Mass., where she was associated with John D. Long, later governor. In November 1864 she consented to undertake the instruction of a little deaf child. The man-ual method—using finger spelling and signs— was at that time universally used in the schools for the deaf in the United States. She knew that in Germany deaf children were taught to speak and to read speech from the lips, but she knew nothing of the method employed. She obtained the consent of the parents of her pupil to at-tempt to teach the child to speak. Encouraged by her success with this pupil, in June 1866 she opened a small private school for deaf children in Chelmsford, with her first pupil as one of these. She and one assistant took the entire care of these children both in and out of school hours. At the end of a year the little school num-bered eight pupils.

On Oct. 1, 1867, she assumed the principal-ship of the new Clarke Institution for Deaf Mutes, now The Clarke School for the Deaf, which was to be opened in Northampton, Mass., being established by the endowment of John Clarke of that city. This was the first school for teaching deaf children under the oral method in the United States. Its establishment was obtained through the influence of Gardiner Green Hubbard [q.v.], whose own little daughter, later the wife of Alexander Graham Bell [q.v.], had been taught orally by a private teacher under her mother's direction. Schools for the deaf in the country violently opposed this new dream of "visionary enthusiasts," but from the first she quietly and unobtrusively carried on her work. Her teachers were inexperienced but eager to follow suggestions and try experiments. Soon after the school at Northampton was opened, Alexander Graham Bell was for some months a member of the staff of Clarke School. His marvelous knowledge of phonetics and his personal magnetism were a strong influence in the further development of the methods of the school. At this time Miss Rogers spent a year in Europe, mostly in Germany, studying the methods employed in teaching the deaf there, and returned to continue more enthusiastically the work she had so well begun. In 1884 failure of health obliged her to go to Colorado. In 1886 her resignation was accepted by the official board of the school. She later returned to North Billerica but was never able to resume the burden of teaching. She adapted herself to the situation and became active in supervising the village kindergarten and in various other concerns. The work she had begun has continued to broaden and strengthen. Today schools for the deaf throughout the country to an increasing extent employ the oral method she introduced, and the number of schools using this method exclusively steadily increases.

[Harriet B. Rogers, "Reminiscences of Early Days of Speech Teaching," in *Clarke School and Its Graduates* (1918); C. A. Yale, *Years of Building* (1931); A. G. Bell, *The Growth of Oral Method in America* (1917?); *Deaf-Mute Education in Mass., Report of the Joint Committee of the Legislature* (1867); *Institution for Deaf-Mutes, Annual Report,* 1868–84; personal acquaintance.]   C. A. Y.

ROGERS, HENRY DARWIN (Aug. 1, 1808–May 29, 1866), geologist, educator, third of the four sons of Patrick Kerr and Hannah (Blythe) Rogers, was born in Philadelphia. Of his three brothers, William [q.v.] also became a geologist and James and Robert [qq.v.], chemists. Henry received much of his early education from his father. After conducting a school in Windsor, Md., for a time, in company with his brother William, in 1828 he accepted a position as lecturer in chemistry in the Maryland Institute, Baltimore. Two years later he was appointed professor of chemistry and natural philosophy in Dickinson College, Carlisle, Pa. Becoming disgusted with the narrow bigotry of the trustees, he soon resigned, however, and for

a brief period was employed on a railway survey in New England. An interest in socialism led him in 1832 to accompany Robert Dale Owen [q.v.] to London, with no more definite plans than "to be useful." Fortunately, he soon became associated with friends who introduced him to the Geological Society of London, where he met De la Beche, Lyell, and others, and quickly became converted to a more strenuous calling.

Returning to the United States in 1833, he gave lectures on geology at the Franklin Institute in Philadelphia, and in 1835 was appointed to the chair of geology and mineralogy in the University of Pennsylvania. This same year he was also made director of the geological survey of New Jersey, and in 1836 he accepted a like position with the newly organized geological survey of Pennsylvania. The work of the New Jersey survey was practically finished in 1838, and the final report issued in 1840; that of Pennsylvania came to an untimely end in 1842 through lack of appropriations by the state legislature. Rogers was unwilling, however, to leave the work in its unfinished condition and continued it at his own expense until he was able in 1847 to present his final report, though through legislative indifference it was not printed until 1858. In the meantime, he moved to Boston, where the final revision was prepared, funds being supplied by legislative action in 1851–55. Finding that the work of publication could be carried out more satisfactorily by an Edinburgh firm than in the United States, he went to that city in 1855, and while there was appointed Regius Professor of Natural History in the University of Glasgow, a position he held until his death. This appointment marked the beginning of the Glasgow University school of geology, though as to his success as a teacher, expressed opinions are divided.

Of his geological work in New Jersey, little need be said, since but a brief time was devoted to it. The work of the Pennsylvania survey cannot be passed over so lightly, however, since it is upon this and what grew out of it that his fame as a geologist largely rests, as well as that of his brother William, with whom he worked in hearty cooperation. His report was beyond question the most important document on the geology of America that had appeared up to that time, with the possible exception of the final reports of the New York survey. In it the two brothers advanced noteworthy ideas, previously announced to the Association of American Geologists and Naturalists (see *Proceedings and Transactions, 1840–42,* 1843) regarding the structures of the Appalachian Mountains. These mountains, they showed, were not as had been commonly supposed, uplifted by an intrusion of molten material, but consisted of a series of parallel ridges characterized by predominant southeastern dips, and that they were true folds in the strata, in some cases so sharp and abrupt that the northwestern limb was bent back under the southwestern, or inverted. This view has been proved to be essentially correct. Their ideas as to the cause of the folding—that the flexures "are the result of an outward, billowy movement proceeding from beneath"—have not, however, stood the test of time, indeed were never generally accepted; nor were those they put forward on the subject of glaciation. An objection raised by Rogers to the use of geographical names for the geological systems led him to adopt a wholly fanciful and, as it proved, impractical, scheme in which he represented the Paleozoic time as a geological day and subdivided it according to successive stages, as *primal, auroral, matinal, levant,* and so forth.

Rogers' health, never of the best, began failing soon after he went to Edinburgh, causing him to spend much time in the south of England and on the Riviera. In the fall of 1865, he returned to America, but in April 1866 went back to his University work at Glasgow, only to be taken seriously ill and die on May 29 following. He is described as dignified, quiet, and unassuming, even shy, but admired by all who knew him intimately. As a lecturer, he displayed varied knowledge and no little skill and grace of expression. In March 1854 he was married in Boston to Eliza S. Lincoln, a half-sister of the wife of his brother William; they had one child, a daughter.

[*Life and Letters of William Barton Rogers* (2 vols., 1896), ed. by his wife; J. W. Gregory, *Henry Darwin Rogers: An Address to the Glasgow Univ. Geological Soc.* (1916), with bibliography; G. P. Merrill, *Contributions to a Hist. of Am. State Geological and Natural Hist. Surveys* (1920) and *The First One Hundred Years of Am. Geology* (1924); M. L. Ames, *Life and Letters of Peter and Susan Lesley* (1909), II, 511; *Proc. Am. Acad. Arts and Sci.,* vol. VII (1868); William Sabine, in *Proc. Royal Soc. of London,* vol. XVI (1868); *Am. Jour. Sci.,* July 1866; *Popular Sci. Mo.,* Dec. 1896.]
G. P. M.

ROGERS, HENRY HUTTLESTON (Jan. 29, 1840–May 19, 1909), capitalist, was the son of Rowland and Mary Eldridge (Huttleston) Rogers, both of early New England ancestry. His middle name is often given as Huddleston, which appears to have been the earlier form in the family; to this spelling his son and namesake returned. He was born at Mattapoisett, Mass., but was brought up at Fairhaven, near by, where in boyhood he carried newspapers and delivered

groceries. He later served for a time as a railroad brakeman and baggageman. He was twenty-one when the newly discovered oil fields in Pennsylvania drew fortune seekers to that region. Rogers and a friend, Charles P. Ellis, went together to the Oil City district, each having about $600 in savings. They presently built a small refinery at a cost of $1,800, borrowing the additional funds necessary. On a visit to his home town in 1862, Rogers was married to Abbie Palmer Gifford. In Pennsylvania he met several men destined to become leaders in the oil industry, among them Charles Pratt [*q.v.*], who in 1866 asked Rogers to become associated with him in his refinery business in Brooklyn. There Rogers devised the machinery by which naphtha was first successfully separated from the crude oil—an epochal invention for the industry (*Current Literature,* July 1909). A patent (No. 120,539) was granted on Oct. 31, 1871.

When the Rockefellers organized the Standard Oil Company in 1874, they took over the Pratt business and with it Rogers, now recognized as both an expert oil man and an able executive with a genius for organization. He was made chairman of the manufacturing committee of the new corporation, a little later a trustee, and before 1890 he was vice-president. He conceived the idea of long pipe lines for transporting oil, and organized the National Transit Company, the first corporation with such an object. This was his favorite promotion, and he remained president of the company long after the actual technical management of the oil business itself had been given over by him to others so that he and William Rockefeller [*q.v.*] might devote their time to the operation of the huge financial machine known to Wall Street as "Standard Oil." Either personally or in behalf of this trust, Rogers was interested in several businesses other than oil—gas, copper, steel, banking, and railroads. In 1884 with associates he formed the Consolidated Gas Company, and thereafter for several years he was instrumental in gaining control of great city plants, fighting terrific battles with rivals for some of them, as in the case of Boston. Almost the whole story of his gas interests was one of warfare, as was his connection with copper. During the '90's, when he was virtually the directing head of Standard Oil, he became interested in Anaconda and other copper properties. In 1899 he formed the first $75,000,000 section of the gigantic trust, Amalgamated Copper, which was the subject of such acrid criticism then and for years afterward. In the building of this great trust, some of the most ruthless strokes in modern business history were dealt—the $38,000,000 "watering" of the stock of the first corporation, its subsequent manipulation, the seizure of the copper property of the Butte & Boston Consolidated Mining Company, the using it as a weapon against the Boston & Montana Consolidated Copper and Silver Mining Company, the guerrilla warfare against certain private interests, the wrecking of the Globe Bank of Boston. Standard Oil's interest in steel properties led to Rogers' becoming one of the directors of the United States Steel Corporation when it was organized in 1901. He was long the transportation magnate of Staten Island, being the principal owner of its railroads, traction lines, and ferries. He was a director of the Santa Fé, St. Paul, Lackawanna, Union Pacific, and several other railroads. He was a close associate of E. H. Harriman [q.v.] in the latter's extensive railroad operations, and when Harriman became interested in the insurance business, Rogers, who had long been a trustee of the Mutual Life, was drawn with him into the scandal and governmental investigation of 1905, but as usual emerged almost unruffled. He sustained his worst tactical defeat, however, in an ouster suit brought by the State of Missouri in 1905, in which he, at first defiant, was forced to testify and admit the Standard's secret ownership of certain subsidiary oil companies (218 *Missouri Reports,* 1; 116 *Southwestern Reporter,* 902; see also 224 *United States,* 270). His last great individual enterprise was the building of the remarkable, low-grade Virginian Railway from the West Virginia coal fields to Norfolk. It was an achievement unique in business annals for one man to build a $40,000,000 railroad on his own resources and credit, and that, too, partly in a time of financial stress, the panic of 1907. But the strain of doing it proved fatal to him. He was at his desk on May 18, 1909, but the next morning, in New York City, suddenly died of an apoplectic stroke. His first wife had died May 21, 1894, leaving four children. He afterward married Emelle (or Emelie) Augusta Randel, the divorced wife of Lucius Hart, who, together with a son and three daughters, survived him.

Rogers was a tall, handsome man of distinguished presence and a curious duality of nature. In business he was known as a man of cold steel; away from business he was democratic, a faithful friend, a wit and raconteur. Even the bitterest of his enemies testified to the almost hypnotic charm of his presence when he chose to exercise it. To the end of his life some of the humblest of the citizens of his boyhood home remained his

intimate friends and called him "Hen." His summer home was there, and there at week-ends he found his happiest relaxation. He paved Fairhaven's streets, he gave it a town hall, grammar and high school buildings, a handsome public library, a Masonic lodge building, a costly Unitarian church and parsonage. There he founded the Atlas Tack Company, the largest concern of its kind in America. His fondness for Mark Twain's writings led to an acquaintance with the humorist, and finding the latter in difficulties because of the failure of his publishers, Rogers practically took charge of his affairs and remained his business manager and counselor until death.

[*Who's Who in America,* 1908–09; obituaries in all New York evening and morning papers, May 19, 20, 1909; N. Y. *World,* Mar. 12, Sept. 5, 1907; all New York newspapers of Jan. 6–8, 1906, when the Missouri suit against Standard Oil was being tried; *Harper's Weekly,* May 29, 1909; *Nation* (N. Y.), May 27, 1909; *Current Literature,* July 1909; *World's Work,* May 1905; Thomas W. Lawson, *Frenzied Finance* (1905), the most violent of all the criticisms of Rogers; Ida M. Tarbell, *The Hist. of the Standard Oil Company* (2 vols., 1904); R. I. Warshow, *The Story of Wall Street* (1929); *Dedication of the Memorial Monument to Henry Huttleston Rogers, Jan. 29, 1912. Town Hall, Fairhaven, Mass.* (n.d.); George Huddleston, comp., *Huddleston Family Tables* (1933); information in regard to the spelling of his middle name from his son, Col. Henry H. Rogers.]   A. F. H.

ROGERS, HENRY J. (Mar. 10, 1811–Aug. 20, 1879), a pioneer in the development of telegraphic communication and an inventor, was born in Baltimore, Md., the son of Col. John H. Rogers. He was educated in St. Mary's College, Baltimore, and immediately applied himself to the art of telegraphy and signaling, which from his early youth had appealed to him strongly. He was engaged in developing a system of marine signals with flags when he was attracted to the work of Samuel F. B. Morse [q.v.] and his electro-magnetic telegraph. As a result, about 1843, he obtained employment with Morse in the construction of the demonstration telegraph line between Baltimore and Washington, sponsored by the federal government, and when this line was opened for public business under the direction of the Post Office Department, he was appointed telegraph operator at Baltimore. When the government refused to buy Morse's invention at his stipulated price of $100,000 and the privately owned Magnetic Telegraph Company was organized, May 15, 1845, Rogers was a subscriber to the new company and one of the incorporators. In 1848 he joined the North American Telegraph Company, which used the telegraph invented by Alexander Bain. Its line extended from New York to Washington but the system failed to work properly until Rogers introduced certain modifications. He continued with the company as superintendent until 1852 when, as a result of the successful infringement suit brought by the Morse interests, it was absorbed by the Morse company. Rogers then became superintendent of the House Printing Telegraph Company, organized about 1852, and operating between New York and Washington. In 1855 he severed his connections with it, in order to devote his time to perfecting his marine signaling system, which he had patented on Sept. 27, 1844. He succeeded in having the system adopted by the United States Navy, but failed, after making two trips to Europe, to secure its adoption by any foreign power.

At the outbreak of the Civil War, he was called to Washington and rendered important service in the establishment of field telegraph lines, particularly for the Army of the Potomac. He served also as secretary of the Potomac flotilla and as a navigation officer at the Washington Navy Yard. While in Washington, May 17, 1864, he patented his semaphore telegraph system. At the close of the war he became superintendent of the Bankers' and Brokers' Telegraph Line between New York and Washington, but eighteen months later relinquished this position in order to accept a similar one with the Southern and Atlantic Telegraph Line. He continued in this capacity, with headquarters in New York, until 1873, when he retired to his home in Baltimore. There he engaged in writing a history of the telegraph, but his death prevented the completion of the work. In addition to his two signaling systems, he devised a code of flare signals for use at night and a system of insulation for telegraph lines patented on Dec. 3, 1872. He was married to a Miss McGlennan of Baltimore, and at the time of his death in that city was survived by his widow and four sons.

[J. D. Reid, *The Telegraph in America*, 1879; *Shaffner's Telegraph Companion*, Jan. 1855; S. I. Prime, *The Life of Samuel F. B. Morse, LL.D.* (1875); E. L. Morse, ed., *Samuel F. B. Morse: His Letters and Jours.* (1914); *Baltimore American and Commercial Advertiser* and *Sun* (Baltimore), Aug. 21, 1879; Patent Office records.]   C. W. M.

ROGERS, HENRY WADE (Oct. 10, 1853–Aug. 16, 1926), educator and jurist, was born in Holland Patent, N. Y. He was adopted at an early age by an uncle for whom he was named, Henry W. Rogers of Buffalo, N. Y., later of Ann Arbor, Mich. From the University of Michigan Rogers received the degrees of B.A. in 1874 and M.A. in 1877. Admitted to the bar in the latter year, he practised law for a short time in Minnesota and then in New Jersey. In 1882 he became Tappan Professor of Law at the University of Michigan and in 1886, dean of its law department. His administration was vigorous and successful, and at the time of his retirement this law school was the largest in point of numbers in the United States. His administrative skill so impressed the trustees of Northwestern University, Evanston, Ill., that he was chosen president of that institution in 1890.

At Northwestern, Rogers united a loosely joined federation of schools under separate boards of trustees into an organized whole. He urged the creation of a scientific department and effected the introduction of courses in political science and government. He secured funds for the erection of needed new buildings, including the Orrington Lunt Library. During his administration, the net resources of the University increased more than a hundred per cent., and the enrollment of students was nearly doubled. At times he was forced to work against some opposition, to which he was sensitive, but he surmounted all obstacles and left the University upon a sound basis.

In 1900, feeling that he had accomplished what he could for the institution, he tendered his resignation and immediately went to the Yale School of Law as a lecturer. Here he served until 1921: from 1901 to 1921 as a professor, and from 1903 to 1916 as dean. He continued to teach for eight years after his appointment in 1913 as judge of the federal circuit court of appeals sitting in New York City. His judicial career was terminated only by his death, although he was then planning to retire from the bench to become the first research professor in the newly created Institute of Research in Law at the University of Michigan.

Several commentators upon his career have expressed the view that Rogers' greatest work was done as dean of the Yale School of Law. His administration was marked by the adoption of the case method of legal instruction, and the college-degree requirement for admission, and by the restriction of the faculty to full-time teachers. These steps, initially advocated by the younger group of his faculty, were whole-heartedly and skilfully supported by Rogers so that they were ultimately accepted without friction by a group of older faculty members at first strongly opposed to the changes. Among these men was Simeon Eben Baldwin [*q.v.*], who for more than fifty years had been the guiding force of the faculty. Rogers later nominated Baldwin for the governorship of Connecticut (1910) and for the presidency (1912), and Baldwin recommended Rogers to President Wilson for appointment to the federal bench. To successive groups of Yale men Rogers was a striking, even a portentous, figure, because his classroom methods reduced the most strong-minded of his students to a state somewhat akin to panic. Except as he occasionally employed a touch of sarcasm, his manner was all mildness and his personal contacts were most friendly, yet his skilful, merciless, and persistent cross-examination caused his students to work harder for him, probably, than for any other instructor. When he was appointed judge he had had little legal and no judicial experience, but he at once showed himself a competent, though possibly not great or original, jurist. His written opinions evinced much labor and learning. Besides the law, his chief interests were the Democratic party and the Methodist Episcopal Church. He acted as delegate and chairman at various Democratic conventions, he was president of the Association of American Law Schools in 1906, chairman of the American Bar Association's committee (later council) on legal education and admission to the bar from 1906 to 1920, member of the National Conference of Commissioners on Uniform State Laws in 1910, and chairman of the World's Congress on Jurisprudence and Law Reform of the Chicago exposition of 1893. He was president of the General Laymen's Association of the Methodist Episcopal Church after 1920, chairman of the judiciary committee in the General Conferences from 1908 to 1920, member of the committee on Organic Union of the Methodist Episcopal Church with the Methodist Episcopal Church South from 1916 to 1920, chairman of the committee on international relations of the Federal Council of Churches, 1908, and trustee of the Church Peace Union of the Carnegie Foundation after 1913. He was the author of several legal treatises, including *Illinois Citations* (1881) and *The Law of Expert Testimony* (1883, 1891); associate editor of *Johnson's Universal Cyclopædia* (8 vols., 1893–97); contributor to the tenth edition of the *Encyclopædia Britannica* (1902), to the *American Supplement* (1897); and author of the article on *Injunctions* in the *Cyclopedia of Law and Procedure* (vol. XXII, 1906); as well as author of many articles in popular magazines and law reviews.

Rogers was married on June 22, 1876, to Emma Ferdon Winner of Pennington, N. J., who survived him. He died at his summer home at Pennington, near Trenton, in his seventy-third year.

[B. A. Hinsdale, *Hist. of the Univ. of Mich.* (1906); A. H. Wilde, *Northwestern Univ., A Hist.* (1905), vol. I; *Yale Shingle* (Law School Annual), 1903–11; *Reports to the President of Yale Univ.*, 1926–27; *New Haven Journal-Courier* and *N. Y. Times*, Aug. 17,
1926; *In Memory of Henry Wade Rogers,* memorial booklet, privately printed, containing the funeral address of Aug. 19, 1926, addresses at a memorial service of Nov. 21, 1926, a sketch, and tributes; *N. Y. Law Journal*, Mar. 23, 1928; *Who's Who in America*, 1925–26; *Asso. of the Bar of the City of N. Y., Year Book*, 1927.]   C. E. C.

ROGERS, ISAIAH (Aug. 17, 1800–Apr. 13, 1869), architect, was born in Marshfield, Mass., the son of Isaac and Hannah (Ford) Rogers. His father, a shipbuilder, was descended from John Rogers, an early settler of Marshfield. Isaiah was educated in the local schools. His family wished him to be a farmer, but at the age of sixteen, much against their will, he left for Boston, where he apprenticed himself to a carpenter named Shaw. When his apprenticeship was over, he went South and spent the years 1820 and 1821 in Mobile, Ala. While there he won a competition for the first Mobile Theatre, a barn-like, undistinguished building, finished in 1824. In 1822 he returned to Boston and entered the office of Solomon Willard [*q.v.*], the eminent architect, sculptor, and master mason. Willard later supplied granite for many of Rogers' buildings; in 1842 they took a five-year lease together on one of the Quincy quarries; and as a mark of his affection for the older man Rogers named his son after him.

Rogers' name first occurs in the Boston directory in 1826, and it was probably about this time that he started his own architectural practice. His first large commission was the Tremont Hotel in Boston, the first example of the luxurious, elaborately planned American hotel with extensive plumbing. Its corner stone was laid July 4, 1828, and it was opened in 1829. Probably as a result of his success in this building, Rogers was chosen architect of the new Astor House in New York, where he lived from 1834 to 1842. The Astor House was somewhat similar in general style to the Tremont, but, much larger, it carried luxury and complicated mechanical equipment to a still higher level. Its corner stone was laid July 4, 1834, and it was opened in 1836. His other New York work included the Bank of America (Wall and William Streets), 1835, the façade of which was later reconstructed as the entrance to Pine Lodge Park, Methuen, Mass.; the very similar Merchants' Bank; the Lafayette Place Reformed Dutch Church, 1836; the Astor Place Opera House, later altered into the Mercantile Library and called Clinton Hall, 1847; and especially the Merchants' Exchange, 1836–42. This lavish building, which was unprecedented at that time, in that it cost over a million dollars, had a great interior rotunda and a magnificent Ionic colonnade which Philip Hone called "worthy . . . of Palladio or Michelangelo" (diary note of July 12, 1842, *The Diary of Philip Hone*, 1927, edited by Allan Nevins, II, 611). It has since been incorporated in the present National City Bank. At about the same time Rogers designed the graceful and original Boston Merchants' Exchange.

Rogers was the father of the modern hotel. It was in his work that the combination of lavish public rooms, numerous bedrooms (some in suites), and elaborate mechanical equipment was first made. The list of his hotels includes the Bangor House, Bangor, Me.; the Exchange Hotel, Richmond, Va., 1841, an exquisite design; the Battle House, Mobile; the Charleston Hotel, Charleston, S. C., with its superb Corinthian frontispiece; the magnificent second St. Charles Hotel at New Orleans, *c.* 1851; the second Galt House, Louisville, Ky., *c.* 1865; the enormous Maxwell House, Nashville, Tenn., begun in 1859, during the Civil War used for barracks, and not finally opened till 1869; and the famous Burnet House in Cincinnati, opened in 1850, which the *Illustrated London News* called the best hotel in the world (Williamson, *post*, p. 100).

It was probably to superintend the building of the Burnet House that Rogers moved to Cincinnati, where he lived thereafter. In that city he designed, among other work, St. John's Protestant Episcopal Church, a Romanesque building; the Longview Insane Asylum, with an interesting plan; and considerable alterations to the Ohio State Capitol. In 1855 he designed the Egyptian Judah Touro memorial gate to the Jewish cemetery in Newport, R. I. He was associated at various times with Henry Whitestone, with his son Solomon Willard Rogers, and with A. B. Mullett. He was something of an inventor, and between 1841 and 1863 patented three improvements in iron bridge design and a burglar-proof safe. From 1862 to 1865 (and nominally till 1868, the dates are confused and contradictory) he was supervising architect of the Treasury Department in Washington, being the first formal incumbent of this position. During his administration little important work was done, because of the Civil War, but he completed the west side of the Treasury Building, following the original design of Robert Mills [*q.v.*].

Once the ideas of the Greek Revival are accepted, Rogers can be appreciated as one of the greatest of the designers of his time. The austerity of the Tremont and Astor House exteriors, the recessed vestibule and superb rotunda of the New York Merchants' Exchange, the interest-

ing diagonal towers of St. John's Church, Cincinnati, all show an imaginative mind, an appreciation of true classic dignity, and a thoroughly trained taste. Unlike many of his contemporaries, he succeeded in keeping his classicism alive during his later life, refusing to accept the ugliness of contemporary fashion.

Rogers was married at twenty-three to Emily W. Tobey, of Portland, Me.; they had at least two children. Rogers was for years subject to acute heart attacks, and died as the result of one at the age of sixty-eight.

[A photograph of Rogers and many illustrations of his work appear in Montgomery Schuyler, "The Old 'Greek Revival,'" pt. 4, in the *Am. Architect*, May 3, 1911; later research has rendered doubtful some of the attributions in this otherwise valuable article. See also W. H. Eliot, *A Description of Tremont House, with Architectural Illustrations* (1830); *Ann. Reports of the Commissioner of Patents*, 1841, 1856, 1865; W. W. Wheildon, *Memoir of Solomon Willard* (1865); *The Biog. Encyc. of Ohio* (1876); J. H. Drummond, *John Rogers of Marshfield and Some of His Descendants* (1898); I. N. P. Stokes, *The Iconography of Manhattan Island* (6 vols., 1915–26); Jefferson Williamson, *The Am. Hotel, an Anecdotal Hist.* (1930); J. M. Howells, *Lost Examples of Colonial Architecture* (1931); R. H. Thayer, *Hist., Organization and Functions of the Office of Supervising Architect of the Treasury Dept.* (1886); Darrell H. Smith, *The Office of the Supervising Architect of the Treasury* (1923); *Cincinnati Daily Gazette*, Apr. 15, 1869.]   T. F. H.

ROGERS, JAMES BLYTHE (Feb. 11, 1802–June 15, 1852), chemist, educator, was born in Philadelphia, the son of Patrick Kerr and Hannah (Blythe) Rogers. The father was himself a physician, chemist, and teacher of note. Born in Ireland in 1776, he was employed in a counting-house in Dublin when the Irish rebellion of 1798 broke out, and, having written newspaper articles inimical to the government, he found it advisable to emigrate to the United States. He settled in Philadelphia; married in 1801 Hannah, daughter of James Blythe, a native of Glasgow and a Londonderry publisher; received the degree of M.D. from the University of Pennsylvania in 1802; practised in Philadelphia and Baltimore; and in 1819 succeeded Dr. Robert Hare [*q.v.*] as professor of natural philosophy and chemistry at the College of William and Mary, which position he held until his death in 1828.

James was the eldest of four brothers, the others being William Barton, Henry Darwin, and Robert Empie [*qq.v.*], all of whom became distinguished scientists. Their tastes were similar, they worked much together, and formed, it has been said, a "family group scarcely to be excelled for native powers and acquirements, in the history of science, in this or any age or country" (F. A. Walker, in *National Academy of Sciences, Biographical Memoirs*, vol. III, 1895, p.

3). James received his early education from his father and in the Baltimore schools, studied at the College of William and Mary (1820–21), and in 1822 received the degree of M.D. from the University of Maryland. After several years' experience, he found the practice of medicine distasteful. From boyhood he had been keenly interested in chemistry and had become proficient in delicate and complicated analysis. Accordingly, when the Baltimore firm of Tyson & Ellicott offered him the superintendency of its chemical works in 1827, he accepted the position. While engaged in his duties there he was appointed professor of chemistry in Washington Medical College, Baltimore. About 1829 he and his brother Henry became lecturers at the Maryland Institute, where until recently William Rogers had also served. During the latter part of his stay in Baltimore, he made investigations, with George W. Andrews and William R. Fisher, which resulted in an interesting contribution to forensic chemistry—"Minutes of an Analysis of Soup Containing Arsenic," published in the *Journal of the Philadelphia College of Pharmacy* (July 1834). He also carried on experiments with James Green, an instrument maker, which likewise produced valuable results, recorded in "Experiments with the Elementary Voltaic Battery" (*American Journal of Science and Arts,* April 1835). In 1835 he was called to the professorship of chemistry in the medical department of Cincinnati College. He had married in 1830 Rachel Smith of Harford County, Md.

Rogers remained in Cincinnati until 1839, declining in the meantime the position of melter and refiner in the branch mint at New Orleans. In 1837 he became associated with his brother William in the work of the Virginia Survey. In 1840 he took up his residence in Philadelphia and assisted his brother Henry, who was directing the Pennsylvania geological survey. He succeeded John K. Mitchell in 1841 as professor of chemistry in the Medical Institute of Philadelphia, and in 1844 was elected to a similar position in the Franklin Institute. He was made a member of the American Philosophical Society in 1846, and the following year succeeded Robert Hare, whom his father had succeeded at William and Mary twenty-eight years before, as professor of chemistry in the University of Pennsylvania.

With Robert Empie Rogers he published in 1846 *A Text Book on Chemistry,* and also an important article, "On the Alleged Insolubility of Copper in Hydrochloric Acid . . ." (*American Journal of Science and Arts,* November 1848). Much of his work was so bound up with that of his brothers that it is impossible to designate and

evaluate it. As a clear and interesting lecturer on scientific subjects he had few superiors in his day. Always of delicate constitution, he died of albuminuria in his fifty-first year, survived by his wife, two sons, and a daughter. His brother Robert succeeded him as professor of chemistry at the University of Pennsylvania.

[Joseph Carson, *A Memoir of the Life and Character of James B. Rogers, M.D.* (1852), and *A Hist. of the Medic. Department of the Univ. of Pa.* (1869); E. F. Smith, *James Blythe Rogers* (1927); W. S. W. Ruschenberger, "A Sketch of the Life of Robert E. Rogers, M.D., LL.D., with Biog. Notices of His Father and Brothers" in *Proc. Am. Philosophical Soc.,* vol. XXIII, 1886; *Life and Letters of William Barton Rogers* (2 vols., 1896), ed. by his wife; H. A. Kelly and W. L. Burrage, *Am. Medic. Biogs.* (1920).]   H. E. S.

ROGERS, JAMES HARRIS (July 13, 1856–Dec. 12, 1929), inventor, the son of James Webb and Cornelia (Harris) Rogers, was born in Franklin, Tenn. His father was a clergyman and chaplain during the Civil War on the staff of Gen. Leonidas Polk [*q.v.*]. James's earliest education was received from private tutors. In 1866 his father, having given up the ministry, took the family to Europe, and for a year young Rogers studied in St. Charles College, London. From his earliest boyhood he was intensely interested in the science of electricity and through study and experimentation soon acquired a knowledge of the subject remarkable for one so young.

Beginning his research work while living in France in 1867, he continued it in New York, where the family took up residence in 1868, and later in Peekskill, N. Y. Here, in cooperation with an older brother, he perfected a system of printing telegraph patented Aug. 20, 1872. Rogers continued his experimental work in New York for the succeeding five years, devising a number of interesting improvements in multiplex telegraphy. In 1877, when twenty-one years old, he went to Washington, D. C., where, upon the recommendation of Joseph Henry [*q.v.*], secretary of the Smithsonian Institution, he was appointed chief electrician of the United States Capitol. He carried on this work for the next six years, at the same time pursuing his electrical researches, one of the most interesting results of which was the invention of a system of secret telephony, for which Rogers received United States patents granted Dec. 20, 1881 (No. 251,292) and Jan. 10, 1882 (No. 252,257). Upon resigning his position at the Capitol in 1882, he devoted his full time to research in Washington, eventually, 1895, establishing a laboratory at Hyattsville, Md., where he lived until his death. In the course of these years he was granted some fifty patents for inventions relating to telephony, telegraphy, electric lighting, high frequency currents, and the transmitting of sounds through metal pipes. Probably the most interesting and valuable of these inventions was his system of printing telegraphy, for which he was granted patents between 1887 and 1894, and his underground and subsea radio transmission system, for which he received patents between 1917 and 1921. His printing telegraph system was in many respects a forerunner of the modern method in that a key operator was eliminated and messages were written on a typewriter. By the use of the principle of visual synchronism messages were transmitted at what was then phenomenal speed—approximately two hundred words a minute. About 1908 Rogers turned his attention to wireless telegraphy and to the possibility of transmission through the earth and sea. After undertaking a bit of experimental work at that time, he turned to other things until 1916, when he resumed his investigations and made such progress that with his underground antenna he could pick up messages from across the ocean. Although his discoveries had not yet been patented, in 1917 he offered them to the government. His offer was accepted and patents were issued to him later. Thereafter, until his death, he continued his researches in this same field, considerably interrupted, however, by litigation instituted to defend his patent rights. Among other recognitions of his work, he was awarded the Inventor's Medal of the Maryland Academy of Sciences. He never married.

[*Who's Who in America*, 1926–27; *Electrical Engineer*, Feb. 13, 1895, p. 149; *Scientific American*, Dec. 28, 1889; *Evening Star* (Washington), Dec. 12, 1929; *Washington Post*, Dec. 13, 1929; *Sun* (Baltimore), Dec. 13, 1929; information from relatives; Patent Office records.]

C. W. M.

ROGERS, JOHN (Dec. 1, 1648–Oct. 17, 1721), founder of the Rogerenes, was born in Milford, Conn., the son of Elizabeth (Rowland) and James Rogers who emigrated probably from England, settled at New London, Conn., about 1660, and became one of the richest merchants and landowners in Connecticut. The son was converted by the Seventh-Day Baptists of Newport, R. I., in 1674; he converted his father and brothers to the same creed, and elders from Rhode Island baptized them and admitted them into the Newport church. Having started to study the Bible independently, he gradually developed novel opinions, in which the Rhode Island Baptists could not follow him. Though still accepting the Calvinist doctrine of a new birth, he opposed salaried clergy, the use of meeting houses, formal prayers, and all connection between church and state. He freed his slaves and advocated non-resistance; and he refused to use medicine, believing that diseases should be cured by prayer and anointing with oil. He afterward abandoned the Seventh-Day Sabbath, holding religious services on Sunday but declaring labor on that day to be lawful. Rogerene services were held on the family farm at Great Neck in New London. He toured New England to propagate his doctrines but made few converts outside his own family. He wrote thirteen pamphlets in defense of his opinions, of which *The Book of the Revelation of Jesus Christ* (1720) is perhaps the most important. They are filled with involved theological arguments and do not show any great eloquence or learning. His methods of asserting his opinions were often lacking in tact and good taste; but the courage and firmness with which he endured half a century of persecution cannot be praised too highly. If his character had not been consistently blackened by orthodox historians, he would be remembered as a pioneer of religious freedom.

The state and ecclesiastical authorities, notably Gurdon Saltonstall [*q.v.*], were bitterly hostile to the new sect. The Rogerenes were repeatedly fined for non-attendance at meeting, laboring on the Sabbath, refusing payment of the minister's rates, non-attendance at military training, and entertaining Quakers. Rogers was imprisoned seven times, his various sentences totaling fifteen years; he was whipped twice, on the second occasion receiving seventy-six stripes on a charge of blasphemy. The Rogerenes retaliated by marching into the meeting house in New London during service and making public protests. They seem to have had the sympathy of their neighbors; Rogers was elected to various official positions in the town, juries acquitted him whenever possible, and the government had difficulty in finding officers who would enforce payment of fines. In 1670 he had married Elizabeth, the daughter of Matthew Griswold of Lyme. While under religious conviction he told her of some sexual misdemeanor he had committed before marriage. After his conversion she returned with their two children to her own family, who in 1676 persuaded the General Court to give her a divorce, alleging as sufficient reason what Rogers had confessed to her and accusing him of the most revolting vices. In 1699 Rogers took as a second wife a maid-servant, Mary Ransford, refusing to have any legal ceremony performed. The marriage was unhappy, and there were lawsuits between Mary Ransford and the Rogers family. In 1703 the county court imprisoned her for having a child without being legally married; she was rescued and sent to Block Island, where in 1710 with Rogers' approval she married Robert Jones. In 1714, after unsuccessful attempts to recover his divorced wife Elizabeth, Rogers married Mrs. Sarah Cole, a Quaker widow of Oyster Bay. In 1721 he caught smallpox in Boston and died after his return to New London. He was succeeded as leader of the Rogerenes by John Rogers, Jr., his son by Elizabeth (Griswold) Rogers, who had been brought up by his mother but had at the age of fourteen voluntarily returned to his father. The sect became extinct during the nineteenth century.

[See J. R. Bolles and A. B. Williams, *The Rogerenes* (1904); J. S. Rogers, *James Rogers of New London, Ct., and His Descendants* (1902); F. M. Caulkins, *History of New London* (1852); for the slanders on Rogers' moral character see a letter from William Leete to John Winthrop, Jr., *Mass. Hist. Soc. Colls.*, 4 Ser., Vol. VII (1865), p. 582; these slanders were repeated by most of the older historians of New England.]

H. B. P.

ROGERS, JOHN (Oct. 30, 1829–July 26, 1904), sculptor, was born at Salem, Mass., the son of John Rogers and the grandson of Daniel Denison Rogers, both merchants of Boston. He was descended from the Rev. Nathaniel Rogers who settled at Ipswich, Mass., in 1636, through the latter's son John, who was president of Harvard College in 1682–84. His mother, Sarah Ellen Derby, was the daughter of John Derby, a Salem merchant. His early education was obtained in the Boston public schools and was followed by a period as clerk in a local dry-goods store. After trouble with his eyes had put an end to the study of engineering, he spent some eight years in the occupation of machinist. Part of this time he lived in Manchester, N. H., where his statue of Lincoln was later erected, and part, after a trip to Spain in the search of health, in the Middle West. Eventually he had charge of a railroad repair shop in Hannibal, Mo. From the time he had seen a Boston craftsman moulding clay, he had spent many leisure hours with that pliant medium, and had exhibited at various New Hampshire fairs. Toward the end of 1858 he even went to Europe for a visit to Paris and a few months' training in the Roman studio of the English sculptor, Spence. Finding himself without an interest in the neo-classicism of that environment, however, he returned to America. He had learned little, perhaps, except the way to reproduce clay groups in plaster form, and he determined to continue in his original calling. He was in the city surveyor's office in Chicago when opportunity arrived with unmistakable steps. For a local charity fair in the interest of

the United States Sanitary Commission, he exhibited "Checkers up at the Farm." The interest aroused was so great that he went to New York at the end of 1859 with the "Slave Auction." Although it was a sensational success in the stormy days of *Uncle Tom's Cabin* and Abolition oratory, Rogers yet had to have it peddled from door to door, so hesitant were the art dealers of the city to risk antagonizing their Southern patrons. For several years his situation in New York was financially precarious, but before the war had ended he was prospering.

From the Paris Exposition of 1867, where several bronze figures were shown, and the Centennial Exhibition at Philadelphia in 1876, where he had twenty-nine groups on view, to the World's Fair at Chicago, in 1893, marked by his seated Lincoln, and the award of a gold medal, Rogers was the recipient of critical as well as popular acclaim. He was a member of the National Academy after 1863, and of the National Sculpture Society. The "Rogers groups" may be conveniently divided into three classes. There are the Civil War groups, historically important, and containing some of Rogers' best portraits—the Lincoln in the "Council of War" is said by the Lincoln family to be the best likeness ever made. Then there are the literary and dramatic groups, marked by the spacing of a theatrical performance, and including the series for which Joseph Jefferson posed in his character of Rip Van Winkle, and the miniature scenes from Shakespeare. Perhaps a certain naïve tenderness is the chief charm of these fragile compositions. Then there are the *genre* groups, which include many of his most popular works. He perhaps never surpassed the "Checkers up at the Farm," but the "Charity Patient," with the drapery suggestive of a Tanagra figurine, the "Coming to the Parson," with the cat and dog motif poking gentle fun at the absorbed young lovers, and "Fetching the Doctor," where something of the movement and mass of monumental sculpture is caught, reveal the facility of this folk-artist. Occasional groups or figures were cast in bronze. There are also the equestrian statue of General Reynolds, at the City Hall, Philadelphia, and the seated Lincoln at Manchester to show his skill in work of heroic size. The horse of the former monument is especially notable. But it is not by forcing Rogers into competition with craftsmen of other types that one can best appreciate his work. His was not a monumental style. Nor was it primarily a style of exquisite grace, as the miniature proportions he preferred might lead one to suppose. It was rather the direct embodiment of what he saw, and knew, and thought about his environment. Such abstract elements of plastic beauty as occur are incidental.

Rogers married in 1865 Harriet Moore Francis, of New York City, the daughter of Charles Stephen Francis [q.v.]. They had five sons and two daughters. By 1877 he had established a home in New Canaan, Conn., where he spent his time when he was absent from his New York studio, long at 14 West Twelfth Street. After 1893 a nervous affection in his hands forced him to give up his work as sculptor. He died in New Canaan, July 26, 1904, and was buried in the Lakeview Cemetery. He has been described as a person of very gentle, but determined character, about whom friends of equal simplicity and sincerity liked to gather. His theory of plastic art seems to have been that the telling of a story should be the first consideration in creative work, emotion, whether pathos or humor, being a natural accompaniment. Opposing as he did the belief then current that the nude was the basis of plastic beauty, he held that it had no place in the art of a time in which the nude body was not habitually seen. The total number of his groups is uncertain. One writer gives eighty-seven as a fair estimate, though as yet no complete series has been collected. With the "gelatine mould" and bronze "master cast" as means of reproducing groups accurately and cheaply, the sculptor was able to sell over 100,000 copies during his lifetime. The prices asked in a catalogue published in 1876 vary from five to fifty dollars. The majority of the groups were made of red plaster around a metal frame; they were then dipped in gray paint, and averaged upward to twenty inches high. For the repair of the groups when the surface paint cracked, bottles of "refinishing color" were sold by the master craftsman. He patented the designs, sold pedestals and garden urns as accessories, and freely advertised his products.

In the galleries of the New York Historical Society and of the Essex Institute, Salem, the largest collections of Rogers groups are available to the public. The Metropolitan Museum, New York, and the Brooklyn Museum own a number of bronze "master casts." The cycle of criticism of Rogers' work seems now complete. Delighted wonder attended the exhibition of his early work, but in the nineties the tone of the critics was patronizing, a note which had not altogether disappeared when Taft wrote his *History of American Sculpture* in 1903. More recently, both those who value native sincerity in art, and those who are coming to agree that the

anecdote is a legitimate phase of plastic beauty, have encouraged a new appreciation of America's sculptor laureate in the age of horse-hair covered furniture, involved bric-a-brac, and festooned draperies.

[J. J. Jarves, *The Art Idea* (1864); H. T. Tuckerman, *Book of the Artists* (1867); Lorado Taft, *The Hist. of Am. Sculpture* (1903); Suzanne LaFollette, *Art in America* (1929); W. P. Eaton, "Catching up to John Rogers," *Am. Mag. of Art*, Sept. 1920; W. O. Partridge, "John Rogers, the People's Sculptor," *New Eng. Mag.*, Feb. 1896; *Descriptive Cat. . . . of Group Statuettes from the Studio of Mr. John Rogers* (1895); Mabel Beard, "Up from the Junk Pile," *N. Y. Herald Tribune*, Nov. 22, 1931; "America Discovers a Neglected Folk Art of Its Own," *N. Y. Times*, Nov. 8, 1931; *Who's Who in America*, 1903–05; *N. Y. Times*, July 27, 1904; information as to certain facts supplied by the sculptor's daughter, Miss K. R. Rogers.]

W. S. R.

ROGERS, JOHN ALMANZA ROWLEY (Nov. 12, 1828–July 22, 1906), Congregational clergyman, educator, was born in Cromwell, Conn., the son of John C. and Elizabeth (Hamlin) Rogers. He attended Williams Academy, Stockbridge, Mass., until his parents moved to Ohio, and then entered Oberlin College. After receiving the degree of A.B. in 1851, he prepared for the ministry in Oberlin Theological Seminary, supporting himself by teaching in Oberlin Academy and, during the long vacations, in New York City. He graduated in 1855 and the following year married Elizabeth Lewis Embree of Philadelphia, a Quaker girl.

On his wedding trip he was asked to take a group of orphans to Roseville, Ill. After preaching in the Congregational church of that town, he was invited to become its pastor and was there ordained. He remained in Roseville for about two years, and then, hearing that a friend had given up missionary work in Kentucky because of hardship and danger, he felt impelled to go there himself. The spirit and ideals of anti-slavery Oberlin had made a deep impression upon him, and he felt that nothing could help Kentucky so much as a similar Christian college. A few years before, John Gregg Fee [q.v.] had established an anti-slavery church in what came to be known as Berea, Madison County, Ky., and in 1855 had opened a school. Rogers chose this place for his labors and in April 1858 moved to Berea with the indorsement and financial support of the American Missionary Association. Here he and his wife began teaching fifteen pupils in a room the sides and roof of which were of split clapboards. Rogers made desks, maps, and charts, and introduced such startling innovations as music, pictures, and lectures. The school proved popular, and before the close of the term its enrollment had greatly increased. The following term two additional teachers were employed. Rogers was one of the little group which drew up a constitution for a college, completed and signed in July 1859, a stipulation of which was that the college should be "under an influence strictly Christian, and, as such, opposed to sectarianism, slaveholding, caste, and every other wrong institution or practice." John Brown's raid on Harpers Ferry inflamed the whole South and in December 1859 Rogers and ten others were ordered by an armed mob to leave the state. They appealed to Governor Magoffin, who answered that he could not protect them. They then left the state, but continued to make payments on land they had bought for the site of the college.

After serving for a time as traveling secretary of the American Missionary Association, in New York and New England, Rogers became pastor of the Presbyterian church in Decatur, Ohio, with the understanding that he might leave at a month's notice and return to Kentucky. In 1865 the exiles went back to Berea and reopened the school. Rogers conducted it and was also associated with Fee in the pastorate of the church. A college charter was obtained and the institution grew rapidly. Rogers was instrumental, in 1868, in having the trustees call Edward H. Fairchild, then head of the preparatory department at Oberlin, to the presidency, but remained as professor of Greek until 1878, and served as trustee up to the time of his death. After resigning his professorship, he was pastor of a church in Shawano, Wis., for five years. He then retired to Hartford, Conn. His death occurred at the home of a daughter-in-law in Woodstock, Ill. John Raphael Rogers [*q.v.*] was his son.

[J. A. R. Rogers, *Birth of Berea College* (1903); *Berea College* (1883); *Oberlin College: The Alumni Cat. of 1926* (1927); *Berea Quart.*, Oct. 1926; *Chicago Tribune* and *Courier-Jour.* (Louisville), July 24, 1906.]

J. W. R.

ROGERS, JOHN IGNATIUS (May 27, 1843–Mar. 13, 1910, lawyer, was born in Philadelphia, the son of Matthew and Catharine (Dimond) Rogers, who had emigrated from County Kerry, Ireland (Campbell, *post,* p. 514). He attended the public schools of his native city and graduated from the Central High School. Later, he studied law and in 1865 was admitted to the bar. Specializing in corporation and real-estate law, he was selected to administer the legal affairs of the Building Association League. In this connection he was largely instrumental in formulating and securing the approval of state laws dealing with the incorporation, and relief from certain taxation, of state

building associations. In the year 1869 he was elected to the state House of Representatives, but was later defeated for the state Senate. Politically an ardent Democrat, in 1881 he was one of the founders of the Democratic Committee of Thirty-one which cooperated with the Committee of One-Hundred in electing a mayor of Philadelphia. In the year following, he declined nomination for the office of register of wills.

From his youth he took an active interest in state military affairs, enlisting as a private in the Philadelphia City Troop in 1873 and seeing active service in the serious Pittsburgh labor riots of the year 1877. As poet of this celebrated local organization, he prepared and read an original ode at the troop's centennial celebration, Nov. 17, 1874. In 1883 he was appointed by Governor Pattison colonel and judge-advocate general of the National Guard of Pennsylvania; and in 1887 and 1891 was reappointed to this office by succeeding governors. He was active in organizing the bureau of military justice and in securing adoption by the legislature of a revised military code (Act of Apr. 13, 1887). At the time of his resignation, Oct. 6, 1893, he was considered the foremost authority on military law in the state of Pennsylvania.

For many years Rogers was connected with professional baseball, and in 1882, became the principal stockholder and directing head of the Philadelphia National Baseball Club. As counsel for the club, he secured many legal decisions affecting to this day the status of baseball players. Noted as an eloquent speaker as well as a facile writer, he was in much demand as an orator at banquets and public gatherings. He was one of the founders of the Catholic Club of Philadelphia, and an active member of the Friendly Sons of St. Patrick, the Historical Society of Pennsylvania, and other local organizations. While on a business and pleasure trip in the West, he died suddenly from heart disease at Denver, Colo. He was survived by his widow, Elizabeth (Henkles) Rogers, of Germantown, to whom he was married June 20, 1876, and four sons and a daughter.

[L. M. Williamson and others, *Prominent and Progressive Pennsylvanians of the Nineteenth Century* (1898), vol. II; *A Biog. Album of Prominent Pennsylvanians* (1889), vol. II; J. H. Campbell, *Hist. of the Friendly Sons of St. Patrick* (1892); *Who's Who in Pa.,* 1904; *Public Ledger* (Phila.) and *North American* (Phila.), Mar. 14, 1910; *Phila. Inquirer,* Mar. 20, 1910.]

C. D. R.

ROGERS, JOHN RANKIN (Sept. 4, 1838–Dec. 26, 1901), governor of Washington, son of John and Margaret Ann (Greene) Rogers, was born at Brunswick, Me. His mother was a descendant of John Greene who settled in Rhode Island in 1637. At an early age John Rankin went to Boston to learn the druggist's trade, and from 1856 to 1861 he practised it in Mississippi, managing stores at Jackson and Terry. Opposed to the secession movement, he moved to Cumberland County, Ill., where he taught school and farmed until 1870. He then returned to Maine and for about five years was again engaged in the drug business. Removing to Kansas in 1876, he devoted himself to agriculture and helped organize the Farmer's Alliance. As a Greenback Republican he secured some local offices in Harvey County. His career as a publicist began in 1887 when he established and edited the *Kansas Commoner*.

In 1890 Rogers went to the state of Washington and established himself at Puyallup, Pierce County, where he dealt in real estate and conducted a mercantile business. His first and outstanding literary work, *The Irrepressible Conflict; or, An American System of Money* (1892), attracted wide attention. The following year he published a novel, *The Graftons; or Looking Forward*, reprinted in 1898 as *Looking Forward*. It had appeared originally in the *Kansas Commoner* in 1889 and is a typical newspaper serial for a populist organ. In 1894 he was elected to the lower house of the legislature and in the session of 1895 he introduced bills to redistribute the burden of taxation so as to relieve the small property holder, to improve conditions for workers in coal mines, and to broaden the scope of public education. The last-named measure, the only one of the three which passed, was the unique "Barefoot Schoolboy Law," which provided a maximum state tax of four mills to subsidize the county schools to the extent of at least six dollars for each child of school age.

A coalition of Populists, Silver Republicans, and Democrats elected him governor in 1896. His executive program, decidedly Populist, emphasized restraint in expenditures and more centralized administration for the various state institutions. After a hard struggle he defeated the plan to construct a state capitol building at a cost of $822,951 and negotiated instead the purchase of the Thurston County court house. Additional tax levies on the basis of his "Barefoot School Boy" principles and the furnishing of school textbooks by the state, free or at cost, were among his urgent recommendations to the legislature. The latter scheme, adopted in part, was not successful. When a pernicious lobby fought his measures for the control of railroads and rates he retaliated by calling public attention to its operations. Himself an indefatigable party worker, he was suspicious of orthodox machine politics. Amounting almost to an obsession was his belief in the sanctity of public opinion; no measures, even those in the interest of salutary reforms, would endure, he believed, without a decided mandate from a substantial majority of the people. That the people appreciated this confidence was revealed in the state elections of 1900, when he was reëlected governor by a substantial vote though all the rest of the offices went to orthodox Republicans.

He was in some respects a striking figure, slender, over six feet tall, with bold features set off by a large drooping mustache. His deep voice carried well; his speeches, marked by wide reading and an especial acquaintance with history, were forceful but a little heavy and tedious. On Mar. 17, 1861, he married Sarah L. Greene, of Illinois, by whom he had three sons and two daughters. He died at Olympia from an attack of lobar pneumonia.

["Washington," in *Appletons' Ann. Cyc.*, 1896–1901; obituary, *Ibid.*, 1901, p. 464; *Steel and Searle's Legislative Souvenir Manual*, 1895–96; G. S. Greene and L. B. Clarke, *The Greenes of R. I.* (1903); *Spokesman-Review* (Spokane), Dec. 27, 1901, Jan. 2, 1902; *Seattle Daily Times*, Dec. 27, 1901.]   H. J. D.

ROGERS, JOHN RAPHAEL (Dec. 11, 1856– Feb. 18, 1934), inventor, son of the Rev. John Almanza Rowley Rogers [*q.v.*] and Elizabeth Lewis (Embree), was born in Roseville, Ill. His father was connected with Berea College, Kentucky, in its early days, and after spending three years as a student there, John went to Oberlin College, from which he was graduated with the degree of A.B. in 1875. He then began teaching in the public schools of Michigan and later accepted a position in Berea College. From 1877 to 1881 he was superintendent of schools at Lorain, Ohio. For the next two years he was engaged in railroad engineering work in Iowa and Michigan, at the end of which time he returned to Lorain to teach, remaining there until 1888.

Meanwhile, he had become interested in mechanical type setting, having, as early as 1881, begun experiments with the view of finding a way to space the lines of type, that is, to "justify" them, mechanically. He worked steadily on this problem in his spare time for seven years, and on Sept. 4, 1888, obtained a patent (No. 389,108) for a machine making stereotype matrices. Thereupon, he gave up his teaching position in Lorain, moved to Cleveland, Ohio, and organized the Rogers Typograph Company to manufacture this machine. Two years later, however, his Typograph came into competition with the Mergenthaler Linotype, and through a suit brought against Rogers' company, the

Mergenthaler company obtained an injunction upon the production of a slug. Prior to this, Rogers had devised a form of double-wedge space band and applied for a patent. This invention brought him into a three-cornered interference suit with Ottmar Mergenthaler [q.v.] and another inventor, Jacobs W. Schuckers, who had filed applications for patents involving similar principles about the same time. The wedge-spacing mechanism was essential to each inventor's machine, and Rogers bought Schuckers' application. After some years of litigation, credit for the broad principle of the double-wedge was awarded to Schuckers and the right to utilize it became the property of the Rogers Typograph Company. Since the Linotype also required the double-wedge space band, the Mergenthaler company finally bought all the assets of the Rogers company, and in July 1895 the two were consolidated. Rogers then entered the employ of the Mergenthaler Linotype Company in Brooklyn, N. Y., as consulting engineer and chief of its experimental department, in which capacity he served for the remainder of his life.

Rogers must be given much credit for broadening the scope and increasing the usefulness of Mergenthaler's original one-letter Linotype. He considered thousands of ideas submitted by machinists and operators and developed and refined those that were worth while, making them commercially profitable. In the course of his many years he patented between 400 and 500 devices in the field of composing machines. He was one of the few inventors whose ability yielded due financial reward, and this he used largely for the education of young people. He was for many years a member of the board of directors of the American Missionary Association and a trustee of Oberlin College and of Berea College. He was married twice: first, on Dec. 25, 1878, to Clara Ardelia Saxton of Oberlin, who died in 1932; second, to Mrs. Marion Rood Pratt of Cleveland, Ohio, who with two adopted daughters survived him. He died in Brooklyn, N. Y., and was buried in Berea, Ky.

[*Who's Who in America*, 1930–31; *Printing Equipment Engineer*, Mar. 1934; *N. Y. Times*, Feb. 19, 1934; *Oberlin Alumni Mag.*, Dec. 1924; *Necrological Record of Oberlin Alumni* (1934); Patent Office records; information from the Mergenthaler Linotype Company.]   C. W. M.

ROGERS, MOSES (*c.* 1779–Oct. 15, 1821), early steamboat captain, was born in New London, Conn., the eldest of seven children of Amos and Sarah (Phillips) Rogers. The family, which included among its members many mariners and fishermen, traced its American ancestry to James Rogers who was living in New London

as early as 1660. Moses learned to manage a sailboat in boyhood and by 1800 was in command of a sailing vessel on Long Island Sound. On Feb. 18, 1804, he married Adelia Smith, by whom he had three sons and two daughters. He became greatly interested in steamboat experiments, especially those of John Stevens [q.v.], in some of which he may have had a part. It is frequently stated that he commanded Fulton's *Clermont,* but no original record has come to light which proves this assertion. In any event, he could have commanded it for only a few trips in the fall of 1807 before he was selected by John and Robert L. Stevens [q.v.] to command their steamer, the *Phoenix.* The monopoly of Hudson steam navigation granted to the Fulton-Livingston interests made it necessary to send the *Phoenix,* in 1809, by Sandy Hook and Cape May to the Delaware River for service, and Rogers was captain on this, the earliest ocean voyage of a steam vessel. He continued as captain while the *Phoenix* plied between Philadelphia and Bordentown, N. J., the first steamer on the Delaware and the western link of a stage-coach-steamboat route from New York to Philadelphia. In 1815 he commanded the *Eagle* on the first voyage made by steamer from New York to Baltimore, and later he became part owner of a bi-weekly line between these ports. He also took out patents in 1814 and 1815 for a horse-power ferry-boat which was adopted on several ferry-lines in New York harbor and evidently used in other places.

In 1818, seeing the future *Savannah* under construction in New York, Rogers persuaded Scarborough & Isaacs, a Savannah shipping firm, to purchase it, fit it with engines, and experiment in the use of steam on the ocean. Rogers superintended the building of the engines, paddle wheels, and accompanying machinery. The paddle wheels he constructed so that they could be quickly taken from the water and placed on board in case it was desired to use only sail, an innovation dictated by his experience on the maiden trip of the *Phoenix* when the paddle wheels were badly damaged by storm. After having made the journey from New York to Savannah, Rogers left the latter city on May 22, 1819, for Liverpool. With him on this voyage, as navigator, went Stevens Rogers (Feb. 13, 1789–Nov. 30, 1882), also of New London, designer of the *Savannah's* rigging, who had been associated with him in the *Phoenix* and the *Eagle* and later became his brother-in-law. This first voyage of a steamship across the Atlantic can scarcely be called the first crossing of the ocean by steam, since the passage consumed twenty-nine days and eleven hours, of which time sails were used for twenty-six days and three hours. The voyage was continued to Stockholm and St. Petersburg, where the *Savannah* was visited by many of the nobility, including the Prince of Sweden and the Emperor of Russia. On the stormy voyage home sails were used until the ship was in the Savannah River. The owners were forced to sell the *Savannah,* and Rogers formed new connections with a company about to operate steamers on the Great Peedee River between Georgetown and Cheraw, S. C. He superintended the construction of the *Peedee* in 1820, and while in command of it the following year was stricken with malarial fever. He died and was buried in Georgetown. Though his *Savannah* undertaking did not bear immediate fruit in promoting transatlantic steamship service, Rogers deserves credit for mechanical ingenuity and courageous seamanship.

[The best source of information is J. E. Watkins, "The Log of the Savannah," in *Ann. Report of the Board of Regents of the Smithsonian Institution . . . 1890* (1891), based on the original logbook, preserved in that institution, and on contemporary newspaper references; obituary notice reprinted from the *Georgetown Intelligencer* shows 1821 rather than 1822 to be the correct date of Rogers' death. See also J. S. Rogers, *James Rogers of New London, Ct., and His Descendants* (1902), and A. D. Turnbull, *John Stevens, An Am. Record* (1928).]   O. W. H.

ROGERS, RANDOLPH (July 6, 1825–Jan. 15, 1892), sculptor of the "Columbus doors" of the Capitol at Washington, was born at Waterloo, N. Y., the son of John and Sara (McCarthy) Rogers. The father was a carpenter from the neighborhood of Syracuse, who in successive stages was moving west. He eventually settled in Ann Arbor, Mich., where the future sculptor lived from his eighth to his eighteenth year, a period marked by some education in the common schools and by some clerical experience in a general store. For the next five years he worked in the wholesale dry-goods store of John Stewart in New York City. Long an amateur in the various artistic media, he had been paid ten dollars for a wood engraving of a log cabin and flags by an Ann Arbor paper, and had thereby supplied the party emblem for Harrison's campaign in 1840; now he attracted the attention of his employers by his modeling of the children of one of them, Lycurgus Edgerton, and by a bust of Lord Byron. As a result Stewart and Edgerton lent their clerk the funds for a period of study in Italy. From 1848 to 1851 he worked at the Academy of St. Mark in Florence under Lorenzo Bartolini, celebrated as a neo-classicist of ability. With the proceeds of the sale of an ideal bust called "Night" and a kneeling figure, "Ruth,"

made at the close of the period, he repaid his benefactors their loans to him and for the following two years was established in a studio of his own in Rome, modeling his most popular figure, "Nydia," Bulwer-Lytton's blind girl of Pompeii, prior to his return to America in 1853. The commission for a statue of John Adams for Mt. Auburn Cemetery in Cambridge, and for the bronze doors to face the corridor leading from Statuary Hall to the new House wing of the Capitol at Washington fell to his lot at this time. In 1855 he was again in his studio in Rome, where he centered his activities for the rest of his life, save for occasional professional trips to America. A short visit in the fall of 1857 was marked by his marriage to Rosa Gibson of Richmond, Va., who became the mother of his nine children.

In 1861 the "Isaac" was modeled, and the Washington Monument in Richmond, left incomplete by Thomas Crawford, was finished with two historical figures, and six allegorical figures in place of the eagles originally planned. The Colt funereal monument in Hartford, Conn., "The Angel of the Resurrection," followed in 1862. During the winter of 1863, which he passed in Cincinnati, he received the commission for the first of his military monuments, "The Soldier of the Line." An amazing number of orders for portrait busts, nineteen in the winter of 1866 alone, as well as for medallions, bas-reliefs, and other private commissions, kept him busy until his great opportunity came in 1867 with the order for colossal soldiers' and sailors' monuments for Providence and for Detroit. These were masses of granite, fifty feet in height, decorated with bronze figures and reliefs. Toward the close of his active career came the soldiers' monument at Worcester, Mass., the seated Lincoln in Fairmount Park, Philadelphia, and the Seward in Madison Square, New York City. His last ideal works were the "Lost Pleiad," which has vied in popularity with the "Nydia" of his early days, the "Genius of Connecticut" for the state capitol at Hartford, and the "Last Arrow," an equestrian Indian group. After 1882 the sculptor had to give up his work because of paralysis. Between 1886 and 1888 he forwarded most of the casts representing his life work to the Museum of Art and Architecture of the University of Michigan at Ann Arbor. He died in Rome, Jan. 15, 1892, and, having become a member of the Roman Catholic Church in his later years, was buried with his wife in San Lorenzo Cemetery, the grave marked by his finest funereal monument, representing a freed soul rising with lightness, dignity, and grace.

Randolph Rogers is described as having been

a large, powerful man of great vigor and of un-sparing industry. He was of distinguished ap-pearance, with the massive forehead, the strong features, and the long beard of the patriarch—an indispensable member of the American colony in Rome. He has been depicted as a convivial friend and amateur actor, the companion of Greenough and Crawford, entertaining in his studio Hawthorne one day and royalty the next, going his whole-souled, generous way in a some-what heroic fashion. In 1873 he was chosen pro-fessor of sculpture at the Academy of St. Luke in Rome, and a councilor of the Academy in 1875. He was decorated with the order of Cavaliere della Corona D'Italia in 1884. His "Ruth" and "Nydia" attracted much attention at the Centen-nial Exhibition in Philadelphia in 1876, and as recently as 1931 the exhibition of a bust of his wife in the art museum of Grand Rapids occa-sioned appreciative comment in the local press.

The University of Michigan is the center for any present-day study of Rogers' work. The set of original casts there is nearly complete, al-though the models of the "Columbus doors" are duplicates. Rogers' style is that of the neo-classic period, his subject matter is narrative in char-acter, his modeling approaches realism. Of his popular successes, the "Nydia" is at the Chicago Art Institute, the "Lost Pleiad" at the art mu-seum in San Francisco, and the "Ruth" in the Metropolitan Museum in New York. The doors at Washington are now placed at the main en-trance of the rotunda, and wear well as narrative rather than as decorative or creative art. They follow in general the designs Ghiberti used for his second pair of doors on the Baptistry at Flor-ence. With borders marked by mouldings, tro-phies, and niches, eight panels and a culminating lunette tell the story of Columbus' adventures clearly and dramatically. But perhaps Rogers at his best is represented by the "Michigan," a heroic figure on the top of the Detroit monu-ment, or by the heroic negro figure of "Emanci-pation" on the same monument.

[Sources include: A manuscript biography of Rogers by his wife; J. J. Jarves, *The Art Idea* (1864); H. T. Tuckerman, *Book of the Artists* (1867); Nathaniel Hawthorne, Preface to *The Marble Faun* (1860); Lo-rado Taft, *The Hist. of Am. Sculpture* (1903); M. L. D'Ooge, *Cat. of the Gallery of Art . . . in the Univ. of Mich.* (n.d.); C. E. Fairman, *Art and Artists of the Capitol* (1927); *N. Y. Times*, Jan. 16, 1892.]

W. S. R.

ROGERS, ROBERT (Nov. 7, 1731 o.s.–May 18, 1795), colonial ranger, was born in the fron-tier village of Methuen, Mass., the son of James and Mary Rogers. As he grew to manhood on his father's farm near Rumford, now Concord, N. H., he developed a remarkable physique, early devoted himself to hunting, Indian trading, and exploring the northern wilderness, and became a typical roving frontiersman. In January 1755 he was discovering his exceptional talents as a recruiting officer in raising men for William Shirley's expedition to Nova Scotia, when, to escape prosecution on the charge of counterfeit-ing New Hampshire currency, he entered the New Hampshire regiment, and he soon became a captain on William Johnson's Crown Point expedition. His boldness in procuring intelli-gence by scouting enemy forces and positions and by capturing prisoners commended him to John-son, and he remained in the services of the colo-nies during the winter. In March 1756 Shirley appointed him captain of an independent com-pany of rangers, paid from British contingent funds, and in 1758 Abercromby promoted him to be major of nine such companies, the scouting arm of the British army. Valuable though these companies were, their independence and lack of discipline diminished their usefulness. Rogers himself sometimes preferred spectacular and hazardous exploits to a more reasoned course. Nevertheless, he made scores of raids in winter and summer and participated in several bloody engagements, enlivened with such dashing cour-age, incredible hardihood, and humorous pranks, that he became famous alike in England and the colonies, the most romantic figure of the war. He was with Loudon at Halifax in 1757, with Abercromby at Ticonderoga in 1758, with Am-herst at Crown Point in 1759, when he destroyed the Saint Francis Indians in a daring raid, and again in 1760 in the final campaign about Mon-treal. Later that year he was sent west as far as Detroit and Shawneetown to receive the sur-render of all French posts ("Journal of Robert Rogers . . . on His Expedition for Receiving the Capitulation of Western French Posts," *Bulletin of the N. Y. Public Library*, April 1933).

During the next fifteen years he proved him-self incapable of coping with the problems of peace and civilization. He saddled himself with debts, amounting in time to £13,000. He failed to utilize opportunities in Portsmouth opened by his marriage on June 30, 1761, with Eliza-beth Browne, the daughter of the Rev. Arthur Browne. In 1761 he served as captain of an in-dependent company against the Cherokee in South Carolina, where the governor and council recommended him as superintendent of southern Indians; in 1763, as captain of a New York in-dependent company, he accompanied Dalyell's force to Detroit and aided in the defense of that post against Pontiac. The want of principle dis-played by his illicit trading with Indians and his incapacity for administration kept him from receiving further employment in America, and in 1765 he sailed for England to solicit preferment. There he published his *Journals* and *A Concise Account of North America*, both in 1765, and a crude play, *Ponteach: or the Savages of America. A Tragedy,* anonymously in 1766, one of the first dramas written by a native New Englander. He was lionized in the public prints. Though his proposal to lead an expedition to discover the Northwest Passage was refused, he was successful in gaining appointment to the command of the fort at Michilimackinac.

For two years, with his wife, he lived in that desolate post. There he commissioned Jonathan Carver [*q.v.*] to undertake the exploratory journey into the present Minnesota and seems to have been the first person to use in writing or in print the word Ouragon (Oregon). Disregarding his implicit instructions from Johnson and Gage, he tried to administer his territory, and especially the Indian trade, in his own interests, and schemed for a separate civil and military establishment. He was finally arrested on a charge of treasonable dealings with the French but acquitted for want of evidence. The journal he kept from Sept. 21, 1766, to July 3, 1767, was printed by William L. Clements in the *Proceedings of the American Antiquarian Society* (Oct. 1918). In England again in 1769, after vain efforts to gain reimbursement or employment, he brought unsuccessful suit against Gage for assault and imprisonment and was finally thrown into a debtor's prison, from which his brother James rescued him by assuming his chief debts. In 1774—so he later asserted—he served under the Dey of Algiers. He returned to America in 1775 and for a time courted both the Americans and British. Washington suspected his motives and in 1776 imprisoned him as a spy. Escaping to the British, he raised the Queen's American rangers but was utterly defeated in a skirmish near White Plains and deprived of his command. Thereafter he was employed in recruiting, but the same dishonesty and dissipation that had wrecked his other ventures rendered him useless for this service. In 1778 the New Hampshire legislature granted his wife's petition for divorce, and she continued to have the custody of their only child. In 1780 he fled to England to escape condemnation. Fifteen years later, still receiving half-pay, he died in a cheap London lodging-house and was buried at St. Mary, Newington.

[Manuscript copy of Rogers' journal of the march from Montreal to Detroit, 1760–61, is in the Canadian archives; among the Treasury Solicitor Papers in the Public Record Office in London is a copy of his court-martial, in connection with his King's Bench action against General Gage; additional manuscript material can be found in the Amherst Papers in the Public Record Office, in the Loudoun Papers in the Huntington Lib., San Marino, Cal., and in the Gage and British Headquarters Papers in the William L. Clements Lib., Ann Arbor, Mich.; see also biog. sketch by Allan Nevins in *Ponteach* (Caxton club ed. 1914); M. M. Quaife, "Robert Rogers," *Burton Hist. Coll. Leaflet,* Sept. 1928; Arthur Pound, *Native Stock* (1931); T. C. Elliott, "Jonathan Carver's Source for the Name Oregon," *Quart. of Ore. Hist. Soc.,* Mar. 1922, esp. p. 66; birth date from *Vital Records of Methuen, Mass.* (1909) and verification with the manuscript records.]

S. M. P.

ROGERS, ROBERT EMPIE (Mar. 29, 1813–Sept. 6, 1884), chemist, educator, son of Dr. Patrick Kerr and Hannah (Blythe) Rogers, was born in Baltimore, Md. His middle name was of his own choosing, adopted in his youth out of regard for the Rev. Adam Empie, president of the College of William and Mary (1827–36). Robert was the youngest of the celebrated Rogers brothers, scientists, the other three being James Blythe, William Barton, and Henry Darwin [*qq.v.*]. He received his early education from his father, who in 1819 became professor of natural philosophy and chemistry at William and Mary; after the father's death in 1828, he was taken in charge by his brothers James and William. His first work was in the field of engineering, and in 1831–32 he was connected with railroad surveying parties in New England. He then entered the University of Pennsylvania and graduated with the degree of M.D. in 1836, his thesis, *Experiments upon the Blood* (1836), showing that at this early age he possessed rare manipulative skill and the spirit of a true investigator.

He did not become a practising physician, however. While at the University he had spent much time in the chemical laboratory of Robert Hare [*q.v.*], and he now became chemist to the first Pennsylvania geological survey, of which his brother Henry was the head. Much of his work was routine, although he and Martin H. Boyé [*q.v.*] made an independent analysis of limestones. In 1842 he became professor of general and applied chemistry in the University of Virginia, a position involving the kind of work best suited to his tastes and ability—teaching and investigating. His teaching was characterized by dexterity in experiment and lucidity in exposition; moreover, he was sincerely interested in the everyday life of his students, and in turn was beloved by them. His investigations during this period were mostly done in conjunction with his brother William. Together they devised a new process for preparing chlorine (still commonly used), improved processes for making formic acid and aldehyde, and perfected a method of determining the carbon in graphite. They studied the volatility of potassium and sodium carbonates, the decomposition of rocks by meteoric water, and the absorption of carbon dioxide by liquids, the last named investigation being a helpful contribution to the analysis of mineral waters. At about this time, in collaboration with his brother James, he studied the alleged insolubility of copper in hydrochloric acid, and also published *A Text Book on Chemistry* (1846), a compact work compiled from contemporary books by English authors.

James died in 1852 and Robert succeeded him as professor of chemistry in the medical school of the University of Pennsylvania, becoming dean four years later. In 1855 he edited *Physiological Chemistry,* a translation by G. E. Day of Karl Gotthelf Lehmann's work. In the succeeding years he engaged in expert chemical work and for a time during the Civil War performed numerous duties as assistant surgeon in the West Philadelphia military hospital. In this institution he lost his right hand while showing a laundress how to use an ironing machine. He speedily learned to write with his left hand, however, and to use with remarkable skill what remained of his right arm. On Feb. 21, 1863, occurred the death of his wife, Fanny Montgomery, daughter of Joseph S. Lewis of Philadelphia, whom he had married Mar. 13, 1843. On Apr. 30, 1866, he married Delia Saunders. His interest in applied chemistry led him to make a study of petroleum, and through unfortunate speculations in 1864 in connection with the Humboldt Oil Company he sustained a considerable financial loss. Because of his knowledge of precious metals and their ores he was appointed in 1872 to investigate the waste of silver in the Philadelphia mint; soon afterward he made helpful suggestions about refining which were adopted with profit. In 1875 he prepared the plans for the equipment of the refinery of the mint in San Francisco; and that same year, under instructions of the Director of the Mint, he investigated the Virginia and California mines in Nevada, for the purpose of estimating their probable total yield of gold and silver. In 1877 he resigned his position at the University of Pennsylvania to accept the professorship of medical chemistry and toxicology in Jefferson Medical College, Philadelphia, which position he held until just before his death. He was a member of many scientific organizations and served them in various official capacities. In 1840 he shared in the organization of the Association of American Geologists and Naturalists (later the American Association for the Advancement of Science);

he was also an original member of the National Academy of Sciences.

[W. S. W. Ruschenberger, "A Sketch of the Life of Robert E. Rogers with Biog. Notices of His Father and Brothers," in *Proc. Am. Philosophical Soc.,* vol. XXIII (1886); E. F. Smith, in *Biog. Memoirs, National Acad. Sci.,* vol. V (1905), which includes bibliog., and *Chemistry in America* (1914), which includes bibliog.; *Jour. of Chemical Educ.,* Apr. 1932; H. A. Kelly and W. L. Burrage, *Am. Medic. Biogs.* (1920); *Life and Letters of William Barton Rogers* (1896); *Phila. Press,* Sept. 7, 1884.]   L. C. N.

ROGERS, ROBERT WILLIAM (Feb. 14, 1864–Dec. 12, 1930), Orientalist, was born in Philadelphia, the son of Dr. Samuel and Mary (Osborne) Rogers. Irish and Welsh strains mingled in his ancestry, but the Irish, of which he was most proud, dominated. He was educated at the Central High School in Philadelphia and at the University of Pennsylvania, where he graduated in 1886 with the degree of bachelor of arts; in 1887 he received the same degree from Johns Hopkins University. His interest in Oriental studies was awakened when he was in his fifteenth year. While reading John Stuart Blackie's *On Self-Culture, Intellectual, Physical, and Moral* (1874), he came across the statement that the Book of Job in the Old Testament was the greatest book in all literature. He determined, therefore, to read it for himself. Finding in it much he could not understand, he acquired the commentary on Job in Lange's series. Since it contained many Hebrew words, he sought the help of a neighboring Lutheran minister and began the study of Hebrew. This study he continued while at college, adding, at Johns Hopkins University, the study of Assyrian under Prof. Paul Haupt [*q.v.*]. When in 1887 Prof. J. Rendel Harris left Hopkins for Haverford College, Rogers followed him thither as instructor in Greek and Hebrew. Continuing his Oriental studies, he received from Haverford the degree of doctor of philosophy in 1890. As a boy he had been brought up in the Protestant Episcopal Church, but later allied himself with the Methodist Episcopal, and in 1890 he was admitted on trial to the Philadelphia Conference; in 1894 he was ordained elder. From 1890 to 1892 he was professor of English Bible and Semitic history in Dickinson College, Carlisle, Pa. In 1893 he was called to the professorship of Hebrew and Old Testament exegesis in Drew Theological Seminary, Madison, N. J., a position which he filled until 1929. He was an instructor at the summer sessions of Columbia University from 1915 to 1921. In 1919 he was made professor of ancient Oriental literature in Princeton University, on the Paton Foundation, which position he held conjointly with his professorship in Drew until 1929. On June 3, 1891, he married Ida Virginia Ziegler of Philadelphia, who with two children survived him.

Throughout his life Rogers was an ardent student of Assyriology, Hebrew, and the Old Testament and made his contributions to knowledge in these fields. He spent many of his summers at Oxford and other European centers prosecuting his researches in their libraries. In addition to numerous articles, he was the author of *Outlines of the History of Early Babylonia* (1895); *A History of Babylonia and Assyria* (2 vols., 1900; 6th ed., rewritten, 1915); *The Religion of Babylonia and Assyria* (1908); *Cuneiform Parallels to the Old Testament* (1912); *The Recovery of the Ancient Orient* (1912); *The History and Literature of the Hebrew People* (2 vols., 1917), comprising a manual for teachers and a textbook for students; *Great Characters of the Old Testament* (1920); *A Book of Old Testament Lessons* (2 vols., 1921), a lectionary; *A History of Ancient Persia* (1929). Rogers' work, while intelligent and accurate, was that of an interpreter rather than a discoverer of new material or one who blazes new paths. His *History of Babylonia and Assyria* was, when published, not only the most competent history of these nations in any language but so interestingly written that it found many enthusiastic readers beyond the circle professionally concerned with the subject. As a lecturer, he was often in demand in various parts of the United States, and at one time visited Japan and China, in both of which countries he delivered courses of lectures to continually increasing audiences. He had the gift of making the ancient world live again until his listeners shared with him something of the thrill which he found in the story of ancient life. Although he fully accepted the modern critical view of the Old Testament, he possessed such tact and consideration for the normal growth of his students that he escaped the ecclesiastical censure visited by his Church upon some of its other Old Testament scholars.

His contributions to scholarship were rewarded by recognition from many institutions. In addition to the degree from Haverford College, he received that of Ph.D. from the University of Leipzig in 1895; and numerous honorary degrees. He was a member of Oriental and archeological societies, both American and foreign, and towards the close of his life was elected a member of the American Philosophical Society. In 1929, owing to physical infirmities, he resigned both his professorships and retired to a farm near Chadds Ford, Pa., which he named

"Omagh Farm." Here he was living at the time of his death.

[*Who's Who in America*, 1930–31; *Methodist Who's Who*, 1915; *Methodist Rev.*, May–June, 1931; *Christian Advocate*, May 2, 16, 1929, and Dec. 25, 1930; *N. Y. Times*, Dec. 13, 1930.]   G. A. B.

ROGERS, STEPHEN (January 1826–May 23, 1878), surgeon, was born at Tyre, N. Y. His father, a farmer of very limited means, could give his son few opportunities for study and until the age of seventeen Stephen was employed on the farm, educating himself meanwhile by extensive reading. Later, by working in a store and hiring himself out as a farm laborer, he saved enough money to obtain a scanty education in nearby schools. He read freely in the library of a local physician, spent some time in hospitals in New York, and heavily in debt, accepted an appointment as surgeon to the Panama Railroad, then being built (1849–55). Five years of arduous work in the tropics seriously impaired his health, but he recovered after a prolonged convalescence in Havana, Cuba. During this period he became thoroughly acquainted with Spanish and his knowledge of this language, combined with his professional skill, secured for him a post as surgeon to the Southern Railroad of Chile, with headquarters in Santiago. While there, in 1857, he married the daughter of Samuel F. Haveland. The degree of M.D. had been granted to him by the New York Medical College in 1856, before he went to Chile.

Returning to New York in 1865, he practised surgery in that city and made several contributions to medical jurisprudence while connected with the coroner's office. These were contained in papers read before the Medico-Legal Society of New York, a society in which he took a great interest, serving as president in 1871. His most important medical contribution was a paper on ruptured extra-uterine pregnancy (*Transactions of the American Medical Association*, vol. XVIII, 1867). In it he not only gave a careful description of the signs and symptoms of this condition but also advocated immediate surgical treatment. This paper was enlarged and published as a monograph, *Extra-uterine Foetation and Gestation, and the Early Signs Which Characterize It* (1867). Other papers include an early report on excision of the scapula (*American Journal of the Medical Sciences*, October 1868), which was reprinted separately that same year; on the use of quinine in treating tropical malaria (*Transactions of the Medical Society of the State of New York*, 1862); and a timely protest against the hypodermic use of the same drug (*New York Medical Journal*, September

1874), also printed separately. In 1875, his health again somewhat impaired, he was appointed United States commissioner to the International Exhibition of Chile. While there, he resumed his practice as a surgeon in Santiago, but died three years later while on a visit to Valparaiso.

Dignified in manner and military in bearing, Rogers was much beloved by his associates. He was a scholarly, able surgeon, esteemed in both Chile and New York. Honorary degrees were conferred upon him by the University of Havana (1857) and the University of Chile (1857) and he held membership in the New York Academy of Medicine and the Obstetrical Society of Berlin, Germany. For a short period he was professor of physiological and microscopic anatomy in the New York Medical College.

[William Shrady, in *Bull. Medico-Legal Soc. of N. Y.*, Dec. 1878; *Boletin de la Esposición Internacional de Chile en 1875* (1875), pp. 466 ff.; *Am. Gynecology*, Sept. 1903, p. 266; H. A. Kelly and W. L. Burrage, *Am. Medic. Biogs.* (1920).]   H. R. V.

ROGERS, THOMAS (Mar. 16, 1792–Apr. 19, 1856), inventor, locomotive builder, son of John and Mary (Larrabee) Rogers, was born on his father's farm in Groton, Conn. He was descended from James Rogers who was in New London, Conn., as early as 1660, and was a great-great-grandson of John Rogers, 1648–1721 [*q.v.*], founder of a sect known as the Rogerenes. At the age of sixteen, after receiving a common-school education, Thomas became a carpenter's apprentice and then learned blacksmithing from an uncle. When twenty years old he left home and settled in Paterson, N. J., just at the beginning of the War of 1812. After serving throughout that struggle, he returned to Paterson and soon found employment in a shop that made wooden looms. He also learned pattern making and in the course of four years saved some money with which, in 1819, he purchased the manufacturing rights for a newly imported power loom. He and John Clark then organized the firm of Clark & Rogers and began the manufacture of the new loom, undertaking, also, the spinning of cotton. The business was immediately successful; a second partner, Abraham Godwin, was taken into the company in 1820; the plant was enlarged in 1822; and nine years later Rogers withdrew with $38,000 as his share of the profits.

With this capital he began the construction of a new textile machine manufacturing plant in Paterson, which he called the "Jefferson Works." Upon its completion in 1832 he organized the Rogers, Ketchum & Grosvenor Machine Works and, with Rogers as president, the company began operations. During the first year, in addition to textile machinery the company began making railroad car wheels and boxes and other railroad castings. These were of such good quality that Rogers was soon approached by the leaders in railroad enterprises with the urgent request that he engage in the construction of locomotives. After three years he acceded to these requests and late in 1836 publicly announced in the *American Railroad Journal* (Dec. 24) that his company "was prepared to receive orders for locomotives and tenders." In the meantime, the company had constructed additional buildings and also had imported from England machine tools of all kinds. Rogers, furthermore, had made a close study of the "McNeill," the first locomotive on the Paterson & Hudson River Railroad, imported from England in 1833, and from this had prepared his first design. Immediately following its announcement, the company began the construction of a locomotive intended for the New Jersey Railroad & Transportation Company. The task was an extremely trying one for Rogers, but after many months the locomotive was completed and on Oct. 6, 1837, made a successful trial trip. It was immediately purchased by the newly organized Mad River & Lake Erie Railroad, given the name "Sandusky," and shipped to Ohio, although not a foot of track had been laid. Since it was the first locomotive west of the Alleghany Mountains, its gauge was made the standard for Ohio. In this locomotive the driving wheels were made with cast-iron centers and hollow spokes, and the crank and connecting rod were counterbalanced by adding sufficient extra weight to the section of the wheels opposite the crank. For these improvements Rogers was responsible; he did not patent them, but in order to insure their being public property, he filed specifications in the patent office on July 12, 1837. Three additional locomotives similar to the "Sandusky," each with a single pair of driving wheels, were completed by Rogers, Ketchum & Grosvenor by the middle of 1838. In 1839 Rogers designed and built a new type of locomotive, and, in 1842, produced the "Stockbridge," with cylinders outside of the frame. Two years later, he produced the type of locomotive which was subsequently adopted generally throughout the United States. This had two pairs of coupled driving wheels and was remarkable in that it was the first example of the use of equalizing beams between the driving wheels and front swiveling truck. Always progressive, Rogers took the lead in adopting improvements that others regarded with distrust. Thus to him belongs the credit of introducing the shifting link valve motion on locomotives in the United States; he was the first, also, in 1850, to apply the wagon top boiler. In his twenty years of locomotive building, as in his earlier manufacturing work, he was extremely successful and was actively connected with his company to the day of his death. A skilful workman himself, he always insisted on first-class work being maintained in his shops. Accordingly, the Rogers locomotives had a high reputation for efficiency, safety, and durability, and were used in all parts of the United States, in Cuba, and in South-American countries as well. Rogers married Marie Small of Paterson, N. J., and at the time of his death in New York City he was survived by five children.

[J. S. Rogers, *James Rogers of New London, Ct., and His Descendants* (1902), which is in error as to date of death; J. L. Bishop, *A Hist. of Am. Manufactures* (3rd ed., 1868), vol. III; C. A. Shriner, *Paterson, N. J.* (1890); Angus Sinclair, *Development of the Locomotive Engine* (1907); M. S. Forney, *Locomotives and Locomotive Building ... Origin and Growth of the Rogers Locomotive and Machine Works, Paterson, N. J.* (1886); *Am. Railroad Jour.,* Dec. 24, 1836; death notice, *N. Y. Times,* Apr. 21, 1856.]   C. W. M.

ROGERS, WILLIAM ALLEN (May 23, 1854–Oct. 20, 1931), cartoonist, son of William Allen and Elizabeth (Smith) Rogers, was born at Springfield, Ohio. An early aptitude for drawing won him a position with a farm-implement company, making fancy scrolls on plows and mowing machines. At fourteen he was selling cartoons to a group of Middle-Western newspapers, and thus became the first American cartoonist to be syndicated. In 1873 he joined the staff of the original *Daily Graphic* in New York City, served on this paper till 1877, and then commenced a long association with *Harper's Weekly*. At that time newspaper photography was impracticable, and all illustration was the work of an artist who actually sketched the event as it was happening. It was customary, in making a sketch of an inauguration or a parade, to visit the scene somewhat in advance, make a careful drawing of the setting, and fill in the principal figures later. Naturally, the artist had to work rapidly. In making a death-bed sketch of President Garfield, Rogers had only a few moments in which to absorb and record the scene. On the back of a paper bag he indicated the outline of the dying president, the attendant doctors and relatives, then elaborated these from photographs. The original drawing is with many others, now in the permanent collection of the New York Public Library.

Rogers' career as a political cartoonist began on Oct. 2, 1880. Thomas Nast happened to be absent from Harper's office, and Rogers leapt into the breach by making a pungent cartoon on the Garfield-Hancock campaign, depicting the moribund Democratic party receiving a transfusion of blood from the "stalwart" general. With that cartoon Rogers laid the cornerstone of his reputation, and for the next forty years his pictorial commentary on political events and the news of the day—woman's suffrage, vivisection, silver, Zeppelins, Wall Street, cold storage, Tammany Hall—appeared in *Harper's Weekly, Harper's Monthly Magazine, Life, Puck,* and the *New York Herald*.

In these cartoons Rogers gave a direct and simplified "pictorializing of opinion," which could be easily apprehended by the commonest intelligence. Caricaturist he was not; there is no trace of distortion in the lineaments or physique of his characters. Both his line and his viewpoint, while far from saccharine, lack the savagery of Nast and Daumier, and one has the feeling that Rogers was essentially a well-tempered, healthy, and sympathetic human being. Only during the World War did he lose his balance. In 1914 James Gordon Bennett sent his editors a cable from Europe saying, "Tell Rogers there is only one issue in this war. It is the issue between civilization and savagery" (*A World Worth While,* p. 256). Rogers responded with a series of war cartoons, afterward published in a volume entitled *America's Black and White Book: One Hundred Pictured Reasons Why We are at War* (1917), in which he brutally and often hysterically assailed Germany's leaders and war ideals. So powerful and effective were these cartoons, however, that the French government awarded Rogers membership in the Legion of Honor at the close of the war.

If Rogers had not gained fame as a political cartoonist he would still be affectionately remembered as an illustrator of children's books. As a boy, Booth Tarkington was of the opinion that the illustrator of *Toby Tyler* "must be a pretty fine man." The stories of James Otis and Kirk Munroe were enriched by Rogers' gentle, humorous drawings as they appeared serially in *Harper's Young People* and later in book form. Between 1920 and 1922 Rogers was director of the Illustrators' School for Disabled Soldiers, financed by the Federal Board for Vocational Education. Thereafter he was on the staff of the *Washington Post,* and also found time to write his memoirs, *A World Worth While* (1922)—an autobiography that reveals his essential belief in the goodness of life and humanity. His other published works include:

Danny's Partner (1923), *The Miracle Mine* (1925), and *The Lost Caravan* (1927). On Oct. 20, 1931, Rogers succumbed to a heart malady after a brief illness in his home at Washington, D. C. He had married, on Apr. 10, 1879, Sarah Butler of Springfield, Ohio. A son and a daughter survived him.

[In addition to Rogers' autobiography, see Frank Weitenkampf, "Wm. Allen Rogers in 'A World Worth While,'" *Bull. of the N. Y. Pub. Lib.*, Mar. 1933; *Who's Who in America*, 1928–29; *N. Y. Times*, Oct. 21, 1931; Mar. 10, 1933.]   H. M. R.

ROGERS, WILLIAM AUGUSTUS (Nov. 13, 1832–Mar. 1, 1898), mathematician, astronomer, and physicist, was born at Waterford, Conn., the only son in a family of three children. His parents, David Potter Rogers and Mary Anna (Rogers) were both descended from James Rogers, who was in New London, Conn., as early as 1660. David Rogers was for a time master of a fishing vessel, but later became interested in farming. His son William prepared for college at De Ruyter and at Alfred Academy, N. Y., taught school for a short time at New Market, N. J., and in 1854 entered Brown University, where he received the degree of M.A. in 1857. He was at once appointed tutor and instructor in mathematics in Alfred Academy, in 1859 became professor of mathematics at Alfred University, and the following year was made professor of industrial mechanics there. Here he remained for the succeeding decade, with three absences on leave: to pursue advanced mechanics at Yale, to study practical astronomy under Professor Bond at Harvard Observatory, and to serve in the navy for fourteen months toward the close of the Civil War. In 1865, he built and equipped an astronomical observatory at Alfred University, erecting, among other instruments, an up-to-date nine-inch equatorial refractor.

In 1870 he accepted an assistantship at Harvard Observatory under Joseph Winlock and was placed in charge of the newly erected eight-inch meridian circle. His chief work was the observation of the catalogued stars between 50 degrees and 55 degrees north declination, as a part of the general scheme of the Astronomische Gesellschaft to secure the most accurate positions of all the brighter stars in the sky. In 1877, when Edward C. Pickering [*q.v.*] assumed the directorship of the Observatory, Rogers was made assistant professor of astronomy. He held this position, directing the work of a large corps of assistants, until 1886, when he resigned to become professor of physics and astronomy at Colby University. So valuable were his services in the work of the star catalogue that he

was prevailed upon to continue its supervision until its completion in 1896.

His work with the meridian circle, requiring the greatest precision, led him to seek still greater refinement in apparatus than was then available. He became proficient in the etching of lines on glass for reticles, and in the making of more accurate screws and the determination of their errors. In 1879 he was sent by the American Academy of Arts and Sciences to Europe to obtain copies of the imperial yard and of the French meter. During his twelve years at Colby, he organized a physical laboratory which was a model for accurate measurements and the determination of physical constants. His resignation as professor there was accepted by the trustees to take effect Apr. 1, 1898, in order that he might assume the directorship of the new physical laboratory at Alfred University, the erection and the equipment of which he had planned and directed during the previous year, but his death in March 1898 frustrated this plan.

Rogers was a man of genial disposition, unassuming and modest, but courageous in his convictions. His industry and perseverance were illimitable, and he considered no task too great where accuracy was required. Like his parents and grandparents he was devoutly religious, and belonged to that class of Baptists who strictly observe the sabbath beginning at sunset on Friday. He maintained an active interest in civic matters, and greatly enjoyed sports. During his final illness, when it was impossible for him to go to the lecture room or laboratory, he met his classes in his home. In 1857 he married Rebecca Jane Titsworth of Shiloh, N. H., who assisted him in connection with the reduction and publication of his numerous astronomical observations. Three sons were born to them. His many scientific papers appeared in ten volumes of the Harvard *Annals,* and in numerous publications of the several academies of which he was a member. His researches on the value of the yard and meter, and changes therein, are among the most important ever made. He was closely associated with Albert A. Michelson and Edward W. Morley [*qq.v.*] in the application of optical methods to the determination of minute changes in length, and he undertook researches in meteorology for the special purpose of learning more about the coefficient of expansion as applied to metal objects and thermometers. He was an honorary fellow of the Royal Society of London, a fellow of the Royal Microscopical Society and of the American Association for the Advancement of Science, member of the American Microscopical Society (president 1887), of the American Academy of Arts and Sciences, and of the National Academy of Sciences.

[W. L. Stevens, in *Science*, Apr. 1, 1898; E. W. Morley in *Nat. Acad. Sci. Biog. Memoirs*, vol. IV (1902); S. I. Bailey, *The Hist. and Work of Harvard Observatory* (1931); J. S. Rogers, *James Rogers of New London, Ct., and His Descendants* (1902); *Bangor Daily Whig and Courier*, Mar. 2, 1898.]   L. C.

ROGERS, WILLIAM BARTON (Dec. 7, 1804–May 30, 1882), geologist and educator, son of Patrick Kerr and Hannah (Blythe) Rogers, was born in Philadelphia, Pa. He was the second of four brothers, all of whom became distinguished scientists, the other three being James Blythe, Henry Darwin, and Robert Empie [*qq.v.*]. William was educated under the tutelage of his father, in the public schools of Baltimore, and at the College of William and Mary, where his father became professor of natural philosophy and chemistry in 1819. For a time, with his brother Henry, he conducted a school at Windsor, Md., and in 1827 became a lecturer at the Maryland Institute. While connected with this institution, he presented to the governors, at their request, a plan for a proposed high school. On the death of the father in 1828, William succeeded to his professorship, but in 1835 was called to the chair of natural philosophy in the University of Virginia. This same year he was also commissioned state geologist in the newly organized survey of the state.

In 1848, becoming dissatisfied with his position at the University for various reasons, and "longing for an atmosphere of more stimulating power," he resigned, but was induced to reconsider and remain five years longer. He then removed to Boston. Some years before, he and his brother Henry had formulated provisional plans for a polytechnic school. Under the stimulus of the Boston atmosphere and with the opportunities for the establishment of such a school in the rapidly improving Back Bay district before him, Rogers so successfully advocated the project that in 1861 the legislature passed an act incorporating the Massachusetts Institute of Technology. The following year he was elected its first president. This position he held until 1870, when ill health caused his resignation. In 1878, with improved health, he again became president, continuing as such until 1881, when he resigned but remained as professor emeritus of geology and physics. He died on May 30 of the following year as he was beginning the delivery of diplomas to the graduating class.

Rogers' early predilection was toward chemistry and physics with particular reference to their industrial application. One of his earliest publications had to do with the greensand marls of Virginia and their fertilizing value (see *Farmers' Register*, August and November 1834, May 1835). As state geologist of Virginia, with a small group of assistants, one of whom was his brother Henry, he entered upon his duties in 1835, continuing as such until by legislative enactment the geological survey was abolished in 1842. Annual reports were submitted, but no provision made for a final report, and but for the energetic action of Maj. Jed Hotchkiss in bringing them together and publishing them with a map in 1884 under the caption *A Reprint of Annual Reports and Other Papers on the Geology of the Virginias,* the results would have been largely lost. Rogers' chief claim to recognition as a scientist rests not, however, on his career as state geologist, but rather on his joint work with his brother Henry on the structure of the Appalachian chain. At the time of his removal to Boston, he was working largely on physical problems and in 1861 was appointed by Governor Andrew state inspector of gas meters, a position he accepted with reluctance after having recommended another, but in which he rendered important service in the way of improved standards of measurement.

He was a man of broad views, a true philosophic spirit, and an all-round scientist. His greatest achievements, however, were in connection with the establishment and administration of the Massachusetts Institute of Technology. He possessed oratorical powers of a high order, a voice of commanding quality, and had a rare gift of diction and poetic expression. In personal appearance he was distinguished and impressive. He was a member of many scientific organizations: was chairman of the Association of American Geologists and Naturalists in 1845 and 1847; corresponding secretary of the American Academy of Arts and Sciences from 1863 to 1869; and an original member of the National Academy of Sciences, which he served as president from 1878 to 1882. On June 20, 1849, he was married to Emma Savage of Boston; they had no children.

[*Life and Letters of William Barton Rogers* (2 vols, 1896), ed. by his wife, which contains bibliog. of his writings; W. S. W. Ruschenberger, "A Sketch of the Life of Robert E. Rogers, with Biog. Notices of His Father and Brothers," in *Proc. Am. Philosophical Soc.,* vol. XXIII (1886); *Proc. Am. Acad. of Arts and Sci.,* vol. XVIII (1883); *Proc. Am. Asso. for the Advancement of Sci.,* vol. XLVIII (1899); *In Memory of William Barton Rogers* (Soc. of Arts, Mass. Inst. of Tech., 1882); F. A. Walker, in *Nat. Acad. Sci., Biog. Memoirs,* vol. III (1895); *Popular Sci. Monthly,* Sept. 1876; *Phila. Press,* May 31, 1882.]   G. P. M.

ROGERS, WILLIAM CROWNINSHIELD (July 26, 1823–July 2, 1888), clipper-ship captain, was born at Salem, Mass., the eldest son of

Richard Saltonstall and Sarah (Crowninshield) Rogers. Through his father he was descended from Rev. John Rogers, president of Harvard College in 1682–84; through his mother he was a grandson of Jacob Crowninshield [q.v.]. He attended the Salem Latin School and in 1839 entered Harvard College. In the spring of his junior year he left, apparently because of a weakness which had developed in his lungs, and went to sea as supercargo. He made several voyages, principally to the East Indies, in ships of N. L. Rogers & Brother, of which firm his father was a member. Thereafter, for several years, he commanded the *Thomas Perkins,* one of the "lucky ships" of Salem, and was one of few successful masters who had never served as seaman or subordinate officer on a vessel. In this ship he made a passage during 1849 from New York to San Francisco in 126 days, a remarkable feat for a full-built ship of that type. Leaving the *Perkins,* he took command in 1851 of the new clipper ship *Witchcraft,* of 1310 tons, one of the largest and handsomest clippers then afloat. Sailing from New York, Apr. 4, 1851, he ran to San Francisco in 103 days, net sailing time, the shortest passage but one that had been made up to that time. He was dismasted and compelled to put into Rio de Janeiro for repairs, making the run from that port to San Francisco in 62 days, a record which is believed to be still unbeaten. At the outbreak of the Civil War, Rogers enlisted and was assigned to the command of the clipper barque *Wm. G. Anderson,* with the rank of volunteer lieutenant. On Apr. 12, 1862, he was placed in command of the U. S. S. *Huntsville.* On Feb. 11, 1864, he was attached to the Eastern Gulf Squadron, in command of the U. S. S. *Iuka.* He was promoted to volunteer lieutenant-commander, Oct. 24, 1864. From June 15, 1865, to July 16, 1866, when he resigned from the service, he was engaged in shore duty.

With the death of his father, Rogers was left financially independent. He had retired from business before the war, because of his health, and did not thereafter engage in it actively, although he was a silent partner in the Boston branch of the London banking house of J. S. Morgan & Company and continued to be interested in a number of enterprises. He was instrumental in bringing about the consolidation of several small lines to form the Eastern Railroad Company, in which matter he acted as cotrustee with W. B. Bacon and Willard P. Phillips. In 1865 he received the degree of A.B. from Harvard. On July 6, 1871, he married Mary Ingersoll Bowditch. His only child, William Bowditch Rogers, was born on the Island

of Madeira, Sept. 14, 1874. His wife died at Funchal twelve days later. Rogers died of pleurisy in London on the 2nd day of July, 1888.

[Sources include: *Bull. of the Essex Inst.,* vol. XXI (1889); *Salem Gazette* and *Boston Evening Transcript,* July 3, 1888; *Salem Reg.,* July 5, 1888; *New-Eng. Hist. and Geneal. Reg.,* July 1851, Jan. 1859; *War of the Rebellion: Official Records* (*Navy*), ser. 1 and 2; A. H. Clark, *The Clipper Ship Era* (1910); G. G. Putnam, *Salem Vessels and Their Voyages* (1930); and marine columns of the *N. Y. Herald.*]   C. C. C.

ROHÉ, GEORGE HENRY (Jan. 26, 1851–Feb. 6, 1899), medical educator and psychiatrist, was born in Baltimore, Md., the son of John and Mary (Fuchs) Rohé, both immigrants from Bohemia. He was educated in the Baltimore public schools, began the study of medicine under the preceptorship of Dr. A. F. Erich, and graduated M.D. at the University of Maryland in 1873. He then studied and practised dermatology in Boston under Dr. Edward Wigglesworth, 1840–1896 [q.v.], served as assistant physician to the Boston Dispensary for Skin Diseases in 1876, and the following year returned to Baltimore to become assistant to his former preceptor, now professor of gynecology in the College of Physicians and Surgeons, where Rohé also served as lecturer on skin diseases. He entered the United States Signal Service in 1878, but three years later, settled once more in Baltimore, became professor of obstetrics in the College of Physicians and Surgeons, with which institution he was connected, in one capacity or another, until 1890. During this period he was editor of the *Medical Chronicle* (1882–85), associate editor of the *Independent Practitioner* (1882) and the *Annual of Universal Medical Science* (1890), author of *A Text Book of Hygiene* (1885) and *Practical Notes on the Treatment of Skin Diseases* (2 vols., 1885–86), and co-author with G. A. Liebig of *Practical Electricity in Medicine and Surgery* (1890).

In 1890 he was appointed health commissioner of Baltimore and proved a capable executive, but resigned the following year to become superintendent of the Maryland State Asylum for the Insane, at Catonsville. Four years later, when a new state asylum was erected at Sykesville, he was put in charge, and in the new institution made a departure from previous practice by putting no locks or fastenings on either windows or doors. Dr. A. L. Gihon, who inspected this asylum, reported: "Here then the problem has been solved, so far as human intelligence can do it, of the humane treatment of those unfortunates, whose minds have gone adaft" ("A Modern Madhouse," *Philadelphia Medical Journal,* Nov. 5, 1898, p. 976). Rohé was in advance of his time in his decided opinions with regard to the indeterminate penal sentence. He is quoted as saying, "A prisoner who shows no evidence that he will cease to be a menace to the community should certainly remain where he can do no mischief; and, on the other hand, there is no common sense in continuing to confine one who has experienced an honest change of heart" (*Journal of the Alumni Association of the College of Physicians and Surgeons, Baltimore,* April 1901, p. 7). He was quite convinced that "if the State were to spend more money on modern insane asylums, less money need be spent on jails and penitentiaries" (*Ibid.*). He pointed out in several papers the connection between mental and pelvic diseases and advocated surgical treatment for the relief of certain forms of insanity in women. He was noted among his medical colleagues for his supreme confidence in himself, and there was literally almost no position or duty which he did not consider himself competent to undertake. He was president of the American Association of Obstetricians and Gynecologists and of the Medical and Chirurgical Faculty of Maryland in 1893–94, and of the American Public Health Association, 1898–99. He was attending a meeting of the National Prison Congress at New Orleans, of which he was a prominent member, when death came to him suddenly, Feb. 6, 1899, from heart disease. He had known the danger of his condition for more than a year, but had refused to curtail his activities. He was survived by his wife, Mary Laudemann (Coffin) Rohé, whom he had married Jan. 18, 1890, and by their only child, a daughter.

[E. F. Cordell, *The Medic. Annals of Md.* (1903); *Jour. Alumni Asso., Coll. of Physicians and Surgeons, Baltimore,* Apr. 1899, Apr. 1901; H. A. Kelly and W. L. Burrage, *Am. Medic. Biogs.* (1920); *Md. Medic. Jour.,* Feb. 11, 1899; *Pub. Health Papers and Reports,* vol. XXV (1900); *Am. Jour. of Insanity,* Apr. 1899; *Buffalo Medic. Jour.,* Mar. 1899; H. M. Hurd and others, *The Institutional Care of the Insane in the U. S. and Canada,* vol. IV (1917); *Trans. Am. Asso. Obstetricians and Gynecologists,* vol. XI (1899); *Who's Who in America,* 1899; *Sun* (Balto.), Feb. 7, 1899.]   J. J. W.

ROLETTE, JEAN JOSEPH (Sept. 23, 1781– Dec. 1, 1842), pioneer fur trader on the Wisconsin and Upper Mississippi, was Canadian born, his grandfather having emigrated from Normandy about the middle of the eighteenth century. His father, Jean Joseph Rolette, and his mother, Angélique (Lortie), destined him, their eldest son, for the priesthood, and sent him to the Jesuit college at Quebec. Young Joseph, however, preferred a fur-trading career and in 1805 left for the West, spending one year opposite Detroit, in British territory. In 1806 he formed a partnership with a Scotchman, Murdoch Cameron, for trade at Prairie du Chien and on the Upper Mississippi, then entirely within the British sphere of influence. Lieut. Zebulon M. Pike [*q.v.*], sent in 1805 to recover this region for the United States, found Rolette on the Upper Mississippi, and later dined with him at Prairie du Chien. Rolette married in 1807 Marguerite Dubois, ward of Julien Dubuque, and by her had three daughters. During the War of 1812, like all his fellow traders, he served the British cause. He participated in the capture of Mackinac in 1812 and was in the British force that recaptured Prairie du Chien in 1814. After the latter expedition he was sent to Mackinac to announce the victory.

Following the American reoccupation of Prairie du Chien, Rolette was distrusted by the officers at Fort Crawford and for one winter was imprisoned on an island in the Mississippi. He was pardoned by Calhoun, when secretary of war, and became a citizen of the United States in 1823. Three years previously he had accepted the agency for the American Fur Company under Astor. He was a most successful trader. The Indians called him *Zica* (the pheasant) because he traveled so rapidly, and also *Ah-kay-zaup-ee-tah* (five more) because of his demands when trading. Many stories are told of his humor, vivacity, and good temper. By the *voyageurs* he was known as "King" Rolette, and when appointed (in 1830) chief justice for Crawford County he aided in keeping good order among the French-Canadians of Prairie du Chien. Nevertheless he had a reputation among the chief traders of this region for sharp practice, and his dealings were watched with suspicion. Astor trusted him, and at one time Rolette took his family to visit Astor in New York. His first wife died in 1817, and two years later he married Jane Fisher, a very young girl. He was reputed to be wealthy, but after his death there was much difficulty in settling his estate. He was survived by two daughters and a son, together with his widow, who later became the wife of his former clerk, H. L. Dousman.

[*Wis. Hist. Soc. Colls.,* esp. IX (1882), 293, 465, X (1888), 479; Joseph Tassé, *Les Canadiens de l'Ouest* (Montreal, 1878), I, 143–211; Juliette Magill Kinzie, *Wau-bun* (ed. of 1930); Elizabeth Fisher Baird's narratives in *Wis. Hist. Soc. Colls.,* XIV (1898), 55, and XV (1900), 219; MSS., including Rolette's will and papers relating to the administration of his estate, in Wis. Hist. Lib., Madison.]   L. P. K.

ROLFE, JOHN (1585–1622), colonist, was the son of John and Dorothea (Mason) Rolfe and was christened on May 6, 1585, at Heacham, in Norfolk, England. He was married, probably in 1608, and in June 1609 sailed for Virginia with his wife in the *Sea Adventure.* The vessel was wrecked on the Bermudas, and the voyagers were stranded many months. While there a daughter was born to him but soon died. The company built two pinnaces and in them escaped to Virginia, where his wife died. In 1612 he began experimenting with the native tobacco, which was unpalatable to Europeans. His methods of cultivation proved so successful that he produced a leaf as "pleasant, sweet, and strong" as any "under the sunne" (Hamor, *post,* p. 34). Immediately the staple of Virginia became tobacco, whose influence in shaping the economic, social, and even religious life of the colony can hardly be exaggerated. When in 1613 Pocahontas [*q.v.*] was brought captive to Jamestown, he fell in love with her and, having obtained the consent of Thomas Dale and of Powhatan [*qq.v.*], married her in April 1614. This union brought peace with the Indians for eight years, during which time the English established themselves firmly. In 1616 Rolfe took his wife to England, where she died leaving one son. While in England he wrote a description of Virginia for the King and Sir Robert Rich (no. 208, Duke of Manchester's Manuscripts in Public Record Office, London; *Southern Literary Messenger,* June 1839). He returned to Virginia in May 1617. He was secretary and recorder of the colony from June 1614 to 1619; and in 1621 he was appointed to the Council of State. His third wife was Jane, the daughter of William Pierce, or Pyers. In 1622 Bermuda Hundred, where Rolfe had his home, was wiped out in an Indian massacre, and here he seems to have met his death. His wife and daughter survived.

In the planting of England's first permanent settlement in America his part was vital, since failure might have resulted had it not been, on the one hand, for the peace that followed his marriage with Pocahontas and, on the other, the prosperity resulting from his experiments with tobacco.

[Ralph Hamor, *A True Discourse of the Present State of Va.* (1615; facsimile reprint 1860); Alexander Brown, *The Genesis of the United States* (2 vols., 1890); John Smith, *The Generall Historie of Va.* (1624); William Strachey, *The Hist. of Travaile into Virginia Britannia* (1849).]   T. J. W.

ROLFE, WILLIAM JAMES (Dec. 10, 1827– July 7, 1910), teacher, philologist, was born in Newburyport, Mass., the eldest child of John and Lydia Davis (Moulton) Rolfe and eighth in descent from Henry Rolfe, who, with his wife and son, emigrated from England in 1635 and settled in Newbury. His father was a hatter. Rolfe spent an active, happy boyhood in Haverhill and Lowell, graduated from the Lowell High School, learned proof-reading from the editor of the *Lowell Daily Courier,* spent a year in the counting-room of a cotton-mill, and attended Amherst College for three years as a member of the class of 1849. During the long winter vacations he taught country schools to defray his expenses. He greatly enjoyed his years at Amherst, but in 1848 he departed, feeling that it would be a waste of time to stay longer. He always cherished a strong affection for his college and received honorary degrees from it in 1865 and 1887.

After serving a short apprenticeship at Kirkwood Academy in Maryland, he was for twenty years a schoolmaster in his native state: first as principal and sole teacher at Day's Academy, Wrentham (1848–52)—a strenuous but educative experience—and afterward as principal or master of the Dorchester High School (1852–57), the Lawrence High School (1857–61), the Salem High School (1861–62), and the Cambridge High School (1862–68). What made his work significant was his introduction into the school curriculum of regular instruction in English literature. He had felt keenly the lack of such instruction in his own youth and found a sympathetic response among his pupils. For several years he did not realize that he was the pioneer of a sweeping reform in American secondary education. His work, however, came early to the attention of Cornelius Conway Felton and Francis James Child [*qq.v.*] and won their approbation, and in 1859 Harvard College conferred on him the honorary degree of A.M. In 1868 Rolfe retired from regular teaching and made the first of his many voyages to Europe. For the rest of his long life, he continued to live in Cambridge, devoting himself to various literary activities, but chiefly to the preparation of school books. He taught in the summer sessions of several universities, was president of the Martha's Vineyard Summer Institute (1882–88) and of the Emerson College of Oratory, Boston (1903–08). Until well advanced in years he was an enthusiastic traveler and tramper. In particular, he had an intimate and affectionate knowledge of every trail and summit in the White Mountains.

Thanks to methodical habits of work and to the care with which he guarded his not too robust health, he accomplished an astonishing amount of work. He had the passion for accuracy and thoroughness of a born textual critic, but because these qualities were expended on the editing of school books Rolfe has not received quite the recognition that he deserves. He was appreciated, however, by Child and H.

H. Furness [*q.v.*] in the United States and by Tennyson, Browning, Furnivall, and Halliwell-Phillipps in England. In 1907 he reckoned that he had written or edited 144 volumes in addition to his voluminous contributions to newspapers and periodicals. His first venture was *A Handbook of Latin Poetry* (1866), edited in collaboration with J. H. Hanson. This was followed by a series of science textbooks done in collaboration with J. A. Gillet and by the *Satchel Guide for the Vacation Tourist in Europe* (1872), which underwent annual revisions for many years. From 1869 to 1893 he was co-editor with J. R. Nichols [*q.v.*] of the *Boston Journal of Chemistry* and its successor, *Popular Science News.* He produced a long series of school editions of various English classics: *The Complete Works of Alfred, Lord Tennyson* (12 vols., 1895-98) and the "Cambridge edition" of *The Poetic and Dramatic Works of Alfred, Lord Tennyson* (1898); *The Poetical Works of Sir Walter Scott* (1888), based on a thorough, and much needed, collation of the original editions; and two school editions, each in forty volumes, of Shakespeare (1871-84 and 1903-06). No other editions of Shakespeare have been so widely used in the United States, and the originality, pithiness, and sound scholarship of his annotations have been often praised. A true child of his time, Rolfe idolized Shakespeare and expurgated what he wrote. His innumerable notes on Shakespeare, published for the most part in the *Critic,* the *Literary World,* and the *Nation,* are always exact and pointed. He also published *A Life of William Shakespeare* (1904). The original manuscript of this work was stolen, and Rolfe rewrote it completely.

He was married July 30, 1856, to Eliza Jane Carew, of Dorchester, who had been one of his pupils. She died Mar. 19, 1900. Their three sons outlived him. Rolfe died at the home of a son on Martha's Vineyard and was buried in Newburyport. Sound of mind and happily occupied to the end, he seems not to have anticipated death at the age of eighty-two. The last of his characteristic letters to the *Nation* was published June 30, 1910; the last to the New York *Evening Post* appeared on July 7, the day of his death.

[*A Bibliog. of William James Rolfe* (Cambridge Pub. Lib., 1907); *Emerson Coll. Mag.,* Rolfe Memorial Number, Nov. 1910, including Rolfe's autobiography; W. J. Rolfe and Edward Hitchcock, *Amherst Coll.: The Class of 1849* (1899); *Obituary Record of Grads. of Amherst Coll. for the Academic Year Ending June 28, 1911* (1911); *Amherst Coll.: Biog. Record . . . 1821-1921* (1927); F. W. Stearns, "Two Amherst Philologists," *Amherst Grads. Quart.,* Jan. 1912; *Who's Who in America,* 1899-1911; *Nation* (N. Y.), July 14, 1910; *Boston Transcript* (obituary and editorial), July 8, 1910.]   G. H. G.

ROLLINS, ALICE MARLAND WELLINGTON (June 12, 1847–Dec. 5, 1897), author, daughter of Ambrose and Lucy Jane (Kent) Wellington, was born in Boston. Her father, a descendant of colonial New Englanders, was a graduate of Harvard College and a lawyer; her mother was the daughter of Col. William Kent, a member of the New Hampshire legislature. Alice was taught at home by her father until she was fourteen, when she was sent to the Everett School in Boston and later to Lasell Seminary. A year abroad completed her formal education. She taught for several years, then, in 1876, married Daniel M. Rollins, of New York City, then connected with the firm of Henry Foster & Company, merchants trading with Brazil. Because of her husband's business relations, she traveled much in South America and Europe, and for a time lived in Brazil.

She began writing shortly after her school days were over. She was long a reviewer for the *Critic,* and contributed to almost all the leading periodicals of the day, including those for children and young people. Her first published book was *My Welcome Beyond and Other Poems* (1877), followed in 1878 by another volume of verse, *The Ring of Amethyst.* She next wrote several books for children, among them, *The Story of a Ranch* (1885), *All Sorts of Children* (1886), and *The Three Tetons: A Story of the Yellowstone* (1887). Her novel, *Uncle Tom's Tenement* (1888), based on New York tenement life, was an outgrowth of her essays on the subject and was credited with some reform influence. In 1889 she published another volume of verse, *From Snow to Sunshine.* In *From Palm to Glacier . . .* (1892) she related her experiences in Brazil, Bermuda, and Alaska. Two later volumes, *Aphorisms for the Year* (1894) and *Unfamiliar Quotations* (1895) are compilations. Her more mature poetic work is represented by *The Story of Azron* (1895), while *Little Page Fern and Other Verses* (1895) and *The Finding of the Gentian* (1895) are respectively books of verse and stories for children. Her verse is without especial distinction of idea or phrase, introspective, sad without being morbid, and often inspired by love of nature. Her prose is smooth, well phrased, and shows some humor and good description. Of all her books, *Uncle Tom's Tenement* probably received most attention from reviewers and was most read. During her long final illness she was writing a series of stories, of which those completed were published in the *Ladies' Home Journal* (1897-98). Shortly before her death she penned her last poem, *"Vita Benefica,"* which was published in the *Century Magazine* (February 1898). During her later years she lived at Lawrence Park, Bronxville, N. Y., where she died. She was very active there in social and club life. One son survived her.

[F. E. Willard and M. A. Livermore, *American Women* (1897); *Critic*, Dec. 11, 1897; *Literary World*, Dec. 11, 1897; *Ladies' Home Jour.*, Mar. 1898; *N. Y. Tribune*, Dec. 6, 1897.]   S. G. B.

ROLLINS, EDWARD HENRY (Oct. 3, 1824–July 31, 1889), politician, legislator, railroad financier, was born at Rollinsford, N. H., eldest of the six children of Daniel and Mary (Plumer) Rollins. On both sides of the family he was of good colonial stock, his father being a descendant of James Rawlins who came to New England in 1632, and settled at Ipswich, Mass. Edward spent his youth on his father's farm and once declared that no one knew better "the sorrows of hill-farm husbandry than I did until my twenty-first year." His early education was scanty, and while he began preparation for Dartmouth, lack of means obliged him to relinquish his ambition for a college education. He was an omnivorous reader, however, and overcame many of his early handicaps, writing and speaking with facility and vigor. After leaving home he spent several years as clerk in a Concord drug store, school-teacher, and employee of a wholesale drug firm in Boston. In 1847 he bought a drug business in Concord, N. H., with which he was associated until 1861. On Feb. 13, 1849, he married Ellen Elizabeth West.

His business prospered, his store became a rendezvous for local politicians and party workers, and the proprietor, an anti-slavery Whig, was soon a rising politician. He was a state committeeman for the Whig party in its moribund years, 1850–53, and passed via the Know-Nothing route into the new Republican organization. He was elected to the lower house of the legislature in 1855 and became speaker a year later. He performed important services in the merger of Know-Nothings, Free Soilers, Whigs, and anti-slavery Democrats into a coherent and enthusiastic party. The even balance of party strength and the fact that New Hampshire elections came in the spring made the state a pivotal one in national affairs and the work of Rollins attracted much attention. He was chairman of the Republican state committee from 1856 to 1861, resigning in the latter year because of his election to Congress.

He served three consecutive terms in the House and proved himself a conscientious committeeman, a stalwart supporter of war measures, and an indefatigable worker for the interests of his state and constituents. After the expiration of his third term he was again elected chairman of the state committee, serving from 1868 to 1872, and exercising a great influence on campaigns and policies when no longer a member. A textbook on party methods and practices could be written from his experiences in keeping New Hampshire in the Republican column. A profound believer in Republican principles, opposed to conciliation with the South, a conservative with scant tolerance for reform in any guise, but personally honest and fearless, he was distinctly a product of the era. He was a skilful manager of caucuses and conventions, an adept distributor of patronage and spoils, but emerged unsmirched from the political scandals of the period.

In 1869, through the influence of Oakes Ames [*q.v.*], a personal friend, he became assistant treasurer of the Union Pacific Railroad and secretary of its board of directors; two years later he was promoted to the post of treasurer. He had no connection with the Crédit Mobilier organization but his relationship to the railroad company caused increasing opposition to his candidacy for the United States Senate, and after his election for the term 1877–83 he deemed it advisable to sever it. In the Senate he followed much the same course he had pursued earlier in the House. His failure to secure a reëlection, due to the popularity of the doctrine of rotation which he had done much to foster and to the increasing restiveness of other leaders under the dominance of the Rollins machine, was a severe disappointment and led to his gradual retirement from active politics.

On his return to Concord he became increasingly active in New Hampshire business affairs, heading the banking firm of E. H. Rollins & Sons. From 1886 to 1889 he was president of the Boston, Concord & Montreal Railroad. A paralytic stroke from which he never recovered was probably the result of severe work over a long period of years. He retained an interest in farming, was a breeder of choice live stock, and did much for the agricultural improvement of the state. He died at Isles of Shoals, N. H., survived by four children, one of them being Frank West Rollins [*q.v.*].

[J. O. Lyford, *Life of Edward H. Rollins* (1906), based on Rollins' correspondence and other papers; J. R. Rollins, *Records of Families of the Name Rawlins or Rollins, in the U. S.* (1874); *Biog. Dir. Am. Cong.* (1928); *Granite Monthly*, Sept. 1877; *Concord Evening Monitor*, Aug. 2, 1889; *Independent Statesman* (Concord), Aug. 1, 8, 1889.]   W. A. R.

ROLLINS, FRANK WEST (Feb. 24, 1860–Oct. 27, 1915), banker and politician, was the fourth of the five children of Edward Henry [*q.v.*] and Ellen (West) Rollins. He was born in Concord, N. H., and like his father was devoted throughout his life to the upbuilding of the interests of his native state. Having received his early education in the Concord public schools and under private tuition, he was a student in the Massachusetts Institute of Technology from 1877 to 1880. He then studied law at Harvard (1880–81) and in a Concord office, was admitted to the New Hampshire bar in 1882, but having little taste for the profession, soon entered the investment banking business of E. H. Rollins & Sons. On Dec. 6, 1882, he married Katharine W. Pecker of Concord.

He was notably successful in business, and a public-spirited citizen, serving on numerous administrative boards and directorates, charitable and educational. In 1894 he was elected for a term in the New Hampshire Senate, serving as president of that body. Four years later he was elected governor of the state, holding office from 1899 to 1901. In his inaugural message he anticipated later policies by urging a comprehensive system of good roads and a thorough study of highway construction in relation to development of the economic and scenic resources of the state. He was an efficient but unspectacular executive, although on Apr. 6, 1899, his Fast Day proclamation stirred a local tempest by calling attention to the decadence of the churches in rural New Hampshire and implying the decadence of rural New England in general.

In 1898, at a gathering of natives of New Hampshire in Boston, he initiated a movement which subsequently spread throughout the country—that of "Old Home Week." He regarded himself as the father of this characteristically American institution and several of his addresses on the subject were subsequently collected and published. A more important activity, which he furthered while governor, and also as a private citizen, was conservation. Deeply interested in forestry, he gave generously of time and money to preserve existing forests in the White Mountains and to develop interest in reforestation in the state at large. As in the matter of highways, subsequent developments owed much to his initial efforts.

He had numerous literary interests, accumulated a valuable library, contributed articles and stories to local journals, and published several novels and collections of stories; *The Lady of the Violets* (1897) was probably his best-known work. While his literary efforts enjoyed some temporary popularity, they were minor incidents in his career. He died in Boston, survived by his wife and one son.

[J. R. Rollins, *Records of Families of the Name Rawlins or Rollins, in the U. S.* (1874) ; C. R. Corning, "Governor Rollins," *Granite Monthly*, Sept. 1899; *Who's Who in America*, 1914–15 ; *Daily Patriot* (Concord), Oct. 28, 1915 ; *Boston Transcript*, Oct. 28, 1915.]
W. A. R.

ROLLINS, JAMES SIDNEY (Apr. 19, 1812–Jan. 9, 1888), congressman, was born at Richmond, Ky., the son of Anthony Wayne Rollins, a native of Pennsylvania and prominent physician, and Sallie (Rodes) Rollins. His grandfather, Henry Rollins, was a native of Ireland. James Sidney attended Richmond Academy, spent two years at Washington College, and graduated in 1830 with highest honors from the Indiana University. Rejoining his family in Columbia, Mo., he read law for a time in the offices of Abiel Leonard, then served in the Black Hawk War. In 1834 he completed his legal education at Transylvania University. He developed a large practice, but the routine and delay of the law irked him, and as early as 1836 he turned to public affairs. By inheritance and by conviction a Whig, he edited the *Columbia Patriot* and in 1838 was elected to the legislature from a strongly Whig county. As a legislator he achieved marked distinction in the decade 1838–48. His lifelong interests were education and public improvements. He sponsored in 1839 legislation which gave form and substance to the state university, while his effective and eloquent leadership of the cause of higher education resulted in public grants and in private donations which secured the location of the institution at Columbia. Through successive sessions he urged upon politically hostile and indifferent colleagues the desirability of internal improvements, of wider educational opportunities, and of social legislation. He was an ardent supporter of Clay, and by 1848 he had become the recognized leader of the Missouri Whigs, the minority party in the state. As candidate for governor in 1848 he secured the largest vote ever cast for a Whig. He echoed no popular slogans and had no effective political organization, but his eloquence and presentation of issues attracted many followers.

After several years of successful practice, Rollins returned in 1854 to the legislature, when the issue of slavery in the territories was a threat to the maintenance and integrity of his party. Although a slave-owner, he believed and maintained that it was the right and duty of Congress to prohibit slavery in the territories. He was again a candidate for governor in 1857, receiving the support of former Whigs, Native Americans, and many Benton Democrats (*Weekly Jefferson Inquirer*, May 2, 1857). His defeat by

230 votes ended a brilliant but futile party leadership of twelve years. As the crisis of 1860 approached, he supported the Bell-Everett ticket and became a candidate for Congress. As a border-state moderate in a slave-owning constituency he was willing fully to recognize the complaints of the South but refused to sanction secession. Both he and John B. Henderson, his opponent, emphatically disavowed any antislavery sentiment, and Rollins won. He was reëlected easily in 1862, as a Conservative-Unionist. Primarily concerned with preserving the Union, with or without slavery, he had the confidence of Lincoln and gave the government loyal and courageous support. He opposed confiscation, the Emancipation Proclamation, military government, and had grave doubt of the compensated emancipation plan for loyal slave-owners in Missouri. "I am for the Constitution and the Union as our fathers made them—I want no change" (*Congressional Globe,* Appendix, 37 Cong., 3 Sess., p. 106). By 1865, however, he realized that slavery must be abolished, and he supported the resolution submitting the Thirteenth Amendment. Singularly free from the intolerance and fanaticism of some border-state politicians, he opposed the proscriptive and punitive spirit and measures both in Missouri and in the nation.

In 1866 a crisis in the affairs of the University induced Rollins to reënter the legislature where he remained until 1872. The institution was in a dismal plight. The Republican majority was hostile toward it; the resources were almost exhausted, and public opinion generally indifferent. He met the difficult situation with tact and enthusiasm, and, by judicious concessions, was instrumental in securing the enactment of five significant statutes, 1867–72, relating to the University and to the newly created College of Agriculture. By these measures the institution was placed upon a solid and permanent foundation. Opposed to radical Republicanism, he aided in the restoration of the state Democracy in 1867–68, although he was never in complete accord with the Democratic party. His conciliatory policy, wisely dictated in behalf of educational legislation, was unpopular with many. With Carl Schurz and B. Gratz Brown he was a leader in the Liberal Republican movement. His lifelong ambition to be governor was finally frustrated in 1872 when the former Confederate element defeated him in the Democratic state convention. He retired from active politics in that year. Of tall and commanding presence, with resonant voice and facile rhetoric, he captivated his audiences and was easily one of the

first citizens of the state for half a century. He died after a lingering illness, survived by his wife, Mary E. Hickman, whom he had married on June 6, 1837, and by seven of their eleven children.

[Sources include: W. B. Smith, *Jas. Sidney Rollins Memoir* (1891), containing selections from his speeches and letters; *Hist. of Boone County, Mo.* (1882); W. E. Smith, *The Francis Preston Blair Family in Politics* (2 vols., 1933); *Mo. Republican,* Jan. 10, 1888; Rollins Papers in the possession of Rollins' son, C. B. Rollins, Columbia, Mo.]   T.S.B.

ROLLINSON, WILLIAM (Apr. 15, 1762–Sept. 21, 1842), engraver, was born in Dudley, Worcester, England, eldest son of Robert and Mary (Hill) Rollinson. On May 10, 1782, he was married, in Birmingham, to Mary Johnson, ten years his senior, and on Nov. 29, 1788, he sailed for America. During the voyage he improvised tools and engraved ornaments and monograms on jewelry for officers and passengers. He wrote in his diary, "By when I arrive in America it will bring my hand in and I shall be capable of turning cypher cutter in general to the United States" (Reid and Rollinson, *post,* p. 13). Arriving in New York Feb. 15, 1789, he soon was employed in ornamenting silver buttons for the coat worn by Washington at his inauguration. Other similar work followed, and in about a year he returned to England to bring over his wife and child.

In the American spirit of turning one's hand to anything, he soon began, with no experience, to engrave on copper, and chose for his first effort the subject then most popular with engravers—a portrait of George Washington. For *The Self-Interpreting Bible* (1792), edited by the Rev. John Brown, he engraved seven plates, pronounced "crude" by Stauffer (*post*), who adds that he improved rapidly. About 1796 he changed from line to stipple engraving, doing work for magazines, as also an engraving of Archibald Robertson's portrait of Alexander Hamilton (1804). He engraved bookplates, maps, and certificates. A noted plate is the aquatint view of New York from Long Island (1801) from a drawing by John Wood. Though he "had no knowledge of . . . processes used by those brought up to the profession," he "had perseverance and ingenuity to surmount all difficulties" (Dunlap, *post,* I, 188). He naturally turned to banknote engraving, developing a method of ruling lines by machine to prevent counterfeiting. Engaging W. S. Leney [*q.v.*] to engrave his vignettes in order to improve the artistic element of his products, he took his place among those who perfected methods of banknote engraving, specially cultivated in the United States by many capable engravers.

Tall, and of great bodily strength, Rollinson was "easy going, bright and jovial" (Brand, *post,* p. 4). He was a Mason, a volunteer fireman, a member of the Society of Mechanics and Tradesmen, and a lieutenant of artillery. Three of his grandsons entered the ministry: William Rollinson Whittingham [*q.v.*], Episcopal bishop of Maryland, Richard Whittingham, and William Rollinson.

[Rollinson's diary of his voyage to America is in the possession of his great-grandson, Charles Rollinson. A portrait by F. S. Agate, mentioned by Dunlap, has not been found, but the late D. M. Stauffer possessed a silhouette of him. Two portraits were reproduced with an article by R. W. Reid in the *Masonic Outlook,* Feb. 1931. See also D. M. Stauffer, *Am. Engravers upon Copper and Steel* (2 vols., 1907); R. W. Reid and Charles Rollinson, *William Rollinson, Engraver* (privately printed, 1931); Mantle Fielding, *Am. Engravers upon Copper and Steel* (1917); W. F. Brand, *Wm. Rollinson Whittingham, Fourth Bishop of Md.* (2 vols., 1883); Wm. Dunlap, *A Hist. of the Rise and Progress of the Arts of Design in the U. S.* (3 vols., 1918), ed. by F. W. Bayley and C. E. Goodspeed; *Evening Post* (N. Y.), Sept. 22, 1842.]   F. W.

ROLSHOVEN, JULIUS (Oct. 28, 1858–Dec. 7, 1930), painter, was born at Detroit, Mich., the son of Frederick and Maria Theresa Hubertina (Hellings) Rolshoven. As a youth he had training in art at Cooper Union and the Plessman Academy, New York. In 1878 he registered at the Düsseldorf, Germany, Academy as a pupil of Hugo Crola. A year later he was studying at Munich under Professor Ludwig Loefftz. There, with other young Americans, he came under the spell of the technique and teaching of Frank Duveneck [*q.v.*]. He was of the group of "Duveneck Boys," which included John W. Alexander, John H. Twachtman, Ross Turner, J. Frank Currier, and Harper Pennington, who painted at Florence, Italy. Of his character it has been said: "Rolshoven, too, was endowed by nature with the artistic temperament, making it especially difficult for him to adapt himself to routine work" (Norbert Heermann, *Frank Duveneck,* 1918, p. 46). In 1882 he became a pupil of Tony Robert-Fleury and Adolphe William Bouguereau in Paris. He exhibited his landscape and genre paintings at the Salon and the Société Nationale des Beaux-Arts, Paris; the Munich Secession; Chelsea Art Club, London, and other exhibitions. In 1890 he established at Paris life classes which drew an international attendance, and from 1896 to 1902 he continued in London.

Rolshoven was married first in 1887, at Florence, to Anna Eliza Chickering. She died in 1897, and in 1915 he was married to Harriette Haynes Blazo. Throughout his long residence in Europe he kept up his contacts with Detroit where his mother lived into her ninety-third year. In 1912 an exhibition of some eighty of his paintings from North Africa made a favorable impression on the Detroit public. Many American collectors acquired his paintings, and he was represented in his life-time in the Detroit Institute of Arts by "The Refectory of San Damiano, Assisi"; in the Cincinnati Art Museum, by "Chiogga Fishing Girl" and "Church of St. Francis at Assisi"; by canvases in the museums of Brooklyn, Baltimore, Minneapolis, and Santa Fé.

During a visit to the West in 1914 he became impressed by the landscape and Indians of New Mexico, and during the disturbed war years he was a member of the artist colony at Taos. An exhibition of his New Mexican pictures was held at Detroit in 1923. In 1924 he was awarded the Richard S. Greenough memorial prize of the Newport, R. I., Art Association. After the war he gave residential addresses in three cities, Detroit, Paris, and Florence. He held membership, as an associate, in the National Academy of Design and in the National Arts Club, New York; the Secession, Munich; the Society of Arts and Letters, Paris; the Foreign Arts Club and the Bene Merensa Società di Belle Arti, Florence; the International Fine Arts Congress; the Taos Society of Artists, and the Detroit Fine Arts Society. The extensive list of organizations of which he was a member revealed something of Rolshoven's personality. He was an internationalist, believing that the American artist should associate with the artists of other countries, should experience no inferiority complex in such association, and should demand from the American public at least as generous treatment as that accorded to the foreign artist.

Rolshoven died in New York City while on his way to the bedside of his mother in Detroit, who outlived him by about four hours. A memorial exhibition of his works was held at the Detroit Institute of Arts. He had received during his career such honors as the second medal of the Paris Exposition, 1889; honorable mention, Paris, 1900; a bronze medal, Pan-American Exposition, Buffalo, 1901; silver medal, St. Louis Exposition, 1904; and medals from seasonal exhibitions of Munich, Berlin, Brussels, Florence, and Chicago. His self-portrait is in the gallery of artist portraits at the Uffizi, Florence.

[See: *Bull. of the Detroit Inst. of Arts,* Apr. 1931; *Biog. Sketches of Am. Artists* (1924); pub. by the Mich. State Lib.; *Am. Art Annual,* 1931; *Art News,* Dec. 13, 1930; *Who's Who in America,* 1920–21, 1928–29; *N. Y. Times,* Dec. 8, 1930; information from F. W. Robinson, Asst. Curator, Cincinnati Art Museum.]   F. W. C.

RÖLVAAG, OLE EDVART (Apr. 22, 1876–Nov. 5, 1931), author and educator, was born on the island of Dönna, Helgeland, Norway, the son of Peder Jakobsen and Ellerine Johanna (Olson) Rölvaag. He attended school between the ages of seven and fourteen and read diligently in the local library. After some years of fishing—the traditional occupation of his people—he decided to emigrate and, forfeiting the command of a beautiful boat, secured a ticket from an uncle in South Dakota. He landed in New York in August 1896, worked three years as a farm hand, and then entered Augustana College, a Norwegian Lutheran preparatory school in Canton, S. Dak. After four years at St. Olaf College, Northfield, Minn., he was graduated with honors in 1905. After a year of graduate study at the University of Oslo, Norway, he was appointed professor of Norwegian at St. Olaf College, and in 1916 became head of the department. In the summer of 1926 he suffered a complete breakdown, caused by heart disease, from which he only partially recovered. On Dec. 31, 1926, he was created by King Haakon of Norway a knight of the Order of St. Olaf. He taught again during the first semester of 1927–28, during the second semester was a guest of the Norwegian government at the Ibsen centennial, and returned to teaching in 1928–29. On Aug. 31, 1931, he resigned, intending to devote himself entirely to literary pursuits, but he died at his home in Northfield early in November of that same year. He married Jennie Marie Berdahl of Garretson, S. Dak., on July 9, 1908. Of his four children only two survived him.

Rölvaag's childhood in Norway left a deep imprint on his literary work. This land of contrasts, with its dark winter and its midnight sun, stimulated his imagination and gave him his passionate love of the sea. His later reading added an intense cultural patriotism which determined much of his activity. He deplored the tendency of Norwegians in America to drift away from their racial culture, and sought to stem it by determined propaganda. During the World War he was stung into activity by the "Americanizers," and between 1918 and 1922 published three Norse readers and a collection of essays, *Omkring Fædrearven* ("Concerning our Heritage"). From its founding in 1925 he was secretary of the Norwegian-American Historical Association.

He wrote his first novel as a senior in college, an idyllic (and unpublished) effort entitled *"Nils og Astri, eller Brudstykker av norsk-amerikansk Folkeliv"* (". . . Fragments of Norwegian-American Popular Life"). In 1912 ap-

peared *Amerika-Breve* ("Letters from America"), professing to be letters written to father and brother in Norway by one P. A. Smevik and collected by Paal Mörck. This essentially autobiographical novel, like all his earlier books published in Minneapolis, was an attempt to reveal the gradual accommodation of the immigrant to his new surroundings. In 1914 appeared the more ambitious *Paa glemte Veie* ("On Forgotten Paths"), still under the pseudonym Paal Mörck. The war years left their deposit of bitterness in *To Tullinger* ("Two Simpletons"), 1920, which has been translated and amplified in English as *Pure Gold* (1930). Another novel appeared in 1921, *Længselens Baat,* published in English as *The Boat of Longing* (1933). It was inspired by Rölvaag's grief over the distressing death of his youngest child, and embodied more of the tremendous scenery of Norway and of his own lyric magnificence than any of his other books. Its purpose was to depict the tragic effect of American city life on the soul of a sensitive immigrant.

Rölvaag's earlier works were first issued in Minneapolis. National and world-wide fame came to him with the series begun by *I de Dage* ("In Those Days"), published in Norway in 1924, and *Riket grundlægges* ("The Kingdom is Founded"), 1925, both translated in 1927 with the aid of Lincoln Colcord and published in America under the title, *Giants in the Earth*. The scene is South Dakota of the seventies. In the persons of Per Hansa and Beret Holm, Rölvaag embodied the glory and the tragedy of the immigrant pioneer. The book's success both in Norway and America was instantaneous and phenomenal. American critics were unanimous in acclaiming the integrity of Rölvaag's art and the validity of his interpretation of the frontier. The *Nation* (July 13, 1927, p. 41) called it "the fullest, finest, and most powerful novel that has been written about pioneer life in America." Vernon Parrington and Carl Sandburg gave it high commendation, the former praising Rölvaag's work for its "creative realism and brooding imagination." Within a few years of the book's publication in English it was translated into Swedish, Finnish, Dutch, German, and Hungarian. Two sequels followed: in 1928, *Peder Seier* (English version, *Peder Victorious,* 1929), and in 1931 *Den signede Dag* ("The Blessed Day"), translated in the same year as *Their Fathers' God*. These were well received, although their concern with the less impressive problems of the second generation in the land deprived them of the epic sweep of *Giants in the Earth*.

Artistically Rölvaag found his models among the classic novelists of Norway, especially Jonas Lie, with later impulses from Knut Hamsun and Sigrid Undset. He fused in his work the scrupulous truth of detail demanded by modern realism with an essentially optimistic view of life.

[*Who's Who in America*, 1930–31; Lincoln Colcord, Introduction to *Giants in the Earth* (1927) and "Rölvaag the Fisherman Shook His Fist at Fate," *Am. Mag.*, Mar. 1928; Kristine Haugen, "Glimt fra Rolvaags Liv," *Decorah-Posten* (Decorah, Iowa), Dec. 8, 1931; obituaries in *Northfield News*, Nov. 13, 1931, *N. Y. Times*, Nov. 6, 1931, and *Publishers' Weekly*, Nov. 14, 1931; P. H. Boynton, "O. E. Rölvaag and the Conquest of the Pioneer," *English Journal*, Sept. 1929; Jörgen Bukdahl, "*Riget grundlægges*," in *Det skjulte Norge* (Copenhagen, 1926); Henry Commager, "The Literature of the Pioneer West," *Minn. Hist.*, Dec. 1927; Einar I. Haugen, "O. E. Rölvaag: Norwegian American," *Studies and Records* (Norw.-Am. Hist. Asso.), vol. VII (1933); Addison Hibbard, "Analysis of O. E. Rölvaag's *Pure Gold*," *Creative Reading: Discussions in Current Lit.* (Cambridge, Mass.), Feb. 15, 1930; J. E. Olson, "Rölvaag's Novels of Norwegian Pioneer Life in the Dakotas," *Scandinavian Studies and Notes*, 1927; Vernon Parrington, editor's introduction to *Giants in the Earth* (Harper's Modern Classics, 1929), reprinted in Parrington's *Main Currents in Am. Thought*, vol. III (1930); Georg Strandvold, "Rolvaags Præriesaga," *Decorah-Posten*, Dec. 11, 1931–Jan. 29, 1932; Aagot D. Hoidahl, "Norwegian-American Fiction since 1880," *Studies and Records* (Norw.-Am. Hist. Asso.), vol. V (1930); partial bibliog. of Rölvaag's writing in *Giants* (Parrington ed.), pp. 467–68.]   E. I. H.

ROMAN, ANDRÉ BIENVENU (Mar. 5, 1795–Jan. 28, 1866), governor of Louisiana, was born in St. Landry Parish, the son of Jacques Étienne and Marie Louise (Patin) Roman and the grandson of Jacques Roman who emigrated to Louisiana from Grenoble, France, before 1741. He was early taken to St. James Parish, where his father established a sugar plantation. After graduating from St. Mary's College at Baltimore in 1815, he was married in 1816 to Aimée Françoise Parent and established himself on a plantation in St. James Parish. They had five children. His public life began in 1818 with his election to the Louisiana House of Representatives, where he retained his seat, often without opposition, for many years, during four of which he served as speaker. This service was interrupted in 1826 for two years, while he acted as parish judge. This office he resigned, however, to return to the lower house, where he was again discharging the duties of speaker when he was elected governor. His two gubernatorial terms, with the four years' interval required by law, embraced the period from 1831 to 1843, a period of disaster when the state was scourged by epidemics and flood. Under the governor's insistence a board of public works and a fund for internal improvements was created by law. Under this act many of the water courses were cleared of their obstructions and numerous improvements accomplished. The board effected also the incorporation of the New Orleans drainage company. Roman accepted the presidency of that company after his retirement from office and held it long enough to render important service to the city in planning a system of drainage to relieve it of the immense swamp lying behind it. Since Roman headed the list of private subscribers who sponsored the opening of Jefferson College in St. James Parish, and since he obtained its incorporation in 1831, he may justly be regarded as the founder of that institution. The construction of the state penitentiary at Baton Rouge, based on modern ideals of prison management, was due to him, and the incorporation in 1834 of the New Orleans chamber of commerce won his hearty indorsement. His natural solicitude for the planting interests prompted the formation of a state agricultural society, of which he later became the zealous president. An experimental farm was created in St. James Parish, but, as adequate support was not forthcoming, both the farm and society ceased to exist. His suggestions and exertions, continued through both terms, gave the first practical impetus to the establishment of public common schools in the state. Equally important on the negative side was his courageous use and threat of use of the veto power against plunging the state into debt by unsound railroad legislation, an action that brought upon him general and severe condemnation. His historical interest led him to obtain a small appropriation for the copying of manuscripts in the Paris archives on the colonial history of the state. His second term was notable for financial derangements, during which he insisted on Louisiana paying her bonds. In spite of his effort to retire quietly to his plantation after his second term, he was recalled to public life for special services. In 1845 and 1852 he was called to state constitutional conventions; in 1848 he was sent to Europe as agent for two banks to obtain extension of time for payment of interest and renewal of the bonds.

A Whig in politics, moderate in his attitude toward the abolition movement, he opposed disunion strenuously; but as a delegate to the state secession convention of 1861 he yielded to the majority. He even accepted appointment from the Confederate provisional government on the commission created to confer with the United States for peaceable separation. Although he was too old to enter military service, he remained faithful to the Confederacy, refusing to protect his property by the oath of allegiance after the occupation of the state by federal troops. At the close of the war, about six weeks before his death, destitute and despondent, he accepted from Governor Wells a petty office, recorder of deeds and mortgages in New Orleans. The qualities of good judgment and unflinching firmness could scarcely be denied him, and he has been conceded to be one of Louisiana's ablest governors.

[Mrs. Eugene Soniat-du-Fossat, *Biog. Sketches of La. Governors* (1885) ; Arthur Meynier, *Louisiana Biographies* (1882) ; J. F. Condon, "Annals of Louisiana," App. to F. X. Martin, *The Hist. of La.* (1882) ; Alcée Fortier, *A Hist. of La.* (1904), vols. III, IV ; C. E. A. Gayarré, *Hist. of La.*, vol. IV (1886) ; W. H. Sparks, *The Memories of Fifty Years* (1870) ; "A. B. Roman of Louisiana, Agriculturist," *De Bow's Southern and Western Review*, Oct. 1851 ; S. C. Arthur and G. C. H. de Kernion, *Old Families of La.* (1931) ; *New Orleans Times* and *New Orleans Bee*, Jan. 29, 1866, *Daily True Delta* (New Orleans), Jan. 30, 1866.]

E. L.

ROMANS, BERNARD (*c.* 1720–*c.* 1784), civil engineer, naturalist, cartographer, author, and captain of artillery, was born in the Netherlands about 1720. He studied engineering in England and about 1757 was sent to North America by the British government on professional work. In 1766 he was appointed deputy surveyor of Georgia, but went to East Florida to survey Lord Egmont's estates on Amelia Island and the St. John's River, and was thus enabled to make observations in the northern part of the peninsula. In January 1767, he petitioned for a grant of land in the province; in that year and the next he took up lands at Savannah and on the Ogeechee River, and in 1769 he acquired a tract on Nassau River in Florida, and subsequently extended his investigations to the middle and western parts of the peninsula.

In 1769–70 Romans was appointed principal deputy surveyor for the Southern District by the surveyor general, William Gerard De Brahm [*q.v.*], at a salary of £30 a year; but since De Brahm was suspended by Gov. James Grant in October 1770, Romans failed to receive his salary and brought suit. Nevertheless, he went on a voyage of nearly a year's duration at his own expense, selling his Florida land in 1771. He thus completed his exploration of the Florida and Bahama banks and the west coast as far as Pensacola. There he was employed by Gov. Peter Chester and John Stuart [*q.v.*], superintendent of Indian affairs, to assist in the survey of West Florida and to prepare maps. Finding that Romans understood botany, Chester obtained permission from England to pay him £50 or £60 a year to make botanical discoveries, and the surveyor thus became the king's botanist in the province. Having voyaged as far as New Orleans, he sailed for Charlestown in February

1773, to resume employment under Stuart in South Carolina. His vessel capsized on the journey, and, after his arrival at his destination, for some reason Stuart declined his service.

Romans thereupon proceeded to New York to get subscribers for a book he planned to write on the Floridas. In the following August he was elected a member of the Marine Society of that city and attended a meeting of the American Philosophical Society in Philadelphia, before which he described two Florida plants, previously unknown, presented a paper on an improvement in the mariner's compass, and exhibited a navigation chart for the Florida waters. In January 1774 he was made a member of the society; he was then in Boston seeing about the engraving of his maps and endeavoring to obtain more subscribers for his book. Meanwhile he had found time to contribute an article on indigo to the *Royal American Magazine* (January 1774). On Mar. 9 he met the Rev. Ezra Stiles [*q.v.*] in Newport, R. I., with whom he later talked at length about Indians, Stiles recording in his diary that "Capt. Romans" had traveled among all the tribes "from Labradore to Panama" (*The Literary Diary of Ezra Stiles*, 1901, I, 524–25). At the end of March the busy author was in New York, when he wrote an article on the cultivation of madder for the *Royal American Magazine* (April 1774).

Settling shortly afterward in Hartford, Romans was appointed in April 1775 a member of the Connecticut committee to take possession of Ticonderoga and its outposts. He disagreed with the other leaders about the mode of attack, went on to Fort George, then in the custody of an invalided officer and one assistant, and on May 12 seized it single-handed. He behaved "very genteel and civil" toward his prisoner, permitting him to go to Connecticut. After accepting employment with the New York committee of safety to construct fortifications on the Hudson near West Point, he gave allegiance to the provincial congress on Sept. 18. He complained of his difficulties while building Fort Constitution, opposite West Point (Sept. 30, 1775–Feb. 9, 1776), and criticized the committee's plan. Although signing himself "Colonel," he failed to receive his commission from the provincial congress, resented the countermanding of his orders, and refused to serve as "an overseer" instead of as "sole director" of his plan. By direction of the Continental Congress he was paid up to Feb. 9, 1776.

Returning to Philadelphia, Romans was commissioned in February 1776 captain of a company of Pennsylvania artillery for service in

Canada. In November, Gen. Horatio Gates deputed him to inspect the works at Fort Anne and Skenesboro. Later he retired to Wethersfield, Conn., where he married Elizabeth Whiting, Jan. 28, 1779. His son Hubertus was born on Oct. 23 of that year. About July 1780, Romans was ordered to South Carolina to join the southern army. His vessel was captured and conducted to Montego Bay, Jamaica, where he was kept prisoner. At the end of the Revolution he was put on board ship for some port of the United States, having with him a large sum of money. He is said to have died at sea. His widow tried unsuccessfully to obtain a pension, and died in New York, May 12, 1848, at the age of eighty-nine years.

Romans' most noted book is *A Concise Natural History of East and West Florida,* of which vol. I was published in New York in 1775, and issued in a second edition in 1776. A second volume was projected but never published. The appendix to the *History,* containing contributions from De Brahm and other navigators, was published in 1789 as *The Complete Pilot for the Gulf Passage,* and reprinted in 1794 as *A New and Enlarged Book of Sailing Directions,* and again in 1797 with a slight change in title. The first volume of Romans' *Annals of the Troubles in the Netherlands* appeared at Hartford in 1778, and the second volume at the same place in 1782. These he compiled and translated "from the most Approved Historians." His printed maps include plans of Pensacola Harbor, Mobile Bar, and Tampa Bay, printed in the Appendix to the *Concise Natural History;* "A Map of the Whole Navigation, Showing Lieut. Cook's Tracks," in John Hawkesworth's *A New Voyage Round the World* (vol. I, 1774); *Part of the Province of East Florida* (1774), reprinted in the *Concise Natural History; A Map of the Seat of Civil War in America* (1775), showing Boston and the neighboring region; "A General Map of the Southern British Colonies in America," in *The American Military Pocket Atlas* (1776); *A Chorographical Map of the Northern Department of North America* and *A Chorographical Map of the Country Round Philadelphia,* both advertised for sale in 1778.

[W. H. Siebert, *Loyalists in East Florida, 1774–85* (1929), vol. II; P. L. Phillips, *Notes on the Life and Work of Bernard Romans* (1924); A. D. Candler, *The Colonial Records of the State of Ga.,* vol. X (1907); Secretary of State's Letter Book A . . . Florida MSS. (MSS. Div., Lib. of Cong.), pp. 176–77, 190–91, 224; *Jours. of the Provincial Cong.,* State of N. Y., vols. I, II (1842); *Conn. Hist. Soc. Colls.,* vol. I (1860); *Am. Archives,* 4 ser. II–VI (1839–46), 5 ser. I (1848); *Pa. Archives,* 5 ser. III (1906); *New-Eng. Hist. and Geneal. Reg.,* Apr. 1866, p. 124; *N. Y. Daily Tribune,* May 13, 1848.]
W. H. S—t.

ROMAYNE, NICHOLAS (September 1756–July 21, 1817), physician, was the eldest son of John Romeyn, a New York silversmith, and his wife Juliana McCarty. His brother Jeremiah and several of his close relatives were Dutch Reformed clergymen (W. B. Sprague, *Annals of the American Pulpit,* vol. IX, 1869). Nicholas, who altered the spelling of his name, received his early education at the Hackensack Academy under Peter Wilson [*q.v.*] and entered the medical school of King's College, New York, in 1774. He secured the M.D. degree at Edinburgh in 1780, writing a thesis on the formation of pus, *De Generatione Puris* (Edinburgh, 1780), and continued his education for a time on the Continent. Returning to America, he settled first in Philadelphia, then after the evacuation, in New York, where he married Susan, daughter of Isaac Van Dam, merchant, of the Island of St. Eustatia (*Collections of the New York Historical Society,* Publication Fund Series, vol. XXXVII, 1905, p. 389).

He was one of the original board of regents of the University of the State of New York from 1784 to 1787, and when the trustees of Columbia College were independently chartered in 1787, he was made an original member of this board, resigning in 1793. In 1785 he was elected professor of the practice of physic in the revived Medical School of Columbia College, holding the title until 1787, and in 1791–92 he was lecturer in chemistry, anatomy, and the practice of physic; but this faculty having performed but small service, Romayne was mainly occupied from 1787 in the instruction of private classes. Being a man of learning and wide culture, he attracted many students, and in time he had a medical school of his own. In 1791 he addressed the regents of the University, asking their protection and direction for the school, and shortly afterward he and six associates, young physicians, addressed a second memorial describing their proposed plans for instruction. The regents were favorably disposed, and granted a charter to Sir James Jay [*q.v.*], Romayne, and others as the College of Physicians and Surgeons. The Columbia trustees made immediate objection, representing that they were engaged in establishing a medical department according to their charter, and the Romayne proposal was suspended. Romayne then approached the trustees of Queen's (now Rutgers) College at New Brunswick, N. J., for a degree-conferring arrangement, and was able to secure degrees from that institution for some of his students in 1792 and 1793. The Queen's affair, however, placed him under the ban of his profession in New York, and he went to Europe for further study and observation. Here he was made a licentiate of the Royal College of Physicians in London and a fellow of the Royal College of Physicians in Edinburgh.

Romayne's next appearance was as a speculator in Western lands, implicated in the Blount conspiracy of 1797. The scheme having failed, Romayne, conceiving that his countrymen looked upon him with suspicion, left the country (C. R. King, *post*, III, p. 258). In 1806, "by a sudden and singular change of sentiment," he was called from his retirement and honored by election as first president of the medical society of the city and county of New York (Hosack, *post*, p. 92). In 1807 the College of Physicians and Surgeons, dormant since 1791, was revived and Romayne was made president and trustee, and in 1808 professor of the institutes of medicine; during 1807–08, in the absence of a professor, he gave lectures in anatomy. He made the *Address Delivered at the Commencement of the Lectures* in the school, published in New York in 1808. It was not long, however, before difficulties arose. In 1811 he and several of the professors resigned, and Romayne was back at Queen's College for degree-granting connections. Some of the more distinguished members of the faculty had stood by him, and again in 1812 Queen's established a faculty of medicine and appointed these men to professorships, making Romayne professor of the institutes of medicine and forensic medicine. The school was carried on, as before, in quarters in New York City. Twenty-one students, including Joseph Rodman Drake [*q.v.*], received the Queen's degree, but in 1816 the school was closed. Dr. Hosack said "it fell in its own weakness" (*post*, p. 34). Romayne died in New York the next year at the age of sixty-one. Samuel Latham Mitchill is quoted as having said of him: "His superior attainments in literature and medicine elevated him with high notions, and filled him with contemptuous notions of some who had been less fortunate in education than himself" (Hosack, *post*, pp. 90–91).

[Sources include: David Hosack, *An Inaugural Discourse, Delivered at the Opening of Rutgers Medic. Coll. . . . N. Y.* (1826); *A Communication from the Regents of the Univ., Transmitting a Report of a Committee of the Regents . . . Appointed to Visit the Coll. of Physicians and Surgeons* (1826); manuscript minutes of the Trustees of Columbia and the Coll. of Physicians and Surgeons; J. G. Curtis, "The Genesis of the Coll. of Physicians and Surgeons," *Columbia Univ. Quart.*, Supp. to Dec. 1907; J. C. Dalton, *Hist. of the Coll. of Physicians and Surgeons* (1888); John Shrady, *The Coll. of Physicians and Surgeons* (n.d.); James Thacher, *Amer. Medic. Biog.* (1828), II, 25–29; W. H. S. Demarest, *A Hist. of Rutgers Coll.* (1924); Rutgers College, *Cat. of the Officers and Alumni* (1916); C. R.

King, *The Life and Correspondence of Rufus King*, II (1895), III (1896). Although Romayne's death date is usually given as July 20, 1817, the *N. Y. Columbian* of July 21, 1817, says he "died this morning at 10 o'clock."]   M. H. T.

ROMBRO, JACOB (Oct. 10, 1858–Nov. 28, 1922), editor, author, labor leader, best known under his pen name, Philip Krantz, was born in Zuphran, Province of Wilna (then a part of the Russian Empire), although some biographers give Khodaki, Podolia, as his birthplace. His parents were Baruch Rombro and Bella Rosa (Uger). When he was fourteen years old, he entered the Rabbinical Seminary in Zhitomir, Volhynia, but a year later the Seminary closed its doors, and he then attended the Realschule in Krementchug, graduating in 1879. The next two years he spent at the Technological Institute at St. Petersburg. While still a student at the Realschule he became interested in the Revolutionary movement which was fermenting in Russian educational institutions, and was sentenced to be imprisoned for a year in Charkov for political propaganda, and to remain under the supervision of the police. After the assassination of Alexander II in 1881 he was compelled to leave the country, on account of his alleged affiliations with the conspirators Grinevetzki, Zheliabov, Sophia Perovskaya, and others. He settled in Paris, where he continued his studies at the Sorbonne. Here he commenced his prolific literary career with a lengthy treatise on Spinoza in *Razsviet*, and wrote continuously for other Russian magazines, including *Russki Evrey, Woskhod, Kievskaya Zarya*, an association which he maintained even later in London and New York. Here, too, began his propagandist activity for the ideals of Social Democracy among the Jewish working classes, and he was among the founders of a Jewish *Arbeiter Verein* which during its existence was an active center of Socialism for the many emigrants from Czarist Russia, consisting mainly of workers and students.

In 1883 Rombro went to London where he was asked by Morris Winchevsky [*q.v.*] to contribute to his Yiddish weekly socialist journal *Der Polischer Yidel*. Speaking of Winchevsky's request to write for his paper a description of the riots against the Jews in Russia, Rombro said (Wiener, *post*, p. 223): "It was a hard job for me, and it took me a long time to do it. I never thought of writing in the Jewish Jargon, but fate ordered otherwise, and, contrary to all my aspirations, I am now nothing more than a poor Jargon journalist." His evil plight was his people's gain, however, since for the remainder of his life he devoted his many talents to their enlightenment, his medium being Yiddish. With-in two years he had mastered that language to such a degree that he was able to accept the editorship of the newly founded *Arbeiter Freund,* a socialist monthly. In 1888 he helped to found a Jewish Social-Democratic group, at whose request he supplied a Yiddish translation (London, 1889) of Lassalle's *Das Arbeiter-Programm.* The following year he was chosen by the Jewish workers of London as delegate to the first International Socialist Congress in Paris.

In 1890 he came to the United States, having been invited to act as editor of a new Social-Democratic weekly, the *Arbeiter Zeitung,* his associates being Abraham Cahan, Louis Miller, and M. Zametkin. In addition to editorials and articles on socialism, he furnished numerous translations of popular fiction. As the first socialist paper in Yiddish, the *Arbeiter Zeitung* had a marked influence both on the development of the Jewish labor movement and the Yiddish press in the United States. Rombro's editorship continued for several years after the paper, under the name *Abend-Blatt,* had been converted into a daily in 1894 and had become the official organ of the Socialist-Labor party. In 1892 Rombro was also appointed editor of the newly established *Zukunft,* a Yiddish monthly devoted to socialism, belles-lettres, and popular science. Either as editor or contributor, he was associated with practically every Jewish socialist periodical published in America during his lifetime, and at the time of his death was on the staff of the *Jewish Daily Forward* in New York City.

Rombro played an important part in the development of socialist ideas among the Jewish working classes, but he was far from being a blind partisan. He treated events of general interest without bias. During the last twenty years of his life he took no active part in the socialist movement, but his pen was always at its service. He was much more the teacher of social and political progress than the agitator, believed in evolution rather than revolution, advocated peaceful arbitration rather than the use of force, and died an avowed opponent of the Bolshevist régime. His wide erudition and mastery of many languages helped him in his rôle as interpreter to the Jewish masses of Western sociology, science, history, and culture, and aided him in his endeavor to adjust the newly arrived immigrants from Eastern Europe to American institutions and practices. His writings are characterized by great earnestness and a flowing style. Among his Yiddish books, some of which went into sev-

eral editions, were a history of Socialism, a history of the French Revolution, a history of civilization, and a popular astronomy, as well as a method for the study of English, a "History of All America: . . . of all the countries in the New World," and a series of biographies which appeared in book form, of Aristotle, Bar Kokhba, Josephus Flavius, Mohammed, Don Isaac Abravanel, Baruch Spinoza, Shabbethai Zebi, Lessing and Mendelssohn, the Rothschilds, and Meyerbeer. He married Eva Gordon; his death occurred in New York City.

[Zalmen Reisen, *Lexicon fun der Yiddisher Literatur,* vol. III (Wilna, 1929) ; Leo Wiener, *The Hist. of Yiddish Literature in the Nineteenth Century* (1899) ; Morris Winchevsky, "Reminiscences," being vol. X of his collected Yiddish works (New York, 1927) ; *Am. Jewish Year Book,* 1904–05 ; *N. Y. Times,* Nov. 29, 1922.]   I. S.

ROMEIKE, HENRY (Nov. 19, 1855–June 3, 1903), originator of press clipping service, was born in Riga, Russia. He was of mixed German and Lithuanian stock, the son of Albert and Henriette (Szabries) Romeike. After a fragmentary common-school education in Memel, East Prussia, he was apprenticed to the dry-goods trade at the age of thirteen, but two years later ran away and went to Berlin. There he worked in dry-goods shops for about ten years, but he did not like the business, and finally gave it up and drifted about Europe two or three years, looking for something congenial. During a conversation over a newspaper with a chance acquaintance on a park bench in Paris in 1883, he was struck by the idea that persons of prominence might like to be supplied in a comprehensive way with clippings of newspaper articles regarding themselves. Romeike was almost entirely without funds, and he therefore had great difficulty in getting copies of newspapers sufficient to launch his business. He introduced it by making personal calls on the individuals he wished to serve, leaving small batches of clippings with each. He found that the suggestion pleased many of them, and his business slowly developed. But after about a year in Paris, he decided that the English read more newspapers than the French, and removed to London, though he continued to serve his French customers. Here he took in a partner named Curtice. His clipping bureau was the first in England, and it found many clients there, eventually acquiring patronage even among the nobility and royalty. But reports of advancement in America and the prosperity of its daily newspapers again made him restive, and in 1885 he sent Samuel Leavitt to the United States to make a survey. Leavitt reported that there was more newspaper reading done there than in England, and under Romeike's direction, he established a clipping bureau in New York. Romeike sold his interest in his London business to his partner Curtice and came to New York. In America, even more than in the other countries, he seemed to have filled a long-felt want, and his business, after a slow and modest start, presently brought him emolument and even a measure of fame. Politicians, persons of social prominence, actors, writers, and musicians quickly took to the new idea, and professional and even business men followed them. Romeike was credited with having made America more self-conscious. His novel business brought about the coining of a new slang verb; an article or a book compiled from press clippings was said to be "romeiked." His service was extended to many foreign countries, and not a few titled personages were among his patrons. Romeike was married in London, Sept. 26, 1884, to Jane Sarah Mary Ganther; on July 12, 1892, he was married in New York to Suzanna Dayes. There were two children by the latter union, but the marriage was annulled in 1902. Romeike died about a year later, at the early age of forty-eight.

[Sources include: *Who's Who in America*, 1901–02; obituaries in all New York newspapers, June 4, 1903; *Baltimore Herald*, June 6, 1903; *Utica* (N. Y.) *Observer*, June 8, 1903; *Collier's Weekly*, June 20, 1903. A scrap-book of letters and clippings in the possession of Romeike's brother, Albert Romeike, of New York, was also consulted.]   A. F. H.

RONDTHALER, EDWARD (July 24, 1842–Jan. 31, 1931), bishop of the Moravian Church, was born at Schoeneck near Nazareth, Pa., the great-grandson of Emanuel Rondthaler who had been a Moravian pastor in Sarepta, Russia, emigrated, and then became pastor at York, Pa. The boy's father was Edward Rondthaler, also a Moravian pastor. His mother was Sarah Elizabeth (Rice) Rondthaler of Bethlehem, Pa. In early childhood his parents were sent in succession to take charge of the churches at Graceham, Md., and at Philadelphia, and his elementary education was acquired in private schools in the latter city. In 1853 he was sent to Nazareth Hall for five years and then entered the Moravian College and Theological Seminary, at Bethlehem, Pa., of which his father had been president at the time of his death in 1855. Edward received his bachelor's degree in divinity in 1862. For a year after graduation he studied theology and philosophy at the University of Erlangen, Bavaria, and returned to America in 1864 to become a teacher at Nazareth Hall. In 1865 he was ordained a deacon and given his first charge at Brooklyn, N. Y., where a burned

church edifice had very nearly extinguished the life of a small congregation. He was married on Oct. 1, 1867, to Mary E. Jacobson of Bethlehem, who with a son survived him. In six years his sympathetic and forceful attitude had reunited the congregation and rebuilt the church, and when he left Brooklyn in 1873 he was considered one of the most promising young men in the Moravian group. He remained in Philadelphia for four years and was then called to Salem, N. C., to the pastorate of the mother congregation of the southern province, where for the rest of his long life he devoted himself to the revival of the physical and spiritual forces that had been sadly weakened by the Civil War and the later Reconstruction. From 1884 to 1888 he was the head of the Salem Academy and, after that, president of the provincial governing board for thirty-five years. During this time he continued his increasingly arduous duties as pastor of what he called the "Home Church." Through his administrative genius a group of half a dozen disunited and struggling churches was changed into a closely knit federation of four times the number of members, practically dominating the life, both social and spiritual, of the Wachovia region. On Apr. 12, 1891, he was consecrated a bishop, the ceremony being conducted by three bishops, Van Vleck, Levering, and Bachman.

His strength lay in his ability to control and to inspire those who came into contact with him. His devotion to spiritual ideals and his uncanny ability to sense the potentialities of an economic situation were combined with an infinite tact and patience. He used these gifts at a critical time in the development of Winston-Salem to reorganize and direct social forces that otherwise might have worked themselves out in futile cross-purposes. Moreover, he possessed a magnificent voice of great range and power, which enlarged his audience and widened his circle of influence. When Winston-Salem, the largest industrial city in North Carolina, had grown out of the little village of Salem, his directing share in the unusual development of the community was recognized at a great civic assembly, at which with the presentation of a loving cup he was proclaimed the "first citizen." Yet what he prized above all social honors was scholarship; and when he had passed the usual span of life he still laid aside knotty administrative problems to find rest in the plays of Aristophanes or in the solution of problems in calculus. In 1928 he published *The Memorabilia of Fifty Years,* a series of papers he had issued at the close of each year, in which he discussed local and international affairs from 1877 to 1927. After his death there was published an *Appendix to the Memorabilia of Fifty Years* (1931).

[Biog. in *Appendix to the Memorabilia, ante*; *Winston-Salem Journal*, Feb. 1, 1931; *Twin City Sentinel* (Winston-Salem), Feb. 1, 1931; *Moravian*, Feb. 4, 1931.]   A. G. R.

ROOD, OGDEN NICHOLAS (Feb. 3, 1831– Nov. 12, 1902), physicist, son of Rev. Anson Rood and Alida Gouverneur (Ogden), was born in Danbury, Conn., and died in New York City. His father was a Congregational clergyman whose ancestors, of Scottish origin, had settled in Massachusetts in early colonial days; and his mother, daughter of Uzal Ogden [*q.v.*] and a descendant of John Ogden who was one of the founders of Elizabeth, N. J., belonged to an aristocratic family of New York. Young Rood entered Yale College at seventeen years of age, but soon afterwards transferred to the College of New Jersey (Princeton), where he graduated in 1852. Already he had begun to show a predilection for experimental science; and during the next two years, except for several months at the University of Virginia, he pursued a postgraduate course in the new Sheffield Scientific School at Yale. From 1854 to 1858 he was in Germany studying physics and chemistry at Berlin and Munich under Liebig, Magnus, and Dove, and at the same time devoting much of his leisure to the cultivation of painting and music, for both of which he had talent. In Munich he married Mathilde Prunner.

Returning to the United States with his bride in 1858, he accepted the post of professor of chemistry in a small denominational college at Troy, N. Y. Here, despite an uncongenial environment and scant facilities, he threw himself into his new work with enthusiasm and during the five or six years he was at Troy contributed a series of notable papers to the *American Journal of Science*. These studies included investigations of the polarization of light produced by the passage of light through a block of glass that had been strained in the process of annealing, the after-images that are perceived by looking at a bright surface through the open sectors of a revolving disk and the connection between the sensation of color and the persistence of vision, stereoscopic phenomena, especially stereoscopic lustre (which he had begun to study in Germany under Dove), photography and the duration of electric sparks, and spectrometry. He was one of the first to adapt the microscope to photography and to take binocular pictures with that instrument.

In 1864 he was made professor of physics in Columbia College, New York City, and here spent the rest of his life, becoming identified with the institution as one of its leading spirits and soon being recognized as one of the foremost scientific investigators of his day. He had little taste for the complicated problems of mathematical physics; on the other hand he had a positive genius for experimenting and a consummate ingenuity in the use of simple contrivances for obtaining results of the highest precision and value. "He delighted in the *tour de force* required to push the sensibility of an apparatus to its limit or in the invention of some novel device for determining the hitherto unmeasurable. At one time he devised a means for determining details which the microscope failed to reveal; at another he modified and defined Bunsen's photometric device so as to greatly enhance its sensitiveness. Where Wheatstone measured intervals of time not greater than a millionth of a second, he carried the determination to times as much smaller relatively as a quarter of a minute is smaller than an hour" (Nichols, *post*, p. 468). While Rood was always keenly interested in optics, especially in physiological optics, there is scarcely any part of the physics of his generation that he did not touch and enrich by his work. He was continually improving old methods and devising new ones. His modification of the Sprengel airpump enabled him to produce and measure high vacua far in excess of any that had been obtained before. An exceedingly important experimental device which he developed is the flicker photometer by which the brightness of light of different colors can be compared; this instrument has become indispensable in heterochromatic photometry. Towards the end of his life Rood investigated with characteristic curiosity and ingenuity the properties of the X-rays discovered by Röntgen in 1895. During these latter years also he devised a remarkable method of measuring prodigiously great electrical resistances.

In 1879 he published a notable book entitled *Modern Chromatics with Applications to Art and Industry*, which was translated into French, German, and Italian and soon after republished in England. It contains the mature conclusions and results of the author's numerous contributions to the physics of the color sensations and has become almost a classic in its field. For "lucidity and simplicity of treatment" and for the admirable style in which it is written it deserves to be ranked with Helmholtz's popular scientific lectures or with Tyndall's *Heat* (1863) and *Sound* (1867). The difficult subject of color and color-mixing is treated from both the standpoint of the physicist and that of the artist, and it is this rare combination that lends the book so much charm and gives it so much authority.

Rood has been described as "striking in appearance and in manners, possessing and possibly affecting certain peculiarities, working behind locked doors, sometimes living with his family and sometimes not, in part a recluse, although not averse to congenial company or an evening at the Century Club" (*Popular Science Monthly,* January 1903). In 1865, soon after the foundation of the National Academy of Sciences, he was elected a member of that body. He was an honorary member of the American Water Colour Society and at the annual meetings his paintings were frequently on exhibition. He was a vice-president of the American Association for the Advancement of Science.

[*Columbia Univ. Quart.,* Dec. 1902; *Am. Jour. Sci.,* Jan. 1903; *Science,* Dec. 5, 1902; *Physical Rev.,* May 1903; E. L. Nichols in *Nat. Acad. Sci. Biog. Memoirs,* vol. VI (1909), bibliog.; F. P. Keppel, *Columbia* (1914); *Who's Who in America,* 1901–02; W. O. Wheeler, *The Ogden Family in America* (1907); *N. Y. Times,* Nov. 13, 1902.]　　　　J. P. C. S.

ROOSA, DANIEL BENNETT ST. JOHN (Apr. 4, 1838–Mar. 8, 1908), physician, son of Charles Baker Roosa and Amelie Elmer (Foster) of Bethel, N. Y., was of sturdy Colonial descent, his four great-grandfathers (Duryea, Foster, Heard, and Roosa) having served in the Continental Army. All four names appear in the early history of New York State. As a boy he attended the lower schools in his native village and later the academies of Monticello, N. Y., and Honesdale, Pa. His freshman year at Yale, 1856, was marred by ill health, and he was forced to give up his college course. The following year, however, with characteristic perseverance, he entered the Medical Department of the University of the City of New York (now New York University), from which he was graduated M.D. in 1860. His first appointment was as assistant house surgeon of the New York Hospital, but he left it shortly, after the outbreak of the Civil War, to become assistant surgeon to the 5th New York Volunteers. He served for three months at this time and reënlisted in 1863 for the last part of the war. Between 1861 and 1863 he studied abroad in the ophthalmological clinics of Berlin and Vienna. In 1863 he was appointed professor of diseases of the eye and ear in the University of the City of New York and at the close of the Civil War assumed his duties, serving in this capacity until 1874, and thereafter until 1882, as professor of ophthalmology. For several years he was also professor of diseases of the eye and ear at the University of Vermont.

A man of large vision, Roosa was one of the first to conceive the idea of organizing a medical school for post-graduate work. He was responsible for the founding in 1883 of the New York Post-Graduate Medical School, to which, as president, he devoted the last twenty-five years of his life. This institution is his monument. He possessed a strong and inspiring personality; his militant, pioneer spirit was tempered with sympathy and calm judgment. In his determined struggle to make legally equal homeopaths, osteopaths, and others who had passed the State Regents' medical examinations, he displayed courage, enthusiasm, and steadfastness of purpose. His oratorical skill made him a prominent figure in promoting legislation in regard to many other matters affecting the interests of the medical profession, such as the transfer of chronic insane from county asylums to state institutions, measures for the prevention of blindness, and the raising of standards of academic requirements for medical students. He was one of the founders of the American Otological Society, and its president 1874–76; president of the International Otological Congress in 1876 in New York City, of the Medical Society of the State of New York in 1879, of the New York Academy of Medicine in 1893–94; and vice-president of the International Congress of Ophthalmology at Edinburgh in 1894. His most important publications include: *A Vest-Pocket Medical Lexicon* (1872); *A Practical Treatise on Diseases of the Ear* (1873), long used as a standard textbook; *A Doctor's Suggestion to the Community* (1880); *Determination of the Necessity for Wearing Glasses* (1887); *The Old Hospital and Other Papers* (1889); *A Clinical Manual of Diseases of the Eye* (1894); *Defective Eyesight* (1899), a large number of short articles, and two valuable translations: *The Diseases of the Ear* (1864), from the German of A. F. von Tröltsch, and, in collaboration with Charles E. Hackley, *Treatise on the Diseases of the Eye* (1868), from the German of Carl Stellwag von Carion.

Roosa was twice married, first to Mary Hoyt Blake, who died in 1878, and later, July 8, 1879, to Sarah Elizabeth (Haughwout) Howe, widow of Col. Francis E. Howe. There were no children. Roosa died very suddenly and painlessly of heart complications in Bright's disease, having been vigorous and active until almost the very moment of his death. He was survived by his second wife.

[*Who's Who in America,* 1908–09; *Who's Who in N. Y.,* 1907; H. A. Kelly and W. L. Burrage, *Am. Medic. Biogs.* (1920); *N. Y. Geneal. and Biog. Record,* Oct. 1902; D. W. Howe, *Howe Geneals.* (1929); *Gen.*

Alumni Cat., N. Y. Univ., Medic. Alumni (1908); T. J. Harris, "Early History of the American Otological Society," *Annals of Otology, Rhinology, and Laryngology,* June 1926; *Contributions to the Science of Medicine and Surgery by the Faculty . . . N. Y. Post-Graduate Medic. School* (1908); *Post-Graduate,* Apr. 1908; *N. Y. Tribune,* Mar. 9, 1908.]   G. L. A.

ROOSEVELT, HILBORNE LEWIS (Dec. 21, 1849–Dec. 30, 1886), organ builder and inventor, a first cousin of Theodore Roosevelt [*q.v.*] and the son of Silas Weir and Mary (West) Roosevelt, was born in New York City. His grandfather, Cornelius Van Schaack Roosevelt, had been a prominent merchant and philanthropist, and a founder and director of the Chemical National Bank. In Hilborne Roosevelt's youth the dividing line between the gentleman and "mechanic" was strictly drawn, and his interest in the details of organ building was frowned upon by his family; nevertheless, in opposition to their wishes he entered the shop of Hall & Labagh, New York City, and later made several trips to Europe to study organ construction there. He became a pioneer in the development of the electric organ and in the application of new electrical devices to organ manufacture, and in April 1869 he took out the first patent for an electric organ action (No. 88,909). In 1872 he opened his own factory on Eighteenth Street, New York City, and by 1881 his success as an organ builder necessitated the removal of the business to larger quarters. He added factories in Philadelphia and Baltimore, and constructed some of the largest church organs then known in the United States, among them those of the Garden City (L. I.) Cathedral, and of Grace Church and Trinity Church in New York City. The organ he constructed for the main building of the Philadelphia Centennial Exhibition in 1876, later acquired by the Massachusetts Charitable Mechanic Association, attracted much attention, as it combined the best points of European voicing with some effects never before produced ("The Roosevelt Centennial Organ Scheme," *Roosevelt Organ Journal,* July 1876). It is said to have been the first electric-action organ built in America.

Roosevelt did not confine his attention solely to organ building. Widely known among the creative electricians of his day, he was largely interested in the Bell Telephone Company, and invented several telephone devices, including the automatic switch-hook, on which he received royalties for a number of years. On Feb. 1, 1883, he married Kate, daughter of William Watson Shippen, of Hoboken, N. J. After his untimely death at the age of thirty-seven, his organ business was continued by his brother, Frank H. Roosevelt, until 1893, when the stock and patents were sold to the Farrand & Votey Company of Detroit. In Hilborne Roosevelt the creative rather than the commercial impulse predominated. He was primarily an inventor, and he spent thousands of dollars in electrical experiments and in developing the principle of the electric valve. To him the initial impetus of all subsequent improvement in American organ building is largely due.

[H. C. Lahee, *The Organ and Its Masters* (1902); Alfred Dolge, *Pianos and Their Makers,* vol. I (1911); Hilborne L. Roosevelt, *Manufacturer of Church, Chapel and Chamber Organs* (1883); C. B. Whittlesey, *The Roosevelt Geneal., 1649–1902* (1902); *N. Y. Tribune,* Dec. 31, 1886.]   F. H. M.

ROOSEVELT, NICHOLAS J. (Dec. 27, 1767–July 30, 1854), inventor, engineer, was born in New York City, the youngest child of Jacobus and Annetje (Bogard) Roosevelt. His father, a shopkeeper in New York, had been admitted as a freeman of that city on Feb. 22, 1748, and was a private in the New York colonial troops. Nicholas was educated in New York and developed a great love for mechanics. As early as 1782, when he was living on the farm of Joseph Oosterhaudt, near Esopus, N. Y., he built a model boat, propelled by paddle wheels over the sides. The wheels were turned by hickory and whalebone springs which unwound a cord wrapped around the wheel axles.

After the evacuation of New York by the British, Roosevelt returned there to pursue his mechanical interests. In 1793 he became a director of the New Jersey Copper Mine Association, organized to rework the abandoned Schuyler copper mine, an enterprise which was given up eighteen months later. Meanwhile he had become much interested in steam engines and their manufacture and succeeded in inducing his associates to purchase some land on Second River, now Belleville, N. J., and erect a metal foundry and shop. Following the completion of these works, called Soho after the establishment of Boulton and Watt in England, Roosevelt's associates retired and left him to carry on the enterprise alone. Sanguine and ambitious, he at first had some success, building engines for various purposes, including those for the Philadelphia water works. He also contracted to erect a rolling mill and supply the federal government with copper drawn and rolled for six 74-gun ships which were to be built. After he had gone to great expense to complete this contract, a change in federal administration caused the abandonment of ship construction and a consequent great financial loss to Roosevelt. About 1797 he entered into an agreement with Robert R. Livingston and John

Stevens [*qq.v.*] to build a steamboat on joint account, the engines for which were to be constructed at his foundry. The work of building this experimental boat was slow and tedious and it was not until the middle of 1798 that steam was applied to the machinery. At first the boat was not successful, but on a trial trip, Oct. 21, 1798, after improvements had been made, the *Polacca,* as it was named, attained a speed equivalent to three miles an hour in still water. During the construction of this vessel Roosevelt tried to induce Livingston to use paddle wheels over the sides, but Livingston would have nothing to do with such a plan. In 1801 Livingston was appointed United States minister to France and the whole undertaking was dropped.

By this time Roosevelt's business was in such chaotic condition that he was compelled to abandon his works entirely. In 1809, however, he became associated with Robert Fulton [*q.v.*] in the introduction of steamboats on Western rivers, and in 1811 built at Pittsburgh the steamboat *New Orleans.* In this he descended the Ohio and Mississippi rivers from Pittsburgh to New Orleans in fourteen days. In the belief that he was entitled to a patent for use of vertical paddle wheels, he now applied for such a patent which was granted him on Dec. 1, 1814. The following January he applied to the New Jersey legislature for protection as the inventor of such paddle wheels, but the legislature decided, primarily because of the objections of Fulton and Livingston, that "it was inexpedient to make any special provision in connection with the matter in controversy before the body" (Latrobe, *post,* p. 31), and there the matter rested. Roosevelt soon retired from active work and resided for the remainder of his life with his family in Skaneateles, Onondaga County, N. Y. He married Lydia Latrobe, daughter of the elder Benjamin Henry Latrobe [*q.v.*] of Baltimore, Md., Nov. 15, 1808, by whom he had nine children, six of whom died in their early youth.

[C. B. Whittelsey, *The Roosevelt Geneal. 1649–1902* (1902) ; J. H. B. Latrobe, *A Lost Chapter in the Hist. of the Steamboat* (1871) ; William Nelson, "Josiah Hornblower and the First Steam Engine in America," in *Proc. of the N. J. Hist. Soc.,* 2 ser. VII (1883) ; G. H. Preble, *A Chronological Hist. of the Origin and Development of Steam Navigation* (1883) ; Patent Office records.]   C. W. M.

ROOSEVELT, ROBERT BARNWELL (Aug. 7, 1829–June 14, 1906), political reformer, writer, pioneer in conservation, was born in New York City, the fourth son of Cornelius Van Schaack and Margaret (Barnhill) Roosevelt. Christened Robert Barnhill, he later adopted Barnwell as his middle name. His father was a wealthy banker and merchant, a descendant of Claes Martenszen van Rosenvelt who was an early settler of New Amsterdam. His mother was a member of a prominent family of Quaker merchants of Philadelphia. In his early youth Roosevelt showed a diversity of interests that characterized him throughout his life. He was fond of hunting, yachting, and other forms of outdoor sport, and showed a precocious interest in politics and in English composition. After receiving an excellent preparatory education he studied law and was admitted to the bar on attaining his majority. In 1850 he married Elizabeth Ellis of New York who bore him two sons and two daughters, and during most of his life he resided on East Twentieth St., next door to his brother Theodore, the father of President Theodore Roosevelt.

He quickly attained a prominent position at the bar, at the same time giving much attention to writing and to public affairs. During his more than twenty years of practice he was counsel in an unusual number of cases in which the public interest was involved. At the beginning of the Civil War he identified himself with the group of Democrats who strongly supported the Union cause, and was a founder of the Loyal National League and of the Union League Club, both important propagandist organizations. In 1864 he became secretary of the Citizens' Association and represented it in proceedings before courts and legislative committees. One of his prosecutions resulted in abolishing the offices of the incompetent health wardens and in establishing a model board of health. He was also instrumental in creating a paid fire department. He later became associated with Charles G. Halpine [*q.v.*] in the editorship of the *New York Citizen,* the official organ of the association, and by his editorials helped to arouse the city against the "Tweed ring." He was one of the organizers of the famous Committee of Seventy which overthrew the ring, assuming the special task of leading the opposition among independent Democrats. In 1872 he had practically the sole responsibility for managing the successful mayoralty campaign of the reform ticket. He was elected to the Forty-second Congress (1871–73) and signalized his brief service by exposing a corrupt ring operating in the District of Columbia.

Roosevelt's early writings dealt with hunting, fishing and outdoor life—fields that were then almost wholly unexploited. His first three books, *Game Fish of the Northern States of America, and British Provinces* (1862), *Superior Fishing* (1865), and *The Game Birds of the Coasts and*

Lakes of the Northern States of America (1866), had an important influence in creating the cult of the hunter-naturalist. Foreseeing the eventual destruction of all game and fish unless measures for conservation were undertaken, he assiduously promoted the work of state and international sportsmen's associations. In 1867 he secured from the New York legislature the passage of a law, widely copied in other states, creating the state fishery commission. As chairman or member of that body for twenty years he supervised the introduction and perfecting of artificial methods of propagating fish and the protection of streams against indiscriminate dumping of sewage and mill wastes. His later writings were: *Five Acres Too Much* (1869), and *Progressive Petticoats* (1874), both of which were satires; *Love and Luck* (1886), a novel; *Fish Hatching, Fish Catching* (joint author with Seth Green, 1879), *Florida and the Game Water-Birds of the Atlantic Coast and the Lakes of the United States* (1884); and a memorial edition (1869) of the *Poetical Works of Charles G. Halpine* (*Miles O'Reilly*).

In 1872 Roosevelt received a large inheritance and retired from the bar to become a director of several railroad and industrial companies and to supervise widely dispersed investments. He was a commissioner of the Brooklyn bridge, 1879–81; a member of the Board of Aldermen, 1882, devoting his attention chiefly to securing the passage of a pure-food ordinance; minister to the Netherlands, 1888–89; chairman of a relief committee during the Spanish-American War; and a member of committees formed to aid the Boers. After the death of his wife in 1887 he married Mrs. Marion T. (O'Shea) Fortescue, on Aug. 18, 1888. During his later years he was the leader of various Democratic reform associations which carried on an unequal contest with Tammany Hall. He wanted to be mayor of New York, but his uncompromising zeal for reform deprived him of the support of Tammany and his thoroughgoing support of Democratic policies prevented his indorsement by the Republicans. In the presidency of his nephew, Theodore Roosevelt [*q.v.*], whose party allegiance he disapproved, he lived to see the frequent expression of the principles of conservation and of political reform which seem to have been the dominant interests of his life. He died at Sayville, L. I.

[The most complete sketch of Roosevelt is in the second number of the *New Amsterdam Year Book, 1898*. Briefer accounts are in C. B. Whittlesey, *The Roosevelt Genealogy, 1649–1902* (1902); *Who's Who in America*, 1906–07; *Biog. Directory of the Am. Cong., 1774–1927* (1928); M. A. Hamm, *Famous Families of N. Y.* (1901), vol. II; *N. Y. Herald*, June 15, 1906.

The Roosevelt House in New York City has a collection of his scrapbooks, letters, and other materials, including his Political Black Book.]   E. C. S.

ROOSEVELT, THEODORE (Oct. 27, 1858–Jan. 6, 1919), twenty-sixth president of the United States, was born at No. 28 East 20th St., New York City, the son of Theodore and Martha (Bulloch) Roosevelt. Of the four children, Anna was older, and Elliott and Corinne were younger than he. In his *Autobiography* he stated that his ancestor, Klaes Martensen van Roosevelt, came from Holland to New Amsterdam as a "settler" about 1644; in various genealogies the name appears as Claes Martenszen van Rosenvelt and the date as 1649 (Whittlesey, Clemens, Johnson, *post*). Thereafter, six generations of Roosevelts before his own were identified with Manhattan, and the more recent of them were well-to-do. Robert Barnwell Roosevelt [*q.v.*] was his uncle. His mother, the daughter of James Stephens Bulloch of Roswell, Ga., and a descendant of Archibald Bulloch [*q.v.*], first president of the Provincial Congress of Georgia, was of the aristocracy of the Old South. His parents maintained in their brownstone residence a home of dignity, culture, and restraint; they were established in, though not highly valuing, the society of New York. Handicapped in childhood by asthma, and always by defective eyesight, Theodore rebuilt his body from sheer determination, teaching himself to ride, shoot, and box, though his early interests were more in natural history than sport. His parents gave him tutors and travel as a child and sent him to Harvard. He made Phi Beta Kappa there, but was not thrilled by academic opportunity, and was graduated in 1880, lacking a career but free to choose one.

Law, which he undertook to read, failed to interest him; so he turned to the history of the United States, beginning, with the publication in 1882 of *The Naval War of 1812; or, the History of the United States Navy During the Last War with Great Britain,* a literary and historical career of which he never tired. A free-lance historian, he later dreaded the possibility that he might be forced to enlist among "these small men who do most of the historic teaching in the colleges" (Bishop, *post*, II, 140). Chance, however, saved him from this fate, for a local Republican boss needed an eminently respectable candidate for the 21st Assembly district. Roosevelt was sent to Albany for three sessions, 1882–84, and won acceptance as a leader on his merit. Here his freedom served him well. Irritating to his seniors, he was attractive to reporters in search of news. He attacked misbehavior as he chose, saw to it that the newspapers had his side of every story, and supported with zest laws for the relief of workingmen and for the better government of New York City. His associates saw him as "a light-footed, agile, nervous yet prompt boy, with light-brown, slightly curling hair, blue eyes and an eyeglass, and ready to rise and speak with a clear, sharp, boyish voice" (*Frank Leslie's Illustrated Newspaper,* May 10, 1884, p. 183).

His father had died in 1878. Beginning late in 1883, Roosevelt risked more than $50,000 of his patrimony in ranch lands in Dakota Territory, which he retained until 1887 (Hermann Hagedorn, *Roosevelt in the Bad Lands,* 1921). He lost most of his investment, but gained far more in access to the open air, in valuable experience in the ways of men and cattle, and in solace after the death of his young wife. On Oct. 27, 1880, he had married Alice Hathaway Lee, daughter of George C. Lee of Chestnut Hill, Mass. She died on Feb. 14, 1884, shortly after the birth of their daughter Alice Lee (later Mrs. Nicholas Longworth), and only a few hours after the death of Roosevelt's own mother. These tragic events darkened the year of his last fight in the legislature at Albany and his earnest effort to block the nomination of James G. Blaine for the presidency. Still under twenty-six, he won place as delegate at large to the Chicago Republican National Convention, where he stood by George F. Edmunds [*q.v.*] until the end. The ranch occupied his summer. He was discouraged by the nomination of Blaine and Logan, but came east at last to engage in what was described as a "most remarkable performance in the crow-eating line" (New York *World,* Oct. 19, 1884). He supported the ticket and always despised the Mugwumps. In quick succession he wrote *Hunting Trips of a Ranchman* (1885); *Thomas Hart Benton* (1886); *Gouverneur Morris* (1888); *Ranch Life and the Hunting-Trail* (1888); *Essays on Practical Politics* (1888); and the first two volumes of *The Winning of the West* (1889). He returned to practical politics in 1886, when he entered a thankless contest to run against Abram S. Hewitt and Henry George for mayor of New York. After finishing third in this election he hastened to London where, on Dec. 2, 1886, he was married to Edith Kermit Carow, in St. George's Church, Hanover Square (S. L. Gwynn, *The Letters and Friendships of Sir Cecil Spring Rice,* 1929, vol. I, p. 48). In 1888 he supported a winning presidential ticket and stood in line for a minor reward in national politics.

Harrison made him a civil-service commis-

sioner in May 1889, and Roosevelt was soon convinced that the spoilsmen were alarmed at his arrival in Washington. There was some reason to fear that civil-service reform had died a-borning, for politicians tried to evade the specific requirements of the Pendleton Act of 1883. The commissioners were inconspicuous until Roosevelt brought a glare of happy publicity into his petty office. For six years he lived in and learned his Washington. The Roosevelts kept simple but open house on a side street, the Adams-Hay circle accepted them, Lodge and Spring Rice were in and out. The mysteries of high policy and "backstage" intrigue were open before their eyes. Already set to the notion that in ethics lay the cure of politics, Roosevelt wrote and spoke as a lay evangelist, and applied great energy to the task of keeping out the crooks and protecting the competent. This philosophy remained with him for life (*American Ideals and Other Essays, Social and Political,* 1897). The personal conflicts that were its consequence made good news stories in which he was generally as right as he always looked (*The Strenuous Life; Essays and Addresses,* 1900).

The municipal election of 1894 brought him back to New York the following year, still with no fixed career, but with *The Wilderness Hunter* (1893) added to his list, and *The Winning of the West* (vols. III, IV, 1894–96) nearly done. Writing at the same time and following in the tracks of Frederick J. Turner [*q.v.*], he missed the point that Turner raised in *The Significance of the Frontier in American History* (published separately in 1894), and remained of the school of Francis Parkman, ever interested in heroic events and literary narrative. As president of the American Historical Association in 1912, he expounded his theory at length (*History as Literature, and Other Essays,* 1913). In New York a reform mayor, William L. Strong, organized a non-political administration in 1895. Roosevelt took the presidency of the board of police commissioners, and for two years learned to command men. He was doubtless overzealous and accomplished relatively little, but, with Jacob A. Riis [*q.v.*] as his Boswell (J. A. Riis, *Theodore Roosevelt, the Citizen,* 1904), he penetrated the lowest levels of slum life, observed an unholy alliance of graft, politics, and crime, and again by his ability to turn his daily routine into pungent news brought public attention to a focus on the cesspool.

He envied the career of his friend Henry Cabot Lodge, while Lodge was more than willing to assist him into one. There was chance of this after the election of McKinley in 1896, but it took laborious wire-pulling before McKinley could be persuaded to offer Roosevelt a place as assistant secretary of the navy. Roosevelt took this gladly, for it brought him back to Washington and to official society. In the Navy Department, with an easy-going chief, John D. Long [*q.v.*], he was as jingo as Lodge, and hoped with Leonard Wood [*q.v.*] that war would come out of Cuba. He burned the naval appropriations in target practice, and showed the ambitious Dewey how to let politics aid merit (*Autobiography of George Dewey, Admiral of the Navy*, 1913, pp. 167–68). On an afternoon (Feb. 25, 1898) when Secretary Long was out of town he, as acting secretary, cabled Dewey in the event of war to "see that the Spanish squadron does not leave the Asiatic coast, and then offensive operations in Philippine Islands" (*Ibid.*, p. 179). Roosevelt, resigning on May 6, turned to active service in the field. Wood and he organized the first volunteer cavalry regiment, procured its equipment, and secured its inclusion in the expeditionary force mobilizing at Tampa. The Rough Riders, dismounted of necessity, fulfilled his expectations. In the fighting before Santiago they took Kettle Hill (July 1, 1898); and when Wood was promoted to higher rank Roosevelt became their colonel. Richard Harding Davis [*q.v.*] chronicled their glory, as did Roosevelt himself in *The Rough Riders* (1899). For the rest of his life he attended reunions of his men, found them jobs, and occasionally kept them out of jail. With no army career to risk, Roosevelt took a lead in the "round robin" of July, directing public attention to the precarious situation of the troops in the tropics, because of health and sanitary conditions. This insubordination caused acute irritation in the War Department; but most of the army was evacuated in August for hospitalization at Montauk Point, and he, now "Teddy" to everybody in spite of his intense dislike of the nickname, came home an authentic hero of the war. His sudden popularity, and his expansive grin beneath his spectacles and army hat, upset the plans of Thomas Collier Platt [*q.v.*] for the approaching campaign. Platt yielded gracefully to his nomination for the governorship. Roosevelt took his escort of Rough Riders up and down the state and was elected over Augustus Van Wyck by a small majority. He was inaugurated in January 1899.

He would have been less than human if he had not now suspected that even higher place might come within his reach. He advanced practical reform as much as seemed possible without breaking with Platt, the most important contribution, in his own opinion, being a tax on

corporation franchises. The abundant testimony (displayed in the libel suit of William Barnes in 1915) leaves it still uncertain whether he or Platt was boss; but there is no doubt that after two years of Roosevelt in Albany, Platt was ready for his promotion to any office outside the state. Roosevelt feared that he would be side-tracked as vice-president, but it suited Platt to encourage the boom; and the fact that Roosevelt was unacceptable to McKinley and Hanna was good reason for his indorsement by Quay. He was soon torn between his judgment that the vice-presidency was destructive of a future, and his desire to prove that he could not be kept off the ticket. He was nominated at Philadelphia in June 1900, with no negative voice but his own, and with McKinley prudently keeping hands off. His canvass matched that of Bryan in vivacity, making it possible for McKinley to remain at home in both dignity and safety. But when elected Roosevelt despaired of the future, talked of reading law under Justice White (Thayer, *post*, p. 153), and looked with reluctance to the tame life of president of the Senate. Just before his forty-third birthday, through the assassination of William McKinley, he became twenty-sixth president of the United States.

He took his oath of office in Buffalo, Sept. 14, 1901, pledging himself "to continue, absolutely unbroken, the policy of President McKinley for the peace, the prosperity, and the honor of our beloved country"; and suspecting that there were many who feared for the office in the hands of "this crazy man" (Thomas Beer, *Hanna*, 1929, p. 236). Since the basic pledges of the Republican party had been fulfilled, and since McKinley had given no more than a suggestion of a future course, this pledge was less informing than comforting to timid minds. Roosevelt might well have followed his urge as a reformer, exercising his great skill as an administrator, without breaking with the business statesmen. Yet there were new philosophies abroad, calling for more than an ethical approach to government. A younger generation of political leaders, among whom Robert M. La-Follette [*q.v.*] was best known, were leading crusades for fair play and governmental control, and were using the ideas of Populism which were now becoming respectable since there was no danger that the People's party would establish them. Roosevelt disliked the technical detail now at the bottom of reform, but there was a chance for a flexible president to place himself at the head of a national movement for the reorganization of the American pattern. For his first term he kept McKinley's advisers in his cabinet, and announced no change in doctrine. Yet from the moment that he moved his family into the White House, with Alice and the five younger children—Theodore, Kermit, Ethel, Archibald, and Quentin—there was a new virility in the Executive Mansion and a new technique in the office of the president.

Quick administration was one of the changes. Roosevelt trusted his subordinates and cleared his desk, thus saving time to play where his predecessors felt forced to labor over bundles of official papers. He played beyond the speed of his secretarial advisers and soon surrounded himself with a group of agile companions—the "tennis cabinet"—for hikes, or rides, or games. Toward the end of his presidency, when the army complained of an order to keep physically fit, he rode (Jan. 13, 1909) one hundred miles over rough Virginia roads to shame it. From his playmates of the open he obtained a view of the workings of the government that was obscured by red tape from their superiors. At his hospitable table he sampled with insatiable curiosity the wit of the procession of visitors to Washington, meeting prize-fighter or royalty with equal ease. There was new dignity and formality in White House life, after the residence of several simpler predecessors; the paragraphers smiled at the cockades and livery on the White House coachmen. Decisions flowed from his desk, more often right than wrong, but always swiftly. Washington, under his eye and hand, turned into a world capital, with new monumental beauty and fresh, if somewhat disturbing, importance. There were changes in the diplomatic corps as Europe realized this fact. The French appreciated his tastes, and sent him Jusserand, who could both talk and tramp with him. The British fumbled after the death of Pauncefote, but in 1907 found him James Bryce, a mountain climber whose knowledge of American life was nearly as encyclopedic as his own. The Foreign Office also allowed Cecil Spring Rice, who was an honorary member of the Roosevelt household, to slip in and out of Washington and to maintain a revealing contact with the Roosevelt mind. The Germans, after Von Holleben, gave him his old friend Speck von Sternburg, with whom he had been intimate in Washington as a young man. Through these experiences, Roosevelt sat, mobile and watchful, rarely holding to a lesser advantage at the cost of a greater one, and bringing informed opportunism to a new level of national dignity.

He took over the presidency in the midst of readjustments caused by the war with Spain.

Hay had nearly completed a new isthmian canal treaty with Great Britain, allowing the United States a free hand. This superseded both the old Clayton-Bulwer Treaty (1850) and Hay's own first agreement with Lord Pauncefote, which the Senate had wrecked in 1900. Roosevelt, then governor, had opposed it; but he approved the new treaty, signed Nov. 13, 1901, and the Senate gave assent within a month. In the following June, Congress, by passing the Spooner Act, approved the Panama route for the canal, if an agreement could be made in "a reasonable time" with Colombia; otherwise, the canal was to be built in Nicaragua. Under Roosevelt's immediate direction the Hay-Herran Treaty was soon negotiated; it was ratified by the United States Senate on Mar. 17, 1903, but on Aug. 2 was rejected by Colombia. The Colombians objected to certain limitations upon their sovereignty and sought more money, though it would appear that they expected this to come out of the payment of $40,000,000 from the United States to the New Panama Canal Company rather than from the Treasury itself. Roosevelt, enraged at the "inefficient bandits," apparently did not consider turning to Nicaragua, and regretted that in his official position he could not stir up secession in Panama. Representatives of the New Panama Canal Company, who had long been active propagandists for the Panama route, did the necessary stirring. Roosevelt was prepared to interpret an old treaty of 1846 with New Granada (now Colombia) as warranting the preservation of peace on the isthmus by the United States, even against Colombia when trying to put down insurrection. Panama seceded Nov. 3, 1903, received prompt recognition from the United States, and within the month negotiated in its own name the treaty that Colombia had rejected. "I took the canal zone and let Congress debate, and while the debate goes on the canal does also," said Roosevelt later, on one of the many occasions when he felt prodded to defend the summary action (*New York Times*, Mar. 24, 1911). He guided every step in the construction of the canal (J. B. and Farnham Bishop, *Goethals, Genius of the Panama Canal*, 1930). On Apr. 20, 1921, in the administration of Harding, the Senate ratified a treaty with Colombia, whereby $25,000,000 was paid that aggrieved republic though without the formal apology that Wilson had favored. (On the entire affair, see Bishop, I, chs. xxiv, xxv, xxxv; Hill, *post*, ch. iii; Pringle, *post*, pp. 301–38, and the references cited there.)

Panama was only one among Roosevelt's problems. China was in disorder; and so near to

China lay the Philippines that the safety of the islands was involved. Hay continued to press discreetly for the extension of the doctrine of the "Open Door." The Latin-American republics were troubled by the consequences of economic penetration and their own recklessness, and, in the United States, capital was for the first time showing serious desire for the profits to be obtained in the exploitation of backward economic nations. In 1902 there was European intervention in Venezuela that bore on both the Monroe Doctrine and canal strategy. Roosevelt had announced that the Monroe Doctrine did not guarantee the Latin republics immunity from punishment after misbehavior, but it was no accident that Dewey was in Caribbean waters at the end of 1902 when intervention began with a "pacific blockade." Later, Roosevelt remembered an informal verbal "ultimatum" to Von Holleben which has not been corroborated (Hill, pp. 123–25; Bishop, I, 222–24). The Venezuelan claims were compromised or submitted to arbitration, and the blockade was lifted, but the dilemma remained. Should the Monroe Doctrine be abandoned, or should the United States permit the doctrine to protect defaulters and assume, itself, their liabilities? When in 1904 the Dominican Republic was threatened with intervention Roosevelt persuaded it to invite him to set up a financial receivership, with an American comptroller to collect and disburse its revenues. The Roosevelt corollary to the Monroe Doctrine, now advanced, asserted the interest of the United States in so guiding the affairs of weaker neighbors that they might avoid clashes likely otherwise to involve the Monroe Doctrine. Roosevelt's Dominican convention, submitted in February 1905, lacked Senate confirmation for two years (until February 1907) but his comptroller began work at once. The Senate resented but could not block his action.

He settled the old Alaskan boundary dispute on his own terms, by an adjudication under a convention signed on Jan. 24, 1903; and he recognized no American limits to American interests, but took a hand with Germany and France at Algeciras (S. B. Fay, *The Origins of the World War*, 1930, vol. I, 185, 189, 191). His cautious and friendly pressure upon Russia and Japan resulted in the Peace of Portsmouth, Sept. 5, 1905 (Dennett, *post*). Behind this diplomatic play the defenses of the United States were being modernized. Roosevelt had no confidence in arbitration as a substitute for preparedness. Elihu Root, as secretary of war, continued the army reforms of the McKinley ad-

ministration, set up a general staff (1903), and returned to law in New York. The navy, new for the war with Spain, became newer each year until it could assemble a battle fleet of sixteen units. It was most likely to be tested in the Orient. Japan was sensitive, feeling its new strength, and finding the position of Orientals in the United States humiliating to them and at the same time unacceptable to American labor interests and Pacific Coast opinion. San Francisco, in 1906, engaged in discussions over the proper status of adult Japanese in attendance with American children in the lower grades of the schools, until Roosevelt was drawn into the discussion because of Japanese protest. Openly he soothed Japan, procured a "gentlemen's agreement" to prevent the emigration of Japanese laborers, and exercised coercive pressure on the San Francisco schoolboard; privately he was uneasy lest Japan might have overt action in mind. Against this background, and because no one yet knew how effective any fleet could be in long-range operations, he sent the whole fleet to the Pacific, and then around the world, on a practice cruise. He asked no permission for the demonstration, and left Congress no option but to pay the bills. The tour was a triumph of accurate administration. The fleet kept to its schedule, was greeted with enthusiastic hospitality in Japan, and, on Feb. 22, 1909, was welcomed back at the Capes of the Chesapeake, whence Roosevelt had dispatched it Dec. 16, 1907. "Speak softly," he liked to say, "and carry a big stick, you will go far" (Roosevelt to Henry L. Sprague, Jan. 26, 1900, Pringle, p. 214).

But the embarrassments due to too big a stick, or to one too often displayed, were visible in Latin America where recent events seemed to set a pattern of North American aggression inconsistent with the altruistic promise of the Monroe Doctrine. South American jurists insisted that their own courts ought to be final over aliens, and Drago of Argentina had recently added a protest against the forcible collection of debts. These matters were scheduled for debate by the third Pan-American conference to be held at Rio de Janeiro in July–August 1906, and were likely to want a hearing at The Hague in 1907. To explain away the illusion of a North American menace, Root, now secretary of state after the death of Hay, was sent on tour among the southern neighbors.

Roosevelt's freedom of action in foreign affairs was in sharp contrast to presidential limitations at home, where the industrial revolution was remaking American society. He had need of such a technique as would recognize the existence of Congress, of the courts, and of a public opinion faster than which it was hazardous to go. This technique he never found. He threw aside obstacles until, by their mere accumulation, they jammed his progress. Always a boxer, he clung to his maxim: "Don't hit at all if it is honorably possible to avoid hitting; but *never* hit soft" (Bishop, II, 437). He knew that the best defence is to hit one's adversary first; but this sometimes made it hard for his friends to work with him, and embittered his enemies more than was necessary. He maintained that no utterance purporting to be from him was true unless he authorized as well as uttered it. He contradicted many who tried to interpret him; and from denial passed easily to the lie direct. The cartoonists recalled the biblical story of Ananias and devised a club to which none was eligible until he had been called a liar by Theodore Roosevelt. As the membership grew, it included some who were merely indiscreet or inconvenient. E. H. Harriman and the Bellamy Storers, Alton B. Parker, "Ben" Tillman and William E. Chandler, Delavan Smith, George Harvey, Thomas Collier Platt, William J. Long, Poultney Bigelow were added to the list of the Ananias Club, until unseemly altercation became a jest rather than a discredit. Yet behind these costly quarrels lay the fact that Roosevelt was trying to dominate a government of checks and balances in which the coordinate branches were as constitutional as was the President himself. No President since Thomas Jefferson had ranged his mind over so broad a field. None since Andrew Jackson had been so certain that he had a special mandate.

The domestic wrangle grew steadily more acrimonious, with the direction of Roosevelt swerving cautiously towards the left. Republicans of the school of McKinley sensed this, and feared and fought him. Radical aspirants tried to steal his glory. The fight involved a new hypothesis of the control of industrial society in order to save individual economic freedom. Through the four Congresses of his presidency the Republican party controlled the federal government. There was no effective Democratic opposition. But the key positions were held by conservative leaders, who were more apt to distrust Roosevelt's applications of the "square deal" than to cooperate with him. Joseph G. Cannon [*q.v.*], speaker in the last three of his Congresses, was "stand-pat" and unashamed. Nelson W. Aldrich [*q.v.*], and his elderly and seasoned coadjutors in the Senate, made no pretense of favoring a new theory of government.

Furthermore, Roosevelt's relations with those who saw with him were hindered by the roughness of his technique.

Though president by accident, Roosevelt assumed headship of the Republican party in 1901. Before he moved into the White House he was in contact with Booker T. Washington [*q.v.*] on the problem of negro appointments; and shortly thereafter he slipped into the political error of inviting the negro educator to a meal in the White House (Oct. 16, 1901). This undermined his effort to break the Solid South by annoying the white South. He annoyed the negroes by summary dismissal of negro soldiers after the Brownsville, Tex., riot (Aug. 13–14, 1906), which also brought the fiery Foraker upon his trail (J. B. Foraker, *Notes of a Busy Life,* 1916, vol. II). But he kept to his task; occasional negroes received federal appointment, while he held the Southern white Republicans as well, so that the votes of their delegations to national conventions in 1904 and 1908 were at his disposal. He had greater difficulty with Senator Marcus A. Hanna [*q.v.*], who was chairman of the Republican National Committee and understood both business men and organized labor. In 1903 Roosevelt took from the Ohio convention an indorsement of himself over Hanna's undisguised opposition, on the ground of impropriety. But Hanna was ill; he died in 1904, leaving to conservative Republicans no possible leader. His supporters were ready for peace, and Roosevelt was willing to pay something for an undivided front in a campaign in which he hoped for election in his own right. His fear of missing this was far greater than any of the obstacles. Nominated at Chicago without opposition, he put the national committee in its place, appointing a member of his cabinet, George B. Cortelyou, as chairman. The canvass against Judge Alton B. Parker [*q.v.*], choice of the anti-Bryan Democrats, was without clear issue. The easy victory gained, Roosevelt issued on election night, Nov. 8, 1904, a disclaimer of a third term for himself, holding to the merit of the two-term tradition and conceding that for its purpose his fractional term constituted a first term. He later regretted the pledge, but it gave him freedom.

Among the specific domestic problems that confronted him in both terms, the tariff was a vexatious embarrassment. From the liberal western Republicans came the "Iowa idea" that the tariff made life too easy for the trusts and needed to be revised. This was anathema to protectionists, and though Roosevelt approved it the time never seemed ripe for action. The sharp fight that delayed his Cuban reciprocity bill

(Dec. 17, 1903) indicated the risk that would be run in a general revision. As his second term ended, this revision was indicated as the first thankless task for his successor.

The trusts, however, were fair game. The Republican party had no official policy respecting them, while there was enthusiastic public approval for every exposure of their bad behavior. The "muck-rakers" were raging, but Roosevelt had preceded them, demanding at Pittsburgh, July 4, 1902, that trusts be subjected to public control in the public interest. His speeches were popular in both parties, revealing a cleavage that cut across party lines. They had political value in covering the threatened tariff defection in the West, where Speaker David B. Henderson (Sept. 16, 1902) declined even to submit his record to his Iowa district, and left politics. Through Attorney-General Philander C. Knox [q.v.], Roosevelt attacked the Northern Securities Company as a conspiracy in restraint of trade, and on Mar. 14, 1904, procured its dissolution by the Supreme Court (*Northern Securities Company* vs. the *United States,* 193 *United States,* 197), so that he was a "trust-buster" in time for the campaign. He urged, and Congress added to the cabinet in 1903, a secretary of commerce and labor, whose bureau of corporations was to be the eye of the government in matters of business. The Elkins Law (Feb. 19, 1903) forbade one form of vicious favoritism, the rebate of freight rates. The expedition act (Feb. 11, 1903) gave the government power to hasten to trial its prosecutions under the interstate commerce and anti-trust acts. But there was more enthusiasm than certainty in trust control. Most efforts were based on resentment rather than understanding, and politicians were impatient of the scientific harness with which economists were likely to hamper their freedom of action. The guides to sound decisions lagged behind the desire for correction. But in 1906 the interstate commerce act was strengthened; while the unpopularity of business, increased by the "muck-rakers," made possible sweeping laws for the protection of the consumer of food and drugs. So violently did the orgy of exposure and denunciation proceed that when David Graham Phillips [q.v.] launched his series on "The Treason of the Senate" in Hearst's *Cosmopolitan Magazine,* March 1906, Roosevelt himself tried to call a halt. First in the privacy of the Gridiron Club, Mar. 17, 1906, then publicly, Apr. 14, 1906, he spoke to the text of "The Man with the Muck Rake," and emphasized the need for constructive law. The "muck-rake" period gradually died out, but he

was left unpopular with business and the party stalwarts. A financial reverse in Wall Street in 1907, caused by gross speculation, was termed the Roosevelt panic, and he was described as an enemy of business and of his class. But he was on his way to another extension of government control, this time over natural resources.

More than most presidents, Roosevelt knew the West. In 1902 he approved the Newlands Act for a reclamation service, and the conviction grew on him that the national endowment had been squandered. To call attention to the problem, and to the inadequacy of existing law, he made enlargements of the forest reserves, withdrawing land from entry whether suitable for forests or not when he had reason to think that a useful resource lay within its area. He named a public lands commission in 1903, drafting civilian experts who knew the land, and placing at their service the clerical staff of the government ("Report of the Public Lands Commission," 1905, 58 Cong., 3 Sess., *Senate Document No. 189*). There was a similar inland waterways commission in 1907 ("Preliminary Report," 60 Cong., 1 Sess., *Senate Document No. 325*). On May 13, 1908, he assembled at the White House a conference of governors of most of the states, and elder statesmen of every persuasion, to discuss the inclusive theme of natural resources; and in June he named a conservation commission with Gifford Pinchot at its head. The report of this body in three volumes (60 Cong., 2 Sess., *Senate Document No. 676*) roused resentment because of its intrusion upon a field of action that Congress had left untouched. Congress forbade its wide circulation as a public document and rebuked Roosevelt by prohibiting further use of public funds upon any investigation not authorized in advance by law. Roosevelt avowed in retort that he was free to do as he pleased in that "twilight zone" lying between the prohibitions of the law and duties required by specific enactments. His presidency ended in open defiance on the part of Congress, which restricted the secret-service appropriations lest they be used to trail congressmen.

Blocked though Roosevelt was, the "Roosevelt policies" gained repute, and the question of a third term died hard. His decision to sponsor actively the candidacy of his secretary of war, William Howard Taft [q.v.], seems to have been due to his desire to quiet suspicions of his own intentions. By the use of traditional methods, which four years later Roosevelt condemned, the nomination of Taft was effected. Roosevelt was happy in the hope that his administrative team would be held together. He had in both terms escaped the ineptitudes of a cabinet made for politics. His official family had worked well in harness. Taft, after his election in 1908, preferred to select his own cabinet, and Roosevelt left office somewhat disappointed, it may be, but still cordial.

The activities of the presidency, many as they were, could not keep Roosevelt busy. He had continued to write. He had traveled much, breaking a precedent when he left the country to visit the canal in 1906; and breaking it still more by reading Milton and Tacitus in odd moments. His letters were voluminous, and his talk was incessant. His enemies called him "quack," "demagogue," and "liar"; and even "drunkard" until he quieted this by a libel action at Marquette, Mich., in 1913. But his intimates loved him with an unreasoning devotion (L. F. Abbott, ed., *The Letters of Archie Butt,* 1924; *Taft and Roosevelt. The Intimate Letters of Archie Butt, Military Aide,* 2 vols., 1930). To the ordinary voter he had become the prophet of the "square deal."

Out of office in 1909, he had to find work. His comfortable estate (probated at under a million) yielded less income than he required. He took a post with the *Outlook* as contributing editor, sold literary work to the *Metropolitan Magazine* and the *Kansas City Star,* and received generous royalties from the publishers of his books, describing himself as "an elderly literary man of pronounced domestic tastes." But before taking up letters as an ex-President he arranged a hunt (*African Game Trails: An Account of the African Wanderings of an American Hunter-Naturalist,* 1910). There were only occasional echoes from the jungle while he was buried in it; but on his emergence at Khartum, Mar. 14, 1910, there began a progress of unexpected sparkle. He discussed intimate problems of colonial government with a pungency that made men gasp (*African and European Addresses,* 1910); visited the Kaiser to tell him that he alone among European sovereigns could carry his ward in New York; rebuked the Vatican and snubbed its critics; lectured formally at the Sorbonne, at Oxford, and at Christiania in return for his Nobel Prize; counted the birds in New Forest with Sir Edward Grey; and represented the United States at the funeral of Edward VII, where he had the time of his life. On June 18, 1910, he returned home to a triumphant reception (*New York Times,* June 19, 1910).

Already he had learned of the growing breach between the conservative and insurgent groups in the Republican party, and tales told on Taft were reaching him. He said that all he wanted was privacy, but it was not in his nature to abstain from political activity. He soon entered the unsuccessful fight for a direct primary law in New York and made it clear that in state affairs he would support the progressives (*New York Times,* June 30, Aug. 17, 1930). In the late summer he began a speaking tour in the West. On Aug. 31, at Ossawatomie, Kan., he declared that "property shall be the servant and not the master," and that the Constitution if too rigid to conform to the needs of life must be amended (*New York Tribune,* Sept. 1, 1910; Roosevelt, *The New Nationalism,* 1910). In the autumn he did more speaking, and asserted his leadership in New York, where he was elected temporary chairman of the Republican state convention and brought about the nomination of Henry L. Stimson for the governorship, though he was unable to bring about his election in November. His meetings with Taft had been unsatisfactory (Pringle, pp. 536, 538). By the summer or early autumn of 1911 the unhappy estrangement of the two friends had become complete. Roosevelt might have forced the nomination of LaFollette, the most conspicuous member of the progressive group that was seeking to block the renomination of Taft in 1912, but he did not believe that LaFollette could command the movement and allowed himself to be persuaded that the "Roosevelt policies" were lost unless he reëntered politics. His reëntry was staged to follow an appeal from seven Republican governors (Howland, *post,* pp. 212–13); he declared to a reporter that his hat was in the ring (*New York Times,* Feb. 23, 1912) and on Feb. 25 released his acceptance of the memorial (*Ibid.,* Feb. 26, 1912). Taking the aggressive by advocating direct primaries instead of conventions, he rolled up majorities wherever he could enter primary contests and demonstrated that he was the choice of the Republican rank and file. By his advocacy of the initiative, referendum, and recall, however, he had alienated the conservative leaders, among them his old friend Henry Cabot Lodge; and the administration controlled the party machinery, as it had four years before. Elihu Root steered the convention that seated Taft delegates in disputed cases and renominated him. In vain Roosevelt shouted "naked theft!" His delegation became the nucleus of the Progressive party which met Aug. 5, 1912, to nominate him for president and Gov. Hiram Johnson of California for vice-president on a platform that embraced most of the programs of liberal reform. He led Taft in November, but only succeeded in opening the breach through which Woodrow Wilson marched to victory as minority president. (For the entire campaign and its controversies, see Pringle, pp. 525–71, and references.)

Shot by a fanatic in Milwaukee, Oct. 14, Roosevelt recovered in time to finish his canvass, but the days of his youth were gone. In 1914 he tried one more major expedition, and one too many. Visiting the republics of La Plata he plunged into the blank spaces of the map (*Through the Brazilian Wilderness*, 1914), where he found the "River of Doubt," but whence he narrowly escaped with his life. He never recovered from the tropical infections, and was already blind in one eye, the consequence of a boxing accident while in the White House. He returned to his desk (*A Book-Lover's Holidays in the Open*, 1916) to watch the world at war. Roosevelt was a neutral until his old suspicions of Germany were revived, his sympathies with the Allies aroused, and he had persuaded himself that had he been president he would have stopped the war. The diplomatic course of President Wilson was generally offensive to him. Army officers told him stories, he supported the National Security League, and with tongue and pen sought to arouse the country (*America and the World War*, 1915; *Fear God and Take Your Own Part*, 1916; *The Foes of Our Own Household*, 1917). He was convinced that the Progressive party was dead and in 1916 he had a moment of hope that the Republican breach might be healed behind him, again a candidate. Between Hughes and Wilson he had to support Hughes, though each time he spoke he alienated the German vote which Hughes must gain to win.

When war came at last, his four sons were soon at the front while he besieged the War Department and overcame aversion to besiege the White House for permission to raise a volunteer division and to command one of its brigades. Despite the incumbrances of age, accident, disease, and the lack of professional military training, he found no justice in the refusal to accept his service. Bitter, he stayed at home to talk and write (*The Great Adventure; Present-Day Studies in American Nationalism*, 1918), until in January 1918, he rushed to Washington "to tell the truth and speed up the war." It may be that the way was being paved for his return as the presidential candidate of a united party in 1920. But, on Jan. 6, 1919, he died peacefully in his sleep. His career had personalized the American recognition of a changing world. His flaws were on the surface and undisguised; his human values were timeless.

[His official biography, J. B. Bishop, *Theodore Roosevelt and His Time Shown in His Own Letters* (2 vols.,

1920), was begun under his direction and is in fact largely autobiographical; it supplements *Theodore Roosevelt: An Autobiography* (1913). All of his writings, cited above, are highly personal, and his earlier biographers found it easier to accept his estimate of himself than to reconstruct events from the evidence of working documents. His books, articles, journalistic releases, speeches, letters, and state papers are so numerous as to have defied complete collection; but selections from his works began to be assembled as early as *Sagamore Ed.* (15 vols., 1900); and *Executive Ed.* (14 vols., 1901); among subsequent but incomplete collections are *Elkhorn Ed.* (28 vols., 1906–1920), and *National Ed.* (20 vols., 1926) in which the Roosevelt Memorial Asso., Hermann Hagedorn, ed., cooperated with the publishers. This association maintains an invaluable collection of Rooseveltiana at the Roosevelt Birthplace in New York City. His letter files he deposited in the Lib. of Cong., subject to reasonable restrictions that have permitted their examination to 1909. J. H. Wheelock, *A Bibliography of Theodore Roosevelt* (1920), is reasonably complete to its date. Tyler Dennett, *Roosevelt and The Russo-Japanese War* (1925); A. L. P. Dennis, *Adventures in Am. Diplomacy, 1896–1906* (1928); and H. C. Hill, *Roosevelt and The Caribbean* (1927), have made careful use of his papers in correcting part of the record. H. F. Pringle, *Theodore Roosevelt; A Biography* (1931), is a thoroughly judicious work with an excellent bibliography. W. F. McCaleb, *Theodore Roosevelt* (1931), has used the manuscripts but is inaccurate and shows bias. Roosevelt's presidency was lived under the observation of J. F. Rhodes, who covered it inadequately in *The McKinley and Roosevelt Administrations, 1897–1909* (1922); and under the admiring gaze of Mark Sullivan, *Our Times* (vols. II–V, 1927–33). Among the genealogies are W. M. Clemens, *The Ancestry of Theodore Roosevelt; A Genealogical Record from 1649* (1914); F. M. Smith, *Roosevelt Arms and Family History* (1909); C. B. Whittlesey, *The Roosevelt Genealogy, 1649–1902* (1902); A. P. Johnson, *Franklin D. Roosevelt's Colonial Ancestors* (1933).

The biographies that appeared during his life are little more than compilations of the growing newspaper legend, tinctured often with uncritical hero-worship: T. W. Handford, *Theodore Roosevelt, the Pride of the Rough Riders, an Ideal American* (1897); Murat Halstead, *The Life of Theodore Roosevelt* (1902); R. C. V. Meyers, *Theodore Roosevelt, Patriot and Statesman* (1901); F. E. Leupp, *The Man Roosevelt, A Portrait Sketch* (1904); J. A. Riis, *Theodore Roosevelt the Citizen* (1904); James Morgan, *Theodore Roosevelt, the Boy and the Man* (1907); Sydney Brooks, *Theodore Roosevelt* (1910); Max Kullnick, *From Rough Rider to President* (1911); C. G. Washburn, *Theodore Roosevelt; the Logic of his Career* (1916). A more useful group of works followed his death: L. F. Abbott, *Impressions of Theodore Roosevelt* (1919); H. C. Lodge, *Theodore Roosevelt* (1919); W. D. Lewis, *The Life of Theodore Roosevelt* (1919); W. R. Thayer, *Theodore Roosevelt, An Intimate Biography* (1919); J. B. Bishop, ed., *Theodore Roosevelt's Letters to His Children* (1919); W. A. White, *Political Adventures of Theodore and Me* (1920); H. J. Howland, *Theodore Roosevelt and his Times; A Chronicle of the Progressive Movement* (1921); Corinne R. Robinson, *My Brother, Theodore Roosevelt* (1921); Anna R. Cowles, ed., *Letters from Theodore Roosevelt to Anna Roosevelt Cowles 1870–1918* (1924); *Selections from the Correspondence of Theodore Roosevelt and Henry Cabot Lodge* (2 vols., 1925); Earle Looker, *The White House Gang* (1929), *Colonel Roosevelt, Private Citizen* (1932); L. D. Einstein, *Roosevelt, his Mind in Action* (1930); Owen Wister, *Roosevelt, The Story of a Friendship, 1880–1919* (1930). Among the journalists who enjoyed his friendship and recorded his *dicta* are: A. W. Dunn, *Gridiron Nights* (1915); J. J. Leary, *Talks with T. R.* (1920); H. H. Kohlsaat, *From McKinley to Harding; Personal Recollections of our Presidents* (1923); O. K. Davis, *Released for Publication; Some Inside Political History of Theodore Roosevelt and his Times, 1898–1918* (1925); C. W. Thompson, *Presidents I've Known and Two Near Presidents* (1929). An interesting collection of cartoons is Raymond Gros, ed., *T. R. in Cartoon* (1910).] F. L. P.

ROOT, AMOS IVES (Dec. 9, 1839–Apr. 30, 1923), apiarist, was born on a farm near Medina, Ohio, the son of Samuel Homer and Louisa (Hart) Root and a descendant of John Roote who settled at Farmington, Conn., in 1640. His early days were spent on the farm and in the local schools, with two winter terms in an academy at Wellsville, Columbiana County. A nervous and sickly boy, he decided to follow some other occupation than farming. He entered the employ of a local jeweler and at the age of twenty-one started a watch-repair shop of his own which soon expanded into a jewelry manufacturing business.

One day in August 1865 a stray swarm of bees passing through the air attracted his attention, and from that time on he was a student and breeder of the bee. In 1869 he began the manufacture and sale of beekeepers' supplies, later abandoning his jewelry business, after seventeen years, to give his entire attention to the bee industry. He perhaps did more than any other man in America to commercialize beekeeping. By 1876 he had twenty men working on bees and bee supplies. Later the work of the A. I. Root Company required a force of a hundred or more employees. Root himself, primarily a business man, did very little scientific work, but he popularized the results of the scientific work of C. C. Miller and Lorenzo L. Langstroth [*q.v.*], introducing the Langstroth method throughout the world. He built and perfected the first comb foundation machine and the first simple hive without porticos, and was the first to put out comb honey section boxes holding a pound of honey. In January 1873 he began the publication of a monthly periodical, *Gleanings in Bee Culture,* which he edited till 1890. From 1865 to 1887 he wrote profusely on the general subject of bees, *ABC of Bee Culture* (1877; subsequent revisions under slightly altered title) being perhaps his best-known book. In the late eighties his health broke down and he found it necessary to spend a large amount of time out of doors. He established a vegetable garden of about ten acres, experimented with new plants, and was one of those responsible for the introduction of the Grand Rapids lettuce. He was author or co-author of several books on such subjects as strawberry, potato, and tomato culture, and from his press at Medina issued other volumes on agricultural subjects, for some of which he supplied editorial additions. Ability to write, business tact, and above all a restless energy and intensity of spirit characterized him. Brought up in a God-fearing family, he drifted in his early manhood into the skepticism of Ingersoll and Tom Paine, but in the seventies was converted, returned to his Congregational allegiance, and almost immediately took up Sunday-school work. In 1875, he started the "Our Home" page in *Gleanings in Bee Culture,* in response to his burning desire to help human beings live better and happier lives. He was one of the founders of the Anti-Saloon League. To foreign missionaries he sent *Gleanings in Bee Culture* free of charge. For a long time he offered to send a bee smoker to any reader who would quit the use of tobacco. In 1909 he began a crusade in his paper against whiskey advertisements in newspapers. During much of his early life he was in poor health, but about 1895, having established a successful business, he began to allow himself more leisure and thus regained his health and with it the quiet spirit which marked his later life. He married Susan Hall on Sept. 30, 1861, and for many years his son was associated with him in business.

[Paper read by A. R. Webber before the school children of Medina on the day of the funeral of A. I. Root (MS. in the possession of E. R. Root); Root's autobiography, *Gleanings in Bee Culture,* July 1923–Oct. 1928; E. R. Root, "A Son's Memories of A. I. Root," *Ibid.,* June 1923; *Ohio State Journal* (Columbus), May 1, 1923; *Who's Who in America,* 1922–23; J. P. Root, *Root Geneal. Records* (1870); correspondence with E. R. Root and personal interviews with apiarists and horticulturists in Ohio.] J. I. F.

ROOT, ELISHA KING (May 10, 1808–Aug. 31, 1865), mechanic, inventor, was the son of Darius and Dorcas (Sikes) Root and a descendant of Thomas Root who settled in Hartford, Conn., in 1637. Born on his father's farm at Ludlow, Mass., he received a common-school education and then became a machinist's apprentice. Upon completing his apprenticeship, he worked at his trade in various shops in Ware and Chicopee Falls, Mass., and in 1832, when twenty-four years old, went to Collinsville, Conn., to work for the Collins Company, manufacturers of axes. He began there as a lathe hand in the repair shop but because of his unusual and mechanical aptitude very soon became foreman. He remained with this company for seventeen years, the last four as superintendent, and during this time, through his inventions and improvements in axe-manufacturing machinery and methods, he converted the Collins establishment from a primitive shop into a modern factory, thereby enabling the company to increase its business greatly and attain virtual control of the American axe market.

In 1849 Root was offered positions by four

different manufacturers, and accepted the superintendency of the newly established Colt Armory at Hartford, Conn., at a very large salary. He then removed with his family to Hartford and in the course of the next five years designed and built the Colt Armory as well as most of the machinery for it. In this plant the principle of interchangeable parts was adopted and automatic or semi-automatic machinery was substituted for most of the handwork. Even before the armory was completed in 1855, Root had devised and patented much of the automatic machinery, one of the most ingenious of his devices being a drop hammer, patented Aug. 16, 1853. In addition, he devised machines for boring and rifling gunbarrels, for stock-turning, for splining, and for making cartridges, and worked out the whole system of jigs, fixtures, tools, and gauges. It is said that many of the machines devised by Root are still running, and are on a par in accuracy and economy of production with those produced today (1934). Every process in the Colt Armory showed his influence. It is said that his drop-hammer inventions of 1853 and 1858 put the art of die-forging on its present basis; his form of drop hammer remained in vogue until the present board drop was developed. Besides his inventions bearing on the manufacture of firearms, Root patented a cam pump (1856), designed especially for use in raising water from the Connecticut River to a reservoir from which the workmen's village built up around the armory was supplied.

Upon the death of Colt [*q.v.*] in 1862, Root became president of the armory and continued in this capacity until his death in 1865, receiving, it is said, the highest salary paid in the state of Connecticut. He was one of the ablest mechanics New England ever produced and the success of both the Collins and Colt companies was in a large measure due to him. Furthermore, many of the most famous of America's later tool builders received their mechanical training under his supervision. "The credit for the revolver belongs to Colt; for the way they [the revolvers] were made, mainly to Root" (Roe, *post*, p. 169). Root married, first, Charlotte R. Chapin of Springfield, Mass., on Oct. 16, 1832; after her death, he married Matilda Colt of Hartford, Oct. 7, 1845. At the time of his death in Hartford he was survived by his widow and four children, one of whom was a son by his first wife.

[J. P. Root, *Root Geneal. Records, 1600–1870* (1870); J. L. Bishop, *A Hist. of Am. Manufactures,* vol. II (1864); J. W. Roe, *English and American Tool Builders* (1916); *Hartford Daily Courant,* Sept. 2, 1865; Patent Office records.]   C. W. M.

ROOT, ERASTUS (Mar. 16, 1773–Dec. 24, 1846), lawyer and politician, was born at Hebron, Conn., the son of William and Zeruiah (Baldwin) Root. His paternal ancestor, Thomas Root, emigrated to America about 1637 and was one of the first settlers of Hartford, Conn. Erastus graduated from Dartmouth College in 1793, taught for a while, published in 1796 *An Introduction to Arithmetic for the use of Common Schools* (reputed to be the first to use the decimal system in coinage), and then read law with Sylvester Gilbert of Hebron. He began practice at Delhi, N. Y., but soon went into politics. Between 1798 and 1844 he served several terms in the state Assembly and Senate, and presided over the latter body as lieutenant-governor of the state in 1823 and 1824. In 1821 he represented Delaware County at the state constitutional convention, where he was a leader in the movement to broaden the suffrage and democratize the state government. In 1824 he brought suit against Charles King and Johnston Verplanck, editors of the *New York American,* for libel, because they had printed an article stating that he had appeared before the Senate in an intoxicated state during his term as lieutenant governor (*New York American,* Aug. 25, 1824). The basis of the case was political and was probably attributable to Root's blocking the passage of an electoral law. The controversy was bitter, and after Root had won a verdict in the circuit court the case was carried to the court of errors, where the first judgment was affirmed (4 *Wendell,* 113, 1829).

In the twenties Root had been a leader in the anti-Clintonian wing of the Democratic party. In 1830 he hoped for the Democratic nomination for the governorship but failed to receive it. He was offered the nomination by the Working Men's party but declined it. While in the legislature, he debated frequently, but showed special interest in certain reforms such as the abolition of capital punishment and negro slavery. He was a representative in Congress from New York during the years 1803–05, 1809–11, 1815–17, and 1831–33. Having become dissatisfied with his party in 1830, he refused to support Jackson in 1832 and later became an avowed Whig. In Congress he showed an interest in most subjects, but was always on the alert to protect the interests of his state. According to a contemporary historian, "though a little uncouth in his manner, and rough, and . . . sometimes rude in his expressions, his wit was keen and his sarcasms severe and biting. He seized with great force and effect upon . . . those points most likely to make an impression on the popular ear . . . and his attacks upon his opponents were severe almost to ferocity. . . . He had much parliamentary tact, and although . . . reckless in his expressions . . . and though irregular in his habits, of highly cultivated intellect" (Hammond, *post,* I, 372). He was one of the chief figures of his day in the political history of the state and was rated among the most able politicians of the time. He was married, on Oct. 4, 1806, to Elizabeth Stockton of Walton, N. Y., by whom he had five children. He died suddenly in New York City, in December 1846, while on his way to Washington.

[See: G. T. Chapman, *Sketches of the Alumni of Dartmouth Coll.* (1867); J. D. Hammond, *The Hist. of Pol. Parties in . . . N. Y.* (2 vols., 1842); C. Z. Lincoln, *The Const. Hist. of N. Y.* (1906), vol. I; D. S. Alexander, *A Pol. Hist. of the State of N. Y.* (vols. I and II (1906); D. R. Fox, *The Decline of Aristocracy in the Politics of N. Y.* (1919); *N. Y. American,* June 17, 19, 20, 1826; David Murray, *Delaware County, N. Y.* (1898); *Biog. Dir. Am. Cong.* (1928); J. P. Root, *Root Geneal. Records* (1870); *N. Y. Herald,* Dec. 25, 1846.]   M. L. B.

ROOT, FRANK ALBERT (July 3, 1837–June 20, 1926), newspaper publisher, author, was born in Binghamton, N. Y., the son of Albert Berthoud and Marinda (Boyden) Root. He served an apprenticeship in a printer's shop at Wellsboro, Pa., and in 1853 set out as a journeyman. Four years later, Apr. 21, 1857, he arrived in Kansas Territory, with which region he was thereafter chiefly identified. Between 1857 and 1861 he worked successively on the *Herald of Freedom* (Lawrence), the *Chindowan* (Quindaro), the *Weekly Highlander* (Highland), and the *Champion* (Atchison).

Between 1861 and 1863 he was assistant postmaster at Atchison, then became express messenger and later local mail agent at Latham Station, Colorado Territory, and after that, mail agent on the Denver division of the Overland Stage Line. On Oct. 21, 1864, at Atchison, Kan., he married Emma Clark, daughter of John Hawkins and Margaret (Allen) Clark. He was associated with F. G. Adams in publishing the *Free Press* (Atchison), 1865–68, and after the *Free Press* was consolidated with the *Champion,* was associated with John A. Martin [*q.v.*] until 1869. He was owner or part owner successively after 1869 of the *Telegraph* (Waterville), the *Courier* (Seneca), the *Express* (Holton), and the *Times* (North Topeka), and at the last two places held the office of postmaster. He established the *Review-Express* at Gunnison, Col., and conducted it from 1880 to 1886, then returned to Topeka, Kan., where he published the *Mail* (North Topeka) from 1886 to 1893.

Root traveled extensively, in addition to frequent changes from one paper to another, thus acquiring a quantity of first-hand information on the West. He possessed a natural talent for descriptive writing, and wherever he went recorded carefully his observations in diaries or in voluminous letters to newspapers. He thus accumulated data which later served him in his most distinctive achievement. After retiring from active publishing in 1893 he devoted his time largely to gathering additional information from participants in the making of the West, and from other sources, and embodied much of this material in an authentic book, *The Overland Stage to California* (privately printed, Topeka, 1901), published in association with William E. Connelley.

[F. W. Blackmar, *Kansas* (1912), II, 606; *Topeka Daily Capital* and *Topeka Daily State Journal,* both June 21, 1926; *Who's Who in America,* 1920–21; *Trans. Kan. State Hist. Soc.,* vols. I–II (1881); Root Papers, the property of George Allen Root, deposited with the Kansas State Historical Soc., Topeka, Kan., including diaries, scrapbook of newspaper letters, clippings, autobiographical sketch, letters containing information on the overland stage and kindred subjects, and a manuscript (unfinished) of a volume of memoirs.]   J. C. M.

ROOT, FREDERIC WOODMAN (June 13, 1846–Nov. 8, 1916), teacher, composer, organist, and conductor, was born in Boston, Mass., the eldest of eight children of George Frederick [*q.v.*] and Mary Olive (Woodman) Root. Both parents, of English descent, came from several generations of New England ancestors, and both were musicians. Frederic began the study of piano with his father at the age of five and at thirteen he was placed under Benjamin Colman Blodgett, one of the most distinguished organists and educators of his time. He also began the study of voice with his father, and when he subsequently went to New York for further training, he studied piano with William Mason and Robert Goldbeck, organ with James Flint and E. A. Bowman, and voice with Carlo Bassini. In 1858 his father became a partner in the music house of Root & Cady in Chicago and in 1859 removed his family there. Frederic continued his education in the new home and when still quite young he began assisting his father in various ways—conducting choruses at "conventions" and especially at the "normal institutes" so characteristic of this period. The proficiency of the enthusiastic young musician was further recognized when, in 1864, he was made editor and arranger for the publications of Root & Cady.

In 1863 Root became organist of the Third Presbyterian Church of Chicago and in 1865 of the Swedenborgian Church, where (except for two years in Europe) he remained until 1884. In 1869–70 he was abroad for further study and travel, devoting much of his time to the study of voice under Vannuccini in Florence, Italy. Hitherto his main interest was centered on instrumental music (piano and organ), but during his sojourn abroad he turned his attention to voice production, in which field he later became a most successful teacher and brought out many important singers. When the firm of Root & Cady went out of existence at the time of the Chicago fire, he devoted considerable time to composition and to writing for musical magazines, especially the *Song Messenger,* which he edited for many years. He was in great demand as a lecturer and became one of the pioneers in shaping the musical taste of the early women's clubs. From 1884 to 1886 he was choral director of the First Baptist Church, but he returned to the Swedenborgian church as organist until 1890. He was the first director of the Mendelssohn Club (1879–85) and in 1885 served as music critic of the *Chicago Herald.* In 1889 he organized and conducted a festival chorus of four hundred voices in a series of concerts given by Gilmore's Band and in 1893, during the Columbian Exposition in Chicago, he directed the chorus in connection with the Folklore Congress. In 1895 he resumed his organ work and was successively organist at the Auditorium and at the First Church of Christ, Scientist. He was a member and president (1904–05) of the Chicago Literary Club, a charter member of the Cliff Dwellers, and member of other social organizations. He died in Chicago in 1916. He had married, Apr. 30, 1874, Fanny, daughter of Samuel Sherwood Smith of Cincinnati, who, together with a daughter and two sons, survived him. Among his most important books are *The Technic and Art of Singing, The Polychrome Lessons in Voice Culture, Introductory Lessons in Voice-Culture,* and numerous collections of exercises, studies, and songs. His compositions are limited largely to church music and songs. Of these the best undoubtedly are the following sacred songs: "Love Never Faileth" and settings of four poems by Mary Baker Eddy—"O'er waiting harp-strings of the mind," "Blest Christmas morn," "Saw ye my Saviour" and "Shepherd, show me how to go."

[*Who's Who in America,* 1916–17; *Internat. Who's Who in Music* (1918); *Grove's Dict. of Music and Musicians, Am. Supp.* (ed. 1928); *Etude,* Jan. 1917; *Chicago Evening Post,* Nov. 8, 1916; information as to certain facts from members of the family.]

F. L. G. C.

ROOT, GEORGE FREDERICK (Aug. 30, 1820–Aug. 6, 1895), music educator, composer, was born in Sheffield, Mass., the son of Frederick Ferdinand and Sarah (Flint) Root, and a descendant of John Roote who was one of the first settlers of Farmington, Conn. When George was six the family moved to North Reading, Mass. In 1838 he went to Boston for study with the choirmaster and organist, A. N. Johnson, and soon he became his instructor's assistant in teaching, and also his assistant as organist at the Winter Street and Park Street churches. While in Boston he met Lowell Mason and helped him in his work at the Boston Academy of Music. In 1844 he moved to New York to become singing teacher at Abbott's school for young ladies, and organist of the Mercer Street Presbyterian Church. He was soon invited to teach also at the Rutgers Female Institute, as well as at Miss Haines's school for young ladies, the Union Theological Seminary, and the New York State Institution for the Blind. In August 1845 he married Mary Olive Woodman, an accomplished singer, sister of J. G. Woodman, an organist and composer.

In the autumn of 1850 Root went abroad, where he remained until the following summer, studying in Paris with two singing teachers, Giulio Alary and Jacques Potharst. Following his return to America he established in 1853 the New York Normal Institute, in association with William Bradbury, "to afford thorough musical instruction, and especially to qualify teachers of music" (advertisement in *Dwight's Journal of Music,* Jan. 22, 1853). The principal teachers at the first session were Lowell Mason, Root, Bradbury, and Thomas Hastings; the assistants were Root's brother-in-law, J. C. Woodman, and John Zundel, organist of Brooklyn's Plymouth Church. Root's success in training teachers led him to follow Mason's example in holding "musical conventions," gatherings of teachers in various parts of the country, who came from different towns in their districts to learn the latest methods of class instruction in singing. For many years this was one of Root's principal activities, and in many ways it was his most important contribution to the musical development of America. In 1859 he moved to Chicago, for he had already taken a financial interest in a music store (the firm of Root & Cady) which his younger brother, E. T. Root, had founded the year before. The fire of 1871 ruined the firm, and its book-catalogue, plates, and copyrights were sold to the John Church Company of Cincinnati, with whom Root maintained connections in Chicago under the firm of George F. Root & Sons. He continued his normal courses, principally in the summer months, when teachers were on vacation. Some of his classes were held in the building of the University of Chicago. In 1886 he took another trip abroad and spent most of his time during a several months' visit in England, observing the English tonic-sol-fa methods.

Root's career as a composer was more spectacular than his work as teacher, even though his most permanent cultural contribution was made through his "normals" and his teachers' conventions. His first composing was undertaken to provide a musical playlet for the pupils in his classes. To this end he wrote "The Flower Queen" in 1851, for which the verses were supplied by Fanny Crosby, then one of his pupils at the New York Institute for the Blind. The cantata was soon published, and much to the composer's surprise, met with a ready sale. Impressed with the success of Stephen Foster's songs, and newly aware of his own facile gift for melody, Root tried writing songs of his own, in similar vein. Under the pen name of "Wurzel" he published "Hazel Dell," and "Rosalie, the Prairie Flower." Later, as he became further involved in musical education for the people, he dropped his *nom de plume* and did not hesitate to associate himself with a style of music that was frankly popular. In the years between 1853 and 1855 he composed "The Shining Shore," an evangelical hymn that has been the best known of his sacred songs. His first Civil War song, "The First Gun is Fired," was unsuccessful, but his second venture, "The Battle Cry of Freedom," composed within a few hours after he had read Lincoln's proclamation calling for troops, was sung throughout the North. "Tramp, Tramp, Tramp, the Boys are Marching" was almost equally popular. He also composed sentimental songs relating to incidents in the war, such lyrics as "Just Before the Battle, Mother," and "The Vacant Chair." His compositions number more than two hundred individual songs, and he compiled more than seventy song collections, musical entertainments for schools, and educational works on music. His work as a composer belongs to a past generation, yet it exerted a powerful influence in its time.

[Root published an autobiography in 1891 under the title: *The Story of a Musical Life*. See also: W. S. B. Mathews, *A Hundred Years of Music in America* (1889); F. J. Metcalf, *Am. Writers and Compilers of Sacred Music* (1925); J. T. Howard, *Our Am. Music* (1930); G. P. Upton, *Musical Memories* (1908); *Grove's Dict. of Music and Musicians, Am. Supp.* (ed. 1928); J. P. Root, *Root Geneal. Records, 1600–1870* (1870); *Chicago Daily Tribune*, Aug. 8, 1895.]

J.T.H.

ROOT, JESSE (Dec. 28, 1736 o.s.–Mar. 29, 1822), jurist and member of the Continental Congress, was born at Coventry, Conn., the eighth and youngest child of Ebenezer and Sarah (Strong) Root and the descendant of Thomas

Roote or Root who emigrated from England about 1637 and settled in Hartford. The boy was educated in the common school of Coventry and, showing himself able and industrious, continued to college. In 1756 he graduated from Princeton University, then known as the College of New Jersey. On May 18, 1758, he was married to Mary Banks of Newark, N. J. They had nine children. He had returned to Connecticut to study theology with the Rev. Samuel Lockwood of Andover and was licensed to preach by the Hartford south association on Mar. 29, 1757. On account of the death of his brother in 1758 and of the illness of his father, who died in 1760, he did not long continue his ministerial work. Furthermore, he was not at all sure that he was fitted for it, and when at the time of the settlement of his father's estate Judge Trumbull suggested that he might make a good lawyer, he found that others, notably Judge Eliphalet Dyer of Windham, agreed with the suggestion. Thus in February 1763 he was admitted to the bar at Windham but chose Hartford in which to practise.

For the next thirty-four years he was continually in the public service and soon found opportunity to defend the colonies with both tongue and pen as a member of the Council of Safety. On Dec. 30, 1776, he received a captain's commission from Governor Trumbull and three days later set out for the army at Peekskill with a company of volunteers he had raised in Hartford. He soon rose in rank to be lieutenant-colonel and then adjutant-general. In December 1778 he presented his credentials in the Continental Congress and sat in that body until the end of 1782. From 1780 to 1789 he was a member of the state Council, the upper house of the legislature under the old constitution, and was for a time its chairman. In 1789 he was appointed assistant judge of the superior court and in 1798 succeeded to the duties of chief justice. In the same year he published *Reports of Cases Adjudged in the Superior Court and Supreme Court of Errors . . . 1789 to . . . 1793* and added a second volume in 1802. In 1807 he returned to private life, believing that men of high office should in the public interest retire while at the height of their powers. For two years, 1807 and 1808, however, he was a member of the legislature, and in 1808 a presidential elector. Likewise in 1818 he was a member of the convention to frame the new state constitution; yet he esteemed it no less an honor to hold the office of school visitor in his own town of Coventry and filled it punctiliously to the last days of his life. He had nine children, all born in Coventry, a wealth of friends, and was beloved and respected for his charity and public works. In stature he was tall, with an easy yet dignified manner. He was characteristically punctual in all business and presided on the bench with both firmness and complaisance. He died at his home in Coventry after a brief illness and lies buried there in the Nathan Hale Memorial Cemetery.

[*Christian Spectator,* July 1824; J. P. Root, *Root Geneal. Records* (1870); J. H. Trumbull, *The Memorial Hist. of Hartford County, Conn.* (1886), vol. I; *Connecticut* (1904), vols. II, III, ed. by Forrest Morgan; *General Cat. of Princeton Univ.* (1908); F. B. Heitman, *Hist. Register and Dictionary of the U. S. Army* (1903), vol. I; *Jour. of the Continental Cong.,* vols. XII, XXIV (1908–22); Thomas Day, *Reports of Cases . . . in the Supreme Court of Errors . . . Conn.,* vol. I (1817), p. xxxii; *Conn. Courant* (Hartford), Apr. 2, 1822.]   W. G. L.

ROOT, JOHN WELLBORN (Jan. 10, 1850–Jan. 15, 1891), architect, was born in Lumpkin, Ga., the son of Sidney and Mary (Clark) Root. His father, a descendant of Thomas Root or Roote, one of the first settlers of Hartford, Conn., was a native of Vermont. As a lad, despite an eager wish to become an architect, he had been apprenticed to a jeweler. In his twenties he left the North and settled in Georgia, opened a dry goods store in Lumpkin, and married the daughter of Judge James and Permelia (Wellborn) Clark. The Clarks were a brilliant family, not without eccentricity. Judge Clark wrote voluminously, and carefully destroyed what he had written. An uncle of Mary Clark Root, John Wellborn, for whom the architect was named, was well-to-do and at one time a member of Congress; in middle life he suddenly gave all his wealth to the church and devoted himself to preaching to the poor.

John Wellborn Root's talents showed early. He was a precocious musician as well as a draftsman, and is said to have made recognizable portraits at the age of seven. In the house in Atlanta to which the family moved during his boyhood he had a special studio room. When the Civil War began, Sidney Root invested all his spare capital in blockade runners and made a fortune trading with England. After the capture of Atlanta, John was sent to Liverpool where his father had many friends. He was put in school at Claremont, nearby, and in June 1866 matriculated at Oxford. He also continued to study music, especially the organ. Soon after the close of the war, however, the Roots settled in New York, where the father lost his fortune almost as swiftly as he had made it, and John entered the University of the City of New York as a sophomore in the civil engineering department. He graduated in 1869 at the head of his class and was Commencement orator. Since the

family fortunes were by this time insufficient to allow him to be sent to Paris, he entered the architectural office of James Renwick the younger [*q.v.*], where he stayed for a year without pay; then he got a job in the office of J. B. Snook, the designer of the old Grand Central Station. In 1871, Peter B. Wight [*q.v.*], who had seen some of Root's drawings in New York, invited him to Chicago to become head draftsman for the firm of Carter, Drake & Wight.

Here in 1872–73 Root met another young draftsman, Daniel H. Burnham [*q.v.*], and an instant sympathy developed between the two. In July 1873 they went into partnership. The panic of that year almost at once wiped out their first prospect, a new suburb, and for a while their progress was difficult. They could only give part time to the partnership, spending the rest in other offices earning their office rent; at one time Root helped out by serving as organist in the First Presbyterian Church. Late in 1874 their first big job, the house for John B. Sherman, came to the office through a real estate friend of Root's, and after 1875 their rise was rapid and the firm of Burnham & Root became well known. Burnham was the job-getter and developed the primary plan idea, while Root designed the exteriors—sometimes following rough sketches of his partner's, often developing the whole himself. His engineering training stood him in good stead; although he was never a brilliant mathematician, he had the creative engineering mind. Thus, in order to save space in the cellar of the ten-story Montauk Building he devised the system of grillage foundations, by which the weights on piers are spread over sufficient area by means of steel rails (he later used rolled beams) set criss-cross and embodied in concrete—a method more economical than the cut stone foundations formerly used. This method has since become standard practice except where loads are extraordinarily heavy.

Root's design was in many ways epoch-making. Though—like most of the work of his period, even that of the rebel, Louis Sullivan [*q.v.*]—it was superficially based on the Romanesque of H. H. Richardson [*q.v.*], it was all essentially personal and, as far as Root could make it, modern, honest, and structurally true. His business buildings showed a continually growing grasp of the fundamentals: the verticality, the uniformity, the composition of the whole became ever more important, the dressing of Romanesque detail less and less so. The climax was the Monadnock building. Its simplicity was the result of a suggestion by Burnham, but the superb working out of that simplicity, the beauty of proportion, the masterly handling of the simple base and the slight outcurving of the cornice, were all Root's and these created a building that more than a generation later still seems modern.

The cooperation between Burnham and Root was superb. Each, in his way, idolized the other, and to Burnham's freely expressed admiration for his partner's talents is due in no small measure their success. Moreover, Root himself was exceedingly popular. He loved playing the piano, chiefly extemporizing, and his playing was widely appreciated; it was much more than a mere amateur's talent. Next to music, his chief recreation was sailing. He was witty and something of a Bohemian; as an amateur actor he was widely sought; and this personal popularity helped his professional reputation. He was one of the founders of the Western Association of Architects, and was instrumental later in its merging with the American Institute of Architects, of which he was secretary at the time of his death. When Chicago was finally settled upon as the location for the World's Columbian Exposition, it was natural that Root, as the foremost Chicago architect, should be appointed consulting architect (August 1890); on Sept. 4, 1890, at his request, this appointment was changed to include his partner. While to the latter belongs the credit for the formation of the board of architects and the generalship of the whole; to Root must go much of the credit for the final choice of a lakeside site and the settlement of the basic plan. The World's Fair activity was the climax of his life. It was after a dinner to the architects that he caught a cold which rapidly developed into the pneumonia from which he died.

John Root married Mary Louise Walker in 1880; already a victim of tuberculosis, she died six weeks after the wedding. On Dec. 12, 1882, he married Dora Louise Monroe. They had three children, two daughters and a son who became an architect. Root was co-author with Russell Sturgis, Bruce Price, Donald G. Mitchell, and others, of *Homes in City and Country* (published in 1893, after his death), to which he contributed "The City House in the West."

[Harriet Monroe, *John Wellborn Root* (1896), with many illustrations of his architectural work, and many quotations from his writings and lectures; Theodore Starrett, "John Wellborn Root," *Architecture and Building*, Nov. 1912; Montgomery Schuyler, *Am. Architecture* (1892); J. P. Root, *Root Geneal. Records* (1870); Charles Moore, *Daniel H. Burnham* (2 vols., 1921); *Chicago Daily Tribune*, Jan. 16, 1891; information from Harriet Monroe.]   T. F. H.

ROOT, JOSEPH POMEROY (Apr. 23, 1826–July 20, 1885), physician, diplomatist, son of John and Lucy (Reynolds) Root, was born in Greenwich, Mass. His father was descended from John Roote who settled in Farmington, Conn., about 1640. After his early schooling was completed, he attended the Berkshire Medical College, Pittsfield, Mass., graduating in 1850. The following year he moved to New Hartford, Conn., and in September married Frances Evaline Alden, by whom he had five sons. He joined the practice of politics to that of medicine, and was elected as a Whig to the Connecticut legislature in 1855. Moved by his social and political convictions to throw himself into the anti-slavery movement, he joined a company of emigrants (the Beecher Bible and Rifle colony) starting for Kansas in March 1856. He settled at Wyandotte, and at once began an active part in the affairs of the distracted territory. He was chairman of the Free-State Executive Committee, and in August 1857 was elected to the Kansas Senate under the Topeka constitution. He was one of the pioneer corps who located the public road from Topeka to Nebraska City, and he was sent East as an agent to obtain arms and aid for the free-soilers.

He contributed editorially to the Wyandotte papers, the *Register* (1857) and the *Gazette* (1858). In December 1859 he was elected lieutenant-governor of the new state on the Republican ticket. In 1861 he was chosen one of the officers of the first annual meeting of the Kansas State Temperance Society. During the Civil War he was surgeon of the 2nd Kansas Cavalry (as it was finally designated) and was medical director of the Army of the Frontier. In 1866 he presided over the Republican state convention. On Sept. 15, 1870, President Grant appointed him minister to Chile, an act which recognized his services and at the same time eliminated him from active participation in state politics. He presented his credentials on Dec. 2, 1870, and since diplomatic duties were not pressing, he gave much time to a general interest in Chilean affairs. He traveled extensively. Once he crossed the Andes into Argentina and reported the trip to the Department of State in the form of a treatise on the cause of earthquakes. Later he accompanied the minister of foreign affairs to southern Chile to investigate the Indians. Improvements in transportation fascinated him; he was enthusiastically in favor of an intercontinental railroad, he urged subsidies by the United States to West-Coast steamship lines, and he undertook on his own account to have Chile establish a system of towboats in the Straits of Magellan.

Root won great popularity with the Chileans for his efforts during a frightful smallpox epidemic in 1872. He served on the Santiago Board of Health and contributed his services to hospitals and private patients, laboring to improve the sanitary treatment of the disease. In recognition of his work a street in Santiago, the "Calle de Root," was named for him. He was recalled in June 1873 to make a place for Cornelius Logan [q.v.]. In 1874 he was elected a vice-president of the Temperance Convention which forced the Republican convention to adopt an anti-liquor plank. Governor St. John appointed him surgeon-general of Kansas. In 1876 he published *Catechism of Money,* advocating greenbackism; in this same year he was named a member of the Chilean Centennial Commission. In 1884 he was a delegate to the Republican National Convention. Except for two years (1877-79) when he was on the staff of a sanitarium at Clifton Springs, N. Y., he lived at Wyandotte until his death. He took a lively interest in the Kansas Historical Society and contributed several manuscript writings to its archives, among them a memoir of his experiences in Kansas in 1856.

[*Topeka Capital,* July 22, 1885; *Weekly Commonwealth* (Topeka), July 23, 1885; *The U. S. Biog. Dir., Kan. Vol.* (1879); J. P. Root, *Root Geneal. Records* (1870); H. C. Evans, *Chile and Its Relations with the U. S.* (1927), p. 96, where Root's given name appears incorrectly as Thomas; *Trans. Kan. State Hist. Soc., 1901-02* (1902); D. W. Wilder, *The Annals of Kan.* (1886); *Papers Rel. to the For. Relations of the U. S., 1871-73*; Root's dispatches (3 vols.) in the Archives of the Dept. of State.]   G. V. B.

ROPES, JAMES HARDY (Sept. 3, 1866–Jan. 7, 1933), theologian, New Testament scholar, was born in Salem, Mass., the son of William Ladd Ropes, librarian of Andover Theological Seminary, and Harriet Lawrence (Peirson) Ropes. Graduating from Phillips Academy, Andover, in 1885, with first honors in classics, and from Harvard College in 1889, *summa cum laude,* he spent a year under the United States Geological Survey in New England and the West. In 1893 he graduated from Andover Theological Seminary, receiving the foreign fellowship. He then spent two years in Germany in study of the New Testament and of early church history at the universities of Kiel, Halle, and Berlin, traveling also in England, Russia, and Italy. He was instructor in New Testament criticism and interpretation in the Harvard Divinity School, 1895–1901; assistant professor, 1898–1903; Bussey Professor, 1903–10, succeeding in this chair Prof. Joseph Henry Thayer [q.v.]. From 1910 he held the Hollis Professorship of Divinity. He was ordained a minister of the Congregational Church in 1901. On Nov. 23, 1897, he married Alice, daughter of Edward Jackson Lowell of Boston, by whom he had a daughter and a son.

In 1910 he suggested a combination of the institutions of learning in and about Boston to give the public the benefit of selected college courses. He was chairman of the joint committee which carried out this plan, and in charge of university extension from 1910 to 1922. He was a member of the corporation of Radcliffe College, 1905–12, and of the corporation of Simmons College; a trustee from 1899 of Phillips Academy, Andover, and of Andover Theological Seminary (until the separate incorporation of the latter in 1907); and president of the board of trustees of the Academy from 1929 until his death. During his connection with this institution he effected a reorganization of the school, which was termed a masterpiece, showing real genius, and putting him in the forefront of those interested in the betterment of secondary education. He was of greatest service to the Harvard Divinity School and to Andover Seminary at the time of the removal of the latter to Cambridge in 1908. The schools entered into closer affiliation in 1922, but were separated by a decree of the supreme court in 1926, Andover Seminary removing, in 1931, to Newton. He was a fellow of the American Academy of Arts and Sciences, a member of the American Oriental Society, of the Society of Biblical Literature and Exegesis, and of the Archæological Institute of America. From 1921 he was editor of the *Harvard Theological Review.*

Besides many articles in professional journals, he published *Die Sprüche Jesu die in den Kanonischen Evangelien nicht überliefert sind* (1896); *The Apostolic Age in the Light of Modern Criticism* (1906); *A Critical and Exegetical Commentary on the Epistle of Saint James* (1916); *The Text of Acts* (1926); *The Singular Problem of the Epistle to the Galatians* (1929). The qualities essential to the interpreter of the New Testament were preëminent in Ropes, thoroughness, perspective, solidity of judgment, restraint of imagination, and religious insight. His colleages, whether in the theological school or in the faculty of arts and sciences, knew his absolute sincerity and selflessness. His work on the *Review* was characterized by punctilious care in the supervision of every smallest detail, whether of form or substance. The appreciation in which under his leadership it came to be held at home and abroad was extraordinary. His *Text of Acts,* awarded the British Academy's medal for Biblical studies, is the most comprehensive survey of all the manuscripts extant, with the object of finding out by a comparison of progressive variations the most probable text from which those known to us have been derived. His scholarship, the prescience of his mind, and the perfection of his self-discipline make this book the model of a critical edition.

[*Who's Who in America*, 1932–33; *Class of 1889, Harvard Coll. . . . Seventh Report* (1914) and *Eighth Report* (1919); *Harvard Theological Rev.*, Jan. 1933; *Harvard Univ. Gazette*, Apr. 1, 1933; *Boston Transcript*, Jan. 9, 1933; personal acquaintance.]
E. C. M—e.

ROPES, JOHN CODMAN (Apr. 28, 1836– Oct. 28, 1899), military historian, was born in St. Petersburg, Russia, the son of William and Mary Anne (Codman) Ropes. His father, a merchant and ship-owner of Salem, had gone to Russia a few years before to establish a branch house. In 1837 the family removed to London for a similar purpose and in 1842 returned to Boston. The boy began preparation for college at Chauncy Hall School but in 1850, on account of a spinal trouble resulting from an injury in infancy, had to leave school for treatment. A year later he was able to resume his studies under a private tutor, William W. Goodwin [*q.v.*], and in 1853 he entered Harvard College, where he graduated in 1857. He then entered the Harvard Law School, graduated in 1861, and entered upon the practice of law in Boston. With John C. Gray [*q.v.*] he edited the *United States Law Review* from 1866 to 1869. From boyhood he had been intensely interested in military affairs, and hence it was a keen disappointment to him that his physical disability prevented his entering the army at the opening of the Civil War. Being unable to do this, he followed the course of operations with close and intelligent observation. He often visited the army in the field, living in camp with his friends, generally with the 20th Massachusetts Infantry, the regiment of his brother Henry, who was killed at Gettysburg. Much of his Civil War correspondence is contained in *War Letters, 1862–1865 of John Chipman Gray . . . and John Codman Ropes* (1927).

After the war he turned his taste for historical study to military subjects and in 1876 was a founder of the Military Historical Society of Massachusetts. Among his writings on the Civil War, the most important were *The Army under Pope* (1881) in the Campaigns of the Civil War Series and his *Story of the Civil War* (2 vols. 1894–98). At his death, the latter was completed only to include the campaigns of 1862. Later his friend William R. Livermore wrote and published an additional volume (1913). Even before he went to college he had read much

on Napoleon, for whose military genius he always had a great admiration. This study he always continued, and he wrote extensively upon the Napoleonic campaigns. Of these writings, perhaps the most important are *The First Napoleon* (1885) and *The Campaign of Waterloo* (1892) with *An Atlas of the Campaign* (1893). His style was clear and lively; he habitually took the view of the higher commanders and discussed operations in terms of corps and divisions, rarely going into the tactical details of smaller units. In his work on the Civil War, in spite of his strong Northern sympathy, he presented the Southern views with fairness. His judgments of commanders and their plans were positive, but he generally presented the evidence on both sides, giving the reader a basis for disagreement. His writings were based upon careful study of the best sources of information and enjoy a high reputation.

His interest in military affairs was by no means an indication of a militaristic turn of mind. Quite the contrary, he was unqualifiedly opposed to war, theoretically; he believed that the Spanish-American War could have been avoided, and in the controversies resulting from it he was definitely an anti-imperialist. Yet he accepted war as a fact and considered it useful to trace its intellectual element and the logical processes of its conduct. He was an active member of Trinity Church in Boston, where he served for many years as a vestryman. He was a student of theology and planned, had he lived, to write a series of essays on theological subjects. Personally, he was much loved and admired by his large circle of friends. His spinal trouble caused a slight deformity, but this was not particularly noticeable and did not prevent ordinary physical activity. He continued always in the practice of law, gradually withdrawing, however, from court work to office practice; he visited his office even on the last day of his life. He was never married.

[*A Memoir of the Life of John Codman Ropes* (1901) with sketches and addresses by numerous associates; personal information from Mrs. Albert T. Leatherbee of West Roxbury, librarian of the Military Historical Society of Massachusetts; *Daily Evening Transcript* (Boston), Oct. 29, 1899.]
O. L. S., Jr.

ROPES, JOSEPH (Dec. 15, 1770–Sept. 29, 1850), privateersman and merchant, was born in Salem, Mass., the son of David Ropes, a noted privateersman of the Revolution who was killed in battle in 1781, and Ruth Hathorne, a kinswoman of Nathaniel Bowditch and Nathaniel Hawthorne. While still a boy he ran away to sea and made a voyage to the West Indies. His pay was four dollars a month at first, but the life suited him and he rose steadily from cabin boy to shipmaster. In 1794 he commanded the ship *Recovery* and in 1797 the ship *John.* He made many voyages to China, the East Indies, Arabia, and the Isle of France. In 1809 he took command of the *America,* of 473 tons, 114 feet long, with 30 feet breadth of beam, a large vessel in those days and one of the fastest ships of her time. She made a voyage to the Mediterranean and was the first American merchantman to visit Constantinople. Ropes remained here ten months and was received by the Sultan, who wished to negotiate through him a commercial treaty with the United States.

When the War of 1812 broke out the *America* was converted into a privateer. Her upper deck was removed, her sides fortified with oak, and her yards and royalmasts lengthened. She carried 20 guns and 150 men. Ropes commanded her on her first cruise and sailed from Salem Sept. 7, 1812. He cruised in the chops of the English Channel. He was a strict disciplinarian and quelled a mutiny on board the ship. Although he fell in with no war vessels and fought no battles, he captured six prizes during the cruise valued at $158,000. When the *America* returned to Salem about the end of the year Ropes gave up his command and retired permanently from a seafaring life. Why he did so in war-time, at the end of a successful cruise, is not known. He was, however, chosen captain of a company of Sea Fencibles—an artillery force for coast defense. After the war he settled down into the life of a useful and public-spirited citizen. He served as selectman of the town and for several terms in the state legislature. He was director of a bank and of an insurance company, and one of the founders of the East India Marine Society. He had married, Feb. 3, 1801, Sarah, daughter of Zachariah Burchmore, another Salem privateersman. They had two daughters.

[*Hist. Colls. of the Essex Inst.,* vols. IV (1862), VII (1865), and XXXVII (1901); E. S. Maclay, *A Hist. of Am. Privateers* (1899); *Salem Reg.,* Oct. 3, 1850.]　　　　　　　　　　　　　　　G. W. A.

RORER, DAVID (May 12, 1806–July 7, 1884), lawyer, legal writer, was the son of Abraham Rorer who lived on a farm in Pittsylvania County, Va. On the foundation of a country-school education, he studied law in the office of Nathaniel H. Claiborne [*q.v.*] and was admitted to the Virginia bar before he was twenty years old. Accompanied by a slave, he set out on horseback in the fall of 1826 for Little Rock, Ark. In 1827 he married Martha (Daniel) Martin, by whom he had two sons and two daughters. On the western frontier he practised law, superintended the construction of a military highway, investigated the condition of the Indians, and dabbled in politics, eventually becoming prosecuting attorney. In the autumn of 1835 he resigned that office, went to St. Louis, and thence in the following spring to the pioneer settlement of Burlington on the west bank of the Mississippi River in Michigan Territory. At Burlington he made his home during the remainder of his life. There his first wife died in 1838, and in the following year he married Delia Maria Viele; two daughters by this marriage survived him. Within the first three years of his residence in Burlington, that town became successively the capital of Wisconsin Territory and of the Territory of Iowa. Rorer plotted the town, drafted the charter and some of the ordinances, contributed most generously toward the erection of a church, suggested the sobriquet "Hawkeyes" for the inhabitants of Iowa, participated in a convention to petition Congress for the creation of Iowa Territory, and ran as an independent Democrat for the office of delegate to Congress. As a consequence of the bitter partisanship of that candidacy he engaged in a street fight and fatally shot a newspaper editor who abused him (J. C. Parish, *Robert Lucas,* 1907, p. 181). That was the end of his political career, for which he had little talent or inclination.

For approximately four decades Rorer was one of the most active members of the Iowa bar. Colleagues and rivals knew him as a thorough scholar, a vigorous advocate, and a close reasoner who could on occasion be eloquent without oratorical vacuity. Though reared as a slave owner, he early perceived the evils of negro bondage and manumitted his own slaves. He was associated with three notable fugitive slave cases. In the first trial before the Iowa territorial supreme court in 1839, his argument that Iowa was free territory according to the Ordinance of 1787 and the Missouri Compromise convinced the court that prohibition of slavery in a territory annihilated slave property, and Ralph, by living in Iowa with the consent of his master, had become free (*Iowa Reports,* 1 *Morris,* 1)—a judgment contrary to the Dred Scott decision seventeen years later. In behalf of a Missouri slave owner, however, he won a verdict in 1850 for the recovery of several fugitive slaves "harbored and concealed" among the Quakers near Salem, Iowa (*Ruel Daggs* vs. *Elihu Frazier et al.*). Although Iowa was free soil, he maintained that the state was bound to respect federal law. Five years later he defended an alleged fugitive slave named Dick and won his release by lack of identification. During the Civil War he was energetic in support of the Union and advocated immediate emancipation as a salutary and effective measure.

Beginning in 1853, Rorer was continuously employed for the next quarter of a century as a railroad attorney, as solicitor, first, of the Burlington & Missouri River Railroad Company, which he had helped to organize in 1852, and in the same capacity after its consolidation with the Chicago, Burlington & Quincy, Dec. 31, 1872. As a result of his extensive experience in railroad litigation and to gratify his taste for research, he wrote three exhaustive works: *A Treatise on the Law of Judicial and Execution Sales* (1873), *American Inter-state Law* (1879), and *A Treatise on the Law of Railways* (2 vols., 1884). The scope and detail of these works indicate the author's grasp and accuracy; the publication of second editions of the first two is evidence of their popularity and usefulness to the legal profession.

[E. H. Stiles, in his *Recollections and Sketches of Notable Lawyers and Public Men of Early Iowa* (1916), and in *Annals of Iowa*, July 1907; accounts of the fugitive slave cases, *Ibid.*, July 1899, Apr. 1903; A. M. Antrobus, *Hist. of Des Moines County, Iowa* (1915), I, 399; *Biog. Rev. of Des Moines County, Iowa* (1905); *Weekly Hawkeye* (Burlington), July 10, 1884.]

J. E. B.

ROSA, EDWARD BENNETT (Oct. 4, 1861–May 17, 1921), physicist, was born in Rogersville, N. Y., the son of Edward D. and Sarah Gilmore (Rowland) Rosa. His father was a descendant of Albert Heymans Roosa who came from Holland and settled near Newburgh, N. Y., in 1660. Edward graduated from Wesleyan University, Middletown, Conn., at the head of the class of 1886, and after two years of teaching pursued advanced studies at the Johns Hopkins University, from which he received the doctorate of philosophy in 1891. There, under the direction of H. A. Rowland [*q.v.*], he began the work on electrical measurements which later gave him world-wide recognition. Son of a Methodist minister, he was endowed with a strict moral sense and a confidence in his own judgment which never wavered. Training in banking and bookkeeping strengthened the sense of exactitude which found expression in his later activities in scientific and public affairs.

In 1891 he returned to Wesleyan as associate professor of physics, and from 1892 to 1903 he held a professorship there. He was notably successful as instructor and administrator, but also continued his investigative work. Jointly with Professor Wilbur O. Atwater [*q.v.*], he devised apparatus and made measurements which showed that the physical law of conservation of energy applied to animal processes as it does to inanimate ones, and thus gave a scientific basis for study of problems of nutrition.

In 1902, on leave of absence from Wesleyan, he took charge of the electrical work of the National Bureau of Standards, which had been established in 1901. All his energies thereafter were directed to the development of that institution. In fact, he became a martyr to its welfare, in the trying period of readjustment after the World War, for he died suddenly at his desk in 1921, as a direct result of over-exertion in preparing data regarding the status of personnel in the Bureau of Standards and other scientific organizations of the government.

Rosa's first decade of service in the Bureau was devoted to the establishment of precise electrical units and standards and the building up of a staff capable of carrying on the specialized work in electrical measurements which he developed, while the second decade was marked by an intensive practical application of these facilities, including work on many military problems which arose during the war. His fundamental work on electrical measurements included precise determination of the value of the ampere as measured by the mechanical forces exerted between coils carrying current, and a determination of the relation between electrical units derived from magnetic effects and those derived from electrostatic forces. Both of these were done with the collaboration of N. Ernest Dorsey. From the latter relation between units, it is possible to predict the velocity of light, and it has been found that the electrical measurements of Rosa and Dorsey gave a result nearer the true value than had been obtained up to that time by direct measurements on light itself. Rosa also took a leading part in the researches and the negotiations which led to the establishment of the present international system of electrical units, being secretary of the International Committee on Electrical Units and Standards which had jurisdiction over this work.

His later activities included studies of many engineering problems arising in the operation and the regulation of public-utility services. He urged effectively the principle of solving such problems by scientific study carried on jointly by the utilities and regulatory authorities, with consequent agreement on just and reasonable rules and practices. One outgrowth of this method of cooperative action was the enlargement and reorganization of the American Engineering Standards Committee, which has since become the American Standards Association. His final work was an analysis of federal governmental expenditures, showing the immense costs of war and of preparation for war, in contrast with small expenditures for productive functions of the government. The widespread publication of these analyses played a great part in promoting intelligent discussion of government finances, and in developing public support for the limitation of armaments which was begun at the Washington Conference of 1921.

Rosa's writings were largely detailed technical studies, appearing in appropriate periodicals and in the publications of the Bureau of Standards. The more important among them were the following: "A New Respiration Calorimeter and Experiments on the Conservation of Energy in the Human Body" (*Physical Review,* September, October 1899), with W. O. Atwater; "A New Determination of the Ratio of the Electromagnetic to the Electrostatic Unit of Electricity" (*Bureau of Standards Bulletin,* vol. III, 1907, pp. 433–604), with N. E. Dorsey; "Formulas and Tables for the Calculation of Mutual and Self-Inductance" (*Ibid.,* vol. VIII, 1911, pp. 1–237), with F. W. Grover; "A Determination of the International Ampere in Absolute Measure" (*Ibid.,* pp. 269–393), with N. E. Dorsey and J. M. Miller; "The Silver Voltameter" (*Ibid.,* vol. IX, 1912–13, pp. 151–207, 209–282, 493–551, and vol. X, 1914, pp. 475, 536), with G. W. Vinal and A. S. McDaniel; and "Expenditures and Revenues of the Federal Government" (*Annals of the American Academy of Political and Social Science,* May 1921). Rosa was married on Mar. 22, 1894, to Mary, daughter of William W. Evans of Harrisburg, Pa.; they had no children.

[F. W. Nicolson, *Alumni Record of Wesleyan Univ., Middletown, Conn.* (1931); *Who's Who in America,* 1920–21; *Science,* June 24, 1921; *N. Y. Times,* May 18, 1921; family records; official records, Bureau of Standards; personal acquaintance.]   G. K. B.

ROSATI, JOSEPH (Jan. 12, 1789–Sept. 25, 1843), Roman Catholic prelate, was born at Sora in the Kingdom of Naples. Early in life he was destined for the Church, and on May 30, 1801, received clerical tonsure. His classical studies were completed in 1807 in the Diocesan Seminary, and on June 23 of that year he entered the Congregation of the Mission in Rome. He took his vows Apr. 1, 1808, and in the fall commenced his theological studies under Father Andrew James Felix Bartholomew de Andreis [*q.v.*]. On Feb. 10, 1811, during the last year of his course, he was raised to the priesthood. After four years in home mission work through the Papal States, he received a note from De Andreis asking him whether he would join the Louisiana Mission recently organized

at the instance of Bishop Du Bourg [*q.v.*]. He replied emphatically in the affirmative, and with six companions embarked, Oct. 21, 1815, for Marseilles, whence they later sailed for America. They reached Baltimore July 26, 1816, and Bardstown, Ky., Dec. 4 following. Here, at St. Thomas' Seminary, Rosati began in earnest to learn English while helping the local clergy minister to their scattered flocks. In November 1817 he succeeded De Andreis, who had gone to Missouri, as professor of theology in the Seminary, serving in this capacity until, with the Louisiana band, he started for "the Barrens" (Perryville, Mo.) in the following year. They reached their destination on Oct. 1, 1818, and almost at once opened St. Mary's Seminary in temporary quarters.

This institution of classical and theological learning, the first of its kind west of the Mississippi and the nursery of many pioneer Catholic missionaries in the Middle West, may be said to be, under the fostering care of Bishop Du Bourg, Rosati's own creation. He it was who devised the plan of the institution and superintended its construction, while teaching the most important courses and acting as pastor to the Catholics of the surrounding country. Upon him likewise devolved, after the death of De Andreis, Oct. 15, 1820, the superiorship of his Congregation in America. On Nov. 26, 1822, scarcely nine months after the completion of the seminary building, he received the pontifical brief appointing him Bishop of Tenagra and vicar apostolic of Mississippi and Alabama. His representations to Rome (he sent back the brief) and Du Bourg's plea that the creation of the new vicariate was a premature and ill-advised step, resulted only in having the title changed: on July 14, 1823, Pius VII appointed Rosati coadjutor to the Bishop of Louisiana, and forbade him further resistance. Accordingly, he received episcopal consecration at Donaldsonville, La., Mar. 25, 1824, and for two years continued his multitudinous functions at "the Barrens," while caring for the interests of the Catholics in Upper Louisiana. On Nov. 4, 1826, he was notified of Du Bourg's resignation and the division of Louisiana into two dioceses, New Orleans and St. Louis, both of which he was to administer for a time. Pope Leo XII desired him to accept the See of New Orleans, but he himself wished to remain in St. Louis; finally on Mar. 20, 1827, the matter was settled according to his wishes, although he continued to administer Lower Louisiana until the consecration (June 24, 1830) of Rev. Leo De Neckere, Bishop of New Orleans. During these four years Rosati could scarcely do more than attend to the routine work; nevertheless, this period saw the establishment of the Ladies of the Sacred Heart in St. Louis (1827); the building of St. Mary's College at "the Barrens" (1827); the opening of the St. Louis Hospital (Nov. 26, 1828) by the Sisters of Charity from Emmitsburg, Md.; and the erection of St. Louis College by the Jesuits (1829).

In the fall of 1830 Rosati settled in St. Louis and for ten years labored strenuously in the vast territory under his spiritual care. Among the many churches he erected, the cathedral of St. Louis (built 1831–34) remains as a lasting monument of these strenuous days of religious growth. On Apr. 27, 1840, he left St. Louis to attend the provincial Council of Baltimore, and thence proceeded to Rome. Sent as Apostolic Delegate to negotiate an arrangement between the Haytian Republic and the Holy See, he stopped at Philadelphia on his way to consecrate Peter Richard Kenrick [q.v.], whose appointment as his coadjutor he had obtained in Rome. His difficult and laborious mission resulted in the draft of an agreement with which he returned to Rome. Since he had won the favor of the authorities of Port-au-Prince, he was sent to Hayti once more by the Pope to complete the work. While on his way thither, he was seized by illness in Paris, and advised to return to Rome, where he died.

[Rosati MSS. (17 vols.) in archives of Kenrick Seminary, Webster Groves, Mo.; "Vita di Monsig. Giuseppe Rosati" (MS.), archives of the Congregation of the Mission, Collegio Leoniano, Rome; "Necrologia di Monsig. Rosati," in *Diario di Roma*, Nov. 7, 11, 1843; "Necrologia di Monsig. Giuseppe Rosati," in *Annali delle Scienze Religiose*, vol. XVIII, fasc. lii (1844); R. H. Clarke, *Lives of the Deceased Bishops of the Cath. Church in the U. S.* (1872); J. G. Shea, *The Hierarchy of the Cath. Church in the U. S.* (1886); J. E. Rothensteiner, *Hist. of the Archdiocese of St. Louis* (1928), vol. I; *Life of the Very Rev. Felix De Andreis . . . Chiefly from Sketches by the Rt. Rev. Joseph Rosati* (1900); F. G. Holweck, "The Arkansas Mission under Rosati," *St. Louis Cath. Hist. Rev.*, July–Oct. 1919; *Cath. Expositor and Lit. Mag.*, Dec. 1843.]   C. L. S.

ROSE, AQUILA (c. 1695–1723), poet, was born and educated in England. Misfortune of some kind induced him to enlist as a common sailor, and, after visiting various cities on the Mediterranean, he chanced to come to Philadelphia and remained there, being too ill for further duty aboard ship. The date of his arrival is unknown but must have been sometime before Gov. William Keith's visit to the Indians at Conestoga (July 1717), which he commemorated in verse. While convalescing he made friends, James Logan, 1674–1751 [q.v.], among them, and a place was found for him as compositor in the printing office of Andrew Bradford

[q.v.]. He married Maria ——, and was esteemed for his amiable disposition and accomplishments. When he petitioned the Assembly for the right to operate a ferry on the Schuylkill, the corporation of Philadelphia objected to granting the ferry franchise to a private party, but an amicable arrangement was made. The corporation established the ferry and leased it to Rose for twenty-one years, stipulating that he improve the approaches and erect a house and boatsheds. In 1722 he was made clerk of the Assembly. The next year, while retrieving a boat washed from its moorings in a freshet, he took a chill, became desperately ill, and died. The day of his death was given by Samuel Keimer [q.v.] in his *Elegy on the Much Lamented Death of the Ingenious and Well-Beloved Aquila Rose* (1723) as the 24th of Fourth Month (*i.e.*, June) and by Elias Bockett, in *A Poem to the Memory of Aquila Rose* (London, printed for the author, 1723–24), as the 22nd of August. The latter date has the support of Rose's son Joseph, who was apprenticed to Benjamin Franklin in 1730 and in 1740 published *Poems on Several Occasions, By Aquila Rose: To Which Are Prefixed, Some Other Pieces Writ to Him. and to His Memory after His Decease.* The small, neatly printed octavo contains two translations from the *De Tristibus* of Ovid (Bk. I, Elegies ii and iii); lines to Richard Hill [q.v.]; the aforementioned poem, "To his Excellency Sir William Keith, Bart. on his Journey to Conestogoe, and Treaty with the Indians there"; three carriers' addresses for New Year's Day, 1720, 1721, and 1722; seven other short pieces in couplets or quatrains, and several addressed to him or to his memory, including a reprint, with a separate title-page, of Bockett's elegy. Rose's poems are the work of a cultured amateur, the best versifier in English that Philadelphia could show before the younger Thomas Godfrey [q.v.]. His own estimate of their worth may be inferred from the fact that, with good opportunity to publish his work, he refrained from doing so.

[The Library of Congress and the Hist. Soc. of Pa. have each a copy of the *Poems on Several Occasions*. See also the headnote to the reprint of Keimer's *Elegy* in Samuel Hazard's *Reg. of Pa.*, Nov. 1828; J. F. Fisher, "Some Account of the Early Poets and Poetry of Pa.," *Memoirs of the Hist. Soc. of Pa.*, vol. II, pt. 2 (1830); J. T. Scharf and Thompson Westcott, *Hist. of Phila.*, vol. I (1884); F. H. Williams, "Pa. Poets of the Provincial Period," *Pa. Mag. of Hist. and Biog.*, Apr. 1893; M. K. Jackson, *Outlines of the Lit. Hist. of Colonial Pa.* (1906).]   G. H. G.

ROSE, CHAUNCEY (Dec. 24, 1794–Aug. 13, 1877), railroad builder, financier, and philanthropist, was born at Wethersfield, Conn., and died at Terre Haute, Ind. He was the grandson of John Rose who emigrated from Scottish Highlands early in the eighteenth century, and the son of John and Mary (Warner) Rose. His education was brief and limited to that furnished by the common schools of his native village. In 1817 he visited Indiana, Illinois, Missouri, Kentucky, Tennessee, and Alabama, looking for a place to establish himself. Favorably impressed with Terre Haute and its people he returned there in April 1818, but the following year went to Rosedale, where he built and operated a grist and saw mill. In 1825 he moved back to Terre Haute and immediately became active in the affairs of this pioneer village as a merchant, farmer, and contractor. His native energy combined with thrift, forethought, and upright business methods brought him a deserved prosperity and considerable wealth.

Rose was greatly interested in securing railroad facilities for Terre Haute. A road had been projected from Richmond, Ind., to Springfield, Ill., but in spite of many difficulties, he succeeded in diverting it to Terre Haute. It is an evidence of his strong-willed and self-reliant character that he also successfully fought an attempt to get a land grant from the government to build the road and, largely by his own efforts, financed the building operations by private subscription. The Terre Haute & Richmond Railroad (later the Terre Haute & Indianapolis) was organized in 1847 with Rose as its first president. This office he resigned in 1853 after the portion of the road lying between Terre Haute and Indianapolis was built and in running order. His efforts and his money were important factors in bringing other railroads to, or through, Terre Haute. Among these were the Evansville & Crawfordsville Railroad, which was completed between Evansville and Terre Haute in 1853; an extension of the Crawfordsville branch, which later became known as the Logansport Division of the Terre Haute & Indianapolis; and an extension of the Evansville road to Danville and Chicago, known as the Evansville, Terre Haute & Chicago Railroad. It was only on account of advancing years that he took no active part in the completion of the St. Louis, Vandalia & Terre Haute Railroad in 1870, although the preliminary surveys had been made under his direction.

Rose gave way the greater part of his fortune to philanthropic causes, the most of it during his lifetime. Among the objects of his generosity were the Indiana State Normal School and Wabash College; he also helped many young women who wished to attend the Normal School,

his annual outlay for this purpose often exceeding $5,000. His largest gifts in Terre Haute were to the Providence Hospital, the Rose Ladies Aid Society, the Rose Dispensary, the Chauncey Rose School (formerly the Rose Orphan Home), and the Rose Polytechnic Institute. This last institution was one in which he was greatly interested towards the close of his life, the more so, perhaps, because he had felt the need of trained engineers in various industrial enterprises. The school was incorporated in September 1874 as the Terre Haute School of Industrial Science and the name was changed later, over his protest, to the Rose Polytechnic Institute. In March 1883, it was formally opened under the presidency of Charles O. Thompson [q.v.]. Rose made gifts to the school during his lifetime and left it a specific bequest in his will. It was also made the residuary legatee of the Rose estate. He was unmarried and outlived a sister and six brothers, none of whom left any children.

[*Rose Polytechnic Institute Memorial Volume* (1909); *Saturday Evening Mail* (Terre Haute), Aug. 18, 1877; H. W. Beckwith, *Hist. of Vigo and Parke Counties* (1880); *A Biog. Hist. of Eminent and Self-Made Men of the State of Ind.* (1880), vol. II; Blackford Condit, *The Hist. of Early Terre Haute from 1816 to 1840* (1900); C. C. Oakey, *Greater Terre Haute and Vigo County* (1908), vol. I; *Terre Haute Gazette*, Dec. 16, 1899; Loren Hassam, *A Hist. Sketch of Terre Haute, Ind.* (1873); W. H. Smith, *The Hist. of the State of Ind.* (1903), vol. I; *Indianapolis Sentinel*, Aug. 16, 1877.]   J.B.P.

ROSE, EDWARD (fl. 1811–1834), guide, was the son of a white trader among the Cherokee. His mother was a half-breed Cherokee, negro woman. Irving says he was once a Mississippi River pirate (*Astoria, post*, chap. xxiv). He may have gone up the Missouri with the party led by Manuel Lisa [q.v.] in 1807 or with the Missouri Fur Company's expedition in 1809. He had been living among the Crows for two or three years when Wilson Price Hunt [q.v.] engaged him at the Arikara village in June 1811 as hunter, guide, and interpreter, but, becoming suspicious, paid him off at a Crow village near Big Horn Mountain on Sept. 2. In May 1812 Rose joined Lisa's expedition to the upper Missouri.

In 1823 Joshua Pilcher [q.v.] called Rose "a celebrated outlaw who left this country in chains some ten years ago" (Chittenden, *post*, II, 685). For whatever reason, he apparently returned to the Crows and remained with them until his popularity aroused factional jealousy. He then lived among the Arikara for several years. In 1823 he became interpreter to William H. Ashley [q.v.] of the Rocky Mountain Fur Company, whom he vainly cautioned against the Arikara just before the defeat of June 2. The Arikara called a warning to Rose before opening fire. When Col. Henry Leavenworth [*q.v.*] arrived to punish the hostiles Rose was made an ensign and on Aug. 11 was the only man willing to visit the village after the bombardment. Leavenworth called him "a brave and enterprising man" (Robinson, *post,* p. 225). In 1825 he was interpreter to Gen. Henry Atkinson [*q.v.*] on his treaty-making expedition up the Missouri and at a conference with the Crows quelled a dangerous brawl with his rifle-butt. Late in 1832 Zenas Leonard [*q.v.*] with his party encountered Rose in a Crow village at the mouth of Stinking River, where he ranked as a chief, had four wives, and helped recover some stolen horses. In November 1834 the "old negro" performed his most famous exploit in leading the storm of a Blackfoot fortification, himself killing five (Leonard, *post,* pp. 264–67; *Rocky Mountains, post,* chap. xxii; Parkman, *post,* chap. x; Bonner, *post,* chap. xiv, but see also *James Clyman, American Frontiersman,* 1928, ed. by C. L. Camp). Rose's death apparently occurred before 1837. According to one account he and some companions blew themselves up with a keg of gunpowder near Fort Cass, while beset by Arikara. Chittenden, however, states that Rose's grave is "on the banks of the Missouri nearly opposite to the mouth of Milk river" (*post,* II, 688; see also *Rocky Mountains,* chap. xxii). Chittenden remarks that while Rose "bore a bad reputation," everything definitely known of him is entirely creditable (*post,* II, 685). He was powerfully built, taciturn and moody, nicknamed, from a scar, *Nez Coupé.* Of surpassing courage and sagacity, he was also renowned as buffalo-stalker and interpreter. Irving admits that he not only strengthened the Crows against the Blackfeet but also established a tradition of friendship for the whites.

[Overland journals, Astor Papers, Baker Lib., Boston; H. M. Chittenden, *The Am. Fur Trade of the Far West* (1902), vols. I, II; Washington Irving, *Astoria* (1836), esp. chap. xxiv and *The Rocky Mountains* (1837), later ed. as *The Adventures of Capt. Bonneville; Leonard's Narrative; Adventures of Zenas Leonard* (1904), ed. by W. T. Wagner; "Official Correspondence pertaining to the Leavenworth Expedition of 1823," ed. by Doane Robinson, *S. D. Hist. Soc. Colls.,* vol. I (1902); J. C. Luttig, *Journ. of a Fur-Trading Expedition to the Upper Missouri* (1920), ed. by S. M. Drumm; T. D. Bonner, *The Life and Adventures of James P. Beckwourth* (1856); D. H. Coyner, *The Lost Trappers* (1847) of doubtful authenticity; Francis Parkman, *The California and Oregon Trail* (1849), chap. x.]   K. W. P.

ROSE, ERNESTINE LOUISE SIISMONDI POTOWSKI (Jan. 13, 1810–Aug. 4, 1892), reformer, was born in Piotrkow, Russian Poland, of Jewish parentage. Her father was a rabbi, strict in religious observances to the point of asceticism; but she, precocious and independent-minded, revolted early against orthodox Judaism. When Ernestine was sixteen her mother died, and soon afterward the daughter left home. For some years she traveled on the continent, spending considerable time in Prussia and France and interesting herself in the cause of the oppressed wherever she went. In 1832 she was in England, where she met Elizabeth Fry, Robert Dale Owen, and other congenial spirits. In 1835 she presided at the organization in England of the Association of All Classes of All Nations, which made no discrimination regarding sex, religion, race, party, or condition. At about this time she married William E. Rose, an English gentile of wealth and culture who sympathized with her views; and, coming to the United States to live, in 1836 they made their home in New York City.

Her alien race, nationality, and the deistic views she now professed roused considerable feeling against her; but this merely increased her already extensive sympathies and stimulated her zeal for the cause of all humanity, and she threw herself heartily into the various reform movements of the country. Paying her own expenses, she traveled through the eastern states and as far west as Michigan, lecturing to large audiences on religion, free schools, the science of government, abolition, and woman's rights. During the Civil War she worked with the Women's National Loyal League. Her special interest seems to have been in obtaining justice for women, and for this she worked untiringly. During the eleven years of campaigning for the married women's property bill in New York State, 1837–48, she petitioned the legislature almost annually, and five times she addressed it on the subject of the measure. Beginning in 1850, for nineteen years she attended practically every New York state and national convention relating to woman's rights; and she played an important part in many of them. As a public speaker she was pointed, logical, and impassioned (for examples see *Speech of Mrs. Rose . . . at the Anniversary Paine Celebration, 1850,* and *An Address on Woman's Rights, Delivered before the People's Sunday Meeting in Cochituate Hall . . . Oct. 19, 1851,* 1851). In a time when it was easy to be led off by fanatical 'ologies and 'isms, her remarkably keen mind picked out the fundamentals and helped her colleagues to maintain a steady course. In 1869 she and her husband returned to England, where she spent most of her remaining years working, as much as broken health permitted, for the causes that she loved. She died at Brighton.

[E. C. Stanton, S. B. Anthony, and M. J. Gage, *Hist. of Woman Suffrage*, esp. vols. I, III (1881–87); I. H. Harper, *The Life and Work of Susan B. Anthony* (3 vols., 1898–1908); Henry Lewis, "Ernestine Rose, First Jewish Advocate of Women's Rights," *Forward* (N. Y.), June 19, 1927; *Woman's Jour.*, Aug. 13, 1892; *Times* (London), Aug. 6, 1892; private information; death date from *Times, ante*.]   M. W. W.

ROSE, JOHN CARTER (Apr. 27, 1861–Mar. 26, 1927), jurist, reformer, author, was born in Baltimore, Md., the son of Mary Elizabeth Hall and John Rose and a descendant of Robert Rose who left Ipswich, England, in 1634 and settled at Wethersfield, Conn. He received his early education in the primary schools of Baltimore and attended the Baltimore City College from 1873 to 1876. He began the study of law in the office of his cousin, Thomas W. Hall, a Baltimore lawyer, and in 1882, when he was twenty-one, he graduated from the law school of the University of Maryland. On Oct. 19, 1886, he married Grace Harvey Beatson, the daughter of George Harvey Beatson of Baltimore. During his first years at the bar Rose wrote editorials for the Baltimore *Sun* on public questions. Early in his career he aligned himself with a reform group who were working to eliminate the political abuses prevailing throughout the state, and for ten years he served as counsel to the Reform League, of which he was a charter member. Largely through his efforts many of the aims of this organization, such as the adoption of the Australian ballot, were realized, and upon the passage of a new election law in 1896, he became counsel to the Supervisors of Election of Baltimore City. In 1890 he acted as supervisor of the census for Maryland.

Rose's prominence as a reformer resulted in his appointment by President McKinley as district attorney (May 1898), an office which he held through successive administrations until his elevation to the district judgeship by President Taft on Apr. 4, 1910. He had built up a lucrative practice and the acceptance of the latter office, which he had neither sought nor desired, entailed financial sacrifices. He possessed unusual arithmetical ability and an almost infallible memory, and his grasp of the fundamental principles of the law, coupled with an extensive knowledge of economics, political science, and history, made him an unusually able member of the federal judiciary. During the twelve years that he held the office of district judge he was never reversed in a criminal case and seldom in a civil action. He delivered many notable opinions, including *United States* vs. *Curry* (201 *Fed.*, 371), which resulted in an amendment of an act of Congress because of his criticism of its basic unfairness, and *The Virginia* (264 *Fed.*, 986), a landmark in admiralty law. He enjoyed the confidence and respect of the members of the United States Supreme Court, and it was at the request of one of the justices that he undertook, in the last year of his life, a revision of his *Elementary Treatise on the Jurisdiction and Procedure of the Federal Courts* which was first published in 1915. Rose also enjoyed the friendship of Roosevelt and, as a member of the "tennis cabinet," was frequently consulted concerning public papers. His wit, and the speed with which he grasped the essential elements of a case, made his courtroom a disciplinary chamber, where circumlocution and long arguments were banned, where he was feared, sometimes disliked, but always respected. It is to his credit that he maintained his poise and sense of proportion during the war hysteria of 1917–18 and during the supposed "Red" menace that immediately followed. In December 1922, he was promoted by President Harding to the United States circuit court of appeals for the fourth circuit. In 1925 Rose was elected president of the Maryland State Bar Association. He died of heart trouble in his sixty-sixth year at Atlantic City and was buried in Baltimore. Three of his four children survived him.

[*John Carter Rose Memorial Proc.* (1928); *Report of the Thirty-Second Ann. Meeting of the Md. State Bar Asso.* (1927); E. F. Cordell, *Univ. of Md., 1807–1907* (1907), vol. II; *Who's Who in America*, 1926–27; the *Sun* (Baltimore), Mar. 26, 27, 28, 1927; information as to certain facts from Douglas H. Rose, II, and Morris A. Soper; personal acquaintance.]   H. C.

ROSE, JOSEPH NELSON (Jan. 11, 1862–May 4, 1928), botanist, was born on a farm near Liberty, Union County, Ind., the son of George W. Rose and Rebecca Jane (Corrington). The Rose family came originally from Monmouth County, N. J., to southern Indiana. George W. Rose was born and brought up near Fairfield, Ind. He was drafted for service during the latter part of the Civil War, and was sent to camp at Vicksburg, Miss., where he died, leaving two infant sons. The Corrington family, of English origin, settled in New Jersey before the American Revolution. Joseph Corrington removed to Cincinnati, Ohio, in 1792, and his grandson Joseph Corrington was the maternal grandfather of Joseph Nelson Rose.

The latter received his early education in the common schools of Union County and was graduated from the Liberty High School in 1880. In the fall of that year he entered the preparatory department of Wabash College and in 1881 the college proper, from which he was graduated with the degree of A.B. in 1885. He at once re-entered Wabash as its first post-graduate student, receiving the degree of A.M. in 1887 and that of Ph.D. in 1889. During the last two years he acted as assistant in botany to Prof. John M. Coulter [*q.v.*], whose influence undoubtedly inspired his future career. On Aug. 8, 1888, he married Lou Beatrice Sims, of Delphi, Ind., the daughter of Joseph Allen Sims, originally of Culpeper, Va., and Susanna (Hawkins) Sims. He was the father of five children, four of whom, with their mother, survived him.

In August 1888 Rose accepted a position as assistant botanist in the United States Department of Agriculture, Washington, D. C., under Dr. George Vasey. His studies thus far had been upon fungi, pines, the flora of Indiana, and the *Umbelliferae* of North America, the last a difficult family of phanerogams upon which he published monographically, both then and later, for the most part jointly with Coulter. It fell to Rose's lot to report upon the rich botanical collections brought out of Mexico by Edward Palmer, and for the next twenty years his numerous published papers related primarily to the flora of that country. They include a series entitled "Studies of Mexican and Central American Plants," published in *Contributions from the United States National Herbarium* (1897–1911). These consist largely of synoptical studies and revisions in many families of flowering plants, increasing attention being given to several groups of succulents, especially *Agave* and the families *Crassulaceae* and *Amaryllidaceae*. Meanwhile, in 1896, the National Herbarium had been returned by the Department of Agriculture to the United States National Museum, under the custody of the Smithsonian Institution, and Rose was transferred to the Museum as assistant curator. During the next fifteen years he made nine trips of botanical exploration to Mexico, visiting nearly every state in the Republic and collecting many thousands of specimens, hundreds of which represented species new to science. Besides herbarium material large series of living plants of *Cacti* and *Crassulaceae* (live-forevers) were forwarded to Washington for greenhouse cultivation, marking the beginning of important living collections which later were to form the basis of monographic studies. His first paper on *Crassulaceae,* published jointly with Dr. N. L. Britton in 1903, contained descriptions of many new species. This was followed two years later by a joint systematic treatment of the entire family as represented in North America. Subsequently, up to 1927, he published many other papers upon the

American members of this group, on which he was the acknowledged authority.

Rose's studies of the *Cactaceae* found expression similarly. His special interest in this family appears to have developed principally through field-work in the mountains of Mexico. His first paper appeared in 1907 and during the next two years about a dozen more were published, several of them written in collaboration with Britton. In 1912 Rose was furloughed from his position as associate curator in the Museum (to which he had been promoted in 1905) to accept appointment as research associate of the Carnegie Institution of Washington for the purpose of preparing, in collaboration with Britton, a monographic treatment of the *Cactaceae* of the world. Setting about this task with characteristic patience, quiet enthusiasm, and thoroughness, he visited Europe at once, to study historic museum material and to acquaint himself with the species cultivated in all the important gardens. In 1913 he collected in the West Indies. Between 1914 and 1918 he made four trips of exploration, covering a large part of South America and assembling an extraordinarily rich collection of herbarium material and of living plants. The final results of this extended investigation are contained in a beautifully illustrated monograph of four volumes by Britton and Rose entitled *The Cactaceae* (1919–23). This is an exceedingly important treatise, not only because it presents a well-considered new classification of this difficult family, but also because it has been influential in bringing into present general favor a fascinating and intricate group of plants which are almost exclusively American.

In 1923 Rose returned to the National Herbarium as associate curator, and besides continuing his studies of succulents undertook, again jointly with Britton, a revision of the North American leguminous plants of the families *Mimosaceae* and *Caesalpiniaceae,* the results of which have mostly appeared since his death. His published work includes nearly 200 titles, among them many important papers written in association with no fewer than twelve botanists. This spirit of cooperation was an outstanding well-recognized characteristic—a reflection of his invariable tolerance, helpfulness, and remarkably even temperament, and a judicial attitude which though deliberately critical was always friendly and unbiased. Despite rapidly failing strength he continued steadily at work to the very day of his death. His name and work are fittingly commemorated in four genera of plants named in his honor.

[William Trelease, "Joseph Nelson Rose, 1862–1928," *Science*, LXVII, 598–99 (June 15, 1928); Alwin Berger, "Joseph Nelson Rose," *Zeitschrift für Sukkulentenkunde*, III, 281–83 (July 1928); J. J. Verbeek Wolthuys, "In Memoriam, Dr. Joseph Nelson Rose," *Succulenta*, X, 125–27 (July 1928); H. Wegener, "Dr. Joseph Nelson Rose," *Desert*, I, 105 (Jan. 1930); *Who's Who in America*, 1928–29; *Evening Star* (Washington, D. C.), May 5, 1928.]   W. R. M.

ROSE, URIAH MILTON (Mar. 5, 1834–Aug. 12, 1913), jurist, was born at Bradfordsville, Marion County, Ky., the son of Dr. Joseph and Nancy (Simpson) Rose. At the age of five he was studying Latin and his father gave him the best educational advantages available up to the time of his own death in 1849. The small estate which Dr. Rose had accumulated now went into the hands of an administrator, and Uriah had to shift for himself. Fortunately R. H. Roundtree, an able and kindly lawyer, took an interest in him and found a place for him as deputy county clerk. He studied law at night and saw it administered at first hand daily by some of the most celebrated lawyers and jurists of the state. In September 1853 he graduated in law at Transylvania University and on Oct. 25 following married Margaret T. Gibbs. He set out in December of the same year for Batesville, Ark., where he formed a law partnership with William E. Gibbs, a brother-in-law, hoping to recover his lost health riding the circuits. First he had to master the highly technical common-law pleading then in vogue in Arkansas, but his graceful courtesy and refinement of manner disarmed the rough-and-tumble lawyers of the frontier, and he was soon able to meet the best lawyers of the state on terms of equality. In 1860 Governor Conway appointed him chancellor in Pulaski County. He hesitated to accept the post, but did so on the advice of friends and held the office until the Federals captured the state capital. He had opposed secession, but at the outbreak of war cast in his lot with the state and remained loyal to it to the end. In the fall of 1865 he moved to Little Rock and formed a partnership with George C. Watkins, formerly chief justice of Arkansas. After the death of Judge Watkins in 1867, Rose's name stood first in that of the leading law firm of the state. In this year he published *Digest of the Arkansas Reports* (1867), covering the first twenty volumes of reports. In 1874 he went to Washington to lay before President Grant the claims of Elisha Baxter [*q.v.*] in the Brooks-Baxter war over the governorship.

In 1872 Rose began a series of travels which took him all over Europe, the West Indies, Mexico, and Hawaii. He was a good linguist, reading German and speaking French fluently. He collected a library of some eight thousand volumes in different languages and was familiar with most of it. He exercised a powerful influence over the Arkansas bar, leading it toward sobriety and higher moral standards, and adding dignity to the profession. He was frequently in demand for addresses at bar association meetings and as an after-dinner speaker. A happy success on such an occasion when he proposed a toast in honor of President Theodore Roosevelt at the time of the latter's visit to Little Rock led to his appointment as delegate to the Second Peace Conference at The Hague in 1907. In 1891 he published *The Constitution of the State of Arkansas,* with notes; his occasional addresses were collected and published after his death as *Addresses of Uriah M. Rose* (1914). He served as president of the Arkansas Bar Association, 1899–1900, and of the American Bar Association, 1901–02. After his death his statue was placed by the state in the Statuary Hall of the National Capitol, an honor accorded to few private citizens. He died in his eightieth year, survived by his widow and eight of their ten children.

[Memoir by G. B. Rose in *Addresses of U. M. Rose* (1914); W. E. Hemingway, *In Memoriam: U. M. Rose* (n.d.); Fay Hempstead, *Hist. Rev. of Ark.* (1911), vol. I; J. M. Moore, in *Proc. . . . Bar Asso. of Ark.*, 1914; *Case and Comment*, Nov. 1913, Jan. 1914; *Ark. Gazette* (Little Rock), Aug. 12, 1913.]   D. Y. T.

ROSE, WALTER MALINS (Nov. 25, 1872–Feb. 12, 1908), legal annotator and digester, was born in Toronto, Canada, the son of Henry J. Rose. The family moved to Ontario, Cal., where Walter attended Chaffey College. In 1895 he received the degree of A.B. from Stanford University and the following year graduated from the law school of Cornell University, winning also the Boardman thesis prize. In September 1896 he was admitted to the California bar and entered into practice with Robert Hayne in San Francisco. Three years later he was admitted to practice before the United States Supreme Court, but owing to ill health, he was forced to relinquish his practice and moved to Arizona. Between 1899 and 1901 he published a twelve-volume work, with an additional index volume, entitled *Notes on the United States Reports,* treating cases reported from 2 *Dallas* to 172 *U. S.* The work purported to show "the present value as authority of the cases therein reported as disclosed by all subsequent citations in all the courts of last resort, both Federal and state." Clearly it was an ambitious undertaking for one so recently called to the bar. His classification of material followed a chronological arrangement, in outline, of points of law determined

in Supreme Court decisions, with subsequent cit-
ing cases listed. The citations of each annotated
case were arranged under the respective points
of law involved, and by a further classification,
cases affirming a principle were treated separately from those qualifying or denying it. Both the
conception and the method were new and afforded a distinct departure in the field of legal authorship. In 1917 a revised edition of the work
was published by Charles L. Thompson.

Rose's next undertaking was an application of
the new method to the case law of a single state.
In a five-volume work, *Notes on Texas Reports,*
published in 1902, he presented a "chronological
series of annotations of the decisions of the Supreme Court and the various civil and criminal
appellate courts of Texas, showing their present
value as authority as disclosed by all the subsequent citations" thereof. A posthumous edition
was published in 1910 and there have been later
supplements. In 1903 he published a three-volume *Digest of the United States Reports from
the Beginning to the October Term, 1902*—a task
for which his previous labors had especially fitted
him. This was followed in 1907 by his *Code of
Federal Procedure,* in three volumes, based upon
Robert Desty's manual relating to the same subject but with material rearranged "along more
modern and satisfactory lines." His "Code" provisions were taken from the Constitution, acts
of Congress, court rules, and decisions, all topi-
cally arranged. He also published monographs
on leading cases.

About 1906 he moved to Los Angeles and established himself in active practice. He served
as counsel for various corporations and in the
relatively brief interval before his death was
unusually successful. He died suddenly, at the
age of thirty-five, after an operation for appendicitis. His wife was Mary (Holt) Rose, of Holt,
Ky., whom he had married on Oct. 19, 1899.
She, with a son, survived him.

[*Who's Who in America,* 1908–09; *Cornell Alumni
News,* Feb. 19, 1908; *Stanford Alumnus,* Mar. 1908;
Times (Los Angeles), Feb. 13, 1908.]   C. S. L.

ROSECRANS, SYLVESTER HORTON
(Feb. 5, 1827–Oct. 21, 1878), Roman Catholic
prelate, was born in Homer, Ohio, son of Crandall Rosecrans, a native of Wilkes-Barre, Pa.,
and Jemima (Hopkins) Rosecrans. On his father's side he was descended from Harmon Rosenkrans who emigrated from Norway to New
Amsterdam about 1657; his mother was a descendant of Stephen Hopkins [*q.v.*] of Rhode
Island, a signer of the Declaration of Independence. In 1845, while a student in Kenyon College, Sylvester, influenced by the conversion of

his brother William Starke Rosecrans [*q.v.*] to
Catholicism and the instructions of Rev. J. B.
Lamy [*q.v.*], also entered the Catholic Church.
He then transferred from Kenyon to St. John's
College, Fordham, N. Y., from which he was
graduated a year later. After studying theology
at Mount St. Mary's Seminary of the West (Cincinnati) and at the Propaganda in Rome, where
he was awarded a doctorate in divinity, he was
ordained a priest on July 16, 1852. As a curate
at St. Thomas' Church and at the cathedral in
Cincinnati, as a teacher and finally rector of the
collegiate department of the archdiocesan seminary, and as associate-editor with Father Edward Purcell of the *Catholic Telegraph,* Father
Rosecrans won local renown and the favor of
Archbishop Purcell [*q.v.*], at whose suggestion
he was named titular bishop of Pompeiopolis
and coadjutor of Cincinnati by Pope Pius IX.
Although consecrated by Purcell, Mar. 25, 1862,
he humbly continued to teach for two years and
published a small volume, *The Divinity of Christ*
(1866). As the brother of General Rosecrans
he attracted wide attention during the Civil War,
and seconded the bold patriotism of his ordinary,
for which he was severely criticized by the anti-
war editor of the powerful *New York Freeman's
Journal.* A man of spirit, he showed courage in
1865 when he was wounded by burglars on his
refusal to surrender a church collection.

In 1867 he was given the pastorate of St. Patrick's Church, Columbus, in preparation for his
elevation to the new see of Columbus (Mar. 3,
1868). During his tenure of ten years, there
was a marked growth in the diocese because of
the heavy Irish and German immigration. In
addition to about forty churches, he built St.
Joseph's Cathedral; established the *Catholic Columbian* in 1875, to which he himself was a regular contributor; fostered religious confraterni-
ties, especially much-needed temperance societies; instituted St. Aloysius Seminary (1871);
and, through the various religious communities
which he encouraged to enter the diocese, promoted a number of convents, monasteries, and
orphanages. Beloved by the bishops of the province, Rosecrans was a scrupulously orthodox, dependable, and unambitious ecclesiastic, rigorous
with himself, lenient with his priests, and honored by his people irrespective of their racial
antecedents.

[Allen Rosenkrans, *The Rosenkrans Family in Europe and America* (1900); R. H. Clarke, *Lives of the
Deceased Bishops of the Catholic Church in the U. S.,*
vol. III (1888); J. G. Shea, *The Hierarchy of the Catholic Church in the U. S.* (1886); G. F. Houck, *The
Church in Northern Ohio and in the Diocese of Cleveland* (1887); J. H. Lamott, *Hist. of the Archdiocese of
Cincinnati* (1921); *Catholic Encyc.,* XIII, 192; M. J.

Kelly and J. M. Kirwin, *Hist. of Mount St. Mary's Seminary of the West* (1894) ; L. W. Mulhane, "Maj.-Gen. William Starke Rosecrans," in *Records of the Am. Catholic Hist. Soc.*, Sept. 1924 ; *Cleveland Leader*, Oct. 22, 1878.]   R. J. P.

ROSECRANS, WILLIAM STARKE (Sept. 6, 1819–Mar. 11, 1898), soldier, was born in Kingston township, Delaware County, Ohio, the eldest son of Crandall and Jemima (Hopkins) Rosecrans. He was a descendant, in the sixth generation, of Harmon Hendrick Rosenkrans, who came to America about 1657. The family had been represented in Ohio since about 1809. His great-grandfather had served as a captain in the Revolutionary War, and his father with the same rank in the War of 1812. His mother was a descendant of Stephen Hopkins [*q.v.*], one of the signers of the Declaration of Independence. He received his preparatory education in the public schools, entered the United States Military Academy in 1838 and was graduated in 1842. He was commissioned brevet second lieutenant of engineers and his first duty was on the fortifications of Hampton Roads, Va. In 1843, after having been promoted second lieutenant, he was brought back to West Point, where he served four years as assistant professor in the departments of engineering and of natural and experimental philosophy. On Aug. 24, 1843, he was married to Ann Eliza, the only daughter of Judge Adrian Hegeman of New York City. For the next ten years he was assigned to various posts in New England, and became a first lieutenant, but resigned his commission on Apr. 1, 1854. He began civil life as an engineer and architect in Cincinnati, Ohio, where he remained for a year, and then was engaged in coal mining and river navigation in western Virginia. He returned to Cincinnati in 1857 as head of an oil refining company.

On Apr. 19, 1861, he became a volunteer aide-de-camp to General McClellan, then commanding in Ohio. He was made colonel and chief engineer of the department of Ohio, and also appointed colonel of the 23rd Ohio Volunteer Infantry in June, but almost immediately was commissioned brigadier-general in the regular army. In McClellan's campaign in western Virginia he commanded a brigade, and won the battle of Rich Mountain in July, one of the first battles of the Civil War. He succeeded McClellan as commanding general of the department of the Ohio, and later as chief of the new department of western Virginia, he continued the operations which ended, late in the fall, in the complete expulsion of the Confederate forces, and the formation of the state of West Virginia. In May 1862, he commanded the left wing of Pope's Army of the Mississippi which formed a part of Halleck's command in a movement upon Corinth, the important railway junction of northern Mississippi. In June, when Pope was called east, Rosecrans succeeded him in command. His reduced force constituted the left wing of the army in the region of Corinth, now under the command of Grant, who had succeeded Halleck. Early in September the Confederate general, Price, moved up and occupied Iuka, on the Memphis and Charleston Railway twenty miles southeast of Corinth. General Van Dorn, cooperating with him, was at Holly Springs, fifty miles southwest, and Grant planned to concentrate upon Price before the two Confederate forces could effect a junction. Rosecrans attacked Price, but failed to cut off his retreat to the south, and returned to Corinth. Price and Van Dorn joined forces and attacked his entrenched position there on Oct. 3, 1862. The battle was hotly contested, and losses were heavy on both sides. The advantage was with the Confederates on the first day, but on the second they were decisively defeated and driven back to Holly Springs. Rosecrans followed, but was unable to bring the enemy to battle again. He was now promoted major-general of volunteers and ordered to relieve Buell in Kentucky, his command finally being reorganized as the Army of the Cumberland, with three army corps.

After the battle of Perryville in Kentucky, the Confederate forces under General Bragg had fallen back into Tennessee and were concentrating at Murfreesboro. Rosecrans joined Buell's army on Nov. 2, and, after reorganizing the army, advanced to Nashville where he remained for a month, accumulating supplies to provide against probable interruption of communications. Late in December he moved out against Bragg, and the two armies met on Stone River, just west of the town, on Dec. 29. Both moved to the attack two days later, each army advancing the left wing. Bragg gained the first success and rolled up the Federal right, but Rosecrans, by great exertion, established a new line which held against all attacks. Fighting continued for the next two days, and on Jan. 3, 1863, Bragg retreated to Shelbyville, twenty-five miles south. Here the armies faced each other for six months, undertaking only minor operations.

On June 23 Rosecrans began an advance, and in nine days very skilfully maneuvered Bragg out of his positions at Shelbyville and Tullahoma, and back into Chattanooga. For some time Rosecrans had felt that he had been hampered in developing the efficiency of his command by the headquarters in Washington. During the six months of waiting at Murfreesboro there arose an unfortunate controversy between Rosecrans, Halleck, and Stanton over Halleck's offering a major-generalship either to Grant or to Rosecrans depending upon which of the two first won an important victory. A testy and untactful letter to headquarters, referring to this auctioning-off of military honors, brought Rosecrans into decided disfavor in Washington. Now, as after the battle of Murfreesboro, Halleck constantly pressed Rosecrans to advance, and as before, Rosecrans steadily declined to move until he considered the time ripe. At last, on Aug. 16, he came forward, made a feint up the Tennessee River above Chattanooga, then crossed in force below that place and maneuvered Bragg out of it. Rosecrans followed him, his lines greatly extended, but Bragg, having been reinforced, turned to face him and defeated him badly in the hard-fought and bloody battle of Chickamauga on Sept. 19 and 20, 1863. Rosecrans had to fall back to Chattanooga where he was besieged. The disaster at Chickamauga was brought about on the field by an officer who executed to the letter an order from Rosecrans which was obviously in error and which opened up a wide gap in the Federal line.

The army was in a most desperate situation and all the resources of the North were turned to its relief. Strong reinforcements which Rosecrans had previously requested were now put in motion toward Chattanooga and Grant was placed in command of all the western armies. The error at Chickamauga cost Rosecrans his command. He was relieved on Oct. 19, and was assigned to command the department of the Missouri. In December 1864, he was sent to Cincinnati, Ohio, to await orders, and remained on this status or on leave until Mar. 28, 1867, when he resigned his commission in the regular army. On Mar. 13, 1865, he received the brevet rank of major-general for his services at Murfreesboro. Rosecrans was generally regarded as an able commander and has been called the "greatest strategist of the war . . ." (Cist, *post*, p. 235). He accomplished an incredible amount of work, and in campaign seemed to be able to do without sleep. He had a hot temper, which he was not always able to control, and was often hasty and indiscreet in speech. He especially resented interference from above with his plans, and seemed to persist the more obstinately in his own decisions. These characteristics brought him into conflict with his superiors, as in the Tullahoma and Chickamauga campaigns, and ultimately led to his relief. He was, however, well liked in the army and was affectionately called "Old Rosy" by the soldiers.

In 1868 and 1869 he was minister to Mexico. He returned to Ohio, declined the Democratic nomination for governor, and soon afterward went west to engage in mining operations first in Mexico and later in California. From 1881 to 1885 he was a representative in Congress from California, and became chairman of the committee on military affairs. By special act of Congress he was commissioned a brigadier-general on the retired list of the regular army, Mar. 2, 1889. Upon leaving Congress he was appointed register of the treasury and served until 1893. He then returned to California and took up his residence on his ranch at Redondo, near Los Angeles, where he remained until his death. He took an active interest in civic affairs and was particularly energetic in trying to induce Americans to invest in Mexico. He was buried at Rosedale Cemetery, Los Angeles, but was reinterred in 1902 with much ceremony at Arlington National Cemetery, Washington, D. C., the president being the principal speaker on the occasion. He was survived by three of his eight children. While at West Point he had been converted to the Roman Catholic church and converted his brother, Sylvester Horton Rosecrans [*q.v.*], to that faith.

[Allen Rosenkrans, *The Rosenkrans Family in Europe and America* (1900); Timothy Hopkins, *John Hopkins . . . and Some of his Descendants* (1932); G. W. Cullum, *Biog. Reg. . . . Officers and Grads., U. S. Mil. Acad.* (1891); *Biog. Dir. Am. Cong.* (1928); L. W. Mulhane, "Major-Gen. Wm. Starke Rosecrans," *Records of the Am. Catholic Hist. Soc.*, Sept. 1924; Joseph Taggart, *Biog. Sketches of the Eminent Am. Patriots* (1907); H. M. Cist, *The Army of the Cumberland, in Campaigns of the Civil War*, vol. VII (1882); *War of the Rebellion:Official Records (Army)*, *passim*; San Francisco *Bulletin*, Mar. 11, 1898.]

O. L. S., Jr.

ROSELIUS, CHRISTIAN (Aug. 10, 1803–Sept. 5, 1873), lawyer, son of Johann Conrad and Anna Marie (Wacker) Roselius, was born near the German city of Bremen. He was baptized Johann Christian, but in later life did not use his first name. His parents were poor, and at the age of sixteen he went without money to Bremen, where four years later, by the sale of future services, he secured passage to New Orleans on the Dutch brig *Jupiter*. He served an apprenticeship as a printer in his adopted city and in 1825 started a magazine, *The Halcyon*, which was destined to a short existence. By hard study he sought to overcome his deficiencies of education, adding a speaking command of French and English to his native German and acquiring proficiency in Latin. Beginning the study of law in the office of Auguste D'Avezac [q.v.] in company with Alexander Dimitry [q.v.], he developed a passion for French civil law and its ancient background and thus acquired an important legal equipment for Louisiana practice. He married the directress of a school for girls and himself resorted to teaching while struggling for a beginning at law. He was admitted to the bar in 1828 and was engaged in the active practice of law with little interruption during the rest of his life. He attained the front rank of the Louisiana bar, ranking with Pierre Soulé and Edward Livingston.

In 1840 he was elected to the state legislature, and the following year was named state attorney general for a two-year term. He served as a member of the state constitutional convention in 1845. He was an important participant in drawing and subsequently executing the will of John McDonogh [q.v.], the wealthy benefactor whose name has become closely associated with the New Orleans public schools. In the pursuit of his profession he acquired a competence but tended to reduce it by a generous munificence. He was ready with hand and purse to help the unfortunate, including kinsmen whom he aided on one of his visits to his native country. A Whig in politics, he opposed secession as a member of the state convention that voted such a step on the eve of the Civil War. In 1863 he declined appointment to the highest judicial office in the reconstructed state government, expressing a refusal to serve on a court subject to military interference. He was a member of the board of administrators of the University of Louisiana (later to become Tulane University) at New Orleans, 1847–55; professor of civil law in the University, 1850–73; and dean of the law department, 1865–72. He took great interest in his law teaching, preparing written lectures on the status of civil law in Louisiana that were marked for clarity and methodical organization; his name is closely connected with the development of this law school.

Of ordinary height, Roselius was rather spare and angular and had a physical appearance that suggested a greater age than was his. He was more forceful than attractive as a public speaker. His private library was rich in Shakespeare and the Latin classics, which he read constantly. He owned a spacious home in Carrollton, a suburb of New Orleans in his day, and his hospitality was enjoyed by not a few distinguished visitors to the city. He died at New Orleans, and his funeral was held at a Lutheran church on St. Charles Avenue with interment in the old St. Louis cemetery. Of his three children, one daughter survived him.

[*Berühmte Deutsche Vorkämpfer für Fortschritt, Freiheit und Friede in Nord-Amerika* (Cleveland, 1888); *Sketches of Life and Character in Louisiana* (1847) by a member of the New Orleans bar (J. S. Whitaker); *Green Bag*, Mar. 1890; *New Orleans Daily Picayune*, Sept. 6, 1873; *New Orleans States*, Dec. 10, 1922 (devoted chiefly to the Roselius home in the Carrollton suburb); names of parents from Bremen records through the courtesy of Dr. R. L. Jaeger, German consul at New Orleans.]   H. C. N.

ROSENBERG, ABRAHAM HAYYIM (Oct. 17, 1838–Aug. 5, 1925), author, Biblical scholar, was born in Karlin (Pinsk), Russia, the son of Uzziel Yaffa Rosenberg and Leah Lieberman. His father, a Hebrew scholar, tutored him in Hebrew and the Talmud, his acquaintance with secular studies beginning only at the age of twenty-two, after he had already lost his first wife and was the father of four children. He entered the Rabbinical Seminary in Zhitomir, and after his graduation served as district Rabbi in Pinsk from 1872 to 1881. Here he married his second wife, Clara Bercinsky. In 1881 he accepted the post of district Rabbi in Nikolayev, and was also instructor of Jewish history and religion at the classical gymnasium in the same city. He was exposed to petty police persecution on account of his liberal views, and moved from the city in 1888, accepting a Rabbinical post in Poltava. Still further subjected to police hostility, he quit the country and emigrated to the United States in 1891.

He started his literary career by writing articles in the field of Jewish learning and sketches of Jewish life which were published in the Russian magazines, *Russkiy Evrey, Voskhod, Razsviet, Evreiskia Zapiski,* and in the Hebrew journals, *Ha-melitz, Ha-karmel, Ha-eshkol.* He was also the author of a Jewish history in Russian. His chief field of study, however, was the Bible. While still in Russia he had conceived the idea of publishing a Hebrew cyclopedia of Biblical literature, containing an historical and geographical description of the persons, places, and other subjects mentioned in the Old Testament. He was able to publish this *magnum opus,* to which he devoted his life, only many years later in America. Settling down in the ghetto of New York City he deliberately chose to maintain himself with the aid of a small printing press in a basement, his main concern being the printing of his cyclopedia. Indeed, the first two volumes were set up by himself, appearing in 1898 and 1899. The whole work, consisting of ten volumes, entitled *Ozar ha-shemoth,* was published by a group of admirers two years before his death, and won wide recognition, definitely establishing Rosenberg's reputation as a Biblical scholar.

Apart from his chief interest, Rosenberg devoted time to other branches of both Hebrew and Yiddish literature. In 1891 he was editor of the Hebrew weekly *Ha-ibri,* published by Kathriel Sarasohn, an editor of the Hebrew literary monthly *Ner ha-maarabi* in 1895. He also contributed numerous articles to *Ha-leom, Ha-pisgah, Ha-yom, Ha-modia le-hodashim* and other Hebrew periodicals. He began to write Yiddish after coming to the United States, and contributed popular historical articles to the Yiddish press and longer works published in installments. These include a history of ritual murder cases and a discussion of agriculture among Jews in times of the prophets and the Talmud. Several books in Yiddish, including a life of the patriarch Abraham and an account of the expulsion of the Jews from Spain, *Gerush Spanien,* came from his pen. His most ambitious undertaking in Yiddish was the translation and adaptation of Johann Gustav Vogt's *Weltgeschichte* in twelve volumes, to which he added much new material and an additional section devoted to Jewish history and literature and published in 1918.

[Hutchins Hapgood, *The Spirit of the Ghetto* (1902); Salomon Wininger, *Grosse Jüdische National-Biographie,* vol. V; Zalmen Reisen, *Lexicon fun der Yiddisher Literatur,* vol. IV (1929); *Am. Hebrew,* Aug. 14, 1925; M. Tausner, in *Hadoar,* a Hebrew weekly published in New York City, Aug. 14, 1925.]

I. S.

ROSENBERG, HENRY (June 22, 1824–May 12, 1893), merchant, banker, philanthropist, christened Heinrich, was born in the mountain village of Bilten, Canton Glarus, Switzerland, the second child of Johan Rudolf Rosenberger, shoemaker, and Waldburg (Blum) Rosenberger. He was early apprenticed as a fabric printer and was later transferred to a store in Glarus, where he met his employer's son, John Hessly. Failing to obtain a desired clerkship, in 1843 he emigrated to the seaport village of Galveston in the Republic of Texas, where this son employed him in his little dry-goods store at eight dollars a month. Three years later Rosenberg bought out his employer.

The story of Rosenberg's life is closely connected with the history of Galveston's development. He participated in directing capacities in nearly every enterprise that contributed to its expansion. By 1859 he owned the largest retail dry-goods store in Texas. In 1874 he organized the Galveston Bank & Trust Company, of which from 1882 he was sole owner until his death. He was also actively interested in the First National Bank, the Galveston City Railway Company, the Gulf, Colorado & Santa Fé Rail-

way Company, serving as its president from 1874 to 1877, and the Galveston Wharf Company. He served as president of the Board of Harbor Improvements (1869–73) and as alderman (1871–72, 1885–87). Childless, he took a great interest in child welfare, and in 1886 gave to the city the Rosenberg School; for many years, also, he was connected with the directorate of the Galveston Orphans' Home. He was a vestryman of Trinity Episcopal Church, and in 1882 contributed about half the cost of Eaton Chapel. He also renovated the little church in Bilten in which he had been christened and confirmed. From Apr. 13, 1866, to Sept. 6, 1869, he was vice-consul for Switzerland, and from the latter date to his death, consul. On June 11, 1851, he married Letitia Cooper of Galveston, a native of Virginia, who died in 1888; on Nov. 13, 1889, he married Mary Ragan Macgill of Hagerstown, Md., who had been practically an adopted daughter. He had no children. He is described as a ruddy-faced gentleman of benevolent countenance, with short beard, short, rotund figure, always well but unostentatiously dressed, cane in hand, and flower in lapel.

His will placed him at the head of Texas philanthropists up to that time. He made provision for the maintenance of an orphanage in Bilten, but more than sixty-two percent of his estate, valued at something over one million one hundred thousand dollars, he turned back in bequests to Galveston. Among these were buildings for the Island City Protestant and Israelitish Orphans' Home, and for Grace Episcopal Church; sites and buildings for the Letitia Rosenberg Woman's Home and for the Young Men's Christian Association—the first such building in Texas; a charity fund for the German Lutheran Church; seventeen drinking fountains for men and beasts. A foreigner from a liberty-loving country seeking freedom and a livelihood in the seven-year-old Republic of Texas, where he doubtless heard heroic stories of the Texas Revolution, he also left $50,000 for a Texas Heroes' Monument, which was designed by Louis Amateis [*q.v.*]. A residuary legacy provided for the endowment of a free public library. The residuary assets promised to be about $400,000; but through the excellent management of Maj. A. J. Walker, executor, the assets at his death in 1904 had almost doubled, and the Rosenberg Library opened in that year, by far the wealthiest library in the state. Under the judicious policies of the directors, the assets had increased by 1930 to nearly a million dollars, and the book collection to about 85,000 volumes. Rosenberg was buried in Loudon Park Cemetery, Baltimore, Md. In

1906 a bronze statue of him, executed by Louis Amateis, was placed by the citizens of Galveston in front of the library.

[*Henry Rosenberg, 1824–1893* (1918), pub. by the Rosenberg Lib.; J. H. Brown, *Indian Wars and Pioneers of Tex.* (n.d.); scrapbook of clippings chiefly from the *Galveston News* and *Galveston Tribune,* 1871–1904, and manuscripts and other data collected by Frank C. Patten, librarian, for the Rosenberg Library.]

O. F. R.

ROSENBLATT, JOSEPH (May 9, 1882–June 19, 1933), cantor, concert artist, was born in a small South Russian town, Biélaya Tzerkov (White Church), near Kiev, capital of the Ukraine, the tenth child of Raphael Shalom and Chäyé Sarah (Prylutzky) Rosenblatt. His father was a synagogue precentor of some ability. At eight years of age Joseph was already touring Central Europe, officiating as boy-cantor in synagogues of Germany and Austria and giving sacred concerts. His chief protector, Dr. Bloch, editor of the Vienna *Wochenschrift,* was extremely active in fostering and glorifying this wonder-boy. At fourteen, Rosenblatt began to compose, and in 1900, when he was eighteen, he received his first appointment, that of cantor of the Munkácz synagogue in Hungary. Soon after, in competition with forty others, he won the coveted position of chief cantor in Pressburg, a major Austrian city. In 1906 he became the chief cantor at the largest Hamburg synagogue, one of the most prominent positions in the Jewish cantorate, but even this success did not stop his ardent studies in music.

His fame brought him at last, in May 1912, an invitation to officiate at the Ohab Tzedek Congregation of New York and he then emigrated to America, destined soon to become one of the most beloved singers of the country of his adoption. Possessing a nature of rare kindliness and generosity, he was easily persuaded to tour the United States in 1916 for the benefit of sufferers in the World War. His first great triumph took place on May 19, 1918, however, when a concert of classical, secular, and synagogal music at Carnegie Hall, New York, brought him enthusiastic acclaim from the public and the press. He immediately received lucrative and flattering offers from the Chicago Opera Company and other operatic organizations; but his strong Orthodox convictions, as well as a noble conception of his duties to Levitical functions and the worldly behavior appropriate to the same, made him firmly refuse all offers of operatic appearance. A Jewish paper to which he had given financial support failed in 1926, involving him in a heavy indebtedness. He then resigned his position as cantor that he might earn money on the concert stage to meet his obligations. In 1923 he gave brilliant concerts in almost every European country. In 1928 he again gave concerts in Europe, and in 1929, in South America. Finally, in March 1933 he was able to realize his life-dream, that of visiting and concertizing in Palestine. His career was cut short, however, by his death, in Jerusalem, after a short illness, when he was at the height of his artistic power and fame. He was buried on the Mount of Olives, twenty thousand people attending his funeral. His wife, Taube (Kaufman) Rosenblatt, member of a prominent family of Brzesko, Austria, whom he married in 1900, and eight children survived him.

Rosenblatt left a number of compositions, among them a choral setting for Psalm CXIII, dedicated to President Harding; an effective synagogal *Uvnucho Yomar* for cantor and choir; and a collection of his own cantorial recitatives, published in Hamburg and New York. Of these synagogal songs the most interesting is *"Elohai neshomo"* (My Lord, the soul, you have given me) and *"K'gavno."* They have a modal freshness and a spiritual charm that come from the true Hebrew melodic instinct and the fineness of the composer's soul. As a singer, he was famous for the ease, flexibility, power, and brilliance of his tenor voice. He was endowed with a natural vocal virtuosity, faultless pitch, and a *falsetto* that was world-known.

[*Musical America,* June 22, 1918, July 1933; *Am.-Jewish Chronicle,* May 24, 1918; *Musical Courier,* June 24, 1933; *N. Y. Times,* June 19, 1933.]   L. S.

ROSENFELD, MORRIS (Dec. 28, 1862–June 22, 1923), poet, was born in Bokscha, Suwalki, at that time part of Russian Poland, the son of Ephraim Leib Rosenfeld and his wife, Rachel Wilchinsky. His ancestors for several generations had been fishermen; his father a military tailor. He received at home the education allotted to Jewish boys of humble family, and studied Hebrew and the Talmud. When his father moved to Warsaw later, he acquired some knowledge of Polish and German. At the age of eighteen he was married to Bella Guttenberg, and with the birth of his first child began a bitter struggle for a livelihood. In 1882 he went to London and learned the tailoring trade. After a short stay in England he proceeded to Amsterdam, Holland, where he tried his hand at diamond-grinding. In 1886 he emigrated to the United States, where he remained until his death.

For fourteen wretched years he eked out a miserable existence as a presser and tailor in the sweatshops of New York City, and their squalor and oppression are well reflected in his plaintive muse. But earlier in London he had already composed melodious threnodies which touched the hearts of his readers, themselves the toilers and oppressed. At the end of a long day with the needle he would take up the pen, and sing the sorrows and woes of the underdog. Two years after his arrival in New York City he printed his first collection of folk and revolutionary songs, *Die Glocke*; another collection, *Die Blumenkette,* appeared in 1890; and, in 1917, *Dos Liderbuch.* He also made occasional contributions to the Yiddish press, but Yiddish journalism was then in so precarious a state financially that he was unable to live from his pen and continued to work in the sweatshop. Here he would probably have remained had it not been for Leo Wiener of Harvard University, who was drawn by the unusual talent displayed in *Dos Liderbuch.* Wiener at once introduced him to the outer world in 1898 by publishing his *Songs from the Ghetto,* containing some of Rosenfeld's poems with a prose translation, glossary and introduction. This booklet aroused a great interest in the poet both in America and abroad, and he was enabled to devote himself entirely to literature. He became editor and contributor to several Yiddish papers; wrote poetry and prose sketches; gave readings at Harvard and the University of Chicago, at Wellesley and Radcliffe colleges, and in many cities in Europe.

Morris Rosenfeld stands out as the most original poet in Yiddish literature. His fiery talents express themselves in many fields but his genius is at its highest in his depiction of the sad fate of the poor and oppressed. Himself one of the submerged tenth, he was the mouthpiece of the victims of a dehumanized society. Dramatic action and lyric indignation are welded into one in his poems, among which "My Boy," "Whither," "Despair," "Songs of Labor" or "Sephirah," "On the Bosom of the Ocean," "The Jewish May," "The Candle Seller," are already considered classics. Wiener characterizes the poet in these terms: "It was left for a Russian Jew at the end of the nineteenth century to see and paint hell in colors not attempted by any one since the days of Dante; Dante spoke of the hell in the after-life, while Rosenfeld sings of the hell on earth, the hell that he has not only visited, but that he lived through . . ." (Wiener, *post,* 130). Rosenfeld lived to see his poems translated into many languages: English, German, Hebrew, Russian, Roumanian, Polish, Bohemian, Hungarian, and many of his songs were set to music. Adolf von Sonnenthal, the great Viennese actor, included Rosenfeld's poems in his program of dramatic recitals.

During the last few years of his life his health was seriously impaired and he lived a lonely existence. He was stricken with paralysis and died soon after his sixtieth birthday. His funeral was attended by thousands of the working class and he was buried in the plot of the Workingmen's Circle at Mount Carmel Cemetery, New York City. His wife and children survived him.

[Leo Wiener, *The Hist. of Yiddish Literature in the Nineteenth Century* (1899); foreword by Alex. Harkavy, *The Works of Morris Rosenfeld* (3 vols., 1908); M. Pines, *Di Geshichte fun der Yiddisher Literatur* (1911), vol. II; Zalmen Reisen, *Lexicon fun der Yiddisher Literatur,* vol. IV (1929); *N. Y. Times,* June 22, 25, 1923.]   I. S.

ROSENTHAL, HERMAN (Oct. 6, 1843–Jan. 27, 1917), author, librarian, was born in Friedrichsstadt, province of Courland, then part of Russia, a son of Moritz Rosenthal and Pauline Birkhahn. He was educated at the district school in Bausk and the progymnasium in Jakobstadt, both in Courland. He soon acquired a phenomenal command of Hebrew, German, and Russian, and was equally at home in the literature of all three languages. At the age of sixteen he commenced writing poetry of his own and translating into German the poems of famous Russian poets. In 1870 he published a collection of poems, *Gedichte,* while he was employed in a printing establishment in Krementchug, Russia. During this period he was also a contributor to *Hameliz* and other Hebrew periodicals, and in 1872 he published a humorous story, *Die wunderliche Kur.* Four years later he assisted in founding a Russian daily, *Zarya,* in Kiev. He served in the Russian Red Cross during the Russo-Turkish war and received the society's medal for distinguished services.

Soon after his arrival in the United States in 1881 Rosenthal began to carry out a long-cherished plan to found agricultural colonies for Russian Jews who had been compelled to emigrate to the United States due to the repressions of the Czarist régime, and, along with Michael Heilprin [*q.v.*], became one of the pioneers of Jewish colonization in the United States. While still in Russia he had been deeply interested in the promotion of culture among the Jews, and in the United States he desired to further these efforts along economic lines. He succeeded in founding the first agricultural colony of Russian Jews in Louisiana in December 1881. Soon afterward he organized another in South Dakota, and in 1891 took a prominent part in the administration of a settlement in Woodbine, N. J. He also identified himself with other movements and societies for the furtherance of liberty and enlightenment, but his chief services were enlisted on behalf of his co-religionists. As German poet, English essayist, Hebrew and Russian scholar, he used all four languages to fight for his ideals, to ease the burden of the oppressed, and to shed light upon the history and achievements of the Jews in Russia and Poland. In 1887 and 1888 Rosenthal was in the book trade, but gave up business to become chief statistician for the Edison Electric Company. At the request of James Jerome Hill [*q.v.*], he went to Japan, China, and Korea, 1892–93, to investigate economic conditions and trade in the interests of the Great Northern Railway. In 1894 he was appointed chief of the discharging department of the Immigration Bureau at Ellis Island. In 1898 he accepted the post of chief of the Slavonic division at the New York Public Library, which he held until his death.

Rosenthal was a contributor to the *Staatszeitung* and the *Outlook* in New York, and to other periodicals. Together with Abraham Hayyim Rosenberg [*q.v.*], he edited a Hebrew monthly, *Ha-modia le-hodashim,* from 1900 to 1902. In 1900 he became a member of the editorial board of the *Jewish Encyclopedia* as chief of the Russian department, and his historical knowledge, his brilliant style, and linguistic proficiency were of high value to this great enterprise. He rendered into German verse the book Ecclesiastes, *Worte des Sammlers* (1885); Song of Songs, *Lied der Lieder* (1893); was the author of *Spätherbstnebel, Poems* (1906); *Report on Japan, China and Corea* (1893); *A List of Russian, other Slavonic and Baltic Periodicals in the New York Public Library* (1916); and translated into English Hugo Ganz' *The Land of Riddles* (1904), and the *Memoirs of a Russian Governor, Prince Serge Dmitriyevich Urussov* (1908). In June 1864 he was married to Anna Rosenthal of Vilna. Their two sons survived him.

[*Who's Who in America*, 1916–17; *The Jewish Encyc.*, vol. X; *Library Jour.*, Feb. 1917; *Am. Hebrew,* Feb. 2, 1917; J. D. Eisenstein, *Ozar zikhronothai* (1929); *N. Y. Times*, Jan. 31, 1917.]   I. S.

ROSENTHAL, MAX (Nov. 23, 1833–Aug. 8, 1918), lithographer and mezzotint engraver, was born in Turck, near the city of Lodz, in what then was Russian Poland. He was the youngest of six children of Wolf and Rebecca Rosenthal. His father was a chemist and glass manufacturer, his mother a talented amateur sculptor, and his eldest brother, David, an artist, who is said to have surreptitiously painted altar pieces for churches near his home. When he was twelve, young Rosenthal was sent to Paris to study art and escape conscription in the Im-

perial Russian Army, which recognized the Jewish rule of regarding a boy as of age at thirteen. In Paris he was apprenticed to Martin Thurwanger, a lithographer, and in 1849 was brought by Thurwanger to the United States, where color lithography was struggling in the darkness of ignorance. Though his master remained only eighteen months, Rosenthal decided to stay with his elder brother, Louis, who was living in Philadelphia. He studied in the school of the Pennsylvania Academy of the Fine Arts and afterwards worked for a time in the establishment of Napoleon Sarony in New York. When Louis Rosenthal started his own business about 1850, Max returned to Philadelphia to work for him and subsequently entered into partnership with him, working chiefly in chromolithography, then a comparatively new field. Within a short time Max Rosenthal produced the illustrations for C. W. Webber's *The Hunter-Naturalist* (1851) and in the same year made some color lithographs for H. L. Stephens' *The Comic Natural History of the Human Race* (1851). For Matthias W. Baldwin, the locomotive builder, he produced large color lithographs of some of his locomotives. His large view of the interior of Masonic Hall, Philadelphia, published in 1854, attracted great attention as a remarkable example of pen lithography and the largest piece of chromolithography produced in the United States up to that time. During the first years of the Civil War, Rosenthal followed the Army of the Potomac, making sketches of the camps which he published in lithographic reproductions. About 1870 he began to make a series of lithographic portraits for such collectors as Dr. Thomas Addis Emmet and David McN. Stauffer of New York, and E. Coppee Mitchell and Ferdinand J. Dreer of Pennsylvania; these, about two hundred in all, were copies of portraits of distinguished Americans of whom no engraved portraits existed. About 1882 he began to etch, and before he retired from that field had produced about a hundred and fifty portraits of eminent American and British officers of the Revolutionary period. It was not until 1892, however, that he began the really important work of his artistic life. In that year he began experiments in mezzotint engraving and, having mastered it, devoted most of his remaining years to the production of important mezzotint engravings. He won so conspicuous a place among American engravers in this field that his reputation is likely to rest upon these achievements, though he turned to painting toward the end of his career. The majority of his mezzotint plates were portraits.

usually of eminent American statesmen, generals, and jurists. In 1859 Rosenthal had been married in Philadelphia to Caroline Rosenthal, who, though of the same name, was not related to him; their son Albert became a portrait painter.

[*Who's Who in America,* 1918–19; *Who's Who in Pa.* (1904); D. McN. Stauffer, *Am. Engravers Upon Copper and Steel,* vol. I (1907); *The Print Connoisseur,* Sept. 1921; *List of Portraits, Lithographs, Etchings, Mezzotints by Max Rosenthal and Albert Rosenthal* (1923); Harry T. Peters, *America on Stone* (1931); obit. notice in *Public Ledger* (Phila.), Aug. 9, 1918.]
J. J.

ROSENTHAL, TOBY EDWARD (Mar. 15, 1848–Dec. 23, 1917), genre and portrait painter, born in New Haven, Conn., was the son of Jacob and Ernestine (Germanus) Rosenthal. The family moved to New York in 1857 and to San Francisco in 1861, where Toby began the study of drawing and painting under Henri Bacon and Fortunato Arriola. In 1865 he was sent to Munich, where he continued his art education at the Bavarian Royal Academy for some seven years under Alexander Straehuber, Karl Raupp, and Carl von Piloty. He took a studio in Munich and exhibited there frequently, taught classes in painting and design, became a trustee of the Kunstgenossenschaft, and in all respects was thoroughly imbued with the methods and ideals of the Munich school. In 1880 he married Sophie Ansbacher of Nürnberg. He made occasional visits to the United States and from time to time sent pictures to the American exhibitions.

One of the earliest of his figure pieces to elicit more than casual attention from the public was his "Sebastian Bach and his Family at their Morning Devotions" (1870), purchased by the Leipzig museum. "Elaine," exhibited in Boston, New York, and Philadelphia in 1875 and 1876 and subsequently acquired by the Art Institute of Chicago, aroused still greater interest; for this work the artist was awarded a medal at the Centennial Exhibition of 1876 in Philadelphia, where his "Young Monk" was also shown. One of the critics characterized "Elaine" as "a good loud translation of our household Tennyson into the dialect of Munich" (quoted in Isham, *post,* p. 378), and another writer could not find in it any trace of "a lofty or subtle insight for beauty personal to the artist" (*Ibid.*). Still another commentator (*Art Journal,* vol. I, 1875, p. 126) considered that "the wisdom of choosing so sad a subject" was doubtful. Nevertheless, in 1876 the picture was a strong popular favorite, for Rosenthal's vein of sentimentality appealed to a very large element of the pub-

lic. His "Vacant Chair," which was sold for $650 in New York in 1909; his "Trial of the Escaped Nun, Constance de Beverley" (1883), a motive taken from Sir Walter Scott's *Marmion*; his "Dancing during the Empire," and a number of similar compositions were received with pronounced approbation both in Germany and America. He was given a medal at one of the international exhibitions held in Munich, and he received the cross of the Bavarian Order of St. Michael. Isham commends his workmanship but points out that, while he had mastered the Munich technique thoroughly, he had also accepted the mental and emotional viewpoint of the school, so that one will not find in his works a trace of anything distinctly American. He died in Munich in the seventieth year of his age.

[*Am. Art News,* Jan. 5, 1918; *Boston Transcript,* Dec. 29, 1917; *Am. Art Annual,* 1918; Samuel Isham, *The Hist. of Am. Painting,* 1905; *Zeitschrift für Bildende Kunst,* vol. XIX (1884), p. 263; *Who's Who in America,* 1910–11; obituary in *Berliner Tageblatt und Handels-Zeitung,* Dec. 24, 1917.]
W. H. D.

ROSENWALD, JULIUS (Aug. 12, 1862–Jan. 6, 1932), merchant and philanthropist, was the son of Samuel and Augusta (Hammerslough) Rosenwald. He was born in Springfield, Ill., almost directly across the street from the house where Abraham Lincoln lived, and he was undoubtedly influenced by the strong Lincoln tradition. He was educated in the public schools of Springfield, and in 1879 began his business career with Hammerslough Brothers, wholesale clothiers of New York City, remaining with that concern until 1885. He then became president of Rosenwald & Weil, a Chicago clothing firm, continuing in that capacity until 1906. From 1895 to 1910 he was vice-president and treasurer of Sears, Roebuck & Company; from 1910 to 1925, president; and until his death, chairman of the board of directors. On Apr. 8, 1890, he married Augusta Nusbaum of Chicago, who died May 23, 1929; to this union were born five children—two sons and three daughters. On Jan. 8, 1930, he married Adelaide (Rau) Goodkind, mother of the wife of his eldest son.

Rosenwald built up a great establishment through seeing the possibilities of the mail-order business, appreciating his own limitations, and surrounding himself with experts. He will be remembered, however, as a philanthropist and humanitarian. He attended the religious services of Chicago Sinai Congregation, of which he was vice-president, regularly; and he freely confessed that he derived his social vision and social passion from that source. His good works covered a wide range. He was one of the leaders and pioneers who brought about the Federation of Jewish Charities in Chicago in 1923. As a member of the American Jewish Committee, he helped to protect the Jew against unjust discrimination. Feeling that the Jewish problem in Russia must be worked out in Russia itself, he contributed six million dollars to further a plan for the colonization of Jews in that country. Through his far-sightedness, the Hebrew Union College of Cincinnati, and the Jewish Theological Seminary of America, in New York City, were put on a firm financial footing, though not endowed. In helping the former, he paid a tribute to Isaac M. Wise [q.v.]; in assisting the latter, he memorialized a warm friend, Louis Marshall [q.v.]. Though never a Zionist and not sympathetic with any form of Jewish nationalism, he gave to the Hebrew University of Jerusalem and to other cultural agencies in Palestine, and aided in the relief of the unfortunate of that country. He believed that Jews are a people and not a nation; he interpreted Judaism in terms of service to humanity.

His philanthropies transcended the prejudices of race, creed, country, and nationality. The most of his gifts were made through the Julius Rosenwald Fund, which he created in 1917. Its chartered purpose was the "well-being of mankind." In 1929 its capital amounted to $30,000,000, and his will provided that principal as well as interest should be spent within twenty-five years after his death. He helped to establish colleges in Assyria and Constantinople. Immediately after the World War, he fed the hungry children of Germany; later, he established a dental clinic in Berlin. His contributions to work for the advancement of the negro were doubtless the outstanding feature of his philanthropy. Feeling that it was wrong to give without causing others to give, and especially without insisting that those who were to be helped make an effort in their own behalf, he contributed part of the total cost (about $3,850,000) of twenty-five negro Young Men's Christian Association, and three negro Young Women's Christian Association buildings in twenty-five cities with approximately 2,000,000 negro population. Like Booker T. Washington, he felt that the salvation of the negro lay in education. He also contributed $3,-660,000 toward the total cost of $23,200,000 for 4,500 negro public schools in the South; 339 of these were built in 1929.

As a citizen of Chicago, Rosenwald was socially minded and gifted with civic vision. He was one of the founders of the Municipal Voters League. As a member of the Committee of Fifteen, he was fearlessly active in banishing the

"red light district." The Public Efficiency Bureau found him among the most conscientious in trying to minimize graft and corruption. During the race riots in Chicago he served valiantly to restore peace and good will. He was an ardent champion of the Chicago Planning Commission, and president of the Jewish Charities of Chicago. He gave to the city, in 1929, an industrial museum, to be known as the Museum of Science and Industry founded by Julius Rosenwald. His gifts to the University of Chicago amounted to almost five million dollars, but money was the least part of his contribution to this institution, for he later gave his thought, his vision, his energy, and his enthusiasm during more than twenty years of service on its board of trustees.

Rosenwald had no sympathy with jingoism and chauvinism, he abhorred war, but both in war and in peace he served his country. In 1916 President Wilson appointed him a member of the Advisory Commission of the Council of National Defense and chairman of the committee on supplies. At the request of the secretary of war, he went on a special mission to France in 1918, and was a member of the Second National Industrial Conference in 1919. His Americanism was manifest in his abounding faith in the common man; he believed that the common sense of the common man was uncommonly good. He loved maxims, some of which he created; others, many of which motivated him, he appropriated. He did not believe in endowments, feeling that endowments for specific purposes intended for a blessing, may, and frequently have, become a curse. He sought to influence foundations not to tie up great sums in perpetuity. His articles, "Principles of Public Giving" and "The Trend Away from Perpetuities" (*Atlantic Monthly*, May 1929, December 1930) created history in the realm of philanthropy. In season and out of season, he would say: "I believe that large gifts should not be restricted to narrowly specified objects, and that under no circumstances should funds be held in perpetuity. . . . I have confidence in future generations and in their ability to meet their own needs wisely and generously" (*Ibid.*, May 1929, p. 606). He died in Chicago, survived by his wife and all his children.

[B. C. Forbes, *Men Who Are Making America* (1917); Edwin Wildman, *Famous Leaders of Industry*, 2 ser. (1921); *Who's Who in American Jewry*, 1928; *Who's Who in America*, 1930–31; L. L. Mann, *Julius Rosenwald, A Memorial Tribute* (1932); *Jour. of Negro Hist.*, Apr. 1932; Graham Taylor, in *Survey*, Feb. 1, 1932; *N. Y. Times*, Jan. 7, 8, 1932.] L. L. M.

ROSEWATER, EDWARD (Jan. 28, 1841– Aug. 30, 1906), Nebraska journalist and politician, was born in the village of Bukowan,

Bohemia. His parents, Herman and Rosalia (Kohn) Rosenwasser, were of German Jewish descent, but were Bohemian rather than German in sentiment. Edward went to school in Prague until he was thirteen, learned German of a tutor, and in 1854 came with his parents and their eight other children to the United States. The Rosenwassers settled in Cleveland, changed their name to Rosewater, and were speedily absorbed into the main currents of American life.

The boy Edward found work, first as a store clerk, later as a book-keeper, and after 1858 as a telegrapher. When the Civil War broke out he was stationed in the South, where he remained until 1862. He then entered the United States military telegraph corps, and served with Frémont in West Virginia, with Pope during his disastrous Virginia campaign of 1862, and with the War Department at Washington. In 1863, he yielded to the persuasions of Edward Creighton [q.v.] and accepted a position with the Pacific Telegraph Company at Omaha, Nebr. Through his connection with this company, and later with other western telegraph lines, Rosewater learned much about the sources of news. He established a news bureau to contribute items from the Rocky Mountain area, and became an agent of the Associated Press.

With this background, his transition to the newspaper world was easy. After a brief connection with the *Omaha Daily Tribune,* he made his real début into newspaper work with the establishment of the *Omaha Daily Bee* in 1871. That year, as a member of the Nebraska legislature, he had advocated the creation of a school board for the city of Omaha. Such a measure passed the legislature, but had to be submitted to the voters of the city for their approval. To insure ratification of the project at the polls, Rosewater established the *Bee,* a sort of tabloid newspaper "not much larger than a full-page theater program," as a medium for his arguments. The *Bee* was at first distributed without cost, but its spicy editorials and its well-chosen telegraphic news won such hearty support that when the campaign for a better school system was won the *Bee* lived on. Enlarged to the usual newspaper size and offered to subscribers as an afternoon daily, it outstripped its local competitors and soon became one of the outstanding newspapers in the United States. Rosewater was always among the first to adopt the latest improved methods of publication, he maintained unabated his keen sense of news values, and he fought valiantly through his editorials for the rights of the common man. Had the *Bee* been less vigorous in its denunciation of railway abuses, probably Rosewater would have won in 1901 the seat in the United States Senate that he coveted.

Rosewater was a loyal citizen of Omaha and contributed in many ways to the material advancement of that city. The *Bee* building, an eight-story fire-proof structure erected in 1887–88, was long regarded as one of the architectural triumphs of the West. The Trans-Mississippi Exposition, held at Omaha in 1898, was originally projected by Rosewater, and he, more than any other man, was responsible for its conspicuous success. He was married on Nov. 13, 1864, to Leah, daughter of Loeb and Ella Colman, of Cleveland, Ohio, by whom he had five children. Shortly before his death he handed over to his two sons, Victor and Charles, the active management of the *Bee.* He died suddenly, in August 1906, without having shown previously any signs of failing health.

[*Omaha Daily Bee,* Sept. 1, 2, 1906; J. S. Morton, Albert Watkins, and G. L. Miller, *Illus. Hist. of Nebr.,* I (1905), 744–46, using material furnished by Rosewater himself; A. C. Edmunds, *Pen Sketches of Nebraskans* (1871); *Who's Who in America,* 1903–05; additional information from Victor Rosewater, Esq., of Philadelphia.] J. D. H.

ROSS, ABEL HASTINGS (Apr. 28, 1831–May 13, 1893), Congregational clergyman, was born in Winchendon, Mass., the seventh of the nine children of Phineas and Betsey (Marshall) Ross. The family lived at different times on farms in Winchendon, Gardner, and Ashburnham, and the boy's life was one of poverty and hard labor. Lacking financial backing, he gained his education by his own indomitable persistence. After some study at Winchendon Academy, he entered the preparatory department of Oberlin in 1851 and the college in 1853, graduating from the latter in 1857. Returning to New England, he continued his studies at Andover Theological Seminary, from which he was graduated in 1860. Ordained in the Congregational Church at Boylston, Mass., on Oct. 17, 1861, he served as pastor there until 1866, being absent for several months during the Civil War in the service of the Christian Commission. His other pastorates were at the First Church, Springfield, Ohio, 1866–73; Plymouth Church, Columbus, Ohio, 1873–75; and Port Huron, Mich., 1876–93, where he died. From 1871 to 1891 he was lecturer on church polity at Oberlin Theological Seminary and from 1882 to 1886, Southworth Lecturer on Congregationalism at the Andover Theological Seminary.

Ross was an authority on the history and polity of the Congregational denomination and one of its best known and most influential leaders. He early realized the imperfections of the denominational organization and the loss of power resulting therefrom, and he labored for a generation to correct them. "There can be no doubt," it has been said regarding his service to Congregationalism, "that our churches owe more to him than to almost any other man of his generation for their growing sense of a common life and of the need and the possibility of a more perfect union in their fellowship and their activities" (W. H. Ryder, in *Andover Theological Seminary Necrology*, 1892–93, p. 90). He was a strong advocate of an ecumenical Congregational council which should be advisory in its nature but destitute of authority, and like the local and national councils of the denomination, should not infringe on the independency of the churches. His views on this subject set forth in his article "An Ecumenical Council of the Congregational Churches" (*Congregational Quarterly*, April 1874) bore fruit in the International Congregational Council in London in 1891, in the proceedings of which he had a prominent part. He was a constant contributor on social, denominational, and religious subjects to the reviews and quarterlies, and was the author of twenty-three books and pamphlets. His *Church-Kingdom* (1887), comprising his Southworth Lectures at Andover, is of permanent value, and his *Pocket Manual of Congregationalism* (1889) ranks as one of the best treatises on the polity of that order. Other publications of his worthy of mention are *The Ohio Manual; Statement of the Historical, Doctrinal and Ecclesiastical Position of the Congregational Churches* (1877); *The Church of God; a Catechism* (1881); *Sermons for Children* (1887); *Immanuel Catechism for Infant Classes* (1893). His literary work was marked by clearness of definition and lucidity of statement and when on controversial ground he was fair and good tempered. His simple and sincere manner and kindly spirit gained him a wide circle of friends. On Oct. 15, 1860, he married Mary Maria Gilman, an Oberlin classmate, who survived him.

[*Congregational Year Book*, 1894; *Congregationalist*, May 18, 1893; *Advance*, May 18, 1893; *Detroit Tribune*, May 15, 1893; information from the secretary of Oberlin College and several of Ross's friends.]

F. T. P.

ROSS, ALEXANDER (May 9, 1783–Oct. 23, 1856), fur trader, explorer, author, was born in Nairnshire, Scotland, the son of Alexander Ross, a farmer. He received a good education and on his emigration to Canada in 1804 obtained employment as a schoolteacher. At Montreal, in May 1810, he met Wilson Price Hunt [*q.v.*], with whom he engaged as a clerk of Astor's Pacific Fur Company and in September sailed from New York on the *Tonquin*. He aided in the building of Fort Astoria, and later of Fort Okanogan, of which he was several times in charge. In 1813 he married an Indian woman, an Okinagan, by whom he had several children and to whom he remained devotedly attached. In 1814, following the sale of Astoria, he joined the North West Company and in 1816 was second in command at Fort George. He was a member of the expedition that in July 1818 founded Fort Nez Percés, popularly known as Fort Walla Walla, where he remained in charge for more than five years. For a time after the absorption of the North West Company by the Hudson's Bay Company he continued at his post. In the fall of 1823 he resigned and started east but was persuaded to lead an expedition into the Snake River country. Leaving Flathead House, at the present Eddy, Mont., on Feb. 10, 1824, he penetrated the present Idaho as far as the mouth of Boise River, unexpectedly encountering six American trappers, led by Jedediah S. Smith [*q.v.*]. By November he was back at his starting place. In the spring of 1825, with his wife and children, he again started east but halted at the Red River colony, where he was to reside for the remainder of his life. On the site of the present Winnipeg he received a grant of 100 acres of land. He was appointed the colony's first sheriff and retained the post for many years. His *Adventures of the First Settlers on the Oregon or Columbia River* was published in London in 1849. Six years later came *The Fur Hunters of the Far West* in two volumes and in 1856 *The Red River Settlement*. Many years after his death a few of his letters were published by George Bryce in *Transactions of the Historical and Scientific Society of Manitoba* (No. 63, 1903) and his journal of the Snake Country expedition in 1824 was edited by T. C. Elliott in the *Quarterly of the Oregon Historical Society* (December 1913). He died in "Colony Gardens," now a part of Winnipeg. His widow, familiarly known in her later days as "Granny Ross," survived him by thirty years.

Ross was a man of exceptional abilities and was greatly esteemed by all who knew him, white and red alike. For the first fourteen years of the white man's occupation of Oregon he was an energetic and influential participant in the activities of the region, and for the history of a considerable part of the period he remains almost the sole first-hand authority. The captious criticism of his writings in Bancroft (*post*, esp. I, 579 and II, 238) has been generally disregarded by later students.

[Autobiog. material in own writings, esp. letters edited by Bryce, *ante*; H. J. Morgan, *Bibliotheca Canadensis* (1867); H. H. Bancroft, *Hist. of the Northwest Coast* (2 vols., 1884); H. M. Chittenden, *The Am. Fur Trade of the Far West* (1902), vols. I, III; H. W. Scott, *Hist. of the Oregon Country* (1924), vols. I–III, comp. by L. M. Scott; *Canadian Mag.*, June 1917; *Queen's Quarterly*, July 1903.]   W. J. G.

ROSS, ALEXANDER COFFMAN (May 31, 1812–Feb. 26, 1883), song writer and jeweler, was born in Zanesville, Ohio, one of twelve children of Elijah and Mary (Coffman) Ross. Elijah Ross, who like his wife had been born in Pennsylvania, settled in Zanestown, afterwards Zanesville, in 1804. He was a gunsmith and during the War of 1812 was ordered to remain at home to repair guns, swords, and military accoutrements. The son became familiar at an early age with the repair and manufacture of guns in the little shop kept by his father, soon learned to handle tools, and at seventeen was apprenticed to a jeweler of the town. After completing his knowledge of his trade in New York, he returned to Zanesville and on Apr. 2, 1838, married Caroline Granger, by whom he had three children. He died in Zanesville. As a boy he had supplemented the elementary education he received at home by reading as widely as possible, especially on scientific subjects; and although he was a jeweler by trade until his retirement in 1863, he never lost his early interests. An amateur photographer, he took in 1839 what he believed to be the first daguerreotype taken in the United States west of New York; he afterwards made improvements in his process and took good daguerreotype portraits as early as 1843. He was a lover of music as well; in New York he had been a member of an orchestra led by Ureli C. Hill [*q.v.*] and later was influential in bringing many musical troupes to Zanesville. He also had a fondness for the circus and was quick to pick up the popular songs that in those days were sung by the clowns.

It was his interest in both popular songs and politics that brought him his chief distinction. In the presidential campaign of 1840, which has been popularly known as the "Log Cabin and Hard Cider Campaign" but was preëminently also the campaign of music and song, he took an active part. For a Zanesville club, organized in enthusiastic support of Harrison and Tyler, Ross wrote to the tune of "Little Pigs" the famous "Tippecanoe and Tyler, Too," contriving the chorus in church, it is said, while the sermon was being given. Soon afterward, at a great Whig meeting in Lafayette Hall, New York, at which he was present, the chairman called for some one to sing a song before the speaking began. Ross volunteered and, answering the questions of the crowd as to his identity with "I am a Buckeye, from the Buckeye state," sang his song, the chorus of which was as follows:

For Tippecanoe and Tyler, too—Tippecanoe and Tyler too;
And with them we'll beat little Van, Van, Van,
Van is a used-up man;
And with them we'll beat little Van.

It was followed by a storm of cheers, encored over and over again, and almost overnight became throughout the country the most popular song of the campaign.

[C. B. Galbreath, in *Ohio Archaeological and Hist. Quart.*, Jan. 1905; J. N. Granger, *Launcelot Granger of Newbury, Mass., and Suffield, Conn.: A Geneal. Hist.* (1893); *Cincinnati Enquirer*, Feb. 26, 1883; letters from the Ross family.]   C. B. G—h.

ROSS, ARAMINTA [See TUBMAN, HARRIET, *c.* 1821–1913].

ROSS, BETSY (Jan. 1, 1752–Jan. 30, 1836), legendary maker of the first stars-and-stripes, was born in Philadelphia, the eighth of the seventeen children of Samuel and Rebecca (James) Griscom, and a great-grand-daughter of Andrew Griscom, a carpenter, who emigrated from England to West Jersey in 1680 and later moved to Philadelphia. The building business that he established was continued by Betsy's father. She is supposed to have attended the Friends' school in South Fourth Street and early evinced an aptitude for fine needlework. She also evinced considerable independence of mind, for on Nov. 4, 1773, she eloped to Gloucester, N. J., with John Ross, son of the Rev. Æneas Ross of New Castle, Del., and was there married to him. The next May the Society of Friends disowned her, with evident reluctance, for marrying out of meeting. For a number of years she attended Christ Church and later, with her third husband, became a loyal member of the Society of Free Quakers.

Ross opened an upholsterer's shop on Arch Street, on the site of what is now No. 233, and the young couple lived on the premises. On Jan. 21, 1776, Ross, then a soldier in the militia, was killed by an explosion of gunpowder on a wharf that he was patrolling. Throughout the uncertain years that followed Mrs. Ross continued to carry on the business. The well-known story of her making the first stars-and-stripes at the behest of Washington, Robert Morris, and George Ross, is based on a family tradition that was first made public by her grandson, William Canby, in a paper that he was permitted to read before the Historical Society of Pennsylvania in March 1870. That making flags was a part of her business is attested by the minutes of the Pennsylvania State Navy Board, which, on May 29, 1777, ordered the payment to her of £14/12/2 for "making ships' colours, etc." (*Pennsylvania Archives*, 2 ser., vol. II, 1874, p. 164), but other documentary evidence has not been found. The stars-and-stripes was adopted as the national flag June 14, 1777, by a resolution of the Continental Congress (*Journals of the Continental Congress, 1774–89*, vol. VIII, 1907, p. 464). Whatever her connection with the flag, it could hardly have been as important or romantic as her descendants supposed. On June 15, 1777, at Old Swedes' Church, Wicaco, she married Capt. Joseph Ashburn, by whom she had two daughters. The brigantine *Patty*, of which he was first mate, was captured at sea by the British. Ashburn died Mar. 3, 1782, in the Old Mill Prison, Plymouth, England. Word of his death was brought to his widow by his fellow prisoner, John Claypoole, who had been a life-long friend of them both. Betsy and he were married May 8, 1783. They had five daughters. Claypoole died Aug. 3, 1817, and Betsy spent the last years of her long life in the home of one of her daughters. Her remains now rest in Mount Moriah Cemetery.

[E. S. Parry, *Betsy Ross, Quaker Rebel* (1930); Lloyd Balderston, *The Evolution of the Am. Flag* (1909), from materials collected by Geo. Canby; G. H. Preble, *Hist. of the Flag of the U. S.* (2nd rev. ed., 1880); Byron McCandless, "The Story of the Am. Flag," *Nat. Geographic*, Oct. 1917; Morton Pennypacker, "Capt. John Hulbert and His Flag of 1775," *N. Y. Hist.*, Oct. 1933; A. J. Wall, "The Flag with an Eagle in the Canton," *N. Y. Hist. Soc. Quart. Bull.*, Oct. 1933; Joseph Jackson, "Arch Street's Place in the Annals of Old Phila.," *Public Ledger* (Phila.), Nov. 30, 1913; J. W. Jordan, *Colonial Families of Phila.*, II (1911), 1250–51; R. I. Graff, *Geneal. of the Claypoole Family of Phila.* (1893), pp. 68–76; *N. Y. Times*, May 28, 1933; *Evening Star* (Washington), June 14, 1933.]   G. H. G.

ROSS, EDMUND GIBSON (Dec. 7, 1826–May 8, 1907), journalist, United States senator, was born at Ashland, Ohio, the son of Sylvester F. and Cynthia (Rice) Ross. When he was about ten years old he was apprenticed to a printer at Huron, and, after learning the trade, he traveled for some years as a journeyman printer. In 1848 he married, at Sandusky, Fanny M. Lathrop, the daughter of Rodney Lathrop of New York. He lived for a time at Janesville, Wis., and for four years at Milwaukee, where he was foreman of the job printing office of the *Sentinel*. Although born a Democrat, Ross, in his own words, was "baptized in politics in the old Abolition party of 1844." Joining the Republican party in 1856, with the spirit of a crusader he led a colony of free-state settlers, heavily armed, to Kansas, driving an oxteam all the way. Here he began a period of great activity against the pro-slavery party. In 1857 he and his brother bought the Topeka *Kansas Tribune*, and two years later

founded the *Kansas State Record* (Topeka), which they sold in 1862. He was a member of the Wyandotte Constitutional Convention of 1859 from Wabaunsee. In 1862 he enlisted in the 11th Kansas Regiment and later recruited a company and became its captain. A brave and dashing soldier, he was promoted to major in 1864, and served on the Missouri border until the war ended. In 1865 he became editor of the Lawrence *Tribune*.

The following year he was appointed to the United States Senate to succeed James H. Lane [*q.v.*], who, mentally deranged, partly because of criticism of his support of President Johnson, had committed suicide. Interestingly enough, Ross was one of his critics. The appointment was popular and in 1867 the legislature elected him to fill out the term. He entered the Senate an intense Radical and an earnest opponent of Johnson. He voted for all the radical measures of reconstruction, including the tenure-of-office act, of which, however, he was quite doubtful. When Johnson removed Stanton in January 1868, Ross voted for the Senate resolution declaring the act illegal. After the President's impeachment, however, he was insistent that Johnson should have a fair trial and voted on many questions with the known opponents of conviction, notably in connection with the admission of evidence for the defense. The rumor spread among the Radicals that Ross was "shaky," and he was continually importuned by them, flooded with letters and telegrams from Kansas. At this time he rather favored conviction, but the character of the pressure upon him made him doubtful. In answer to a telegram of instruction from Kansas, he replied: "I have taken an oath to do impartial justice . . . and trust I shall have the courage and the honesty to vote according to the dictates of my judgment and for the highest good of the country" (*Scribner's, post*, p. 521). His final conclusion to vote against conviction for lack of evidence, was reached in face of the belief that he would thereby secure his own political destruction. He said later: "I almost literally looked down into my own grave. Friends, position, fortune, everything that makes life desirable to an ambitious man, were about to be swept away by the breath of my mouth, perhaps forever" (*Ibid.*, p. 524). The burst of bitter denunciation which followed the first vote fell most heavily on Ross. He was a "poltroon and traitor," it was said; "littleness had borne its legitimate fruit"; "Kansas repudiates you as she does all perjurers and skunks," were the words of a telegram from his home state (Dewitt, *post*, p. 545). Charges of corruption were made and every species of pressure known to politicians was exerted. Ross "bore the ordeal with the fortitude of a stoic and the inscrutability of a sphinx" (*Ibid.*, p. 574), and again voted "not guilty." Immediately thereafter he demanded an investigation of the charges against him, but none was ever made. Several times, however, he defended his position in the Senate (*Congressional Globe,* 40 Cong., 2 Sess., pp. 2598–99, 4513–17). During the remainder of his term, which ended in 1871, he was an independent. He favored the absolute repeal of the tenure-of-office act, and supported the Fifteenth Amendment although he believed that Congress had power to grant negro suffrage.

At the conclusion of his term he returned to Kansas and published a weekly newspaper at Coffeyville. In November 1879 he began to edit the Lawrence *Standard* and in February of the following year bought the Leavenworth *Press* and merged the two. He left the Republican party in 1872, partly because of its treatment of him, but also because of his dislike of the protective system and the character of Grant's administration. For the rest of his life he was a Democrat, although he violently opposed Bryan and free silver. In 1876 he was a Democratic candidate for elector and in 1880 for governor, but was badly beaten. Two years later he moved to New Mexico and became again a journeyman printer. Cleveland appointed him governor of the territory in May 1885, and he filled the position for four stormy years of struggle with what he asserted was a corrupt ring, antagonizing Democrats as well as the Republican legislature. In 1893 he was an unsuccessful candidate for reappointment. He spent the rest of his life in Albuquerque. Shortly before his death a messenger brought him greetings from the governor and legislature of Kansas, expressing appreciation of his conduct in the impeachment trial. He was utterly fearless, honest, and of good ability, but lacked tact, was brusque and headstrong, and, in the words of an opponent, "rejoiced in opposition." Two sons and three daughters survived him.

[Information concerning Ross himself appears in his *Hist. of the Impeachment of Andrew Johnson* (1896) and in articles by him in *Forum*, July 1895, and *Scribner's Mag.*, Apr. 1882. See also D. M. Dewitt, *Impeachment and Trial of Andrew Johnson* (1903); D. W. Wilder, *The Annals of Kan.* (1886); *Trans. Kan. State Hist. Soc.*, vols. I, II (1881); R. E. Twitchell, *The Leading Facts of New Mexican Hist.*, II (1912), 496–502; *Albuquerque Morning Jour.*, May 9, 10, 1907.]

J. G. deR. H.

ROSS, ERSKINE MAYO (June 30, 1845–Dec. 10, 1928), federal judge, son of William Buckner Ross and Elizabeth Mayo (Thom), was born in Belpré, Culpeper County, Va., the fourth of five children. On his father's side his ancestry was English, and on his mother's, Scotch. As a boy he attended the Virginia Military Institute, and while enrolled as a cadet there participated in various engagements in the Civil War. He graduated in 1865, and on Sept. 11 of that year, together with Otis Allen Glazebrook and Alfred Marshall, organized the Alpha Tau Omega college fraternity in Richmond, Va. Projected as a national organization, it was the first such fraternity to be formed after the Civil War (W. R. Baird, *Baird's Manual, American College Fraternities,* 12th ed., 1930). The thirty-first congress of the fraternity, held in Los Angeles in 1929, was known as the Ross Memorial Congress.

In 1868 Ross began the practice of law in Los Angeles. He soon obtained a commanding position in the legal profession of Southern California, in 1879 was elected justice of the state supreme court for the short term, and in 1882 was reëlected for the full term of twelve years. He resigned this position in 1886 to engage in private practice as a partner of Stephen M. White [*q.v.*], but within a year was appointed by President Cleveland to the federal district court of the southern district of California, and in 1895 advanced to the United States circuit court. This latter position he held until his resignation thirty years later, when he was nearly eighty years of age. His service on the federal bench is thus one of the longest on record (see letter from President Coolidge at the time of his retirement, *Los Angeles Times,* Dec. 11, 1928).

Ross's decisions were recognized for their clarity, impartiality, and fearlessness, and were seldom reversed by the higher courts. On Sept. 5, 1893, in the case of Chum Shang Yuen, a Chinese laborer resident in California, who had failed to register in accordance with the provisions of the so-called Geary Act of May 5, 1892, Ross upheld the validity of this act, and ordered the deportation of the defendant (57 *Fed. Reporter,* 588). The decision led to a bitter quarrel between the Judge and Richard Olney [*q.v.*], attorney general of the United States, who was opposed to the enforcement of this particular section of the act, but in California the decision was exceedingly popular. On July 22, 1895, Judge Ross declared the so-called Wright Irrigation law unconstitutional under the "due process" clause, thereby invalidating some millions of dollars worth of bonds, and throwing the water laws of California into great confusion (68 *Fed. Reporter,* 948). His decision confirming the title of Leland Stanford Junior University to its endowment made possible the continuation of that great educational institution (69 *Fed.*, 25; 161 *U. S.*, 412). Of greater significance both from a legal and a social point of view was his decision, at the time of the Pullman strike in 1894, in the case of W. H. Clune and three associates, that a concerted action of a number of individuals to prevent the transportation of trains with Pullman cars was an unlawful conspiracy punishable as such, and in contempt of the Court's order against interference with the transportation of mail and interstate commerce (62 *Fed. Reporter*, 834). In his charge to the Grand Jury in connection with this case he stated that "no man has a legal or moral right while continuing in the employment of another to refuse to do the work he is employed and engaged to do" (p. 835).

Ross was a charter member of the California Club, one of the five founders of the city of Glendale, and a horticulturist of note. The suburb of Glendale known as Rossmoyne perpetuates his name. On May 7, 1874, he married Ynez Hannah Bettis; one son was born of this marriage. After the death of his first wife, he married, June 1, 1909, Ida Hancock, widow of Henry Hancock of Los Angeles; she died in 1913. Ross died in Los Angeles, leaving by his will nearly a quarter of a million dollars to various philanthropic and educational institutions, including $100,000 as a prize foundation to the American Bar Association.

[J. C. Bates, *Hist. of the Bench and Bar of Cal.* (1912); Willoughby Rodman, *Hist. of the Bench and Bar of Southern Cal.* (1909); O. T. Schuck, *Hist. of the Bench and Bar of Cal.* (1901); *An Illustrated Hist. of Los Angeles County, Cal.* (1889); *Am. Bar Asso. Jour.*, Feb. 1929; *Los Angeles Times*, Mar. 17, 1925, Dec. 11, 1928; scrapbook deposited by Judge Ross shortly before his death with the librarian of the Los Angeles County Law Library.]   R. G. C.

ROSS, GEORGE (May 10, 1730–July 14, 1779), jurist, signer of the Declaration of Independence, eldest son of the Rev. George Ross and his second wife, Catherine Van Gezel, was born at New Castle, Del. His father, a graduate of the University of Edinburgh, prepared for the Presbyterian ministry, but, deciding during his studies that this Church was too censorious and hypocritical, he took orders in the Church of England, came to America as a missionary, and for many years served as rector of Immanuel Church, New Castle. George received a classical education and studied law with his step-brother, John, of Philadelphia. Following his admittance to the bar in 1750, he established himself at Lancaster, Pa., his ability as a lawyer soon winning him an extensive practice. One of his first clients was a beautiful and accomplished lady of Scotch-Irish descent, Anne Lawler, whom

he married Aug. 17, 1751, and by whom he had two sons and a daughter.

Excepting for twelve years' service as prosecutor for the Crown in Cumberland County, his political career began with his election to the provincial Assembly in 1768. During his seven years in that body he gained a reputation for his deep interest in Indian problems and for his championship of the Assembly in disputes with the governor. His growing political influence secured his election to the Provincial Conference at Philadelphia in July 1774, and to the First Continental Congress in the same year, though at this time he was generally recognized as a Tory. The following year, however, witnessed his conversion to the ranks of the Whigs, and as a member of the Assembly, of the Pennsylvania committee of safety, and of the Second Continental Congress to November 1775, he was one of the most untiring workers for the patriot cause in Pennsylvania. During this period he also saw brief service as a colonel of associators, and in 1776 assisted in negotiating a treaty to pacify the Indians of northwestern Pennsylvania. He was vice-president of the Pennsylvania constitutional convention of 1776, aided in drawing up the declaration of rights, and otherwise played a conspicuous part in the convention's deliberations. On July 20, 1776, the convention elected him to Congress, but illness compelled his withdrawal in January 1777. For several years after its inauguration he was a firm friend of the new state government, but in 1779, like many of his lawyer brethren, he began to feel that the evils of the times demanded constitutional revision.

On Mar. 1, 1779, he was commissioned judge of the admiralty court of Pennsylvania, although he had been serving in that capacity earlier, and as such had sat in the famous case of the sloop *Active*. Though his sympathies were with the plaintiff, Gideon Olmsted [*q.v.*], the jury found the Connecticut captors entitled to only one fourth of the prize and Ross held that he was bound by law to confirm this verdict. When the committee on appeals of Congress reversed his judgment he defied that body and declared he would submit to no usurpation of the power of his court. In an elaborate vindication of his action he contended that the court of appeals had authority to set aside the decree of a judge in a question of law, but there its power ended; that under Pennsylvania's law the verdict of the jury was conclusive upon the facts without an appeal (*U. S.* vs. *Judge Peters*, 5 *Cranch*, 115 at p. 120). In the midst of the controversy between Congress and the state of Pennsylvania, which dragged on for more than thirty years, Ross died suddenly, in Philadelphia, from a violent attack of the gout. Noted for his genial manner and good humor, he loved conviviality, and on his death bed complacently remarked that he was going on a long journey to a cool place—"there were most excellent wines there"—and he should fare deliciously.

[*Hist. Papers and Addresses of the Lancaster County Hist. Soc.*, vol. I (1897); H. P. Read, *Rossiana* (1908); *Pa. Archives*, 1 ser. VI, VII (1853), 2 ser. III (1875); *Minutes of the Provincial Council of Pa.*, vols. X–XII (1852–53); *Pa. Mag. of Hist. and Biog.*, IV (1880), 230, 257–58; vol. XVI (1893), pp. 385–98; *Pa. Evening Post* (Phila.), July 16, 1779.] J. H. P.

ROSS, JAMES (July 12, 1762–Nov. 27, 1847), lawyer, United States senator, son of Joseph and Jane (Graham) Ross, was born near Delta, York County, Pa. His grandfather, Hugh Ross, of Scotch ancestry, came to America from northern Ireland about 1723. James studied the classics at Slate Ridge Presbyterian Church school and at an academy in Pequea, Pa. At the age of eighteen he was induced by the Rev. John McMillan, a close friend of the Ross family, to go to western Pennsylvania, where he taught Latin and Greek in McMillan's academy near Canonsburg (now Washington and Jefferson College, Washington, Pa.). He had originally intended to enter the ministry, but while he was at Canonsburg, Hugh Henry Brackenridge [*q.v.*], a Pittsburgh lawyer, persuaded him to take up law, and in 1782 encouraged him to continue his studies at Philadelphia. He returned to Washington County in 1784 and was admitted to the bar. Specializing in land cases, he soon acquired a large practice, and in 1795 moved to Pittsburgh. He was attorney for President Washington's estates in western Pennsylvania and numbered among his clients prominent and wealthy business men.

His first connection with state politics was as a member of the Pennsylvania constitutional convention in 1789–90. A member of the committee that drafted the new frame of government, he was a stanch Federalist and attracted attention by his zealous advocacy of a clause for religious liberty similar to that in the federal Constitution. During the Whiskey Insurrection (1794) he used his influence to restrain popular fury against the federal government. President Washington appointed him one of the federal commissioners to treat with the insurgents and his efforts were in a large measure responsible for the amicable settlement of the uprising, and the saving his friend Brackenridge from prosecution for treason. In 1794 the Pennsylvania legislature elected him to the United States Senate in place of Albert Gallatin [*q.v.*],

who was disqualified on account of the residence requirement. Reëlected in 1797, he served until 1803, and in 1799 was president *pro tempore* of the Senate. A firm believer in Hamiltonian ideas and policies, he worked diligently, though unsuccessfully, in 1800, to keep Pennsylvania in the Federalist ranks and to insure a national victory for his party by urging the passage of an act under which the legality of electoral votes for president and vice-president would have been decided by a grand committee composed of the chief justice and six members from each house of Congress. Under the Republican administration he defended Federalist legislation against Jeffersonian attacks, notably the excise law and the Judiciary Act of 1801, asserting that the repeal of the latter would erect Congress into "a complete tyranny" and render the judiciary totally subservient to Congress (*Annals of Congress*, 7 Cong., 1 Sess., p. 166). A series of resolutions introduced by him on Feb. 16, 1803, following Spain's withdrawal of the right of deposit at New Orleans and designed to embarrass the administration and provoke war with Spain, demanded the immediate seizure of the mouth of the Mississippi River, the fortification of its banks, and then negotiations for navigation advantages. In 1799, 1802, and 1808 he was Federalist candidate for governor of Pennsylvania, but the high tide of Jeffersonianism, his liberal religious views, and his refusal to canvass the state conspired in each instance to defeat him. From 1816 to 1833 he was president of the Pittsburgh select council, but otherwise he was not active in politics after 1808, his law practice and land speculations, which proved highly profitable, engaging his attention. He was distinguished for his polished manner, his legal learning, and his forensic ability, and displayed an independence of judgment which sometimes cost him political preferment. His wife, whom he married on Jan. 13, 1791, was Ann, daughter of George Woods, of Bedford, Pa. He died at Allegheny City, now a part of Pittsburgh, survived by one son.

[J. I. Brownson, *The Life and Times of Senator James Ross* (1910); Boyd Crumrine, *Hist. of Washington County, Pa.* (1882); Thomas Mellon, "Reminiscences of the Hon. James Ross," in *Western Pa. Hist. Mag.*, July 1920; *Annals of Congress*, 1794–1803; *Pa. Mag. of Hist. and Biog.*, XIII (1889), 4; *Biog. Dir. Am. Cong.* (1928); *Daily Morning Post* (Pittsburgh), Nov. 30, 1847.] J. H. P.

ROSS, JOHN (Oct. 3, 1790–Aug. 1, 1866), Cherokee chief, was born near Lookout Mountain, Tenn., the son of David and Mary (McDonald) Ross. His Indian name was Coowees-coowe or Kooweskowe. His father was a

Scotchman of Loyalist sympathies who had settled among the Cherokee at the close of the American Revolution, and his mother was also Scotch but of one-fourth Cherokee blood. He was taught at home by a private tutor and later attended the Kingston academy in Tennessee. In 1809 he was sent by the United States Indian agent on a mission to the western Cherokee, who had removed to what was then the wilderness region of Arkansas. During the War of 1812 he served as adjutant of a Cherokee regiment in the army of Andrew Jackson and fought in the battle of Horseshoe Bend against the Creeks. In 1817 he became a member of the national council of the Cherokee, and, made president of that body in 1819, he served until 1826. He helped draft the Cherokee constitution of 1827 and in that year was elected assistant chief. In 1828 he was elected principal chief of the eastern Cherokee and held this position until 1839. Many times he was in Washington with a Cherokee delegation to oppose removal. He became the leader of the Cherokee party opposed to westward removal, and, in spite of Major Ridge [q.v.] and the treaty party, he resisted the efforts of the federal government to force them to leave their fertile lands. After all his efforts had failed, in 1838–39 he led his people to their new home in what is now Oklahoma and helped make the constitution of 1839, uniting the eastern and the western Cherokee under one government. Chosen chief of this united Cherokee Nation in 1839, he held office until his death, though his right to it was disputed by the Southern wing of Cherokee and by the government of the United States for a time during the period of the Civil War. At the outbreak of the Civil War he sought to keep the Cherokee neutral but in October 1861 signed a treaty of alliance with the Confederacy, which was repudiated in 1863.

He was married in 1813 to a full blood Cherokee woman called Quatie, who died at Little Rock, Ark., in 1839 on the way to Indian Territory. In 1845 he was married to Mary Bryan Stapler of Wilmington, Del., a white woman of the Quaker faith who was many years his junior. She died in 1865. He was of aristocratic training and manner. His home near Park Hill resembled the "mansion houses" of the Old South and was surrounded by fields cultivated by his numerous slaves. When Northern troops invaded Indian Territory in 1862, he went to Philadelphia, which he continued to make his home. He died in Washington, D. C., where he had gone to assist in making the Cherokee treaty of 1866. He has had many violent critics as well as many warm defenders. That he had great ability as a statesman and diplomat cannot be questioned, and the fact that he was for nearly forty years the head of his nation is evidence that he possessed the confidence of a majority of his people.

[Papers in files of Office of Indian Affairs, Washington, D. C., and in possession of Univ. of Okla., the Okla. Hist. Soc., and various members of Ross family in Okla.; John Howard Payne MSS. in Newbury Lib., Chicago; A. H. Abel, *The Slaveholding Indians* (3 vols., 1915–25); R. C. Eaton, *John Ross and the Cherokee Indians* (1921); F. H. Hodge, *Handbook of Am. Indians*, pt. II (1910); Emmet Starr, *Hist. of the Cherokee Indians* (1921).]   E. E. D.

ROSS, LAWRENCE SULLIVAN (Sept. 27, 1838–Jan. 3, 1898), Confederate soldier, governor of Texas, was born at Bentonsport, Iowa. His father, Capt. Shapley P. Ross, and his mother, Catherine (Fulkerson) Ross of Virginia, moved to Texas about 1839, where Captain Ross was Indian agent. Young Ross was graduated from Wesleyan University, Florence, Ala., in 1859. He spent his vacations in service against the Comanche Indians on the Texas frontier, and was once dangerously wounded. In 1859 Governor Houston made him captain of a company of rangers employed to guard the border and to crush the Comanches. In one engagement he rescued a white woman, Cynthia Ann Parker, who had been captured at Parker's Fort in 1836 and who later became the mother of Quanah [q.v.]. Ross killed Chief Peta Nocona in a hand-to-hand combat. Gen. Winfield Scott then offered him a commission in the United States Army and Governor Houston made him an aide-de-camp with the rank of colonel. He entered the Confederate service as a private, was made major of the 6th Texas Cavalry in September 1861, and was promoted to the rank of colonel in May 1862. As a result of his skill in covering the retreat of General Van Dorn from Corinth, Miss., he was made a brigadier-general on Feb. 5, 1864. He returned, penniless, to his home in 1865 at the age of twenty-seven, with a long record of 135 military engagements behind him and facing the prospect of earning a livelihood on the Texas frontier. He engaged in farming with marked success in the Brazos bottom and soon bought a plantation, where he reared and educated his children.

He served two arduous years as sheriff of McLennan County, having been elected in 1873 when lawlessness in Texas was at its height. As a member of the state constitutional convention of 1875, he advocated a policy of retrenchment but urged long terms and adequate salaries for judges. As a state senator from 1881 to 1885, he supported the policies of Governors Oran Milo Roberts and John Ireland, 1827–1896 [*qq.v.*], for economy in government, improvement in elementary and higher education, and a stricter enforcement of the laws. During the two terms Ross served as governor, 1887–1891, Texas enjoyed unusual peace, progress, and prosperity. He led and advised the legislature in passing laws which prohibited dealing in cotton futures, enlarged the powers of the land commissioner, and closed the sale of public lands to corporations. A beginning was made in the regulation of railroads and in the fight for the railroad commission which was established during the administration of his successor. He was the first governor to occupy offices in the new capitol building.

Ross served as president of the Agricultural and Mechanical College of Texas at College Station from 1891 until his death. Governor Culberson offered him an appointment as railroad commissioner in 1895, and he accepted, but the news of his contemplated withdrawal from the college aroused such great opposition from friends and patrons that he reconsidered and declined the new office. His death resulted from an illness contracted from exposure while enjoying his favorite sport, fox hunting, on the Trinity River. He was buried in Waco and his funeral was attended by a crowd estimated at thirteen thousand people. He was married at Waco in 1859 to Elizabeth Tinsley. His widow and six children survived him. In his public life he made no pretense of being an effective speaker, but was endeared to Texans because of his common sense, patriotism, and inflexible honesty.

[Sinclair Moreland, ed., *Governors' Messages, Exec. Series, Archives and Hist. Dept., Tex. State Lib. Coll.* (1916); D. G. Wooten, *A Comprehensive Hist. of Tex.* (1898), vol. II; *House and Senate Jour.,* 1881–91; S. S. McKay, *Debates in the Texas Constitutional Convention of 1875* (1930); *Confed. Mil. Hist.* (1899), vol. XI; F. M. Clarke, "A Chapter in the Hist. of Young Territory," *Quart. of Tex. State Hist. Asso.,* July 1905; Elizabeth Brooks, *Prominent Women of Tex.* (1896), p. 67; *Houston Daily Post,* Jan. 4, 1898; *Dallas Morning News,* Jan. 6, 1898.]   S. S. M.

ROSS, MARTIN (Nov. 27, 1762–1827), Baptist clergyman, was born in Martin County, N. C., third of the ten children of William Ross, a Scotchman from Virginia. His childhood and youth were probably those of the normal farmer's son. Entering the Revolution as a boy, he served until its close. In January 1782 he joined the neighboring Baptist Flat Swamp Church. The next year he married Deborah (Clayton) Moore, widow of James Moore, and in 1806, Mary Harvey, widow of Miles Harvey, each of whom bore him children. Licensed to preach in 1784, he was pastor of Skewarkey, Martin County (1787–96), Yoppim, Chowan County (1796–1806) and Bethel, near Hertford on the road to Edenton (1806–27). Francis Asbury in 1804 found him "much thought of," left him "in great affection," visited him again in 1806 (*The Journal of the Rev. Francis Asbury,* 1821, III, 132, 189). Cool and competent Thomas Meredith (*post*) declared him "dignified," "chaste and instructive in his conversation," in all private relations "amiable and exemplary," a "mild and humane master," "a useful citizen," of a hospitality "plain but cordial and substantial," in his ministerial character combining "those qualities which were useful, rather than dazzling."

Without discouraging or undervaluing the remarkable emotional revivals of his day, Ross emphasized the formation of churches and the discipline of members, and in 1826 wrote the circular letter of the Chowan Association on discipline. While the lowly and illiterate were asserting themselves in loud and lengthy "sermons" and even sensible men were contending against pay for preachers, he openly deplored his early lack of formal education, read and reflected much, gave useful advice publicly to other preachers, and boldly argued on grounds of professional usefulness as well as Scripture that preachers ought to "live of the gospel" (circular letters, Kehukee Association, 1791, Chowan Association, 1809). Finding the Baptists of the Kehukee Association out of line with "that missionary spirit which the great God is so wonderfully reviving amongst the different denominations of good men in various parts of the world" (Hassell, *post*, p. 721), he promoted a famous meeting at Cashie Meeting-house (near Windsor) in June 1805, where the pioneering "Philanthropic Missionary Society" was formed. Three years later he was working for a "Meeting of General Correspondence," composed of delegates from the Kehukee and its daughter associations. His proposal (modified the next year to conform to the Virginia manner) led to a joint meeting of all North Carolina Associations each year from 1811 to 1820, with missions apparently the main interest. In 1826 he began working for a North Carolina Baptist State Convention, which he apparently intended should foster ministerial education as well as missions. Though ill health and domestic affliction blocked him in this endeavor, in 1830, under the immediate leadership of Thomas Meredith, his neighbor, friend, and successor at Bethel, the Convention was constituted. This powerful organization today recognizes him as its father.

[N. C. Chowan Baptist Association, *Minutes,* especially 1828, containing Thomas Meredith, "Memoir of Elder Martin Ross"; C. B. and Sylvester Hassell, *Hist. of the Church of God* (copr. 1886), which largely follows Lemuel Burkitt and Jesse Read, *A Concise Hist. of the Kehukee Baptist Asso.* (1803) and Joseph Biggs, *Concise Hist. of the Kehukee Baptist Asso.* (1834); J. D. Hufham, "The Baptists in N. C.," in *N. C. Baptist Hist. Papers,* July 1898; N. C. Baptist State Convention, *The Growth of One Hundred Years* (1930); G. W. Paschal, *Hist. of N. C. Baptists* (1930), vol. I.]   C. C. P.

ROSSER, THOMAS LAFAYETTE (Oct. 15, 1836–Mar. 29, 1910), soldier and engineer, was born on his father's farm in Campbell County, Va., the eldest son of John and Martha Melvina (Johnson) Rosser. When the boy was thirteen, John Rosser, experiencing reverses, emigrated to the sparsely settled Sabine River country in Texas. Here Thomas, working with his father and a few slaves in developing the frontier plantation, grew up; a stalwart youth, six feet, two inches tall, endowed with extraordinary strength and endurance. By rigid economies his parents sent him, at sixteen, to a school at Mount Enterprise, Tex. On July 1, 1856, he entered West Point, becoming a member of the five-year class that was graduated in May 1861 without him for, at the outbreak of the Civil War, he resigned. George A. Custer [*q.v.*], who entered in 1857, was an intimate friend.

Hastening South, Rosser was assigned to the Washington Artillery as first lieutenant, serving creditably at first Manassas. Promoted captain, he was severely wounded in May 1862 on the Peninsula. On his return to duty, General Stuart obtained his commission as colonel of cavalry, giving him the 5th Virginia Regiment, which he commanded brilliantly for fifteen months. Leading the van when Pope's headquarters were captured at Catlett's Station, distinguishing himself at second Manassas, South Mountain, and in many cavalry engagements, he abundantly demonstrated the abilities which caused Stuart to pronounce him "a fine artillerist as well as bold Cavalier" (*Official Records,* 1 ser., vol. XII, pt. 2, p. 737).

On May 28, 1863, he married Betty Barbara Winston, of Hanover Court-House, and in September, following the Gettysburg campaign, was promoted brigadier-general. Assuming command of the noted Laurel Brigade at Buckland Mills in October, he roundly defeated Custer, who thenceforth became his perennial rival. Rosser contributed decisively to the Confederate victory at Trevilian (June 11, 1864), and in October went to the Shenandoah Valley to command Early's cavalry. Largely outnumbered, he suffered defeat by Custer at Woodstock (Oct. 8). But though beaten again at Cedar Creek (Oct. 18), he kept his troops keen by independent operations, and was promoted major-general on Nov. 1, 1864. In December he raided New Creek, W. Va., taking 700 prisoners, 3,000 horses and cattle, and destroying the railroad shops at Piedmont. The following month, with 300 picked men, he crossed the snow-covered mountains and surprised and captured two entire regiments at Beverly, W. Va. After Pickett's defeat at Five Forks (Apr. 1, 1865), Rosser's division held the Southside Railroad open during the following night, and behaved with desperate valor throughout the subsequent retreat, twice successfully attacking pursuing Union cavalry and taking many prisoners. At Appomattox Rosser charged through the Union lines with two cavalry divisions and escaped to Lynchburg, thus avoiding surrender with Lee's army. He was captured, however (May 2), near Hanover Court-House.

Hard-pressed after the war to support his family, in 1871 Rosser found employment with the Lake Superior & Mississippi Railroad and in 1872 with the Northern Pacific. By ability and energy he soon became chief engineer of the latter, superintending construction to Livingston, Mont. In the Indian country his friendship was renewed with Custer, whose troops often guarded Rosser's surveyors. After a period as chief engineer of the Canadian Pacific (1881–86), Rosser, having acquired a competence, in 1886 purchased a fine property, "Rugby," near Charlottesville and became a gentleman farmer. Commissioned brigadier-general, United States Army, by President McKinley in 1898, he commanded a brigade of Northern volunteers at Chickamauga throughout the Spanish-American war. In 1905 he was appointed postmaster at Charlottesville, and was filling this office when he died. Two daughters and a son survived him. Rosser was a gifted cavalry leader of the audacious American school. Many of his operations deserve attentive study, while his courage and resolution throughout a stormy life compel enduring admiration.

[J. M. Hanson, "Thomas Lafayette Rosser," in *Cavalry Journal,* Mar.–Apr. 1934; W. N. McDonald, *A Hist. of the Laurel Brigade* (1907); H. B. McClellan, *The Life and Campaigns of Major-General J. E. B. Stuart* (1885); J. W. Thomason, Jr., *Jeb Stuart* (1930); C. A. Evans, ed., *Confed. Mil. Hist.,* III (1899), pp. 658–60; E. L. Wells, *Hampton and His Cavalry in '64* (1899); *War of the Rebellion, Official Records (Army),* 1 ser., esp. vol. XLIII, pts. 1, 2, and vol. XLVI, pt. 1; Frederick Whittaker, *A Complete Life of Gen. George A. Custer* (1876); letters to the author from Thomas L. Rosser, Jr., Malcolm E. Rosser, and from officials of the Northern Pacific and Canadian Pacific Railroads; obituaries in *Confederate Veteran,* Aug. 1910; *Times Dispatch* (Richmond), Mar. 30, 1910.]

        J. M. H.

ROSSITER, THOMAS PRICHARD (Sept. 29, 1818–May 17, 1871), historical and portrait painter, born in New Haven, Conn., was the son of Harry Caldwell and Charlotte (Beers) Rossiter and a descendant of Edward Rossiter, who came to America in 1630 and settled in Connecticut. He began the study of drawing and painting in New Haven under Nathaniel Jocelyn, and by the time he was twenty had taken a studio and begun the painting of portraits. In 1840 he sailed for Europe in company with A. B. Durand, J. F. Kensett, and J. W. Casilear. After studying six months in London and traveling through England and Scotland, he spent a year with Kensett in Paris, where he studied in a life class made copies in the Louvre. In the fall of 1841 he went with Thomas Cole by way of Switzerland to Rome; there he took a studio in the Via Felice and passed five consecutive winters studying in the museums and painting, his summers being given to travel in Italy, Germany, and Switzerland. After his return to America in 1846, he settled in New York, where, on Oct. 15, 1851, he married Anna Ehrick Parmly, and the same year, with Kensett and Louis Lang, moved into a new studio in Broadway which had been planned and built especially for them. In the spring of 1853, he again set forth on extended travels abroad and in December took a studio in Paris, where he stayed almost three years. He exhibited in the Salon of 1855 and received a gold medal. He had previously (1849) been elected to the National Academy of Design.

In the summer of 1856 he returned to New York and was kept busy painting portraits until October 1857, when he began several large historical compositions, notably his well-known "Washington and Lafayette at Mount Vernon, 1776," also called "Palmy Days," which was bequeathed to the Metropolitan Museum, New York, in 1905. This large painting, finished in 1859, depicts Washington in a dark blue coat and knee-breeches, standing on the veranda of his house in conversation with Lafayette. Mrs. Washington and Nellie Custis are seated at a table, with a little girl beside them; on the lawn is a boy with a colored nurse and two dogs. In the distance, beyond a line of trees, is the Potomac. The landscape part of the work was done by Louis R. Mignot [*q.v.*]. In 1860 Rossiter left the city and moved to Cold Spring, N. Y., a beautifully situated village on the east bank of the Hudson, where he lived in a house that he designed and constructed for his professional purposes. There he made another historical picture entitled "The Prince of Wales and President Buchanan with Other Dignitaries at the Tomb of Washington, 1860," now in the National Gallery of Art, Washington. The painter's other contributions to Washingtoniana are "Washington in his Library at Mount Vernon" and "Washington's First Cabinet." He devoted much time towards the end of his life to a series of pictures of the life of Jesus. In earlier years he had made a number of large biblical illustrations, such as "The Return of the Dove to the Ark," "The Jews in Captivity," "The Parting of Ruth, Orpha and Naomi," and "Rebecca at the Well," the last being in the Corcoran Gallery of Art, Washington. He died suddenly in 1871 at his home on the Hudson, leaving three children.

[H. T. Tuckerman, *Book of the Artists* (1867); H. W. French, *Art and Artists in Conn.* (1879); Samuel Isham, *The Hist. of Am. Painting* (1905); *The Metropolitan Museum of Art: Cat. of Paintings* (1926); *The Nat. Gallery of Art: Cat. of Colls.* (1922); *Cat. of Paintings in the Corcoran Gallery of Art* (1908); *Bull. of the Metropolitan Museum of Art,* Nov. 1905, p. 10; death notice in *N. Y. Daily Tribune,* May 19, 1871.]

        W. H. D.

ROSSITER, WILLIAM SIDNEY (Sept. 9, 1861–Jan. 23, 1929), statistician, publisher, was born at Westfield, Mass., the only child of Samuel E. Chadwick and Margaret Harvey (Rossiter). When the boy was five years old his parents were divorced, the mother being given custody of the child, and four years later his name was changed to that of his mother's father. His mother soon removed to Washington where she lived for many years with two unmarried sisters. The influence of a family friend, Julius H. Seelye, drew Sidney to Amherst College in 1880. After graduating (1884) he entered the business office of the *New York Tribune* and continued for sixteen years in newspaper work or publishing.

In 1900 he was given charge of printing and publishing for the Census Bureau, his duties being those of a liaison officer between the Bureau and the Government Printing Office. The appointment proved a turning point in his life. His new duties brought him into intimate contact with a group of statisticians who were interpreting the population statistics of the Census of 1900; this experience gave him what was virtually post-graduate training in economics and statistics; he wrote the reports on printing and publishing for the censuses of manufactures of 1900 and 1905, and in time the human significance of population statistics became perhaps his main intellectual interest. His lack of formal statistical training proved no handicap, for it emboldened him to go beyond the actual meaning of his figures. William Rush Merriam [*q.v.*], the director of the Census, leaned heavily on him, and Merriam's successor, Simon Newton Dexter North [*q.v.*], made him his chief clerk and acting director. Rossiter's management of the Census printing and his magazine articles on the subject led to his appointment in 1908 by President Theodore Roosevelt to investigate the increasing cost of government printing. His report (*House Document 974, 60 Cong., 1 Sess.*), besides contributing to the resignation of the Public Printer, made constructive recommendations which have influenced the subsequent administration of the Government Printing Office.

While superintending the publication of the names of heads of families recorded at the census of 1790, he prepared *A Century of Population Growth from the First Census of the United States to the Twelfth, 1790–1900* (Department of Commerce and Labor, Bureau of the Census, 1909), which contained an estimate of the proportion of English, Scotch, Irish, German, Dutch, and French blood in the population of the United States, based upon classification of families according to the stock indicated by the last name. Although he failed to allow adequately for the effects of translating or transforming foreign into English names and so overstated the proportion of English blood, he presented in this study an approximate solution of a problem previously thought insoluble, and his estimate in improved form is now used in determining immigrant quotas from European countries to the United States.

When Director North resigned, in 1909, as the result of a departmental controversy, Rossiter resigned also, and for some years thereafter divided his time between the drygoods business of R. H. Stearns & Company in Boston and the Rumford Press of Concord, N. H. The latter enterprise throve under his management until it absorbed all his energies. During the twenty years of his connection with it as treasurer, vice-president, and president, its employees increased ten-fold, the value of its capital twenty-fold, and the quality of its publication was equal to the best. In 1918 he persuaded the secretary of commerce to invite the American Statistical Association and the American Economic Association to cooperate with the director of the Census by appointing a joint advisory committee. Rossiter became its chairman and retained that post until his death. He had long

made his summer home in Vermont, first at Greensboro and later at Morgan, and in 1911 he printed "Vermont: an Historical and Statistical Study of the Progress of the State" in the *Publications of the American Statistical Association*. This had been planned as a state document and prepared with the cooperation of the federal Census Office. It was followed by several less technical articles and addresses, all contributing to the organization of state councils and the New England Council, which aimed to deal constructively with social and economic problems in that group of states. He was chairman of the New Hampshire Council and an active member of the New England Council. In 1922 he was president of the American Statistical Association and in this same year published *Increase of Population in the United States, 1910–1920* (Census Monograph No. 1). He was a loyal member of his college class, attended forty-eight of the annual reunions held for fifty years after graduation, and prepared and published the annual class record. On Oct. 21, 1891, he married Nellie C. Budd of New York; they had one child, a daughter. He died in Concord, N. H.

[Memorial volume containing Rossiter's published articles, placed by his class in the Amherst College Library; *Amherst Coll. Biog. Record* (1927); *Class of Eighty-four of Amherst Coll.: The Class Book* (1894); *Who's Who in America, 1928–29*; *N. Y. Herald Tribune*, Jan. 24, 1929; *Concord Daily Monitor* (Concord, N. H.), Jan. 24, 1929; personal acquaintance.]
W. F. W.

ROTCH, ABBOTT LAWRENCE (Jan. 6, 1861–Apr. 7, 1912), meteorologist, brother of Arthur Rotch [*q.v.*], was born and died in Boston, Mass. His father, Benjamin Smith Rotch, was a great-grandson of William Rotch [*q.v.*], the noted Nantucket merchant; his mother, Annie Bigelow (Lawrence), was a daughter of Abbott Lawrence [*q.v.*] of Boston, founder of the Lawrence Scientific School at Harvard. Rotch was therefore born to the possession of ample means and into a tradition of public service. He received his preliminary education from tutors and in private schools, then entered the Massachusetts Institute of Technology. Before his graduation in 1884 he conceived and carried into execution plans for the erection of an observatory on the summit of Great Blue Hill, ten miles south of Boston, for the study of weather phenomena. His purpose was to establish an institution free from official control, where investigation might be independent of prescribed duties and requirements. The building was completed by the close of 1884, and observations were begun Feb. 1, 1885. Rotch maintained the observatory at his own expense until his death in 1912, when he bequeathed it, with an endowment of $50,000, to Harvard University.

The study of cloud heights, directions, and velocities as carried on at Blue Hill is one of the best of American contributions to knowledge of the clouds. Rotch suggested the use of daily maps at local Weather Bureau stations, and defrayed the expenses connected with the issue of the first such map, at the Boston weather station in May 1886. An extensive traveler and an expert mountain climber, he visited and studied the equipment of nearly all European high-level observatories. He made the ascent of Mont Blanc six times, reaching the famous Vallot cabin five times and the summit thrice. He made two balloon ascensions from Paris, Nov. 12 and 14, 1889, in which modern instruments were used. On July 4, 1910, he took part in the International Balloon Ascensions at Strassburg.

He was much interested in the development of aeronautics, was one of the founders of the Aero Club of America, and also a prime mover and president of the Aero Club of New England and the Harvard Aeronautical Society. He was a firm believer in the ultimate success of flight through the air at a time when such belief was regarded as fantastic. He was a friend of Professor Samuel P. Langley [q.v.] and of the Wright brothers. These and others interested in aviation were welcomed spectators of the kite flights at Blue Hill in the late nineties. He was the pioneer in the United States in exploring the free air. In 1894 at Blue Hill he first used a kite to lift recording instruments; he was the first to obtain meteorological data by means of kites flown from the deck of a moving steamer (1901), by sounding balloons made the first observations in the United States at heights of five to ten miles (1904), and was the first to make trigonometric measurements of the flight of pilot balloons (1909). It was in large measure the success of his exploration of the free air that led Léon Teisserenc de Bort to found a private observatory for the study of dynamic meteorology at Trappes, near Paris, and, indirectly, led to the founding of the aeronautical observatory near Berlin under Richard Assmann. The important discovery by Teisserenc de Bort of the isothermal region, beginning about twelve kilometers above sea level in temperate latitudes, later named the stratosphere, may thus be considered in part a result of Rotch's work.

With Teisserenc de Bort in 1905 he cooperated in fitting out an expedition to explore the atmosphere over the tropical and temperate parts of the Atlantic Ocean, thus securing data which later were of great service in discussions of the best routes for transatlantic flying. With Andrew Henry Palmer he prepared and published *Charts of the Atmosphere for Aeronauts and Aviators* (1911), a first attempt at mapping the conditions of the upper air. He wrote two books, *Sounding the Ocean of Air* (1900) and *The Conquest of the Air* (1909), and contributed many papers to scientific periodicals; the bibliography of his publications comprises 183 titles. For more than a decade (May 1884–April 1895) he was associate editor of the *American Meteorological Journal.* He also edited the Blue Hill observations which after 1887 were regularly published in the *Annals of the Astronomical Observatory of Harvard College.*

Rotch was personally known to the leading meteorologists of Europe, for he made it a point to attend all meetings of the International Meteorological Committee, and on many occasions was the sole representative of the United States. His work was known and appreciated abroad more than at home. He was exceedingly modest, preferring to remain unnoticed, but always encouraging others and giving his assistants fullest credit. From 1888 to 1891 and from 1902 to 1906 he held the title of assistant in meteorology at Harvard, and in 1906 he became the first professor of meteorology there, in both these capacities serving without salary. For many years he was a trustee of the Massachusetts Institute of Technology and from 1899 was librarian of the American Academy of Arts and Sciences. Just before his death he was chosen as exchange professor for 1913 at the Sorbonne.

Rotch married, Nov. 22, 1893, Margaret Randolph Anderson of Savannah, Ga., a descendant of Thomas Jefferson. He was survived by his wife, two daughters, and a son.

[R. M. Lawrence, *The Descendants of Maj. Samuel Lawrence* (1904); Alexander McAdie, *The Founder of the Blue Hill Observatory* (1914); memoirs by R. DeC. Ward, in *Proc. Am. Acad. Arts and Sci.*, vol. XLVIII (1913), *Harvard Graduates' Mag.*, June 1912, and *Science*, May 24, 1912; Frank Waldo, "The Blue Hill Meteorological Observatory," *Pop. Sci. Mo.*, July 1901; *Quart. Jour. Royal Meteorological Society*, vol. XXXVIII (1912); *Who's Who in America*, 1912–13; *Technology Review*, May 1912; *Nature* (London), Apr. 25, 1912; *Boston Transcript*, Apr. 8, 1912.]
A. M.

ROTCH, ARTHUR (May 13, 1850–Aug. 15, 1894), architect, was born in Boston, the son of Benjamin Smith and Annie Bigelow (Lawrence) Rotch and brother of Abbott Lawrence Rotch [q.v.]. He was a grandson of Abbott Lawrence [q.v.] and a great-great-grandson of William Rotch [q.v.] of Nantucket. His immigrant ancestor on his father's side was an earlier William Rotch, who was in Salem before 1692 and went to Provincetown, Mass., in 1719, and whose son Joseph, moving to Dartmouth, on Buzzard's Bay, in 1765 to become a whaler, was one of the founders of the town of New Bedford. Arthur was educated at Mr. Dixwell's school in Boston and then at Harvard, from which he was graduated in 1871. He had long been interested in architecture, and in the fall entered the school of architecture of the Massachusetts Institute of Technology, where he remained two years, leaving to go to Paris and enter the École des Beaux Arts. In Europe he spent a leisurely period of almost seven years, traveling and studying not only architecture but painting—water color and decorative—as well. During this time he is said to have had charge of part of the restoration and redecoration of the château of Chenonceaux. Shortly after his return to Boston, he formed, in 1880, a partnership with George T. Tilden. Rotch and Tilden's work, which was principally domestic and ecclesiastical, comprised large houses in Boston, Washington, Bar Harbor, and Lenox, and the Churches of the Messiah and the Ascension in Boston, and of the Holy Spirit in Mattapan, Mass. It also included the art museum at Wellesley College, the Rindge Manual Training School at Cambridge, the gymnasium of Phillips Exeter Academy at Exeter, N. H., and public libraries at Bridgewater and Groton, Mass., and Eastport, Me. Rotch married, Nov. 16, 1892, Lisette de Wolf Colt, with whom he took an extended trip abroad. He had been for some time troubled with severe rheumatism, and the European trip did not help him; a trip south in the winter of 1893–94 was equally fruitless. He died the following summer at his summer home in Beverly, Mass.

Rotch is important for reasons far more significant than his own architectural work, which is often tentative and inconclusive. It is true that it is frequently more polished, more advanced than other work of the time, which was still trying vainly to follow the creative genius of H. H. Richardson [q.v.] and achieving for the most part only a pallidly picturesque incoherence; Ventfort Hall, at Lenox, is notably good Jacobean for the early nineties, and the Mattapan church, in the mid-eighties, remarkable in its attempt to achieve both academic polish and simple, direct picturesqueness. But Rotch's most important contribution was to the taste of his time and to architectural education. A man of large means, he stinted neither time nor money in aiding his beloved profession. He

was a trustee of the Boston Museum of Fine Arts (incidentally, an accomplished water colorist and a frequent exhibitor both in Boston and New York), and he was influential in the founding of the Rotch Traveling Scholarship endowed by his father in 1884 to enable draftsmen or architects under thirty who have worked two years in a Massachusetts office to have two years of study abroad. Moreover, he furnished the architectural library of Massachusetts Institute of Technology, and when the Harvard School of Architecture was founded in 1893 he financed its entire first year at his own expense. On his death he left $25,000 to the Boston Museum of Fine Arts and $40,000 to the school of architecture of the Massachusetts Institute of Technology.

[Daniel Ricketson, *The Hist. of New Bedford, Bristol County, Mass.* (1858); Z. W. Pease, "Arnold's Garden," in *Old Dartmouth Hist. Sketches*, No. 48 (1919), and Julia W. Rodman, "Samuel and Elizabeth Rodman, Their Forebears and Associates," *Ibid.*, No. 54 (1926); C. H. Jones, *Geneal. of the Rodman Family, 1620 to 1886* (1886); *Vital Records of New Bedford, Mass.* (2 vols., 1932); *Vital Records of Nantucket, Mass.*, vol. II (1926); C. E. Banks, *The Hist. of Martha's Vineyard*, vol. III (1925); *Am. Architect*, May 5, 1920; *Mass. Inst. of Technology, Ann. Report of the President and Treasurer* for 1892 and 1895; *Eleventh Report of the Class of 1871 of Harvard Coll.* (1921); obituaries in *Am. Architect and Building News*, Aug. 18, 1894, and *Boston Transcript*, Aug. 16, 1894.]

T. F. H.

ROTCH, THOMAS MORGAN (Dec. 9, 1849–Mar. 9, 1914), pediatrician, first cousin of Arthur and Abbott Lawrence Rotch [*qq.v.*], was born in Philadelphia, the son of Rodman and Helen (Morgan) Rotch. His father came of a New Bedford family, being a great-grandson of William Rotch [*q.v.*]; his mother was a collateral descendant of John Morgan [*q.v.*], the founder of the University of Pennsylvania medical school. Rotch was graduated by Harvard College in 1870 and by the Harvard Medical School in 1874. During the last year of his medical course he served, as was customary at the time, as house officer at the Massachusetts General Hospital. On June 4, 1874, he married Helen, daughter of his uncle, William J. Rotch of New Bedford. His internship was followed by two years of study abroad, particularly in Berlin, Vienna, and Heidelberg; he returned to Boston in 1876, a well-educated physician.

Rotch began at once the practice of pediatrics, a "specialty" unknown before his time; no other physician in the United States had yet attempted to limit his practice to patients in the first two years of life. Entering boldly into a field where the death rate was highest, he established in 1881 and became medical director of the West-End Nursery and Infants' Hospital, the first hospital in the United States to admit only patients within so restricted an age limit. As early as 1878 he began teaching pediatrics at the Harvard Medical School. The faculty of that institution were soon impressed by the value of his studies and in 1888 a chair of Diseases of Children was founded with Rotch as the incumbent. He was made a full professor in 1893; his title was changed to professor of pediatrics ten years later, and he held the latter position until his death. His book, *Pediatrics: the Hygiene and Medical Treatment of Children,* one of the first to be written on that branch of medicine, was published in 1896.

Rotch realized, early in his career, that the high death rate of infants was largely due to bad nutrition. He soon devised a "percentage" method of artificial feeding (*Archives of Pediatrics,* August 1887) based on a careful estimation of the caloric value of milk. Varying the formula of cow's milk to meet the requirements of the infant and compounding a product free from impurities, he placed the feeding of infants upon a scientific basis. Later he used the Röntgen ray as a means of studying the bone development of growing children, and in 1910 published *Living Anatomy and Pathology: the Diagnosis of Diseases in Early Life by the Roentgen Method.* He was a member of many medical associations, and served as president of the American Pediatrics Society in 1891. His work was recognized abroad and in 1902 he addressed the British Medical Association on American methods in the modification of milk for infants (*British Medical Journal,* Sept. 6, 1902). His paper led to the establishment of a milk laboratory in London, and in 1903 Rotch was appointed consulting physician to an infants' hospital in that city.

Rotch's only child, a son, died in 1902, shortly after graduating from Harvard College, and on Apr. 18, 1903, in consideration of the gift of a fund raised by the father's friends to provide a new building, the name of the West-End Nursery and Infants' Hospital was changed to Thomas Morgan Rotch, Jr., Memorial Hospital for Infants. The new building, erected on the grounds of the Harvard Medical School, was completed in the year of Rotch's death.

[J. C. Warren, in *Harvard Graduates' Mag.,* June 1914; *Tenth Report of the Class of 1870 of Harvard College* (1920); *Boston Medic. and Surgic Jour.,* Apr. 9, 1914; L. E. Holt, in *Archives of Pediatrics, 31:* 161, 1914; Abraham Jacobi, in *Trans. Am. Pediatrics Soc.,* vol. XXVI (1914); *Twenty-first Ann. Report of the West-End Nursery and Infants' Hospital, Now Thomas Morgan Rotch, Jr., Memorial Hospital for Infants, Jan. 1903–Jan. 1904* (1904); *Boston Herald,* Mar. 10, 11, 1914; *Boston Transcript,* Mar. 10, 1914.]

H. R. V.

ROTCH, WILLIAM (Dec. 4, 1734 o.s.–May 16, 1828), whaling merchant, was born in Nantucket, Mass., the son of Joseph and Love (Macy) Rotch. He was the grandson of William Rotch who was in Salem, Mass., before 1692. On Oct. 31, 1754, he married Elizabeth Barney, the daughter of Benjamin Barney of Nantucket. With his father he amassed wealth in the whale fishery, continuing at Nantucket after the elder man had removed to New Bedford, Mass. Although he suffered a loss of $60,000 by the Revolution, his abhorrence of war led him on one occasion to cast a large consignment of bayonets into the sea. British depredations afloat and ashore during hostilities threatened the very existence of the island town, until a committee led by Rotch obtained promises of future safety from the King's officers at Newport and New York, a procedure that brought about the impeachment of the delegation by the Massachusetts authorities for high treason, although they were not convicted. In 1783 Rotch's ship *Bedford* entered the Thames flying the American flag, probably the first display of "the rebellious stripes of America" in any British port.

When, after the Revolution, the American whale fishery was virtually ruined through the heavy duty imposed on sperm oil by Great Britain, he attempted to establish an enterprise in England. He had fruitless interviews to that end in 1785 with Pitt and Lord Hawkesbury, who refused concessions yet relented after the Quaker merchant had succeeded in founding a prosperous business in Dunkirk, France. When certain civil and religious questions affecting the Friends required decision by the French National Assembly Rotch's earnest plea before that body, where he persisted in wearing his hat, drew a friendly reply from Mirabeau. The subsequent Reign of Terror drove him back to America in 1794. When he was eighty he wrote a brief record of his experiences in these eventful years, *Memorandum Written by William Rotch* (1916 and in *New-England Historical and Genealogical Register,* July 1877–Oct. 1878). Meantime his son, William Rotch, Jr., had removed to New Bedford, where he engaged in maritime and other commercial ventures of an extensive character, and thither the father repaired to live in retirement but to contribute from his ripe experience an impetus to the whaling industry, in which New Bedford long stood preëminent. The Rotch ships had been known the world over. Their owner had made numerous friends among prominent merchants and men in public life in this country and abroad. To his imposing "Mansion House" came a stream of distinguished guests, including the Duc de la Rochefoucauld. A friend of the colored race, the wealthy merchant did not hesitate to dine with a negro ship captain. He was an influential factor in the Yearly Meeting of Friends and became a loyal patron of the Friends school in Providence, R. I., in later years the Moses Brown School. Tall and dignified, attired in Quaker garb, he commanded the profound respect of his townsmen, who admired his generosity and his liberal views.

[Autobiographical sketch, *ante;* manuscript copies of letters in Mass. Hist. Soc.; *Vital Records of Nantucket, Mass.,* vols. II, IV, V (1926–28); Augustine Jones, *William Rotch of Nantucket* (1901); Daniel Ricketson, *The Hist. of New Bedford, Mass.* (1858); R. W. Kelsey, *Centennial Hist. of Moses Brown School* (1919); C. E. Banks, The Hist. of Martha's Vineyard, vol. III (1925); birthdate from statement of birthdate in *Vital Records, ante,* vol. II, as 10th mo., 4th day, 1734.]
W. M. E.

ROTHERMEL, PETER FREDERICK (July 8, 1817–Aug. 15, 1895), artist, the last American painter in the art tradition of the Peales, Sully, and Inman, was born in Nescopeck, Luzerne County, Pa., the son of Peter Rothermel, a native of northwestern Pennsylvania and a descendant of early settlers. Young Rothermel received a common school education, supplemented, at the insistence of his father, by the study of surveying, but at twenty years of age, following his own inclination, went to Philadelphia and became a sign painter. A few years later, through the influence of a friend, James McMurtrie, he began the study of drawing under John R. Smith, but before the end of his first quarter of tuition, enrolled in the classes of the Pennsylvania Academy of the Fine Arts. He studied subsequently under Bass Otis [*q.v.*], the teacher of Inman.

For a time the young painter worked at portraits, but his first success came with the painting of "De Soto Discovering the Mississippi," which was purchased by the Art Union. Edward Carey, a patron, advised him to go abroad, but Rothermel refused to leave his old mother, and argued his conviction that all Americans went to Europe too early. In 1847 he became a director of the Pennsylvania Academy of the Fine Arts, and as chairman of its committee on education endeavored to raise the standard of its schools, urging the purchase of casts from Greek and Roman sculpture for use in the antique class, the opening of the library of the Academy to artists and students, and the inauguration of school prizes and public lectures on art. He was also active in the promotion of the Artists' Fund Society.

In 1855 Rothermel resigned his post, and the following year set out for Europe, traveling at his own expense, although James L. Claghorn, art connoisseur and later president of the Academy, urged upon him a list of fifty patrons for whom he might paint pictures. In London Rothermel made sketches of the actor, Edwin Forrest [*q.v.*], to be used in his painting, "King Lear," then journeyed through Belgium, up the Rhine, and across the Alps to Florence and Genoa. For two years he resided in Rome, completing "King Lear" and "St. Agnes," the latter bought by Count Conchilef. His "Virtuoso" went to St. Petersburg; a preliminary study for "King Lear," his "Rubens and Van Dyck," and his "Fountain Gen-net-z-zano" were bought by members of the Russian nobility. By way of Venice and Munich, Rothermel traveled back to Paris, where he exhibited in the Salon of 1859. Shortly afterward he returned to America.

His most ambitious canvas, "The Battle of Gettysburg," was begun only after three years of preliminary research and sifting of the conflicting stories told by participants in the battle; the actual painting required a year and a half, and the picture was completed in 1871. It represented Pickett's charge on the afternoon of the third day. This heroic work, exhibited at Chicago, was rescued from the great fire by a young artist who carried it to Pittsburgh. For some time it hung in Memorial Hall, Philadelphia; it was exhibited in London in the eighties, and was finally installed in the Hall of Trophies in the Capitol at Harrisburg, for which it had been ordered by the Pennsylvania legislature. Rothermel's work was colorful, though inclined to the photographic, and his compositions were filled with well-handled figure groups. He contributed to the major exhibitions of his day, including the Centennial Exhibition at Philadelphia in 1876. Many of his paintings, including "Paul at Ephesus," "The State House on the Day of the Battle of Germantown," "Desdemona," and "The Bather," are to be found at the Pennsylvania Academy of the Fine Arts.

He married Caroline, the daughter of John Goodhart of Philadelphia, and had three children. In 1877 he removed from Philadelphia to his country home, "Grassmere," near Linfield, Montgomery County, Pa., where he died eighteen years later.

[*Public Ledger* (Phila.), Aug. 16, 1895; *N. Y. Tribune,* Aug. 16, 1895; H. T. Tuckerman, *Book of the Artists* (ed. of 1882); C. E. Clement and Laurence Hutton, *Artists of the Nineteenth Century and Their Works,* vol. II (1879); J. D. Champlin and C. C. Perkins, *Cyc. of Painters and Paintings,* vol. IV (1887); *Catalogue of the Permanent Collection . . . Pa. Acad. of the Fine Arts* (1902); J. W. Jordan, *Encyc. of Pa. Biog.,* vol. VI (1916); Mantle Fielding, *Dict. of Am. Painters, Sculptors, and Engravers* (1926).]
D. G—y.

ROTHROCK, JOSEPH TRIMBLE (Apr. 9, 1839–June 2, 1922), physician, botanist, forester, was born in McVeytown, Mifflin County, Pa., the son of Dr. Abraham and Phoebe Brinton (Trimble) Rothrock and a descendant of Abraham Rothrock who emigrated from the Palatinate to Berks County, Pa., early in the eighteenth century. Prepared in the village school, Freeland Seminary (now Ursinus College), and Academia, a preparatory school in Juniata County, Joseph entered the Lawrence Scientific School at Harvard in 1860. Meanwhile a period spent for the sake of his health as axeman on the Philadelphia & Erie Railroad had given him a keen interest in botany and forestry, and through the kindly interest of William Darlington [*q.v.*], a distant kinsman, he was accepted by Asa Gray [*q.v.*] as a special student and assistant. At the outbreak of the Civil War he enlisted in the 131st Pennsylvania Infantry, and on July 1, 1863, was commissioned captain, 20th Pennsylvania Cavalry. He fought at Antietam and Fredericksburg, where he was wounded. Honorably discharged, June 6, 1864, he returned to Harvard, and received his degree of B.S. in July.

The following winter he spent at the medical school of the University of Pennsylvania, but in 1865–66, under appointment from the Smithsonian Institution, he accompanied the exploring expedition to British Columbia and Alaska headed by Robert Kennicott [*q.v.*] and Maj. Frank Pope. His plant collections were lost in the Fraser River, but his "Sketch of the Flora of Alaska" was published in the *Report* of the Smithsonian Institution for 1867. He received the degree of M.D. from the University of Pennsylvania in that year and immediately became professor of botany at the Pennsylvania State Agricultural College. In 1869 he moved to Wilkes-Barre, where he established a medical practice and was instrumental in founding the Wilkes-Barre Hospital, but hard work again undermined his health, and in 1873 he became botanist and surgeon to the government survey in Colorado, New Mexico, and California, under Lieut. G. N. Wheeler. His report (*United States Geographical Surveys West of the 100th Meridian*, vol. VI, 1878), enumerated and described 1,168 species belonging to 637 genera, representing 104 natural orders of plants. The plant genus *Rothrockia* and at least six species perpetuate his fame as a botanist.

After a year as principal of a young ladies' academy in Wilkes-Barre, he accepted a post at the University of Pennsylvania, where he was professor of botany from 1877 to 1904. In 1877, he was appointed Michaux lecturer on forestry

by the American Philosophical Society. In 1880, he spent nine months as a student at the University of Strassburg. Deeply impressed by the German forest-conservation policies, he came home dedicated to the task of arousing public opinion to the need of protecting the forests. He was one of the founders of the Pennsylvania Forestry Association and its president in 1886. In 1893, Governor Pattison appointed him to a commission to study the forests of Pennsylvania; and he was the author of its report. Following the submission of this document to the legislature in March 1895 the division of forestry in the state department of agriculture was created, with Rothrock as its first commissioner, and when in 1901 a separate department of forestry was created, he was again the first commissioner. This post he held until 1904, and remained on the advisory board after his retirement. He inaugurated the policy of purchasing lands at the head waters of rivers for flood control, established tree nurseries to facilitate reforesting on both private and public lands, organized the fire wardens, and founded the State Forest School at Mount Alto to train workers in the forest service.

Some of Rothrock's other interests are suggested by his book, *Vacation Cruising in Chesapeake and Delaware Bays* (1884). In 1880 he cruised to the Bahamas and the West Indies in his yacht *White Cap*, collecting valuable scientific material for the University. As early as 1876, he began to take delicate boys to the woods for camp life, and in time founded the School of Physical Culture in Luzerne County, Pa. In 1902, he opened an informal camp for tubercular patients on the State Forest Reserve near Mount Alto; it proved successful and in 1907 was put under the newly created state department of health. He married, May 27, 1868, Martha E. May, daughter of Addison and Elizabeth Shafer May, and they had five children. His associates describe him as a man small in stature, abounding in energy, and with great charm of manner. He wrote of himself in an autobiographical sketch, "I am an Episcopalian, and politically a Republican when my conscience will endure it" (Kelly, *post*, p. 213). He died at his home in West Chester, Pa., survived by two sons and a daughter.

[*Biog. and Portrait Cyc. of Chester County, Pa.* (1893); autobiog. material in address by Rothrock, *Bull. Chester County Hist. Soc.*, Sept. 27, 1913; "Exercises in Appreciation of Dr. Joseph Trimble Rothrock," *Ibid.*, Mar. 19, 1914; *A Tribute to Dr. Joseph Trimble Rothrock, by His Friends* (1923); H. A. Kelly, *Some Am. Medic. Botanists* (1914); J. W. Harshberger, *The Botanists of Phila. and Their Work*

(1899); *Who's Who in America*, 1922–23; *Public Ledger* (Phila.), June 3, 1922.]   M. P. S.

ROTHWELL, RICHARD PENNEFATHER (May 1, 1836–Apr. 17, 1901), mining engineer, editor, was born at Oxford, Ontario, son of the Rev. John Rothwell. The father was a native of County Meath, Ireland, where the family (probably originally Scottish) held large estates under a grant from William and Mary. He graduated from Trinity College, Dublin; became a clergyman of the established church; married Elizabeth Garnett of Athearn Castle; and emigrated to Canada. Richard entered Trinity College, Toronto, but after a year there transferred to the Rensselaer Polytechnic Institute at Troy, N. Y., and was graduated as a civil engineer in 1858. He then went to Paris and entered the Imperial (now National) School of Mines, where, two and a half years later, he received the degree of engineer of mines. After pursuing specialized courses at the mining academy in Freiberg, Saxony, he entered the employ of W. T. Henley, a manufacturer of wire rope and telegraph cable in North Woolwich, England, where he showed ability and firmness of character. In connection with the wire business he was in France for a time examining some copper deposits. Declining an offer to be assistant superintendent at the wire works in England because he did not wish to give up mining engineering, he returned to Canada and examined iron-ore lands for the English owners of the Bessemer-steel rights.

In 1864, at the age of twenty-eight, he came to the United States and opened an office as engineer at Wilkes-Barre, taking up work also at the near-by towns of Eckley and Drifton, the latter of which he surveyed and laid out. Much of his work was for the anthracite operators, but he also designed for the Hazard Manufacturing Company what was then the largest wire-rope-making plant in the world. The machinery showed ingenuity and novelty in invention, and remained in operation for many years. At his suggestion the first underground locomotives in the anthracite mines were adopted in 1869, near Mauch Chunk, Pa., by the Lehigh Coal & Navigation Company. Some of the maps which he made after topographical surveys in several states between Massachusetts and the Gulf were accepted by national and state geological surveys. On the subject of ventilation and fires in coal mines he wrote a number of articles for the *American Journal of Mining* (later *Engineering and Mining Journal*). These were based on his experience in connection with mine explosions, disasters, in which he had displayed personal courage and leadership, on one occasion being overcome by gas while leading a rescue party.

In 1871 Rothwell joined with Eckley B. Coxe [*q.v.*], Martin Coryell, and Rossiter W. Raymond [*q.v.*] in founding the American Institute of Mining Engineers. Perhaps the conception came from him; at all events he was chairman at the preliminary meetings in Wilkes-Barre. Despite his modesty he held at various times high office in the Institute, being president in 1882. He also contributed many technical papers to its published *Transactions*. His practice as a consulting engineer grew so rapidly that in 1873 he moved his office to New York and made long trips from there. The next year he joined Raymond as editor of the *Engineering and Mining Journal* and later took over its ownership from Raymond. For many years these two able and courageous editors maintained a high standard of technical journalism; their paper became the leading organ of the mining engineering profession and led the way to free publicity for technical improvements. They had a friendly disagreement over the question of the coinage of silver which led to Raymond's withdrawal as editor in 1890; thereafter he was a special contributor. Rothwell's somewhat positive views on silver were published in a book, *Universal Bimetallism, and an International Monetary Clearing-House . . .* (1893), which incidentally cost his paper some subscribers. As head of the Scientific Publishing Company, of New York, which pioneered in the exchange of technical information, he began issuing in 1893 a voluminous annual compilation called *The Mineral Industry; its Statistics, Technology and Trade*. This book set an example in liberalizing the publicity policy of the mining industry and in 1898 won its author the gold medal of the Société d'Encouragement pour l'Industrie Nationale de France. Rothwell's greatest service to the engineering profession was his intelligent and persistent emphasis on the need of American industrial corporations publishing their technical experience. A short time before his death he became president of the United Correspondence Schools of New York.

Among his inventions and improvements in American engineering practice were his wire-rope machine and its accessories, a cylindrical roaster for ores, a pressure-filter, a method of mining soft ore, coal-breakers for reducing anthracite, and methods of chlorinating gold ores. He was a member of many technical and professional societies, both in America and Europe. On May 29, 1862, he married Bertha Hillebrand of Baden, Germany; she and their daughter survived him. Shortly before his death Rothwell established, partly from money left by a business associate, Sophia Brauenlich, the Sophia Fund. The object of this Fund is the care of friendless girls under six years of age and the securing of their adoption by suitable persons.

[R. W. Raymond, in *Trans. Am. Inst. of Mining Engineers,* vol. XXXI (1901), with bibliog. of Rothwell's publications; *Engineering and Mining Jour.,* Apr. 20, 1901; *Biog. Record Officers and Grads. Rensselaer Polytechnic Inst.* (1887); *Bulletin de la Société d'Encouragement pour l'Industrie Nationale de France,* July 1898; *Who's Who in America,* 1899-1900; *N. Y. Times* and *N. Y. Tribune,* Apr. 18, 1901; dates of birth and marriage verified by office of the Sophia Fund.]

P. B. M.

ROULSTONE, GEORGE (Oct. 8, 1767-1804), the first printer in Tennessee, was born in Boston and probably learned his trade there. While still in his nonage he launched the *Salem Chronicle and Essex Advertiser,* which ran from March till August 1786. He is next heard from three years later, in Fayetteville, N. C., where he was employed on the *Gazette,* later the *North Carolina Chronicle.* When William Blount [*q.v.*] became governor of the Territory of the United States South of the Ohio, he foresaw the advantage of a newspaper favorable to himself and persuaded Roulstone to accompany him across the mountains to the new country. Since Knoxville, which was to be the territorial capital, was as yet hardly more than a name, Roulstone set up his press temporarily at Hawkins Court House (Rogersville) and issued there, Nov. 5, 1791, the first number of the *Knoxville Gazette.* It was a three-column, four-page sheet, published fortnightly, but because of the difficulty of obtaining paper and other supplies in the wilderness it was subject to variations in format and date of issue. Paine's *Rights of Man* was run as a serial in the early numbers. The first issue printed at Knoxville appeared Oct. 10, 1792. Roulstone was a man of more than ordinary capacity and judgment, and his paper made friends for himself and for Blount. Except during 1798, or a part of that year, he continued to publish the *Gazette* until his death early in 1804. As the territorial printer he produced the volume of *Acts and Ordinances of the Governor and Judges of the Territory of the United States South of the River Ohio* (1793); two volumes (1794-95) of the acts passed at the first and second sessions of the Territorial Assembly, and the journals of the legislature. After the admission of Tennessee as a state he continued as public printer until his death. Other issues of his press, known only from advertisements in the *Gazette* are: *A Sermon on Psalmody, Preached at Salem Church at the*

Opening of the Presbytery of Abingdon, October 12, 1786, by Hezekiah Balch, A.M., Pastor of Mt. Bethel Church, Greenville (1794); *The Sermon Given at Knoxville, February 25, 1794, in the Presence of the Governor William Blount and Assembly of the Territory South of the Ohio, by Samuel Carrick, A.M., Pastor of the Church in Knoxville* (1794); and *Toplady's Translation of Zanchius on Predestination* (1795). His most important production was the *Laws of the State of Tennessee* (1803). Roulstone was clerk of the Legislative Council, one of the five commissioners of the city of Knoxville, and postmaster of the town. To facilitate the delivery of his paper he also maintained a private post. He was a trustee of Blount College (later the University of Tennessee), of which Samuel Carrick [*q.v.*] was the first head. His widow, a daughter of Devereaux Gilliam of Nashville, was public printer for a few years after his death, and married William Moore, public printer in 1808, who continued the *Gazette.*

[See J. G. M. Ramsey, *The Annals of Tenn.* (1853; 1926); Wm. Rule, ed., *Standard Hist. of Knoxville, Tenn.* (1900); D. C. McMurtrie, *Pioneer Printing in Tenn.* (Springfield, Ill., 1931; reprinted from *Nat. Printer Journalist,* Nov. 1931); *Proc. Am. Antiquarian Soc.,* n.s., XXVIII (1918), 299, XXXV (1925), 87-89. A file of the early issues of the *Knoxville Gazette* is in the library of the Tenn. Hist. Soc.]

G. H. G.

ROUND, WILLIAM MARSHALL FITTS (Mar. 26, 1845-Jan. 2, 1906), journalist and prison reformer, was born at Pawtucket, R. I., the son of a Baptist minister, Daniel Round, and his wife, Elizabeth Ann Fitts. He attended the public schools and studied for a while at the Harvard Medical School, but ill health prevented his graduation. Brown University in 1892 bestowed upon him the honorary degree of master of arts. Shortly after his attendance at Harvard he entered upon journalistic work, being connected at different times with the *Boston Daily News,* the New York *Independent,* the *Golden Rule* (Boston), and other papers. In 1872 he was appointed United States commissioner to the world's fair to be held in Vienna the following year, and there had charge of the New England department. Five years later (1877) he married Ellen Miner Thomas, grand-daughter of Hon. Charles Miner [*q.v.*] of Wilkes-Barre, Pa.

Interested in plans for social betterment, Round was chosen in 1881 a member of the executive committee of the Prison Association of New York, and in 1882 became its corresponding secretary. Among the purposes of this body were the amelioration of conditions of prisoners, improvement in government and discipline of prisons (county, municipal and state), and assistance to released prisoners; it also possessed legal powers of inspection of county jails and prisons. Round threw himself into the work with persistence and vigor. His are among the most relentless and illuminating descriptions that have been written of the overcrowding, idleness, filth, and political corruption of county jails; and improvement followed his efforts. At the same time he gave strong support to movements for the indeterminate sentence, the development of systems of parole, establishment of suitable prison industries, and mitigation of severe physical punishments in penal institutions. He even advocated curtailment or abolition of the almost universal county jail—a proposal which not till later took the form, in a few states, of state farms for misdemeanants. In 1883 he assisted in the reorganization of the National Prison Association, the name of which was changed in 1908 to American Prison Association; for a few years he was its secretary.

In 1887 he was called by Frederick G. Burnham as advisor in connection with a plan for establishing a farm school for unmanageable boys, and was subsequently the virtual director of the Burnham Industrial Farm at Canaan, N. Y., for several years. He introduced the cottage housing system, and what was then called the "mill" system by which, through good conduct, extra privileges might be earned. In part, his ideas were drawn from the system established by Wichern at the Rauhe Haus near Hamburg and from that of F. A. Demetz at Mettray, France. Among the employees at Canaan, Round founded the non-sectarian Order of St. Christopher, as a training order for workers in public institutions. After leaving the Burnham Industrial Farm he lived for a while at College Point, Long Island, and there had charge of a small orphan asylum. Because of failing health he resigned his position as secretary of the Prison Association of New York in 1900.

Earlier in his life, under the pen name of Rev. Peter Pennot, Round had published several novels, among which were: *Achsah: a New England Life Study* (1876), *Torn and Mended, a Christmas Story* (copyright 1877); *Child Marian Abroad* (1878); *Hal, the Story of a Clodhopper* (1880); and *Rosecroft, a Story of Common Places and Common People* (1881). In the latter part of his life his work was in Boston, and there in 1903 he was associated with Edward Everett Hale [*q.v.*] in the publication of the *Lend a Hand Record*. His work was done in the pioneer days of the effort to reach a scientific approach to the problems of delinquent conduct, but many of his ideas have stood the test of later

social and psychological analysis. He died at Acushnet, Mass., survived by his wife; there were no children.

[Annual reports of the Prison Association of N. Y., 1882–1900, and especially the memorial notice in *Prison Asso. of N. Y., Sixty-first Ann. Report*, 1905–06; *Who's Who in America*, 1906–07; *Hist. Cat. Brown Univ.* (1905); N. R. Nichols, *Round-Rounds Geneal., Descendants of John Round of Swansea, Mass.* (1929); *N. Y. Daily Tribune*, Jan. 17, 1892; *Boston Transcript* and *N. Y. Tribune*, Jan. 6, 1906; names of parents from records of Brown Univ.] W. D. L.

ROUQUETTE, ADRIEN EMMANUEL

(Feb. 13, 1813–July 15, 1887), priest and poet, was born in New Orleans, a younger brother of François Dominique Rouquette [*q.v.*], and the son of Dominique and Louise (Cousin) Rouquette. When he was five, his father died, and when he was eight, he was sent to the Collège d'Orléans, but he frequently ran away to live with the Choctaw Indians in the back parishes. Later, to overcome his truancy and to perfect his neglected English, his mother sent him to Transylvania University in Kentucky. After her death, when he was sixteen, his guardian shipped him off to Paris, where he matriculated at the Collège Royal, but later went to the Collège Royal at Nantes, and finally graduated (1833) from the College of Rennes in Brittany.

He had always been moody, introspective, vacillating, a romantic dreamer and psychologically maladjusted, and upon his return to Louisiana he soon drifted back into a life with the Indians on Bayou Lacombe. Tradition says he fell in love with a beautiful Indian maiden, Oushola (the bird singer), and that grief over her sudden demise so prostrated him that he left the country. At any rate, he went back to Paris and began to study law. Fantastically unfitted for so practical a profession, he soon neglected his studies and divided his time between student dissipations and the courts, where he listened enthralled to the oratory of the great French *avocats*. At last, when overcome by homesickness and dissatisfaction with his futile mode of living, he was so impressed by the Lenten lectures of an eloquent ecclesiast, Father de Ravignan, that he collected a small library on church history and returned to New Orleans in 1836, intending to study. Soon, however, he left the city and went back to the Indians in St. Tammany Parish.

He continued to lead this rudderless life, writing occasional poetry for his own amusement, until, encouraged by the success in France of a small volume of verse by his brother Dominique, he sailed for Paris and published *Les Savanes* (1841), a collection of his own poems. It was enthusiastically received by French poets and critics, Brizeux, Barthélemy, Deschamps, and even Sainte-Beuve; while in England Thomas Moore hailed him as "the Lamartine of America." Despite this praise, he returned to New Orleans again, only to find it as hard as ever to adjust himself to his surroundings. In this restless mood he was easily persuaded by Abbé Perché that the church could afford him a refuge from his *mal de siècle.*" He began his studies with avidity and in 1846 took holy orders. Almost immediately he sprang into fame as an orator by reason of the eloquent sermons he preached in the St. Louis Cathedral of New Orleans, but his new duties complicated his life and he longed for solitude, pouring out his desire in a rambling, mystical book, *La Thébaïde en Amérique, ou Apologie de la Vie solitaire et contemplative* (1852). He had previously published in English, *Wild Flowers: Sacred Poetry* (1848).

During the late 1850's he preached a series of anti-slavery sermons which made him many powerful enemies. This was the last straw which made unbearable the burden of adjusting himself to life in a city, so he asked permission to devote himself to ministering to the Indians. He joined the Choctaws, whose entire confidence he won, and was christened by them "Chahta-Ima" (Choctaw-like). In time he built several small, crude wooden chapels in St. Tammany Parish. He still gave a great deal of time to writing, continued to contribute to *Le Propagateur Catholique,* and in 1860 brought out a long volume of mystical verse, *L'Antoniade, ou la Solitude avec Dieu,* in which he contended that all the accomplishments of genius were born of poverty and solitude.

During the Civil War the Indians took refuge in the deepest swamps and the Abbé kept them alive by bringing them food and quinine, through the Northern lines, in pirogues. Some years later, inspired by Châteaubriand, he published *La Nouvelle Atala* (1879), an account of the spiritual adventures of a preposterously idealized Indian maiden. Toward the end of his life he viciously attacked George W. Cable [*q.v.*], who had aroused the intense resentment of the Creoles by his books. Rouquette called his diatribe *Critical Dialogue between Aboo and Caboo* (1880), signed it with the pseudonym "E. Junius," and included a "poem" in the Creole dialect making charges against Cable that were both untrue and vulgar. It was a sign of his declining powers; in 1885, while at work upon a dictionary of the Choctaw language, he lost his reason and was taken to the Hôtel-Dieu in New Orleans, where he died—the last of the "Black robe" fathers—on July 15, 1887.

[E. L. Tinker, *Les Écrits de Langue Française en Louisiane au XIXe Siècle* (1932), with comprehensive bibliog.; J. A. Reinecke, "Les Frères Rouquette," *Comptes Rendus de l'Athénée Louisianais,* Jan., Apr., July 1920; J. W. Davidson, *The Living Writers of the South* (1869); Susan B. Elder, *Life of Abbé Adrien Rouquette* (1913), not very reliable; C. P. Dimitry, "The Rouquette Family," *New Orleans Times-Democrat,* Nov. 20, 1892, condensed in *Old Families of Louisiana* (1931), ed. by S. C. Arthur and G. C. H. de Kernion, A. N. De Menil, *The Literature of the La. Territory* (1904); *N. Y. Freeman's Jour.,* Aug. 6, 1887; *New Orleans Times-Democrat,* July 16, 1887.]

E. L. T.

ROUQUETTE, FRANÇOIS DOMINIQUE

(Jan. 2, 1810–May 1890), poet, was born at his parents' summer place on Bayou Lacombe, Louisiana. His father, Dominique, was a native of France, from near Bordeaux, who came to New Orleans about 1800, set himself up as a wine merchant, and married a Creole, Louise Cousin. Young Dominique played so much with the Choctaw children in the nearby Indian camps that he learned their language at an early age and could shoot a bow and arrow with the best of them; and as soon as his brother Adrien [*q.v.*] was old enough to walk he took him along on these excursions. At the age of seven the elder boy was sent to the Collège d'Orléans, where he stayed for five years and exhibited the lack of emotional control that is so often considered a peculiarity of poets. Then, at twelve, he crossed the ocean alone and matriculated at the Royal College of Nantes in Brittany.

In due course he graduated and in 1828 returned to New Orleans, but his relatives persuaded him to go to Philadelphia to study law in the office of William Rawle [*q.v.*], then the leader of the Pennsylvania bar. A dreamer and unconquerably indolent, he soon tired of this profession and went back to Bayou Lacombe to divide his days between idly wandering with the aborigines and writing occasional verse. He was forever falling in love, and then going to France to get over it. In 1839, during one of these visits, he published in Paris a thin volume of poems in praise of life among the Indians, which he called *Meschacébéennes,* the ancient name of Mississippi. Châteaubriand had created a vogue for this type of literature, and Rouquette's little book was an immediate success. Hugo, Béranger, Barthélemy, as well as lesser critics, praised it enthusiastically and predicted a future for its author.

He returned to New Orleans in the same year, and in 1846, married Laura Verret. He had wasted most of his patrimony on his gay trips to Paris and so, to make a living, began to write poems and articles for *L'Abeille* and *Le Propagateur Catholique,* and in time opened a boys' school in New Orleans. When this venture ceased to pay in 1849 he took his family to Fort Smith, Ark., and opened another school; but the citizens of that frontier town were more interested in having their sons learn how to fight Indians and ride wild horses than in having them taught to read and write. Rouquette was soon forced to convert the school into a grocery store, but he was so impractical that this too failed, and he went back to New Orleans in 1851. Meanwhile (1850), he had published a translation, *The Arkansas,* by J. B. Bossu, Rouquette's only work in English. In 1852 he opened still another school at Bonfouca, in St. Tammany Parish, where he made his older pupils teach the younger ones while he went away for two or three days at a time to smoke, read, and write poetry under the oaks of Matassa. This was his last attempt to support his family; his wife soon died of consumption, and his two sons were turned over to his nephew, Cyprien Dufour, to be reared.

In 1856 Rouquette published a second collection of poems under the title, *Fleurs d'Amérique.* The French critics received it as enthusiastically as they had the *Meschacébéennes.* Émile Deschamps wrote: "Your *Fleurs d'Amérique* have all the grace, all the perfume, all the freshness of their living models"; and most flattering letters arrived from Méry and from Eugène Guinot of *Le Pays.* For the rest of his life Dominique drifted without bag or baggage from the house of one relative to that of another, repaying hospitality with poems for birthdays, baptisms, and weddings, which he sang at the feasts. When he was older he wandered the streets of his city, in broken shoes and wrinkled, patched clothes, always with a blanket around his shoulders, a palm-leaf fan in one hand and a stick in the other. Sitting on someone's doorstep, he scribbled poetry on a piece of brown manilla paper and then found some friend to buttonhole on the corner, to whom to recite with flashing eyes the lines he had just finished. His many women relatives would walk blocks rather than meet him on the street, for he always insisted upon enveloping them in the folds of his musty old blanket as he kissed them and asked solicitously after the health of each member of their families. He never failed to present them with a grimy little caramel wrapped in yellow straw paper, a supply of which he carried in his pocket together with loose tobacco and his very rank pipe. Had he lived in the days of the troubadours when poets had patrons, he would have had fame and

riches; but born too late, he died in penury, even though his verses had been much praised by some of the best critics in France. On May 10, 1890, he was buried under the grass of Bonfouca.

[E. L. Tinker, *Les Écrits de Langue Française en Louisiane au XIXe Siècle* (1932); Alcée Fortier, in *Comptes Rendus de l'Athénée Louisianais,* July 1890; J. A. Reinecke, "Les Frères Rouquette," *Ibid.,* Jan., Apr., July, 1920; C. P. Dimitry, "The Rouquette Family," *New Orleans Times-Democrat,* Nov. 20, 1892; E. A. Alderman and J. C. Harris, *Lib. of Southern Lit.,* vol. X (1909); Charles Testut, *Portraits Littéraires* (1850); "Dominique Rouquette," *L'Avant-Coureur* (St. Charles Parish), Dec. 17, 1859, printing the letters from the French critics, Méry, Eugène Guinot, and Émile Deschamps; congratulating Rouquette on his *Fleurs d'Amérique.*]   E.L.T.

ROUSSEAU, HARRY HARWOOD (Apr. 19, 1870–July 24, 1930), engineer and naval officer, was born at Troy, N. Y., the son of William White and Jeanette (Parker) Rousseau. After graduating as valedictorian from the Troy High School he entered Rensselaer Polytechnic Institute and completed the civil engineering course in 1891. During the next seven years he engaged in structural engineering work in Albany, in Brooklyn, and with the Pittsburgh Bridge Company. In October 1898, he entered the civil engineer corps of the navy as lieutenant, serving in the Bureau of Yards and Docks, 1899–1903, and subsequently at the Mare Island Navy Yard, California. Being personally known by Secretary of the Navy Metcalf, a Californian, and by President Roosevelt, under whom he had occasionally served as aide, he was appointed chief of the Bureau of Yards and Docks in January 1907, with the temporary rank of rear admiral.

That same year the President made him a member of the new Isthmian Canal Commission headed by Lieut.-Col. George W. Goethals [*q.v.*]. On this commission he served until it went out of existence in 1914, after 1908 being in charge of the second division of the chief engineer's office with the title of assistant to the chief engineer. In this capacity he had special supervision of the "design and construction of canal terminals, including dry-docks, ship repair shops, piers, coaling plants, fuel oil plants, breakwaters, and floating cranes." Goethals, with whom he worked in perfect harmony, placed a high value upon his technical training, experience, and administrative ability, and considered him, together with Col. Harry F. Hodges [*q.v.*], one of his "indispensable" subordinates. The Navy Department "desired his return to duty at Washington, and on one occasion the Secretary of the Navy especially requested . . . his relief from duty on the Isthmus in order that the Navy Department might avail itself of his services" (J.

B. Bishop, *The Panama Gateway,* 1913, p. 182), but he remained at Panama until the terminal works were completed in 1916, within the estimated cost and time. Congress by special act, Mar. 4, 1915, authorized his advancement from lieutenant commander to rear admiral.

After his return from Panama he was a member of the commission on navy yards and naval stations, 1916–20, that made a study of the coasts of the United States with a view to locating naval and aviation bases. Goethals also secured his services for the Shipping Board, during the World War, and he was assistant general manager and head of the shipyard plants division of the Emergency Fleet Corporation from 1917 to 1919, with many additional naval duties as project manager in charge of expenditure of naval funds for improvements in shipyards, member of the government Munitions Board, and a member of the Port Facilities Commission. He was awarded the Navy Cross for "exceptionally meritorious service in a duty of great responsibility."

While acting on many important naval and other government boards, his chief post-war duty was as government receiver, 1924–27, during litigation over Naval Petroleum Reserve No. 1 (the Elk Hills suit), and subsequently as director of naval petroleum and oil shale reserves until his death. In this later period he was also chief coordinator of the budget, administering, under the director of the budget, all federal coordinating agencies, a duty which required great application and labor and is thought to have broken his strength. His death occurred on the steamship *Cristobal* en route to Panama for an inspection of the Panama Railway, of which he had been a director since 1907. His funeral services were held in St. Thomas' Episcopal Church, Washington, of which he was a vestryman, and he was buried in Arlington National Cemetery. During his canal service he published two articles on engineering work there: *The Isthmian Canal* (Government Printing Office, 1909), a paper presented at the twentieth annual session of the Trans-Mississippi Commercial Congress, and "Terminal Works, Dry docks, and Wharves of the Panama Canal" (*Transactions of the International Engineering Congress,* 1915, vol. I, pt. 2, pp. 371–432). He was married at Panama in 1908 to Gladys Fargo Squiers, daughter of Herbert G. Squiers, United States minister to Panama, and was survived by his widow and three sons. Of undoubted engineering ability, Rousseau has been characterized personally as a man of reserved yet kindly nature, keen sense of humor, and unusual social charm.

[F. T. Chambers, "Harry Harwood Rousseau," *Trans. Am. Soc. Civil Engineers,* vol. XCV (1931); J. B. and F. Bishop, *Goethals, Genius of the Panama Canal* (1930); *Who's Who in America,* 1930–31; *N. Y. Times,* July 25, 27, 1930.]   A. W—t.

ROUSSEAU, LOVELL HARRISON (Aug. 4, 1818–Jan. 7, 1869), soldier, congressman from Kentucky, was born near Stanford, Lincoln County, Ky., of inconspicuous parentage. His father, who had removed to Kentucky from Virginia, died in 1833 and left a large family with scanty resources. The boy managed to attend the common schools for a short time, but soon he was forced to the pounding of rock in the construction of the turnpike from Lexington to Lancaster. On becoming of age he settled in Louisville, where he took up the study of law, and, proceeding feverishly without the aid of a teacher for fourteen hours a day, he acquired a great deal of information but undermined his health. In 1840 he moved across the Ohio into Indiana and settled in Bloomfield, where he was admitted to the bar the next February. He served as a Whig in the state House of Representatives during 1844 and 1845. On the outbreak of the Mexican War he became a captain in the 2nd Indiana Infantry. He participated in the battle of Buena Vista and was mentioned for gallantry in the engagement. On June 23, 1847, he was honorably mustered out, and four days after his return he was elected to the state Senate. However in 1849, a year before his term of office had expired, he returned to Louisville. His constituency refused to let him resign, so theoretically he still served Indiana.

In Louisville he established a reputation as an able criminal lawyer. In 1855 he helped to quell the riot that broke out there, incident to the Know-Nothing movement. Five years later he was actively back in politics with a seat in the Kentucky Senate. So vigorous was his opposition to secession that he resigned from the Senate in 1861 and began to raise troops for the Union. To keep from violating the neutrality Kentucky had announced, he set up his training camp across the river from Louisville, in Indiana, and called it Camp Jo Holt. His efforts were largely responsible for saving the state for the Union. On Sept. 9, he became colonel of the 3rd Kentucky Infantry, and on Oct. 1 he was promoted to be brigadier-general of volunteers. He played a prominent part at the battle of Shiloh and later at Perryville so distinguished himself that he was promoted to be major-general of volunteers on Oct. 8, 1862. He fought in the Chickamauga engagement and also in the battle of Nashville. He took part in many minor activities in Alabama, Mississippi, and western Tennessee. He was an excellent soldier, handsome in appearance, and beloved by his men. In January 1865 the Radical element in Kentucky supported him for the federal Senate, and he was barely defeated by James Guthrie. A few months later he was elected to the federal House of Representatives by a majority of almost a thousand votes. Shortly before the meeting of Congress he resigned from the army, on Nov. 30, 1865. Forsaking his radicalism, within less than a month he was in the thick of the Reconstruction debates, boldly opposing the Freedmen's Bureau Bill and other legislation and policies that appeared to him extreme. As he listened to the vindictive speeches of his fellow members of Congress who had fought only with their tongues during the war, he lost his temper, and at times his better judgment, and made bitter comments. Josiah B. Grinnell, of Iowa, replied in a tone which greatly enraged him, and, upon the former's delay in offering an apology, in the corridors of the Capitol he beat the Iowan in the face with a cane. The House, urged on by Thaddeus Stevens, reprimanded Rousseau, whereupon he resigned his seat on July 21, 1866, and stood for reëlection (*Address of Hon. Lovell H. Rousseau to his Constituents, 1866*). His Kentucky constituency returned him, and he served until Mar. 3, 1867. The same month he reëntered the army and was made a brigadier-general with the brevet rank of major-general in the regular army and was soon dispatched to Alaska to receive that territory from the Russians. The next year he was summoned to Washington to testify in the Johnson impeachment proceedings. He arrived too late, and on expressing a desire not to be returned to Alaska he was put in charge of the department of Louisiana. He died in New Orleans the following year and was buried in the Arlington National Cemetery.

[*Am. Annual Cyc. . . . 1869* (1870); Lewis and R. H. Collins, *Hist. of Ky.* (2 vols., 1874); *Biog. Cyc. of . . . Ky.* (1896); F. B. Heitman, *Hist. Register and Directory of the U. S. Army* (1903), vol. I; *Ky. Statesman* (Lexington), Jan. 14, 1869.]   E. M. C.

ROWAN, JOHN (July 12, 1773–July 13, 1843), jurist, congressman and senator from Kentucky, was born near York, Pa., the son of William and Eliza (Cooper) Rowan. His father, having lost his modest fortune during the Revolution, removed to Kentucky about 1783 and settled at Louisville. Soon thereafter he removed to a site on the Green River, now called Calhoun, where he remained only for a short time before finally settling in Bardstown. There John received his formal education in the cele-

brated school of James Priestley [*q.v.*], before going on to Lexington to study law. He received his license in 1795 and, beginning the practice of his profession immediately, he became in time an able criminal lawyer and a celebrated orator. In 1799 he represented Nelson County in the constitutional convention that drew up Kentucky's second constitution, and five years later he became secretary of state under Gov. Christopher Greenup [*q.v.*]. In 1806, he was elected to Congress as a Republican from his old home, in spite of the fact that he was now living in Frankfort, in another district. When Aaron Burr sought his assistance in the court procedure in Frankfort in 1806, he refused on the ground that he was a congressman elect. The next year, when he entered the Tenth Congress, he moved a set of resolutions to bring about an investigation of the alleged Spanish intrigues of Harry Innes [*q.v.*], a federal judge in Kentucky. Rowan was made chairman of the committee of investigation but was unable to find evidence sufficient to warrant impeachment proceedings. From 1813 to 1817 he represented Nelson County in the Kentucky House, and in 1822 and 1824 he represented Jefferson County. In 1819 he was appointed to the court of appeals, the highest state court, but a year on the bench convinced him that the work of a judge was too confining, so he resigned in 1821. By this time his sympathy with the relief party had led him into a disagreement with the extreme conservatism that characterized the court. In 1823–24 he led the fight against the old court, though in the end it turned out to be futile. The state always reposed great confidence in his ability and integrity. In 1820 the legislature appointed him with John J. Crittenden [*q.v.*] to adjust the troublesome boundary dispute with Tennessee; and three years later it gave him and Henry Clay the task of protecting the state's interests in the complicated dispute with Virginia over the occupying claimants laws. In 1839 the United States made use of his services by appointing him on the commission set up to adjust the claims against Mexico. In the meantime, in 1824, the legislature had elected him to the federal Senate for the term from 1825 to 1831. While in this position he took a prominent part in its deliberations, directing his efforts especially toward amending the federal judiciary system and abolishing imprisonment for debt. He also took part in the Webster-Hayne debate.

His ability as an orator obtained for him the commission from the legislature to make the commemorative address on the battle of Tippecanoe, and his interest in history brought about in 1838 his election to the presidency of the newly formed Kentucky Historical Society, a position he held until his death. In further recognition, a new county was created and named for him. He died in Louisville, where he had made his home part of the time, but he was buried in the family cemetery near his Bardstown home, the famous "Federal Hill" of today, the home in which he entertained Lafayette and many other celebrated people, and where tradition erroneously holds that Stephen Collins Foster wrote "My Old Kentucky Home." He married Annie, the daughter of William Lytle, federal surveyor-general and large landholder in Ohio, and the aunt of William Haines Lytle [*q.v.*]. They had eight children.

[Lewis and R. H. Collins, *Hist. of Ky.* (2 vols. 1874); W. E. Connelley and E. Coulter, *Hist. of Ky.* (1922), vols. I, II; *Biog. Encyc. of Ky.* (1878); *Biog. Cyc. of the Commonwealth of Ky.* (1896).]

E. M. C.

ROWAN, STEPHEN CLEGG (Dec. 25, 1808–Mar. 31, 1890), naval officer, was born near Dublin, Ireland, of Protestant parents, and was named for his maternal grandfather. His father's name was John Rowan. Having been severely burned at an open fire in a Wexford hotel, where the family stopped en route to America, Stephen was left with his grandparents, and was ten years old when he joined his parents, brother, and sisters at Piqua, Ohio. He was appointed a midshipman in February 1826, while studying at Oxford, Ohio, and made his first cruise on the *Vincennes*, 1826–30. This sloop was the first American man-of-war to circumnavigate the globe. After two years at New York on a revenue-cutter, he spent four years in West Indies waters as passed midshipman and master on the schooner *Shark* and the sloop *Vandalia*. The *Vandalia* received news of the Dade massacre, at Pensacola, hurriedly provisioned the ship for three months, and sailed for Florida to cooperate in the Seminole War. Rowan subsequently commanded dangerous boat expeditions on the Withlacoochee River, in Charlotte Harbor, and on Miakka River.

He was promoted to the rank of lieutenant in 1837 and the following year was ordered to the coast survey. He served from 1841 to 1844 in the *Delaware* on the Brazil and Mediterranean stations, and in July 1845 became executive officer of the *Cyane* on the Pacific Station. News of imminent war with Mexico reached the squadron at Mazatlán, and the *Cyane*, under Capt. S. F. Du Pont, proceeded to Monterey where it cooperated with Commodore Sloat in the capture of the city on July 7, 1846. Rowan was ordered to build earthworks, blockhouse,

and stockade, a task which would have presented unlimited difficulties for many a seaman, but which he accomplished quickly and effectively. He was then ordered to take a detachment of marines and seamen and occupy San Diego where the *Cyane* blockaded the port until provisions were exhausted. She later sailed for San Francisco and then returned to San Diego, where Rowan, commanding a battalion of seamen and marines, joined the army under Stockton and Kearney. He fought in the battles, Rio San Gabriel and the Mesa, and helped to retake Los Angeles. Later at Mazatlán, he led a boat expedition to San José to relieve Lieutenant Heywood's detachment, besieged by Mexicans and nearly starved. During the ten years following the Mexican War, he served two tours of duty as ordnance inspector at the New York navy yard, commanded the supply-ship *Relief*, and the receiving-ship *North Carolina*. He was made commander on Sept. 14, 1855.

At the beginning of the Civil War, he was in command of the steam-sloop *Pawnee*, which supplied the chief defense of Washington during Lincoln's inauguration, and cooperated in the unsuccessful attempts to relieve Fort Sumter, and to burn the Norfolk navy yard. In May 1861 he directed against the batteries at Aquia Creek the first shot fired from a naval vessel in the war. The *Pawnee* joined Stringham's squadron in August and helped to capture two forts and about 600 men at Hatteras Inlet. Rowan's most distinguished service was rendered on Feb. 8, 1862, when, commanding a flotilla of nondescript vessels in the North Carolina sounds, he cooperated with General Burnside in the capture of Roanoke Island and destruction of a Confederate gunboat. The next day he made a dashing attack at Cobb's Point on the Pasquotank River, destroyed the fort and captured or routed the Confederate squadron, and took both Elizabeth City and Edenton. He assisted the army, on Mar. 14, to capture New Bern, taking seven small forts mounting thirty-four guns. He was promoted to the rank of captain on July 16, 1862, and the same day, as a reward for his gallantry, was made a commodore. He next commanded the *New Ironsides*, South Atlantic Blockading Squadron, and was under fire fourteen times in Charleston harbor from July 18 to Sept. 8, 1863, being struck 164 times. In August 1864, he was detached to command for two months all naval forces in North Carolina sounds and he was then placed on waiting orders. On July 25, 1866, he was promoted to rear admiral.

He was in command of the Norfolk navy yard, 1866–67, Asiatic Squadron, 1867–70; and the New York navy yard, 1872–76; governor of the Naval Asylum at Philadelphia in 1881, superintendent of the Naval Observatory in 1882, and president of various important naval boards. He was commissioned vice admiral on Aug. 15, 1870, and retired in 1889. He died at the Ebbitt House, Washington, D. C., and was buried in Oak Hill Cemetery, Georgetown, beside his wife, Mary (Stark) Rowan, born in Norfolk, Va., whom he had survived about fifteen years. Their only child who lived was Maj. Hamilton Rowan of the United States Army. The elder Rowan published his recollections of the Mexican War in the *Proceedings of the United States Naval Institute*, volume XIV, 1888.

[Letter of Mar. 20, 1931, from Capt. Stephen Clegg Rowan, U. S. Navy, a grandson; autobiographic memoranda and official papers, Naval Records and Library, Navy Dept.; *War of the Rebellion: Official Records (Navy)*, 1 ser., vol. VII; L. R. Hamersly, *The Records of Living Officers of the U. S. Navy and Marine Corps* (4th ed., 1890); S. C. Ayres, *Sketch of the Life and Services of Vice Admiral S. C. Rowan* (1910); J. T. Headley, *Farragut and Our Naval Commanders* (1867); *Evening Star* (Washington, D. C.), Mar. 31, 1890.]   C. L. L.

ROWELL, GEORGE PRESBURY (July 4, 1838–Aug. 28, 1908), advertising agent, publisher, was born at Concord, Essex County, Vt., the son of Samuel and Caroline E. (Page) Rowell, and a descendant of Thomas Rowell, a seventeenth-century emigrant from England. When he was thirteen, his family settled on a farm near Lancaster, N. H., where he was entered in Lancaster Academy. During the winters of 1854–56 he taught school and "boarded round." In 1856 he secured a job in a Boston store, but lost it in the panic of 1857, and returned to teaching. The next year he started collecting bills for the *Boston Post*. Soon he began to sell advertising space in the paper, and was earning $14.00 per week when, on Sept. 1, 1862, at Lancaster, he married Sarah Burnside Eastman.

Rowell's first independent enterprise was the introduction in Boston of a scheme of theatre program advertising which he had noted in New York. The success of this plan encouraged him in 1865 to launch an advertising agency with his friend Horace Dodd. Net profits for the first year were five times the capital of $2,000 which the partners had invested in equal shares. Their success was due to Rowell's novel list system whereby columns of space, engaged from country weeklies by the year, were retailed to advertisers at $100 for a one-inch advertisement inserted four times in 100 papers. He soon sold out the Boston office to Dodd and set up the new firm of George P. Rowell & Company in New York, Apr. 1, 1867. Since the "list system" was by that time widely imitated, he credited the immediate success of his new venture more largely to his unique reputation for prompt payment to publishers and his assumption of responsibility for collecting from advertisers. He placed large quantities of patent medicine and lottery advertising, and at one time originated and unsuccessfully advertised Ripans Tabules, which, though advocated for various ills, were a dry form of a common household remedy—rhubarb and soda—sold at a fabulous price. In later years, however, his views changed, and he extolled "Truth in Advertising" campaigns. In 1869 *George P. Rowell and Company's American Newspaper Directory* first appeared, listing geographically and by class 5,411 United States publications and 367 periodicals in Canada. The second edition, in 1870, was considerably more ambitious, including brief histories of over fifty well-known advertisers, and an "American Newspaper Rate-Book," but the following year the simpler form was resumed and continued with slight variations until the final edition in 1908, when it was absorbed by *N. W. Ayer & Son's American Newspaper Annual*. The most significant result of its publication was the deflation of false circulation figures formerly customary among publishers.

In 1871 Rowell decided to take four months of vacation every year, and did so almost invariably the rest of his life. He had sold a quarter interest in the business to Charles Nelson Kent, a boyhood friend who proved an able partner. At the Centennial Exhibition in Philadelphia, 1876, he erected for public use a building to house the eight thousand or more newspapers donated regularly by their publishers during the period of the fair. In 1880 he bought "Prospect Farm" near Lancaster, N. H., and for six years seldom visited his office. His activities during this time included an unsuccessful campaign for the state legislature, the founding of the Percy Summer Club as a fish and game preserve, and a money-losing experience as the owner-editor of the village newspaper.

At Boston in 1866 Rowell and Dodd had started a house organ called the *Advertiser's Gazette* which was continued in New York until sold in 1878 to an unsuccessful publisher who had soon discontinued it. On July 15, 1888, Rowell began the publication of *Printers' Ink,* a journal for the advertising trade. Though soon imitated by many other publications, it remained a leading periodical in its field, and representative of the best long-time interests of advertising. It fought with the Post Office Department in the interest of equitable rates for advertisers and publishers, advocated better ethics among advertisers and agencies, and successfully promoted in 1911 the statute against misleading advertising which was later adopted by a number of states.

In the autumn of 1890 Rowell was divorced by his first wife, by whom he had had one daughter, and on Jan. 27, 1891, he married Mrs. Jeannette (Rigney) Hallock, daughter of Thomas Rigney of New York City. He sold his business to his employees in 1892, was forced to resume control some years later to avert bankruptcy, and sold out finally in 1905. In that year he wrote his reminiscences in a series of fifty-two informal papers, published weekly in *Printers' Ink*, and later in book form under the title, *Forty Years an Advertising Agent* (1906). His health broke during a trip to Switzerland and Egypt in the winter of 1907–08, and in August following, at Poland Springs, Me., he died.

[G. P. Rowell, *Forty Years an Advertising Agent* (1906); Roland Rowell, *Biog. Sketch of Samuel Rowell and Notices of Some of His Descendants* (1898); *Who's Who in America, 1903–05*; *Daily Patriot* (Concord, N. H.), Aug. 29, 1908; *Printers' Ink,* Sept. 2, 1908; information as to certain facts from Rowell's daughter, Persis Eastman Martin.]   W. M., Jr.

ROWLAND, HENRY AUGUSTUS (Nov. 27, 1848–Apr. 16, 1901), physicist, son of the Rev. Henry A. Rowland and his wife, Harriet (Heyer), was born in Honesdale, Pa. His father, grandfather, and great-grandfather were all clergymen and graduates of Yale; his mother was descended from a New York family. The boy was sent to Phillips Academy, Andover, to be prepared for Yale College, but evinced so much greater interest in natural science than in literature and kindred subjects that he was permitted to enter the Rensselaer Polytechnic Institute at Troy, N. Y., instead. He was graduated with the degree of civil engineer in 1870. During the next two years he did some field work and taught natural science at Wooster University, Ohio; but in the spring of 1872 he returned to Rensselaer as instructor in physics, becoming assistant professor in 1874. In 1875 he was chosen by President Daniel Coit Gilman [q.v.] to become the first professor of physics in the new Johns Hopkins University. After a year in Europe, spent partly in purchasing apparatus and investigating laboratories and partly in the laboratory of Von Helmholtz at Berlin pursuing certain researches of his own which he had long had in mind, he assumed his academic duties in Baltimore.

In Rowland were combined to a marked degree the scientist's grasp of fundamental principles, the engineer's understanding of practical mechanics, mathematical aptitude, and manual dexterity. His greater contributions to experimental physics were of three kinds: those which involved distinctly original concepts, those concerned with the accurate measurement of certain physical constants, and those in which his engineering talent was most conspicuous. His first important investigation, carried on at Troy, was inspired by Faraday's researches and especially by his concept of magnetic lines of force. Rowland put the physical concept into mathematical language, deducing the consequences of his own theory and testing them by actual experiment. The resulting paper, "On Magnetic Permeability, and the Maximum of Magnetism of Iron, Steel, and Nickel," he sent to Clerk Maxwell in England, who had it published in the *Philosophical Magazine* of August 1873. This investigation provided the basis for subsequent study of both permanent and induced magnetization and the starting point for all calculations for the design of dynamos and transformers. A second important experiment grew out of a question which had occurred to Rowland in his student days, before he was familiar with Faraday or other writers on electrical theory; namely, whether a moving charged conductor would have an effect upon a magnet similar to that of an electric current. By direct experiment in the laboratory of Von Helmholtz during his winter in Berlin, 1875–76, he answered this question in the affirmative (*"Bericht betreffend Versuche über die elektromagnetische Wirkung elektrischer Convection,"* *Monatsberichte der Berliner Akademie,* Mar. 16, 1876). This experiment is of very great significance in connection with the modern theory of electrons.

Another notable contribution resulted from his interest in the study of the spectrum of the sun and the spectra of the elements. Dissatisfied with the cumbersome apparatus necessitated by the gratings of Fraunhofer and Lewis Morris Rutherfurd [q.v.], which were made on plane surfaces, he combined the principle of the grating with that of the concave mirror, eventually producing gratings ruled on concave surfaces and thus obviating many of the experimental difficulties inherent in the use of plane gratings. He was always interested in the mechanism of electric currents, as is shown by many of his early experiments, and it was in the course of testing some of his deductions as to the nature of a current that Dr. E. H. Hall was led to the discovery of what is called the "Hall Effect" ("Preliminary Notes on Mr. Hall's Recent Discovery," *American Journal of Mathematics,* 1879). The cause of terrestrial magnetism was another problem which attracted Rowland from early youth; he persistently believed that terrestrial magnetism is in some way connected with the rotation of the earth, and one of his last experiments was an attempt to discover whether a piece of matter in rapid rotation would give rise to a difference of potential.

In the field of measurements, he obtained values that are still accepted for the mechanical equivalent of heat (this he considered one of his principal achievements), the ohm, the ratio of the electric units and the wave-lengths of various spectra. When he first went to Johns Hopkins, he insisted upon the establishment and equipment of an adequate workshop in which the apparatus for original research could be produced, and not the least of his contributions to his science were the machines he himself devised. To produce gratings for spectrum analysis more accurate than any previously known, he designed a ruling machine with a screw from which, by a process he devised, errors and irregularities had been virtually eliminated; this was the fundamental part of the machine, but the other details were also finished with a skill almost inspired. His ability to foresee difficulties and guard against them was conspicuously evident in the design of this machine. As a young man, in the early seventies he made for himself a small direct-current dynamo with an original system of automatic regulation, and the existence of this machine was one reason why, in the decades that followed, certain fundamental patents on dynamos could not be secured in the United States. Consulted in regard to the installation of the electrical equipment at the Niagara Falls Power Plant, he became interested in the theory of alternating currents, and after months spent in working out the mathematical formulæ involved, felt himself fully equipped to undertake the design of almost any machine involving the use of such currents. He designed many types of measuring instruments, several of which were adopted for commercial use. He also devised a successful printing telegraph.

Rowland's teaching was less by precept than by example. Passionately interested in his own research, he paid little attention to most of the students in his laboratories, and was a severe critic of those who attracted his notice, though his ardor in itself was a stimulating influence to the talented. He was co-author with J. S. Ames of a textbook, *Elements of Physics* (1900). Outside the University, he found great pleasure in nature, and made hobbies of photography, fishing, sailing, and fox-hunting. He

was a useful citizen, fearless when public questions were involved. As a man, he was remembered by associates as "the embodiment of unselfishness, high ideals, patience and enthusiasm." On June 4, 1890, he married Henrietta Troup Harrison of Baltimore, who with two sons and one daughter survived him. He died in April 1901, after an illness of many months.

[*The Physical Papers of Henry Augustus Rowland* (1902) contains a biog. memoir by T. C. Mendenhall which is printed also in *Nat. Acad. Sci. Biog. Memoirs*, vol. V (1905). See also J. S. Ames, "Henry Augustus Rowland," *Johns Hopkins Alumni Mag.*, Jan. 1916; *Who's Who in America*, 1899–1900; H. B. Nason, *Biog. Record Officers and Grads. Rensselaer Polytechnic Inst.* (1887); *Science*, May 3, 1901; *Nature*, May 2, 1901; the *Sun* (Baltimore), Apr. 17, 1901.]

J. S. A.

ROWLAND, HENRY COTTRELL (May 12, 1874–June 6, 1933), physician, author and traveler, was born in New York City, the son of George and Maria Townsend (Durfee) Rowland. He was a descendant of Henry Rowland, who settled in Fairfield, Conn., in the seventeenth century, and of Thomas Durfee, who settled in Portsmouth, R. I., about 1660. After attending private schools in New York City and Stamford, Conn., and studying for one year at Williams College, he went to Yale and graduated from the Yale School of Medicine in 1898. After graduation he enlisted in the navy as an able seaman on the United States auxiliary cruiser, *Yankee,* and participated in the bombardment of Santiago; the next year he transferred to the army medical service as acting assistant surgeon on a hospital ship, made two voyages to the Philippine Islands, and took part in the insular campaign of 1898–1900. From 1900 to 1905 he practised surgery in New York City. In 1903 he published his first book, *Sea Scamps: Three Adventurers of the East,* a collection of eight short stories. These were followed in 1904 by a novel, *To Windward,* an entertaining, though crudely written story whose action was laid on board ship and in the wards of a city hospital. From that time on, for nearly thirty years, he was a prolific writer of articles, short stories, and novels of mystery and seagoing adventure. On June 22, 1910, he married Mary Fulton Parkinson, in London. When the outbreak of the World War found them living in Vermenton, France, Rowland offered his services to the Allies; for two years he was physician to the war sufferers at Vermenton and Accolay, and during 1916 director of the local military auxiliary hospital at Accolay. The next year he carried on publicity and propaganda for the Allies in the United States, and in 1918 acted as an accredited special agent of the intelligence department of the United States Navy and as war correspondent for *Collier's Weekly.* After the war he established his home in Washington, D. C., and resumed his practice of writing in the winter and traveling in the summer. He died in Washington, survived by his wife and two children.

Rowland's unquenchable zest for adventure shaped both his stories and his life. In 1905 he sailed as a surgeon aboard the *Endymion* in a transatlantic yacht race, went ashore for a few days, found France to his liking, and began a sojourn there that lasted fourteen years. In 1907 he and two friends crossed the English Channel in a motor boat, cruised inland across Europe through rivers and canals from the mouth of the Seine to the Black Sea, and were wrecked in a violent storm off the Bosporus (*Across Europe in a Motor Boat,* 1908). In 1924, with a friend, he sailed to Central and South American ports on a five-thousand-mile cruise in a ketch of his own design and construction, writing several serial stories while on board. These travels and his profession furnished him with the literary materials he most prized. He had a lively, vigorous style, and he acquired great skill in shaping and weaving incidents into plot, though he regarded the study of technique as belonging to the later years when the search for physical adventure becomes impossible (*Woman's Home Companion,* August 1925, p. 112). For Rowland, however, no quiet years in which to achieve a finished technique intervened between adventurous living and death.

[D. H. Hurd, *Hist. of Fairfield County, Conn.* (1881); W. F. Reed, *The Descendants of Thos. Durfee of Portsmouth, R. I.* (2 vols., 1902–05); *Obit. Record Grads. Yale Univ.,* 1933; obituaries in *N. Y. Times,* June 7, 1933, in *Washington* (D. C.) *Post,* June 7, 1933, and editorial and obituary in *Evening Star* (Washington, D. C.), June 6, 1933; *Who's Who in America,* 1932–33; *Bookman,* Oct. 1912.]   V. L. S.

ROWLAND, THOMAS FITCH (Mar. 15, 1831–Dec. 13, 1907), inventor, manufacturer, was born in New Haven, Conn., the son of George and Ruth Caroline (Attwater) Rowland. His first Rowland ancestor in this country is said to have been Henry, who was in Fairfield, Conn., as early as 1649; he was also a lineal descendant of Thomas Fitch [*q.v.*], a colonial governor of Connecticut. Thomas received his early education in New Haven and at the age of thirteen entered his father's grist mill as the miller's boy. Upon the construction of the New York & New Haven Railroad through New Haven a few years later, the grist mill was demolished and Rowland entered the employment of the railroad, becoming the first apprentice in the machine

shop. While in this service he fired the third passenger train that was sent over the railroad from New Haven to New York. In 1850 he gave up this work to accept an appointment as second assistant engineer of the steamboat *Connecticut,* plying between Hartford and New York; but when control of the company owning this vessel changed hands in 1852 and all of the employees were discharged, he obtained a job with the Allaire Works of New York, an old established engine-building concern. A year or two later Rowland left this company and in the succeeding six or eight years was variously employed about New York in the designing and construction of steamboat machinery.

In 1859, in association with Samuel Sneden, a prominent builder of wooden vessels, he established a business at Greenpoint, L. I., for the construction of wooden and iron steamships and for structural iron works. The first contract the new firm obtained was with the Croton aqueduct department for a wrought-iron water-pipe, 7½ feet in diameter and a quarter of a mile long. It was to be located on top of the high bridge over the Harlem River for the purpose of carrying water from the aqueduct to the new reservoir in Central Park. This work, requiring 450 tons of wrought-iron plate and 400 tons of castings, was successfully carried out. The partnership was severed in 1860 and Rowland thereafter continued business alone under the name of "The Continental Works." At the outbreak of the Civil War he began the manufacture of gun carriages and mortar beds for the navy department and fitted out most of the steamers purchased from the merchant service, which vessels took part in the capture of Port Royal and were known as the "Porter Mortar Fleet." In 1861 Rowland contracted with John Ericsson [*q.v.*] for the building of an iron-clad floating battery, afterwards known as the original *Monitor.* Upon its completion he built the monitors *Montauk, Catskill,* and *Passaic,* the double-turreted monitor *Onondaga,* and the light-draft gunboats *Cohoes* and *Muscoota.* In the 1870's he built a number of ferryboats for the Union Ferry Company, New York, and constructed steamboats for Cuban waters. He also began the design and manufacture of steam engines and boilers especially adapted for use in the oil industry, and was engaged in designing and constructing gas-manufacturing plants in various parts of the country. For many years he experimented in the art of iron and steel welding and about 1887 designed the process and apparatus used by his company in the manufacture of the Fox corrugated and Morison suspension furnaces widely used for many years in the internal furnace type of boiler. At the same time he incorporated his business as the "Continental Iron Works," and served as the president until his death. He married, in 1855, Mary Elizabeth Bradley of New Haven, Conn., and was survived by three sons. He died in New York City.

[J. L. Bishop, *A Hist. of Am. Manufactures* (1868), vol. III; *Trans. Am. Soc. of Mech. Engineers,* vol. XXIX (1908); *Trans. Am. Soc. of Civil Engineers,* vol. LXII (1909); *N. Y. Tribune,* Dec. 14, 1907; Patent Office records.]   C. W. M.

ROWLANDS, WILLIAM (Oct. 10, 1807–Oct. 27, 1866), clergyman and editor, was born in London, the eldest of the four children of Thomas and Mary (Jones) Rowlands. Both parents were natives of central Wales. After the death of his father, a thrifty milk dealer, in 1814, and of his mother five years later, William, the only surviving child, was cared for by relatives in Wales. If his formal education ended after four years of study at Ystradmeurig and Llangeitho, he had by then gained command of both English and Welsh. From 1824 to 1829 he taught school at Merthyr Tidfil and Pontypool, meanwhile preaching occasionally in Calvinistic Methodist chapels. He was not ordained, however, until 1832. Having come into a small inheritance, he gave up teaching in 1829 and bought a printing establishment, where, among other things, he issued a monthly Sunday-school paper of which he was editor. He married on Aug. 25, 1829, Ann Jacob of Cardiff, whose substantial dowry and his own sanguine temperament led him to overexpand his business activities. By the autumn of 1833 he was bankrupt. Misfortune crowded upon him; the church forbade his preaching; in September 1834 he lost his wife, and, eighteen months later, his only child. His reinstatement in the ministry was but partial solace for all his troubles. He was obliged to begin his life anew and America seemed to offer the fairest future.

Rowlands arrived in New York in the summer of 1836. Not yet thirty, vigorous and energetic, he was conscious of his ability both as preacher and as editor. At once he began preaching to the Welsh community in New York City. Here and in Oneida County, N. Y., he ministered for the rest of his life save for a two-year pastorate at Scranton, Pa. (1856–58). Less eloquent than some of his colleagues, he gained an abiding reputation among the Welsh-Americans for the clarity, the vigor, and the deep sincerity of his preaching. In his pastoral work he was equally successful, for his quick sympathy and ready understanding won him the confidence and affection of his parishioners. His greatest influence, however, was exerted through the religious press. In 1836 no Welsh newspaper or periodicals existed in America. Believing there was need for a religious publication among his countrymen, in January 1838 he issued the first number of *Y Cyfaill* ("The Friend"), a monthly periodical which survived until December 1933. Rowlands' intention to make his paper independent in both religion and politics proved impossible. Soon the Congregationalists and the Baptists founded religious periodicals of their own and *Y Cyfaill* then became the accepted organ of the Calvinistic Methodists. A Democrat who joined the Republicans only in 1861, Rowlands rigorously excluded partisan politics from his paper. Though opposed to slavery, he refused to support abolition, which Robert Everett [*q.v.*] was urging in *Y Cenhadwr*. He condemned the liquor trade roundly and continuously. Though *Y Cyfaill* in Rowlands' lifetime never reached a circulation of two thousand, its influence was deep and widespread. Through it he shaped the thinking of a large proportion of the Welsh-Americans.

Even his active work as pastor and editor did not exhaust his energies. Besides numerous pamphlets, including a short history of his denomination in America, he published a volume of sermons: *Dammeg y Mab Afradlon* (1860). He became a life member of the American Tract Society (1851) and a life director of the American Bible Society (1852). On May 17, 1838, he married Catherine Parry of Remsen, N. Y. By her he had thirteen children, of whom only five survived their father. His indefatigable activity continued almost unabated until his death in Utica.

[Howell Powell, *Cofiant—William Rowlands* (Utica, 1873); biog. material scattered through the first thirty volumes of *Y Cyfaill*; R. D. Thomas, *Hanes Cymry America* (Utica, 1872); *Utica Daily Observer,* Oct. 27, 1866.]   P. D. E.

ROWLANDSON, MARY WHITE (c. 1635–c. 1678), Indian captive and author, was born about 1635, probably in England, the daughter of John White, wealthiest of the original proprietors of Lancaster, Mass. About 1656 she married Joseph Rowlandson, the first minister of Lancaster, to whom she bore four children. For twenty years following her marriage, she led the hard, uneventful life of a frontier housewife; but on Feb. 10, 1675/76, during King Philip's War, the Indians attacked Lancaster, burnt the village, and carried away captive Mrs. Rowlandson and her three surviving children, of whom the youngest died from exposure shortly after. For eleven weeks, while the Indians wandered about in north central Massachusetts and southern New Hampshire in an effort to avoid the colonial forces, she remained a captive. She suffered, as the Indians did, from lack of food, but the prospective ransom and her skill in making shirts and knitting stockings apparently won her comparatively good treatment. On May 2, 1676, after considerable diplomatic bargaining in which the blusterings of the government probably counted for less than the influence of John Hoar (Shurtleff, *post,* and H. S. Nourse, *The Hoar Family in America,* 1899), she was returned to her friends for a payment of twenty pounds; soon afterward her two children were released. In 1677 the family moved to Wethersfield, Conn., where Mr. Rowlandson had been called as minister. After his death in 1678, the town voted his widow an "allowance of £30 per year so long as she remains a widow among us" (Stiles and Adams, *post,* p. 328). The town records fail to show how long the allowance was paid or the date of Mrs. Rowlandson's death.

The Soveraignty & Goodness of God, Together with the Faithfulness of His Promises Displayed; Being a Narrative of the Captivity and Restauration of Mrs. Mary Rowlandson was first published in Cambridge in 1682. Designed by the author "to be to her a memorandum of Gods dealings with her" and *"to declare the Works of the Lord,"* this was one of the most widely-read pieces of seventeenth-century prose. A London edition under a slightly different title appeared within a few months; apparently two second editions came out the same year in Cambridge, and some thirty editions and reprints have been issued since then. No first edition is known. Historians have praised the *Narrative* for its picture of Indian life (J. G. Palfrey, *History of New England,* vol. III, 1864, p. 183) and for "its pure, idiomatic and sinewy English" (M. C. Tyler, *A History of American Literature,* vol. II, 1878, p. 139); it illustrates as well the contempt felt by the colonists for the Indians and admirably fulfills its author's intentions, for Mary Rowlandson in even the darkest hours of her captivity was able to strangle the doubts of God's mercy that assailed her, to assert repeatedly her utter and submissive confidence in God, and finally to believe "as *David* did, *It is good for me that I have been afflicted"* (*Narrative,* p. 73).

[See C. H. Lincoln, ed., *Narratives of the Indian Wars,* 1675–1699 (1913); the excellent ed. of H. S. Nourse and J. E. Thayer, *The Narrative of the Captivity and Restoration of Mrs. Mary Rowlandson* (1903; reprinted in 1930 without bibliog.), a facsimile of a second ed. of 1682; Jos. Willard, ed., *Narrative of the Captivity and Removes of Mrs. Mary Rowland-*

son (1828). See also A. L. White, *Geneal. of the Descendants of John White* (2 vols., 1900); H. S. Nourse, "Mrs. Mary Rowlandson's Removes," in *Proc. Am. Antiq. Soc.,* n.s., vol. XII (1899), *The Early Records of Lancaster* (1884), and *Lancastria,* vol. I (1900); S. G. Drake, *The Old Indian Chronicle* (1867) and *Biog. and Hist. of the Indians of N. America* (7th ed., 1837); N. B. Shurtleff, ed., *Records of the Gov. and Company of the Mass. Bay,* vol. V (1854); H. R. Stiles and S. W. Adams, *The Hist. of Ancient Wethersfield* (1904), vol. I.]
                        L. H.

ROWSE, SAMUEL WORCESTER (Jan. 29, 1822–May 24, 1901), painter, illustrator, and lithographer, was born at Bath, Me., one of six children of Edward and Mercy (Blake) Rowse. The family, its name more usually spelled Rouse, is genealogically interesting, coming down from Capt. Augustus Rouse of the *Dunkirk* (concerning whose settlement in Boston see H. W. Foote, *Annals of King's Chapel,* vol. I, 1882, p. 233). Samuel was baptized June 23, 1822 (Records of the Winter Street Congregational Church, Bath). The family a little later moved to Augusta, where after common schooling young Rowse was apprenticed to a local engraver. This occupation brought him to Boston, where he learned lithography, probably in the shop of Tappan and Bradford (Peters, *post*). In the work of his early years in Boston there have been identified a portrait of Richard Fletcher, justice of the supreme court of Massachusetts, and several minor pieces delineated for Tappan and Bradford. Among his illustrations were those for Louise Chandler Moulton's *This, That, and the Other* (edition of 1856). A reticent, reserved man, who never married, Rowse had a brief stage experience, appearing in *King Richard III* at Boston. Convinced that his talent did not lie in that direction, he resumed the making of delicate, well-characterized crayon drawings through which he gained a national and international reputation. Among his familiar portraits are those of James Russell Lowell, Ralph Waldo Emerson, and Nathaniel Hawthorne. His studio for many years was in the old Studio Building, Tremont Street, where his closest friend and professional associate was Eastman Johnson [*q.v.*]. In 1872 Rowse visited England, where he became acquainted with John Ruskin, of whom he later said, "He wanted me to hold the brush while he painted" (Peters, *post*). Having moved to New York in 1880, Rowse made his home at Morristown, N. J., where he died after amassing a considerable estate. He was an occasional exhibitor in his later years, but his celebrity among collectors rests upon his early portraits.

[A MS. on the Maine Rouses, prepared by W. J. Rouse, M.D., was owned in 1931 by Miss Mary Pelham Hill, of Topsham, Me. Other sources are Bath, Me., Church Records, 1795–1829, compiled by Mary P. Hill and deposited in MS. at the New England Hist.

Geneal. Soc., Boston; H. T. Peters, *America on Stone* (1931); C. E. Clement and Laurence Hutton, *Artists of the Nineteenth Century* (1884); Theodore Bolton, *Early Am. Portrait Draughtsmen in Crayons* (1923); E. W. Emerson, *The Early Years of the Saturday Club, 1855–1870* (1918); *N. Y. Tribune*, May 26, 1901.]

F. W. C.

ROWSON, SUSANNA HASWELL (*c.* 1762–Mar. 2, 1824), novelist, actress, educator, was born in Portsmouth, England, of a family which produced several British and American naval officers and at least two other authors, her cousin Anthony Haswell [*q.v.*] and her brother, Lieut. Robert Haswell (F. W. Howay, *Washington Historical Quarterly*, April 1933). Her mother, Susanna Musgrave (or Musgrove), died giving birth to her daughter. When the child was about five, her father, Lieut. William Haswell, who was stationed in Massachusetts and had remarried there, returned to England for her; and the clearest recollection of her childhood was that of the stormy passage, ending in shipwreck, vividly narrated in her novel *Rebecca*. Her girlhood was happily spent at her father's home in Nantasket, where at ten she surprised their summer neighbor, James Otis, by her familiarity with Spenser, Shakespeare, and Homer and Virgil in Pope's and Dryden's translations. In 1775 her father's estate was confiscated and his family interned at Hingham and later Abington, until he was exchanged in 1778 and they all returned to England. In 1786, encouraged by the success of Fanny Burney and Harriet and Sophia Lee, she published her first novel, *Victoria*, dedicated to the Duchess of Devonshire and favorably noticed (January 1787) by the *Critical Review* and the *Monthly Review*. Later in the year, she married William Rowson, then in the hardware business in London and trumpeter in the Royal Horse Guards, a personable young man and a fair musician but of no great stability of character. Her next few works, *The Inquisitor or Invisible Rambler* (1788), *Poems on Various Subjects* (1788), and *Mary, or the Test of Honour* (1789), added little to her reputation. But early in 1791 (Vail, *post*) she produced the novel, *Charlotte, a Tale of Truth,* which was to make her famous. Supposedly based on an actual amour of her kinsman, Col. John Montrésor [*q.v.*], this book, sentimental and didactic, yet unusually unified and direct for her and treating a situation of universal appeal with genuine pathos, captivated the American fancy when reprinted in Philadelphia in 1794 and became the chief American "best-seller" before *Uncle Tom's Cabin,* passing through more than 160 editions before 1905. *Mentoria, or the Young Lady's Friend,* a collection of didactic tales and essays, came later in 1791, followed by *Rebecca, or the Fille de Chambre* (1792), largely autobiographical and second-best among her novels despite its disorderly plot. In 1792 William Rowson failed, and the family turned for support to the stage, in which Mrs. Rowson had already shown her interest by the versified critique, *A Trip to Parnassus* (1788). In the winter season of 1792–93 the Rowsons played in Edinburgh and other cities but were stranded when Thomas Wignell [*q.v.*], recruiting in England for his company at the New Chestnut Street Theatre, Philadelphia, met and engaged them. From the end of 1793 to 1796 they acted, mostly in minor parts, in Philadelphia, Baltimore, and Annapolis. For the Philadelphia company, Mrs. Rowson wrote *Slaves in Algiers,* acted June 30, 1794, and the musical farce *The Volunteers,* Jan. 21, 1795, and adapted Massinger's *The Bondman* as *The Female Patriot,* June 19, 1795. (For bibliographical details, see Vail, *post.*) Her appeal to contemporary interest and to American patriotic sentiment (shown in these plays and in her verse address, "The Standard of Liberty," recited at Baltimore, Oct. 29, 1795) aroused her fellow-countryman, William Cobbett [*q.v.*], to a coarse satire, *A Kick for a Bite* (1795), that led her to allude to him in the preface to *Trials of the Human Heart,* published later in the same year, as "a kind of loathsome reptile." In 1796 the Rowsons went to the Federal Street Theatre, Boston, for which Mrs. Rowson wrote a comedy, *Americans in England* (1796), first presented on Apr. 19, 1797, and later assigned to John Hodgkinson [*q.v.*], who performed it as *The Columbian Daughter, or Americans in England.*

In the spring of 1797 she left the stage to devote the rest of her life to conducting a select school for young ladies in or near Boston. In this career she was notably successful, furnishing her pupils with musical training under competent foreign instructors and infusing them with her own fine qualities of character. She did not relinquish her interest in letters, serving from 1802 to 1805 as editor of the *Boston Weekly Magazine,* to which she contributed in serial form her novel "Sincerity" (separately published as *Sarah, the Exemplary Wife* in 1813), poems, and the greater part of an essay series, "The Gossip." After 1805 she continued to write for the magazine's successor, *The Boston Magazine,* for *The Monthly Anthology and Boston Review,* and J. T. Buckingham's *New England Galaxy.* A collection of her poems and songs—more than thirty of the latter were separately published between 1794 and 1824—was issued as *Miscellaneous Poems* (1804). *Reuben and Rachel,* a very poorly organized historical novel tracing the fortune of certain descendants of Christopher Columbus through three centuries and numerous countries, appeared in 1798. Another novel, left in manuscript at her death and printed in 1828 as *Charlotte's Daughter, or The Three Orphans,* is a sequel to *Charlotte Temple,* in which Lucy, Charlotte's illegitimate daughter, narrowly escapes an incestuous marriage with her half-brother, a theme perhaps suggested by William Hill Brown's *The Power of Sympathy* (1789) and *Ira and Isabella* (1807). More than thirty editions, mostly under the title *Lucy Temple,* were issued. Most of her later publications, however, were textbooks or monitory works for young women.

Herself childless, Mrs. Rowson devoted a mother's care successively to her husband's younger sister, Charlotte; to his illegitimate son, William; and to at least one adopted daughter. In her later life, while her husband held a government clerkship, she was able to contribute to many philanthropic enterprises, serving as president of the Boston Fatherless and Widows Society. She died in her house in Hollis Street, Boston, Mar. 2, 1824. William Rowson survived her and remarried, dying at Boston in 1842.

[See esp. R. W. G. Vail, *Susanna Haswell Rowson, the Author of Charlotte Temple: A Bibliographical Study* (1933), an invaluable bibliog., and Elias Nason, *A Memoir of Mrs. Susanna Rowson* (1870), based in part on a memoir by her friend Samuel L. Knapp, printed in the preface to *Charlotte's Daughter* (1828). An obit. notice appeared in the *Evening Gazette,* Mar. 6, 1824. Other sources of value are J. T. Buckingham, *Personal Memoirs and Recollections of Editorial Life* (1852), vol. I, pp. 83–85; Eliza S. Bowne, *A Girl's Life Eighty Years Ago* (1887); Wm. Cobbett, *A Kick for a Bite* (1795); F. W. Halsey, ed., intro. to *Charlotte Temple* (1905); and John Spargo, *Anthony Haswell, Printer-Patriot-Ballader* (1925), which gives the best account of the Haswell family.]   M. E.

ROYALL, ANNE NEWPORT (June 11, 1769–Oct. 1, 1854), traveler, author, was born in Maryland. Her father, William Newport, may have been an illegitimate son of one of the Calverts (see letter of Lord Baltimore to Governor Sharpe from London 1767, Porter, *post,* p. 19), and all that is known of her mother is that she had relatives in Virginia named Anderson. After a wandering childhood, spent chiefly in frontier Pennsylvania, Anne returned to Virginia and entered in menial capacity the household of William Royall, scholar, gentleman farmer, Revolutionary veteran, and ardent Mason. Royall became interested in his dependent, undertook her education, and in 1797 was married to her. At his death, sixteen years later, he left her the bulk of his property, but after ten years of litigation, spent by her chiefly in the South, his

other heirs succeeded in breaking the will, leaving her penniless at the age of fifty-four. During the illness and poverty she suffered in the following months she was assisted by friendly Masons and, in her disappointing struggle for a government pension as wife of a Revolutionary officer, by no less an advocate than John Quincy Adams.

In 1824 she started out to earn her living by traveling over the United States and publishing accounts of her journeys. She was an ardent pro-Mason and anti-Evangelical, for which she suffered both adulation and assault. Her attitude against the Presbyterians led to her trial and conviction in Washington in 1829 on the trumped-up, obsolete charge of being a common scold. After this unpleasant experience she found it difficult to travel, so, aided by her life-long friend, Mrs. Sarah Stack, she embarked on the proprietorship and editorship of a small, independent newspaper in Washington. Her two papers, *Paul Pry* (Dec. 3, 1831–Nov. 19, 1836) and *The Huntress* (Dec. 2, 1836–July 24, 1854) ran in succession from 1831 to a few months before her death. She was a vigorous editor, noted for her ability to uncover graft in any department of government. She advocated the veto of the United States Bank charter, Sunday mail transportation, non-partisan tariff regulations, no nullification, sound money, tolerance for Roman Catholics, no union of church and state, territorial expansion, internal improvements, liberal appropriations for scientific research, and state rights in the matter of slavery. She attained a kind of unenviable fame throughout the country, many enemies, a few stanch friends. In 1848 her pension was at last awarded, but after various fees were paid it proved to be only a trifle. In her last years she was often miserably poor. She died at her home on B Street, now part of the grounds of the Library of Congress and was buried in the Congressional Cemetery.

Between 1826 and 1831 she published ten volumes of travels, of which the first, *Sketches of History, Life and Manners in the United States, by a Traveller* (1826) is probably in all respects the best. It was followed by *The Black Book, or a Continuation of Travels in the United States* (3 vols., 1828–29), *Mrs. Royall's Pennsylvania* (2 vols., 1829); *Mrs. Royall's Southern Tour* (3 vols., 1830–31), and *Letters from Alabama* (1830). All bear the faults of hasty execution and reveal the gaps in the author's early education, which her later wide reading never filled. She was given to personalities of doubtful taste, and the violent expression of both her sympathies and antipathies is often tiresome. Withal, she was a tireless traveler, a shrewd observer, a careful verifier of facts, and a strictly honest writer. Her own vigorous, aggressive personality pervades her work; she is always readable and nearly always reliable. There is scarcely a city or town of any importance in the United States of 1826–30 that her keen observant pen did not sketch. Her "pen portraits" include nearly 2,000 of the great and near-great of her day. She was the author of a novel, *The Tennessean* (1827), which in plot, execution, and characters is one of the worst ever written in America. She tried her hand at drama with a play, *The Cabinet, or Large Parties in Washington,* the text of which has disappeared, but which was given one performance at the Masonic Hall in Washington. Her works deserve to survive as valuable sources for the study of the social history of the United States. In her journalism as well she was always vigorous and straightforward, but often amateurish and ungrammatical. She was grossly personal, given to tirades against her opponents, and long praises of her benefactors. She was steadfastly loyal to her cause, or to anyone who befriended her. Her kindness to "fallen women" in an age without charity and her devastating generosity in her brief periods of prosperity show the violence of her likes and dislikes, and her sincere consistency in both. At once pathetic and admirable, the Miss Flite of the Capitol, with tongue and eyes that were a terror to any dishonest congressman, "Godless Anne Royall," yet with more true charity about her than the "saints" against whom she railed, she is a figure to be included in some lesser national gallery.

[S. H. Porter, *The Life and Times of Anne Royall* (1909), and in *Columbia Hist. Soc. Records,* vol. X (1907); Heber Blankenhorn, "The Grandma of the Muckrakers," *American Mercury,* Sept. 1927; R. L. Wright, *Forgotten Ladies* (1928); *Evening Star* (Washington), Oct. 2, 1854.]   J. H. B—h.

ROYCE, JOSIAH (Nov. 20, 1855–Sept. 14, 1916), philosopher and teacher, was the youngest child and only son of Josiah and Sarah Eleanor (Bayliss) Royce, who crossed the continent to California in the "gold rush" of 1849. Both parents were English by birth, the father having been born in Ridlington, Rutlandshire, in 1812, and the mother in Stratford-on-Avon in 1819. The father emigrated to Canada, the mother to the United States, both in childhood; and they met and were married at the latter's home in Rochester, N. Y. In 1848 they moved to eastern Iowa, the point of departure for their journey to California, which began on Apr. 30 of the following year. The little family, now including Mary, a child of two years of age, met with the adventures and risks characteristic of this great migration. They reached Council Bluffs on June 4, and Salt Lake City on Aug. 20. They lost their way in the Carson desert, and were forced to retrace their steps for many miles to the Humboldt Sink, but eventually, in a state of exhaustion, reached the Carson River at the foot of the Sierras on Oct. 12. Here they met a rescuing party of the United States Government Relief Company, abandoned their wagon and proceeded on muleback, camping in the open, and crossing the divide just in time to escape the first heavy snowfall of winter. They finally reached Weaverville, Cal., on Oct. 24, approximately six months from their date of departure. After a brief sojourn here and at Sacramento the family passed three years in San Francisco, where they arrived Jan. 1, 1850. After unsuccessful ventures in store-keeping and merchandising in the vicinity of Sacramento, a more permanent settlement was made in Grass Valley, Nevada County, a relatively populous and pleasant mining town in the foot-hills of the Sierras. A second daughter, Harriet, had been born in San Francisco, and a third, Ruth, during their subsequent wanderings. The fourth child and only son, Josiah, was born in Grass Valley on Nov. 20, 1855.

The record of this Odyssey was preserved in the diary of the mother, Sarah Eleanor Royce. She was a remarkable woman, combining a profound and vital spirituality with intellectual interests and attainments. Through many years of hardship and uncertain family fortunes, in an environment which tended to reduce life to elementals, she clung firmly to her faith and ideals and did what she could to preserve the standards of life to which she was accustomed. The young Josiah was indebted to his mother not only for his inheritance but also for his early education, religious and secular. Finding no adequate school in Grass Valley, she organized one and taught it herself, in her own house. When Josiah reached the age of eleven, however, the family returned to San Francisco, where he entered the Lincoln Grammar School, and in 1869, the Boys' High School. Here he was most fortunate both in his associates and in his teachers. A number of his classmates afterwards distinguished themselves in their several professions, among them Albert A. Michelson [*q.v.*], the celebrated physicist. The principal, Theodore Bradley, and many of his staff, were men of marked individuality; the spirit of the school was stimulating, its methods and curriculum were progressive. The young Royce, already an omnivorous reader, spent many of his out-of-school hours in the Mercantile Library. The extremely modest circumstances of his family life combined with his personal traits to limit his social contacts with his contemporaries, but even at this early age he showed remarkable intellectual gifts, especially in the field of mathematics, where he soon outstripped his teachers. After some further preparatory instruction in Oakland, he matriculated at the recently established University of California in Berkeley in the fall of 1871.

The influence of the California environment upon the growing boy was intellectual and moral rather than physical. For bodily activities, except walking, he had neither capacity nor taste. His mother and his three sisters protected him from any lessons which he might otherwise have learned from physical hardship. Nor did he acquire the pioneer's readiness and self-sufficiency in dealing with his fellows. In social situations he was timid, sensitive, and conscious of himself (to quote his own reminiscence) as "redheaded, freckled, countrified, quaint." At an early age he formed the habit of thoughtful solitude. But the influence of California was nevertheless deeply imprinted on his soul. His interest in its romance, and his memory of early experience, bore fruit in two books: *California . . . A Study of American Character* (1886), in the American Commonwealth Series; and his only novel, entitled *The Feud of Oakfield Creek* (1887). He judged himself to be a "born non-conformist," and California ripened this tendency. The majestic scenery with which he was surrounded in boyhood and youth encouraged the cosmic sweep of his imagination, and filled him with awe. In 1879, referring to his intention of dealing with problems of life, he said he would deal with them independently and reverently—"independently, because I am a Californian, as little bound to follow mere tradition as I am liable to find an audience by preaching in this wilderness; reverently, because I am thinking and writing face to face with a mighty and lovely Nature, by the side of whose greatness I am but as a worm" (*Fugitive Essays*, p. 7).

But while his genius and his circumstances combined to render him detached and shy, nevertheless (or perhaps for this very reason), he felt a wistful need of social relations; and the belief that a man's fullest development can be found only in the life of the "community" became the central article of his creed and a major topic in his philosophizing. The lack of an established social order in a pioneer community was calculated to call attention to the need of it. To California, also, Royce owed his profound Americanism. He never acquired the cosmopolitanism of eastern scholars, and his philosophical

development consists essentially in the interaction of his instinctive (and incorrigible) Protestantism and moral individualism with the pantheistic and esthetic doctrines which he acquired from his German teachers, Lotze, Schelling, Schopenhauer, Fichte, and Hegel.

The University of California of Royce's student days provided no instruction in philosophy, but Joseph LeConte, geologist and pioneer Darwinian, and Edward Rowland Sill [*qq.v.*], poet and essayist, were his beloved teachers. They supplied him with nourishing philosophical pabulum in the name of science and literature. At the same time, like other eager American youths of his generation, he read Herbert Spencer and John Stuart Mill for himself. But with his lively intellectual interest, his feeling for literature, and his exceptional memory, his education was mainly a voyage of discovery in which he himself supplied both the motive power and the guiding hand. He had discovered *Faust* and other literary classics in his high-school days, and had read widely in history. His graduation thesis on the theology of the *Promethus Bound* of Aeschylus (*California University Bulletin,* June 1875) illustrated the characteristically philosophical method of his studies, whatever their subject matter. It was to the friendly interest excited by the high quality of this thesis that the young scholar owed the opportunity of studying in Europe after receiving his bachelor's degree in 1875. He spent the next year mainly at Göttingen and Leipzig, where through the lectures of Lotze, Wundt, and Windelband, and through his studies of Kant, Schopenhauer, and others, his thought received a spiritualistic-idealistic impress which it never lost. In 1876 Daniel Coit Gilman, who had been the president of the University of California during Royce's undergraduate days, invited him to be one of the first twenty fellows appointed at the new Johns Hopkins University. Here he received the degree of Ph.D. in 1878, with a dissertation (read and approved by President Noah Porter of Yale) entitled, "Of the Interdependence of the Principles of Knowledge," and on the basis of examinations set by Prof. George S. Morris of the University of Michigan.

Royce's fellowship at the Johns Hopkins had been in literature, the field of his examinations for the doctorate had been the history of philosophy, together with German literature in the eighteenth and nineteenth centuries, and he began his teaching career as an instructor in English at the University of California, where he spent the next four years. This literary emphasis of his early studies and teaching colored his writings, his first literary ventures including critical essays on Schiller, Shelley, George Eliot, and Browning (republished posthumously in *Fugitive Essays,* 1920). But it was the philosophy of his authors which most deeply interested him. His permanent attraction to Schelling and others of the German Romantic movement was due to their union of philosophy and literature. In his teaching of rhetoric he found an opportunity of introducing logic, and of preparing a *Primer of Logical Analysis for the Use of Composition Students* (1881). He had long since found his vocation in philosophy, and he schooled himself in its technicalities by continuous reading and thinking. In an entry of his diary for July 25, 1880, he remarked: "The use of writing a diary is that every day vies with its neighbors in saying something for itself. A day like this that has nothing to say, is ashamed." He counted that day lost that did not see some step forward in his soul's progress toward speculative truth. His reading during this California period embraced a reëxamination of Kant and Hegel, together with a study of contemporary writers such as William James, Charles S. Peirce, Shadworth Hodgson, and the psychologists Wundt and Bain. He improved his knowledge of mathematics. He wrote copiously on philosophical subjects and provisionally draughted a systematic treatise to be called "Outlines of Critical Philosophy," or "The Work of Thought." In an article on "Mind and Reality," which appeared in *Mind* in January 1882, he announced his adhesion to the philosophical school of post-Kantian idealism and sketched several of his most characteristic doctrines.

In proportion as Royce grew in philosophical attainment he felt his isolation. At California he had no philosophical students to teach, and no philosophical colleagues to confirm his intellectual faith and criticize his ideas. In the summer of 1877 he had visited William James in Cambridge, and at a crucial moment had received encouragement to undertake the doubtful venture of philosophy. He heard James's lectures at the Johns Hopkins during the following winter, and he corresponded with him when he went to California. For the next thirty years the affectionate friendship of these two men conspicuously illustrated the philosopher's favorite theme of unity in difference. James began in 1880 to look for an opportunity for Royce in the East. Finally his own leave of absence for the year 1882–83 provided the opportunity of calling Royce to Harvard as his substitute. The probable absence of George Herbert Palmer in the following year made it possible that the appointment would be extended for two years. There was little prospect of permanence. But Royce took the risk, and with his wife, Katharine Head Royce, whom he had married on Oct. 2, 1880, and their eldest son, then an infant, he crossed the continent to Cambridge in the summer of 1882. At Harvard Royce remained during the balance of his days. He began his teaching with some misgivings, doubting his ability to enter into sufficiently "close relations" with his students. He soon earned however, the good opinion of his students, his colleagues, and of President Eliot. He was appointed to an assistant professorship in 1885, to a professorship in 1892, and finally, upon the retirement of George Herbert Palmer in 1914, to the Alford Professorship of Natural Religion, Moral Philosophy and Civil Polity.

During the earlier years of his career Royce's development was greatly influenced by his association with James. As James's substitute in 1882–83 he was obliged to teach psychology, even "advanced psychology." He also taught psychology at the Massachusetts Institute of Technology (in addition to his Harvard work), conducted experiments (on invention) in the Harvard psychological laboratory, took part actively in the work of the American Branch of the Society for Psychical Research, and in 1903 published his *Outlines of Psychology.* But the influence of his colleague and friend was much more central than this. In July 1879 James had published in *Mind* an article entitled "The Sentiment of Rationality," in which he undertook to analyze the motives which induce men to reason, construing thought as an expression of will and emotion. Royce, influenced by Fichte, Schopenhauer, and the Romanticists, found himself on common ground. He conceived his essay on "Mind and Reality" to be a sequel to James's "Sentiment of Rationality," and thought of James and himself as collaborators in inaugurating a new method of philosophizing, of which the cardinal principle should be the essentially active and creative character of the knowing mind. This partnership did not last long. It soon became clear that whatever they might say, James and Royce meant very different things. When James spoke of a "sentiment" of rationality or a "will" to believe, he referred to natural minds. To Royce, on the other hand, consciousness was a universal principle, governed by its own inward dialectical necessities. As early as 1883 he wrote down in his diary a criterion of truth which in slightly different terms he often reaffirmed. A given statement is true, he said, when "the contradictory of this statement would involve this statement itself." The mind thinks what, if it is to think at all, it cannot avoid thinking without contradicting itself. It is under this dialectical compulsion that the mind escapes the scepticism of the passing moment, and the relativities of a merely human experience—all of which is widely removed from James both in matter and in doctrine. For Royce the mind is absolutely compelled to affirm the being of an Absolute; for James the mind is doubtfully inclined to believe in a world of change and chance, where God is only one of many. On this issue they fought for decades, exchanging first words and letters, then articles, and finally books. The feud was inherited by their pupils. Royce the protagonist of monism, or the essential and necessary oneness of things, and James the friend of pluralism, or of manyness and differences, have became symbolic of long-lived and good-humored philosophical controversy. But though the breach was wide the affinities and connections were never wholly forgotten. Towards the close of their careers Royce was still building bridges such as "The Eternal and the Practical," or "absolute pragmatism," and inviting James to cross over; while James, though he still rejected monism, made it clear that the only monism that really tempted him was that morally "richer and thicker" variety provided by his colleague Royce.

The first of Royce's major philosophical works was *The Religious Aspect of Philosophy,* published in 1885, and summing up the philosophical tendencies and influences of his early years. He turns to religious problems because, as he tells us, these first "drove the author to philosophy." Having ceased long since to be connected with any "visible religious body," he does not pride himself on the fact (like the fox who lost his tail), but proposes to set forth a religious view of the world which, though it does not imply, is nevertheless consistent with, a more positive creed. The method of the book is a variant of the method of doubt, and the argument falls into two main parts. The first part is an appeal to the thinker to play the nobler part and "postulate" what is not given in experience. Common sense postulates an external world, science postulates the simplicity and orderliness of nature, hence why should religion not postulate that goodness at the heart of things which "satisfies the highest moral needs"? But in the second part of the argument the author supports postulate by proof. Doubt itself implies the possibility of error. What, then, is error, and what are its conditions? Error attaches only to judgments, and judgments refer to objects. They are erroneous only provided they are in some sense inadequate or inap-

propriate to their own objects, that is, to objects which they themselves select and consciously identify. The object referred to must be given, and the judgment entertained must be recognized as, relatively to that object, erroneous. But most human cognitive situations are incomplete, because their objects are not given. This is the case, for example, with one man's knowledge of another's mind, or with his knowledge of past and future. Since even in these cases his judgments are either true or false, there must be a more comprehensive knowing, embracing this man's judgment, but transcending his temporal and other limitations so as to embrace the missing objects. This universal knower, affirmer of all judgments, experiencer of all objects, and thus uniquely qualified to bring judgments and their objects together, is the famous "Absolute." Although this is only one of many ways of arriving at such a conclusion, it is Royce's most original contribution to its proofs. The general metaphysical implications are evident. They are idealistic, since all reality is essentially the act, idea, or experience of a mind; they are monistic, since there is one such mind to which all others are related as parts to whole, and which stands not only as the ultimate being of metaphysics, but as the object of worship and the standard of value.

In the next of Royce's constructive treatises these moral and religious implications assume a crucial importance. In 1895 he delivered before the Philosophical Union of the University of California an address on "The Conception of God." This was afterward published (1897) together with discussions of Royce's address by G. H. Howison, Joseph LeConte, and S. E. Mezes. To this volume Royce also contributed a supplementary essay on "The Absolute and the Individual," which contained a critical comparison of the Thomist and Scotist doctrines of the principle of individualism. Howison, expounding his so-called "personal idealism," attacked the monistic trend of Royce's thought as failing to provide for the autonomy of the moral individual, thus appealing to Royce against himself. For despite his argument for an all-enveloping mind, here reiterated and strengthened, Royce was not prepared to abandon, or even to disparage, the human prerogatives of freedom and responsibility. And yet how shall these prerogatives be reconciled with a metaphysical Absolute? In *The Conception of God* the author attempted to meet the difficulty by insisting that the principle of individuation is choice or preference, that the Absolute is an individual consisting ultimately in a sheer act of will, and that this Absolute Will is parcelled out among human beings, each of which wills independently within its own province.

At the same time that Royce was thus restating, amplifying, and applying his characteristic metaphysical doctrines he found time to give numerous public lectures, and to renew his literary interests. From these activities there resulted, in 1892, the most brilliantly written and the most widely read of his works, *The Spirit of Modern Philosophy* (see also his *Lectures on Modern Idealism* published posthumously in 1919). This book is, on the one hand, a work of historical narrative and exposition, distinguished by its imaginative sympathy, its playful humor, and by paragraphs of sustained eloquence. The author's beloved Romanticists, together with Kant, Hegel, and Schopenhauer, are treated with peculiar tenderness and insight. But the book serves also, on the other hand, to make clear Royce's own historical orientation; in particular, his view of the limits of science. By subordinating the "world of description" to the "world of appreciation," he argues the inadequacy of the new positivistic and evolutionary school, in which he, like all English and American students of his day, was widely read.

In 1899 and 1900 Royce delivered the Gifford Lectures at the University of Aberdeen, and these lectures in their published form, under the name of *The World and the Individual* (1900, 1901), constitute the most important of his systematic works. In the first volume the author pays his respects to rival philosophical tendencies, mysticism, realism, and "critical rationalism," the last serving as a sort of blanket designation for diverse forms of empiricism and materialism. Against all of these doctrines, affirming as they do that being is above or beyond experience, or a mere possibility of experience, Royce argues an unqualified idealism, according to which reality belongs exclusively to the conscious life of an all-enveloping mind. The constructive portion of the book gives to this characteristic doctrine a new and significant development. In *The Religious Aspect of Philosophy* Royce had used the term "thought" to designate the processes of the Absolute, while in *The Conception of God,* the emphasis had been shifted to "will." In the present book the term "purpose" plays a mediating rôle. Thought is essentially purposive. The key to its nature is found in the double meaning of ideas. An idea's "internal meaning" consists of the universals or ideal possibilities which constitute *what* is judged; its "external meaning" consists in the particular object to which it refers, and which constitutes that which is judged *about*. This object, while it lies beyond the idea, is embraced within mind as the experience to which the idea points as its own "fulfilment." The second volume of *The World and the Individual* is devoted to cosmological and practical applications. The author introduces the interesting speculation that the so-called unconscious parts of nature belong to minds whose "time-rate is slower or faster than those which our consciousness is adapted to read or to appreciate" (*Ibid.,* II, 240). The practical applications pursue the general line of thought already adopted in *The Conception of God.* The reality of the human individual must somehow be reconciled with the doctrine of the Absolute. This can be done, the author believes, by making the Absolute *consist* of human or other finite individuals; which it embraces, supplements, and completes, but does not supersede. Each finite individual makes his unique and indispensable contribution to the whole. But if this notion is to be adhered to consistently, it is evident that Royce is confronted by the ancient "problem of evil" in an aggravated form. Pain and sin, like everything else, make their contributions: what, then, becomes of the pity or remorse which condemns them? Royce's answer, the inevitable and universal answer of pantheism in its last line of defense, is that the supreme value of the world lies in moral conflict, struggle, and overcoming; and that what in the limited, finite view is reprobated, is in the higher view accepted as affording the necessary resistance to the moral will.

After 1900 Royce's interests developed in opposite but complementary directions—toward a more technical and specialized treatment of logic, and toward a more popular treatment of moral, social, and religious problems. Both of these tendencies reacted upon his central philosophical doctrines. Royce was one of the first Americans after Charles S. Peirce [*q.v.*] to enter the field of symbolic logic and the philosophical foundations of mathematics. He wrote a number of technical papers on these subjects and on the allied subject of scientific method, the most important being the "Principles of Logic," contributed to the *Encyclopædia of the Philosophical Sciences* in 1913 (original German edition in 1912); and "The Relations of the Principles of Logic to the Foundations of Geometry," published in the *Transactions of the American Mathematical Society,* vol. VI (1905). The effect of his logical and mathematical studies was to give additional emphasis and a more vigorous formulation to his favorite principle of non-contradiction, and to provide him with an interpretation of infinity. The difficulty of infinity was inherent in his system. Reality is a "self-representative" system, like the ideally perfect map which must contain itself. Every fact of experience is the fulfilment of a purpose; but this fulfilment is itself a fact which fulfils another purpose, and so on, *ad infinitum*. Such an endlessly repetitive process was regarded by F. H. Bradley and others as a vicious regress, which must somehow be escaped. To Royce, however, it signified the fact that reality is infinite, and infinite neither in the bad sense, nor in the edifying sense, but in the sense of modern mathematics. In the "Supplementary Essay," appended to the first volume of *The World and The Individual,* he gave a masterly exposition and philosophical interpretation of the views of Cantor, Bolzano, and others, who had defied infinity as a multitude or series having parts which may be placed in one-to-one correspondence with the whole; as, for example, the odd numbers may be placed in one-to-one correspondence with the positive integers.

Royce had always applied his philosophy to the concrete moral issues of his day (see his *Race Questions, Provincialism, and Other American Problems,* 1908). A series of public lectures on ethics, given before various audiences and finally in 1907 before the Lowell Institute in Boston, were published in 1908 as *The Philosophy of Loyalty.* The book had a wide appeal. Its central thesis is the salvation of the individual through loyalty to a cause. To escape a conflict of loyalties, the maxim of loyalty to one's own cause is supplemented by the maxim of "loyalty to loyalty," by which the loyal individual will indirectly support the whole realm of causes. A fuller development of the same ideas appeared in a set of lectures delivered at Manchester College, Oxford, and published under the name of *The Problem of Christianity* (2 vols., 1913). These lectures contained Royce's final interpretation of that Christian faith which in the person of his mother had been so powerful an influence in his childhood, and contained at the same time his most thorough treatment of the subject of religion (see also *The Sources of Religious Insight,* 1912). He selected as the three central Christian ideas, the Pauline Church, the "lost" state of the natural man, and atonement. These ideas he interpreted in terms of the "community," as being the supreme object of the individual's loyalty, by estrangement from which man is lost, and by whose spirit and service he is restored.

The effect of these ethical and religious studies, embracing in addition to major works numerous special essays and addresses, was to bring the metaphysical Absolute into nearer relation to man. The Absolute assumes the form of a personified "Beloved Community," to which the individual man was bound by a sort of patriotic fervor, or blend of self-sacrifice and self-aggrandizement. But even the more technical aspects of Royce's metaphysics were modified by the new emphasis. From Peirce he borrowed the notion that there is a kind of object, namely a sign, which cannot as such be either perceived or conceived but must, if it is to be apprehended at all, be "interpreted." Whereas perception and conception are "dyadic" relations (involving only two terms, subject and object), interpretations are triadic, involving a sign, an interpreter, and a second mind to which the interpretation is communicated. Thus, Royce argues, interpretation involved a *community* of two or more minds. Already, in his *Studies of Good and Evil* (1898), he had emphasized the dependence of self-consciousness on social relations; and in the second volume of *The World and the Individual* had adopted the view that nature is a social product, or a construction dictated by the exigences of stable and cooperative human intercourse. In *The Problem of Christianity* this view receives confirmation and restatement. As from the beginning of Royce's whole development, knowledge is creative of being; but knowledge is now construed as a social affair —a community of interpretation.

The moral issues of the World War stirred Royce profoundly, and won him to a vigorous public support of the cause of the Allies. At a mass-meeting held in Tremont Temple, Boston, on Jan. 30, 1916, he electrified a great audience by the daring, candor, and solemnity of his address. His humanity was shocked by the cruelty and waste of war and he devoted much thought and ingenuity to the problem of its prevention. The obvious depth and sincerity of his feeling, and his moral courage embodied in physical gentleness, won him a new and reverent regard during his last days. For he had begun to fail from 1912, and the emotional strain of the war years told heavily upon him. He died on Sept. 14, 1916, leaving a widow and his two younger sons, Edward and Stephen. Immediately after his death his addresses on war and peace were published under the title of *The Hope of the Great Community* (1916), a title admirably summarizing both his deepest and his latest interests.

After the death of James, Royce had become the most influential American philosopher of his day. For twenty-five years he was the leading exponent in America of that post-Kantian idealism which at the close of the nineteenth century numbered more adherents among students of philosophy than any rival tendency. Within this idealistic school he represented the voluntaristic wing. His method, it is true, was rationalistic. He believed it possible to *prove* ultimate truths, and had a growing fondness for the technical apparatus of logic. But the truth which he proved was a voluntaristic truth. He proclaimed the priority of action to passivity, of appreciation to description, of interpretation to perception and conception, of purpose and choice to necessity, and of moral to intellectual or even esthetic categories. He stands, therefore, closer to Fichte than to any other of the immediate followers of Kant; and belongs with Rickert, Windelband, and Münsterberg among Fichte's later followers. Such a classification does not, however, do him justice. He was distinguished from German neo-Fichteans not only by his profound metaphysical passion, but also by the English and American strains in his inheritance. With all of his *a priori* metaphysics, he was also something of a British empiricist; and with all his doctrinal monism and pantheism, he was profoundly American in his individualism and moral dualism. A mere doctrinal classification of Royce is inadequate, furthermore, because he was so much more than a doctrine. He was a man of rich experience and varied talents, with an exceptional understanding of music, and a vivid appreciation of literature. He was a scholar and a teacher. His historical scholarship was of that breadth and depth which is attainable only by men happily endowed with extraordinary memories. He was a teacher who both respected and did honor to his vocation. Through his voluminous writings and numerous public lectures he was a teacher of the general public, the more acceptable because his teachings provided a positive support for moral and religious conviction. His success as a teacher in the stricter sense was proportional to the seriousness and alertness of his students. Of the limitations of the average undergraduate mind he was not sufficiently aware, and his lectures were too discursive to be easily followed. With smaller groups of advanced students, and especially with his seminary, frequently attended by younger colleagues from scientific and other departments of the University, he was a truly great teacher. His learning gave him inexhaustible resources of allusion and comparison; his dialectical skill made him invincible in discussion; his sympathy and humor enabled him to interpret, amplify, and

confirm the poorest efforts of his younger associates. His peculiar genius lay in finding some grain of significance in the feeblest thinking, and some basis of agreement with his most remorseless critics.

His defects as a thinker and writer flowed mainly from one source, namely, a tendency to prolixity. He had a prodigious capacity for work, was a wide reader, and a voluminous writer. There was, apparently, some connection between his prodigality of effort and the quality of the product. In 1883 he remarked in his diary, "As usual I spin out the business a trifle too long." He lacked dexterity, intellectually as well as physically. His processes of mind were powerful, massive, but laborious. As a colleague expressed it: "He needed considerable sea-room." His style sometimes reached great heights of eloquence, but was never wholly free from a certain grandiose quality. Similarly, his thinking was marked by profusion and sheer power, rather than by refinement, pointedness, or focal illumination. He carried big guns but they were too big to hit the center of a small target.

Royce was an original and unique individual. His body was of medium stature, round and youthful in appearance, and with slight muscular development. His great dome-like head and Socratic features gave him an appearance which, without physical attractiveness, served none the less as a medium of spiritual beauty. He was faithful, brave, generous, and above all unworldly and high-minded, as became the philosopher that he was in person as well as by profession.

[Brief accounts by Royce himself of his parentage and early life are to be found in his *California* (1886), pp. 240–46, and in his *The Hope of the Great Community* (1916), pp. 122–36. The narrative of his mother, Sarah Royce, based on her diary of 1849, has been edited by R. H. Gabriel and published under the title, *A Frontier Lady: Recollections of the Gold Rush and Early California* (1932). The author has also had access to Royce's own diaries; to the unpublished correspondence between Royce and William James; and to the recollections of his wife and sister. A bibliography of Royce's published works and of articles on his philosophy by Benjamin Rand, is in the *Philosophical Review*, May 1916; and of his unpublished works, by Jacob Loewenberg, *Ibid.*, Sept. 1917. The following expositions and criticisms of Royce's philosophy are especially recommended: "Papers in Honor of Josiah Royce on his Sixtieth Birthday," *Philosophical Review*, May 1916; Jacob Loewenberg, editor's introduction to *Fugitive Essays, by Josiah Royce* (1920); Gabriel Marcel, "La Métaphysique de Josiah Royce," *Revue de Métaphysique et de Morale*, May–June, July–Aug. 1918; Jan.–Feb., Mar.–Apr. 1919; M. J. Aronson, *La Philosophie Morale de Josiah Royce* (1927); George Santayana, *Character and Opinion in the United States* (1920), ch. iv. For more personal materials, see G. H. Palmer, in *Harvard Graduates' Mag.*, Dec. 1916.]

R.B.P.

ROYE, EDWARD JAMES (Feb. 3, 1815–Feb. 12, 1872), fifth president of Liberia, was born in Newark, Ohio. His father, John Roye, who had been born in Kentucky, was thrifty and on his death in 1829 left his son some personal property and land. The boy was educated in the public schools of Ohio. He taught school a few years in Chillicothe. He then started in business as a sheep-trader and shop-keeper and lived in various parts of the Middle West. On the death of his mother in 1840, he began to consider the possibility of emigrating to some foreign country in order to escape American prejudice. He first chose Haiti and began to study French at Oberlin, but he finally changed his mind and went to Liberia.

He arrived there with a stock of goods in 1846. His energy soon made him the leading merchant in the country; he exported African products to England and to the United States and was rated in 1870 as the richest man in Liberia. In 1849 he was speaker of the House of Representatives, and he served as chief justice from 1865 to 1868. Three times he was candidate for the presidency, was finally elected, and in January 1871 was inaugurated president. He immediately announced a progressive policy. He wished to undertake a complete financial reconstruction, some measures for general education, and an improved system of roads (*Inaugural Address of President Edward James Roye,* 1870). For these purposes Liberia needed capital, and he began to negotiate for a loan from Great Britain. He went to England in 1870 to settle a boundary dispute and conducted negotiations for the loan. Unfortunately, he made the initial mistake of yielding too much to Lord Granville, agreeing to a rectification of the boundary that practically gave back to England land Liberia had formerly bought. He returned to Liberia before finishing the matter of the loan but left negotiations in the hands of two Liberians and a white man, David Chinery, who was consul for Liberia in London. A loan for $500,-000 was finally negotiated on very severe terms, carrying interest at seven per cent. and issued at thirty per cent. below par with three years' interest deducted. He hastily agreed to the terms without consulting the legislature and ordered certain goods to be charged against the loan. As a final result, Liberia actually received something like $89,515 cash, while her bonds were issued for at least $400,000. The result of all these negotiations caused great resentment in Liberia against him. He was also accused of embezzling some of the money and foolishly made matters worse by seeking to extend the two-year term of the presidency by edict. Public indignation was excited to fury, and the people, rising in insurrection, overpowered him and his friends, seized his house, and imprisoned him with one of his sons. In October 1871 he was deposed from his office, an executive committee was appointed to carry on the government until a new president was elected and Joseph J. Roberts [*q.v.*] was recalled from retirement. He was then summoned to trial before the supreme court but escaped during the night, either because of carelessness or connivance, and tried to reach an English steamer in the harbor. He was drowned in the attempt to ride the breakers in a native canoe.

[*African Repository,* Apr. 1870, July, Aug. 1872; *Fifty-fifth Annual Report of the Am. Colonization Soc. . . . 1872* (1872); H. H. Johnston, *Liberia* (1906), vol. I; T. H. B. Walker, *Hist. of Liberia* (copr. 1921).]

W. E. B. D–B.

ROYSTER, JAMES FINCH (June 26, 1880–Mar. 21, 1930), philologist, university administrator, was born at Raleigh, N. C., the second son of Wisconsin Illinois and Mary Wills (Finch) Royster. Prepared at the Raleigh academy, in 1897 he entered Wake Forest College, where the enthusiasm of Benjamin Sledd awoke a continuing interest in linguistic and literary studies. Grounding himself on Latin and Greek, the young student displayed an increasing ability in Germanic philology, particularly Old English and Middle English. He was graduated from Wake Forest in 1900. He entered the graduate school of the University of Chicago, where he was strongly influenced by John M. Manly. After eighteen months at the University of Berlin, 1902–03, he became an instructor in English at the University of Colorado, 1904–05, where he met his future wife, Carrie Belle Lake, to whom he was married on June 17, 1908. An assistant in English at the University of Chicago in 1906–07, he won his doctorate in 1907, his dissertation, an edition of an unpublished *Middle English Treatise on the Ten Commandments* (1911) being characteristically workmanlike. He was immediately called to the University of North Carolina, where he served as associate professor of English, and where his two children were born. Linguistic articles marked by commonsense methods, editorial work on *Studies in Philology,* and the fostering of graduate study increased his reputation; and in 1914 the University of Texas called him as professor of English with a view to modernizing its literary curriculum. Although his research interests were linguistic, he battled what he regarded as philological antiquarianism in the name of modern letters, but, feeling that academic conservatism was too strongly entrenched to be routed, he welcomed a recall to the University of North Carolina in 1921 as Kenan professor of English philology. At Chapel Hill he was in his element, a member of perhaps the most brilliant group of literary scholars in the South including Edwin Greenlaw, then dean of the graduate school, and Thornton Shirley Graves. As dean of the college of liberal arts, 1922–25, he steadily labored for a humane and vigorous curriculum. Upon the translation of Greenlaw to The John Hopkins University in 1925, he was appropriately made his successor as dean of the graduate school, with the task of maintaining and extending the brilliant work of his predecessor in fostering university research work. Under the Greenlaw-Royster régime Chapel Hill became notable as the flourishing center of graduate study. His devotion to the institution led to over-work, and the death of his beloved wife in 1928 shook a personality already suffering from strain. Appointed to the directorship of the American University Union in London, he left to take up his duties in the summer of 1929, broke down in mental health after reaching England, and returned to die at Richmond, Va., from self-inflicted burns.

Inevitably his writing suffered from his administrative labors; an occasional article on Chaucerian or similar problems was all he could find time for. He left behind him no body of writing fully representative of his great powers. Besides various textbooks characteristic articles are "Old English Causative Verbs" (*Studies in Philology*, July 1922) and the revolutionary "I'll Not Trust the Printed Word—" (*Ibid.*, July 1917). His best platform was the classroom.

[Personal recollections; family letters; *Who's Who in America*, 1928–29, *Studies in Philology*, July 1930, October 1931, p. v; *New York Times*, Mar. 22, 1930.]

H. M. J.

RUBLEE, HORACE (Aug. 19, 1829–Oct. 19, 1896), editor and diplomat, was born in Berkshire, Franklin County, Vt., the son of Alvah and Martha (Kent) Rublee. Attracted by reports of rich farming land in the Middle West, his father journeyed to Wisconsin in 1839 and settled at Sheboygan, where his family joined him the following year. The boy's early education was obtained in the district schools of Vermont and Wisconsin. Lacking the rugged physique necessary for his father's occupations, lumbering and farming, he taught school near his home until, at the age of twenty, he decided to go to college. In 1850 he entered the University of Wisconsin, then in its first year as a prepara-

tory school, housed in one small building, with a faculty of one teacher. While attending the university he supported himself by setting type on one of the Madison newspapers, but his constitution was not equal to the strain of study and work, and he was compelled to withdraw from college on account of poor health. Returning to his home in Sheboygan, he again taught in a district school. He began his newspaper work by reporting the sessions of the state legislature during 1852 and 1853 for the *Wisconsin Argus*, a Democratic weekly paper that published a daily edition while the legislature was in session. In the spring of 1853, during the temporary absence of its editor, Rublee became editorial writer on the *Wisconsin State Journal*, a Madison daily, established the previous year by David Atwood [*q.v.*]. The following year Rublee bought a half-interest in the paper, which he retained until he went abroad in the diplomatic service fifteen years later.

His political activities began with the movement against the extension of slavery that led to the birth of the Republican party. At the first state convention of that party, held in Madison on July 13, 1854, Rublee was one of the secretaries. During 1856–57 he was state librarian. In 1856 or 1857 he married Kate Hopkins of Washington County, N. Y., one of whose brothers, James C. Hopkins [*q.v.*], became United States judge for the western district of Wisconsin. From 1859 to 1869, Rublee served as chairman of the Wisconsin Republican state committee, and in 1868 was a delegate to the Republican National Convention that nominated General Grant for the presidency.

President Grant appointed him minister to Switzerland in 1869, a post that he held for seven years. Studious in his tastes, he acquired a considerable knowledge of the German language and literature during his residence in Switzerland. After resigning his diplomatic position, he returned to Wisconsin in 1877 and again became chairman of the Republican state committee. When the Republican state convention adopted a weak plank on "Greenbackism," Rublee, as chairman of the state committee with the support of some of the other Republican leaders, issued an address to the Republican voters demanding the resumption of specie payments. He carried the Republicans to victory on this issue.

During 1877 he contributed articles to the *Evening Wisconsin*, the leading Republican evening newspaper in Milwaukee. He went to Boston in 1879 to act as temporary editor of the *Daily Advertiser*, but, although urged to remain in journalism in the East, soon decided to return to Wisconsin. In 1881 he organized a company to purchase the *Daily Milwaukee News,* a Democratic morning paper. With Rublee, a stanch Republican, as editor, its name was changed to the *Republican and News.* The following year the company bought the *Milwaukee Sentinel,* then the oldest as well as the most important morning paper in the state. It was in his connection with the *Sentinel,* from 1883 until he died in 1896, that Rublee won distinction as editor and editorial writer. He made it more than a party organ; it was the leading newspaper of the commonwealth, and his editorials were quoted by other newspapers both within and without the state. At his death he was survived by two sons.

[A. M. Thomson, *A Political Hist. of Wis.* (1902); *The Columbian Biog. Dict. . . . Wis. Vol.* (1895); H. P. Myrick, in *Proc. Wis. Press Asso.,* 1897; *Papers Relating to the Foreign Relations of the U. S.,* 1870-76; *Milwaukee Sentinel* and *Milwaukee Jour.,* Oct. 19, 1896.]   W. G. B.

RUDGE, WILLIAM EDWIN (Nov. 23, 1876–June 12, 1931), printer and publisher, was born in Brooklyn, N. Y., son of William Edwin and Lavina (Knapp) Rudge. He attended the public school and at twelve or thirteen entered his father's printing office at Nassau and Liberty streets, New York, where he learned his trade, meanwhile taking a three-year course in engineering at Cooper Union. His father soon suggested that the boy take over three presses in the plant and work for himself. This was the beginning of "The Printing House of William Edwin Rudge." In 1895, the plant was moved to 83 Murray St., where an electric motor was substituted for foot-power on the presses. The father became ill in 1900, and the son succeeded to the business. A fire at the Murray Street shop in 1905 necessitated another removal, to 218 William St. In 1921, the plant was moved to Mount Vernon, N. Y., which for some time had been Rudge's place of residence. Here, in a picturesque rural setting, a one-story, graystone building, once used for glass manufacture, was gradually remodeled and furnished with equipment capable of doing high quality work.

Before 1912, Rudge had done general commercial printing. About that time he became associated with the group of typographers, designers, collectors, and others who founded the American Institute of Graphic Arts. He became sensitive to art, design, and quality, and set for himself the ideal of producing books and printed matter in the most beautiful form. For design of books he secured the services of such men as Frederic W. Goudy, Bruce Rogers,

Frederic Warde, and W. A. Dwiggins. At his press in Mount Vernon he assembled a library on the graphic arts, consisting of histories and source books, together with examples of fine printing from the best presses.

Rudge produced many works of outstanding merit, notably, Joseph Pennell's *Adventures of an Illustrator* (1925), Mary Vaux Walcott's *North American Wild Flowers* (5 vols., 1925), with faithful reproductions of water color sketches, produced by the "Smithsonian Process," a method perfected by Rudge, consisting of four-color printing on all-rag, uncoated paper; Robert Bridges' *The Testament of Beauty* (1929); the *Private Papers of James Boswell* (1928), edited by Geoffrey Scott and Frederick Pottle; books by Hervey Allen, Ford Madox Ford, Cass Gilbert, Christopher Morley, Arthur Symons, and wood-engraving by Timothy Cole. He was constantly critical of his own work and always experimenting with new methods and processes in the hope of achieving finer results. "Expense, profit, all the limitations of the ordinary printer, have been brushed aside by the largeness of imagination which touched everything he did" (*Saturday Review of Literature,* July 25, 1931, p. 15). He received many medals and awards; his work ranks with that of the foremost American printers and is highly regarded by fellow craftsmen of all countries. He was a member of the advisory board at New York University for the course given by the American Institute of Graphic Arts, and an officer of many organizations connected with the graphic arts. In 1925, Herbert Hoover, then secretary of commerce, appointed him to represent the printing industry at the International Exposition of Modern Decorative and Industrial Art in Paris. He made friends easily and kept them. He displayed a keen interest in his employees, with the result that several young men who began with him became designers of national reputation. On Apr. 18, 1906, he married Lillie May Gould of Mount Vernon, N. Y. His two sons followed their father as printers.

[*American Printer,* June 5, 1920; N. Y. *Evening Post,* Jan. 4, 1923; *San Francisco Printer,* Dec. 1930; *Typothetae Bulletin,* July 1, 1931; *Bookbinding Magazine,* July 1931, p. 41; *Inland Printer,* July 1931; "The First Reader," *N. Y. World Telegram,* June 16, 1931; *Publishers' Weekly,* June 20, 1931; *Sat. Rev. of Lit.,* July 25, 1931; *News-Letter* (American Institute of Graphic Arts, July 1931); *Chicago Evening Post,* Sept. 25, 1931; *N. Y. Times,* June 13, 1931; *Who's Who in America,* 1930–31.]   J. A.

RUFFIN, EDMUND (Jan. 5, 1794–June 18, 1865), agriculturist and publisher, was born in Prince George County, Va., the son of George and Jane (Lucas) Ruffin. He was educated at home until his sixteenth year when he entered the College of William and Mary for a brief and unprofitable period ending in his suspension for neglect of classroom work. He served as a private in the War of 1812, but saw no active fighting, and, after six months of drill and camp duty at Norfolk, returned home to marry, in 1813, Susan Travis of Williamsburg and assume charge of the Coggin's Point farm which the recent death of his father had left to him. Here he began the agricultural experiments which were to bring him fame and to restore his section to prosperity.

Agriculture in Virginia at this time was at low ebb. The continual planting of a single crop on the same lands, and the use of bad methods in plowing and planting had depleted the soils, ruined the planters, and sent thousands of emigrants from the state. With little knowledge, either practical or theoretical, Ruffin set to work to discover the fundamental trouble and to find a remedy. After early failures, he observed that sorrel and pine always grew on poor lands and that calcareous earths were absent. Adopting a suggestion from Sir Humphrey Davy's *Elements of Agricultural Chemistry* (1815), he began experimenting with marl in various quantities upon his fields. Favorable results led to the conclusion that soils, once fertile but reduced by harmful cultivation, had become "acid" and had, thereby, lost their power to retain manures. This condition he now believed could be corrected by the application of calcareous earths (marl) and that a fertility equal to or greater than the original could then be acquired by the use of fertilizers, crop rotation, drainage, and good plowing. The experiences of the next few years were to prove the practical correctness of his conclusions.

In October 1818, Ruffin presented his theories and results before the Prince George Agricultural Society and three years later printed them in enlarged form in the *American Farmer* (Dec. 28, 1821, vol. III, 313–24). By 1832, they had grown into a volume of 242 pages, published under the title, *An Essay on Calcareous Manures*. This work ran through five editions and grew to nearly five hundred pages. Still further to advance the cause of agriculture, Ruffin began, in June 1833, the publication of an agricultural journal, the *Farmer's Register*. It appeared monthly, first from "Shellbanks" and then from Petersburg. The editor, himself, wrote nearly half of the articles offered but he also reprinted the best articles from foreign sources and presented the ideas and experiences of the most enterprising local planters. For ten

years this journal rendered invaluable service to the whole South and then failed because of the editor's activities for banking reform, especially the publication of another periodical, the *Bank Reformer* (Sept. 4, 1841–Feb. 5, 1842).

Ruffin early took a hand in the organization of agricultural societies. He was one of the founders of the Prince George society and one of the leaders in the move to associate local societies for the purpose of opposing protective tariffs. In 1841 he was appointed a member of the first Virginia State Board of Agriculture and served as its first corresponding secretary. In 1842 he became agricultural surveyor of South Carolina, publishing after a year's work the excellent *Report of the Commencement and Progress of the Agricultural Survey of South Carolina* (1843), which became a landmark in the agricultural history of the state. When the Virginia State Agricultural Society was organized in 1845 he was elected as its president but declined to serve under the impression that his work had not been sufficiently appreciated in his native state. He accepted this honor, however, in 1852 and two years later became commissioner for the society in an effort to put it on firm financial foundations and enlarge its usefulness. His work toward the establishment of experimental farms and agricultural education was particularly notable.

In 1843 Ruffin moved to a new estate, "Marlbourne," in Hanover County, where he made his home until retirement in 1855. He wrote and spoke much on agricultural improvement in these years for newspapers, farm journals, and agricultural societies. His *Address on the Opposite Results of Exhausting and Fertilizing Systems of Agriculture* (1853), given before the South Carolina Institute, and his *Premium Essay on Agricultural Education* (1853), presented to the Southern Central Agricultural Association, were of high merit. In 1855 he gathered together a number of articles and issued them in book form under the title, *Essays and Notes on Agriculture*. His *Notes on the Cane-brake Lands* (of Alabama) were published in 1860, and his *Agricultural, Geological and Descriptive Sketches of Lower North Carolina, and the Similar Adjacent Lands* in 1861.

Ruffin was always interested in politics. He served for three years in the Senate of Virginia (1823–26) but resigned in disgust at the methods employed by politicians. He early became a Whig but drifted over into the Democratic ranks as the struggle over slavery and state rights developed. He was from the first an ardent defender of slavery and was one of the first secessionists in Virginia. He wrote much for the Richmond and Charleston newspapers, *DeBow's Review,* and the *Southern Literary Messenger.* His views on slavery were brought together in four pamphlets: *Address to the Virginia State Agricultural Society on the Effects of Domestic Slavery on the Manners, Habits, and Welfare of the Agricultural Population of the Southern States, and the Slavery of Class to Class in the Northern States* (1853), reprinted in part as an appendix to the second pamphlet, *The Political Economy of Slavery* (n.d., probably 1858); *African Colonization Unveiled* (n.d.), printed also in instalments under varying titles in *De Bow's Review* for April, July, September, October, November 1859 and November 1860; and *Slavery and Free Labor Described and Compared* (n.d.), printed also in the *Southern Planter,* December 1859–January 1860. In 1860 he published a book entitled *Anticipations of the Future,* designed to show the necessity of secession and the glories of an independent South.

An advocate of direct trade with Europe, he attended three Southern commercial conventions and served as chairman of the Virginia delegation at the one held in Montgomery, Ala., in 1858. He originated the League of United Southerners, and secured and presented one of John Brown's pikes to the governor of each Southern state. He was invited to sit in three seceding conventions and as a volunteer with the Palmetto Guard of Charleston was permitted to fire the first shot from Morris Island against Fort Sumter (Craven, *post,* pp. 217, 270). He was with his company as a "temporary" private at the first Battle of Manassas (Bull Run) and fired the shot that blocked the bridge over Cub Run. He spent the war period wandering about from one of his plantations to another as "Yankee" invasions necessitated but returned to Charleston from time to time to "aid" in her defense. With the collapse of the Confederacy, he ended his own life at "Redmoor" in Amelia County on June 18, 1865, and was buried in the family graveyard at "Marlbourne." Three of his eleven children survived him.

[H. G. Ellis, "Edmund Ruffin: His Life and Times," in *John P. Branch Hist. Papers of Randolph-Macon Coll.,* June 1910, vol. III, 99–123; W. P. Cutler, "A Pioneer in Agricultural Science," in *Yearbook of U. S. Dept. Agriculture, 1895* (1896), pp. 493–502; *DeBow's Review,* Oct. 1851, pp. 431–36; E. G. Swem, *An Analysis of Ruffin's Farmer's Register with a Bibliography of Edmund Ruffin* (*Bulletin of Va. State Lib.,* XI, July–Oct. 1918); A. O. Craven, *Edmund Ruffin, Southerner* (1932); MS. Diary of Ruffin, 1856–65 (14 vols.) in Lib. of Cong.; obituary in *Richmond Times,* June 20, 1865.]   A. O. C.

RUFFIN, THOMAS (Nov. 17, 1787–Jan. 15, 1870), jurist, the eldest child of Sterling and Alice (Roane) Ruffin of Essex County, Va., was born at "Newington," King and Queen County, Va. Prepared for college at Warrenton, N. C., he entered the junior class of the College of New Jersey, and, graduating in 1805, immediately began the study of law under David Robertson, a learned Scotch lawyer in Petersburg. In 1807 he followed his father to North Carolina and continued his studies under Archibald D. Murphey [*q.v.*]. Admitted to the bar in 1808, he settled in Hillsboro, where on Dec. 9, 1809, he married Anne, the daughter of William Kirkland.

He rose rapidly at the bar, and in 1813, 1815, and 1816, as an ardent Jeffersonian Republican, he represented the borough of Hillsboro in the House of Commons, serving as speaker in 1816. He never held a purely political office again, although he was a Crawford candidate for elector in 1824. At the close of his legislative term he was elected superior court judge, but resigned two years later and returned to practice in order to make good a security debt. He habitually attended two courts a week for forty-three weeks in the year—a herculean task in the day of bad roads; was reporter of the supreme court for a short time (1820–21); and by 1825 was at the head of the profession in the state. In that year he returned to the bench, but in 1828 he again resigned, this time to become president of the state bank, which had become heavily involved. A year later the bank was safe, and he was elected associate justice of the supreme court, becoming chief justice in 1833. He resigned in 1852 and retired to his farm in Alamance County, where he had made his home for many years. In 1858, by almost unanimous election of the legislature, he was called back to the supreme court, but served for only one year. He represented North Carolina at the peace conference in 1861, as an ardent supporter of the Union, and sought in every way to secure the adoption of a compromise that would preserve it. He returned to North Carolina still denying any constitutional right of secession, but eager for a revolutionary separation from the North. Without being a candidate, he was elected to the secession convention, where he voted for the Badger ordinance of revolution; offered a compromise between that and outright secession; and, both failing, voted for the ordinance of secession, and thereafter spared no effort in support of the war. In 1866 he opposed, on constitutional grounds, the right of the "Johnson" convention to submit a new constitution and was largely responsible for its rejection. Bitterly opposed to congressional reconstruction, he was no less opposed to the use of violence to undo it, and the

Ku Klux movement excited in his mind only horror. His last years were spent in Hillsboro where he died.

It is as a judge that Ruffin is chiefly known and remembered, and in the quarter-century of his service he established a reputation extending wherever English law is known. Constantly cited as an authority in American state and federal courts, he was quoted as well at Westminster (J. M. Vanfleet, *The Law of Collateral Attack,* 1892, Section 634; *Steel* vs. *Dixon,* 17 *Chancery Division,* 825). In constitutional law, authorities rank him with Marshall and Lemuel Shaw [*qq.v.*] as a pioneer. In common law and equity he was equally noted—a rare combination. His opinions, 1460 in number, embrace almost every topic of civil and criminal law. They are noted for their breadth of view, fullness of discussion, force of reasoning, strength and simplicity of language, lack of citation of authority, and the almost inevitable character of their conclusions. Though respecting precedent, he was not hampered by it in administering justice. He was responsible for two important departures in equity from English precedents: one, the rejection of the doctrine of part performance as a basis for decreeing the specific execution of a verbal contract for sale of land; the other, the discarding of the doctrine of vendor's lien upon land sold upon credit. In *Hoke* vs. *Henderson* (15 *N. C.,* 1) the first case of its kind in the United States, he held, contrary to the doctrine later adopted by the federal courts and those of every other state, that the holder of an office had an estate in it of which he could not be divested except by the abolition of the office. This remained the rule in North Carolina until 1903, when it was reversed (134 *N. C.,* 131). In *Raleigh and Gaston R. R. Co.* vs. *Davis* (19 *N. C.,* 451) he laid down the doctrine, then new, that the legislature had the power to provide for condemnation of a right of way for railroad purposes without the owner's being entitled to jury trial for assessment of damage. His opinion in *State* vs. *Mann* (13 *N. C.,* 263) illustrates his relentless logic as applied to slavery. As executive officer of the court he greatly improved its procedure and that of the courts below.

Ruffin was also an agriculturist of some note, operating profitably two plantations many miles apart. Like his kinsman, Edmund Ruffin [*q.v.*] of Virginia, he believed in scientific agriculture and kept abreast of every new development. For six years (1854–60) the active president of the state agricultural society, he exerted a powerful influence in extending agricultural knowledge. He rose to eminence by unremitting labor rather than by brilliance of mind. In appearance and manner he was austere and seemingly cold, but in reality his was a fiery nature in severe restraint. Of dominating will, he was inclined to be dictatorial, and he disliked opposition. His whole outlook on life was serious, but he had a genial human side, as the number of his devoted friends gave evidence. He was deeply religious, a devoted member of the Episcopal Church, and several times a delegate to its General Convention. Actively interested in the University of North Carolina, he was a trustee from 1813 to 1831 and again from 1842 to 1868, when reconstruction terminated the old board's existence. Thirteen of his fourteen children survived him.

[*The Papers of Thomas Ruffin* (4 vols., 1918–20), ed. by J. G. deR. Hamilton; W. A. Graham, *Life and Character of the Hon. Thomas Ruffin* (1871); Walter Clark, "Thomas Ruffin," in *Great Am. Lawyers,* vol. IV (1908), ed. by W. D. Lewis; Francis Nash, "Chief Justice Thomas Ruffin," *Charlotte Daily Observer,* Mar. 19, 1905; S. A. Ashe, *Biog. Hist. of N. C.,* vol. V (1906); 13–43, 51, 57 *N. C. Reports; Daily Standard* (Raleigh), Jan. 18, 1870.]   J. G. deR. H.

RUFFNER, HENRY (Jan. 16, 1790–Dec. 17, 1861), Presbyterian clergyman, educator, author, was born in Shenandoah County, Va., son of David and Ann (Brumbach) Ruffner. Having come to the Valley in 1739, the Ruffners— a German-Swiss people, big-bodied and heavy-fisted—moved on in 1796 to the wild Kanawha country, where, also, they bought land, started manufacturing, and helped build schools and churches. Prepared at Dr. McElhenney's Academy near by, Henry, in 1813, graduated from Washington College, Lexington, Va. After a year of theology and a year of travel he was licensed to preach and returned for mission work in the Kanawha country. On Mar. 31, 1819, he married Sarah, daughter of Capt. William Lyle, a farmer living near Lexington.

For thirty years thereafter he was identified with Washington College, first as teacher (thrice acting as president), and then (1836–48) as president and teacher. Under him the school took on the characteristics of a modern college, especially architecturally, though competition with the new Virginia Military Academy kept its numbers small. Meantime, his unusual energy was finding other outlets. From 1819 to 1831 he preached regularly at the Timber Ridge Church. At the educational convention in Lexington in 1842 he was the moving spirit and submitted " 'the most valuable document on general education issued in Virginia since the early days of Thomas Jefferson, viz., an elaborate plan for the organization of an entire educational system of public instruction' " (Ambler, *post,* p. 277, quoting the United States

Commissioner of Education). From 1840 to 1847 he was preparing "The Early History of Washington College" (*Washington and Lee Historical Papers*, vol. I, 1890), in which appear his views on "the general management of literary institutions and the subject of liberal education." Out of a debate in the Franklin Literary Society of Lexington on the advisability of dividing Virginia into two states at the Blue Ridge, grew his *Address to the People of West Virginia ... Showing that Slavery is Injurious to the Public Welfare, and that it May be Gradually Abolished, Without Detriment to the Rights and Interests of Slaveholders, by a Slaveholder of West Virginia* (1847). In it he argued for confinement of slavery to the region east of the Blue Ridge and its gradual abolition there on broad grounds of public policy. This "Ruffner Pamphlet" became important politically, especially in 1859.

With the reluctant consent of the trustees, Ruffner left Washington College in 1848 for the Kanawha mountains. There he hoped to recover fortune and health at farming and mining; but after a few years he returned to preaching, this time in what is now Malden, W. Va. Meanwhile, as "literary recreations," he had written and published "Judith Bensaddi," a romance which appeared in revised form in the *Southern Literary Messenger*, July 1839, with the statement that the first version had been published in a Philadelphia periodical ten years before; two Calvinistic treatises, *A Discourse on the Duration of Future Punishment* (1823) and *Against Universalism* (1833); and *The Fathers of the Desert* (2 vols., 1850). As an exponent of its energy and hard sense and of its views on slavery and education, ante-bellum western Virginia had no better representative than Henry Ruffner. Two of his four children survived him, one of whom was William Henry Ruffner [*q.v.*].

[William Henry Ruffner, "Hist. of Washington Coll., now Washington and Lee University," in *Washington and Lee Hist. Papers*, nos. 5, 6 (1895, 1904), a continuation of Henry Ruffner's *Early Hist. of Washington Coll.*; C. H. Ambler, *Sectionalism in Va.* (1910); *Southern Lit. Messenger*, Dec. 1838, Jan.-Apr. 1839, containing his "Cincinnati Address" and his "Notes on a Tour from Va. to Tenn. ... 1838."] C. C. P.

RUFFNER, WILLIAM HENRY (Feb. 11, 1824–Nov. 24, 1908), Presbyterian clergyman, educator, was born in Lexington, Va., son of Henry [*q.v.*] and Sarah (Lyle) Ruffner. His boyhood was spent on his father's farm near Lexington and in Washington College, from which he graduated in 1842 and to which he returned for the degree of M.A. in 1845 after a year as manager of his father's salt work in the Kanawha country. From 1845 to 1846 he studied at Union Theological Seminary, then located at Hampden-Sidney, Va., and from 1846 to 1847, at Princeton Theological Seminary. After traveling as colporteur and preaching to country churches in the Valley, he spent two leisurely years as chaplain of the University of Virginia (1849–51). During this time he planned a series of discourses by Presbyterian ministers on the evidences of Christianity, which were published (Bruce, *History of the University of Virginia*, vol. III, 1921, p. 136), and studied moral philosophy under William Holmes McGuffey [*q.v.*], who, Ruffner said later, "resolved my intellectual forces into common sense." On Sept. 3, 1850, he married Harriet Ann Gray, by whom he had four children. He was ordained, Jan. 14, 1852, by the Presbytery of Philadelphia, and became pastor of the Seventh (Tabernacle) Presbyterian Church of Philadelphia.

Despite marked success in this work, a chronic throat trouble compelled his resignation in 1853. For sixteen years thereafter he was principally a successful farmer, first in Rockingham County and then at "Tribrook," near Lexington, preaching only occasionally. From 1865 to 1876, he served Washington College as trustee. Sharing Henry Ruffner's reasoned anti-slavery views, he opposed both abolition and secession; but after Lincoln's call for troops in 1861 he heartily supported the Southern cause. During Reconstruction his attitude, while entirely self-respecting, was conciliatory and constructive. Though in 1866 he deemed a state system of general public education impracticable, in 1867 he openly advocated state provision for the education of negroes. A state system of public schools having been made mandatory by the constitution, in 1869 he energetically sought from the Conservative majority in the legislature election as state superintendent, receiving convincing support from his friends and neighbors, notably Gen. Robert E. Lee. He was elected on Mar. 2, 1870.

Quickly and with but little assistance Ruffner drew the school law—which became a model for other Southern states—and secured its enactment. For twelve years thereafter he gave unremitting attention to the details of administration, believing that "there is more in the right execution of any plan than in the plan itself." Quite as important were his eleven annual *Reports* and his miscellaneous writings, through which he built up a philosophy of public education that prevailed over the strong individualistic beliefs and the antipathy to education of the negroes at the expense of the whites. Especial commendation has been given his solution to the

Ruger

problem of the relation of church and state in the educational field, which has been described as "co-operation without alliance" (Sadie Bell, *The Church, the State, and Education in Virginia,* 1930, chapters x, xi). For these services he has frequently been called the "Horace Mann of the South." In the clash between the bondholders and the schools over state revenues Ruffner was a moderate Readjuster; but when the Readjusters became radical, he adhered to the Conservatives. Consequently, he was not reëlected superintendent either by the former in 1882 or by the latter in 1886. Meantime as *ex officio* trustee of the new Agricultural and Mechanical College he had drawn up a plan for the institution, earnestly recommending emphasis upon advanced technical training. He was first president of the State Female Normal School, at Farmville, which he had helped to secure and which he endeavored to organize along practical lines, serving from 1884 to 1887. Thereafter, his unusual energy and versatility found outlet for ten years principally in making extensive physical surveys for large corporations. Among his published reports in this field were *A Physical Survey Extending from Atlanta, Georgia . . . to the Mississippi River* (1883), in collaboration with J. L. Campbell; *Report on the Landed Property of the Buena Vista Company* (1889); and *A Report on Washington Territory* (1889). He also edited his father's "Early History of Washington College" and continued it down to 1848 (*Washington and Lee Historical Papers,* no. 5, 1895; no. 6, 1904). To all his work Ruffner brought a strong mind, a progressive disposition, good judgment, and absolute honesty. Characteristically, when his superintendency took him into politics, he had sought and obtained his demission from the ministry. He died in Asheville, N. C.

[Ruffner Papers in Hist. Foundation of the Presbyt. and Reformed Churches, Montreat, N. C.; O. K. Lyle, *Lyle Family* (1912); *Va. Jour. of Educ.,* Jan. 1909; E. L. Fox, "William Henry Ruffner and the Rise of the Public Free School System of Va.," in *The John P. Branch Hist. Papers of Randolph-Macon Coll.,* June 1910; C. C. Pearson, "William Henry Ruffner: Reconstruction Statesman of Va.," in *South Atlantic Quart.,* Jan., Apr. 1921 and *Readjuster Movement in Va.* (1917); *Asheville Gazette,* Nov. 25, 1908.]

C. C. P.

RUGER, THOMAS HOWARD (Apr. 2, 1833–June 3, 1907), soldier, was born in Lima, Livingston County, N. Y., the son of Thomas Jefferson Ruger and Maria (Hutchins) Ruger. His father, an Episcopal minister, moved to Janesville, Wis., when the lad was thirteen years of age. The latter received academic schooling in preparation for the United States Military Academy and entered in his seventeenth year.

As a cadet he was reticent and retiring, unusually diligent and careful of speech, and, though without college training, was graduated number three in the class of 1854. Within a year he resigned his commission in the corps of engineers to practise law at Janesville.

Upon the outbreak of the Civil War, he was commissioned lieutenant-colonel of the 3rd Wisconsin Infantry, and became colonel a few months later. He participated creditably in the Maryland and Shenandoah operations of 1861–62, and distinguished himself at the battle of Antietam. He was promoted to the rank of brigadier-general of volunteers on Nov. 29, 1862, and ably commanded a brigade in the Army of the Potomac throughout the Rappahannock and Pennsylvania campaigns of 1862–63. At Gettysburg, where he succeeded to the command of a division, his brilliant service won him the brevet of brigadier-general, United States Army. On Aug. 15, 1863, he was ordered to New York City to suppress draft riots. In the following October he was transferred to a brigade in the West, and took part in all of Sherman's operations. He commanded a division in the Tennessee campaign against Hood, and in the subsequent operations in North Carolina from February to June 1865. He was brevetted major-general of volunteers for his services at the battle of Franklin, Tenn., on Nov. 30, 1864.

Following the war, he commanded the department of North Carolina for a year, and served as provisional governor of the state of Georgia from January to July 1868. He had been appointed colonel of the 33rd Infantry, Regular Army, on July 28, 1866, and was transferred to the 18th Infantry in 1869. During the years 1871–76, he served as superintendent of the United States Military Academy, where he maintained a high standard of scholarship and discipline. Until the year 1878 he commanded the department of the South, and until 1885, the district of Montana—taking command during the latter year of the important infantry and cavalry school at Fort Leavenworth, Kan. He became a brigadier-general on Mar. 19, 1886, and a major-general on Feb. 8, 1895. He commanded various military departments during this period and successfully conducted an expedition against hostile Indians in the Northwest. He also suppressed serious railway riots in Sacramento and San Francisco, Cal. He was retired from active military service by operation of law on Apr. 2, 1897, and spent two years traveling with his family on the continent of Europe. Upon his return, he made his home in Stamford, Conn., and lived the rest of his life very quietly in the enjoyment of

Ruger

his books and his garden. He was survived by his wife, Helen Lydia Moore, to whom he had been married in 1857, and their two daughters.

[Who's Who in America, 1906–07; G. W. Cullum, Biog. Reg. . . . Officers and Grads., U. S. Mil. Acad. (1891); O. O. Howard, biographical sketch in Ann. Reunion, Asso. of Grads., U. S. Mil. Acad., 1908 (1908); J. D. Cox, The March to the Sea (1906), and Atlanta (1909), vols. IX and X in Campaigns of the Civil War; N. Y. Times, June 4, 1907.]   C. D. R.

RUGGLES, SAMUEL BULKLEY (Apr. 11, 1800–Aug. 28, 1881), lawyer, descended from John Ruggles who settled in Roxbury, Mass., in 1635, was born in New Milford, Conn., the son of Philo and Ellen (Bulkley) Ruggles. His father, a lawyer, removed to Poughkeepsie, N. Y., in 1804. The boy gave evidence of precocity, and by private tutoring was prepared for college at the age of twelve. He was admitted to the sophomore class at Yale and graduated in 1814. He then passed several years at Poughkeepsie, studying in his father's law office, and finally, after admission to the bar in 1821, began practice in New York City. He was successful in his profession, but long before he had reached his fortieth year he had retired from active practice to devote his time to public interests.

As early as 1831, when little thought had been given in New York to the providing of breathing spaces in city blocks, Ruggles was working out a plan by which a subdivision could be developed with a small park as its central feature, to be held in perpetuity by the surrounding lot-owners. He had bought land (lying between Third and Fourth Avenues, Twentieth and Twenty-second streets) as farm acreage, and through a costly process of leveling and filling converted it into a desirable residential district. He realized little profit from his investment, but in Gramercy Park the community had a permanent object-lesson in the beauty and value of small parks, which became the more impressive as the city was closely built around it in the course of years. In 1931 the centenary of the park was observed, with tributes to its founder (see editorial, New York Times, May 16, 1931). Ruggles was also active in promoting the creation of Union Square, one of the earliest of the city's public parks. Later he was one of the Croton Aqueduct commissioners. His election to the lower house of the state legislature in 1838 and his selection as chairman of the Ways and Means Committee gave his zeal for public service a wider scope. His Report upon the Finances and Internal Improvements of the State of New York (1838) was epoch-making in New York's canal policy. Ruggles was one of the few men after the time of DeWitt Clinton [q.v.] to make a

sincere, broadly conceived effort to formulate a canal policy for the future. As canal commissioner 1839–58 and president of the commission from 1840, he carried far beyond the state boundaries his inquiries into traffic conditions and the products then needing the Erie Canal for transport to the seaboard (see his Report . . . in Respect to the Enlargement of the Canals for National Purposes, 1863).

His familiarity with the transportation problems of the day made it natural that he should have a part, with James Gore King [q.v.] and other New Yorkers, in the building of the New York & Erie Railroad. He continued his statistical studies over a long period, publishing many pamphlets on economic themes. His chief public service in later years was rendered as delegate of the United States to the International Statistical Congress at Berlin in 1863 and at The Hague in 1869 (see his report, Internationality and International Congresses, 1869), and to the International Monetary Conference at Paris in 1867. His reports on the last-named conference were published under the titles, International Coinage (1867) and International Coinage: Supplemental Report (1870). On the complicated issue of bimetallism he was far more at home than were most of his countrymen. He had been interested in banking since 1839, when he had helped to found the Bank of Commerce.

In one other field Ruggles was for years distinctly in advance of his times. While he was serving as trustee of Columbia College (1836–81) the opposition of some of his colleagues, in 1854, to the election of Oliver Wolcott Gibbs [q.v.] to the chair of chemistry because of his Unitarianism, called out from Ruggles a ringing protest, The Duty of Columbia College to the Community (1854). The conflict seems to have set clearly within his vision the development of the college into a university. From that ideal he never wavered and in 1880, while he was still a trustee, he took part in the erection of the School of Political Science, headed by Dr. John W. Burgess, in the conviction that the University had at last arrived. Ruggles was married, May 15, 1822, to Mary Rosalie Rathbone, who died in 1878. They had two sons and a daughter. Ruggles died at Fire Ireland, N. Y., as the result of a paralytic stroke.

[Samuel Orcutt, Hist. of the Towns of New Milford and Bridgewater, Conn. (1882); Charles King, Progress of the City of N. Y. during the Last Fifty Years (1852); J. B. Pine, The Story of Gramercy Park, 1831–1921 (1921); Portrait Gallery of the Chamber of Commerce of the State of N. Y. (1890), comp. by George Wilson; J. W. Burgess, Reminiscences of an American Scholar (1934); H. S. Ruggles, The Ruggles Family (1917), vol. II; F. B. Dexter, Biog. Sketches

Grads. Yale Coll., vol. VI (1912), which gives year of birth as 1799; *N. Y. Times*, Aug. 29, 1881; data supplied by John Ruggles Strong, a grandson of Ruggles.]
                                                    W. B. S.

RUGGLES, TIMOTHY (Oct. 20, 1711–Aug. 4, 1795), soldier, judge, and Loyalist, son of Rev. Timothy and Mary (White) Ruggles, was born in Rochester, Mass. The founder of his family in America was Thomas, who settled in Roxbury in 1637; his descendants were substantial men and office holders. Young Timothy graduated from Harvard in 1732. Because of his combative energy and bluff wit he seemed ill-suited to the ministry, and became an advocate practising at Rochester and representing that town in the General Court in 1736. In that year he moved to Sandwich, where he married Bathsheba (Bourne) Newcomb, a rich widow, and became proprietor of a tavern. He was a leading lawyer in Barnstable and adjacent counties, and for eight years between 1739 and 1752 was in the legislature.

About 1753 he moved to Hardwick, in Worcester County, where in 1686 his family had acquired a large tract of land. Here he lived in elegant style, keeping a well-stocked stable, hounds, and a deer park, though in his personal habits, especially in eating and drinking, he was most temperate. He was a justice of the peace and member of the legislature almost continually until 1770, and in 1762 serving as speaker. Commissioned colonel in 1755 of one of the Massachusetts regiments which served under Sir William Johnson, he took part in the hard-fought battle of Lake George, contributing to the defeat of Baron Dieskau, fought subsequently in the campaigns of 1756 and 1757, and in 1758 was commissioned a brigadier-general under Lord Amherst and shared in the invasion of Canada. In 1760 he left the service, receiving substantial grants from King and province. In the meantime, 1757, he had been appointed judge of common pleas for Worcester County, and in 1762 he became chief justice, an office he held down to the Revolution.

Ruggles' personality was distinctive and forceful. Young John Adams, who later came to detest his politics, made this diary entry in 1759: "Ruggles's grandeur consists in the quickness of his apprehension, steadiness of his attention, the boldness and strength of his thoughts and expressions, his strict honor, conscious superiority, contempt of meanness, &c. People approach him with dread and terror" (*The Works of John Adams*, vol. II, 1850, p. 67). He was very tall, dark, bold of countenance, given to no silly talk; his speech was blunt, often witty, sometimes profane. He was known as "the Brigadier," and became the subject of many ancedotes, not all authentic. In Mercy Otis Warren's dramatic piece, *The Group*, he figures as Brigadier Hateall. Ruggles was not of the Otis faction; when the people of Boston almost unanimously elected James Otis [*q.v.*] to the General Court, Ruggles prophesied that "out of this election will arise a d—d faction, which will shake this province to its foundations" (*Ibid.*, vol. X, 1856, p. 248).

As the movement toward revolution began to develop, Ruggles lost popularity and influence. At the Stamp Act Congress of 1765 he was elected president over Otis by a single vote, but Otis dominated the scene. Ruggles would not sign the petitions drawn up, alleging scruples of conscience. Thomas McKean [*q.v.*] of Pennsylvania reflected on Ruggles' sincerity, and the Brigadier replied with what McKean interpreted as a challenge, but no duel was fought. Returning to Boston, Ruggles was censured by the legislature and was not allowed to place his reply in its journal. He remained a strong supporter of Gov. Thomas Hutchinson [*q.v.*], threatening, it is said, to put in jail every man who signed the non-importation agreement of 1774. In that year he was made a member of the Council by the King's *mandamus*, but seems not to have taken the oath of office (Stark, *post*, p. 136). At this time a Committee of Correspondence was formed at Hardwick, and Ruggles was obliged to take refuge in Boston. There in December 1774 he strove to form an association of Loyalists pledged not to "acknowledge or submit to the pretended authority of any Congress, Committees of Correspondence, or any other unconstitutional assemblies of men" (Sabine, *post*, II, 244).

In November 1775 General Howe appointed Ruggles to command three companies of volunteers, to be called the Loyal American Associators (Jared Sparks, *The Writings of George Washington*, vol. III, 1834, p. 162, note), but it is doubtful if Ruggles ever fought in the field against the American army, although it appears that he was present for a short time with the British on Long Island. His name was fourth on the list of those banished from Massachusetts by the Act of 1778; his estates were confiscated, and in 1783 he moved to Nova Scotia, where he received a large grant in the wilderness. To the clearing of this tract he devoted the remainder of his life. He died on his estate at Wilmot, and was buried in the church near by. His three sons followed him into exile, but his four daughters remained in the States. One, Bathsheba, wife of Joshua Spooner, caused her husband to be murdered in 1778; apparently insane, she was convicted and hanged, July 2, 1778, after a most sensational trial.

[Lorenzo Sabine, *Biog. Sketches of Loyalists of the Am. Rev.* (1884), vol. II ; J. H. Stark, *The Loyalists of Mass.* (1910) ; E. A. Jones, *The Loyalists of Mass.* (1930) ; H. S. Ruggles, *Gen. Timothy Ruggles* (1895) ; *Am. Quart. Reg.*, May 1841, p. 406 ; C. C. Baldwin, in *Worcester Mag. and Hist. Jour.*, May 1826 ; W. T. Davis, *Hist. of the Judiciary of Mass.* (1900) ; D. H. Hurd, *Hist. of Worcester County, Mass.* (1889), I, xviii ff. ; L. R. Paige, *Hist. of Hardwick, Mass.* (1883) and *An Address at the Centennial Celebration in Hardwick, Mass.* (1838) ; Herbert Parker, *Courts and Lawyers of New England* (1931), vol. I.]   C.F.

RUMFORD, BENJAMIN THOMPSON, COUNT [See THOMPSON, BENJAMIN, 1753–1814].

RUMSEY, CHARLES CARY (Aug. 29, 1879–Sept. 21, 1922), sculptor, poloist, was born in Buffalo, N. Y., the son of Laurence Dana and Jennie (Cary) Rumsey. A maternal uncle, Seward Cary, had a local reputation as a sculptor, but Charles's father achieved prosperity in tanning and railroads. The boy's preliminary education was received at the Nichols School, Buffalo. He early began to develop what later became his two major interests—indicated by his exhibition of a sculptured figure at thirteen and by his friendship with Devereux Milburn, the poloist. Between 1893 and 1895 Rumsey resided in Paris and received instruction from Paul Bartlett [*q.v.*]. Later he entered Harvard University, from which he graduated in 1902, having in the meantime continued his training in sculpture at Boston under Bela Lyon Pratt [*q.v.*]. Between 1902 and 1906 he was again in Paris. During this period, while he was enrolled at the Julian and Colarossi academies, Emmanuel Frémiet became his chief advisor. In 1906 he returned to America and from this time until his death, resulting from an automobile accident, he practised his profession in New York and vicinity. His wife, Mary Harriman, the daughter of Edward H. Harriman, whom he had married May 26, 1910, and three children survived him.

Always enthusiastically interested in amateur athletics and at one time the amateur boxing champion of France, for years he devoted his leisure time to polo. From 1913 he was a member of every United States polo team to compete in international cup matches, and in 1921 was classed as an eight-goal man, only two below the highest rating in the modern game. At the time of his death he was competing in the preliminaries for the international matches of that year. During the World War he attained the rank of captain of cavalry.

Rumsey's most certain fame as a sculptor rests on his bronzes depicting polo ponies and their

riders. In this particular field he unconsciously achieved masterpieces. His patrons for such figures included H. P. Whitney, August Belmont, Thomas Hitchcock, Jr., and J. E. Madden. For the last named he modeled "Nancy Hanks," set up in the equine cemetery at Lexington, Ky. In the other phases of his sculpture Rumsey's work is marked by the zeal of the experimenter and the ability to find inspiration from outstanding sculptors of animals, especially, perhaps, from Barye and even Myron. Notable among his monumental works is the equestrian "Pizarro," awarded a medal at the Panama-Pacific International Exposition in 1915, and later given by the sculptor's widow to the city of Lima, Peru, where Pizarro's bones are deposited (*New York Times*, Dec. 8, 1934). Other heroic figures include the "Dying Indian" given to the Brooklyn Museum, the "Centaur," the "Bull," and "Victory." The last of these marks the war memorial erected in Brooklyn for Brownsville and vicinity, from which district Rumsey enlisted. As examples of his decorative and experimental works may be mentioned the "Buffalo Hunt," a frieze designed to decorate the end of the Manhattan Bridge, the frieze for three sides of the stadium in Rice Memorial Playground, Pelham Park, N. Y., and, in colored cement, the "Pagan," the central figure in the courtyard of his studio at Wheatley Hills, Long Island. Commissions for fountain figures were receiving attention from the sculptor at the time of his death.

An important exhibit of Rumsey's works was held in 1917 at the Sculptor's Gallery in New York City, when the critical public had its first opportunity to form an opinion of his growing facility. Five years after his death, the Société Nationale des Beaux-Arts held a retrospective exhibition in Paris, at which some ninety-four examples of his compositions in bronze and colored cement were shown. In 1930 Rumsey was included in the exhibition of works by current American sculptors at the Brooklyn Museum. To his friends his vitality and versatility were constant sources of amazement. His supple vigor and recklessness as rider added to his personal charms. As a sculptor he infused his own love of life and movement into his compositions, attaining a rhythm and dynamic power which gave them individuality in spite of the evident influences of Rodin, Bourdelle, and Maillol.

[*Harvard Coll. Class of 1902 . . . Sixth Report, June 1922* (1922) ; *N. Y. Times*, Apr. 15, 1917 (mag. section), Sept. 22, 1922 ; *Boston Transcript*, Dec. 19, 1914 ; N. Y. *Evening Post*, Saturday Mag., Apr. 21, 1917 ; *Exposition Rétrospective de l'Oeuvre de Charles Cary Rumsey, 1879–1922 . . . Société nationale des Beaux-Arts Exposition* (Paris, 1927) ; W. H. Fox, "Two Important 'Works by American Sculptors," in *Brooklyn Museum Quart.,* July 1930 ; Arsène Alexandre, "Charles Cary Rumsey," in *La Renaissance de l'Art Français,* June 1927 ; *Public Ledger* (Phila.), Nov. 5, 1922 (mag. section) ; *Who's Who in America,* 1922–23.]

W. S. R.

RUMSEY, JAMES (March 1743–Dec. 20, 1792), inventor, son of Edward and Anna (Cowman) Rumsey, was born on his father's farm at Bohemia Manor, Cecil County, Md. Information regarding the first forty years of his life is scanty. He had an elementary schooling, learned blacksmithing, and is said to have served in the Revolutionary War. He was living in Baltimore in 1780 and two years later, in partnership with a friend, began operating a grist mill at Sleepy Creek, Md. This enterprise lasted less than a year, however, because Rumsey paid no attention to the business and spent his time dreaming of "impossible things." In 1783 he went to Bath, now Berkeley Springs, W. Va., and, with another friend, opened a general store and engaged in the building trade as well, for Bath even then was popular as a health resort. He was busy with these concerns throughout 1783 and 1784 and had the honor of building a house and stables for General Washington on his lands at Bath.

Meanwhile, he had been working in secret on a mechanically propelled boat, at the same time endeavoring to interest capital in his undertaking. While he failed to secure any money, the House of Delegates of the Virginia Assembly in June 1784, by resolution, indicated a sympathetic interest in his boat plans; Washington, after seeing a model of Rumsey's craft, gave him a kindly worded certificate in September; in November, the Virginia legislature granted him the exclusive rights to build his special boats and navigate the waters of the state with them; and two months later, the Maryland legislature granted him a similar privilege. In gaining these advantages, however, Rumsey had neglected his family and business, and by the summer of 1785 he was in bad repute and much in debt. Accordingly, he was glad to accept a position as superintendent of construction of canals for the Potomac Navigation Company, of which General Washington was president. He held it for only a year, however, giving it up because he was dissatisfied with the "pay and emoluments" allowed him (Washington, *Diaries, post,* III, 85).

He now became engrossed in perfecting a steamboat. It is said that he had considered the use of steam power for a boat as early as 1783, but it was not until the winter of 1785 that he actually began to experiment with a steam engine. He worked in secret on his plans throughout 1786 and 1787, but because of the publicity which John Fitch [*q.v.*] was getting in Philadelphia with his project, Rumsey was urged by Washington and others to come out in the open and demonstrate his plans. This he did on Dec. 3, 1787, and again on Dec. 11, exhibiting on the Potomac River, near Shepherdstown, W. Va., a boat propelled by streams of water forced out through the stern, a steam engine being employed to operate the force pump. Having no money to proceed with his experiment and being unable to secure any locally, Rumsey went to Philadelphia in the spring of 1788 and presented his case to the American Philosophical Society, whereupon, on May 9, a number of the members formed the "Rumseian Society," to promote Rumsey's several projects. These included, in addition to his steamboat, an improved steam boiler; an improvement in a saw mill; an improvement in a grist mill; and a plan for raising water by means of a steam engine. Because Fitch held the public's interest in America, the Society immediately sent Rumsey to England to patent his improvements and to interest English capital. He soon secured English patents on his boiler and steamboat, and through his friends, similar patents were granted him by the United States in 1791. For over four years he labored abroad to perfect his second steamboat but throughout that time had the most disheartening experiences, due mostly to the lack of money. Even the Rumseian Society failed him. By the winter of 1792, however, the completion of the *Columbia Maid,* so christened by Rumsey, was in sight; but just a few months before it was finished Rumsey died in London, at the age of forty-nine. His friends in England buried him in St. Margaret's churchyard, near Westminster, but the grave is unmarked.

Rumsey published two pamphlets in 1788 bearing on his steamboat work: *A Plan Wherein the Power of Steam is Fully Shewn ...* and *A Short Treatise on the Application of Steam.* Rumsey was married twice, his second wife having been Mary Morrow. At the time of his death he was survived by his widow and three children, one a daughter by his first wife.

[Letters of Rumsey are in the MSS. Division of the Library of Congress; papers in the suit of *McMechen* vs. *Rumsey,* brought against the Rumsey estate, are in the Va. State Library, and letters from these are printed in *William and Mary Quart.,* Jan.-July 1916. See also *House Report No. 324, 27* Cong., 2 Sess., and *No. 403, 29* Cong., 1 Sess.; Ella May Turner, *James Rumsey* (1930) ; J. L. Bishop, *A Hist. of Am. Manufactures,* vol. I (1861) ; G. M. Beltzhoover, *James Rumsey* (1900) ; J. C. Fitzpatrick, *The Diaries of George Washington* (1925), vols. II, III ; U. S. Nat. Museum records ; Patent Office records.]   C. W. M.

RUMSEY, WILLIAM (Oct. 18, 1841–Jan. 16, 1903), jurist and author of legal works, was born at Bath, N. Y., a son of David and Jane (Brown) Rumsey. He attended schools in Steuben County, N. Y., and then entered Williams College in the class of 1861. He was awarded his degree, though in April of his senior year he left college to become a first lieutenant on the staff of his uncle, Gen. Robert B. Van Valkenburgh of the New York militia. In October he was appointed adjutant of the 1st New York Light Artillery. Promoted to captain and then major, he served on the staff of Gen. William W. Averell [q.v.]. He was twice wounded—at Fair Oaks and at Moorfield—and was brevetted lieutenant-colonel, Mar. 13, 1865, for gallantry in action. He wished to remain in the army after the war, but his father persuaded him instead to travel in the Orient and recuperate from a severe attack of inflammatory rheumatism which had resulted from wounds and exposure. While abroad he was for a time secretary to General Van Valkenburgh, who was then the American minister to Japan.

Early in 1868 he returned to America and began studying law in his father's office. Before the close of the year he was admitted to the bar. Favorable reputation came rapidly. When his father became a justice of the state supreme court, in 1873, William succeeded to his extensive practice; and in 1880, when his father retired from the bench, he was elected to the vacant justiceship, which he held continuously for twenty-one years. He was nominated by the Republicans for judge of the court of appeals in 1888, and was narrowly defeated. After 1895 he sat on the appellate division of the supreme court (first and fourth departments) until 1901, when he resigned to engage in private practice in New York City. Besides his duties on the bench, he aided in formulating the code of civil procedure and the proposed code of evidence, from which experience grew his three-volume work, *The Practice in Actions and Special Proceedings in the Courts of Record in the State of New York* (1887–90). It immediately became the recognized standard on the subject. A second edition under the title, *The Practice in Civil Actions in the Courts of Record in the State of New York under the Code of Civil Procedure,* appeared in 1902–04. It was rendered valueless, however, by the civil practice act of 1920 which repealed the code on which the work was based.

Rumsey was deeply read in legal history. He possessed a phenomenal memory which enabled him to recall accurately the minute details of the development of legal principles. With such an equipment he was able to do his work without drudgery and in an amazingly short time. In general he was conservative; but he did not hesitate to develop—as in the case of *Roberson* vs. *Folding Box Company* (64 *App. Div.*, 30), which sustained a new common-law "right of privacy"—significant extensions of the law, which followed logically from principles already established. On Feb. 1, 1877, he married Ella Moore of Brooklyn, N. Y. He was survived by his widow, two daughters, and a son.

["Proc. in the Appellate Division of the Supreme Court, Fourth Department," 76 *App. Div. Reports,* 631–35; Edward Patterson, in *Asso. of the Bar of the City of N. Y., Annual Report,* 1904; F. B. Heitman, *Hist. Reg. and Dict. U. S. Army* (1903), vol. I; *Who's Who in America,* 1901–02, incorrect in some details; *N. Y. Herald* and *N. Y. Tribune,* Jan. 17, 1903; information as to certain facts from members of Rumsey's family and from his partner, John S. Sheppard.]

E. C. S.

RUNCIE, CONSTANCE FAUNT LE ROY (Jan. 15, 1836–May 17, 1911), composer, pianist, was born in Indianapolis, Ind., the daughter of Robert Henry Faunt Le Roy, a Virginian in the service of the United States Coast Survey as astronomer, and Jane Dale (Owen) Faunt Le Roy, daughter of Robert Owen [see *Dictionary of National Biography*] and sister of David and Robert Dale Owen [qq.v.]. Constance seems to have inherited musical gifts from both her parents; her father was an amateur composer and her mother, from whom she received her first music lessons, a finished performer on the piano and the harp. After a childhood spent in New Harmony, Ind., a village purchased from the Rappists by her grandfather, she was taken in 1852 to Stuttgart, Germany, for five years' training in piano and composition. On Apr. 9, 1861, she married the Rev. James Runcie, an Episcopal clergyman who had officiated at intervals in the little church in New Harmony, where the family had settled once more on returning to the United States. After her marriage she went with her husband to his rectorship in Madison, Ind., and in 1871 to St. Joseph, Mo., where she lived until her death, surviving her husband, who died in 1889, by almost a quarter century. In 1897 an accident deprived her of her hearing. She died in Winnetka, Ill., survived by her two sons and two daughters.

Her music is seldom heard today; but she was well known in her time, and her life and her music were characteristic of the period and environment in which she lived. According to tradition, no musical composition that she submitted to a publisher was rejected. It is said (*Musical America, post*) that William Mason [q.v.], the pianist, once remarked to the composer, "I thought when hearing your music it was that of a man. It is both virile and dramatic." Among her songs the most widely used were "I've Wandered Far Away," "Invocation to Love," "Das Vöglein Singt," and "Take My Soul, O Lord." Besides much published music, she left the manuscript of a romantic opera, *The Prince of Asturia*. She also tried her skill as a writer, published *Poems, Dramatic and Lyric* (1888), and completed two unpublished novels. In addition to her musical activities, she is credited with being the founder of one of the first regularly organized women's clubs in the United States, the Minerva Society, formed in New Harmony, Sept. 13, 1859. The quaint Rappite house in which the club was first organized later became the property of the Indiana Federation of Women's Clubs. In St. Joseph she founded a literary and musical club that still continues and bears her name, the Runcie Club.

[Faunt Le Roy sometimes appears as Fauntleroy. Information about Mrs. Runcie's life has been supplied by her daughter, Elinor Dale Runcie. Printed sources are Stella Reid Crothers in *Musical America*, Aug 21, 1909; A. H. Estabrook, "The Family History of Robert Owen," *Ind. Mag. of Hist.*, Mar. 1923; W. S. B. Mathews, *A Hundred Years of Music in America* (1889); E. E. Hipsher, *American Opera and Its Composers* (1927); *Who's Who in America*, 1910–11; obituary in *N. Y. Times*, May 18, 1911.] J.T.H.

RUNKLE, JOHN DANIEL (Oct. 11, 1822–July 8, 1902), mathematician, educational administrator, son of Daniel and Sarah (Gordon) Runkle, was born at Root, Montgomery County, N. Y., and spent his early life on a farm. Although handicapped at this time in his efforts to secure an education, he persevered, and at the age of twenty-five was able to enter the newly established Lawrence Scientific School at Harvard. In the Harvard catalogue of 1848–49 his name stands alone as "student in mathematics." He was a member of the first graduating class of the Lawrence Scientific School, receiving the two degrees of S.B. and M.A. simultaneously in 1851; after his graduation he sent two of his four younger brothers to Harvard. In 1852 he contributed papers to the *Astronomical Journal* on the elements of Thetis and Psyche (June 26, July 24, 1852). In 1856 his *New Tables for Determining the Values of the Coefficients in the Perturbative Function of Planetary Motion*, were published in the Smithsonian Contributions to Knowledge, and other tables followed in 1857. In 1858 he began the publication of the *Mathematical Monthly*, but the time was not yet ripe for such a journal and only three volumes appeared (October 1858–September 1861). In 1849 he had begun a connection with the *Nautical Almanac*, a relationship which continued in one form or another for thirty-five years. Benjamin Peirce [*q.v.*] thought so highly of him in

his early relations with this publication that in the preface of his *System of Analytic Mechanics* (1855) he said that Runkle had been influential in causing him to publish the work.

In 1862 Runkle married Catharine Robbins Bird. In that same year the Massachusetts Institute of Technology was founded and he became its first secretary. He was professor of mathematics from 1865 to 1868 and from 1880 to 1902, when he was made professor emeritus. In 1868, when illness incapacitated President William Barton Rogers [*q.v.*], Runkle became acting president, and from 1870 to 1878 he was president. In 1871 he conducted an expedition of students to Colorado and Utah for the purpose of observing mines and the processes of mining. In 1872 he established the Lowell School of Practical Design. After resigning his presidency of the Massachusetts Institute of Technology, he spent two years in Europe; during this time he investigated technological schools, and upon his return presented his findings in three papers: "Technical and Industrial Education Abroad" (*Massachusetts Institute of Technology; Abstract of the Proceedings of the Society of Arts*, 1881); "The Manual Element in Education" (*Forty-fifth Annual Report of the Massachusetts Board of Education, 1880–81*, 1882); and "Report of Committee on Industrial Education," in *Fifty-fourth Annual Meeting of the American Institute of Instruction . . . 1883* (1884). His *Manual Element in Education* (1882) was reprinted separately. He also wrote a textbook, *The Elements of Plane Analytic Geometry* (1888), and a report published under the auspices of the Massachusetts Institute of Technology on *The Russian System of Shop-Work Instruction for Engineers and Machinists* (1876).

[*Proc. Washington Acad. of Sci.*, vol. V (1903); *Proc. Am. Acad. Arts and Sci.*, vol. XXXVIII (1903); *Technology Rev.*, July 1902, Apr. 1925 (portr.); *Quinquennial Catalogue of Harvard Univ.* (1925); *Who's Who in America*, 1901–02; *Boston Transcript*, July 10, 1902.] D.E.S.

RUPP, ISRAEL DANIEL (July 10, 1803–May 31, 1878), historian, translator, was born in East Pennsboro (now Hampden) Township, Cumberland County, Pa., the fourth of the fourteen children of George and Christina (Boeshor) Rupp, and was a grandson of Johann Jonas Rupp, a native of Reihen, near Sinsheim, Baden, who emigrated to Pennsylvania in 1751 and in 1772 bought the land on which Israel Daniel was born. He was baptized in the Reformed faith by the Rev. John Winebrenner [*q.v.*] and got his first taste of book-learning from a pious German schoolmaster, Peter Blaeser. He learned English a few years later; Dutch he picked up from his maternal grandfather; and from a Rev. Mr. Vorhoof he acquired the rudiments of French and Latin. Altogether he learned to read eight or nine languages. A German biography of Franklin first awoke his interest in history, which, fed by strong family feeling and love for his native soil, became the preoccupation of his life. In August 1823 he was prostrated by a severe illness, and on his recovery his father allowed him to leave the farm and map out a career for himself. He studied for a while with his physician, Asa Herring, and in 1825 opened a subscription school first at Silver Spring and then at Mechanicsburg. On July 19, 1827, he married Caroline Aristide, daughter of a French physician. They had five daughters and three sons and lived to celebrate their golden wedding.

It was in the year of his marriage that he formed his plan for a great history of Pennsylvania and began his long quest for materials. For some twenty of the next thirty-three years he was a schoolmaster, and according to tradition a very good one, in Cumberland, Dauphin, Lebanon, and Lancaster counties, and perhaps elsewhere; but whenever teaching was not sufficiently peripatetic for his purposes he took to the road in other capacities. At one time he was an itinerant book-seller, and at various times he was an insurance agent. He was a delegate to political conventions, electioneered for John Quincy Adams throughout the German counties in 1828, and, after his hero's defeat, took to the stump in behalf of James Brown's magnificently complicated "American system of syntax"—probably with even less success. Later he went about the state with Josiah Holbrook [q.v.] organizing county, township, and family lyceums. In 1830 he wandered as far west as Cincinnati and there published his *Geschichte der Märtyrer, nach dem ausführlichen Original des Ehrw. Johann Fox und anderer kurz gefasst, besonders für den gemeinen deutschen Mann in den Ver. Staaten von Nord-America aus dem Englischen übersetzt* (new ed., 1832), the first of the eleven works, several of great bulk, that he translated from English into German or from German and Dutch into English. (For a complete list see Seidensticker, *post*.) The next year saw him ensconced as postmaster at Rupp's, Pleasant Township, Marion County, Ohio, but in 1832 he was back in his native state. He edited the Carlisle *Herald* in 1833 and the *Practical Farmer* in 1837. At Harrisburg, whither he was frequently drawn by the state library and archives, he not only taught school but reported the doings of the Senate for the newspapers and wrote speeches for members of both houses of the legislature.

All the while he lost no opportunity to consult books, documents, and public records of all kinds, and he was a constant practitioner of the genial art of pumping information out of magistrates, parsons, and old inhabitants with long memories. His affability and his willingness to receive as well as to impart information made him welcome everywhere.

His *History of Lancaster County* (1844) was the first of six volumes devoted to the history of twenty-three counties of the state. His other historical works were an *Early History of Western Pennsylvania* (1846), *A Collection of Thirty Thousand Names of German . . . Immigrants in Pennsylvania . . . 1727 to 1776* (1856; rev. ed., 1876; a new ed. in prep. by W. J. Hinke), and *A Brief Biographic Memorial of Joh. Jonas Rupp* (1875). His textbooks were *The Lyceum Spelling-Book* (1836), *The Geographical Catechism of Pennsylvania and the Western States* (1836), and *The Farmer's Complete Farrier* (1843; 1847). He edited *The Practical Farmer* (Mechanicsburg, 1837) and *He Pasa Ekklesia: An Original History of the Religious Denominations at Present Existing in the United States* (1844). Even during his lifetime his publications became rare and were much sought after. He laid an enduring foundation for the study of Pennsylvania local history and made the subject popular. Though his books are written in a rough, homespun style, are sometimes poorly arranged, and are peppered with some of the most fantastic of typographical errors, they are generally accurate, show much acumen in separating fact from fancy, and preserve a vast quantity of information that would otherwise have been lost or left all but inaccessible in widely scattered archives. Among his unpublished writings is a diary kept with conscientious care for half a century. In April 1860 he removed to Philadelphia, where he spent the rest of his life. With his simple tastes, industrious habits, and rugged health, he was able by his writing to keep his family in decent comfort and to find much leisure for historical studies. In 1866 he visited Colorado, which he described in delightful letters to the *Reformed Church Messenger*. A week before his death he suffered an apoplectic stroke.

[W. H. Egle, "Our Hist. Writers: I. Daniel Rupp," *Hist. Mag.*, Feb. 1871, and obit. notice, *New Eng. Hist. & Geneal. Reg.*, Jan. 1879; Oswald Seidensticker, "Memoir of Israel Daniel Rupp, the Historian," *Pa. Mag.*, Jan. 1891.]   G. H. G.

RUPP, WILLIAM (Apr. 17, 1839–Apr. 3, 1904), clergyman, theological professor, editor, was born in Lowhill Township, Lehigh County, Pa., son of Solomon and Maria (Frey) Rupp, and eldest of eight children. He was of German ancestry, a lineal descendant of George and Ursula (von Peterholtz) Rupp who came from Alsace about 1750 and settled in Lehigh County. His father was a carpenter and a farmer. Industry, thrift, and domestic piety were the characteristics of the community in which his boyhood was passed. His formal education was begun in the Allentown Seminary. In 1862 he graduated with highest honors from Franklin and Marshall College, and in 1864, from the Theological Seminary of the (German) Reformed Church, then located at Mercersburg, Pa. Since he was only fifteen years old when his father died, his education must have been largely of his own choosing and direction, and significant entries in his diary show that he suffered many privations for the sake of it. He was married on Nov. 16, 1865, to Emma A. Hambright, daughter of Adam F. Hambright of Lancaster, Pa. Eleven children were born to them.

On Feb. 6, 1865, he was ordained to the ministry by the Lebanon Classis of the Reformed Church, and for the next twenty-eight years he served in the active pastorate with comparatively small rural congregations for his field of labor. Thus he had the leisure he craved for further study, some of the subjects he pursued being Hebrew, Greek, and French; Homer, Shakespeare, and Goethe; ancient philosophy and patristic literature; botany and geology. In recommending his practice to his fellow ministers he naively added: "And some degree of such study [the physical and moral laws of the universe] is even required to teach men how to leave such subjects wisely alone" (*An Inaugural Service: Rev. William Rupp, D.D.*, 1894, p. 79). He preached in both English and German, but preaching in the popular sense was not his forte; nevertheless it was through his sermons and in greater degree through his articles in the church periodicals that he became known as a thinker and writer of great force and influence. Thus he was unwittingly qualifying for his election to the chair of practical theology in the theological school of his denomination at Lancaster, Pa.

He entered upon the duties of his office Jan. 1, 1894. The theme upon which he rang the changes throughout his inaugural address was expressed in these words of his own underscoring: "*And the ministry which presents Christ in His full adaptation to the spiritual needs of men at any place or time will be the ministry for the times*" (*An Inaugural Service*, p. 36). He accepted the Christological principle as fundamental to all right thinking in speculative theology and put his faith in it, also, as the determin-

ing factor in practical theology. He contended against traditionalism for a more rational faith —biblical, scientific, liberal—but kept free from what he called the "common rationalism of popular protestantism." His courses in sociology and ethics were regarded as a contribution of great value to the philosophy and practice of the Christian life. His most important writings will be found in the pages of the *Reformed Church Review*, for which he wrote his first article in 1871, later becoming associate editor (1893), and finally, sole editor (1897). Much of his writing was thought-provoking; some of it stirred up a wholesome intellectual strife. He rendered a noteworthy service to his Church in a critical period of controversy and left his impress upon the trend of contemporary theological thought.

[*Franklin and Marshall College Obit. Record*, June 1904; H. H. Rupp, "Excerpts from the Diaries of Wm. Rupp," in *Bull. of the Theological Sem. of the Reformed Church*, Oct. 1930; *An Inaugural Service* (Phila. 1894); files of *Reformed Church Rev.*, 1871-75, 1883-1904; *Reformed Church Messenger*, Apr. 14, 1904.]

G. F. M.

RUSH, BENJAMIN (Dec. 24, 1745 o.s.–Apr. 19, 1813), physician, patriot, humanitarian, was born on a plantation near Philadelphia, in the agricultural community of Byberry, the fourth of the seven children of John and Susanna (Hall) Harvey Rush. He was descended from John Rush, a yeoman from Oxfordshire, who came to Byberry in 1683. His father, a gunsmith and farmer, died when Benjamin was but five years old. At eight he was sent to school with an uncle by marriage, Samuel Finley [*q.v.*], and then to the College of New Jersey (now Princeton), where he received the A.B. degree in 1760. Upon returning to Philadelphia Rush first thought of studying law, but changed his mind in favor of medicine. He was a student under Dr. John Redman from 1761 to 1766 and, in addition to this apprenticeship, attended the first lectures of Dr. William Shippen and Dr. John Morgan in the College of Philadelphia.

During these years he displayed an interest in public affairs, was swayed by Whitefield's preaching, and aroused to youthful patriotism by the Stamp Act controversy; but revivals and politics were forgotten in the zest of professional adventure. On Dr. Redman's advice, he sailed in 1766 to complete his medical education at the University of Edinburgh. There he sat under such masters as Monro, *Secundus*, Joseph Black, and John Gregory, and became the friend and disciple of the great William Cullen. He also found time in the society of fellow students to doubt and debate all things, and so became something of a republican and a philosopher as well as a physician. He received his doctor's degree in June 1768, and immediately went to London for further training in St. Thomas's Hospital. In London he was on friendly terms with Benjamin Franklin, in whose society he learned, among many things, the art of being agreeable.

After a short visit to Paris, Rush returned to Philadelphia in 1769, and at once began to practise medicine. Although he claimed to be without influential friends, he had already arranged an appointment as professor of chemistry in the College of Philadelphia, the first such chair established in the colonies. While holding it Rush published the first American text in that subject, *A Syllabus of a Course of Lectures on Chemistry* (1770, reissued 1773). His practice grew, at first largely among the poor; but within five years he had a very fair income. Rush attracted attention by his unusual ability and training, and also as the practitioner of a new "system." Instead of that of the famous Dr. Hermann Boerhaave, he preached the system of his master, Cullen, with such a scorn for the "old school" that he alienated many of his colleagues. He began writing almost at once, and in 1772 published anonymously one of the first American works on personal hygiene, *Sermons to Gentlemen upon Temperance and Exercise* (London, 1772).

Meanwhile he had become a member of the American Philosophical Society and cultivated other than purely professional interests. In 1773 he published *An Address to the Inhabitants of the British Settlements in America, upon Slave-keeping,* and in 1774 helped to organize the Pennsylvania Society for Promoting the Abolition of Slavery. Maintaining his interest in the quarrel between the colonies and the mother country, he wrote articles for the local press, and associated with such patriot leaders as Thomas Paine, John Adams, and Thomas Jefferson. When war began he offered his services in the patriot cause. While waiting for action, he was married, on Jan. 11, 1776, to Julia Stockton, eldest daughter of Richard Stockton of Princeton. In June he was elected to the Provincial Conference, in which he was a leader in declaring for independence, and a month later was made a member of the Continental Congress. He thus became a signer of the Declaration of Independence.

In April 1777 he was appointed surgeon-general of the armies of the Middle Department. Finding the medical service in a deplorable condition he protested to General Washington, accusing Dr. Shippen, the director general, of maladministration. Washington referred the matter to Congress, which decided in favor of Shippen, and Rush resigned in consequence. Washington's defeats near Philadelphia, in addition to his own personal experiences, now led Rush to question the general's ability; and caused him to be associated indirectly with the Conway Cabal (Rush Manuscripts, XXIX, 136, Ridgway Library). He finally wrote an anonymous letter to Governor Patrick Henry of Virginia, urging that Washington be replaced by Gates or Conway. Henry forwarded this to Washington, who recognized Rush's excellent hand and accused him of personal disloyalty. (Rush's letter, dated Yorktown, Jan. 12, 1778, is printed in John Marshall, *The Life of Washington,* 2 ed., 1832, vol. I, note 12, pp. 29, 30.)

This affair ended Rush's military career, and he returned to his practice in Philadelphia. In the new University of the State of Pennsylvania, opened in 1778, he began to deliver lectures in 1780. In 1783, he became a member of the staff of the Pennsylvania Hospital and served in that capacity for the rest of his life. Here he saw something of the needs of the sick and the poor, and this aroused again his interest in social reform. Stirred, moreover, by the idealism of the Revolution, he now became a sponsor of the various ameliorative movements which were to remould America in the ensuing century. He established the first free dispensary in the country (1786), became president of the Pennsylvania Society for Promoting the Abolition of Slavery (1803), condemned public and capital punishments, and demanded real "penitentiaries" by way of prison reform. His advocacy of temperance was so effective that he has been formally recognized as the "instaurator" of the American temperance movement. His republican enthusiasm led him to favor an improved education for girls, a comprehensive system of schools culminating in a national university, and a theory of education which gave greater freedom to children and encouraged their training in science and utilitarian subjects rather than in the traditional disciplines. Practising what he preached, he persuaded the Presbyterians to found Dickinson College (1783), and served as one of its trustees. Most of his essays on social reform appeared in magazines of Philadelphia, and were later collected and published in 1798 under the title of *Essays, Literary, Moral and Philosophical.* While these were extravagantly praised by contemporaries as masterpieces of prose, they have long since been subjected to a similarly extreme neglect by American readers.

For a brief period in 1787, Rush once more

resorted to the newspapers in the cause of nationalism, this time to urge the acceptance of the new federal Constitution. As a result he was elected to the Pennsylvania ratifying convention, in which he and James Wilson led the successful movement for adoption. In 1789 these two men inaugurated a campaign which secured for the state a more liberal and effective constitution—the last achievement of Rush's political career. His only direct reward was a later appointment by President Adams as treasurer of the United States Mint (1797–1813). After 1789 Rush devoted himself primarily to his profession. The College of Philadelphia, now re-established, was merged in 1791 with the University of the State of Pennsylvania to form the University of Pennsylvania. Since the medical faculties of both schools were retained, there was some shifting of academic chairs. Rush had succeeded, upon the death of Dr. Morgan in 1789, to the chair of theory and practice in the college; in January 1792 he became professor of the institutes of medicine and clinical practice in the new university, and in 1796 succeeded Dr. Adam Kuhn as professor of theory and practice as well. In addition to the university connection, he was associated with those who organized the Philadelphia College of Physicians in 1787, although he resigned from this body in the course of the first yellow-fever controversy.

Three aspects of Rush's medical work deserve attention: his "system" of theory and practice; his specific contributions to medical science; and his influence as a teacher. He had inherited from Cullen a complicated nosology, a distrust of natural healing powers, and a corresponding confidence in the use of special remedies for each species of disease. He probably also acquired from Cullen, as well as from the general medical philosophy of the day, the view that all theory should be organized, on rational principles, into a "system" that would make practice simple and intelligent (William Cullen, *First Lines of the Practice of Physic*, 1796, pp. 9–52). Cullen had urged that each generation formulate new systems, in order to keep pace with advancing scientific knowledge; and during the eighties two of his ablest pupils, John Brown of Edinburgh and Rush, began to take him at his word. It happened that Cullen's pathology had emphasized the rôle of the nervous system and nervous energy, rather than the old conceptions concerning the humors and solids. Exaggerating this point, Brown concluded that all diseases were due either to an excess or to a lack of nervous stimulation, and thus indicated either "depleting" or stimulating remedies (John Brown, *The Ele-

ments of Medicine*, 1788, *passim*). This view soon had a wide following in Europe, and Rush in America was so impressed that he decided to carry "Brunonianism" one step further to its logical conclusion. It is impossible to describe his system briefly without over-simplification, but the essential principle was the reduction of Brown's two types of disease to one. All diseases, he decided, were due to one "proximate" cause, a state of excessive excitability or spasm in the blood vessels, and hence in most cases called for the one treatment of "depletion" through bleeding and purging. Thus, as he himself declared, there was after all but one disease and one type of treatment (Manuscript Lectures on the Practice of Physic, 1796, I, Lecture No. 31, University of Pennsylvania Library). This conception was so simple, and so completely the antithesis of the nosology in which he had been trained, that it came to hold for his speculative mind all the fascination of an ultimate panacea. It was, literally, too good to be true, but he confidently proclaimed it when the initial volume of his *Medical Inquiries and Observations* was published in 1789.

The system was soon pronounced fanciful by various critics, who also declared that its author's fondness for depletion led him to dangerous extremes in practice. He seems to have averaged about ten ounces in ordinary bleedings, but often took more, and was actually willing to remove as much as four-fifths of all the blood in the body (*Medical Inquiries and Observations*, 3 ed., 1809, vol. IV, 353). Rush scorned the first criticism on the ground that reasoning and deduction were essentials in scientific method, and claimed that his treatment succeeded in practice. The real test of this claim seemed to have come in the epidemic of yellow fever which descended upon Philadelphia in 1793. Rush worked with desperation and devotion for three months, while several thousand of his fellow citizens, including members of his own household, died of the "yellow monster." His treatment, he declared, was practically always effective when employed promptly. But the only supporting data he offered were aggressive and dogmatic assertions as to his diagnoses and cures. He wrote a justly famous account of the epidemic as a whole, but failed to keep an exact record of his own cases. In a word, while correct in his view that hypotheses have their place in medicine, he was largely blind to his obligation to check them against the facts. Vital statistics of a sort were already available but he did not use them. The way was thus open for a lay critic, William Cobbett, to point out the correlation between the increasing employment of Rush's treatment and the increasing mortality rate—the more bleeding, the more deaths! The doctor's system, Cobbett observed, is "one of the great discoveries . . . which have contributed to the depopulation of the earth" (*The Rush-Light,* New York, Feb. 28, 1800, p. 49). The pamphleteer's motives were not above suspicion, and Rush's treatment was not the only variable involved; yet it was indeed impossible to reconcile his claims with the stark fact of the mortality tables. He was not guilty of deliberate misrepresentation, but rather the victim of a certain credulity about diagnoses and cures which characterized much of his work.

The epidemic had several immediate effects, so far as Rush was concerned. His view that its "remote" cause was unsanitary conditions antagonized many citizens, and particularly those doctors who ascribed the disease to importation and contagion. Both this issue and that relating to treatments, were taken into the newspapers, and Rush again found himself the center of controversy. Nevertheless, his published accounts of the epidemic, and of those which followed it, won for him recognition by several European governments and learned societies. The chief essay is *An Account of the Bilious Remitting Yellow Fever, as it Appeared in the City of Philadelphia, in the Year 1793* (1794).

It has been remarked that Rush was an observant man, but not a good observer. His shortcomings as a systematic observer have been noted; it remains to point out that he was indeed an observant man in special fields of medicine. There is reason to believe that he was the pioneer worker in experimental physiology in the United States. He was the first American to write on *cholera infantum,* and the first to recognize focal infection in the teeth. He was probably the first to advocate the study of veterinary medicine. His repudiation of current nosology was valuable, in that he strove to reduce the confusion of treatments associated therewith—he favored purging the *materia medica* as well as his patients. Most notable were his contributions to psychiatry, made while working with the insane at the Pennsylvania Hospital, where he inculcated a scientific and fairly humane attitude toward this class of patients. His famous work, *Medical Inquiries and Observations upon the Diseases of the Mind* (1812) shows some appreciation of what would today be known as mental healing and even of psycho-analysis. He was, finally, the first medical man in the country to achieve a general literary reputation.

Rush, therefore, was probably the best-known American physician of his day, though his reputation as a scientist was exaggerated because of his popularity as a teacher. He was hated by his enemies, but there is overwhelming evidence that he was admired by his students to a degree rare in the history of any of the professions. His classes grew ever larger, and his fame spread throughout the country, especially in the South and West. His son James declared that while before 1790 Rush's classes numbered from sixteen to forty-five annually, by 1812 he had had 2872 in his medical classes, and, including private students, 3000 in his lifetime (cited by Goodman, *post,* pp. 132, 162). No wonder he contributed, more than any other one man, to the establishment of Philadelphia as the leading American center of medical training during the first half of the nineteenth century.

Rush was well and active until a few days before his death on Apr. 19, 1813. He was buried in Christ's Church graveyard in Philadelphia and here his wife was buried thirty-five years later. Of his thirteen children six sons, among them James and Richard Rush [*qq.v.*], and three daughters survived him. He died a professing Christian, but without strict denominational attachments. He was at various times a member of the Episcopalian and the Presbyterian churches, accepted the Universalists' view of salvation, and has been claimed by the Unitarians. In fact his education so broadened his mind as to destroy any spirit of denominationalism, without weakening a generally pious outlook which was the result of early training. His piety, however, was complacent and inconsistent at times; and his occasional use of theological arguments in medical reasoning was a survival of medievalism in method entirely foreign to his abler contemporaries. The truth is that Rush had an able and versatile, but not a fundamentally critical mind.

[The majority of Rush's manuscripts are in the Ridgway Branch of the Philadelphia Lib. Co.; others are in the Pa. Hist. Soc., the Univ. of Pa., the Philadelphia Coll. of Physicians, the Girard Estate, the N. Y. Academy of Medicine, the N. Y. Hist. Soc., the Lib. of Cong., and in the private possession of Mr. Lynford Biddle of Chestnut Hill, Philadelphia. Important printed sources are: E. C. Burnett, ed., *Letters of Members of the Continental Cong.,* vols. I–III (1921–1926), containing selections from his diary and correspondence; *A Memorial Containing Travels through Life or Sundry Incidents in the Life of Dr. Benjamin Rush. . . . Written by Himself* (1905); H. G. Good, *Benjamin Rush and His Services to Am. Education* (1918); sketches in various collections of American medical biography, of which the most detailed is that by Samuel Jackson in S. D. Gross, ed., *Lives of Eminent Am. Physicians and Surgeons of the Nineteenth Century* (1861), pp. 2–85; and the most reliable, that by Francis Packard, in H. A. Kelly and W. L. Burrage, eds., *Diction-*

ary of Am. Medical Biography (1928); the favorable essay of David Ramsay, *An Eulogium upon Benjamin Rush, M.D.* (1813); the critical essay by Victor Robinson, "The Myth of Benjamin Rush," *Medical Life*, Sept. 1929, vol. XXXVI, pp. 445–48. A list of Rush's publications and a general bibliography are in Good, pp. 259–75; and an almost complete list is in the *Index Catalogue of the Lib. of the Surgeon-General's Office, U. S. A.*, XII (1891), pp. 398–400. N. G. Goodman, *Benjamin Rush, Physician and Citizen, 1746–1813* (1934), the latest and most complete study, is well documented and contains an excellent bibliography. A death notice appeared in *Poulson's American Daily Advertiser*, Apr. 21, 1813.]   R. H. S—k.

RUSH, JAMES (Mar. 15, 1786–May 26, 1869), physician and psychologist, was born in Philadelphia, seventh of the thirteen children of Dr. Benjamin Rush [*q.v.*] and his wife, Julia (Stockton), and brother of Richard Rush [*q.v.*]. He graduated from the College of New Jersey (Princeton) in 1805, and was granted the degree of M.D. at the University of Pennsylvania in 1809. He then followed his father's example by continuing his medical training at Edinburgh, where he was as much influenced by current philosophical thought as by strictly professional interests. Upon returning to Philadelphia in 1811, he began to practise medicine, and gave some private lectures, though, contrary to certain statements regarding him, he never held a regular chair. Personally attractive and of some means, he gave considerable time to social life, and on Oct. 19, 1819, married Phoebe Anne Ridgway, daughter of Jacob Ridgway, a wealthy Philadelphia merchant. She eventually inherited an estate of more than a million dollars and became something of a leader in local society, though tradition has it that, having come from "north of Market Street," she always experienced some opposition in her social aspirations.

Rush gradually gave up his practice and came to devote himself largely to social and scientific interests. In 1827 he published in Philadelphia *The Philosophy of the Human Voice,* in which a medical approach to the subject was followed by a detailed treatise on elocution. Although unattractive to the modern reader, this work achieved popularity in an age of declamation, and went through six editions by 1867. In 1834 he published *Hamlet, a Dramatic Prelude, in Five Acts.* During his younger years, he had worked occasionally on psychological studies, only to abandon them in middle age; but the death of his wife on Oct. 23, 1857, led him to retire from social life and to return to his earlier interests. He finally published his *magnum opus,* a two-volume *Brief Outline of an Analysis of the Human Intellect* (1865), which proved to be a learned and rather original work, but one that was verbose and almost unreadable. It is of some

interest, however, in that it expressed a relatively early American concern with the development of psychology as an objective science. "The mind," he observed, "has been and still is regarded as the working of a *spiritual something* in the brain, and therefore not to be investigated, as a physical function of the senses and the brain conjoined. This appears to be the principal cause why the problem of the mind has not been finally solved, on the clear and assignable data of observation and experiment: for who has ever experimented upon Spirit? And certainly Thinking and Wrangling, in the metaphysical way of demonstration, have never been able to show . . . any thing within, or round about it" (vol. II, p. 475). This general point of view he claimed to have held since the beginning of the century.

Rush really represented that mid-stage in the modernization of a science in which one theorizes about avoiding theory and establishing facts; and he was apparently unaware that the final stage, that of systematic inductive procedures, was already being attained by the German psycho-physicists of the time. Rush died, a childless, embittered recluse, in his old home on Chestnut Street in 1869; his last book, *Rhymes of Contrast on Wisdom and Folly* (1869), expresses ironic condemnation of the younger generation and all its wicked works. He left his estate to the Library Company of Philadelphia, to establish the Ridgway Branch of that institution, stipulating that every ten years during the half-century following his death, the Library Company should publish an edition of 500 copies of each of his books, to be sold at cost (*Provisions of the Last Will and Testament of Dr. James Rush, relating to the Library Company of Philadelphia,* 1869). He added, furthermore (*Ibid.,* p. 27), "Let it not keep cushioned seats for time-wasting and lounging readers, nor places for everyday novels, mind-tainting reviews, controversial politics, scribblings of poetry and prose, biographies of unknown names, nor for those teachers of disjointed thinking, the daily newspapers."

[*Provisions,* cited above; *A Memorial . . . of Dr. Benjamin Rush . . . Written by Himself* (1905); MSS. in the Ridgway Branch, Library Co. of Phila.; *Public Ledger* (Phila.), May 28, 1869.]   R. H. S—k.

RUSH, RICHARD (Aug. 29, 1780–July 30, 1859), lawyer, diplomat, and statesman, was born at Philadelphia, Pa., the second son and third child of the celebrated physician, Benjamin Rush [*q.v.*], and Julia (Stockton) Rush. The boy grew up in a cultivated household, and at the age of fourteen was ready for entrance into the College of New Jersey (now Princeton), from which his father and his maternal grandfather had graduated. In college he was the youngest member of his class, and, while not a distinguished student, showed great interest and ability in debating. After finishing his course he studied law in the office of William Lewis, a well-known legal luminary of Philadelphia, and was admitted to the bar in December 1800. His early years of practice were not particularly brilliant, but during them Rush met many interesting persons who came to his father's house, and read widely in law, history, government, and literature. His reputation as a speaker began to be established when in 1807 he made an eloquent speech on the sinking of the *Chesapeake* at a public meeting in the State House yard in Philadelphia. In 1808 he defended William Duane, the editor of the *Aurora,* against the charge of libel for an attack upon Gov. Thomas McKean of Pennsylvania, and thus made his first important political contacts. He refused, however, to be a candidate for Congress at this time.

In January 1811, he was appointed attorney-general of Pennsylvania, the beginning of nearly twenty years of uninterrupted office-holding. An ardent Republican, he warmly opposed the renewal of the charter of the Bank of the United States, and in November, having attracted the favorable attention of President Madison, to whom he long remained devoted, he became comptroller of the treasury. On July 4, 1812, the administration put him forward to defend the war with Great Britain in an address at Washington. Rush's temperament, in general, was not belligerent, and the cool and objective character of his mind was ill-suited to whipping up the war-spirit. The speech is almost apologetic in tone, far too argumentative to be a great war speech, but it seemed to be well received, and encouraged him to more political pronouncements, which helped to make him better known. In February 1814, he was offered the choice of the offices of secretary of the treasury, or of attorney-general, and chose the latter. In this post he was charged with the duty of editing the *Laws of the United States* from 1789 to 1815 (5 vols., 1815), which he performed in authoritative fashion. On the inauguration of Monroe, Rush was made secretary of state, pending the return of John Quincy Adams from Europe to assume that office. In this capacity, he negotiated the famous Rush-Bagot convention (Apr. 28, 1817), establishing a limitation of naval armaments on the Great Lakes, one of the earliest treaties of this kind in the history of the United States. On Oct. 31, 1817, he was appointed minister to Great Britain.

Rush was undoubtedly amongst the most efficient and amongst the best liked of American ministers to the Court of St. James's. A man of high breeding, emphatically a gentleman, he moved with ease in the British society of the period, and his genuine regard for the British people, coupled with wide intellectual interests and a tact that was almost unfailing, gave him a wide measure of success. He was confronted with a great variety of difficult problems at the very outset, a number of important disputes with Great Britain left over by the War of 1812 not having yet been liquidated. These included the fisheries question, the matter of compensation for the slaves carried off by the British in the war, and the troublesome problem of the northwestern boundary. The convention of Oct. 20, 1818, did not really settle all of these, only the question of the slaves being put in the way of a final solution. But Rush negotiated a treaty of joint occupation of Oregon which served as a basis of understanding for nearly thirty years, and he secured important concessions on the fisheries problem. In 1819 he dealt with great wisdom with the issue raised by Andrew Jackson's recent invasion of Florida, and the execution of two British subjects, Ambrister and Arbuthnot. British public opinion was exceedingly inflamed, and Lord Castlereagh, the foreign secretary, afterwards told the minister that war might have been brought about if he had but lifted a finger (*Memoranda of a Residence at the Court of London,* 1845, p. 152). In his conversations with Castlereagh, Rush set forward the American point of view with remarkable candor, and yet without offense. His description of his interview with Castlereagh on this occasion may be regarded as a model of diplomatic manners.

Rush played an important rôle in the diplomatic negotiations which led up to the enunciation of the Monroe Doctrine. In the summer of 1823, French troops had invaded Spain, and George Canning, the British foreign secretary, had received certain intimations from Sir Charles Stuart, the British minister in Paris, with regard to a projected congress on the affairs of South America. Suspecting that such a congress might pave the way for the re-conquest of the Spanish colonies, Canning asked if it might not be possible for Rush to join him in a joint prohibition of such action. Rush had, of course, no instructions. After carefully pondering the matter, he decided that he could not accept the proposal, barring British recognition of the independence of the colonies. When Canning stated his inability to act on this basis, Rush, despite new and pressing overtures from Canning, refused to commit himself. The dispatches which he wrote in August and September 1823 were an important factor in persuading James Monroe and John Quincy Adams to take the strong stand which they assumed in the memorable message of Dec. 2. The message was not well received in England. In particular, that part of it (directed against Russia in the northwest, and not concerned with the Spanish colonies) which forbade new colonization by European powers in the American hemisphere, was most unacceptable to Canning. Rush had to do what he could to defend it, and, acting under instructions, he brought it forward in the new discussions on the northwest question which took place in 1824. He did not, however, succeed in persuading the British commissioners to acquiesce in it.

In the course of his long stay in England, Rush examined many different aspects of British institutions. He made a special study of the British navy, and it was his desire, when John Quincy Adams became president in 1825, that he might become secretary of the navy in the new administration. At Adams' insistence however, he accepted the office of secretary of the treasury, and discharged the duties of this post with extraordinary fidelity, never having been absent from office a single day in the course of four years, except for one week's illness. In this period of his life he was a protectionist, though of a rather mild type. He was no doubt partly influenced by the opinion of his state, and also apparently by the infant industry argument. He desired, however, to institute a warehouse and drawback system, not unlike that which existed in Great Britain. He played no prominent part in connection with the tariff of abominations in 1828, but does not seem to have been hostile to that measure. In 1828 he accepted a place on the ticket with John Quincy Adams, as a candidate for vice-president, but went down to crushing defeat with the rise of the Jacksonian Democracy. At this period came one of Rush's rare lapses from the urbanity which was characteristic of him. On his appointment to the Treasury, he had been the object of a slashing attack by John Randolph, who stigmatized his appointment as the worst since Caligula had made his horse a consul (Powhatan Bouldin, *Home Reminiscences of John Randolph, of Roanoke*, 1878, p. 317). Rush was stung by this, and other attacks, into publishing under the pen name of Julius an attack upon Randolph, splenetic in the extreme. He declared his willingness to avow his authorship, and accept a challenge

to a duel, if Randolph cared to take the pains to look into the matter (Julius, *John Randolph, Abroad and at Home,* 1828, p. 13).

For some years after 1828 Rush was in private life. In 1829 he was sent abroad by the towns of Georgetown and Alexandria and the city of Washington to negotiate a loan of one and a half million dollars for the Chesapeake & Ohio Canal. Received with considerable coolness in Great Britain, despite his many personal friendships there, he finally succeeded in getting very favorable terms from the Dutch bank of the Crommelins. His efforts were not as gratefully received as he thought they should have been by those who sent him. In the Anti-Masonic agitation Rush took a prominent part, and he was the first choice of the new political group for the presidency. He declined to run, however. The struggle over the Bank in 1832 brought him back into the Democratic party. He sympathized strongly with President Jackson on this issue. In 1835, together with Gen. Benjamin Chew Howard of Baltimore, he was commissioned to settle a boundary dispute between the states of Ohio and Michigan, which threatened to result in an appeal to force. He succeeded in preventing an armed clash, though not in settling the question. In the summer of 1836 he sailed for England to secure the Smithson bequest to the United States. James Smithson, an Englishman, had died without issue, and had left the whole of his estate, on the death of a nephew, to the United States. The estate had become tied up in the chancery court, however, and it required much time and patience to liquidate the matter. Rush conducted his mission with efficiency and patience, and made use of his stay in Great Britain to resume many old connections, and to make new ones (*Occasional Productions, Political, Diplomatic, and Miscellaneous,* 1860, pp. 219–57). He was also extremely successful in disposing on very favorable terms of the British securities which composed the Smithson estate, and, in August 1838, brought back to this country in English gold coin the sum of upwards of £104,000, which was used to establish the Smithsonian Institution. He always retained a great interest in this establishment, of which he was elected a regent, a post which he held to his death (Cyrus Adler, "The Relation of Richard Rush to the Smithsonian Institution" in *Smithsonian Miscellaneous Collections,* vol. LII, 1910, pp. 235–51).

The next public service to which this interesting man was called (Mar. 3, 1847) was that of minister to France, in the administration of President Polk. From 1838 to 1847 he had lived quietly on his estate outside of Philadelphia, but though now sixty-seven years old, he cheerfully accepted political office once more. He arrived in France in the closing days of the July monarchy, and was a witness to the stirring events of the February revolution, which he described with much skill (*Occasional Productions,* pp. 355–82). After a brief period of reflection, he decided to recognize the republic then set up, without waiting for instructions from Washington, and despite the reserve of all the other members of the diplomatic corps. He followed with obvious mistrust the course of the red republican revolt of July, but seems to have witnessed without extravagant regret the election of Louis Napoleon as president in December 1848. He was recalled with the entry of the Whigs into power in 1849.

This was Rush's last political office. He lived for ten years more, and still entertained an interest in public affairs. He approved the compromise measures of 1850, but was, in general, sympathetic with the attitude of the Democratic party towards slavery. He much feared the dissolution of the Union, censured the extravagance of the anti-slavery agitation, and voted for Buchanan in 1856. He died in Philadelphia on July 30, 1859. He had married Catherine E. Murray on Aug. 29, 1809; of their ten children, three sons and two daughters survived him.

Of the men of the second rank who played a rôle in politics in the Middle Period, Richard Rush is decidedly one of the most attractive. He no doubt betrays a certain conventionality of mind, in the general character of his political thought, but he was by no means unwilling to accept personal responsibility, or to act on his own initiative when the occasion required. He had singularly few enemies; indeed, outside of the feud with the acid Randolph, and one youthful political altercation in Pennsylvania, his life was remarkably free from personal controversy. Laborious to a degree, of judicious mind, of wide intellectual interests, and of engaging manners, he played worthily every rôle to which he was called. A certain fastidiousness may have had something to do with the limited character of his political success, as compared with that of other men decidedly his inferiors in capacity. In appearance he was distinctly impressive. He had remarkable eyes, a broad and high forehead, and an air of scholarship that was decidedly attractive. His writings are not literary masterpieces, but they are usually interesting, and reveal a keen observer of men and things. The most important are his *Memoranda of a Residence at the Court of London,* the first edition

of which (1833) covered only two years, a second edition (1845) comprising the rest of his mission; and *Occasional Productions, Political, Diplomatic and Miscellaneous,* published by his executors in 1860.

[In addition to the works mentioned in the text, see an excellent account of Rush's career down to 1840, in the *U. S. Mag. and Democratic Rev.,* Apr. 1840, pp. 301–25. C. K. Webster, *The Foreign Policy of Castlereagh, 1815–1822* (1925); Dexter Perkins, *The Monroe Doctrine, 1823–1826* (1927); W. C. Ford, "John Quincy Adams and the Monroe Doctrine," in *Am. Hist. Rev.,* July 1902; J. M. Callahan, "Agreement of 1817. Reduction of Naval Forces upon the Great Lakes," in *Ann. Report of the Am. Hist. Asso. for the Year 1895* (1896); Beckles Willson, *America's Ambassadors to England, 1785–1928* (1928), and *America's Ambassadors to France, 1777–1927* (1928); *A Memorial . . . of Dr. Benjamin Rush . . . Written by Himself* (1905); *Am. State Papers. Foreign Relations,* vols. IV, V (1834, 1858); obituaries in *Daily National Intelligencer* (Washington), *Public Ledger* (Philadelphia), Aug. 2, 1859; Trescott Papers, Lib. of Cong.; his diplomatic dispatches in the State Department.]   D. P.

RUSH, WILLIAM (July 4, 1756–Jan. 17, 1833), the first native American sculptor, was of direct descent in the fourth generation from John Rush, who had commanded a troop of horse in Cromwell's army, and came to Pennsylvania in 1683. William, born in Philadelphia, was the son of a ship-builder, Joseph Rush, coroner of the city from 1780 to 1785, and Rebecca (Lincoln) Rush, of the same family as Abraham Lincoln; his father was a first cousin of Dr. Benjamin Rush [*q.v.*]. The boy was early apprenticed to Edward Cutbush, from London, England, a wood-carver, whom within three years Rush surpassed in creating the figures which were then much in demand for the prows of ships. He is said to have served in the Revolution, and on Dec. 14, 1780, he married Martha Wallace of Philadelphia. Intelligent, industrious, and gifted, at once artist and craftsman, he established for himself a thriving business. His laurel-crowned "America" adorned the prow of the United States frigate *America.* For the frigates *Constellation* and *United States* he carved figures representing respectively "Nature" and the "Genius of the United States." It is recorded that London wood-carvers enthusiastically copied his "Indian Trader," on the ship *William Penn,* and that Hindus reverenced his "River God," on the ship *Ganges.* In "Suggestions of William Rush to Naval Constructor Joshua Humphreys, for designs for figureheads for naval vessels," dated Apr. 30, 1795 (*Pennsylvania Magazine of History and Biography,* April 1907), are mentioned various emblems dear to Rush: the cardinal virtues, the flaming torch, the Goddess of Liberty supported by Law and Justice, "the American Eagle Darting upon and Destroying the Vitals of Tyranny, with the shackels of Despotism."

Rush's once famous figureheads have now vanished, except for the well-known life-size statue of Washington, now in Independence Hall, Philadelphia, intended originally as the figurehead for a ship to be named *Washington*. Many of his other carvings remain, however. Among these are the naïve figures of "Comedy" and "Tragedy" loaned to the Pennsylvania Museum of Art; and several important works preserved at Fairmount Park, Philadelphia. These last include "Wisdom" and "Justice," colossal figures made to crown a triumphal arch in front of Independence Hall in honor of Lafayette's visit in 1824, and now in the assembly room of the Fairmount water works. At Fairmount, also, is a bronze replica of Rush's most notable work, the "Spirit of the Schuylkill," the first public fountain figure erected in the United States. The original wood carving was placed in Centre Square, now Penn Square, to commemorate the founding of the Philadelphia water system. Critics of opposing camps agree as to the grace, refinement, and good proportion of this female figure in symbolic rippling drapery, girdled with sedge and holding up a bittern spouting water. This work is often called the "Nymph with Bittern," and (mistakenly) "Leda and the Swan." A belle of the day "consented to pose" for the sculptor—an episode later celebrated in a painting by Thomas Eakins [*q.v.*]. Similar in conception to the "Spirit of the Schuylkill," but more commonplace in design and execution, are the two carvings in wood of reclining draped figures, now placed outside the Fairmount water-works buildings, and entitled respectively "Schuylkill Enchained," and "Schuylkill Released." A life-size group in wood, "Liberty Crowning the Bust of Washington," was exhibited at the Metropolitan Museum, New York, in 1927. From internal evidence, according to the Museum authorities, it may safely be attributed to Rush. He worked in clay as well as in wood and greatly regretted that he had not time to try marble. It is said that when orders pressed, he would stand over an apprentice, directing him where to cut, Rush's belief being that, whatever material is used, the artist must clearly visualize within it the form he wills to release, and that the rest of the work is merely mechanical. He studied nature carefully, as his work shows.

The Pennsylvania Academy owns a plaster cast of his symbolic self-portrait, carved in pine, his shoulders shaped in the semblance of a rough log, with a pine branch over it. Despite a touch of the grotesque in the vigorous treatment, it presents a noble, kindly head, in harmony with the few facts known of him as a public-spirited citizen. After initial attempts (1789–91), the painter Charles Willson Peale [*q.v.*] and a small group of others including Rush were finally able in 1805 to found the Pennsylvania Academy of the Fine Arts, the earliest organization of the kind in the United States, Rush serving as one of the directors from that time until his death. He was also an influential member of the city council for a period stated as "more than a quarter of a century" (Taft, *post*, p. 23). In 1812 he exhibited at the Academy a group of his later works, of which Dunlap lists busts of Linnæus, William Bartram, and the Rev. Henry Muhlenberg, together with figures of "Exhortation," "Praise," and "a Cherubim." To this number others have added two busts of William Penn, a self-portrait, busts of Voltaire, Franklin, Rousseau, and Lafayette, and figures of "Architecture," "Agriculture," and "Christ on the Cross." Other titles of works by Rush are "Winter," "Commerce," "Peace," and "War."

[J. T. Scharf and Thompson Westcott, *Hist. of Phila.* (1884), vol. III; *Pa. Mag. of Hist. and Biog.*, July 1907; *A Memorial . . . Incidents in the Life of Dr. Benjamin Rush . . . as well as a Short Hist. of the Rush Family in Pa.* (privately printed, 1905); C. H. Hart, *Browere's Life Masks of Great Americans* (1899); J. M. Beck, in *Fairmount Park Art Asso.: 50th Anniversary* (1922); Wilfred Jordan, in *Art and Archaeology*, June 1921; William Dunlap, *Hist. of the Rise and Progress of the Arts of Design in the U. S.* (Goodspeed ed., 1918), inaccurate in some details; Lorado Taft, *The Hist. of Am. Sculpture* (1904), Suzanne LaFollette, *Art in America* (1929); C. R. Post, *A Hist. of European and Am. Sculpture* (1921); F. D. Whittemore, *George Washington in Sculpture* (1933).]   A. A.

RUSK, JEREMIAH McCLAIN (June 17, 1830–Nov. 21, 1893), congressman, governor of Wisconsin, secretary of agriculture, was born on a farm in Morgan County, Ohio, the son of Daniel Rusk and Jane Faulkner, both natives of Pennsylvania and children of Scotch-Irish immigrants to Maryland. Both his grandfathers had fought in the Revolution shortly after their arrival in America. Jeremiah's common-school education was meager. At the age of sixteen, after the death of his father, he managed his mother's farm; later he drove a stage and became a railway construction foreman. In 1853 he removed to Wisconsin, settling in Viroqua, Vernon County, as tavern keeper. To this business he soon added the ownership of a stage line and a good farm, and in time the part ownership of a bank. His extraordinary activity, sound practical judgment, and personal popularity made his numerous business enterprises uncommonly successful.

Equal or greater success waited on his political ambitions. In 1855 he was elected sheriff of his county, and two years later, coroner. In 1861, he was elected to the state Assembly, resigning in 1862 to become major in the 25th Wisconsin Infantry, a regiment he had recruited. He rose in rank from major to lieutenant-colonel, won distinction for his soldierly conduct at "The Crossing," in the battle of Salkehatchie River, February 1865 (*War of the Rebellion: Official Records, Army,* 1 ser. XLVII, pt. 1, p. 387), and at the close of the war was brevetted colonel and brigadier-general. After his return to Wisconsin, he was elected state bank controller in 1865 and reëlected in 1867. In 1871 he went to Congress as successor to C. C. Washburn, and served for three terms.

He declined diplomatic appointment in 1881, but was that year elected governor of Wisconsin. He set a record for length of service as governor of his state: he was elected three times and one of his terms was extended by statute, so that he was in office seven years. During this period he made his deepest impression upon the people of the state, earning the title of affection: "Uncle Jerry." His governorship, strong in every respect, was marked by two highly dramatic episodes—the feeding of 1700 desperate railway workers left stranded without pay by a bankrupt railway company, and the quelling of the industrial strike riots in Milwaukee in May 1886. In the first case Rusk enforced the remedy, "bread, not bayonets." In the second, after his repeated warnings that violence and property destruction would not be tolerated, he gave the order to fire, which put an end to the rioting. His most characteristic remark, known to millions, was uttered in connection with that grim incident: "I seen my duty and I done it."

His devotion to duty was acclaimed so universally as to make him appear to many an available candidate for the presidential nomination in 1888. In consequence, when Harrison upon his inauguration found himself with a new office to fill in the secretaryship of agriculture, he called Rusk to that position, afterwards saying of him: "He not only filled the measure of the man I wanted, but enlarged it" (Casson, *post,* p. 2). Rusk's service was noteworthy for at least two achievements: he secured the inspection of all American meat exports, with the consequent eradication of cattle and swine diseases complained of by importing countries, and thus prepared the way for the removal of European restrictions on such imports; and he at once popularized the new department's activities and policies by engaging the interest of the newspapers.

After Mar. 4, 1893, he retired to his farm, where he died eight months later.

Jerry Rusk was a character to inspire legend. Tall (six feet, three inches), broad, and well set up, he was physically fit for any emergency. His democratic ways, cheery manner, spontaneous humor, and great good sense, coupled with his loyalty and dependableness, endeared him not only to business and political associates, but to the people of Wisconsin generally. Though practically uneducated and never a reader, he was a clear, straightforward, logical thinker and writer on every day business and administrative subjects. His was fundamentally the active, not the reflective type of mind. In politics he was a strict party conformist, and a conciliator of factional differences.

On Apr. 5, 1849, in Ohio, Rusk married Mary Martin, by whom he had three children. She died in January 1856, and in December of that year, at Viroqua, he married Elizabeth M. Johnson, by whom he had two children.

[Henry Casson, *Uncle Jerry* (1895), the only general biography, is diffuse and eulogistic, but presents the main facts of Rusk's life. It contains an introduction written by Benjamin Harrison, also speeches on Rusk by John C. Spooner. An attack in violent language on Rusk as secretary of agriculture was printed anonymously at Lincoln, Nebr., Aug. 1, 1892. Volumes of pamphlets and newspaper clippings by and about Rusk are in the Wis. State Hist. Library. Rusk's letters are in the Keyes, Fairchild, and LaFollette collections, in the same institution, and Mary E. Rusk, a daughter, has deposited there such papers as were left in the Viroqua home. A brief notice appears in *Biog. Dir. Am. Cong.* (1928) and an obituary in the *Madison Democrat,* Nov. 22, 1893.]   J. S.

RUSK, THOMAS JEFFERSON (Dec. 5, 1803–July 29, 1857), soldier, chief justice of Texas, and senator, was born in Pendleton District, S. C., the son of John and Mary (Sterritt) Rusk. His father, a stonemason, had emigrated from Ireland in 1791 and settled on land belonging to John C. Calhoun. His mother taught him to read the Bible and other literature, and Calhoun furnished him law books, allowed him to use his office, and obtained him a position in the office of William Gresham, clerk of the district court. Rusk studied in this office and worked in a grocery store until 1825, when he removed to Clarksville, Ga., and began the practice of law. There he remained for ten years, was unusually prosperous in his profession, was married in 1827 to Mary F. Cleveland, the daughter of John Cleveland, and became the partner of his father-in-law in the mercantile business. He invested heavily in a gold-mining company, the managers of which embezzled its funds and fled to Texas. He was financially ruined and pursued them to Nacogdoches only to find that they had squandered the funds. Well pleased with the new country, he decided to settle there and engage in farming and stock-raising. He became interested in the quarrel with Mexico, was elected captain of a company of troops, and joined Austin at San Antonio. He was soon made colonel and was authorized to raise men, arms, and food in East Texas.

In the convention of 1836 he took an active part, signed the declaration of independence for Texas, aided in the drafting and adoption of the constitution of the republic, and was elected on Mar. 16 secretary of war in the provisional government. When the convention adjourned, the situation looked gloomy for the Texas cause. It is claimed that President Burnet sent him to influence Houston to stop the retreat toward Nacogdoches and to fight Santa Anna, and that he succeeded in this delicate mission (but see Samuel Houston sketch). At San Jacinto Rusk fought bravely and led successful charges after Houston was wounded. He took command of the Texas army after the battle and served several months, was made secretary of war in Houston's cabinet, but soon resigned to enter the practice of law at Nacogdoches. As a member of the House of Representatives in the Second Congress of the republic he took a leading part in the enactment of laws concerning the courts. He was elected major-general of militia and after the adjournment of Congress cleared East Texas of hostile Indian tribes by October 1839. This aggressive policy was contrary to the wishes of President Houston but met the full approval of his successor, M. B. Lamar. Congress had elected Rusk chief justice of the supreme court in 1838, and he presided over its first session from January to June 1840.

After four years of service to the Republic of Texas, usually without pay, he returned to Nacogdoches to resume the practice of law; but threats of a Mexican invasion of Texas had created a demand for a counter-invasion of Mexico, and in 1843, over the veto of President Houston, he was made major-general to lead the campaign. Houston, desiring an armistice, withheld his commission for five months and hampered the proposed expedition in other ways. Rusk finally resigned in disgust. He favored the annexation of Texas to the United States and was president of the Texas convention that confirmed annexation and formulated the constitution of 1845.

He was elected to the Senate of the United States in 1846, 1851, and 1857. There he and Houston worked harmoniously for the interests of Texas. He was seldom absent from his post

and was considered the working member of the Texas delegation. He enjoyed the renewed friendship with Calhoun, but this intimacy served to handicap him in his relations with President Polk. He declined a commission as major-general but as a senator gave full support to the administration in the war with Mexico. He worked consistently for the improvement of the mail and transportation service. He was a leader in the long fight for government support of a Southern Pacific railroad. He fought steadfastly for the Rio Grande boundary as opposed to the Nueces River and voted finally for the present arrangement as provided in the compromises of 1850. He sponsored the final settlement of the debt of Texas in 1854. He favored the Kansas-Nebraska bill, and he denounced the principles and methods of the Know-Nothing group at every opportunity. He served for several terms as chairman of the committee on post offices and post roads and in March 1857 was elected president *pro tempore* of the Senate. He was the choice of many delegates as nominee for president in the Democratic convention of 1856 but was unwilling to have his name entered. He is said to have declined an offer to enter Buchanan's cabinet as postmaster-general. He was a man of large and impressive figure, with deep-set, dark eyes. His good judgment, unfailing courtesy and tact made him one of the popular men in the federal Senate. He was a forceful speaker but not an orator, and his most effective work was done in committees. His fondness for home life and retirement caused him to resign several important offices and to decline to seek several others. He had seven children, two of whom died in infancy. His devotion to his family, including his brother David, many years his junior, attracted the notice of Houston and other contemporaries. His wife died of tuberculosis in 1856. Her loss brought him a despondency, which resulted in his suicide the following year at his home in Nacogdoches.

[*Texas Almanac* (Galveston), 1857–61; D. G. Wooten, *A Comprehensive History of Texas* (2 vols., 1898); S. H. Dixon and L. W. Kemp, *The Heroes of San Jacinto* (1932); Marquis James, *The Raven* (1929); J. D. Lynch, *The Bench and Bar of Texas* (1885); R. W. Stayton, "Thomas J. Rusk," *Texas Law Review*, Oct. 1925; E. C. Barker, "The San Jacinto Campaign," *Quart. of the Texas Hist. Asso.*, Apr. 1901; L. F. Blount, "A Brief Study of Thomas J. Rusk, 1835–1856," *Southwestern Hist. Quart.*, Jan., Apr. 1931; H. S. Thrall, *A Pictorial Hist. of Texas* (5th ed., 1879); S. S. McKay, "Texas and the Southern Pacific Railroad, 1848–1860," *Ibid.*, July 1931; C. B. Sterrett, "The Life of Thomas J. Rusk," manuscript thesis in Univ. of Texas Lib.]   S. S. M.

RUSS, JOHN DENNISON (Sept. 1, 1801–Mar. 1, 1881), a pioneer teacher of the blind in the United States, physician, penologist, was born in Essex, Mass., the son of Dr. Parker and Elizabeth (Cogswell) Russ. His earliest American ancestor was Henry Rust who came to Hingham, Mass., some time between 1633 and 1635. John's father was the first of his line to adopt the name Russ. Graduated in arts from Yale College in 1823, the son chose his father's profession and in 1825 received from Yale the degree of M.D. After a year spent in European hospitals, he entered upon the practice of his profession in New York City. In 1827, however, the young physician, fired with a desire to aid the Greek patriots in their struggle for independence, sailed for Greece in charge of a shipload of food sent by American sympathizers. For nearly three years he remained there as distributor of food and organizer of hospitals. In this work he was closely associated with that other philanthropic physician, Samuel G. Howe [q.v.], later, in Boston, to become devoted as was Russ in New York to the interests of the blind. Russ returned to New York in 1830 and resumed the practice of his profession. On his way back he had married, in England, a widow, Eliza Phipps Jenkins, whose children he adopted, giving them his name. His wife died in 1860, having borne him no children, and in 1872 he married Elsie Birdsell, who survived him.

In 1830–31 New York City was visited by epidemics of cholera and of ophthalmia and Russ was drawn into public hospital work. Thus his attention was directed to the prevalence of blindness due to ophthalmia among children and he was moved to seek means for their education. He joined with another physician, Samuel Akerly, and a well-known Friend, Samuel Wood, in establishing a school under the name of the New York Institution for the Blind, which was opened Mar. 15, 1832, with three pupils; Russ himself served as teacher. Soon the enrollment increased, the accomplishments of the pupils were exhibited, a house was procured for the school, and the board of managers appointed Russ superintendent. His enthusiasm and ardor, along with innate intelligence and remarkable sensing of the needs of the blind, gave the institution immediate success. With only meager assistance, he taught a growing number of pupils, busying himself, also, with the invention of devices for use in their work, and managing the business affairs of the school until his retirement in the spring of 1835.

Practising his profession all the while, Russ next rendered humanitarian service in connection with prison reform. One of the organizers in 1843 of the Prison Association of New York,

he became its secretary and from 1845 to 1853 served in this capacity and as investigator of conditions in the city and state prisons. His reports were comprehensive in character and had considerable effect. In 1851 he was one of the corporators of the New York Juvenile Asylum (now the Children's Village of Dobbs Ferry) and became its first executive. He served as superintendent from 1853 to 1858. An instinct for discovering fields of service and generously giving himself in them was further shown in his professional contacts. It is reported that as a physician Russ answered every call of distress but payment for attendance he never exacted, the patient making return therefor or not according to his own conscience and ability.

After his retirement from active public work in 1858, he again turned his attention to the needs of the blind. He invented a phonetic alphabet, but since it proved unwieldy, he atttempted again, as he had done thirty years before, to improve the Braille system of writing and reading by embossed points. Through almost a decade he studied this subject and sought to promulgate his findings, with seemingly no encouragement or evidence of interest on the part of educators of the blind. About this time, however, the superintendent of the New York Institution, William B. Wait [q.v.], was carrying on similar studies, without any apparent connection with the experiments of Russ, and he was able to promulgate the so-called New York Point System, a variant of the embossed dot system of Louis Braille. The last years of Russ's life were spent in retirement on an estate which he purchased and developed at Pompton, N. J., and there he died. His body lies in the family tomb at Essex, Mass.

[Robert Crowell, *Hist. of the Town of Essex* (1868); A. D. Rust, *Record of the Rust Family* (1891); L. E. Richards, ed., *Letters and Journals of Samuel Gridley Howe* (2 vols., 1906, 1909); *Obit. Record Grads. Yale Coll.*, 1881; H. A. Kelly and W. L. Burrage, *Am. Medic. Biogs.* (1920); *N. Y. Tribune*, Mar. 3, 1881; records of the N. Y. Institution for the Blind; reports of the Prison Asso. of N. Y.; *In Memoriam, John Dennison Russ* (n.d.); letters of John D. Russ in the possession of the family.]   E. M. V–C.

RUSSELL, BENJAMIN (Sept. 13, 1761–Jan. 4, 1845), journalist, was born at Boston, Mass., eldest son of John Russell, a mason. While yet attending the public school, he frequented the printing office of Isaiah Thomas [q.v.] and learned to set type. On Apr. 19, 1775, with several schoolmates he followed a detachment of troops to Cambridge and because of sudden developments in the preparations for war was unable to return home; after spending three months in doing errands for officers quartered in the

Harvard Yard and in acting as clerk for a company of Connecticut troops, he encountered his father, received a thrashing, and next day was taken to Worcester and apprenticed to Isaiah Thomas, who had recently removed the *Massachusetts Spy* there from Boston. At the time of the Declaration of Independence, he impulsively enlisted in the army but, being not yet sixteen years old, was released; in 1780, however, Thomas was drafted and employed Russell as his substitute. He joined the army at West Point, was a member of the guard at the execution of Major John André, but served in no engagement. At the end of his six months' enlistment he returned to continue his apprenticeship, from which Thomas reluctantly relieved him in 1781 when he reached his twentieth year, and he became a full-fledged journeyman. Equipped with two years' experience as journeyman, some familiarity with writing (gained mainly by making surreptitious contributions to the *Spy*), and a young wife to whom he had been married two months, he decided in November 1783 to set up a newspaper in Boston, but difficulty in obtaining equipment delayed until Mar. 24, 1784, the publication of the first number of *The Massachusetts Centinel and the Republican Journal*, to be issued twice a week by William Warden and Benjamin Russell. At the end of the second year, Russell became sole owner and editor and so continued until 1828, when he retired from journalism. The title was soon shortened to the *Massachusetts Centinel* and in 1790 changed to the *Columbian Centinel*.

Russell soon proved his ability as a journalist, not only by energetic news gathering, vigorous writing, ingenious typography, and novel incipient cartoons, but by associating himself and his paper with mechanics and merchants and by taking an active part in politics. Thus he soon became an important citizen, and his paper the most enterprising and influential in Massachusetts. With him as voluntary contributors were associated such men as Fisher Ames, John Lowell, George Cabot, Stephen Higginson, and Timothy Pickering [*qq.v.*]. Though the first number of the *Centinel* bore the motto "Uninfluenced by party, we aim only to be just," Russell was naturally a thoroughgoing Federalist. He denounced Shays's rebellion and all disorder, was strongly nationalistic, and vigorously urged ratification of the Constitution. He joyously acclaimed the adherence of each state, was leader among the Boston mechanics who influenced the Massachusetts convention in favor of ratification, and in the next issue after that event uttered a column of ecstatic verse. He gave the

administrations of Washington and Adams unqualified support and, as the Federalist party took shape, made the *Centinel* its leading organ in New England. The proceedings of the first session of Congress he printed gratis, though later when funds were available Washington asked for and paid the cost. During the French Revolution and the Napoleonic Wars no other American paper was so noted for its "foreign intelligence" and the accurate details of the movements of forces and operations in Europe. It was said that Russell had the map of all the seats of conflict in his head and could trace and define every league of ground traversed by Bonaparte from the Battle of Marengo to Waterloo. To "Major Ben's" office Louis Philippe and Talleyrand, during their residence in Boston, regularly went for news, and the former gave Russell an atlas of which the editor made constant use. Russell thought the election of Jefferson a national calamity; no act of his administration or Madison's won the approval of the *Centinel*, and during this period of verbal violence no paper was more vituperative in denouncing the Republicans and all their works. He reluctantly supported De Witt Clinton [*q.v.*] against Madison and bitterly opposed the War of 1812. But the influence of Russell and his paper in national politics declined with the Federalist party, and it was still further weakened when the editor took a leading part with old political enemies in honoring Monroe on his visit to Boston in 1817. If he thus destroyed his influence, however, he gained renown by coining the phrase, "era of good feelings." He is also among those who have been credited with the invention of the word *gerrymander* (Buckingham, *post,* p. 91).

As a citizen, Russell was public-spirited and generous. Though associated with the well-to-do, he was always proud of being a mechanic; he was president of a printers' mutual protective society and in 1795 founded the Massachusetts Charitable Mechanic Association, of which he was president from 1808 to 1817. He held many public offices, especially after his retirement from journalism. For several years he was president of the Boston board of health, successively member of the school committee, member of the Common Council, and alderman. From 1805 until 1821 and 1828 until 1835, he was a member of the Massachusetts House of Representatives; he was twice elected senator from Suffolk County (1822 and 1825) and ended his political career as a member of the Executive Council in 1836 and 1837. He was married on Sept. 21, 1783, to Esther Rice of Worcester, Mass., daughter of Lemuel and Abigail Rice. After her death, he married Guest Campbell, a widow, in 1803. He had two sons and a daughter.

[The fullest account of Russell's life, with a portrait, is in J. T. Buckingham, *Specimens of Newspaper Literature* (1850), vol. II. See also Frederic Hudson, *Journalism in the United States from 1690 to 1872* (1873); D. A. Goddard, *Newspapers and Newspaper Writers in New England, 1787–1815* (1880); Francis Baylies, *Eulogy on the Hon. Benj. Russell* (1845); C. A. Cummings, "The Press and Literature of the Last Hundred Years," in Justin Winsor, *Memorial Hist. of Boston,* vol. III (1881); Joel Munsell, *The Typographical Miscellany* (1850); Isaiah Thomas, *The Hist. of Printing in America* (2 vols., 1874); A. H. Ward, *A Geneal. Hist. of the Rice Family* (1858). Brief obit. notices are to be found in the *Boston Daily Atlas,* Jan. 6, 1845; and *Boston Daily Advertiser,* Jan. 7, 1845.]   F. W. S—t.

RUSSELL, CHARLES TAZE (Feb. 16, 1852–Oct. 31, 1916), religious leader, generally known as "Pastor Russell," was born at Pittsburgh, Pa., the son of Joseph L. and Eliza (Birney) Russell, both of Scotch-Irish descent. His education was confined to that offered in the common schools, supplemented by some work with private tutors. Received at an early age into the Congregational church of which his parents were ardent members, he revolted against the doctrine of eternal punishment and after several years' study of the Bible became convinced that there was no scriptural authority for it. Meanwhile he was supporting himself by selling shirts. In 1872 he believed himself to have discovered through his studies that the second coming of Jesus would be in invisible form in the autumn of 1874. These conclusions he embodied in a booklet, *The Object and Manner of Our Lord's Return,* which obtained wide circulation. In 1878 he became pastor of an independent church in Pittsburgh, and in the following year he began to publish a magazine, *The Watch Tower and Herald of Christ's Presence,* which was issued later as *Zion's Watch Tower* and still later under its original title. Appearing semi-monthly, with no advertisements, and devoted entirely to religious topics, it ultimately obtained an Anglo-American circulation of 45,000 copies, besides being translated into fifteen foreign languages. In 1881 Russell published his most important work, *Food for Thinking Christians,* reissued in 1886 as *Millennial Dawn,* vol. I, with the subtitle, "The Plan of the Ages," later incorporated in a six-volume series of Studies of the Scriptures. It attained a circulation of over five and a half million copies. All of Russell's publications after 1884, embracing numerous pamphlets in addition to Studies of the Scriptures, were issued by the Watch Tower Bible and Tract Society organized in that year.

Gradually he began to establish branch church-

es throughout the United States and later in Canada, England, and Europe, until there were more than 1200 congregations of which he was regarded as the pastor. In 1909 his wife, Maria Frances Ackley, whom he had married in 1879, brought suit for divorce, alleging immoral conduct on Russell's part with female members of the church. The divorce was granted and though appealed five times by Russell was always sustained. This unpleasantness led to the transfer of his headquarters to Brooklyn, N. Y., where in the same year he bought the old Bethel Chapel under the Brooklyn Bridge. This soon became too crowded for his following, and he moved to more expansive quarters uptown, establishing the "Brooklyn Tabernacle." In 1910 he traveled to Palestine, where his speeches exerted some influence on the nascent Zionist movement. The next year he was in further trouble, owing to the sale in his church (at sixty dollars a bushel) of so-called "Miracle Wheat" alleged to possess new and very marvellous agricultural properties; exposed by the *Brooklyn Daily Eagle,* he sued the paper for $100,000 damages in October 1911 but lost the case. In the midst of these difficulties he sailed away for a trip around the world, during which he devoted some time to a study of missionary work in the Orient. On his return, he was given a great ovation in the Hippodrome by thousands of New York Jews. The scandals connected with his name do not seem to have materially lessened his influence. During all the later years of his life, aside from special trips, he averaged annually over thirty thousand miles of travel in visiting his various pastorates, including that of the "London Tabernacle," one of the strongest centers of Russellism. He died suddenly from heart failure on a train in Texas, his last words being, "Please wrap me in a Roman toga" (*Watch Tower,* Dec. 1, 1916, p. 365) —a request fulfilled so far as possible by means of an improvised toga made out of Pullman sheets. The essence of his teaching lay in the doctrine that the world since 1874 has lived in the "Millennial Age" or "Day of Jehovah," to be marked shortly by an international revolution of the working classes reducing society to chaos, after which will occur the resurrection of the dead, a last judgment occupying a thousand years, and finally the establishment of the messianic kingdom on earth.

[See *Watch Tower,* June 1, 1916, for Russell's account of the development of his theology; *Ibid.,* Dec. 1, 1916, for a biog. sketch, reprinted in the 1924 ed. of *The Plan of the Ages*; obituaries in the *N. Y. Times* and *N. Y. Tribune,* Nov. 1, 1916; files of the *Brooklyn Daily Eagle,* Sept., Oct., 1911, esp. Sept. 23, Oct. 19; M. S. Czatt, *The International Bible Students: Jehovah's Witnesses* (1933).]   E. S. B.

RUSSELL, CHARLES WELLS (Mar. 16, 1856–Apr. 5, 1927), lawyer, diplomat, government official, was born at Wheeling in what is now West Virginia, the son of Charles Wells and Margaret Wilson (Moore) Russell. He attended Georgetown University (Washington, D. C.) from 1870 to 1873 and received the degree of LL.B. there in 1883 and that of LL.M. in 1884. Meanwhile, on Feb. 19, 1879, he married Lucy Floyd Mosby, sister of Col. John S. Mosby [*q.v.*]. There were three children, two of whom predeceased him. After the death of his first wife he married, on Oct. 1, 1885, her sister, Lelia James Mosby. The following year he was appointed to a position in the federal Department of Justice and was given charge of many of the French spoliation cases. From 1893 to 1895 he was the legal adviser of the joint commission of Congress, headed by A. M. Dockery, appointed to investigate the status of the laws organizing the federal executive departments; he then engaged in general practice in Washington. In the winter of 1897–98 he investigated conditions in Cuba for the Washington authorities, assisted the Evacuation Commission in Porto Rico, and successfully resisted, before the United States–Spanish Treaty Claims Commission, claims arising out of the destruction of the battleship *Maine*.

Reëntering the Department of Justice in 1902 as special assistant to the attorney general, he was detailed to investigate the French Panama Canal Company's title, which was accepted pursuant to his recommendation, and he later arranged the details of transfer, visiting Paris twice in the course of the proceedings. His next important assignment was to defend an action against the American commander at Havana, Gen. John R. Brooke [*q.v.*], brought by the Countess O'Reilly to enforce her slaughter-house monopoly there (*O'Reilly de Camara* vs. *Brooke*, 209 *U. S.*, 45). Successful in this, he continued in charge of insular matters for the Department until 1905, when he became assistant attorney general, serving until 1910. It was during this latter period that he was detailed to investigate and prosecute peonage in the South. He prepared a report on the subject in which he recommended: "That an incessant fight be made against peonage in every district in which it is to be found; . . . that Federal supervision of the interstate labor-supplying business of places like New York, Philadelphia, Pittsburg, and Chicago be provided for by law;" and that "the definition of legal peonage be made broad enough to include the holding of persons in servitude, whether in liquidation of an indebtedness 'or otherwise'" (*Report of Hon. Charles W. Rus-sell, Assistant Attorney General, Relative to Peonage Matters . . . Oct. 10, 1907*, 1908). His prevailing argument on demurrer in the cases at Muskogee, Okla., involving allotments of the five civilized tribes, was considered of sufficient importance to be published by the Government Printing Office (*Suits at Muscogee . . . Argument on Demurrer by Charles W. Russell, Assistant Attorney General*, 1909).

On Dec. 21, 1909, Russell was appointed envoy extraordinary and minister plenipotentiary from the United States to Persia. During his four years of service there, the crisis resulting from the invasion of Persian sovereignty by certain European powers became acute, and the Persian government approached that of the United States, through the Persian legation at Washington, with a request for assistance in obtaining the services of American financial experts. As a result, W. Morgan Shuster, of Washington, D. C., went to Persia as treasurer general, with four other Americans, and served from May to December 1911. Russell met the party on its arrival and was in close touch therewith during the whole of the tense period which followed. Persian rights were for the time protected and it is probably due to the experience of the Medjlis (national elective assembly) during that period and the support given by the Americans, that Persia was able to maintain her integrity until after the World War, when a new era dawned.

While in Persia, Russell published *The Secret Place and Other Poems* (Washington, 1911) and *Iranian Rest and Other Lyrics* (Teheran, 1912). Toward the close of his mission, which ended in September 1914, he was designated as the President's representative at the Shah Amed's coronation ceremonies. After his return to the United States, Russell edited *The Memoirs of Colonel John S. Mosby* (1917). The narrative is in the first person as if by Mosby himself; but there are notes and an introduction by Russell. He also published *Poems* (1921), apparently a complete collection of his verse. He died at his home in Washington, D. C.

[*Reg. of the Dept. of State, Sept. 20, 1911* (1911); *Who's Who in America*, 1926–27; W. M. Shuster, *The Strangling of Persia* (1912); *Evening Star* (Washington, D. C.), Apr. 7, 1927.]   C. S. L.

RUSSELL, DAVID ALLEN (Dec. 10, 1820–Sept. 19, 1864), soldier, the son of David Abel and Alida (Lansing) Russell, was born in Salem, N. Y. His father was a congressman from New York from 1835 to 1841. David was appointed a cadet to the United States Military Academy in 1841 and was graduated in 1845, number thirty-eight in a class of forty-one members. He was commissioned brevet second lieutenant in the 1st Infantry and assigned to duty at Fort Scott, Kan., being promoted to the rank of second lieutenant on Sept. 21, 1846. During the Mexican War he served in General Scott's army, participated in the battle of Cerro Gordo and minor engagements, and was brevetted first lieutenant for meritorious conduct. After the Mexican War he served in garrisons and on frontier duty in Oregon and Washington where he was engaged in hostilities with the Yakima Indians in 1855 and 1856. He was promoted to first lieutenant on Jan. 1, 1848, and to the rank of captain on June 22, 1854.

At the beginning of the Civil War he served in the defenses of Washington, D. C. As colonel of the 7th Massachusetts Volunteers he commanded with distinction in the Peninsular and Maryland campaigns during the summer and autumn of 1862. He became a brigadier-general of volunteers in November 1862 and was assigned to the command of a brigade in the VI Corps in the Army of the Potomac, participating in the battle of Fredericksburg in December, and in the battle of Gettysburg in July 1863. At Rappahannock Station, Va., on Nov. 7, 1863, he led his brigade in a gallant charge against Confederate intrenchments which resulted in the capture of a large number of prisoners, some artillery, and eight battle flags. In recognition of his heroic services on this occasion, he was designated by General Meade to go to Washington and present the captured battle flags to the secretary of war. He had also to recover from a wound which he had received in the charge. He resumed command of his brigade in January 1864 and continued in that capacity until May, when he was assigned to the command of a division.

He fought in all the battles of Grant's Virginia campaign of 1864 from the Wilderness to Petersburg. Early in July 1864, his division accompanied the VI Corps in a hurried move to repel Early's raid on Washington and afterwards joined Sheridan's army in the Shenandoah Valley. At Winchester on Sept. 19, 1864, while leading one of his brigades at a critical moment of the battle, he received a wound in the breast. He concealed the wound from his men, and remained in the saddle, urging them forward, until, a little later in the day, he was killed by a fragment of shell which passed through his heart. For his gallant and meritorious conduct he was four times given brevet grades in the regular army, the last being that of major-general at Winchester. General Wright, in command of the VI Corps, wrote in his official report that Russell

was "an officer whose merits were not measured by his rank, whose zeal never outran his discretion, whose abilities were never unequal to the occasion, a man tenderly just to his friends and heartily generous to his foes" (*War of the Rebellion: Official Records, Army*, 1 ser., XLIII, part I, 151).

[G. W. Cullum, *Biog. Reg. . . . Officers and Grads.*, *U. S. Mil. Acad.* (1891); *Dedication of the N. Y. Auxiliary State Monument on the Battlefield of Gettysburg* (1926); N. V. Hutchinson, *Hist. of the Seventh Vol. Infantry* (1890); *Battles and Leaders of the Civil War* (1887–88), vols. III, IV; records of the Pension Bureau and Adj.-General's office, Washington, D. C.; *Albany* (N. Y.) *Evening Jour.*, Sept. 26, 1864.]

S. J. H.

RUSSELL, IRWIN (June 3, 1853–Dec. 23, 1879), poet, was the son of Dr. William McNab Russell, a native of Ohio but of Virginian extraction. While still young, Dr. Russell had established his practice in Port Gibson, Miss., and there had married Elizabeth Allen, a native New Yorker of New England extraction, who had taught for several years in the Port Gibson Female College. Irwin was born in Port Gibson, but his family soon moved to St. Louis, whence, however, they returned to Port Gibson at the outbreak of the Civil War. Irwin, though always of frail physique, had early displayed precocity. At four he could read, and at six he could understand Milton's poetry. Food was scarce during the Civil War, and the growing boy was certainly undernourished. At the end of the war the family returned to St. Louis, where Irwin remained till 1869, when Irwin graduated with credit from St. Louis University. He then went to Port Gibson to study law in the office of Judge L. N. Baldwin. By special act of the legislature of Mississippi he was admitted to the bar at the age of nineteen. Meanwhile he had several times run away from his studies—once to New Orleans, and once to Texas with his chum Austin Wharton. While on these trips he lived in sailors' boarding houses and frequented Mississippi steamboats, with many of whose captains he was on terms of intimacy. He thus acquired an unusual penetration into human character and motives, but also a fondness for strong drink, which remained one of his besetting weaknesses. In 1877 he became Judge Baldwin's assistant. He had always been more interested in literature than in the law, however, and had already produced considerable verse. His first poem, "A Chinese Tale," a juvenile effort on the origin of foot-binding, appeared in 1869. "Ships from the Sea" received a great deal of attention locally when it was published in the *Port Gibson Standard* of Oct. 13, 1871. One of the first of Russell's poems in negro dialect, "Uncle Cap

Interviewed," appeared in January 1876 in the "Bric-à-Brac" department of *Scribner's Monthly*. Many of his poems appeared in *St. Nicholas, Appleton's Journal, Popular Science Monthly, Puck*, and other periodicals. Much of his work was published anonymously or under various pen names. He was one of the first to recognize the literary possibilities offered by the negro, and his mastery of negro dialect and character was acknowledged by such connoisseurs as Joel Chandler Harris and Thomas Nelson Page.

In 1878 an epidemic of yellow fever reached Port Gibson. Immediately there was an exodus from the town, but out of sixteen hundred people, between six and seven hundred remained. Dr. Russell stayed to tend the sick, and his son became his assistant. For several months they toiled night and day to alleviate the suffering. The girl Russell is said to have loved, Dora Donald, died in the epidemic. In the latter part of December, Russell went to New York, where he was welcomed by such literary notables as Henry Cuyler Bunner, Richard Watson Gilder, and Robert Underwood Johnson, but despite the interesting book shops of the city and the literary life there, he did not find New York conducive to writing. In May 1879 his father died as a result of the exertions he had made during the epidemic, and there ensued a period of deep despair for the poet. In August, sick and practically penniless, he reached New Orleans, having worked his way down as a fireman. He soon secured a connection with the *New Orleans Times*, but the hardships he had undergone proved too much for his physique, and without appealing for aid from his friends or his family, he died in a cheap boarding house on Dec. 23. With a premonition of death, not ten days before, he had published in the *New Orleans Times* his melancholy poem, "The Cemetery." He is chiefly significant historically as a pioneer in the use of negro dialect for literary purposes, but his was an authentic poetic voice even if a minor one.

[Russell's one volume of verse, *Poems by Irwin Russell*, was compiled and published posthumously in 1888 with a preface by Joel Chandler Harris. It was added to and republished in 1917, under the title, *Christmas-Night in the Quarters and Other Poems*, with a good sketch of the author by Maurice Garland Fulton. Articles by A. A. Kern in the *Tex. Rev.*, Oct. 1916 and by C. C. Marble, in the *Critic*, Oct. 27 and Nov. 3, 1888, are illuminating. See also W. M. Baskervill, *Southern Writers: Biog. and Crit. Studies* (1897), vol. I; M. W. Musgrove, "Memories of Irwin Russell," *Daily Picayune* (New Orleans), Sunday, June 2, 1907; *New Orleans Times*, Dec. 24, 1879.]

H. L.

RUSSELL, ISRAEL COOK (Dec. 10, 1852–May 1, 1906), geologist, was born of New England ancestry at Garrattsville, N. Y., the son of Barnabas and Louisa Sherman (Cook) Russell.

He spent the first twelve years of his life near his birthplace and then went with his parents to Plainfield, N. J. He was educated in the schools of Clinton, N. Y., the Hasbrook Institute at Jersey City, the University of the City of New York, where he received the degree of B.S. and C.E. in 1872, and the School of Mines at Columbia College. On completing his university training Russell went as photographer of the United States Transit of Venus Expedition to New Zealand and Kerguelen Island, an experience that opened to him the field of physiography, afterwards the subject of much of his study. In 1878, after two years as assistant professor of geology in the School of Mines at Columbia, he joined the Wheeler survey for geological exploration in New Mexico under the direction of John J. Stevenson [q.v.], and the following year traveled in Europe.

In 1880 he was appointed to the newly established United States Geological Survey and assigned to the Great Basin division under G. K. Gilbert [q.v.], later one of the most distinguished of American geologists. After a year as assistant to Gilbert, he was given independent work investigating the Quaternary history of a series of desert basins in northern Nevada and adjacent parts of California and Oregon. His four years' study of these areas saw the light in a massive monograph published by the government under the title *Geological History of Lake Lahontan of Northwestern Nevada* (1885), which remains a classic of the science. Transferred in 1885 to the Southern Appalachian province, he labored diligently on the difficult problem of the structure of an area of much-metamorphosed rocks. In 1888 he began an extensive correlation of the Triassic formation of the United States, an undertaking which, being interrupted, resulted in the publication of a correlation of the Atlantic provinces only, "Correlation Papers: The Newark System," in the *United States Geological Survey Bulletin No. 85* (1892). In 1889 he began a series of expeditions to Alaska. On the first of these, made for the United States Coast and Geodetic Survey, he studied the northern section of the eastern boundary; and during two succeeding summers, under the joint auspices of the United States Geological Survey and the National Geographic Society, he explored the glaciers and the slopes of Mount Saint Elias, making two attempts, the second of which very nearly succeeded, to conquer the summit of the mountain. (See "An Expedition to Mount Saint Elias" in the *National Geographic Magazine,* May 1891, and "Second Expedition to Mount Saint Elias in 1891" in the *Thirteenth Annual*

Report of the United States Geological Survey,
1893, pt. 2.)

When in 1892 he became professor of geology
at the University of Michigan, he continued to
devote his summer vacations to exploration,
mainly in the northwestern United States and in
northern Michigan. In addition to numerous
technical reports he wrote five popular volumes
described as "Reading Lessons for Students of
Geography and Geology." The first of these,
Lakes of North America, appeared in 1895; later
came *Glaciers* (1897), *Volcanoes* (1897), and
Rivers of North America (1898), and finally a
general geographic study entitled *North America* (1904). He was recognized as an authority
in the geography of North America, particularly
Alaska and the northwestern states and territories, and as a geologist of high repute in the
field of dynamical geology, especially glaciology.
He served as vice-president of the American
Association for the Advancement of Science
(Section E), as president of the Michigan Academy of Science, and as president of the Geological Society of America. Russell was married on
Nov. 27, 1886, to Julia Augusta Olmsted, of
Cambridge, Mass., by whom he had three daugh-
ters and a son. He died of pneumonia in Ann
Arbor, Mich.

[See Bailey Willis in *Bull. of the Geological Soc. of
America,* vol. XVIII (1907), which gives a complete
bibliog. of Russell's publications; W. P. Lombard and
M. L. D'Ooge in *Science,* Oct. 5, 1906; G. K. Gilbert
in *Jour. of Geology,* Nov.-Dec. 1906; C. A. Davis in
Ninth Report of Mich. Acad. of Sci., 1907; W. H.
Hobbs in *Michigan Technic,* Feb. 1907; *Who's Who in
America,* 1906–07; obituary in *Detroit Free Press,* May
2, 1906.]   W. H. H.

RUSSELL, JOHN HENRY (July 4, 1827–
Apr. 1, 1897), naval officer, was born at Frederick, Md., the son of Robert Grier Russell and
Susan Hood (Worthington) Russell. He entered the navy as midshipman in 1841, made one
cruise in the Pacific, was then attached to the
sloop *St. Mary's* in the Gulf of Mexico, and participated in the capture of Corpus Christi and
in the blockade of Vera Cruz. Commissioned
passed midshipman on Aug. 10, 1847, he entered
the United States Naval Academy that autumn
and was graduated in 1848. In 1853 he was assigned to the North Pacific Exploring Expedition under Cadwalader Ringgold [*q.v.*] serving as acting lieutenant and navigator in the
sloop *Vincennes.* When the expedition reached
China, Russell, under Robert Milligan McLane
[*q.v.*], the American commissioner, was present at an interview with the Chinese imperial
commissioner. After two years spent in Arctic
and North Pacific waters, Russell returned to
San Francisco. He was commissioned master

on Sept. 14, 1855, and lieutenant the following
day.

At the outbreak of the Civil War he was on
ordnance duty at the Washington navy yard.
He was immediately sent to the Norfolk yard to
assist in saving the Union vessels there from
capture by the Confederates, and had command
of the last boat to leave the yard on Apr. 21, 1861.
He was then assigned to the frigate *Colorado.*
On the night of Sept. 13, 1861, he commanded a
boat expedition of a hundred sailors and marines
to destroy the privateer *Judah* at Pensacola.
Though she was protected by shore batteries
and a force of a thousand men, Russell approached boldly in the night and, after a severe
hand-to-hand fight in the early morning, succeeded in burning her to the water's edge. Admiral Porter called it "the most gallant cutting-
out affair that occurred during the war" (Porter, *post,* p. 51). Gideon Welles extended him
the special recognition of the navy department,
and President Lincoln thanked him personally.
The Maryland legislature also gave him a vote
of thanks.

He was then given command of the steamer
Kennebec in Farragut's squadron. In the celebrated passage of the forts below New Orleans,
the *Kennebec,* being slow and near the end of
the line, failed to pass the forts and withdrew
from action, but Russell was present at the surrender of both forts and received the garrison
of Fort Jackson on board his ship. He participated in all the operations of Farragut's squadron up the Mississippi to Vicksburg. Commissioned lieutenant commander on July 16, 1862,
he commanded the *Kennebec* in the blockade of
Mobile and the *Pontiac* in the South Atlantic
Blockading Squadron. In 1864 he was sent to
the Pacific Coast where he commanded the
Cyane until the end of the war. In September
1869 he won distinction for rescuing during a
great storm in the Gulf of California the passengers and crew of the steamer *Continental.*
After the war he rose successively through the
grades to the rank of rear admiral on Mar. 4,
1886. He retired voluntarily in August 1886,
after forty-five years of active service. He married Cornelia Pierpont Treadway in 1864 and
had three children. He was a capable officer and
seaman, as well as a man of unflinching courage;
his spectacular exploits won him the confidence
and esteem of his superiors and paved the way
for subsequent promotions.

[Family information from a son; *War of the Rebellion: Official Records (Navy),* 1 ser., vols. III–V, XV,
XVI, XVIII–XX; *Senate Exec. Doc. No. 22,* 35 Cong.,
2 Sess., p. 340; L. R. Hamersly, *The Records of
Living Officers of the U. S. Navy and Marine Corps*
(4th ed., 1890); D. D. Porter, *The Naval Hist. of the*

Civil War (1886); *Jour. of the Proc. of the House of Delegates* (Md.), Dec. 1861 (1861); *Army and Navy Jour.*, Apr. 3, 1897; *Evening Star* (Washington, D. C.), Apr. 2, 1897.]   L. H. B.

RUSSELL, JONATHAN (Feb. 27, 1771–Feb. 17, 1832), orator and diplomat, son of Jonathan and Abigail (Russell) Russell, was born at Providence, R. I.; on his father's side he was a descendant of John Russell who was in Charlestown, Mass., as early as 1640. He was graduated in 1791, with highest honors, from Rhode Island College (later Brown University) and studied law, practising it little but becoming a moderately successful merchant. On July 4, 1800, in the Baptist Meeting House in Providence, he delivered an oration which seems to have coincided with the opinions of the political revolution of that year; it was published and went through more than twenty editions. In 1810, having become prominent as a leader of the Jeffersonian party, he was appointed chargé d'affaires at Paris by Madison, and by appointment of July 27, 1811, filled the same office in London. From January 1814 to October 1818 he served as United States minister to Sweden and Norway, at Stockholm.

In 1814, Russell joined John Quincy Adams, James A. Bayard, Henry Clay, and Albert Gallatin [*qq.v.*] at Ghent, to engage in the negotiation of the treaty of peace with Great Britain; in the course of the negotiations he alone voted with Clay against Gallatin's proposal to concede the free navigation of the Mississippi in exchange for express recognition of the right to the Northeastern fisheries. After four years in Sweden, he was recalled by Monroe, and returned to America by way of Germany and Italy. Of this tour he kept an interesting journal, which was printed a century later in the *Proceedings of the Massachusetts Historical Society* (vol. LI, 1918). In 1819 he settled at Mendon, and in the following year was elected to the General Court in May, to the constitutional convention at Boston in October, and to the United States House of Representatives in November. Here he served one term (1821–23).

In 1822 he had a controversy with John Quincy Adams, who believed that Russell, as the tool of Clay, was seeking to destroy Adams' reputation in the West by pointing him out as one of the majority of the Ghent commissioners who had been ready to trade free navigation of the Mississippi for the restoration of the Northeastern fisheries. Russell published what purported to be a copy of his letter of Feb. 11, 1815, to Secretary Monroe, setting forth his dissent from the majority; Adams secured the original letter from President Monroe, accused Russell of treachery, and published *The Duplicate Letters, the Fisheries and the Mississippi: Documents Relating to the Transactions at the Negotiation of Ghent* (1822), calling attention to the differences in phrasing between Russell's "copy" and the original. Although he later found sufficient reason to forgive Clay, he wrote of Russell more than a year after the latter's death, "He is gone to his account, and is sufficiently punished in this world for his perfidy" (Adams, *Memoirs, post,* IX, 3). For many years, to "Jonathan Russell" an opponent was current political slang in New England for overwhelming him in a dispute. This controversy with Adams is supposed to have been the cause of Russell's retirement from public life, although as late as March 1829, "a broken down man" as the result of "two or three paralytic shocks," he was said to have been expecting a foreign post from Jackson (*Ibid.*, VIII, 111).

Russell was married on Apr. 3, 1794, to Sylvia Ammidon of Mendon, Mass., by whom he had four children, and on Apr. 2, 1817, to Lydia Smith, who also bore him four children. She was the daughter of Barney Smith, Boston merchant and owner of the Hutchinson house on Milton Hill, and in 1829, after the death of Smith, the Russells moved from Mendon into that house. Here, after several years of broken health, Russell died. His remains were ultimately buried in Forest Hills.

[The Russell Papers are in the Library of Brown Univ., Providence, R. I. See also "Journal of Jonathan Russell, 1818–1819," *Proc. Mass. Hist. Soc.*, LI (1918), 369–498, with miniature by Dumont, and engraving by Bance; "Letters to Jonathan Russell," *Ibid.*, XLVII (1914), 293–310, and LIV (1922), 76–80; *Memoirs of John Quincy Adams* (12 vols., 1874–77); J. G. Metcalf, *Annals of the Town of Mendon* (1880); A. K. Teele, *The Hist. of Milton, Mass.*, 1640–1887 (n.d.); *Hist. Cat. Brown Univ.* (1914); *Biog. Dir. Am. Cong.* (1928); J. R. Bartlett, *Geneal. of . . . the Russell Family . . . Descendants of John Russell of Woburn* (1879); *Boston Daily Advertiser and Patriot*, Feb. 20, 1832. Negatives of photographs of a bust of Jonathan Russell, by Trentanove, made in Rome in 1819, are in the Mass. Hist. Soc.]   S. M.

RUSSELL, JOSEPH (Oct. 8, 1719 o.s.–Oct. 16, 1804), merchant, ship-owner, was born in the township of Dartmouth, Mass., the son of Joseph and Mary (Tucker) Russell. His great-grandfather, John Russell, is counted as his first American ancestor, although tradition has it that John Russell was the son of Ralph Russell of Pontypool, Monmouthshire, who emigrated to New England and is said to have established the first iron works in America at Raynham, Mass., in 1652. The part of Dartmouth in which Joseph Russell was born has since become the city of New Bedford, and the village out of which the city grew originated on his farm. In 1760 he sold an acre of land to one John Loudon, who was by trade a caulker and probably supported himself by work on Russell's vessels. Other workers followed Loudon in purchasing lots and building dwellings on them, and in 1765 Joseph Rotch [q.v.], attracted by the deep water and other advantages for shipping, bought ten acres for business and dwelling houses. The resulting village was called Bedford (later New Bedford) because the family name of the English dukes of that title was Russell, and Joseph Russell was nicknamed "the Duke" as a consequence.

Russell was also prominent in the development of the whaling industry. Capturing whales by posting lookouts on shore and sending boats after those seen was practised early in Southampton, L. I., and from there spread to New England settlements, though operations conducted from shore were gradually paralleled and finally supplanted by deep-sea whaling, in which vessels that constantly grew in size and made increasingly long voyages served as a base. As early as 1755 Russell owned ships that made whaling voyages or traded with the West Indies; he kept a store for the sale of imported goods, and he was a pioneer in the manufacture of spermaceti candles, paying a Captain Chaffee, who had been in the business in Lisbon, the then very large salary of £100 a year to superintend the process. In the Revolution (in which his sentiments are indicated by his naming one of his vessels *No Duty on Tea*) he not only lost his capital through the cessation of American maritime commerce but had most of his ships and buildings burned by the British when they raided New Bedford in 1778. After the Revolution, however, he rapidly recovered. His prominence and initiative are shown by his engaging George Claghorn, the builder of the frigate *Constitution,* to construct a ship for him of the extraordinary burden, for that day, of 175 tons; it was this vessel, the *Rebecca,* that in 1791–93 made the first whaling voyage around Cape Horn to the Pacific hunting grounds.

He was a Quaker and strict in adhering to Quaker practices, but he did not lack independence. Though he refused to allow his famous ship *Rebecca* to be launched with a figure-head, he had also refused in 1772 the demand of his sect that he free his two negro slaves. Of slender build and medium height, he nevertheless was physically equal to the rough life of his period and gave many evidences of his endurance and resourcefulness. In 1744 he married Judith Howland, who was also of an old Dartmouth Quaker family. They had five sons and six daughters, several of the sons being partners in their father's business and prominent citizens of New Bedford.

[Daniel Ricketson, *The Hist. of New Bedford, Bristol County, Mass.* (1858); L. B. Ellis, *Hist. of New Bedford and Its Vicinity, 1602–1892* (1892); B. B. Russell, *The Descendants of John Russell of Dartmouth, Mass.* (1904), reprinted from *New England Hist. and Geneal. Reg.,* Oct. 1904, Jan. 1905.]

S. G—n.

RUSSELL, LILLIAN (Dec. 4, 1861–June 6, 1922), comic opera prima donna, internationally famous beauty, was the daughter of Charles E. and Cynthia (Howland) Leonard and was named Helen Louise. Her father was a newspaper and book publisher, and her mother an ardent and well-known feminist. The future toast of Broadway, one of five daughters, was born in Clinton, Iowa. In 1865 the family removed to Chicago, where "Nellie" was educated at the Convent of the Sacred Heart and at Park Institute, a finishing school. Ambitious to become an opera singer, she studied singing in New York under Leopold Damrosch [q.v.], and in 1879 made her first stage appearance in the chorus of Edward E. Rice's *Pinafore* company. The following year saw her real début. Tony Pastor [q.v.] had heard her sing at a friend's house, and offered her seventy-five dollars a week to appear at his Bowery variety theater. She first appeared there on Nov. 22, 1880, billed as "Lillian Russell, the English Ballad Singer," and made a favorable impression with her clear young soprano voice and vivacious personality. The stage name then chosen was retained for the remainder of her professional career.

After further study, both vocal and dramatic, and a California tour as the lead in *Babes in the Wood,* she returned to New York to achieve her first real success as D'Jemma in Edwin Audran's *The Great Mogul: or, the Snake Charmer,* which opened on Oct. 29, 1881. She played in a series of successful comic operas, including Gilbert and Sullivan's *Patience* and *The Sorcerer,* and by the spring of 1883 was receiving $150 a week with the McCaull Opera Company. In 1880 she had married Harry Braham, conductor of Rice's *Pinafore* orchestra, but separated from him shortly thereafter. In June 1883, she eloped to London with Edward Solomon, an English Jew who wrote comic operas. At the time she was playing in *The Princess of Trebizonde,* and her departure was entirely unexpected. Braham then divorced her in New York, and she and Solomon were married in Hoboken on May 10, 1884. There was one child of this marriage, a daughter. Subsequently it developed that Solomon had never been legally separated from his first wife. Lillian Russell left him in 1886, and later brought suit in New York for an annulment, which was granted on Nov. 16, 1893. Her attorney was the notorious Abe Hummel.

She made her London début at the Gaiety Theatre, on July 16, 1883, playing in *Virginia and Paul,* by Solomon. From the time of her return to the United States in 1884, the popularity of "airy, fairy Lillian" mounted rapidly. Beauty of face and figure and an excellent natural voice —not highly trained, nor adapted to grand opera —were her chief assets. An unfailing *flair* for publicity added to her box-office appeal. She kept herself constantly in the public eye—in one season she signed five contracts and broke four of them; in another, she sought a permanent injunction restraining any manager from requiring her to appear in silk tights. Probably the most difficult parts she sang were Fiorella in Offenbach's *The Brigands* (1889), and the title rôle in the same composer's *The Grand Duchess* (1890). She specialized in the type of comic opera in which only the soprano lead was of importance, and in which practically no dramatic ability was required.

On Jan. 21, 1894, Lillian Russell was married, in Hoboken, to John Haley Augustin Chatterton, known on the stage as Signor Perugini and then playing as her leading man in *The Princess Nicotine.* In May of the same year both announced that they would never live together again, and on Oct. 23, 1898, Perugini finally obtained a divorce. The next year a new phase of Lillian Russell's career began. She joined the burlesque company of Weber and Fields, and played with them for several seasons in such offerings as *Fiddle-dee-dee* and *Whoop-dee-doo.* She left the company only when it was broken up by a quarrel between Weber and Fields. After an appearance as Lady Teazle in a musical version of *The School for Scandal* in 1904–05, and a brief interlude in vaudeville, she tried straight comedy. Her first venture in this field, *Barbara's Millions,* which reached Broadway on Oct. 8, 1906, was a complete failure. Said a critic the next day: "Singers, as a rule, are incompetent to act. Miss Russell furnishes no exception to the rule" (*New York Tribune,* Oct. 9, 1906, p. 7). Later she appeared in *Wildfire,* a melodrama of the race-track, which was a tremendous success, first on the road and then in New York. In 1912 she joined the Weber and Fields Jubilee Company to appear in *Hokey-Pokey.* At the end of its run she was married in Pittsburgh, on June 12, to Alexander Pollock Moore, publisher of the *Pittsburgh Leader* and, after her death, ambassador to Spain. Her professional career, except for occasional vaudeville engagements, was ended.

The last ten years of her life saw such varied activities as the writing of beauty articles for the woman's page of the *Chicago Herald* and the *Chicago Daily Tribune,* and Liberty Loan and Red Cross work during the World War years. In 1920 she took the stump for Warren G. Harding, who sent her abroad in 1922 on a special mission to investigate immigration problems. She submitted a report favoring future restriction and temporary suspension of immigration. Her death in Pittsburgh was due to complications following a fall on shipboard while returning to the United States.

[The material about Lillian Russell is confined chiefly to periodicals of the period of her popularity. The Robinson Locke Dramatic Collection in the N. Y. Pub. Lib. contains 6 vols. of clippings devoted to her. Her own "Reminiscences" appeared in *Cosmopolitan,* Feb.–Sept., 1922. Two useful articles are in the *Literary Digest,* Apr. 22 and June 24, 1922. Material for this sketch has been drawn also from *Who's Who in America,* 1922–23, the files of the *N. Y. Tribune,* 1880–1906, esp. issues of June 8, 1883, Apr. 2, Sept. 24, Oct. 1, 1886, Feb. 10, 1891, Aug. 30, Nov. 15, 17, 1893, Jan. 20, 22, May 16, 1894, May 21, 1897, June 24, July 1, Oct. 23, 1898, Oct. 9, 1906, and from obituaries in the *N. Y. Herald,* June 6, 1922, *N. Y. Times,* June 6, 1922, *World* (N. Y.), June 7, 1922, and *Times* (London), June 7, 1922.]
             L. P. B.

RUSSELL, Mother MARY BAPTIST (Apr. 18, 1829–Aug. 6, 1898), founder of the Sisters of Mercy in California, was born in Newry, Ireland, and baptized Katherine. She was the daughter of Margaret Mullan by her second husband, Arthur Russell, a sea-captain in the Norway trade who on his marriage had turned to the less hazardous occupation of brewer. Margaret Mullan reared six children by a first husband, John Hamill, a wealthy Belfast merchant, of whom two became distinguished nuns; another, a South American patriot; and still another, a royal judge in Roscommon. Of the Russells there were also six, of whom Sarah and Elizabeth became nuns; Charles a member of Parliament, an attorney general of England, Lord Chief justice, and finally Baron Russell of Killowen; and Matthew, a Jesuit litterateur. Left fatherless, they were carefully trained by a spiritual mother and an uncle, Dr. Charles William Russell [see *Dictionary of National Biography*], later president of royal Maynooth, who took his guardianship most seriously. Katherine, her mother's first freeborn child after the enactment of Catholic emancipation, was educated in schools of Killowen and Belfast and inured to hardship as a volunteer nurse in the famine and cholera days, when in 1848 she joined the Institute of Mercy at Kinsale. Having attracted attention as a student and a nurse, she made her final vows of profession,

Aug. 2, 1851, and took the name in religion of Sister Mary Baptist. In 1854 she was named superior of a colony of eight selected nuns and novices who enlisted for the archdiocese of San Francisco at the solicitation of Rev. Hugh Patrick Gallagher [*q.v.*]. Fortunately, Gallagher's party, which included Levi S. Ives [*q.v.*] and a number of Presentation nuns, missed the ill-fated *Arctic* and sailed from Queenstown on the *Canada* (Sept. 23, 1854), for New York. Thence they journeyed via Panama to the straggling town of San Francisco, where they arrived on Dec. 8, 1854—in time to suffer from Know-Nothing abuse.

With the assistance of Archbishop Alemany, Mother M. Baptist established a convent and school. Within a year, she was given charge of the county hospital where cholera victims were isolated. With their Irish experience, these nurses were most successful in combatting the disease. Hostility to the nuns ended in gratitude. Two years later, she bought the building and christened it St. Mary's Hospital; it became one of the largest institutions of its kind in the country. In the course of time, as superior (1854–67; 1870–76) and as guiding counselor to other superiors, she established orphanages for boys and girls, a Magdalen Asylum, a home for destitute aged, a retreat house for the community, a branch house at Sacramento (1857), a convent school and orphanage at Grass Valley (1863), St. Peter's and St. Brendan's schools in San Francisco, St. Anthony's school in Oakland, and St. Hilary's Sanitarium in Marin County (1897). She took charge of the smallpox hospital in the epidemic of 1868, fed hundreds of unemployed in the hard years of 1893 and 1894, and furnished nurses at the Presidio during the Spanish-American War. Her devotion and disinterested spirit of boundless charity won people of all classes. In 1878 she made a journey to Ireland for novices. She had the loyal devotion of the growing Irish colony in California and when, worn out by a life of labor, obedience to rule, and soliciting campaigns for her charities, she died, the *San Francisco Chronicle* (Aug. 10, 1898) declared that "no dead sovereign ever had a prouder burial than Mother Mary Russell, whose life of self-denial and good works has crowned her in a city's memory."

[Matthew Russell, *The Three Sisters of Lord Russell of Killowen* (1912), reprints his *Life of Mother Mary Baptist Russell* (1901); Mother Austin Carroll, *Leaves from the Annals of the Sisters of Mercy* (n.d.); C. G. Herbermann, ed., *Diary of a Visit to the U. S. A. in the Year 1883 by Charles Lord Russell of Killowen* (1910); *San Francisco Chronicle*, Aug. 7, 10, 1898, and *San Francisco Examiner*, Aug. 7, 8, 10, 1898.]

R. J. P.

RUSSELL, OSBORNE (June 12, 1814–*c.* 1865), trapper, Oregon and California pioneer, and author, was born probably in Hallowell, Me. Of his parents nothing is recorded. Though he had little schooling, his studious and observant turn of mind gave him in time a practical education. At sixteen he ran away to sea but at New York, with the remainder of the crew, deserted his vessel; he then engaged with a fur company operating in Wisconsin and Minnesota, where he remained for nearly three years. At Independence, Mo., in April 1834 he joined Nathaniel J. Wyeth [*q.v.*] in his second expedition for the mountains, took part in the building of Fort Hall, Idaho, which was begun in July, and later served as a trapper and hunter. For the next six or seven years, part of the time under James Bridger [*q.v.*] and at other times with two or three companions or alone, he trapped over a wide region, experiencing rather more than his share of desperate adventures. In 1842 he went to Oregon with Dr. Elijah White's emigrant party, reaching the falls of the Willamette in September. He took an active part in political affairs; on May 14, 1844, he was chosen one of the three executive committeemen of the Provisional Government, and in the following year he was a candidate for governor, but toward the close of the campaign apparently threw his influence to George Abernethy [*q.v.*], who was elected. In 1848, hearing of the gold discoveries in California, he started for the placers and in September arrived in Hangtown (which his *Journal of a Trapper* calls Gallowstown), later Placerville. For a time he panned gold; later with a partner, Gilliam, he kept a provision store and boarding house, and still later operated two trading vessels between Sacramento and Portland. When his partner absconded with all the firm's money and one of the vessels, he was financially ruined, and he spent the remainder of his life in trying to pay off his creditors. He died in the county hospital at Placerville.

Through all his wanderings in the beaver country he kept a journal. At some time between 1843 and 1848 he sent it to New York for publication, but it did not appear until 1914 at Boise, Idaho, under the title, *Journal of a Trapper Or Nine Years in the Rocky Mountains, 1834–1843*. As a precise and intimate first-hand account of the daily life of the trapper explorer the book has no equal. Russell is characterized by Burnett, who knew him well, as a man of education, refined feelings, and virtuous habits, and as one who "always remained true to his principles." Burnett gives him the title of judge, a distinction apparently won by the part he took in a vigilance court at Placerville, which sentenced three murderers to be hanged.

[Publisher's note in 1921 ed. of *Jour. of a Trapper*; P. H. Burnett, *Recollections and Opinions of an Old Pioneer* (1880), pp. 161–62; incidental references in H. H. Bancroft, *Hist. of Oregon* (1886); C. H. Carey, *Hist. of Oregon* (1922), and H. W. Scott, *Hist. of the Oregon Country* (6 vols., 1924).]   W.J.G.

RUSSELL, SOL SMITH (June 15, 1848–Apr. 28, 1902), actor, was born in Brunswick, Mo., the son of Charles Elmer Russell, keeper of a small country store, who had been at one time an itinerant physician and preacher, and of Louisa Mathews, daughter of Edwin Mathews, a teacher of music in Cincinnati, Ohio. He was named for the actor, Sol Smith [*q.v.*], who was his uncle by marriage. During his boyhood and youth, he lived with his parents in St. Louis, Mo., and Jacksonville, Ill., but soon after the outbreak of the Civil War he ran away from home and remained with a Union regiment for several months as a drummer boy, not being allowed to enlist because of his youth and the absence of formal parental consent. His departure from home, however, was the beginning of a long professional career on the stage. Joining a company at the Defiance Theatre in Cairo, Ill., he made slow advancement from small beginnings; he often appeared in a variety of parts in one evening, besides singing between the acts and drumming in the orchestra.

This opening engagement struck the keynote of his career. He could turn his mind, his hands, his agile body to almost anything that would amuse an audience. Soon afterwards he was acting and singing his songs in stock companies and on tours through the Middle West; he joined the Peak family of bell ringers, and in 1868 the Berger family, giving character bits and songs, and proving so popular with the Bergers that they were later advertised as the "Berger Family and Sol Smith Russell Concert Troupe." After a season in 1867 with the stock company at the Chestnut Street Theatre in Philadelphia, he spent three seasons touring in his own monologue entertainment. His first New York engagement was at Lina Edwin's Theatre in 1871; and after a season of twenty-six weeks at the Olympic Theatre, nineteen weeks at the Howard Athenaeum in Boston, and various other engagements, he joined Augustin Daly's company at the Fifth Avenue Theatre in New York, making his debut there on Aug. 25, 1874, as Mr. Peabody in *What Could She Do, or Jealousy,* a version of Emile Augier's *Gabrielle.* The theatre records show that he appeared in three other characters that season, Trip in *The School for Scandal,* the present Mrs. Peters in *Moorcroft,*

or the Double Wedding, by Bronson Howard, and Colander in *Masks or Faces,* written by Tom Taylor and Charles Reade and later the basis for Reade's novel, *Peg Woffington.* He made his first starring appearance in 1880 in *Edgewood Folks,* a comedy *pasticcio* designed by J. E. Brown with the assistance of William Seymour especially to fit him, in which he sang a number of songs and made ten changes of costume. After a season in 1884–85 as leading comedian at the Boston Museum, he continued starring without further interruption in a succession of comedies of homely life, his rôles inspired by and invested with his own quaint personality. They included *Felix McKusick,* by J. E. Brown; *Pa,* by C. W. Walters; *Bewitched* and *Peaceful Valley,* by E. E. Kidder; *The Tale of a Coat,* rewritten to order for him by Dion Boucicault, and a dire failure; *April Weather,* by E. E. Kidder; and *A Bachelor's Romance,* by Martha Morton. Once in a while he escaped from these characters to act in his own inimitable and characteristic manner, such old-time stage favorites as Dr. Pangloss in *The Heir-at-Law,* and Bob Acres in *The Rivals*; and during the season of 1897–98 he made an especial feature of a triple bill consisting of *Mr. Valentine's Christmas, The Taming of the Shrew,* and *The Spitfire.* He was an intimate friend of James Whitcomb Riley, whose poems he recited with humor and pathos. He made his last appearance on the stage in Chicago, Jan. 7, 1901, in the title rôle of *The Hon. John Grigsby,* a comedy by Charles Klein. After a lingering illness with locomotor ataxia, he died in Washington, having acquired a considerable fortune through hard work and thrift. Tall and slight in appearance, deliberate in action, he had a dry, crackling comedy manner that was irresistible in its appeal to an audience. His first wife was Louise Berger; after her death he married Alice M. Adams (daughter of William T. Adams [*q.v.*], known to boy readers as Oliver Optic), who with their two children survived him.

[E. A. Dithmar, *Memories of Daly's Theatres* (1897); *Famous Am. Actors of Today* (1896), ed. by F. E. McKay and C. E. L. Wingate; J. B. Clapp and E. F. Edgett, *Players of the Present* (1901), pt. III; *Illustrated American,* June 17, 1893; *Boston Transcript,* June 29, 1895; *St. Louis Republic,* Mar. 12, 1899; *N. Y. Dramatic Mirror,* Nov. 20, 1897; obit. notices in *Phil. Record, Boston Herald, Boston Jour.* and *Boston Globe,* Apr. 29, 1902, and *N. Y. Dramatic Mirror,* May 3, 1902; letter by William Seymour in *Boston Herald,* July 1, 1923; *Who's Who in America,* 1899–1900.]
     E.F.E.

RUSSELL, WILLIAM (Apr. 28, 1798–Aug. 16, 1873), educator, was born in Glasgow, Scotland, the son of Alexander and Janet (Jamieson) Russell. After a period of preparatory study in a local grammar school, he matriculated in 1811 at the University of Glasgow. He did not receive a degree upon completing his studies, because he could not afford the journey to Oxford or Cambridge, which alone had the privilege of granting degrees at that time. He had decided to devote his life to teaching, but before he was able to establish himself in his native city, a pulmonary ailment made it necessary for him to seek a warmer climate. Accordingly, he sailed for Georgia early in 1817. He seems to have improved here sufficiently to take employment as a tutor in the home of Judge John McPherson Berrien of Savannah. Later in the year he revisited Glasgow, and was convinced that the Scottish climate was too severe for his health.

Returning to Savannah in 1818, he conducted a private school for about two years in connection with the Chatham Academy. In 1821 he was appointed principal of the Academy and on Aug. 22, married one of the teachers, Ursula Wood, daughter of the Rev. Luke and Ann (Pease) Wood of Somers, Conn. It is probable that his wife influenced him to remove, in 1822, to New Haven, where they conducted a school in the New Township Academy building. In 1825 he became headmaster of the Hopkins Grammar School; he also gave private lessons in elocution and oratory to students at Yale College. Suffering a recurrence of his ailment, he resigned and moved to Boston, where, for five years, he gave instruction in elocution in several schools and to students attending Harvard College. In 1826 he became first editor of the *American Journal of Education,* carrying on his editorial work at night. During this period he gave many lectures on educational topics before teachers' institutes, reading circles, and lyceums, and took an active part in the discussions of the Transcendentalists in Boston and neighboring towns. Late in 1830 he removed to Philadelphia, with Amos Bronson Alcott [*q.v.*], and the following year established a school for girls in connection with the academy at Germantown. He organized the first teachers' association in Philadelphia (1831) and founded a *Journal of Education* there a year later. In 1833 he withdrew from the Germantown academy and established a school for girls in Philadelphia, where he remained until 1838. Returning then to Boston, he again taught elocution and later, in partnership with James E. Murdoch [*q.v.*], opened a school of speech. From 1842 to 1844, he resided in Andover, teaching elocution and oratory at Phillips Academy, the theological seminary, and Abbot Academy. He also lectured at the Theological Institute, East Windsor, Conn., a con-

nection which he maintained for about twenty years. Although he removed to Medford, Mass., in 1846, he did not sever his affiliations with these various institutions; in fact, he lectured periodically at others as well, among them Brown University, Union Theological Seminary, and Princeton.

In 1849, he founded the Merrimack Normal Institute, at Merrimack, N. H., a private normal school which he conducted successfully until 1852. The year following he taught in the normal school at Providence, R. I. In response to an invitation from the town of Lancaster, Mass., he opened the New England Normal Institute there on May 11, 1853, but because of failing health, closed it in 1855. During the two years of its existence, it became an important center of Pestalozzianism in the United States. He resided in Lancaster until his death, devoting his later years to lecturing and writing for various teachers' journals. He was one of the organizers of the American Institute of Instruction, and did much to further its important work.

Russell was a voluminous writer. His publications include: *A Grammar of Composition* (1823), *Suggestions on Education* (1823), *Manual of Mutual Instruction* (1826), *Lessons in Enunciation* (1830), *Rudiments of Gesture* (1830), *Exercises in Elocution* (1841), *The American Elocutionist* (1844), *Orthophony, or the Cultivation of the Voice* (1845), *Elements of Musical Articulation* (1845), *Pulpit Elocution* (1846), *Harper's New York Class Book* (1847), *Primary Reader* (1847), *Exercises on Words* (1856), *Teaching a Profession* (1858).

[*Papers Read at a Reunion of McGaw Normal Institute, Aug. 19, 1885 . . . a Memorial of the Life, Work, and Character of Professor William Russell* (Manchester, N. H., 1885); A. P. Marvin, *Hist. of the Town of Lancaster, Mass.* (1879); *Am. Jour. of Educ.,* Mar. 1857; W. S. Monroe, *Hist. of the Pestalozzian Movement in the U. S.* (1907); Charles Northend, *The Annals of the Am. Institute of Instruction . . . 1830-1883* (1884); W. I. Addison, *The Matriculation Albums of the Univ. of Glasgow from 1728 to 1858* (1913), p. 259; *Boston Transcript,* Aug. 18, 1873.]
R. F. S.

RUSSELL, WILLIAM EUSTIS (Jan. 6, 1857–July 16, 1896), governor of Massachusetts, was born at Cambridge, the ninth child and fourth son of Charles Theodore and Sarah Elizabeth (Ballister) Russell. He was descended from William Russell who settled in Cambridge in 1645. Having received his early education in the public schools, he entered Harvard College, from which he was graduated in 1877. His career in college was distinguished by the fact that he campaigned for Tilden, although his classmates, or their fathers, were overwhelmingly Republican. He led his class at Boston University Law School, where, in 1879, he received the first *summa cum laude* degree ever given there. He was admitted to the bar in April 1880.

Having begun the practice of law with his father, an old Democrat and a former mayor of Cambridge, Russell easily drifted into politics. At twenty-four, he was elected to the common council without his knowledge, defeating the regular nominee by one vote in a "sticker" campaign. In 1882 and 1883 he was elected to the board of aldermen. Four times (1884–87) he was chosen mayor on a non-partisan ticket, enforcing during his incumbency the "pay-as-you-go" policy in municipal finances. Cambridge voted for local prohibition while he was mayor, and although opposed to this policy, Russell strenuously enforced the decision of the electorate. A street-car strike added to his difficulties. In 1886 he declined the Democratic nomination to Congress from the fifth district.

When only thirty-one, he received the first of his five Democratic nominations for governor. Defeated in 1888 and 1889, he was elected in 1890, 1891, and 1892. His terms were notable, not so much for what he performed, as for what he prevented; for during all three years his hands were tied by a Republican legislature and council. All his vetoes were sustained, however, although he vainly urged personal responsibility as against commission government. Remaining startlingly youthful in appearance, Russell won friends and adherents by his tact, adaptability, memory for names and faces, and peculiar charm of manner. To these qualities were added firmness in decision, extraordinary energy in the search for facts, and a directness of statement that appealed to the most varied types of audiences. Though devoid of the usual arts of the political orator, he was adept in politics and a dangerous opponent on the stump. He was a tireless and intelligent foe of protection, with the unusual power of making a tariff speech interesting. He was the first governor to campaign through the small towns and to stay over night in the annual state troop encampments.

Although in 1894 he had retired from politics to the practice of law, his remarkable victories in a Republican state, his forcible defense of Cleveland in the *Forum* for May of that year, his addresses, and especially his speech at "Monticello," Apr. 13, 1896, with its courageous opposition to free silver and its call to duty to the Democratic party, had given him national prominence and caused him to be talked of widely for the presidency. In June 1896, at the personal request of Cleveland, he accepted election as a delegate to the Democratic National Convention at Chicago, where, with William C. Whitney and other leading gold Democrats, he conducted a vigorous, though unsuccessful fight against free silver.

Returning to Cambridge exhausted with the struggle and the heat, he set out, July 13, for B. F. Dutton's fishing camp at St. Adelaide, on the Little Pabos, in the Province of Quebec. The morning after his arrival he was found dead in his cabin, with a book by his side. Rumors that he died from sleeping medicine were utterly without foundation. President Cleveland attended his funeral at Cambridge. On June 3, 1885, at Cambridge, Russell had married Margaret Manning Swan, by whom he had three children.

[*Speeches and Addresses of William E. Russell* (1894), ed. by C. T. Russell with introduction by T. W. Higginson; C. C. Everett, *Memoir of the Hon. William Eustis Russell* (1898), also found in *Pubs. of the Colonial Soc. of Mass.*, vol. V (1902); C. E. Norton, *The Public Life and Services of William E. Russell* (1896), reprinted in *Harvard Grads. Mag.*, Dec. 1896; *Harvard Coll. Class of 1877, Seventh Ann. Report*, June 1917; *Boston Daily Advertiser*, July 17, 1896; information from Francis Peabody, and P. P. Chase; information and suggestions from Charles Warren, formerly private secretary and law partner of Russell.] S. M.

RUSSELL, WILLIAM HENRY (Oct. 9, 1802–Oct. 13, 1873), politician, California pioneer, was born in Nicholas County, Ky., the son of Robert Spottswood and Deborah (Allen) Russell and grandson of Gen. William Russell. He practised law in his native county and in 1830 represented it in the legislature; about this time he married Zanette Freeland of Baltimore. He early came to the attention of Henry Clay, who befriended him, and it is said that for a time he was Clay's secretary. In 1831 he emigrated to Callaway County, Mo., and in the following year served in the Black Hawk War; in 1841 he was appointed United States marshal of the District of Missouri, which included the Indian Country. He had by this time acquired the courtesy title of "colonel." His term ended in 1845, and in May 1846, near Independence, Mo., he joined a wagon-train of California emigrants, among whom was Edwin Bryant, later the author of *What I Saw in California* (1848), in which Russell figures. He was elected captain of the company but near Fort Laramie was displaced. With Bryant and seven others he continued the journey on muleback by way of Fort Bridger to the site of the future Salt Lake City and then across the Great Salt Desert, the first to follow Frémont's track of the year before. Arriving at Sutter's Fort on Sept. 1, and proceeding to Yerba Buena and Monterey, Russell joined Frémont's California Battalion with the rank of major and was one of the peace commissioners who framed the treaty of Cahuenga, Jan. 13, 1847. Frémont [q.v.] a few days later appointed him secretary of state. On the downfall of the Frémont administration in March, Russell left for the east by way of Santa Fé, reaching the Missouri settlements in July and thence going to Washington; he was one of Frémont's principal witnesses in the court-martial, which began in November. In 1849 he returned to California and practised law at San José and elsewhere until at least 1854. Later he went east again and in 1861 was appointed consul at Trinidad, Cuba. By 1865 he was back in the United States, and two years later sought vainly to get the post of consul-general at Havana. He died in Washington and was buried in Oak Hill Cemetery.

Russell appears as "Col. R——" in one passage in Parkman's *The California and Oregon Trail* (1849, ch. x) and in many passages in other Western books of the time. He was a large man, expansive in manner, boastful and bombastic in speech. His egotism sometimes made him the sport of his companions. In a story often told about him, he is said to have mistaken the chorus of "tu-whoo's" from a flock of owls for a challenge of "Who are you?" and to have thundered back, "Col. William H. Russell, of Kentucky—a bosom friend of Henry Clay!" Ever after he was known as "Owl" Russell. He was, however, a man of many substantial and endearing qualities, and was widely popular. He is sometimes confused with William Hepburn Russell [q.v.], the founder of the Pony Express.

[Anna Russell des Cognets, *William Russell and His Descendants* (1884); W. H. Davis, *Seventy-Five Years in California* (1929); H. H. Bancroft, *Hist. of California*, vol. V (1886); L. H. Garrard, *Wah-To-Yah and the Taos Trail* (1850), chs. XXIII–XXV; *Appletons' Ann. Cyc.*, 1873; *Daily Nat. Republican* (Washington, D. C.), Oct. 14, 1873; information from Ludie J. Kinkead and Mrs. Jouett T. Cannon, Frankfort, Ky.]
W. J. G.

RUSSELL, WILLIAM HEPBURN (Jan. 31, 1812–Sept. 10, 1872), freighter and founder of the Pony Express, was born in Burlington, Vt., the son of William Eaton and Myrtilla (Hepburn) Russell, and grandson of Benjamin and Betsy (Eaton) Russell. His father, a soldier in the War of 1812, died in 1814; some years afterward the widow married a Colonel Bangs, with whom she moved to Missouri. Beginning work as a clerk at sixteen, Russell in time became a merchant and for a period was a partner in a bank at Richmond, Mo. On June 9, 1835, at Lexington, Mo., he married Harriett Elliott Warder, daughter of the Rev. John Warder. By the late forties he was engaged in freighting on government contracts and on Dec. 28, 1854, he joined Alexander Majors [q.v.] and W. B. Waddell in a partnership, with its operating center at Leav-

enworth, which four years later became the firm of Russell, Majors & Waddell. From the first, the business grew rapidly; in 1857 it underwent a vast expansion when the contract was obtained for supplying the army ordered to Utah. In May 1859 Russell and John S. Jones, as an independent venture, started a stage line from Leavenworth to Denver, but it was taken over by the firm within a year; in February 1860 the Central Overland California and Pike's Peak Express Company was chartered, with Russell as president, and first-class coaches began running through to California. Though Northern sentiment demanded that the bulk of the Pacific mail should be carried over the central route, Southern dominance in Washington had in 1857–58 dictated the giving of the contract to the Butterfield Company, operating from Memphis, Tenn. Determined to prove that the use of the central route was not impracticable, Russell persuaded the reluctant Majors to join him in the operation of a Pony Express; on Apr. 3, 1860, with all preparations made, riders set out simultaneously from Sacramento and a point opposite St. Joseph, and relays of dauntless men and swift horses speeded the mail across the western half of the continent in the incredible time of ten days. Russell, now perhaps the most talked-of man in the United States, was hailed as the "Napoleon of the West."

His period of glory, however, was a brief one. Going to Washington to obtain funds for his ruinously expensive venture, he became involved in the greatest financial scandal of the time. The government was bankrupt and could not fulfil its obligations; John B. Floyd [q.v.], the secretary of war, when pressed for payment, availed himself of the services of Godard Bailey, a clerk in the Interior Department, who abstracted $870,000 in bonds from the Indian Trust Fund and turned them over to Russell, substituting for them acceptances given by Floyd to Russell. When the transaction became known in mid-December, both the House of Representatives and the District of Columbia grand jury took action. At the end of December Floyd resigned. On Jan. 30, 1861, Floyd, Russell, and Bailey were indicted; Russell, who on Jan. 18 had made a statement before a select committee of the House, protested his innocence, and in March the criminal court, evidently with the intent of leaving the matter to Congress, dismissed the last of the three indictments. The Civil War came on, and the case was swallowed up in the rush of preparation for the conflict, though for many years thereafter it was to reappear in litigation. On Apr. 26, Russell was succeeded as president of the stagecoach company by Bela M. Hughes. With the completion of the overland telegraph, on Oct. 24 the Pony Express came to an end; on Mar. 21, 1862, the company was disposed of at public sale to Ben Holladay [q.v.], and some time later Russell transferred his interest in the freighting business to Majors. Each of the partners lost a fortune. Russell attempted a new start in New York City, where he seems to have engaged in several speculative enterprises. In the summer of 1872, while in Washington, he fell ill and was taken to the home of a son, a banker of Palmyra, Mo., where shortly afterward he died, survived by his wife and five children.

[B. M. Little, *Brief Sketch of the Nat. Old Trails Road* (Lexington, Mo., 1928); L. R. Hafen, *The Overland Mail* (1926); *Collectors Club Philatelist*, Jan., Apr. 1929; W. E. Connelley, *A Standard Hist. of Kansas and Kansans* (5 vols., 1918); *Cong. Globe*, 36 Cong., 2 Sess., pp. 874 ff.; obit. notice in *St. Louis Daily Globe*, Sept. 14, 1872; information from Floyd C. Shoemaker, Columbia, Mo., Frank H. Sosey, Palmyra, Mo., and Mrs. W. J. Boyer, Wilmington, Del.]   W. J. G.

RUSSWURM, JOHN BROWN (Oct. 1, 1799–June 17, 1851), first superintendent of public schools in Liberia and governor of the Colony of Maryland, was born at Port Antonio, Jamaica. He was the son of a white American and a colored woman. When his father left the island, he put the boy in school in Canada. The father afterward married a white woman in Maine, who learned of the existence of the boy, then called John Brown. She insisted that he join the family and assume his father's name. After the death of the father and her remarriage, she still cared carefully for the boy. He was sent to school in Maine and eventually entered Bowdoin College, where he graduated in 1826. He was reported by his classmates to have been a young man of sound intelligence, a great reader with a special fondness for history and politics (Cleaveland, *post*, p. 354). He was probably the first person of acknowledged African descent to finish an American college course. He settled in New York City, where in 1827 he established one of the first colored papers in the United States, *Freedom's Journal*. His paper espoused the abolitionists' cause and opposed emigration to Africa; but after a time he changed his mind and said: "We consider it mere waste of words to talk of ever enjoying citizenship in this country" (*African Repository*, Dec. 1851, p. 357).

Thereupon, he emigrated to Liberia in 1829 to become superintendent of public schools and to carry on trade. From 1830 to 1834 he acted as colonial secretary, editing and publishing at the same time the *Liberia Herald*. In 1836 he was appointed governor of the Maryland Colony at Cape Palmas, a position he held until his death in 1851. The Maryland Colony was established under the auspices of the Maryland State Colonization Society. The territory there was obtained through James Hall, a friend and schoolmate of Russwurm. The president of the society bore the testimony as to how well Russwurm discharged his difficult duty in averting the perils of the surrounding savage tribes, in quieting the controversies of civilized and angry white men, and resisting unreasonable popular clamor among the colonists (Cleaveland, *post*, pp. 353–54). Although the Maryland Colony was distinct from Liberia, Russwurm worked in careful collaboration with Joseph J. Roberts [q.v.] of Liberia and was instrumental in the final union of the two colonies. Even before an actual union, they acted together in foreign affairs and established a common customs tariff. Russwurm encouraged agriculture and trade, built a stone jail that could also be used as a fort, took a census in 1843, and established a court with presiding justices. He married a daughter of Lieutenant-Governor McGill of Monrovia and at his death in 1851 left four children.

[*African Repository*, esp. July 1846, Nov., Dec. 1851; Nehemiah Cleaveland and A. S. Packard, *Hist. of Bowdoin College* (1882); *General Cat. of Bowdoin College* (1912); Archibald Alexander, *A Hist. of Colonization on the Western Coast of Africa* (1846); H. H. Johnston, *Liberia* (1906), vol. I; W. E. B. Du Bois, "The College-bred Negro," *Atlanta Univ. Pubs.*, no. 5 (1900).]   W. E. B. D–B.

RUST, RICHARD SUTTON (Sept. 12, 1815–Dec. 22, 1906), Methodist Episcopal clergyman, educator, was born in Ipswich, Mass., the son of Nathaniel Rust, Jr., and his second wife, Mary (Sutton) Kimball. He was descended from Henry Rust who emigrated from England and settled in Hingham, Mass., as early as 1635. Richard's father, a cordwainer and dealer in boots and shoes, died when the boy was but six years old; his mother, when he was nine. He tried working on an uncle's farm, then cabinetmaking, but, eager for an education, he bought back a part of his time of apprenticeship and entered Phillips Academy, Andover, Mass. Expelled with several students who refused to resign from an anti-slavery society, he became a student at Canaan, N. H., in an academy which admitted negroes. When local opposition closed this, he went to Wilbraham Academy, Wilbraham, Mass., and from there to Wesleyan University, Middletown, Conn., from which he received the degree of A.B. in 1841. While a student he earned money by giving anti-slavery lectures. He was received into the New England Conference of the Methodist Episcopal Church on trial in 1844, and ordained elder in 1846. During a pastorate in Worcester, Mass., he founded and edited *The American Pulpit* (1845–48), a collection of sermons including a few of his own. Transferred to the New Hampshire Conference in 1846, he became principal of the New Hampshire Conference Seminary (now Tilton School) and state school commissioner. He made some improvements in the school system, but soon returned to preaching. In 1841 he married Sarah A. Hubbard; after her death he married, in 1875, Elizabeth A. Lownes.

Rust's early concern for the negro became his dominating interest. Transferred to the Cincinnati Conference in 1859, he was made president of Wilberforce University, a school for negroes, serving until it was sold to the African Methodist Episcopal Church in 1863. For the next two years he was president of Wesleyan Female College, Cincinnati. He shared the intense local interest in the early Contraband Relief Association, later the Western Freedmen's Aid Commission, of which he became corresponding secretary in 1865. When, finally, the many relief societies were united into the American Freedman's Union Commission, Rust became a member of the western branch of the executive committee. He soon grew dissatisfied with the work of this large, undenominational body, however, for he was sectarian in his interests, violently prejudiced against the "Romanists," and insisted that the mission of the teacher sent to the South was to evangelize as well as educate. He therefore helped to organize the Freedmen's Aid Society of the Methodist Episcopal Church, at Cincinnati, in 1866, served as its general field agent for two years, and then as corresponding secretary for over twenty years. He vigorously directed and helped in the work of securing funds, overseeing schools in operation and suggesting improvements, selecting sites for new schools, planning buildings, and keeping the needs of the society constantly before the laity. One of these schools, Rust University at Holly Springs, Miss., was renamed for him. It was estimated in 1882 that the teachers sent out from these institutions had taught more than three-fourths of a million children. When, in 1892, he finally retired, he was still alert, impressive though grizzled in appearance, and forceful in address. He died in Cincinnati in his ninety-second year. His publications include: *Freedom's Gifts: or Sentiments of the Free* (1840), a compilation, including two contributions of his own; *Method of Introducing Religion into Common Schools* (n.d.); and *The Freedmen's Aid Society of the Methodist Episcopal Church* (1880); he also edited and con-

tributed to *Isaac W. Wiley, Late Bishop of the M. E. Church, a Monograph* (1885).

[J. M. Buckley, *A Hist. of Methodists in the U. S.* (1896); A. D. Rust, *Record of the Rust Family Embracing the Descendants of Henry Rust* (privately printed, 1891); Matthew Simpson, ed., *Cyc. of Methodism* (5th ed., 1882); *The Biog. Encyc. of Ohio of the Nineteenth Century* (1876); *Ann. Cat., Rust Univ.*, 1889–90; *Wiley Coll. Announcements, 1924–25*; *Alumni Record of Wesleyan Univ., Middletown, Conn.* (1921); *Am. Freedman*, Apr. 1866.]   H. R. S.

RUTER, MARTIN (Apr. 3, 1785–May 16, 1838), Methodist clergyman, educator, and missionary to Texas, son of Job and Sarah Ruter, was born in Charlton, Mass., but at the age of eight went with his parents to central Vermont, where he lived in the towns of Bradford and Corinth. Here he came under fervid Methodist influence; his father's house was a stopping place for itinerant ministers, and for a time Martin boarded in the home of Margaret (Appleton) Peckett, who had been a housekeeper for John Wesley. When he was fifteen years old he delivered an exhortation to a throng of people at a quarterly meeting which so impressed the presiding elder, John Broadhead, that he took the boy with him as an assistant on the circuit. The next year, in spite of his youth, Ruter was admitted to the New York Conference on trial. He was ordained deacon in 1803, and elder in 1805, becoming that year a member of the New England Conference. In the meantime he had labored with noticeable success on circuits in New Hampshire and Massachusetts and had had a year of missionary service in Montreal, Canada. Until 1816, when he was stationed at Philadelphia, his ministry was to churches in New England. During this period he came to be held in increasingly high esteem for both his spiritual and intellectual qualities, and rose to a place among the leaders of the denomination, being sent to the General Conference for the first time as early as 1808.

After 1818, when he was put in charge of the Wesleyan Academy, New Market, N. H., the establishment of which by the New England Conference he had fostered, his major work until almost the end of his life was that of furthering the educational interests of the denomination. He stayed at New Market two years and was then chosen by the General Conference of 1820 to open the western branch of the Book Concern at Cincinnati. Following eight years' successful management of this enterprise, he was appointed first president of Augusta College, Augusta, Ky. The desire to be directly engaged in the work of evangelization was ever uppermost with him, and in 1832 he resigned to undertake a pastorate in Pittsburgh, but two years later was persuaded to accept the presidency of Allegheny College, which had recently come under Methodist control. A preacher at fifteen, he himself had had little schooling, but by persistent private study he had become a broadly, if not a deeply, learned man. He had a good command of the French language, acquired when he was in Montreal; he was well versed in the classics; his knowledge of Hebrew, Chaldaic, and Syriac was such that he was called to the professorship of Oriental languages at Cincinnati College in 1821, and in 1824 he published *An Easy Entrance into the Sacred Language: Being a Concise Hebrew Grammar, Without Points.* He had an aptitude for mathematics, published *The Juvenile Arithmetick and Scholar's Guide; Wherein Theory and Practice Are Combined* (1827), and taught astronomy. In addition he prepared a primer, a speller, and a small treatise on the conjugation of French regular verbs. He published a church history in 1832, based on the works of George Gregory, a second edition of which appeared in 1834 under the title *A Concise History of the Christian Church,* long used as a textbook in Methodist Conferences. As early as 1820 Transylvania University conferred upon him the degree of D.D., said to have been the first awarded to an American Methodist. The incident created a furor in Methodist circles, since a degree after one's name was considered an adornment comparable with gold and costly apparel. His reputation for both learning and goodness gave prestige to the institutions with which he was connected; he proved himself an able administrator and set high educational ideals.

The crowning work of his life was brief but potent in effect. Always apostolic in zeal, he resigned the presidency of Allegheny in June 1837 to superintend missionary work in Texas. In less than a year, having labored indefatigably and laid a foundation "which, had there been no other service of his lifetime to his church, would have assured him a permanent place as a maker of Methodism in America" (Smith, *Martin Ruter, post,* pp. 103–04), he died of typhoid pneumonia, a martyr to his devotion. He was buried in Washington, Tex., on the banks of the Brazos; later his body was moved to Navasota, where in 1901 a shaft of Vermont granite was erected as a memorial. His second wife, Ruth Young of Concord, N. H., whom he married in April 1809, and seven children survived him; his first wife, Sybil Robertson of Chesterfield, N. H., to whom he was married in June 1805, died in 1808.

[*Vital Records of Charlton, Mass.* (1905); *Minutes of the Ann. Conferences of the M. E. Ch. 1829–39* (1840); T. O. Summers, *Biog. Sketches of Eminent Itinerant Ministers* (1858); W. B. Sprague, *Annals Am.*

Pulpit, vol. VII (1859); E. A. Smith, *Allegheny—A Century of Education* (1916) and *Martin Ruter* (1915); Macum Phelan, *A Hist. of Early Methodism in Texas* (1924); P. N. Garber, *The Romance of Am. Methodism* (1931).]   H. E. S.

RUTGERS, HENRY (Oct. 7, 1745–Feb. 17, 1830), Revolutionary officer, landed magnate, and philanthropist, the son of Hendrick and Catharine (de Peyster) Rutgers, was the last descendant in his direct line of the Dutch immigrant, Rutger Jacobsen Van Schoenderwoert, who came to Fort Orange in 1636, and who rose to affluence by investing the profits of prosperous breweries in merchandise and Manhattan real estate. Coming to manhood during the pre-revolutionary period of opposition to Great Britain, he joined his clan in supporting the Sons of Liberty, formidable agitators who met at the Rutgers farm. His formal education was completed on graduation from King's College with the class of 1766. Relieved from the necessity of an active business career, he devoted his mature life to caring for his property, a considerable tract in what was to become New York's lower East Side around Chatham Square, and performing the duties of the public-spirited citizen. These activities were prefaced by an interlude of soldiering in the Revolution, during which he was mentioned as a captain at the battle of White Plains. Military interests continued until 1795 when he resigned the command of the 1st Regiment of New York militia (manuscript letter of Mar. 3, 1795, to Gov. DeWitt Clinton in the Rutgers University Library).

His interests were manifold, ranging from local and state politics to the patronage of numerous educational and religious projects. He was a member of the state assembly in 1784 and in 1800 was again a successful candidate for that body as a member of the group formed by Aaron Burr for use in building his own and the Jeffersonian fortunes. His continued interest in local politics was evidenced by his prominence in raising a fund of $28,000 for the construction of the first Great Wigwam of Tammany Hall in 1811.

Many educational institutions felt the benefit of his advice and support. He gave the land for the second free school, established for the city's poor, and frequently met deficits out of his own pocket. He succeeded Governor Clinton as president of the Free School Society in 1828 and served until his death. He was a regent of the University of the State of New York from 1802 to 1826, a trustee of Princeton University from 1804 to 1817, and of Queen's College from 1816 to 1821. Four years later Queen's College petitioned the New Jersey legislature for a change of name. This move was simultaneous with the election of Philip Milledoler [*q.v.*], pastor and personal friend of Rutgers, as president, and the name of Milledoler's erstwhile elder, now an octogenarian, was given to the struggling institution. So far his donations had not been considerable, and the honor was probably conferred in a combined desire to compliment a prominent member of the Dutch Reformed Church (he was then president of its Board of Corporation) and to share in the benefactions of one whose generosity had been proverbial and might, through gift or bequest, become perennial. The last hope was not largely realized, as his known gifts thereafter consisted of $200 for the purchase of a bell and $5,000 in cash.

He added to lifelong devoutness a rather high catholicity and generosity in matters religious. When he broke up the Rutgers farm, called the "Bouwery," into long-time leaseholds, he offered several lots for the building of churches, including in his tender the Baptists and Presbyterians as well as his own Dutch Reformed. He was at various times an elder in the First Presbyterian Church and in the Market Street Dutch Reformed Church, for which last he gave the site. The Rutgers Street Presbyterian Church, opened in 1798, was also built on land which he gave. In spite of continued disbursements, so great that at his death it was asserted that "it may be questioned, whether any one individual in our country has given so much in the whole amount, to objects of general charity," he died worth the very respectable sum of $907,949. Gilbert Stuart's portrait of Washington hung in the Rutgers mansion for many years.

[E. H. Crosby, "The Rutgers Family of N. Y.," *N. Y. Geneal. and Biog. Record,* Apr. 1886; Frederick Brückbauer, *The Kirk on Rutgers Farm* (1919); W. H. S. Demarest, *A Hist. of Rutgers College, 1766–1924* (1924); Wm. McMurray, *A Sermon Occasioned by the Death of Col. Henry Rutgers* (1830); I. N. P. Stokes, *The Iconography of Manhattan Island,* vol. III (1918); *N. Y. Daily Advertiser,* Feb. 18, 1830.]   L. E. E.

RUTHERFURD, LEWIS MORRIS (Nov. 25, 1816–May 30, 1892), astrophysicist, was born at Morrisania, N. Y. He was the son of Robert Walter and Sabina (Morris) Rutherfurd and a great-grandson of Lewis Morris, 1726–1798 [*q.v.*], signer of the Declaration of Independence and Maj. Walter Rutherfurd, a British army officer who served in the French and Indian War, and married Catherine, daughter of James Alexander [*q.v.*]. Rutherfurd entered Williams College in the sophomore class at the age of fifteen. While an undergraduate he assisted in the preparation of lecture experiments in chemistry and physics. After graduation he studied law under

William H. Seward and was admitted to the bar in 1837. On July 22, 1841, he married Margaret Stuyvesant Chanler, by whom he had seven children. He gave up his law practice in 1849 and for the next seven years, largely on account of his wife's health, resided in France, Germany, and Italy. He had already been in the habit of devoting much of his leisure time to the study of chemistry, mechanics, and astronomy, and while in Florence he profited greatly from an intimacy with Amici, who was experimenting on the achromatism of microscope objectives.

On his return to New York in 1856, Rutherfurd built a small observatory in his garden on Second Avenue at Eleventh Street and fitted up a study and machine shop in the house. Here he started his pioneer work in astronomical photography and spectroscopy. His first photographs of the moon were secured in 1858 at about the same time that the experiments of De la Rue were meeting with success. Impatient with the unsatisfactory results obtained in photographing with a visual telescope, he devised a combination of lenses which would convert the instrument into a photographic telescope. This he tried out with reasonable success, in 1860, at a solar eclipse in Labrador. His first scientific paper, dated July 28, 1862 (*American Journal of Science,* September 1862), confirmed Clark's discovery of the companion of Sirius and gave a series of measures of position.

The laboratory experimentation of Kirchhoff and Bunsen in spectroscopy was attracting great attention. Turning his attention to this field, Rutherfurd followed up the observational work of Fraunhofer and succeeded in observing the general characteristics of the spectra of the sun, moon, and a number of stars. In his paper, dated Dec. 4, 1862 (*Ibid.,* January 1863) he attempted, for the first time, a classification of stellar spectra, which agrees essentially with that published later by Secchi. During this investigation he realized that the spectroscope could be used to determine the color curve of a telescope objective and, using this discovery to test his work as it progressed, he succeeded, in 1864, in finishing an objective, 11¼ inches in diameter, designed solely for photography. A 13-inch telescope which could be converted from a visual to a photographic instrument by the addition of a third lens was finished in 1868. With these instruments he made many fine photographs of the sun and moon.

Realizing the value and convenience of obtaining a photographic record of the relative positions of stars, Rutherfurd inaugurated a long program of photographing numerous star fields.

The measurement of the plates was carried out on an engine which he devised and built. In the first design the micrometer wire was carried entirely across the plate by a very long screw. Later, however, a glass scale was added, making it necessary to use the screw for measuring short distances only, and thus greatly reducing the errors inherent in the screw. Troubled by the possibility that the photographic film might not stay fixed in position and thus vitiate the measures, Rutherfurd experimented and found that treatment with dilute albumen secured this necessary condition (*Ibid.*, December 1872). He is to be credited with overcoming the mechanical difficulties of making an efficient spectroscope of hollow prisms filled with liquid maintained at uniform density. It was with a spectroscope of this type that he secured a photograph of the solar spectrum showing many new lines. He also devised the now well-known method of connecting the prisms so that they all automatically come to the angle of least deviation. During 1870 he built an engine with which he succeeded in ruling interference gratings, which was superior to all others down to the time of Henry A. Rowland [*q.v.*]. Rutherfurd was a trustee of Columbia College for more than twenty-five years and took a leading part in establishing the department of geodesy and practical astronomy in 1881. In 1883 he made an unconditional gift to the college of his entire observatory equipment, following this gift in 1890 with that of all his negatives and twenty folio volumes of plate measures. The work of measurement and reduction was later carried on by John K. Rees [*q.v.*] and Harold Jacoby.

[Livingston Rutherfurd, *Family Records and Events, Compiled Principally from the Original Memorials in the Rutherfurd Collection* (1894); B. A. Gould, in *Nat. Acad. Sci. Biog. Memoirs*, vol. III (1895); J. K. Rees, in *Contributions from the Observatory of Columbia Univ.*, no. 1 (1906); J. K. Rees and others, *Lewis Morris Rutherfurd: A Brief Account of His Life and Work; Discussion of Some of His Stellar Photographs* (2 vols., 1898–1906); *Astronomy and Astrophysics*, Oct. 1892; *Mo. Notices of the Royal Astronomical Soc.*, vol. LIII (1893); *Astronomical Jour.*, June 13, 1892; *N. Y. Times*, June 1, 1892.]   R. S. D.

RUTLEDGE, EDWARD (Nov. 23, 1749–Jan. 23, 1800), signer of the Declaration of Independence, governor of South Carolina, was born in Charlestown (now Charleston) or in Christ Church Parish across the bay, being the seventh and youngest child of Dr. John and Sarah (Hext) Rutledge, and the brother of John Rutledge [*q.v.*]. He was admitted in 1767 to the Middle Temple and called to the English bar in 1772. He returned home in January 1773, and a few months later represented the printer, Thomas Powell, in the noted *habeas corpus* proceedings before Assistant Justice Rawlins Lowndes [*q.v.*]. His public life began when he was elected in July 1774 to the First Continental Congress. Aggressive but not radical, he bent his efforts toward procuring a bill of rights and a plan of permanent relief, and supported so vigorously the stand of his brother John that he brought upon himself one of the choicest compliments distributed by John Adams who called him "a perfect Bob-o-Lincoln—a swallow, a sparrow, ... jejune, inane and puerile" (*Works,* vol. II, 1850, p. 401). Despite his youth and the lack of the eloquence and finish in his speeches that he later acquired, his winning personality and soundness of thought brought him growing esteem. He was elected to the first and second provincial congresses of 1775 and 1776, and in the same years to the Continental Congress, where, after the departure of his brother and of Christopher Gadsden [*q.v.*], he was the leader of the South Carolina delegation. Restrained more by the opinion of his constituents than by his own, he staved off action on the resolution for independence for nearly a month. On July 2, however, the South Carolina delegation voted for it under his influence. Rutledge felt that confederation should have been achieved before independence, but opposed building a strong government, and in August repudiated the proposed plan as dangerous, fearing especially the "low Cunning, and those levelling Principles" of the New England States (letter to John Jay, June 29, 1776, Burnett, *post,* I, 518).

In November 1776 he returned home to take part in the defense of the state and to look after his private affairs. The state gained a captain of artillery but lost a delegate in Congress whose service in the critical years to come would have been of the greatest value. In 1778 he was elected to the state House of Representatives from Charlestown, and by that body in 1779 to Congress, but did not reach Philadelphia. He was in the fight at Beaufort in February 1779, and was captured at the fall of Charlestown. From September 1780 to July 1781 he was one of the St. Augustine "exiles," but was exchanged in time to take his seat in the legislature in January 1782. He drew up the bill proposing the confiscation of the properties of Loyalists, and favored the measure as necessary to finance the state, but used his influence to moderate its effect.

The years following the Revolution brought honors in public life and success in law practice to the genial and charming gentleman. He added to his property and obligations by investing in plantations in partnership with his brother-in-law, Charles Cotesworth Pinckney [*q.v.*].

From 1782 to 1796 he represented Charleston in the House of Representatives as well as in the state conventions of 1788 and 1790. His efficient work brought him an increasing burden, especially in matters of finance, until in the session of 1792 he was chairman of nineteen committees. He was stiffly conservative and rarely conceded anything to the democratic elements in the state. An influential Federalist, he was presidential elector in 1788, 1792, and 1796, voting in the last-named year for Thomas Pinckney and Jefferson. In 1796 and 1798 he was elected from Charleston to the state Senate, and in the latter year became governor. At the time of his election, however, his health was broken. He performed his duties with care but in great physical distress, and died in Charleston nearly a year before the end of his term. He was twice married, first, on Mar. 1, 1774, to Henrietta, the daughter of Henry Middleton [q.v.], by whom he had three children. She died on Apr. 22, 1792, and on Oct. 28, he married Mary (Shubrick) Eveleigh.

[David Ramsay, *The Hist. of S. C.* (1809), vol. II; J. B. O'Neall, *Biog. Sketches of the Bench and Bar of S. C.* (1859), vol. II; John Sanderson, *Biog. of the Signers* ... vol. III (1823); A. S. Salley, Jr., *Delegates to the Cont. Cong. from S. C.* (1927); M. L. Webber, "Dr. John Rutledge and His Descendants," *S. C. Hist. and Geneal. Mag.,* Jan. 1930; see also *Ibid.,* Apr. 1911, pp. 49–50, Jan. 1916, pp. 4–6, 11–13, Jan. 1926, pp. 2–9, July 1926, pp. 153–55; E. C. Burnett, *Letters of Members of Cont. Cong.,* I, II, IV (1921, 1923, 1928); *Jour. of Cont. Cong.,* IV–VI (1906); John Drayton, *Memoirs of the Am. Rev.* (1821), vol. I, pp. 131–41, 167–76; *Correspondence of Mr. Ralph Izard of S. C.* (one vol., 1844); U. B. Phillips, "The S. C. Federalists," *Am. Hist. Rev.,* July 1909; Register of Mesne Conveyance, Charleston, K7, 293; Inventories, D, 1800–1810, 19, Will Book C, 640–42, Charleston courthouse; manuscript journals of S. C. House and Senate; *Charleston City Gazette,* Jan. 25, 1800.] R. L. M.

RUTLEDGE, JOHN (Sept. 1739–July 18, 1800), statesman and jurist, the eldest son of Dr. John and Sarah (Hext) Rutledge, and a brother of Edward Rutledge [q.v.], was born in Charlestown (now Charleston), S. C., or in Christ Church Parish nearby, when his mother was just turned fifteen years of age. John received his early education from his father, who died in 1750, from the Anglican minister of Christ Church, and from a tutor of the classics in Charlestown. After studying in the Middle Temple he was called to the English bar in February 1760, and returned to an immediate and brilliant success in Charlestown. In 1761 he was elected to the Commons House from Christ Church Parish and represented it in the provincial bodies until the Revolution placed him in the governor's chair. In this compact and vigorous assembly, with its traditions of rule by the planters and

their allies, and of legislative dominance under imperial supervision, his political philosophy was matured, and it changed but little thereafter.

In 1762 the twenty-three year old lawyer, as chairman of a committee, presented a powerful indictment of the action of Governor Boone in the noted dispute over the election of Christopher Gadsden [q.v.]. In the Stamp Act Congress of 1765 he was chairman of the committee which wrote the memorial and petition to the House of Lords. In the heated discussions of July 1774 he proved acceptable to the cautious merchants as well as to the aggressive planters, and was sent to the First Continental Congress. There he based his arguments solely on English constitutional precedent, of which he was the foremost exponent in the province, and, like Joseph Galloway [q.v.], was bent on maintaining self-government without breaking up the empire. With the rest of the South Carolina delegation he wished a complete embargo, but the northern delegates wanted a boycott only on trade with Great Britain, thus leaving their income practically untouched, while destroying that of South Carolina. Rutledge led the successful fight to except rice from the boycott list, and this achievement, with his attitude toward colonial rights, carried him a long step toward the political leadership of South Carolina. He was reëlected to the Second Continental Congress and his efforts for the establishment of regular governments in the colonies culminated in the advice of Congress to South Carolina Nov. 4, to take such action if it should seem necessary. The next day he set out for Charlestown, keenly ambitious to play a part in the coming reorganization. He was elected to the Council of Safety, and during December and January became second in influence only to the president, Henry Laurens [q.v.]. He was one of the large committee which wrote the South Carolina constitution of 1776, and when the Provincial Congress, by its adoption of that instrument, became the General Assembly he was elected president. The following December he was reëlected for the regular term of two years.

The trust of the troubled commonwealth in the young lawyer was due in part to the completeness of his identification with the opinions and interests of its rulers; in part to his political training and abilities; in part to certain personal qualities: his courage, tact—although he was intolerant when aroused—his unremitting industry, and his intensity of conviction and purpose. The new government passed through its first tests with fine success. The British attempt upon Charlestown was repulsed in June and the Cherokees were subdued in July, and for more than two years the state suffered no invasion and enjoyed some prosperity. Meanwhile, a liberal movement in the state gained momentum, and found expression in March 1778 in a revision of the constitution which substituted a senate elected by the people for the legislative council, the creature of the House, and disestablished the Anglican Church. Profoundly distrusting democracy, Rutledge protested against even so short a step toward it, vetoed the new constitution, and resigned. His rival, the more liberal though cautious Rawlins Lowndes [q.v.], was elected to fill out his term, and the constitution was reënacted. But when the state faced invasion in January 1779, Rutledge was elected governor and took the field in a desperate effort to supply Lincoln and Moultrie with men. The organized power of the state was exhausted, however, and Congress was unable, even unwilling, to send adequate forces to protect the outlying states. When the British commander in May slipped behind Lincoln in a dash upon Charlestown, the governor proposed a parley, and after a conference with the Privy Council made an offer of neutrality. Rutledge's purposes in the affair are obscure, and the whole matter is involved in contradictions (see McCrady, post, 1775–1780, pp. 360–81). Immediate danger passed because of a dispute over terms and the approach of Lincoln, but in March 1780 Charlestown was besieged by land and sea in overwhelming force. The Assembly adjourned to meet no more for two years, after hastily granting the governor and "such of his council as he could conveniently consult, a power to do everything necessary for the public good, except the taking away the life of a citizen without a legal trial" (Ramsay, Revolution of South Carolina, post, II, 47–48). A month before the fall of the city, Rutledge slipped out and strove to gather militia for its relief, but in May it was surrendered with practically all of the Continental troops and the militia and civil leaders of the state as well.

The destruction of Gates's army at Camden in August seemed to most people merely confirmation of the conviction that the war in South Carolina was over, but Governor Rutledge retired to the North Carolina border towns and did not for a moment despair. Realizing that without regular troops the British could not be driven out of South Carolina, he laid siege to Washington and Congress by letter and in person. He pinned great hopes upon General Greene, but at the same time encouraged Thomas Sumter, Francis Marion [qq.v.], and other militia officers who had escaped the physical and moral débâcle of Charlestown and Camden, to wage detached and intermittent warfare, in order to wear down the British and to bring into the field men who would not enter the regular service. Accordingly, a new set of military leaders appeared in the state, and were rapidly promoted as they showed enterprise and ability. In August 1781 he was back in South Carolina and by a well planned coup impressed a large quantity of indigo which he sold at Philadelphia for sadly needed army supplies. At the same time he set about a skilful restoration of civil government, working to a large extent through the militia officers. A proclamation suspending the use of currency and forbidding suits for debt was followed on Sept. 27 by an offer of pardon, with a long list of exceptions, to those who had joined the British, on condition that they appear in thirty days for six months' militia service. Finally, on Nov. 20, he issued a call for election of members of a legislature to meet in January.

The Assembly thanked the governor in glowing terms for his service, though a more significant tribute was the prompt enactment of each of his recommendations, including a confiscation proposition which probably prevented even harsher measures. He laid down the office in which the constitution forbade him to succeed himself on Jan. 29, and a few days later took his seat in the ranks of the House as a member for St. Andrew's Parish. He had already been elected to Congress, however, and attended from May 1782 to September 1783. The next year he began his judicial career with his election to the chancery court of the state, and from 1784 to 1790 sat in the House of Representatives. His votes were conservative but not illiberal.

With Charles Cotesworth Pinckney, Charles Pinckney, and Pierce Butler [qq.v.], he was elected to the Federal Convention of 1787, and became chairman of the committee of detail. His speeches and motions reflected the needs of his hard-pressed state and of the planters in the somewhat isolated lower South, or were designed to win concessions necessary for ratification. He fought for wealth as part of the basis of representation, for assumption of state debts, against restrictions on the slave trade, and—unchanged in his attachment to legislative supremacy—for election of the president by Congress, and of Congress by the legislatures. The first electoral vote of South Carolina was cast for Washington and Rutledge, and the latter was appointed senior associate justice of the Supreme Court. He accepted the appointment but delayed taking his seat, and later resigned to accept the office of chief justice of the state, to which he was elected in February 1791. On June 12, 1795, he wrote

Washington indicating his wish to be appointed chief justice of the Supreme Court in place of John Jay who was about to resign. Washington wrote at once offering the place. At the same time the text of Jay's treaty was published with its discriminations against the southern states and France and in favor of Great Britain. On each score it ran counter to Rutledge's deepest feeling, and in a public meeting in St. Michael's Church in Charleston, he outdid the other leaders of the city in the bitterness of his attack. As a result his nomination was rejected by the Senate in December. In the interim Rutledge had held one term of the Supreme Court but the intermittent insanity, of which he had occasionally shown signs since the death of his wife in 1792, definitely ended his public career. He was survived by eight of the ten children borne him by Elizabeth, the daughter of Frederick Grimké, whom he married on May 1, 1763.

The most gifted and devoted leader of the ruling group of eighteenth-century South Carolina, John Rutledge embodied, perhaps, more perfectly than any other man, the ideas of his class.

[For general accounts, see Edward McCrady, *The Hist. of S. C. in the Rev., 1775-1780* (1901), *1780-1783* (1902); Henry Flanders, *The Lives . . . of the Chief Justices*, 1 ser. (1855); manuscript paper by St. J. R. Childs. For his early life, see *S. C. Hist. and Geneal. Mag.*, Jan. 1930; Flanders, pp. 433-42; David Ramsay, *The Hist. of S. C.* (1809), vol. II, pp. 510-11; E. A. Jones, *Am. Members of the Inns of Court* (1924). For his public life, 1761-76, see manuscript journals of the Commons House; *Jour. of Cont. Cong.*, vols. I, III (1904, 1905); E. C. Burnett, *Letters of Members of Cont. Cong.*, vol. I (1921); John Drayton, *Memoirs of the Am. Rev.* (1821), vol. I, pp. 131-41, 166-79; *Colls. of the S. C. Hist. Soc.*, vol. III (1859). For his career as president and governor, see A. S. Salley, Jr., *Jour. Gen. Assembly*, Mar.-Apr. 1776 (1906), Sept.-Oct. 1776 (1909), 1782 (1916); William Moultrie, *Memoirs of the Am. Rev.* (1802), vol. I, pp. 192-218, vol. II, pp. 407-14; David Ramsay, *The Hist. of the Rev. of S. C.* (1785), vol. I, pp. 132-38, vol. II, pp. 45-48; *Hist. of S. C.*, vol. I, pp. 469-70; R. W. Gibbes, *Doc. Hist. of the Am. Rev., 1776-1782* (1857), pp. 129-32, 223, 1781 and 1782 (1853), pp. 32, 130-35, 162, 175-78, 182, 184-85, 191; *The State Records of N. C.*, XIV (1896), pp. 805, 819-22, XV (1898), p. 368; *S. C. Hist. and Geneal. Mag.*, Oct., 1916, Jan., Apr., July 1917, Jan. 1926; McCrady, *The Hist. of S. C. in the Rev., 1780-1783*, p. 511. For the period 1782-1800, see Burnett, *Letters*, VI (1933); manuscript journal of House of Reps. of S. C.; Flanders, pp. 599-600, 621-42; Max Farrand, *The Records of the Federal Convention* (3 vols., 1911); Charles Warren, *The Supreme Court in U. S. Hist.* (rev. ed. 1932), vol. I.] R. L. M.

RYAN, ABRAM JOSEPH (Feb. 5, 1838-Apr. 22, 1886), Catholic priest, poet of the Confederacy, was the son of Matthew and Mary (Coughlin) Ryan, who emigrated from Clonmell, Ireland, to Norfolk, Va., some time between 1828 and 1838. From there they soon moved to Hagerstown, Md., where Abram was born. While claims to his birthplace have been put forth in behalf of Norfolk and also in behalf of

Rathkeale and Limerick, Ireland, and while various dates have been given for his birth, the baptismal record in Hagerstown, the Vincentian records at Germantown, Pa., and a letter of Feb. 21, 1859, in which he notes his age as twenty-one years, all indicate that he was born at Hagerstown on Feb. 5, 1838. Seeking their fortunes in the West, the Ryans settled in St. Louis, Mo., where a daughter, Ellenor (d. 1856), entered the community of the Sisters of St. Joseph of Carondelet as Sister Mary Herman. Abram attended the Christian Brothers' school and studied theology at Niagara University, Niagara Falls, N. Y., under the Vincentian Fathers, whose novitiate in Germantown, Pa., he entered in 1854. Two years later, Nov. 1, 1856, he took his solemn vows. After completing his work in theology, he taught at Niagara University and at the diocesan seminary at Cape Girardeau, Mo., until, on Sept. 1, 1862, he joined the Confederate service as a free-lance chaplain.

An impulsive, mystic person of deep spiritual sense and humanitarian interests, Father Ryan shrived the dying on the battlefield and carried the wounded to safety, through the years of "victory and defeat until the Conquered Banner was furled at Appomattox." At Gratiot prison in New Orleans, when the chaplain fled and no other minister would accept the assignment, it was Ryan who appeared and ministered to the smallpox victims. Of himself he had no thought; and of death he had no fear. Touched by a Celtic melancholy, after a favorite younger brother was killed in his gray uniform, Ryan wrote "In Memory of My Brother" and "In Memoriam." When the war was over, he wrote the beautiful, pathetic verses of "The Conquered Banner" to the measures of a Gregorian hymn (see *Freeman's Journal*, New York, May 19, 1866), and the "Sword of Robert E. Lee," which were long sung in households and schools of the Southland. These were followed by "The Lost Cause," "Gather the Sacred Dust," "March of the Deathless Dead," and similar lyrics. He thus became the recognized poet of the Confederacy, described by Robert Taylor of Tennessee in his lecture on "The Blue and Gray" as "the Tom Moore of Dixie, whose spirit shall keep watch over the Stars and Bars until the morning of the Resurrection."

After the war, Father Ryan lived for a time near Beauvoir, Miss., in terms of friendly intimacy with the family of Jefferson Davis. Irreconcilable and unreconstructed until the North joined in relief work during the cholera plague in the South in 1878, he finally sang forgiveness in the poem "Reunited." For a time, he edited the ephemeral *Pacificator* in Augusta, Ga., where he was stationed as a curate at St. Patrick's Church, and later, *The Banner of the South,* in which he was apparently assisted by John Quinn, an Irish schoolmaster. Ill health compelled him to discontinue the paper five years later, though as a pastor in New Orleans he again edited a Catholic weekly, *The Star.* He was constantly on the move and served in his priestly capacity at Biloxi, Miss., Nashville, Knoxville, and Clarksville, Tenn., Macon, Ga., and finally at Mobile, Ala., where he was pastor of St. Mary's Church (1870–83). He made frequent lecture tours through the United States, and into Canada and Mexico, at times for the relief of Southern orphans and widows or of the victims of recurrent plagues. His audiences were as greatly interested in seeing him as in hearing him; he is described as somewhat stooped, with black hair reaching to his shoulders, pensive, sad, unworldly. His poems, collected and published in 1879 (*Father Ryan's Poems*), passed through several editions, and selections were included in various anthologies. They were followed by a scarcely known but beautifully written book of devotions, *A Crown for Our Queen* (1882). Going to the Franciscan monastery in Louisville for religious quiet, he died there, leaving an incomplete manuscript on the life of Christ. His remains were interred in Mobile, where a monument has been erected by the children of the South through a dime collection which the *Mobile Register* promoted.

[C. W. Hubner, *Representative Southern Poets* (1906); M. L. Rutherford, *The South in Hist. and Lit.* (1906); *Proc. of the Ceremony of Unveiling of the Monument Erected . . . to the Memory of the Rev. Father Abram J. Ryan* (1913); *Records Am. Catholic Hist. Soc.,* Mar. 1928; *Irish Mo.* (Dublin), Dec. 1891; *Commonweal,* Sept. 18, 1929; *America,* Dec. 3, 1927; *Cath. World,* Jan. 1928; *Lit. Digest,* May 31, 1913; *Southern Bivouac,* Aug. 1886; *Courier-Jour.* (Louisville, Ky.), Apr. 23, 1886; *Daily Register* (Mobile, Ala.), Apr. 23, 1886.]
　　　　　　　　　　　　　　　　R. J. P.

RYAN, ARTHUR CLAYTON (Dec. 28, 1879–June 22, 1927), missionary, was born on a farm at Grandview, Louisa County, Iowa, eldest of the eight children of Charles Hammond and Nettie (Lockwood) Ryan. After preparation at the Wilton (Iowa) Academy he entered Grinnell College. While a student there, he married, Dec. 24, 1907, Edith, daughter of Henry and Sarah (Hubbard) Hoover of Muscatine. Later he attended Oberlin College, returning to Grinnell in 1909 to receive the degree of A.B. He graduated from Oberlin Theological Seminary in 1911; during his final year there he was appointed as a missionary by the American Board of Commissioners for Foreign Missions.

On May 11, 1911, at Oberlin, he was ordained to the Congregational ministry, and in September set sail for Turkey. On his arrival he was stationed at Talas, near Cæsaraea. He spent the following year in language study and in travel through Central and Southern Anatolia, familiarizing himself with the country and the general work of the mission. When the missionaries at Constantinople were overwhelmed with relief work among both Moslem and Christian refugees who had fled to the neighborhood of the capital as a result of campaigns and changes in boundaries during the Italo-Turkish and Balkan wars, he was transferred to that station, September 1912. Assigned to relief work, he acted during 1913 and 1914 as agent of the American and British Red Cross societies in their attempt to rehabilitate devastated Thrace. His great energy and ability led to his appointment as secretary of the Constantinople chapter of the American Red Cross, a position which he held until the end of the Dardanelles campaign, while simultaneously engaged in mission activities. In March 1916 he left for the United States by way of Switzerland, and immediately after his arrival threw himself with characteristic vigor into the work of raising funds for the Near East Relief. With headquarters in Chicago, he not only campaigned for this organization, but also aided in the home promotion work of the American Board. In August 1919 he returned to Constantinople and was occupied with the delicate task of reclaiming mission property seized by the Turkish government during the war when, in October 1920, he was appointed secretary of the Levant agency of the American Bible Society. Though his office was in Constantinople, he spent most of the next four years in travel throughout Eastern Europe and Nearer Asia, studying the problems connected with translating, publishing, and distributing the Scriptures.

While on a year's furlough in the United States in 1924, he was called to the Society's headquarters in New York to fill temporarily the vacant office of general secretary. So deeply did his ability, thoroughness, and capacity for work impress the board of managers that they chose him unanimously to hold the position permanently. For two years he was engaged in the most intense activity, for he had administrative charge not only of the central organization but also of publicity and the task of interesting individuals, churches, and other bodies in supporting the Society's work. Traveling extensively through the country, he made frequent and effective addresses both on the activities of the organization and on his own experiences abroad.

In promoting the expanding program of the Society he proved himself both a good administrator and a most capable manager of campaigns for contributions. While apparently in the prime of life and abounding in vigor, he fell ill of pneumonia and died at his home in Scarsdale, N. Y., after only two days of sickness, survived by his wife and two children.

[*Missionary Herald,* Sept. 1927; *Bible Society Record,* vol. LXXII, p. 84; *N. Y. Times,* June 24, 1927; *Congreg. Year Book, 1927* (1928); records of the Am. Board of Commissioners for Foreign Missions, Boston; information furnished by Mrs. A. C. Ryan and Charles H. Ryan.]   W. L. W., Jr.

RYAN, EDWARD GEORGE (Nov. 13, 1810–Oct. 19, 1880), jurist, one of the most colorful and striking figures in the history of the bar of Wisconsin, was born at "New Castle House," near the village of Enfield, in the county of Meath, Ireland, the son of Edward and Abby (Keogh) Ryan. He was educated at Clongowes Wood College, where he spent seven years. In 1830, after having studied law for two years, he emigrated to the United States and completed his preparation for the bar in the city of New York, supporting himself meantime by teaching. He was admitted to the bar on May 13, 1836, and in the same year went to Chicago. In 1842, he was married to Mary, the eldest daughter of Hugh Graham, who died in 1847; and in 1850, to Caroline Willard Pierce of Newburyport, Mass. He removed to Racine, Wis., in 1842, and in December 1848, to Milwaukee. While living in Racine, he was elected a delegate to the first constitutional convention, held in 1846, and took a prominent part in the deliberations of that body. His great abilities quickly won for him a place among the leaders of the bar. He was a law partner of James G. Jenkins and Matthew H. Carpenter [*qq.v.*], and appeared upon one side or the other in nearly every important case down to the time he went upon the bench.

Upon the resignation of Chief Justice Luther S. Dixon [*q.v.*], Governor Taylor, on June 17, 1874, appointed Ryan to succeed him. While his surpassing abilities as advocate and lawyer were well known and everywhere recognized, grave doubts were expressed as to the propriety of the appointment because of his violent and uncertain temper. A contemporary, William F. Vilas [*q.v.*], said: "His passion burned, when lighted, like a flaming volcano, shaking him with fearful violence, and belching the hot lava of his wrath on everything and everybody which stood in opposition" (50 *Wis.,* 31). This trait was the great defect of his character and undoubtedly limited his usefulness as a lawyer and citizen, although it did not mar his work as a judge. He wrote the

opinion for the court in many important cases, two of which deserve special mention—*Attorney General* vs. *The Railroads* (35 *Wis.,* 425) and *State ex rel. Drake* vs. *Doyle* (40 *Wis.,* 175). The first involved the power of the state legislature to regulate the rates to be charged by railway companies. The question was then comparatively new and the issues at stake were very important. The court's opinion lays down principles of law which have been followed from that time forward. The second case mentioned involved the right of a state to prescribe the conditions upon which foreign corporations might transact business in the state. This opinion is also a landmark in constitutional law. Though he was a brilliant advocate and profound lawyer and had won the highest laurels in the forum, his work as a justice of the supreme court placed him in the first rank of jurists and furnishes his principal claim to fame.

Judge Ryan was a profound scholar and classicist and had an intimate knowledge of contemporary literature. As a writer his style was clear and lucid, and possessed unusual force; his logic was faultless. His *Address Delivered Before the Law Class of the University of Wisconsin* (1873) is a legal and literary classic, and is probably more often referred to and quoted than any other similar production. He was of a deeply religious nature. Born and reared in the Roman Catholic faith, he subsequently became a member of the Episcopal Church. Among his papers was found a prayer, apparently much used by him, which in simple beauty and pathos compares favorably with many to be found in books of devotion. He moved to Madison while a member of the supreme court, and died in that city, survived by three sons.

["Death of Mr. Chief Justice Ryan," 50 *Wis.,* 23; J. W. Hinton, *Memorial Address on Edward G. Ryan, Late Chief Justice of Wis.* (1880), pamphlet in Wis. State Lib.; J. R. Berryman, *Hist. of the Bench and Bar of Wis.* (1898); P. M. Reed, *The Bench and Bar of Wis.* (1882); J. B. Winslow, "Edward George Ryan," in W. D. Lewis, *Great Am. Lawyers* (1909), vol VI; G. E. Roe, *Selected Opinions of Luther S. Dixon and Edward G. Ryan* (1907); *Milwaukee Daily Sentinel,* Oct. 20, 1880.]   M. B. R.

RYAN, JOHN DENNIS (Oct. 10, 1864–Feb. 11, 1933), capitalist, copper miner, was born in Hancock, Mich., the son of John C. and Joanna Ryan. His father was a mining expert and prospector, a pioneer in the Lake Superior copper district, but the son for a number of years showed little interest in mining. Nor did he accept the college education which his parents offered him. At seventeen he went to work in a general store owned by an uncle in one of the Michigan copper towns, and for the next eight years was a clerk,

At twenty-five he went to Colorado, and obtained work as a traveling salesman of lubricating oils. A part of his territory was in Montana, and there he met and sold oils to Marcus Daly [*q.v.*], the copper magnate, who more than once offered him a position. But Ryan, so far satisfied with his job, refused. Not until he married an old playmate, Nettie Gardner of Hancock, Mich., in 1896, did ambition begin to stir within him. He was then thirty-two and earning $200 a month. He now began buying stock in Daly's bank and trust company in Montana, and in the course of several years became an important factor in its affairs.

Around the turn of the century, the Montana copper busines was in a turmoil. The Amalgamated Copper Company had been organized by H. H. Rogers and the Rockefellers, and had taken over the Daly-Haggin-Tevis holdings in the Anaconda properties, being opposed by William A. Clark and later by Frederick Augustus Heinze [*q.v.*]. The rival factions waged political as well as litigious and physical warfare. Rogers asked Ryan to take charge of affairs in Montana for the Amalgamated. Ryan made so many friends among the voters that Heinze's faction sustained a serious political defeat, and Heinze was forced to sell out to the Amalgamated in 1906. When Rogers died in 1909, Ryan was elected his successor as president of Amalgamated. He dissolved the corporation, turning it back again into the Anaconda Copper Mining Company. The great expansion in the use of copper, especially for electrical purposes, was now in full swing, and under Ryan's direction Anaconda became one of the greatest industrial enterprises in existence. At his death it was the world's largest producer of copper and fabricator of copper products, and its assets were said to be more than $700,000,000. The company, with its great buying power, was able to take over, often at low prices, and to put on a paying basis, valuable properities in Mexico and South America, including the Chile Copper Company, which owned one of the largest known bodies of copper ore. In 1922 the American Brass Company, America's largest consumer of copper ore, was also absorbed. Ryan organized the Montana Power Company, and sold it several years later to a subsidiary of the Electric Bond and Share Company for more than $82,000,000. While at the head of his company he brought about the first important use on the North American continent of hydro-electric power for railroads—namely, in the electrification of the Chicago, Milwaukee & St. Paul Railway through the Rocky Mountains. His power company also supplied

most of the current for domestic use in Montana and for nearly all the mines of the state. In 1926 he was accused by the Interstate Commerce Commission of making contracts with the Chicago, Milwaukee & St. Paul (of which he was a director) so advantageous to his copper company that they aided in bringing about the insolvency of the road.

The World War had greatly increased the use of copper, and the Anaconda's profits had mounted enormously. Ryan resigned its presidency in 1917, however, in order to serve as a member of the war council of the American Red Cross. Shortly afterward, he became director of the Bureau of Aircraft Production (May 1918), assistant secretary of war (August 1918), and chairman of the Aircraft Board, his particular task being the stimulation of lagging aircraft production. Under his direction, $1,000,000,000 was spent in aviation. Following charges that not one fighting plane of American manufacture reached the front, Ryan, before a congressional investigating committee after the armistice, vigorously defended his administration. On Nov. 21, 1918, he had resigned his government post. He was then elected chairman of the board of directors of the Anaconda Company, which place he held until his death. He was also president of the United Metals Selling Company, and chairman of the boards of the Andes Copper Mining Company, the Chile Copper Company, and the Chile Exploration Company. He was a director in several banks and corporations. For his church activities and benefactions, Pope Pius XI made him a Knight of St. Gregory the Great in 1923. He died in New York City. His only surviving child was a son, John Carlos Ryan.

[*Literary Digest,* Mar. 21, 1914, p. 605; May 23, 1914, pp. 1247–48; "Investigation of Chicago, Milwaukee & St. Paul Railway Co.," 131 *Interstate Commerce Commission Reports,* 615–72; *War Expenditures. Hearings before Sub-Committee No. 1 (Aviation) of the Select Committee on Expenditures in the War Department. House of Representatives, Sixty-sixth Congress* . . . Serial 2 (3 vols., 1919–20); *Who's Who in America,* 1932–33; obituaries in *N. Y. World-Telegram, N. Y. Evening Post,* Feb. 11, 1933; *N. Y. Times, N. Y. Herald-Tribune,* Feb. 12, 1933.]

A. F. H.

RYAN, PATRICK JOHN (Feb. 20, 1831–Feb. 11, 1911), Catholic prelate, son of Jeremiah and Mary (Toohey) Ryan, was born in Thurles, Ireland, where he attended the Christian Brothers' school before going to Naughton's School in Rathmines, Dublin. As a schoolboy, he presented an address to Daniel O'Connell, a prisoner in Richmond Bridewell, and won the latter's approval as a youthful orator of promise. In 1852 he was graduated as a deacon from St. Patrick's College, Carlow, and emigrated to St. Louis,

Mo., where he completed his theological training and was ordained a priest, Sept. 8, 1853. As a curate at the cathedral, rector of the church of St. John the Evangelist, builder of the Church of the Annunciation, spiritual adviser of Confederate prisoners, of whom he was said to have converted several hundred, and as a preacher of exceptional power, Father Ryan won popular favor and the good will of Bishop Peter R. Kenrick [*q.v.*]. In 1866 he accompanied the latter as theologian to the Second Plenary Council of Baltimore, where he was selected as one of the official preachers. In 1868 he was invited by Pius IX to preach the English Lenten sermons. During Kenrick's absence at the Vatican Council, Ryan and Henry Muehlsiepen as vicar generals administered the diocese. On the nomination of the American bishops at the Council, he was named coadjutor bishop of St. Louis with the titular see of Tricomia (1870), but was not consecrated by Kenrick until Apr. 14, 1872.

As a coadjutor, he was exceedingly active, especially since Archbishop Kenrick, said to be somewhat annoyed by the promulgation of papal infallibility, rarely officiated in public for several years. Preaching and lecturing on all occasions, Ryan, described as the Chrysostom of the West, became recognized as one of the greatest preachers in the Church and one of the leading orators in the country. He was a tall, well-built, powerful figure with a leonine head crowned with auburn hair. He had a resonant but mellow voice, a sense of humor, striking ability as a raconteur, and was sane and tolerant in his utterances. In 1871 he addressed the legislature of Missouri on "Arts and Sciences"; in 1877 he gave a series of lectures in St. Louis, published in 1878 under the title *What Catholics do not Believe,* which had wide circulation; he was invited by Cardinal McCloskey to preach at the dedication of St. Patrick's Cathedral in New York (1879). Invited to Rome in 1883 in preparation for the Third Plenary Council of Baltimore, he returned in 1884 as titular archbishop of Salamis. At the Council, he was an active figure and preached the opening sermon. On June 8, 1884, he was transferred to the metropolitan see of Philadelphia, the second largest in the United States (see *St. Louis Globe-Democrat,* Aug. 18, 1884).

Again, it was as an orator and preacher that he gained renown—at the funerals of Archbishops Corrigan, Hennessy, and Kenrick, at the foundation of the Irish Church in Rome, at the centennial celebration of the Church in Baltimore, at the Republican National Convention of 1900, at the McKinley memorial service in Philadelphia,

and at numerous other ecclesiastical and civil functions. In 1896 he arbitrated a riotous street-car strike. On behalf of President Cleveland, he presented a copy of the Constitution of the United States to Pope Leo XIII; President Theodore Roosevelt appointed him to the Board of Indian Commissioners because of his interest in the Indians and his connection with various Catholic Indian missionary enterprises. As the spiritual leader of a third of the population of Philadelphia, he was potent in public affairs and commanded the respect of all classes in the community. He did not hesitate, however, to speak boldly when Catholic interests were at stake. Because of his reputation in Rome, priests of his careful training were elevated to bishoprics. He was uncompromising in urging pastors to build parochial schools; he cooperated in the foundation of the Roman Catholic High School endowed by Thomas Cahill, of the Central Catholic High School for Girls, and of an Industrial Home at Eddington, donated by the Drexels (1886). The establishment of the Protectory for Homeless Boys near Morristown (1896) he regarded as his crowning work. With the assistance of various communities of nuns, he fostered a number of other charitable institutions. During his régime, churches increased from 127 to 297, including two negro churches and about eighty racial churches for Poles, Slovaks, Lithuanians, Greeks, and Italians. He was simple and unusually democratic in his manner of living; approachable, though somewhat condescending in manner; emotional, but not contentious. A cultured man rather than a learned scholar, he was deeply interested in the local Catholic colleges, acted as editor-in-chief of the *American Catholic Quarterly Review* from 1890 to his death, published several lectures, and was honored with degrees by a number of institutions.

[R. F. Crowley, *The Episcopal Silver Jubilee of the Most Rev. P. J. Ryan* (1897); *Am. Catholic Who's Who,* 1911; *Who's Who in America,* 1910–11; J. L. J. Kirlin, *Life of the Mt. Rev. P. J. Ryan* (1903); *Catholicity in Phila.* (1909); *Cath. Encyc.,* XIII, 282; John Rothensteiner, *Hist. of the Archdiocese of St. Louis* (1928); F. J. Zwierlein, *The Life and Letters of Bishop McQuaid* (1925–27); files of Ryan's diocesan *Cath. Standard and Times,* esp. Feb. 1911; *Records of the Am. Catholic Hist. Soc.* from 1884, esp. Mar. 1911; *N. Y. Freeman's Jour.,* Aug. 20, 1887; *Am. Cath. Quart. Rev.,* Jan. 1896, Oct. 1903, Apr. 1911; *Rev. of Reviews,* Oct. 1900; *Harper's Weekly,* Sept. 8, 1906; *Outlook,* Feb. 25, 1911; *Catholic World,* Mar., Apr., 1911; *America,* Feb. 18, 1911; *Phila. Inquirer* and *Public Ledger* (Phila.), Feb. 11–18, 1911; information from associates.]   R. j. P.

RYAN, STEPHEN VINCENT (Jan. 1, 1825–Apr. 10, 1896), Catholice prelate, son of Martin and Catherine (McCarthy) Ryan, recent immigrants from County Clare, Ireland, was born near Almonte, Lanark County, Ont., where some selected Irish peasants had been settled as an experiment in British colonization. Discouraged over agriculture in the cold North, the family in 1828 found its way to Pottsville, Pa., where Stephen received his early training and experienced a vocation for the priesthood. He entered St. Charles Borromeo Seminary in Philadelphia, but on joining the Congregation of the Mission (Lazarists, Vincentians) in 1844 he was enrolled at St. Mary's Seminary at the Barrens, Mo., where he completed his theological studies and on June 24, 1849, was ordained a priest by Archbishop Peter R. Kenrick [q.v.] of St. Louis. An instructor at St. Mary's Seminary from 1849 to 1851, and later a professor and rector of the Lazarist College of St. Vincent at Cape Girardeau, Mo., in 1857 at a general synod in Paris he was elected visitor general of his order in America. In addition to managing its churches and seminaries for years, he established in 1867 a new motherhouse and novitiate of the order at Germantown, Pa., and St. John's College in Brooklyn. On the death of his fellow Vincentian, Bishop John Timon [q.v.] of Buffalo, he was elevated, against his will, to that see by Pope Pius IX and consecrated on Nov. 8, 1868. (See *New York Freeman's Journal,* Nov. 21, 1868.) As bishop, he found himself in continual disagreement with Bishop Bernard McQuaid [q.v.] of Rochester. There were not only diocesan boundary disputes (which were not settled by Rome to the satisfaction of McQuaid until Ryan's death) but marked differences over matters of policy. As a liberal who was in harmony with Archbishop John Ireland [q.v.], he disagreed with the rigorous McQuaid on the school question, on the affair of Edward McGlynn [q.v.], on the candidacy of Sylvester Malone [q.v.] for a regency of the University of New York, and on episcopal "autocracy" in handling priests out of joint with the administration. Indeed, he supported Fathers Louis A. Lambert [q.v.] and James M. Early against McQuaid, who winced under the criticism of the independent *Catholic Union and Times,* a diocesan paper founded by Ryan in 1872 as the *Catholic Union* of Buffalo and merged in 1881 with the *Catholic Times* of Rochester as the *Catholic Union and Times.* He was sufficiently interested in Catholic education to publish a sound pastoral on the eve of his *ad limina* visit to Rome (*New York Freeman's Journal,* Sept. 14, 1878), to improve vastly Our Lady of Angels Seminary at Niagara, to promote secondary schools, and to build a number of parochial schools. In other ways, too, he developed his diocese and saw its population and its priesthood

double during his régime. A controversialist of considerable ability, he published *Claims of a Protestant Episcopal Bishop to Apostolic Succession and Valid Orders Disproved* (1880) as a result of a controversy with Bishop A. C. Coxe [q.v.] of Western New York, and a substantial article on *Early Lazarist Missions and Missionaries* (1887).

[Patrick Cronin, *Memorial of the Life and Labors of Rt. Rev. Stephen Vincent Ryan* (1896); files of *Cath. Union and Times,* esp. Apr. 1896; ann. official Cath. directories; J. N. Larned, *A Hist. of Buffalo* (1911); F. J. Zwierlein, *The Life and Letters of Bishop McQuaid* (3 vols., 1925–27); *Buffalo Courier,* Apr. 10, 1896.]   R. J. P.

RYAN, THOMAS FORTUNE (Oct. 17, 1851–Nov. 23, 1928), financier and promoter, was born on a small farm in Lovingston, Nelson County, Va., of southern Irish stock. According to an obituary notice (Baltimore *Sun,* Nov. 24, 1928), his father was George Ryan and his mother's maiden name was Fortune. His early life followed the accepted pattern of the American success story. He was left orphaned and penniless at fourteen, and at seventeen made his way to Baltimore. The lanky, angular country boy walked the streets for days until he was finally hired as an errand boy in the dry-goods commission house of John S. Barry. In 1872, at the age of twenty-one, Ryan went to New York, where he started as a messenger, or "pad-shover," in a Wall Street brokerage firm. Soon, largely with the financial aid of Barry, whose daughter, Ida M., he married on Nov. 25, 1873, he became a partner in a firm of his own, Lee, Ryan and Warren; and in 1874 he purchased a seat on the Stock Exchange. For a decade he carried on his brokerage work with skill and silence. He became a Tammany man, a contributor to Tammany funds, and a member of the general committee of the Hall. He was at thirty-three a slender, long-legged, long-armed young man, over six feet in height, fashionably dressed, with a knack for making the right contacts.

His opportunity for carving out a real fortune came with the struggle for street-railway franchises in New York City. In 1883 he organized the New York Cable Railroad, a paper organization which entered a three-cornered fight with Jacob Sharp and William C. Whitney [q.v.] for the control of the Broadway surface franchise from Union Square to the Battery. Sharp won, by distributing a half million in cash to the "boodle aldermen." Ryan and Whitney stood ready to parcel out three quarters of a million in bribes, but only half was in cash and the rest in stock Ryan's next step was to persuade Whitney and Peter A. B. Widener [q.v.], in December

1884, to pool their resources and continue the fight for the franchise. Ryan was in direct charge of operations, pushing legal suits against Sharp, and inaugurating a state legislative investigation. Sharp, seeing that all was lost, sold his stock to the Ryan syndicate, but the matter had gone too far to be hushed up. The legislature annulled the franchise; Sharp was sentenced to four years' imprisonment for bribery but died, uttering incoherent accusations, before appeal could be taken. The syndicate, after a two-year court fight waged through Elihu Root, succeeded in having the annulment declared unconstitutional, and bid in the franchise and the property of Sharp's railroad for $25,000. Using this as their basis they extended their properties until by 1900 the Metropolitan Street Railway Company (incorporated in 1893) controlled practically every line in the city. The methods used in this process have served as a model in public-utility promotion. The Metropolitan Traction Company, which was organized (1886), in Ryan's own words, as a "great tin box" to hold the securities of the various companies of the syndicate, is considered to have been the first holding company in the United States. Franchises were acquired through political influence; small lines were bought up, their stock was watered, and then exchanged at absurdly inflated valuations for the stock of the Metropolitan; other roads were leased at excessive rentals, the members of the syndicate securing large sums for negotiating the leases and meanwhile buying into the stock of the leased road, whose dividends were guaranteed through the fixed rentals; when new lines had to be constructed or old lines overhauled the work was done at fantastic costs by companies under the control of the syndicate members; the Metropolitan securities were boosted in value by artificially maintained dividends, and when in 1899 the stock had been pushed to $269 the insiders unloaded on an enthusiastic public. In 1902, when disaster to the roads was impending, Ryan persuaded Jacob H. Schiff, of Kuhn, Loeb & Company, to join him in a reorganization, the Metropolitan Securities Company.

In 1905 Ryan found himself threatened by the competition of the new subway system, which August Belmont had been shrewd enough to finance. Ryan first sought to persuade and then determined to frighten Belmont into merging his enormously profitable Interborough Rapid Transit Company with the Metropolitan. When Belmont attempted to extend his subway franchises, Ryan bid for the franchise himself, offering to give transfers that would be good on his surface lines as well, thereby achieving a "unified" city transportation system. He took care to accelerate public enthusiasm for his proposal by the efforts of Lemuel E. Quigg [q.v.], one of the most skilful, and one of the earliest, publicity agents. Belmont finally surrendered in 1905, and the two systems were consolidated and further overcapitalized in a new $200,000,000 corporation. Ryan invested his financial methods with an air of respectability by calling in, as the president of the new Interborough-Metropolitan Company, Theodore P. Shonts, a member of Roosevelt's Panama Canal Commission. In 1906 Ryan retired from his traction interests, leaving behind him doom and collapse. The Metropolitan went into receivership in 1907. In 1908 Frederick W. Whitridge, the receiver for the Third Avenue System, estimated that of a thirty-five million dollar Ryan bond issue fifteen million could not be accounted for at all, and the other twenty million had been spent recklessly on padded construction contracts and in the distribution of political plums. Soon the remaining Ryan traction companies went into bankruptcy. Robert M. LaFollette stated on the floor of the Senate, Mar. 19, 1908, that "the Metropolitan Interborough Traction Company cleaned up, at the lowest estimate, $100,000,000 by methods which should have committed many of the participants to the penitentiary" (*Congressional Record,* 60 Cong., 1 Sess., p. 3568). Ryan was always the financial executive, and even before Whitney died in 1904 he had become the controlling person in the syndicate, which became known as the "Ryan crowd." Whitney called him "the most adroit, suave and noiseless man" that American finance had known, and had prophesied in 1901 that if he lived Ryan would become one of the wealthiest men in the country. In 1905, before he withdrew from the Metropolitan, his fortune was at a low estimate in excess of $50,000,000, and his power extended over resources in banking, public utilities, and industrial enterprises totalling over a billion dollars.

Early in the nineties he and Whitney organized the American Tobacco Company with a capitalization of twenty-five million dollars. In 1898 it was recapitalized at over seventy million; in 1904, after several mergers, it was again recapitalized at a total, including bonds, of over $250,000,000. Through a series of mergers it secured virtually complete monopolistic control of the industry, and on May 29, 1911, it was ordered dissolved by the federal government (*United States* vs. *American Tobacco Company,* 221 *United States Reports,* 106). Since the Ryan-Whitney syndicate was never completely trusted by the Wall Street banking houses it was essential, at a relatively early date, to secure control of some banks. In 1898 Ryan and Whitney gained control of the State Trust Company, which was closely tied up with the American Surety Company. Its board of directors was changed and it was used as a source of loans as well as a bank of deposit for the Metropolitan. In 1900 one of the stockholders petitioned for an investigation, charging gross violations of the banking laws. One investigation was ended as soon as it was begun; another, by the state superintendent of banks, Frederick S. Kilburn, resulted in a report, on which no action was taken. The New York *World,* however, obtained and published a copy of the Kilburn report (Mar. 12, 1900). It implicated Ryan, Root, and others in the syndicate in attempts to use the funds of the trust and surety companies to cover up and facilitate the operations of the Metropolitan. Particular instances of loans, such as that for $100,000 to the lobbyist Louis F. Payn, seemed to indicate that they were intended as concealed payments. There was a great scandal, and a bill was finally pushed through the state legislature amalgamating the State Trust Company with the Morton Trust Company, another Ryan venture; when the Morton Trust was in 1910 merged with the Guaranty Trust Company, Ryan took a prominent part in the latter. In 1903 Ryan organized the National Bank of Commerce. In the same year he gained control of the Seaboard Air Line Railroad, after ruthlessly breaking John Skelton Williams [q.v.], who had originally organized it.

In 1904 Ryan secured control of the Washington Life Insurance Company. In 1905 he astounded the financial world by buying James Hazen Hyde's controlling block of shares in the Equitable Life Assurance Society. Ryan acquired stock that was normally worth $7,500,-000 for $2,500,000, despite the fact that Harriman was willing to pay twice that sum. Harriman never forgave Ryan, and the incident was the beginning of a feud between them. Harriman "did not think that Ryan was a suitable man to have control of the Equitable, with its $400,000,-000 of assets" (George Kennan, *E. H. Harriman,* 1922, vol. I, 413). Ryan's own statement of his motives in buying the stock ran in terms of a desire to save it from a receivership (*North American Review,* August 1913, pp. 163–64). The Armstrong legislative committee, investigating the insurance business in 1905, elicited from John Tatlock, Ryan's president of the Washington Life Insurance Company, the information that during 1905 Ryan invested several millions of its assets in the stock of his other properties, and had placed its deposits in his own banks. In

the outcry that was raised when he bought the Hyde stock Ryan moved adroitly to place the voting power of the stock for five years in the hands of three trustees, including former President Cleveland. He placed Paul Morton [q.v.], formerly of Theodore Roosevelt's cabinet, in the chairmanship of the company.

Perhaps the most glamorous of Ryan's ventures were his enterprises in the Congo. King Leopold of Belgium invited him to head a syndicate to reorganize financially and develop industrially his African properties. After a series of conferences between the two the Société Internationale Forestière et Minière du Congo ("Forminière") was organized, Ryan receiving for the promotion one-quarter of the stock. The original objective was rubber, but nothing much came of that, due to cheaper production costs in other fields. But diamond, gold, and copper mines were developed. Ryan said in an interview in June 1910, "I sleep like a baby. I don't remember ever having been in better health or spirits. . . . I am interested not only in the industrial development of the Congo but also in its social and moral conditions" (*Collier's,* Dec. 30, 1911, p. 22). In America his influence was considered in certain quarters far from moral. William Jennings Bryan and the silver Democrats attributed the nomination of Judge Alton B. Parker for the presidency in 1904 largely to Ryan's influence. In the 1912 convention of the Democratic party, to which Ryan was a delegate from Virginia, Bryan attacked Ryan and Belmont for coming "with their paid attorneys" to "seek secret counsel with the managers of this party," and accused them of attempting to control the nominations (*Proceedings,* p. 131). He introduced and forced through a resolution by which the convention declared itself "opposed to the nomination of any candidate for president who is the representative of or under obligation to" Ryan, Belmont, or Morgan (*Ibid.,* p. 129).

After 1910 Ryan increasingly retired from the active management of his far-flung enterprises. His home was at 858 Fifth Avenue in New York City; a third of the block had been turned into a private garden containing expensive statuary. His collection of Limoges enamels was one of the finest in the world, and he had a magnificent collection of tapestries, bronzes, and other art objects. His first wife died on Oct. 17, 1917; she had borne him five sons, of whom three survived him. On Oct. 29, 1917, he was married to Mary Townsend (Nicoll) Lord Cuyler, a widow and the sister of De Lancey Nicoll [q.v.]. Ryan's benefactions and those of his first wife to the Catholic church were very extensive, amounting in all to about twenty million dollars. His estate, when he died, was estimated to be over two hundred million dollars.

[For Ryan's street railway activities and banking ventures, see B. J. Hendrick, "Great American Fortunes and Their Making. Street-Railway Financiers," in *McClure's Mag.,* Nov., Dec. 1907, Jan. 1908; B. J. Hendrick, *The Age of Big Business* (1919), ch. V; C. E. Russell, "Where Did You Get it, Gentlemen?" in *Everybody's Mag.,* Aug.–Dec. 1907, Jan., Mar. 1908; A. H. Lewis, in *Cosmopolitan,* July 1908, pp. 141–52; *State of N. Y. Public Service Commission, First District. Investigation of Interborough Metropolitan Co.* (5 vols., 1908); H. J. Carman, *The Street Surface Railway Franchises of N. Y. City* (1919); W. N. Amory, *The Truth about Metropolitan* (2 ed., 1906); Garrett Garet, "How Failure Pays," in *Collier's,* Dec. 30, 1911. For the American Tobacco Co., see H. R. Seager and C. A. Gulick, *Trust and Corporation Problems* (1929); *Report of the Commissioner of Corporations on the Tobacco Industry,* vol. I (1909), vol. II (1911). For Ryan's activities in insurance, see *State of N. Y. Assembly Document No. 41. Report of the Joint Committee . . . Appointed to Investigate the Affairs of Life Insurance Companies* (1906); and *Testimony Taken before the Joint Committee . . .* (1905), vols. V, VI; as well as Ryan, "Why I Bought the Equitable," *North American Review,* Aug. 1913. For the Congo, see I. F. Marcosson, *An African Adventure* (1921), pp. 225–35; for the episode in the Democratic National Convention of 1912, see *Official Report of the Proceedings* (1912), pp. 129–138. For personal details, see *Who's Who in America,* 1928–29; obituaries in *N. Y. Times,* and *Sun* (Baltimore), Nov. 24, 1928.]
               M. L.

RYAN, WALTER D'ARCY (Apr. 17, 1870–Mar. 14, 1934), illuminating engineer, was born at Kentville, Nova Scotia, the son of James William and Josephine (Rasuse) Ryan. He was educated at Kentville Academy, Professor Currey's School and St. Mary's College at Halifax, Memramcook College at Memramcook, N. B., and the Royal School of Cavalry at Quebec. In 1892 he became a student engineer at Lynn, Mass., in the shops of the Thomson-Houston Electric Company, which that year was merged with other organizations into the General Electric Company. After varied and intensive experience he became a commercial engineer and investigated the use of power for operating metal-cutting and wood-working machinery.

In the late nineties he determined to specialize in electric illumination, and upon his representations the General Electric Company, on Jan. 1, 1899, established at Lynn an illuminating engineering laboratory. Five years later Ryan was formally appointed illuminating engineer, the first person in the electrical profession to be so designated. Under his direction electric illumination was developed into both a science and an art. The scientific side embraced a photometric and spectro-photometric studies of lighting units and efficiencies and methods of light distribution. Globes and reflectors were developed by scientific procedure and various instruments were introduced for making light measurements. Both arc and incandescent searchlights benefited from these laboratory studies. The artistic aspect of electric illumination, greatly facilitated by the appearance, about 1913, of high capacity incandescent lamps, found expression in spectacular applications of light, with contrasting shadow effects, in combination with color. The first disclosure to the public of these artistic possibilities occurred in 1915, during the Panama-Pacific International Exposition at San Francisco. There Ryan departed from prevailing conventional practices by illuminating the façades of the buildings from concealed sources—from which procedure arose the art of floodlighting of public buildings, business structures, monuments and statuary. He had previously supervised the lighting of the expositions at Buffalo in 1901 and St. Louis in 1904, and subsequently carried out many other spectacular lighting displays, notably the lighting of the Brazilian Centennial Exposition in 1922 at Rio de Janeiro and of "A Century of Progress" in 1933 at Chicago.

From 1909 until his death in 1934, Ryan's headquarters and those of the Illuminating Engineering Laboratory were at the main works of the General Electric Company in Schenectady. Between 1920 and 1930 he introduced the revolutionizing conception of high-intensity street lighting. He was constantly engaged in educational work in his chosen field, and from 1917 until his death was lecturer in illuminating engineering at Rensselaer Polytechnic Institute. Among the more significant of his published papers were *Light and Illuminating Engineering* (General Electric Company, 1903); "Luminous and Flame Arcs versus Open and Enclosed Carbon Arcs for Street Illumination" (*Proceedings of the National Electric Light Association,* vol. I, 1910); "Illumination of the Panama-Pacific Exposition" (*Scientific American Supplement,* June 12, 1915); "Building Exterior, Exposition and Pageant Lighting" (*Illuminating Engineering Practice,* University of Pennsylvania lectures, 1917); "Illumination of the Panama-Pacific International Exposition" (*Proceedings of the American Institute of Electrical Engineers,* vol. XXXVI, 1917); "Lighting the Exposition" (*Architectural Forum,* July 1933). He was actuated in his work by the precision of the engineer combined with the imagination of the artist. Both were sustained by an intense energy, a contagious enthusiasm, and great affability of disposition. These qualities made him a leader of men in all the technical associations of his profession, particularly in the Illuminating Engineering Society, of which, in 1906, he was one of the founders. On June 13, 1932 he was appointed a consulting engineer of the General Electric Company. He died at his home in Schenectady, survived by his wife, Katharine (Haskins), a son, and three daughters.

[French Strother in *World's Work,* July 1915; A. A. Willoughby, in *American City,* Mar. 1915; *Scientific American,* Feb. 20, 1915; F. M. Todd, *The Story of the Exposition* (1921), II, 343; obituary in *N. Y. Times,* Mar. 15, 1934; records of the General Electric Company, Schenectady, N. Y.; personal acquaintance.]

J. W. H.

RYBNER, MARTIN CORNELIUS (Oct. 26, 1853–Jan. 21, 1929), composer, pianist, teacher, the son of Johan William Rybner and Charlotte (Gosch), was born in Copenhagen, Denmark. He was educated at the University of Copenhagen and studied music at the Royal Conservatory, where his teachers included Niels Wilhelm Gade and J. P. Hartmann in composition, Tofte and Ferdinand David in violin, Neupert, Reinecke, Von Bülow, Rubinstein, and Liszt in piano. After his débuts in Copenhagen and in Leipzig as a concert violinist and a concert pianist, he made successful tours in Scandinavia, Germany, France, England, and Italy, earning merited recognition. He was awarded several decorations and was appointed court pianist to the King of Denmark and the Grand Duke of Hesse. He established himself in Baden-Baden, as the director of its choral society, in 1875. In 1886 he was appointed director of the College of Music and the Philharmonic Society of Karlsruhe, in Baden, and, in addition to these responsibilities, in 1902 became Felix Mottl's assistant conductor at the Karlsruhe Opera, where in 1903 he conducted the first performances in Germany of Massenet's oratorio *Marie Madeleine* and Klose's "Grand Mass." The following year, when Edward MacDowell [*q.v.*] resigned the professorship of music at Columbia University, Rybner was called as his successor and held the position, in which he won the friendship and esteem of his pupils, until 1919, when he resigned it to devote his time to composition and recital work. After 1924 he also taught composition at the New York College of Music.

As a composer his output comprised a number of meritorious works, including a three-act ballet, "Prince Ador" (Karlsruhe, 1903), a symphonic poem, *Friede, Kampf und Sieg,* a *Fest-Ouverture* in C major, two marches for orchestra, a piano trio, a violin concerto in G minor, and a festival cantata for solo, chorus, and orchestra. In addition he wrote mixed choruses, songs and duets, violin and 'cello pieces, and some excellent Wagner concert-transcriptions for piano, including "Siegmund's Love Song," "Wotan's Farewell and Fire Music," "Siegfried's

Funeral March," and the "*Liebestod*" from *Tristan und Isolde.* He was also the author of a pedagogic work, *Phases of Piano Study,* and an appreciation, "Niels Wilhelm Gade: On the Centenary of His Birth" (*Musical Quarterly,* January 1917). His wife was Claudine Pezel de Corval; their daughter, Dagmar de Corval Rybner, became an accomplished pianist, after 1912 being active in New York as a solo artist and in duet with her father until his death.

[*Who's Who in America,* 1928–29; *Musical America,* Feb. 2, 1929; *Musical Courier,* Jan. 24, 1929; *Sun* (N. Y.), Jan. 22, 1929.]

F. H. M.

RYDBERG, PER AXEL (July 6, 1860–July 25, 1931), botanist, was born in Odh, Vestergötland, Sweden, the son of Adolf Fredrik and Thekla Elfrida (Otterstrom) Rydberg. Graduating from the royal gymnasium at Skara in 1881, he left Sweden for the United States the following year. At this time he planned to become a mining engineer, but a serious accident suffered in an iron mine in Michigan soon put an end to this ambition, and he turned to teaching as a profession. For six years, 1884–90, he taught mathematics at Luther Academy, Wahoo, Nebr., meanwhile entering the state university, where he graduated in 1891 and where he renewed his boyhood interest in botany. For the next four years he was actively engaged in the work of the botanical survey of Nebraska and spent the summers in botanical exploration in Nebraska and South Dakota for the United States Department of Agriculture, teaching at Luther Academy in the winter. His first two important botanical works, the *Rosales* (part of the projected "Flora of Nebraska") and the *Flora of the Sand Hills of Nebraska,* appeared in 1895. In the same year he received his master's degree from the University of Nebraska, spent the summer in Montana under the auspices of the United States Department of Agriculture, and then went to New York, where he registered as a graduate student at Columbia University. While at Columbia he was a professor at Upsala Institute in Brooklyn (which later became Upsala College, first at Kenilworth, then at East Orange, N. J.) and continued his summer fieldwork in Montana. In 1898 he received from Columbia University the degree of Ph.D., his dissertation being *A Monograph of the North American Potentilleae,* a large quarto volume. In 1899 he became a member of the scientific staff of the newly organized New York Botanical Garden, and it was to the work of this institution that he devoted the remaining thirty-two years of his life, studying plants in the herbarium and publishing the results of his studies. His field trips, though few, extended from New York to North Carolina and California; he revisited Sweden only once, in 1901. A member of various scientific societies, he was not particularly active in any of them except the Torrey Botanical Club of New York City; it was in publications of the Torrey Club that nearly two-thirds of his papers first appeared, the remainder being mostly in publications of the New York Botanical Garden. The total number of his contributions to botanical science exceeds one hundred and sixty. His most important books are *Catalogue of the Flora of Montana and the Yellowstone National Park* (1900), *Flora of Colorado* (1906), *Flora of the Rocky Mountains* (1917; second edition, 1922), and the posthumously published *Flora of the Prairies and Plains* (1932). In the course of his studies on the flowering plants of North America, he described as new at least a hundred genera and seventeen hundred species. How many of these will stand the test of time, must long remain uncertain. His work was done in such a painstaking and conscientious manner, however, that later generations of botanists may reasonably be expected to appreciate it even more than his contemporaries. In his lifetime two genera (Rydbergia and Rydbergiella) and various species were dedicated to him.

On Nov. 11, 1903, he married the daughter of one of his cousins, Alfrida Amanda Rydberg, who with their son and two of their three daughters survived him. His health failed gradually for several months before his death, which occurred in New York, but he continued work on the proofs of his last book until the day before the end. Throughout his life in America he was active in Lutheran affairs, at first in churches of the Augustana Synod, later in a church of the Missouri Synod.

[*Who's Who in America*, 1930–31; *Am. Men of Sci.* (1927), ed. by J. M. and Jacques Cattell; *Jour. of N. Y. Botanical Garden*, Oct. 1931; obituary in *N. Y. Times*, July 26, 1931; personal acquaintance.]   J. H. B—t.

RYDER, ALBERT PINKHAM (Mar. 19, 1847–Mar. 28, 1917), painter, was born in New Bedford, Mass., one of four sons of Elizabeth (Cobb) Ryder and Alexander Gage Ryder, custom-house officer and coal dealer. His father was a native of Yarmouth, Mass., and a descendant of Samuel Rider, first known in America about 1638. The boy studied in the Middle Street grammar school in New Bedford and in his teens, having been given a box of colors and brushes, set out to experiment in picture making, early discovering the futility of the attempt to rival nature. When the family moved to New York City about 1868, he began the serious study

of art under William E. Marshall [*q.v.*], painter and engraver, pupil of Thomas Couture; in 1871 he entered the antique class of the National Academy of Design and there two years later exhibited a picture, "Clearing Away," the first of a long series of contributions to the Academy's annual exhibitions. From 1878 to 1887 he also sent regular contributions to the exhibitions of the Society of American Artists, of which he was a member, omitting only one exhibition. Although he was made an Academician in 1906, surprisingly small attention was paid to his early work. It was Daniel Cottier, the picture dealer, who first discovered its unusual distinction and beauty and found a market for it, Sir William Van Horne and Thomas B. Clarke being among the earliest patrons (Sherman, *post*, p. 18).

Since Ryder's life was as simple as it was uneventful, even a very small income was sufficient for his needs. The artist, he thought, needs but a roof, a crust of bread, and his easel; "all the rest God gives him in abundance" (quoted in Sherman, p. 21). He himself was so unsophisticated that he once kept a check for a large sum in a cupboard for several months and marveled at the financial knowledge of the friend who told him how to use it; he gave away some of his best pictures (one of them to a blacksmith), would share his last dollar with a beggar, and in other ways manifested the unworldliness that is one of the traditional traits of genius. His Fifteenth Street studio—an attic where for years he lived, worked, ate, and slept in perfect contentment—was encumbered with dusty furniture, packing boxes, frames, trunks, heaps of old magazines and papers, unwashed dishes, tin pails, oil cans, milk bottles, teacups, and empty cereal packages. Yet from this dust and disorder came strange and fascinating visions that are of the rarest achievements of poetic painting. He never married and, though he had many friends among artists and amateurs of art, lived almost like a recluse, occupied with painting, music, and poetry (which he sometimes tried, not altogether successfully, to write). In 1893 he went abroad with Cottier and Olin Warner [*q.v.*], the sculptor, but he was apparently not much interested in the old masters and travel did not appeal to his taste. He preferred long solitary walks in the park, occasional visits to Cape Cod, where he could make studies of moonlight on water, and for the rest, undisturbed seclusion in his own familiar, untidy studio in Fifteenth Street. His vivid though fragmentary record of his esthetic experiences in youth and maturity, "Paragraphs from the Studio of a Recluse," published in *The Broadway Magazine*, September 1905, makes it clear that his mode of living was due not at all to misanthropy but to deep absorption in his work and to a conviction that the artist must sacrifice everything but his own integrity. Brooding for years over a tiny picture, never wholly satisfied with what he had done, he worked with the utmost patience and care, often hampered, too, by an affection of the eyes, the result of poisoning from vaccination in childhood. Commenting both on his slowness and on his inability to achieve satisfaction, he once wrote to a friend: "Have you ever seen an inch worm crawl up a leaf or twig, and there clinging to the very end, revolve in the air, feeling for something to reach something? That's like me. I am trying to find something out there beyond the place on which I have a footing." (See Sherman, p. 28.) His most productive years and his best work came between 1873 and 1898. After that his inspiration seemed to wane somewhat, and the dull tone of much of the later work is in marked contrast with the rich, enamel-like quality of his earlier painting. In 1915, after a serious illness that obliged him to spend several months in a hospital, he went to stay with friends at Elmhurst, L. I., and there spent his last years in seclusion, leaving many paintings unfinished at his death.

In accordance with precedent, the death of the artist was followed by a memorable outburst of cordial appreciation. So rare is imaginative work of a high order in modern painting, so strong the appetite for ideal as opposed to realistic art that he was proclaimed as one of the elect who see nature en beau, not as literalists see it but with "richer enthralments." He has been likened at times to George Fuller [q.v.] and Matthew Maris, and particularly to Adolphe Monticelli and William Blake, "whose faults are manifest to the most casual and obtuse critic, but whose fascination is felt only by the peculiarly receptive" (Isham, post, p. 394). Certainly, a cold analysis of its qualities cannot do justice to a charm that is amenable to no rigid academic formula, overleaps the barriers of pictorial conventions, and is wholly spontaneous and original. In his seventy years Ryder produced hardly more than a hundred and fifty pictures, but not one was perfunctory. Although his small marines, structurally and technically, represent him at his best (Sherman, p. 51), he painted not only marines and pastoral landscapes and an occasional still life (some of these with great fidelity to reality) but symbolic and "literary" pictures as well. It is worth noting that such subjects as "Macbeth and the Witches," "Ophelia," "Jonah and the Whale," "The Race Track" (sometimes called "Death on a Pale Horse"), though they offer plentiful opportunity for melodrama or sentimentality, under his treatment are marked instead by genuine poetic feeling, delicate or powerful but never insincere. This is due in part to the intensity of his vision and in part to the firmness of the design. For, though content with a mere blur of white to represent a girl's dress and neglectful of craftsmanship in other ways, he was a master of design. A boat lying firmly beached beneath a rock in the moonlight not only conveys an inexplicable emotion but forms part of a satisfying pattern. "The Flying Dutchman," which Isham calls "a swirl of delicately matched old ivory and violet grays," is at the same time a symbol of the vastness and portentousness of the sea and a richly beautiful arabesque. Unfortunately, all of Ryder's work has suffered with the years from the cracking and dulling of the pigment. His technical methods, painstakingly slow as he was, were those of a man indifferent to the permanence of his work, as he was indifferent to mere skill and to a literal reproduction of nature.

A year after his death a noteworthy memorial exhibition of his work was opened at the Metropolitan Museum of Art, New York. American museums throughout the country contain his paintings in permanent collections. In the Museum of the Brooklyn Institute are no less than nine examples; the Metropolitan Museum has his "Toilers of the Sea," "The Curfew Hour," "The Bridge," and "Smugglers' Cove." The Albright Art Gallery, Buffalo, is fortunate in the possession of his "Temple of the Mind," formerly in the Clarke collection. Others may be seen in the Phillips Memorial Gallery and the National Gallery of Art, Washington, where there is a fine "Moonlight at Sea."

[The best source is F. F. Sherman, Albert Pinkham Ryder (1920); F. N. Price, Ryder (1847–1917) A Study of Appreciation (1932), gives a vivid impression of Ryder but is wholly uncritical. See also The Rider Family of Yarmouth (1913), no. 66 in Lib. of Cape Cod Hist. and Geneal.; Who's Who in America, 1916–17; obituary in N. Y. Times, Mar. 29, 1917; Lewis Mumford, The Brown Decades (1931); Suzanne La Follette, Art in America (1929). Among mag. articles the most useful are those by Henry Eckford, in Century, June 1890; Duncan Phillips, in Am. Mag. of Art, Aug. 1916; Marsden Hartley, in Seven Arts, May 1917; R. E. Fry, in Burlington, Apr. 1908; Anon., Art Amateur, July 1884; H. E. Schnakenberg, in The Arts, Nov. 1924; Elliott Daingerfield, in Scribner's, Mar. 1918; J. L. French, in Broadway, Sept. 1905; W. de S. Beck, in International Studio, Apr. 1920; Walter Pach, in Scribner's, Jan. 1911; F. J. Mather, Jr., in Nation, Apr. 12, 1917. Important items are the Metropolitan Museum Cat., Loan Exhibition of the Works of Albert P. Ryder (1918), and D. M. Cheney's reminiscences in New Bedford Standard, June 10, 1917. See also Samuel Isham, The Hist. of Am. Painting (1907); C. H. Caffin, The Story of Am. Painting (1907); Leo Stein, in New Republic, Apr. 27, 1918; Cat. of the Thos. B. Clarke Coll. (1899); Cat. of Am. Paintings Belonging to Wm.

T. Evans (1900); W. H. Downes and F. T. Robinson, in *New England Mag.*, Apr. 1896; *Lit. Digest,* June 7, 1930, and newspaper articles far too numerous to mention, many of them of unusual interest.]   W. H. D.

RYERSON, MARTIN ANTOINE (Oct. 26, 1856–Aug. 11, 1932), capitalist, philanthropist, art collector, was descended from Dutch ancestors who came to America about 1646. His father, Martin Ryerson, born near Paterson, N. J., went to Michigan at sixteen, where he worked for Indian traders at Grand Rapids and Muskegon and laid the foundation of a substantial fortune by purchasing large timber tracts near Muskegon. As his third wife he married Mary A. Campau of Grand Rapids and there young Martin was born. In childhood he accompanied his parents to Chicago, where an office of the lumber company had been opened in 1851. He attended the Chicago public schools until he was twelve, when his parents placed him in a boarding school in Paris. He remained in school abroad for seven years, going to Geneva when the Franco-Prussian War broke out. On his return to the United States he entered the Harvard Law School, where he was graduated in 1878.

He began practice with the Chicago law firm of Dexter, Herrick & Allen, but a severe illness and his father's urging soon persuaded him to forsake the confinement of a law office for the lumber business. He took charge of the Chicago office and on his father's death in 1887 assumed control of the business of Martin Ryerson & Company. He was also a director of the Elgin National Watch Company and of leading Chicago banks, and a trustee of the O. S. A. Sprague Memorial Institute from its beginning. In the early nineties he retired from active business with a fortune sufficient to allow him to devote most of his time and money thenceforth to the Art Institute, the Field Museum, and the University of Chicago.

His connection with the Art Institute began when he became governing member in 1887. He served as trustee from 1890 until his death, as vice-president, 1902–25, and president, 1925–26, and was then made honorary president. He was a serious student of art, and with Charles L. Hutchinson [*q.v.*], president until his death in 1924, formulated the policies of the Institute, maintained its standards of acquisitions, and fostered its educational departments. He built and endowed its Ryerson Library for the study of art, and by his will bequeathed it his fine collections, previously loaned—not only of paintings, but of prints, textiles, tapestries, porcelains, and furniture—together with a considerable endowment. He was one of the incorporators of the Field Museum of Natural History, a trustee from its organization in 1893, and first vice-president from 1894 until his death; to it he gave freely and generously of his fortune both during his lifetime and in his will. He was a member of the original board of trustees of the University of Chicago selected in 1890; in 1892 he became president of the board and served in that capacity until his voluntary retirement in 1922. He was made an honorary trustee in 1931. Here again, the record is eloquent of his sound judgment, his insight into educational policies, his zeal for promoting the artistic and material interests of the young institution. Together with his friend Charles L. Hutchinson, who served as treasurer, he established artistic standards and architectural ideals which influenced the design of the University buildings and the plan of its quadrangles, while under his chairmanship the University grew from a modest beginning to a corporation whose assets exceeded $50,000,000. His gift of Ryerson Physical Laboratory in memory of his father was supplemented by funds for equipment and research to assist the work of Albert A. Michelson [*q.v.*] and his colleagues, and by his will, after the death of his widow the University was to share with the Art Institute and the Field Museum the sum of approximately six million dollars. Notable among his many other gifts were those of a park (the farm on which he was born) and a public library to his birthplace, Grand Rapids, Mich.

Ryerson was married, Oct. 26, 1881, to Caroline Hutchinson, daughter of Charles and Emily (Smith) Hutchinson, formerly of Gloversville, N. Y. There were no children.

[*Mich. Pioneer and Hist. Soc. Colls.,* vol. I (1877), XIII (1889); *Bull. Art. Inst. of Chicago,* Sept.–Oct. 1932, Jan. 1933; *Field Museum News,* Dec. 1932; *Univ. Record* (Univ. of Chicago), Oct. 1932; A. W. Ryerson and A. L. Holman, *The Ryerson Geneal.* (1916); *Who's Who in America,* 1932–33; T. W. Goodspeed, *A Hist. of the Univ. of Chicago, 1891–1916* (1916); *Chicago Tribune,* Aug. 12, 23, 1932; *N. Y. Times,* Aug. 12, 1932.]   E. A. D.

RYLAND, ROBERT (Mar. 14, 1805–Apr. 23, 1899), Baptist clergyman, educator, was the son of Josiah and Catharine (Peachey) Ryland of "Farmington," King and Queen County, Va. From 1820 to 1823 he was a student at Humanity Hall Academy, conducted by Peter Nelson in Hanover County, and in 1826 he was graduated from Columbian College, Washington, D. C. Entering the Baptist ministry, he accepted a call to the Second Baptist Church in Lynchburg, Va. When, in 1832, the Baptists established at Richmond the Virginia Baptist Seminary to educate young men for the ministry, he was placed in charge. No detail of direction was too minute for his watchful care. He recruited likely students as he drove through the state, combining the mission of preacher and teacher. When the Seminary was chartered as Richmond College in 1840, he was made president and continued to direct its affairs with fidelity to two principles he had adopted—to keep the college out of debt and to make no educational claims that he was not able to substantiate. When the Civil War interrupted its logical development, the faculty, student body, buildings, and endowment attested his successful and constructive leadership.

In addition to his college work, he labored among the negroes of Richmond, serving as pastor of the First African Church from 1841 to 1865, during which time nearly four thousand members were added to the church roll. The catechism he wrote for his unlettered members required only two answers, "yes" or "no," with a passage of scripture to be memorized to support the answer. Many of the leaders of the negroes in Richmond in the early decades of their struggle up from slavery had been taught their standards in life by him and gratefully acknowledged their indebtedness. When the war was over, he resigned in the belief that the church would prefer a preacher of the negro race, an arrangement not hitherto permitted under Virginia law.

Before the war, in an address published under the title *The American Union* (1857), he had advised against the defense of slavery as right in the abstract, though he saw in the institution a means used by God to teach the negroes the Christian religion. He favored colonization in Africa, was opposed to disunion, counseled compromise on the part of the South, and recommended abstinence from all agitation on the subject of the "peculiar institution." He supported the Confederacy, however; devoted his time and resources to the care of wounded soldiers; invested his own savings in the Confederate cause, and advised the investment of the endowment funds of Richmond College in Confederate bonds. In 1866, feeling that younger minds should direct the affairs of a college to serve the new generation, he resigned the presidency of Richmond College. Subsequently, he accepted a position to teach in the National Theological School for negro preachers in Richmond, and was connected, also, with the Richmond Female Institute, a Baptist school for girls. In 1868 he moved to Kentucky to become president of the Shelbyville Female College, served a similar institution at Lexington (1871–78), and another at New Castle (1878–81). He spent succeeding years with a daughter in Lexington, and in 1893, when nearly ninety years old, became chaplain of Southwest Virginia Institute, at Bristol, acting in that capacity for four years.

His published books and pamphlets include *Baptism for the Remission of Sins* (1836); *A Scripture Catechism for the Instruction of Children and Servants* (1848); *Lectures on the Apocalypse* (1857); *The Virginia Baptist Educational Society: The Society—The Seminary—The College* (1891); and "A Sketch of the Life of the Late Rev. Robert Baylor Semple," in the *Virginia Baptist Preacher* (Richmond), April 1852. His first wife, whom he married in 1830, was Josephine, daughter of Thomas Norvell of Richmond; she died in 1846, and he later married Betty Presley Thornton, daughter of Anthony and Ann Thornton of Caroline County. There were four children by the first marriage and three by the second.

[Papers and letters of Ryland are in the possession of the Va. Baptist Hist. Soc., Univ. of Richmond; his *Va. Baptist Educ. Soc.: the Soc.: the Sem.—the Coll.*, with intro. by C. H. Ryland, gives an account of his services as president of Richmond Coll.; see also, H. A. Tupper, *The First Century of the First Baptist Church of Richmond, Va.* (1880); G. B. Taylor, *Va. Baptist Ministers* (4 ser., 1913); M. C. A. Cabell, *Sketches and Recollections of Lynchburg* (1858); *Times* (Richmond), Apr. 25, 1899; G. B. Taylor, *Life and Times of James B. Taylor* (copr. 1872).]   M. H. W.

RYNNING, OLE (Apr. 4, 1809–September 1838), immigrant leader and author, was born at Ringsaker, Norway, the son of the Rev. Jens Rynning and his wife, Severine Cathrine Steen. His father, then curate at Ringsaker, later minister at Snaasen, was noted for his writings on scientific subjects. Ole was tutored privately for matriculation at the national university in Christiania, where he studied from 1830 to 1833. He then opened a private school at Snaasen and soon became interested in the economic conditions of Norwegian farmers and laborers. The Gordian knot of their difficulties could be cut, he believed, by emigration, and in 1837 he set out for America as the leader of a group of eighty-four emigrants who sailed from Bergen for New York on Apr. 7, aboard the bark *Ægir*. Celebrating the Norwegian national holiday in mid-ocean, these country people of western Norway voiced, in an emigrant song that Rynning wrote for them, the pull of destiny westward and sounded an undertone of affection for the viking North.

The *Ægir* reached New York, on June 9, and a week later the immigrants started for Illinois. From Chicago, Rynning and three companions made their way to the Beaver Creek region in Iroquois County, where they selected a settlement site to which about fifty of the immigrants came later. The low land of the vicinity, dry in the late summer, was flooded the next spring; ultimately the colony was devastated by malaria; and in 1840, the last of the Norwegian pioneers of 1837 departed from it. Meanwhile, Rynning had written a work that became known throughout Norway as the "America Book." He had gone away on a trip to explore the surrounding country-side and had been caught in a blinding blizzard. When he was found both his feet were frozen and lacerated. While confined to his bed he wrote *A True Account of America for the Information and Help of Peasant and Commoner,* reading each chapter aloud to his neighbors and inviting their criticisms. He met misfortune with simple courage and rose above local circumstance to take a broad view of the American scene. He completed his book in February 1838, and the next spring, Ansten Nattestad, a member of the colony, journeyed back to Norway by way of New Orleans, taking the manuscript with him. It was published at Christiania late in the year and created a sensation among the common folk of Norway. No book like it had appeared in that country before. Compact and informative, "the work of a keen observer," as Prof. Edward Channing has said, it is one of the most interesting of all immigrant guide-books (*A History of the United States*, V, 1921, p. 469). A second edition appeared in 1839, and for many years the book stimulated Norwegian emigration. "Many who were scarcely able to read," said one immigrant, "began in earnest to practice in the 'America-book'" (*Billed-Magazin,* Apr. 17, 1869).

In thirteen concise chapters Rynning discussed such topics as the climate, soil, and products of America; the cost of provisions and of land; the American government; the religious situation; the problem of language and of education; the fortunes of the earlier settlers from Norway; and the prospects for immigrants. He disposed of many absurd rumors about America with quiet common sense and gave much shrewd advice. He praised the ideas of general freedom and equality, but denounced the slavery system and predicted that the United States ultimately would witness a separation of the North and South or violent civil disputes. A fourteenth chapter, in which he criticized the Norwegian state church, was excised by a state-church dean who, unluckily, read the proof.

Rynning regained the use of his feet, but in September 1838 he fell victim to the epidemic then scourging the Beaver Creek colony and died. Only one of his neighbors was well at the time; he chopped down an oak and from it hewed a crude coffin; in this, Rynning's body was placed and buried in an unmarked grave on the prairie. Of this captain of people in dispersion, Nattestad, who knew him well, said, "When sickness and suffering visited the colonists, he was always ready to comfort the sorrowing and to aid those in distress so far as it lay in his power. Nothing could shake his belief that America would become a place of refuge for the masses of people in Europe who toiled under the burdens of poverty" (*Billed-Magazin,* Feb. 20, 1869).

[Rynning's *Sandfærdig Beretning om Amerika* was reprinted by R. B. Anderson under the title *Student Ole Rynnings Amerikabog* (1896); the original and an English translation are given in T. C. Blegen, ed., *Ole Rynning's True Account of America* (Norwegian-Am. Hist. Asso., *Travel and Description Series,* vol. I, 1926). The original text of Rynning's emigrant song is presented, with an English translation, by Blegen and Martin B. Ruud in *Norwegian-American Studies and Records,* vol. VIII (1934). For further information see Anderson, *The First Chapter of Norwegian Immigration 1821–1840* (1895); Blegen, *Norwegian Migration to America, 1825–1860* (1931); Knud Langeland, *Nordmændene i Amerika* (1888); B. J. Muus, *Jens Rynnings Æt* (1894); articles on Jens and Ole Rynning in J. B. Halvorsen, *Norsk Forfatter-Lexikon 1814–1880,* vol. IV (1896); Ole K. Nattestad, *Beskrivelse over en Reise til Nordamerica* (Drammen, 1839), translated by Anderson in *Wis. Mag. of Hist.,* Dec. 1917; and Svein Nilssen's reports of interviews with Ansten and Ole K. Nattestad in *Billed-Magazin* (Madison, Wis.), vol. I, Feb. 13 and 20, 1869.]   T. C. B.

SABIN, CHARLES HAMILTON (Aug. 24, 1868–Oct. 10, 1933), banker, was born at Williamstown, Mass., a son of Thomas and Cordelia (Eldridge) Sabin. Growing up on a farm, he obtained his schooling chiefly at the Greylock Institute in South Williamstown, from which he was graduated at the age of seventeen. He first found employment in a flour store in Albany, N. Y., but by the time he was twenty-one he held a clerkship in the National Commercial Bank of Albany, which he left for a subordinate position in the Park Bank. After seven years with the Park Bank, he was made cashier in 1898 of the Albany City National Bank. To that institution he brought so much new business—the deposits were doubled in four years—that he again attracted the attention of the directors of the National Commercial Bank, who elected him vice-president in 1902. During the panic year of 1907, when the position had rather an uncertain future, he was called to the presidency of the National Copper Bank of New York City and held it for three years, until a merger with the Mechanics and Metals National Bank was accomplished. At that time he took a vice-presidency in the Guaranty Trust Company, then in a period of rapid expansion, and in 1915 was promoted to the presidency. Under his direction the Guaranty Trust Company took a leading part both during and after the World War in enlisting the interest of American capital in financial and economic conditions abroad, publishing a series of pamphlets on the subject. In the foreword to *The Solvency of the Allies*, Sabin wrote in 1919: "This is a time when all thought of profits should be forgotten and the simple necessities of the situation faced. Our first and single duty now is to help restore the world to normal conditions." In 1921 he gave up the presidency to become chairman of the board, and with the exception of a part of one year he held that position until his death. He also held directorships in various corporations. His distinction lies in the fact that he was a "career man," who owed little to circumstances and almost everything to his own adaptability and energy, and that he represented the New York bankers in dealing with the tremendous and imperfectly undertsood problems of international finance that followed the war. Although, like other individual bankers, he was overshadowed by his institution, it was he who held the helm through the stormy years 1915–21.

In New York in the later years of his life he devoted much time and thought to the advancement of the Boys' Club on the East Side founded by E. H. Harriman. A polo enthusiast and a devotee of golf, he engaged actively in outdoor sports to the last. He died of cerebral hemorrhage at his Long Island country home in the Shinnecock Hills. He had been married first on Dec. 29, 1897, to Mabel Whitney of Albany, from whom he was divorced in 1915; and second, on Dec. 28, 1916, to a daughter of Paul Morton [*q.v.*], Pauline (Morton) Smith, who took a prominent part in the campaign for the repeal of the Eighteenth Amendment. His second wife, with a son by his former marriage, survived him.

[*Who's Who in America*, 1932–33; *N. Y. Times*, Dec. 29, 1916, and Oct. 12, 1933; *N. Y. Herald Tribune*, Oct. 12, 1933; brief article and portrait in *Bankers Mag.*, Oct. 1921.]

W. B. S.

SABIN, JOSEPH (Dec. 6? 1821–June 5, 1881), bibliographer and bibliophile, was born probably at Braunston, Northamptonshire, England. He was educated in the schools of his native village and of Oxford but never attended the university. At fourteen he was apprenticed to Charles Richards, a prominent book dealer of Oxford, to learn the bookbinding trade. He had been at the bookbinder's bench only a few months, when his employer realized that he would be far more valuable in the salesroom. After three years as assistant salesman, he became general manager and had charge of the buying of books. He was always ready to place his rapidly accumulating knowledge of books at the disposal of customers and, in spite of a somewhat brusque manner and a decided impatience with pretentious mediocrity, he won and held the respect of his patrons, who learned to trust his judgment implicitly. While serving as apprentice he became interested in the temperance question and all his life was ready to write and speak in advocacy of the cause. During the last year of his apprenticeship, which ended in 1842, he became acquainted with the family of Mr. Winterborn, an architect and builder of Oxford, with one of whose sons he formed a partnership to carry on the business of a bookseller and auctioneer, and to one of whose daughters he was married in 1844. In 1844 he published anonymously his first regular book, *The Thirty-nine Articles of the Church of England, with Scripture Proof and References*.

In 1848 he sold his business and sailed on the ship *West Point*, with his wife and two sons, for New York City. From New York he soon removed to Philadelphia, where he obtained employment with George S. Appleton. He settled his family on a farm he purchased on Chestnut Hill, since 1854 within the corporate limits of the city. While with Appleton he introduced half binding in calf and morocco, then unknown in America. In 1850 he was employed by Cooley & Kesse, book auctioneers at 191 Broadway, and later by their successors, Lyman & Rawdon. He devoted much time to the preparation of sales and auction catalogues, of which he issued about 150 during his life. His first important catalogue, for the collection of Samuel Farmar Jarvis, was issued in 1851. That year he was engaged by the rival firm of Bangs, Brother & Company, with whom he remained five years, cataloguing among other collections the extensive library of Americana brought together by E. B. Corwin. The sale of this library drew attention to Americana and started Sabin on his life work, *Dictionary of Books Relating to America, from its Discovery to the Present Time* (14 vols., 1868–84), known as well by the fly-leaf title, "Bibliotheca Americana." In 1856 he opened a second-hand book store on Canal Street, New York, but after a year he returned to Philadelphia and at No. 27 South Sixth St. developed a good business with the South, where an active group of collectors was then to be found. The breaking out of the Civil War brought this business to an abrupt close. In 1861 with H. A. Jennings he opened an auction room on Fourth Street in New York. Probably in 1865 he retired and devoted himself to the handling of rare books and prints, at No. 84 Nassau St., working steadily on his "Bibliotheca Americana," for which he issued a prospectus on Dec. 5, 1866. He also was interested in publishing *Sabin & Sons' American Bibliopolist* and the *Sabin's Reprints*. He became known, not only in this country but in Europe, as an expert in all matters relating to books and prints. In twenty years he made thirty trips to Europe in quest of rare books and managed to attend all the more important sales of this period.

In 1879 he determined to give all his time to the *Dictionary* and gave up the business, which was, however, carried on under the firm name of J. Sabin's Son. His "Bibliotheca Americana" occupied most of his active hours during the last years of his life, exhausted all his spare funds, and left him a poor man. He undertook to give with accuracy the title of every book and pamphlet, in every language, relating in any way to America. The entries are arranged alphabetically by author, and, in addition to a complete bibliographical description, some idea is given of the character of the work as related to America. The work was begun in 1856, but the first part of volume I was not published until 1867 (issued in parts; vol. I dated 1868). Twelve volumes had been published when he died.

[Since Sabin's death the *Dictionary of Books Relating to America* has been continued, vols. XV–XX (1885–92) ed. by Wilberforce Eames and since then by R. W. G. Vail; the largest collection of Sabin's catalogues is in the N. Y. Public Lib. and the next in Lib. of Cong.; S. A. Allibone, *A Critical Dictionary of Eng. Lit.*, vol. II (1870); *Publishers' Weekly*, June 11, 1881; *N. Y. Times, N. Y. Tribune, World* (N. Y.), and *Commercial Advertiser* (N.Y.), for June 6, 1881.]

H. H. B. M.

SABINE, LORENZO (July 28, 1803–Apr. 14, 1877), historian, was born in Lisbon, N. H., spent twenty years in Eastport, Me., and died in Boston Highlands, Mass. His mother was Ann (or Harriet) Clark, the daughter of John Clark. His father was Elijah R. Sabin, as the name was then spelled, a Methodist clergyman and in 1811 chaplain of the House of Representatives of Massachusetts. He was the descendant of William Sabin who was in Rehoboth, Mass., as early as 1643. When Lorenzo was fifteen years of age his father died in Savannah, Ga., where he had gone because of illness; and from that time the boy provided his own livelihood and whatever education he received, and occasionally he aided his five younger brothers and sisters. For a time he was apprenticed to Lincoln & Edmonds, Boston publishers, but the poverty of the family sent him forth in 1821 to seek his fortune on "the eastern frontier of the union." In Eastport, Me., which had been incorporated in the limits of the United States, he obtained a small clerkship, and there after a short time he set up trade on his own account. Within a year he was bankrupt, but, undiscouraged by his fail-

ure, after a second period of clerking and of keeping the books of the Passamaquoddy Bank, he again ventured an independent business. Of his activities during the years that followed he later wrote that he "built and owned vessels, fitted out fishermen, and was a petty dealer in codfish and molasses" (*Proc. Mass. Hist. Soc., post.* p. 378). This life he pursued for fifteen years, combining with it a variety of activities. In 1834 and 1835 he was a member of the Maine House of Representatives. He was also deputy commissioner of customs, and for a short time edited the *Eastport Sentinel*. About 1848 he removed to Framingham, Mass.

In his local community he was known as an indefatigable reader and, as a young man, he was the prime source of vitality in a forum that achieved some small fame. His keen curiosity about all aspects of his occupation, his unremitting study, and his persistent efforts to formulate his ideas acceptably laid the foundation for his later historical publications. The proximity of Eastport to the Canadian border had brought him into contact with the descendants of many of the American Loyalists, and the interest thus roused resulted in his most valuable historical work, *The American Loyalists or Biographical Sketches of Adherents to the British Crown in the War of the Revolution* (1847), a work that drew upon many family records and recollections as well as on more easily accessible public material. The second and enlarged edition of the study in two volumes, *Biographical Sketches of Loyalists* (1864), is still in frequent use. In 1847 he also contributed a *Life of Commodore Edward Preble* to Jared Sparks's Library of American Biography Series. One of his early ambitions had been to obtain a place in the pages of the *North American Review* and this he seems first to have achieved by an article on "The Whale Fishery" in January 1834. Another article on "American Forest Trees" appeared in April 1837. His business had given him an abundant knowledge not only of Maine forests but also of the fisheries of the northeast coast, which he incorporated in articles for that journal between 1843 and 1846. Of these perhaps the most important were on "Fisheries" (July 1843), "Our Commercial History and Policy" (October 1843), and the "American Fisheries" (April 1846). Other articles in the same magazine were "The Forest Lands of Maine" (April 1844), "Simcoe's Military Journal" (October 1844), "British Colonial Politics" (January 1845), and "Life and Works of John Adams" (July 1857). Some of these articles may have attracted the attention of the administration to him for, in

1852, he was called to Washington, and for a year worked, under the direction of the department of the treasury, on problems connected with the fisheries. The result of this work appeared as *Report on the Principal Fisheries of the American Seas* (1853).

Elected as a Whig to complete the congressional term of Benjamin Thompson, he served in the federal House of Representatives from Dec. 13, 1852, to Mar. 3, 1853. In 1857 he became secretary of the Boston board of trade, a position he held for ten years. The annual reports of the board during his term constitute a genuine contribution to the history of the period. He also published *Notes on Duels and Duelling ... with a Preliminary Historical Essay* (1855), several addresses for special occasions, and numerous articles. His historical work is characterized by his industrious research, a love for the past, and great interest in the personal aspects of historical problems. Of him the *Boston Evening Transcript* wrote: "Probably no man living has so accurate and general a knowledge of the individual history of the period of the Revolution as Mr. Sabine has acquired" (quoted in *New England Historical & Genealogical Register,* April 1860, pp. 179–80). Little is recorded of his family life. We know only that he was three times married: on Nov. 20, 1825, to Matilda F. Green, on July 13, 1829, to Abby R. D. Deering, and on Sept. 17, 1837, to Elizabeth M. Deering. Of his five children but one survived him.

[E. E. Hale, "Memoir of the Hon. Lorenzo Sabine," *Proc. Mass. Hist. Soc.,* vol. XVII (1880); *New Eng. Hist. and Gen. Reg.,* Oct. 1878; *Daily Evening Transcript* (Boston), Apr. 16, 1877.]   E. D.

SABINE, WALLACE CLEMENT WARE (June 13, 1868–Jan. 10, 1919), physicist, was born in Richwood, Ohio. He was the son of Hylas and Anna (Ware) Sabine and a descendant of William Sabine or Sabin who was settled in Rehoboth, Mass., in 1643. According to family tradition, each of his four names represented one of the four racial strains that were joined in him: Scotch, Dutch, English, and French. His English forebears were Quakers and his French forebears probably Huguenots, and, though he subscribed to no religious creed, his moral qualities were such as one might expect from such a lineage.

He was graduated A.B. from Ohio State University in 1886, having been a student of Thomas Corwin Mendenhall [q.v.], and the same year enrolled as a graduate student in mathematics and physics at Harvard. Here he received the degree of A.M. in 1888, the next year was made an assistant in physics, and rose through the

various grades thereafter to a professorship in 1905. He never became a candidate for the doctorate, although he possessed remarkable aptitude for research requiring a high degree of experimental skill. His published papers were remarkably few and remarkably significant. Giving most of his time and strength to teaching rather than to research, he was apparently content for some years to remain obscure himself while setting his pupils in the way of distinguished achievement. In 1895, however, upon the completion of the Fogg Art Museum, designed by Richard Morris Hunt [q.v.], its auditorium proved to be "monumental in its acoustic badness," and Sabine was designated by President Eliot to remedy the defect. As a result of the interest thus aroused and the consequent experimentation, "so far as the properties of auditoriums are concerned, Sabine in less than twenty years brought architectural acoustics from the empirical state, in which success with any new structure was a happy accident and failure was a misfortune often made ridiculous by such attempted remedies as the stringing of wires in the overhead space, to the status of a reasoned science and a precise art" (Hall, *post.* p. 12).

After the death of Professor Nathaniel Southgate Shaler [q.v.] in 1906, Sabine was made dean of the Lawrence Scientific School, and in 1908 of the Harvard Graduate School of Applied Science, which was initiated under his influence. After about seven years this school disappeared in a merger between Harvard and the Massachusetts Institute of Technology for applied science teaching, an arrangement which Sabine approved. In the spring of 1917 he gave a course of lectures on architectural acoustics at the Sorbonne and soon afterward devoted himself, without official status but very effectively, to a study of aerial warfare and the promotion of a better understanding between England, France, and Italy as to the means and methods of such warfare. Returning to America in the fall of 1917, he placed the experience and knowledge he had thus gained at the service of the government, and from that time until the end of the World War he, though still as a civilian, held an important office in the military air service, being "the final authority to select from the samples sent from overseas" instruments to be reproduced in the United States. He divided his time between this service and teaching at Harvard, going back and forth weekly between Cambridge and Washington, though his health had been seriously broken since the fall of 1916. He survived the war, but died soon after its close.

Sabine married, Aug. 22, 1900, Dr. Jane

Downes Kelly, a physician of established reputation who continued in practice after marriage. Two daughters were born to them. After his death his most significant writings were brought together in a volume with the title *Collected Papers on Acoustics* (1922), published by the Harvard University Press.

[E. H. Hall in *Memoirs Nat. Acad. Sci.*, vol. XXI (1927), with bibliography of Sabine's fifteen published papers; W. D. Orcutt, *Wallace Clement Sabine: A Study in Achievement* (1933); *Who's Who in America*, 1918–19; *Boston Transcript*, Jan. 10, 1919.]

E. H. H.

SACAGAWEA (*c.* 1787–Dec. 20, 1812), interpreter of the Lewis and Clark expedition, was born in a Shoshone village of which her father was the chief, probably in the neighborhood of Lemhi, Idaho. In the fall of 1800 she was captured with several others at the Three Forks of the Missouri by a war party of Hidatsas. Taken to the Hidatsa village at the mouth of Knife River, she and another girl were later sold to Toussaint Charbonneau, a Canadian living with the tribe, who married, according to Indian rites, both of them. In the winter of 1804–05, when Meriwether Lewis and William Clark [*qq.v.*] were at Fort Mandan, Charbonneau was engaged as an interpreter to the expedition, with the understanding that Sacagawea was to accompany him. On Feb. 11, 1805, at the fort, she gave birth to her first child, a boy. Less than two months later, on Apr. 7, the expedition set forth; and Sacagawea, with her infant strapped to her back, went with it, sharing all the hardships and privations of the journey. Her services were inestimable; without the aid she obtained from the Shoshones it is hardly possible that the expedition could have proceeded beyond the headwaters of the Salmon. On the return the Charbonneaus remained with the Hidatsas. Clark had become deeply attached to the boy, John Baptist, whom he nicknamed "Pomp" and for whom doubtless he named Pompey's Pillar (originally Tower) on the Yellowstone; and he offered to take the lad, when weaned, to educate as his own child. A few years later, probably in the fall of 1809, Sacagawea, with her husband and child, arrived in St. Louis. Under Clark's patronage Charbonneau tried farming for a time, but the venture was unsuccessful. Leaving the boy with Clark, the Charbonneaus took passage with the expedition led by Manuel Lisa [*q.v.*] that left St. Louis in April 1811, and returned to the Hidatsas. In August 1812, with an infant daughter, Lizette, they rejoined Lisa at his new post, Fort Manuel, on the Missouri near the present boundary of the two Dakotas. On Dec. 20, 1812, John C. Luttig, Lisa's clerk, entered on his journal the record: "this Evening the Wife of Charbonneau a Snake Squaw, died of a putrid fever she was a good and the best Women in the fort, aged abt 25 years she left a fine infant girl" (Luttig, *post*, p. 106). She was buried in the grounds of the fort, and her infant was taken to St. Louis and placed under the guardianship of Clark.

No other American woman has been honored with so many memorials as Sacagawea. A river, a peak, and a mountain pass in Montana bear her name; a bronze statue of her was exhibited at the St. Louis exposition of 1904; there is another bronze statue in Portland, Ore.; a statue at the capitol in Bismark, N. Dak.; a boulder with bronze tablet at Three Forks, Mont.; a monument at Armstead, Mont.; a public fountain at Lewiston, Idaho, and a cement shaft at the grave assumed to be hers on the Shoshone reservation. Her character and services have evoked many tributes. Though Lewis mentions her in one instance (July 29, 1805) somewhat disdainfully, Clark gives many evidences of a deep regard for the woman whom he whimsically nicknamed "Janey." To Brackenridge (*post*), a fellow-voyager on the expedition of 1811, she was "a good creature, of a mild and gentle disposition, greatly attached to the whites, whose manners and dress she tries to imitate," and she has been described as a "modest, womanly, unselfish, patient, enduring little Shoshone squaw" who "proved time and again the inspiration, the genius of the occasion" (Wheeler, *post*, vol. I, p. 124).

Though the Luttig entry has been generally accepted as the authentic death record of Sacagawea, the matter is still warmly controverted. The theory has been advanced that Sacagawea returned to her people, among whom she lived until she was nearly one hundred years old, and that she is identical with the woman known as "Bazil's mother," interred Apr. 9, 1884, in the Shoshone burial grounds (Hebard, *post*). This theory has been reflected in a bill before Congress and in an effort to compel a decision from the Commissioner of Indian Affairs. The controversy also includes a lively disputation over the heroine's name.

[The spelling of Sacagawea's name in this article follows the precedent of Lewis, Clark, and Ordway. See *Original Jours. of the Lewis and Clark Expedition* (7 vols., 1904–05), ed. by R. G. Thwaites; J. C. Luttig, *Jour. of a Fur-Trading Expedition . . . 1812–1813* (1920), ed. by Stella M. Drumm; H. M. Brackenridge in *Early Western Travels*, vol. VI (1904), ed. by R. G. Thwaites; O. D. Wheeler, *The Trail of Lewis and Clark* (2 vols., 1904); Doane Robinson, in *S. Dak. Hist. Colls.*, XII (1924), 71–84; Grace R. Hebard, in *Jour. Am. Hist.*, Sept. 1907, and *Sacajawea, a Guide and Interpreter of the Lewis and Clark Expedition* (1933); manuscript articles by Dr. Chas. A. Eastman and J. E. Rees.]

W. J. G.

SACCO, NICOLA (Apr. 22, 1891–Aug. 23, 1927) and Bartolomeo Vanzetti (June 11, 1888– Aug. 23, 1927), principals in the Sacco-Vanzetti case, were both natives of Italy. Sacco, who was christened Ferdinando but took the name of an elder brother when the latter died, was born at Torre Maggiore, province of Foggia, in Southern Italy. His father, Michele Sacco, was a substantial owner of vineyards and olive orchards. In April 1908 he emigrated to the United States, where in 1912 he was married; he had a son and a daughter. With the exception of an absence in Mexico (1917–18) to avoid the draft, Sacco at the time of his arrest in 1920 had been for eleven years employed as a skilled edger in a shoe factory at Milford, Mass., where he was known as a steady workman absorbed in his family, his work, and his garden. During his residence in Massachusetts Sacco first became interested in Socialism and later, like Vanzetti, came under the influence of Luigi Galleani, a philosophical anarchist of the school of Blake and Tolstoy. Vanzetti, whose parents, Battista and Giovanna Vanzetti, were of well-to-do farming stock, was born at Villafalletto, province of Cuneo, Piedmont, and, following his mother's death, emigrated to New York in June 1908. Of a reflective temperament and a roving disposition, he never married and sampled a variety of employments in different parts of the country before 1915, when he settled in Plymouth, Mass. There he remained, save for a visit to Mexico in 1917–18 to avoid the draft, and was at the time of his arrest in 1920 engaged as a fish peddler.

In the winter of 1919–20 a wave of anti-radicalism swept the United States. In Massachusetts several members of the Galleani group were deported or imprisoned and the press was full of the machinations of the "Reds." At the height of this campaign, on Apr. 15, 1920, the paymaster and guard of a shoe factory were shot dead in the main street of South Braintree, Mass., and robbed of some $16,000. The shots were fired by two men of foreign appearance who were immediately driven away in a car by their accomplices. It was with this brutal crime that Sacco and Vanzetti, arrested on May 5, were charged. Their joint trial began on May 31, 1921, at Dedham, before Judge Webster Thayer. No money had been traced to the defendants nor was there any evidence that either of them had ever been in possession of the car in which the murderers made their escape. The prosecution relied on two main points: (1) evidence of eye-witnesses identifying the defendants as participants in the crime; (2) the fact that on arrest the defendants

made to the police false statements as to their movements and circumstances, from which a guilty consciousness of murder might be inferred. The defence sought to meet the first of these points by the evidence of the defendants themselves and of numerous other witnesses placing them elsewhere at the time of the crime. To the second it replied that the nervousness and admitted falsehoods of the defendants were explained by their consciousness, not of murder, but of radicalism and their fear of sharing the fate of some of their fellow radicals. At the time of their arrest they were actually obtaining a car in order to dispose of incriminating Socialist literature in their possession. On July 14, both defendants were found guilty of murder in the first degree.

After the trial, applications for a re-hearing were made to Judge Thayer, partly on the ground of fresh evidence, partly on the ground that the question of radicalism, unavoidably introduced by the defence, had been improperly capitalized by the prosecution and the presiding judge. It was claimed that the district attorney's cross examination, ostensibly directed to disprove, was really calculated to emphasize and exploit the defendants' evasion of military service and their unpopular opinions for the double purpose of prejudicing them in the eyes of the jury or, if they were acquitted, of providing the federal agents with materials for a deportation order against them. These motions were all denied and the supreme court of Massachusetts, whose power of review is limited to questions of law, refused to intervene. Meanwhile, the spontaneous confession in 1925 of a condemned criminal named Madeiros (or Medeiros) exonerating the defendants had led to the discovery (1926) of much corroborative detail pointing to the theory that the murder was the work of a gang of professional bandits from Providence, R. I. Sacco and Vanzetti were now defended by a prominent and conservative Boston lawyer, William G. Thompson, whose courageous, powerful, and disinterested presentation of their case aroused doubts of their guilt in many minds. Meetings of protest took place all over the world and such famous names as Mazaryk, Einstein, Anatole France, and Romain Rolland were associated with petitions for the men's release. In Massachusetts, however, opinion remained predominantly hostile. To the native New England element Sacco and Vanzetti were aliens and agitators; to the Catholics they were renegades in religion. Both elements were united to resent outside intervention with local institutions, and to citizens the vindication of those institutions appeared of greater importance than the guilt or innocence of the accused. Nevertheless, so insistent was the demand for an impartial review that on June 1, 1927, Gov. Alvan T. Fuller of Massachusetts announced the appointment of an advisory committee to report to him on the fairness of the trial and the justification for the conviction. (The death sentence had been imposed on Apr. 9, 1927.) The members of this committee were President A. Lawrence Lowell of Harvard University, President Samuel W. Stratton of the Massachusetts Institute of Technology, and a former probate judge, Robert Grant.

On Aug. 3 the Governor, who had meanwhile conducted his own inquiry, announced that both he and the advisory committee were unanimous in finding the trial fair and the defendants guilty. But the committee's report, published a few days later (*New York Times,* Aug. 7, 1927), was at once the object of serious and detailed criticism, particularly in regard to its treatment of the charge of prejudice against Judge Thayer. The defence unsuccessfully attempted to persuade the federal courts to intervene and demonstrations in favor of the defendants continued both at home and abroad. As the day fixed for the executions drew nearer, Boston was placed under something resembling martial law and on Sunday, Aug. 21, 1927, over 150 persons were arrested for picketing near the State House. After midnight of Aug. 22, that is, in the first hours of Aug. 23, both defendants were electrocuted.

During his long imprisonment Vanzetti had devoted himself to reading and improving his command of English; and a number of his letters written during this period have been published. Unless they can be thought to have been deliberately concocted for the purpose, these letters may be thought to provide some psychological confirmation of the material evidence against his having committed a murder for profit. For they display him as a man of considerable native intelligence striving after education and as an idealist with an unexpected vein of realistic humor. Throughout his imprisonment he was supported by the belief, eloquently expressed in a passage from his statement on receiving sentence, that he was promoting the cause he had at heart: "Now we are not a failure. . . . Never in our full life could we hope to do such work for tolerance, for joostice, for man's understanding of man as now we do by an accident. Our words—our lives—our pains—nothing! The taking of our lives—lives of a good shoemaker and a poor fish-peddler—all! That last moment belongs to us—that agony is our triumph" (Ehrmann, *post,* p. 245).

An opinion as to the guilt of Sacco and Vanzetti must depend on the consideration of a mass of detail which it is impossible to summarize in this article. Communists came to value the case as a proof of their thesis that no "Capitalist" society can afford justice to its opponents in the class war. Others, not subscribing to this general proposition, felt grave misgivings in the particular instance.

[*The Sacco-Vanzetti Case* (5 vols., 1928–29), a transcript of the record; *The Letters of Sacco and Vanzetti* (1928), ed. by Marion Frankfurter and Gardner Jackson; Fernand Collin, *L'affaire Sacco et Vanzetti* (Louvain, 1927); Eugene Lyons, *The Life and Death of Sacco and Vanzetti* (1927); Felix Frankfurter, *The Case of Sacco and Vanzetti* (1927); O. K. Fraenkel, *The Sacco-Vanzetti Case* (1931); H. B. Ehrmann, *The Untried Case* (1933).]   S. G—s.

SACHS, JULIUS (July 6, 1849–Feb. 2, 1934), educator, was born at Baltimore, Md., the son of Joseph and Sophia (Baer) Sachs. He took the degrees of A.B. and A.M. at Columbia in 1867 and 1871. After studying in Germany at the universities of Würzburg, Berlin, Göttingen, and Rostock from 1867 to 1871, he returned to America with the degree of Ph.D. from Rostock. In 1871, in a deliberate attempt to raise the standard of secondary education in the United States, he established a preparatory school in New York City, the Sachs Collegiate Institute School of Boys, of which he remained the head for more than thirty years. In spite of his youth, he was unusually well-equipped for such a venture and the moment a singularly propitious one, for colleges and universities, having raised their own standards, had begun to make demands that few private and no public schools of the time could properly meet. The Sachs Collegiate Institute had a widespread influence on American educational standards and methods. It was not only a model school for boys but also a training school for teachers under wise and considerate leadership. There was no paltering with educational nostrums, no attempt merely to interest a student, but a sincere belief that the only durable satisfaction for the student is proportional to his own thoughtful labor.

Sachs's own scholarly investigations were not made impossible by his other activities. His "Observations on Plato's Cratylus" (*Transactions of the American Philological Association,* 1878) was the first of a long series of learned articles, the most notable being "Observations on Lucian" (*Ibid.,* 1880), "Notes on Homeric Zoology" (*Ibid.,* 1886), and "Echoes of Greek Epic Poetry in Vase Paintings" (a lecture delivered before the New York Society of the Archaeological Institute of America, Mar. 6, 1893). He also contributed many articles on educational subjects to the *Educational Review* from 1905 to 1918. In 1912 he published a very complete study, *The American Secondary School and Some of Its Problems.*

Sachs was a man of fine appearance, great vigor of mind and body, and exceptional intellectual equipment. His career seems almost consciously to have been shaped on that of Hermann Sauppe of Göttingen, under whose influence he had come in 1869 and whom he described as "a master of his craft, ready to share his resources as a practical teacher and an investigator with the young aspirants, a veritable professor of the teaching method" (Sachs, "Reminiscences of German University Days," article prepared for *Teachers College Record,* March 1917, printed separately, but not published in that issue). Throughout the years his leadership as a teacher and scholar was clearly recognized by his election to head the Schoolmasters' Association of New York, 1889, the American Philological Association, 1890–91, the Headmasters' Association of the United States, 1899, and the New York Society of the Archaeological Institute of America, 1900–03. In 1902 he was invited to join the faculty of Teachers College in Columbia University as professor of secondary education, an opportunity greatly to extend his influence. His success in this work until his retirement in 1917 is amply attested by numbers of mature students and especially by very sincere tributes at the time of his death from President Nicholas Murray Butler, Dean Frederick J. E. Woodbridge, and others. On June 23, 1874, he married Rosa Goldman of New York, with whom, at their fiftieth wedding anniversary, he established at Columbia the Julius and Rosa Sachs Endowment Fund, designed to promote scholarship in the field of secondary education. They had a daughter, and a son who became a surgeon.

[*Cat. of the Sachs Collegiate Inst. School of Boys* (1906); *Teachers Coll. Record,* Mar. 1934; "In Memoriam: Memorial Services for Dr. Julius Sachs, Held in Milbank Chapel, Teachers College, Columbia University . . . May 15, 1934" (MS.); *Who's Who in America,* 1932–33; *N. Y. Times,* Feb. 3, 1934; personal acquaintance.]   F. L. T.

SACHS, THEODORE BERNARD (May 2, 1868–Apr. 2, 1916), physician, was born of Jewish parents, Bernard and Sophia Sachs, at Dinaberg, Russia. His father, a well-to-do merchant, gave him a good education in the Kherson High School and the University of Odessa, from which he was graduated in law in 1891. He then emigrated to America and settled in Chicago, where he became a sewing-machine operator for a clothing manufacturing firm and thus supported himself while he attended the College of Physicians and Surgeons (later affiliated with the University of Illinois). He graduated in 1895 and, after two years as intern and house physician at Michael Reese Hospital, established his office in the Jewish quarter of Chicago's west side. From the first he had an especial interest in tuberculosis. In 1900 he established in the Jewish Aid Dispensary the first clinic in Chicago devoted exclusively to patients suffering from pulmonary tuberculosis, and awoke a storm of protest by denouncing the neglect of tuberculous patients at the county institutions at Dunning and Oak Forest. In 1905 he was attending physician to a camp for tuberculous patients at Glencoe, the first of its kind in the state; later there were established a camp at Dunning and the Edward Sanitarium at Naperville, where he was director and examining physician from its foundation to his death. He was in the forefront of the campaign successfully waged in 1909 for the establishment of the Chicago Municipal Tuberculosis Sanitarium, begun in 1911 and completed in 1915. As secretary of the first board of directors and later its head, he exercised much influence upon the plans of the buildings and upon the organization of its services. A corrupt city government, however, made efficient administration impossible and brought accusations of inefficiency and dishonesty against the board of directors. Sachs submitted his resignation on Mar. 20, 1916, and two weeks later committed suicide by morphine poisoning at the Edward Sanitarium, leaving a letter addressed to the people of Chicago that called for an inquiry into the affairs of the sanitarium and protested against its exploitation by politicians. A report of the finance committee of the Chicago city council later exonerated the sanitarium board of charges of any misuse of public funds. In the midst of his municipal work Sachs was director and president of the Chicago Tuberculosis Institute, secretary of the United Hebrew Charities, and attending physician to several hospitals. In 1915–16 he was president of the National Association for the Study and Prevention of Tuberculosis. The most notable of his few articles are *Tuberculosis in the Jewish District of Chicago* (1904), *Children of Tuberculous Parents* (1908), and *The Examination of Employees for Tuberculosis* (1912). He was greatly assisted in his investigations and writings by his wife, Lena Louise Wilson of Chicago, whom he married Jan. 4, 1900.

Sachs had exalted ideas of professional responsibility and of citizenship, an unusual capacity for initiative and for organization, and an untiring industry that made him ruthless in the prosecution of inefficiency. Yet he was an oppressively serious person, with an habitual expression of sadness. He was usually preoccupied, overwrought and nervous, and frequently highly irritable; furthermore, though lavish in sacrifice of his personal interest and with total disregard of pecuniary gain, he loved honors, which he sought and earned. It was probably on account of these personal qualities that, in spite of his ability and sincerity, he never achieved the support of the medical profession of Chicago but always met either apathetic unconcern or secret opposition.

[*Alumni Record, Univ. of Ill.* (1921); *Proc. Inst. of Medicine of Chicago, 1916–17* vol. I (1917); S. A. Knopf, *A Hist. of the Natl. Tuberculosis Assoc.* (1922); *Medic. Times* (N. Y.), June 1916; *Jour. of the Outdoor Life*, May 1916; *Ill. Medic. Jour.*, Apr. 1916; H. A. Kelly and W. L. Burrage, *Am. Medic. Biographies* (1920); obituary in *Chicago Daily Tribune*, Apr. 3, 1916.]   J. M. P—n.

SACHSE, JULIUS FRIEDRICH (Nov. 22, 1842–Nov. 14, 1919), antiquary, author, the son of Johann Heinrich Friedrich and Julianna Wilhelmina (Bühler) Sachse, was born, lived, and died in Philadelphia. His father, a pupil of Thorwaldsen's, was an artist and designer in bronze and other metals. After attending the old Lutheran Academy, Sachse became a haberdasher and maker of men's shirts. He received several medals for work of his manufacture which he exhibited at fairs in Vienna, Paris, and Philadelphia. On May 15, 1864, he married Emma Caroline Lange, who with their five children survived him. About 1890 he retired from business in order to devote himself to research, writing, and photography. He joined numerous historical societies and was one of the founders, in 1891, of the Pennsylvania-German Society, of which he was treasurer 1891–1913, president 1913–14, and a member of the executive committee until his death. To its *Proceedings* he contributed eleven monographs and translations. He was one of the editors of the *American Journal of Photography* and in 1913 was made librarian and curator of the Grand Lodge of the Free and Accepted Masons of Pennsylvania. As the latter post gave him access to a large amount of historical material, he produced a number of books and articles on Masonry in Pennsylvania, of which the one of most general interest is *Benjamin Franklin as a Freemason* (1906). He was employed as a photographer by the *Ladies' Home Journal* and by the publishers of various illustrated books; perhaps his most beautiful work in this field was a series of studies, made in his own hothouse, of

the development of the night-blooming Cereus. His various books, which he always issued privately, were lavishly embellished with photographs, zincographic facsimiles, and pen-and-ink drawings, which he made with much skill; and he was more than generous in providing illustrations for his friends' publications. The subject to which by temperament he was most strongly attracted, and which he made peculiarly his own, was the history of the Seventh Day Baptists of Ephrata and of their predecessors, the band of millenarians, led by Johannes Kelpius [*q.v.*], who settled on the Wissahickon near Germantown in 1694. In its pursuit he made a number of trips to Europe and unearthed, there and in Pennsylvania, an astonishing quantity of books, pamphlets, papers, documents, and other relics more or less relevant to the subject. This collection he later gave to the Seventh Day Baptist Historical Society. The chief literary products of this investigation were *The German Pietists of Provincial Pennsylvania 1694–1708* (1895), *The German Sectarians of Pennsylvania 1708–1800* (2 vols., 1899), *The Music of the Ephrata Cloister* (1903), and *Justus Falckner, Mystic and Scholar* (1903). He also published various articles on certain ramifications of the subject and translations of some of his important sources. The chief merits of his historical work were his unflagging enthusiasm and his faculty for discovering materials. In spirit he was hardly an historian at all but a romantic discoverer of the past. As a scholar he was almost wholly self-trained. In form and substance his works leave much to seek, but they have done more than the writings of anyone else to awaken interest in Pennsylvania German history. Much of his influence was due to his engaging personal qualities. He was in bad health for some four months before his death, although active until the very end.

[C. F. Randolph, "Julius Friedrich Sachse, Litt. D.," *Sabbath Recorder*, Mar. 15, 1920; *Who's Who in America*, 1920–21; *Public Ledger* (Phila.), Nov. 16, 1919; H. M. M. Richards, obituary, *Proc. Pa.-German Soc.*, vol. XXXI (1925); portrait, *Ibid.*, vol. XXV (1917); letter from his daughter, Miss Emma Florence Sachse, June 27, 1932.]   G. H. G.

SACKETT, HENRY WOODWARD (Aug. 31, 1853–Dec. 9, 1929), lawyer, was born at Enfield, near Ithaca, N. Y. The son of Solon Philo Sackett, a physician, and his wife, Lovedy K. Woodward, he was descended from Simon Sackett who came from England to New England in 1631. Henry attended the Ithaca Academy and Cornell University, where he graduated in 1875. After teaching for one year, he began the study of law in New York and at the same time, for the *New York Tribune,* wrote special reports of cases in process of adjudication before the court of appeals and the state supreme court. He was admitted to the bar in 1877 and shortly thereafter became associated with Cornelius A. Runkle, whom he later succeeded as counsel for the *Tribune,* a position he continued to hold with this paper and its successor, the *New York Herald Tribune,* until his death. In 1888 he formed a law partnership with Charles Gibson Bennett, which in later years became the well-known firm of Sackett, Chapman, Brown & Cross, corporation lawyers and attorneys for estates.

In the course of his service as counsel for the *Tribune,* Sackett became a leading authority on the law of libel. During the last years of his life he was special lecturer on that subject in the School of Journalism of Columbia University. As a defender of the freedom of the press he exerted a substantial influence. In 1914 the crucial cases of *Burdick* vs. *U. S.* and *Curtin* vs. *U. S.* (*236 U. S.,* 79, 96) came, on appeal, before the United States Supreme Court. George Burdick, city editor of the *Tribune,* and W. L. Curtin, a reporter on the same newspaper, had each been fined $500 for contempt of court in refusing to divulge confidential information involving prominent persons in a smuggling case. In an effort to induce them to testify, President Wilson offered pardons to both men, but the pardons, tendered in the Grand Jury room, were rejected. Sackett delivered the closing argument before the Supreme Court, which handed down a decision in favor of his clients. He argued that the exercise of the presidential pardoning power in the present case would "tend to destroy some of the most essential safeguards of free government. It would pervert the grand jury . . . and would tend to destroy to a dangerous degree the separation of powers between the executive and the judicial branches of the government and in practical effect would arm the executive with summary powers which ought to be possessed only by the judicial branch." (*236 U. S.,* 81–82.)

In 1897 Governor Black appointed him to his staff with the rank of colonel. Thereafter he was commonly known by his military title. For thirty years he was a trustee of Cornell University. By his will he made the University his beneficiary to the extent of eleven-twelfths of his residuary estate. He had long been interested in the extraordinary scenic beauties of the Cornell campus, particularly in what he conceived to be their spiritual influence on the observer's mind. In 1927 he gave to the University $200,000 for the conservation of these natural and picturesque values and for making them comfortably acces-

sible to students and the general public. He was trustee and vice-president of the American Scenic and Historic Preservation Society, commissioner for Fire Island State Park, president of the Andrew H. Green ("father of greater New York") Memorial Association, and president of the Empire State Society of Sons of the American Revolution. He was married on Nov. 17, 1886, to Elizabeth Titus who died in 1926. They had no children.

[C. H. Weygant, *The Sacketts of America* (1907); *N. Y. Herald Tribune,* Dec. 10 and editorial, Dec. 11, 1929; *Cornellian Council Bulletin,* Jan. 1930; *Who's Who in America,* 1928–29; *N. Y. Times,* Dec. 10 and 20, 1929.]

W. A. H.

SADLIER, DENIS (1817–Feb. 4, 1885), Catholic book publisher, was born in the shadow of the Rock of Cashel in County Tipperary, Ireland. His father, James, died in Liverpool en route to America but his mother courageously continued the journey, arriving in New York with her family in January 1830. For two years Denis and his brother James attended St. Peter's School in Barclay Street. They then entered the book-binding shop of Arthur & Company, and in 1836 established a similar concern of their own in Carmine Street under the name of D. & J. Sadlier & Company. They soon entered the publishing field, bringing out in 1837 an edition of Alban Butler's *Lives of the Saints* and in 1838 a quarto Bible. As the business grew rapidly, they continually moved to larger quarters until finally, in 1860, they located in Barclay Street, with a branch in Montreal. As job printers, contrivers of designs for churches, publishers of Bibles, prayer books, school texts, and a Household Library of 164 titles, and as compilers of the official, annual *Sadlier's Catholic Directory* (1864–96), the firm of Sadlier became a national Catholic institution. It also published from June 1857 to December 1881 the *New York Tablet,* which attracted numerous writers of distinction. In 1869, on the death of James, who had supervised the publication department, Denis carried on the business alone. He passed through the panic of 1873 unscathed, but in 1879, under the pressure of financial troubles, he assigned all properties, including the dower of his wife, Julia Browne, whom he had married in 1841, as a pledge to his creditors; by 1884, however, the business was readjusted and continued for several years.

In 1850 Sadlier established a residence in the anti-Catholic neighborhood of Harlem, where he became popular enough to be chosen a public school trustee, then a most unusual honor for a Catholic citizen. A passionate, intense man of marked business integrity and of liberal charities, a stout Democrat with no ambition for political office, a trustee of Manhattan College, and a self-trained reader of good books, he won recognition in both the business and the social life of New York. In 1864 he moved to Wilton, Westchester County, where he died. At the obsequies in St. Patrick's Cathedral, Monsignor Quinn declared that it was Sadlier's "chief object in life to preserve the Catholics of America from the temptation to peruse such [bad] literature by giving them attractive Catholic books," and added, "There is hardly a Catholic book which does not bear the well-known imprint of the name which has become a household word throughout the length and breadth of the English speaking Catholic world."

[*Sadlier's Cath. Directory,* 1886; *N. Y. Freeman's Jour.,* Sept. 15, 1877, Feb. 14, 1885; the *Sun* (N. Y.), Feb. 5, 6, 1885; information as to certain facts from Anna T. Sadlier (1854-1932) of Ottawa, Canada.]

R. J. P.

SADLIER, MARY ANNE MADDEN (Dec. 31, 1820–Apr. 5, 1903), author, was born at Cootehill, County Cavan, Ireland. After the death of her father, Francis Madden, a prosperous merchant, she emigrated, in 1844, to Montreal. Here, in November 1846, she married James Sadlier, manager of the local branch of the New York publishing house of D. & J. Sadlier, by whom she had six children. In 1860 she removed to New York, where her husband died in 1869.

A voluminous writer of short stories, essays, and translations for *La Belle Assemblée* (London), the *New York Tablet,* the *New York Freeman's Journal,* the *Boston Pilot,* D'Arcy McGee's *The American Celt,* and *The Literary Garland,* she became a favorite among Catholic readers. In all, she wrote about sixty novels dealing with Irish historical episodes and with the social, religious, and educational problems of the Irish in America. To the latter she strongly recommended pride of background, reconciliation with the customs of the New World, Americanization without secularization, and compromise between the old folks and their American-born children. Thus she performed a real service beyond mere entertainment, and as social studies some of her books retain a pronounced value.

Among her best-known works were *The Blakes and the Flanagans* (1855, 1858), translated into German by J. P. Bachem as *Alt-Irland und Amerika* (1857), dealing with the school question; *Willie Burke* (c. 1856); *The Fate of Father Sheehy* (1863), a story of Tipperary; *Con O'Regan* (1864, 1885), a tale of emigrant life in America; *Aunt Honor's Keepsake* (1866), which stressed the need of saving the Irish orphans for

the old faith; *Bessy Conway* (c. 1865), based on the problems of Irish immigrant girls; *Eleanor Preston* (c. 1865); *Alice Riordan* (1851); *Confessions of an Apostate* (1868); *Maureen Dhu* (1870), a picturesque story of the Claddagh in Galway; *New Lights; or, Life in Galway* (1855, 1885); *MacCarthy More* (1868, 1885); *The Red Hand of Ulster* (1850), a stirring tale of the rising of the Northern Earls against Elizabeth; *The Confederate Chieftains* (1860, 1895), a story of the rebellion of 1641, which went through several editions; *Purgatory: Doctrinal, Historical and Poetical* (1886), a compilation dedicated to her son, Francis Xavier, who died a Jesuit in 1885; *Catechism of Sacred History and Doctrine* (1864), in which she collaborated with Mother Angela [*q.v.*]; and *Stories of the Promises* (1895), in collaboration with her daughter Anna Teresa Sadlier (1854-1932), an author of numerous short stories and books. She edited the *Poems of D'Arcy McGee* in 1869, and in 1885 she published *Life of the Blessed Virgin, Mother of God,* translated from the French of Matthieu Orsini, in a volume which also contained her translation of Francis de Ligny's life of Jesus Christ. In 1895 she was awarded the Laetare Medal by Notre Dame University as an outstanding lay contributor to the general work of the Church, and in 1902 she received a special blessing from Pope Leo XIII in recognition of her illustrious services for the Catholic Church. The closing years of her life she lived in Montreal with her children.

[*Catholic Encyc.,* XIII, 323; *The Messenger,* May 1903; *Gazette* (Montreal), Apr. 6, 1903; W. S. Wallace, *Dict. of Canadian Biog.* (1926); *A Round Table of Representative Am. Catholic Novelists* (1897); list of pubs. under Sadlier's advertisements in *Sadlier's Cath. Directory,* 1865 ff., from which approximate dates of publication can be determined; especially, information from the late Miss Anna T. Sadlier of Ottawa, Canada.]

R. J. P.

SADTLER, JOHN PHILIP BENJAMIN (Dec. 25, 1823–Apr. 28, 1901), Lutheran clergyman, college president, was born in Baltimore, the son of Philip Benjamin and Catharine Sadtler. His father, a German by birth, was a goldsmith and an amateur of optics. Sadtler graduated from Pennsylvania College (later Gettysburg College) in 1842, stayed on at Gettysburg as a student in the theological seminary under Samuel Simon Schmucker [*q.v.*], and was licensed by the Maryland Synod in 1844. By his marriage Oct. 9, 1845, to Schmucker's daughter, Caroline Elizabeth, he became a member of one of the most influential of Lutheran ministerial families. He was pastor of churches in and near Pine Grove, Schuylkill County, Pa., 1845–49; at

Shippensburg, 1849–53; of St. Peter's, Middletown, 1853–56; and of St. John's, Easton, where he succeeded Charles Frederick Schaeffer [q.v.], 1856–62. In the latter year, seeking a somewhat milder climate for the sake of his wife's health, he accepted the principalship of a girls' school at Lutherville, Md., a suburb of Baltimore. The school and the village where it was located owed their existence to the enterprise of John Gottlieb Morris [q.v.]. Sadtler was a good teacher and administrator, and by conducting Lutherville Seminary prosperously through the Civil War years and the hard times that followed he gained the reputation of a financial wizard. He declined the presidency of Pennsylvania College, of which he was a trustee 1862–77, but was induced a few years later to succeed Frederick Augustus Muhlenberg [q.v.] as the second president of Muhlenberg College at Allentown, Pa. He took charge Jan. 1, 1877, and with his formal inauguration later in the year the college became the property of the Lutheran Ministerium of Pennsylvania. Its future was still dim. The students, drawn mostly from humble Pennsylvania-German homes, were not always the most likely candidates for a higher education; the teachers were some of them men of genuine ability, but they were hampered by insufficient books and apparatus, long hours, and the necessity of giving instruction in two or more departments; the institution was heavily in debt and had little ready money. Sadtler, however, was devoted to the college and was confident of its growth, and he was the kind of man who inspires the devotion and confidence of others. During his administration the debt was reduced, endowment funds were received, students increased slightly in number, and the work of the college improved measurably. In 1885 he was crippled permanently by a fall on the ice, and, fearing that he could no longer fulfill all the duties of his position, he retired at the end of the year. Theodore Lorenzo Seip [q.v.] was his successor. For the rest of his life Sadtler made his home in Baltimore. He contributed articles to the *Evangelical Review* and the *Workman*, was president of the Society for the History of the Germans in Maryland, and was as active as his health would permit in the work of the church. He died while on a visit to Atlantic City. He was survived by his wife, two daughters, and seven sons (the *Sun, post*), one of them Samuel Philip Sadtler [q.v.], the chemist.

[Biog. sketch by G. T. Ettinger in S. E. Ochsenford, *Muhlenberg Coll.* (1892); the *Sun* (Baltimore), Apr. 29, May 2, 1901; obituary in *Fifteenth Ann. Report of the Soc. for the Hist. of the Germans in Md.*, 1900–01; A. R. Wentz, *Hist. of the Gettysburg Theol. Sem.* (1926).]
           G. H. G.

SADTLER, SAMUEL PHILIP (July 18, 1847–Dec. 20, 1923), teacher, chemist, author, was born in Pinegrove, Schuylkill County, Pa., the son of J. P. Benjamin Sadtler [q.v.] and Caroline Elizabeth (Schmucker). Both his father and his maternal grandfather, Samuel Simon Schmucker [q.v.], were Lutheran ministers. His early education was obtained at Easton, Pa., and he graduated from the Easton High School in 1862. The same year he entered Pennsylvania (now Gettysburg) College, Gettysburg, where he was graduated in 1867, his course having been interrupted in 1863 by the battle of Gettysburg. During his senior year his attention was turned from classical studies toward the study of science, which he determined to choose for his life work. In the fall of 1867, therefore, he went to the newly established Lehigh University, where for a year he studied chemistry, physics, and mineralogy, and in the fall of 1868 he became a student at Harvard, pursuing advanced work under Wolcott Gibbs [q.v.], one of the most distinguished chemists in America. In January 1870 he received the degree of S.B. from Harvard and a month later sailed for Germany to complete his chemical education.

After spending one year at the University of Göttingen he was granted the degree of Ph.D. and returned to America to accept the professorship of chemistry and physics at Pennsylvania College, which he held from 1871 to 1874. In the latter year he was called to the professorship of general and organic chemistry in the University of Pennsylvania, and in 1878 became professor of chemistry at the Philadelphia College of Pharmacy. These chairs he held concurrently until 1891, when he relinquished that at the University of Pennsylvania to open an office as consulting chemical expert. He continued as professor at the College of Pharmacy, however, until 1916, when he was made professor emeritus. Associated with him in his consulting office, which he maintained until his death, was his son, Samuel S. Sadtler. As expert he prepared chemical testimony in at least fifty cases of important patent litigation.

In 1877 Sadtler published *Chemical Experimentation: Being a Hand-Book of Lecture Experiments in Inorganic Chemistry . . . for the Use of Lecturers and Teachers*. For many years, from 1883 until his death, he was chemical editor of *The Dispensatory of the United States*. In 1891 he published the first edition of his *Hand-Book of Industrial Organic Chemistry*, which went through several editions and was translated into German and Russian. In 1892, with Prof. Henry Trimble, he brought out the first edition of *A Text-Book of Chemistry Intended for . . . Pharmaceutical and Medical Students* (parts I and II), better known in the enlarged edition of 1895. The third edition (1900) appeared under the names of Sadtler and Dr. Virgil Coblentz, and the sixth edition (1927) was entitled, *Pharmaceutical and Medical Chemistry*. Sadtler was an active member of the Committee on Revision of the *United States Pharmacopœia*. He contributed many articles to chemical journals and delivered many addresses on chemical and other technical subjects. He was a founder and the first president (1908–09) of the American Institute of Chemical Engineers and was a member of the American Philosophical Society, the American Association for the Advancement of Science, the Franklin Institute, and many other professional and scientific bodies. An active layman in the Lutheran Church, he was president of the General Council Board of Publication in 1906, and from 1919 to his death was president of the Board of Publication of the United Lutheran Church. He married Mary Julia Bridges of Baltimore on Dec. 17, 1872, and was the father of two sons and two daughters.

[*The Alumni Record of Gettysburg Coll.* (1932); *The First Century of the Phila. Coll. of Pharmacy* (1922); *Who's Who in America,* 1922–23; *Am. Jour. Pharmacy,* July 1916; *Industrial and Engineering Chemistry,* Feb. 1924; *Lutheran,* Dec. 27, Jan. 3, 1924; *Pub. Ledger* (Phila.), Dec. 21, 1923; information from family.]

A. R.

SAENDERL, SIMON (Sept. 30, 1800–Feb. 22, 1879), Catholic priest and missionary, first superior of the Redemptorists in the United States, was a native of Malgerzdorf, Lower Bavaria. He was ordained in 1825 and entered in 1829 the order of the Redemptorists. In the latter year the Rev. Frederick Rese [*q.v.*], then vicar general at Cincinnati, visited Vienna and persuaded the Redemptorists to send missionaries supported by the Leopoldine Foundation to his diocese. Father Saenderl, as superior, with two other priests and three lay brothers left Vienna in 1832 and arrived at Cincinnati on July 17. In the autumn of 1832 he was sent to Green Bay, Wis., where he dedicated a church on Nov. 1 and for a year ministered to the French inhabitants and to the Menominee Indians, with whom he had considerable success. The plan had been to establish a Redemptorist center at Green Bay but, finding economic conditions unfavorable, the Redemptorists left there, Saenderl going as missionary to the Ottawa Indians at Arbre Croche, Mich., where he studied Indian languages and worked on a dictionary. He officiated at this mission from 1833 to 1835, and again

from 1836 to 1839. In the interim, with the new superior, Joseph Prost, he again visited Green Bay, walking for nine miles over the ice in order to reach there. His desire for a community life led him to leave Arbre Croche; his superior, however, sent him in 1841 to Rochester, N. Y., to minister to the German Catholics, and after two years there he was at Pittsburgh for a few months. After 1843 he became involved in strife with his superiors concerning a murderer, whom he attended to the scaffold (*United States Catholic Magazine,* March 1844, pp. 195–98). He finally left for Toronto, where he had a small mission, and later ministered at Monroe, Mich., and several neighboring towns. Becoming involved in new controversies, however, he was in 1848 suspended from the order. In 1852, after visits to the Holy Land and Austria, he joined the Trappist order, professed on Easter, 1853, and was made master of German novices. After joining the Trappists he shut himself from the world in their convent at Gethsemane, Ky., where he passed his remaining years. He was a quiet, simple man, and, though inclined to controversy, was of a saintly personal character, and devoted to his mission work. On coming to America he was too inexperienced for his responsibilities in establishing the order in a new country but is important for his position as the first superior.

[Rev. J. F. Byrne, "The Redemptorists in America," in *Records Am. Cath. Hist. Soc.,* June 1930–Mar. 1932; Rev. Theodore Roemer, "The Leopoldine Foundation and the Church in the U. S. (1829–1839)," in *U. S. Cath. Hist. Soc. Monograph Series,* vol. XIII (1933); A. I. Rezek, *Hist. of the Diocese of S. Ste. Marie and Marquette* (2 vols., 1906–07); *Berichte der Leopoldine Stiftung* (50 annual issues, 1831–80), of which an English translation, not yet published, is being made by Father P. L. Johnson, St. Francis. Wis.]

L. P. K.

SAFFORD, JAMES MERRILL (Aug. 13, 1822–July 3, 1907), geologist and educator, the son of Henry and Patience (Van Horne) Safford, was born in Zanesville, Ohio. His immediate ancestors were from New England, descendants of Thomas Safford who emigrated from England to America in 1630 and in 1641 settled at Ipswich, Mass. James passed his youth and received his early training in Zanesville. He was graduated from the Ohio University at Athens, receiving the degree of A.B. in 1844, and then took a special course at Yale. While here, in 1847, he was called to the professorship of chemistry and the natural sciences at Cumberland University, Lebanon, Tenn., where he remained until 1872. He then became professor of chemistry in the medical school of the University of Nashville, retaining this professorship when, two years later, the school was combined with the medical department of Vanderbilt University. In 1875 he was also chosen professor of geology and natural history at Vanderbilt, a position he continued to hold until he retired as professor emeritus in 1900. His teaching is said to have been characterized by simplicity, clearness, and thoroughness. He was eminently practical and avoided all unessential technicalities and doubtful hypotheses. The students all liked him.

In 1854 he was made state geologist of Tennessee, serving in that capacity by successive reappointments until 1860, when the office was abolished. Under an act of 1871 he was again appointed and served until 1900. As a geologist he was eminently successful, particularly when the time and the conditions are considered. There were no good maps; much of the state was still a wilderness; travel was by foot or on horseback over none too good dirt roads. In 1856 he published his first report, *A Geological Reconnoissance of the State of Tennessee,* following it in 1869 with his *Geology of Tennessee,* a volume of 550 pages with a geological map and seven plates. In securing the data for this book, he is said to have had no instruments except a compass and a pocket level; over much of the area surveyed he was obliged to travel on foot, covering some 11,000 miles in this manner: yet "for compactness and clearness, this work is not excelled, perhaps not equalled, by any other official report published in this country" (Stevenson, *post,* p. 524). The enterprise was carried on, also, under financial conditions that would have been ridiculous had they not been pitiful. By the act of 1854 his salary was fixed at $1,500 a year, payable quarterly with no allowance for expenses or assistance. The act of 1871, under which he was appointed for his second period of service as state geologist, stipulated that that official should receive $300 a year, but for a part of the time the legislature failed to make the necessary appropriation. In 1874 Safford was coeditor with J. B. Killebrew of an *Introduction to the Resources of Tennessee,* and in 1884 he contributed to the *Reports of the Tenth Census* (vol. V) a discussion of the physical geography and agricultural features of the state.

He is described as "a man among men, everywhere commanding respect by his common sense, his integrity, and his manly recognition of others" (*Stevenson,* p. 524). That he was not more widely known among his collaborators was due to his geographic isolation and inability to attend the society meetings of his fellow workers. Further than this, he shrank from public speaking and debates and disliked controversy. He preferred putting his views on paper and letting

them be taken at their face value. He was married in 1859 to Catherine K. (Howard) Owen, and passed his later days with a daughter in Dallas, Tex., where he died.

[S. M. Culbertson, *The Ohio Valley Saffords* (1932); E. S. Safford, "The Saffords in America, June 1923" (MS. in Lib. of Cong.); J. J. Stevenson, in *Bull. Geol. Soc. of America,* Jan. 30, 1909; J. T. McGill in *Trans. Tenn. Acad. Sci.,* vol. II (1917); *Who's Who in America,* 1906–07; *Nashville Banner,* July 4, 1907.]

G. P. M.

SAFFORD, TRUMAN HENRY (Jan. 6, 1836–June 13, 1901), astronomer, mathematician, and teacher, eldest of eight children of Truman Hopson and Louisa (Parker) Safford, was born at Royalton, Vt. He was descended from Thomas Safford who became a freeman of the Massachusetts Bay Colony in 1630; his great-grandfather, John Safford, born at Preston, Conn., in 1729, was among the original grantees of Royalton (1781); his grandfather, Nathan, is said to have carried the town's assessment list in his head. Both parents were well qualified to direct his development. His father, a farmer, took a lively interest in public affairs while his mother before marriage had been a teacher. Delicate health prevented his regular attendance at school, but his father's library offered opportunities to his liking. At two years he knew his letters and at six he showed extraordinary skill and speed in lengthy mental and written computations. Stimulated by a visit to Dartmouth College, he computed an almanac for 1846 for Bradford, Vt., and for 1847 he computed almanacs for Bradford, Cincinnati, Philadelphia, and Boston. At this period skeptics subjected him to severe mental tests: one examination lasting three hours was discontinued only when, after multiplying mentally 365,365,365,365,365,365 by itself in about one minute, he confessed that he was tired. How his results were obtained he never completely disclosed, but his processes showed gain by practice and loss by neglect. Though urged to do so, his parents always refused to employ his talents for their own financial profit.

In 1847 President Everett and Professor Benjamin Peirce [*q.v.*] of Harvard became interested in him, and the family moved to Cambridge, Mass., where after fitting for college he graduated from Harvard with honor in 1854. For twelve years thereafter he was a member of the staff of Harvard Observatory and after the death of Professor George P. Bond [*q.v.*] was acting director for about a year. Volumes IV and V of the *Annals* were completed and published under his supervision. In 1866 he became professor of astronomy at the old University of

Chicago and director of the Dearborn Observatory, but the Chicago fire of 1871 put an end to public support of this observatory and for the five years following he was occupied with astronomical work connected with United States geographical surveys.

In 1876 he became Field Memorial Professor of Astronomy at Williams College, and this position he held until his death. He took part at various times in teaching physics and mathematics and also acted as librarian. With the Repsold circle of the Field Memorial Observatory, established in 1882, he made the observations for *The Williams College Catalogue of North Polar Stars* (1888). His astronomical interests lay mainly in the fields of the older astronomy and his many papers on orbits, ephemerides, positions of stars, proper motions, methods of reduction, instrumental and personal corrections to observations, the proper motion of Sirius before and after discovery of its companion, etc., appeared in the *Astronomical Journal,* the *Sidereal Messenger,* the *Proceedings of the American Academy of Arts and Sciences,* and other scientific journals of the United States, England, and Germany. He also published *Mathematical Teaching and Its Modern Methods* (1887), *The Development of Astronomy in the United States* (1888), an address at the fiftieth anniversary of the observatory at Williams College; and a paper on "The Psychology of the Personal Equation" (*Science,* Nov. 26, 1897).

He married at Cambridge, Mass., Mar. 8, 1860, Elizabeth Marshall Bradbury, and to them were born six children. Five of these, with their mother, survived him. He suffered a paralytic stroke some years before his death, which occurred at the home of a son in Newark, N. J.

[E. M. W. Lovejoy, *Hist. of Royalton, Vt.* (1911); M. D. Gilman, *The Bibliog. of Vt.* (1897); *Williams Alumni Rev.,* June 1926; *Littell's Living Age,* Jan. 8, 1848; *Ladies' Repository,* Apr. 1849; *Science,* July 5, 1901; *Observatory,* Aug. 1901; *Mo. Notices of the Royal Astron. Soc.,* vol. LXII (1902); *Proc. Am. Acad. Arts and Sci.,* vol. XXXVII (1902); S. I. Bailey, *The Hist. and Work of Harvard Observatory* (1931); *N. Y. Times,* June 14, 1901.]   J. M. P—r.

SAFFORD, WILLIAM EDWIN (Dec. 14, 1859–Jan. 10, 1926), botanist, ethnologist, and philologist, was descended from Thomas Safford, who emigrated from England in 1630, and was in Ipswich, Mass., by 1641. Later ancestors lived in Vermont, but his grandfather, Eliel Todd Safford, married Ann Tyler Harrison, of Prince William County, Va., and died at Parkersburg, Va. (now W. Va.), in 1840. The latter's son, William Harrison Safford (Feb. 19, 1821–Apr. 20, 1903), born in Parkersburg, married Anna Marie Pocahontas Creel, daughter of Dr. David Creel of Wood County, Va. (now W. Va.), and moved to Ohio in 1848, settling in Chillicothe. He was a distinguished jurist and the author of *The Blennerhasset Papers* (1861). William Edwin Safford, born in Chillicothe, was the fifth of ten children. From his home surroundings, and notably through the influence of his mother, Safford grew up with a strong interest in natural history, and from his association with German children in school early acquired an idiomatic knowledge of that language which led later to his special linguistic studies. His enthusiasm for the natural sciences was further fired by the requirement of reading aloud, as a youth of sixteen, the writings of Darwin and Huxley to his vigorous-minded grandfather Creel, who died at the age of ninety-two.

In 1876 Safford entered the United States Naval Academy, and on completing the four-year course was assigned in the autumn of 1880 to the *Powhatan.* A cruise to Panama next spring afforded him a first view of the tropics. On the return voyage he chanced to meet Alexander Agassiz at Key West, and, adopting willingly enough that famous scientist's advice, resolved to fit himself for scientific collecting on future cruises. He was later detailed to post-graduate studies in botany and zoölogy at Yale (1883–85) and in marine zoölogy at Harvard (1885). There followed a voyage around Cape Horn and a long cruise in the southern Pacific, during which Safford's botanical and ethnological bent found full play, and then a detail of two years as instructor in modern languages at the Naval Academy. In 1890 he was detached from duty and appointed commissioner to Peru and Bolivia (1891–92) for the World's Columbian Exposition, his researches in South America centering in ethnology. He returned to the navy in 1893 and saw service in the Spanish-American War, after which there followed immediately a colorful year as vice-governor of newly acquired Guam. He resigned from the navy in August 1902, when ranking as lieutenant, to accept appointment as assistant botanist in the United States Department of Agriculture, and was promoted in 1915 to economic botanist, a position which he held up to the time of his death. From George Washington University he received the degree Ph.D. in 1920. He was married, Sept. 14, 1904, to Clare, daughter of Chief Justice Decius S. Wade, of Montana, and was survived by his wife, a son, and a daughter.

Safford's life in the navy, though uncongenial in some ways, gave him an exceptional opportunity of observing man and nature in strange places. An omnivorous student of the history of exploration, he gained a first-hand knowledge of South Sea peoples that was matched by his knowledge of ancient American cultures. The period from 1902 onward, when for the first time he was really free to write, proved one of great productiveness. His remarkable breadth of interest is well shown in a series of articles published in the *Plant World* (Sept. 1902–Dec. 1904), brought together in book form under the title, *A Year on the Island of Guam* (1904, later republished); in *The Chamorro Language of Guam* (n.d., preface 1909), reprinted from the *American Anthropologist* (1903–05); and especially in a volume entitled, *The Useful Plants of the Island of Guam* (*Contributions from the United States National Herbarium,* vol. IX, 1905), which is classic. The last is virtually a handbook of the island, but its usefulness is by no means restricted to Guam, since it contains detailed information regarding many widely distributed plants and plant products of the Pacific region. It at once established Safford's reputation as an ethnobotanist. There now followed at frequent intervals many important ethnobotanical papers, of which only a few may be mentioned: "An Aztec Narcotic, *Lophophora Williamsii*" (*Journal of Heredity,* vol. VI, 1915, pp. 291–311); "*Lignum Nephriticum*" (*Annual Report of the Smithsonian Institution . . . 1915*); "Food Plants and Textiles of Ancient America" (*Proceedings of the Second Pan-American Scientific Congress,* 1917, vol. I); "Narcotic Plants and Stimulants of the Ancient Americans" (*Annual Report . . . of the Smithsonian Institution . . . 1916*); "Daturas of the Old World and New" (*Ibid., 1920*); "Foods Discovered with America" (*Scientific Monthly,* Aug. 1925), "Peyote, the Narcotic Mescal Button of the Indians" (*Journal of the American Medical Association,* Oct. 15, 1921); and "The Potato of Romance and of Reality" (*Journal of Heredity,* 1925, vol. XVI). It was Safford's special facility with Nahuatl and other ancient American tongues and with Polynesian dialects which contributed so largely to the value of this work.

At the same time Safford was publishing systematic papers on certain groups of tropical American plants, for example, the genus *Dahlia,* the cactus family, the bull-horn acacias and their ant inhabitants, and an important long series upon the family *Annonaceae,* besides dictionary work, notes of exploration and travel, biographical sketches, and numerous botanical articles for Bailey's *Standard Cyclopedia of Horticulture* (6 vols., 1914–17). The taxonomic papers are noteworthy, especially those upon *Annonaceae,* but in Safford's complete bibliography of about

100 titles it is those subjects of ethnobotanical scope in which his genius found full expression. To the art of masterly exposition he brought a wealth of observed fact and of deep and varied erudition derived from almost innumerable historical sources. The complicated story of the potato was his last published paper. On Mar. 17, 1924, he was stricken with paralysis, but partially recovered and continued at work almost to the day of his death, which resulted from pneumonia with attendant heart complications.

Safford was intensely dynamic, with a genius for friendship, "one who loved nature profoundly but humanity not less" (Smith, *post*). He was witty and jovial, keenly inquisitive of all things, trained to acute perception that amounted almost to intuition, and extremely fluent in self-expression. Of his generation there were few better deserving of that old term of distinction—naturalist.

[W. C. Barnes, "William E. Safford," in *Science,* new ser., vol. LXIII, Apr. *23,* 1926; D. C. Peattie, "Dr. William Safford," in *Am. Botanist,* vol. XXXII, Apr. 1926; T. H. Kearney, "William Edwin Safford," and E. F. Smith, "William Edwin Safford, the Man," *Jour. of Heredity,* vol. XVII, Oct. 1926; *The Official Record, U. S. Dept. of Agriculture,* vol. V, no. 3, p. 4, Jan. 20, 1926; editorial in *Evening Star* (Washington), Jan. 11, 1926; *Who's Who in America,* 1926–27; S. M. Culbertson, *The Ohio Valley Saffords* (1932); E. S. Safford, compiler, "The Saffords in America, June 1923" (typed MS., Lib. Cong.); records of Navy Dept.; personal recollections and family sources.]
W. R. M.

SAGE, BERNARD JANIN (Feb. 5, 1821–Sept. 2, 1902), lawyer, author, was born near New Haven, Conn., of New England parentage. Through his mother, *née* Lewis, he was connected with the Louisiana family which furnished Gov. Francis T. Nicholls [*q.v.*] to the latter state. Despite an early ambition to become a sailor, Bernard accepted a school training and studied law. In early manhood he entered the law office of Thomas H. Lewis in New Orleans, and in time became the owner of a sugar plantation. His marriage was said to have been prevented by the death of his fiancée and he remained a bachelor. He loved music, was somewhat pedantic, and was given to puns. He received praise for financial encouragement to young men seeking an education.

Sage was a Whig in ante-bellum politics and in 1860 supported the Bell-Everett ticket, but after the outbreak of the Civil War he served the Confederacy. He was a master in the Confederate navy, with special duties of an executive or secret nature, and was sent abroad by President Davis on special missions. After the fall of the Confederacy, he made a documentary and interpretative study in Europe of the treaty of

1783 recognizing the independence of the United States. This study, supporting the state-rights view of the origin of the Union, he expected to use in his capacity of counsel for the defense in the projected trial of Jefferson Davis. The results of the study were published in book form under the pseudonym "P. C. Centz, Barrister," the name being an adaptation, with initials, of "Plain Common Sense." The first edition appeared in London in 1865 under the title *Davis and Lee,* and the book was subsequently issued in America with the title changed to *The Republic of Republics* (4th ed., 1881). Upon its first appearance, it was referred to in the Southern press as a brilliant work by a British lawyer. It presented the argument that Davis and Lee, who were taught the doctrine of state rights at West Point, could not be considered traitors for being loyal to their respective states in the war. Sage maintained that primary allegiance was to the state, that the Union and the Constitution were formed of and by the states, and that secession, as well as the subsequent conquest of the South by the North, was a legitimate act or step under international law involving no violation of national law. Thus Davis could be defended, against any charge of treason, on the grounds of history and international law without an implication of protest as to the outcome of the war.

For a few years after the war Sage was a resident of Washington, D. C., but he spent the last thirteen years of his life in New Orleans. In 1890 he contributed the chapter on Louisiana to *Why the Solid South*, edited by Hilary A. Herbert. As the result of financial reverses he lost his plantation and became dependent, in his last days, upon the kindness of friends. He died of apoplexy in New Orleans and was buried in the Nicholls cemetery lot at Thibodaux, La.

[*Daily Picayune* (New Orleans), Sept. 3, 1902; *Times-Democrat* (New Orleans), Sept. 3, 1902; A. B. Booth, *Records of La. Confed. Soldiers and La. Confed. Commands* (1920), vol. III, bk. 2, p. 432; *The Republic of Republics* (4th ed., 1881); information from Frank Nicholls, Thibodaux, La.]　　H. C. N.

SAGE, HENRY WILLIAMS (Jan. 31, 1814–Sept. 18, 1897), merchant, lumber manufacturer, and philanthropist, was born in Middletown, Conn., a descendant of David Sage who emigrated from Wales, and settled in Middletown about 1652. Henry's father was Charles Sage, who was shipwrecked on the Florida coast in 1838 and killed by Indians; his mother, Sally (Williams) Sage. Most of his youth was spent in Bristol, Conn., until 1827, when the family moved to Ithaca, N. Y. This removal thwarted his early ambition to enter Yale College. He still cherished the hope of a professional career,

however, and for a time studied medicine with Dr. Austin Church of Ithaca; but circumstances conspired to make him a business man. Ill health interrupted his medical studies, and in 1832 he found it expedient to enter the employ of his uncles, who, under the firm name of Williams & Brothers, were merchants and owners of transportation lines over the waterways of central New York. He revealed abilities of a high order, and in five years became proprietor of the business. Soon he was one of the substantial and influential men of the region and in 1847 was elected on the Whig ticket to the legislature.

Appreciating the demand for lumber that the rapid development of the country would create, he undertook to supply it on an extensive scale. Buying in 1854 a large tract of timber land around Lake Simcoe, Canada, he manufactured it there, and soon after, with John McGraw, began to draw upon the Michigan forests, his manufacturing establishment being at Winona. In 1857 he moved to Brooklyn, where he was intimately associated with Henry Ward Beecher in the affairs of Plymouth Church. Returning to Ithaca in 1880, he made that city his home until his death seventeen years later.

Sturdy in frame, with a full beard, clean-shaven upper lip, firm mouth, and shrewd eyes, Sage was in appearance the typical successful business man of the Victorian era. Deprived of a college education, he found time for private study, and was especially interested in religion, psychology, and philosophy. The furtherance of education became, moreover, in his later years, one of his chief concerns, and, since he was a friend of Ezra Cornell [*q.v.*], Cornell University was the principal object of his thought and benefactions. In 1870 he was elected to the board of trustees and in 1875 succeeded Cornell as chairman, serving until his death. In 1870 he offered to erect a college for women, and although there was opposition to making the university a coeducational institution, his offer was accepted and Sage College, a woman's dormitory, with lecture rooms and other equipment, was opened in 1874. He exerted his influence against the sale of the national lands held by the college, at a time when the trustees were sorely tempted to dispose of them, thereby "saving the future of the university . . . and making it possible for it to become one of the representative universities of the land" (Hewitt, *post,* p. 430). He furnished the funds for the erection of a chapel, dedicated in June 1875, established the Sage School of Philosophy at a cost of more than a quarter of a million of dollars, gave $560,000 to the library and its endowment, made a substantial gift to the museum of archeology, and otherwise contributed to the financial needs of the institution. No less valuable was the business sagacity which he exercised in the administrative work of the university during more than twenty-five years of its early history. His benefactions were not confined wholly to Cornell, but schools, libraries, and churches, in various parts of the country, were aided by him. In 1871 he founded the Lyman Beecher Lectures on Preaching at the Yale Divinity School. His wife was Susan Elizabeth (Linn) Sage, who died in 1885. Both are buried in the apse of Sage Chapel at Cornell.

[*Geneal. Record of the Descendants of David Sage* (1878); W. T. Hewitt, *Cornell Univ., a Hist.* (1905); *Memorial Exercises in Honor of Henry Williams Sage* (1898); *Cornell Era,* Sept. 25, 1897; *Albany Jour.,* Sept. 18, 1897; *Brooklyn Eagle* and *N. Y. Tribune,* Sept. 19, 1897.]   H. E. S.

SAGE, MARGARET OLIVIA SLOCUM (Sept. 8, 1828–Nov. 4, 1918), philanthropist, was born in Syracuse, N. Y., the daughter of Joseph and Margaret Pierson (Jermain) Slocum. She was the descendant of Anthony Slocombe or Slocum, an English Quaker who emigrated to Massachusetts before 1637. Her father was a well-to-do merchant, a state assemblyman, and agent of the government to introduce American agricultural implements and methods into Russia. After studying in local schools until she was eighteen, she attended Mrs. Emma Willard's school, the Troy Female Seminary, now Russell Sage College, from which she graduated in 1847. Later, because of the financial reverses of her father, she taught at Chestnut Street Seminary, later Ogontz School, of Philadelphia for two years and thereafter from time to time as her health permitted. She spent her vacations at the Jermain estate near Troy, where she was especially welcome for her enlivening social qualities. In 1869 she became the second wife of Russell Sage [*q.v.*], who laid the foundation for his financial success in Watervliet and Troy. They had no children. During her married life she was a devoted wife; she lived the conventional existence of a well-to-do church member. In the *North American Review* of November 1905 she published an article "Opportunities and Responsibilities of Leisured Women," which reflects many of her religious and social ideas. She grasped many contemporary ideas: she believed in woman's suffrage, in practical education such as manual training schools for the children of wage-earners, in specialization in education for the self-supporting woman. She identified herself with every community in which she lived, and, especially after the inheritance of her husband's fortune made it possible, she gave liberally and discriminatingly to each of those communities. She died in New York City.

Upon her husband's death in 1906 she inherited by his will practically the whole of his fortune, something more than $63,000,000, and at once she began to distribute this money. The wide range of the objects of her charity is indicative of the character and variety of her interests. She was especially interested in the Woman's Hospital of New York, in the New York Exchange for Woman's Work, and in home and foreign missions. She gave the money to found the Russell Sage Institute of Pathology in connection with the city hospital of New York on Blackwell's Island, as well as to support the American Seamen's Friend Society, Home for the Friendless, Mount Sinai Hospital, and various relief, social, and educational agencies. She made substantial donations to the Y. W. C. A., to naval and railway Y. M. C. A. building projects, and to the international Y. M. C. A. She also bought 70,000 acres on Marsh Island in Louisiana for a bird refuge and made large bequests to the Botanical and Zoölogical Gardens, the American Natural History Museum, and the Metropolitan Museum. The enumeration in her will of eighteen colleges, the Northfield Seminary, the Northfield Training School, Tuskeegee Normal and Industrial Institute, the Idaho Industrial Institute, bespeak her interest in education. She made an initial gift of $250,000.00 to Emma Willard School for practical arts, which was supplemented until it totalled $1,000,000 and resulted in the founding of Russell Sage College in 1918.

Perhaps her greatest distinction was her gift of $10,000,000 to the Russell Sage Foundation for the improvement of social and living conditions in the United States. Established in April 1907, it was empowered by a liberal charter to use any means that should seem expedient to its members or trustees. Although Robert De Forest, her attorney and the president of the Charity Organization Society of New York City, advised her wisely in regard to this endowment, nevertheless it must be remembered that she was a woman of vigorous opinion and always acted from firm conviction. Desirous of helping the unfortunate, she was convinced that the wisest aid was to provide for the less fortunate a good environment, protect them from the unscrupulous, and give them opportunity for self-support and individual responsibility. The Sage Foundation, at that time heralded as the largest single gift to philanthropy in the history of the world, received a third of all her gifts and bequests.

[*Emma Willard and Her Pupils* (copr. 1898) ; C. E. Slocum, *Hist. of the Slocums,* vol. II (1908) ; Henry Whittemore, *Hist. of the Sage and Slocum Families* (1908) ; *Survey,* Nov. 9, 23, 1918, Apr. 3, 1909; *World's Work,* Nov. 1906; *Bird Lore,* Feb. 19, 1915; *N. Y. Times,* Nov. 4, 5, 7, 14, 1918; *Troy Record,* Nov. 14, 1918.]   E. E. W.

SAGE, RUSSELL (Aug. 4, 1816–July 22, 1906), congressman and financier, came of pioneer New England stock, being a descendant of David Sage who was living in Middletown, Conn., as early as 1652. His father, Elisha Sage, veteran of the War of 1812, his mother, Prudence (Risley) Sage, and five children were emigrating by ox train from Connecticut towards Michigan when Russell was born, in the covered wagon, in Verona township, Oneida County, N. Y. Observing that the land was good, Elisha Sage settled in Oneida County, and there Russell grew to the age of twelve, working on the farm and getting a few bits of primary schooling. In 1828 he went to work in his brother Henry's store in Troy, N. Y. Notwithstanding his long hours, he attended a night school, paying a dollar and a half of his monthly salary of four dollars to learn arithmetic and bookkeeping; meanwhile, he also studied markets and read newspapers omnivorously. Before he reached manhood he began to do trading on his own account and at twenty-one, with the capital thus acquired, he bought out the store of his brother Elisha Montague, and a year or so later resold it at a profit. He then (with a partner) started a wholesale grocery business in Troy. The firm had its own sailing vessels on the Hudson, and traded in other things than groceries—Vermont and Canadian horses, for example, fresh and cured meats, and grain.

In 1845 Sage was elected alderman of Troy and later treasurer of Rensselaer County. In 1848 he was a delegate to the National Whig Convention. He was nominated for congressman in 1850 and defeated, but ran again successfully in 1852. He was reëlected representative in 1854, but retired at the end of that term. In Congress he advocated the Homestead Law and free soil for Kansas, but his most noteworthy act was a resolution asking that the government take over the old mansion, "Mount Vernon," and make it a permanent memorial to Washington (*Congressional Globe,* 33 Cong., 1 Sess., pp. 52–54; Dec. 15, 1853). This was one of the first moves toward its restoration and preservation.

Leaving Congress in 1856, Sage continued to build up his fortune, adding banking to his other activities. A chance meeting with Jay Gould [*q.v.*] in a railroad station was a momentous incident in his life, for it led to a close association

and to Sage's interest in railroad affairs. He had already loaned some money to the La Crosse Railroad, a small line in Wisconsin, and was compelled to advance more to save the first loans. The road was eventually expanded into the Chicago, Milwaukee & St. Paul system, in which promotion Sage made large profits. He was for years a director and vice-president of the corporation. By 1863 he was giving most of his attention to stocks and finance, and he decided to move to New York. His first wife, Maria Winne of Troy, whom he had married in 1841, died in 1867, and on Nov. 24, 1869, he married again, in Troy, his second wife being Margaret Olivia (Slocum) Sage [*q.v.*], who outlived him.

Sage is credited with being the originator of "puts and calls" in the stock market about 1872. His fortune was greatly increased by advances in the value of securities under the skilful manipulation of his ally, Jay Gould. The methods used in their campaign to gain control of the New York elevated lines in 1881 were bitterly criticized by the press and business men. Cyrus W. Field [*q.v.*], whom they had taken in with them to court public confidence, was eventually ruined, but Gould and Sage came through unscathed and with the desired control. Sage was one of the shrewdest and most conservative of all great financiers. Though at times a large operator, he was never a plunger. He preferred small, sure profits or those which resulted from manipulation, and his occasional speculative purchase was usually based on very canny foresight. He was caught short only once in his life, in the little Wall Street panic of 1884, when he lost fully $7,000,000. He was, at one time or another, stockholder and director of many railroad corporations. He was actively concerned in the organization of the Atlantic & Pacific Telegraph Company, and in its consolidation with the Western Union.

During the last quarter century of his life he was best known as a money lender. At one time he is said to have had $27,000,000 out on call loans. He might have from five to eight millions in cash bank deposits in the morning, and loan nearly all of it before the day was over. His frugality was proverbial; he loved to chaffer, even over the price of an apple, and there was no epicureanism in him. He preferred comfort rather than elegance; plain food and cheap clothing satisfied him as well as the richest. His homes on Fifth Avenue and Long Island were comfortably furnished, however; he indulged himself in a love of good horses, and did not question his wife's expenditures. His philanthropies, such as the education of more than forty Indian children and the presentation of a dormitory to Troy Female Seminary, were popularly credited to Mrs. Sage's prompting. In 1891 Sage was seriously injured in his office by a bomb exploded by one Henry W. Norcross, who had first demanded $1,200,000. Norcross and a clerk were killed, but Sage, despite his years, fully recovered. He died at his home on Long Island at the age of ninety, and his fortune at that time was estimated at $70,000,000.

[Among many newspaper references to Sage, see obituaries in all New York newspapers of July 23, 1906; *N. Y. Times,* Dec. 27, 1881, Dec. 5, 1891, Jan. 11, 1899; *World* (N. Y.), Apr. 27, July 10, 1902; *N. Y. Daily News,* Jan. 30, 1904; R. I. Warshow, *Jay Gould; the Story of a Fortune* (1928); Henry Clews, *Twenty-eight Years in Wall Street* (1887); *Who's Who in America,* 1906–07; Henry Whittemore, *Hist. of the Sage and Slocum Families* (1908); *Bench and Bar,* Sept. 1906; *N. Y. Geneal. and Biog. Record,* Oct. 1906.]

A. F. H.

ST. ANGE DE BELLERIVE, LOUIS (*c.* Oct. 1698–Dec. 27, 1774), soldier, commandant of St. Louis, and acting governor of Upper Louisiana, was born in Montreal, Canada, son of Robert Groston de St. Ange and Marguerite Crevier de Bellerive, and baptized Oct. 16, 1698. The family was of the nobility, and possibly the name St. Ange was taken from the district in Canada known as *la côté de St. Ange.* The father, who seems to have come from the province of Champagne in France, went to Canada in 1687 as a sergeant and married there in 1692. Having been sent with his father to the Missouri, in 1724 Louis went in command of one detachment with Étienne Venyard, Sieur de Bourgmont [*q.v.*], on an expedition westward for the purpose of making an alliance with the Padouka Indians. That accomplished, they returned to Fort Orleans on the Missouri. St. Ange was later stationed at a new fort established near the mouth of the Kansas River and in 1736 was appointed to succeed Jean Baptiste Bissot, Sieur de Vincennes [*q.v.*], on the Wabash River with the rank of captain. Remaining at this post for twenty-eight years, he took part in the French resistance to the English, who were crowding out the French in the Ohio Valley; and in 1764, when the treaty of Paris had ended the conflict, he conducted the evacuation of Fort Chartres as successor to Neyon de Villiers, the commandant. He retained this command for about fifteen months, until the English commander, Capt. Thomas Stirling, came to take possession on Oct. 10, 1765. A few weeks later, with his few soldiers and most of the white inhabitants, St. Ange moved across the Mississippi River to St. Louis.

At this time the territory west of the river had been transferred from France to Spain in the secret treaty of San Ildefonso, but it was incumbent upon France to govern the country until Spain should take possession. This portion of what was called the Illinois Country was never surrendered to the English and continued under the command of St. Ange until 1770, when Don Pedro Piernas arrived as the Spanish authority. St. Ange then took service as a captain in the Spanish army, but he was now advanced in years and remained in St. Louis until his death. During this time his wise counsel was much sought not only by the people, who depended on him as their friend and able intermediary with the Spanish authorities, but by the Spanish lieutenant-governor as well. He died a bachelor at the home of Madame Marie Thérèse (Bourgeois) Chouteau, where he had lived for some time.

[Cyprien Tanguay, *Dictionnaire Généalogique des Familles Canadiennes,* vol. IV (1887); W. B. Douglas, "The Sieurs de St. Ange," *Ill. State Hist. Soc. Pubs.,* no. 14 (1910); *Wis. Hist. Soc. Colls.,* vol. XVII (1906); Baron Marc de Villiers du Terrage, *La Découverte du Missouri et l'Histoire du Fort d'Orléans* (1925) and *Les Dernières Années de la Louisiane Française* (1904); Pierre Margry, ed., *Découvertes et Établissements des Français dans l'Ouest,* vol. VI (1886); J. P. Dunn, "Docs. Relating to French Settlements on the Wabash," *Ind. Hist. Soc. Pubs.,* vol. II (1895); C. W. Alvord, "The Critical Period 1763–1765," *Ill. State Hist. Lib. Colls.,* vol. X (1915); will of St. Ange. MS. in possession of *Mo. Hist. Soc.,* printed in F. L. Billon, *Annals of St. Louis* (1886), pp. 125–27.]

S. M. D.

ST. CLAIR, ARTHUR (Mar. 23, 1736 o.s.– Aug. 31, 1818), soldier, governor of Northwest Territory, was born in Thurso, Caithness County, Scotland. He is often erroneously said to have been the son of Margaret Balfour (Wedderburn) and James St. Clair, an officer in the French army, and the grandson of the Baron of Rosslyn. He was probably the son of William Sinclair, a merchant, and the great-grandson of James Sinclair, second Laird of Assery. His mother may have been Elizabeth (Balfour) Sinclair (John Henderson, *Caithness Family Hist.,* 1884, p. 335; L. A. Morrison, *The Hist. of the Sinclair Family,* 1896, p. 43). It is said that he enjoyed the advantages of an incomplete term at the University of Edinburgh and an unsuccessful apprenticeship under William Hunter, the celebrated anatomist of London. In 1757 he became an ensign in the British army and served with Amherst in Canada. On May 15, 1760, he married Phoebe Bayard, of Boston, a niece of Gov. James Bowdoin [*q.v.*]. They had seven children. He resigned from the army in 1762 with the commission of lieutenant, and, later, with a legacy of £14,000 from the Bowdoin estate and his own military service claims he purchased an estate of some 4,000 acres in the Ligonier valley of western Pennsylvania. As the largest resident property owner in Pennsylvania west of the mountains, he was placed in an anomalous position, when Governor Penn in 1771 made him the agent of colonial government in this frontier country. As justice of the county court of Westmoreland County after its formation in 1773, he was obliged to extend the form but not the substance of government into the Pittsburgh area, at the same time that John Connolly, captain of the militia and after 1774 justice of the district of western Augusta County, Va., sought to extend the substance as well as the form of Virginian control over the same region. St. Clair was unsuccessful before the superior military force and greater popular appeal of the Virginians, who rebuilt and garrisoned the fort abandoned by the British in 1772 and prepared for the surveying and occupation of the Kentucky country. Supported by the fur traders, he refused to cooperate in these and other actions offensive to the Shawnee Indians and thus probably relieved Pennsylvania of the vengeance of that tribe in Dunmore's War of 1774. He favored rewarding the Delaware Indians for their neutrality in the face of frontier insults but acquiesced in the refusal of Penn and the legislature to establish and garrison a satisfactory trading post at the Delaware town of Kittanning.

As the Revolutionary War came on, he was made a member of the Committee of Safety of Westmoreland County, but he was powerless to extend Pennsylvania control over the Pittsburgh area, as the Virginia committee sent John Neville [q.v.] to occupy the fort and as Virginia's commissioners undertook most of the financial burdens and diplomatic manipulation at the treaty of Pittsburgh in 1775, by which the outstanding issues of Dunmore's War were settled and a Loyalist-Indian uprising prevented. At this treaty he occupied the minor position of secretary to the relatively insignificant commissioners of the Continental Congress. In 1775 he was sent as colonel to take part in the retreat of the American army from Canada. In the winter of 1776–77, as brigadier-general, he was with Washington in the campaign and the battles of Trenton and Princeton. In the spring of 1777, as major-general, he was ordered to the defense of Fort Ticonderoga, which was popularly considered as impregnable. His evacuation of the post, probably as the result of factors beyond his control, filled the public mind with such dismay that he was recalled by Congress from service in the field. Although he was completely exonerated by a court martial in September 1778 (*Proceedings of a General Court Martial . . . for the Trial of*

Major General St. Clair, Aug. 25, 1778, 1778, and reprinted in *New York Historical Society Collections,* vol. XIII, 1881), he was not, for the rest of the war, placed in a position to render conspicuous service.

On his return to civil life he entered Pennsylvania politics as an anti-constitutionalist. As a member of the council of censors in 1783, he unsuccessfully opposed the constitution of 1776, and he wrote the majority report recommending a new constitutional convention in order to abolish the unicameral legislature and other radical features. Elected state delegate to the Continental Congress he served from Nov. 2, 1785, to Nov. 28, 1787, and was president in 1787. With the creation of the Northwest Territory in 1787, he was appointed governor and served until 1802. As administrator of Indian affairs he was obliged to defend the treaties made with the tribes in 1784 and 1785, which deprived them of much land north of the Ohio, and which the Indians claimed had been forced upon them by fraud and military compulsion. They insisted upon a treaty to make the Ohio River the boundary and to be drawn up at a grand council in which all the tribes were fairly represented. At the treaty of Fort Harmar in 1789, however, he met only part of the Indians concerned, permitted those present to weaken their strength by quarreling among themselves, and finally manipulated the tribes into an apparent acceptance of the earlier and much hated treaties. The resulting dissatisfaction led into a war in which he, as major-general and commander of the federal army, was surprised and overwhelmingly defeated on Nov. 4, 1791, on a branch of the Wabash about a day's march from the site of Fort Wayne. The defeat was administered by a confederated Indian army with the Miami, Little Turtle [q.v.], which was inferior in numbers to the American army.

St. Clair was under positive and unalterable orders to erect a chain of military posts from Fort Washington, near the mouth of the Miami, to the rapids of the Maumee in the heart of the country of the then powerful Miami confederacy. Few military enterprises have been more poorly planned and executed. He was originally directed to set out from Fort Washington in July, but he did not do so until September. The result was that the frosts destroyed the grass, which was the only source of food for the horses and cattle. The delay was caused in part by the prolongation of the peace mission of Thomas Proctor, until the final and unsuccessful outcome of which St. Clair was obliged to postpone all offensive movements. Blundering in the quartermaster's department resulted in the failure to provide adequate supplies and arms. The morale of the army, two-thirds of which was militia and from which many had deserted, was also undermined by the fact that during their six months' service they received their monthly pay of three dollars but once, by short rations, and by the rigorous and non-military services required of them by St. Clair. St. Clair himself was not so experienced in frontier and Indian warfare as was his second in command, Gen. Richard Butler [q.v.], though he seems to have been more able. He declined to accept Butler's opinions and advice on certain technical matters, and the resulting estrangement continued throughout the campaign. At no time during the expedition did St. Clair have sufficient knowledge of the numbers and location of the Indians opposing him. The disaster was most humiliating, and, although he was exonerated from blame by Washington and by a committee of the House of Representatives, he resigned from the army and devoted himself to his duties as governor of the Northwest Territory. His ambitions for advancement in Federalist politics were, of course, checked.

In governing the frontiersmen of the Northwest Territory, he sought to enforce the spirit and the letter of the highly centralized and undemocratic Ordinance of 1787. With an overbearing manner and a paternal zeal too uncomplimentary to his frontier citizens, he objected to much proposed legislation that was aimed to decentralize the functions and control of local institutions. He objected to statehood as premature and sought to gerrymander the territory into smaller territories so as to postpone statehood indefinitely. The result was a movement by the local Jeffersonians in 1801 to remove him from office, and, at the same time, to create the state of Ohio. They were successful in the latter but failed in the former, until St. Clair at the constitutional convention of 1802 denounced as a nullity the Ohio enabling act of Congress. He was thereupon removed from office by Jefferson. He retired to his home, the "Hermitage," near Ligonier, Pa., where he developed his estate and built an iron furnace to manufacture stoves and castings. Owing to generous lending of money, signing notes for friends, and the failure of the Republican Congress to reimburse him for moneys advanced for government use while he was the Federalist governor of the Northwest Territory, he lost the whole of his fortune. In 1812 he published in defense of himself, *A Narrative of the Manner in which the Campaign against the Indians in . . . [1791] was conducted under the command of Major General St. Clair, together with . . . the Reports of the Committees appointed to inquire into the causes of the failure thereof.* His later years were spent in poverty and political oblivion, and he died in the log cabin that was his home on Chestnut Ridge.

[St. Clair Papers in Ohio State Lib., Columbus, Ohio; some papers in Lib. of Cong.; papers of proceedings of the treaty of Fort Harmar, Draper Coll., Frontier Wars MSS., vol. XXIII, pp. 75–143, State Hist. Soc. of Wis., Madison; *Territorial Papers of the U. S.,* vols. II, III, "The Territory Northwest of the River Ohio" (1934), ed. by C. E. Carter; *Pa. Archives,* 1 ser. vol. IV (1853); *American State Papers: Military Affairs,* vol. I (1832); *Military Jour. of Maj. Ebenezer Denny* (1859); W. H. Smith, *The St. Clair Papers* (2 vols., 1882); Ellis Beals, "Arthur St. Clair, Western Pennsylvania's Leading Citizen," *Western Pa. Hist. Mag.,* Apr., July 1929; R. C. Downes, "The Statehood Contest in Ohio," *Miss. Valley Hist. Rev.,* Sept. 1931 and *Frontier Ohio,* Ohio Arch. and Hist. Soc. Series, vol. II (in proof 1934); birthdate from statement of contents of register of baptisms in Thurso (Henderson, *ante*), and dependent on validity of above statement of parentage.]   R. C. D.

ST. DENIS (DENYS), LOUIS JUCHEREAU de (Sept. 17, 1676–June 11, 1744), French explorer, colonizer, commandant, was born in Canada at Beauport, Que., of which his father Nicolas was seigneur; his mother was Marie-Thérèse Giffard. After a Canadian boyhood he joined at the age of twenty-two the expedition of Pierre le Moyne, Sieur d'Iberville [q.v.], when he founded Louisiana, and in 1700 accompanied Jean Baptiste le Moyne, Sieur de Bienville [q.v.], on a trip of exploration to the Red River of Louisiana. Somewhat later (1702–05) he was in charge of a post on the lower Mississippi, while the capital of the colony was at Biloxi. He engaged in several expeditions into the Indian country and in 1710 again mounted Red River to the country of the Natchitoches Indians, where he traded with these and neighboring tribes in what is now Texas. In 1711 a Spanish missionary in that region wrote to the French officer at Mobile offering opportunities to trade with the Texas Indians. In 1713 Cadillac, then governor, sent St. Denis to open a route across Texas and begin the Indian trade. Once more ascending Red River to the Natchitoches, he founded a post there and crossed to the Rio Grande but was detained by the Spaniards at the presidio of San Juan Bautista until orders could come from Mexico. During his detention he wooed the commandant's grand-daughter, Mañuela Sánchez Ramón, and Feb. 17, 1716, they were married— a romantic incident unduly magnified by Gayarré (*post*) and older historians of Louisiana. Meanwhile he had been sent to Mexico, where he was kept in prison until he persuaded the authorities to allow him to accompany as guide a Spanish expedition which in 1716 was sent to found missions in the region north of Mexico. Because of this service he has been accused of bad faith or double dealing; apparently at that time he attempted to be all things to all men, Spanish as well as French. Returning to Mobile and reporting his success to Cadillac, he was furnished with new goods and in 1717 went back via Natchitoches to San Juan, where his goods were seized. Going to Mexico city to protest, he was a second time imprisoned but finally escaped on Sept. 5, 1718, arriving at Natchitoches early the next year. His escapades and smuggling enterprises created an international incident when the king of France asked his agent at Madrid to find out secretly what Spain meant to do with this adventurer; but as the two nations were at peace no further attempt was made to restrain his trading incursions. He arrived at Natchitoches from Mobile in 1719; there his wife joined him, and there he spent the remainder of his life, a thorn in the side of the Spanish in Mexico. When the news of his death reached Mexico city the governor of that time exclaimed in effect, "St. Denis is dead, thank God! Now we can breathe easier."

An incident of his later years was the repulsion in 1731 of an attack by the rebellious Natchez Indians upon Fort St. Jean at Natchitoches, which he commanded. Four years later the fort was moved to the site of the present Natchitoches, where, "fortified by all the sacraments of the church," St. Denis was buried within the walls of the old church building, his Spanish wife beside him. He had great influence with the Indians of Texas and Louisiana, for he spoke their languages and they trusted him; and he maintained for a quarter of a century an outpost for France on the Spanish border which was useful in commercial and diplomatic affairs.

[G. P. Garrison, *Texas* (1903), first correctly outlined St. Denis's history after its gross exaggeration by Charles Gayarré, *Hist. of La.*, vol. I (1854). See also Cyprien Tanguay, *Dictionnaire Généalogique des Familles Canadiennes*, vol. I (1871); L. G. Bugbee, "The Real Saint-Denis," *Texas Hist. Assoc. Quart.*, Apr. 1898; Charmion C. Shelby, "St. Denis's Second Expedition to the Rio Grande 1716–1719," *Southwestern Hist. Quart.*, Jan. 1924; C. E. Castañeda, "Silent Years in Tex. Hist.," *Ibid.*, Oct. 1934; H. E. Bolton, *Tex. in the Middle Eighteenth Century* (1915); S. C. Arthur and G. C. H. de Kernion, *Old Families of La.* (1931); C. W. Hackett, ed., *Pichado's Treatise on Limits of La. and Tex.*, vol. I (1931).]   L. P. K.

SAINT-GAUDENS, AUGUSTUS (Mar. 1, 1848–Aug. 3, 1907), sculptor, owed his salience in American art to a dual significance in his work. It was rooted primarily in intrinsic gifts and then in the influence which he exercised upon his contemporaries. He was a recognized *chef d'école*, long leading and accelerating the movement liberating sculpture in the United States from an arid convention. There had been distinguished men before him and one of them, whom he came to know in his young manhood, J. Q. A. Ward [*q.v.*], an artist of very high abilities, had already pointed the way promising escape from a thin academic hypothesis. But it was left to Saint-Gaudens to effect the essential modernization of a school, to gather up the elements of progress and illustrate their potency through large and varied achievement.

He was wont to say that "no one ever succeeded in art unless born with an uncontrollable instinct toward it," and he had such an instinct. How he came into possession of it is a mystery. He sprang from a family of French shoemakers, settled in the little town of Aspet, some fifty miles from Toulouse. Bernard Paul Ernest Saint-Gaudens, his father, was taught the trade in an elder brother's factory at Carcassonne. He seems to have been of a roving disposition for he is presently found in London and subsequently, for full seven years, in Dublin. It was in Dublin that he married Mary McGuinness, who was native Irish, and there, in a house on Charlemount Street, Augustus was born. Two elder brothers died young, but later there were younger ones. Within six months of his birth the family had taken ship for the United States, landing in Boston. Shortly afterwards they were established in New York, where Bernard Saint-Gaudens was for years to flourish as a maker of shoes. It was in the workroom that Augustus, making pen drawings of the shoemakers, first disclosed his "uncontrollable instinct." His father was wholly sympathetic. Augustus tells how, when he was thirteen and had finished his modest schooling, he was informed that it was time to go to work and asked what he would like to do. "I don't care," he said, "but I should like it if I could do something which would help me to be an artist" (*Reminiscences*, I, 38). Promptly Bernard apprenticed him to one Avet, a pioneer stone-cameo cutter and a hard taskmaster. Later he was employed by Jules Le Brethon, a shell-cameo cutter. This experience at the lathe was doubly valuable for it not only nurtured his artistic aptitude but gave him a craft with which he was to eke out a livelihood while engaged in the struggle of a young and unknown sculptor.

He describes himself as "a terrific worker" at this time, cameo cutting all day and studying drawing at Cooper Union at night. There followed a period of drawing from the nude at the National Academy of Design. He developed rapidly in his work and had, besides, sublime confidence in himself. He was only nineteen when the wise and kind Bernard asked him if he wouldn't like to see the Paris Exposition, that of 1867. He sailed in February, with his passage paid and a hundred dollars in his pocket, launched upon a strenuous career. The first necessity was a means of self-support. His skill as a cameo cutter won it for him at once, with Lupi, an Italian in the Rue des Trois Frères. He could not as readily obtain entrance into the École des Beaux-Arts. That required a paper from the American Legation, which turned up nine months after his application for it had been made. While waiting he frequented a small school in the Rue de l'École de Médecine. "Here," he says, "I modeled my first figures from the nude, and laid an excellent foundation for the future" (*Ibid.*, I, 69). When at last he was accepted at the Beaux-Arts he chose the *atelier* of Jouffroy. He confesses that he was not a brilliant pupil and did not shine in the competitions. But Jouffroy grounded him well and the whole atmosphere of this period of pupilage stimulated the talent stirring within him without fixing it in any mould, the master's or that of any one else. The antique interested him and helped him but could not land him in a formula. Already he was sympathetic also to the naturalistic elements in the Renaissance and when, at the time of the Franco-Prussian War, he left for Rome, he continued, even under the tremendous pressure of that city's august tradition, to be his own man. Rome enchanted him, as it was to do all his life long. "It was as if a door had been thrown wide open to the eternal beauty of the classical" (*Ibid.*, I, 104). Yet it is significant that he began in Rome not with an Apollo or a Venus but with a Hiawatha.

At this point it is well to pause upon some consideration of Saint-Gaudens as a man. He had been a lively boy and from his youth up he was the same energetic and resilient type, sensitive, gay, full of humor, incurably independent, and avid of experience. Born when he was, divers great personalities and events came to touch his imagination. He could recall seeing Rachel act and hearing Brignoli sing. He could recollect the repercussions of the Civil War and one of the vividest pictures in his memory was of himself as a lad falling into line at the City Hall to see the body of Lincoln lying in state. His first period in Paris, as has been noted, was terminated by the War of 1870, and in Rome he watched the famous entry of Victor Emmanuel II. The sensations of life crowded in upon him and fertilized his mind and character. Through it all he worked like a demon. There never was a more industrious artist, one readier to tackle arduous tasks and to see them through in the highest spirits. In

the *atelier Jouffroy* he used to electrify, and possibly amuse, his comrades by singing the Marseillaise (*Ibid.*, I, 78) and often at his work he was wont to sing. He drew upon unusual stores of resolution and perseverance. The story of Saint-Gaudens is not by any means one of swift growth and facile triumph but, on the contrary, one of persistent effort and hard-won success.

Some of his severest tests were to come in Rome, where he was dogged by illness and economic difficulties. There, to be sure, the dealer Rossi paid him well for the cameo cutting which was ever in reserve as a crutch, but when the "Hiawatha" was about ready to be cast in plaster he lacked the money to have the work done. But it was in Rome, too, that fortune began to smile. There he had the first of the friendly encounters which were frequently to smooth his path. Montgomery Gibbs appeared upon the scene, to make the casting of the "Hiawatha" possible, and to order portraits of his two daughters in return (*Ibid.*, I, 113). Through the Gibbs family also there came about commissions for copies of the busts of Demosthenes and Cicero, for William M. Evarts, and the opportunity to make a bust of that eminent personage. He attacked the Evarts problem in New York, on the occasion of a visit home, but it was not long before he was in Europe again, to meet in Rome Augusta F. Homer, who on June 4, 1877, at Roxbury (now part of Boston), Mass., was to become his wife. The Evarts bust best suggests the strain that was to run like a leading motive throughout the sculptor's career, the strain of portraiture. But side by side with it, subordinated to it only by fate and not by choice, ran his interest in imaginative design. The "Hiawatha," in marble, now at Saratoga, offers one early testimony to this. The "Silence," a figure in the Masonic Temple in New York, offers another. In Rome also he made a study for a slave holding the young Augustus on the top of a column, setting a laurel crown upon his brow. Saint-Gaudens was ever to have his dreams, his vein of poetic feeling. From his boyhood he remembered climbing a hill on Staten Island, to find that there were other hills farther away, the source of his "first feeling of the ever-mysterious beyond." When for a time Europe was left behind him and he was settled in a prosaic studio in New York he would "turn on the water at the little wash-basin, let it run continuously with a gentle tinkle, and thus recall the sound of the fountain in the garden at Rome" (*Ibid.*, I, 157). Only a poet could have done that. In the life he now began to organize at home the artist above all others whose influence he recognized, whose friendship was most important to him, was

John La Farge [*q.v.*]. But the making of portraits was to prove a portentous factor.

Two full-length statues fell to his lot, the "Admiral Farragut" for Madison Square in New York and the "Captain Randall" for Sailors' Snug Harbor, Staten Island. To keep replenished the poetic fire in him there was also the large relief, "Adoration of the Cross by Angels" which John La Farge got for him to do, in association with certain paintings of his own, in the chancel of St. Thomas's Church, in New York (burnt in 1905). Of the relief La Farge said, "there is a breath of Italy in it" (*Ibid.*, I, 201), by which he must have meant its grace, its tenderness. Quite other traits were requisite in the "Farragut," the first production in which Saint-Gaudens was authoritatively to affirm his ability and leadership. He needed now force, directness, insight into the springs of character, and the power to express character in monumental design. Richer in these things than perhaps he himself knew, he leapt into something like fame. The "Farragut," exhibited in the plaster at Paris in 1880 and unveiled in 1881, when Saint-Gaudens was in his early thirties, was to prove a landmark in his life and in the history of American sculpture; in the former because it decisively disclosed his mastery, and in the latter because it did so much to further what might be called the humanization of a national art. Gone was the old convention. Some trace of idealism, it is true, remained, in the symbolical figures depicted in relief on the pedestal. But the surmounting admiral, set four-square as though upon his quarter-deck, challenged all the formulas of the academy. He was placed realistically before the world, a living embodiment, and, moreover, the whole design struck a new and vital note. Here was racy characterization joined to original composition, a public memorial with the stamp of creative art upon it. It was the better because Saint-Gaudens had the collaboration of Stanford White [*q.v.*] in the pedestal. This was a happy augury. The two were thenceforth to be similarly allied upon numerous occasions, White's genius for a pedestal being akin to his friend's genius for a statue. They worked together in extraordinary harmony. But what is peculiarly prefigured in the "Farragut" is Saint-Gaudens' function as interpreter of major figures in American life, especially those of the Civil War. It is impossible, of course, to traverse in detail the conception and development of each project in this field, interesting as it would be to describe, for example, the long struggles from which the "Farragut" emerged and the slow, infinitely painstaking way in which, at home or abroad, Saint-Gaudens worked out his many

problems. But treating the subject at large emphasis may justly first be placed upon the historical content of the sculptor's work.

Curiously, it did not rest, at the outset, upon exhaustive research. He was not, until he had reached his prime, a great reader. One hears little in the *Reminiscences* of the sources of his inspiration for portraiture. But some subtly clairvoyant quality seems to have served him well. One feels it in "The Puritan" (1885), which began with some thought of a particular personality (Deacon Samuel Chapin) but ended as the embodiment of a type. One feels it far more in those commemorative figures for which Saint-Gaudens could find authentic documentation. Thus it is in the standing "Lincoln" in Lincoln Park, Chicago, which came within six years of the "Farragut," and the seated "Lincoln" for the Chicago Lake Front, which dates from 1907. Thus it is likewise with the equestrian "General John A. Logan" (1897), at Chicago, and the "Shaw Memorial" opposite the State House, Boston, which, long delayed, was unveiled in the same year. Thus finally it is with the equestrian "Sherman," of 1903, in Fifth Avenue Plaza, New York. These works are nothing if not eloquently expressive of the different individualities portrayed. If they are beautiful as monuments they are also intensely human as records. Allusion has been made to the sculptor's clairvoyance in these matters, his dependence upon some mysterious *flair* for the secrets of personality. The time came when he went more deliberately into the subject. His son assigns this time to the early nineties, the period immediately following the Stevenson relief (1887) and the Sherman bust (1888). Both men profoundly stirred Saint-Gaudens and spurred in him "a desire to comprehend the mental significance of the man before him," so that afterwards he would begin a portrait "by reading all possible biographies of the subject, or, if the person he planned to model was alive, keeping him in a constant state of conversation" (Homer Saint-Gaudens, in *Reminiscences*, I, 388–89). He would spare no pains to build his portrait from within and this, as it happened, was at one with his habit of work, which was slow, even hesitant, subject not only to his own criticism but to that which he asked of his friends, ever anxious as he was to get at "the last word" of truth. On the other hand, the hypothesis of a piercing, half-unconscious, imaginative penetration to the heart of a problem, directing and governing all his other resources, still holds. His statues carry conviction because they are spiritually "of the centre," based on a spontaneous, inner understanding of what he was doing. That he was himself possibly aware of this is dimly suggested by one of his axioms: "Conceive an idea. Then stick to it. Those who hang on are the only ones who amount to anything" (*Ibid.*, II, 19). He hung on. With the saying just quoted there may well be bracketed another: "After all, it's the way the thing's done that makes it right or wrong, that's about the only creed I have in art" (*Ibid.*, I, 344).

The way in which the thing was done meant, with Saint-Gaudens, a singular union of delicacy and strength. Perhaps the best introduction to a study of his technique is to be had through consideration of the portraits in low relief which he began to model as far back as the seventies, the "Rodman Gilder" (1879), the "Bastien-Lepage" (1880), the "Homer Saint-Gaudens" (1882). That passion for the classical which so stirred him on his first sojourn in Rome and which never really left him, was transmuted into something very suave yet free and bold, something akin to the realism of the Renaissance masters. His early medallions, so exquisitely touched, so tender in the modulation of surfaces, are also vitalized portraits, as declarative of personality as the figures which he was later to do in the round. The outstanding example is the "Bastien-Lepage" and its great merit, it should be remarked, lies not alone in its truth and subtle modeling but in the feeling for design which pervades it. The placing of the head and shoulders within the rectangle, the disposition of the painter's palette and brushes, to say nothing of the hands themselves, point to a trait constant in Saint-Gaudens, his solicitude for simple—and charming—composition. It embraced also, of course, the matter of lettering which always went with the subject, though this might amount to nothing more than the name of the sitter, the date, and the artist's signature. The inscription was made part and parcel of the whole. In the Paris studio in which the big "Stevenson" for Saint Giles' Cathedral, Edinburgh, was carried to completion (1887–1902) a friend sat with the sculptor and watched an assistant working over the letters under criticism and instructions that might, in their minute concern, have been evoked over the handling of the figure itself. It has been told that the 1052 letters composing this inscription were modeled twelve times over. Sometimes the medallions were more or less elaborately conceived, as in the case of "The Children of Jacob H. Schiff," with its dog and the gracefully decorative festoons flung from one pilaster to another, but as a rule Saint-Gaudens reduced his design to the sparest elements. The simplicity of unity belongs also to the reliefs which he executed on a large scale,

such as the "Shaw Memorial" and the "Dr. James McCosh" (1889).

Portraiture, it is obvious from the foregoing, incessantly engaged him, yet more attention should be given to Saint-Gaudens as an imaginative artist in the broadest sense than he commonly receives. The lure of that "ever mysterious beyond" was with him all his life. It was surely not a predilection for bald prose that moved him in his early manhood to make the "Hiawatha" and the "Silence," and those productions of his immaturity foreshadow the gusts of purely creative invention which were repeatedly to visit him. In one of his letters from Paris, written in 1898, there is a passage warmly tinctured by this recurrent emotion. "I have been having a desire lately to do a nude," he says, "suggested by a man in the street; a working-man coming home from work carrying his child (who had rushed out to meet him) astride his shoulders. I want to make a Venus carrying a winged figure of Love on her shoulders in some such fashion, and the little God of Felicity and Misery shooting his bow" (*Ibid.*, II, 192–93). There were so many portraits to do that it would seem as if all his dreams of sailing off into the blue were bound to be frustrated. As a matter of fact he had more than one opportunity to turn his thoughts into idealistic paths. There was the relief of the "Adoration of the Cross," for St. Thomas's. There were the angels for the Morgan tomb at Hartford, Conn.—which by coincidence were also lost by fire (1882). The angelic figure haunted Saint-Gaudens and left a distinct mark upon his art. He divined it with great feeling in the lovely figures for the Morgan tomb and again in the celebrated "Amor Caritas" (1887) which represents him in the Luxembourg. The truly spiritual visage and the slender uplifted arms in that bronze are illustrative of his gift for etherealized beauty. The drapery shows his technical skill also, that and his command over line and over light and shade. Even a condensed survey of his imaginative works must take account, further, of the nude "Diana" modeled in 1892 for the tower of Madison Square Garden in New York, and of the symbolical groups for the Boston Public Library which were left unfinished at his death. One of the last things upon which he worked was the head for the Christ forming part of the Phillips Brooks monument in Boston. Of all this idealistic work of his it is to be said that it is touched with nobility. There is nothing in it that is earth-bound, that is sensuous, that partakes of the super-sophistication so often encountered in modern sculpture. Saint-Gaudens was puzzled when he tried to philosophize life but some indefinable groping toward the light brought him to a state of mind in which he saw things with a certain loftiness. "In one of my blue fits the other day," he once wrote, "I felt the end of all things, and, reasoning from one thing to the other and about the hopelessness of trying to fathom what it all means, I reached this; we know nothing (of course), but a deep conviction came over me like a flash that at the bottom of it all, whatever it is, the mystery must be beneficent; it does not seem as if the bottom of all were something malevolent. And the thought was a great comfort" (*Ibid.*, II, 120). Once he said to his friend Dr. Henry Shiff that "beauty must mean at least some goodness" (*Ibid.*, II, 203).

He was a meditative man, with whom reverie had a curiously grave undertone and it is characteristic that, despite his natural gayety, his imaginative work has a marked seriousness about it. There is no gross strain in the "Diana," only a spare, refined elegance. Nowhere is his art purer, more elevated, than in the "Adams Monument" (1891), in Rock Creek Cemetery, Washington, his one essay in the grand style. The bronze figure, seated in its heavy drapery on granite, against granite, has taxed the ingenuity of observers eager to find a title for it and to identify the artist's symbolical purpose. Some have sought to invest it with the meaning of Eastern philosophy, of Buddha. Others have attached to it a Christian symbolism. Henry Adams, who commissioned the monument for his wife's grave, was inclined to call it "The Peace of God." Saint-Gaudens himself, pressed for an explanation, suggested "The Mystery of the Hereafter," adding that his idea was to express something "beyond pain, and beyond joy" (*Ibid.*, I, 362–63). The bronze remains enigmatic. This silent form, muffled as in unearthly garments, is "a mysterious, sphinx-like presence, strange and massive with something of terror, but more of solemn dignity and beauty, in its broad simple lines" (Cortissoz, *Augustus Saint-Gaudens*, p. 30). Simplicity! It is the keynote to the sculptor's art, the most durable of the elements which he drank in when Rome opened for him the door to "the eternal beauty of the classical." In the "Adams Monument" he "conceives an idea" in its quiddity and never wavers from his central inspiration but, like your genuine poet, he leaves something that defies analysis in his work. He swathes his figure in a robe itself free from teasing details and in arranging its folds, in carrying them to a hood-like formation around the head and arm, he attains to an effect of heroic majesty. It is impossible to avoid superlatives in touching upon this monument. The truth is that nothing quite like it for tragic power has been put forth in American or European sculpture in recent times. The French Dubois, for whom Saint-Gaudens had unmeasured admiration, might have given it a more antique accent. His countryman, Rodin, might have made it more palpitant, more romantic. But neither of them could have produced so poetically the atmosphere of the "ever mysterious beyond," and neither of them could have left it more impressively stamped with the distinction of style. Saint-Gaudens did many fine things. The standing "Lincoln" at Chicago, for example, is a masterpiece of characterization and of plastic design. The "Sherman," in New York, is one of the few great equestrian monuments of modern times, if not the greatest of them all. But for creative energy and originality, for spiritual force and for the sure fusion of dramatic purpose with technical authority and breadth, the "Adams Monument" is Saint-Gaudens' best bid for immortality.

That bid was established primarily upon an imaginative conception but the technical authority just mentioned had much to do with it and with the ever-widening scope of the sculptor's influence. A distinguished French critic, Paul Leroi, once exclaimed over what he called the beautiful integrity of Saint-Gaudens' work. "It is work well done," he said. "It is true; it is sincere; . . . he has never made any sacrifices to réclame" (*Ibid.*, p. 24). His contemporaries in the United States were quick to recognize this and his example reacted upon the whole body of American sculpture. Explaining in his *Reminiscences* why the "Shaw Memorial" had taken him an unconscionable time to complete, he says: "My own delay I excuse on the ground that a sculptor's work endures for so long that it is next to a crime for him to neglect to do everything that lies in his power to execute a result that will not be a disgrace. There is something extraordinarily irritating, when it is not ludicrous, in a bad statue" (*Reminiscences*, II, 78–79).

He not only endeavored to improve existing conditions by making good statues but in divers other ways did what he could to keep American art on the side of the angels. An old Parisian comrade of his, Bion, once called him a "righter of wrongs." It was an apt designation. A sketch of his life would be incomplete without some reference to the share he took in the general development of artistic matters. In 1877, when he was but twenty-nine, he plunged with avidity into the controversy between the older and the younger generations in the National Academy of Design that then came to a head, and he acted as one of the founders of the Society of American Artists. This organization crystallized the newer ideas arising from contact with Paris, it assembled under a liberal program many of the finest talents thrown up in American art, and Saint-Gaudens was a constructive leader in its campaign. He was all for progress and the world well lost. As time went on he steadily participated in the various projects looking to advance. He taught, devotedly, at the Art Students' League (c. 1888–97). He took promising young artists into his studio, as helpers, always admonishing them "to develop technique and then to hide it." When the Chicago Exposition of 1893 was toward he went on with Richard Morris Hunt and Charles F. McKim to confer with Daniel H. Burnham [qq.v.], who wanted him to supervise the entire sculptural aspect of the fabric. He could not do this but in an advisory capacity he watched over the modeling of the "Columbus" before the Administration Building by Mary Lawrence (later Mrs. Tonetti) and it was on his suggestion that Daniel Chester French made the stately "Liberty" in the lagoon and that Frederick W. MacMonnies did his famous fountain. The satisfaction that he had in this work by MacMonnies, who had begun professional life in his studio, was like Saint-Gaudens in its generosity. He was wonderfully appreciative of his juniors when he felt that they were on the right track. One of them, a total stranger to him, had on a certain occasion just put a fine relief into place. Saint-Gaudens on seeing it promptly ferreted out the young man's address and drove to it, post haste, in a cab. "I am Mr. Saint-Gaudens," he said to the astonished sculptor who opened the door, "and I've come down to tell you what I think of the beautiful work you have done" (Cortissoz, *Augustus Saint-Gaudens*, pp. 73–74).

When Charles F. McKim was founding the American Academy in Rome Saint-Gaudens labored to promote its interests, even bringing himself to what was, for him, the agonizing point of making speeches in support of them. It is pertinent to borrow some sentences from one of these, as throwing light upon his point of view: "In the repeated attacks that are made on the Roman Academy and on the École des Beaux Arts and in the incessant cry for greater freedom in the development of the artistic mind, there is a certain amount of truth. But in such reaction the pendulum swings too far and the real question is lost sight of. There is a middle ground on which to stand. It seems to be rarely realized that the very men who are shown as examples against the

schools were, if not actually brought up in the School of Rome, all men of thorough academic training. Only after such training does the mind become sufficiently mature and the individual personality so developed as to be able to indulge in unqualified freedom and liberty of expression" (*Reminiscences,* II, 262). In such ideas he may be said to have stated his artistic testament. He knew that the "divine fire," as he recognized it in sculptors so varied as Houdon, Rude, and Dubois, in such painters as Baudry and Puvis de Chavannes, was indispensable. But so, he believed, was rigorous training, the technical power without which the divine fire glows in vain. When Dubois died and a friend wrote to Saint-Gaudens expressing his sympathy, the sculptor replied: "I agree with what you say about Dubois. I agree with both hands and all my heart. He . . . has had more to do with keeping a high standard among those who believe, as you say, in 'thorough discipline' than any other man in a century at least" (*Ibid.,* II, 49–50). Thorough discipline was his own watchword. If the long list of the works with which he enriched American sculpture embraces so many affirmations of beauty it testifies also to his devoted craftsmanship.

His struggles toward achievement were arduous to the point of exhaustion. "People think a sculptor has an easy life in a studio," he said to a friend as in his workshop they threaded a maze of clay models, plaster casts, scaffolds and ladders in which assistants were at work. "It's hard labor, in a factory" (Cortissoz, *Augustus Saint-Gaudens,* p. 78). Yet the strain of constant effort was lightened in many ways. The work was itself a joy, accompanied by song. It involved inspiring contacts with men like La Farge, White, Henry Adams, Stevenson, John Hay, Sherman, William Dean Howells, John Sargent, Bastien-Lepage, indeed a veritable host of distinguished friends. He had delightful relations with Theodore Roosevelt over what the President called his "pet crime," the reformation of the United States coinage. In 1905 they put their heads together with the result that Saint-Gaudens made his memorable designs for the twenty-dollar gold piece and other coins. It is interesting to observe that he was, according to his wont, endlessly thoroughgoing in the enterprise, seeking to reconcile the practical issues involved with his dream of reviving something of the spirit of the ancient Greek coins and that of the Renaissance medals. There is a peculiarly felicitous touch in the circumstance that, after having erected here and there monuments in memory of heroes in American history he should have rounded out his career with work destined for widespread circulation amongst his fellow countrymen.

The full stream of his activities had flowed through many channels and scenes. His work had been done variously in Rome, in Paris, in New York, involving travels too frequent and too complicated for the tale of them to be set forth in anything less than an exhaustive biography. But one aspect of the subject of the sculptor's locale is of an importance requiring special comment. This was his discovery, in 1885, of the place in Cornish, N. H., which was thenceforth to be his headquarters, a sanctuary to which it was always good to return. "Aspet," as he called it, out of ancestral memories, he gradually formed into a beautiful estate, embellishing the old house that he had found there, erecting studios, and slipping into a life serener than that which he knew in the city or abroad. He knew misfortune at "Aspet." Fire, which had destroyed the relief at St. Thomas's and the angels for the Morgan tomb, destroyed also one of the Cornish studios, in 1904, and some of his most cherished possessions were lost—the drawing he had made of his mother, the portraits of himself by Bastien-Lepage, John Sargent, and Kenyon Cox, with innumerable precious papers, including his letters from Robert Louis Stevenson. The ruined "Parnell" for Dublin and the seated "Lincoln" could be done over again but these other things could only be mourned. He bore the disaster with courage. High courage, in fact, was in his blood. "Life is a battle, bitter or friendly, but nevertheless a battle," he wrote, "and to my mind a wholesome one" (*Reminiscences*, I, 292). He fought it unflinchingly. A friend who knew him well met him in Paris when he had received the first intimations of the illness that was ultimately to prove fatal. He was worried and confessed it but in his demeanor there were only cheerfulness and a kind of sweet resolution. He faced the end with a brave heart. Shortly before it came, in his retreat at Cornish, he watched the sunset behind Ascutney Mountain. "It's very beautiful," he murmured, "but I want to go farther away" (*Reminiscenes*, II, 359).

He went away at fifty-nine, in the full tide of his creative powers, the studios teeming with activity. Though the fight for health had fatigued him, recovery would have found him, in technical grasp and in imaginative fervor, well abreast of his task. In that event the groups for the Boston Public Library, to name only one of his last commissions, would have undoubtedly ranked high in his *œuvre*. Yet he could have legitimately rested upon his laurels for he had

put forth an imposing series of statues and reliefs, erecting in them a standard to which the sculptors of the United States could gratefully repair. They have persistently recognized him as their chief and early and late he was the recipient of honors testifying to their confidence. While he was still a young aspirant in Europe he was appointed to the jury for the American exhibition in the Paris exposition of 1878 and this was prophetic of the distinctions to be bestowed upon him. His fellow artists loved to pay him tribute and tokens of appreciation flowed in from other sources. Princeton, Harvard, and Yale all conferred degrees upon him. As it was at home so it was abroad. The Luxembourg acquired the "Amor Caritas," and he was allied with the Legion of Honor as a matter of course. In Paris he was hailed as a master, having extraordinary success in the Salon, where, in 1900, he received the Grand Prix. In London he was elected to the Royal Academy. In his own country, where so many notable productions keep his name and fame alive, there is also a special monument to his genius. "Aspet" was handed over to a board of trustees by his widow and his son Homer and as the Augustus Saint-Gaudens Memorial, crowded with replicas of the works in bronze and plaster, it annually draws thousands of visitors. These pilgrims can thus study at full length the sculptor's purely artistic traits. All that is missing is the handsome *gaillard* charm of the man, the blithe spirit, the puissant driving force, the rich quality and *élan* of one of the most endearing personalities ever known to American art.

[The canonical source of information is *The Reminiscenes of Augustus Saint-Gaudens* (2 vols., 1913) edited and amplified by his son, Homer Saint-Gaudens. There is a comprehensive bibliography in *Index of Twentieth Century Artists*, May 1934. Other publications include: Royal Cortissoz, *Augustus Saint-Gaudens* (1907), and *The Painter's Craft* (1930), pp. 403–12; Kenyon Cox, *Old Masters and New: Essays in Art Criticism* (1905), and *Artist and Public and other Essays and Art Subjects* (1914); C. L. Hind, *Augustus Saint-Gaudens* (1908), special extra number of *The International Studio*; C. R. Post, *A Hist. of European and Am. Sculpure*, vol. II (1921), pp. 240–43; Lorado Taft, *The Hist. of Am. Sculpture* (1924); Adeline Adams, *The Spirit of Am. Sculpture* (1929); W. H. Law, *A Chronicle of Friendship, 1873–1900* (1908), pp. 215–26, 273–75, 387–95, 401–02, 477–86, 499–506; Maitland Armstrong, *Day Before Yesterday: Reminiscences of a Varied Life* (1920); Louis Réau, *L'Art Français aux États-Unis* (1926), pp. 177–81; C. H. Caffin, *Am. Masters of Sculpture* (1903); obituary in *N. Y. Times*, Aug. 4, 1907.]   R. C.

ST. JOHN, ISAAC MUNROE (Nov. 19, 1827–Apr. 7, 1880), commissary-general of the Confederate States Army, and engineer, the eldest child of Isaac Richards and Abigail Richardson (Munroe) St. John, was born in Augusta,

Ga., where his father was then in business. He was a descendant of Matthias St. John who came to Dorchester, Mass., before 1632. A few years after the child's birth the family removed to New York City. He entered Yale in 1841 and was graduated in 1845, the youngest member of his class. He began the study of law in New York City but gave up these studies to become assistant editor of the *Baltimore Patriot,* Baltimore, Md. In 1848, he gave up journalism to become a civil engineer. Until 1855 he was on the engineering staff of the Baltimore & Ohio R. R., and then moved to Georgia, where, for five years, he was in charge of construction divisions of the Blue Ridge R. R.

When the Civil War began, St. John was in South Carolina, and he at once entered the Confederate service as a private of the Fort Hill guards of that state. He was soon transferred, however, to Magruder's army of the peninsula for engineering duty, became chief engineer of that army, and, in February 1862, was commissioned captain of engineers. The energy and ability which he displayed in Magruder's army attracted the attention of the Confederate war department, and he was promoted to major on Apr. 18, 1862, and assigned to duty in Richmond as chief of the nitre and mining bureau. He efficiently performed the difficult task of supplying the Confederacy, which was blockaded on all sides, with nitre for the manufacture of gunpowder, and with metals for the construction of implements of war. His accomplishments were recognized by his successive promotions to lieutenant-colonel and colonel. Near the end of the war, when the problem of feeding the Confederate armies had become acute, St. John was selected to direct this important activity. On Feb. 16, 1865, he was appointed commissary-general with the rank of brigadier-general, and at once organized an efficient system for collecting and storing supplies and for forwarding them to the armies. He continued on this duty after the evacuation of Richmond and until the final collapse of the Confederacy. An article on the "Resources of the Confederacy" appeared under his name in the *Southern Historical Society Papers,* March 1877.

After the war he returned to his profession of civil engineering. From 1866 to 1869 he was chief engineer of the Louisville, Cincinnati, & Lexington R. R. and then for the next two years he was city engineer of Louisville, Ky. He made the first topographical map of Louisville and planned the first complete sewerage system of that city. In 1871 he declined reëlection as city engineer and became consulting engineer of the

Chesapeake & Ohio R. R. In 1873 he was chief engineer of the Elizabeth, Lexington & Big Sandy R. R. He died suddenly of apoplexy while in residence at the "Greenbrier," White Sulphur Springs, W. Va. His wife was Ella J. Carrington, the daughter of Col. J. L. Carrington of Richmond, Va. They were married on Feb. 28, 1865, and had six children.

[O. St. John Alexander, *The St. John Geneal.* (1907); *Obit. Record of Grads. of Yale College,* June 1880; M. J. Wright, *Gen. Officers of the Confed. Army* (1911); *Memorandum Relative to the Gen. Officers . . . of the Confed. States, Sen. Doc.* 244, 60 Cong., 1 Sess. (1908); Special Orders of the Adjutant and Inspector General's Office, Confed. States, Lib. of Hist. Section, Army War College; *Courier-Jour.* (Louisville, Ky.), Apr. 10, 1880.]   S. J. H.

ST. JOHN, JOHN PIERCE (Feb. 25, 1833–Aug. 31, 1916), governor of Kansas, prohibitionist, the son of Samuel and Sophia (Snell) St. John, was descended from Matthias St. John who was made a freeman in Dorchester, Mass., in 1634. Born in Brookville, Franklin County, Ind., he lived on a farm, acquired a scanty education, and learned to hate liquor when his father became a victim of alcoholic drink. When he was twelve he began to earn a living for himself, and during the next fourteen years he worked at various occupations, made an unfortunate marriage with Mary Jane Brewer at the age of nineteen, and participated in the gold rush to California. He was admitted to the bar at Charleston, Ill., and at the same place, Mar. 28, 1861, was married to Susan J. Parker, his first wife having secured a divorce. After the Civil War, during which he won the rank of lieutenant-colonel in the 143rd Illinois Regiment, he practised law for a time at Independence, Mo., but in 1869 removed to Olathe, Kan.

He made his first appearance in public life as a Republican member of the Kansas Senate of 1873–74, where he worked for strict liquor regulation. The woman's crusade, the temperance movement started by Francis Murphy [*q.v.*], and the rise of anti-liquor organizations in Kansas produced the moment when a temperance candidate could profit most from his principles, and St. John was elected governor in 1878. At that time he was forty-six years old. He was slightly above medium height, well proportioned and vigorous physically, with deep-set, piercing eyes, dark hair, and a rather thin face festooned with a long and drooping but carefully kept moustache. The outstanding event of his first administration (1879–81) was the submission to the electorate of a constitutional amendment prohibiting the manufacture and sale of intoxicating liquor for beverage purposes. By reason of his oratorical ability and his prestige as governor, he became the leader in the fight for the amendment. In the election of 1880 it was adopted, and he was re-elected. Credit for the adoption of the first constitutional prohibitory amendment in history has ordinarily been assigned more to him than to any other person. His second term was chiefly occupied with a moderately successful attempt to enforce prohibition. In 1882 he made a fight for a third term, but was defeated, owing mainly to objection to the third term, a reaction against prohibition, credence given to an unsubstantiated charge that he favored railroad corporations, and the jealousy of a number of influential politicians who secretly combined against him. His principle of prohibition, however, was sustained in the election of local officials and the state legislature.

By 1882 St. John had become a character of national significance, largely through his connection with the adoption of constitutional prohibition in Kansas. After his defeat for a third term—the first Republican gubernatorial defeat in Kansas—he was practically expelled from his party, and devoted himself to lecturing on prohibition. In 1884 he accepted the nomination of the National Prohibition Party for president and drew fifteen times as many votes as any candidate of this party had ever received before. His campaign was centered in New York, in the hope of securing the balance of power in this pivotal state. Grover Cleveland carried the state by a plurality of 1,149 votes; if the Republicans had carried New York, the electoral vote would have stood 218 for Blaine and 183 for Cleveland. St. John received 25,016 votes in New York, and both major parties agreed that his vote was drawn almost exclusively from Republican ranks. For this reason, although any one of a number of factors might have been influential in producing the result in this state, St. John at the time was held responsible for the election of the first Democratic president since the Civil War, and the abuse and vilification heaped upon him by the Republicans knew no bounds. He was the only third party candidate between 1860 and 1912 who could plausibly be credited with turning an election.

In 1896 he broke with the Prohibition party, and from this time was a free lance in politics. His temperance lectures were less in demand, and he turned to mine speculation and real estate, but he was never successful in financial ventures. During his last years he again became popular as a prohibition speaker, and found himself restored to public favor in Kansas. He died at Olathe, survived by one son, a daughter having died in 1903.

[Senate and House Journals of the State of Kan., 1873–74, 1879–83; Correspondence of the Governors of Kan., 1879–83 (MS.), Kan. State Hist. Soc., Topeka; St. John's scrapbooks (13 vols.), in the possession of Miss May Parker, Olathe, Kan.; *Hist. of the State of Kan.* (1883), ed. by W. G. Cutler; D. W. Wilder, *The Annals of Kan.* (1886); Orline St. John Alexander, *The St. John Geneal.* (1907); *Who's Who in America,* 1914–15; *Emporia Gazette,* Sept. 1, 1916; Edna Tutt Frederikson, "John P. St. John, the Father of Constitutional Prohibition," doctoral dissertation (1931), Univ. of Kan.]   E. T. F.

ST. LUSSON, SIMON FRANÇOIS DAUMONT, Sieur de (d. 1674), French soldier and explorer, went to Canada in 1663 with the Commissioner Gaudais-Dupont. The next year he received a grant of land and thereafter acted as agent for the intendant Jean Talon. In 1668 he asked permission to return to France, probably with Talon, and came back with him to New France in 1670. In his second term of service (1670–73) Talon made extensive plans for enlarging New France and for exploring the interior of the continent of North America. Consequently, when news reached him in the year of his return of the discovery of copper on Lake Superior and of new alliances with the tribes around the upper Great Lakes, he determined to send an expedition, headed by St. Lusson, to take formal possession of this distant territory for the king of France and explore for mines near Lake Superior. It was October 1670 before the flotilla got under way. This was late for an expedition to so distant a destination, and St. Lusson was forced to camp with his men on the north shore of Lake Huron, spending the winter in hunting excursions. Early in the spring he sent Nicolas Perrot [*q.v.*] to Green Bay to summon the chiefs of the tribes there to the ceremony, while he himself proceeded to Sault Ste. Marie, where there was a Jesuit mission. On June 14 the pageant of annexation took place. Aided by the Jesuit missionaries, St. Lusson marched in state from the mission house and, in the presence of representatives from fourteen different tribes, performed a feudal ceremony of taking possession in the name of Louis XIV of all land "discovered and to be discovered." With the chanting of Latin hymns, the raising of a cross and the arms of France, and an oration to the Indians, the ceremony was concluded. He later advanced into the Lake Superior region but found no mines.

After his return to Quebec he served in Acadia and then went to France, where at Dieppe in May 1672 he sold a ship for Talon and sent gifts to the king of a young moose, a fox, and wild geese from Canada. Probably he went back the next year to Canada, where a son was christened in June 1673. Since his wife, Marguerite Bérin, remarried in 1675, it is supposed that he died in

1674. His fame rests on the great ceremony of annexation in 1671.

[See Louise P. Kellogg, ed., *Early Narratives of the Northwest* (1917) and *The French Régime in Wis. and the Northwest* (1925). The text of St. Lusson's official report is in *Wis. Hist. Colls.*, vol. XI (1888), reprinted from E. B. O'Callaghan, *Docs. Relative to the Colonial Hist. of the State of N. Y.*, vol. IX (1855), where Talon's report also appears, and in Pierre Margry, *Découvertes et Établissements des Français dans l'Ouest*, vol. I (1876), pp. 92–99. Perrot's account is in E. H. Blair, *Indian Tribes of the Great Lakes and Upper Miss. Region* (1911), vol. I. The account of the Jesuits is in R. G. Thwaites, ed., *The Jesuit Relations and Allied Docs.*, vol. LV (1899). See also Benjamin Sulte, "Les Français dans l'Ouest en 1671," *Proc. and Trans. Royal Soc. of Canada*, 3 ser., vol. XII (1919); *Le Bulletin des Recherches Historiques*, May 1931.]

L. P. K.

SAINT-MÉMIN, CHARLES BALTHAZAR JULIEN FEVRET de (Mar. 12, 1770–June 23, 1852), artist and engraver, was born in Dijon, France, the son of Bénigne Charles Fevret de Saint-Mémin and Victoire Marie de Motmans, a Creole from Santo Domingo. Privately educated in Dijon until he was fourteen, he entered the École Militaire in Paris, graduated in 1785, and in 1788 became an ensign in the French guards with the intention of following a military career. The French Revolution, however, obliged the family to flee to Switzerland. In 1793 he and his father left Switzerland for the West Indies to prevent the sequestration of Madame de Saint-Mémin's estate in Santo Domingo, but in New York they learned of the negro rebellion and went no farther. In need of money, they first started a vegetable garden, and when this venture failed Saint-Mémin turned to account his artistic ability, formerly a mere pastime.

His first American work (done in 1796) was a panoramic pencil sketch of New York, which he afterwards engraved and colored, getting his knowledge of the engraver's art from an encyclopedia. After executing several other landscapes, he turned to the more lucrative branch of portraiture. With a physionotrace, invented in 1786 by Gilles-Louis Chrétien, he secured an exact profile of the sitter on red paper (which later faded to a soft pink) and then drew in the features, hair, and clothing with black and white crayon. Afterwards, by means of a pantograph, he reduced the large profile to the size of a miniature about two inches in diameter and recorded it directly on a copper plate with graver and roulette. Both machine and tools he made himself, using the instructions of an encyclopedia and his own ingenuity. After a short partnership with an engraver named Valdenuit, he continued to work alone in New York until 1798, when he moved first to Burlington, N. J., where his mother and younger sister had established a girls' school, and later to Philadelphia. From 1804 to 1809 he lived successively in Baltimore, Annapolis, Washington, Richmond, Va., and Charleston, S. C. The following year he returned to France. Coming back to New York in 1812, he gave up engraving because of his impaired eyesight and painted portraits and landscapes in oils. Two years later, with his mother and sister, he returned to France, where from 1817 until his death he served as director of the museum at Dijon.

Nothing is known of Saint-Mémin's portraits in oils. Of his water colors there exist three portraits of women, owned by the Maryland Historical Society, and five profile portraits of Osage Indians probably done in Washington in 1804 (Lockwood, *post*). Most of the crayon portraits are in private collections. The eight hundred and more profile engravings include portraits of practically all distinguished Americans of the first part of the nineteenth century, as well as a portrait of Washington that is said to be the last one done from life. Saint-Mémin himself made the two identical groups of these in American collections, writing the name of the subject and the date of the engraving on each print. One of these (privately owned) was photographed and published with biographical data pertaining to the subject of each profile in *The St.-Mémin Collection of Portraits . . . To Which Are Prefixed a Memoir of M. de St. Mémin* (1862). The other collection is in the Corcoran Gallery of Art, Washington, together with some small engravings of public buildings executed for a proposed asylum for French refugees on the Susquehanna River, several silhouettes, and a line map entitled "Plan of the Siege of Savannah."

[Philippe Guignard, *Notice Historique Sur la Vie et les Travaux de M. Fevret de Saint-Mémin* (1853); J. H. Morgan, "The Work of M. Fevret de Saint-Mémin," in *Brooklyn Museum Quart.*, Jan. 1918; Frederick Houston, "Collecting the Portraits of St. Mémin," *House and Garden*, Nov. 1924; Alice Van Leer Carrick, "Saint-Mémin and His Profiles," *House Beautiful*, Nov. 1928, reprinted in *Shades of Our Ancestors* (1928); L. V. Lockwood, "The St. Mémin Indian Portraits," *N. Y. Hist. Soc. Quart. Bull.*, Apr. 1928; Theodore Bolton, *Early Am. Portrait Draughtsmen in Crayons* (1923), inaccurate in some details; critical study and hist. of the landscapes in I. N. P. Stokes, *The Iconography of Manhattan Island* (6 vols., 1915–28).]

F. N.

SAINT-MÉRY, MOREAU de [See MOREAU DE SAINT-MÉRY, MÉDÉRIC-LOUIS-ELIE, 1750–1819].

ST. VRAIN, CERAN DE HAULT DE LASSUS de (May 5, 1802–Oct. 28, 1870), Santa Fé trader, pioneer merchant, soldier, was born at Spanish Lake, near St. Louis, Mo., the son of Marie Felicité Chauvet (Dubreuil) and Jacques Marcellin Ceran DeHault DeLassus de St. Vrain, an officer in the French navy who had come to America and settled near Ste. Genevieve, Mo., in 1793–94. At an early age the son embarked in the fur trade. He was in Taos, N. Mex., on Mar. 21, 1825, having just finished a troublesome journey of five months to that place. About this time he dissolved partnership with François Guerin, with whom he had conducted an expedition to the southwest outfitted by Bernard Pratte & Company of St. Louis. On Aug. 29, 1826, Gov. Antonio Narbona of New Mexico issued a passport at Santa Fé to St. Vrain and William S. Williams [q.v.] to the state of Sonora for private trade. At this time St. Vrain, in partnership with Paul Baillio since the previous June, was engaged in equipping trappers. He sold his interest to Sylvestre Pratte in the fall of 1826 and worked for Pratte as his clerk until the latter's death, Sept. 1, 1828. About Jan. 1, 1831, he formed a partnership with Charles Bent [q.v.], under the name of Bent, St. Vrain, & Company, which lasted until Bent's assassination and was surpassed in importance only by the American Fur Company.

Like most of the Santa Fé traders, he became a citizen of Mexico. In 1844, for valuable services in maintaining the peace on the Mexican frontier, he and Cornelio Vigil received a land grant from the Mexican government comprising four million acres in the fertile valleys of the Huerfano, Apishapa, Purgatoire, and other tributaries. The title to this land was confirmed by the United States government after Vigil's death, application for confirmation being made by St. Vrain as manager of Vigil's estate and probably as surviving partner. At the time of the Taos anti-American revolt during the Mexican War, he was the organizer and captain of a company of volunteers. When the Apaches and Utes made war on the ranches and villages, 1854–55, he was appointed lieutenant-colonel of volunteers. In June 1861 he was appointed colonel of the first New Mexico cavalry, but he resigned on October 12, 1861, "on account of age" and was succeeded by Kit Carson.

He had married Luisa Branch of Mora, N. Mex., and had two sons and a daughter. He was a large powerful man, whose sturdiness of character, courage, and honesty made a deep impression on the southwest. In books written by western visitors he is described as a polite gentleman and an amiable fellow traveler and is pictured as an outstanding figure. When he died at Mora, his funeral was attended by officers from Fort Union and more than two thousand other persons.

[Information from St. Vrain's daughter; Baptismal Reg., Old Cathedral, St. Louis; W. B. Douglas, "Geneal. of family of De Lassus and St. Vrain" (MS.), and Bent and St. Vrain Collection (MSS.), in Mo. Hist. Soc.; T. M. Marshall, "St. Vrain's Expedition to the Gila in 1826," Southwestern Hist. Quart., Jan. 1916; Annie H. Abel, The Official Correspondence of James S. Calhoun While Indian Agent at Santa Fé (1915); Benj. M. Read, Illustrated Hist. of N. Mex. (1912); R. E. Twitchell, The Leading Facts of New Mexican Hist., vol. II (1912); Le Baron B. Prince, A Concise Hist. of N. Mex. (1912), and Hist. of the Ark. Valley, Colo. (1881); Louis Houck, A Hist. of Mo. (1908), vol. I; F. L. Billon, Annals of St. Louis (1886); L. H. Garrard, Wah-To-Yah and the Taos Trail (1850); Mo. Republican (St. Louis), Nov. 17, 1870.]   S. M. D.

SAJOUS, CHARLES EUCHARISTE DE MÉDICIS (Dec. 13, 1852–Apr. 27, 1929), physician, was born at sea while his parents, Count Charles Roustan de Médicis-Jodoigne of Florence, Italy, and his wife, Marie Pierette (Cort), were traveling to France. When he was two years old his father died; eight years later his mother married Charles Sajous, and the youth assumed the surname of his stepfather. He began his medical studies at the University of California, but finished them at Jefferson Medical College, Philadelphia, from which he graduated in 1878. After serving a term as resident physician at the Howard Hospital in Philadelphia, he began practising laryngology in that city. From 1880 to 1882 he was professor of anatomy and physiology in the Wagner Free Institute of Science, and from 1881 to 1890, clinical lecturer on laryngology in Jefferson Medical College. In 1891, having become greatly interested in the new field of endocrinology, he went abroad to study the subject in the European clinics. He remained in France and Germany for several years engaged in this pursuit and throughout the rest of his life the study of the physiology and therapeutics of the ductless glands chiefly absorbed his energies. In 1897–98, after his return to America, he was professor of laryngology and dean of the faculty of the Medico-Chirurgical College of Philadelphia. From 1909 to 1922 he held the chair of therapeutics in the medical college of Temple University. Here he had an opportunity to expound his views on endocrinology which was further extended when in 1921 he was appointed professor of applied endocrinology in the Post Graduate School of the University of Pennsylvania. This position he held until his death.

Sajous was a voluminous writer and an indefatigable editor. In 1885 he published Hay Fever and Its Successful Treatment by Superficial Organic Alteration of the Nasal Mucous Membrane, and in the same year, Lectures on the Diseases of the Nose and Throat. From 1888 to 1896 he undertook editorial charge of the Annual of the

Universal Medical Sciences, published by the F. A. Davis Company of Philadelphia, and during the nine years of its existence not only edited but contributed innumerable articles to the forty-five volumes of this work. In 1898 he assumed the editorship of a somewhat similar project published by the same firm, at first called the *Annual and Analytical Cyclopædia of Practical Medicine* and later, *Sajous's Analytic Cyclopædia of Practical Medicine,* of which ten editions, in from six to nine volumes each, were issued before his death. He was the author of *The Internal Secretions and the Principles of Medicine* (2 vols., 1903–07), in which he reviewed all the available literature on endocrinology and set forth his own views on the subject. This book also went through a number of editions, but it is marred by the uncritical enthusiasm with which its author indorsed the views of many writers whose statements were not based upon exact scientific observation. From 1911 to 1919 he was managing editor of the *New York Medical Journal.* He was the first president of the Association for the Study of the Internal Secretions, a member of the American College of Physicians, the American Therapeutic Society, and the American Philosophical Society, and a fellow of the College of Physicians of Philadelphia. In 1926 he published *The Strength of Religion as Shown by Science.* He married, Jan. 30, 1884, Emma Christine Bergner of Philadelphia. Their only child, Louis Theodore de Médicis Sajous, graduated in medicine at the University of Pennsylvania in 1909 and was closely associated with his father in his studies in endocrinology. He died Jan. 16, 1929, and three months later his father died, from cardio-renal disease, at his home in Philadelphia.

[Victor Robinson, in *Medic. Life,* Jan. 1925, with full bibliog. to that date; *N. Y. Medic. Jour.,* Dec. 9, 1911; *Medic. Jour. and Record,* May 15, 1929; *Jour. Am. Medic. Asso.,* May 4, 1929; J. M. Anders, in *Trans. Coll. of Physicians of Phila.,* 3 ser. LII (1930); *Pa. Medic. Jour.,* June 1929; *Who's Who in America,* 1928–29, inaccurate in the spelling of names; *Pub. Ledger* (Phila.), Apr. 28, 1929; personal acquaintance.]
F. R. P.

SALISBURY, ALBERT (Jan. 24, 1843–June 2, 1911), educator, eldest of six children of Oliver and Emily (Cravath) Salisbury, both of New England stock, was born in Lima, Rock County, Wis. His father was a farmer, sheep-raiser, and nursery-man, and the son served an apprenticeship in all these callings. His mother, a teacher before her marriage, supplemented effectively the instruction he gained in the little district school. At eighteen he began attendance at Milton Academy, continuing till he enlisted in December 1863 as private in the 13th Wisconsin

Infantry. He saw service in the Army of the Cumberland, and for three months after the ending of the Civil War, in Texas. For a time after his return to Wisconsin he was farmer, nurseryman, and teacher in a rural school. Then, as was to have been expected of a man who had taken his Latin textbooks with him when he went to the war, he continued his studies. Milton Academy had now become Milton College, and here he was graduated A.B. in 1870. In that same year he became principal of the Brodhead, Wis., high school, and three years later, instructor of history and the first conductor of teachers' institutes for the state normal school at Whitewater, Wis. Through his service for nine years in the latter capacity he was largely instrumental in shaping in Wisconsin that form of training teachers in service.

In 1882 he resigned his Whitewater positions and began work for the American Missionary Association as superintendent of schools for the freedmen of the South and the Indians of the West, but in 1885 returned to the Whitewater Normal School as its president, in which office he remained until his death. He was a man of commanding presence and both from the chapel platform and through conference with individuals exerted a strong influence on the lives of his students. A vigorous force in community and state, he urged the establishment of a state institution for the feeble minded and the improving of the rural schools. As chairman of committees of the Wisconsin Teachers' Association which had espoused both these causes, he investigated conditions, reported them by voice and pen, and agitated vigorously and persistently for reform of the prevailing ills. After several failures, he was instrumental in securing, in 1895, the establishment of a state institution for the feeble minded. In the fall of 1900 he was one of those who participated by invitation in the "Teachers' Visit to Europe" under the auspices of the National Civic Federation. After his return in the spring of 1909 he rendered a report to the National Education Association on teacher training in Great Britain. As author and editor his chief works were: *Historical Sketch of Normal Instruction in Wisconsin, 1846–76* (1876); *Orthoepy and Phonology* (1879); *The Duty of the State to the Feeble-Minded* (1890); *Historical Sketches of the First Quarter-Century of the State Normal School at Whitewater* (1893); *The Rural School Problem* (1897); *Theory of Teaching and Elementary Psychology* (1905); *School Management: a Textbook for County Training Schools and Normal Schools* (1911). He was an active member and for long one of the trustees of the

Congregational Church of Whitewater. He was twice married: on Nov. 20, 1866 to Abba A. Maxson who died in 1881, and in 1883 to Agnes Hosford, who, with three children of his first marriage, survived him.

[*Bull. of the State Normal School, Whitewater, Wis.,* Jan. 1912; *Who's Who in America,* 1910–11; *Whitewater Register,* June 9, 1911; *Milwaukee Free Press,* Feb. 19, 1905; *Milwaukee Sentinel,* June 3, 1911; typewritten autobiographical sketch in possession of Salisbury's widow (Whitewater, Wis.).]   W. J. C.

SALISBURY, EDWARD ELBRIDGE (Apr. 6, 1814–Feb. 5, 1901), Orientalist and teacher, was born in Boston, Mass. His father, Josiah, was of English ancestry, of a noted family; his mother, Abby (Breese) Salisbury, was of Huguenot descent. His early education was given him by his father, who, having been connected with the mercantile business of the family, then for a time a clergyman in Boston, had retired to private life. Fitted for college at the Boston Latin School, he went to Yale, where his brother-in-law, Theodore Dwight Woolsey [*q.v.*], became professor of Greek in 1831. After graduating, in 1832, he spent several years in advanced study in New Haven, paying especial attention to Hebrew and the cognate languages. In 1836 he married his cousin, Abigail Salisbury Phillips, daughter of Edward Phillips of Boston, and with her proceeded to Europe, where for nearly four years he studied Oriental languages, especially Arabic with De Sacy and Garcin de Tassy in Paris, and Sanskrit with Bopp in Berlin. On his return to America in 1841 he was appointed professor of Arabic and Sanskrit at Yale; but before assuming the duties of the office he spent the year 1842–43 in Europe, studying chiefly Sanskrit in Bonn and Paris.

When he began his work at Yale, in 1843, he was the only scholar of his kind in America, and he at once began to supply what was greatly needed. It was given to him to open the wide field of Oriental studies in this country, to arouse interest in great literatures and in chapters of history hitherto little known, and to prepare the way for scientific research in the two chief domains which his chair included. In the early years of the American Oriental Society (founded in 1842) he was one of its main pillars. He contributed to its first volume, and provided at his own expense fonts of Oriental type. "For some ten years he was virtually the Society, doing its work and paying its bills. He gave it standing and credit in the world of scholars" (*In Memoriam, post,* p. 6). In the *Journal* of the Society he published papers dealing with Arabic, Sanskrit, Persian cuneiform, Assyrian, and Phoenician, as well as an able essay on the genuineness of the Nestorian monument of Singan-fu. He was in constant correspondence with American missionaries in the East, who provided him with valuable material.

In 1854 he relinquished the professorship of Sanskrit to his former pupil, William Dwight Whitney [*q.v.*], retaining, however, the chair of Arabic until 1856. It was after the latter date that he did his principal work on research and publication. The following papers, printed in the *Journal of the American Oriental Society,* deserve especial mention: "Contributions from Original Sources to Our Knowledge of the Science of Muslim Tradition" (1859; vol. VII); "Materials for the History of the Muhammadan Doctrine of Predestination and Free Will" (1863; vol. VIII); "The Book of Sulaimân's First Ripe Fruit, Disclosing the Mysteries of the Nusairian Religion" (1864; vol. VIII). While his tastes were chiefly literary and historical, nevertheless his philological attainments were of a very high order. His knowledge of the Arabic language was thorough and accurate, and he was well acquainted with the literature which up to that time had been made available. In his later years he gave much time to studies in the fields of art and history. His eyesight failing, he devoted himself to genealogical research, with the skilful assistance of his second wife, Evelyn McCurdy Salisbury, daughter of Judge Charles J. McCurdy of Lyme, Conn.; his first wife had died in 1869. First published were his *Family-Memorials* ... (2 vols., 1885); then the *Family-Histories and Genealogies* ... (5 vols., 1892), dealing with his wife's family.

Salisbury's public-spirited benefactions were many. To Yale University he gave large sums for buildings, books, and collections; also (thirty years before his death) his own very valuable library, containing a large part of De Sacy's library and collection of Arabic manuscripts. It was only through funds contributed by him that Yale was enabled to secure for its faculty Professors William Dwight Whitney and James Dwight Dana [*q.v.*]. He was elected a member of the Société Asiatique in 1838, a corresponding member of the Imperial Academy of Sciences and Belles Lettres, Constantinople, in 1855, and a corresponding member of the Deutsche Morgenländische Gesellschaft in 1859.

[*Obit. Record Grads. Yale Univ.,* 1901; *New Eng. Hist. and Geneal. Reg.,* Oct. 1901; E. W. Hopkins, "Memorial Address in Honor of Professor Salisbury" (presented Feb. 16, 1901, at Yale Univ.), pub. in his *India Old and New* (1901), reprinted in abstract, "In Memoriam," in the *Jour. Am. Oriental Soc.,* vol. XXII, pt. I (1901); E. M. Salisbury, in *Family-Histories and Geneals.* (1895); *Biog. Memoranda Respecting All Who Ever Were Members of the Class of 1832 in Yale*

Coll. (1880), ed. by E. E. Salisbury; Salisbury's "Jour. of Travels in Europe," MS., in the Yale Lib.] C. C. T.

SALISBURY, JAMES HENRY (Oct. 13, 1823–Aug. 23, 1905), physician, was born at Scott, N. Y., the son of Nathan and Lucretia (Babcock) Salisbury, both of English colonial ancestry. After attending Homer Academy near his birthplace, he received the degree of bachelor of natural science from Rensselaer Institute of Troy, N. Y., in 1846, his medical degree from Albany Medical College in 1850, and the degree of M.A. from Union College in 1852. Appointed assistant chemist of the New York state geological survey at Albany in 1846, he became chief chemist in 1849. In 1851–52 he also lectured on elementary and applied chemistry at the state normal school. During this period he wrote *Anatomy and Histology of Plants* (1848) and *History and Chemical Investigations of Maize* (1849), the latter a voluminous pamphlet issued by the state agricultural society.

Although he later settled at Newark, Ohio, for practice, his chief interest was still in research. In addition to *Ancient Earth and Rock-Writing* (1863), a book on the mound builders written in collaboration with his brother, C. B. Salisbury, and such books as *An Account of Some Experiments and Observations on the Influence of Poisons and Medicinal Agents upon Plants* (1854), *Some Experiments on Poisoning with Vegetable Alkaloids* (1862), *Experiments Connected with the Discovery of Cholesterin and Seroline* (1863), and *Histology and Anatomy of the Spleen* (1866), his early work included the analysis of various fruits and vegetables and, in the field of phytopathology, a book on *Blight in Apple, Pear, and Quince Trees and Decay of their Fruit* (1863). Influenced by his work in plant pathology he conceived the idea that human disease was also largely due to fungus infestation. In 1862 he wrote an article (*American Journal of the Medical Sciences,* July 1862) attributing measles in the army camps to fungi found on straw, and a second (*Ibid.,* October 1862) on experimental inoculation with straw fungi for prevention of the disease. Later he identified certain "algoid vegetations" as the causative agents in malaria, syphilis, gonorrhea, variola, vaccinia, and typhoid fever, and reported these investigations in detail in *New Algoid Vegetations* (1868) and *Microscopic Examinations of Blood* (1868). Similarly, in *Original Investigations in Diphtheria and Scarlet Fever* (1882), he affirmed that the two diseases were nearly related and that both were due to what he called "mucor malignans," a fungus he found in the blood and excretions of patients. It is evi-

dent that he was groping vaguely about in the dawn of the germ theory of disease, near to the solution of some of its problems but always falling short of realization. By the time germ causation was well established, his interests were elsewhere and he shared none of the honors. He was then advocating the preponderant influence of food and drink in the production of disease, including in his list abnormal growths and mental alienation. He wrote two books in support of this idea, *Brief Statement of the So-Called "Salisbury Plans" of Treating by Alimentation* (1887) and *Relation of Alimentation and Disease* (1888). Meanwhile he had assisted in the organization of the Charity Hospital Medical School in Cleveland, where from 1864 to 1866 he was professor of physiology, histology, and pathology. From about 1880 he lived in New York City. He died suddenly from a cerebral hemorrhage at his summer home in Dobbs Ferry, N. Y. He had been married on June 26, 1860, to Clara Brasee of Lancaster, Ohio, daughter of John T. Brasee. A final estimate of his work marks him as an able microscopist and a painstaking investigator; his articles, which received serious consideration when published, are scholarly and well illustrated with charts. Of all his researches those in medicine are the least useful, although a little later he might have achieved world fame through them.

[*Who's Who in America,* 1903–05; anonymous, *Sketch of Life of James H. Salisbury* (1884), with portrait; *Albany Medic. Annals,* Nov. 1905, pp. 777–79; H. A. Kelly and W. L. Burrage, *Am. Medic. Biogs.* (1920); obituary in *N. Y. Tribune,* Aug. 24, 1905.]

J. M. P—n.

SALISBURY, ROLLIN D. (Aug. 17, 1858–Aug. 15, 1922), geologist and educator, was born at Spring Prairie, Walworth County, Wis., the son of Daniel and Lucinda (Bryant) Salisbury. He attended the public schools, graduating from the state normal school at Whitewater in 1877, and after a year of teaching entered Beloit College, where Thomas Chrowder Chamberlin [*q.v.*] was professor of geology. Soon after his graduation in 1881 he became Chamberlin's assistant in his work for the United States Geological Survey, thus beginning a quasi-official connection which lasted until 1910. In 1882, when Chamberlin resigned from Beloit, Salisbury replaced him, attaining the rank of professor in 1884. Here—except for the year 1887–88 which he spent in study abroad, especially at Heidelberg— he continued until 1891, when he became professor of geology at the University of Wisconsin. The following year he accompanied Chamberlin to the new University of Chicago, as professor of geographic geology, and there spent the rest of his life. He was head of the department of geography from 1892 to 1919, and from then until he died Chamberlin's successor as head of the department of geology. In addition, he was dean of the University Colleges, 1894–96, and dean of the Ogden Graduate School of Science from 1899 until his death. He was closely associated with Chamberlin in the management of the *Journal of Geology* from its foundation in 1893, and for the last four years of his life was the responsible editor.

As a teacher Salisbury took high rank. His master, Chamberlin, said that his "greatest service to science lay in his singular success in stimulating and training young talent, not only for the teaching of science but for research." As dean of the Ogden School he came in touch with thousands of young minds to whom he imparted "effective impulses toward sound scholarship and the higher life" (Chamberlin, *post*, p. 481). It has been stated that at one time fully a third of the state geologists of the country had been his pupils. He required a great deal of his students and was harshly critical of failure, but eagerly spent himself to further the development of those in whom he saw promise. He was a lucid writer, and for ease of comprehension, even by those who were not geologists, had few equals.

Salisbury limited his geological researches chiefly to glacial and Pleistocene deposits, and in his field became a leading authority. During his year at European universities in 1887–88 he studied particularly the glacial deposits of the North German lowlands, and he subsequently made an extended trip through South America. For the purpose of studying glacial action at close hand, he took part in the Peary Relief Expedition of 1895. From 1891 to 1915 he was geologist in charge of the Pleistocene division of the Geological Survey of New Jersey, and in 1919 he was appointed a member of the board of commissioners in charge of the Illinois Survey. His most notable contributions in his special field were "Preliminary Paper on the Driftless Area of the Upper Mississippi Valley" (*Sixth Annual Report of the United States Geological Survey . . . 1884–'85*, 1885), in which he collaborated with Chamberlin, and his articles on "Surface Geology of New Jersey" in the *Geological Survey of New Jersey: Annual Reports of the State Geologist*. With Chamberlin he was also the author of *Geology* (3 vols., 1904–06), in the American Science Series.

Salisbury was a man of exceptional presence, straightforward, unpretentious, possessing culture, refinement, and marked conversational ability. Though a lover of children and family life,

he never married. From his college days he was regarded almost as a son by the Chamberlins and for years looked upon their house as his real home. He was stricken with coronary thrombosis on May 31, 1922, and died in the following August.

[The "D." in Salisbury's signature was merely a letter, standing for no name (Keyes, *post*, p. 97). Sources include *Who's Who in America*, 1922–23; E. S. Ames, in *Univ. Record* (Univ. of Chicago), Oct. 1922; Charles Keyes in *Pan-American Geologist*, Sept. 1922; T. C. Chamberlin, in *Jour. of Geol.*, Aug.-Sept. 1922; H. D. Densmore, in *Wis. Mag. of Hist.*, Sept., Dec. 1931; *N. Y. Times*, Aug. 17, 1922; *Chicago Herald and Examiner*, Aug. 16, 17, 1922; personal acquaintance.] G. P. M.

SALM-SALM, AGNES ELISABETH WINONA LECLERCQ JOY, Princess (Dec. 25, 1840–Dec. 21, 1912), whose part in the Mexican adventure of Emperor Maximilian made her internationally conspicuous, was born on a farm in Franklin County, Vt., or possibly in Philipsburg, Que., where part of her girlhood was spent. The daughter of William and Julia (Willard) Joy and the grand-daughter of Micah Joy, a Revolutionary soldier, she was descended from Thomas Joy [*q.v.*]. Her adventurous spirit, which found vent in escapades which lived long in local tradition, took her to Washington early in the Civil War, where, under the name of Agnes Leclercq, she was married, Aug. 20, 1862, to a German soldier of fortune, Felix Constantin Alexander Johann Nepomuk, Prince Salm-Salm (1828–1870), a colonel on Gen. Louis Blenker's staff. Her energy and cleverness secured for him the colonelcy of the 8th New York Infantry, and later of the 68th. Accompanying her husband, she became a notable figure in camp, field, and hospital—the toast of the officers and the talk of the men. Her husband was brevetted brigadier-general of volunteers at the close of the war, and was appointed military governor of Atlanta.

Upon being mustered out, he embarked in February 1866 for Mexico, where the Austrian archduke, Maximilian, was struggling to maintain himself as emperor in the face of the forces headed by President Juarez. Salm-Salm became Maximilian's chief aide, and his wife followed him to Mexico and shared all his anxieties. When Querétaro fell by treason and Maximilian and his suite were captured and threatened with summary execution, she braved all obstacles and dangers to go to their rescue. When intercession failed, she plotted the Emperor's escape, offering his keeper large bribes of money or anything else within her gift; failing, she clasped the knees of President Juarez, praying for mercy, but without success. Before his execution Maximilian decorated her with the Grand Cordon of the Order of San Carlos, and later his brother, the Austrian emperor, pensioned her. Salm-Salm next became a major in the Prussian Guards, and in the ensuing war with France was killed (1870). The Princess, experienced in army relief work in America, obtained from General von Steinmetz permission to accompany his staff on horseback and to carry on a relief work in camps and field hospitals like that since developed under the Red Cross. Generals von Goeben and Fransecky thanked her personally and in the name of the army for her services; she received the Prussian Medal of Honor and was recommended for the Iron Cross, a decoration reserved for men. The Empress Augusta gave her an onyx brooch.

Left a widow at thirty, after a decade of breathless activity, she went to Rome to consult Pope Pius IX with regard to entering a convent, but he told her that she had no vocation to be a nun, and she eventually settled down to the routine of German social life, residing first at Bonn and later at Karlsruhe. In 1875, at Stuttgart, she published *Zehn Jahre aus Meinem Leben,* three volumes covering her decade of war service. It was published in English as *Ten Years of My Life* (2 vols., London, 1876; Detroit and New York, 1877). In 1876 she married the secretary of the British legation at Berlin, Charles Heneage, from whom she later separated. She revisited America in 1899, bringing the flags of the Prince Salm-Salm's regiments and being warmly greeted by Carl Schurz and other wartime friends; in 1899–1900 she came again, seeking funds for an ambulance corps for the Boers. Twelve years later she died at Karlsruhe. Her appeal to Juarez is the subject of a historical painting by Manuel Ocaranza (1873), owned formely by Gen. Mariano Ruiz, Mexico City. She also figures in the drama *Juarez and Maximilian* by Franz V. Werfel, produced in Vienna, Berlin, and New York (1925–26), and in several novels.

[*Ten Years of My Life* (1876), mentioned above; Prince Felix Salm-Salm, *My Diary in Mexico in 1867* (2 vols., London, 1868); German edition (3 vols., Stuttgart, 1868), repr. 1928 as *Maximilian von Mexico . . . Blätter aus dem Tagebuch des Prinzen Felix zu Salm-Salm,* ed. by Otto Hellinghaus; J. R. Joy, *Thomas Joy and His Descendants* (1900), with portrait; *Almanach de Gotha,* 1894 and later issues; Sara Y. Stevenson, *Maximilian in Mexico* (1899); Eagon Cæsar, Count Corti, *Maximilian and Charlotte of Mexico* (2 vols., 1928); J. L. Blasio, *Maximilian, Emperor of Mexico, Memoirs of His Private Secretary* (1934), ed. by R. H. Murray; *Metropolitan,* Aug. 1899; *N. Y. Times,* Dec. 22, 1912.]　　J. R. J.

SALMON, DANIEL ELMER (July 23, 1850–Aug. 30, 1914), veterinarian, was born at Mount Olive, N. J., the son of Daniel Landon and Eleanor (Flock) Salmon. After a preparatory education in the public schools of Mount Olive and in Chester Institute nearby, he entered Cornell University in 1868 with the first freshman class and became interested in the veterinary department. Graduating in 1872 with the degree of bachelor of veterinary science, after a course which included six months at the Alfort Veterinary School in Paris, he married Mary Thompson Corning of Ithaca, N. Y., and settled in Newark, N. J., for the practice of veterinary medicine. In 1876 he received the degree of doctor of veterinary medicine from Cornell. In 1875, on account of impaired health, he had moved to Asheville, N. C. Two years later he delivered a course of lectures on veterinary medicine at the University of Georgia, and in the same year he began special study of the disease of swine. After sharing in a campaign carried on by the state of New York in 1879 for the eradication of contagious pleuro-pneumonia of cattle, he accepted an appointment with the United States Department of Agriculture to investigate diseases of domestic animals in the southern states, with special reference to Texas fever. Early in 1883 he was asked to organize in the Bureau of Agriculture a veterinary division, which in the following year became the Bureau of Animal Industry. He was made chief of the bureau and held the post until a controversy with the department head caused his resignation in December 1905.

The period of his incumbency marks an epoch of notable achievement. His early contacts with contagious pleuro-pneumonia and Texas fever led him to concentrate the attention of the bureau upon them, with the result that these two serious menaces to the cattle industry were soon under complete control. Other investigations concerned the cause and prevention of fowl cholera, contagious diseases of swine, and nodular disease of sheep. In his earlier career Salmon had been a skilful laboratory technician, but the exactions of administrative duties early took him away from the details of research. In addition to a genius for the selection of assistants, he had great administrative ability and professional vision. As head of the bureau he directed its policies and planned the work of his assistants and found time to write nearly one hundred articles, either alone or in collaboration with others, which collectively cover the whole field of veterinary research of the period. In the field of public health administration he was responsible for the inauguration of a nation-wide system of meat inspection, for a quarantine system for imported live stock, and for the inspection of exported cattle and the ships carrying them. In 1906 he accepted an invitation from the government of Uruguay to organize the veterinary department of the University of Montevideo and remained there five years. Returning to the United States, he took up the manufacture of veterinary biological products. In 1913 he assumed the management of a laboratory for the production of serum for the prevention of hog cholera in Butte, Mont. He died there of pneumonia and was buried in Rock Creek Cemetery in Washington. After the death of his first wife he married on Nov. 15, 1904, Agnes Christina Dewhurst of New York. He had been president of the American Public Health Association and of the American Veterinary Medical Association and was a member of many foreign and American scientific societies.

[For a list of Salmon's publications, see C. W. Stiles and Albert Hassall, *Index-Catalogue of Medic. and Veterinary Zoology* (36 nos., 1902–12). See also *Who's Who in America,* 1914–15; D. E. Salmon, *The U. S. Bureau of Animal Industry . . . 1884–1900* (1901); *Cornell Veterinarian,* Oct. 1914; *Am. Veterinary Rev.,* Oct. 1914; H. A. Kelly and W. L. Burrage, eds., *Am. Medic. Biogs.* (1920); *Evening Star* (Washington, D. C.), Sept. 3, 1914.]   J. M. P—n.

SALMON, LUCY MAYNARD (July 27, 1853–Feb. 14, 1927), educator, historian, was born in Fulton, N. Y. Her parents, George and Maria Clara (Maynard) Salmon, were both natives of Massachusetts. She attended Falley Seminary in Fulton and had a year of preparation at the Ann Arbor (Mich.) high school before she entered the University of Michigan, from which she received the A.B. degree in 1876. After five years spent in McGregor, Iowa, where she was principal of the high school, she returned to the University of Michigan for graduate work in history. There she studied under Charles Kendall Adams and took the A.M. degree in 1883. Her thesis, the "History of the Appointing Power of the President," was published in the first volume of the *Papers of the American Historical Association* (1886). For three years then she taught history at the Indiana state normal school and returned to graduate study, this time to Bryn Mawr College. As fellow in history, 1886–87, she worked under Woodrow Wilson, then in his second year of teaching at Bryn Mawr. In 1887 she went to Vassar College, first as associate professor, and two years later as professor of history, and made that the center of her life work. She was still in active teaching at the time of her death.

While she wrote and published a number of books and articles, it was as teacher that her greatest influence was felt. The present day theory of making the student the chief agent in his own instruction was the cardinal principle of her teaching, and from this she never wavered.

The project method, dear to the progressive school in recent time, was years ago made notable by her use of the special topic in her own history classes. Under her teaching the library was the laboratory of the student of history. She made it her special concern to see that the college library was well equipped with original sources for research. In the field of history teaching her influence spread far beyond her own class-room. She was a member of the committee of seven of the American Historical Association, 1896–99, whose report *The Study of History in Schools* (1899), formed the standard guide for the teaching of history in secondary schools for the next generation. She was founder and the first president of the Association of History Teachers of the Middle States and Maryland, 1903–04. She was an active life member of the American Historical Association and served, 1915–19, as the first woman elected to its executive council. In the field of historical scholarship her most significant influence was in her fresh view of what constitutes historical material. To her the matter from which history is to be written was not primarily the consciously significant document, the Constitution of the United States or Magna Carta, but the daily newspaper, a railway time-table, the place name of a region, something of ordinary observation on Main Street or in the back yard. She was profoundly interested in the material of every-day living as significant for interpretation of the past. Her volume, *Domestic Service* (1897) was written as an examination of the common sphere of the household for the elucidation of historical and economic forces. The study of the newspaper as historical material was the most extensive of her published work. The two companion volumes, *The Newspaper and the Historian* and *The Newspaper and Authority,* both published in 1923, are undoubtedly the works by which her quality as historical scholar will be measured. She took active part in the civic life of Poughkeepsie and consistently impressed upon her students the ideals of good citizenship, whether the civic unit be the college campus or the home town or the nation. No one who knew her could fail to recall her continuous and consistent devotion to peace. Even in wartime she remained quietly and steadily loyal to this principle. In 1926, the year before her death, her former students and other friends established at Vassar the "Lucy Maynard Salmon Fund for Research," and under this fund the first publication was her posthumous volume, *Why is History Rewritten?* (1929). Another posthumous volume, *Historical Material,* was published in 1933.

[*Who's Who in America*, 1926–27; *Vassar Miscellany News*, Feb. 19, 1927; *New York Times*, Feb. 15, 1927; *Am. Hist. Rev.*, Apr. 1927; *Addresses at the Memorial Service for Lucy Maynard Salmon, Held at Vassar College*, Mar. 6, 1927 (1927); *Proc. of the Assn. of Hist. Teachers of the Middle States and Maryland*, No. 25 (1927), No. 31 (1933) with an appreciative notice and a portrait; MS. bibliography in Vassar College Library; personal association over a long period of years.]
          C. M. T.

SALMON, THOMAS WILLIAM (Jan. 6, 1876–Aug. 13, 1927), physician, psychiatrist, pioneer in mental hygiene, was born in Lansingburg, Rensselaer County, N. Y. His father, Thomas Henry, a physician, and his mother, Annie (Frost), were natives of England. Salmon's formal education was obtained in the village schools and academy. Graduating from the Albany Medical College in 1899 with the degree of M.D., he spent a year in private practice, at Brewster, N. Y., and served temporarily at the Willard, N. Y., state hospital for mental disorders. During an epidemic of diphtheria in that institution he made with W. L. Russell one of the earliest studies of human carriers, the results of which were printed in the report of the state commission in lunacy (October 1904), and published separately the following year (*Report of an Epidemic of Diphtheria in the Willard State Hospital*).

In 1903 he entered the United States Public Health Service. As a result of a medical trip on a revenue cutter, he proposed and drew plans for a hospital ship for fishermen at sea, which was afterwards provided (see *Modern Hospital*, June 1914). In 1905 he was assigned to the immigration service at Ellis Island, New York Harbor. There, for six years, during one of which (1911) he was on leave of absence as chief medical examiner for the New York state commission in lunacy, his interest and efforts were directed to measures for preventing an influx of the mentally unfit from foreign countries, and for dealing adequately with the problem of mental disorders in the immigrant population. His work at Ellis Island, his writings, and his representations at Washington contributed much to what is best in the present laws, regulations, and methods relating to this problem. In 1912 he made for the National Committee for Mental Hygiene an extremely productive survey of the treatment of mental disorders throughout the country. He was appointed medical director of this committee in 1915 and became the leading spirit and guide in a widespread movement for improvement in the treatment and prevention of mental disorders. He was one of the founders and a member of the first editorial board of the magazine *Mental Hygiene*. The excellent statistical studies of the insane and feeble-minded, which are now conducted by the federal Bureau of Census, were established under his initiative and guidance.

During the World War he mobilized the psychiatric resources of the country, and enabled the United States Army to adopt remarkably effective measures for preventing the admission of recruits who were nervously and mentally unfit and for dealing with mental disorders and disabilities among the soldiers. He was awarded the distinguished service medal, and retired to the reserve corps with the rank of brigadier-general. He then directed his attention to the mentally disabled ex-service men, and the superior hospital and out-patient service provided for their care was in great measure due to his capable, indefatigable efforts.

In 1921, he resigned his position with the National Committee to become professor of psychiatry at Columbia University and a consulting psychiatrist. At Columbia he reorganized his department and added greatly to its teaching and research resources by securing from the state the establishment, at the medical college, of a psychiatric institute and hospital. Salmon was an interesting and convincing speaker and made many addresses. He published numerous articles in current journals; edited, with Norman Fenton, the section on "Neuropsychiatry," in volume X (1929) of *The United States Army in the World War*, and wrote the chapter on immigration in W. A. White and S. E. Jelliffe, *Modern Treatment of Nervous and Mental Diseases* (1913), and the chapter on mental hygiene in M. J. Rosenau, *Preventive Medicine and Hygiene* (1913). In 1899 he married Helen Potter Ashley; four boys and two girls were born to them. He died by accidental drowning.

[*Who's Who in America*, 1926–27; *Mental Hygiene*, Oct. 1927; bibliog. of ninety titles, *Ibid.*, Jan. 1928; *N. Y. Times*, Aug. 15–19, 1927; personal acquaintance.]
          W. L. R.

SALOMON, HAYM (*c.* 1740–Jan. 6, 1785), merchant, banker, Revolutionary financier, was born at Lissa, Poland, of Jewish-Portuguese ancestry. In his youth he traveled widely, acquired an excellent knowledge of foreign languages, and, returning to Poland about the age of thirty, became an ardent advocate of Polish independence. In 1772 he fled to England and thence to New York, where he opened a brokerage and commission merchant's business. His previous association with the cause of liberty in his native country drew him naturally to the side of the American Whigs and later to the movement for American independence. During the British occupation of New York his activities led to his arrest as a spy (Sept. 22, 1776) and consequent imprisonment. The British, however, put him to use as an interpreter and assigned him to the Hessian general, Heister, who placed him in the commissary department. There he made use of his increased freedom to induce Hessian soldiers to resign or to desert. Paroled after a brief imprisonment, he resumed his business as merchant and continued to act as an under-cover desertion agent among the Hessians. On Jan. 2, 1777, he married Rachel, daughter of Moses B. Franks, an influential Jewish merchant.

In August 1778 Salomon was again arrested, charged with being an accomplice in a plot to burn the King's fleet and to destroy British warehouses around New York. He was confined in the dreaded prison, the Provost, and condemned to death, but on Aug. 11, by turning to advantage a string of golden guineas which he had concealed on himself, he bribed his jailer and escaped to the American lines, leaving his family behind in the city. Fourteen days later found him in Philadelphia addressing a memorial to Congress setting forth his services to the cause and asking for some employment, but to no avail. With the assistance of friends he thereupon opened an office as dealer in bills of exchange and other securities. The business prospered, and within the next few years he became a leading broker in the city and one of the largest depositors in the Bank of North America, to which he was a subscriber. He was paymaster-general for the French forces in America and most of the war subsidies of France and Holland passed through his hands. As almost sole broker for the office of finance in the sale of bills of exchange he contributed much to maintain the bankrupt government's credit. The diary of Robert Morris shows no less than seventy-five transactions with Salomon between August 1781 and April 1784. Original checks and vouchers presented before a later committee of Congress show that he advanced in specie to the superintendent of finance at various times a total of $211,678. In addition he held government obligations of various sorts amounting to $353,729.33, six promissory notes to the amount of $92,600, making an aggregate indebtedness against the government of $658,007.43, as shown by his papers and later recognized by committees in Congress. To calculate the full extent of Salomon's financial assistance there should be added to the above figures advances of more than $20,000 to pay the salaries of men holding government posts in order to keep them in the service, and untold additional advances during the war to army officers,

to foreign agents, and for the outfitting of soldiers (*Senate Report No. 93, 38* Cong., 1 Sess., June 24, 1864). These liberal advances in specie and equally liberal investments in Revolutionary paper furnish a singularly outstanding example of unselfish devotion to the American cause, particularly when it is remembered that the family was left practically penniless at his death.

Following the war Salomon suffered heavy financial reverses. His plans to return to New York in 1785 as a factor, broker, and auctioneer were interrupted by his sudden death, undoubtedly hastened by an impaired constitution owing to his imprisonment by the British. In the settlement of his estate all assets, including Revolutionary securities, were given a value of $44,732 against an indebtedness of $45,292. Repeated efforts were made by the heirs to secure a settlement of the Salomon claim from the government. Although the case was considered by Congress at least ten times between 1848 and 1926 and a Senate committee in 1864 recognized the claim as one of "undeniable merit," all such efforts proved unsuccessful.

[Most helpful in reconstructing the story of Salomon, which had dropped from sight for many years, is *Senate Doc. No. 178,* 69 Cong., 2 Sess., Dec. 20, 1926, containing the committee report of June 24, 1864, a sketch by Salomon's son, Haym M., a biographical sketch by H. B. Adams, and an invaluable bibliography by J. H. Hollander. Much of the same material is in *Pubs. of the Am. Jewish Hist. Soc.,* No. 2 (1894). Major instances of congressional consideration of the family claim may be found in the following: *House Report No. 504,* 30 Cong., 1 Sess. (1848) ; *Senate Report No. 219,* 30 Cong., 1 Sess. (1848) ; *Senate Report No. 177,* 31 Cong., 1 Sess. (1850) ; *Senate Report No. 127,* 36 Cong., 1 Sess. (1860) ; *Senate Report No. 65,* 37 Cong., 2 Sess. (1862) ; and *Senate Report No. 93,* 39 Cong., 1 Sess. (1864). Salomon's story has been the subject of a novel, H. S. Baron, *Haym Salomon, Immigrant and Financier of the American Revolution* (1929). C. E. Russell, *Haym Salomon and the Revolution* (1930), gives all the entries concerning the subject to be found in Robert Morris's unpublished diary. See also M. C. Peters, *Haym Salomon, The Financier of the Revolution* (1911), and *The Jews Who Stood by Washington* (1915) ; Isaac Markens, *The Hebrews in America* (1888) ; Simon Wolf, "Are Republics Ungrateful?," *Reform Advocate,* Feb. 20, 1892; article by Herbert Friedenwald, in *The Jewish Encyclopedia* (1925), vol. X ; *Pa. Journal and Weekly Advertiser* (Philadelphia), Jan. 8, 1785.]   J. H. P.

SALTER, WILLIAM (Nov. 17, 1821–Aug. 15, 1910), Congregational clergyman, author, and historiographer, was born in Brooklyn, N. Y., the son of William Frost Salter, owner of the ship *Mary and Harriet,* upon which William played as a youth, and of Mary (Ewen) Salter who had come to New York with her husband from Portsmouth, N. H. He was a descendant of John Salter, mariner, who emigrated from England about 1680 and settled in Rye, N. H.

In 1840 he graduated from the University of the City of New York and then entered the Union Theological Seminary, but at the end of two years transferred to Andover, where he was graduated in 1843. Stirred by the need of religious and educational facilities on the frontier, he, with ten other Andover graduates, went to the Territory of Iowa under the auspices of the Home Missionary Society. The Iowa Band, as this group came to be known, proceeding by train, boat, and wagon, arrived at a point on the eastern bank of the Mississippi, opposite Burlington, on Oct. 24, 1843. Soon thereafter Salter preached his first sermon at Keosauqua, in a little room over the blacksmith shop, and on Nov. 5, 1843, was ordained at Denmark. Becoming missionary pastor in Maquoketa, he served there during a part of the years 1844–46, frequently riding a circuit and preaching whenever he could gather a few persons. In April 1846 he became pastor of the First Congregational Church of Burlington, and continued as such until his death sixty-four years later.

In the critical years previous to the Civil War he conducted an underground railway station for the assistance of runaway slaves. During the conflict he served as army chaplain in the Christian Commission and ministered to Union and Confederate wounded in several hospitals. Returning to Burlington at the close of the war, he resumed his parish work and writing. During his long pastorate, he was in intimate touch with many of the prominent Iowa pioneers, and his published works include a number of biographical sketches among which are: *Sermon with Reference to the Death of James G. Edwards* (1851); *Augustus C. Dodge* (1887); and *James Clarke, Third Territorial Governor* (1888). During the period of the Civil War he published *Our National Sins and Impending Calamities* (1861) and *The Great Rebellion in the Light of Christianity* (1864). In the religious field he wrote: *On Some Objections to the Old Testament—Their Origin and Explanation* (1853); *The Progress of Religion in Iowa for Twenty-five Years* (1858); *Studies in Matthew* (1880); *The Christian Idealism of R. W. Emerson* (1886); *Cooperative Christianity* (1888). His major works are: *The Life of James W. Grimes* (1876); *Iowa: The First Free State in the Louisiana Purchase* (1905); and *Sixty Years and Other Discourses* (copr. 1907). He was married on Aug. 25, 1846, to Mary Ann Mackintire of Charlestown, Mass.

[W. T. Salter, *John Salter, Mariner* (1900); J. L. Hill, *Rev. William Salter, D.D., 1821–1910* (n.d.), reprinted with bibliog. added from *Annals of Iowa*, Jan. 1911; Ephraim Adams, *The Iowa Band* (1870); P. D. Jordan, "The Discovery of William Salter's Almanac-Diary," *Annals of Iowa*, Oct. 1930, and "The Life and Works of James Gardiner Edwards," in *Jour. of the Ill. State Hist. Soc.*, Oct. 1930; *Who's Who in America*, 1908–09; *Register and Leader* (Des Moines), Aug. 16, 1910; diary, covering the period 1843–1851, marriage book, containing a list, with dates, of all marriages performed, 1843–1910; and Civil War diaries, containing his experiences as chaplain, in private hands.] P. D. J.

SALTER, WILLIAM MACKINTIRE (Jan. 30, 1853–July 18, 1931), Ethical Culture lecturer, philosopher, author, was the son of Rev. William [*q.v.*] and Mary Ann (Mackintire) Salter, of Burlington, Iowa. His early religious and educational training was stimulated by his Congregational father who put the boy to the study of Latin at the age of ten and introduced him to Greek two years later. When he was fourteen, he entered Knox College, Galesburg, Ill., where he became skeptical with respect to orthodox religion. This skepticism expressed itself in his graduating oration in 1871, "Is Orthodoxy in Theology Necessary for the Christian?"; which led some Knox trustees to question, but not deny, the right of the candidate to the degree of bachelor of arts. He entered the theological department of Yale College in the fall of 1871, where he searched theology and sacred writings for a justification of orthodoxy, but gradually, he relates, "one article after another of my former faith became wrapped in uncertainty." In 1873 he left Yale for the Harvard Divinity School, thinking that "I might at least hold on to enough to be a Unitarian minister if I could not be an Orthodox one." During the summers of 1872–73 he preached at Somesville, Me., and from Aug. 16, 1874, to July 4, 1875, in the Unitarian Church at Wayland, Mass. While in the latter place he attempted to formulate his own creed in a series of sermons beginning with "Man's Need of Religion," but found, after re-entering Harvard in 1875, that "solid grounds for distinctive Christian faith in any form had slipped away." He was granted the degree of bachelor of divinity in 1876 and appointed Parker Fellow of Harvard at the University of Göttingen.

While in Germany he turned his attention from the Christian fathers to the pagan philosophers, studying Plato, Aristotle, and others, not alone for themselves, but with the thought of tracing pagan influence on the development of Christian doctrine. His health failed, however, and he returned to the United States, where he herded sheep in Colorado from February 1878 to October 1879. While tending his flocks he prepared a pamphlet, *On a Foundation for Religion* (1879), based upon the "enthusiasm of humanity" which John Robert Seeley's *Ecce Homo,* a volume much beloved by him, described. In 1879 he met Felix Adler and heard him describe a new type of religious movement which laid stress on human service and not upon theological arguments and explanations. During 1881–82 he was a student at Columbia University. In 1881 he affiliated himself with Dr. Adler's ethical culture movement and later wrote: "I moved slowly—perhaps I always do, I have to weigh and ponder—but at last I had no choice: I joined the pioneer with heart and soul, and count myself blessed that for twenty-five years, in whatever limited and fragmentary way, I responded to his high example" (autobiographical sketch, MS., 1926). His rise in the movement was rapid; from 1883 to 1892 and again from 1897 to 1907 he was lecturer for the Chicago society, and from 1892 to 1897 for the Philadelphia society. He was a special lecturer on Nietzsche at the University of Chicago from 1909 to 1913.

On July 19, 1913, he sailed for Europe and, after traveling in Italy and the Austrian Tyrol, settled down in Munich to begin work on his book, *Nietzsche the Thinker* (1917). Interrupted by the World War, he returned to the United States to study, lecture, and write at "Hilltop," his home on Silver Lake, N. H. He completed his book, upon which his fame as a scholar rests, contributed articles on Nietzsche and the World War to magazines, and in the winter of 1920–21 lectured on Nietzsche at Johns Hopkins University. Although gentle and lovable, Salter possessed great moral strength. He pleaded for a fair trial for the bombers of the Chicago Haymarket riots when public opinion was against him, and he remained unswervingly pro-German and anti-British during the World War. In addition to about eighty printed lectures, he published: *Die Religion der Moral* (Leipzig, 1885), *Moralische Reden* (Leipzig, 1889), *Ethical Religion* (1889), *First Steps in Philosophy* (1892), *Anarchy or Government* (1895), *Walt Whitman* (1899), and *Burgess's Political Philosophy as Indicated in His Recent "The Sanctity of Law"* (1929). On Dec. 2, 1885, he was married to Mary S. Gibbens, of Cambridge, Mass.; a daughter by this marriage died and they adopted a boy.

[Material for this sketch was taken from MSS. in private hands; the lib. of the Ethical Culture Soc. of N. Y. contains Salter's Ethical Culture MSS., and the lib. of Knox Coll., his Nietzsche and World War material. See *Proc. and Addresses of the Am. Philosophical Asso.,* vol. V (1931); *Who's Who in America,* 1930–31; *Standard,* Nov. 1931; *N. Y. Times,* July 19, 1931.]
P. D. J.

SALTONSTALL, DUDLEY (Sept. 8, 1738–1796), naval officer, was born at New London, Conn., the fifth of fourteen children of Gen. Gurdon Saltonstall and Rebecca (Winthrop) Saltonstall. He was a direct descendant of Richard Saltonstall and the grandson of Gurdon Saltonstall [*qq.v.*]. In 1765 Dudley was married to Frances, the daughter of Dr. Joshua Babcock, of Westerly, R. I., and they had seven children.

Saltonstall took to the sea early in life, was a privateersman in the French and Indian War, and commanded merchant vessels before the Revolution. At an early period of this contest he commanded the fort at New London and in the fall of 1775, when the first Continental fleet was assembled, he was given command of the ship *Alfred,* flagship of Commodore Esek Hopkins [*q.v.*]. John Paul Jones was first lieutenant. Early in 1776 this fleet cruised to the Bahamas and captured the island of New Providence. Upon the return voyage the fleet took two small prizes off Block Island, and later engaged the British frigate *Glasgow,* but failed to capture her. For allowing her to escape and for other reasons Hopkins was eventually dismissed from the navy, but Saltonstall was exonerated and, on Oct. 10, 1776, was appointed fourth on the list of captains. In 1777 he was ordered to command the new frigate *Trumbull,* but she did not get to sea for two years. However, in some manner unexplained, he sailed in another ship of the same name and reported the capture of two British transports.

Saltonstall is best remembered for his connection with the disastrous Penobscot expedition of 1779. The British having taken possession of Bagaduce, now Castine, in Penobscot Bay, the State of Massachusetts fitted out an expedition for its recapture. The force comprised a fleet of nineteen naval vessels and privateers carrying more than 200 guns and 2,000 men, commanded by Saltonstall in the Continental frigate *Warren,* of 32 guns, with about twenty transports conveying the troops under Gen. Solomon Lovell. The militia contingent which Lovell had been able to recruit within the short time allowed him consisted of less than 1,000 men. The expedition arrived in Penobscot Bay on July 25. Three British sloops of war, mounting altogether 56 guns, lay in Bagaduce harbor and would readily have surrendered to the American force. Saltonstall, however, did nothing; the urging of his officers could not move him. The army made a successful landing but could not take the fort without the assistance of the navy, which could only be rendered from an anchorage in the harbor. There followed nearly three weeks of delay and aimless discussion, waiting for reinforcements which could not possibly have arrived in time. Then, on Aug. 13, a British fleet appeared in the bay. The troops were hastily reëmbarked on the transports and the whole American fleet fled ignominiously up the river. Two of the ships were taken by the British; all the others were destroyed to prevent capture. Saltonstall was dismissed from the navy. Later in the war he was successful in privateering and afterwards returned to the merchant service. He died of yellow fever at Mole St. Nicolas, Haiti, the exact day and month being unknown.

[Leverett Saltonstall, *Ancestry and Descendants of Sir Richard Saltonstall* (1897); F. M. Caulkins, *Hist. of New London, Conn.* (1860), pp. 509, 531; G. W. Allen, *A Naval Hist. of the Am. Rev.* (2 vols., 1913), and authorities there cited; note furnished by L. F. Middlebrook, Esq., of Hartford, Conn.]   G. W. A.

SALTONSTALL, GURDON (Mar. 27, 1666 o. s.–Sept. 20, 1724 o. s.), clergyman, colonial governor, was born in Haverhill, Mass., the eldest son of Nathaniel and Elizabeth (Ward) Saltonstall, the grandson of Richard Saltonstall [*q.v.*], and the great-grandson of Nathaniel Ward [*q.v.*]. His father also was a Massachusetts magistrate. He graduated from Harvard College in 1684 and was ordained minister of the church at New London, Conn., in 1691. Through his orthodoxy, learning, and unusual eloquence he soon rose to a position of prominence among the clergy of the colony; because of his practical wisdom he became the confidant and advisor of his leading parishioner, Fitz-John Winthrop, later the governor. Only two years after his ordination the Assembly asked him to go to England with Winthrop to represent the colony in a dispute over the New York governor's claim to command the Connecticut militia. Flattering though the invitation was, he declined to go. During Winthrop's governorship, 1698–1707, both he and the Assembly relied more and more upon Saltonstall's help in drafting state papers and in adjusting disputes within the colony and with its neighbors. Upon Winthrop's death the Assembly, at a special meeting called for Dec. 17, 1707, o. s., asked Saltonstall to leave the pulpit and assume the governorship. Such a step was unprecedented, even in Puritan New England, and it has few parallels in all American history. At the time, the deputy governor, Robert Treat [*q.v.*], was eighty-five, and none of the magistrates had so fully the public confidence as had the New London minister. His patrician ancestry, his dignity of bearing, which amounted almost to pompousness, his wealth and orthodoxy were just the attributes that eighteenth-century Connecticut expected and demanded of its governors. Yet Saltonstall had not advanced to leadership through the regular apprenticeship of the magistracy as law and custom demanded, and his choice as acting governor of the tradition-bound colony was an outstanding tribute to his abilities—and perhaps to his political management. When he accepted the call, the Assembly amended the law to permit his election by the freemen in the following May even though he had not previously been nominated a magistrate. These proceedings of the Assembly met the approval of the voters, and he was annually reëlected until his death.

As governor, he faced the usual problems of his times: warfare with the French and Indians, boundary disputes with neighboring colonies, the defence of the colony's charter from threatened cancellation in England. In these and similar crises the governor's adroit management fully justified the confidence placed in him. It is not altogether a coincidence, however, that the most lasting decisions reached during the administration of this learned divine had to do with church government and higher education. In the solution of these problems his influence was felt long after his death. One of the first acts of the Assembly after his election was to call upon the churches of the colony to appoint delegates to a synod at Saybrook, which was to draw up a system of ecclesiastical discipline. The result of this meeting was the Saybrook platform of 1708, which, with its indorsement of the Savoy Confession and its provision for consociations of churches and associations of ministers, set the course for Connecticut Congregationalism for generations to come. Under the governor's leadership the Assembly approved the platform, and he had it printed in 1710 at the New London press he had recently caused to be established (*A Confession of Faith . . . by Delegation at Say-Brook*). Even before his translation to the governorship, he had been interested in the founding of a college in Connecticut. Though never a trustee, he was one of the ministerial leaders in the movement that led to the chartering of the Collegiate School in 1701. As governor he actively protected the institution, soon named Yale College, from the factional jealousies and Anglican defections that endangered its early career. During the controversy over the location of the college, he used the great influence of his office to support the majority trustees in their decision to settle permanently at New Haven. His attitude so angered the ministerial leaders of the Hartford faction, Timothy Woodbridge and Thomas Buckingham, that they obtained their own election to the Assembly in 1719 in a strenuous effort to bring about his defeat for reëlection. The unedifying spectacle of two clergymen entering the political arena for the purpose of driving another minister from the highest public office of the colony ended with the complete victory of the governor. In 1722 his firm but temperate leadership was again invoked when the conversion to Anglicanism of Timothy Cutler, Samuel Johnson [qq.v.], and others intimately associated with the college threatened the very foundations of conservative Puritanism upon which it had been built.

In his religious and political views Saltonstall was thoroughly conservative, and some of the bolder spirits of the colony showed restlessness under the restraining influence of his administration. His years in office were marked by a number of personal and factional attacks. But he successfully overrode all opponents, and at his death, which came suddenly through apoplexy, was sincerely mourned throughout New England. Cotton Mather outdid himself in eulogy, likening his old friend to a *"Silver Basket of a comely Body, carrying in it the Golden Apples* of a well-furnished and well-disposed Soul," and adding "We will not call him a *Star,* but even a *Constellation* of the most fulgid Endowments" (Sibley, *post,* pp. 283–84, from Mather, *post*). Saltonstall was married three times: to Jerusha, the daughter of James Richards of Hartford, to Elizabeth, the daughter of William Rosewell of Branford, and to Mary, the daughter of William Whittingham and the widow of William Clarke of Boston. His third wife and seven of his ten children survived him. A contemporary portrait by an unknown artist, presented to Yale by his son, hangs in the Gallery of Fine Arts in New Haven.

[*The Public Recs. . . . of Conn.,* IV–VI (1868–72); Eliphalet Adams, *Discourse on the Death of the Hon. Gurdon Saltonstall* (1724); Cotton Mather, *Decus ac Tutamen. A Brief Essay . . . in Commemoration of . . . Gurdon Saltonstall* (1724); F. B. Dexter, *Doc. Hist. of Yale Univ.* (1916); Benjamin Trumbull, *A Complete Hist. of Conn.* (1797); F. M. Caulkins, *Hist. of New London, Conn.* (rev. ed. 1895); Leverett Saltonstall, *Ancestry and Descendants of Sir Richard Saltonstall* (1897); J. L. Sibley, *Biog. Sketches of Grads. of Harvard Univ.,* vol. III (1885); Edwin Oviatt, *The Beginnings of Yale* (1916); Williston Walker, *The Creeds and Platforms of Congregationalism* (1893).]   L. W. L.

SALTONSTALL, RICHARD (*c.* 1610–Apr. 29, 1694), Massachusetts colonist, born at Woodsome, Almondbury, Yorkshire, England, and baptized Oct. 1, 1610, was the eldest son of Sir Richard Saltonstall and Grace, daughter of Robert Kaye. His father, the nephew of Sir Richard, Lord Mayor of London, was an original patentee and Assistant of the Massachusetts Bay Company. Richard, Jr., was admitted fellow commoner at Emmanuel College, Cambridge, in 1627 and, in 1630, accompanied his father to Massachusetts Bay, where they established the settlement of Watertown. After being admitted freeman, May 18, 1631, young Saltonstall returned to England, studied law, and on July 4, 1633, married Muriel, daughter of Brampton Gurdon of Suffolk. With their first child, the Saltonstalls returned to New England in 1635 and settled in Ipswich.

Richard was prominent in local affairs as an important property holder, proprietor of the only gristmill in town, and deputy, 1635–37. After the removal of John Winthrop, Jr., Saltonstall's name appeared first on all town petitions and the townspeople referred to him as the "Worshipful Mr. Saltonstall." His residence in Ipswich was interrupted by three sojourns in England (1649–63; 1672–80; and 1686–94), during which he was appointed in 1650, a commissioner of a High Court of Justice to repress the enemies of the Commonwealth, and, in 1654, a trustee for settling sequestrated estates in Scotland (C. H. Firth and R. S. Rait, *Acts and Ordinances of the Interregnum,* 1911, II, 362, 885). Saltonstall undertook these journeys to England for the sake of his wife's health and, also, to oversee the family property which, contrary to the usual practice of the New England colonists, was retained.

In colony affairs he occupied important offices, serving as an Assistant, 1637–49, 1664, and 1680–82. As a magistrate he kept court at Ipswich, Newbury, and Piscataqua. In military affairs he served as a sergeant-major in Colonel Endicott's regiment, and he was an alternate commissioner of the New England Confederacy in 1644 and substitute agent of the Colony to England in 1660. He was one of that liberal Ipswich group, which included Bellingham, Simon Bradstreet, and Nathaniel Ward [q.v.], whose members were able, by virtue of their piety and devotion, to defy successfully arbitrary methods in government. In a manuscript, no longer extant, Saltonstall condemned the proposed Life Council as sinful and contrary to the charter, which condemnation caused trouble for the author. In 1643 the Ipswich group remonstrated with Governor Winthrop with respect to his policy of extending aid to Charles de LaTour in his quarrel with his rival D'Aulnay, Acadian official, and hinted at the neutrality of Ipswich in the event of hostilities. Saltonstall petitioned the Confederacy, in 1645, against unneutral aid to LaTour as impolitic and dishonorable (John

Winthrop, *The History of New England,* 1853, ed. by James Savage, II, 464–67). His advanced views are also indicated by his formal protest, in 1645, against the slave trade and by his opposition to the course taken by the authorities against Dr. Robert Child, Samuel Maverick [*q.v.*], and others who had petitioned for exemption from the prevailing ecclesiastical restrictions. Governor Winthrop found it difficult to cope with an opponent of unquestioned religious orthodoxy and assured social position.

To the regicides, Whalley and Goffe, Saltonstall gave fifty pounds in 1672 and to Harvard College over four hundred and fifty pounds (*Publications of the Colonial Society of Massachusetts,* vol. XV, 1925, "Harvard College Records," pt. 1, p. 214). As a Harvard overseer he recommended, in 1671–72, an unnamed candidate for the then vacant presidency. He died at Hulme, Lancaster, England, survived by four children. His grandson, Gurdon [*q.v.*], became governor of Connecticut.

[Henry Bond, *Geneals. of the Families and Descendants of the Early Settlers of Watertown, Mass.* (1855); "Early Inhabitants of Ipswich, Mass.," in Abraham Hammatt, *The Hammatt Papers,* nos. 1–7 (1880–99); N. B. Shurtleff, *Records of the Governor and Company of the Mass. Bay* (5 vols., 1853–54); *New Eng. Hist. and Geneal. Reg.,* Apr. 1879, p. 228; Leverett Saltonstall, *Ancestry and Descendants of Sir Richard Saltonstall* (1897); John and J. A. Venn, *Alumni Cantabrigienses,* vol. IV (1926); T. F. Waters, *Ipswich in the Mass. Bay Colony,* vol. I (1905); John Noble, *Records of the Court of Assistants of the Colony of the Mass. Bay* (3 vols., 1901–28).]
N. H. D.

SALTUS, EDGAR EVERTSON (Oct. 8, 1855–July 31, 1921), novelist, essayist, poet, was the son of Francis Henry Saltus and Eliza Howe (Evertson). His great-grandfather, Solomon Saltus, came to New York City from Bermuda in the late eighteenth century and became a successful merchant; on his mother's side he was descended from an old Dutch family. He attended St. Paul's School, Concord, N. H., and entered Yale College with the class of 1876, leaving after one year and returning for a brief time with the class of 1877. He spent three or four years abroad, studying in Paris, Heidelberg, and Munich. In 1880 he received the degree of LL.B. from Columbia College, but he never practised law.

After his marriage to Helen Sturgis Read in November 1883, he turned to authorship, publishing in 1884 a slight but interesting biography of Balzac. While in Germany he had studied under Eduard von Hartmann, and in 1885 he paid tribute to Hartmann's influence in *The Philosophy of Disenchantment,* an account of Schopenhauer and his school. This led to *The Anatomy of Negation* (1886), a study of antitheistic philosophies from the early Asiatic cults to contemporary positivism and atheism. In 1887 his first novel, *Mr. Incoul's Misadventure,* appeared, and by the end of 1894 he had written more than a half dozen others. During this period he also issued a collection of essays and sonnets, *Love and Lore* (1890), made translations from the French, and published an account of the Roman emperors, *Imperial Purple* (1892).

With the exception of *Mary Magdalen* (1891), an historical novel of the time of Christ, Saltus' early fiction dealt with New York society. Adopting an involved and epigrammatic style, he sought to cloak with glamor the melodramatic stories he unfolded, and by writing of murders, suicides, and adulteries, to illustrate the philosophy of disenchantment he had preached. His best work of this period is not in his novels, but in *Imperial Purple,* which, however lacking in historical accuracy, displays all the virtues of his style: his unusual vocabulary, his bizarre and sometimes genuinely epigrammatic mode of expression, and his skill in innuendo.

Between 1894 and 1903 he published little under his own name. In the late nineties he was employed by P. F. Collier & Son. For this firm (see Honce, *post*) he probably compiled *The Lovers of the World* (n.d.) and *The Great Battles of All Nations* (2 vols., 1899); for it he wrote supplementary chapters for the Nations of the World Series. Divorced from his first wife, he married, on Oct. 8, 1895, Elsie Welsh Smith, from whom he soon after separated. There was one daughter by this marriage. In 1903, with the publication of a collection of short stories, *Purple and Fine Women,* he returned to fiction, writing four novels in the next decade. He also wrote *Historia Amoris* (1906) and a history of religions, *The Lords of the Ghostland; a History of the Ideal* (1907). On Aug. 16, 1911, he married Marie Giles, subsequently his biographer. In his later years, despite ill health, he wrote two novels and various shorter pieces, and in *The Imperial Orgy* (1920) sought to do for Russia what, in *Imperial Purple,* he had done for Rome. Throughout his life he spent much of his time abroad. He was converted by his third wife to theosophy, a doctrine that made itself felt in all his later work.

From the first Saltus set himself against the main currents in American literature. His early novels, denounced as shocking by the moralists, were justly criticized by the more discriminating for weakness in characterization and sensationalism in style. Merely because he was a rebel, he attracted the attention of a small and somewhat esoteric group, counting among his admirers James Huneker and Elbert Hubbard. In his later years, and after his death, such critics as Carl Van Vechten and Gorham Munson attempted, with some immediate success, to awaken an interest in his work. The revival they initiated was, however, of brief duration, for it soon became apparent that the stylistic virtues these critics praised were vitiated by Saltus' inability to distinguish between the original and the merely bizarre. His importance, it became clear, was chiefly historical, that of a rebellious and exotic writer who, in his own time, did something to broaden the range of American literature, but without achieving any significance in his own right.

[Marie Saltus, *Edgar Saltus the Man* (1925) has little material on the early years, and is in general unsatisfactory. It may be supplemented by Ethel Saltus Ludington, *Ludington-Saltus Records* (1925); *Yale Seventy-Seven: Their Lives and Letters* (circa 1892); O. J. Bannard and E. P. Howe, *Biog. Record of the Class of 1876, Yale College* (1911); J. G. Huneker, *Steeplejack* (1920), vol. II; *Who's Who in America, 1920–21.* For critical estimates see Ramsay Colles, in *Westminster Rev.,* Oct. 1904; Carl Van Vechten, *The Merry-Go Round* (1918); G. B. Munson, "The Limbo of American Literature," in *Broom,* June 1922. For bibliography see Van Vechten, *op. cit.; Publishers' Weekly,* June 23, 1923; bibliog. by Charles Honce in Saltus' *The Uplands of Dream* (1925).]   G.H.

SAMPSON, MARTIN WRIGHT (Sept. 7, 1866–Aug. 22, 1930), professor of English, a descendant of Alexander Sampson, who came to Boston from England early in the eighteenth century, was born in Cincinnati, Ohio, the son of William S. Sampson, a manufacturer, whose father had settled there about 1830, and of Virginia Ada (Wright) Sampson. Before his graduation, in 1888, from the University of Cincinnati, where his literary and scholarly tastes were encouraged by James Morgan Hart [*q.v.*], he spent a year in study at the University of Munich. In 1890 he received the degree of M.A. from Cincinnati. Meanwhile he had begun the work as teacher of English which, with intervals of study and travel abroad, occupied the remainder of his life: first at the University of Iowa (1889–91), then at Stanford (1892–93), then at Indiana (1893–1906), and finally at Cornell University (1908–30).

His favorite subjects were the English romantic poets, the modern novel, the Elizabethan drama, and the history of the drama. As teacher he had the twofold object of imparting to his students his own keen appreciation and of developing in them as well the scholarly instinct which, not content with mere enjoyment, insists upon full knowledge and understanding. His lectures were informal, and his lifelong interest in other arts than literature furnished him with happy illustrations of the principles of poetry and drama. While at Indiana University, by insisting that no pupil should be graduated who could not write clear and correct English, he raised the standard of English in the high schools of the state. He also founded the university's first dramatic club. At Cornell he gave afternoon readings before the students of engineering, who dropped in from their shops and laboratories bringing their pipes with them. Entertaining them at first with stories by popular authors and with humorous verse, often of his own composition, he gradually introduced more substantial fare, and soon had them listening with genuine interest to Milton and Plato. He encouraged the literary aspirations of the undergraduate by founding the Manuscript Club, a group of students who met at his house on Saturday evenings to read aloud their original stories, poems, and plays. In 1909 he established the Frances Sampson Fine Arts Prize, awarded annually for evidence of appreciation. In 1917 he organized the Cornell unit of the American Ambulance Field Service, the first to reach the front under the American flag. He edited *Camion Letters from American College Men, Volunteer Drivers of the American Field Service in France, 1917* (1918) and just before his death, which resulted from an automobile accident, he completed the editing of *Military Records of Cornell University in the World War* (1930).

Sampson published a textbook, *Written and Oral Composition* (1907), in collaboration with E. O. Holland, and edited a number of works of English and American literature, among them *The Lyric and Dramatic Poems of John Milton* (1901), Webster's *The White Devil and the Duchess of Malfy* (1904), *The Two Gentlemen of Verona* (1912), Middleton's plays (1915), and Henry James's *Daisy Miller* (1927) and *The Ambassadors* (1930). His introductory essays are urbane in style and illuminating as criticism. A collection of tales written originally for his own children, *The Good Giant* (1928), met with public favor. His attitude toward academic problems was entertainingly presented in a one-act satire, *The Soul of a Professor* (published in *Cornell University Plays,* 1932). A volume of his poems, *Voices of the Forest,* was published posthumously in 1933.

He married in 1892 Frances Van Rensselaer Gardiner, who died in 1909. In 1910 he married Julia Dauchy Pattison, by whom he had four children.

[*Who's Who in America,* 1914–15, 1930–31; *Letters of Edward Dowden* (1914); Dowden, Richard Garnett, and W. M. Rossetti, *Letters About Shelley* (1917), ed.

by R. S. Garnett, pp. *232, 233*; *N. Y. Times*, Aug. 24, *1930*; *Cornell Alumni News*, Sept. 18, 1930, Mar. 29, *1932*; personal acquaintance.]   W. S., Jr.

SAMPSON, WILLIAM (January 1764–Dec. 28, 1836), lawyer, Irish patriot, son of Rev. Arthur and Anne (Wilson) Sampson, was born at Londonderry into the privileged caste of Ireland, and was brought up under influences favorable to England. He is said to have attended the University of Dublin, and in 1790 studied law at Lincoln's Inn, London. He was admitted to the Irish bar and obtained a good practice. Experience and observation then brought him—very late, as he afterward regretfully wrote—into the movement for political reform. He contributed articles and poems to nationalist newspapers, defended state prisoners, took the oath of the United Irishmen in open court, and in December 1796 presided over a meeting at Belfast which was called treasonable. After the outbreak of war he collected information regarding the atrocities of the government troops. These activities and the false report that he held a major-general's commission in the French army led to his arrest and continued imprisonment without a trial. He was offered his release on condition that he would submit to official examination and then go into exile in some country at peace with England; and in order to save the life of a friend he accepted the offer. Admission to the United States being denied by Adams' administration, he was sent to Portugal in 1799, and by that country to France. He remained there six years and then spent nearly a year in Hamburg. In 1806, he appeared in London with a passport from the British minister to Hamburg. He was at once arrested and sent at the expense of the British government to New York. His family arrived four years later.

In America Sampson won prominence in the practice of law, the reporting of cases, and propagandist writing. He was admitted to the bar almost immediately after his arrival, and while practising turned his knowledge of stenography to account by publishing a dozen or more verbatim reports of cases which had attracted popular attention. As a lawyer, he achieved high rank chiefly through his eloquence and his vigorous advocacy of personal rights. In one of the first American cases involving organized labor he defended the journeymen cordwainers who were accused of conspiring to raise their wages by means of a closed shop; and, though the decision went against them, his argument clearly stated the principle on which the closed shop has since been justified (William Sampson, reporter, *Trial of the Journeymen Cordwainers*, 1810). In 1813 he successfully interposed as *amicus curiae* to prevent a Catholic priest's being required to disclose secrets imparted to him in confession. To his report of the case, entitled *The Catholic Question in America* (1813), he appended a treatise on the doctrine of penance. Though himself a Protestant, he helped to prosecute Orangemen who had attacked Catholic Irishmen in Greenwich Village, N. Y., in 1824, and he defended Irishmen charged with rioting in Philadelphia in 1831. During the years 1825–30 he resided in Georgetown, D. C., and appeared in several cases before the Supreme Court of the United States.

In 1807 he published *Memoirs of William Sampson* in the form of a series of letters to a friend. Ostensibly an account of his experiences in the Irish rebellion, the volume was really a scathing denunciation of the whole British policy toward Ireland. It was favorably received in America; a second edition, revised and enlarged, was published at Leesburg, Va., in 1817; and a third edition, less complete, at London in 1832.

Sampson best deserves to be remembered as the chief exponent of the early movement to codify the common law. In 1823 he delivered an address before the New York Historical Society (*An Anniversary Discourse . . . Dec. 6, 1823*, 1824) which contained a violent and radical attack on certain barbarities in the common law, and a recommendation that the American people discard its undesirable features and preserve the best by codification. In the controversy that followed, Sampson, by correspondence, brought his proposal to the favorable consideration of jurists and political leaders in many parts of the country. His work was moderately successful during his lifetime and influenced the leaders of the following generation. Among his other writings was a *History of Ireland* (2 vols., 1833), being a continuation of W. C. Taylor's *History of the Civil Wars of Ireland* (2 vols., 1831). He married Grace Clarke in 1790 and had three children; he died in New York City, survived by his widow and a daughter.

[*Dict. of Nat. Biog.*; R. R. Madden, *The United Irishmen*, 2 ser. II (1843), 335–88; introduction to the London edition of Sampson's *Memoirs*; C. C. Beale, *William Sampson, Lawyer and Stenographer* (1907), repr. from *Proc. N. Y. State Stenographers' Asso.*, 1906; E. J. McGuire, "William Sampson," *Jour. Am. Irish Hist. Soc.*, Oct. 1916; L. B. Sampson, *The Sampson Family* (1914); *N. Y. American*, Dec. 29, 1836. Most accounts give the day of Sampson's birth as Jan. 17, but Madden's copy of his tombstone inscription gives Jan. 27.]   E. C. S.

SAMPSON, WILLIAM THOMAS (Feb. 9, 1840–May 6, 1902), naval officer, was born at Palmyra, N. Y., the eldest of seven children of James and Hannah (Walker) Sampson. His great-grandparents had come to America from northern Ireland. With an excellent record in the Palmyra schools, he gained an appointment to the United States Naval Academy, and was graduated first in the class of 1861. After duty earlier in the Civil War as instructor at the Naval Academy at Newport, he joined the monitor *Patapsco* in 1864, as executive officer, and was on her turret when she was blown up while removing mines in Charleston harbor, Jan. 15, 1865, with a loss of sixty lives. He was made lieutenant in 1862, and lieutenant commander in 1866, while serving in the *Colorado* of the European Squadron. Admiral Dewey, his shipmate in the *Colorado,* speaks of Sampson as possessing "a most brilliant mind and the qualities of a practical and efficient officer on board ship," and as being one of the handsomest men he had ever seen (*Autobiography of George Dewey,* 1913, p. 139).

He was at the Naval Academy from 1868 to 1871, and after service on the European station returned to Annapolis as head of the physics department, 1874–78. Not a great reader of general literature or a man of wide interests, he developed in these years of study and teaching an outstanding proficiency in the scientific side of his profession, especially in physics, chemistry, metallurgy, and astronomy. Characteristic of the man and his methods were his academy lectures, delivered quietly but with great clearness, and with such painstaking attention to detail that in his illustrative experiments a former student could "not recall a single failure" (I. N. Hollis, "Rear-Admiral Sampson," *World's Work,* Nov. 1901, p. 1421). After commanding the *Swatara* in the Orient, 1879–82, he was stationed at the Naval Observatory, and in 1884 was a delegate to the International Meridian Conference. He commanded the Newport Torpedo Station from 1884 to 1886 and was also a member of an inter-service board on coast defenses, the naval aspects of which he treated in an article in the *Proceedings of the United States Naval Institute,* April 1889. From 1886 to 1890 he was superintendent of the Naval Academy. After two years in command of the *San Francisco,* he became superintendent of the naval gun foundry at Washington and later chief of the ordnance bureau, 1893–97. During his tenure of this office he was credited with making great advances in guns, explosives, and gunnery practice (Long, *post,* p. 227).

In June 1897 he joined the North Atlantic Squadron in command of the battleship *Iowa.* He was president of the board of inquiry on the *Maine* disaster, and was selected to command the squadron on the eve of the war with Spain, when the health of Admiral Montgomery Sicard [*q.v.*] was judged unequal to the task. This appointment over a dozen capable senior officers gave signal recognition of his high service reputation. Though the Spanish opposition was not such as to try his leadership to the utmost, he met with notable success the constant tests of judgment and severe mental and physical stress of the extended tropical campaign. In deference to departmental orders not to endanger his ships against shore defenses before meeting the Spanish fleet, he gave up his early design of an attack on Havana, and, at the declaration of war on Apr. 21, 1898, left Key West with twenty-six vessels to establish a blockade of the north coast of Cuba. In the later stages of the war, especially, a general supervision of fleet movements was maintained by the departmental strategy board in which Mahan had a guiding hand. Still, much was necessarily left to the command at sea, and it is high tribute to Sampson that the only move criticised later by Mahan was the cruise eastward to Puerto Rico and bombardment of San Juan on May 12, which left Havana open, with the destination of the approaching Spanish squadron as yet unknown.

Upon receiving news of Cervera's arrival at Martinique, also on May 12, Sampson hastened westward, and was joined at Key West by the Flying Squadron from Norfolk, under the command of Winfield Scott Schley [*q.v.*]. This force, now operating under Sampson's orders, was dispatched on May 19 to blockade Cienfuegos, chief southern port of Cuba, where it was expected Cervera would next appear. There was some constraint in the arrangement by which Schley, though two numbers senior to Sampson, was placed under him, and this was increased by Schley's delay in moving eastward from Cienfuegos to Santiago upon receiving news of Cervera's arrival there on May 19, and his still further delay in establishing a close blockade of that port. To the department's anxious query as to when and for how long he could himself blockade Santiago, Sampson replied that he could go at once and blockade indefinitely. He joined Schley at Santiago on June 1, and the combined forces took up their month-long vigil off the port, with ships in close semicircle around the narrow entrance and searchlights at night playing directly upon it. In this blockade Sampson's genius for patient and painstaking organization found full play. His health was not of the strongest, and from the time of the *Maine* inquiry he had been under a heavy burden, his duties including at this time supervision of the whole

Cuban blockade, cooperation with the army, direction of minor operations, and control of over a hundred vessels in his total force. Undoubtedly towards the end he suffered some slackening of physical and mental powers.

On the morning of July 3, Sampson in his flagship, the *New York,* had gone about seven miles eastward for a conference with General Shafter. He had signaled, "Disregard movements of flagship," but had not turned over the command to the next in rank, Schley; he was in sight of the squadron, and probably within signal range of the nearer units. When the suspense was ended by the coming out of Cervera's squadron at 9:35 A. M., the *New York* hastened back toward the battle, but though under fire from the entrance forts and in position to control later operations, she did not actually fire on any of the larger enemy ships. Schley, meantime, in the fast cruiser *Brooklyn,* was conspicuous in the action, and the early newspaper dispatches gave him chief credit for the victory. Sampson's first message— "The fleet under my command offers the nation as a Fourth of July present the whole of Cervera's fleet" (*Annual Report of the Navy Department,* 1898, *post,* p. 505) was ridiculed. Popular opinion made Schley the hero, though the department and the service in general strongly supported Sampson. Politics also entered into the long and bitter controversy which ensued, and the provisional promotions of Aug. 10, 1898, advancing Sampson eight numbers and Schley six, were not confirmed by the Senate. Both became permanent rear admirals by the Personnel Act of 1899, but Sampson, with manifest injustice, never received special recognition for his excellent work throughout the war. Actually, the question of command in the battle was not vital, since no squadron orders of consequence were issued. In his final decision in the matter, President Roosevelt stated that "technically Sampson commanded," but that his real credit rested "upon the excellence of the blockade; upon the preparedness of the squadron . . . and the standing orders in accordance with which they instantly moved to the attack" (Long, *post,* II, 208). Sampson published an article on the Atlantic fleet in the Spanish-American War in the *Century Magazine,* April 1899.

The hostility of the press correspondents was unquestionably due largely to Sampson's austere, uningratiating manner. He was reticent by nature, and gave an initial impression of coldness. With subordinates he was uniformly courteous, and he won their devotion, but he was not quick to praise. For a time after the Santiago victory it was planned to send a force under Sampson to the Spanish coast, but the plan was abandoned and after the close of hostilities he brought his fleet on Aug. 20 to New York. From September to December 1898, he was in Cuba with the Puerto Rico Evacuation Commission, and subsequently continued in command of the Atlantic fleet until October 1899. Thereafter until his death he was in charge of the Boston navy yard. His death from paresis occurred in Washington, D. C., and he was buried in the National Cemetery at Arlington. He was married in 1863 to Margaret Sexton Aldrich of Palmyra, and in 1882 to Elizabeth Susan Burling of Rochester, N. Y. By his first marriage he had four daughters, and by his second, two sons.

[*Who's Who in America,* 1901–02; L. B. Sampson, *The Sampson Family* (1914); L. R. Hamersly, *The Records of Living Officers of the U. S. Navy and Marine Corps* (6th ed., 1898), *Biog. Sketches of Distinguished Officers of the Army and Navy* (1905); W. A. M. Goode, *With Sampson Through the War* (1899); E. S. Maclay, *A Hist. of the U. S. Navy* (1902), vol. III; J. D. Long, *The New Am. Navy* (2 vols., 1903); *Ann. Report of the Navy Dept., 1898, Append. to the Chief of Bur. of Navigation* (1898); articles on Sampson by Sec. of Navy J. D. Long and Admiral A. T. Mahan, *Fortnightly Review,* Aug. 1902; speeches by Mahan and others at the unveiling of the Sampson Memorial Window, Naval Academy, *Proc. U. S. Naval Institute,* Mar. 1909; *Washington* (D. C.) *Post,* May 7, 1902. For additional material, see the bibliography for the article on Schley.]   A. W—t.

SAMUELS, EDWARD AUGUSTUS (July 4, 1836–May 27, 1908), ornithologist, nature lover, and sportsman, the son of Emanuel and Abigail Samuels, was born in Boston and resided throughout his life in eastern Massachusetts. His father was interested in outdoor life and encouraged him in his studies in natural history, but his schooling was limited to that provided by the city. Early in life he began writing for the press and in 1860 he became assistant to the secretary of the Massachusetts State Board of Agriculture, in which capacity he served for twenty years. His duties allowed him ample time for other pursuits and in 1870 his musical tastes led him to begin the publication of music, which he continued until about 1890. His spare hours, however, were devoted to the promotion of the study of birds and to work for the protection of fish and game. His election as president of the Massachusetts Fish and Game Protective Association in 1885, a position which he held for seven years, was one in which he took the greatest pride. Under his leadership the association increased greatly in numbers and influence, and became an important force in improving the state laws and in developing public sentiment in support of them.

Samuels

While not a scientist in the modern sense of the word, Samuels was a good observer and keenly interested in the habits of animals, especially birds. He felt the lack of any popular book on the birds of Massachusetts, and having a taste for writing, and excellent judgment in selecting what was well written, he published a number of papers in the *Reports* of the State Board of Agriculture intended to meet this need. Meanwhile he undertook the preparation of a volume entitled *Ornithology and Oology of New England,* the first edition of which appeared in 1867. It met with immediate success, and the legislature made a special appropriation to purchase a thousand copies for public libraries throughout the state. New editions were soon called for and in 1870 the fifth edition was issued, under the title *The Birds of New England,* by which the work is most widely known. The technical matter for this very popular and useful book was taken from the publications of Spencer F. Baird [*q.v.*], and there are liberal quotations from Audubon, Wilson, and Nuttall, as well as from the letters of less-known naturalists. But the matter is so well chosen that it probably meets the needs of the reader better than any attempt at original writing could have done. There is no doubt that Samuels' *Birds of New England* did more to stimulate bird study and to increase the public interest in birds in New England than any other publication of the last half of the nineteenth century. Of his subsequent publications, none met with comparable success, but his *With Fly-Rod and Camera* (1890) was very well received and did much to develop and stimulate the love of outdoor life which is now so general. It was perhaps the first publication to suggest the "hunting with a camera," instead of a gun, which has been so marked a feature of twentieth-century field work. Among his associates, Samuels was regarded as one of the best-informed men on all subjects pertaining to the natural history of the New England states. He was approachable and eager to help any one who showed an interest in that field and many a student owes him a debt for help freely and cheerfully given.

He married Susan B. Caldwell, a school-teacher and author of stories for young people, while his sister Adelaide was also a writer of no little reputation. After 1890, his eyesight began to fail and in his later years, he was blind. His affliction was increased by paralysis, which completely prevented his actual writing, but he nevertheless, by dictation, continued his contributions to *Forest and Stream* and similar publications. He died at the home of his daughter, Mrs. John A. Barton, in Fitchburg, Mass.

[*Who's Who in America,* 1908–09; *Boston Transcript,* May 28, 1908; *Forest and Stream,* June 13, 1908; *Auk,* July 1908.]   H. L. C.

SAMUELS, SAMUEL (Mar. 14, 1823–May 18, 1908), mariner, has been called the greatest of American transatlantic packet commanders. He was born in Philadelphia and at eleven, after a disagreement with his step-mother, ran away to become a cabin boy on a coasting schooner. This was the beginning of a lively series of maritime adventures later recounted in his memoirs, *From the Forecastle to the Cabin* (1887). He was shipwrecked on the Florida coast; was sentenced to be flogged while serving on a revenue cutter at Mobile; was shanghaied aboard a Baltimore cotton ship for Liverpool; was chased by West Indian pirates; served on the Texas frigate *Houston*; sailed around the world, fighting cannibals in the Pacific; became an officer at seventeen; and married a girl who was a passenger on a trip from New Orleans to New York. At twenty-one, already a father, he was given the command of a ship bound for the Mediterranean. There he declined a proffered post of admiral in the Turkish navy and rescued from a Constantinople harem a Swedish lady who had been enslaved in Egypt. He survived attacks of banditti near Pisa, pirates near Leghorn, and cholera at Hamburg, and was rescued when washed overboard off the Cape of Good Hope. For three years he commanded Schuchardt & Gebhard's packet *Angelique* between New York and Amsterdam.

His chief fame came from his seventy-eight fast voyages between New York and Liverpool as commander of the packet *Dreadnought*. Built under his supervision at Newburyport, Mass., by a group of New York merchants for their Red Cross Line, this vessel was ready for sea in February 1854. Samuels says of her, "She was never passed in anything over a four-knot breeze. She was what might be termed a semi-clipper, and possessed the merit of being able to bear driving as long as her sails and spars would stand. By the sailors she was nicknamed the 'Wild boat of the Atlantic,' while others called her the 'Flying Dutchman'" (*Forecastle to Cabin,* p. 250). Samuels was a great driver, keeping full sail on his heavily sparred ship long after most others were under reefed topsails. He drove her night and day and always used the short northern passage in spite of the extra danger from gales and ice. He was a firm disciplinarian and left a graphic account of overcoming a particularly tough crew of Liverpool "packet rats" who had sworn to throw him overboard (*Ibid.,* pp. 267–91). He established a packet speed record in

1859, reaching Liverpool in thirteen days and eight hours from New York, but the latest research discredits the story of a run from New York to Queenstown the following year in nine days and seventeen hours (Paine, *post,* p. xvi). Samuels maintained a remarkable regularity of fast voyages between 1854 and 1862, his first eight averaging twenty-four and a half days. Because of the combination of speed and safety, the *Dreadnought's* staterooms were booked a year in advance and she commanded freight rates midway between those of the steamships and the regular sailing packets, her owners offering to refund freight charges if delivery were not made on time.

During the Civil War, Samuels commanded the *John Rice* in 1863, was general superintendent of the Quartermaster's Department at New York in 1864, and commanded the *G. B. McClellan* at the taking of Fort Fisher in 1865. In 1866, he was captain of the steamship *Fulton,* the last of the American liners to Havre, and in December won the first transatlantic yacht race, driving James Gordon Bennett's *Henrietta* from "Sandy Hook to the Needles" just ahead of the *Fleetwing* and *Vesta.* In 1870, in the *Dauntless,* he was beaten by the British yacht *Cambria* in a race from Head of Kinsale to Sandy Hook and in 1887, the *Coronet* beat him in the old *Dauntless.* By that time he had long been ashore, in various business capacities. His Samana Bay Company in 1872 hoped to exploit a concession in Santo Domingo, which, however, was revoked in 1874. He organized the Rousseau Electric Signal Company and the United States Steam Heating & Power Company, served as general superintendent of the Pacific Mail Steamship Company, and in his last years was president of the Marine Journal Company. He died at his home in Brooklyn.

[The chief source for Samuels' career through 1862 is his *From the Forecastle to the Cabin* (1887), reprinted, with a critical foreword, by R. D. Paine in 1924. See also "Capt. Samuel Samuels of the Dreadnought," illustrated, in *Outing Mag.,* Dec. 1905; F. B. C. Bradlee, "The Dreadnought of Newburyport," *Essex Inst. Hist. Colls.,* vol. LVI (1920); A. H. Clark, *The Clipper Ship Era* (1910); O. T. Howe and F. C. Matthews, *Am. Clipper Ships,* vol. I (1926); C. C. Cutler, *Greyhounds of the Sea* (1930); J. H. Morrison, *Hist. of N. Y. Ship Yards* (copr. 1909); J. D. J. Kelley, *American Yachts* (1884); R. F. Coffin, *The America's Cup* (1885); *Who's Who in America,* 1906–07; *N. Y. Herald,* Apr. 1, 1905, May 19, 1908.]   R. G. A.

SANBORN, EDWIN DAVID (May 14, 1808–Dec. 29, 1885), educator, was born at Gilmanton, N. H., the son of David Edwin and Hannah (Hook) Sanborn, and a descendant of John Sanborn (or Samborne), who came from England to Boston in 1632 and later settled in Hampton, N. H. He attended Gilmanton Academy and was graduated from Dartmouth College in 1832. After a period of teaching and the study of law, he entered Andover Theological Seminary in 1834, but in the next year was summoned back to Dartmouth as a tutor. Soon he became professor of Latin and Greek, and in 1837, professor of Latin. In 1859 he assumed a similar chair in Washington University, St. Louis, but returned to Dartmouth in 1863 as professor of oratory and belles-lettres. In 1880 he was appointed to the newly established Winkley Professorship of Anglo-Saxon and English Literature, resigning two years later because of ill health. Sanborn was a voluminous contributor to the periodical press, and was in much demand throughout the state as a speaker on a great variety of occasions. Many of his addresses were printed in pamphlet form. He assisted Fletcher Webster in editing the correspondence of the latter's father, Daniel Webster, and in 1875 he published a *History of New Hampshire.* Twice he was a member of the state legislature, and in 1850 of the constitutional convention.

It was as a teacher of the old school, however, that he showed his greatest strength. His reading was remarkably wide, his memory prodigious, and his power of interesting and inspiring students equaled by that of few teachers of his day. His opinions were pronounced and he was ready at all times to set them forth; he was bluff, abrupt, and downright, saying what was on his mind with little regard for the feelings of others. Eager, brimful of learning, quick at repartee, for more than forty years he inspired generations of undergraduates with some measure of his own vigor and enthusiasm. The students were amused at his peculiarities, but they were drawn to him by the contagion of his personality and held him in sincere admiration. The term "Bully," applied to him in his earlier days, became, in later years, a mark of real affection. He is an example of the college teacher at his best in the days before productive scholarship, in the technical sense, became a requirement of the professor. The Sanborn English House, erected at Dartmouth in 1929 by the use of part of a bequest by his son, Edwin Webster Sanborn, perpetuates his name, and, in its purpose and application, his ideals. In 1837 he was married to Mary Ann, daughter of Ezekiel Webster of Boscawen, N. H., and niece of Daniel Webster: she died in 1864, and in 1868 he married Mrs. Sarah Fenton Clark of Detroit. By his first wife he had four children, one of whom was Katherine Abbott Sanborn [*q.v.*], lecturer and author. He died in New York City.

[See V. C. Sanborn, *Geneal. of the Family of Samborne or Sanborn in England and America* (1899); J. K. Lord, *A Hist. of Dartmouth Coll.* (1913); L. B. Richardson, *Hist. of Dartmouth Coll.* (1932); *N. Y. Daily Tribune*, Dec. 30, 1885. Much of Sanborn's correspondence is preserved in the lib. of Dartmouth Coll.]
L. B. R.

SANBORN, FRANKLIN BENJAMIN (Dec. 15, 1831–Feb. 24, 1917), author, journalist, philanthropist, was born on his ancestral farm in Hampton Falls., N. H., the fifth of the seven children of Aaron and Lydia (Leavitt) Sanborn, and the sixth in descent from John Sanborn, who settled in Hampton in 1640. His father was a farmer and, when his son was born, clerk of the town. The boy's intellectual development was stimulated by his love for Ariana Walker, daughter of James Walker of Peterborough. With her encouragement he completed his preparatory schooling at Phillips Exeter Academy and entered Harvard College as a sophomore in 1852. He enjoyed his college life, but from his teachers he derived far less than from Theodore Parker, whose preaching he attended regularly, and from Ralph Waldo Emerson, on whom he first ventured to call in 1853. On Aug. 23, 1854, he was married to Ariana Walker, who was on her deathbed and succumbed eight days later. Sanborn graduated from Harvard in 1855 and removed to Concord, Mass., where at Emerson's suggestion he had already opened a school.

It was a happy move, for Concord was his spiritual home. Less original than the elder literary men of the village, he was their fellow in vigor and independence of mind and in breadth of interests, and he had a practical sagacity and knowledge of the world that some of them lacked. He was soon in the thick of the abolition movement. As secretary of the Massachusetts Free Soil Association he went on a tour of inspection in the West in the summer of 1856 and, although he did not actually enter Kansas Territory, brought back with him an enduring interest in the problems of that region. The next January he met John Brown in Boston, was captivated by the man, and became his New England agent. He was apprised of Brown's intentions at Harpers Ferry, did what he could to dissuade him, but, when dissuasion proved futile, aided him. Later, he refused to leave Massachusetts to testify before a committee of the United States Senate, grounding his refusal on an appeal to the doctrine of state rights, and on Feb. 16, 1860, the Senate ordered his arrest. Sanborn retreated twice to Quebec but returned on the advice of his friends. The sergeant-at-arms of the Senate delegated the power to arrest him to one Carleton of

Boston, who with four assistants apprehended him at Concord on Apr. 3, 1860. He was released at once on a writ of *habeas corpus* issued by Judge E. R. Hoar; a *posse comitatus* chased the arresting party out of town; and the next day the state supreme court, by a decision written by Chief Justice Shaw, ordered Sanborn's discharge.

To newspaper work, philanthropy, and literature he devoted the greater part of his long life. On Aug. 16, 1862, he married his cousin, Louisa Augusta Leavitt, by whom he had three sons. He succeeded Moncure Daniel Conway [*q.v.*] as editor of the *Boston Commonwealth* (1863–67) and was a resident editor of the *Springfield Republican* (1868–72). He had been a correspondent of the *Republican* since 1856 and remained on its staff until 1914. As a newspaper man he was noted for his blistering criticism of various Massachusetts politicians. In 1863 Gov. John Albion Andrew [*q.v.*] appointed him secretary of the state board of charities. This office was the first of its kind in the United States, and Sanborn made it important and influential. He instituted a system of inspection and report for state charities that has been widely copied, made himself an expert on the care of the insane, and drafted many bills that were enacted into law. He retired as secretary in 1868 but remained on the board and was its chairman from 1874 to 1876; from 1879 to 1888 he was state inspector of charities. He was a founder and officer of the American Social Science Association, the National Prison Association, the National Conference of Charities, the Clarke School for the Deaf, and the Massachusetts Infant Asylum, and for all of them he worked hard and effectively. He lectured at Cornell University, Smith College, and Wellesley College, and joined with William Torrey Harris [*q.v.*] in establishing the Concord School of Philosophy. He knew intimately all the men and women who made Concord famous, was their sympathetic, helpful friend while they lived and their loyal, intelligent editor and biographer after their death. His publications include: *Henry D. Thoreau* (1882); *The Life and Letters of John Brown* (1885), a fourth edition of which was issued under the title *John Brown, Liberator of Kansas and Martyr of Virginia* (1910); *Dr. S. G. Howe, the Philanthropist* (1891); *A. Bronson Alcott: His Life and Philosophy* (2 vols., 1893), with W. T. Harris; *Memoirs of Pliny Earle, M.D.* (1898); *The Personality of Thoreau* (1901); *Ralph Waldo Emerson* (1901); *The Personality of Emerson* (1903); *New Hampshire* (1904); *New Hampshire Biography and Autobiography* (1905); *Michael*

Anagnos (1907) ; *Bronson Alcott at Alcott House, England, and Fruitlands, New England* (1908) ; *Hawthorne and His Friends* (1908) ; *Recollections of Seventy Years* (2 vols., 1909) ; and *The Life of Henry David Thoreau* (1917). He published many magazine articles and did much editorial work on the literary remains of his friends. In some conservative circles his reputation as a subversive thinker lingered even into the twentieth century. He made two extensive visits to Europe and in his latter years enjoyed his membership in the Massachusetts Historical Society. Retaining his faculties to the end, he never lost his passion for liberty and justice or his admiration for the great men whom he had known in his prime. He died at his son's home in Plainfield, N. J., and was buried in Concord.

[Sanborn's writings contain much biog. material, especially his *Recollections of Seventy Years* (2 vols., 1909) and "An Unpublished Concord Jour.," ed. by G. S. Hellman, *Century Mag.*, Apr. 1922. See also : V. C. Sanborn, *Geneal. of the Family of Samborne or Sanborn* (1899), and "Franklin Benjamin Sanborn, A.B.," *New England Hist. and Geneal. Reg.*, Oct. 1917, and *Kan. State Hist. Soc. Colls.*, vol. XIV (1918) ; Lindsay Swift, "Franklin Benjamin Sanborn," *Proc. Mass. Hist. Soc.*, vol. L (1917) ; Ed. Stanwood, memoir, *Ibid.*, vol. LI (1918) ; *The Report of the Secretary of the Class of 1855 of Harvard Coll., July 1855 to July 1865* (1865) ; *Apocrypha Concerning the Class of 1855 of Harvard Coll. and Their Deeds and Misdeeds during the Fifteen years between July, 1865, and July, 1880* (1880) ; *Springfield Republican*, Feb. 25, 27, 1917 ; Alexander Johnson, "An Appreciation of Franklin B. Sanborn," *Survey*, Mar. 10, 1917 ; W. E. Connelley, "Personal Reminiscences of F. B. Sanborn," *Kan. State Hist. Soc. Colls.*, vol. XIV (1918) ; H. D. Carew, "Franklin B. Sanborn, an Appreciation," *Granite Mo.*, Nov. 1922.]
G. H. G.

SANBORN, KATHERINE ABBOTT (July 11, 1839–July 9, 1917), author, teacher, and lecturer, was born in Hanover, N. H., the eldest daughter of Edwin David Sanborn [*q.v.*] and Mary Ann (Webster) Sanborn and the descendant of John Samborne, an English emigrant who settled in Hampton, N. H., about 1640. She was usually called Kate and most of her writing appeared under that name. Her mother was the daughter of Ezekiel Webster, the gifted brother of Daniel Webster, and of this relationship she was always proudly conscious. Her father, professor of Latin, gave more than forty years of service to Dartmouth College, interrupted by four years of teaching at Washington University in St. Louis. The family and community life in which she grew up was intellectually invigorating and socially stimulating. Books and lectures abounded, distinguished writers and scholars were frequent guests, and there was an unfailing supply of young men to entertain a lively girl.

She was taught by her father and his colleagues along the lines of the college curriculum,

and she studied music in Andover, Mass., and elocution in Boston. Her chief education, however, was from reading and conversation; and in her writing she always retained much of the casual, anecdotal manner of the ready talker. She was almost inevitably a writer and teacher, beginning to publish at the age of eleven and opening a school in her father's house before she was twenty. From 1859 to 1863, during her father's years in St. Louis, she taught girls in Mary Institute, connected with Washington University. Later she taught elocution at Packer Collegiate Institute in Brooklyn, where she formed a close friendship with Anne Charlotte Lynch Botta [*q.v.*]. Her wit and wide knowledge of books attracted many to the "talks" on current literature that she gave first in Mrs. Botta's drawing room and later in various clubs and schools. In this line of lecturing she was among the pioneers, and likewise she was among the early organizers of women's clubs. She was always avid for novel experiences and susceptible to new influences. She wrote constantly for periodicals, and her *flair* for journalism was shown even in the titles of her lectures and publications, such as "Hunting Indians with a Taxicab," "Are Women Witty?" The gifts of quick association and retentive memory made her an excellent raconteur and determined her interest in anthologies and quotation calendars, of which she edited many. For three years, from 1880 to 1883, she taught English literature at Smith College. Although a stimulating and suggestive teacher, she had not the sound scholarship and intellectual patience necessary for real college work. On leaving Smith she made an extended lecture tour in the West and extended her travels to Alaska.

A break in health sent her to the country and she settled in Metcalf, Mass., for the remainder of her life. The records of her experiences *Adopting an Abandoned Farm* (1891) and *Abandoning an Adopted Farm* (1894) are delightfully humorous and may be counted as among the early contributions to "back to the land" writings. Lightly as she wrote them, the experiences were not all easy or remunerative, and the wise may read many a warning and much sage advice under the flow of wit. This is true also of her *A Truthful Woman in Southern California* (1893). Her last serious work, *Memories and Anecdotes* (1915), written too late to show her qualities at their best, abounds in clever turns and apt quotations and exhibits many of her chief characteristics, her redundancy, her lack of continuity, her wide and delighted reading, her love of people, and her unfailing zest in life. "Refreshing" was the word chosen by her friend,

Edna Dean Proctor, as most applicable to her. "A stout, buxom, red-headed woman, with hair all a-flying" a country neighbor is quoted as saying of Kate Sanborn. She was a purely New England product, with Yankee versatility and adaptability, and she went "all a-flying" down many new paths that later and soberer feet have worn to smoothness and even to monotony.

[*Memories and Anecdotes, ante*; E. W. Sanborn, *Kate Sanborn* (1918); V. C. Sanborn, *Geneal. of the Family of Samborne or Sanborn* (1899), esp. p. 429; *New York Times*, July 10, 1917; *Daily Evening Transcript* (Boston), July 9, 1917.]   E. D. H.

SANBORN, WALTER HENRY (Oct. 19, 1845–May 10, 1928), judge, descended from William Sanborn who came to Boston from England in 1632, was born at Epsom, N. H., the son of Henry Frederick and Eunice (Davis) Sanborn. He attended the local district school and academy, taught in the country districts after he was fifteen, and graduated from Dartmouth College as class valedictorian in 1867. For three years following he was principal of the high school at Milford, N. H., then went to St. Paul, Minn., and studied law in the office of his uncle, Gen. John B. Sanborn. He was admitted to the bar Jan. 28, 1871, and joined his uncle in a partnership which lasted more than a score of years. On Nov. 10, 1874, he married Emily F. Bruce of Milford, N. H.; two sons and two daughters were born of this marriage.

While his professional interests were always paramount with him, he also found time for other duties. From 1878 to 1880 and again from 1885 to 1892 he served in the St. Paul City Council; during the latter period he also had office in state and county bar associations. He had entered the Masonic order, becoming interested especially in the Knights Templars, and in 1889 was their Grand Commander for Minnesota.

In 1891 Sanborn was selected by President Harrison as one of three judges of the newly created circuit court of appeals for the eighth circuit. His commission was dated Mar. 17, 1892, and he exercised it for the remainder of his life—more than a generation. On June 4, 1903, he became presiding judge of the circuit. Notable administrative work which he did in his judicial capacity included conducting receiverships of the Union Pacific Railway (1893–98), the Chicago and Great Western (1908–09), the St. Louis & San Francisco (1913–14), and the Denver & Rio Grande (1918–19). The best exemplification of his work, however, is found in his opinions, and the bar of the circuit soon learned that it had in him a master builder of the law. Among the earliest of his significant opinions was that in the Omaha Bridge Cases in 1892 (51 *Fed. Reporter*, 309), when he upheld the right of the Rock Island Railway to use the Union Pacific bridge across the Missouri. In *U. S. vs. Trans-Missouri Freight Association* (58 *Fed. Reporter*, 58), 1893, he held the Sherman Anti-trust law inapplicable to an agreement between competing railways to maintain freight rates recommended as reasonable by a committee of their own choosing. His ruling was reversed by a vote of five to four in the Supreme Court (166 *U. S.*, 343), but he was able to say that a majority of the judges (including those of his own court) who had passed on the case were of his view, and a decade later (1903), in *Whitwell vs. Continental Tobacco Company* (125 *Fed. Reporter*, 454), he maintained a somewhat similar position, holding the same act inapplicable to a corporation and its employee with an arrangement for special rates on its products to purchasers who refrained from handling those of its competitors. The large number of personal injury cases which came to his court enabled him to specialize in that field. His discussion (*Chicago, St. Paul, Minneapolis, and Omaha Railway Company vs. Elliot,* 55 *Fed. Reporter*, 949) of what constitutes the proximate cause of an injury is probably unexcelled in judicial opinions in English; masterly expositions of the "fellow servant doctrine" are found in *City of Minneapolis vs. Lundin* (58 *Fed. Reporter*, 525), *What Cheer Coal Co. vs. Johnson* (56 *Fed. Reporter*, 810), and *Gowen vs. Harley* (56 *Fed. Reporter*, 973), all rendered in 1893. An important precedent on contributory negligence is found in *Union Pacific Railway Company vs. Jarvi* (53 *Fed. Reporter*, 65), 1892; the employer's duty to warn minor employees of latent dangers, in *Bohn Manufacturing Company vs. Erickson* (55 *Fed. Reporter*, 943). He held the Federal power of naturalization exclusive, and his opinion in *City of Minneapolis vs. Reum* (56 *Fed. Reporter*, 576), 1893, is a valuable contribution to the literature of that subject. With a strong intellect, highly trained, deep learning gathered by long and exhaustive study, and a clear and incisive style of expression developed by extensive judicial service he has had few superiors on the American bench. In 1927 the Bar Association of St. Louis gave him a testimonial dinner in celebration of his service of thirty-five years.

[C. E. Flandrau, *Encyc. of Biog. of Minn.* (1900), vol. I; H. J. Boswell, *Am. Blue Book: Attorneys of Minn.* (1923); *Walter Henry Sanborn: A Testimonial Vol.* (Bar Asso. of St. Louis, 1927); *Who's Who in America*, 1926–27; J. B. Sanborn, *Sanborn Family in the U. S.* (1887); *St. Paul Dispatch*, May 10, 1928.]   C. S. L.

SANDEMAN, ROBERT (Apr. 29, 1718–Apr. 2, 1771), promoter in the American colonies of a religious sect which came to be known as the Sandemanians, was born at Perth, in Scotland, the eldest son of David and Margaret (Ramsay) Sandeman. His father was a merchant, and from 1736 until 1744 Robert was a linen manufacturer in partnership with his brother William. As a young man, probably while at the University of Edinburgh, he came under the influence of John Glas [see *Dictionary of National Biography*], whose daughter Catherine he married in 1737. She died in 1746. He became an elder in the Glassite churches in 1744 and served successively at Perth, Dundee, Edinburgh, and London. The Glassites, or Sandemanians as they were later called in England and America, originated in 1728 as a protest against the established Church of Scotland and formed an independent body, rejecting the Covenant, asserting the independence of church and state, preaching the doctrine that faith is mere intellectual assent, and practising many of the primitive Christian rites. The chief article of their belief was that "the bare Work of Jesus Christ without a Deed or Thought on the Part of Man is sufficient to present the chief of Sinners spotless before God" (Sandeman's epitaph, Edes, *post*, p. 112). Sandeman became widely known by his controversial writings, particularly *Letters on Theron and Aspasio Addressed to the Author*, published in Edinburgh in 1757, a criticism of James Hervey's *Dialogues*. In 1760 he organized the London congregation of the sect.

Perceiving the interest aroused in America by his writings and being in correspondence with Ebenezer White, pastor at Danbury, Conn., and others of the New England clergy, he sailed for America on Aug. 10, 1764, accompanied by James Cargill. At Providence, R. I., he was joined by Andrew Oliphant. He and his associates preached in many towns of New England and within a few years organized congregations at Boston, Portsmouth, N. H., Taunton, Mass., Newtown and Danbury, Conn. In 1764, at Boston, he published *Some Thoughts on Christianity*. By 1767 he had made his home at Danbury, which became the chief stronghold of the sect in America and where remnants of the congregation existed until about 1900.

Sandeman and his followers were vigorously opposed by the leading New England ministers for their defense of "the voluntary principle." They were especially suspect for their rejection of the Covenant of Grace and of the doctrine of justification by faith as an act of regeneration. Sandeman taught that "every one who obtains a just notion of the person and work of Christ ... is justified and finds peace with God simply by that notion" (Letter II, *Epistolary Correspondence, post*). Samuel Langdon [*q.v.*] said of the Sandemanians that they were of "a very malevolent Spirit and high Enthusiasm very much like that of the hottest New Lights, however frigid Sandeman's notions may seem to his readers" (Letter to Ezra Stiles, Sept. 7, 1766, *Literary Diary, post*, II, 171). In 1770 Sandeman was brought before the judge at Danbury and fined £40 for remaining in town four weeks after being warned to depart as an undesirable transient. At the hearing he pleaded that the law was not intended "against harmless strangers but against persons of ungoverned and dishonest conversations" (Walker, *post*, p. 154), and the sentence was never executed. Several of his disciples, however, were ordered out of New Haven in 1777 for the expression of Loyalist views.

Ezra Stiles described Sandeman as "of a middling Stature, dark Complexion, a good Eye, uses accurate Language, but not eloquent in utterance, has not a melodious voice, his expressions governed by Sentiment, his dialect Scotch, not graceful in his Air and Address, yet has something which deforces attention, and this is chiefly by the Sentiments he infuses or excites in his Auditory—generally grave and decent, and not a noisy speaker" (Walker, p. 151). He died at Danbury.

[*An Epistolary Correspondence between S. P. and R. S.* (1760), correspondence between Samuel Pike and Robert Sandeman, begun in 1758; Sandeman's *Discourses on Passages of Scripture with Essays and Letters ... with Biog. Sketch of the Author* (Dundee, 1857); Samuel Langdon, *An Impartial Examination of Mr. Robert Sandeman's Letters on Theron and Aspasio* (Portsmouth, N. H., 1765); Walter Wilson, *The Hist. and Antiquities of Dissenting Churches*, III (1810), 274–75; Andrew Fuller, *Strictures on Sandemanianism* (New York, 1812); H. H. Edes, "The Places of Worship of the Sandemanians in Boston," *Col. Soc. Mass. Pub.*, vol. VI (1904); Williston Walker, "The Sandemanians of New England," *Ann. Report Am. Hist. Asso., 1901* (1902), vol. I; J. G. Sandeman, *The Sandeman Geneal.* (1895); F. B. Dexter, *The Literary Diary of Ezra Stiles* (3 vols., 1901).]   H. W. S.

SANDERS, BILLINGTON McCARTER (Dec. 2, 1789–Mar. 12, 1854), Baptist minister, educator, the eldest son of Ephraim and Nancy Sanders, was born in Columbia County, Ga. Early left an orphan, he was reared in a friendly and pious home. He prepared for college in Kiokee, or McNeil's, Seminary, and entered Franklin College, Athens, Ga., about 1806, but in 1808 transferred to South Carolina College, Columbia, S. C., where he graduated in 1809. After teaching for two years in Columbia County Academy, Ga., he was a successful farmer for about twenty years. In 1817 he served in the lower House of the state legislature, but declined to be a candidate for reëlection. He joined Kiokee Baptist Church in January 1810, being baptized by Abraham Marshall. Some years later, feeling called to preach, he was licensed by Union Church, Warren County, Ga., and on Jan. 5, 1825, was ordained. He continued to farm, but now devoted much time to itinerant preaching and pastoral work. At different times he was pastor of Williams Creek, Pine Grove, Union, Powelton, Shiloh, Greensboro, Penfield, Sugar Creek, Griffin, and other Georgia Baptist churches. Tall and slender, with a tendency to tuberculosis, he was energetic and punctual, with a strong, clear, practical mind, sound judgment, and great moral earnestness. He was neither a great scholar nor a very eloquent preacher, but his practical, pungent sermons were so effective that he was much sought after by the churches of Georgia.

Recognition of his character, business ability, energy, and influence as a preacher led to his selection as first principal of Mercer Institute on its establishment at Penfield in 1832. He continued as head of the institution until 1839 when it was made Mercer University. During this formative period he was financial agent, teacher, and general administrative head of the institution, and has been justly called the real founder of Mercer University, of which for its first few months he served as president. After his resignation (see *Valedictory Address . . . Dec. 16, 1839,* 1840) he was for several years secretary and treasurer of the board of trustees, and remained a member of that body until his death.

Perhaps his chief title to fame is his service to Mercer University, but he occupied other important positions in the Baptist denomination in Georgia and in the public life of his state. He was moderator of the Georgia Association for nine years and clerk for a number of years, was for six years president of the Baptist State Convention and for many years chairman of its executive committee. He edited the *Christian Index* for a year, was a frequent delegate to the Triennial and the Southern Baptist Convention. On Mar. 17, 1812, he married Martha Lamar, by whom he had nine children. After her death in 1822 he married, Feb. 25, 1824, Cynthia Holliday, by whom he had thirteen children. Two children of the first marriage and eight of the second survived their father, who died at Penfield after a long illness. He was one of the most important of the Baptist preachers and educators of Georgia during the first half of the nineteenth century.

[C. D. Mallary, *Living and Dying unto the Lord: A Discourse in Commemoration of Elder Billington M. Sanders* (1854), which is the authority for year of death, sometimes erroneously stated as 1852; W. B. Sprague, *Annals Am. Pulpit,* vol. VI (1860); B. D. Ragsdale, *Story of Ga. Baptists* (1932); S. G. Hillyer, *Reminiscences of Ga. Baptists* (1902); J. H. Campbell, *Ga. Baptists, Hist. and Biog.* (1874); Wm. Cathcart, *The Bapt. Encyc.* (1881); *Hist. of the Bapt. Denomination in Ga., with Biog. Compend.* (1881); minutes of Ga. Association and Baptist State Convention.]

W.J.M.

SANDERS, CHARLES WALTON (Mar. 24, 1805–July 5, 1889), educator, was born at Newport, N. Y., one of ten children of Jacob and Lydia (Martin) Sanders, and a direct descendant of John Sanders, who came to Salem, Mass., from Wiltshire, England, in 1630. His father was a farmer in modest circumstances, but was desirous of educating his children, and at the age of four Charles was sent to a local school where he acquired as much knowledge as his teacher could impart. When he was nine his father moved to Homer, Cortland County, N. Y., where the son finished his slender country-school education. He became a licensed teacher in 1821, and at the age of twenty-four was elected inspector of common schools, serving for several years. He taught seventeen years in the schools of Homer and Cortland County. In 1837 or 1838, meaning to capitalize the experience and observation resulting from his years of country-school teaching, he moved from the back-country to the metropolis, and plunged into the writing and compilation of spellers and readers for elementary schools. The next twenty-five years saw an amazing succession of more than forty titles of primers, spellers, a series of six graded readers, grammars, speakers, charts, and cards for teaching children, school singing-books, all bearing the name of the author on the cover, title-page, and every left page throughout every volume. An advantageous association with the leading educational publisher of the day, combined with the solid merits of the books, brought such popularity that 13,000,000 Sanders' readers were reported sold between 1838 and 1860, and the author at one time received about $30,000 yearly in royalties.

In preparing his textbooks, he had in mind certain definite aims, to the achievement of which he brought industry, originality, and the instincts of a born teacher, sharpened by years of experience with under-privileged country children. Previous to his time, reading-books had been composed of selections from the masters of English literature, often pedantic, and in most cases beyond the easy comprehension of children. Characteristics which contributed to the worth and popularity of the Sanders' readers were:

careful grading, pictures, moral and ethical tone; the simplicity and interest, as well as literary merit, of the contents; emphasis on articulation and inflection in teaching reading and in class exercises. Much of the matter in the first, second, and third readers was Sanders' own. By putting a few songs with music at the end of each reader, he has shared credit for introducing singing into the public schools. In his public school music interests he was associated with William Batchelder Bradbury [q.v.]. He maintained close touch with his constituency for many years by spending three months annually in visiting and lecturing before schools and teachers' meetings, and in giving entertaining illustrative readings. He was present at the organization of the New York State Teachers' Association, in 1845. He was interested in the early temperance movement, and was a steadfast Republican until Cleveland claimed his vote in 1884. On Aug. 2, 1842, he was married to Elizabeth Barker, the daughter of John and Anna Barton Barker, of White Plains, N. Y., and had three children. He died in New York City.

[W. R. Cutter, *Geneal. and Family Hist. of Central N. Y.* (1912), vol. III; C. W. Sanders, *Geneal. of the Cortland County, N. Y., Branch of the Sanders Family* (1908); S. A. Allibone, *A Critical Dictionary of English Literature,* vol. II (1870); *State of N. Y., Dept. of Public Instruction, 37th Annual Report, 1891* (1891); *N. Y. Times,* July 6, 1889.]   J.I.W.

SANDERS, DANIEL CLARKE (May 3, 1768–Oct. 18, 1850), preacher and educator, was born at Sturbridge, Mass., the fourth child and only son of Michael and Azubah (Clarke) Sanders. After the death of his father in 1773, his mother married Capt. Ebenezer Fisher of Needham, where the boy was prepared for college under the direction of Rev. Samuel West. He entered Harvard, graduating in 1788. Burdened with the formidable debt of one hundred dollars, he immediately took employment "keeping a common school in Watertown." Soon afterward he became preceptor of the grammar school in Cambridge. Here he studied theology under the guidance of Rev. Thomas Prentiss of Medfield. Licensed by the Dedham Association in 1790, he preached as a candidate and as a supply in various pulpits in Massachusetts, New Hampshire, and Vermont. In 1794 he was ordained as pastor in Vergennes, Vt., where two years earlier he had married Nancy, daughter of Dr. Jabez Fitch. In 1799 he accepted a call to preach in Burlington, where he also kept a private school until the organization of the University of Vermont. He was made a trustee of that embryo institution in January 1800, and in October became its first president.

His duties while directing the new university during its first fourteen years were varied and onerous. He managed its lands and finances, supervised in part the erection of its first building, and for some years carried the entire burden of instruction, continuing meantime his pastoral duties until 1807. Though students increased from four the first year to over fifty in 1813, the university was in financial trouble. Hostilities on Lake Champlain during the second war with Great Britain disrupted its activities. In the spring of 1814 the trustees suspended instruction, leased the university building to the government for use as barracks, and dismissed all salaried officers, including the president. Sanders at this time was almost overwhelmed with misfortunes: his book, *A History of the Indian Wars with the First Settlers of the United States, Particularly in New England,* published anonymously at Montpelier in 1812, had aroused bitter criticism because of its strictures on colonial bigotry and cruelty to the natives (see *Historical Magazine,* February 1858); his wife was a victim of occasional attacks of insanity; five of his eight children had recently died in an epidemic. Now he was without employment and with few resources save a claim on the University for arrears of salary.

After preaching for a time in New York City he reluctantly accepted a call (May 1815) to become pastor of the First Congregational Church of Medfield, Mass., where his parents and grandparents had been born and where he had preached his first sermon. During the fourteen years of his pastorate here he gained a wide reputation as a thoughtful and eloquent speaker. A moderate man, averse to theological controversies, he attempted unsuccessfully to guide his church through that stormy period. After the stricter Calvinists had seceded, he found it impossible to stay with the thorough-paced Unitarians and resigned his pastorate in the spring of 1829, though he continued to reside in Medfield until his death.

The last phase of his career was devoted to occasional preaching and to public life. He was a delegate to the state constitutional convention of 1820–21; represented the Medfield district in the Massachusetts House, 1833–36; and during the same years was one of the selectmen of his town, where later he held other minor positions. His last years he spent caring for his invalid wife, whose death in 1850 he survived by only two months. He published a number of sermons, one of which, *A Sermon, Preached in Medfield . . . Near the 166th Anniversary of the Incorporation of the Town* (1817), was the first historical sketch of Medfield.

Sanders

Sanders

[W. S. Tilden, *Hist. of the Town of Medfield, Mass.* (1887); *Vital Records of Sturbridge, Mass., to the Year 1850* (1906); A. M. Hemenway, *The Vt. Hist. Gazetteer*, vol. I (1868); *Vt. Alumni Weekly*, Oct. 10, 1923; J. A. Savage, *First Congreg. Church*, reprint from *Medfield, Mass.: Proc. at the Celebration of the 250th Anniversary of the Incorporation of the Town* (1902); copy in Univ. of Vt. Library of an autobiography and journal (MSS.) of Sanders.] P. D. E.

SANDERS, DANIEL JACKSON (Feb. 15, 1847–Mar. 6, 1907), Presbyterian clergyman, educator, editor, the son of William and Laura Sanders, was born in slavery near Winnsboro, S. C., on the plantation of Thomas Hall, a Methodist preacher. His owner permitted him to learn the letters of the alphabet, and before he became free he had learned to spell and to read. At the age of nine years he was given his first instruction in the shoemaker's trade; he served as an apprentice for five years, making such remarkable progress that at the end of three years his master was able to collect pay for his services. In 1866 he left his master's home and set out for Chester, S. C., taking with him only a small shoemaker's kit. As he worked he secured tutelage from a Mr. W. B. Knox, and in 1869 and 1870 attended Brainerd Institute, at Chester, where he proved so apt a pupil that after two years of study he was made a tutor in the school. By 1871 he was prepared to enter Western Theological Seminary at Allegheny, Pa., where in 1874 he graduated with honors. He then became pastor of the Chestnut Street Presbyterian Church in Wilmington, N. C. Here he assembled the colored Presbyterians, who until then had been worshipping in the galleries of the churches of their former owners, into the northern Presbyterian Church (Presbyterian Church in the United States of America).

Because of his religious attitude, his forensic power, and sound logic, Sanders soon became a leader in the educational world. He was elected principal of the public schools in Chester, S. C., and in 1875, principal of the city schools in Wilmington, N. C. This position he resigned shortly in order to go abroad to raise money for the work of the Board of Missions for Freedmen. He spent over a year in Scotland and England and raised a large sum of money for the Board. In addition, he raised $6,000 as an endowment for an African scholarship fund to prepare men at Biddle University, a Presbyterian institution at Charlotte, N. C., for mission work in Africa. Upon his return from Europe he resumed his pastorate.

Feeling that the church needed an organ of publicity, he began on Jan. 1, 1879, the publication of the *Africo-American Presbyterian,* which had a wide influence in building up the Presbyterian cause among the colored people. This publication he edited until his death. On Sept. 16, 1880, he married Fannie Price, and of this union nine children were born. In 1891, he was elected president of Biddle University, of which he had been a trustee for fourteen years. He was its first colored president. His unusual executive ability and untiring interest in the expansion of the university enabled it to make rapid advancement. As a teacher of theology and church government he was well liked by his students, who called him "Zeus." He continued as president of Biddle (which later became Johnson C. Smith University) until his death.

Sanders was the first colored moderator of both the Yadkin and Cape Fear presbyteries, he served as a stated clerk in the Atlantic and Yadkin presbyteries and the Catawba Synod, and three times was delegate to meetings of the Alliance of Reformed Churches Holding the Presbyterian System—at Toronto, Liverpool, and Washington. He was many times a member of the General Assembly, where his voice was heard and given recognition. With an extremely simple philosophy of life to guide him he commended himself each day to God and did his best in each day's work. He died at the age of sixty.

[*Johnson C. Smith Univ. Alumni Jour.*, D. J. Sanders Edition, Apr. 1928; *Africo-American Presbyterian*, Mar. 15, May 3, 1888; *Minutes of the Gen. Assembly of the Presbyt. Ch. in the U. S. A.*, 1870–1907; *Who's Who in America*, 1906–07; *Charlotte Daily Observer*, Mar. 7, 1907; information as to certain facts from Mrs. D. J. Sanders and a son, Brooks Sanders.] D. B. P.

SANDERS, ELIZABETH ELKINS (Aug. 12, 1762–Feb. 19, 1851), author and reformer, was the daughter of Thomas and Elizabeth (White) Elkins. She was born in Salem, Mass., and spent her entire life there, living to be called "our most delightful old lady" by a writer on Salem life (Silsbee, *post*, p. 95). Friends and relatives united to praise her powers of mind and her magnanimous spirit. On Apr. 28, 1782, she married Thomas Sanders, who after a period spent in the counting-room of her relative, Elias Hasket Derby [*q.v.*], East India merchant, became one of the most successful business men in Salem. In a handsome house on Chestnut Street she reared her two sons and three daughters, dispensed hospitality, and devoted her leisure to wide reading. The elder son, Charles, is remembered at Harvard University as the donor of Sanders Theatre.

Mrs. Sanders took an active part in all movements for bettering the condition of the unfortunate or the oppressed. She gave liberally of her wealth, and frequently contributed to local papers articles approving prison reform, measures for reclaiming delinquents, and greater educational opportunities for the poor. She lent her aid also to the health reformers, and protested against doctors who were too liberal in their use of drugs. Her most ardent championship, however, was reserved for the cause of the American Indians, whom she regarded as "the dethroned monarchs of the land." In 1828 she published, anonymously, *Conversations Principally on the Aborigines of North America,* a little volume in the form of talks between a mother and her children, setting forth her views on the lack of justice and humanity with which the Creeks had been treated by General Jackson. Influenced by the writings of Charlevoix and of William Bartram [*qq.v.*], she argued that the simplicity of primitive races was especially favorable to the development of lofty sentiments, and urged more considerate treatment of all Indians. The following year, in a somewhat similar volume entitled *The First Settlers of New-England,* she dealt with the conquest of other tribes. In this book she elaborated her statements concerning the unchristian conduct of the usurpers toward the natives, and contended that while wrongs at home remained unredressed it was absurd to expend vast sums to maintain missions in foreign lands.

This disapproval of foreign missions found further expression in magazine articles, later published in pamphlet form as *A Tract on Missions* (1844), *The Second Part of the Tract on Missions* (1845), and *Remarks on the "Tour Around Hawaii," by the Missionaries, Messrs. Ellis, Thurston, Bishop, and Goodrich, in 1823* (1848). Mrs. Sanders insisted in these works that missionaries to heathen lands accomplished no good results. As a stanch Unitarian she was especially indignant with those who carried "the appalling dogmas of Calvinism" to virtuous and happy Polynesians. She praised Melville's *Typee* (1846) for revealing the "scandalous and wicked transactions" of missionaries in the Sandwich Islands, and defended it against critics who wished to suppress the book. Besides her controversial works she published one other volume, *Reviews of a Part of Prescott's 'History of Ferdinand and Isabella,' and of Campbell's 'Lectures on Poetry'* (1841).

[M. C. D. Silsbee, *A Half Century in Salem* (1887); *Vital Records of Salem,* vols. I (1916), III (1924); *Ancestry and Descendants of Sir Richard Saltonstall of New England* (1897); *Salem Gazette,* Feb. 21, 1851; information from family.]   B. M. S.

SANDERS, FRANK KNIGHT (June 5, 1861–Feb. 20, 1933), Biblical scholar, author, was born at Batticotta, Jaffna, Ceylon, son of the Rev. Marshall Danforth and Georgianna (Knight) Sanders. He was of old New England ancestry running back to Robert Sanders, a resident of Rhode Island in 1736; to Richard Knight, who came from England in 1635; and to Roger Williams and Chad Brown of early Rhode Island fame. He prepared for college in the academy at Lakeville, Conn., and in the preparatory department of Ripon College, Ripon, Wis., from which institution he was graduated with the degree of A.B. in 1882.

After his graduation he went out as an instructor to Jaffna College, of which his father was the first principal, although he died before the teaching work of the college was actually begun. Returning to the United States, Sanders entered the Yale Divinity School, in 1886, where he came under the vital instruction of William Rainey Harper [*q.v.*], a contact which proved determinative in Sanders' career, leading him to graduate work in Semitic languages and Biblical studies. In 1889 he received the degree of Ph.D. For the next sixteen years he was a member of Yale faculties, serving as instructor in Semitic languages, as Harper's successor in the Woolsey chair of Biblical literature in Yale College (1891–1901), and as dean of the Divinity School and professor of Biblical history and archæology (1901–05). On Jan. 6, 1902, he was ordained, in New Haven, to the Congregational ministry.

Sanders' administrative gifts were such that he was inevitably called to fill executive positions. From 1905 to 1908 he was secretary of the Congregational Sunday-School and Publishing Society, with headquarters in Boston; from 1908 to 1914 he served as president of Washburn College, Topeka, Kan.; from 1914 to 1927 he was in New York as director of missionary preparation for the Foreign Missions Conference of North America. Throughout his entire career, however, from his days as student assistant with Dr. Harper to the last weeks of life, he maintained personal teaching relations through the conduct of correspondence courses. For years, too, he conducted "The Senior Bible Class" department in the *Sunday School Times* and frequently served as special lecturer in important schools and colleges. He was a voluminous writer. Of his published books his *History of the Hebrews,* first issued in 1914 and revised and enlarged as late as 1928, had the widest circulation. Among his other works are *The Student's Life of Christ* (copr. 1906), *Historical Notes on the Life of Christ* (copr. 1907); *The Program of Christianity* (1919), *Old Testament Prophecy* (1921), *Old Testament History* (1922). With various associates he was co-editor or co-author of some forty volumes. He understood the art of multiplying efficiency through collaboration, but never used the services of another without giving recognition; to him an associate, however young and unknown, was a "colleague." In writing and lecturing, he had rare ability to make Biblical characters and events living and vital without transgressing the limits of sound historical criticism.

He entered whole-heartedly into the life of the Church and various religious societies. There was never an interruption in his active interest in the Young Men's Christian Association; at Jaffna he founded the first college association in the East and in later years in America served on state committees and the national council. When the nation-wide Religious Education Association was founded in 1903, he was chosen its first president. As chairman of the Commission on Inter-Church Relations which consummated the union of Congregational and Christian Churches in 1931 ("the first union of two denominations in the United States in which there had been no previous historic relationship") he made a contribution to American church history. He was a member of the Society of Biblical Literature and Exegesis, the American Oriental Society, the Archaeological Institute of America, and the American Academy of Political and Social Sciences. A man of intense vitality, tall, of muscular build, his black hair and moustache only just graying at seventy-one, he worked always at high speed, getting the heart of an important new volume in an evening's rapid, selective reading, and formulating notes for a well-ordered lecture with similar rapidity. He was a rare companion in time of leisure, a stimulating fellow-worker, a mediator of the newer Biblical scholarship and the old faith. On June 27, 1888, he was married to Edith Blackman of Whitewater, Wis., who with two sons and a daughter survived him. He died at his home in Rockport, Mass.

[Letters, family documents, and personal acquaintance; *Who's Who in America*, 1932–33; *Boston Herald, Boston Transcript,* Feb. 21, 1933; *N. Y. Herald Tribune,* Feb. 22, 1933; *Ripon Alumnus,* Mar. 1933; *Congregationalist,* Mar. 2, 9, 1933; *Yale Univ. Obit. Record,* 1933; *Congregational Year Book,* 1933.]
H. T. F.

SANDERS, GEORGE NICHOLAS (Feb. 27, 1812–Aug. 12, 1873), promoter, revolutionist, Confederate agent, was born in Lexington, Ky., the son of Lewis Sanders, who was locally noted as a breeder of fine horses, and of Ann (Nicholas) Sanders, daughter of Col. George Nicholas [*q.v.*]. As a youth, he was associated with his father as a trader in stock. In November 1843, at Ghent, Ky., he engineered a political meeting which authorized him to correspond with presidential candidates on their attitude towards the annexation of Texas. About 1845 he went to New York City where he engaged in political wire-pulling and financial promoting, furthering his ends, in political conventions and the lobbies of hotels, legislatures, and Congress, by fair means and foul. His numerous enemies insisted that as agent of the Hudson's Bay Company he had reaped questionable rewards when he adjusted its claims in the Oregon country, but he was nevertheless in perpetual debt. His correspondence with Stephen A. Douglas indicates that he was a go-between for Eastern capitalists who were speculating in Chicago real estate. As the agent of George Law [*q.v.*], he made a deal whereby Law took over forty thousand antiquated muskets from the war department to sell to the French revolutionists of 1848, but Sanders arrived in Paris too late to conclude the sale.

Committed by conviction as well as by financial interest to the revolutionary cause in Europe, he became, in the early fifties, the leader of a movement known as "Young America" (M. E. Curti, in *American Historical Review,* October 1926). He contended that a crusade for European republicanism would divert attention from sectional controversies, open European markets to American surplus, and fulfil the American mission of furthering the cause of democracy and freedom throughout the world. Seizing on Stephen A. Douglas as the most likely Democratic politician to sponsor such a policy, Sanders in 1851 acquired the *United States Magazine and Democratic Review* (thereafter simply the *Democratic Review*), and in a series of vindictive articles beginning in January 1852 excoriated the political rivals of Douglas, erratically championed the program of "Young America," and greatly added to the number of his enemies.

In 1853 he received a recess appointment to the London consulship. He went over before the appointment was confirmed and his house became the headquarters of Kossuth, Garibaldi, Herzen, Ledru-Rollin, Mazzini, and other exiles. He engaged in wild dreams and bizarre plots, promising the revolutionaries American financial support, sending their secret communications to the Continent in the dispatch bags of the American embassy, and writing fulminating letters to London newspapers advocating the assassination of Napoleon III. He also influenced Buchanan and Soulé in issuing the Ostend Manifesto (J. B. Castleman, *Active Service,* 1917, p. 135; A. A. Ettinger, *The Mission to Spain of Pierre Soulé,*

1932). As a result of his reckless activities and of bitter attacks at home, the Senate refused to confirm his appointment. Victor Hugo, Garibaldi, and Mazzini wrote him affectionate letters and regretted the blow to European liberalism which his departure meant. In 1857 he was given a recess appointment as navy agent at New York, which was confirmed.

During the Civil War, Sanders played an audacious rôle as a Confederate agent in Europe and Canada. His grandiose imagination led him to plot various schemes to outwit the Federal blockade. He was also a member of the Niagara Peace Conference in 1864, to which he came disguised as a Welsh miner (E. C. Kirkland, *The Peacemakers of 1864,* 1927, pp. 71–72). Although he probably had no connection with the assassination of Lincoln, President Johnson, on May 2, 1865, offered $25,000 for his arrest (D. M. DeWitt, *The Assassination of Abraham Lincoln,* 1909, p. 101).

Sanders spent much of the later part of his helter-skelter life in Europe. During the siege of Paris he was deep in the counsels of the radicals, and his enthusiastic friends gave him a great popular ovation at the Hôtel de Ville. Half idealist, half charlatan, impulsive and prodigal, he had the talent of making and keeping warm friends and bitter enemies. He was a large-framed, powerful man with radiant blue eyes, dishevelled hair, and unkempt appearance. After a courtship conducted by correspondence, he married, a week after their first meeting, Anna Reid, editor of a weekly literary paper in New York. Her unusual accomplishments added much to the lavish entertainments for which her husband was noted.

[M. E. Curti, "George N. Sanders, Patriot of the Fifties," *So. Atlantic Quart.,* Jan. 1928; sketch by a friend, W. M. Corry, in *The Biog. Encyc. of Ky.* (1878); *The Political Corresp. of the Late Hon. George N. Sanders* (1914); G. F. Milton, *The Eve of Conflict* (1934); *N. Y. Times,* Aug. 13, 1873; copies of letters from Sanders to Douglas, through the courtesy of G. F. Milton. A collection of Sanders MSS. is in the possession of Dudley Holland, Greenwich, Conn.]
M. E. C.

SANDERS, JAMES HARVEY (Oct. 9, 1832–Dec. 22, 1899), agricultural journalist, was born in Union County, Ohio, of colonial Virginia ancestry. He received a common-school education and some academy training in Ohio, and in 1852 accompanied his family to southeast Iowa, settling on farm property near Talleyrand, Keokuk County. Notwithstanding his incomplete education, he added school teaching to his work on the farm. Having married Martha Rodgers of Ohio, he moved to Sigourney, the county seat, where he engaged for a time in banking and pro-

moting a new railway. Becoming interested in journalism, however, he purchased the *Sigourney News* in 1863 and thus began a notable career as a publisher and editor.

In May 1869, he began publishing the *Western Stock Journal,* the first periodical devoted to animal husbandry. The following year the *National Livestock Journal* was established at Chicago, and in November 1870 the two consolidated, with Sanders as associate editor though he continued to reside in Iowa. In the financial crisis of 1873 he lost all his savings, and for a year thereafter served as editor of the *Spirit of the Times,* a New York journal mainly interested in promoting the trotting horse and the race track. After a year in the East he went to Chicago, where he and S. G. Brabrook purchased the *National Livestock Journal,* Sanders becoming its editor in January 1876. In his hands this monthly periodical was extremely successful. His son, Alvin H., born in 1860, gave him valuable assistance after 1876. In October 1881, he disposed of his interests in the *National Livestock Journal* and in December began the publication, at Chicago, of the *Breeders' Gazette,* a weekly, thus launching on its career the most important livestock journal of its day. He had a keen conception of what was necessary in a high-class livestock journal to secure the support of intelligent stockmen. In 1888 he accepted a commission from the United States Department of Agriculture to go to Europe and investigate the health of herds from which cattle were being exported to America. He gave up the editorial cares of the *Breeders' Gazette* to his son in 1888, thus terminating his active service in journalism, although his name appeared as joint editor of the periodical until 1891.

Sanders was a great lover of farm animals, especially the horse. In 1868 he purchased in Ohio the noted Percheron stallion, Victor Hugo, and later the imported horses Dieppe, Diligence, and Tempest, paying $3,000 for Dieppe and $2,500 for Diligence. He was the author of the *Norman Stud Book* (1876), the first book of its kind devoted to French draft horses in America; a second edition was entitled the *Percheron-Norman Stud Book.* When in France in 1883, he rendered valuable assistance to French horsemen by establishing the *Percheron Stud Book* (*Hippique Percheronne Français*). He was a great student of heredity and his library contained the works of noted scientists in this field. In 1881 he published in cooperation with Kentucky breeders, a register of pedigrees, the *Breeders' Trotting Stud Book.* In 1885 he brought out *Horse-Breeding,* and in 1887, *The Breeds of Livestock and the Principles of Heredity,* both of which circulated extensively at home and abroad. Sanders died at his own hand (*Commercial Appeal*, Memphis, Dec. 23, 1899) in Memphis, Tenn.

[*Breeders' Gazette*, Dec. 27, 1899; A. H. Sanders, *At the Sign of the Stock Yard Inn* (1915); A. H. Sanders and Wayne Dinsmore, *A Hist. of the Percheron Horse* (1917); W. E. Ogilvie, *Pioneer Agricultural Journalists: James Harvey Sanders* (1927); *A Biog. Cat. of the Portrait Gallery of the Saddle and Sirloin Club* (1920), pp. 68–70; *Commercial Appeal* (Memphis), Dec. 23, 1899.]   C. S. P—b.

SANDERS, THOMAS (Aug. 18, 1839–Aug. 7, 1911), telephone financier, was born in South Danvers, Mass., then part of Salem, of a family settled in Salem and Gloucester since the seventeenth century. His father was George Thomas Sanders and his mother, Mary Ann (Brown). He was educated in the common schools. Keenly interested in fine animals, he rode horseback all his life, and very early went into the business of breeding horses on a farm near East Brookfield, Vt. In 1870 he sold this farm, taking a smaller place near by at Williamstown, and moved to Haverhill, Mass. There he established a successful leather business and continued also his interest in horses. He acquired a beautiful estate in Haverhill, which he called "Birchbrow," where he and his family kept open house to their friends during the rest of his life.

Sanders married Susan Bradley Howe of Haverhill on June 6, 1866. The eldest of their eight children, George, was born deaf, and it was while seeking the best possible means of education for this boy that Sanders was introduced by Miss Sarah Fuller, principal of the School for the Deaf in Boston, to the young instructor in Visible Speech, or lip-reading, Alexander Graham Bell [*q.v.*]. In the fall of 1873 Sanders engaged Bell to teach his son, and for several years thereafter Bell lived with the child and his grandmother in Salem, going often to Boston for his other work. In Mrs. Sanders' house Bell conducted experiments that led up to the invention of the telephone, in connection with these experiments giving little George manual training coördinated with his regular lessons. Deeply grateful for the extraordinary results of Bell's teaching, though skeptical of the practical value of his scheme of "talking by telegraph," Sanders undertook to give the inventor whatever money he needed for his experiments.

Sanders advanced the money required during the period of experiment and early organization of the telephone enterprise, putting more than $110,000 into it before he got a dollar back, but by an agreement signed Feb. 27, 1875, with Bell and Gardiner Greene Hubbard [*q.v.*], who contributed executive ability and business acumen to the combination, he received an equal share in the ownership of Bell's inventions. When the Bell Telephone Company was formed with Hubbard as trustee in July 1877, Sanders was made treasurer. When his own resources gave out, he enlisted the financial support of George L. Bradley and others, thus bringing about in 1878 the formation of the New England Telephone Company, of which Sanders was treasurer and then president. Soon he and Bradley enlisted the support of the Forbes interests and secured the union of the telephone organizations in 1879 into the National Bell Telephone Company, with William H. Forbes as president. Sanders continued as a director of the Telephone Company until his death.

Meantime, he was actively interested in a silver and antimony mine in New Brunswick, and he also invested $250,000 in a silver mine at Ouray, Colo., but the repeal of the silver-purchase clause of the Sherman Act in 1893 caused him severe losses. At Haverhill and also in Vermont he continued his interest in fine breeding. He did a great deal in the development of the Morgan horse, Merino sheep, and Jersey cattle. He was the organizer of the Vermont Livestock Company, a regular exhibitor at the Vermont State Fair, a member of the Essex Agricultural Society, and a life member of the New England Agricultural Society, and was active in all these organizations. It was while driving up to his Vermont farm that he was suddenly taken ill and died of a heart attack in Derry, N. H., at the age of seventy-two.

[Thomas Sanders, "The Early Days of the Telephone" (MS.), address before the Fortnightly Club of Haverhill, Mar. 23, 1903; W. C. Langdon, "The Early Corporate Development of the Telephone," *Bell Telephone Quart.*, July 1923, and "Two Founders of the Bell System," *Ibid.*, Oct. 1923; D. W. Howe, *Howe Geneals. . . . James of Ipswich* (1929); *Boston Transcript*, Aug. 8, 1911, which contains a number of errors; Thomas Sanders Collection, Am. Telephone Hist. Library, N. Y. City; information from the family, esp. George T. and Charles Bradley Sanders.]   W. C. L.

SANDERS, WILBUR FISK (May 2, 1834–July 7, 1905), pioneer lawyer, senator, was born at Leon, Cattaraugus County, N. Y., the son of Ira Sanders, a farmer from Rhode Island, and Freedom (Edgerton) Sanders, of Connecticut. Wilbur attended public school and an academy at Phelps, N. Y., taught school for a while, and in 1854 went to Akron, Ohio, where he continued teaching while studying law with his uncle, Sidney Edgerton [*q.v.*]. In 1856 he was admitted to the bar and into partnership with his uncle. On Oct. 27, 1858, he married Harriet P. Fenn; to this union five children were born. With the outbreak of the Civil War in 1861 Sanders enlisted in the Federal army, and in October was commissioned first lieutenant, 64th Ohio Infantry. In 1862 he became acting assistant adjutant general on the staff of Gen. J. W. Forsyth but his health failed, and in August he resigned.

The next spring he accompanied Sidney Edgerton, who had been appointed territorial chief justice, to Bannack, in what was then eastern Idaho. In this mining camp, which was soon to become the first capital of Montana, he began the practice of law. The country was terrorized by "road agents" who held up stages and wagon trains and killed with reckless freedom, and when a particularly atrocious murder in December 1863 aroused some miners to arrest the murderers, Sanders was the only lawyer who dared undertake the prosecution. Despite threats by friends of the accused, he secured the conviction and speedy execution of the criminals. He was subsequently one of the organizers of the Vigilantes, who cleared the country of outlaws.

He was a leader in the movement to form a separate territory from eastern Idaho, and after the organization of the territory of Montana in 1864, in a region peopled largely by Irish and Southern Democrats he promoted the Republican party and bitterly opposed the policies of the territorial secretary, Thomas Francis Meagher [q.v.], who was also acting governor. He was Republican candidate for delegate to Congress in 1864, 1867, 1880, and 1886, and each time was defeated. He was a delegate to the Republican National Convention in 1868, 1872, 1876, and 1884, and from 1873 through 1879 he sat in the territorial legislature. When Montana was admitted as a state in 1889, the legislature elected Sanders one of the first United States senators, and he drew the short term (Jan. 1, 1890–Mar. 3, 1893). The election was contested, but Sanders and the other Republican candidate were seated by the Senate. Here he urged legislation allowing citizens the right to cut timber from the public domain and sought federal money for irrigation projects, to make the Missouri River navigable to Great Falls, and for various state purposes. His vagueness on the question of silver doubtless lost him support in Montana, and at the end of his term the Republican legislature did not reëlect him.

In spite of his political activities Sanders was an eminent lawyer. His practice extended to all sorts of cases, from the Davis will case, involving millions of dollars, to a fight against an attempt of labor unions to boycott Chinese, and another against the city of Helena for persecuting the Salvation Army. He was founder and for many years president of the Historical Society of Montana, organized the Montana Bar Association, and was active in many other such organizations. His power of sarcasm and ridicule aroused dread in his opponents. He spoke bitterly against the rising Populists and in the Republican state convention of 1896 savagely attacked the free-silver stand of the majority. In one of his last speeches he criticized the technical rulings of the supreme court in language so violent that newspapers did not dare print his address. Yet people said that in his later years his tongue was not so sharp, and his courage, honesty, personal generosity, and kindness were widely extolled at the time of his death by friends and life-long opponents.

[*Biog. Dir. Am. Cong.* (1928); *Progressive Men of the State of Mont.* (n.d.); *Contribs. to Hist. Soc. of Mont.*, vols. I–VIII (1876–1917); A. K. McClure, *Three Thousand Miles Through the Rocky Mountains* (1869); Granville Stuart, *Forty Years on the Frontier* (1925), vol. II; *Montana Daily Record* (Helena), July 7, 8, 12, Oct. 6, 1905; *Boston Herald*, July 8, 1905; *Billings Gazette*, Sept. 29, 1896; T. J. Dimsdale, *The Vigilantes of Montana* (1866); N. P. Langford, *Vigilante Days and Ways* (1890), vol. II; *Who's Who in America*, 1903–05; *Report of the . . . Am. Bar Asso.*, 1905; Tom Stout, *Montana* (1921), vol. III; *Proc. Mont. Bar Asso., 1903–14* (n.d.).]   P. C. P.

SANDERSON, JOHN (1783–Apr. 5, 1844), author and teacher, was born near Carlisle, Pa. His father, William Sanderson, was a farmer who served as a soldier in the American army throughout the Revolution. His mother, Agnes McClellan (Buchanan) Sanderson, is said to have been descended from the Douglas family of Scotland. Since schools in the country districts were few and inadequate at that time, John was educated by private tutoring. In 1806 he went to Philadelphia to study law, but soon became a teacher and assistant principal in the Clermont Academy. He married Sophie, the daughter of John T. Carré, the head of the school, with whom for a number of years he was associated in teaching. He became distinguished for his mastery of the classics and later of the English language and of French literature.

Sanderson developed a gift for writing and became a popular contributor to several publications of his day, especially the *Aurora*, the *Portfolio*, and the *Knickerbocker*. After the retirement of William Duane [q.v.] he seems to have been for some months the editor of the *Aurora*. There is no question that he bought an interest in the paper from Duane in 1822 which he sold to Richard Penn Smith the following year (receipt from Sanderson to Smith, July 15, 1823, Historical Society of Pennsylvania). Meanwhile, in 1820, with his brother, Joseph M. Sanderson, he published the first two volumes of the *Biography of the Signers to the Declaration of*

Independence that was later completed in seven additional volumes (1823–27) by Robert Waln, Jr., and others. He was an ardent champion of classical training at a time when the public schools afforded no opportunity for the study of Greek or Latin, and in an able pamphlet he insisted that the ancient languages should not be excluded from the curriculum of Girard College (*Roberjot's Remarks on Mr. Biddle's Discourse,* n.d.).

His health declining, he gave up teaching for a time. In 1835 he went abroad and spent nearly a year in Paris, where he was well received in literary circles. During this period he wrote a series of articles later brought together and published as *Sketches of Paris: in Familiar Letters to His Friends; by an American Gentleman in Paris* (1838). Marked as it was by vivid descriptions of personalities and events, a keen sense of humor, and kindly understanding, this work was widely read. It was published in London with the title, *The American in Paris* (2 vols., 1838), and was translated into French by Jules Janin and published in Paris in 1843. A rather brief stay in England furnished material for "The American in London," a part of which appeared in the *Knickerbocker.*

In the autumn of 1836 Sanderson returned to America. The educational system of Pennsylvania had been recently assured of state aid, and its public schools were expanding under the impetus of intelligent interest and support. The Central High School of Philadelphia was opened in 1838, Dr. Alexander Dallas Bache [*q.v.*], the great-grandson of Benjamin Franklin, became its first principal the following year, and in September 1840 Sanderson, who had been Bache's teacher, became professor of Greek and Latin and assisted in the department of English and belles-lettres. His culture and experience, a certain originality of approach, together with unusual charm of personality, made him an inspiring teacher, and in this position he continued until his death.

[J. T. Scharf and Thompson Westcott, *Hist. of Phila.* (1884), vol. II; Henry Simpson, *The Lives of Eminent Philadelphians* (1859); F. S. Edmonds, *Hist. of the Central High School of Phila.* (1902); R. W. Griswold, *The Prose Writers of America* (1847); obituary by J. L. Hart, in *Proc. Am. Phil. Soc.,* Apr.–June 1844; editorial in the *U. S. Gazette* and obituary in *Public Ledger* (Phila.), Apr. 6, 1844; family records.]

A. L. L.

SANDERSON, ROBERT (1608–Oct. 7, 1693), silversmith, was born in England and emigrated to America as a young man. He and his wife, Lydia, were among the first settlers in Hampton, N. H., in 1638. The following year he became a landholder and a freeman of Water-

town, Mass., and in this village his first child was born. In 1642, after the death of his first wife he married Mary, the widow of John Cross, of Middlesex County, Mass. She lived until 1681 and bore Sanderson four children. His third wife, Elizabeth, and three sons of his second marriage, all silversmiths, survived him.

Although his fame as a silversmith has suffered because of his association with John Hull [*q.v.*], whose many sided activities made his name better known, Sanderson deserves a place in the front rank of the New England silversmiths (Bigelow, *post,* p. 110). Having learned and practised his trade in England before coming to America, he was undoubtedly sought out for instruction by those who aspired to his craft. He was probably Hull's first teacher, through whom the principles of his art descended to Jeremiah Dummer, 1645–1718, John Coney, and the two Reveres [*qq.v.*]. For the splendid tradition of the New England masters in exquisite workmanship and in a fine feeling for form and line, Sanderson, with his surviving work as evidence, must claim some credit. His mark consisted of his initials in crude capitals, surmounted by a rose or sun in outline, or by a sun in full splendor.

In 1652 John Hull was appointed to establish a mint in the colonies. He immediately chose Sanderson as his partner and the two men worked together for many years. The workshop was doubtless often left in the hands of Sanderson because of Hull's many public activities, trading and land interests. The following year Sanderson moved to Boston where he lived the rest of his life. He became a deacon of the old First Church in 1668.

[Benjamin Worcester, *The Sanderson Homes at Piety Corner* (1899); Henry Bond, *Geneal. of the Families . . . of the Early Settlers of Watertown, Mass.* (2nd ed., 1860); *Pubs. of the Colonial Soc. of Mass.,* vol. VII (1905); *Historic Homes and Places and Geneal. . . . Middlesex County, Mass.* (1908); *The Diaries of John Hull, Trans. and Colls. of the Am. Antiquarian Soc.,* vol. III (1857); F. H. Bigelow, *Hist. Silver of the Colonies and Its Makers* (1917); Hollis French, *The Walpole Soc., A List of Early Am. Silversmiths* (1917); S. S. Crosby, *The Early Coins of America* (1875); *New-England Hist. and Geneal. Register,* Jan. 1898.]

K. A. K.

SANDERSON, SIBYL (Dec. 7, 1865–May 16, 1903), dramatic soprano, was born in Sacramento, Cal., the daughter of Silas W. Sanderson, a jurist who was at one time justice of the supreme court of California, and later chief counselor of the Union Pacific R. R. Sibyl Sanderson was educated in the public schools of San Francisco, and after her father's death was taken with her three sisters to Paris by her mother. In January 1886 she entered the Paris Conservatory, where she studied under Massenet, Sbriglia and Marchesi. It is said also that she had some lessons from Jean de Reszké. Two years later, under an assumed name, she made her operatic début at The Hague in Massenet's *Manon*. Massenet was so much impressed with her voice that he wrote *Esclarmonde* for her, and in this opera she made her Paris début at the Opéra Comique in 1889. Following this engagement she sang at the Théâtre de la Monnaie in Brussels and was the leading prima donna for two seasons. A few years later Massenet composed *Thaïs* for her, and the work was presented at the Paris Grand-Opéra in 1894. Enthusiastic in his praise, Massenet called her an "ideal" Manon and an "unforgettable" Thaïs (*Mes Souvenirs,* p. 178). Meanwhile, in 1893, Sanderson had created the title rôle of Saint-Saëns' *Phryné*. In spite of her tremendous popularity in Paris, and in other foreign cities—Brussels, St. Petersburg, Moscow—she was received coldly in London and never found favor in America. She sang for two seasons at the Metropolitan Opera House in New York under the régime of Maurice Grau [*q.v.*] —first in 1895, and again in 1901. It is said that "her voice was pure and sweet, but small, and cold; as an actress she was completely lacking in emotional warmth; but her personal beauty and charm of manner were extraordinary" (*Baker's Biographical Dictionary,* p. 811). Her first American failure may be attributed to the fact that she was suffering from a cold during her visit. Her chief rôles during her American engagements were Manon, Michaela, and Juliette.

Her domestic affairs gained her as much publicity as her singing. After a long engagement she was married, on Dec. 1, 1897, to a wealthy Cuban planter, Antonio Terry, following his divorce from his first wife. She suffered a stroke of paralysis soon after her marriage and lived quietly at her husband's château at Chenonceaux, France, until his death in 1899. A daughter was born to them but she died shortly after birth. From 1899 until her death frequent rumors were circulated about her possible marriage to others. The summer of 1903 had been set as the time for her marriage to Count Paul Tolstoi, a cousin of the Russian novelist. Her friendship with Massenet also caused comment. It was common gossip in Paris that "Massenet composed *Le Jongleur* to answer the flings of the boulevardiers that his inspiration required the spur of Sibyl Sanderson's charms" (Krehbiel, *post,* p. 124). She died of pneumonia in Paris at the age of thirty-eight, and her body was cremated at the Cemetery of Père la Chaise.

[*Who's Who in America,* 1901–02; *Grove's Dict. of Music and Musicians, Am. Suppl.* (1930); *Baker's Biog.*

Dict. of Musicians (3rd ed., 1919); J. M. Green, *Musical Biog.* (1908), vol. II; H. C. Lahee, *Famous Singers of To-day and Yesterday* (1898); Jules Massenet, *Mes Souvenirs* (1912); *Musical Courier,* May 20, 1903; Henri de Curzon, obituary in *Le Guide Musical,* May 31, June 7, 1903; *N. Y. Times,* May 17, 1903; *Record-Union* (Sacramento, Cal.), May 17, 1903; H. E. Krehbiel, *More Chapters of Opera* (1919).]   J.T.H.

SANDHAM, HENRY (May 24, 1842–June 21, 1910), painter and illustrator, was born in Montreal, Canada, the son of John Sandham, a house-decorator, and Elizabeth (Tait) Sandham, both British subjects. He was educated in the public schools of Montreal, and became assistant in William Notman's photographic studio, where he was eventually promoted to a partnership. His success in retouching portraits led him to make experiments in painting which were measurably encouraging. He then tried his hand at landscapes, making sketches along the St. Lawrence. His work was seen by John A. Fraser, later art editor of the *Century,* who did much towards helping him. On May 23, 1865, he married Agnes Fraser, daughter of John Fraser, a Canadian journalist; four of their six children died before reaching maturity. Within a few years he had attained some reputation in Canada as portrait painter and landscapist; in 1879 (Morris, *post,* p. 22) he was one of the few artists chosen to form the Royal Canadian Academy of Arts; and about that time Princess Louise selected his "Beacon Light, St. John Harbor" for the National Gallery collection at Ottawa.

After a visit to England and France in 1880 he went to Boston, where he became a successful illustrator. He made drawings for a number of books, including Edgar Allan Poe's *Lenore* (1886), F. J. Stimson's *King Noanett: A Story of Old Virginia and the Massachusetts Bay* (1896), and Helen Hunt Jackson's *Ramona* (1900). He also illustrated the last-named author's *Glimpses of California and the Missions* (1902), going to California for the purpose. In 1909 he illustrated A. R. H. Moncrieff's *Adventures in America.* Among the drawings he made for the *Century* were those which accompanied George Kennan's papers on Siberia, in 1888–89. He contributed illustrations to other periodicals, designed bookplates and Easter cards, and wrote and illustrated a paper on Haiti for *Harper's New Monthly Magazine,* August 1899. A volume published about 1920, *Pictures of Canadian History* (n.d.), contains a number of his drawings.

Sandham's first large historical picture, "The Dawn of Liberty," delineating the fight on Lexington Common in 1775, now hangs in the town hall of Lexington. It was first shown at the Boston Art Club, of which Sandham was vice-president. Subsequent essays in historical painting comprise his "Founding in Maryland," exhibited at the World's Columbian Exposition, Chicago, 1893, showing Calvert and his colonists taking formal possession of the grant in the name of Lord Baltimore, and a very large composition called "The March of Time," twelve by twenty-one feet, containing forty-six life-size figures, many of them portraits of veterans of the Civil War, shown marching across Boston Common during a reunion of the Grand Army of the Republic in 1889. This work was exhibited at the Boston Art Club in 1890, with some ninety other pictures by Sandham, and was later acquired by the National Gallery of Art in Washington.

In 1901 Sandham left Boston and went to London, where he lived until his death nine years later. He was buried at Kensal Green. He had exhibited at the Royal Academy and the Paris Salon and had received medals in London, Philadelphia, Boston, and Lisbon. A memorial exhibition of his works was held at the Imperial Institute, London, in June 1911.

[F. T. Robinson, *Living New England Artists* (1888); Will Jenkins, "A Canadian Artist in the Azores," *Internat. Studio*, Jan. 1903; *Am. Art Annual,* vol. X (1913); *Boston Transcript,* June 23, 1910; E. M. Morris, *Art in Canada* (n.d., *c.* 1911); cat. of sale coll., Leonard's Gallery, Boston, Jan. 1901; cat. of exhibition at Toronto, Ont., Mar. 1898; cat. of exhibition at Boston Art Club, 1890; cat. of memorial exhibition, London, 1911; W. S. Wallace, *The Dict. of Canadian Biog.* (1926); *Who Was Who, 1897–1916* (London, 1920); *Dict. Nat. Biog., Second Supp.* (1912).]   W. H. D.

SANDLER, JACOB KOPPEL (Aug. 6, 1856–Feb. 23, 1931), composer, son of Isaac Moses and Bathsheba (Ostrowsky) Sandler, was born in Bialozerkove, Russia. He studied Hebrew and sang in the choir of his local synagogue, ruining his voice by singing soprano parts after adolescence. His musical training was limited to learning how to read, write, and harmonize a melody. When he was seventeen, friends carried him off to Kiev to enter him in the conservatory, but his parents brought him back and married him to a bride of fifteen, Rebecca Sherman. Thereafter, he earned a meager living as the leader of an itinerant synagogue choir. When his six growing children lacked educational opportunities in the Pale of Settlement of Czarist Russia, and his parents had emigrated to America, he followed them, landing in New York in February 1888.

An unworldly idealist without competitive spirit, always yielding to life with self-critical humor, he could scarcely provide for his family, which joined him a year later. After brief periods as an unsatisfactory operator in a shirt factory, and as an even more unsatisfactory pedler of goods sold on the instalment plan, he found employment in his favorite pursuit, that of directing a synagogue choir. The precarious living this work afforded he eked out as chorus director in a Yiddish theater of New York's Ghetto, receiving a salary of from eight to ten dollars a week when the play was successful. Sandler wrote the required irrelevant songs and choruses for such worthily forgotten pieces as *The Princess Oath,* and *Die B'ne Moishe.* When the latter drama proved an expensive failure, M. Horowitz Halevi undertook to write another to be entitled "Brocha, or the Jewish King of Poland." He asked Sandler for the incidental music, including a lament by a girl who was being crucified. That same night Sandler wrote several numbers, and in the early hours of the morning turned to his Hebrew Bible for inspiration for the lament. He found it in the first words of Psalm XXII, *"Eili, Eili, lama azavtani"*—"My God, my God, why hast Thou forsaken me?" Halevi's play was produced in April 1896 at the Windsor Theater in the Bowery, and Sandler's inspired *"Eili, Eili,"* gave it the phenomenal run of three months. Then the play was forgotten, and the song led an obscure half life in the Ghetto of New York.

Later Sandler drifted away from the uncongenial commercialism of the theater, and, after supplementing his uncertain earnings as a synagogue musician by serving as salesman or messenger, he spent the last eleven years of his life in a minor but secure position in the office of the *New York Times.* Meanwhile, his *"Eili, Eili,"* virtually forgotten in America, had been carried back to Russia, the land of its spiritual origin. In 1909, M. Shalit, a pupil of Rimsky-Korsakoff, arranged it for publication by the St. Petersburg Society for Jewish Folk Music. In this form it was brought back to the United States by Kurt Schindler as a Jewish folk melody, and was first sung by Jacob Medvedieff on Dec. 26, 1915, and later by Sophie Braslau at the Metropolitan Opera House. One of Sandler's daughters who was in the audience gave her father the exciting news of the resurrection of his song after almost twenty years of oblivion. Then began a contest, waged not by the unassuming Sandler but by others, to prove him the composer of this *soi-disant* folk song. What Sandler himself craved was not the fortune in royalties that had been paid to publishers by singers, violinists, and phonograph companies, but the credit of authorship of the sublime lament. A lawsuit to establish his copyright proved unsuccessful, but in the last years of his life concert programs gave him credit for the song. Few, however, knew Jacob Koppel Sandler, who died as he had lived, humbly, obscurely, leaving the poetry and beauty of his soul imperishably enshrined therein.

[*N. Y. Times*, Mar. 1, 1931; Meyer Beer (Joseph Kotchock), in *Am. Jewish News*, Mar. 21, 1919; J. G. Huneker, in *N. Y. Times*, May 4, 1919; B. A. Bergman, in *Jewish Tribune*, Aug. 19, 1921; Grenville Vernon, in *Musical Observer*, Jan. 1922.]   D. deS. P.

SANDS, BENJAMIN FRANKLIN (Feb. 11, 1812–June 30, 1883), naval officer, was born in Baltimore of an old Maryland family, the son of Benjamin Norris and Rebecca (Hook) Sands. In his infancy the family moved to Louisville, Ky., where he lived until he was sixteen. After a year's schooling in Washington, under the care of his uncle, Maj. J. H. Hook, he entered the navy as midshipman Apr. 1, 1828. He had a Brazilian cruise in the *Vandalia*, 1828–31, followed by a year in the West Indies in the *St. Louis* and then by several months' study at Norfolk, with promotion to passed midshipman, June 14, 1834. During the next seven years he was employed in coast survey work, chiefly in New Jersey, spending his winters in Washington and summers in field expeditions. In these he was frequently accompanied by his wife Henrietta Maria, sister of Gen. William H. French [*q.v.*], whom he married in Washington, Nov. 15, 1836. He was promoted to lieutenant in 1840. A Mediterranean cruise in the *Columbia*, 1842–44, preceded three years in the Bureau of Charts and Instruments at the Naval Observatory. As executive of the *Washington* during the last summer of the Mexican War, he participated in operations at Laguna and Tabasco, and thereafter became executive of the *Porpoise*, African Squadron, which he commanded on the homeward voyage, January to April 1850. During the next eight years he was again on survey and hydrographic duty, commanding the steamer *Walker* in the Gulf of Mexico. His scientific bent appears in the invention of a deep-sea sounding apparatus and other devices useful in this work. He was made commander in 1855, and was chief of the Bureau of Construction from 1858 to 1861.

In February 1861 he conveyed secret instructions to the ships at Pensacola, Fla., and in April went with the expedition sent to evacuate the Norfolk, Va., navy yard, where he had charge of the party that fired the ships and ship-houses. After a year on the Pacific coast in the survey steamer *Active*—a remote assignment probably due to the department's early suspicion of officers from border states—he was made captain in July 1862, returned east in October, and served as senior officer on the Cape Fear River and Wilmington blockade till late in 1864, first in the *Dacotah* and after December 1863 in the fast side-wheeler *Fort Jackson*. In his autobiog-

raphy, *From Reefer to Rear Admiral* (copyright 1899), Sands says that during this duty he never fully undressed or enjoyed a whole night's sleep, the strain telling severely on his health. His division captured some thirty steamers and twenty-three sailing vessels. There were engagements with shore defenses and a raid, Apr. 21, 1864, on salt works near Wilmington which netted a hundred and sixty prisoners. Sands also claims to have originated the idea of an additional outer line of blockaders. In October 1864, preparatory to operations against Fort Fisher, his ship was attached to the second division under Capt. Joseph Lanman [*q.v.*], but Sands understood he was still in charge of the blockade and disputed vainly the award of $14,000 prize money to Lanman. His ship was in both attacks on Fort Fisher, Dec. 24–25, 1864, and Jan. 13–15, 1865. Afterward, until July 1865, he commanded the second division, West Gulf Squadron. The surrender of the last Confederate troops occurred on his ship, June 2, and on June 5 he hoisted the flag at Galveston, Tex.

Made commodore in 1866 and rear admiral in 1871, he had charge of the Naval Observatory from 1867 to 1874. His maintenance of hearty cooperation between officer and civilian personnel did much to assure continued control of the observatory by the navy, and his experience and interest stimulated its progressive development. The "Great Equatorial," then the largest refracting telescope in the world, was added to the equipment, and expeditions were organized to observe the eclipses of Aug. 7, 1869, and Dec. 22, 1870, the reports of which appeared under Sands's name. After his retirement on July 11, 1871, he lived in Washington, D. C., where he died. His funeral was in St. Matthew's Catholic Church and his interment in Mount Olivet Cemetery. He had three daughters and five sons, the three eldest sons serving in the navy during the Civil War.

[The chief source is Sands's autobiography. See also *War of the Rebellion: Official Records (Navy)*, esp. vols. VIII, X, XI; L. R. Hamersly, *Records of Living Officers of the U. S. Navy and Marine Corps* (ed. 1890); obituaries in *Evening Star* (Washington), July 2, 1883, and *Army and Navy Jour.*, July 7, 1883. Information on the family has been supplied by a grandson, W. F. Sands, Washington, D. C.]

            A. W—t.

SANDS, COMFORT (Feb. 26, 1748–Sept. 22, 1834), merchant, Revolutionary patriot, was born on the Cowneck, now Sands' Point, Long Island, N. Y., fifth of the eight children of John and Elizabeth (Cornell) Sands. He was descended from James Sands who emigrated from England to Plymouth, followed Anne Hutchinson to Westchester County and Rhode Island,

and in 1661 settled on Block Island. After a good elementary schooling, Comfort started at twelve as a clerk at Cowneck, went to New York City as a clerk for his brother, and in May 1769 opened a store of his own in Peck Slip. He prospered rapidly in the West Indian business and within six years was credited with a considerable fortune. He identified himself prominently with the Revolutionary movement in New York from the outset. In 1765 he was in the group that seized and burned ten bales of stamped paper from a brig. He participated in the non-importation agreements and served on most of the important committees. He was a member of several of the provincial congresses and state assemblies, and he sat in the New York constitutional convention. In 1776, as a member of the Committee of Public Safety, he sent three vessels to the West Indies for supplies. Unlike some other merchants, such as Thomas Buchanan and Lewis Pintard [qq.v.], he did not remain in New York City during the British occupation. In 1776 he and his family barely escaped capture, when the redcoats destroyed the fine new home he was building near New Rochelle. For the next seven years, he was steadily on the move, sometimes in or near Philadelphia, at other times at Poughkeepsie, and other places in upstate New York. This absence did not prevent him from serving steadily as auditor-general of New York, province and state, from 1776 to 1782. His functions included the analysis of claims against the state, and he did not hesitate to deduct a private account from the amount paid a state creditor, "Stop 7/6 for a pr. Shoes he Owes me 'for'" (Knight, *post,* p. 135). In 1778 he served on a commission at New Haven to regulate the price of labor and commodities for the army, and at the close of the war he was, with two others, in charge of the exchange of state and federal securities.

His fortunes, somewhat disturbed by the Revolution, were soon restored. He and his brother Joshua formed a partnership for foreign trade and also purchased, at the sales of confiscated Loyalist property, an extensive tract in Brooklyn. In 1784 he was, with Alexander Hamilton, one of the founders and directors of New York's first bank, the Bank of New York. He was president of the Chamber of Commerce from 1794 to 1798. The Anglo-French wars stimulated his commerce to such an extent that his bank deposits between 1795 and 1797, it is said, amounted to $3,443,873. The wars were not an unmixed blessing, however, and so many of his ships were seized by the French and British that in June 1801 he was declared a bankrupt, but the final

settlement left a surplus of $118,000. He later retired to a country estate in New Jersey. He was described as "tall, of a clear florid complexion and prominent features; in character he was firm, open and unsuspecting, generous to friends, relatives and dependents, and liberal of his time and property in all matters pertaining to the public good" (Wilson, *post,* p. 198). On June 3, 1769, he was married to Sarah Dodge and, after her death, he was married on Dec. 5, 1797, to Cornelia Lott who survived him. He had eighteen children: ten sons and five daughters by the first marriage, and one son, Robert Charles Sands [q.v.], and two daughters by the second. The census of 1800 showed that he owned one slave. He died in Hoboken, N. J.

[Temple Prime, *Descent of Comfort Sands* (1886); George Wilson, *Portrait Gallery of the Chamber of Commerce of the State of N. Y.* (1890); *Catalogue of Portraits in the Chamber of Commerce of the State of N. Y.* (1924); E. C. Knight, *N. Y. in the Revolution as Colony and State, Supplement* (1901); L. C. Hatch, *The Administration of the Amer. Rev. Army* (1904); J. A. Scoville (pseud. Walter Barrett on title page), *Old Merchants of N. Y.,* 3 ser. (1865); *N. Y. Geneal. and Biog. Record,* July 1915, Jan. 1924.]   R. G. A.

SANDS, DAVID (Oct. 4, 1745–June 4, 1818), Quaker preacher, abolitionist, was born at Cowneck, Long Island, N. Y., the son of Nathaniel and Mercy Sands, who were members of the Presbyterian Church. When David was fourteen the family moved to Cornwall on the Hudson, at that time a sparsely settled farming community. He possessed a keen mind and seized every opportunity to promote his education, often studying by firelight in the evening. At about twenty years of age, with his father's help, he started a mercantile business in Cornwall, which took him frequently to New York City. Meantime he had come under the influence of itinerant Quaker preachers and members of the Quaker Society in Cornwall and in New York City. In his twenty-first year he became a member of the Society of Friends, joining the meeting at Nine Partners, N. Y. He was married in 1771 to Clementine Hallock of Nine Partners, and they settled for life in Cornwall. He began to give religious messages in Quaker meetings in 1772 and quickly revealed a rare gift for public speaking. He was officially recorded a minister in the Society of Friends in 1775 and immediately began what proved to be a life-long itinerant service.

The most effective contribution he made was on his second journey through the New England colonies. The first preparatory journey was in 1775–76. This was followed in 1777 by extensive services in the New England sections, where there were settled Quaker meetings, followed by a journey into pioneer sections of what is now the state of Maine. Much of his pioneer work was in the regions bordering on the Kennebec River, two years after Benedict Arnold's famous expedition. During the years 1777–79 Sands traveled on horseback four successive times through the Kennebec settlements, often cutting the paths for his horse to travel in. He left behind in these regions a long line of Quaker meetings, whose establishment was mainly due to his labors, and he is historically the founder of Quakerism in central Maine. His numerous visits to New England likewise led to an expansion of Quakerism in Massachusetts and New Hampshire. He paid a fifth visit to the Kennebec Valley in 1795 continuing through the settlements in northern and eastern Maine and sailing from Halifax for England. The years from 1795 to 1805 were spent in itinerant ministry in Europe. He visited during these ten years many groups of Quakers in Great Britain and Ireland and on the Continent. He was permitted to have an interview with King George III and was received with much kindness and friendly feeling. He was in Ireland in the agonizing period during the "Great Rebellion." His travels in Germany and France were also extensive and were marked by profound religious influence. He represented in the later part of the eighteenth century a strong reaction against Quietism and in the direction of an evangelical awakening. There was an evangelical note in his preaching that was at that time new in Quaker circles. With this religious intensity was joined a strong human sympathy for slaves and a passion for the overthrowing of the system of slavery. In his old age he made a final journey through New England and the provinces of Ontario and Quebec. He died in his own home.

[*Journal of the Life and Gospel Labours of David Sands* (1848); *The Annual Monitor for 1819* (1819); *Quaker Biographies,* ser. 2, vol. I (n.d.); R. M. Jones, *The Society of Friends in Kennebec County* (1892), *The Quakers in the American Colonies* (1911), and *The Later Period of Quakerism* (1921).]   R. M. J.

SANDS, JOSHUA RATOON (May 13, 1795–Oct. 2, 1883), naval officer, was born in Brooklyn, N. Y., son of Ann (Ayscough) and Joshua Sands, collector of the port of New York and twice United States representative, and nephew of Comfort Sands [*q.v.*]. Entering the navy in June 1812, he saw active service on Lake Ontario in the engagement with the *Royal George* off Kingston, Nov. 9, 1812, the attack on Toronto in April following, and the capture of Fort George in May. During the rest of the war he was in the *General Pike,* in a shore battery, and then in the *Superior.* Promoted to lieutenant

in 1818 after three years in the Mediterranean, he fought two duels—the first at Valparaiso, Oct. 7, 1823, with Lieut. T. S. Hamersley, which caused injury to neither participant but led to Sands's court martial and long confinement in his ship; the second at Rio, Aug. 20, 1830, in which Sands, then executive of the *Vandalia,* killed his opponent, Surgeon H. Bassett, but was completely exonerated. (See B. F. Sands, *From Reefer to Rear Admiral,* 1899.) Through the Mexican War he commanded the small steamer *Vixen,* participating in operations at Alvarado, Tabasco, Laguna, and elsewhere, and served as governor at Laguna until the investment of Vera Cruz, where with other vessels the *Vixen* carried a reconnaissance close under the fortress. After the capture of Tampico and Tuxpan, he returned home in 1847 in the *St. Mary's.* In 1851 he commanded the *St. Lawrence,* carrying American exhibits to the London world's fair. In 1857 in the *Susquehanna* he assisted in Atlantic cable-laying operations and later lay several months at Grey Town, Nicaragua, where on Dec. 24, 1857, he captured a remnant of the filibusters of William Walker [*q.v.*]. In August his ship, ravaged by yellow fever, landed over a hundred patients in New York. In 1859–61 he commanded the Brazil station in the *Congress.*

Promoted to captain in 1854, he was retired in this grade in December 1861, but was made commodore (retired) in 1862 and rear admiral in 1866. He was lighthouse inspector on the lower Great Lakes, 1862–66, and port admiral at Norfolk, Va., 1869–72. Thereafter he lived chiefly in Baltimore, Md., where he died at the home of his daughter. His funeral was at St. Ann's Episcopal Church, Brooklyn, and his burial in Greenwood Cemetery. He was married first in 1826 to Mary, daughter of John Stevens of Hoboken, N. J., who died in 1828; second in 1830 to her younger sister Henrietta, who died in 1847; and third to Ellen Ann Crook of Baltimore, described as a handsome girl of nineteen. He had a son John (1840–1914) by his second wife, and a son and two daughters by his third. Admiral A. T. Mahan [*q.v.*], once a young aide on his staff, pictures him interestingly in *From Sail to Steam* (1907) as of slight frame, handsome and active, with a reputation for high courage, "not of particular distinction" but with the salt savor of the old navy.

[Temple Prime, *Descent of Comfort Sands* (1886); records of St. Ann's Church, Brooklyn, N. Y.; death notice in *The Sun* (Baltimore), Oct. 3, 1883, and obituaries in *Evening Star* (Baltimore), Oct. 3, 1883, and *Army and Navy Jour.,* Oct. 6, 1883; C. O. Paullin, "Dueling in the Old Navy," *Proc. U. S. Naval Inst.,* vol. XXXV (1909); record of court martial, *Am. State Papers* (*Naval Affairs*) (1860), vol. II, pp. 487–605;

T. H. S. Hamersly, *Gen. Reg. U. S. Navy . . . 1782 to 1882* (1882); L. R. Hamersly, *Records of Living Officers U. S. Navy and Marine Corps* (eds. 1870, 1878).]
A. W—t.

SANDS, ROBERT CHARLES (May 11, 1799–Dec. 16, 1832), author and journalist, was born in New York City, the son of Cornelia (Lott) and Comfort Sands [*q.v.*]. It was probably from his mother that he inherited his love of learning. At seven he began the study of Latin and became so proficient in the classical languages that in October 1812, he was admitted to the sophomore class of Columbia College, where he distinguished himself both in the classics and in other branches of learning. At Columbia he made the acquaintance of James Eastburn, and their friendship became in time one of the most intimate in early Knickerbocker literature, rivaled only by the more picturesque friendship of Joseph Rodman Drake and Fitz-Greene Halleck. In college they established in succession two short-lived literary periodicals. As New York at this period offered little financial opportunity to a young man with literary ambitions, Sands in 1815 began the study of law. During the next four years his legal studies were both arduous and extensive, but he found time to form with Eastburn and two other friends an association known as the "Literary Confederacy." In addition to writing and circulating a manuscript periodical called the "Aeronaut," the members of this organization, in its social life so typical of early literary New York, contributed to the *New-York Daily Advertiser* in 1817 a series of essays called "The Neologist" and in 1819 to the *Commercial Advertiser* another called "The Amphilogist." In 1817 Sands published *The Bridal of Vaumond,* a metrical romance in the manner of Scott dedicated to Washington Irving, which was attacked for its immaturity by the *Analectic Magazine,* February 1818. With Eastburn he had begun another poem, *Yamoyden,* based on the life of the Indian chief, Philip. Before it was finished, Eastburn died, and Sands edited and completed it as a memorial to his friend, publishing it in 1820.

In the same year he was admitted to the bar but after a few years withdrew to devote himself to literature. In 1821 the "Literary Confederacy" began to publish a periodical called *St. Tammany's Magazine,* its contents consisting largely of literary parody and burlesque. In 1824 Sands became for a short period editor of the *Atlantic Magazine;* and when in 1825 the magazine merged with the *New York Review,* under the editorship of William Cullen Bryant [*q.v.*], he was engaged as an assistant. In May 1826 the magazine was discontinued. In 1827 he

joined the editorial staff of the *New-York Commercial Advertiser,* a position he held until his death. In the meantime other literary schemes had also occupied his attention. His study of the Spanish language and history resulted in a biographical sketch of Hernando Cortés, which was translated into Spanish and prefixed to an edition of Cortés' letters published under the title *Historia de Méjico* (1828). In the same year he joined with Bryant and Gulian C. Verplanck in the publication of an annual called *The Talisman,* to which he contributed some of his best work. In 1830 he edited the *Life and Correspondence of John Paul Jones,* and in 1832 he contributed to the *Tales of Glauber-Spa* his best short story, "Boyuca." In the midst of his literary labors his life was suddenly cut short by an apoplectic stroke. He was unmarried and lived during the latter part of his life at the family home in Hoboken, where he died. He mingled freely in New York society, where "his warmth and kindness of disposition," writes his friend Verplanck (*post*), "attracted and strongly attached to him many intimate friends, whom he loved with an unwavering constancy and affection." His reputation as a poet must rest primarily on his contributions to *Yamoyden* and "The Dream of the Princess Papantzin," published in *The Talisman* (1829). The former, modelled on Scott, is as a whole diffuse and unsymmetrical; yet it contains detached passages fraught with genuine feeling that bear some claim to poetry. Historically, it is important for its early use of the American Indian. "The Dream of the Princess Papantzin," a blank verse poem founded on a Mexican legend, is on the whole inferior to the best portions of *Yamoyden.* Much of the prose is in a satirical or mock-heroic vein, with here and there a Rabelaisian touch typical of early Knickerbocker literature. His best serious work in prose is undoubtedly "Boyuca," a by-product of his Spanish-American studies.

[*The Writings of Robert C. Sands in Prose and Verse* (2 vols., 1834) contains an excellent biog. sketch by G. C. Verplanck. Other biog. articles may be found in *N. Y. Mirror,* Dec. 29, 1832; *Knickerbocker,* Jan. 1833, Mar. 1834. For geneal. material, see Temple Prime, *Descent of Comfort Sands* (1886). Reviews of *Yamoyden* may be found in *Lit. and Sci. Repository,* Jan. 1821; *N.-Y. Jour. and Belles-Lettres Repository,* Dec. 1820; *North Am. Rev.,* Apr. 1821; *American* (N. Y.), Dec. 11, 1820; *Lit. Gazette,* Jan. 27, 1821; Nathan Drake, *Evenings in Autumn* (1822), vol. I. For obituaries see *N.-Y. American,* Dec. 17, 1832; *N.-Y. Daily Advertiser,* Dec. 18, 1832; *N. Y. Commercial Advertiser,* Dec. 17, 1832. Much reliable manuscript material is preserved in the N. Y. Hist. Soc.]   N. F. A.

SANDYS, GEORGE (Mar. 2, 1577/78–Mar. 4, 1643/44), colonist and poet, was born at Bishopsthorpe, near York, seventh and youngest son of Edwin Sandys, archbishop of York, and his wife Cicely, daughter of Sir Thomas Wilford; Sir Edwin Sandys was his brother. Save that he had three noble godparents, that he entered St. Mary Hall, Oxford, Dec. 5, 1589 (he appears to have taken no degree), and that he was admitted to the Middle Temple Oct. 23, 1596, little is known of his youth or early manhood. In 1610 he left England on an extended foreign tour, visiting France, Italy, Turkey, Egypt, and Palestine; and after returning home published *A Relation of a Iourney Begun An: Dom: 1610* (1615), an authoritative account of his travels which proved popular and influential. Early interested in colonial enterprise, he was a shareholder in the Virginia Company under its third charter (1611) and in the Bermudas Company, disposing of his shares in the latter organization in 1619, after an unsuccessful effort to obtain the governorship of the islands. In April 1621, however, upon Southampton's recommendation, he was appointed treasurer of the Virginia colony, and that autumn accompanied Governor Wyatt (who had married his niece, Margaret Sandys) to Jamestown, remaining in Virginia until 1628 or later.

His duties as treasurer consisted not only in accounting to the Company in England for all quitrents and other annual revenues, "but also in carrying out that body's directions for promoting the cultivation of . . . the 'staple commodities'" (P. A. Bruce, *Institutional History of Virginia*, 1910, II, 602). He was, however, no book-suffocated scholar or clerk: besides his cultural accomplishments he possessed initiative, an observant practicality, and exceptional industry. He commanded a punitive force against the Tappahannock Indians; he offered to lead an expedition in search of a route to the South Sea; he built the first water-mill in America; he sponsored iron manufacture, engaged in the making of glass, and after the massacre of 1622, devoted considerable effort to reviving silk culture and grape culture; and he is credited with having introduced ship-building into the colony. He was made a member of the council, September 1624, and was reappointed in 1626 and 1628. He managed successfully the 1500 acres with which his office was endowed and acquired other property, about which he sometimes quarreled with the colonial council. Best remembered of all his achievements, however, was his *Ovid's Metamorphosis Englished by G. S.* (1626) in verse, the first five books of which he had translated and seemingly had published before sailing for Virginia. A second complete edition, handsomely printed and illustrated, was issued in 1632, and

included a translation of Book I of Virgil's *Æneid*.

A member of the commission for the better plantation of Virginia, 1631, and having "spent the ripest of his years in the public employment" (*Calendar of State Papers, post,* p. 138) there, he applied for the secretaryship of the Crown's special commission "to govern the plantations"; his petition failing, he settled permanently in England, and was shortly made a gentleman of the privy chamber to King Charles. At court he became intimate with Lucius Cary, second viscount Falkland, and subsequently spent part of his time at Carswell, home of Sir Francis Wenman (who had married the poet's niece, Anne Sandys), where he could associate easily with the circle which gathered about Falkland at Great Tew, Oxfordshire. His closing years, however, were passed mainly at Boxley Abbey, near Maidstone, Kent, the residence of his niece Margaret, widow of Francis Wyatt, whither he "retired himself for his poetry and contemplations." In 1636 he published, under special license from the King, the first of his celebrated poetic renditions of the scriptures, *A Paraphrase vpon the Psalmes of David and vpon the Hymnes Dispersed throughout the Old and New Testaments,* to a second augmented edition of which (1638) Sidney Godolphin, Carew, Waller, and others contributed commendatory verses while Henry Lawes added music. Favorably as this volume impressed individual poets and churchmen—it was one of the three books which comforted Charles I during his imprisonment at Carisbrooke—Sandys' *Psalmes* were not generally adopted in divine service, doubtless, as Richard Baxter observed, in consequence of their not being "fitted to the usual tunes" (*Poetical Fragments,* 4th ed., 1821, p. v). Meanwhile, he had not lost interest in, or connection with, Virginia, and during the 1630's, as a result of his friendly relations with the King, he acted as an unofficial London representative of the colonial liberal party. In 1640, when the Virginia Assembly sought the restoration of their ancient charter rights, Sandys was appointed agent of the colony in England. Instead of presenting the Assembly's petition to the King, Sandys proffered it to Parliament, which renewed the original charter. Perturbed by this action, Charles supplanted Governor Wyatt with the royalist Sir Francis Berkeley, who forthwith convened a new assembly at Jamestown. Under Berkeley's domination this body protested against the renewal of the charters, assuring the King— as most histories erroneously assume to be the truth—that Sandys in presenting the former petition to the Commons "had mistook his instructions" (Alexander Brown, *English Politics in Early Virginia History,* 1901, pp. 96–105). Except for the publication of *Christs Passion* (1640), translated from the Latin of Grotius, and *A Paraphrase vpon the Song of Solomon* (1641), his last years were uneventful. He died, presumably unmarried, at Boxley Abbey and was buried in Boxley Church, the register of which with understandable pride designates him *"Poetarum Anglorum sui saeculi facile princeps."* By numerous of his distinguished associates he had long been esteemed no less for his unfailing nobility of character, his modesty, gentle disposition, and piety, than for his indubitable poetic talents.

The first man in America to devote himself seriously to literature and scholarship, Sandys, hampered as he was by distraction, hardship, and danger, with his *Ovid* nevertheless succeeded in accomplishing a work of real magnitude, acclaimed by his contemporaries, and passing through eight editions before the close of the century. The infrequency of his original compositions may account for a subsequently diminished interest in his writings, but his decasyllabic couplets show a deftness, a metrical freedom and variety, that had no little share in developing the capacity of heroic verse; his style is direct and prevailingly simple, often vigorous, picturesque, and eloquent. Speaking of his later versification, which is smoother and more harmonious than that of the *Ovid,* Joseph Warton observed that Sandys did more to polish and tune the English language by his *Paraphrases* than either Denham or Waller had done; Dryden, who objected that Ovid's poetry is evaporated in Sandys' hands from a too close adherence to the original, elsewhere paid tribute to "the ingenious and learned Sandys, the best versifier of the former age"; and Pope, who liked the *Ovid* "extremely," declared that "English poetry owes much of its present beauty" to Sandys' translations.

[Richard Hooper, *The Poetical Works of George Sandys* (2 vols., 1872); A. W. Ward and A. R. Waller, *The Cambridge Hist. of English Lit.,* vol. VII (1911); Alexander Brown, *The Genesis of the U. S.* (2 vols., 1890), and *The First Republic in America* (1898); Thomas Fuller, *The Hist. of the Worthies of England* (1840), ed. by P. A. Nuttall, III, 434; W. N. Sainsbury, *Calendar of State Papers, Colonial Ser., 1574–1660* (1860).]   A. C. G., Jr.

SANFORD, EDMUND CLARK (Nov. 10, 1859–Nov. 22, 1924), psychologist and college president, was born in Oakland, Cal., the son of Jennie (Clark) and Edmund Philo Sanford. His father was a descendant of Thomas Sanford, an early emigrant from England whose name appears on a bridge built at Milford, Conn., as a memorial to those who founded the town in 1639;

his mother was born in Farmington, Conn., where five generations had preceded hers. Young Sanford was trained as a clerk in his father's drug store, the only one in Oakland, and had his early education in the public schools of Oakland. He received the degree of A.B. from the University of California in 1883 and went to Oahu College, Honolulu, where for two years he taught the classics, mathematics, and ancient history. In 1885 he entered the Johns Hopkins University as a graduate student in psychology and received the degree of Ph.D. in 1888. After a year, 1888–89, as instructor in psychology at Johns Hopkins, he went to Clark University. Made assistant professor of psychology in 1892 and professor of experimental and comparative psychology in 1900, he resigned in 1909 to become the second president of Clark College. In 1920, after the resignation of President Granville Stanley Hall [*q.v.*] of Clark University, he left the presidency of Clark College to become professor of psychology and education in Clark University, a position he held at his death. On Dec. 28, 1901, he married Florence Bartling, of Oakland, who died Dec. 1, 1922. They had no children.

Before the days of Hugo Münsterberg and Edward Bradford Titchener [*qq.v.*], Sanford ranked easily as one of the best three experimental psychologists in the United States. In 1902 he was president of the American Psychological Association, but his relative importance diminished rapidly during his years of administrative work as president of Clark College. On the *American Journal of Psychology* he served as acting editor, 1888–89; associate editor, 1895–1920, and cooperating editor, 1920–24. During his connection with Clark University, he supervised the writing of twenty-four Ph.D. theses. The seventy-seven titles of his own bibliography include poems, songs, essays, addresses, and humorous speculations as well as scientific articles. The latter are remarkably excellent in quality but few in number. His one book, *A Course in Experimental Psychology* (2 vols., 1894–98), was first published in six installments in the *American Journal of Psychology* between April 1891 and April 1896 and concerned itself entirely with the field of sensation, though it comprised only half of what the writer planned eventually to include. As the only laboratory manual in English for a time, it gained wide use in academic circles. Titchener and other equally competent fellow psychologists comment on his artistic skill in the investigation of minor problems. Ill throughout most of his life, he lacked the necessary vigor and enthusiasm for sustained research on fundamental problems. It is possible, too, that he was overwhelmed by the dominating personality of Stanley Hall, with whom he worked for many years, and that he avoided the basic problems in which Hall delighted. Sanford is described as a man of unfailing courtesy and gentleness, with great poise of personality and an unusual ability to make lasting friendships.

[L. N. Wilson, ed., "Edmund Clark Sanford, Nov. 10, 1859–Dec. 22, 1924," *Clark Univ. Lib. Pubs.*, no. 1 (1925), with bibliog.; W. H. Burnham, *Pedagogical Seminary and Jour. of Genetic Psych.*, Mar. 1925; E. B. Titchener, *Am. Jour. Psych.*, Apr. 1925; C. E. Sanford, *Thomas Sanford* (2 vols., 1911); *Who's Who in America*, 1924–25; *Boston Post*, Nov. 23, 1924.]

C. M.

SANFORD, EDWARD TERRY (July 23, 1865–Mar. 8, 1930), jurist, was born at Knoxville, Tenn., the son of Edward Jackson Sanford, who had moved there from Connecticut in 1852, and Emma (Chavannes) Sanford, of Swiss descent. On his father's side he was descended from Thomas Sanford who was in Dorchester, Mass., as early as 1634, and later settled at Milford, Conn. Sanford was graduated B.A. and Ph.B., 1883, at the University of Tennessee, received the degrees of B.A., 1885, and M.A., 1889, at Harvard, and that of LL.B., 1889, at the Harvard Law School. He then traveled in Europe for more than a year. Meanwhile, in 1888, he had been admitted to the Tennessee bar and on his return to America he began practice with a Knoxville law firm. On Jan. 6, 1891, he married Lutie Mallory Woodruff, who bore him two daughters, one of whom predeceased him. From 1897 to 1923 he was a trustee of the University of Tennessee, and from 1909 until his death, of the George Peabody College for Teachers. He was a man of unusual culture, with a deep appreciation of music, literature, and the fine arts, and, in the words of one of his colleagues, "was born to charm" (285 *U. S.*, xlviii). His first important official position was that of assistant attorney general of the United States, to which he was appointed by President Theodore Roosevelt in 1907. After he had served about a year in that capacity, he was appointed judge of the United States district court for the middle and eastern districts of Tennessee, where he served until President Harding nominated him as justice of the Supreme Court on Jan. 24, 1923, to succeed Justice Pitney. After confirmation he took the oath on Feb. 5 and his seat on the bench on Feb. 19.

As a district judge, Sanford seemed "sometimes . . . to be slow in coming to a decision" (285 *U. S.*, xlvi). As a justice of the Supreme Court he delivered the opinion of the Court in only 130 cases during his seven years' service,

but some of the cases in which he wrote opinions were of more than average importance. As a district judge he had frequent occasion to administer the Federal Bankruptcy Act, and two of his seven opinions on the Supreme Court enumerated by the Chief Justice as outstanding construed that act: *Meek* vs. *Banking Co.*, 268 *U. S.*, 426 (1925) and *Taylor* vs. *Voss*, 271 *U. S.*, 176 (1926). He wrote the opinion, dissented from by Justices Holmes and Brandeis, in *Gitlow* vs. *New York*, 268 *U. S.*, 652 (1925), upholding a conviction for publishing a Communist Manifesto; and also that in *Whitney* vs. *California*, 274 *U. S.*, 357 (1927), in which all concurred, affirming a conviction for "criminal syndicalism" by reason of membership in the Communist Party. On the other hand, in *Fiske* vs. *Kansas*, 274 *U. S.*, 380 (1927), he wrote the opinion reversing such a conviction where the organization to which the accused belonged was not shown to have advocated unlawful measures; and he dissented from the majority in *U. S.* vs. *Schwimmer*, 279 *U. S.*, 644 (1929), denying citizenship to a pacifist. In *Liberty Warehouse Co.* vs. *Grannis*, 273 *U. S.*, 70 (1927), he wrote the opinion holding that a federal court could not render a "declaratory judgment"—a declaration of rights in an *ex parte* controversy—though such a proceeding was authorized by a state law passed at the active urge of many eminent lawyers. Probably his most important opinion was in what is known as the "Pocket Veto" case, 279 *U. S.*, 655 (1929), holding inoperative a bill passed by Congress and referred, less than ten days before its adjournment, to the President who neither signed nor returned it. This disposed of a question open for a hundred and forty years.

[*Proc. of the Bar and Officers of the Supreme Court of the U. S. in Memory of Edward Terry Sanford* (1931), found also in 285 *U. S. Reports*; *Who's Who in America*, 1928–29; J. A. Fowler, in *Am. Bar Asso. Jour.*, Apr. 1931; C. E. Sanford, *Thomas Sanford* (2 vols., 1911); *Class of 1885, Harvard Coll., Secretary's Report No. VII* (1910) and *No. IX* (1925); *N. Y. Times*, Mar. 9, 1930.]

C. S. L.

SANFORD, ELIAS BENJAMIN (June 6, 1843–July 3, 1932), Congregational clergyman, was of Puritan ancestry, a descendant of Thomas Sanford who was in Dorchester, Mass., as early as 1634 and later settled in Milford, Conn. The son of Rev. Isaac Sanford, a Methodist minister, and Lovisa Ann (Weeks) Sanford, he was born at Westbrook, Conn. Prepared for college chiefly at the Goshen (Conn.) Academy, he entered Wesleyan University in 1860, receiving the degree of A.B. in 1865. He was licensed as a Methodist preacher and received into the New York East Conference in 1865, the year of his graduation, and began his ministry as pastor of the Methodist Church in Thomaston, Conn. In 1867, he transferred to the Congregational body, becoming pastor of the First Church of Cornwall, Conn. While there, he married (Oct. 10, 1870) Martha Sanford of Thomaston, a distant relative. Becoming interested in religious journalism, he assumed in 1873 the associate editorship of a new publication, *Church Union,* launched in the interest of Christian unity, but soon left it to become editor of the *Alliance,* of Baltimore, Md., a short-lived publication. In 1882, he took charge of the *Golden Rule,* of Boston, forerunner of the *Christian Endeavor World.* After occupying this editorial post for a few months, he was forced by serious illness to give up all work for a time, after which he returned to the pastorate, becoming minister of the Congregational church in Westbrook, Conn., his native town, where he remained until 1894.

In 1895, Sanford was chosen secretary of a new organization known as the Open and Institutional Church League, designed to promote a more adequate church program, especially in social service, and interchurch cooperation in carrying it out. Five years later, when increasing interest in church cooperation had led to the organization of the National Federation of Churches and Christian Workers, he became its general secretary. This organization, despite its name, had no official relation with the denominations, but it paved the way for an official federation. In 1905 a Conference on Interchurch Federation was held in Carnegie Hall, New York, as a result of which, under the organizing genius of Sanford, the constitution for the Federal Council of the Churches of Christ in America was formulated. Owing chiefly to Sanford's persistent and persuasive urging, the constitution had been ratified by the group of interested denominations by 1908, in which year the Council came into formal existence. At the outset, Sanford was elected its corresponding secretary, a position which he held until 1913, when failing health forced him to resign. He was then elected honorary secretary, in which office he continued until his death in 1932. The intervening years he spent in retirement at Middlefield, Conn.

During this period of retirement from active labors, Sanford wrote the history of the formative period of the church federation movement, under the title, *Origin and History of the Federal Council of the Churches of Christ in America* (1916), and also *A History of the Reformation* (1917). He had previously published *A History of Connecticut* (1887), *A Concise Cyclopedia of Religious Knowledge* (1890), and *Church Federation—Inter-Church Conference*

on Federation . . . 1905 (copyright 1906), of which he was editor.

[The first chapter of Sanford's *Origin and Hist. of the Fed. Council of the Churches of Christ in America* is largely autobiographical. See also C. E. Sanford, *Thomas Sanford* (2 vols., 1911); F. W. Nicolson, *Alumni Record of Wesleyan Univ.* (1931); *Hartford Courant,* July 4, 1932; unpub. correspondence in the files of the Fed. Council of the Churches of Christ in America.]   S. M. C.

SANFORD, HENRY SHELTON (June 15, 1823–May 21, 1891), diplomatist, founder of Sanford, Fla., was born at Woodbury, Conn. A descendant of Thomas Sanford who was in Dorchester, Mass., as early as 1634 and later settled in Milford, Conn., he was the only son of Nehemiah Curtis and Nancy Bateman (Shelton) Sanford. From his father, a manufacturer, he inherited an ample fortune. He attended Washington (later Trinity) College, Hartford, for two years, but was obliged by ill health to abandon his formal studies in 1841. Six years later he began his diplomatic apprenticeship as an attaché at St. Petersburg. In 1848 he went to Frankfort as acting secretary of legation, and the following year to Paris as secretary of legation, a post which he held until early in 1854, acting as chargé d'affaires in 1853. In connection with this service he published *The Different Systems of Penal Codes in Europe; also a Report on the Administrative Changes in France* (1854). He resigned after the arrival of the new minister, John Young Mason [*q.v.*], when the latter discarded the plain civilian dress prescribed by Secretary Marcy.

In 1861 Sanford was appointed minister resident to Belgium, where he served for eight years, enjoying cordial relations with the court, discharging special duties in the purchase of military supplies, and observing the activities of Confederate agents. On May 20 and July 20, 1863, at Brussels, he signed on behalf of the United States the Scheldt Treaties relating to import duties and to the capitalization of the Scheldt dues. In 1868 he signed a naturalization convention with Belgium, a consular convention, and an additional article, concerning trademarks, to the commercial treaty of July 17, 1858. On Sept. 21, 1864, in Paris, he married Gertrude E. du Puy of Philadelphia, by whom he had seven children.

After his return to the United States in 1870 he bought a large tract of land on the St. John's River in Florida, establishing himself in a commodious house on a plantation which he called "Belair," and setting out extensive orange groves. Three miles from "Belair" he built a sawmill and a store, the beginnings of the town of Sanford. The place was at first regarded as a "Yankee nest" and there was some local bitterness against Sanford's early attempt to bring in negro laborers, whereupon he established a colony of Swedish immigrants at New Upsala, near by. In 1880, interesting British capital, he formed a company to promote the development of the Sanford region; he was also concerned in the building of the South Florida Railroad.

Shortly after the creation, in 1876, of the International Association for the Exploration and Civilization of Central Africa, under the leadership of Leopold II, King of the Belgians, Sanford was appointed a member of its executive committee. It was through his exertions as the Association's representative that on Apr. 22, 1884, the United States recognized the flag of the Association "as that of a friendly government." This was the earliest form of recognition, and King Leopold was much gratified. He had already, in 1878, made Sanford a grand officer of the Order of Leopold. At the Conference of Berlin (1884–85), Sanford sat as associate delegate of the United States with John A. Kasson [q.v.], American minister to Germany, and with Kasson he signed the General Act of the Conference, establishing the status of the Congo Free State. In 1890 Sanford discharged his last diplomatic service and participated for the last time in the affairs of Africa, when, on July 2, at Brussels, he signed with Edwin H. Terrell, minister to Belgium, the General Act between the United States and other powers for the repression of the slave trade and the restriction of commerce in firearms and liquor in Africa. He died in the following year, at Healing Springs, Va. The title "General," by which he was commonly known, was derived from the fact that the state of Minnesota had enrolled him as a major-general in its militia during the Civil War, in recognition of his gift of a pair of field pieces to the 1st Minnesota Volunteers.

[C. E. Sanford, *Thomas Sanford* (2 vols., 1911); *Some Account of Belair* (1889); *Am. Jour. of Internat. Law*, vol. III (1909), Supp., "Official Docs."; D. C. Boulger, *The Reign of Leopold II* (1925), vol. I; R. S. Thomson, *Fondation de l'État independent du Congo* (1933); J. S. Reeves, "The International Beginnings of the Congo Free State," *Johns Hopkins Univ. Studies in Hist. and Pol. Sci.*, 12 ser. (1894); *Papers Relating to Foreign Affairs*; archives of the Department of State; W. W. Folwell, *A Hist. of Minn.*, II (1924), 87; information from the Registrar of Trinity College; obituary in *N. Y. Tribune*, May 23, 1891.]   M. B. G.

SANFORD, NATHAN (Nov. 5, 1777–Oct. 17, 1838), legislator and jurist, was descended from Robert Sanford, an early settler of Hartford, Conn., through his son Ezekiel, who was one of the first settlers of eastern Long Island. The son of Thomas Sanford and his wife Phebe (Baker?), widow of Theophilus Howell, Nathan

was born at Bridgehampton, L. I. He received his early education at Clinton Academy, Easthampton, and at Yale, although he did not graduate. In New York City he studied law in the office of the elder Samuel Jones, and was admitted to the bar in 1799. In 1802 he became a leader of the Tammany faction of the Jeffersonian Republican party and during the next twenty-nine years was almost continuously in public office. He was United States commissioner of bankruptcy in 1802, and from 1803 to 1815 held the lucrative post of United States attorney for the district of New York, from which he was thought to have derived $100,000 annually in fees (*The Diary of Philip Hone*, 1927, ed. by Allan Nevins, II, 526). He was a member of the assembly in 1808–09 and 1811, being speaker in 1811 until forced to retire on account of illness, was state senator, 1812–15, and United States senator, 1815–21. Though a candidate for reëlection to the Senate he was thrust aside by his party in favor of Van Buren (Hammond, *post*, I, 561). As a member of the state constitutional convention of 1821 he introduced and promoted the adoption of the resolution which abolished property qualifications for the suffrage. On the retirement of James Kent [q.v.], Aug. 1, 1823, he became chancellor and served until Jan. 24, 1826. He was an unsuccessful candidate for vice-president in 1824, and two years later once more became United States senator, serving from Jan. 31, 1826, to Mar. 3, 1831.

As chancellor, Sanford's opinions were characterized by clarity, good sense, and the absence of attempts to parade his legal learning. In his eleven years in the Senate he took little part in the debates on great questions, confining his attention to administrative problems and to measures for improving the organization of the government. He urged the creation of a department of the interior and the expansion of the attorney-general's office into a department of justice. He advocated the vigorous policy of collecting the French spoliation claims afterward followed by Jackson. In 1830 he presented a report on the currency (*Register of Debates in Congress*, vol. VII, App., pp. cxxxi–cxxxvii) which was the basis of subsequent legislation. He proposed constitutional amendments to require the choice of presidential electors by districts and to allow the president to remove judges with the consent of two-thirds of each house of Congress.

Besides his interests in law and public affairs he was a student of foreign languages and delighted in reading the Latin poets. He was married three times—on May 9, 1801, to Eliza Van Horne of New York, who died in 1811; on Apr.

14, 1813, to Mary Isaacs of New Haven; and subsequently to Mary Buchanan of Baltimore, each of whom bore him one or more children. He died, at Flushing, L. I., from a pulmonary affection of long standing, having carried on an active existence, to the wonder of physicians, for a quarter of a century after he had lost the use of one lung.

[B. F. Thompson, *Hist. of Long Island* (3rd ed., 1918), vol. IV; J. T. Adams, *Hist. of the Town of Southampton* (1918); D. S. Alexander, *A Pol. Hist. of the State of N. Y.,* vol. I (1906); *Legal and Judicial Hist. of N. Y.* (3 vols., 1911), ed. by Alden Chester; J. D. Hammond, *The Hist. of Pol. Parties in the State of N. Y.,* vols. I, II (1842); *Biog. Dir. Am. Cong.* (1928); C. E. Sanford, *Thomas Sanford* (1911), II, 1339; death notice in *N. Y. American,* Oct. 18, 1838.]

E. C. S.

SANGER, CHARLES ROBERT (Aug. 31, 1860–Feb. 25, 1912), chemist, was born in Boston, the son of George Partridge Sanger [*q.v.*] and Elizabeth Sherburne (Thompson) Sanger. His great-grandfather, Zedekiah Sanger, was minister at Duxbury and South Bridgewater; his grandfather, Ralph Sanger, minister of Dover; and his father, a judge of the court of common pleas and United States district attorney for Massachusetts. His mother came of a family of Portsmouth, N. H., sea captains.

Early in Sanger's boyhood his father moved to Cambridge, and he was fitted for college at the high school there. Entering Harvard College in 1877, he displayed much interest in chemistry, was prominent in student activities, and was elected permanent class secretary in his senior year. Graduated in 1881, he spent the next year in research work with Prof. Henry Barker Hill [*q.v.*] at Harvard, and the succeeding year in similar work at the universities of Munich and Bonn. He then returned to Harvard to continue his researches with Professor Hill and was granted the degree of doctor of philosophy in 1884. He remained at Harvard as an assistant until 1886, when he was appointed professor of chemistry at the United States Naval Academy, Annapolis. In 1892 he was made Eliot Professor of Chemistry at Washington University, St. Louis. He was called back to Harvard in 1899 as assistant professor of chemistry, to give the course on qualitative analysis previously given by Professor Hill. Later, he also initiated a course on industrial chemistry. Upon the death of Hill in 1903, Sanger was promoted to a full professorship and appointed director of the chemical laboratory.

In his work with Hill, Sanger made notable contributions to the chemistry of pyromucic acid and its derivatives. His most important investigations, however, were concerned with the de-

tection of arsenic in the tissues and excreta of persons exposed to arsenic-containing wallpaper. He improved the well-known Berzelius-Marsh test for arsenic and was able to demonstrate a marked correlation between the degree of exposure to such wallpaper, the amount of arsenic in the excreta, and the intensity of the morbid symptoms. In cases where arsenic was present in wallpapers but where the formation of dust was precluded by a covering of paint or other paper, he was able, nevertheless, to demonstrate the absorption of arsenic by persons exposed to such wallpapers, and thus to confirm the conclusion of Gosio that in some way a gaseous effluvium containing arsenic was given off from them. Later, he improved the Gutzeit method for the detection of arsenic and antimony until it surpassed in delicacy even the above mentioned Berzelius-Marsh method. (For papers dealing with this subject, see *Proceedings of the American Academy of Arts and Sciences,* vol. XXVI, 1891; XXIX, 1894; XLIII, 1908.) His last researches were concerned with the preparation and properties of pyrosulphuryl chloride and chlorosulphonic acid, the action of sulphur trioxide on silicon tetrachloride, and the detection of fluorine.

Sanger was quiet, scholarly, and methodical, and phenomenally accurate and careful in all his observations and deductions. He was vice-president of the Northeastern Section of the American Chemical Society in 1902–03. He was also a Fellow of the American Academy of Arts and Sciences and was editor of its *Proceedings* in 1909–10. On Dec. 21, 1886, he was married to Almira Starkweather Horswell, who died Jan. 6, 1905, leaving three children. On May 2, 1910, he married Eleanor Whitney Davis. He died at Cambridge, Mass.

[*Proc. Am. Acad. Arts and Sciences,* vol. XLVIII (1913); *Harvard Coll., Class of 1881, Fiftieth Anniversary* (1931); *Harvard Grads. Mag.,* June 1912; *Who's Who in America,* 1912–13; *Boston Transcript,* Feb. 26, 1912.]

A. B. L.

SANGER, GEORGE PARTRIDGE (Nov. 27, 1819–July 3, 1890), lawyer and editor, son of the Rev. Ralph and Charlotte (Kingman) Sanger, was born at Dover, Mass., where his father was a minister for more than half a century. He was descended from Richard Sanger, who settled as a blacksmith in Sudbury, Mass., in 1646. George received his preliminary education under his father and at Bridgewater Academy, taught in country school, and in 1836 entered Harvard College. He was graduated A.B. in 1840 and for two years had charge of a private school at Portsmouth, N. H. In 1842 he became a proctor at Harvard and enrolled in the law school, and the following year was appointed tutor in Latin. He received the degree of LL.B. in 1844, and upon his admission to the bar in 1846 severed his connection with Harvard (except as a Latin examiner) and entered into a law partnership with Stephen H. Phillips of Salem. Later, for some time, he lived in Charlestown. On Sept. 15, 1846, he married Elizabeth Sherburne Thompson of Portsmouth, N. H., who bore him five sons, one of whom was Charles Robert Sanger [q.v.].

From 1848 to 1861 Sanger edited *The American Almanac and Repository of Useful Knowledge,* and from May 1851 to March 1855, the *Monthly Law Reporter.* From 1849 to 1853 he was assistant United States attorney and in 1853–54 was state's attorney for the Suffolk district, with residence in Boston. In 1853–54 he was also captain of the Ancient and Honorable Artillery Company, having previously served as captain of the Charlestown Guards. Appointed judge of common pleas by Governor Washburn in 1854, he served in that capacity until the court was abolished in 1859. During this service, in conjunction with George Minot, he edited the eleventh volume of the *Statutes at Large of the United States of America,* covering the period from 1855 to 1859. Beginning with the twelfth volume (1859–63), he took over the sole editorship of the series, which he held until the completion of the seventeenth volume (1871–73), after which the Department of State assumed exclusive charge of the publication. Meanwhile, in 1859, with Judge William A. Richardson [q.v.], he was designated by the state legislature to revise and edit *The General Statutes of the Commonwealth of Massachusetts* (1860), and after the appearance of the revision of that year, with Richardson supervised the publication of annual supplements down to 1881. He also revised and consolidated the municipal laws and the Boston ordinances, in collaboration with John G. Locke. In 1873 he was elected to the lower branch of the General Court and later in the same year President Grant appointed him United States attorney for Massachusetts. This office he held until after Cleveland became president, retiring in 1886 and resuming practice in Boston. In addition to his public duties, he was the first president of the John Hancock Mutual Life Insurance Company, organized in 1863. His career, if not spectacular, was creditable and marked by unusual industry and satisfactory service.

[J. C. Rand, *One of a Thousand* (1890); Abner Morse, *The Geneal. of the Descendants of Several An-*cient *Puritans,* I (1857), 129; *Green Bag,* Aug. 1890; *Boston Daily Advertiser,* July 4, 1890.]   C. S. L.

SANGSTER, MARGARET ELIZABETH MUNSON (Feb. 22, 1838–June 4, 1912), author, editor, daughter of John and Margaret (Chisholm) Munson, was born at New Rochelle, N. Y. Her father, a Wesleyan Methodist, was born in England in 1786; her mother was of Scotch Covenanter parentage. The austere atmosphere of the Munson home was due to the serious mother, twenty years her husband's junior, for John Munson was of a cheerful, spontaneous temperament. When Margaret was three, the family removed to New York. Under her mother's instruction, she became able to read at the age of four almost any book, and at six she recited at Miss Halstead's private school Pitt's speech on the Stamp Act. John Munson's restlessness and real-estate changes caused the family to remove to Paterson, N. J., when Margaret was eight. There she attended Passaic Seminary, a Baptist institution, and became much interested in foreign missions. The only other school in which she was a pupil was that of Monsieur Paul Abadie in Brooklyn, N. Y., where she studied Latin, Greek, and French, and secured a diploma. In 1854 her father died and her mother's brother, David Chisholm, came to live with the family and assumed its responsibilities.

Having filled many blank books with verse and essays, about 1855 Margaret wrote *Little Janey,* the story of a child's life, which was purchased for forty dollars and printed by the Presbyterian Board of Publication. The Board then gave her a commission for a hundred juvenile stories related to assigned pictures. In an effort to earn more money she "wasted" time studying music and painting and teaching embroidery to children. These activities were abandoned when, in October 1858, she was married to George Sangster, a native of Scotland, whom she had met at a Sunday school convention at which he was one of the speakers. He was a widower with two little girls, to whom Margaret became devoted. Though her mother's expertness and her own lack of aptitude had kept her from learning the domestic arts, she soon became a "not unsuccessful housekeeper" (*Autobiography, post,* p. 162). In 1859 a son, her only child, was born. During the Civil War George Sangster became an officer in the Union army and after the war the family settled at Norfolk, Va., where, in spite of existing bitterness between Northerners and Southerners, they made many warm friends. In 1870 they removed to Brooklyn, N. Y., and in 1871 George Sangster died.

In Norfolk Mrs. Sangster had contributed prose and verse to the *Christian Intelligencer, Sunday-School Times, Independent,* and *Hearth and Home.* Faced with the necessity of earning a living, she naturally turned to writing. The editor of *Hearth and Home,* George Cary Eggleston [*q.v.*], engaged her to write a series of articles, and a year later put her in charge of the children's page, formerly conducted by Mary Elizabeth Mapes Dodge [*q.v.*]. Shortly after, she became assistant editor. Within the next three years she was thrice offered the position of dean in women's educational institutions, but preferred to continue in journalism. Questions that came to her office made her feel that she had a "mission to girlhood" and prompted her to write letters and short essays addressed to girls and young women which were published in various magazines. When *Hearth and Home* ceased publication, Dec. 25, 1875, other editorial positions were offered her. She edited the family page of the *Christian Intelligencer,* was literary adviser for Harper & Brothers, postmistress of *Harper's Young People,* and finally editor of *Harper's Bazar* (1889–99). She was also a contributor to the *Christian Herald,* the *Ladies' Home Journal,* and the *Woman's Home Companion.* Though she wrote several novels, most of her volumes of prose and verse are compilations from her magazine articles. Among the best of her works are *Poems of the Household* (1882), *Little Knights and Ladies* (1895), *Home Life Made Beautiful in Story, Song, Sketch, and Picture* (1897), *Cheerful To-days and Trustful To-morrows* (1899), *Winsome Womanhood* (1900), *Lyrics of Love, of Hearth and Home, and Field and Garden* (1901), *Janet Ward, a Daughter of the Manse* (1902), *Eleanor Lee* (1903), *Good Manners for All Occasions* (1904), *What Shall a Young Girl Read?* (1905), *Fairest Girlhood* (1906), *Ideal Home Life* (1910), *Eastover Parish* (1912), *My Garden of Hearts* (1913), a collection of stories and essays issued posthumously. In 1909 she published *An Autobiography: From My Youth Up; Personal Reminiscences.* The tone of all her writings is cheerful, practical, rather sentimental, and very religious. Her prose is clear and direct, her poetry simple and full of fancies which appeal to children. She said of her method that she never waited for inspiration but was a "day-laborer." During her later years she lived at Glen Ridge, and at Maplewood, N. J., where she died. She had been blind for several years but continued her writing with the aid of secretaries. The *Christian Herald* for June 5, 1912, the day after her death, carried her "Home Chats," and the issue of June 12, an arti-

cle, "Choosing a Partner for Life" and a poem by her, "The End of the Day."

[In addition to Margaret E. Sangster's *Autobiog.,* see *Who's Who in America,* 1912–13; F. E. Willard and M. A. Livermore, *A Woman of the Century* (1893); *N. Y. Times,* June 5, 1912; "A Voice That is Still," in *Christian Herald,* June 19, 1912.]   S.G.B.

SANKEY, IRA DAVID (Aug. 28, 1840–Aug. 13, 1908), singing evangelist, son of David and Mary Sankey, was born in Edinburg, Lawrence County, Pa. In a family the members of which were musically inclined he early acquired ability to read music and familiarity with sacred songs and tunes. In 1857 his father was made president of a bank in Newcastle, Pa., in which Ira, after attending the high school, became a clerk. Joining the local Methodist church, he was soon chosen choir leader and superintendent of the Sunday School. Upon the outbreak of the Civil War he served a term of enlistment in the Union army and then returned to Newcastle to be assistant to his father, who had been appointed collector of internal revenue. On Sept. 9, 1863, he married a member of his choir, Fanny V. Edwards, daughter of Hon. John Edwards. Singing had now become one of his chief interests, and his services were frequently utilized at Sunday School conventions and political gatherings in his section of the country. In 1870 he was a delegate to the international convention of the Young Men's Christian Association at Indianapolis. Here his singing attracted the attention of Dwight L. Moody [*q.v.*], who persuaded him to join him in the religious work he was then carrying on in Chicago. He assisted Moody in the remarkable series of meetings held in England, Scotland, and Ireland from 1873 to 1875, and in the years that followed he contributed in no small degree to the success of Moody's evangelistic campaigns in the United States and abroad, the names of the two becoming inseparably associated.

Sankey had had little training in the art of singing, nor was his voice—a strong baritone of moderate compass—at all exceptional; nevertheless, he could move vast audiences profoundly. Generally accompanying himself on a small reed organ, he sang simply but with careful enunciation and much feeling and expression. He had a dramatic sense that enabled him to choose the song best fitted to the occasion, and frequently he prefaced it with words that added to its effect. Although his chief work was to sing the Gospel, he could also make moving verbal appeals and was successful in dealing with individuals in inquiry meetings. Nothing in his personal appearance was of assistance to him. He was bulky in figure, weighing over 220 pounds, his face was adorned with long side-whiskers, and he was somewhat unctuous in manner; yet his audiences, forgetting all this, were captivated by the sweetness and compelling emotion of his singing. Published collections of the songs used in the Moody and Sankey meetings gained almost world-wide popularity. The first of these, *Sacred Songs and Solos,* was published in England in 1873. This was followed by *Gospel Hymns* (nos. 1–6, 1875–91) and other collections. They were compilations from various sources; Sankey wrote comparatively few, though he supplied the music for more; and in the editing he was assisted by others. The successors of the camp-meeting spirituals, they are characterized by a contagious melody, pathetic or ringing, a frequence of march or dance rhythm, and the use of solo effects, climactic catchwords, and the chorus (L. F. Benson, *The Hymnody of the Christian Church,* 1927, pp. 266–67). Neither Moody nor Sankey profited from the immense sale of the hymn books. The royalties, turned over to a board of trustees, went chiefly to the support of the Northfield School which Moody established. In 1906 Sankey published *My Life and the Story of the Gospel Hymns.* His last years were spent in blindness at his home in Brooklyn, N. Y. He was survived by his wife and two sons.

[In addition to references above, see W. R. Moody, *D. L. Moody* (1930); Gamaliel Bradford, *D. L. Moody: a Worker in Souls* (1927); *Who's Who in America,* 1908–09; John Julian, *A Dict. of Hymnology* (1891); *Harper's Weekly,* Aug. 29, 1908; *Outlook,* Aug. 22, 1908; *Current Literature,* Oct. 1908; *N. Y. Times* and *N. Y. Herald,* Aug. 15, 1908; *Brooklyn Eagle,* Aug. 14, 1908.]   H. E. S.

SAPPINGTON, JOHN (May 15, 1776–Sept. 7, 1856), physician, son of Dr. Mark Brown and Rebecca (Boyce) Sappington, was born in Maryland, but when he was a schoolboy his family moved to Nashville, Tenn. He studied medicine under his father and for a time practised with him at Nashville, later moving to Franklin, Tenn., where he practised alone. On Nov. 22, 1804, he married Jane Breathitt, daughter of Gov. John Breathitt of Kentucky. He rode on horseback from his home in Tennessee to Philadelphia, where he attended for one term (1814–15) a course of medical lectures at the University of Pennsylvania. In 1817 he went to Missouri, locating in Howard County. After practising there for two years he moved across the Missouri River to Saline County, where he established his permanent residence, "Fox Castle," near Arrow Rock.

Sappington's life may be said to have been devoted to the cause of quinine. In the early development of the Southern and Western states,

malaria was so prevalent that it was one of the greatest obstacles with which the early settlers had to contend. Soon after quinine (isolated from Peruvian Bark in 1820) became available in the United States, Sappington recognized its specific nature in the treatment of malaria, and strongly advocated its use without recourse to bleeding, vomiting, and purging which, as late as 1850, such a prominent member of the medical profession as Daniel Drake thought necessary. Unable to change the erroneous opinions of his fellow practitioners and realizing the urgent need of making quinine available to people in the intensely malarious districts, he began in 1832 the wholesale distribution of Dr. John Sappington's Anti-Fever Pills. Over one million boxes of these were distributed through the Western and Southern states. He also wrote and published *Theory and Treatment of Fevers* (1844), perhaps the first medical treatise written west of the Mississippi. In it he gave in detail his method of preparing his quinine-containing pills and advocated quinine, properly used, as the only thing necessary to cure malaria. Although living in a frontier community far removed from the seats of medical learning, Sappington's views regarding the treatment of fevers was more in accord with modern medical practice than were those of his more favored contemporaries. Among his friends he numbered Andrew Jackson, Thomas Hart Benton, and Nathaniel Beverly Tucker.

[Sappington manuscript collection in the State Hist. Soc. of Mo.; T. B. Hall, "John Sappington," *Mo. Hist. Rev.,* January 1930; H. L. Conard, *Encyc. of the Hist. of Mo.* (1901), vol. V; Univ. of Pa. records; W. B. Napton, *Past and Present of Saline County, Mo.* (1910); Daniel Drake, *A Systematic Treatise . . . on the Principal Diseases of the Interior Valley of North America* (1854); Robert J. Terry, "Dr. John Sappington, Pioneer in the Use of Quinine in the Miss. Valley," *Proc. of the Celebration of the Three Hundredth Anniversary of the First Recognized Use of Cinchona* (St. Louis, 1931), pp. 165–80.]   T. B. H.

SARGENT, AARON AUGUSTUS (Oct. 28, 1827–Aug. 14, 1887), United States senator, was born in Newburyport, Mass., son of Aaron Peaslee and Elizabeth (Stanwood) Flanders Sargent. He was a descendant of William Sargent who was in Ipswich, Mass., as early as 1633. After attending the common schools, he was apprenticed to a cabinet maker for a short time, and then learned the printer's trade. This he followed for several months in Philadelphia in 1847, and then moved to Washington, where he became secretary to a member of Congress.

In December 1849 he went to California, and for a time found employment in the freight-carrying business between San Francisco and Stockton. In 1850 he was on the Sacramento

Placer Times, but soon moved to Nevada City, Cal., and became a compositor on the *Daily Journal.* Returning to San Francisco, he was compositor on the *Placer Times and Transcript* and the *Alta California,* but soon went back to Nevada City, and not long after bought the *Daily Journal.* As editor and manager, he conducted this paper as a Whig organ, studying law in his spare time. In 1854 he was admitted to the bar. He was nominated for the California assembly by the new American Party in 1852, and from that time he seems to have been dominated by a consuming political ambition which quite subordinated his career as a lawyer. He was active in the organization of the Republican party in California, and for some years was a member of the party's state executive committee.

In 1855–56 he served as district attorney for Nevada County, and in 1857 was the unsuccessful Republican candidate for the attorney-generalship. In 1860 he was a delegate to the Republican National Convention, and was elected representative in Congress, serving from 1861 to 1863. As a member of the select committee on a Pacific railroad, he displayed energy and ability in procuring the enactment of the first Pacific railroad bill to pass Congress. Of this measure he and Theodore D. Judah [*q.v.*], chief engineer of the Central Pacific Railroad, were the authors. At the end of his term, Sargent unsuccessfully sought his party's nomination for the governorship, and then resumed the practice of law. In 1867, he was an unsuccessful candidate for the United States Senate, and in 1868 and 1870 was reëlected to the House of Representatives. After a bitter campaign, he succeeded, in 1872, in supplanting Cornelius Cole as United States senator. In the Senate, Sargent was a member of the committees on naval affairs, mines and mining, and appropriations. He successfully opposed the nomination by President Grant of Caleb Cushing [*q.v.*] to be chief justice of the Supreme Court because of statements contained in a letter from Cushing to Jefferson Davis. At the close of his senatorial term in 1879, Sargent again returned to his law practice. In 1882 President Arthur appointed him minister to Germany, but owing to his outspoken criticism of Germany's unfriendly discrimination against American pork, he became *persona non grata* to the German government and resigned in April 1884. President Arthur immediately offered him the ministry to Russia, but this he declined. Returning to California, he soon became the Republican candidate for election to the Senate. The legislature chosen in 1884 appears to have contained a majority of Sargent supporters, and the public

generally assumed that he would be reëlected with little opposition. The Republican legislative caucus, however, unexpectedly nominated Leland Stanford [*q.v.*], and he was elected. Stanford and Sargent had been close friends and this apparent treachery came as a blow from which the latter never recovered. He died in San Francisco and was buried in Laurel Hill Cemetery. On Mar. 14, 1852, he was married to Ellen Clark; his widow, a son, and two daughters survived him.

Sargent was a man of strong and forceful personality, aggressive in political contests, untiring and persevering in pursuit of his ends. He was a good German scholar, well read on all political topics, and an able debater. He spoke with great rapidity; as a contemporary expressed it, "his volubility was manifest both in tongue and pen" (*Memoirs of Cornelius Cole, post,* p. 235). Closely identified with the militant Pacific railroad interests, he became a masterful machine politician, "placing or displacing men according to the will of a syndicate."

[E. E. Sargent, *Sargent Record* (1899); *Vital Records of Newburyport, Mass.* (1911), I, 342; *San Francisco Chronicle,* Aug. 15, 1887; *San Francisco Evening Bull.,* Aug. 15, 16, 1887; *Biog. Dir. Am. Cong.* (1928); H. H. Bancroft, *Hist. of Cal.* (1890), VII, 291–92, 548–49; *Memoirs of Cornelius Cole, Ex-Senator of the U. S. from Cal.* (1908); C. C. Phillips, *Cornelius Cole* (1917), pp. 262–64; E. C. Kemble, *A Hist. of Cal. Newspapers* (1927).]   P.O.R.

SARGENT, CHARLES SPRAGUE (Apr. 24, 1841–Mar. 22, 1927), arboriculturist, was born in Boston, Mass., the son of Ignatius and Henrietta (Gray) Sargent. His father was a well-known merchant in trade with the East Indies, a descendant of William Sargent who was in Gloucester, Mass., in 1678. Educated in private schools and at Harvard University, from which he graduated in 1862, Charles enlisted on the northern side in the Civil War in 1863, rising through successive grades to the rank of major of volunteers, and was honorably mustered out of the army in 1865. After three years of European travel he married Mary Allen Robeson on Nov. 26, 1873. They had two sons and three daughters, one of whom married Guy Lowell [*q.v.*]. For a time he was occupied with the development of his garden, one of the best in the vicinity of Boston, and with the study of botany. In this he had the advantage of close association with Asa Gray [*q.v.*], by whose friendship his work was undoubtedly influenced. In 1872 he became director of the Harvard Botanic Garden in Cambridge. He was professor of horticulture at Harvard in 1872–73 and professor of ariboriculture from 1879 until his death.

In 1873 he was appointed director of the newly created Arnold Arboretum. Though for a time he also held the directorship of the Botanic Garden, in 1879 he gave it up to devote all his energies to the Arboretum and to work relating to trees and forests. The plans for the Arboretum, worked out in cooperation with Frederick Law Olmsted [q.v.], involved much opposition and long delays in preparation; it was not until the spring of 1886 that the first trees were planted in their permanent groupings. Until his death the development and enlargement of the living collections of the Arboretum was Sargent's chief consideration, although with this was coordinated important research work on ligneous plants, particularly those composing a part of the North American flora. These studies resulted most notably in *The Silva of North America* (1891–1902), fourteen folio volumes with illustrations of every species of tree then known north of Mexico. Before this his appointment as special agent of the Tenth Census (1880) enabled him to explore forested regions throughout the United States and led to collaboration with many of the best field botanists in the country. The results were published in Volume IX of the Tenth Census, *Report on the Forests of North America* (1884), the first complete synopsis of the trees of North America and a splendid foundation for the future work on the *Silva*. This appointment also furnished the opportunity to bring together the Jesup collection of woods of North America, established by Morris K. Jesup [q.v.] and now a part of the exhibits in the American Museum of Natural History in New York, described in Sargent's *The Woods of the United States* (1885).

As a member of the Northern Pacific Transcontinental Survey in 1882–83, he was impressed with the desirability of establishing national parks in the western mountains and took an active part in the effort to secure them. He likewise helped in 1884 to establish a conservation policy in the Adirondack forests of New York. His journeys undertaken for the study of trees included a visit to Japan in 1892, a trip around the world in 1903, and travel in South America in the winter of 1905–06. From 1888 to 1897 he published and edited *Garden and Forest,* a weekly magazine that helped to awaken an interest in arboriculture and forestry in the United States. His own writings include *Forest Flora of Japan* (1894), *Manual of the Trees of North America* (1905), and many articles. He also edited the three volumes of *Plantae Wilsonianae* (1913–17), a description of plants collected by Ernest Henry Wilson [q.v.]. He never engaged in class work or gave public lectures, preferring to do his share of educational work through writing, but he inspired many by his wise counsels and did much to clarify problems in dendrology and landscape gardening.

[No extended biog. of Sargent has yet been written, but there is an excellent account of his life and work, with bibliog. and portrait, in *Jour. of Arnold Arboretum,* Apr. 1927. See also E. W. and C. S. Sargent, *Epes Sargent of Gloucester and His Descendants* (1923); *Who's Who in America,* 1926–27; S. E. Morison, ed., *The Development of Harvard Univ.* (1930); *Class Report: Class of 'Sixty-Two, Harvard Univ., Fiftieth Anniversary* (1912); *Harvard Grads.' Mag.,* June 1927; *Nat. Acad. Sci. Biog. Memoirs,* vol. XII (1929), with bibliog.; *Am. Forestry,* Nov. 1921; obituary in *Boston Transcript,* Mar. 23, 1927.]   J. G. J.

SARGENT, DUDLEY ALLEN (Sept. 28, 1849–July 21, 1924), director of physical culture, physician, was born in Belfast, Me., the son of Caroline (Rogers) and Benjamin Sargent, a ship-carpenter and spar maker who died in 1856. The visit of an itinerant circus in Belfast when he was fifteen and later a gymnastic exhibition by students from Bowdoin College seem to have determined his career. Endowed with unusual strength and agility, he was soon the leader of a group of high-school boys who practised assiduously to master gymnastic and acrobatic feats and attained sufficient skill to give exhibitions in Belfast and neighboring towns. He himself won an engagement with a circus as a result of mastering the exceedingly difficult feat of sitting in a rocking chair balanced on a swinging trapeze. In 1869 he became director of the gymnasium at Bowdoin College. Two years later, though he retained his position as director, he was admitted as a freshman. In 1872 he spent three months of the winter term at Yale College, introducing his plan of physical training, and until his graduation from Bowdoin in 1875 he continued to divide his time between the two institutions. In 1875 he became instructor in gymnastics in Yale College and a student in the Yale Medical School, from which he obtained the degree of M.D. in 1878. The same year, he opened his Hygienic Institute and School of Physical Culture, a private gymnasium in New York, and only a year later he was appointed assistant professor of physical training and director of the Hemenway Gymnasium at Harvard.

During the forty years in which he held the position he exerted a greater influence on the development of physical training in American colleges and schools than any other man. Since he early recognized that the introduction of physical training in colleges and schools was dependent upon an adequate supply of trained teachers, he organized in Cambridge in 1881 the

Sanatory Gymnasium, which became the Sargent School for Physical Education. In 1887 he organized courses in physical training in the Harvard University summer school, which were given under his direction until 1919. He worked unceasingly in the interest of wholesome and nation-wide physical training, and against excesses in athletics, the abuse of military drill in schools, and other unwise measures. He was active in the organization of the American Association for the Advancement of Physical Education (later the American Physical Education Association) and the Society of Directors of Physical Education in Colleges. He served as president of the first in 1890, 1892–94, and 1899–1901, and of the second in 1899. In 1882 he published *A Handbook of Developing Exercises*; in 1887, *Anthropometric Apparatus, with Directions for Measuring and Testing the Principal Physical Characteristics of the Human Body* and an article in *Scribner's Magazine* for July 1887, "The Physical Proportions of the Typical Man." In 1893 he exhibited life-size statues of typical American students at the Columbian Exposition in Chicago. *Health, Strength and Power* appeared in 1904, and in 1906 twelve of his papers and essays were published under the title *Physical Education*. In 1927 appeared *Dudley Allen Sargent: an Autobiography*, edited by L. W. Sargent. He was a man of strong convictions, very loyal to those who shared his views but often intolerant toward those who opposed him. An indefatigable worker, he devoted all his time to professional interests even at the expense of social and family responsibilities. His wife, Ella Fraser Ledyard of Brooklyn, N. Y., whom he had married on Apr. 7, 1881, left him about 1898, and he lived alone during the last twenty-five years of his life. He retired from Harvard at seventy but continued to teach in his normal school until his death. He was survived by his wife and a son.

[*Who's Who in America*, 1924–25; F. E. Leonard, *A Guide to the Hist. of Physical Ed.* (1923); R. T. McKenzie, ed., *Hist. of Physical Ed.* (1927); L. C. Hatch, *Hist. of Bowdoin Coll.* (1927); *Obit. Record Grads. Yale Univ.* (1925); *Jour. Am. Medic. Assoc.*, Aug. 16, 1924; *Boston Transcript*, July 21, 1924; long personal acquaintance.]   G. L. M.

SARGENT, EPES (Sept. 27, 1813–Dec. 30, 1880), journalist, poet, dramatist, advocate of spiritualism, and indefatigable literary worker, was of the sixth generation of his family in America, a descendant of William Sargent who received a grant of land in Gloucester, Mass., in 1678. He numbered among his other early ancestors Gov. John Winthrop and Gov. Joseph Dudley [*qq.v.*]. The poet was the son of Epes

Sargent, a Gloucester ship-master, and his second wife, Hannah Dane Coffin, also of Gloucester. In 1818 the father removed from his native town to Roxbury and began a not wholly successful career as a Boston merchant, after which he returned to the sea. The son entered the Boston Latin School in 1823 and was graduated in 1829 (information from the Headmaster, Public Latin School, Boston, 1931). His course was interrupted for some months while he accompanied his father on a voyage to Russia, and the *Literary Journal,* published in 1829 by students of the Latin School, contained extracts from his letters from St. Petersburg. There is a persistent, but unverifiable, tradition that he attended Harvard College for a short time and contributed to the *Collegian,* on which his elder brother, John Osborne Sargent [*q.v.*], had been a collaborator with Oliver Wendell Holmes and others.

In the early thirties he joined the editorial staff of the *Boston Daily Advertiser,* and later that of the *Boston Daily Atlas.* For some time he was Washington correspondent of the *Atlas,* and thus formed many political acquaintances, particularly among the Whigs. A later result of this experience was his *Life and Public Services of Henry Clay* (1842, and subsequent revisions). After leaving the *Atlas* he devoted himself to miscellaneous literary work. His first plays—*The Bride of Genoa* (written 1836; published 1837) and *Velasco* (written 1837; published 1839) were both produced at the Tremont Theatre, Boston. The last-named tragedy, written for Miss Ellen Tree, was, so far as acting possibilities were concerned, the most successful of his dramatic attempts, and won some slight vogue on the English as well as on the American stage. From about 1839 to 1847 Sargent was engaged in various ventures in New York. He worked with Morris on the *New York Mirror,* with Park Benjamin on the *New World,* founded and conducted for a few months *Sargent's New Monthly Magazine* (January–June 1843), and edited *The Modern Standard Drama* (7 vols., beginning in 1846). In 1847 he returned to Boston and until 1853 was editor of the *Boston Transcript.* On May 10, 1848, he married Elizabeth W. Weld of Roxbury.

Throughout his active career Epes Sargent was a contributor to many magazines and other periodicals; a frequent author of occasional verse, particularly for theatrical occasions; and at times a lecturer. S. G. Goodrich [*q.v.*] in his *Recollections* (1856, II, 275) mentions him as one of those who assisted in the preparation of the Peter Parley books, and later as a writer of verse for the *Token*. His best volume of verse was *Songs of the Sea with other Poems* (1847; 2nd ed. 1849), based largely on experiences during a voyage to Cuba. Some of the sonnets in this collection have merit, but the only piece now remembered is the song, "A Life on the Ocean Wave." Another collection of poems appeared in 1858, and a narrative in verse, *The Woman who Dared,* in 1870. Among his works of fiction were *Fleetwood, or the Stain of Birth* (1845), and *Peculiar, a Tale of the Great Transition* (1864). More miscellaneous are *American Adventure by Land and Sea* (1841); *Arctic Adventure by Sea and Land* (1857, 1860). Plays, besides the two already named, were a comedy, *Change Makes Change,* and a tragedy, *The Priestess* (privately printed, 1854). Sargent edited the works of several English poets, among them Hood, Rogers, Campbell, Gray, and Goldsmith; two miscellanies, *The Emerald* (1866) and *The Sapphire* (1867); and *Harper's Cyclopædia of British and American Poetry,* published posthumously in 1881. He compiled a series of school speakers, one of school readers, and other works for schools. It was the success of these that for a time made his name almost universally known in America. The works mentioned, both original and edited, are but a few of those that bear his name. Large as was the bulk of his literary work, a great part of it was completed before he had passed his early fifties. In the later years of his life he was interested in Spiritualism, devoted much of his waning energy to the exposition of his new faith, and did relatively less of other writing. He was in correspondence with the leading students of Spiritualism at home and in Europe, and wrote, besides many articles for periodicals, *Planchette, or the Despair of Science* (1869), *The Proof Palpable of Immortality* (1875), and *The Scientific Basis of Spiritualism* (1880). His attitude toward the subject and the development of his ideas may be inferred from a comparison between the title of the last of these three works and the subtitle of the first.

Sargent was in poor health during his later years, suffering from a complication of ailments, especially bronchial; but his death resulted from a cancer of the mouth, which was distressingly painful and impaired his power of utterance. While never ranked as great in any department of literature or scholarship he was a writer of taste and sound ideals whose work met the needs of his time, and he was deservedly respected in his day. A contemporary wrote: "A dapper, elegant little man he was, neatly attired, swinging a thin, polished back [black?] bamboo cane, and seeming the embodiment of cheer"—a descrip-

tion not inconsistent with the somewhat less patronizing portrayal given by Poe in his *Literati*.

[Most published sketches are full of misstatements. Sargent left no direct descendants; and his career has sometimes been confused with those of other members of his family. The purely genealogical information in E. W. and C. S. Sargent, *Epes Sargent of Gloucester and His Descendants* (1923) is probably accurate, but the biographical sketch is an untrustworthy compilation; this volume also contains "A List of Publications of the Descendants of Epes Sargent," comp. by Julia M. Johnson. See, further, *The Complete Works of Edgar Allan Poe* (1908), ed. by N. H. Dole, IX, 36–38; E. A. and G. L. Duyckinck, *Cyc. of Am. Lit.* (1875), II, 569–71; *Boston Transcript,* Dec. 31, 1880.]
W. B. C.

SARGENT, FITZWILLIAM (Jan. 17, 1820– Apr. 25, 1889), physician, was born in Gloucester, Mass. His father, Winthrop, was descendant of William Sargent, who came to Gloucester from England before 1678, many of whose descendants distinguished themselves in the civil and military affairs of the colonies and some in literary or artistic paths. His mother, Emily Haskell, was a descendant of William Haskell, who came to New England about 1637. Winthrop Sargent succeeded his father in the management of large shipping interests belonging to his family, but the business failed in 1829, and in the following year he removed to Philadelphia, where he engaged in the commission business. He returned to Massachusetts in 1843, but in 1862 went back to Pennsylvania and lived at Morgan's Corner (now Radnor), near Philadelphia, until his death in 1874.

FitzWilliam Sargent studied at Jefferson College, Canonsburg, Pa., from which he received the degree of B.A., in 1837. Sometime later he entered the medical department of the University of Pennsylvania, from which he graduated in 1843. In the last year of his medical course he served as resident physician in the Wills Eye Hospital of Philadelphia. After graduating, he served two years as resident physician in the Pennsylvania Hospital and then entered on general practice in Philadelphia, paying particular attention to ophthalmology. In 1849 he was elected one of the attending physicians to the Wills Hospital, changing his position to attending surgeon in 1852. He resigned from the Hospital in 1857. He was elected a Fellow of the College of Physicians of Philadelphia in 1852. In 1848 he edited an American edition of *The Principles and Practice of Modern Surgery,* by Robert Druitt, and wrote a little book, *On Bandaging and Other Operations of Minor Surgery,* which went through several editions, being also translated into Japanese and published at Osaka in 1874. It was illustrated by the author. In

1852 he edited the American edition of James Miller's *The Principles of Surgery,* of which a second edition was published in 1856. He also contributed several articles to the *American Journal of the Medical Sciences*. On June 27, 1850, he married Mary Newbold Singer, a daughter of John and Mary (Newbold) Singer. Thereafter he lived principally in Europe. His wife was an accomplished musician and also had considerable talent in drawing and painting. She is said to have had much to do with the cultivation of the artistic genius of their son John Singer Sargent [*q.v.*], born while his parents were living in Italy in 1856. In 1887 while living in Florence, Italy, FitzWilliam Sargent suffered an apoplectic stroke, and in the spring of 1888 the family moved to Calcot, near Reading, England. The following winter was passed in Bournemouth, where Sargent died.

[E. W. and C. S. Sargent, *Epes Sargent of Gloucester and His Descendants* (1923); E. E. Charteris, *John Sargent* (1927); W. C. Posey and S. H. Brown, *The Wills Hospital of Phila.* (1931); H. A. Kelly and W. L. Burrage, *Am. Medic. Biogs.* (1920).]   F. R. P.

SARGENT, FRANK PIERCE (Nov. 18, 1854–Sept. 4, 1908), labor leader and federal official, was born at East Orange, Vt., and died at Washington, D. C. His parents were Charles Edwin and Mary C. (Kinney) Sargent and he was a descendant of William Sargent who was living in Ipswich, Mass., as early as 1633. His early education was received in the common schools, and for one year he attended Northfield Academy, Northfield, Mass. In his teens he worked on a farm and in the mills at Montpelier, Vt., and Manchester, N. H.

In 1878 he went to Arizona for his health, enlisted there in the United States Cavalry, and was active in the Geronimo campaign against the Apache Indians. Honorably discharged in 1880, he went to work for the Southern Pacific Railroad as an engine wiper at Tucson, Ariz. Within three months he became a locomotive fireman, and joined the Brotherhood of Locomotive Firemen, his initiation taking place Oct. 20, 1881, in one of the coal bins in the railroad yards. From 1883 to 1894 he lived in Terre Haute, Ind., and from 1894 to 1902 in Peoria, Ill. He was a delegate to the national convention of the Brotherhood of Locomotive Firemen at Terre Haute in September 1882, and at the Denver convention in 1883 he was elected vice grand master. In 1885, at the Philadelphia convention, he was elected grand master of the order, which office he held until 1902. He was prominent in the Chicago, Burlington & Quincy strike in 1888, and the American Railway Union

strike against the Great Northern Railroad in 1894, and became known as a forceful leader for the firemen, while his moderation and reasonable methods in dealing with employers gained their confidence.

In 1898 he was appointed by President McKinley on the Industrial Commission, from which he resigned. He declined appointment in 1900 as director of the Bureau of Engraving and Printing. On May 7, 1902, he was nominated by President Roosevelt as commissioner general of immigration, and the nomination was confirmed the following day. In this office he was instrumental in the initiation of methods which aimed at the prevention of fraud against intending immigrants, and at the exclusion of undesirable and criminal elements. He also gave especial attention to the prevention of the smuggling of Chinese across the Mexican and Canadian borders. He was hindered, however, in carrying out what he conceived to be the policy of American labor, by the opposition of powerful diplomatic, industrial and political forces, which brought influence to bear upon those in higher authority. After the Chicago and New York anarchistic riots he made a special study of the changing character of the immigration into the United States and called attention to the fact that its sources were no longer so largely among the Germanic races of Northern Europe, but were then, to a great extent, in southern and southeastern Europe and Asia Minor. His reports included recommendations for amendments in the immigration laws to meet the changing conditions, and the delays in securing these were a cause of deep disappointment to him. Later developments more than justified his wisdom, and compelled the adoption of policies more in line with his thought. His writings include: "The Need of Closer Inspection and Greater Restriction of Immigrants" (*Century Magazine,* January 1904); and "Problems of Immigration" (*Annals of the American Academy of Political and Social Science,* July 1904). He had the confidence and friendship of Samuel Gompers [*q.v.*], and had a part in the conferences of Gompers and John Mitchell [*q.v.*] with President Theodore Roosevelt in 1902 which led up to the appointment of the federal commission for the settlement of the great anthracite coal strike. He was also a member of the group chosen to represent the interests of labor in the National Civic Federation. He was a man of large stature and commanding personality, and his winning manner and keen executive ability gained and held for him the loyalty of those associated with him. He was married on Oct. 17, 1881, to

Georgia M. McCullough of Saugus, Mass., who with an adopted daughter survived him.

[E. E. Sargent, *Sargent Record, William Sargent of Ipswich* (1899); *Brotherhood of Locomotive Firemen and Enginemen's Mag.*, Oct. 1908; Samuel Gompers, *Seventy Years of Life and Labor* (2 vols., 1925); A. P. Kellogg, "The National Conference on Immigration," in *Charities and the Commons*, Dec. 16, 1905; *Who's Who in America*, 1908–09; *Evening Star* (Washington, D. C.), Sept. 4, 1908; *N. Y. Times*, Sept. 5, 1908.]
W. R. G.

SARGENT, FREDERICK (Nov. 11, 1859–July 26, 1919), engineer, specialist in the design and construction of electrical generating stations, was born at Liskeard, Cornwall, England, on the farm of his parents, Daniel and Jane (Yates) Sargent. He early developed a taste for mechanics and became an apprentice in the famous engineering works of John Elder & Company on the Clyde, near Glasgow. While serving his apprenticeship, he attended night classes at Anderson's College, Glasgow. In 1880 he came to the United States and found employment designing marine steam engines in the shipbuilding yards on the Atlantic Coast. The following year he was designer for the Sioux City (Iowa) Engine Company and in 1882 went to Milwaukee to join the engineering staff of E. P. Allis & Company. He soon became acquainted with the Western Edison Light Company of Chicago and in 1884 went to work for them; on the organization of the Chicago Edison Company in 1887 he became its consulting engineer, holding this connection with the Edison Company and its successor, the Commonwealth Edison Company, until his death. To the duties of this post he added, in 1889, those of chief engineer of the Edison United Manufacturing Company, with headquarters in New York, and on the reorganization of this concern as the Edison General Electric Company he became its assistant chief engineer. In August 1890 he returned to Chicago to establish himself as a consulting electrical and mechanical engineer, and in 1891 formed the firm of Sargent & Lundy. He was consulting engineer for the World's Columbian Exposition in 1891 and 1892, and his firm after that period was continuously engaged in the design and construction of central generating stations for important companies in various parts of the United States and even in England and in South America. During the World War, he was consulting engineer for the government in connection with the Edgewood Arsenal and other projects.

While his early training had been in the design and construction of reciprocating engines, Sargent was among the first to recognize the great advantages of the steam turbine, and his purchase of the first large turbine for the Fisk Street Station, Chicago, began a new epoch in central station design. He saw the advantages in the use of high pressures and temperatures, took the lead in the introduction of pressures of 400 and 600 pounds, and had recommended the employment of 1200-pound pressures, which were introduced after his death. His mechanical mind indicated the economical and satisfactory solution of serious construction troubles in installations where large fluctuations in the condensing water levels existed.

Sargent had an active mind and a broad outlook; his thinking was always simple, direct, and practical. His designs were usually in advance of the times, but his experimenting was held in restraint by sound practical common sense. A genius in the design and operation of steam electric generating stations, he left his imprint indelibly on the central-station industry of his generation. He was awarded a medal by the World's Columbian Exposition and was a member of the jury of awards for power engineering at the St. Louis exposition of 1904. He was a member of the American Society of Mechanical Engineers, the American Institute of Electrical Engineers, the Western Society of Engineers, and other organizations. He married at Sioux City, Iowa, in 1885, Laura S. Sleep, daughter of William H. Sleep, a manufacturer, of Plymouth, England. His wife, with two sons and a daughter, survived him. He died at his home in Glencoe, Ill.

[*Trans. Am. Soc. Mech. Engineers*, vol. XLI (1919); T. C. Martin and S. L. Coles, *The Story of Electricity*, vol. II (1922); *Who's Who in America*, 1918–19; A. N. Marquis, *The Book of Chicagoans*, 1917; *Power*, Aug. 5, 1919; *Electrical World*, Aug. 2, 1919; *N. Y. Times*, July 27, 1919.]
G. A. O.

SARGENT, GEORGE HENRY (May 5, 1867–Jan. 14, 1931), journalist, bibliographer, was born, lived during many years of his life, and died in the old family farmhouse in Warner, N. H. He was the son of Walter and Addie C. (Morrill) Sargent, being descended on the paternal side from William Sargent, who emigrated from England and was in Ipswich, Mass., as early as 1633. George Henry was educated in the schools of his native town, and, giving up his original intention of entering college, went West in 1887 and began his life work in journalism as a reporter on the *St. Paul Daily Pioneer Press*, of which paper he was city editor from 1890 to 1895. In the latter year he returned East, and joined the staff of the *Boston Evening Transcript*, continuing his connection with that newspaper uninterruptedly throughout the rest of his life, as reporter, writer of special articles, and for over twenty-seven years as the writer of "The Bibliographer" department, every issue of which was from his own hand. In 1914, as the result of an illness which made it inadvisable for him to continue to live and work in the city, he left Boston, and thereafter made his home on his ancestral farm. He carried on his literary work there by correspondence, and through occasional visits to Boston, New York, Philadelphia, New Haven (where he delivered lectures on his special subject), and other cities, maintaining contact with book collectors and dealers. In 1889 he was married to Carrie Florence Dietz of Iowa City, Iowa, and it was largely due to her care that he was enabled to go on with his work through fifteen years of semi-invalidism.

He had many other interests in addition to those of journalism and bibliography, being active in the political affairs of his town and state, and directing the work of the New Hampshire farm where he lived. In face and stature he was the typical and gaunt New England Yankee. His friends and acquaintances were many, and everybody interested in bibliography, not only in the United States but also in England, looked upon him as a leading authority. He was an assiduous worker, and during the years of his labors upon "The Bibliographer" department of the *Boston Transcript,* he never failed to have his articles— usually totaling two columns every Wednesday —ready on time. He died early on a Wednesday morning, and the last installment of his work, mailed a day or two previously, appeared in the *Transcript* that evening. He was, moreover, not merely a looker-on and a casual writer in the field of bibliography, his own collection of books being extensive and valuable. Among his published works, in addition to a number in pamphlet form, were *The French Revolution and Napoleon in Literature and Caricature* (1906), *Amy Lowell, a Mosaic* (1926), *The Writings of A. Edward Newton, a Bibliography* (1927), and *A Busted Bibliophile and His Books* (1928).

[*Who's Who in America,* 1930–31; E. E. Sargent, *Sargent Record, William Sargent of Ipswich* (1899); Karl Schriftgiesser, "George Sargent, 1867–1931," in *The Bookman,* Mar. 1931; *Boston Transcript,* Jan. 14, 1931; *Publishers' Weekly,* Oct. 27, 1923, and Jan. 31, 1931; introduction to *The Fine Lib. of the Late George H. Sargent, Sold . . . at Unrestricted Auction Sale . . . Dec. 19th 1931* (1931); personal acquaintance.]

E. F. E.

SARGENT, HENRY (*c.* November 1770– Feb. 21, 1845), painter, military man, was born at Gloucester, Mass., and baptized on Nov. 25, 1770. Son of Daniel and Mary (Turner) Sargent and brother of Lucius Manlius Sargent [*q.v.*], he was a great-grandson of William Sargent who received a grant of land at Gloucester in 1678. His father was a prosperous and public-spirited merchant. Henry was sent as a young boy to Dummer Academy, South Byfield, and then, the family having moved to Boston, he continued his studies under local teachers. After a period in the counting house of Thomas Handasyd Perkins [*q.v.*], he continued his commercial apprenticeship with his father, but suddenly, as he was attaining his majority, without having previously shown special partiality for the arts of design, he determined to become an artist. An elder brother's efforts in this direction seem to have stimulated him, and his mother encouraged him. John Trumbull [*q.v.*], who visited Boston in 1790, saw some of his work and found it promising.

In 1793 Sargent went to London, where he studied with Benjamin West and had courteous treatment from John Singleton Copley [*qq.v.*]. A letter of Sargent's dated Mar. 27, 1795 (Addison, *post,* p. 279), shows that he found living in London expensive and the painter's profession much depressed. He returned to Boston in 1799, still strongly conscious of "the apathy then existing towards the arts" (Dunlap, *post,* II, 192). Accordingly, in that same year he took a commission in the national army then being raised under command of Alexander Hamilton. This service was brief, but it gave Sargent a taste for military life which motivated his long connection with the Massachusetts militia. In or shortly after 1799 he joined the Boston Light Infantry, which had been organized the year before and of which his brother, Daniel Sargent, was captain. Records of the adjutant-general's office in the Massachusetts State House show that Henry Sargent became first lieutenant of this company Oct. 1, 1804, and captain, Mar. 31, 1807. Of the tall, thin, Yankee build, he was a handsome officer and an efficient drill master. During the War of 1812 his company aided in the fortification of Fort Strong, and on May 31, 1815, he was appointed aide-de-camp to the governor, with the rank of colonel. In 1812, 1815, 1816, and 1817 he was a member of the state Senate.

In the course of the following decade, growing deafness caused him gradually to withdraw from public services and to devote himself entirely to his painting and to mechanical inventions, in which latter field he achieved no great celebrity. His painting was that of a diligent and gifted artist whose talent fell short of genius. His portraits were less masterful than those of his fellow townsman, Gilbert Stuart [*q.v.*], with whom he was personally intimate. Like Copley, whom he somewhat resembled as a painter, Sargent enjoyed intensive elaboration of textures and accessories. He had capacity for doing canvases that required sustained effort. The well-known

"Landing of the Pilgrims," at Pilgrim Hall, Plymouth, attributed to him, is not representative of his best work. Far better are the two conversation pieces, "The Tea Party" and "The Dinner Party," owned by the Museum of Fine Arts, Boston. These have something of the exquisiteness of the so-called Little Dutchmen and they give fascinating glimpses of social life in Boston homes of the early nineteenth century. An altar painting, "The Christ Crucified," which Sargent made for the Church of the Holy Cross, Boston, won contemporary favor. The full-length portrait of Peter Faneuil, in Faneuil Hall, if by Sargent, to whom it is ascribed, must be a copy after John Smibert (see note in Dunlap, *post,* II, 196). Sargent's self-portrait is at the Boston Museum; his likenesses of Jeremy Belknap, D.D., and John Clarke, D.D., both friends of his parents, are at the Massachusetts Historical Society. Continuing to paint at intervals down into old age, he was elected in 1840 an honorary member of the National Academy of Design and in 1845, president of the newly organized Artists' Association of Boston. He had married, Apr. 2, 1807, Hannah, daughter of Samuel and Isabella (Pratt) Welles, of Boston, and they had two daughters who died in infancy and two sons, one of whom was Henry Winthrop Sargent [*q.v.*].

[Wm. Dunlap, *A Hist. of the Rise and Progress of the Arts of Design in the U. S.* (3 vols., 1918), ed. by F. W. Bayley and C. E. Goodspeed; L. M. Sargent, *Dealings with the Dead* (1856), II, 538; H. T. Tuckerman, *Book of the Artists* (1867); C. E. Mann, *The Sargent Family and the Old Sargent Homes* (1919); E. W. and C. S. Sargent, *Epes Sargent of Gloucester and His Descendants* (1923); Albert Welles, *Hist. of the Welles Family* (1876); Julia deW. Addison, in *Art in America,* Oct. 1929; *Museum of Fine Arts, Boston, Cat. of Paintings* (1921).]   F. W. C.

SARGENT, HENRY WINTHROP (Nov. 26, 1810–Nov. 11, 1882), horticulturist and landscape gardener, was born in Boston, the first child of Hannah (Welles) and Henry Sargent [*q.v.*]. Educated at the Boston Latin School and at Harvard College, where he was graduated in the class of 1830 with a creditable record, he first studied law in the office of Samuel Hubbard in Boston but never engaged in the practice of this profession. He next became a partner in the banking house of Gracie and Sargent, New York agents of his uncle, Samuel Welles, a Paris banker. On Jan. 10, 1839, he married Caroline Olmsted, daughter of Maria (Wyckoff) and Francis Olmsted of New York, who survived him. There were three children of this marriage, two of whom predeceased their father. In 1841 Sargent retired and removed to "Wodenethe," an estate of about twenty acres on a plateau overlooking the Hudson just above Fishkill Landing

(now Beacon), N. Y., which soon became famous for its distant views and its vistas cut through the native forest to the Hudson and the mountains, and for its extensive plantation of coniferous trees. In planning it, the owner was without doubt assisted and inspired by his friend and neighbor, Andrew Jackson Downing [*q.v.*], the foremost American landscape gardener of the day.

In 1847–49 he travelled with his family in Europe and the Levant, primarily to gather plants and to study the design of parks and country places. As a result he later published a comprehensive garden guide entitled *Skeleton Tours* (1870), which included the British Isles, the Scandinavian peninsula, Russia, Poland, and Spain. He was a frequent contributor to horticultural papers, especially to the *Horticulturist,* and in 1873 with Charles Downing [*q.v.*] he wrote a supplement to Andrew Downing's *Cottage Residences* (1842). But his most important literary contribution is his supplement to the sixth (1859) and subsequent editions of Downing's *A Treatise on the Theory and Practice of Landscape Gardening* (1841). In this he gave an account of the newer deciduous and evergreen plants and told in considerable detail of the development of his own "Wodenethe" and of the estate of his relative, Horatio Hollis Hunnewell [*q.v.*], at Wellesley, Mass. A second supplement, added in the edition of 1875, gives a brief account of trees and shrubs introduced since 1859. In a period which marks the beginning of the professional practice of landscape architecture in America, this book and its supplement exerted a great influence on popular taste. Sargent's influence may also be seen more directly in the horticultural interests of his kinsmen, H. H. Hunnewell and Charles Sprague Sargent [*q.v.*].

[Emma W. and C. S. Sargent, *Epes Sargent of Gloucester and His Descendants* (1923); *1830, Harvard Univ. Memoirs* (1886); L. H. Bailey, ed., *Standard Cyc. of Horticulture,* vol. III (1915); J. H. Sheppard, *Reminiscences of Lucius Manlius Sargent* (1871); Albert Welles, *History of the Welles Family in England and Normandy, with . . . Some of the Descendants in the U. S.* (1876); obituary in *Gardener's Monthly and Horticulturist,* Dec. 1882; *N. Y. Tribune,* Nov. 11, 1882.]   K. M.

SARGENT, JAMES (Dec. 5, 1824–Jan. 12, 1910), inventor, was the son of William and Hannah (Allen, Allan, or Allyn) Sargent and was born on his father's farm at Chester, Vt., where until he was eighteen he helped with the farm work and obtained something of an education in the district schools. At that time, because of his intense interest in machinery, he went to work in a woolen mill and soon became an expert in the care of machines. A year or so later he became foreman of a woolen mill at Ashuelot, N. H., where he remained until 1848. Meanwhile he became interested in daguerreotyping, mastered the art, outfitted himself, and from 1848 to 1852 was occupied with marked success as a traveling daguerreotyper. During this period he perfected an apple parer he had invented and in 1852 went to Shelburne Falls, Mass., where in partnership with a man named Foster he began manufacturing and selling this device. After five years he became associated with the Yale and Greenleaf Lock Company as a traveling salesman. Making a careful study of lock mechanisms, he soon was able to pick any lock by means of a special micrometer of his own invention that detected variations in the combination wheels. When he became so expert that he could pick even the lock he sold, he experimented in secret to produce a combination lock he could not pick. About 1863 he succeeded and offered the invention to his employer. When the offer was rejected, he resigned his position and in 1869 formed the partnership of Sargent and Greenleaf in Rochester, N. Y., to manufacture the new device. It proved immediately successful. By the use of a powerful magnet within the lock mechanism, other parts of the lock were held sufficiently under control so that not even the micrometer could detect the relative positions of the unlocking devices.

Sargent's business grew rapidly in the succeeding years, especially when he proved that the locks of the United States Treasury were unsafe and obtained the federal business for his company. To improve his invention he substituted a simple mechanical device for the permanent magnet in his combination lock and perfected his first time lock about 1873, the first of which he personally installed in May 1874 on the door of the iron safe of the First National Bank, Morrison, Ill., where it gave satisfactory service for forty years. Until his retirement some years before his death, he not only directed the affairs of his extensive lock business but invented and manufactured such devices as railway semaphore signals, automatic fire alarms, smoke consumers, and glass-lined steel tanks. In his later years he was closely associated with the Pfaudler Vacuum Fermentation Company of Rochester, N. Y., manufacturers of enameled steel tanks, and did experimental work for the Gordon Railway Signal Company; he was also president of the Waterloo Gold Mining Company of California. On Apr. 29, 1847, he married Angeline Morse Foster in Winchester, N. H., and at the time of his death was survived by an adopted daughter.

[A. A. Hopkins, *The Lure of the Lock* (1928); *Who's Who in America,* 1908–09; data from Sargent and Greenleaf, Inc., and the Pfaudler Company, Rochester, N. Y.; obituary in *Democrat and Chronicle* (Rochester), Jan. 13, 1910; Patent Office records.]

C. W. M.

SARGENT, JOHN OSBORNE (Sept. 20, 1811–Dec. 28, 1891), lawyer, journalist, author, was born in Gloucester, Mass., the second child and eldest son of Epes and Hannah Dane (Coffin) Sargent, his mother being the second of his father's three wives, and he one of a total of twelve children by the different marriages. Both his father and his mother were of families long established in New England, and he enjoyed the best social and educational advantages. After attending the Boston Latin School, he entered Harvard College, where he distinguished himself for scholarship and took a prominent part in conducting the *Collegian,* an undergraduate publication. Upon his graduation in 1830 he studied law in Boston and was admitted to the bar in January 1834; but a letter he wrote to the *Boston Daily Atlas,* a Whig newspaper, so impressed the editor that he was engaged to write its political editorials. This led him into politics, and in 1836 and 1837 he was elected to the lower house of the Massachusetts legislature. Offered an associate editorship by the *Courier and Enquirer* of New York in 1838, he left Boston to help conduct it till after the election of Harrison to the presidency. He was now in a position of political influence, but the death of the president changed this, and in 1841 he returned to the practice of law in New York. The candidacy of Taylor brought him back into political journalism, however, for he conducted a publication supporting his candidacy and later went to Washington as joint editor of the *Republic,* the official organ of the administration. Because of a disagreement with the cabinet he withdrew, but on the accession of Fillmore he rejoined the paper and helped to conduct it, refusing appointment as minister to China to do so.

Though in 1853 he resumed the practice of law in New York, he devoted much time to literary interests. He had already assisted in editing the *New England Magazine* for January and February 1835, and he had published *A Lecture on the Late Improvements in Steam Navigation* (1844) and articles on other practical subjects. He now turned towards belles-lettres, rather as a translator than a creator. After 1861 for about twelve years he spent most of his time in Europe publishing a translation of *The Last Knight* (1871) from the German of A. A. von Auersperg, several pamphlets on the legal decision in Minot's case, and *Chapters for the Times*

(1884), anti-Blaine campaign literature. For the most part, however, he devoted himself to translating Horace, on which he expended endless pains. Very little of this was published during his life, most of it appearing in *Horatian Echoes* (1893), for which Oliver Wendell Holmes wrote an introduction. Much of what he wrote apart from this is untraceable because of its journalistic character, and some of his substantial work appeared under the name of his brother Epes [*q.v.*]. More significant even than his important legal documents and influential political arguments was his interest in Horace. He not only translated the urbane Roman's words but realized his ideal of life to a notable extent, investing his own mode of living both with the Horatian spirit and with the amenities and refinements of a later age.

On Jan. 17, 1854, he married Georgiana, daughter of Benjamin Welles of Boston, by whom he had one daughter. He was influential in making the Board of Overseers of Harvard University include persons from outside Massachusetts, and in 1880 he was elected as the second member from outside the state. From 1886–87 on, he offered a prize of one hundred dollars for the best translation from Horace by a Harvard or Radcliffe student, an award made permanent by his daughter in 1892.

[See Emma W. and C. S. Sargent, *Epes Sargent of Gloucester and His Descendants* (1923), biog. sketch and bibliog.; editorial on Sargent's journalistic career, *Boston Herald*, Dec. 30, 1891; Eugene Field on his poetic activities, *Chicago Daily News*, Jan. 12, 1892; biog. sketch in *Horatian Echoes* (1893); obituary in *Boston Transcript*, Dec. 29, 1891. A journal of Sargent's and some correspondence are in the Widener Lib., Harvard Univ.]　　　　　　　　　　　　　　S. G—n.

SARGENT, JOHN SINGER (Jan. 12, 1856– Apr. 15, 1925), portrait, genre, and mural painter, was born in Florence, Italy. He was the son of Dr. FitzWilliam Sargent [*q.v.*], a native of Gloucester, Mass., who attained prominence as a physician in Philadelphia, and of Mary Newbold (Singer) Sargent of the latter city. On the paternal side the family came of English Puritan stock from Devonshire. His mother's ancestry is traced back to Caspar Singer, who came from Alsace-Lorraine to America about 1730, and to the Newbolds, who were from Yorkshire. In 1854 FitzWilliam Sargent was persuaded by his wife, a woman of means and culture, and an excellent musician, to give up his practice and go to Italy. Thus it fell out that John Sargent was born in the Casa Arretini, on the Lung' Arno, near the Ponte Vecchio. His parents wandered from place to place during his childhood. Four daughters were born to them, two of whom died, leaving to John two younger

sisters, Emily and Violet, who eventually survived him; a younger brother died in 1869.

His father saw John as a future admiral in the United States navy, but this plan was thwarted by the boy's manifest bent, which was sagely abetted by his mother. His first crude essays in drawing were made under her supervision. He received some elementary lessons at the Academy of Fine Arts in Florence, where he got a prize. He made sketches in the Boboli Gardens and in the suburbs. Wherever he went he made careful drawings from nature. At Nice (1862), in the Pyrenees (1865), in Spain (1868), in Rome (1869), at Dresden and in Switzerland (1872), his pencil was never idle. Finally, in the summer of 1874, the family moved to Paris, and his career as a painter was definitively decided upon. He began work in the École des Beaux-Arts, taking courses in anatomy, perspective, and decorative design. In October, at the age of eighteen, he entered the atelier of Carolus Duran. Among the things that he acquired there was a facile and fluent technique quite suited to his temperament, an extraordinary dexterity in seizing instantaneous effects. He was not only the cleverest student in the class; he soon bid fair to outstrip his accomplished master. This precocious virtuosity was not altogether pleasing to Carolus, and a time came when there was a certain coolness between master and pupil. Nevertheless, Sargent always recognized his debt to the teaching of Carolus Duran. Velasquez was held up as the beau ideal, the model, to whom all the young men were advised to look for guidance; and that alone might be regarded as a vital item of artistic faith and practice.

Sargent was twenty years old when he made his first visit to the United States (1876), in company with his mother and his sister Emily. His Americanism has been the subject of much debate; those who knew him best testified to his lifelong loyalty to the country of his fathers. Returning to France in the autumn, he painted his "Gitana," now in the Metropolitan Museum, and the "Rehearsal of the Pasdeloup Orchestra at the Cirque d'Hiver" (Boston Art Museum). In 1877 he sent his first picture to the Salon, a portrait of Miss Watts. He passed the summer at Cancale, at a country house near Lyons, and in Switzerland. In 1878 his "En Route pour la Pêche" (Corcoran Gallery) was shown at the Salon. It was painted at Cancale, where he made several other sketches. To the same year is referred an early portrait, that of Mrs. H. F. Hadden, whose sister posed for the full-length figure called "The Lady with the Rose," exhibited at the Salon of 1881. In the fall of 1878 he spent several weeks at Capri, painting with his usual zest. In 1879 his portrait of Carolus Duran appeared; also the portrait of Robert de Civrieux and his dog (Boston Art Museum), "Luxembourg Gardens at Twilight" (Minneapolis Institute of Art), and a replica of the latter work which went into the great collection of John G. Johnson at Philadelphia. He made his second trip to Spain in 1879, and in January 1880 paid his first visit to Morocco. This expedition brought forth the "Fumée d'Ambre-Gris" which Henry James so much admired. The Spanish journey resulted in the production of "El Jaleo," one of the masterpieces of his early period, now in Fenway Court, Boston; several pictures of the Alhambra; a group of fine copies after Velasquez; and the beautiful "Spanish Courtyard" of the McCagg collection.

The life story of a painter so prolific and indefatigable tends to reduce itself to a long descriptive catalogue of his works. Sargent seldom rested; his so-called vacations became sketching-tours. He was blessed with a fine physique, and felt little need of husbanding his strength. Following the Spanish and Moroccan sojourn of 1880 and a visit to Venice, came a period of pleasant activity to which belong the portraits of the Boit children (Boston Art Museum), the Misses Vickers, and Mrs. Henry White, and the thrice-famous "Madame Gautreau" (Metropolitan Museum), around which centered a veritable tempest of unaccountable abuse when it was first exhibited in Paris. The few sane critics were powerless to offset the storm of disparagement. Sargent was astonished and hurt. The outcry was in fact much ado about nothing. The portrait, painted at "Les Chênes," Paramé, not far from St. Malo, was entirely serious and devoid of malice; it depicted the lady in a costume of her own choosing. The episode is generally supposed to have had something to do with Sargent's departure from Paris for London; however this may have been, he decided upon London as his domicile. So far as press criticism was concerned, he was but turning from Scylla to Charybdis. The *Athenaeum* (June 21, 1884, p. 798) called the portrait of Mrs. White hard, metallic, raw in color, and tasteless. In a plebiscite organized by the *Pall Mall Gazette* in 1886 the popular vote declared by a large majority that "The Misses Vickers" was the worst picture in the Academy exhibition; while the *Spectator* (May 1, 1886, p. 581) pronounced it shallow, pretentious, and untrue. In the aristocratic circles of London, however, the exotic style and brilliance of Sargent's portraits, offer-

ing such a novel contrast to the prosaic academic manner of the British painters of the time, soon brought him all the patrons he could desire, and his vogue steadily increased.

He was twenty-eight when, in 1885, he established himself in the Tite Street studio which was to become the scene of his greatest triumphs. The first of these came from the picture called "Carnation, Lily, Lily, Rose," painted at Broadway, Worcestershire, 1884–86, and exhibited at the Royal Academy in 1887. It is now in the Tate Gallery. It depicts two pretty children working in a flower garden in the twilight. The charm of this composition was felt by every one. It became a universal favorite. It was the first of a long series of pictures of children in which the artist revealed the most tender and lovable side of his nature. He did not usually wear his heart upon his sleeve, but when he was happily inspired by a thoroughly congenial subject he did work of remarkable delicacy and pure beauty. The Davis and Meyer groups, the portraits of the Boit children, Beatrice Goelet, the Hon. Laura Lister, and Homer Saint-Gaudens are to be especially remarked as pages of unsurpassed artistry, picturing with sympathy and understanding that exquisite thing, youth, in all its freshness and purity.

In 1887 Sargent was called to the United States to paint some portraits, among them those of Mrs. H. G. Marquand, Mrs. Charles E. Inches, and Mrs. John L. Gardner. The first exhibition of his works ever held was opened at the St. Botolph Club, Boston, in December 1887. It contained several of the above-mentioned portraits, which had been painted in Frederic P. Vinton's studio; "El Jaleo" (bought by T. Jefferson Coolidge); the large square picture of the Boit children; and a few small figure pieces. The picture of the Boit children, dating from 1882, had been seen in the Salon of 1883 under the title of "Portraits d'Enfants," and it was later shown in the Paris Exposition of 1900. In 1919 it was given to the Boston Art Museum by the daughters of Edward D. Boit in memory of their father, an artist-friend of Sargent's. It is one of the important works of his early period, and one of his best. From the Boston sojourn of 1887–88 dates the pronounced American appreciation which was to Sargent a source of so much satisfaction throughout his career. This was the first of a long series of visits to Boston. That city became his American headquarters; several important exhibitions of his works were held there; a great group of his watercolors was acquired by the Museum of Fine Arts; and all his mural decorations were made for the Public Library, the Art Museum, and the Widener Library of Harvard University.

In the spring of 1889 his father died. In the summer the artist, who was never married, took, with his mother and sisters, Fladbury Rectory, near Pershore, Worcestershire, for three months, and there they entertained a number of guests—Edwin A. Abbey, Alfred Parsons, Alden Weir, M. and Mme. Paul Helleu, Flora Priestley, and Violet Paget (Vernon Lee). Sargent painted a portrait of Miss Priestley which was exhibited at the New English Art Club in 1896 and drew an elaborate and fervent critique from the fastidious George Moore (Downes, *post*, pp. 176-77). He also painted a picture of Helleu sketching on the banks of the Avon while his wife reclined on the ground and leaned against his shoulder (Brooklyn Museum). The portrait of Ellen Terry as Lady Macbeth (now in the Tate Gallery), which was exhibited that year, was pronounced "the picture of the year"; it was also called the "best-hated picture of the year."

The next trip to America occurred in 1890. New York, Philadelphia, and Boston were visited in turn. Sargent painted his celebrated picture of Carmencita, the Spanish dancer, now in the Luxembourg. By many judges it is considered his masterpiece. He made the likenesses of three famous American actors, Edwin Booth, Joseph Jefferson, Lawrence Barrett. In Boston he painted a dozen portraits, the most important being the fine full-length group, "Mother and Child" (Mrs. Edward L. Davis and her small son), exhibited at the National Academy of Design in 1890 and afterwards in many other places. In the spring, in New York, Sargent was one of the ushers at the wedding of his close friend Abbey. The trustees of the Boston Public Library commissioned Sargent and Abbey to paint the mural decorations for two of the rooms of the library just then completed. From this time forth a large part of Sargent's time and energy was given to this mural work. He was already tired of so much portrait painting and welcomed the change. He decided to adopt as the subject of his decoration the development of religious thought from paganism through Judaism to Christianity. In 1891 preliminary work was begun in a huge studio built by Abbey for this purpose in Fairford, Gloucestershire. Sargent had been in Egypt and Greece, getting first-hand data about the pagan deities. The first part of his work (a lunette, frieze, and a section of the ceiling) was completed in 1894 and installed in 1895; and he went to Boston to see to the emplacement. While there, as usual, he painted several portraits. His full-length picture of Ada

Rehan was first seen in 1895; to the same year belong his "Coventry Patmore" (National Portrait Gallery, London) and his stylistic "W. Graham Robertson." The outstanding work of 1897 was the portrait group of Mrs. Carl Meyer and her children; but the culminating event was the appearance in 1898, 1901, and 1902 of the Wertheimer family portraits (Tate Gallery, London). It would be difficult to exaggerate the sensation caused by this prodigious series of works. In them he reached the climax of his life as a portraitist. The record of his achievements would not be complete without at least a mention of his large portrait groups of "Lady Elcho, Mrs. Tennant and Mrs. Adeane" (1900), "The Misses Hunter" (1902), "The Ladies Alexandra, Mary and Theo Acheson" (1902), and the "Four Doctors" (1906) belonging to Johns Hopkins University.

Sargent was made a Royal Academician in 1897. His diploma picture, "A Venetian Interior" (1900), is characterized by all of the finest qualities of his art. The room depicted is the grand sala of the Palazzo Barbaro, and the four figures in it are those of the Curtis family of Boston. In 1899 the Copley Hall Sargent loan exhibition in Boston was opened—the most comprehensive showing of his work held during his lifetime. It contained 110 of his pictures. In 1903 the Boston Art Museum sponsored another loan exhibition of twenty portraits, for the most part of Boston and Philadelphia people. His visits to Boston now increasing in frequency and duration, he established a studio in the Pope Building, Columbus Avenue, which he occupied at intervals during the ensuing twenty years. In this time he crossed and recrossed the Atlantic almost every year; these voyages gave him the only real rest periods he allowed himself to take. He found time to make many summer and autumn trips to Italy, Spain, Switzerland, Majorca, Corfu, and other places, but he was always sketching busily. The fateful summer of 1914 found him in the Dolomites, where he continued to paint serenely for a long time after the war had begun. Early in 1916 he came again to America for the purpose of installing the last of the Boston Public Library decorations. That summer he went off on a sketching expedition to the Canadian Rockies and the Glacier National Park. The beautiful landscape, "Lake O'Hara" (Fogg Art Museum, Harvard University), and a group of watercolors were the principal fruits of this tour. Returning to Boston, he worked hard on the scaffoldings in the library until the Christmas holidays, when the completed decorations were at last unveiled to the public gaze. At about the same time another exhibition of his easel paintings was in progress at the Boston Art Museum; and in 1917 his Rocky Mountain pictures were displayed in a loan exhibition at the Copley Gallery in aid of the American Ambulance Hospital at Paris.

Having completed the library decorations, the artist now undertook to decorate the rotunda of the Art Museum. In the midst of the preparatory studies for this commission, the British Government invited him to go to the front in northern France and to record his impressions of the war for the Imperial War Museum in London. He proceeded at once to the British General Headquarters in June 1918. Thence he went to Bavincourt, to Arras, and to various places in the war zone. He saw very little that was paintable; was taken with influenza and spent a wretched week in a casualty clearing station, under canvas, surrounded by wounded soldiers; and went back to England in October. His picture "Gassed"—a pathetic scene which he actually witnessed—was exhibited in the Royal Academy of 1919. Soon after the close of the war he was commissioned to paint for the National Portrait Gallery, London, a large portrait group of twenty-two members of the British General Staff.

The Sargent exhibition of 1924 in New York, assembled by himself, contained seventy-two works. The press reviews served to prove that a hostile bloc was forming, recruited mostly from the ranks of the modernists. Public opinion was sharply divided, but the opposition was aggressive. In July Sargent left for London to carry to completion the mural paintings for the Boston Art Museum and to execute two or three portrait commissions. His death, which occurred in London in April, was due to heart failure. The funeral, Apr. 18, was private, the burial being at Brookwood, Surrey. Imposing memorial services were held in Westminster Abbey, Apr. 24. Memorial exhibitions were held at the Royal Academy, London, the Metropolitan Museum, New York, and the Boston Art Museum. Honorary degrees were conferred on Sargent by the Universities of Oxford, Cambridge, Harvard, Yale, and Pennsylvania. The list of his medals, prizes, and orders would fill a whole page. He declined a knighthood offered by the premier in 1907, saying that he was an American citizen. In 1918 he was asked to be a candidate for the office of president of the Royal Academy, but he did not choose to run. At the post-mortem sale of his pictures and sketches in 1925, at Christie's, London, 237 items brought a total of about $850,000.

As a portrait painter Sargent may be ranked beneath such masters as Titian, Holbein, Velasquez, Rembrandt, and Hals, but he will be rated as the equal of the best British eighteenth-century painters, Reynolds and Gainsborough. The vitality of his personages insures the future fame of the artist. As a painter of genre he is original, piquant, objective, and often has great charm of style. His interiors in Italy and Spain —the "Venetian Interior," the "Spanish Courtyard," the "Hospital at Granada," the "Breakfast in the Loggia" (Freer Gallery)—are delightful, personal, and full of flavor. In landscape he was not so preëminent, though the "Lake O'Hara" is a handsome canvas, and some of his Alpine subjects have excellent points. His water colors, of which there are large groups in the museums of Brooklyn, Boston, New York, and Worcester, are truly superb for their spontaneity, freedom, luminosity, and limpid style. He was doubtless the most masterful water colorist of his time, with the single exception of Winslow Homer.

As to his mural paintings, there is much to be said pro and con. He daringly violated the accepted canons which place a ban on relief and perspective, and as a consequence his walls do not have the plane surface and vertical aspect demanded by sound architectonic principles. In this respect it cannot be said that his Boston Public Library work, his *magnum opus,* compares favorably with Puvis de Chavannes' mural paintings which adorn the same building. Again, Sargent's want of flatness of modeling is in some sort matched by the overwhelming complexity and superabundant quantity of images and symbols. In a word, he is not simple enough. His redundancy is an esthetic sin. On the other hand, it must be allowed that his splendor of effect, however obtained, is most impressive. It is magnificent, if it is not war. Perhaps it is permissible for a man of great talent to disregard the rules of the game, to flout conventions. Sargent's mental attitude towards his subject is singularly objective; he records, he does not judge; one might call him an unbiased historian, viewing the religious faiths of Pagan, Jew, and Christian, from the outside, without preference and without conviction, simply as a great spectacle. There are those who assert that his Christian symbolism betokens sincere religious feeling, but it would be difficult to establish this contention. His fertility of invention is undeniable. Old ideas are used freely, but they are invested with new forms. They are combined and related with ability and ingenuity. The ancient traditions and doctrines are presented with a new accent. Richness and pictorial effectiveness are not wanting; the intellectual and esthetic grasp is firm. If the work has little of the impassioned conviction and ingenuous sentiment of the age of faith, this is hardly to be imputed to the artist as a serious fault; he was of his own time, and he was true to himself; one can but accept gratefully what he had to give.

Sargent was modest, generous, and absolutely sincere. Adulation and flattery were distasteful to him. He underrated his own ability and at times made fun of his own paintings. He was not avaricious, and cared little for luxuries. He was an accomplished linguist and a musician of talent, but found his chief pleasure in his work.

[Evan Charteris, *John Sargent* (1927); W. H. Downes, *John S. Sargent, His Life and Work* (1925); *The Work of John S. Sargent, R.A.* (1903); introductory note by Alice Meynell; Nathaniel Pousette-Dart, compiler, *John Singer Sargent* (1924); A. L. Baldry, in *Studio*, Feb. 15, Mar. 15, 1900; R. V. S. Berry, in *Art and Archaeology*, Sept. 1924; Christian Brinton, *Modern Artists* (1908); F. W. Coburn, in *Am. Mag. of Art*, Feb. 1917, Jan. 1923; Royal Cortissoz, *Art and Common Sense* (1913), and article in *Scribner's Mag.*, Mar. 1924; Samuel Isham, *The Hist. of Am. Painting* (1905); Henry James, *Picture and Text* (1893); Arthur Layard, in *Die Kunst*, vol. XVII, 1907–08; Robert Ross, in *Art Journal*, Jan. 1911; William Starkweather, in *Mentor*, Oct. 1924; Walter Tittle, in *Illustrated London News*, Apr. 25, 1925; J. C. Van Dyke, *Am. Painting and Its Tradition* (1919); Forbes Watson, in *The Arts*, Mar. 1924; E. W. and C. S. Sargent, *Epes Sargent of Gloucester and His Descendants* (1923); *Boston Evening Transcript*, Apr. 15, 24, 1925.]
                                                  W. H. D.

SARGENT, LUCIUS MANLIUS (June 25, 1786–June 2, 1867), author, antiquary, temperance advocate, was born in Boston, the youngest of seven children of Daniel and Mary (Turner) Sargent, and brother of Henry Sargent [q.v.]. His father was a merchant dealing in fishermen's supplies who had moved from Gloucester to Boston and profited so much by his industry, prudence, and popularity that he occupied what was for those days a conspicuously expensive mansion, although his character was notable for thrift and dread of ostentation. Lucius Manlius attended a number of elementary and secondary schools, including Phillips Exeter Academy, from which he passed to Harvard in 1804. He did not complete his course there, for a pamphlet published by him in 1807, *No. 1 of the New Milk Cheese,* pours furious scorn on an official of the college with whom he had had a dispute about the quality of the food at the commons table. He studied law after leaving college and was admitted to the bar on Feb. 19, 1811, but he never practised to any extent, for he inherited a competence and greatly increased it by conservative speculation. He turned to literature as an avocation, publishing *The Culex of Virgil; with a Translation into English Verse* and a collection

of Latin riddles in 1807 and *Hubert and Ellen,* a volume of poems, in 1812. At the Boston peace celebration on Feb. 22, 1815, an ode of his, "Wreaths for the Chieftain," was sung. On Apr. 3, 1816, he married Mary Binney of Philadelphia, by whom he had three children, one of whom attained the brevet rank of brigadier-general in the Civil War. After the death of his first wife in 1824, he married Sarah Cutler Dunn, July 14, 1825.

He wrote constantly for the newspapers and became well known for his literary interests, but he found a more popular subject in temperance reform, which he took up with characteristic assertiveness. From 1830 till the approach of the Civil War he spoke and wrote on this theme so frequently and vigorously that he became one of the most uncompromising and conspicuous leaders in the crusade against liquor. He wrote *The Temperance Tales* (2 vols., 1848), stories of a tract-like nature bearing such titles as "My Mother's Gold Ring," "I Am Afraid There Is A God," "Groggy Harbor," "An Irish Heart," and others to the number of twenty-one, first published in separate issues between 1833 and 1843. These were widely distributed by religious and temperance societies as well as by Sargent himself.

He also achieved prominence as an antiquary. In 1848 he began a series of weekly articles in the *Boston Evening Transcript* entitled "Dealings with the Dead" (published in book form in 1856), which in spite of their name did not lack light touches. Under such pseudonyms as Sigma, Amgis, Saveall, and others, he wrote for numerous other publications, and he aroused considerable interest by attacking the coolie trade of the British in India (*Evening Transcript,* Apr. 16–Oct. 3, 1856) and by assailing Macaulay for statements derogatory to William Penn (*Dealings with the Dead,* I, pp. 231–69). Though he showed enthusiasm for the past, his efforts were generally directed towards blasting something offensive to him out of existence. At seventy-five he published *The Ballad of the Abolition Blunder-buss* (1861), which abuses Emerson and others for their anti-slavery views as violently as his *Temperance Tales* do the saloonkeeper. Even one of his obituaries refers to him as a man of "harsh prejudices," though it acknowledges the urbanity of his manners in ordinary intercourse and the warmth of his attachment to his kindred and friends. In 1842 Harvard conferred the degree of A.M. on him, thereby recognizing his public services and condoning his undergraduate contumacy, for the violence of which he often expressed regret. He was preeminently a good hater, but he was a conspicuous man in his day and helped to develop a sentiment in favor of prohibition, besides making rather valuable contributions to local history.

[Emma W. and C. S. Sargent, *Epes Sargent of Gloucester and His Descendants* (1923); J. H. Sheppard, *Reminiscences of Lucius Manlius Sargent* (1871); *New England Hist. and Geneal. Reg.*, July 1871; obituaries in *Boston Post* and *Boston Daily Advertiser*, June 4, 1867.]   S. G—n.

SARGENT, NATHAN (May 5, 1794–Feb. 2, 1875), journalist, was born in Putney, Vt., the son of Samuel and Mary (Washburn) Sargent, and seventh in a family of eleven children. He was a descendant of William Sargent, who emigrated from Northampton, England, to Charlestown, Mass., in 1638, and settled in that part of the town which in 1649 was set off as Malden. After receiving an academic education in his native town, Nathan studied law with Judge Phineas White of Putney; later, he studied in the office of Stephen Ross, Troy, N. Y., teaching school at the same time. Admitted to the bar in 1818, he immediately moved to Cahawba, Ala., where he practised law and served for some time as judge of the county and probate courts. On Feb. 14, 1821, he married Rosina (Hodgkinson) Lewis, who became the mother of his four children, three of whom died in infancy. In 1826, because of ill health, he moved to Buffalo, N. Y. About 1830 he gave up his profession of law and established in Philadelphia, Pa., the *Commercial Herald*, a Whig newspaper, which he edited for some years. This venture did not pay financially, however, and he became a successful correspondent of the *United States Gazette*, Philadelphia. His first letter, signed "Oliver Oldschool," under which name he became widely known, appeared in that publication on Jan. 3, 1842.

He was an ardent Whig and later a devoted Republican. In an age of letter writers, he wrote from Washington, D. C., where he went to live in the forties, witty, vivid, sarcastic, but gentlemanly reports of the proceedings in Congress and of events at the Capital. His articles were published in many newspapers throughout the North. A kindly nature and unusual ability as a correspondent gained for him a national reputation. He was honest, faithful to his party, and infrequently very partisan. He accepted the American system and reviewed Tyler's veto message on the tariff in 1842 with pain and indignation. He believed it was suicidal for the Whigs to adopt Tyler in 1840. Congress, he said, was the supreme organism in our free government, not the Jacksonian type of executive. Congress should never strike its flag and legislate at the foot of the throne. His pungent articles were introduced in newspapers as editorials during the forties and his editorial quarrels with the leading Democratic editors were greatly enjoyed by the Whigs. He delighted in poking fun at the Democrats to provoke merriment in their opponents. His description of John C. Calhoun as a debater in Congress is illustrative of his poignant style and manner of describing public characters. "Mr. Calhoun," he wrote (Aug. 8, 1842), "utters his sentences with surprising rapidity and great indistinctness, pausing long between each; his voice is sharp, unmusical and unmodulated, he seems, therefore, to throw his sentences out by jerks, and to stop as if he had run plump against a post or period. Every sentence appears to be an embodiment of a maxim, principle, or axiom . . . and his whole speech a string of these connected, if at all, by very distant ties . . . of reasoning; hence he is one of the most difficult speakers to report." The task which he considered most important was to interpret public opinion for his readers. Abraham Lincoln had no warmer supporter than Oliver Oldschool, who considered him the successor of Henry Clay. His party maxim was *Fas est ab hoste doceri* (It is right to learn from the enemy).

He served as sergeant-at-arms of the House of Representatives (1847–51), as register-general of the United States Land Office (1851–53), as commissioner of customs (1861–71), and for years as the president of the Washington reform school. Among his publications were *Brief Outline of the Life of Henry Clay* (1844), reissued under slightly varying titles, and *Some Public Men and Events* (2 vols., 1875). He was survived by his widow and one daughter.

[*New England Hist. and Geneal. Reg.*, July 1875; J. S. and Aaron Sargent, *Sargent Geneal.* (1895); *National Republican* (Washington), Feb. 3, 1875; A. M. Hemenway, *Vt. Hist. Gazetteer*. vol. V (1891), pt. 2, pp. 246–48.]   W. E. S.

SARGENT, WINTHROP (May 1, 1753–Jan. 3, 1820), soldier, territorial administrator, was born at Gloucester, Mass., the son of Winthrop and Judith (Sanders) Sargent. His ancestor, William, had emigrated from England and received a grant of land in Gloucester in 1678. Winthrop graduated from Harvard College in 1771 and at the outbreak of the Revolution enlisted in the Continental Army, earning by meritorious service the brevet rank of major. In 1786 he was surveyor on the Seven Ranges in Ohio and that same year he attended the meeting in Boston at which the Ohio Company was organized. The next year he was elected secretary of this organization, and during the summer rendered valuable assistance to Manasseh Cutler in the purchase of the land which the company proposed to settle. He reached Marietta in July 1788, and took an active part in the planting of the new colony.

On Oct. 7, 1787, he was designated by Congress as secretary of the Territory Northwest of the River Ohio. During the frequent and prolonged absences of Gov. Arthur St. Clair [q.v.], Sargent assumed the executive responsibilities with the same disinterested devotion to public duty that he always manifested. Recent research has cleared him of the criticism formerly made of his course in the organization of Wayne County (Detroit) in 1796. He was St. Clair's adjutant-general in the expedition of 1791 against the Indians and in the defeat at Fort Recovery, Nov. 4, 1791, he was twice wounded. After this defeat, as acting governor he organized the militia to repel anticipated Indian attacks. On Feb. 9, 1789, he married Rowena Tupper, who died in 1790, shortly after the birth of an infant son who did not long survive.

In 1798 Sargent resigned his secretaryship to become the first governor of Mississippi Territory. His Federalism, impartial enforcement of law, and unfortunate connection with one of the factions in the territory led to such criticism that President Jefferson refused to reappoint him in 1801, and he retired to the plantation of his second wife, formerly Mary (McIntosh) Williams, whom he had married Oct. 24, 1798. He died in 1820, on a north-bound steamboat near New Orleans. Two sons survived him.

Sargent's numerous papers reveal the varied intellectual interests which led to his membership in the American Philosophical Society, the American Academy of Arts and Sciences, and the Massachusetts Historical Society. He contributed to the *Memoirs* of the American Academy "List of Forest and Other Trees Northwest of the River Ohio" (vol. II, pt. I, 1793), "Meteorological Observations" (vol. III, pt. 1, 1809), and "An Account of Several Shocks of an Earthquake" (vol. III, pt. 2, 1815); and in 1796 published *Papers Relative to Certain American Antiquities,* later reprinted in the *Transactions of the American Philosophical Society* (vol. IV, 1799). As a public servant he was conscientious, energetic, and patriotic in the discharge of responsibilities placed on him, although his Federalism and his New England training made him unpopular amid the democracy of the frontier and involved him in many unpleasant controversies. His contribution to the West of his day was that of one who modestly aids in the laying of foundations.

[Sargent Papers in Mass. Hist. Soc., Boston, and Ohio State Archaeol. and Hist. Soc., Columbus; *Diary of Col. Winthrop Sargent during the Campaign of* MDCCXCI (1851), repr. in *Ohio Archæol. and Hist. Quart.,* July 1924; with extracts from Jour. of 1793–95; *The Records of the Original Proc. of the Ohio Company* (2 vols., 1917), ed. by A. B. Hulbert; *The Miss. Terr. Arch.,* 1798–1803 (1905), ed. by Dunbar Rowland; *The St. Clair Papers* (2 vols., 1882), ed. by W. H. Smith; *Am. State Papers, Misc.,* I (1834), 233–41; *Papers in Relation to the Official Conduct of Gov. Sargent* (1801), and *Political Intolerance . . . Exemplified in a Recent Removal from Office* (1801), attacks on Jefferson for removing Sargent; Dunbar Rowland, *Hist. of Miss.* (2 vols., 1925); Winthrop Sargent, *Early Sargents of New England* (1922); E. W. and C. S. Sargent, *Epes Sargent of Gloucester and His Descendants* (1923); B. H. Pershing, "Winthrop Sargent," in *Ohio Archæol. and Hist. Quart.,* Oct. 1926, and "Winthrop Sargent: A Builder of the Old Northwest," dissertation (1927), Univ. of Chicago.]

B. H. P.

SARGENT, WINTHROP (Sept. 23, 1825– May 18, 1870), author, grandson of Winthrop Sargent [q.v.] and son of George Washington and Margaret (Percy) Sargent, was born in Philadelphia, Pa., where he received his early education. He graduated from the University of Pennsylvania in 1845 and received a law degree at Harvard two years later. He began the practice of law in Boston, but he enjoyed an income large enough to make him independent of his profession and he was more interested in the history of the American Revolution than in his legal career. On April 22, 1851, he married Sarah Ellery Gray of Boston and soon after his marriage established himself in Philadelphia, where he remained until the outbreak of the Civil War. Shortly after his return to Philadelphia in 1851 he became interested in the military history of the French and Indian War and edited for the Historical Society of Pennsylvania *The History of an Expedition against Fort Du Quesne, in 1755; under Major-General Edward Braddock. . . .* This work, published in 1855, was based upon manuscript sources and edited with a skill not then common in American historiography; it remained for many years the standard work on the Braddock expedition. In 1860 he published an edition of *The Loyal Verses of Joseph Stansbury and Doctor Jonathan Odell, Relating to the American Revolution,* characterized by moderate and very fair-minded notes. At about the same time he ended his labors on Major André, whom he sought to rehabilitate, by the publication of the *Life and Career of Major John André* (1861). Sargent's view was extreme in favor of André. In spite of a florid treatment and other literary defects, his book was long regarded as the definitive work upon the subject.

During the Civil War he lived in Mississippi, where, at Natchez, his father was brutally murdered in 1864. At the close of the war he moved to New York City and began the practice of law, but he was depressed by the death of his father and his own poor health. He soon gave up the law to seek rest in Europe. He died of consumption in Paris in 1870, survived by one son.

[Emma W. and C. S. Sargent, *Epes Sargent of Gloucester and His Descendants* (1923), brief biog. sketch and complete bibliog.; private information from James W. Winter of Paris; obituary in *N. Y. Times,* May 19, 1870.]   F. M.

SARPY, PETER A. (Nov. 3, 1805–Jan. 4, 1865), fur trader, was probably the first white resident of Nebraska. He was born at St. Louis of French parentage, the second son of Gregoire Berald and Palagie (L'Abadie) Sarpy. His father was a merchant and fur trader. Peter was favored with the best educational and social opportunities in St. Louis. His father died in 1824, and his elder brother, John B. Sarpy, was employed in the firm of Berthold & Chouteau, the promoters of the Missouri Fur Company, and later associated with the American Fur Company. At an early age, probably 1823, Peter was employed as clerk of John P. Cabanné, the agent for the Missouri and American Fur companies at Council Bluffs. He was put in charge of the post established at Bellevue on the west bank of the Mississippi. For Cabanné he executed the arrest of the Leclerc party, 1832, and this is one explanation of his military title. He was unusually successful in dealing with the Indians. Nicomi, his Indian wife, the daughter of an Iowa chief, was a strong ally, but her generosity cost him large quantities of supplies.

As a licensed fur trader at the fork of the Missouri and Platte rivers he commanded a post of strategic importance. Situated on the edge of the Indian reservation he carried on a large business with both the natives and the whites. Frémont, returning in 1842, employed Sarpy to build a ship for him and sold his overland equipment at Sarpy's post. Brigham Young on his first expedition sought the trader's assistance, and the latter, after offering supplies and ferrying the party over the river, negotiated with the Indians for a friendly passage and escorted the Mormon leader beyond the point of greatest danger. Sarpy had a significant part in the negotiation of the land session treaties with the Omaha and Oto Indians in 1854. The next year two regiments of Nebraska volunteers were raised for defense against the Indians, and he was made quartermaster of the brigade. To carry the immigrants and travelers he established ferries over the Missouri, the Elkhorn, and Loup rivers. He introduced a steam ferry service between St. Mary, Iowa, and Bellevue, Nebr. He also established a post store at St. Mary chiefly for supplying the

white travelers and settlers, and he founded the St. Mary *Gazette*. He participated in the laying out of the towns of Bellevue and Decatur, Nebr. In 1862 he removed to Plattsmouth, Nebr., where he lived until his death. He was buried in St. Louis. He left no descendants, and his estate, except an annuity for Nicomi during her lifetime, went to relatives in St. Louis. He was a colorful leader, short of stature with a handsome face and piercing dark eyes, a man of prompt action, unfailing courage, and vivid emotions. The Indians called him "White Chief."

[Date of birth from statement of the record in Baptism Register Diocesan Chancery Office, St. Louis, given in a paper on Sarpy before the Nebraska Historical Society in 1921 by the Rev. M. A. Shine, now in possession of Nebraska Historical Society; J. S. Morton, *Illustrated History of Nebraska,* vol. I (1905); H. M. Chittenden, *The American Fur Trade of the Far West* (1902), vol. I; J. C. Frémont, *Report of the Exploring Expedition to the Rocky Mountains* (1845); *Nebr. State Hist. Soc. Proc. and Colls.,* 2 ser., vols. I, II, V (1894–1902); *Nebr. State Hist. Soc. Pubs.,* vol. XX (1922); *Omaha Daily Herald,* Dec. 8, 1874; *Papillion Times* (Hist. ed.), June 18, 1931.]   J. L. S.

SARTAIN, EMILY (Mar. 17, 1841–June 18, 1927), painter, engraver, educator, was born in Philadelphia, the daughter of John Sartain [*q.v.*] and Susannah Longmate (Swaine) Sartain. Her great-grandfather, Barak Longmate, and her grandfather, John Swaine, were both noted English engravers. Samuel and William Sartain [*qq.v.*] were her brothers. Reared in a family devoted to art and literature, Emily's talent developed early and as a girl she accompanied her father on trips to Europe and studied in great art centers. She learned mezzotint engraving from her father and worked with him on portraits and prints, becoming the only woman mezzotint engraver of her day on either side of the Atlantic. After an intensive year of study abroad, she returned to America to attain success in book-portrait work and the engraving of large framing prints. Subsequent study from 1864 to 1870 under Christian Schussele [*q.v.*], at the Pennsylvania Academy of the Fine Arts, four years more in the studio of the French painter, Evariste Luminais, in Paris, and two winters in the galleries of Italy, completed her education in the handling of colors. In 1875 a three-quarter-length portrait of Mlle. Del Sarte was accepted by the Paris Salon together with a genre picture "La Pièce de Conviction" which, under the title of "The Reproof," was awarded a medal the following year at the Centennial Exhibition in Philadelphia. The artist now divided her time between portrait-painting and engraving. In 1881 and again in 1883 she was awarded the Mary Smith prize at the Pennsylvania Academy of the Fine Arts for the best work shown by a woman artist. From

1881 to 1883 she was art editor of *Our Continent,* an illustrated journal published in Philadelphia, and of the de luxe edition of *New England Bygones* by Ella H. Rollins, published in 1883.

In 1886 she accepted the invitation of the board of directors of the School of Design for Women to become principal of the institution, thus beginning her career as an educator. She was made a director of the Philadelphia public schools in 1890, but pressure of work forced her to resign two years later. Her preoccupation with educational work was detrimental to her own personal career as an artist, although she still executed a few oil portraits, and finished two large etchings for New York publishers. For the Columbian Exposition in Chicago in 1893, she acted as chairman of the committee of women artists who decorated the women's room of the Pennsylvania State Building with murals and paintings. She was also the first woman ever appointed to the bureau of judges for an international exposition —a distinction which, however, barred her from awards in Chicago. In 1899 she was invited to London to speak before the International Council of Women on opportunities offered women of America in applied design. The following year she was appointed official delegate to represent the United States in Paris at the International Congress of Instruction in Drawing, rendering a similar service in Berne, Switzerland, in 1904. An exhibit at the Pan-American Exposition at Buffalo in 1901 brought her an honorable mention for oil portraits, and her various services in the interest of art and education brought a long list of medals, certificates and diplomas, including one from the London Society of Literature, Science and Art.

Until the outbreak of the World War she spent the summer months studying in Europe. She was an accomplished linguist in French, Italian, German, and Spanish. After thirty-three years as principal of the School of Design for Women she resigned active work, becoming principal emeritus. During the many years of her public life she had been interested in local as well as in international cultural movements and sponsored the organization of many art and literary clubs in Philadelphia. After her retirement she spent two years in California, then went to Europe, where she established residence in Paris. In 1927 she returned to Philadelphia where she died of acute heart trouble. She is buried in Monument Cemetery.

[A short account of the life of Emily Sartain by her niece, Harriet Sartain, Dean of the School of Design for Women, deposited at Strawberry Manshion in Philadelphia; C. E. Clement, Laurence Hutton, *Artists of the Nineteenth Century* (1907), vol. II; J. D. Champlain, ed., *Cyclop. of Painters and Paintings,* vol. IV

(1887); Mantle Fielding, *Dict. of Am. Painters, Sculptors and Engravers* (1926); *Who's Who in America,* 1926–27; *Public Ledger* (Philadelphia), June 19, 1927.]
D. G—y.

SARTAIN, JOHN (Oct. 24, 1808–Oct. 25, 1897), engraver, publisher, was born in London, the son of John Sartain and Ann (Burgess) Sartain. The father died when John was eight years of age, and four years later the lad, in an effort to help support the family, entered upon his first job with an Italian pyrotechnist and scene artist, who made him "powder monkey" and assistant to the head scene-painter in the "department of steam, smoke and fire" at Charles Kemble's Theatre and at Vauxhall Gardens (*Reminiscences, post,* p. 52). Soon a relative set him the task of tending turnpike, but he was rescued from this occupation by a bequest from his grandmother. He decided then to become an engraver and apprenticed himself for seven years in 1823 to John Swaine to learn heraldry and letter engraving. He practised drawing in his spare time and his talent attracted the attention of William Young Ottley, who was writing an historical sketch of the early Florentine school of painters. Ottley gained Swaine's permission to have the apprentice execute eighteen plates and work up fourteen left previously unfinished. Through this work, published in 1826, Sartain was introduced to the art of the masters and met such distinguished men as Sir Thomas Lawrence and Thomas Sully. When Sartain returned to his apprenticeship, he accepted occasional commissions for engravings, dividing the profits with Swaine. One of these plates, sold to Eliakim Littell [*q.v.*] in 1830, was engraved in mezzotint for Sartain's instructor in miniature, Henry Richter, after that artist's picture "The Tight Shoe."

He was married to Susannah Longmate Swaine, daughter of his employer, on Jan. 11, 1830, and six months later sailed with his bride to America. He secured a letter of introduction to John Vaughn and through him held an exhibition at the Franklin Institute. His first important commission was from Thomas Sully who had him engrave his portrait of Bishop White. Commissions followed from the painters, Jacob Eicholtz and John Neagle [*qq.v.*], and from the Penn Society. He also executed plates for the *Gentleman's Magazine,* the *Casket,* and *Godey's Lady's Magazine.* In 1841 he became associated with *Graham's Magazine,* and through that medium introduced pictorial illustration as a distinctive feature of American periodicals. His prompt success necessitated the turning out of one plate every two weeks in addition to other work which, in 1847, included the owning and editing of a quarto-volume entitled *The American Gallery of Art*. In 1843 Sartain entered upon an ill-starred venture as proprietor of *Campbell's Foreign Semi-Monthly Magazine*. He also had a financial interest in the *Eclectic Museum*, but neither was profitable. After Graham's failure in 1848, however, he joined with William Sloanaker in purchasing for $5,000 the *Union Magazine* and creating under the name, *Sartain's Union Magazine of Literature and Art,* a publication of rare cultural value. The first issue appeared in January 1849. The noted men and women writers of the day, including Longfellow, John Howard Payne, Lucy Larcom, Harriet Martineau and Edgar Allan Poe, whose poem, "The Bells," Sartain was the first to publish, contributed to *Sartain's Magazine*. The venture was, however, a monetary failure, and Sartain spent the next seven and a half years paying off its debts.

When his magazine was discontinued in 1852, the engraver turned to general work, his output of plates being estimated at 1500. He made engravings and vignettes for early banknotes and indulged his versatility further in oil-painting, watercolor, and miniature. In 1855 he attended the international exposition in Paris, being entrusted in 1862 with a second mission to deliver diplomas of honorary membership in the Pennsylvania Academy of the Fine Arts to European notables. Sartain was made chief of the bureau of art for the Centennial Exhibition in Philadelphia in 1875, and was honored by four Italian societies of letters and the arts. In 1886, as chief of the American art department, he began collecting pictures to exhibit at a London exposition. In 1885 he received the Star of Merit (Laureat) of the rajah of Calcutta and in 1892 was made Commander of the Royal Order of Melusine by the princess of Jerusalem, Cyprus, and Armenia. About this time, also, he was made a Freeman of London. For fourteen years he was vice-president of the Philadelphia School of Design for Women, with which his daughter Emily Sartain [*q.v.*] was closely associated. He was a prominent Freemason, a member of the Artists Fund Society (president in 1844) and of the Society of St. George. Sartain's additional skill as an able architectural designer was responsible for the unique arrangement of galleries and rooms at the Pennsylvania Academy of the Fine Arts, of which he was a director and Academician for twenty-three years, and for the design of the monuments to Washington and Lafayette at Monument Cemetery in Philadelphia.

The first important mezzotint produced in the United States was executed by Sartain shortly after his arrival from England. It was after Neagle's painting, "Old Age." His "Christ Rejected" after Benjamin West, and "The Iron-Worker and King Solomon" after Christian Schüssele, are among the largest and finest ever executed in America (see Clement and Hutton, *post*, p. 235). Sartain had eight children of whom three, Samuel, William and Emily [*qq.v.*], were all distinguished. When he died in Philadelphia, Sartain had completed his autobiographical volume *Reminiscences of a Very Old Man,* published in 1899. He is buried in Monument Cemetery.

[John Sartain, *Reminiscences of a Very Old Man* (1899), *Annals of the Sartain Tribe* (privately printed, 1886), Mantle Fielding, *Dict. of Am. Painters, Sculptors and Engravers* (1926); *Bryan's Dict. of Painters and Engravers*, vol. V (1905); C. E. Clement, Laurence Hutton, *Artists of the Nineteenth Century* (1907), vol. II; *A Biog. Album of Prominent Pennsylvanians*, vol. II (1889); *Public Ledger* (Philadelphia), Oct. 26, 1897, Mar. 15, 1908.]   D. G—y.

SARTAIN, SAMUEL (Oct. 8, 1830–Dec. 20, 1906), engraver, the eldest child of John Sartain [*q.v.*] and Susannah Longmate (Swaine) Sartain, was born in Philadelphia, a few months after his parents had come to America. Before the boy was seventeen years of age he won fame among artists by engraving Harlow's portrait of Benjamin West. He had studied the art under his father, and at the Pennsylvania Academy of the Fine Arts. About 1851 he established his own business in Philadelphia, working for various publishers. He was commissioned by the Art Union of Philadelphia in 1854 to engrave the painting "Clear the Track" by Christian Schüssele [*q.v.*], and won for this work a silver medal from the Franklin Institute. Many of his best plates were engraved after works by Peale, Sully, and Neagle. He excelled especially in mezzotint and line engravings, and his skill was sought for illustrating biographical works with portrait-engravings. One of his most important engravings, a portrait of Alexander Johnston Cassatt [*q.v.*], was completed a year before Sartain's death. He also engraved many plates of biblical subjects popular during the period of the Civil War. From these plates enormous editions were printed and sold. In some instances sales were so great that the original plate was worn beyond repair and a duplicate plate had to be substituted to satisfy the demand. Among the most popular were: "Christ Blessing Little Children," after Eastlake; "One of the Chosen," after Guy; "Christ Stilling the Tempest," after Hamilton; and "The Song of the Angels," after Moran. Sartain's patience and technical dexterity were evidenced in his mechanical engraving of the Lord's Prayer on a silver dollar.

An active interest in various phases of scientific research led the artist to establish contact with the Franklin Institute, of which he was manager for thirty years and treasurer for the last fifteen years of his life. He was also an expert amateur photographer, and for many years was vice-president of the Photographic Society of Philadelphia. He was married to Harriet Amelia Judd of Waterbury, Conn., on Dec. 11, 1854. She became one of the leading pioneer women physicians of the country, combining domestic and professional life until her retirement from active work in 1889. They had three children, one of whom died young. Sartain died in Philadelphia.

[Information from the family; *Who's Who in America*, 1903–05; John Sartain, *Annals of the Sartain Tribe* (privately printed, 1886); *Philadelphia and Popular Philadelphians* (1891); Mantle Fielding, *Dict. of Am. Painters, Sculptors and Engravers* (1926); *Public Ledger* (Philadelphia), Dec. 21, 1906.] D. G—y.

SARTAIN, WILLIAM (Nov. 21, 1843–Oct. 25, 1924), painter, was the third son of John Sartain [*q.v.*] and Susannah Longmate (Swaine) Sartain. He was born in Philadelphia, Pa., and received his academic training in the public high school of that city. His early leaning toward art was encouraged by his father, under whom the boy studied drawing and engraving until he entered the classes in the Pennsylvania Academy of the Fine Arts in 1867. In 1864 he produced a plate titled "Young America Crushing Rebellion and Sedition," and in 1866, "Little Samuel," a plate after a painting by James Sant. Although well on the road to success as an etcher of portraits and mezzotints, young Sartain turned definitely to painting at the age of twenty-four and worked for a year under Christian Schussele [*q.v.*].

He went abroad in 1868 to continue his study at the École Nationale Supérieure des Beaux Arts in Paris and under Léon Bonnat, and remained in Europe for eight years. He sketched in Spain, England, Holland, Belgium, Germany, and Italy, spending several winters in Seville and Rome, and the year 1874 in Algiers. He collected a valuable note-book of material from which, in later years, he could develop landscapes and figure compositions. While in Italy and Algiers he painted such subjects as "View in the Street in Algiers," "Arab Cemetery," "Tombs of the Saints at Bouzareah," and made studies of Italian types. It was in 1874 that he completed his "Narcissus," a canvas now owned by Smith College, Northampton, Mass. His first success came when he exhibited some of his work in London in 1875 and was "hung on the line," an honor infrequently bestowed upon foreigners. This recog-

nition encouraged him to make his début in an exhibition at the National Academy of Design in New York City in 1876. With his reputation already established, he returned to the United States the next year and settled in New York. Using the sketch material from his European note-book, he produced "Nubian Scheik" in 1879–80, and "A Chapter of the Koran" in 1883.

In 1879 he began a parallel career as teacher when he was put in charge of all the life classes of the Art Students' League at Cooper Union. He also taught for some years at the Philadelphia School of Design for Women of which his father was vice-president and his sister Emily Sartain [*q.v.*] was principal. By 1880 he was well established in New York, and was in that year elected an Associate National Academician. The following year he received a silver medal in an exhibition in Boston, and in 1884 held a special exhibition of his own at the Williams and Everett's gallery in that city, being warmly received by the critics. In 1887 he won honorable mention in Philadelphia; at the Pan-American Exposition in Buffalo in 1901 he won a bronze medal; and at the Charleston Exposition of 1902 he was granted a silver medal.

Sartain's special interest and talent lay in landscape-painting, and such canvases as "The Valley" (1902) and "The Passing Shower" (1903) illustrate his gift for portraying wide expanses of earth and sky with the simple devices of mass composition and a limited use of color. In 1910 he sent some of his work to the international exposition at Buenos Aires, winning a silver medal and the honor of purchase by the Argentine government. His "Nubian Scheik" was also purchased by the French government for its collection in the Luxembourg. Sartain is further represented in various public and private collections in the United States, including that of the Corcoran Gallery in Washington, D. C., and the Metropolitan Museum in New York City. He was active in American art affairs from the moment he returned to his native land, being a founder of the Society of American Artists, and, later in his life, president of the New York Art Club. He was also an occasional contributor on art subjects to magazines.

Thirty years before his death actually occurred, it was reported that he had died. One of the leading art dealers on Fifth Avenue gave credence to the rumor and enhanced the value of Sartain's pictures by trying to corner the market. Sartain, however, was quietly painting in a New England village. He was never married.

[Information from the family; *Who's Who in America*, 1924–25; Arthur Hoeber, "William Sartain, Painter," *New England Mag.*, Mar. 1903; J. D. Champlain, ed., *Cyclop. of Painters and Painting,* vol. IV (1887); Mantle Fielding, *Dict. of Am. Painters, Sculptors and Engravers* (1926); *Bryan's Dict. of Painters and Engravers,* vol. V (1905); *Art World,* May 1917; *N. Y. Times,* Oct. 26, 1924.] D. G—y.

SARTWELL, HENRY PARKER (Apr. 18, 1792–Nov. 15, 1867), physician, botanist, was born at Pittsfield, Mass., of Scotch ancestry, the son of Eleanor (Crofut) and Levi Sartwell, a mechanic. Of vigorous physique and adventurous spirit, he early left home and went to Utica, N. Y., where he began to study medicine under the tutelage of a local physician. He finished work with his preceptor and was granted a license to practise medicine by the Oneida County Medical Society on Sept. 7, 1811. With a horse, saddle, and bridle, purchased on credit, he started for New Hartford, N. Y., where he soon had a good practice, owing largely to his agreeable personality and his successful treatment of his first patients. In riding about the country on professional business, he found an opportunity to cultivate a boyhood interest in natural history and began to collect various specimens, at this period chiefly minerals. His collection, which became quite extensive, was later acquired by the Penn Yan Academy. During the War of 1812, he served as surgeon in the United States army and at the end of the war settled in Springville, N. Y. He removed thence to Bethel (later Gorham), continuing his practice, and there began the study of botany which later made him widely known. In April 1832 he removed to Penn Yan, N. Y., where he lived and practised his profession until his death. He is said to have been married four times.

A highly respected member of the medical profession in New York and for a time president of the Yates County Medical Society, he was also widely known locally for his knowledge of geology, mineralogy, and natural history, and he contributed liberally to *Catalogue of Plants Found in Oneida County and Vicinity* (1865) by John Alsop Paine [*q.v.*]. At one time he made a considerable collection of insects, which was later destroyed by fire, while his meteorological observations were so completely and carefully prepared that they are now on reference at the Smithsonian Institution. He was also an expert horticulturist. His extensive and thorough knowledge of the subjects he pursued places him unquestionably in the front rank of early American naturalists. The branch he chiefly cultivated, however, was botany. He became acquainted, largely by correspondence, with the leading botanists of his time, both American and European, and often sent them specimens and even quite large collections of plants. The genus

Sartwellia was named for him, and he was regarded as a capable, reliable, and energetic collector. His own most valuable work is *Carices Americae Septentrionalis Exsiccatae,* of which two volumes were published, 1848–50; the third he was engaged on at the time of his death. His herbarium, the work of nearly a half century, consists of about eight thousand specimens, many gathered by exchange with botanists in all parts of the world. It now forms part of the collection of Hamilton College, Clinton, N. Y., which conferred upon him the honorary degree of Ph.D. in 1864.

[*Yates County Chronicle,* Nov. 21, 1867, Nov. 4, 1868, and Oct. 28, 1869; *Amer. Jour. Sci. and Arts,* Jan. 1868; *Ann. Report of . . . Smithsonian Inst.,* 1871; *Am. Ann. Cyc.,* 1867; H. A. Kelly and W. L. Burrage, *Am. Medic. Biogs.* (1920); C. S. Sargent, ed., *The Sci. Papers of Asa Gray* (1889), vol. II; *Buffalo Commercial Advertiser,* Nov. 18, 1867.] C. W. D.

SASLAVSKY, ALEXANDER (Feb. 8, 1876–Aug. 2, 1924), violinist and conductor, was born at Kharkov, Russia, the son of Michael and Anna (Gantz) Saslavsky. He was trained as a violinist by Gorski in Kharkov, and later by Jakob Gruen in Vienna. In 1893 he was graduated from the Vienna Conservatory of Music. During the same year he made a concert tour of Canada, and then went to New York City, where he became one of the first violins of the New York Symphony Society. He was a member of this organization for twenty-five years, and in 1903 he became concert-master and assistant conductor under Walter Damrosch. On one occasion in 1911 he took the orchestra to Spokane, Wash., for a five weeks' engagement and conducted two concerts daily. In 1904 Saslavsky was one of the organizers of the Russian Symphony Orchestra, and for four years acted as its concert-master, until he resigned because of the conflict with his duties as concert-master of the New York Symphony Society. He settled in Los Angeles, Cal., in 1918 and the following year became concert-master of the newly formed Philharmonic Orchestra of that city. He remained in California until his death in San Francisco.

During his entire career Saslavsky was important as a teacher, and for his work in introducing chamber music to a larger public. In 1906 and 1907 he organized two string quartets. He spent his summers in the Northwest, giving chamber-music concerts in Denver, Colo., and other cities. He often appeared as a soloist, both in recital and playing concertos with orchestra. He introduced many new works in his programs, and as soloist with the Russian Symphony Orchestra he gave New York and other American cities first hearings of such compositions as

Mlynarski's violin concerto, a romance and caprice by Rubinstein, and the newly discovered violin *Concerto in C* by Haydn. A contemporary spoke of Saslavsky as an "artist who has worked unceasingly in the interests of true art and artistic ideals . . . a remarkable violinist, possessed of all the necessary attributes a player should possess—a fine, big tone, faultless intonation, complete mastery of the bow, a genuinely artistic sense of interpretation—and, above all, a thorough musician in everything he undertakes . . ." (Saenger, *post,* p. 1270). On June 18, 1906, he was married to C. Izolee Todd of Boston, Mass.

[Material regarding Saslavsky is meager. There is a brief account in *Grove's Dict. of Music and Musicians,* vol. IV (1928) and the *Am. Supp.* (1930), in *Who's Who in America,* 1924–25, and in *Baker's Biog. Dict. of Musicians* (3rd ed., 1919). See also Gustav Saenger, "Alexander Saslavsky, Soloist—Concertmaster—Conductor," *Musical Observer,* Apr. 1913; an obit. article by Alfred Metzger, *Pacific Coast Musical Rev.,* Aug. 11, 1924; and *San Francisco Chronicle,* Aug. 3, 1924.]

J. T. H.

SASSACUS (*c.* 1560–June 1637), chief sachem of the Pequots in 1633, was born probably near Groton, Conn., the son of Wopigwooit, whom he succeeded to leadership in the tribe. About the time of his accession the tribal power declined as a result of war with the Dutch and the defection of the Mohegan chieftain, Uncas [*q.v.*]. Relations with the English settlers, too, were strained; but a treaty of submission staved off a breach with them until the fall of 1636, when an expedition sent from Massachusetts to enforce the terms of the agreement precipitated hostilities. Sassacus tried without success to bring the Narragansetts into league with him, urging that unless a stand were made the white men would soon overrun the whole country. During the ensuing winter and spring his followers made frequent raids upon the Connecticut settlements. Finally, in May 1637, the new colony determined to end the irregular warfare by a vigorous offensive. John Mason [*q.v.*], with a small force, made a sudden attack upon the savage stronghold situated on the Mystic River and, according to his own estimate, slaughtered nearly 700 Indian men, women, and children (Orr, *post,* pp. 21–29). The stroke was decisive. The bands separated and were soon either subjugated or exterminated while Sassacus, himself, fleeing westward, was assassinated by the Mohawks.

[Charles Orr, *Hist. of the Pequot War* (1897); "Letters of Roger Williams," ed. by J. R. Bartlett, *Narragansett Club Publications,* 1 ser., vol. VI (1874); J. W. De Forest, *Hist. of the Indians of Connecticut* (1851); *Bradford's Hist. of Plymouth Plantation* (1908), ed. by W. T. Davis; John Winthrop, *The Hist. of New England,* vol. I (1825), ed. by James Savage; F. W. Hodge, *Handbook of Am. Indians,* pt. II (1910).]

G. P. B.

SATTERLEE, HENRY YATES (Jan. 11, 1843–Feb. 22, 1908), Episcopal clergyman, first bishop of the diocese of Washington, was born in New York City, the second of eight children. The Satterlees were an old English county family of Suffolk and Devonshire. Benedict, the founder of the American line, emigrated to New London, Conn., in 1685. Edward, Henry's grandfather, settled in Albany; his son, another Edward, the bishop's father, a well educated and cultivated man, had marked artistic and literary tastes. His wife, Jane Yates, came of ancestry noted for public service. Her grandfather, Christopher Yates, served on General Schuyler's staff in the Revolution. One of his sons, Joseph Christopher [*q.v.*], was governor of New York from 1823 to 1825. Another, Henry, the bishop's grandfather, served as state senator and as mayor of Schenectady, N. Y. To his mother the bishop chiefly owed his spiritual sensitiveness and strong convictions.

His young boyhood was passed in Albany, but in 1856 the family moved to New York, where he attended the Columbia Grammar School, and, in 1863, received the degree of B.A. from Columbia College. After a serious inclination to a military career, he decided on the ministry, and was prepared at the General Theological Seminary in New York. Ordained deacon on Nov. 21, 1865, he was appointed assistant minister in Zion Parish, Wappinger Falls, the following September. On June 30, 1866, he was married to Jane Lawrence Churchill of New York, and on Jan. 11, 1867, he was ordained priest. Eight years later, he succeeded to the rectorship of the parish. At Wappinger Falls were born his two children.

In 1882 he accepted the rectorship of Calvary Parish, New York City. He rapidly became a power in the community and in the counsels of the Church, giving early proof of that capacity for leadership which marked his later years. Twice he declined elections to the episcopate, in Ohio (1887) and in Michigan (1889). In 1895, he issued the most important of his several books: *A Creedless Gospel and the Gospel Creed.* In it he endeavored to show that Christianity is not a mere human aspiration, but a dramatic self-revealing of God, in the person of Jesus Christ, not only in past history, but in present experience. This creed was the center of his faith and the source of his spiritual power. A few years later he published *New Testament Churchmanship and the Principles upon Which It Was Founded* (1899).

In 1896, he was elected bishop of the newly formed diocese of Washington. His parochial ministry of twenty years, almost equally divided between a country town and the metropolis, had brought him into close touch with every stratum of American life. This experience proved an admirable equipment for his new work. In organizing his diocese, he kept in mind the potential influence which the Episcopal Church in Washington, if fully equipped and wisely led, might wield in the nation's spiritual life. This ideal led to his vision of a national cathedral, fully furnished for its mission by the beauty and majesty of its architecture and the appeal of its spiritual ministrations. He threw himself into the cathedral project with dynamic faith and courage. Yet he was no visionary; practical wisdom marked each step. At his death, no stone of the great building of his dreams was in its place save the foundation stone: but every development of Washington Cathedral, material and spiritual alike, has been in line with his far-seeing plans.

President Theodore Roosevelt, who came into close contact with the bishop, wrote of him: "To an unusual degree, he combined spiritual-mindedness with the purpose to do efficient, practical work and I do not think any one came in contact with him without becoming conscious of a certain elevation of thought and temper, and the power of inspiring others" (Brent, *post*, p. 117). His body now lies beneath the altar of the Bethlehem Chapel, which forms the crypt of the choir and apse of the cathedral and was built in his memory by loving friends.

[C. H. Brent, *A Master Builder; Being the Life and Letters of Henry Yates Satterlee* (1916); *Who's Who in America*, 1908–09; *Living Church*, Feb. 29, 1908; *Churchman*, Feb. 29, 1908; *Evening Star* (Washington), Feb. 22, 1908.]
P. M. R.

SATTERLEE, RICHARD SHERWOOD (Dec. 6, 1798–Nov. 10, 1880), army surgeon, was born in Fairfield, Herkimer County, N. Y., the son of Major William Satterlee, an officer of Connecticut troops in the Revolutionary army, and Hannah (Sherwood) Satterlee. His native town was the seat of Fairfield Academy, with a medical college and faculty which in his day ranked with the best in the country. It is probable that he obtained his education here, though he did not obtain a medical degree. He was licensed to practise in 1818 and moved to Seneca County, N. Y., and shortly thereafter to Detroit, Mich., where, on Feb. 25, 1822, he entered the United States army as an assistant surgeon. In this city in June 1827, he was married to Mary S. Hunt. His early years in the army were spent in routine duty in frontier posts of the Middle West. During the Seminole War in Florida he

served with the brigade of Col. Zachary Taylor who gave him an official commendation for his care of the wounded at the battle of Okeechobee on Dec. 25, 1837. During the Mexican War he landed with the army which took Vera Cruz after a siege, and in the advance to Mexico city he acted as senior surgeon of Worth's division of regulars. He directed the medical service of that division at the battles of Cerro Gordo, Churubusco, Molino del Rey, and Chapultepec and, on July 5, 1847, forwarded to the war department a detailed report upon the health of the army.

After the occupation of Mexico city he was appointed medical director upon the staff of General Scott, and in that capacity was charged with the establishment of a general hospital to care for the bulk of the army casualties. He had been advanced to the grade of major in 1832, and in 1853 was appointed medical purveyor. In this capacity he served through the Civil War. So satisfactory was his service that he was brevetted lieutenant-colonel and brigadier-general. The accompanying citation commended him "for diligent care and attention in procuring proper army supplies as Medical Purveyor and for economy and fidelity in the disbursement of large sums of money" (Hamersly, *post*, p. 741). General Scott gave active support to his candidacy for surgeon-general when a change was made in 1862, but William Alexander Hammond [*q.v.*] was given the place. As a result of a reorganization of the medical department of the army in 1866 he was appointed chief medical purveyor with the grade of lieutenant-colonel. He was in charge of the medical supply depot in New York City until his retirement from active service in 1869.

[A. C. Wildey, *Geneal. of the Descendants of Wm. Chesebrough* (1903); biog. sketch by Albert Allemann, in H. A. Kelly, W. L. Burrage, *Am. Med. Biog.* (1920); W. B. Atkinson, *The Physicians and Surgeons of the U. S.* (1878); R. F. Stone, *Biog. of Eminent Am. Physicians and Surgeons* (1898); H. E. Brown, *The Med. Dept. of the U. S. Army* (1873); T. H. S. Hamersly, *Complete . . . Army Reg. of the U. S., 1779–1879* (1880); *Army and Navy Jour.*, Nov. 13, 20, 1880; *N. Y. Times*, Nov. 11, 1880.]
J. M. P—n.

SAUGANASH (c. 1780–Sept. 28, 1841), Indian sub-chief, was born in Canada. His name is often spelled Sagaunash, and he is also known as "Englishman" or Billy Caldwell. His father was said to be William Caldwell, an Irish officer in the British service, and his mother was a Potawatomi. He was trained by Roman Catholic priests at Detroit, and, in addition to the several Indian dialects that he spoke, he acquired fluency in both French and English. From about 1807 he was closely associatel with Tecumseh [*q.v.*] for some six years as an interpreter and perhaps as a secretary. He opposed the government of the United States and the frontier settlers, but there seems good authority for believing that he used his influence against the perpetration of atrocities. He arrived at Fort Dearborn the day after the massacre of Aug. 15, 1812, and it is certain that he was the means of saving several lives. He was probably at the Battle of the Thames on Oct. 5, 1813, when Tecumseh was killed, and thereafter may have remained for some years in Canada. Under the British government he had the title of "captain of the Indian Department," which he is known to have used in signing documents as late as 1816. About 1820 he made his residence at the present Chicago and avowed his allegiance to the United States. In 1826 he was appointed a justice of the peace. With two other negotiators, he rendered valuable aid to the settlers and the government in 1827 by keeping the Winnebago chief, Big Foot, at peace. In 1828, at a point a few miles north of the mouth of the Chicago River, the government built for him a house, probably the first frame structure erected in the Chicago region. He again exerted his influence for peace in 1832 by dissuading Indians from joining Black Hawk's band. By successive treaties culminating in the one of 1833, at Chicago, the Potawatomi ceded virtually all of their lands east of the Mississippi, and in the summer of 1836 they began their long migration to Western Iowa. Sauganash accompanied them. He died in the vicinity of the present Council Bluffs. Sauganash was more than six feet tall. By reason of his height, his powerful frame, and his erect bearing he was sometimes called the "Straight Tree." He was a man of exceptional intelligence and ability, and he was highly regarded by his white neighbors. Upon his tribesmen he urged the acceptance of the white man's mode of life and was especially interested in the education of the Indian youth. He had but one wife, the sister of the Potawatomi chief, Yellow Hand, and but one child, a son who died before reaching manhood.

[*Handbook of Am. Indians*, ed. by F. W. Hodge, pt. II (1910); C. A. Burley, *Sauganash* (copr. 1920); Mrs. John H. Kinzie, *Wau-Bun, the Early Day in the Northwest*, esp. pp. 186, 253 (1930), ed. by L. P. Kellogg.] W. J. G.

SAUGRAIN DE VIGNI, ANTOINE FRANÇOIS (Feb. 17, 1763–c. May 19, 1820),

naturalist, physician, scientist, philosopher, was born in Paris, France, son of Antoine and Marie (Brunet) Saugrain, the de Vigni in his name, after a Paris custom, merely indicating the place where he was nursed as an infant. His ancestors were librarians, booksellers, and publishers. He was educated in physics, chemistry, and mineral-

ogy. While still a very young man, he went into the service of the king of Spain, and in 1785 and again in 1786 he was in Mexico for the purpose of examining mines and mineral productions. In 1787 in the company of two friends, M. Raquet and M. Picque, he sailed for the United States, remained for a while in Philadelphia, where he enjoyed the intimate friendship of Benjamin Franklin, and in the spring of 1788 traveled westward in the hope of finding a suitable spot for a French settlement. In an attack by Indians opposite the Big Miami, Picque and Raquet were killed, and Saugrain was wounded and taken captive. Escaping, he reached Louisville, Ky., Mar. 29, 1788, but suffered the loss of part of one foot from an infected frost-bite. In April 1790, after a visit to France, he returned with a party of French immigrants, destined for the settlement of Gallipolis, Ohio. After six years in that settlement and some time in Lexington, Ky., and Portage des Sioux, Mo., he reached St. Louis in 1800 and settled there. At St. Louis he was appointed post surgeon by the Spanish lieutenant-governor, Delassus. After the American occupation he was appointed army surgeon by Jefferson and served from June 17, 1805, until he resigned in 1811. When the Lewis and Clark expedition was being fitted out in St. Louis, he supplied gratuitously a medicine chest, thermometers, barometers, and matches.

Besides having the distinction of being the only practising physician in St. Louis when Upper Louisiana was transferred to the United States, he was known far and wide for his chemical laboratories. He made and sold ink, thermometers, phosphoric lights for hunters, barometers, and matches of glass tubes containing phosphorus; he conducted experiments in electricity and had an electric battery. He was also famed for treatment of smallpox by inoculation; in 1809 he introduced the first smallpox vaccine virus brought to St. Louis and publicly offered to vaccinate, free of charge, all indigent persons, paupers, and Indians. Although very small of stature, he was a hero in combat with the Indians. He was high-spirited and full of fire, but at the same time a man of rare good nature. He was married in Kanawha County, Va., Mar. 20, 1793, to Genevieve Rosalie Michau, born in Paris, July 23, 1776. Many of the descendants of their six children became prominent in St. Louis in later years.

[Saugrain died during the night of May 18–19, 1820; see *St. Louis Enquirer, Mo. Gazette* (St. Louis), May 24, 1820. See also "Généalogie de la Famille Saugrain, par Claude M. Saugrain en 1810, Continué par Antoine P. Saugrain en 1865" (chart); Saugrain MS., Mo. Hist. Soc.; H. M. Brackenridge, *Recollections of Persons and Places in the West* (1868, rev. ed.); *The Rec-*

ord of the Celebration of the Two Hundredth Anniversary of the Birth of Benjamin Franklin (6 vols., 1906–08), vols. IV and V, Am. Philos. Soc.; W. V. Byars, *A Memoir of the Life and Work of Dr. Antoine François Saugrain, the First Scientist of the Miss. Valley* (n.d.); N. P. Dandridge, *Antoine François Saugrain (de Vigni)* (1904), reprinted in *Ohio Archaeological and Hist. Quart.*, Apr. 1906; E. F. Bliss, "Dr. Saugrain's Note-Books, 1788," *Proc. Am. Antiquarian Soc.*, n.s., vol. XIX (1909) and "Dr. Saugrain's Relation of his Voyage down the Ohio River . . . in 1788," *Ibid.*, n.s., vol. XI (1898); E. S. Meany, *Wash. Hist. Quart.*, Oct. 1931.]   S. M. D.

SAULSBURY, ELI (Dec. 29, 1817–Mar. 22, 1893), United States senator, brother of Gove and Willard Saulsbury [qq.v.] and son of William and Margaret (Smith) Saulsbury, like his brothers was born in Kent County, Del. He attended the local schools and in 1839, having joined the Methodist Church the year previous, entered Dickinson College at Carlisle, Pa., where he pursued a special course. He seems to have lived on the ancestral farm for a considerable time thereafter. In 1853 he became a member of the state legislature from his native county. Meanwhile, however, he had been studying law both at home and in the office of his brother Willard at Georgetown, Del., and in 1857 was admitted to the bar and commenced practice at Dover. With Willard he was elected delegate to the National Democratic Convention at Chicago in 1864. In 1871, on the expiration of Willard's term in the United States Senate, and of Gove's as governor, Eli, with Willard's help, defeated Gove and was elected United States senator. In spite of their rivalry for office, the three brothers were in practical accord in their political views, which were those of the northern Democrats generally. Eli's first important speech in the Senate (Jan. 30, 1872) was in favor of the removal of political disabilities of former Confederates and against the Civil Rights bill. On Apr. 22, 1874, he spoke against recognition of the Louisiana state ("carpet bag") government and in favor of white supremacy. He served on several committees, rendering his most conspicuous service on the Committee on Privileges and Elections, which passed on the large number of contests from the southern states. He opposed the eight-hour law in 1876 and the contract-labor law in 1885. He supported the anti-polygamy bill in 1882 with evident reluctance and sought to make its penal provisions prospective only. He did not vote on the civil service reform bill in 1882 but in 1888 advocated the selection of civil service employees according to their political affiliations. He opposed the bill to restrict Chinese immigration in 1888 on the ground that it would violate existing treaties, and he was the author of a resolution to

inquire into conditions in Samoa. He favored an international coinage in 1888 and presented many petitions for legislation prohibiting the liquor traffic, but opposed the Blair Educational Bill in 1884 and the international copyright bill in 1888. He was a working senator, and few important measures escaped his participation.

Reëlected twice, Saulsbury, as he neared the end of his third term, encountered an opponent in the person of James L. Wolcott, a former student of law in his office. After bitter strife between their followers, the Wolcott faction prevailed in the Kent County caucuses and, by invoking the unit rule in the county convention, nominated a legislative ticket pledged exclusively to their leader, thus eliminating Saulsbury from the contest. A large number of his followers "bolted" the party ticket, however, to elect the Republican nominees, and that party thereby for the first time secured a senator from Delaware. After the expiration of his term, Mar. 3, 1889, Saulsbury returned to his home in Dover, where he died. He never married.

[*Biog. Dir. Am. Cong.* (1928); J. T. Scharf, *Hist. of Del.* (1888), vol. I; H. C. Conrad, *Hist. of the State of Del.* (3 vols., 1908); W. A. Powell, *A Hist. of Del.* (1928); *Every Evening and Wilmington Daily Commercial*, Mar. 22, 1893.]   C. S. L.

SAULSBURY, GOVE (May 29, 1815–July 31, 1881), physician, governor of Delaware, was the eldest of three brothers who attained political distinction in that state in the middle nineteenth century. They were of Welsh descent, sons of William Saulsbury of Mispillion Hundred, sheriff of Kent County, Del., and his wife, Margaret Smith. Gove, born on the ancestral acres, attended free schools of the vicinity, then Delaware College at Newark. After a period of teaching country schools, he entered the medical college of the University of Pennsylvania, where he was graduated M.D. in 1842, having written a thesis on rheumatism. He at once entered upon the practice of his profession at Dover. In 1843 he joined the Methodist Episcopal Church and eventually became active in its affairs. He was president of the board of trustees of Wilmington Conference Academy and just before his death had been chosen delegate to the Ecumenical Council of Methodism in London, September 1881. On Nov. 1, 1848, he married Rosina Jane Smith of Snow Hill, Md., by whom he had five children, only one of whom survived him.

Saulsbury was a delegate to the National Democratic Convention in 1856, and in 1862 was elected to the Delaware Senate, where he took a prominent part in the sessions of 1863 and 1864. He supported in the latter year a joint resolution to inquire into the enlistment of negroes within the state, and later presented a committee report severely arraigning the Republican governor, William Cannon [*q.v.*], for his policy in furnishing Federal troops. Soon becoming the recognized Democratic leader, Saulsbury was elected speaker of the Senate at the opening of the session of 1865, upon the death of Governor Cannon, Mar. 1, became acting governor, and in the following year was elected governor by a majority of 1312. He served for nearly six years, longer than any other governor of Delaware. During his public service he opposed successively each of the amendments to the Federal Constitution growing out of the Civil War, and each was rejected by the Delaware legislature, in part, no doubt, because of his urgent messages. In 1869 he characterized the reconstruction measures enacted by Congress as "the most flagrant usurpation of power" and in his last message (1871) he referred to the Fifteenth Amendment as having been "adopted by fraud and coercion."

His term as governor expired less than two months before that of his brother Willard [*q.v.*] as United States senator, and the two, as well as the third brother, Eli [*q.v.*], became candidates for the senatorship. Gove held, throughout, his following of fourteen, rising on the third ballot to fifteen, but Eli, on the fourth ballot, with Willard's support, received sixteen votes and was elected, Jan. 17, 1871, on the day of Gove's retirement from the governorship. Gove Saulsbury seems never to have held public office thereafter, although he was a delegate to the National Democratic Convention in 1876 and again in 1880.

[J. T. Scharf, *Hist. of Del.* (1888), vol. I; J. M. McCarter and B. F. Jackson, *Hist. and Biog. Encyc. of Del.* (1882); W. A. Powell, *A Hist. of Del.* (1928); H. C. Conrad, *Hist. of the State of Del.* (3 vols., 1908); *Every Evening and Wilmington Daily Commercial,* Aug. 1, 1881.]   C. S. L.

SAULSBURY, WILLARD (June 2, 1820–Apr. 6, 1892), United States senator, chancellor of Delaware, brother of Gove and Eli Saulsbury [*qq.v.*] and son of William and Margaret (Smith) Saulsbury, was born in Mispillion Hundred, Kent County, Del. He attended local schools, Delaware College at Newark, and Dickinson College, Carlisle, Pa., then studied law under James L. Bartol, later chief justice of Maryland, and Martin W. Bates, later United States senator. Admitted to the bar in 1845, he opened an office at Georgetown, Del., entered politics, and soon acquired a local reputation as an orator. On May 11, 1850, he married Annie Milby Ponder. A daughter and two sons were born of this marriage; one son, John P., became secretary of state of Delaware, and the other, Willard

[*q.v.*], a United States senator. In the year of his marriage Saulsbury was appointed attorney-general of Delaware. His five years of service (1850–55) gave him state-wide acquaintance and reputation, and in 1856 he was chosen a delegate to the National Democratic Convention at Cincinnati which nominated James Buchanan for the presidency. Two years later he was elected to the United States Senate, entering that body in 1859, on the eve of the Civil War. On Apr. 2, 1860, he defended slavery in an elaborate speech (*Congressional Globe,* 36 Cong., 1 Sess., pp. 1480–88). On Dec. 5 following he declared, apropos of the President's message, that Delaware "having been the first to adopt the Constitution, will be the last to do any act or countenance any act calculated to lead to the separation of the states" (*Ibid.,* 36 Cong., 2 Sess., p. 14); he later supported the resolutions of J. J. Crittenden [*q.v.*] "for taking the sense of the people" on proposals which would virtually have restored the compromises of 1820 and 1850. He was exceedingly critical of arrests in Delaware for alleged disloyalty to the Union and he opposed interference by military and naval forces in elections and the suspension of the writ of *habeas corpus.* On Jan. 29, 1862, he spoke against the resolution to expel Senator Bright of Indiana for alleged treason and on Feb. 7, 1863, he proposed a referendum on compensated emancipation in Missouri. In the following year he was a delegate to the National Democratic Convention at Chicago and in the ensuing winter he was reëlected to the Senate. During his service there he was a member of the committees on commerce, mines and mining, patents, and pensions. A candidate for reëlection in 1871, he was opposed by his brothers Gove and Eli, and threw his support to the latter. Two years later, in November 1873, he was appointed by his brother-in-law, Governor Ponder, chancellor of the state, and he held that position for the remainder of his life. His opinions are published in 6 *Delaware Chancery Reports* (edited by his son Willard) and seem amply fortified by authority, the cases being generally well briefed. Especially notable is his opinion in *Green* vs. *Saulsbury* in the appendix to the volume, wherein he defined the jurisdiction of the Orphans' Court and traced its history from its establishment in 1683 at Philadelphia, when "the three lower counties" were a part of Pennsylvania. The bar in each of the counties adopted commendatory resolutions at the time of his death.

[The best account of Saulsbury's life is found in Appendix C to 6 *Del. Chancery Reports,* and was evidently written by his son Willard. See also *Biog. Dir. Am. Cong.* (1928); J. T. Scharf, *Hist. of Del.* (1888);

H. C. Conrad, *Hist. of the State of Del.* (3 vols., 1908) ;
W. A. Powell, *A Hist. of Del.* (1928) ; *Every Evening
and Wilmington Daily Commercial,* Apr. 6, 1892.]
C. S. L.

SAULSBURY, WILLARD (Apr. 17, 1861–
Feb. 20, 1927), senator, was born at Georgetown, Del., the son of Willard Saulsbury [*q.v.*]
and Annie Milby (Ponder) Saulsbury. After
attending private schools and the University of
Virginia (1877–79), he studied for the bar in his
father's office and was admitted in October 1882.
He became associated in the practice of law with
Victor DuPont of Wilmington, with whom he
continued in partnership until the latter's death
in 1888. On Dec. 5, 1893, he married May Du-
Pont, the daughter of his former partner. During his last years he was the head of the firm of
Saulsbury, Morris & Rodney, with offices in both
Wilmington and Washington, D. C. His business achievements included the consolidation of
the Wilmington traction companies and the organization of the Equitable Trust Company of
which he was long a director, as he was likewise
of the Union National Bank.

Scion of a family which had produced several
prominent Democratic leaders, he became active
in the councils of that party. He was chairman
of the county committee from 1892 to 1900, state
committeeman for a score of years and chairman
from 1900 to 1906, and from 1908 to 1920 national committeeman from Delaware. He was a
delegate to four national conventions between
1896 and 1920; in 1896 he was chairman of the
delegation and in 1904, a member of the committee on resolutions. At the convention of 1924 the
Delaware delegation presented his name as a
candidate for the presidency. From 1899 to 1913
he was his party's nominee for the United States
Senate, regularly receiving the entire Democratic vote in the legislature, but not until the
last-named year was he successful, and then only
after a desperate struggle. He was the last Delaware senator elected by the legislature.

In the Senate he soon became known as a leading supporter of President Wilson. He was assigned to the committee on foreign relations, and
became chairman of the committee on the Pacific Islands and Porto Rico. During the recess
of Congress in 1915 he visited the Far East,
reaching China while the twenty-one Japanese
demands were being pressed upon China and acquiring much first-hand knowledge of the situation. He also gave special attention to the needs
of the United States Court for China, and endeavored to strengthen its position in the international community. At the opening of the session of 1916 he was elected president *pro tempore*
of the Senate, a rare honor for so new a member,

and continued as such for the balance of his term.
He was nominated for reëlection to the Senate
in 1918, but the tide had already turned against
the Wilson administration and Saulsbury, as one
of its leading exponents, was defeated, though by
a narrow margin.

After the expiration of his term he resumed
the practice of law. When the Washington Conference on the Limitation of Armaments was in
process of incubation, he was invited by President Harding, with whom his personal relations
in the Senate had been most friendly, to serve on
the Advisory Committee. In 1923 he was a member of the Pan-American Conference at Santiago
de Chile. His last four years were passed quietly; he died at Wilmington, and was buried at
Dover in the churchyard of Christ Church (Episcopal), to which he belonged. He was a man of
polished manners, excellent address, and winsome
qualities. His long experience in practical politics taught him the art of handling men and,
had his lot fallen in an earlier era when his party
was stronger in his native state, he might well
have served for a long period in the Senate and
have become one of the leading statesmen of his
time.

[J. T. Scharf, *Hist. of Del.* (1888), II, 607 ; *Biog.
Dir. Am. Cong.* (1928) ; H. C. Conrad, *Hist. of the
State of Del.* (1908), III, 1048 ; *Who's Who in Amer-
ica,* 1926–27 ; *N. Y. Times,* Feb. 21, 1927 ; *Wilmington
Morning News,* Feb. 21, 1927 ; personal acquaintance.]
C. S. L.

SAUNDERS, ALVIN (July 12, 1817–Nov. 1,
1899), territorial governor of Nebraska, United
States senator, was born ten miles south of Flem-
ingsburg, Ky. His father, Gunnell Saunders, a
native of Virginia, married Mary Mauzy, likewise a Virginian. When Alvin was about twelve
years old the family removed to Springfield, Ill.
Here Alvin attended district school two months
each winter. At nineteen he went west, working
on a farm at Mount Pleasant, Iowa, for a short
time, and then becoming clerk in a dry-goods
store. Realizing the importance of further education, he prevailed on one of the qualified citizens to establish a night school and became a
faithful attendant. In 1839 he was appointed
postmaster of Mount Pleasant, but seven years
later was superseded by an appointee of President Polk's. In 1846 he was the youngest delegate to the convention that framed the constitution under which Iowa was admitted to the
Union. He was elected to the Iowa Senate in
1854 and reëlected in 1858. The first Republican
state convention, at Iowa City, Feb. 22, 1856,
found him one of the participants. He was chairman of the Iowa delegation in 1860 to the national convention that nominated Lincoln and

was active during the campaign in behalf of Lincoln, with whom he had previously formed an acquaintance.

On Mar. 26, 1861, Lincoln appointed Saunders governor of Nebraska territory. He assumed office May 15 and three days later issued a proclamation calling for volunteers. In his first official message to the legislature he advocated a transcontinental railway; as one of the Commissioners for the Union Pacific, he delivered the principal address at the ground-breaking ceremonies, Dec. 2, 1863. In January 1861 he urged the legislature to ask Congress to pass a homestead law, an action taken by Congress May 20, 1862. In 1865 he intimated he would not seek another term, but the legislature, disregarding party affiliations, adopted a resolution sent to the President asking his reappointment. Saunders went to Washington and on Apr. 14, 1865, called upon the President. The signing of his commission was probably Lincoln's last official act. Saunders continued as territorial governor until March 1867, when Nebraska became a state.

In 1868 Saunders was a delegate to the Republican National Convention. The following year he was appointed by the governor as one of the board of regents for the control of the old capitol grounds in Omaha for school purposes, serving as president of the board until it was superseded by the board of education, of which, in 1874, he was a member. In 1877 he was elected United States senator from Nebraska, serving until 1883. Among his special interests in Congress were Indian affairs and the development of inland waterways. He was also interested in numerous business and semi-public enterprises in Omaha. He founded the State Bank of Nebraska in Omaha and served for several years as its president, and assisted in establishing the street railway system and the gas works. He lost heavily during the financial difficulties of 1875, but met all his indebtedness and in time again accumulated a competence. One of the organizers of the Omaha Real Estate Exchange in 1886, he was its first president. He actively promoted the Trans-Mississippi and International Exposition in 1898, and was the resident vice-president. A member of the church of the Disciples of Christ, he was an incorporator and a zealous promoter of Nebraska Christian University (later Cotner University and after 1919 Cotner College), at Bethany Heights, a suburb of Lincoln. He was married in Washington, D. C., Mar. 11, 1856, to Marthena Survillar Barlow of Greencastle, Ind. A son and a daughter were born to them; the latter married the only son of President Benjamin Harrison. Saunders died in his home in Omaha at the age of eighty-two, and was buried in Forest Lawn Cemetery.

[J. S. Morton, *Illus. Hist. of Nebr.*, I (1905), 550–52, with portr.; J. W. Savage and J. T. Bell, *Hist. of the City of Omaha* (1894); *Biog. Dir. Am. Cong.* (1928); *Omaha Daily Bee*, Nov. 2, 1899; L. A. Moomaw, *Hist. of Cotner Univ.* (1916); T. W. Tipton, "Forty Years of Nebraska," *Nebr. State Hist. Soc. Colls.*, 2 ser. IV (1902).]

E. W. L.

SAUNDERS, FREDERICK (Aug. 14, 1807–Dec. 12, 1902), librarian, author, pioneer in work for international copyright, was born in London, England, the son of W. Saunders of the publishing firm of Saunders & Otley. He married Mary Ann Farr of London, Sept. 18, 1833, and for several years during his early manhood worked in his father's office. In 1837 he came to America, primarily to arrange for the publication of Bulwer Lytton's novel, *Rienzi,* but secondarily to launch a movement for an international copyright agreement that would prevent the reprinting of the works of English authors in America without remuneration to the writers. The first man to lay the matter before Congress, he made three separate appeals, one of them backed by a petition signed by fifty-six leading British authors that was carried to Washington by Charles Dickens and placed in the hands of Henry Clay. With the support of all writers in both countries, Saunders was at first confident of success. But, though he succeeded in making thoughtful Americans ashamed of the situation, he was ahead of his time, and two generations passed before the seed he planted and never ceased to nurture, bore fruit. He did not even succeed in getting a valid copyright on *Rienzi*; it was "pirated" by several publishers, and he said that his firm lost £7,000 on the venture. Notwithstanding his ill-success in this matter, he remained in the United States as a member of the staff of the New York *Evening Post* in the days when William Cullen Bryant, John Bigelow, and Parke Godwin were its luminaries. Meanwhile, he had begun publishing books, mostly collections of original essays or compilations. *Memories of the Great Metropolis* (1852); *Salad for the Solitary* (1853), which had a large sale and continued to be read for decades afterward; *Salad for the Social* (1856); *Pearls of Thought* (1858); *Mosaics* (1859); *Festival of Song* (1866); *About Woman, Love and Marriage* (1868); *Evenings with the Sacred Poets* (1869), treating of hymnology from ancient to modern times, and *Pastime Papers* (1885) were his principal works. He edited *Our National Centennial Jubilee* (1877) and, with Henry T. Tuckerman, *Homes of American Authors* (1853). His friend Washington Irving [*q.v.*], who had suggested the founding of the Astor library, was influential in securing for him in 1859 the position of assistant librarian. In 1876 he became librarian and remained at that post for twenty years, meanwhile continuing to write for literary periodicals. He had a part in the negotiations that led to the consolidation in 1895 of the Astor library, the Lenox library, and the Tilden Trust into the great New York Public Library. In 1896, at the age of eighty-nine, he retired by his own request but continued to serve as a trustee of the library until his death. He lived to see the New York Circulating Library, with eleven branches, combined with the other units in 1901. His "Recollections of a Retired Librarian" appeared in the *Critic,* Apr. 17, 1897.

[*Who's Who in America,* 1901–02; obituaries in *Evening Post* (N. Y.), Dec. 13, 1902; *N. Y. Times,* Dec. 14, 1902; scrap album on the Astor library compiled by Saunders, now in N. Y. Pub. Lib.; "A Book-lover's Memories," *N. Y. Times,* July 18, 1895; *Lib. Jour.,* Nov. 1896, Jan. 1903; *Publishers' Weekly,* Dec. 20, 1902.] A. F. H.

SAUNDERS, PRINCE (d. Feb. 1839), negro reformer and author, was the son of Cuff and Phyllis Saunders. He was born either in Lebanon, Conn., or in Thetford, Vt. In Thetford he spent part, at least, of his boyhood and owned property in 1805. He was baptized on July 25, 1784, at Lebanon, Conn. He taught a colored school at Colchester, Conn., was a student in Moor's Charity School at Dartmouth College in 1807 and 1808 under the patronage of Judge Oramel Hinckley of Thetford, formerly of Lebanon, and in November 1808 was recommended by President John Wheelock of Dartmouth as a teacher in Boston. There he taught a school for colored children, and through his influence Abiel Smith, a merchant, left a legacy for the work. He enjoyed the friendship of such men as William Ellery Channing (1780–1842) and William S. Shaw [*qq.v.*], and he founded the "Belles Lettres Society" for young white men and was active in its administration. While in Boston he became engaged to the daughter of Paul Cuffe [*q.v.*], but the engagement was later broken. He was sent from Boston to England by friends as delegate of the Masonic lodge of Africans and probably for other reasons, as he had letters from prominent Americans. He at once stepped into English society, mingling with the nobility, meeting the King, and making the acquaintance of Wilberforce, who was at the time interesting himself in behalf of Hayti and the emperor, Christophe, and had been commissioned by Christophe to send teachers to Hayti.

Saunders was sent with others. He was entrusted with the task of organizing a school sys-

tem on the English Lancastrian plan and was to aid in changing the religion of Hayti from Catholic to Protestant. In the process he was intimately connected with the family life of Christophe. In 1816 he introduced vaccination into Hayti under the direction of Wilberforce and personally vaccinated Christophe's children. He was sent back to England as messenger or envoy by Christophe, probably more than once, and memoirs of the period indicate that this honor added to his social prestige. While in England he published his first volume, *Haytian Papers* (1816), being a translation of laws of Hayti and the Code Henri with his own comments. The frontispiece is a striking engraving of Saunders, which was said by a contemporary to be a "perfect likeness." It shows a face of pronounced African characteristics with the air of a man of the world. In 1818 an American edition of this book was published in Boston by Bingham & Company, without the portrait. He apparently overstepped his authority in London, considering himself more of an ambassador than messenger, and was recalled by Christophe. We find him next in Philadelphia, then a center of activity and culture of the free colored people of America. There he served as lay reader for several months in the African church, later called the African Episcopal Church of St. Thomas and published *An Address . . . before the Pennsylvania Augustine Society* (1818) and *A Memoir . . . to the American Convention for promoting the Abolition of Slavery* (1818). He was a gifted man especially in the use of language. His manners were cultivated, and the stories of his life in England show him to have had a shrewd wit. That he enjoyed the attentions showered upon him is evident. The overthrow and suicide of Christophe in 1820 gave Saunders an opportunity to go back to Hayti under Boyer, and at his death he is spoken of as attorney general. He died at Port-au-Prince, Hayti.

[Dartmouth College Archives; William Bentley Fowle MSS., in possession of Mass. Hist. Soc., Boston; Schomberg Colls., N. Y. Pub. Lib.; records of Lebanon, Conn., and Thetford, Vt.; *Amer. Almanac . . . 1840* (1839), ed. by J. E. Worcester, p. 298; Vernon Loggins, *The Negro Author* (1931); Wm. Douglass, *Annals of St. Thomas' Church* (1862); O. D. Hine, *Early Lebanon* (1880), p. 40; *Emancipator,* July 4, 1839; spelling of name varies, on title page of *Haytian Papers* (*ante*) spelled Sanders and under portrait (*Ibid.*) spelled Saunders.] M. B. S.

SAUNDERS, ROMULUS MITCHELL (Mar. 3, 1791–Apr. 21, 1867), congressman, diplomat, was born in Caswell County, N. C., the son of William and Hannah (Mitchell) Saunders. His mother died soon after his birth and the family moved to Sumner County, Tenn.

Romulus was sent back to North Carolina to be educated and, prepared for college at Caswell and Hyco academies, entered the University of North Carolina in 1809 and was a student there for two years. Returning to Tennessee, he studied law under Hugh L. White and was licensed in 1812. He then went back to his native state and settled in Milton. On Dec. 22, 1812, he married Rebecca Peine Carter, who died after having borne him three sons and two daughters; on May 26, 1823, he married Anna Heyes Johnson, the daughter of William Johnson [*q.v.*], associate justice of the Supreme Court of the United States, by whom he had two sons and four daughters.

Saunders entered public life in 1815 as a member of the North Carolina House of Commons. In 1816 he was a member of the state Senate but returned to the House in 1818 and served until 1821, being speaker in 1819 and 1820. Elected to Congress, he served three terms (1821–27). In 1820 and 1824 he supported William H. Crawford [*q.v.*] for president and voted for him when the election was thrown into the House of Representatives. In 1828 he was elected attorney general of North Carolina, occupying that office until 1831. In 1834 he was appointed a member of the commission on the French Spoliation claims, in connection with which he acquired considerable reputation. Elected a judge of the superior court in 1835, he resigned in 1840 to accept the Democratic nomination for governor. With his opponent, John M. Morehead [*q.v.*], Saunders engaged in the first statewide canvass, and although he proved himself the abler campaigner, he lost the election. The next year he was again elected to Congress and served two terms (1841–45). Here he proved himself an active partisan and won from John Quincy Adams the following characterization: "There is not a more cankered or venomous reptile in the country" (*Memoirs of John Quincy Adams,* 1876, XI, 197). In 1842 he was an unsuccessful candidate for the United States Senate. He was a delegate to the Democratic national convention of 1844 and moved the adoption of the two-thirds rule which defeated Van Buren and became a permanent part of Democratic nominating machinery.

On Feb. 25, 1846, President Polk appointed him minister to Spain and gave him a special commission to negotiate for the purchase of Cuba for $100,000,000. Saunders did not bring up the matter at once, the *Amistad* case and a prolonged discussion of Spanish debts to American citizens making the time inappropriate. He spent most of 1847 in Paris, leaving Thomas C. Reynolds, the secretary, in charge of the legation. A quarrel arose between them in which Saunders appears clearly in the wrong but which led to the dismissal of Reynolds. In July 1848 Saunders broached the Cuban matter and in December received a curt refusal to discuss the question (*House Executive Document 121,* 32 Cong., 1 Sess., p. 57). He resigned May 1, 1849, and returned to Raleigh, which had been his residence since 1831. From 1850 to 1854 he represented Wake County in the House of Commons. In 1852 he was again unsuccessfully a candidate for the United States Senate, but was elected superior court judge, remaining on the bench until 1867. He was a member of the North Carolina code commission of 1852–54, and from 1819 to 1864 served as a trustee of the University of North Carolina. He had excellent abilities but lacked balance. His partisanship and his ceaseless quest for public office made enemies for him, but he always retained a large measure of popularity.

[S. A. Ashe, *Biog. Hist. of N. C.,* vol. III (1905); J. H. Wheeler, *Hist. Sketches of N. C.* (1851), and *Reminiscences and Memoirs of N. C.* (1884); *Alumni Hist. of the Univ. of N. C.* (2nd ed., 1924), ed. by D. L. Grant; *Biog. Dir. Am. Cong.* (1928); *The Works of James Buchanan* (12 vols., 1908–11), ed. by J. B. Moore; *Tri-Weekly Standard* (Raleigh, N. C.), Apr. 25, 1867; *N. C. Legislative Jours.*; *Cong. Globe*; Instructions to Ministers, Spain, vol. XIV and Dispatches, Spain, vol. XXXV (MSS., State Dept. Archives).]

J. G. deR. H.

SAUNDERS, WILLIAM (Dec. 7, 1822– Sept. 11, 1900), horticulturist, landscape gardener, was born at St. Andrews, Scotland. He came of a family of gardeners and received a thorough practical training in the art, together with a course in horticulture, at the University of Edinburgh. In 1848, shortly after his marriage in England to Martha Mildwaters, he removed to America, settling at first in New Haven, Conn. Here he began a series of contributions that continued for nearly forty years to the leading horticultural periodicals of the time, Hovey's *Magazine of Horticulture,* the *Horticulturist,* the *Farmer and Gardener, Philadelphia Florist* and others. In 1854 he formed a partnership with Thomas Meehan [*q.v.*] in Philadelphia for the practice of landscape gardening. He designed the Clifton Park estate of Johns Hopkins and the Ross Winans place in Baltimore; Rose Hill Cemetery, Chicago, and a number of cemeteries and private estates.

In 1862 he was appointed superintendent of the experimental gardens of the newly created Department of Agriculture. He designed the grounds of the Department at Washington and had charge of their development until his death in 1900. In 1863 he designed the national cemetery at Gettysburg and in 1865, at the suggestion of General Grant, selected the site and designed the grounds of the Lincoln monument at Springfield, Ill. In addition to establishing conservatories and greenhouses for the study of plants economically important, he assembled for the Department of Agriculture and established on the Mall an extensive collection of trees and shrubs regarded as adapted to the conditions of the middle Atlantic tidewater. From about 1870 until the realignment of the Mall in 1931 this was considered the most comprehensive arboretum in North America south of the Arnold Arboretum near Boston. As a member of the parking commission, an advisory body created in 1871, he helped to develop the system of street tree planting used in the District of Columbia. He organized and directed the exhibits of the Department of Agriculture at the Centennial Exhibition in Philadelphia in 1876, the New Orleans exposition of 1884, and the Paris exposition of 1889. He was also a pioneer in the introduction of foreign plants. As early as 1866 he introduced the Australian *eucalyptus globulus* into California. In 1870 he imported from Russia and later distributed through the northern states scions of some three hundred varieties of Russian apples, one of which, Yellow Transparent, became a widely planted summer apple. From Japan he introduced the hardy trifoliate orange, the dominant understock for the Satsuma group of oranges, and in 1871 from Bahia, Brazil, the Washington Navel orange, which promptly became the leading commercial variety in California and gave strong impetus to the development of the citrus industry in the southwest.

Furthermore, he sensed the needs and desires of rural people and as early as 1855 outlined an organization for mutual help. One of the seven organizers of the order of Patrons of Husbandry, he wrote its constitution and preamble in 1867, and served as master of the national organization for the first six years. He wrote widely on general horticulture. His published papers include some three thousand titles, among them the first bulletin of the Department of Agriculture (1862), a report on the objects and aims of the United States propagating garden, with a catalogue of the plant material available for distribution.

[*Yearbook U. S. Dept. of Agriculture,* 1900, pp. 625–30, and other Dept. of Agriculture pubs.; L. H. Bailey, ed., *Standard Cyc. of Horticulture,* vol. III (1915); T. C. Atkeson, *Semi-Centennial Hist. of the Patrons of Husbandry* (1916); *Evening Star* (Washington, D. C.), Sept. 11, 1900; manuscript jour. and list of Saunders' important published papers and existing un-published MSS. in lib. of Dept. of Agriculture, Washington, D. C.; personal acquaintance.]   W. A. T.

SAUNDERS, WILLIAM LAURENCE (July 30, 1835–Apr. 2, 1891), editor, historian, was born in Raleigh, N. C. His father was the Rev. Joseph Hubbard Saunders and his mother, Laura, daughter of Dr. Simmons J. Baker of Halifax County, N. C. Prepared for college at the Raleigh Academy, Saunders entered the University of North Carolina in 1850 and was graduated in 1854. He returned to study law under Judge William H. Battle [*q.v.*], was licensed in 1856, and received the degree of LL.B. in 1858. He began practice in Salisbury, N. C., where he also edited the *Salisbury Banner,* but in 1861 he volunteered for military service and during the war rose from the rank of private to that of colonel, at Appomattox being in command of the 46th North Carolina Regiment. He was twice wounded, both times seriously, and always thereafter suffered greatly from the results.

At the close of the war he settled in Florida. He had married, Feb. 3, 1864, Florida Cotten, daughter of John W. Cotten of Edgecombe County, N. C. She died in July 1865, and Saunders soon returned to North Carolina, settling at Chapel Hill, where he watched the course of Reconstruction with passionate interest. When conditions seemed no longer bearable, he assumed direction of the activities of the "Invisible Empire," or Ku Klux Klan, although he was never a regular member of it and was bound by no oath. He began to write regularly for the newspapers, and from 1872 to 1876 was one of the editors of the *Wilmington Journal.* In 1870 he was elected chief clerk of the Senate and held the place until 1874. During this period he was summoned to appear in Washington before the congressional committee which was investigating the Ku Klux activities. His friends urged him to leave the country but he refused and appeared in Washington, where he declined to answer any questions bearing in any way upon the Ku Klux and quietly defied the committee to punish him. He was badgered and threatened for several days without losing his calm poise, and was then released.

In 1876 he moved to Raleigh and with Peter M. Hale established the *Observer,* which he edited with great ability for three years, retiring then on account of ill health. In the same year he became secretary of state and retained that post until his death. During this period he was one of the most influential leaders in the Democratic party. He gave sound advice, planned campaigns, and edited the party handbooks. He played a large part in the reopening of the University of North Carolina, which had been closed by Reconstruction since 1870, and was a trustee from 1875 until his death and for most of that time secretary of the board of trustees. Saunders' greatest achievement, however, was his part in the publication of *The Colonial Records of North Carolina* (10 vols., 1886–90). His influence with Gov. T. J. Jarvis [*q.v.*] made the work possible, and he himself gave to the task of editing and publication eleven years of his life. Apart from the high value of these ten volumes in themselves, their influence in the state and elsewhere in stimulating historical research and the preservation of historical material has been very great.

Saunders was possessed of a keen, alert mind and excellent judgment. Modest, self-effacing, and unselfish, he had a deep passion for service. Quiet and retiring always, he was nevertheless widely popular. He died in his fifty-sixth year.

[S. A. Ashe, *Biog. Hist. of N. C.,* vol. IV (1906); A. M. Waddell, *The Life and Character of William L. Saunders* (1892), also pub. in the *News and Observer* (Raleigh), June 1, 1892; *Alumni Hist. of the Univ. of N. C.* (2nd ed., 1924), ed. by D. L. Grant; *House Report No. 22,* 42 Cong., 2 Sess., pt. 2, pp. 354–62; *Trinity Archive,* June 1896; obituary article in *News and Observer* (Raleigh), Apr. 2, 1891.]   J. G. deR. H.

SAUNDERS, WILLIAM LAWRENCE (Nov. 1, 1856–June 25, 1931), engineer, inventor, was born in Columbus, Ga., the son of the Rev. William Trebell and Eliza (Morton) Saunders. After graduating from the University of Pennsylvania in 1876 with the degree of B.S., he engaged in newspaper work in Philadelphia for two years but gave this up to become an engineer with the National Storage Company, Communipaw, N. J., in the construction of docks. This work involved considerable subaqueous rock excavation for which no satisfactory rock drilling equipment was available. In the course of his four years' work, however, Saunders developed a compressed-air drilling apparatus for submarine use, patented Jan. 9, 1883, which has been in general use in subaqueous work such as that in the Baku oil fields of Russia. Shortly after this, he joined the engineering staff of the Ingersoll-Sergeant Drill Company in Jersey City and had much to do with the development of the rock drill in its diversified forms. Patents granted to him between 1883 and 1898 dealt with the radialaxe system of coal mining, the apparatus for Ingersoll track and bore channelers and gadders for quarrying stone, and the pumping of liquids by compressed air. He was successively engineer, secretary, and vice-president of his company. On its reorganization as the Ingersoll-Rand Company in 1905, he became president and ultimately chairman of the board, an office he held at the time of his death.

Besides being a director in a number of business enterprises he was a government director and department chairman of the Federal Reserve Board of New York and a member of the district committee on capital issues, Federal Reserve Board. Under President Woodrow Wilson he served as a member of the New Jersey harbor commission, the New Jersey board of commerce and navigation, and as chairman of the United States naval consulting board. He was also a member of the advisory committee of the Federal Trade Commission and chairman of the industrial training committee of the National Civic Federation. He was twice mayor of North Plainfield, N. J., his residence for upwards of thirty years, and had long been prominent in New Jersey politics; he served as a member of the New Jersey State Committee, as Wilson's personal representative from New Jersey on the national campaign committee in 1916, and as a delegate to the Democratic National Convention in 1924. In December 1926, through the American Society for the Control of Cancer, he offered a prize of $50,000 for the discovery of the nature of human cancer and an equal amount for the discovery of a positive cure, but after two years, convinced of the futility of the search, he withdrew his offer. He also founded the medal awarded annually by the American Institute of Mining and Metallurgical Engineers in recognition of achievements in mining methods. Throughout his career he maintained his membership in such engineering societies as the American Institute of Mining and Metallurgical Engineers, of which he was president in 1915, and the United Engineering Society, of which he was president, trustee, and a member of the finance committee. He wrote on both engineering and political subjects, and was editor of *Compressed Air Magazine.* In 1903 he edited *Compressed Air Information;* in 1911 with R. T. Dana he published *Rock Drilling,* and in 1912 with G. H. Gilbert and L. I. Wightman *The Subways and Tunnels of New York.* Among his political articles were "Business and Politics and the Anti-Trust Laws," "Right and Strength in Equal Suffrage," and "Government Regulation of Commerce as Affecting Foreign Trade" (*New York Times, post*). He married Bertha Louise Gaston on August 4, 1886. At the time of his sudden death in Teneriffe, Canary Islands, while on a world tour, he was survived by two daughters.

[*Who's Who in America,* 1926–27; *Cassier's Mag.,* June 1907; *Mech. Engineering,* Aug. 1931; *Compressed Air Mag.,* Aug. 1931; *Engineering-News Record,* July 2, 1931; *Mining and Metallurgy,* Aug. 1931; obituary in *N. Y. Times,* June 26, 1931; Patent Office records.]
                                                        C. W. M.

SAUR, CHRISTOPHER [See SOWER, CHRISTOPHER].

SAVAGE, EDWARD (Nov. 26, 1761–July 6, 1817), painter, engraver, was born at Princeton, Mass., the second child of Seth and Lydia (Craige) Savage and a grandson of Edward Savage, of Huguenot descent, who emigrated from Ireland to Massachusetts in 1696. The younger Edward, according to a family tradition which is probably true, learned the goldsmith's trade, and thus probably received some practice in engraving. He was evidently intimate with Paul Revere (*Christian Science Monitor*, June 16, 1924). By 1789 he had attained such proficiency as a painter that he was commissioned by the president of Harvard College to paint a portrait of Washington. The latter recorded in his diary, Dec. 21, 1789: "Sat from ten to one o'clock for a Mr. Savage, to draw my Portrait for the University of Cambridge, in the State of Massachusetts." The picture was delivered at Cambridge probably in August 1790, the artist having in the meantime, while he was in New York, made for John Adams another Washington portrait—not, as has been asserted, a replica of the first one (Hart, *post*, p. 7).

Savage went in 1791 to London, where he is said to have had instruction from Benjamin West and where he engraved several plates in mezzotint and stipple. His journeying seems to have extended to Italy. Returning to the United States, he married at Boston, Oct. 13, 1794, Sarah Seaver, who survived him. His older brother John had become a successful merchant in Philadelphia and thither the young artist went in search of opportunities. In 1795 he exhibited at Philadelphia a panorama depicting London and Westminster in a circle. Leaving Philadelphia about 1801, he joined with Daniel Bowen in opening the New York Museum, exhibiting works of art and curiosities. These were later reassembled at Boston in the Columbian Museum, which, with most of its treasures, was burned in 1803, reërected and again burned in 1807, only to be re-inaugurated and continued until 1825 when it was absorbed by the New England Museum.

Savage's ability as a painter and engraver was disparaged by William Dunlap [*q.v.*] in an account (*post*) the inaccuracies of which have since been corrected (Hart, and Bayley and Goodspeed, *post*). The portraits of George and Martha Washington, now owned by the Boston Museum of Fine Arts, are certainly creditable paintings, and such mezzotints as Savage made after his own portraits in oil of Gen. Anthony Wayne, Dr. Benjamin Rush, and Thomas Jefferson, to say nothing of his familiar stippled plates of "Liberty" and "The Washington Fam-ily," even though they do not evidence supreme technique, do not merit Dunlap's characterization of them as "wretched pictures."

Savage's name is not found in the Philadelphia directory after 1801. His fifth child was born at New York, Mar. 31, 1802; his sixth child, Aug. 22, 1805, at Princeton, Mass., where a seventh and an eighth also were born. Here Savage ended his days. Like many artists of his era, he gave much attention to mechanics and invention. He was a partner from 1809 onward in the Poignaud and Plant Cotton Factory at the nearby town of Lancaster (Blake, *post*, p. 296). Savage himself was effectively portrayed in profile by Saint-Mémin [*q.v.*] and in full face by himself. The self-portrait is in the Worcester Art Museum, where his engraved work is best preserved. In October 1921 the Massachusetts Historical Society, Boston, received from Miss Catharine Colvin of Lake Forest, Ill., who had them from Charles Henry Savage, grandson of the artist, an extensive collection of his miniature portraits, engravings, and other family souvenirs. To the Chicago Art Institute Miss Colvin had previously given an original Savage portrait of Washington, recorded (*Transcript, post*) as painted in 1793, though the artist in that year was in England.

[*A Descriptive Catalogue of an Exhibition of Early Engraving in America* (Mus. of Fine Arts, Boston, 1904); C. H. Hart, *Edward Savage, Painter and Engraver* (1905); Wm. Dunlap, *Hist. of the Rise and Progress of the Arts of Design in the U. S.* (1834); rev. ed., by F. W. Bayley and C. E. Goodspeed, 3 vols., 1918); Frank Weitenkampf, *Am. Graphic Art* (1912); F. E. Blake, *Hist. of the Town of Princeton, . . . Mass.* (1915), vol. I; *Boston Transcript*, Oct. 14, 1921.]

F. W. C.

SAVAGE, HENRY WILSON (Mar. 21, 1859–Nov. 29, 1927), real-estate operator and theatrical producer, was born at New Durham, N. H., the son of Capt. M. Henry and Betsey T. (Woodhouse) Savage. He received the degree of A.B. at Harvard in 1880 and entered the real-estate business in Boston, in which he prospered for more than fifteen years. The turning point in his career came soon after he built the Castle Square Theatre in Boston in 1894. He had no thought at the time of any connection with the stage as a business, the theatre being merely a realty investment. For a while, however, it did not prosper, and during the winter of 1895 the manager of a German company which was playing light operas there stole away on a boat for Europe, leaving his company stranded. The actors sought aid from Savage, and he decided to take over the company himself.

Shortly afterwards he organized his own company to give light opera in English at moderate prices. Thus began the Castle Square Opera Company, one of the most famous organizations of its kind that the American stage has known. It became a school for light opera stars, and whether in Boston or touring the country, as it did from coast to coast, it was everywhere exceedingly popular. It presented not only light opera, but began giving the more tuneful of the grand operas, such as *The Bohemian Girl, Maritana, Martha, Faust, Romeo and Juliet,* and *Der Freischutz,* all in English. Next, Savage daringly ventured upon *Tannhäuser, Lohengrin,* and *Die Meistersinger* in English. By this time the Castle Square Company had become virtually a double organization, one section for grand opera, the other for the lighter pieces. In 1900 Savage's office was in New York; he had taken over the Studebaker Theatre in Chicago, and his operetta troupe was disintegrating into various organizations for the production of newly written musical comedies. Several of these, such as *Tarantella* (1899), *King Dodo* (1900), *The Sultan of Sulu* (1902), and *The Prince of Pilsen* (1903), were first seen at the Studebaker. Meanwhile, from New York and Boston, he was launching *The Yankee Consul* (1903), *Peggy from Paris* (1903), *Woodland* (1904) and others. He also brought out George Ade's highly successful spoken comedies, *The County Chairman* (1903) and *The College Widow* (1904).

For a quarter of a century he was one of America's most successful producers, and with the most varied repertoire, embracing comedy both sung and spoken, grand opera, and an occasional serious drama. The Henry Savage Grand Opera Company continued for several years after 1900, most of the time playing at a top price of one dollar. He did not have the greatest of opera stars, but his company was well balanced, had good voices, and won high praise from critics. Some famous American singers, such as Grace Van Studdiford, Maude Lillian Berri, and Maude Lambert, were graduates from it. One of its singers became a star in Paris, and another in the Russian Royal Opera. In 1904 it gave Wagner's *Parsifal* for the first time in English, and received high acclaim. In 1906 it gave Puccini's *Madame Butterfly* its first American production, also in English; and in 1911 the same composer's *The Girl of the Golden West.* One of the cleverest strokes of Savage's career was his capture of the American rights to Franz Lehar's operetta, *The Merry Widow,* which he first presented in America in 1907, and which scored the most enormous success in light-opera history. It ran in New York and elsewhere for several

years; women's hats and toilet articles were named in its honor, and its lilting waltz songs were played and whistled in every hamlet on the continent, as well as all over the world. In 1921 Savage staged a beautiful revival of this play, with stars in all the principal rôles. Another of his remarkable productions was that of *Everywoman,* a modern imitation of the medieval morality plays, first presented in 1910, and on tours for several years thereafter. He also introduced the Hungarian dramatist Ferenc Molnar to American audiences, presenting his play, *The Devil,* in 1908 with George Arliss in the leading rôle. Some others of his productions were *Madame X, Along Came Ruth, Easy Dawson, The Sho-Gun, Excuse Me, Tom Jones, The Galloper, Cornered, The Little Damozel, Shavings, Mary Jane's Pa, Miss Patsy, Pom-Pom, Have a Heart, Little Boy Blue, The Love Cure, Sari, Head Over Heels, Lady Billy,* and *The Clinging Vine.* His list is notable for wholesomeness and high quality. His last production was *Lass o' Laughter* in 1925. On Oct. 24, 1889, Savage married Alice Louise Batcheler of Boston, and two children survived him. He was long a director of the National Association of Theatrical Producing Managers, and was its president from 1907 to 1909.

[*Who's Who in America,* 1926–27; *Who's Who in Music and Drama,* 1914; *N. Y. Times,* Nov. 30, Dec. 2, 1927; *World* (N. Y.), Nov. 30, 1927; *N. Y. Herald-Tribune,* Nov. 30, 1927; *Boston Transcript,* Nov. 29, 1927; "Grand Opera in English," in *The Theatre,* Feb. 1904; *Robinson Locke Dramatic Collection,* N. Y. Public Lib.; *The New Yorker,* Dec. 10, 1927.] A. F. H.

SAVAGE, JAMES (July 13, 1784–Mar. 8, 1873), antiquary, was born in Boston, one of the eleven children of Habijah and Elizabeth (Tudor) Savage. His father was a merchant descended from Thomas Savage who emigrated from England to Boston about 1635. He was educated at Derby Academy at Hingham, Mass., Washington Academy at Machias, Me., and Harvard College, where he graduated in 1803. He made a voyage to the West Indies in 1805, after which he studied law in the offices of Isaac Parker [*q.v.*] and others till he was admitted to the bar in 1807. He prepared for the press and compiled an index for the *Charters and General Laws of the Colony and Province of Massachusetts Bay,* published by the state in 1814. In 1816, when the third volume of John Winthrop's history of New England was found in manuscript, he was entrusted by the Massachusetts Historical Society with the duty of copying and annotating it. He decided to edit the whole work instead of the new volume only, and his edition, *The History of New England from 1630 to 1649,* appeared in two volumes in 1825–26. Another, with additions and corrections, was issued by him in 1853. This was an important piece of antiquarian scholarship, and he did much other miscellaneous writing and editing, for he was very industrious. He is perhaps best known for his *Genealogical Dictionary of the First Settlers of New England, Showing Three Generations of Those Who Came before May, 1692, on the basis of Farmer's Register.* This work, involving enormous labor, occupied him seventeen years, and was published in four volumes between 1860 and 1862. It is a standard work for the American genealogist.

He happened to see a plan of a London savings bank, and he at once took up the project of providing something similar for Boston. His energy and persistence overcame apathy and opposition, and in 1816 the Massachusetts legislature incorporated the Provident Institution for Savings, one of the first savings banks incorporated in the United States and perhaps the first in the world to be established by the act of a public law-making body. In 1818 he was active in contending that the law made mandatory the provision of elementary schools, and, when a town meeting adopted his view in spite of opposition, he served six years on the body charged with the duty of putting the new schools in operation. From 1811 to 1862 he held a great variety of offices imposing responsibility and labor. He was several times elected to the lower house and to the Senate of the Massachusetts legislature, in addition to service in the Executive Council and as delegate to the Massachusetts constitutional convention in 1820. He also served in the common council, board of aldermen, and school committee of Boston; and he was for fifteen years a member of the board of overseers of Harvard University. He was one of the founders of the Boston Athenaeum, was long active in and for a time president of the Massachusetts Historical Society, and was connected with many other organizations or institutions of a public or semi-public character. In all of these he exerted influence and enjoyed respect, for, though given to rather extreme opinions and violent expression of them, this did not obscure the value of his services. In April 1823 he married Elizabeth Otis (Stillman) Lincoln, the widow of James Otis Lincoln of Hingham, Mass., and the daughter of George Stillman, of Machias, Me. They had one son and three daughters. Savage died in Boston.

[*Letters of James Savage to his Family* (1906); Charles Deane, *Brief Memoir of James Savage, Prepared for the . . . Amer. Acad. of Arts and Sciences* (1874); *Tribute of the Mass. Hist. Soc. to the Memory of . . . James Savage* (1873); J. S. Loring, *The Hundred Boston Orators* (1852), pp. 353–60; *One Hundred*

Years of Savings Bank Service; a Brief Account of Provident Institution for Savings (1916); *New England Hist. and Geneal. Register,* Jan. 1847; *Boston Morning Journ.,* Mar. 8, 1873.]   S. G—n.

SAVAGE, JOHN (Dec. 13, 1828–Oct. 9, 1888), journalist, was born in Dublin, Ireland, where he attended the art school of the Royal Dublin Society, winning the silver medal of the society in 1847. He became infatuated with the "Young Ireland" movement and, when the government closed the art school because of student agitation, he became active in plotting against the authorities. In April 1848 he and J. De C. Young issued an inflammatory publication, the *Patriot,* which was promptly suppressed. Two months later he promoted the *Irish Tribune,* issued by the "Students' Club" to further the old views of Mitchel toward Irish independence. Late in July he fled from Dublin, assisted in the abortive insurrection of September, and then sought refuge in the United States. He arrived in New York City on Nov. 7, 1848. There he met William Erigena Robinson [*q.v.*], who presented him to Horace Greeley [*q.v.*]; within a week Savage was installed as a proof-reader on the *New York Tribune.* Beginning in January 1854 he was the literary editor of the *Citizen,* a newspaper founded by John Mitchel [*q.v.*], which continued publication for one year. He married Louise Gouverneur, a daughter of Captain Samuel Chester Reid [*q.v.*] in August 1854 and for the next three years was hard pressed to earn a living by free-lance journalism. He published in 1856 his *'98 and '48: the Modern Revolutionary History and Literature of Ireland.*

In 1857 he went to Washington and there became the leading editorial writer on the *States,* the organ of Stephen A. Douglas. In Washington he wrote a mediocre tragedy, *Sybil,* produced in various cities in 1858 and published in 1865. *Our Living Representative Men* was a feeble potboiler published in 1860 to take advantage of the imminent presidential campaign; it contained hasty sketches of those men prominently mentioned for the presidential succession in 1861. One of these sketches was elaborated and published in 1866 as *The Life and Public Services of Andrew Johnson.* At the outbreak of the Civil War he was urged to remove the *States,* of which he had become part owner, into one of the southern states. He refused and is said to have joined the 69th Regiment under General Corcoran and to have served with it throughout the war. His most important contribution to the Union cause, however, was a number of tuneful verses designed to inspirit the northern forces. The most successful of these, "The Starry Flag" (later published in a collection of verse by Savage entitled *Faith and Fancy,* 1864), was written on board the United States transport *Marion* during May 1861 as she sailed up the Potomac through the masked batteries of the enemy.

In the spring of 1864 he visited Cuba and in June of that year accepted a position as leading editorial writer on the *New Orleans Times,* remaining until March 1867. It was then that the news of the Fenian movement reached America. Savage's old revolutionary enthusiasm flared up; he offered his services to the cause and came to New York City, where he wrote and lectured on behalf of the Irish. His prominence resulted in his becoming in 1867 the chief executive of the Fenian Brotherhood in America. In this capacity he toured the United States, organizing Irish societies and collecting funds for the Fenian cause; especially successful was his visit to California in 1870. In 1868 he wrote *Fenian Heroes and Martyrs,* which had been preceded by *Poems* (1867). In 1869 he was proposed by President Johnson as United States consul at Leeds, but a Senate committee reported adversely and the matter was tabled. In his declining years he was popular as a lecturer before Catholic colleges and fraternal organizations. Several years before his death he moved to Scranton, Pa. It was at his summer home at Laurelside, near Spragueville, Pa., that he died in 1888, survived by his wife and an adopted daughter.

[*Dict. of Nat. Biog.* (1921–22 ed.); D. J. O'Donoghue, *The Poets of Ireland* (1912); *The Irish Cause on the Pacific: John Savage in Cal.* (1870); obituaries in *N. Y. Tribune, N. Y. Times,* Oct. 11, 1888; information from Hugh O'Reilly and Miles Bryan of New York City.]   F. M.

SAVAGE, MINOT JUDSON (June 10, 1841–May 22, 1918), Unitarian clergyman, author, and lecturer, was born in Norridgewock, Me., the fourth son of James Lambert and Anne Swett (Stinson) Savage, and a descendant of James Savage who came from England to Boston in 1715. Amid circumstances of severe poverty and labor, Minot began attending district school at four years of age. His boyhood was marked by physical infirmity, intermittent schooling, and religious excitement, the last being due to the interest of his parents in Methodist class meetings (though his father was by conviction a Free-Will Baptist) and revivalism. At the age of thirteen, after six weeks of "horror and fear of hell," he joined the church. After finishing high school, he taught in Newark, Del., and Norridgewock, Me., then entered Bangor Theological Seminary, graduating in June 1864. He was at once ordained to the Congregational ministry and on Aug. 29 of the same year married, in Harvard, Mass., Ella Augusta Dodge, sailing with

her in September, via Panama, as a missionary to San Mateo, Cal. He soon transferred his work to Grass Valley, where his ability in preaching, writing, and lecturing began to attract notice. Returning to the East to assist his parents, in 1867 he was settled over the Congregational Church, Framingham, Mass.

In 1869 he removed to Missouri, where he became pastor of the First Congregational Church of Hannibal. Here he soon developed the largest body of that faith in the state. In the meantime, however, he became conscious of growing heterodoxy of belief. A study of church history, Biblical criticism, science, and evolution made it impossible for him longer to hold the old theories. After a severe mental struggle and in spite of the willingness of prominent Congregational churches in Chicago and Indiana to call him, in September 1873 he became minister of the Third Unitarian Church of Chicago. After a year of most acceptable work there, he went to the pulpit of the Church of the Unity, Boston, where he entered on the most influential and productive period of his ministry.

The circle of his hearers, though always large, was not so numerous as that of the readers of his sermons, published for thirty years in tract form and periodically collected in books, of which *The Religion of Evolution* (1876) is perhaps the most distinctive and historically significant. While not the first American theologian to discern and to define the influence of the Darwinian hypothesis on religion, Savage was the first American preacher to attain such prominence and popularity as to bring the issue squarely and clearly to the attention of the Protestant world, especially its clergy. His insistent message was that a frank acceptance of the new world view necessitated by the theory of evolution in science, social philosophy, and religious culture, enhanced and illuminated the true values of Christian faith and ethics rather than destroyed them; though, of course, obsolete and non-essential points suffered by being disclosed as such. His persuasive and eloquent presentation of evolutionist propositions and corollaries, as well as those of Biblical criticism and comparative religion, performed an invaluable service in negotiating understanding and sympathy between Protestantism and science. This service was performed not only by pulpit work but by a prolific output of books, and by lectures and addresses in America and England.

In September 1896 he became minister of the Church of the Messiah, New York City (now the Community Church), where the crowded congregations and sermonic publicity of the Boston period were repeated. To the advocacy of evolutionist optimism and of humanitarian reform, Savage now added that of spiritualistic faith in personal survival after death (see his *Life Beyond Death,* 1899; *Can Telepathy Explain?* 1902). The strenuousness of his exertions brought on Mencken's disease, in spite of which he preached the conference sermon for the International Congress of Religious Liberals, Geneva, 1905. In 1906 failing health necessitated his retirement from the active ministry and the succeeding twelve years of his life were spent in rest, travel, and publication. He died in Boston and his ashes are buried in Mount Auburn Cemetery, Cambridge. Three of his children survived him, a fourth, Philip Henry Savage [*q.v.*], having died in 1899.

As a preacher, he spoke without manuscript, fluently and impressively. His diction was simple but apt, his presentation lucid and logical. He usually addressed the understanding of his hearers rather than the sentiments, yet his own feelings of faith, compassion, reverence, and hope were deep and strong, and occasionally took command of his thought with moving effect. His faith involved such conceptions as the goodness of life, the friendliness of the universe, the significance of man as epitome and culmination of the cosmic processes; and the competence of man, by virtue of his growing intelligence and ethical impulses to adjust himself successfully to cosmic "laws." Conserving the traditional values of Christian piety, trust in Providence, love to an immanent God and love to man, faith in immortality, consecrated exertion against evil in self and society, he added a powerful optimistic emphasis upon human progress.

Typical of his published works, in addition to those previously cited, are *The Morals of Evolution* (1880), *The Evolution of Christianity* (1892), *Social Problems* (1886), *Beliefs about the Bible* (1883), *The Passing and the Permanent in Religion* (1901), *Poems* (1882), and *Hymns* (1898). Several of his hymns have come into general use. To *My Creed* (1887) he affixed a brief spiritual autobiography.

[*Who's Who in America,* 1918–19; *Christian Reg.,* May 30, 1918; *Unity* (Chicago), June 6, 1918; *Boston Transcript,* May 22, 1918; *Springfield Republican,* May 24, 1918; information from a son, the Rev. Maxwell Savage.]　　　　　　　　　　　　　　　C. H. L.

SAVAGE, PHILIP HENRY (Feb. 11, 1868–June 4, 1899), poet, was born in North Brookfield, Mass., second of the four children of the Rev. Minot Judson Savage [*q.v.*] and Ella Augusta (Dodge) Savage. His early associations, clerical and literary, offered little support to the skeptical vigor of his mind and the pagan amplitude of his senses and emotions. The rugged beauty of New England nature, however, meant much to him from the start.

After a few years in the English High School at Boston, and before going to college, he tried traveling salesmanship, oddly mingling, in his letters home, news of the shoe business with descriptions of sunsets and red-winged blackbirds. He entered Harvard College at twenty-one (an age when most men are leaving it), and was graduated with the class of 1893. After that he tried a year of the study of divinity, and another of free-lance poetry writing, before settling at last, in 1895–96, to systematic technical study of his chosen art while serving as instructor in the English department at Harvard. He had himself a keen and painful sense of the difficulty he found in orienting himself to his work. As late as 1895, less than four years from his death, and after the publication of his first book, *First Poems and Fragments* (1895), he wrote a friend: "I see other men in full career, . . . their power of expression running even with their conception, —while I labor and fail. The paltry inspiration that is in some of the *First Poems* does not comfort me. Where are power and beauty? Where, indeed, are simple purity and grace?" (Mason, *post,* p. xxx.) None the less he was slowly finding himself. Already from college he had written his sister Gertrude: "What is true and beautiful is absolute; and what is stupendous and gorgeous and impressive and wonderful is inferior to it" (*Ibid.*). Already he was consciously forming that noble, pure, and exacting taste which is his most distinctive trait, and which gives his best work its incomparably delicate beauty. In one of his note-books he thus truly analyzed himself: "Master of a little beauty which, because it is born and bearer of the divine essence, I will cherish at the expense of most of the concerns of life" (Mason, *post,* p. xxvi). The whole of his short life, outwardly uneventful, was a search for the frail but perfect beauty he was destined to express. In that laborious search he slowly disentangled himself from one after another of the customary interests, the inherited ideas, the traditional beliefs and conventional ways of expression that were not strictly his own.

His last few years were passed as secretary to the librarian of the Boston Public Library. Their most important event was the publication of his *Poems* in 1898. Fine as was the quality of that slender volume, containing a few lyrics possibly as perfect as any in English, the quantity of his best work still remained small when he was stricken with appendicitis and died at the Massachusetts General Hospital in Boston, at the age of thirty-one.

His life was necessarily one rather of high promise than of full achievement. Yet it was long enough to carry him from the instinctive youthful imitation of conventional models to the intellectual independence of the poems "God, thou art good, but not to me" and "What hard, bright Spirit sits beyond the stars?," to the mellow humanity of "A Wreath of Buds and Lavender," and to the poignant simplicity of the verses which may be taken as his epitaph:

"Brother, Time is a thing how slight!
Day lifts and falls, and it is night.
Rome stands an hour, and the green leaf
Buds into being bright and brief.
For us, God has at least in store
One shining moment, less or more.
Seize, then, what mellow sun we may,
To light us in the darker day."

[*The Poems of Philip Henry Savage* (1901), ed. by Daniel Gregory Mason, reprints the two volumes published during Savage's lifetime and offers a biographical and critical Introduction. See also *Who's Who in America*, 1899; *Harvard College: Record of the Class of 1893* (1899); *Christian Reg.,* June 8, 1899; *Boston Transcript,* June 5, 1899.]   D. G. M.

SAVAGE, THOMAS STAUGHTON (June 7, 1804–Dec. 29, 1880), Protestant Episcopal clergyman, physician, missionary, naturalist, was born in upper Middletown (now Cromwell), Conn., son of Josiah and Mary (Roberts) Savage, and a descendant of John Savage who was made a freeman of Middletown in 1654. Although named Thomas Jefferson by his parents, upon beginning his theological studies he dropped the latter name because he believed Jefferson was an infidel, and substituted that of Staughton. His father, who had served as a youth in the Revolutionary army, was a ship-owner, largely interested in the West Indian trade, in which he made a considerable fortune; he was part owner of the celebrated brig *Commerce* of Hartford, wrecked in 1815 on the coast of the Sahara. Thomas' mother was the daughter of Dr. Aaron Roberts, a surgeon in the Revolution. Although of Congregationalist ancestry, young Savage joined the Protestant Episcopal Church while a student at Yale College, from which he was graduated in 1825. Entering the Yale Medical School in 1830, he received the degree of M.D. in 1833. Following his graduation, he undertook an extensive journey, traveling west to Cincinnati, south to New Orleans, and northward along the Atlantic Coast. He then entered the Theological Seminary in Virginia, at Alexandria, from which he graduated; and on Oct. 23, 1836, was ordained priest.

As the first missionary sent to Africa under the auspices of the Protestant Episcopal Church,

Savage arrived at Cape Palmas, Liberia, on Dec. 25, 1836, and established a mission on Mount Vaughan. The next year he visited native villages along the Cavally River, Monrovia, and the "slave factories" at Gallinas River. Serious ill health forced him to return to America, in 1838, where he married Susan Metcalf at Fredericksburg, Va. With his wife he sailed again for Africa and arrived at Cape Palmas on Jan. 23, 1839. His wife died in Liberia three months later. In 1840 he took an easterly voyage as far as Akkra, stopping at many points along the Slave, Ivory, and Gold coasts. On June 2, 1842, he married Maria Chapin of Newbury, Vt., who also died the same year from effects of the Liberian climate. Again, in June 1843, Savage was obliged to return home for rest and recuperation. After a year's absence, he sailed a third time for Africa on May 18, 1844, accompanied by four missionaries, including Elizabeth Rutherford of Providence, R. I., whom he married at Cape Palmas on Dec. 18, 1844. In January 1845 they were transferred to the newly opened station at Fishtown, Liberia, remaining there two years. Savage finally resigned from his missionary work, on account of ill health, in December 1846, but did not sail from Cape Palmas until Mar. 3, 1847.

On the way he was detained in the Gaboon River and spent the month of April at the house of Rev. J. L. Wilson, a Presbyterian missionary. Here he saw the skull of a large ape which he recognized as different from the chimpanzee. Seeking further evidence, he obtained, through chiefs of the Mpongwe tribe, four skulls and other bones of this animal which proved to be the largest of the great apes, the gorilla, previously unknown. Upon his arrival in America, he made this anthropoid known to science, publishing "Notice of the External Characters and Habits of *Troglodytes gorilla,* a New Species of Orang from the Gaboon River" (*Boston Journal of Natural History,* December 1847). Almost equally important was his paper on the chimpanzee, "Observations on the External Characters and Habits of *Troglodytes niger*" (*Ibid.,* April 1843, January 1844) in which he made the earliest step toward the scientific understanding of this animal's behavior, a subject that has now become almost a special branch of psychology. Hardly less interesting are his "Observations on the Species of *Termitidae* of West Africa, Described by Smeathman as *Termes bellicosus* and by Linnaeus as *Termes fatalis*" (*Proceedings of the Academy of Natural Sciences of Philadelphia,* vol. IV, 1850) and "The Driver Ants of Western Africa" (*Ibid.*).

For three years following his return to America, Savage served parishes in Mississippi and Alabama. From 1851 to 1861, and from 1865 to 1867, he lived at Pass Christian, Miss. Removing North in 1868, he was appointed associate secretary of the Episcopal Board of Missions, and from 1869 until his death, he was rector of the Church of the Ascension in Rhinecliff, New York.

[C. C. Adams, *Middletown Upper House . . . 1650 to 1800* (1908); W. A. R. Goodwin, *Hist. of the Theological Sem. in Va.* (2 vols., 1923–24); E. F. Henning, *Hist. of the African Mission of the Protestant Episcopal Church in the U. S.* (1850); *Obit. Record Grads. Yale Coll.,* 1881; *Cat. of Scientific Papers (1800–1863) . . . Pub. by the Royal Soc. of London,* vol. V (1871); *Spirit of Missions,* vol. I (1836) to vol. XVI (1851); *The Churchman,* Jan. 15, 1881; information from family.]   R. K.

SAVERY, WILLIAM (1721–May 1787), cabinet maker, was almost unknown until more than a century and a quarter after his death, although his son William Savery [*q.v.*] had attained distinction before he died, and it is difficult to find the simplest facts about his birth and early life. While he was married, according to the records of the Society of Friends, to Mary Peters, the daughter of Reese Peters, in Philadelphia on Apr. 19, 1746, the records of the Monthly Meeting of that city make no mention of his entrance either into the Society of Friends or of his membership in that Meeting. He is believed to have gone to Philadelphia about 1740, and he is known to have served as assessor of the central wards of that city in 1754 and to have been an agent and collector of taxes for the guardians of the poor of Philadelphia in 1767. The records of the Monthly Meeting show him to have been the father of eleven children, and that he was buried May 28, 1787, when his age was recorded as 65 years. His will, which is dated 9 mo, 8, 1783, was probated Sept. 3, 1787, and in this document he describes himself as "joiner and chair maker." In the Francis White's Philadelphia Directory (1785) he is described as "chair maker."

The discovery of a little printed business label, containing his name and address, attached to a fine specimen of furniture, which is now in the Manor House at Van Cortlandt Park in New York, marked the beginning of his modern fame as a craftsman. In the Palmer Collection of the Metropolitan Museum of Art of New York there are no fewer than three highboys, two lowboys, two, possibly four, tables, and a secretary-desk. These specimens are so extraordinary in the artistic character of their workmanship, that their maker was alluded to as "one of our greatest colonial cabinet-makers" (Halsey, *post,* p. 251).

His shop in Philadelphia, according to his label, was "at the sign of the chair, a little below the Market, in Second Street, Philadelphia" (*Ibid.*), which location, through deeds, has been identified with the present property, No. 17 South Second St. That he did a prosperous business is shown by various documents, which record that in 1766 he received £52 a year as a rental of one house, and that in 1780 he paid taxes on a property valuation of $46,000. While nothing is known of his education or training in his craft, his designs reveal his indebtedness to those early books of design, published in the eighteenth century in England, such as the several volumes by Thomas Chippendale and by Robert Manwaring. The examples of his work in the Palmer Collection prove him to have been an artist. He is supposed to have been self-educated in his trade, but, while undoubtedly owing an obligation to books of design, including those of Batty Langley, he was sufficiently an artist to naturalize and interpret them in an original manner. There is considerable carving in his mahogany pieces, but for the great part his furniture has simple and pure lines, making for dignity and richness. His work, probably with the work of others also, has caused the Philadelphia furniture of the colonial period, especially from 1760 to 1775, to be highly regarded by experts, as "exhibiting the greatest degree of elaboration and ornateness found in American furniture" (Nutting, *post,* p. 452). Skilled artist, as he undoubtedly was, he did not feel it beneath his dignity to repair chairs, and do other odd jobs pertaining to joinery; and it is said that there still is in existence in his handwriting, a bill for sixteen shillings, charged for making a chicken-coop (Hornor, *post,* p. 16). Regarding himself as primarily a chair maker, he excelled in the manufacture of this article of furniture. Some of his chairs, which have been identified, are of great beauty and simplicity, all of them showing an English tendency, but with the added Savery touch that gives them an independent character.

[Records of the Philadelphia Monthly Meeting in the collection of the Penn. Hist. Soc.; A. W. Savary, *A Geneal. and Biog. Record of the Savery Families* (1893); A. H. Savery and F. R. Taylor, *Geneal. and Brief Biog. of the Savery Family of Philadelphia* (1911); F. R. Taylor, *Life of William Savery of Philadelphia, 1750–1804* (1925); R. T. H. Halsey, "William Savery the Colonial Cabinet Maker and his Furniture," *Bulletin of the Metropolitan Museum,* Dec. 1918; W. M. Hornor, Jr., "William Savery, Chair-maker and Joiner," *Bulletin of the Pa. Museum,* Feb. 1928; Wallace Nutting, *Furniture Treasury,* vol. III (1933).]

J. J.

SAVERY, WILLIAM (Sept. 14, 1750 o. s.– June 19, 1804), Quaker preacher, was born at Philadelphia, Pa., the son of William [*q.v.*] and

Mary (Peters) Savery. His mother was of Welsh extraction and his father of French Huguenot. The latter was a cabinet maker of Philadelphia, the producer of some notable pieces of colonial furniture. The younger William served seven years as a tanner's apprentice near Philadelphia, during which time he met Sarah Evans who, on Nov. 19, 1778, became his wife. As a master tanner he operated his own tanneries in Philadelphia and apparently prospered in the business, although at times his absence from home on religious journeys left the burden of affairs on others.

On two rather notable occasions he was present, with other Friends, during treaty negotiations with the Indians. One such occasion was the fruitless attempt, in 1793 near Detroit, to make peace with the western Indians; another, more successful in its outcome, was the council of 1794 with the Six Nations at Canandaigua, N. Y. The report of Savery and his companions concerning the latter occasion led the Friends of Philadelphia into an extensive missionary work among the Seneca Indians.

Aside from his journeys to the Indian country, Savery traveled much "in the ministry" at home and abroad. He visited Quaker centers in various parts of the United States, preaching frequently to large audiences. From 1796 to 1798 he was absent from home, in company with a few other Friends, on a religious pilgrimage to Europe. He visited many of the German states, and preached to the Germans in their own language, apparently with considerable effect. In Holland and France the travelers also found Friends and held meetings with them and with others. In Paris Savery and one of his companions, David Sands, met Thomas Paine, who was born a Friend, but who proved to be not at all amenable to the religious admonitions of his Quaker visitors. Savery also toured Ireland twice in the years 1797–98. The power of his preaching was best exemplified in his meetings in England, where he felt especially called to address those who were not Friends. His fame became so great there that he often spoke to audiences of hundreds and even of a thousand or more people. The buildings were at times crowded to suffocation so that persons in the audience fainted and had to be carried out; yet his hearers would remain quietly through a discourse lasting from one to two hours and were frequently melted to tears by his appeal. The outstanding event of his ministry was the conversion of Elizabeth Gurney (later Fry), whose subsequent ministry to prisoners and influence on prison reform are well known. At the time of Savery's visit to England

she was a rather giddy young girl, very vain and stylish for a Quakeress; but, as she herself testified: "He has caused me to feel a little religion. I have *felt* there is a *God*. I loved the man as if almost he were sent from heaven" (Taylor, *post*, p. 430). She continued under the influence of Savery while he remained in England, and received an impression that changed the whole current of her life.

The preacher who exhibited this remarkable power was a man of average height and of good figure, although somewhat inclined to corpulency. His hearers frequently spoke of his melodious voice, and an English newspaper, the *Bath Chronicle,* after referring to his "good sense, fluency, and even eloquence," added: "He is a man of prepossessing appearance and address, mild and persuasive in his language and manners, and unusually liberal in all his sentiments" (Taylor, p. 424). The most eventful years of his life were past when, in 1798, he ended his work in Europe and returned to Philadelphia. In his home city he carried on his former business, rendered great service in some of the yellow fever scourges of those years, and pursued his religious activities until his death, apparently from dropsy, at the age of fifty-four years.

[The chief secondary authority is F. R. Taylor, *Life of William Savery* (1925); the chief manuscript source is Savery's journal in the possession (1931) of F. R. Taylor, Cheltenham, Pa.; some manuscript and much printed material are at Friends' Lib., Euston Road, London; in the printed version of the journal, *A Jour. of the Life, Travels, and Religious Labors of William Savery* (1837 and later eds.) the reader must allow for large editorial liberties; there are many editions of Savery's sermons, as set down in shorthand at the time of delivery; also *Some Remarks . . .* (1797) by Savery, disapproving the practice of thus reproducing Quaker sermons, which were delivered *ex tempore*; see also, Joseph Smith, *A Descriptive Cat. of Friends' Books* (1867), II, 538–39; A. W. Savary, *A Geneal. and Biog. Record of the Savery Families* (1893); *Poulson's American Daily Advertiser,* June 20, 1804.]   R. W. K.

SAWYER, LEICESTER AMBROSE (July 28, 1807–Dec. 29, 1898), clergyman, Biblical scholar, was born in Pinckney, Lewis County, N. Y., the son of Jonathan and Lucy (Harper) Sawyer. His father was a wagon maker and a soldier of the War of 1812, who died in the service. Leicester was prepared for college privately and graduated as valedictorian of his class at Hamilton College, Clinton, N. Y., in 1828. After a year spent in teaching at Clinton and Philadelphia, he entered Princeton Theological Seminary, from which he was graduated in 1831. He was licensed by the Presbytery of Watertown that same year and on Feb. 23, 1832, was ordained.

After serving several churches in Massachusetts and New York, he became, June 1835, pastor of the North (now United) Congregational Church, New Haven, Conn. Although his pastorate there was attended by marked success, he resigned at the close of two years on account of delicate health and assumed charge of the recently formed Park Street (now Dwight Place) Church in the same city. Retiring from the latter position in 1840, he became president of Central College, Columbus, Ohio. From 1843 to 1854 he was successively stated supply or pastor of Presbyterian churches at Central College and Monroeville, Ohio, and Sacketts Harbor, N. Y. From 1854 to 1859 he was pastor of the Congregational Church at Westmoreland, N. Y., at the end of which time, on account of changes in his theological views, he obtained a letter of retirement from his denomination with the standing of an independent Christian minister. After serving as pastor of the Second (South) Unitarian Church of Hingham, Mass., for the year 1859–60, he retired to Whitesboro, Oneida County, N. Y., where he spent the remainder of his life. From 1868 to 1883 he was night editor of the *Utica Morning Herald,* preparing also for that paper a weekly column headed "Religious Intelligence."

Sawyer was an accomplished classical scholar and a competent and conscientious student of the Bible, in the original languages of which he was well versed. He was one of the earliest American scholars to apply to the study of the Scriptures those literary and historical methods which were later known as the "higher criticism." He translated practically the entire Bible, the work, which appeared in sections at various times, being both a translation and an analytical study. He had the satisfaction of knowing that some of his interpretations which were much criticized at the time were supported by the Revision Committee of 1881. His most noteworthy work in the Old Testament field was that on the Prophets, in which he set forth the then revolutionary conclusion that they contained no reference to Jesus as the Messiah. He published two translations of the New Testament, and in his critical studies reached the conclusion that Jesus was merely a social reformer and that the only genuine portions of the New Testament were five epistles of Paul. The second of these translations, issued in 1891, had a rearrangement of the books, putting what Sawyer regarded as the genuine epistles first and the Gospels last, and an accompanying treatise devoted to an explanation and a defense of this arrangement.

The following are his more important works: *Baptism by Affusion and Sprinkling* (1838);

The Children of Believers Entitled to Baptism (1838); *A Critical Exposition of Mental Philosophy* (1839); *The New Testament Translated from the Original Greek* (1858); *The Holy Bible Translated and Arranged, with Notes* (3 vols., 1860–62); *Daniel, with Its Apocryphal Additions Translated and Arranged* (1864); *The New Testament Translated from the Original Greek* (1891). Sawyer was a well-equipped scholar and an earnest seeker after truth. Although he dealt with matters that were highly controversial, he never sought controversy nor attacked those who disagreed with him. On Sept. 26, 1832, he married Pamelia Bert Bosworth of Smithville, N. Y., who died in 1881. Seven of their ten children survived their parents.

[*Hamilton Lit. Mag.,* Mar. 1899; *Necrological Report . . . Princeton Theological Sem.,* 1899; *Utica Morning Herald,* Dec. 30, 1898; information from a former colleague on the *Utica Morning Herald.*]   F. T. P.

SAWYER, LEMUEL (1777–Jan. 9, 1852), congressman, author, was the youngest of the nine children of Lemuel and Mary (Taylor) Sawyer of Camden County, N. C. Bereft in early life of both parents, he attended local country schools and Flatbush Academy on Long Island, 1793–96. During residence of more than a year in Philadelphia with his brother-in-law, Dempsey Burges, a member of Congress, he devoted irregular study to mathematics and developed habits of extravagance and fondness for gay society which beset him throughout life. Returning to Camden County in 1797, he was both unhappy and unsuccessful in the management of his farm. He early manifested a strong interest in politics, reading, and literary production. In 1799 he attended the University of North Carolina, then studied law for three years—chiefly as an avenue to politics—and achieved local fame as an attorney. He represented Camden County in the House of Commons in 1800. Before casting his vote as Republican presidential elector for Jefferson and Clinton in 1804, he delivered a partisan address in which he hailed Jefferson's election in 1801 as "a greater subject for joy and congratulation than the capture of Cornwallis" (*Raleigh Register and North Carolina State Gazette,* Dec. 17, 1804); and the sitting legislature elected him a member of the Council of State.

Sawyer's stanch Republicanism, attractive personality, and prominent family connection resulted in 1806 in his election to Congress, of which he was a member for sixteen years (1807–13, 1817–23, and 1825–29). He retained popular support despite excessive absence from his seat and infrequent contacts with his constituency due to chronic invalidism. During the first interruption in his congressional career, he sold his farm, resided in Norfolk, Va., and was part owner and business agent of a store in his native county; during the second, he wrote *Blackbeard, A Comedy, in Four Acts; Founded on Fact* (Washington, 1824), which was staged in New York in 1833. In Congress, Sawyer was a consistent supporter of the administrations of Jefferson, Madison, and Monroe. He opposed a naval establishment, advocated rigid economy, and supported the Embargo, though the distress of the lumber trade in his district prompted him to offer, on Nov. 15, 1808, a resolution designed to open trade with the West Indies. In 1810, convinced of the ineffectiveness of non-intercourse and in opposition to Nathaniel Macon [*q.v.*], he urged more vigorous resistance to England. After war began, he proposed, Dec. 16, 1812, a striking increase in the navy. Retaining after the war his belief in economy and strict construction of the Constitution, he opposed the federal policy of internal improvements as unconstitutional and inexpedient, but on Dec. 16, 1825, proposed the use of a war vessel for the exploration of the polar regions of North America, declaring in a widely noticed address that "the time has come when this nation should likewise enter into this glorious career of discovery and human improvement" (*Register of Debates in Congress*, 19 Cong., 1 Sess., p. 814). He voted against the tariff act of 1828. From 1824 he was a Jackson Democrat.

Sawyer was married three times: in August 1810 to Mary Snowden of Camden County, who died in 1812; on Dec. 24, 1820, to Camilla Wertz of Washington, D. C., who died Jan. 27, 1826; and in 1828, to a well-to-do widow, Mrs. Diana (Rapalye) Fisher of Brooklyn, N. Y. Several children by his first two wives died in infancy. After a brief unhappy residence in North Carolina following his retirement from Congress in 1829, Sawyer moved to Brooklyn where he employed much of his leisure in study and writing. He wrote a second drama, *The Wreck of Honor, a Tragedy, in Five Acts* (1826?); a work of fiction, *Printz Hall; A Record of New Sweden* (2 vols., 1839); *A Biography of John Randolph of Roanoke, with a Selection from His Speeches* (1844); and *Auto-biography of Lemuel Sawyer* (1844). Extravagance, questionable conduct, and business incapacity dissipated the money obtained from his third marriage, and his latter years were spent in ill health, unemployment, penury, and unhappiness. From 1850 until his death he held a minor departmental clerkship in Washington, where he died. He was buried in the family burying ground, Lambs Ferry, Camden County, N. C.

[See *Biog. Dir. Am. Cong.* (1928); *Jour. of the House of Commons* (N. C.), 1800, 1804; *Raleigh Reg. and N.-C. State Gazette*, Dec. 2, 1805; *Raleigh Reg. and N.-C. Gazette*, Jan. 12, 1821, Nov. 25, 1828; "Pasquotank Births, Marriages, Deaths, Flesh Marks, and Brands, 1691–1797," in the N. C. Hist. Commission; J. H. Wheeler, *Reminiscences and Memoirs of N. C. and Eminent North Carolinians* (1884); A. H. Quinn, *A Hist. of the Am. Drama from the Beginning To the Civil War* (1923). Although contemporary newspapers give the name of Sawyer's second wife as Wurtz, evidence from records and manuscript sources indicates that the correct spelling was Wertz.]   A. R. N.

SAWYER, LORENZO (May 23, 1820–Sept. 7, 1891), California pioneer and jurist, was born in Leray, Jefferson County, N. Y., the oldest child of Jesse and Elizabeth (Goodell) Sawyer. His first American ancestor was Thomas Sawyer, who emigrated from England to Massachusetts about 1636, settling in Rowley and in 1647 moving to Lancaster. His early life was spent upon his father's farm, and in attending the district school and Black River Institute at Watertown, N. Y. From Pennsylvania, whither his parents had moved, he went to Ohio and finished his schooling. For a time he taught Latin and mathematics at Central College, Ohio, and then studied law in Columbus with Gustavus Swan and with Noah H. Swayne [*q.v.*], afterwards a justice of the United States Supreme Court. In 1846 he was admitted to the Ohio bar, but soon went to Chicago and passed a year in the law office of James A. McDougall, then attorney-general of Illinois and afterwards a United States senator from California. Moving to Wisconsin, he formed a law-partnership with Lieut.-Gov. J. E. Holmes.

In 1850 he crossed the plains with a company of young men from Wisconsin. Arriving in California, he first worked in the mines in El Dorado County, but soon entered upon the practice of law, first in Nevada City, then in Sacramento, and for a few months in 1851 in San Francisco, subsequently returning to Nevada City. In the autumn of 1853 he moved permanently to San Francisco, and the next year became city attorney. In his private practice he was retained in important cases involving alienation of homestead, mining, and water rights. In 1861 he was in Washington, seeking appointment as chief justice of Colorado Territory, but friends persuaded him to return to California, where he began a long career on the bench the following year, when Governor Stanford appointed him judge of the district court of the twelfth judicial district. In 1863 he was elected to the state supreme court and for two years (1868–70) was its chief justice. On Dec. 8, 1869, President Grant nominated him as United States circuit judge for the ninth circuit, and on Jan. 10,

1870, the nomination was confirmed. At the time of Sawyer's death in San Francisco in 1891, he was serving as presiding judge of the newly created circuit court of appeals for the ninth circuit. As a judge, he was called upon to decide important questions relating to the settlement and preservation of land titles. His best-known decision, however, was the *habeas corpus* case in 1889 (*In re Neagle, 14 Sawyer's Reports, 9th Circuit,* 232), afterwards affirmed by the Supreme Court (135 *U. S.,* 1).

In politics Sawyer was first a Whig, then a member of the American Party, but throughout most of his life a Republican. As the first president of the board of trustees of Leland Stanford, Junior, University he delivered an address (1887) at the laying of the University's corner stone in Palo Alto. Though not a man of brilliancy or genius, he was richly endowed with common sense, and was temperate, regular, and rigidly correct in all his habits. No success came to him without hard work. He investigated cases with the greatest patience, and was ready to hear the uttermost word that could be offered in behalf of any cause. Stern and inflexible in his public acts and relations, he was of great gentleness, kindness, and simplicity in his private life. On Mar. 10, 1857, he married Jennie M. Aldrich. She died in 1876, leaving two sons and a daughter.

[H. H. Bancroft, *Chronicles of the Builders of the Commonwealth* (vol. II, 1892); O. T. Shuck, *Bench and Bar in Cal.* (1889); Alonzo Phelps, *Contemporary Biog. of California's Representative Men* (1881); *San Francisco Chronicle,* Sept. 8, 1891; *Evening Bull.* (San Francisco), Sept. 8, 1891; *Green Bag,* Oct. 1891; L. S. B. Sawyer, *Reports of Cases Decided in the Circuit and District Courts of the U. S. for the Ninth Circuit,* 1873–1891; 24–38 *Cal. Reports.*]　　　P. O. R.

SAWYER, PHILETUS (Sept. 22, 1816–Mar. 29, 1900), lumberman and senator, accumulated a large fortune out of the pine lands of northeastern Wisconsin, directed the course of the Republican party in his state for fifteen years, and died a rugged and popular exponent of individualism in business. He was born at Whiting, near Rutland, Vt., but passed his youth at Crown Point, N. Y., to which place his parents, Ephraim and Mary (Potts) Sawyer, took him in infancy. He acquired the rudiments of letters in a few terms of country schools, learned the whole technique of the lumberman in the pineries, and married, in 1841, Melvina M. Hadley, the daughter of a neighbor. Six years later he took his family westward to the vicinity of Oshkosh, Wis., where his home and seat of operations remained until his death. He was a member of the Wisconsin assembly in 1857 and 1861, was twice mayor of

Oshkosh, and attached himself to various Masonic orders. His family mansion, built in the panic year, 1857, became a place of hospitality state-wide in extent; and his fortune, considerable before the Civil War, expanded with the war-time demand for lumber. As his industry evolved from the sawmill and rough-lumber stage to the planing mill and finished woodwork, he amassed profits that he invested in the local banks and the railroads of Wisconsin.

In 1864 he was elected to Congress, thus accomplishing the "redemption" of the fifth Wisconsin district from "the hands of the false Democracy" (*Wisconsin State Journal,* Sept. 16, 1864). With "great energy and practical business talent" he held his seat against only nominal opposition through five terms. He made few speeches but was an able committeeman. Withdrawing from Congress in 1875, he gave his attention again to his business, but did not cease to work in politics with the "Republican regency of Milwaukee." In 1881 he took his seat in the United States Senate, where he remained for twelve years, contributing to the reputation of the Senate as a millionaires' club (*Sunday Sentinel, Milwaukee,* Apr. 6, 1890). In 1885 he received as junior colleague the able young railroad lawyer, John C. Spooner [*q.v.*], who became as effective on the floor as Sawyer was in the committee room. With a family physician to assist him, Sawyer set up an informal pension office that secured passage for many private pension bills. His leadership in Wisconsin politics was impregnable until, in 1890, the party was wrecked by the revulsion against the Bennett law, and the Democrats took possession of the state. Sawyer was replaced by a Democrat in 1893, after he had been compelled by the Democratic administration to make good on the bonds of sundry Republican state treasurers who had, while in office, failed to account for interest received on public deposits. He had also been drawn into significant controversy with the young ex-congressman, Robert M. LaFollette [*q.v.*], who charged him with an attempt at bribery in connection with the treasury interest cases. His explanation of the transaction (*Milwaukee Sentinel,* Oct. 29, 30, 1891) was incapable of either authentication or disproof, but it provided the text for a campaign against boss rule and corruption waged by LaFollette with ultimate success. Sawyer retired to semi-privacy as the "grand old man of Oshkosh," but his hand remained powerful when, after the Democratic interlude, his friends regained power in the state. In his last years the attacks upon him were softened by his reputation for honesty, generosity, and success. He died in Oshkosh, survived by two of his five children.

[The newspapers made Sawyer a legend before he was eighty; see *Daily Northwestern* (Oshkosh), Sept. 19, 1896; *Milwaukee Sentinel*, Mar. 30, 1900. There is a friendly sketch in P. V. Lawson, *Hist. Winnebago County, Wis.* (1908), vol. II. A memorial volume, Horatio Gates, *The Sawyer-Jewell Lineage* (1902), traces his irrepressible vigor to Cerdic the Saxon and King Alfred.]   F. L. P.

SAWYER, SYLVANUS (Apr. 15, 1822–Oct. 13, 1895), inventor, was the son of John Sawyer and was born on his father's farm at Templeton, Mass. From his father, who was a lumberman and mill operator as well as a farmer, he evidently inherited the mechanical ingenuity that he manifested from boyhood. He was never in good health, however, and after obtaining a grade school education he was sent to Augusta, Me., in 1839 to work in the gunsmith shop of his brother-in-law. Poor health soon forced him to relinquish this work and return to his home at Templeton but not before he had gained sufficient knowledge of the gunsmith's art to enable him to repair and make parts for firearms for his friends and neighbors. He also made several inventions, including a small railroad car to be operated by foot power. About 1844 he went to Boston, where he found employment for a short time in a coppersmith's shop. He then spent a year with a manufacturer of locks and house trimmings but was again compelled to return to Templeton because of his health. He had gained a local reputation as a mechanical genius, however, and in the winter of 1845–46 was asked for his advice in the devising of tools to prepare rattan for chair caning and other purposes. After work lasting a year or more on a machine to reduce the eighteen hand operations required to prepare rattan, he felt the need of more experience and obtained employment in the machine shops of Otis Tufts in Boston. In 1849, once more in Templeton, he constructed models of experimental machines and applied for a patent, granted on Nov. 13, 1849, on "machinery for splitting and dressing rattan." When practically applied the device was not satisfactory, but after two years of further experiment he secured a second patent on "machinery for cutting rattan," June 24, 1851. Following this the American Rattan Company was organized and a factory established at Fitchburg, Mass., with Sawyer as superintendent. He continued with the improvement of his rattan machinery and secured additional patents in 1854 and 1855. In 1855, when his company was consolidated with a business rival, he relinquished active connection with it to devote his attention entirely to invention. As early as 1853 he had invented certain improvements in rifled cannon and projectiles (first patented on Nov. 13, 1855), and between 1857 and 1858 he and his brother attempted to demonstrate the practicability of their rifled cannon and projectiles, but nothing came of it. For the succeeding twenty years he continued with a variety of inventions that yielded several patents: dividers and calipers, patented in 1867; a steam generator, 1868; and a shoe-sole machine, 1876. In 1876 he attempted to establish a watch factory in Fitchburg but was compelled by prevailing financial conditions to abandon the enterprise and to turn his attention to the manufacture of watchmakers' tools, particularly a centering lathe, on which he obtained a patent July 10, 1882. In the last few years of his life he gave up all active business and devoted his efforts to horticulture, having a deep interest in progressive farming. He never married. He died in Fitchburg, Mass.

[D. H. Hurd, *Hist. of Worcester County, Mass.* (1889), vol. I; correspondence with Fitchburg Hist. Soc.; Patent Office records; *Boston Transcript*, Oct. 14, 1895.]   C. W. M.

SAWYER, THOMAS JEFFERSON (Jan. 9, 1804–July 24, 1899), Universalist clergyman, editor, and educator, was born in Reading, Vt., one of the ten children of Benjamin and Sally (York) Sawyer. He was a descendant of Thomas Sawyer of Lincolnshire, England, who emigrated to America not later than 1639, and died in Lancaster, Mass., in 1706. Young Sawyer's early life was that of most country boys in his day—six months' labor on the farm and six months' schooling annually. During the year 1822 he lived with the Universalist minister of the town, Samuel C. Loveland, and studied under his direction. He then taught district schools, earning thereby enough money to attend Chester Academy at two different periods, where he completed his preparation for Middlebury College. Entering that institution in 1825, he graduated in 1829 and the same year was ordained to the Universalist ministry at the General Convention, meeting at Winchester, N. H. In April 1830 he became pastor of the Grand Street Universalist Society, recently organized in New York City, which soon afterward established itself in a church edifice on Orchard Street. The following year, Sept. 21, he married Caroline Mehitable (d. 1894), daughter of Jesse and Anna (Kenrick) Fisher of Newton, Mass. She was a woman of considerable literary talent, whose publications include, besides much prose and verse in periodicals, *The Juvenile Library* (4 vols., 1845), and *The Rose of Sharon* (1850–58), an annual;

she also edited from 1861 to 1864 the *Ladies' Repository,* a Universalist monthly. Seven children were born to her.

When Sawyer went to New York, organized Universalism had almost ceased to exist there. For the next fifteen years he was a potent force in its upbuilding. Horace Greeley, who became one of his parishioners in 1831, later said of him that he "was not a brilliant preacher, and never became such; but he possessed qualities more essential to a clergyman than dazzling eloquence —sound judgment, solid learning, immovable integrity, and profound devotion to his Master's cause" (*New York Tribune,* quoted by Eddy, *Life,* p. 252). He was aggressive in the promulgation of Universalist doctrines and quick to take up cudgels in their defense, engaging in numerous public controversies with members of other denominations. The substance of some of these appeared in printed form: for example, *Letters to the Rev. Stephen Remington in Review of His Lectures on Universalism* (1839) and *Review of Rev. E. F. Hatfield's "Universalism as It Is"* (1841). In the interest of the denomination he started and edited, with Philo Price, the *Christian Messenger* (Oct. 29. 1831–Oct. 24, 1835). In November 1835 this was merged with other papers and the *Universalist Union* established, of which Sawyer was an editor for some years.

In 1845 he became principal of Clinton Liberal Institute. A Universalist theological school, for which in General Conventions and elsewhere he had long pleaded, was soon established in Clinton and Sawyer conducted it in connection with his principalship of the Institute. It ceased to exist when he left Clinton, in 1852, but when the Canton Theological School, the beginning of St. Lawrence University, was founded in 1856, he was made first president of the board of trustees, a position he soon resigned. A pioneer advocate of educational institutions under Universalist control, he called the convention held in New York, May 1847, which resulted in the founding of Tufts College. Elected its first president in 1852, he would not accept the position because the trustees could not guarantee him the $2,500 salary for which he asked. From December 1853 to April 1861 he was again pastor of the Orchard Street Church, New York, declining in the meantime the presidency of Lombard University and of St. Lawrence University. Once more he appears in the rôle of an aggressive controversialist, publishing *A Discussion of the Doctrine of Universal Salvation* (1854), a debate with the Rev. Isaac Westcott, a Baptist, in the Broadway Tabernacle; and *Who Is Our God?*

the Son or the Father? (1859), a reply to Henry Ward Beecher. From January 1863 to the end of 1865 he was editor of the *Christian Ambassador.* After relinquishing this position he lived on a farm he had acquired at Star Landing, Woodbridge, N. J., until 1869, when he was called to the Packard professorship of theology at Tufts Divinity School. In 1892 he became professor *emeritus,* having been dean for the ten years preceding, but remained comparatively active until his death in his ninety-sixth year. Among his publications not already mentioned are : *Memoir of Rev. Stephen R. Smith* (1852) ; *The Damnation of the Heathen, and the American Board* (1888) ; and *Endless Punishment in the Very Words of Its Advocates* (1891).

[Richard Eddy, *The Life of Thomas J. Sawyer, S.T.D., LL.D., and of Caroline M. Sawyer* (1900), and *Universalism in America,* vol. II (1894) ; *Cat. of the Officers and Students of Middlebury Coll., 1800 to 1900* (1901) ; *Hist. of Tufts Coll.* (1896), ed. by A. B. Start ; *Universalist Leader,* July 29, 1899 ; *Boston Herald,* Jan. 10, 1897, July 25, 1899.]   H. E. S.

SAWYER, WALTER HOWARD (May 21, 1867–Dec. 21, 1923), engineer, son of John Marshall and Mary (James) Sawyer, was born at Middletown, Conn. Thrown upon his own resources in his youth, he worked his way through school and graduated from Bromfield Academy at Harvard, Mass. Later, he studied engineering in the office of Shedd & Sawyer of Boston and in the evening schools of that city. Between 1885 and 1902 he made preliminary surveys for the New York & Boston Rapid Transit Railroad and for a sewerage system at Newburyport, Mass.; was resident engineer of the hydro-electric development on the Androscoggin River at Rumford Falls, Me., one of the early larger developments of its kind in New England; and was engaged in other hydraulic and sanitary projects in various parts of New England— including a sewer system for Lisbon, Me., hydraulic developments at Hookset, N. H., and Lewiston, Me.—and in work connected with water-rights cases.

In 1902 he was appointed agent and engineer for the Union Water Power Company of Lewiston, Me., with responsible charge of the large water power development at Lewiston and the operation of the extensive storage system of the Androscoggin River, consisting of the Rangeley Lakes system and totalling about thirty billion cubic feet of capacity. He held this position for the remainder of his life, and through it, and through an active consulting practice as well, he exerted a forceful and important influence on the industrial development of Maine. In 1909 he planned and carried out the Aziscohos Reservoir development in the headwaters of the Androscoggin River, the first project of its kind in New England where coöperative use of stored water upon a large scale was involved. This development was possible because of a concentration of head using this storage, totalling some 425 feet, in the hands of four large utility and paper companies; but it required long negotiations and untiring energy to consummate. The reservoir added about ten billion cubic feet of storage to the Androscoggin River system and made it one of the best power streams of the country. In carrying out the project Sawyer invented an adjustable log sluice of novel design and displayed much ingenuity and good judgment in its construction.

He gave much time to research—maintaining a laboratory for this purpose at Lewiston, and devised a method of measurement of water by electro-chemical means, and a method of sewage treatment. He was a pioneer in developing methods of studying the operation of storage reservoirs and was the author of a monograph on ice expansion. He was active in the civic affairs of his home city, Auburn, Me., serving as alderman and upon several commissions; he also formed the Auburn Sewerage District and had a complete sewerage system planned for the city. During the World War he was an active member of the Maine Public Safety Committee and a member of the Federal Milk Commission of New England. He served as president of the Maine Society of Civil Engineers and was prominent in other national and state organizations of this kind. On Apr. 23, 1900, he married Helen F. Hayes of Wellesley, Mass., and he was survived by one daughter. His death occurred in Auburn after a long illness.

[*Trans. Am. Soc. Civil Engineers,* vol. LXXXVIII (1925); *Jour. Boston Soc. Civil Engineers,* Oct. 1924; *Lewiston Evening Jour.,* Dec. 22, 1923.]   H. K. B.

SAXE, JOHN GODFREY (June 2, 1816– Mar. 31, 1887), poet, was born in Highgate, Franklin County, Vt., the second of the four sons of Peter and Elizabeth (Jewett) Saxe. He was of German stock on his father's side and of English on his mother's. His father was a storekeeper, mill-owner, and local politician. Saxe entered Wesleyan University in 1835 but transferred the next year to Middlebury College and graduated thence in 1839. He then read law at Lockport, N. Y., and St. Albans, Vt.; was married Sept. 9, 1841, to Sophia Newell Sollace, sister of one of his college classmates; was admitted to the bar in 1843; served as superintendent of common schools in Chittenden County, 1847–48, and as state's attorney for the county, 1850–

51; owned and edited a weekly paper, the *Burlington Sentinel,* 1850–56; and ran for governor on the Democratic ticket against Hiland Hall in 1859 and against Erastus Fairbanks in 1860. His law practice was never extensive, and he regarded his political activities as a joke. His real interests were, in a modest way, literary. He early gained a Vermont reputation as a wit, punster, and after-dinner poet, and the humorous poems that he contributed to the *Knickerbocker* prepared the way for his volumes of verse. These were: *Progress: A Satirical Poem* (1846); *Humorous and Satirical Poems* (1850); *The Money-King and Other Poems* (1860); *The Fly-ing Dutchman; or, The Wrath of Herr Vonstoppelnoze* (1862); *Clever Stories of Many Nations Rendered in Rhyme* (1865); *The Masquerade and Other Poems* (1866); *Fables and Legends of Many Countries Rendered in Rhyme* (1872); and *Leisure-Day Rhymes* (1875). With true literary tact he dedicated his first volume to Oliver Wendell Holmes and his last to Frederick Locker-Lampson. He contributed to the leading magazines, and several poems were also issued separately. The first of many editions of his collected work was published in 1850, and *Selections from the Poems of John Godfrey Saxe* in 1905. For many years he was one of the most widely read and frequently quoted of American poets. Holmes, Hood, and Praed are his models, but his tone is more popular, and he is inferior to them in originality, polish, and delicacy of sentiment. Less a poet than a humorist using verse as his medium, he owed much of his vogue to his mediocrity.

After selling the *Burlington Sentinel* in 1856, he was sufficiently prosperous and firmly established to depend for his income on his writings and lectures. He made his home in Albany, N. Y., from 1860 to 1872 and then removed to Brooklyn. He was six feet two inches tall, erect in carriage, his kindly face framed in flowing black hair and beard. A wit and humorist in public, in private he was meditative, home-loving, and subject to periods of dejection. He liked to travel, spent twenty-three successive seasons at Saratoga Springs, and visited Europe with his wife in 1867. Five of his six children lived to maturity, but in 1874 his youngest daughter died of tuberculosis; the next year he was severely injured in a railway wreck and his brain was permanently affected; and in the course of the next six years his wife, his two remaining daughters, his eldest son, and his daughter-in-law died, leaving only his son Charles to survive him. Enveloped in hopeless, ever-deepening melancholia, he spent his last years in almost complete seclusion in his son's house in Albany. He died of a heart attack in his seventy-first year.

[*Hist. of Franklin and Grand Isle Counties, Vt.* (1891), L. C. Aldrich, ed.; J. G. Saxe, *Geneal. of the Saxe Family* (priv. printed, 1930); F. C. Jewett, *Hist. and Geneal. of the Jewetts of America* (2 vols., 1908); *Cat. of Officers and Students of Middlebury Coll. . . . 1800 to 1900* (1901); R. W. Taft, *John Godfrey Saxe* (priv. printed, 1900); R. H. Stoddard, "John Godfrey Saxe," *Nat. Mag.,* May 1853; E. C. Stedman and others, "John Godfrey Saxe," *Critic,* Apr. 9, 1887; J. G. and M. S. Saxe, "Saxe—the Vt. Poet," *Bookman,* June 1916; A. W. Peach in *Vermonters* (1931), W. H. Crockett, ed.; *N. Y. Tribune, Daily Press and Knickerbocker* (Albany, N. Y.), *Albany Eve. Jour.* (obituary and editorial), Apr. 1, 1887.] G. H. G.

SAXTON, JOSEPH (Mar. 22, 1799–Oct. 26, 1873), inventor, the son of James and Hannah (Ashbaugh) Saxton, was born in Huntington, Pa. His father was engaged in banking and also was the proprietor of a nail factory. After James had obtained an ordinary education he went to work at the age of twelve in the latter establishment for a short time, and was then apprenticed to a watch-maker for two years. In 1817 he went to Philadelphia in the hope of educating himself. He continued working at his trade in this city for about eleven years, studied engraving on the side, and eventually became associated with Isaiah Lukens, a celebrated machinist. During this time he constructed an astronomical clock with a compensating pendulum and escapement of his own design, and also made the clock for the belfry of Independence Hall. He acquired a wide reputation in Philadelphia for his great ingenuity but, in a desire to enlarge his knowledge, he went to England in 1828 where he soon became connected with the Adelaide Gallery of Practical Science in London and made a name for himself through the construction and exhibition of scientific novelties and apparatus. He met many noted engineers, scientists, and mechanicians, and through these friends was introduced to Michael Faraday and to the meetings of the Royal Society. His association with scientists spurred him to go forward with numerous original experiments. He constructed and exhibited in 1833, before the British Association for the Advancement of Science at Cambridge, a magneto-electric machine which produced a brilliant spark, decomposed water, exhibited an intense light between the charcoal points, and gave a rapid series of heavy shocks. Unfortunately, through his failure at the time to publish a description of this machine, the credit for the invention was given to another. During his residence of nine years in England, Saxton acquired a number of British patents, including a locomotive differential pulley, an apparatus for measuring the velocity of vessels, and a fountain pen.

As early as 1829, he improved the medal-ruling machine so that it was capable of copying without distortion the designs of medals and coins.

He returned to Philadelphia in 1837 to accept the appointment of constructor and curator of the standard weighing apparatus of the United States Mint, having declined the position of director of printing machinery of the Bank of England. During his connection with the mint he designed and constructed the large standard balances used for the verification of the standard weights of the government's assay and coining offices. In 1843 he joined the United States coast survey in Washington, D. C., as superintendent of weights and measures and served in this capacity for the next thirty years. His first work in this new position was the construction of the standard balances, weights, and measures subsequently presented to each state of the Union for insuring uniformity of measures in all parts of the country. He also constructed much of the complex apparatus employed by the Coast Survey, and altered the Survey's dividing engine so that it was completely automatic, driven by a water-turbine of his own design. He also patented an anthracite coal-burning stove, a fusible metal seal, a hydrometer, and an ever-pointed pencil. Saxton was more than a practical mechanical genius but not a profound student of science. According to his biographer, he "possessed more wisdom than learning" (Henry, *post,* p. 314). He was one of the fifty original members of the National Academy of Sciences, and a member of the American Philosophical Society. The Franklin Institute awarded him the John Scott legacy medal in November 1834 for his invention of a reflecting pyrometer. He was married in 1850 to Mary H. Abercrombie of Philadelphia who, with their daughter, survived him.

[Joseph Henry, "Memoir of Joseph Saxton," *Nat'l Acad. of Sciences, Biog. Memoirs,* vol. I (1877); J. R. Eckfeldt and Wm. E. Du Bois, *A Manual of Gold and Silver Coins* (1851); records of the Patent Office; *Evening Star* (Washington, D. C.), Oct. 27, 1873.] C. W. M.

SAY, BENJAMIN (Aug. 28, 1755–Apr. 23, 1813), physician and philanthropist, born at Philadelphia, Pa., was the son of Thomas Say by his second wife, Rebekah (Atkinson) Budd, widow of Thomas Budd and daughter of Samuel Atkinson. A descendant of a French Huguenot family in England and the son of William, who settled in America towards the close of the seventeenth century, Thomas Say (1709–96) began his business life as a harness maker but later opened an apothecary shop and set up as a physician. Although he administered medicines he also claimed to accomplish cures by means of stroking the afflicted part. He was deeply religious, with mystical tendencies. He had a series of visions, an account of the first of which appears in Benjamin's Say's *A Short Compilation of the Extraordinary Life and Writings of Thomas Say* (1796). But in spite of his mysticism he was a good man of business and a public-spirited citizen. He accumulated a comfortable fortune, was active in civic affairs, and was much interested in bettering the condition of the negroes.

There is no definite information as to where Benjamin Say received his medical education. Although he is said to have graduated from the University of Pennsylvania, there is no record in the official registers. Probably his father was his preceptor; at any rate, he followed his example in conducting an apothecary shop in connection with a medical practice. The ledger preserved in the College of Physicians of Philadelphia shows that his practice was both extensive and lucrative. His lack of a degree did not prevent his becoming one of the first junior fellows of the College of Physicians and as such signing the constitution of the college at its adoption on Jan. 2, 1787. He also served as treasurer of the college from 1791 to 1809. He is said to have published a book on "Spasmodic Affections of the Eye" in 1792, but it is not in the library of the Surgeon-General in Washington, D. C., nor in that of the College of Physicians of Philadelphia. His only other publication was *An Annual Oration Pronounced before the Humane Society of Philadelphia* (1799). He was one of the incorporators of the society and its president in 1799. He was also active in the movement to abolish slavery. In 1799 he was elected to the Senate of Pennsylvania but declined to accept a renomination in 1801; in 1808 he was elected representative in Congress from Pennsylvania but resigned in the following year. He and his father were shareholders in the company formed by John Fitch [*q.v.*] to exploit his steamboat. He was also much in horticulture and in 1802 was president of a "Company for the Improvement of the Vine." He married Ann, daughter of Benjamin Bonsall and grand-daughter of John Bartram [*q.v.*], the botanist, on Oct. 1, 1776. By her he had four children, one of whom, Thomas Say [*q.v.*], became a distinguished naturalist. After her death in 1793, he married on Dec. 22, 1795, Miriam Moore, by whom he had two daughters and a son. When he died, in Philadelphia, he left a large estate to his second wife and the six children who survived him.

[H. B. Weiss and Grace M. Ziegler, *Thomas Say, Early Am. Naturalist* (1931), very detailed treatment of the Say family, with bibliog.; W. S. W. Ruschenberger, *An Account of the Institution and Progress of the Coll. of Physicians of Phila. . . . from Jan. 1787* (1887); *Pa. Mag. Hist. and Biog.,* Apr. 1905; death notice in *Poulson's Am. Daily Advertiser,* Apr. 24, 1813; Benjamin Say's account book, 1785–1803, in Pa. Hist. Soc., and ledger, 1796–1804, in Coll. of Physicians of Phila.]

F. R. P.

SAY, THOMAS (June 27, 1787–Oct. 10, 1834), entomologist, conchologist, called "the father of descriptive entomology in America," was born in Philadelphia, of Quaker ancestry. His father, Dr. Benjamin Say [*q.v.*], a member of the Society of Friends, was a physician and apothecary, served as a state senator and for two terms as a member of Congress, and at the time of his death was said to be one of the richest men in Philadelphia. His mother was Ann (Bonsall), daughter of Benjamin Bonsall of Kingsessing and grand-daughter of John Bartram [*q.v.*]. Young Say was educated at the Friends' school at Westtown, a short distance from Philadelphia, but this education was not broad and throughout life he is said to have felt the need of wider training. He then studied pharmacy with his father and started a pharmacy shop with a partner, but the business failed because he too trustfully indorsed the notes of a friend.

As a boy Say had been interested in natural history through his mother's uncle, William Bartram [*q.v.*]. He was one of the original members of the Philadelphia Academy of Natural Sciences (founded in 1812), although he was not present at the first meeting; and from that date he devoted nearly all his time to the study of natural history. After his business failure he lived in the rooms of the Academy, sleeping on the floor and cooking his own meals, thus subsisting at an expense of seventy-five cents a week. He served briefly with the volunteers in 1814 and was a member of the First City Troop for several years thereafter. His great work, *American Entomology,* was planned and begun in 1816, and a ten-page prospectus was issued the following year. In 1818 he visited Georgia and Florida with several other members of the Academy—George Ord, William Maclure, and Titian R. Peale [*qq.v.*]—and in 1819 he was appointed as zoölogist to accompany the expedition to the Rocky Mountains under Maj. Stephen H. Long [*q.v.*], by which large collections were made. He accompanied in the same capacity Long's second expedition, in 1823, which explored the sources of the Minnesota River.

During the next few years he was busily engaged in and out of Philadelphia, where he was made curator of the American Philosophical Society in 1821 and professor of natural history in the University of Pennsylvania in 1822. He held the former post until 1827 and the latter until 1828, although much of the time during these years he was away from the city. In 1824 and 1825, respectively, appeared the first two volumes of his *American Entomology; or Descriptions of the Insects of North America,* and he prepared for the press the first volume (1825) of Charles Bonaparte's *American Ornithology; or the Natural History of Birds Inhabiting the United States.* In 1825, in company with William Maclure, Charles Alexandre Lesueur [*q.v.*], Robert Owen, and others, Say (at the age of thirty-eight) went to Indiana, where Owen had bought the village of New Harmony, intending to found there an ideal community. Like other experiments of the kind, this one soon failed; the founders were involved in lawsuits, which finally were compromised, and Owen returned to Europe. In the meantime, Jan. 4, 1827, Say had married Lucy Way Sistaire, and he maintained his home in New Harmony for the rest of his life. During late 1827 and early 1828 he went to New Orleans and Mexico with Maclure, who was failing in health, and visited Vera Cruz, Jalapa, Mexico City, Tacuba, and Chalco.

In person, Say was six feet tall, and slender; he spoke with a slight lisp. His health had been poor even before he left Philadelphia, owing probably in part to his very frugal diet. In New Harmony he carried the same abstinence to excess. He was very often ill, after his return from Mexico, probably with malaria and surely with obstinate stomach trouble. Nevertheless, he worked on industriously and completed the third volume (1828) of his *American Entomology* as well as the six numbers of his *American Conchology* which were published (1830–34) at New Harmony.

Say's work was almost wholly taxonomic and his writings were almost entirely descriptive. He published practically nothing concerning the habits and life histories of the forms he named and described. That he confined his writing to pure description has been ascribed to his consciousness of his faulty education and to his lack of general reading. His published letters, however, are admirably written, and it is believed that he wrote at least a part of the narrative of Long's expeditions. His descriptive work was excellent, and nearly all his species have been recognized. His collections and library went to the Philadelphia Academy of Natural Sciences after his death, and through neglect, the greater part of his collections was allowed to go to ruin, but Dr. John Lawrence LeConte [*q.v.*], in the Preface to his edition of Say's entomological papers, said: "His descriptions are so clear as to leave scarcely a doubt as to the objects designated." The excellence of his work was early recognized by European zoölogists, and he was made a foreign member of the Linnean Society of London. His earlier papers were published in the *Journal of the Academy of Natural Sciences of Philadelphia* and later ones in the *Boston Journal of Natural History* and the *Annals of the Lyceum of Natural History of New-York.* Others were issued independently by the author at New Harmony. In 1859 J. L. LeConte edited and published in two volumes *The Complete Writings of Thomas Say on the Entomology of North America,* with a biographical memoir by George Ord. The individual titles cover twenty-nine papers, many of them monographic in character. Since the publication of these two volumes, a few other entomological papers of Say's have been found, mainly in agricultural journals. His work on conchology was summarized in 1858 in a volume edited by W. G. Binney, entitled *The Complete Writings of Thomas Say on the Conchology of the United States,* with seventy-five plates. Most of the figures of shells illustrating Say's work were drawn by Mrs. Say; the drawings of insects in his other works were chiefly by himself. His paleontological writings were reprinted in 1896, by G. D. Harris, in the *Bulletins of American Paleontology* (vol. I, no. 5).

[H. B. Weiss and G. M. Ziegler, *Thomas Say, Early Am. Naturalist* (1931); George Ord, "A Memoir of Thomas Say," read before the Am. Phil. Soc., Dec. 19, 1834, and pub. in Preface to LeConte's edition (1859) of Say's entomological writings; B. H. Coates, *A Biog. Sketch of the Late Thomas Say, Esq.* (Phila. Acad. Nat. Sci., 1835); J. S. Kingsley, "Sketch of Thomas Say," *Pop. Sci., Mo.,* Sept. 1882; W. H. Dall, "Some American Conchologists," *Proc. Biol. Soc. of Washington,* vol. IV (1888); F. M. Webster, "Thomas Say," *Entomological News,* Jan.-Apr. 1895; H. S. Barber, "Thomas Say's Unrecorded Journey in Mexico," *Ibid.,* Jan. 1928; Say's correspondence with J. F. Melsheimer, *Ibid.,* 1891–92; S. H. Scudder, "An Unknown Tract on American Insects by Thomas Say," *Psyche,* Jan. 1899; V. Sterki, "A Few Notes on Say's Early Writings and Species," *Nautilus,* July 1907; G. B. Lockwood, *The New Harmony Movement* (1905); *Am. Jour. Sci.,* Jan. 1835; *Poulson's Am. Daily Advertiser,* Nov. 4, 1834.]

L. O. H.

SAYLES, JOHN (Mar. 9, 1825–May 22, 1897), lawyer and writer of law books, was born at Ithaca, N. Y. His father, Welcome, a successful physician, was a member of a Rhode Island family, the founder of which, John, came from England in 1650. His mother was Harriett Elizabeth Sergeant, of Massachusetts, daughter of a noted Presbyterian clergyman and missionary to the Oneida Indians. John began teaching in New York State at the age of fifteen and later taught in Georgia; between school terms he attended college. In 1845 he was awarded the degree of B.A. by Hamilton College, Clinton, N. Y., and in the same year removed to Texas, settling at Brenham. Here he taught school and read law.

He was admitted to the bar in 1846 and three years later became associated in practice with Col. Barry Gillespie, a distinguished lawyer and planter. A later partnership, under the name of Sayles & Bassett, continued for nearly thirty years and was one of the most successful firms in Texas at that time. In 1853–55, he was a member of the Texas legislature. In addition to his work as a lawyer, he served from 1857 to 1860 as a member of the faculty of the law school of Baylor University, which is believed to have been the first law school established in Texas. He was again connected with the school for several years after it was reorganized in 1867. During the Civil War he attained the rank of brigadier-general of militia and rendered distinguished service under Gen. J. Bankhead Magruder [q.v.]. In 1886 he removed to Abilene, in Western Texas, and with his son, Henry, established the firm of Sayles & Sayles.

Though he was an excellent lawyer, his fame rests on the fact that he was the ablest and most prolific writer of law books that Texas has produced. His first volume, *A Treatise on Practice of the District and Supreme Courts of the State of Texas* (1858), consisting largely of his lectures to the law classes in Baylor University, passed through three editions. A complementary volume, *A Treatise on the Civil Jurisdiction of Justices of the Peace* (1867), ran through four editions, the last entitled *Sayles' Guide for Justices* (1894). Another product of his law teaching was *A Treatise on the Principles of Pleading in Civil Actions in the Courts of Texas* (1872). This work formed the basis of three others—*The Rules of Pleading and Practice in the Courts of Record in the State of Texas* (3rd ed., 1882), in preparing which he was aided by his partner, B. H. Bassett; *Revised Statutes of the State of Texas Relating to Organization, Jurisdiction and Practice of the District and County Courts* (1886), in collaboration with his son, Henry Sayles; and, finally, the work of 1872 rewritten and published as the *Precedents and Rules of Pleading in Civil Actions in the County and District Courts of Texas* (1893). In 1871, he brought out *The Probate Laws of Texas*; and in 1876, *A Manual of the Laws of Business*. In collaboration with his son, Henry, he published *Early Laws of Texas* (3 vols., 1888), and *A Treatise on the Laws of Texas Relating to Real Estate* (2 vols., 1891–92). In 1888 there appeared the fourth volume of what was intended to be a four-volume work on the constitution and statutes of Texas. This volume was the third

edition of his *The Constitutions of the State of Texas,* the first and second editions of which had appeared in 1872 and 1884 respectively. The next volume of the series to appear was *The Annotated Statutes, Civil and Criminal, of the State of Texas . . . Supplement for 1889* (1889); the third, *Sayles' Annotated Civil Statutes of the State of Texas* (2 parts), did not appear until 1897, the year of his death. The projected volume on the criminal statutes was not published. At one time Grand Master of Masons in Texas, Sayles was the author of *The Masonic Jurisprudence of Texas* (1879). In 1849 he was married to Mary Elizabeth, only daughter of his first law partner, Col. Barry Gillespie. He had three sons and three daughters.

[Information from a daughter, Mrs. George C. Harris, and a grandson, John Sayles. See J. D. Lynch, *The Bench and Bar of Tex.* (1885); J. C. Townes, *Law Books and How to Use Them* (copr. 1909), p. 185; *Dallas Morning News,* May 30, 1897.]   C. S. P—s.

SAYRE, LEWIS ALBERT (Feb. 29, 1820–Sept. 21, 1900), orthopedic surgeon, was born at Bottle Hill (later Madison), N. J., the son of Archibald and Martha (Sayer) Sayre and a descendant of Thomas Sayre, who was in Lynn, Mass., in 1638. From his grandfather Ephraim, a quartermaster in the Revolution, and his father, a wealthy farmer, prominent in local affairs, he inherited an unusual capacity for physical and mental labor. After attending the local academy for a time and Wantage Seminary at Deckertown, he lived with his banker uncle, David A. Sayre, in Lexington, Ky., and is said to have graduated from Transylvania University in 1839. Though he considered entering the ministry, he began to study medicine under the preceptorship of Dr. David Green of New York and was graduated from the College of Physicians and Surgeons in New York in 1842. His graduation thesis on spinal irritation was of such unusual merit that it was published. Early in his career he gave evidence of that critical open-mindedness which throughout his life inspired respect. As a student he wrote, "I made up my mind that if what I was taught agreed with my experience as to what I found, I would adopt it, and otherwise not" (letter to his son, R. H. Sayre). He was prosector to Dr. Willard Parker [q.v.], 1842–52, and built up his own practice in New York. On Jan. 25, 1849, he married Eliza Ann Hall. They had a daughter, and three sons all of whom became surgeons, among them Reginald Hall Sayre [q.v.].

In 1853 he was appointed surgeon to the Bellevue Hospital and in 1859 to the Charity Hospital on Blackwell's Island. He played an important part in the organization of the Bellevue Hospital

Medical College in 1861 and occupied the first chair of orthopedic surgery in America. He was one of the founders of the New York Pathological Society and was active in the affairs of the New York Academy of Medicine and of the American Medical Association, of which he was president in 1880. During 1860–66, at great personal sacrifice, he served as resident physician of the city of New York, holding the office under four mayors. Under his vigorous and persistent attacks the bad sanitary conditions of the time, particularly those in tenements, were greatly bettered. He advocated compulsory vaccination, was the first American health officer to deal with cholera as a contagious disease, and almost the only one who could have said, "The cholera which has arrived within our harbor, and has been so near our shores . . . was anchored in the bay, and detained there" (*Annual Report of the Resident Physician of the City of New York for 1865*, 1866). He was the acknowledged leader of orthopedic surgery in America. He had been the first American to perform a resection of the hip for morbus coxarius (1854), and he developed a treatment of lateral curvature that became known throughout the world as the Sayre method. When in 1871 he visited Europe and gave demonstrations and lectures in several countries, his fame became international. As delegate of the American Medical Association he attended the international medical convention in Philadelphia in 1876 and the meetings of the British Medical Association in 1877. His demonstrations and lectures were followed by more honors; Charles XV of Sweden made him a knight of the Order of Wasa in 1871, and the British association passed grateful resolutions.

His mental energy carried his constructive thought beyond his own anatomical field of the bones and joints and muscles. Scarcely graduated from medical school, he proposed radical methods of drainage of the pleural cavity and collapse of the lung, methods of diagnosis and treatment looked upon as sound by thoracic surgeons of a later day. He wrote on croup (*Transactions of the Medical Society of the State of New York*, 1864), on lead palsy (*Transactions of the American Medical Association*, vol. XX, 1869), and on abscess of the cellular tissues of the peritoneum. His contributions to his own branch of surgery were often original and strikingly successful. His publications include *Report on Morbus Coxarius or Hip Disease* (1860), *A Practical Manual of the Treatment of Club Foot* (1869), *On Anchylosis* (1874), *Report on Fractures* (1874), *On Disease of the Hip-Joint* (1875), *Spinal Disease and Spinal Curvature*

(1877), and *Lectures on Orthopedic Surgery and Diseases of the Joints* (1876), distinguished for its terseness and for the practicality of its illustrations. Though there was something of the zealot about him—in his lectures he exhorted as well as taught—his zeal was tempered by kindness and honesty. Patients attributed qualities almost supernatural to him and depended on the courage that overflowed from his exhaustless source. Yet neither their intense admiration nor the recognition of the medical world harmed him; he remained a brilliant and resourceful surgeon; just in thought and action.

[T. M. Banta, *Sayre Family, Lineage of Thomas Sayre* (1901); H. A. Kelly and W. L. Burrage, *Am. Medic. Biogs.* (1920); *First Decennial Cat. of . . . Officers . . . Bellevue Hospital Medic. Coll. . . . 1861 to 1871* (1873); *New England Medic. Jour.*, June 1884; *Mag. Western Hist.*, Nov. 1889; J. G. Kuhns and R. B. Osgood, "Am. Explorers in Orthopaedic Surgery," *Crippled Child*, Oct. 1931; Sir Arthur Keith, *Menders of the Maimed* (1919); Daniel Van Pelt, *Leslie's Hist. of the Greater New York* (1898), vol. III; *Medic. Record* (N. Y.), Sept. 29, 1900; *Boston Medic. and Surgical Jour.*, Sept. 27, 1900; *British Medic. Jour.*, Dec. 15, 1900; *Lancet* (London), Oct. 27, 1900; *N. Y. Times*, Sept. 22, 1900; information from Reginald H. Sayre.]
R. B. O.

SAYRE, REGINALD HALL (Oct. 18, 1859–May 29, 1929), surgeon, was born in New York City, the son of Lewis Albert Sayre [*q.v.*] and Eliza Ann (Hall) Sayre. From the Churchill and Maury School he entered Columbia College, where he won a scholarship in chemistry and was graduated with high honors in 1881. In college he was editor of the *Columbia Spectator,* a member of his class crew and of the varsity track team, and champion intercollegiate mile-walker. Although he matriculated in law school his elder brother Lewis persuaded him to study medicine, and he entered Bellevue Hospital Medical College, planning later to join his father in the practice of orthopedic surgery. He wisely elected not the surgical but the medical service under such masters as the elder Austin Flint and Edward Gamaliel Janeway [*qq.v.*] and acquired a catholicity of view that he never lost. He received the degree of M.D. in 1884. With his brother Lewis, who died six years later, he became the trusted associate of his father, whose reputation was international and whose huge practice and spacious offices represented almost an institution. Beginning in 1885 as assistant to the chair of surgery at Bellevue Hospital Medical College, he afterwards became lecturer and orthopedic surgeon there, succeeded his father in 1898 as clinical professor of orthopedic surgery, and twelve years later became full professor. A cosmopolitan in medicine, he was sought as consultant to numerous hospitals within and without New York City. For years he was an officer of the New York Academy of Medicine; he was a charter member of the American Orthopaedic Association and its president in 1903–04, a charter member of the American College of Surgeons, and a lieutenant colonel in the World War in charge of orthopedic instruction to medical officers. Though he wrote little after 1910, his earlier medical writings were significant. They included *The Treatment of Rotary Lateral Curvature of the Spine* (1888), *The Necessity for Thorough Examination in Suspected Pott's Disease* (1893), *The Treatment of Neglected Cases of Rotary Lateral Curvature of the Spine* (1893), and *Posture in the Diagnosis of Disease* (1897). He never married.

Personally a conservative, he possessed, like his more explosive father, remarkable latent force. Like his father, too, he had a delicious sense of humor and the power of vigorous, homely expressions. Though his devotion to his work was marked—he often made ward rounds on Sundays and holidays—he found time to become champion pistol shot of America and captain of four Olympic pistol teams. He also had a great love of horses and could drive with a rein gentle enough for a smart team or fearless enough for Troop A cavalry. The combination of skill and boldness displayed in these recreations was equally apparent in his professional work. His teaching was of the clinical rather than the didactic sort. Quick to appreciate the merit of sound new methods of surgery, he introduced many of them into the United States, and his wide experience and large fund of knowledge won him the deep respect of students and of his medical peers. He once deplored overwork because of its being "so easy to acquire a way of being slipshod and slovenly from lack of time," a characteristic attitude on the part of one who was himself an able, careful practitioner of a specialty that required a high order of artistry.

[T. M. Banta, *Sayre Family, Lineage of Thomas Sayre* (1901); *Who's Who in America, 1928–29; Medic. Jour. and Record* (N. Y.), July 3, 1929; *Jour. of Bone and Joint Surgery,* July 1929; *Bull. N. Y. Acad. of Medicine,* Aug. 1929; *N. Y. Times,* May 30, 1929; information from Miss Mary H. Sayre, a sister; personal acquaintance.]   R. B. O.

SAYRE, ROBERT HEYSHAM (Oct. 13, 1824–Jan. 5, 1907), civil engineer and railroad official, was born in Columbia County, Pa., the son of William H. and Eliza (Kent) Sayre and a descendant of Thomas Sayre who was in Lynn, Mass., as early as 1638. His father was an official of the Lehigh Coal & Navigation Company. Robert received his early education in the common schools and then studied civil engineering under James Nowlin, a mathematician of

considerable reputation. In 1840 he was employed on the enlargement of the Morris Canal, and in the following year joined the engineering corps of his father's company for which, in 1843, he was assigned to make surveys and construct the railroad between the coal mines at Summit Hill and Mauch Chunk on the Lehigh Canal. He also built the switchback railroad and inclined planes into the Panther Creek Valley coal field, exhibiting such ability in this type of work that he was placed in charge of all the railroads and inclined planes of the company and the transportation of coal over them from the mines to Mauch Chunk. At the same time he directed the development of the company's mines and the erection and installation of equipment.

From 1852 until his retirement in 1898, with the exception of three years (1882–85) as president and chief engineer of the South Pennsylvania Railroad, he was in the employ of the Delaware, Lehigh, Schuylkill & Susquehannah Railroad and its successor, the Lehigh Valley system. He held successively the positions of chief engineer, general superintendent, second vice-president, assistant to the president, and vice-president. Convinced by his early experience that the future of the Western Pennsylvania coal region depended upon rail outlets to tidewater, he pushed the construction of the Lehigh Valley Railroad until such an outlet was achieved, building feeder lines from the western coal fields in the period 1852–82, the Easton & Amboy Railroad between 1872 and 1875, and the extensions to Buffalo and Jersey City, 1885–98. He was a pioneer in the introduction of iron bridges to replace wooden structures on the line of the Lehigh Valley Railroad (1857), and in the use of steel rails (1864), the fish-bar track joint, and steel-tired driving wheels and steel fireboxes for locomotives. Few men have had as much influence on the development of a single railroad system as did he.

Besides his railroad interests he was one of the promoters of the Bethlehem Iron Company, of which he became vice-president in 1891, and of the Pioneer Mining and Manufacturing Company of Alabama, and held directorates in a number of other corporations. He was chairman of the board of trustees and of the executive committee of Lehigh University, and to that institution presented a fully equipped astronomical observatory. He was much interested in book collecting and in 1899 built a library addition to his residence at South Bethlehem, Pa., to house some ten thousand volumes. He was married four times: on Apr. 15, 1845, to Mary Evelyn Smith, who died in 1869; on Jan. 12, 1871, to

Mary (Bradford), widow of Richard Brodhead, who died in 1877; on Apr. 15, 1879, to Helen Augusta (Packer), widow of Rollin H. Rathbun; and on May 3, 1882, to Martha Finley Nevin, daughter of the Rev. John W. Nevin [*q.v.*], of Mercersburg. Nine children were born to the first marriage and three to the fourth. Sayre died at South Bethlehem, Pa., survived by his wife and six children.

[T. M. Banta, *Sayre Family* (1901); *The Biog. Dir. of the Railway Officials of America* (1906); M. S. Henry, *Hist. of the Lehigh Valley* (1860), p. 394, portr.; *Who's Who in Pa.*, 1904; *The Biog. Encyc. of Pa. of the Nineteenth Century* (1874); *Public Ledger* (Phila.), Jan. 6, 1907.]   J. H. F.

SAYRE, STEPHEN (June 12, 1736–Sept. 27, 1818), merchant, banker, diplomatic agent, was descended from Thomas Sayre, an early settler of Southampton, L. I. There Stephen was born, tenth and youngest child of John and Hannah (Howell) Sayre. He graduated from the College of New Jersey in 1757 and a few years later went to London, where his handsome person and agreeable manners won him a position in society. His charm, however, concealed an impetuous and rash nature which often involved him in difficulties and which prevented him all his life from any solid accomplishment. He became a member of the mercantile house of Dennys De Berdt [*q.v.*], at that time colonial agent of Massachusetts, and returned to America for a year, collecting debts for the firm, soliciting commissions, and acting also for Charles Townshend, with whom he was a favorite, in the interests of a land scheme which Townshend hoped to promote in the colony of New York.

In 1770 De Berdt died, leaving his firm in financial difficulties, and Sayre organized the banking house of Stephen Sayre & Barth-Coote-Purdon of Oxford Street. He desired De Berdt's position as colonial agent but his candidacy failed. Unofficially, however, he worked constantly for the cause of the colonies. He had already published a pamphlet, *The Englishman Deceived* (London, 1768), which was reprinted in the colonies and widely circulated. He kept in close touch with prominent men both in America and England and was responsible for the beginning of the correspondence of Arthur Lee and Samuel Adams. In 1774, his name headed the list of signers of a petition from Americans in London protesting against the proposed closing of the port of Boston. Meantime (1773), Sayre and William Lee [*q.v.*] had served for a year as sheriffs of London, an unusual honor to be accorded to Americans.

Sayre's outspoken partisanship finally involved him with the authorities and in October 1775 he

was arrested and lodged in the Tower, charged with having plotted to seize the King, take possession of the Tower, and overthrow the government. After five days of close confinement he was admitted to bail and subsequently discharged for lack of evidence. He then sued Lord Rochford for assault and false imprisonment. A verdict was found in his favor, but a point of law prevented the award of damages. By the time the suit was settled the banking house had failed, and Sayre went to Paris intending to sail for America. In May 1777, Arthur Lee appointed him secretary of his mission to Berlin, but the two men quarrelled constantly, and when Lee, unsuccessful, returned to Paris, Sayre stayed behind. After some months in Berlin, he went unofficially to Copenhagen to propose commercial relations with the United States and to further the suggested neutral league. Early in 1779, he moved on to Stockholm, apparently posing as an official agent of the United States, but accomplished nothing. He then returned to Paris, where Franklin told him he had nothing to offer in the way of employment and referred him to Congress for payment for his past services. His next venture was into Russia on various private projects.

At the end of the war he returned home, where he met the South American patriot, Francesco Miranda, then on a tour of the United States; henceforth he was a warm advocate of Miranda's plans and in frequent communication with him. Sayre petitioned Congress for payment for his European services, but without result, and he went again to Europe. His wife, Elizabeth (Noel), a London heiress whom he had married Feb. 18, 1775, died in 1789, and he married in Paris, 1790, Elizabeth Dorone, also a woman of wealth. Returning to America in 1793, he bought a large estate in New Jersey and recommenced petitioning Congress. At length, in 1807, an act was passed granting him pay for the time he spent in Berlin as Lee's secretary, but ignoring his claim for payment for services at Copenhagen and Stockholm. He died at "Brandon," the home of his son in Middlesex County, Va.

[W. B. Reed, *Life and Correspondence of Joseph Reed* (2 vols., 1847); *Letters of Dennys De Berdt* (1911), appearing also in *Col. Soc. Mass. Pubs.*, vol. XIII (1912); W. B. Reed, *The Life of Esther De Berdt* (1853); B. F. Stevens, "Facsimiles of MSS. in European Archives" (MSS. Div., Lib. of Cong.); *Am. State Papers: Claims* (1834); T. M. Banta, *Sayre Family* (1901), with portr.; J. P. Boyd, *The Susquehannah Company Papers*, vol. II (1930); W. S. Robertson, *The Life of Miranda* (2 vols., 1929); death notice in *Richmond Enquirer*, Dec. 10, 1818.]   M. E. L.

SCAMMELL, ALEXANDER (Mar. 27, 1747–Oct. 6, 1781), Revolutionary soldier, was born in that part of the town of Mendon which is now Milford, Mass., and was baptized there on Mar. 22, 1747 o. s. He was the son of Samuel Leslie and Jane (Libbey) Scammell, both of whom emigrated from Portsmouth, England, to Mendon probably in 1737. His father, a physician of standing and affluence, died in 1753 and in his will provided for the care of his two sons by the Rev. Amariah Frost, pastor of the Congregational Church. Alexander was prepared for Harvard College and graduated there in 1769. With such experience in teaching district school as he had already gained during his college course, he taught first in Kingston and then at Plymouth, Mass. In 1772 he went to Portsmouth, N. H., where, with the help of a cousin in government service, he was employed in surveying and exploring for lands and for royal navy timber. He worked with Samuel Holland in surveying and making maps of the region.

The outbreak of the Revolution found him a tall, attractive young man reading law in the office of John Sullivan [q.v.] at Durham, N. H., and hoping to marry Abigail Bishop of Medford, Mass. In this he was, however, to be disappointed by the exigencies of war and the lady's doubts (letters to her in Ballou, *post*, p. 1006, *Historical Magazine, post, New Hampshire Historical Society Collections*, vol. IX, 1889). He became a brigade major in Sullivan's brigade, served in the siege of Boston and in the expedition to Canada the next year, and as aide-de-camp to Sullivan he participated in the Long Island campaign, during which, on the retreat to New York, he was responsible for a blunder that might have been fatal but for the timely arrival of Washington (H. P. Johnston, "The Campaign of 1776," *Memoirs of The Long Island Historical Society*, vol. III, 1878, p. 222). In October 1776 he became brigade major in the division of Gen. Charles Lee [q.v.] and on Dec. 10, 1776, colonel of the third continental battalion to be raised by the state. In 1777 he was with St. Clair at Ticonderoga and was slightly wounded at Saratoga. On Jan. 5, 1778, he was chosen by Congress to succeed Timothy Pickering [q.v.] as adjutant general of the Continental Army and served until Jan. 1, 1781. In that office it became his duty to arrest his old general, Charles Lee, after the battle of Monmouth and in 1780 to take charge of the execution of Major John André. He enjoyed the confidence of Washington, who at the time of his resignation spoke of him in terms of unqualified approval (*The Writings of George Washington*, vol. VII, 1835, ed. by Jared Sparks, p. 314). He resigned to take command of the 1st New Hampshire Regiment,

and he led a party of Continental light horse until on Sept. 30, 1781, he was captured at Yorktown, while reconnoitering as officer of the day. The circumstances of his death at Williamsburg sixteen days later have occasioned some controversy. It has been charged that after his capture he received the wounds from which he died; but the evidence is unconvincing. Contemporary reports of his death are not agreed in making such a charge, and it is not clear by what channels the report of any eye-witness could have found its way back to the American lines.

[Letters in Lib. of Cong., *Historical Mag.*, Sept. 1870, *Mass. Hist. Soc. Proc.*, vol. LII (1919), and "Letters and Papers of . . . John Sullivan," ed. by O. G. Hammond, *N. H. Hist. Soc. Colls.*, vol. XIII, XIV (1930–31); Charles Coffin, *The Lives and Services of . . . John Thomas . . . Alexander Scammell* (1845); Adin Ballou, *Hist. of . . . Milford* (1882); *Vital Records of Milford, Mass.* (1917); *Vital Records of Medford, Mass.* (1907); *Provincial Papers . . . of New-Hampshire*, vol. VII (1873); *State Papers of New-Hampshire*, vols. VIII (1874), XIV (1885), XV (1886); *Mass. Hist. Soc. Colls.*, ser. 1, vol. II (1793), IX (1804), ser. 2, vols. III (1815), IV (1816); *Proc. Mass. Hist. Soc.*, ser. 1, vols. I (1879), XIV (1876), XIX (1882), ser. 2, vols. III (1888), VI (1891), whole ser. vols. XLVI (1913), LII (1919); Henry Lee, *Memoirs* (1812), vol. II, p. 333; *Mag. of Amer. Hist.*, Jan. 1881, p. 21; E. S. Stackpole and Lucien Thompson, *Hist. of . . . Durham, N. H.* (1913), vol. I; *Continental Jour. and Weekly Advertiser* (Boston), Nov. 8, 1781; date of birth from own statement on entrance to Harvard College, Harvard Univerity records through the courtesy of Clifford K. Shipton, Mass. Hist. Soc., Boston.]

K. E. C.

SCAMMON, JONATHAN YOUNG (July 27, 1812–Mar. 17, 1890), lawyer and business man, was born on a farm in Whitefield. Me., the son of Eliakim and Joanna (Young) Scammon. With a farmer's life in prospect, the boy's future was suddenly changed by the loss of two fingers on his left hand. Since he was thus handicapped in the farmer's important business of milking cows, his parents decided to equip him for a profession. He prepared for college and at eighteen entered Waterville (now Colby) College, but left at the end of his first year, probably for lack of means. He studied law in a law office in Hallowell and was admitted to the bar in 1835. Fired by enthusiastic reports of the rapid development of the Mississippi Valley, he started west and, not expecting to settle there, arrived in Chicago in September 1835. Not being greatly impressed with the town, he was preparing to move on when the temporary job of deputy clerk in the circuit court was offered him. He accepted, and Chicago became his home for the remaining fifty-five years of his life. Admitted to the Illinois bar he rapidly won a place of prominence and leadership. Appointed as reporter of the Supreme Court of Illinois in 1839 he compiled four volumes of its reports, *Reports of Cases*

Argued and Determined in the Supreme Court of . . . Illinois (copr. 1840–copr. 1844). Deeply interested in public education, he, probably more than anyone else, was responsible for the establishment of free schools in Chicago. For years he was a member of the board of education and president from 1845 to 1848. One of the city's elementary schools bears his name in recognition of his services. In his early years he was a Whig and later a Republican, being delegate to the Republican National Convention in 1864 and 1872. He served as state senator in 1861.

Throughout his career he was interested in newspaper publishing, in 1844 launching the *Chicago Journal* on its long career, in 1865 helping to found the *Chicago Republican,* which was brought to an end by the fire of 1871, and beginning publication of the *Inter Ocean* in 1872. In the late '40s he became actively interested in banking, insurance, and railroads. He did more than perhaps any other man to obtain better banking laws for Illinois. He established the Marine Bank in Chicago in 1851 and the Mechanics National Bank in 1864, serving as president of each, and he developed the Chicago Fire and Marine Insurance Company, of which also he was president in 1849. He had a prominent part in the development of the Galena and Chicago Union Railroad Company and was instrumental in bringing the Michigan Central Railroad into Chicago. Throughout his long life he continued the practice of law, although, as his career developed, business matters occupied an increasing amount of his time. Robert Todd Lincoln studied law in his office. By the early '50s he had become one of the leading business men of Chicago and a rich man by the standards of wealth of that day. Financial reverses were, however, encountered: temporary in 1857, when, during the panic of that year, his bank failed while he himself was absent in Europe with his family, irreparable in 1874, when the conflagration of 1871, the panic of 1873, and a second devastating fire a year later combined to give him a series of blows from which he never financially recovered. He was instrumental in founding many Chicago societies and charitable institutions, most of which he served as president. Among these were the Chicago Historical Society, the Chicago Academy of Sciences, Hahnemann Medical College, the Hahnemann hospital, the Old Ladies' Home, the old University of Chicago, of which he was one of the most liberal supporters, and the Chicago Astronomical Society, for which he provided funds for a telescope and observatory, which, by contract between the society and the university, was erected on the

grounds of the latter. His name is perpetuated in the new University of Chicago by "Scammon Court" in the School of Education quadrangle, made possible by the gift of land by his widow in 1901. In religion he was a Swedenborgian, very zealous and prominent for years in the national activities of the New Jerusalem Church. He was married twice: first in 1837 to Mary Ann Haven Dearborn, of Bath, Me., who died in 1858, and second, in 1867 to Mrs. Maria (Sheldon) Wright, of Delaware County, N. Y. He died in Chicago.

[T. W. Goodspeed, *The University of Chicago Biographical Sketches,* vol. II (1925) ; *Chicago Magazine,* March 1857, reprinted with additions in *Fergus' Hist. Series,* No. 6 (1876) ; H. L. Conrad, "Early Bench and Bar in Chicago," *Mag. of West. Hist.,* Aug. 1890 ; *Chicago Daily News,* Mar. 17, 1890 ; *Chicago Daily Tribune* and *Chicago Times,* Mar. 18, 1890.] G. B. U.

SCANLAN, LAWRENCE (Sept. 29, 1843–May 10, 1915), Roman Catholic prelate, was born in County Tipperary, Ireland, the son of Patrick and Catherine (Ryan) Scanlan. Educated at St. Patrick's College in Thurles and at the missionary seminary of All Hallows, Dublin, he was ordained a priest on June 24, 1868, and adopted by Archbishop Joseph Alemany [*q.v.*] of San Francisco, who had a rapidly increasing Irish flock. For five years he served as a curate of St. Patrick's Church and at St. Mary's Cathedral in San Francisco, as pastor in a wild mining-camp at Pioche, Nev., four hundred miles from a railroad, and at Petaluma, Cal. In 1873 he was sent as missionary to Utah with headquarters at Salt Lake City, whose frame chapel had been temporarily served since 1866 by such frontier priests as Edward Kelly, J. P. Foley, and Patrick Walsh. A stalwart, militant man of over six feet in height and two hundred pounds, he was especially well suited for arduous visitations on horseback through wild mountainous country, for the privations and coarse food of camps and diggings, and for a free, informal association with the hard but generous miners, railroad laborers, and stockmen to whom he became a hero. At Pioche he learned his business, and the denizens of that boom-town, who boycotted him for his sermons on death, hell, and judgment and for his attempts at moral reform, came to know and love him for his integrity, courage, and zeal for the poor and broken-down. Regardless of creed, they aided him in building a church, a lean-to shanty, and a hospital. His fame preceding him, he was welcomed by about ninety Catholics in Ogden and Salt Lake City and several hundred who were scattered over his parish of 85,000 square miles. If one may judge from the sympathetic messages from Mormon leaders on

Scanlan's death, the friendly relations established by Father Pierre-Jean DeSmet [q.v.] with Brigham Young were maintained, and Mormon elders frequently loaned him the use of their tabernacles. At first single-handed and then assisted by a small corps of self-sacrificing priests, of whom Denis Kiely· became his vicar-general, he labored with astounding activity as vicar-forane, as vicar-apostolic of Utah and a large part of Nevada—consecrated titular bishop of Laranda on June 29, 1887, by Archbishop Patrick W. Riordan [q.v.]—and finally as bishop of the newly created see of Salt Lake City, Jan. 30, 1891.

A true pioneer and builder of the church and state, he laid the foundations of practically every parish in the diocese; he erected over thirty churches and suffered numerous disappointments when populous mining towns in which there were good congregations became ghost towns with deserted churches. He established All Hallows College, soon assigned to the Marist Fathers, in Salt Lake City in 1855; founded academies with the assistance of the Holy Cross Sisters at Salt Lake City, Ogden, Park City, and Silver Reef; built St. John's Hospital at Silver Reef in 1878, the large Holy Cross Hospital in Salt Lake City in 1875, St. Ann's Orphanage, and the Mary Judge Memorial Home for aged and injured miners, and erected the elaborate St. Mary Magdalene's Cathedral which was dedicated by Cardinal James Gibbons in 1909. He also took an active interest in state and civic affairs and in western immigration. When the end came through rheumatism and neuritis, he left a well-ordered diocese and secure foundations for the future church. Buried in the crypt of his cathedral with services by Archbishops Alexander Christie and Edward Hanna, he typified the Irish missionary. He had a brother, Daniel, who remained in Cashel and two clerical nephews, one in Manchester and the other in Australia.

[W. R. Harris, *The Cath. Ch. in Utah, Including an Exposition of Cath. Faith by Bishop Scanlan* (1909); L. J. Fries, *One Hundred and Fifty Years of Catholicity in Utah* (1926); ann. Cath. official directories; *Cath. Ency.,* vol. XV (1912), p. 240; *Who's Who in America,* 1914-15; *Deseret Evening News* (Salt Lake City), May 10-14, 1915.]   R. J. P.

SCARBOROUGH, WILLIAM SAUNDERS (Feb. 16, 1852?–Sept. 9, 1926), president of Wilberforce University, was born in Macon, Ga., the son of Jeremiah and Francis Scarborough. Both his parents knew how to read and write. His father had been set free in 1846 by the railway company that employed him, but his mother was a slave. Her son took her status and, as a slave boy, had to acquire the rudiments of education surreptitiously. A white man, J. C. Thomas, helped educate him. By the time he was ten years old he had not only mastered the three R's but had acquired a knowledge of geography and grammar as well. Being thus qualified to make out passes for its members he was at this early age appointed secretary of one of the most prominent negro societies in Macon. He became a shoemaker's apprentice. The end of the Civil War enabled him to attend a common school, the Lewis High School in Macon, and, for two years, Atlanta University. He then took the regular academic course at Oberlin College from which he was graduated with the degree of A.B. in 1875. While at Oberlin he taught school during vacations at Albany, Ohio, Bloomingburg, Ohio, and other places. After graduation he became a teacher of Latin, Greek, and mathematics at the Lewis High School in Macon, Ga., and then served for a short time as principal of Payne Institute at Cokesburg, S. C.

In 1877 he was appointed a professor· in the classical department at Wilberforce University, Wilberforce, Ohio, with which he·remained affiliated for almost half a century. In 1879 he was appointed the first postmaster of the village. He was elected president in 1908 and served until 1920. During the remaining years of his life he was engaged in literary pursuits. He made a study of the· progress of negro farmers in Virginia for the federal department of agriculture and published some of his results as "Tenancy and Ownership among Negro Farmers in Southampton County, Va.," *U. S. Department of Agriculture, Department Bulletin,* no. 1404 (1916). He had an unusual apitude for languages. Beside his interest in modern tongues he in course of time studied Sanskrit, Zend, Gothic, Lithuanian, and Old Slavonic. In 1882 he was made a member of the American Philological Association, before which he read a paper. He was also a member of the Modern Language Association of America, the American Social Science Association, and the American Spelling Reform Association. He was a communicant of the African Methodist Episcopal Church. He was the author of *First Lessons in Greek* (1881) and the *Birds of Aristophanes* (1886). Among his contributions to periodicals are "Future of the Negro" and "The Educated Negro and Menial Pursuits" in the *Forum* (March 1889, December 1898) and "The Negro Farmer's Progress in Virginia" in *Current History* (December 1926). He also published "The Educated Negro and his Mission" in *The American Negro. Academy Occasional Papers,* No. 8 (1903). In 1881 he was married to Sarah C. Bierce, of Danby, N.

Y., a white woman, who also taught in Wilberforce. They had no children.

[W. J. Simmons, *Men of Mark* (1887); *Journ. of Negro History*, Oct. 1926; *New York Times* for Sept. 12, 1926; *Oberlin College Alumni Cat. of 1926* (1927); *Who's Who in America,* 1924–25 gives birth date as 1854.]   H. G. V.

SCARBROUGH, WILLIAM (Feb. 18, 1776– June 11, 1838), financial backer of the pioneer transatlantic steamship *Savannah,* was born in South Carolina, the son of Lucy (Sawyer) and William Scarbrough. In 1805 he married Julia Bernard of Wilmington, a belle celebrated for her wit and beauty. They had at least three children. In the Beaufort district of South Carolina he owned some 100,000 acres, perhaps inherited, and had 400 slaves working· on his plantations. He was more closely associated, however, with Savannah, where in 1804 he built a handsome house, now a negro school, and he often appeared in public with his coach and six. He engaged in shipping and trade, apparently in partnership with Robert Isaacs.

The event that raised Scarbrough to more than local prominence was his support of the first transatlantic steamship venture. The initiative came from Moses Rogers [*q.v.*]. Scarbrough became interested with a score of other Savannah business men, obtained from the Georgia legislature on Dec. 19, 1818, the incorporation of the Savannah Steamship Company with a capital stock of $50,000, and was one of the directors. Under the supervision of Rogers at New York, the company purchased and equipped the 350-ton vessel, which was named the *Savannah* (see sketch of Daniel Dod). The *Savannah* left New York on Mar. 28, 1819, and reached Savannah in eight days and fifteen hours, using the engine only forty-one and a half hours. The next few weeks were probably the proudest of Scarbrough's life. President Monroe visited the city in May, spent several days as Scarbrough's guest, and was taken on a trip down the Savannah River on the new ship. On her famous trip, she sailed from Tybee Light on the Georgia coast on May 24, 1819, and reached Liverpool on June 20, making the trip in twenty-seven days but using steam for only eighty hours, on eight different days. Her fuel was exhausted soon after a revenue cutter chased her, off Cork, thinking her afire. Leaving Liverpool on July 21, she arrived at St. Petersburg on Sept. 13, touching at Baltic ports and using steam two hundred and thirty-nine hours on eighteen of the days. She anchored in the Savannah River again on Nov. 30, was sent up to Washington in the hope that she might be purchased as a warship, but, failing

in that hope, proceeded to New York, where her engines were removed. She was sold, became a New York-Savannah sailing packet, and was wrecked on Long Island in 1822. The importance of her voyage has often been discounted, particularly by the British, who point out that she was at best an "auxiliary steamer." The chief drawback was the lack of space for fuel in addition to sufficient cargo to make her profitable. The effort was premature; Scarbrough and his associates lost their investment; and permanent transatlantic steam service had to wait almost two decades.

There is little definite information about the later years of Scarbrough's life. It is said that he later went bankrupt, but this was occasioned probably not so much by the *Savannah* as by the yellow fever epidemic of 1820, as well as the fire and the storm of that year, all of which dealt staggering blows to the trade of the little city. He died in New York City, where the arrival of the *Sirius* and of the *Great Western* on Apr. 23, 1838, seven weeks before his death, marked the successful achievement of what he had attempted earlier.

[J. E. Watkins, "The Log of the Savannah," *Ann. Report of the Board of Regents of the Smithsonian Institution ... 1890* (1891); *Ga. Hist. Quart.,* June 1919; F. D. Lee and J. L. Agnew, *Hist. Record of ... Savannah* (1869), pp. 76–77; L. L. Knight, *Georgia's Landmarks,* vol. II (1914); *Hunt's Merchants' Mag. and Commercial Review,* Oct. 1840, p. 297; W. S. Lindsay, *Hist. of Merchant Shipping,* vol. IV (1876); J. H. Morrison, *Hist. of N. Y. Ship Yards* (1909); copy of Scarbrough tombstone inscription in Colonial Park, Savannah, confirming spelling of name, through the courtesy of the Ga. Hist. Soc.]   R. G. A.

SCATTERGOOD, THOMAS (Jan.? 23, 1748–Apr. 24, 1814). Quaker preacher, traveler, was born in Burlington, N. J., the son of Joseph and Rebecca Scattergood. His father died in 1754. His mother gave him a solid education, though it was confined in· the narrow limits of that period. At fourteen he was apprenticed in Philadelphia for training in mercantile business, but at nineteen he became a tanner of leather. In this business he continued successfully throughout the remainder of his life. In 1772 he was married to Elizabeth, the daughter of David Bacon of Philadelphia. His wife died after eight years of married life, leaving one son, and he was married again in 1783 to Sarah, the daughter of John Hoskins of Burlington, N. J.

As a child he was precociously religious and extraordinarily sensitive to inward intimations of duty. He was a conscientious objector to war, and he had many difficulties to face in Philadelphia during the Revolution and the occupation of the city by the British army. He was a Quaker by birthright, and in early life he identified himself by personal conviction with the Society of Friends. When he spoke in public assemblies in his youth, his gift in the ministry was quickly recognized by his elders. He started his life-long travels as an itinerant minister in 1778, his first journey being undertaken in a visit to the meetings of Maryland and Virginia. On a second visit to the meetings in the southern colonies in company with Samuel Emlen and George Dillwyn, he began to keep the diary, which faithfully records the scenes of his labors and the inner states of his mind. This supplied the material for the "Memoirs of Thomas Scattergood," edited by William and Thomas Evans (*Friends' Library*, vol. VIII, 1844, and separately 1845). The *Memoirs* furnish a somewhat unusual opportunity to study the states of mind and spiritual experiences of an over-sensitive soul, almost morbidly honest in his attempts to tell what was going on within him. He belonged in the intimate circle of the Quaker quietists of the last half of the eighteenth century. They reflected the influence of Molinos, Guyon, and Fenelon, and they, further, had profoundly felt in their youth the personal influence of their older Quaker contemporary, John Woolman. In one of his religious journeys in western Pennsylvania Scattergood appointed seven successive meetings, in which he felt that he had no message "divinely given" to him, and consequently he sat through them all in absolute silence. In spite of his inward quietism his outward life revealed a remarkable dynamic driving power. He was almost continuously engaged in public service at home or abroad. He traveled repeatedly over the colonies, where there were Quaker settlements, even to the most remote frontier regions. From 1794 to 1800 he was engaged in extensive religious services in Great Britain, Ireland, and the Orkney Islands, working much of the time in company with contemporary leading Friends, both of England and America. He is generally credited with having been one of the important inspirations for starting Westtown School and the asylum for the insane now called Friends' Hospital. David Sands [*q.v.*] and Scattergood represent two diverse tendencies in the Quakerism of the period. Sands shows the evangelical tendency and Scattergood the profound quietistic tendency. They often traveled together and worked without any conscious disharmony, but they mark in thought the beginning of an important historical divergence. Scattergood died in Philadelphia.

[*Memoirs, ante*; R. M. Jones and others, *The Quakers in the American Colonies* (1911); R. M. Jones, *The Later Periods of Quakerism* (2 vols., 1921).]

R. M. J.

SCHADLE, JACOB EVANS (June 23, 1849– May 29, 1908), laryngologist, was born on a farm near the village of Rauchtown, Clinton County, Pa. His parents, Michael and Phoebe (Sallade) Schadle, were of Revolutionary ancestry of German origin. Graduating from the Millersburg state normal school in 1868, he taught school at Millersburg for six years and at Mifflinburg for one year. At Mifflinburg he met Jane Ray Miller, daughter of Dr. David H. Miller, whom he married in 1878. In 1876 he began the study of medicine with Dr. John S. Crawford of Williamsport, and in 1881 he received his medical degree from Jefferson Medical College in Philadelphia. After a brief period of practice in the village of Pennsdale, near his birthplace, he settled in Shenandoah in the coal region, where he won the appreciation of the community by the skill and courage with which he handled an epidemic of smallpox. After taking a postgraduate course in diseases of the nose and throat under Dr. Charles Euchariste Sajous [*q.v.*], he moved in 1887 to St. Paul, Minn., in order to devote himself exclusively to this specialty, and in a few years he became the leading practitioner of laryngology in that section of the Northwest. He was appointed clinical instructor in laryngology at the University of Minnesota in 1896 and clinical professor in 1897; later he was made professor of rhinology and laryngology, a position he held for the remainder of his life. A skilful operator, he perfected several ingenious instruments for nose and throat work, including a snare for the removal of growths from the nasopharynx, a lymphatome for eradicating adenoid vegetations, and an automatic syringe for intratracheal injections.

From the beginning of his career he was a contributor to journal literature. Two of his early articles are especially noteworthy. In 1885 he reported the successful treatment of five cases of mushroom poisoning by the use of large doses of atropine (*Medical and Surgical Reporter*, Dec. 19, 1885, pp. 713–15), the first recorded use in amanitin poisoning of a treatment which later was universally adopted. In 1888 he reported some observations upon the secondary and remote effects of cocaine (*Medical Register*, vol. V, 1889, pp. 124–25), in which he called attention for the first time to the afterwards generally recognized deleterious effects of cocaine upon the genital system. His chief interests during his professional career, however, were the investigation of the causes and treatment of hay-fever and asthma and of the effects of post-nasal adenoid growths upon the health and development of children. He developed the theory that hay-fever was due to acid secretions from catarrhal inflammation of the maxillary sinus and that extension of the process to the lower respiratory mucous membrane caused asthma. He spent three extended periods of study at German medical centers and was otherwise a confirmed traveler. At the time of his death he had accepted an invitation to present the results of his work on hay-fever and asthma before the International Medical Society in Budapest in 1909. Genial and courteous, with a host of personal friends, he was a public-spirited man prominent in the social and civic life of St. Paul. He died at St. Joseph's Hospital in St. Paul of cerebral thrombosis following a short illness.

[G. M. Gould, *The Jefferson Medic. Coll. of Phila.* (1904), vol. I ; R. F. Stone, *Biog. of Eminent Am. Physicians and Surgeons* (1894) ; *St. Paul Medic. Jour.*, July 1908 ; H. A. Kelly and W. L. Burrage, *Am. Medic. Biogs.* (1920) ; *St. Paul Pioneer Press*, May 30, 1908.]

J. M. P—n.

SCHAEBERLE, JOHN MARTIN (Jan. 10, 1853–Sept. 19, 1924), astronomer, son of Anton and C. Catherine (Vögele) Schaeberle, fourth child of a family of six children, was born in Württemberg, Germany. The family emigrated to America in 1854 and settled in Ann Arbor, Mich., where Schaeberle attended the public schools until at fifteen he entered a machine shop in Chicago as an apprentice. During his three years' apprenticeship he chanced to become interested in astronomy. Fired with enthusiasm, he ground a small mirror and constructed a reflecting telescope upon the roof of his rooming house, where he spent many nights observing the heavens. Convinced that he could make further progress only by mastering the fundamentals of mathematics, he returned to Ann Arbor, finished high school, and entered the University of Michigan, from which he was graduated in 1876 with a degree in civil engineering. During his student days he pursued his astronomical interests even more actively than before. Upon his graduation he became private assistant to James Craig Watson [*q.v.*], and in 1878 was appointed assistant in the observatory. Later he became acting assistant professor at Michigan, where he remained until 1888, when he was called to Mount Hamilton, Cal., as a member of the original staff of the Lick Observatory. For the first five years he had charge of the work with the Repsold meridian circle. With the thirty-six-inch refractor he discovered the faint companion of Procyon, the "Little Dog Star."

A few months after his arrival at the new institution, the solar eclipse of Jan. 1, 1889, total in northern California, occurred. With Edward Singleton Holden and Sherburne Wesley Burnham [*qq.v.*] Schaeberle observed it as a partial eclipse from the observatory. In December of the same year with Burnham he observed a total eclipse at Cayenne, French Guiana, where he obtained good results in spite of adverse conditions. As a consequence, he became interested in eclipse problems and formulated a mechanical theory of the solar corona, which, with some modifications, won and retained many adherents. Because study of the corona suffered greatly from lack of large-scale photographs, he built a long-focus camera, with plate-holder in a movable carriage mounted on a track. When he first used it at the eclipse in Chile, April 1893, he detected a faint comet, which otherwise would not have been seen because of its proximity to the sun. In 1896 he headed an expedition to Japan that was unsuccessful because of clouds. He was also much interested in problems connected with the reflecting telescope, to the theory of which he made definite contributions. He built several reflectors, ranging in size from eight to twenty-four inches in diameter. The last of these, which had a focal length of only three feet, was mounted equatorially and was used for studies of faint extended nebulae and of the sun. The small ratio between focal length and aperture gave such great light-concentrating power that the image of the sun, when focussed upon a moderately thick piece of strap-iron, could melt holes in it within five seconds.

When Holden retired from directorship of the Lick Observatory in 1897, Schaeberle served as acting director until James Edward Keeler [*q.v.*] arrived as Holden's successor. At that time he retired from the Lick Observatory. After a trip around the world he returned to Ann Arbor, where he continued his studies. Throughout his life he was interested in athletics, being particularly adept at swimming and skating, and in music. He never married. He was living in Ann Arbor at the time of his death, which came very suddenly. Though apparently in good health, he was seized with a stroke of apoplexy while doing some light work on the lawn and died instantly under the sky he had studied so diligently.

[*Who's Who in America*, 1924–25 ; *Am. Men of Sci.*, J. M. Cattell and D. R. Brimhall, eds. (3rd ed., 1921) ; *Astronomical Soc. of the Pacific Pubs.*, Dec. 1924 ; *N. Y. Times*, Sept. 20, 1924 ; *N. Y. Herald Tribune*, Sept. 20, 1924 ; information from a nephew, E. A. Schaeberle, Ann Arbor, Mich.]

D. H. M.

SCHAEFFER, CHARLES FREDERICK (Sept. 3, 1807–Nov. 23, 1879), Lutheran clergyman, was born at Germantown, Pa., the youngest son of Frederick David [*q.v.*] and

Rosina (Rosenmiller) Schaeffer. He attended Zion's parochial school in Philadelphia, graduated from the University of Pennsylvania in 1827, studied for the ministry with his father and with his brother-in-law, Charles Rudolph Demme [q.v.], was licensed by the Maryland and Virginia Synod in 1829, and was ordained by the West Pennsylvania Synod in 1831. On Aug. 27, 1832, he married Susanna, daughter of John George Schmucker [q.v.], by whom he had a son and four daughters. After a short period as assistant to his brother, Frederick Christian [q.v.], in New York, Schaeffer was pastor at Carlisle, Pa., 1830–34 and at Hagerstown, Md., 1834–40. Meanwhile his growing reputation as a conservative Lutheran theologian brought him a call to the English professorship in the seminary of the Joint Synod of Ohio at Columbus, Ohio, and in May 1840 he entered on his new duties. A gentleman of broad culture and polished manners, he was ill fitted to thrive in that Grobian environment and before long got into serious difficulties with his students, his German colleague, Johann Friedrich Winkler, and several influential ministers. The board of directors demanded his resignation, which took effect in June 1843, and Schaeffer, his health permanently injured by overwork and malaria, withdrew to Lancaster, Ohio, where he served as pastor until December 1845. Subsequently he was pastor at Red Hook, Dutchess County, N. Y., 1845–51 and of St. John's, Easton, Pa., 1851–56. In that year, after William Julius Mann [q.v.] had wisely declined the position, he was elected to the Ministerium of Pennsylvania's German professorship at the Gettysburg Theological Seminary. His accession to the Gettysburg faculty was a challenge to the liberal element in the General Synod and helped to hasten the breach between the General Synod and the Ministerium of Pennsylvania. Of the other professors in the Seminary, the president, Samuel Simon Schmucker [q.v.], was the great leader of liberal Lutheranism and was intent on carrying his cause through to victory; and the other professor, Charles Philip Krauth [q.v.], was a middle-of-the-road man, a lover of peace, who looked with about equal disfavor on his extremist colleagues. For the next eight years, with the winds of doctrine blowing from three directions at once, Gettysburg was a theological Medicine Hat. The storm broke in 1864 when the Ministerium of Pennsylvania left the General Synod and opened a seminary of its own in Philadelphia. Leaving Gettysburg precipitately, Schaeffer became the first professor and chairman of the faculty of the Philadelphia Seminary,

where, with Mann and Charles Porterfield Krauth [q.v.], his congenial colleagues, he taught until a year before his death.

Schaeffer's literary work was of considerable importance to his denomination. His contributions to the Evangelical Review and to the Bibliotheca Sacra were solid and influential statements of the confessional position; he was the translator of J. F. Kurtz's Manual of Sacred History (1855) and of G. V. Lechler and Charles Gerok's The Acts of the Apostles (1869), Volume IV in the Schaff-Lange Commentary on the Holy Scriptures. His revision (1854) of Philip Frederick Mayer's translation of Luther's Smaller Catechism (1816) was edited by C. F. Welden, A. T. Geissenhainer, and B. M. Schmucker and has become part of the life of the Lutheran Church in America. Later attempts to improve it have only served to exhibit its all but complete accuracy and its unsurpassable beauty of language. He also made a skilful revision of the common version of Johann Arndt's True Christianity (1868) and composed a commentary on the Gospel according to St. Matthew, devotional rather than critical in purpose, which, condensed by his son-in-law, the Rev. Reuben Hill, was published as Volumes I and II of H. E. Jacobs' The Lutheran Commentary (1895). Though a good part of his career was marked by bitter controversy, he was little of a fighter at heart; his uneventful latter years in Philadelphia were, in spite of the affliction of deafness, also his happiest.

[Memorial of Charles Frederick Schaeffer, D.D. (1880), with contributions by Adolph Spaeth, C. P. Krauth, W. J. Mann, and B. M. Schmucker and a bibliog. of his writings; Univ. of Pa. Biog. Cat. of the Matriculates of the Coll. . . . 1749–1893 (1894); L. D. Reed, The Phila. Sem. Biog. Record, 1864–1923 (1923); A. R. Wentz, Hist. of the Gettysburg Theol. Sem. . . . 1826–1926 (1926); Pub. Ledger (Phila.), Nov. 24, 1879.]

G. H. G.

SCHAEFFER, CHARLES WILLIAM (May 5, 1813–Mar. 15, 1896), Lutheran clergyman, was born at Hagerstown, Md., the only child of the Rev. Frederick Solomon Schaeffer (1790–1815) and his wife, Catherine Elizabeth, whose maiden name was either Cremer or Gräber. His father lived the few years of his ministry at Hagerstown, gave proof of eloquence and power, and died of camp-fever contracted while ministering to soldiers quartered near the town. Charles lived his boyhood and youth in the home of his stepfather, the Rev. Benjamin Keller, at Carlisle and Germantown, Pa., and of his grandfather, Frederick David Schaeffer [q.v.], in Philadelphia. He attended the Germantown Academy, graduated in 1832 from the University of Pennsylvania, studied at the Gettysburg Theological Seminary 1833–35, and was licensed in 1835 and ordained in 1836 by the Ministerium of Pennsylvania. In 1837 he married Elizabeth Ashmead of Germantown, who bore him two sons and two daughters and died in 1892. He was pastor at Barren Hill and Whitemarsh (formerly part of the Germantown parish) 1835–41; of Zion's, Harrisburg, 1841–49; and of St. Michael's, Germantown, 1849–75. All these congregations had been served by his grandfather; his uncle, Frederick Christian Schaeffer [q.v.], had preceded him at Barren Hill and Harrisburg, and his stepfather at Germantown. For one-third of his ministerial career Schaeffer was either president or treasurer of the Ministerium of Pennsylvania, and he was a member of many of its committees. He was president of the General Synod in 1859 and of the General Council in 1868, a trustee of Pennsylvania College 1855–73, of Muhlenberg College 1868–76, of the University of Pennsylvania 1859–96, and an editor of the *Lutheran,* the *Foreign Missionary* and the *Philadelphian.* He was an assistant professor in the Philadelphia Theological Seminary from its opening in 1864, and was made Burkhalter professor of church history and pastoral theology in 1874. Though nominally he retired as professor emeritus in 1894, he continued to lecture twice a week and to preside over faculty meetings until the end; three hours before his death he sent directions to his pupils as to their work for the next day. His influence over the Lutheran Church, especially during the last thirty years of his life, was very great.

He was a man of fine intelligence and gracious spirit, prompt, cheerful, and capable in the discharge of every duty, and utterly free from any taint of affectation or self-seeking. In him the rigors of theological orthodoxy were softened and humanized by the devotional spirit. His literary taste was severe and high-bred; in his translations from the German he was able to reproduce not merely the substance but the spirit of the original. His important translations were the *Halle Reports* (1892), consisting of the first three sections of B. M. Schmucker and W. J. Mann's edition of the *Hallesche Nachrichten* (1886); *The Life of Dr. Martin Luther* (1883) by Wilhelm Wackernagel; a thorough revision of the common English version of K. H. von Bogatzky's *A Golden Treasury* (1858); Hans Sachs' *Wittenberg Nightingale* (1883); and a number of hymns, among them three—"Come, O come, Thou quickening Spirit"; "Father, Son, and Holy Ghost"; "O blessed house, that cheerfully receiveth"—that are included in the *Lutheran Common Hymnal* (1917). He contributed

notable articles to the *Evangelical Review* and the *Lutheran Church Review,* and was the author of *The Early History of the Lutheran Church in America* (1857; 1868), which was very good so far as it went, and *Family Prayer for Morning and Evening and the Festivals of the Church Year* (1861), one of the few devotional books of merit that have been composed by Lutheran writers in America. He lived to a patriarchal age with his powers of mind and memory almost unimpaired and died, suddenly but not unexpectedly, at his home in Germantown.

[*Evangelisches Magazin,* 1815, pp. 63–66, 90–91; H. E. Jacobs, "In Memoriam: Charles William Schaeffer," *Luth. Ch. Rev.,* Oct. 1896; L. D. Reed, *The Phila. Sem. Biog. Record, 1864–1923* (1923); A. R. Wentz, *Hist. of the Gettysburg Theol. Sem. . . . 1826–1926* (1926); *Pub. Ledger* (Phila.), Mar. 16, 1896; private information.]   G. H. G.

SCHAEFFER, DAVID FREDERICK (July 22, 1787–May 5, 1837), Lutheran clergyman, was born at Carlisle, Pa., the eldest son of Frederick David [q.v.] and Rosina (Rosenmiller) Schaeffer. He graduated in 1807 from the University of Pennsylvania, studied theology with his father and with the Philadelphia ministers, J. H. C. Helmuth [q.v.] and J. F. Schmidt, assisted his father for a while at Whitpain, Montgomery County, and was called in 1808 to the Lutheran church at Frederick, Md. In accordance with the practice then prevailing in the Ministerium of Pennsylvania, he was licensed by that body at Lebanon June 17, 1808, his ordination not taking place until 1812. On June 28, 1810, he married Elizabeth, daughter of George and Catharine Krebs of Philadelphia, by whom he had six children.

At this period the survival of the Lutherans as a separate denomination depended largely on their success in effecting the transition from worship exclusively in German to worship in both German and English, and on the formation of an inclusive general organization to foster unity of spirit and to guide the home missionary movement. The brunt of the work fell on a few influential ministers, of whom Schaeffer was one of the most conscientious and enlightened. He was one of the organizers of the Maryland Synod in 1820, and at the same time was one of the most active in the formation of the national body, the General Synod. When the first meeting of the General Synod convened in his own church Oct. 21, 1821, he was elected its secretary; he was secretary again in 1825, 1827, and 1829, and president in 1831 and 1833. He founded the first English Lutheran church paper, the *Lutheran Intelligencer,* and conducted it from

1826 to 1831. Until a theological seminary could be started, he trained candidates for the ministry; besides his brothers, Frederick Solomon and Frederick Christian [q.v.], who owed part of their instruction to him, he was responsible for the linguistic and theological education of fourteen ministers, including two who did him much honor, Emanuel Greenwald and Charles Philip Krauth [qq.v.]. When the Gettysburg Theological Seminary was opened in 1826, Schaeffer delivered the charge to its first professor, Samuel Simon Schmucker [q.v.]; the published address is now of considerable doctrinal interest. Though his influence was thus far from being merely parochial, his great reputation actually rests on his strictly pastoral work. For many years he seems to have been an almost perfect embodiment of the ideals of the Christian ministry, and the visible results of his work at Frederick were extraordinary. In spite of opposition he succeeded in introducing English services, and the congregation grew and prospered. He was a man of commanding presence, marked social gifts, and strong intellect. The last year of his life was made unhappy by the illness and death of his wife, by his own broken health, and by difficulties with the Maryland Synod, which disciplined him on a charge of intemperance. He died unexpectedly at Frederick and was buried there.

[Geo. Diehl, "Hist. of the Luth. Ch. of Frederick, Md.," *Evangelical Rev.*, Apr. 1856; W. B. Sprague, *Annals Am. Pulpit*, vol. IX (1869); J. G. Morris, *Fifty Years in the Luth. Ministry* (1878); *Doc. Hist. Ev. Luth. Ministerium of Pa. . . . 1748 to 1821* (1898); A. R. Wentz, *Hist. of the Evangelical Luth. Synod of Md. . . . 1820–1920* (1920).]   G. H. G.

SCHAEFFER, FREDERICK CHRISTIAN (Nov. 12, 1792–Mar. 26, 1831), Lutheran clergyman, was born in Germantown, Pa., the son of Frederick David [q.v.] and Rosina (Rosenmiller) Schaeffer. After attending the Germantown Academy, he studied for the ministry under his father, for whom he acted as vicar at Barren Hill. Though the Ministerium of Pennsylvania withheld a full license from him till he came of age, he was called to Harrisburg in July 1812 and took charge in November. He infused new life into his parish, and in 1814 the town congregation, which had been sharing a log church with the Reformed, began work on Zion Church, a commodious brick building. Almost unique in the experience of Lutheran ministers of that generation was his success in establishing English services alongside the German without incurring opposition and uproar. The prosperity of the Lutheran Church in Harrisburg dates from his pastorate.

In New York, meanwhile, Frederick William Geissenhainer, the successor of John Christopher Kunze [q.v.], had been wrestling with the language problem of the United Congregations, and when he finally resigned in despair he advised them to secure Schaeffer as their pastor. Schaeffer accepted the call thus tendered him and removed to New York in the summer of 1815. At Harrisburg he was succeeded by John George Lochman [q.v.]. Although only in his twenty-third year, he was already a man of note. A handsome presence, a keen and versatile intellect, administrative capacity, and engaging social talents were part of his family heritage. He could preach well in German and with eloquence in English, and through his father's influence he had become thoroughly imbued with the distinctive teachings and spirit of Lutheranism. He resisted the tendency, then very strong in New York, for English-speaking Lutherans to unite with the Episcopal Church; and like his close friend, Samuel Simon Schmucker [q.v.], he was one of the bulwarks of his denomination against the popular rationalism of the time. From 1815 to 1822 he was the sole pastor of the United Congregations. On Dec. 22, 1822, St. Matthew's Church on Walker Street was consecrated for the use of the English portion of the parish, and Geissenhainer was recalled as co-pastor to minister to the Germans. The German majority in the United Congregations grew increasingly hostile in its attitude toward the English, and in 1826 St. Matthew's was sold for debt. Schaeffer then resigned and with Jacob Lorillard, Kunze's son-in-law, organized St. James' Church, of which he was pastor until his death. Only two of his sermons are known to have been published: *"The Blessed Reformation"; A Sermon . . . on Occasion of the Solemnization of the Third Centurial Jubilee in Commemoration of the Reformation* (1817) and *An Address Pronounced at the Laying of the Corner Stone of St. Matthew's Church, New York, October 22, 1821* (1822). A volume of *Parables and Parabolic Stories* (1829) has been ascribed to him. His early death, from tuberculosis, was a severe loss to the Lutherans of New York.

[M. L. Stoever, memoir in *Evangelical Rev.*, Oct. 1856; W. B. Sprague, *Annals Am. Pulpit*, vol. IX (1869); J. G. Morris, *Fifty Years in the Luth. Ministry* (1878); A. L. Gräbner, *Geschichte der Lutherischen Kirche in America* (1892); D. M. Gilbert, *Services Commemorative of the 100th Anniversary of Zion Ev. Luth. Ch., Harrisburg, Pa., Nov. 10–11, 1895* (1896); Peter Anstadt, *Life and Times of Rev. S. S. Schmucker* (1896); *Doc. Hist. Ev. Luth. Ministerium of Pa. . . . 1748 to 1821* (1898); *N. Y. American*, Apr. 1, 1831.]   G. H. G.

SCHAEFFER, FREDERICK DAVID (Nov. 15, 1760–Jan. 27, 1836), Lutheran clergyman, was born in Frankfurt-am-Main, the son of Johann Jakob and Susanna Maria Schaeffer, and the nephew of a superintendent of the Lutheran Church. Orphaned by the death of both parents, he was obliged to leave the Gymnasium at Hanau in 1774 and some months later accompanied one of his uncles to Pennsylvania. He became a school teacher in York County, was befriended and prepared for the ministry by the Rev. Jacob Goering, was licensed by the Ministerium of Pennsylvania in 1786, and was ordained in 1788. While pastor at Carlisle, 1786–90, he did missionary work at several points in York and Cumberland counties and in 1788 founded a Lutheran congregation at Harrisburg. His second charge, 1790–1812, was St. Michael's, Germantown, and its affiliated churches. There he preached occasionally in English and published an *Antwort auf eine Vertheidigung der Methodisten* (Germantown, 1806) as a counterblast to the horde of proselytizing evangelists whom the Second Awakening loosed upon the countryside. In 1812 he was called to succeed the late Johann Friedrich Schmidt as the colleague of J. H. C. Helmuth [*q.v.*] at St. Michael's and Zion's in Philadelphia. After Helmuth's retirement in 1820, Charles Rudolph Demme [*q.v.*] became his assistant and, before long, his son-in-law. He retired in 1834 and spent the brief remainder of his life with his eldest son at Frederick, Md., where he died and was buried.

In the autumn of 1786 he was married to Rosina, daughter of Lewis Rosenmiller of York County, who died less than a year before him. Of their eight children, the four sons who grew to maturity became Lutheran clergymen: David Frederick, Frederick Christian, Charles Frederick [*qq.v.*], and Frederick Solomon. The last, dying before his twenty-fifth birthday, left a reputation for eloquence and power and a son, Charles William [*q.v.*], to carry on the family tradition. The qualities that made Schaeffer one of the most admired and most admirable clergymen of his generation descended without modification to his children and grandchildren.

His eminence was due to solid rather than brilliant parts and to his genius for the pastoral office. A man of devout and holy life, with strong intelligence and perfect tact and gentleness, he was an unending source of comfort and consolation to the sick, the needy, and the bereaved. His sermons were simple and practical, yet did not suffer by comparison with those of Helmuth and Demme, who were famous pulpit orators. He was at his best, probably, in his instruction of children. Despite a somewhat irregular education, he became a scholar. The Hebrew Bible

and the Septuagint were his daily reading; he was a close student of the Book of Concord, which he read in the Latin version; and he was saturated with the devotional writings of the Lutheran Church, the spirit of which was manifest in his own character. Music and geography were his pastimes, and in his younger days he was something of a poet.

[*Zum Andenken an die hundertjährige Jubelfeier in der deutschen evangel. luther. Sct. Michaelis-Kirche in Philadelphia* (1843) ; M. L. Stoever, memoir, *Evangelical Rev.*, Oct. 1854 ; W. B. Sprague, *Annals Am. Pulpit*, vol. IX (1869) ; C. S. Albert, *Hist. of the Luth. Ch. of Carlisle, Pa.* (1876) ; J. G. Morris, *Fifty Years in the Luth. Ministry* (1878) ; D. M. Gilbert, *Centennial of Zion Ch., Harrisburg, Pa.* (1895) ; *Doc. Hist. Ev. Luth. Mininisterium of Pa. . . . 1748 to 1821* (1898) ; death notice in *Poulson's Am. Daily Advertiser*, Feb. 11, 1836.]
G. H. G.

SCHAEFFER, NATHAN CHRIST (Feb. 3, 1849–Mar. 15, 1919), educator and lecturer, was born in Maxatawny Township, near Kutztown, Pa., the son of David and Esther Anna (Christ) Schaeffer and a descendant of George Schaeffer, who settled in Pennsylvania in 1750. His ancestors on both sides were Pennsylvania Germans, respected for their industry, active in promoting the establishment of the normal school at Kutztown, and zealous for the education of their sons. After receiving his early education in a rural school and at Maxatawny Seminary (later the Keystone State Normal School), at sixteen he entered the junior class of Franklin and Marshall College (A.B., 1867) ; he then studied at the Theological Seminary of the Reformed Church at Mercersburg (later at Lancaster) and served as instructor. In 1873 he went abroad to study for two years at Tübingen, Berlin, and Leipzig. Licensed to preach in 1875, he was ordained in 1876 by the German Reformed Church. Throughout his life he was interested in religious education, in the relations between state, church and education, and in church work and Masonry. He organized the Lehigh Classis of the Reformed Church and was called to the missionary field in Japan but declined to enter it.

On returning from Germany in 1875, he was appointed to teach ancient languages at Franklin and Marshall College ; in 1877 he resigned to become principal of the Keystone State Normal School, where he remained sixteen years. He married Anna Ahlum of Applebachsville, Pa., July 8, 1880 ; they had seven children. In 1893 he became superintendent of public instruction in Pennsylvania and held the position until his death. He also served on the Pennsylvania Commission on Industrial Education, on the commission to frame a new state school code, as secretary of the Dental Council, of the Bureau of Medical Education and Licensure, of the National Council of Education, and as lecturer on pedagogy in the graduate school of the University of Pennsylvania (1900–01). At various times he was president of the National Education Association, of the Pennsylvania State Teachers Association, and the Pennsylvania-German Society. He was a popular professional speaker in Pennsylvania and elsewhere. To his friends he became known as the "Pennsylvania Limited," for he could be relied upon to reach the terminal on schedule time. His addresses, with his official reports, constitute the major part of his literary work. Besides these, however, he wrote *Thinking and Learning to Think* (1900), a sketch of the educational system of Pennsylvania (in H. M. Jenkins, *Pennsylvania Colonial and Federal,* 1903, vol. III), and *Bible Readings for Schools* (1897). Fairly representative of his periodical articles are "The Suppression of the Order of Jesuits in the German Empire" (*Mercersburg Review,* January 1875), "Church and State in Germany" (*Ibid.,* July 1875), and "The Literary Activity of the Romans" (*Ibid.,* July 1876). From 1893 to 1919 he edited the *Pennsylvania School Journal.* By local friends and admirers he was extravagantly acclaimed, compared in some respects to Franklin and Lincoln, even likened to Galahad in the days of Arthur, and credited with responsibility for the enormous expansion that occurred in various phases of Pennsylvania education during his incumbency. By others—though they admitted his likable personal qualities, his scholarship, ability and strength of character—he was seen as an extreme conservative under whom, especially in the later years of his superintendency, the schools had been marking time and in many respects hardly holding their own. It is a matter of common knowledge that the schools of Pennsylvania had fallen to a low position in comparison with others. Schaeffer eschewed fads in religion, morals, and education, carrying the tendency to such an extreme that in the eyes of those alive to the problems of the twentieth century the virtue finally became a vice, but he was a gentleman and a scholar of the old school and as such suited the mind and temper of Pennsylvania at the turn of the century.

[*Who's Who in America,* 1918–19; *Report of Superintendent of Pub. Instruction,* 1919, and other ann. reports, 1894–1919; *The Centennial Hist. of Kutztown, Pa.* (1915); E. M. Rapp, address to Hist. Soc. of Berks County, June 1919, MS.; *Pa. School Jour.,* Mar. 1919; *Pa.-German Soc.,* vol. XXX (1924); *Lancaster New Era,* Mar. 17, 1919; *Pub. Ledger* (Phila.), Mar. 16 and 17, 1919.]   T. W.

SCHAFF, PHILIP (Jan. 1, 1819–Oct. 20, 1893), church historian, was born at Chur, the capital of the Swiss canton of Grisons. His father, Philip Schaf [*sic*], was a carpenter in humble circumstances, who died when the child was but a year old; his mother belonged to a family of farmers at Zizers. As a schoolboy in his native town, Philip showed such promise that friends enabled him to continue his education. When he was fifteen he entered the academy of Kornthal, Württemberg, from which, after eight months, he passed to the Gymnasium at Stuttgart. In 1837 he enrolled at the University of Tübingen, where, by nature warmly pious and somewhat mystical, he was more attracted by the evangelical school of Christian Schmid than by the critical school of Ferdinand Baur, although the latter affected lastingly Schaff's historical point of view. In September 1839 he went to the University of Halle, where Friedrich Tholuck was his teacher and friend, and in the spring of 1840, to the University of Berlin. Here he studied under the man who most influenced him, Johann August Wilhelm Neander. In 1841 he received the degree of licentiate of theology, his thesis being the first of his many publications, *Die Sünde wider den Heiligen Geist* (1841). After traveling as a private tutor in southern Europe, he became in 1842 *privat-docent* in the University of Berlin. He was well on his way to a German professorship, when the call to the United States came which changed the current of his life.

Desiring in its theological seminary at Mercersburg, Pa., as successor to F. A. Rauch [*q.v.*] a German scholar of high standing, the Eastern Synod of the German Reformed Church in 1843 engaged Schaff, on the recommendation of Tholuck, Neander, and others. He was ordained to the ministry of the Reformed Church at Elberfeld, Apr. 12, 1844, and in July arrived in the United States. At Mercersburg the villagers, headed by a band, escorted him to Seminary Hill. The noise his coming awakened was not confined to horns and drums, however. In his ordination sermon, he had spoken in reproachful terms of the moral and religious condition of the German emigrants. His remarks became known in the United States, and near and far he was denounced as a defamer of his countrymen. In his inaugural address, furthermore, printed, in enlarged form, in German, and in English as *The Principle of Protestantism* (1845), he set forth the doctrine of historical development, portraying the Reformation, not as a revolution, nor as a restoration, but as a development out of the good forces in the Catholic Church, a development destined to continue, with the possibility of the ultimate union of Protestantism and Catholicism. The address was vigorously criticized, especially because of its alleged leanings toward Puseyism; the classis of Philadelphia adopted resolutions demanding an investigation by the Synod; but in October 1845 the Synod exonerated Schaff of the charges implied in the resolutions.

For nineteen years he remained at Mercersburg, subject to more or less opposition, which was strengthened by his association with John W. Nevin [q.v.] in the development of the controversy-provoking Mercersburg Theology, to the historical and liturgical aspects of which Schaff made substantial contribution. In 1846 he published *What is Church History? A Vindication of the Idea of Historical Development,* and in 1851, *Geschichte der Apostolischen Kirche* (English translation by E. D. Yeomans, 1853), which gave him high rank as a church historian. In 1857 appeared *A Liturgy, or Order of Christian Worship, for the German Reformed Church,* the work of a committee which Schaff headed. He founded and edited (1846–54) *Der Deutsche Kirchenfreund,* the first theological journal in German issued in the United States. During this Mercersburg period he came to be the mediator between the theology of Germany and American scholarship. German theology, he believed, could bear its full fruit only when incorporated into American activity; therefore he endeavored in manifold ways to unite the two. Among the means employed were the works that he edited which appeared later, among them, *A Commentary on the Holy Scriptures* (25 vols., 1865–80), an American edition of John P. Lange's great commentary; and the *Religious Encyclopædia* (3 vols., 1882–84; 3rd edition, 4 vols., 1891), based on the *Real-Encyklopädie* of Herzog, Plitt, and Hauck. He became thoroughly American in interest, though cosmopolitan in spirit and zeal for world-wide Christian union.

In 1865 he resigned his position at Mercersburg after two years' leave of absence, and thereafter resided in New York. For several years, beginning in 1864, he was secretary of the New York Sabbath Committee, an organization aggressively opposed to the secularization of Sunday which many German-Americans favored. He lectured at various theological schools and in 1870 joined the faculty of Union Theological Seminary, transferring his denominational affiliations to the Presbyterian Church. His ecumenical activities were extensive. He was a strong supporter of the Evangelical Alliance, making numerous trips abroad to attend its coun-

cils, and took prominent part in the organization of the American branch. He was also active in the formation of the Alliance of the Reformed Churches. In the work of revising the English Bible, 1881–85, he rendered valuable service, arranging for the organization of the American Committee, selecting its members, and acting as its president. "He had the spirit and habit of universality. He was ubiquitous in person. You could not travel without meeting him or finding that he had been there. . . . He was ubiquitous in reputation. In Glasgow or Durham, or in the little village of the Bavarian Alps, as an American, you would be asked 'Do you know Dr. Schaff?' And he was equally ubiquitous in mind" (*Papers of the American Society of Church History,* VI, 30). The list of publications which bear his name as author or editor numbers eighty or more. He was by nature a historian, however, and his work was marked by thoroughness of research, accuracy, candor, clearness of style, irenic spirit, and keen interest in the bearing of the past on contemporary problems. His most ambitious work was his *History of the Christian Church* (5th edition, revised and enlarged, 7 vols., 1882–92), which remains a lasting monument to his scholarship and industry. Among his other important publications were *Bibliotheca Symbolica Ecclesiæ Universalis: the Creeds of Christendom* (1877); *A Companion to the Greek Testament and the English Version* (1883; 7th edition, revised, 1896); and *Theological Propædeutic* (1893). His death, from a second cerebral hemorrhage, occurred in New York, soon after his return from the Parliament of Religions at Chicago, a trip his doctors had forbidden. He was married in December 1845 to Mary Elizabeth Schley of Frederick, Md.

[D. S. Schaff, *The Life of Philip Schaff* (1897), contains bibliog. of Schaff's publications and references to many sources of information. See also J. I. Good, *Hist. of the Reformed Ch. in the U. S. in the Nineteenth Century* (1911); *Gen. Cat. of the Union Theolog. Sem. . . . 1836–1918* (1919); *Papers of the Am. Soc. of Ch. Hist.,* vol. VI (1894), vol. VII (1895); *N. Y. Times,* Oct. 21, 1893.]   H. E. S.

SCHAMBERG, JAY FRANK (Nov. 6, 1870–Mar. 30, 1934), dermatologist, was born in Philadelphia, Pa., the son of Gustav and Emma (Frank) Schamberg. He attended the public schools and graduated from the University of Pennsylvania in 1892 with the degree of M.D. After serving an interneship in the university hospital for eighteen months, he spent a year in the post-graduate study of dermatology in Vienna, Berlin, Hamburg, Paris, and London, and then began the practice of medicine in Philadelphia. Shortly thereafter he was appointed lecturer on infectious eruptive fevers in the University of Pennsylvania and in 1900 professor of dermatology in the Philadelphia Polyclinic and College of Graduates in Medicine. When this institution was affiliated with the Graduate School of Medicine of the University of Pennsylvania in 1919, he was appointed professor of dermatology and syphilology, a position he held until the time of his death. In the meantime he also held for brief periods the professorship in dermatology and syphilology in the Temple University school of medicine and the Jefferson Medical College. In 1912 he organized the Dermatological Research Laboratories and during the World War, with Dr. John A. Kolmer and Dr. George W. Raiziss, succeeded in synthesizing arsphenamin and neoarsphenamin at a time when supplies of these compounds for the treatment of syphilis were not available. The funds accruing were set aside for medical research and resulted in the establishment of the Research Institute of Cutaneous Medicine, Philadelphia, of which he was director until the time of his death.

In 1912 he served as a member of the Pennsylvania state vaccination commission; in 1920–21 as president of the American Dermatological Association; in 1931 as president of the Philadelphia County Medical Society, and in 1928–29 as chairman of the section on dermatology and syphilology of the American Medical Association. From 1927 to 1934 he served on the editorial board of *Archives of Dermatology and Syphilology*. He was a corresponding member of the dermatological societies of France, Denmark, and the Argentine Republic. He published over a hundred and fifty articles on skin diseases and syphilis and in 1901 described a progressive pigmentary disease of the skin since known as Schamberg's disease (*British Journal of Dermatology*, January 1901). In 1909 he discovered the cause of "grain itch" in collaboration with Dr. Joseph Goldberger, reported in *Epidemic of an Urticarioid Dermatitis Due to a Small Mite . . . in the Straw of Mattresses* (1909). He was also author of *A Compend of Diseases of the Skin* (1898), which went through many editions. With Dr. William Welch he wrote *Acute Contagious Diseases* (1905), republished in collaboration with Dr. John A. Kolmer in 1928 as a textbook on *Acute Infectious Diseases*. In 1908 he published *Diseases of the Skin and Eruptive Fevers* and in 1932, in collaboration with Dr. Carroll S. Wright, *Treatment of Syphilis*. A man of calm demeanor, whose earnestness and cheerfulness were unchanging, he was gifted with an equal enthusiasm for work and for play, and had to an unusual degree the power of stim-

ulating and inspiring his associates. On Oct. 11, 1905, he married May Ida Bamberger •of New York; they had a son and a daughter.

[See *Who's Who in America*, 1932–33; *Pa. Medic. Jour.*, May 1934, p. 671; *Archives of Dermatology and Syphilology*, June 1934; *Jour. Am. Medic. Assoc.*, Apr. 14, 1934; *Pub. Ledger* (Phila.), Mar. 31, 1934. No complete list of Schamberg's writings has as yet (1935) been published.]   J. A. K—r.

SCHARF, JOHN THOMAS (May 1, 1843–Feb. 28, 1898), Confederate soldier, historian, collector of Americana, was born in Baltimore, Md., the son of Thomas G. and Anna Maria (McNulty) Scharf. At the age of sixteen, after an elementary education in St. Peter's parish school and in Calvert Hall, he entered the lumber business of his father, but he soon left it for the more congenial work of fighting for the South in the Civil War. On his second attempt, in July 1861, he succeeded in making his way to Virginia, where he enlisted in the 1st Maryland Artillery. With that unit he went through several campaigns, receiving wounds at Cedar Mountain, at the second battle of Bull Run, and at Chancellorsville. While recovering from the last of these he was commissioned a midshipman in the Confederate navy in 1863. In that branch of the service he participated in some minor engagements, later to be unduly magnified in his history of the Confederate navy, but the lack of activity by the winter of 1864 caused him to resign with the .intention of transferring back to the army. Instead he was sent by the war department on a mission to Canada. He had hardly crossed the Potomac into Maryland, when he was captured. The end of the war prevented his trial as a spy, and in September 1865 he was pardoned by President Johnson. On Dec. 2, 1869, he was married to Mary McDougall of Baltimore, who with three children survived him. After another experience in his father's business he practised law for about four years, served on the editorial staffs of three Baltimore papers, the *Baltimore News, Sunday Telegram,* and *Morning Herald,* was elected in 1877 a member of the Maryland House of Delegates, and held the office of commissioner of the land office from 1884 to 1892. An appointment as special inspector of Chinese immigration at the port of New York took him to that city in 1893, and there he remained to practise law four years later when a Republican administration came into power.

During these years he devoted himself constantly to the writing of local history. The results appeared in articles in the Baltimore *Sun,* in magazines, and in many heavy books. They won for him recognition as an authority on Maryland history. Nearly all his writings were devoted to local history, and his books suffer from the inclusion of biographies of living men and other devices to make them sell. The one outstanding exception is the *History of Maryland* (3 vols., 1879), which in spite of his many prejudices is the most comprehensive treatment of the subject and one which historians still consult. While less significant, *The Chronicles of Baltimore* (1874), in which he anticipated McMaster in the use of newspapers as a main source for writing history, and his *History of the Confederate States Navy* (1887) are of value to the student of history. At one time he was preparing to write the authorized biography of Jefferson Davis. His use of some of the material in a newspaper article angered Davis, and, perhaps for that reason, the work was never completed (Dunbar, Rowland, *Jefferson Davis*, 1922, IX, 510, 574, 576). Less known but perhaps more deserving of memory than his writings was his success as a collector of historical materials. In 1891 he presented to the library of The Johns Hopkins University a collection of Americana, which was one of the largest and best that had been assembled up to that time. Notable in it were some 50,000 pamphlets especially on Southern history, the files of fifteen or more Confederate newspapers for all or portions of the Civil War period, 3000 broadsides, a large assortment of the papers of important private citizens, and a mass of official Maryland records (described in the *Johns Hopkins University Circular*, June 1891, pp. 110–13). Most of the purely local records, such as rent rolls and muster rolls, which were probably acquired while he was commissioner of the land office, have since been deposited with the Maryland Historical Society.

[*Sketch of J. Thomas Scharf* (1879), reprinted from *The Biog. Cyc. of Representative Men of Md. and District of Columbia* (1879); biog. sketch in *The Johns Hopkins Circular, ante*; F. B. Culver, "The War Romance of John Thomas Scharf," *Md. Hist. Mag.*, Sept. 1926; *Sun* (Baltimore), Mar. 1, 1898, Dec. 22, 1929; mother's name from family information.]   W. S. H.

SCHAUFFLER, HENRY ALBERT (Sept. 4, 1837–Feb. 15, 1905), Congregationalist clergyman, missionary, was born in Constantinople, the son of William Gottlieb Schauffler [*q.v.*]; his mother was Mary (Reynolds), who introduced education for women into the Turkish Empire. Sent to the United States, Henry entered Williams College, from which he was graduated as salutatorian of his class in 1859. After two years at Andover Theological Seminary and one year at the Harvard Law School he went back to Constantinople, where he was for two years professor of law at Robert College. He was ordained at Constantinople on June 3,

1865, and for the next five years was an American Board missionary in that city. As a missionary to Catholics in Austria, he was stationed at Prague from 1872 to 1874, and from 1874 to 1881 at Brünn, where he found the field difficult and suffered many hardships; his labors, however, had the important result of securing a fair degree of religious freedom in the empire.

Returning to the United States in 1882, he was employed by the Missionary Society of Cleveland, Ohio, to conduct religious work among the 20,000 Bohemians in that city. His abilities won immediate recognition and he became known as the "Apostle to the Slavs." Within a few years one Polish and four Bohemian churches were established through his efforts, and in 1884 he was made superintendent of its Slavic work throughout the country by the Congregational Home Missionary Society. Churches and missions were planted in many centers of Slavic population; a work of great importance was founded in Chicago; and in 1885, a department for the training of Slavic-speaking ministers was established in Oberlin Theological Seminary. Probably his most important achievement, however, was the Schauffler Missionary Training School in Cleveland, founded in 1886 as the "Bible Readers' School" for the training of Slavic women for mission work among their own people. From small beginnings this school has become a flourishing institution and has broadened its scope till its pupils now represent many nationalities.

Schauffler was characterized by great missionary zeal, marked executive ability, and indomitable persistence. He was master of five languages and had considerable acquaintance with several others. His publications consist chiefly of addresses on the Slavic peoples and mission work among them. On Nov. 25, 1862, he was married to Clara Eastham Gray, who died Sept. 3, 1883; and on July 28, 1892, to Clara Hobart, who had been the first teacher in his Cleveland school. Seven children by the first marriage and three by the second survived him.

[H. M. Tenney, *The Schauffler Missionary Training School* (1915); *Congreg. Year Book*, 1906; *Congregationalist*, Feb. 25, 1905; *Home Missionary*, Apr. 1905; H. P. Schauffler, *Henry Albert Schauffler, a Sketch of His Life by His Son* (1910); *Sketches of the Life and Work of Henry Albert Schauffler, D.D.* (1906); *Andover Theological Sem. Necrology*, 1904–05; *Cleveland Plain Dealer*, Feb. 16, 1905.]

F. T. P.

SCHAUFFLER, WILLIAM GOTTLIEB (Aug. 22, 1798–Jan. 26, 1883), missionary, the son of Philip Frederick and Caroline Henrietta (Schuckart) Schauffler, was born in Stuttgart, Germany. In 1805 his family settled in Odessa,

Russia, where his early education was gained, partly in a German school; he also received private instruction in music and drawing. At fifteen years of age, he was put to work at his father's trade of turner and maker of musical instruments, but, prompted by an insatiable appetite for learning, he soon mastered Russian, French, and Italian, and studied Latin, Greek, and English.

He came early under the influence of "missions" and was converted by an evangelical Catholic, Ignatius Lindl. Urged to enter missionary service by an agent of the Basle Missionary Institute, named Saltet, he was enlisted for work among Moslems by Joseph Wolff. On Feb. 8, 1826, he sailed with Wolff for Constantinople, where he began the study of Turkish and "Islamic controversy." On May 8 he sailed for Smyrna, to begin his missionary activities. A sudden change of plan, however, carried him to America for further education. Arriving in Boston on Nov. 7, he applied, at the suggestion of officers of the American Board of Commissioners for Foreign Missions, for admission to Andover Theological Seminary. There he spent five years, supported by funds of the institution and his own labors, especially as a cabinet maker. His course of study included Greek and Hebrew, but he added, under his own tuition, Chaldaic, Syriac, Arabic, Persian, Turkish, Rabbinic, Coptic, and Ethiopic. Before his career was over, it is said, he could understand twenty-six languages, use ten with facility, and speak extemporaneously in six. He gained experience in preaching by supplying for several months the pulpit of the Park Street Congregational Church in Boston. On Nov. 14, 1831, he was ordained in this church, and commissioned by the American Board as a missionary to the Jews of Turkey.

He spent some time en route in Paris with masters of Arabic, Persian, and Turkish, and visited Stuttgart, Vienna, and Odessa. Arriving in Constantinople on July 31, 1832, he met with no success there, or in Smyrna, to which place he transferred at the end of the year. He then returned to Constantinople to enter government educational service. On Feb. 26, 1834, he married, in Constantinople, Mary Reynolds of the Smyrna Mission. Thereafter, for several years, he engaged in missionary tours and Bible translation. His first Jewish converts were won in 1835. By 1839 he had completed a new translation of the Old Testament into Hebrew-Spanish (Sephardi), which the American Bible Society began publishing in Vienna under his supervision. By 1842, three thousand copies had

been issued, one of which Schauffler presented in person to the Austrian Emperor. A year later, five thousand copies more were printed.

In 1843 Schauffler received a grant of about $2,200 from the Missionary Society of the Established Church of Scotland for his work among the Jews, and he served for a time as chaplain of the Mission to the German (Ashkenaz) Jews. During 1855–56 Jewish missions were transferred to the Free Church of Scotland, and he devoted himself thereafter to the Armenians and Turks under the Turkey Mission of the American Board. He had, in August 1855, represented Armenian missions at a meeting in Paris of the World's Evangelical Alliance, pleading the cause of religious liberty in Turkey. During 1856–57 he aided in the revision of the Turkish New Testament, and began transcribing the Armeno-Turkish Bible into Turkish. Turkey having been at last "opened" by the Crimean War, he visited America in 1857 (arriving in New York Aug. 20) on behalf of Turkish missions. On his way back he secured funds in Edinburgh with which to pay the cost of an English-Turkish lexicon and other literature. Under the auspices of the American and the British and Foreign Bible societies, he translated the New Testament into Turkish (1866), and did further work on the Turkish Old Testament. In 1874 he and his wife left Turkey, and, after spending three years with their son, Henry Albert [q.v.], in Moravia, they proceeded to New York to live with other sons.

In addition to the work of translation, Schauffler wrote "What Drink Did Our Lord Jesus Christ Use at the Institution of the Eucharist?" (Biblical Repository and Quarterly Observer, October 1836), "Resources of the Catholic Church for Carrying on Foreign Missions" (in Elias Loomis' Memoirs of American Missionaries, 1833), and Meditations on the Last Days of Christ (1837). He received several honorary degrees and was decorated by the King of Prussia.

[Autobiog. of William G. Schauffler (1887), ed. by his sons; Missionary Herald, Mar. 1883; H. C. Haydn, Am. Heroes on Mission Fields (1890); C. C. Creegan and J. A. B. Goodnow, Great Missionaries of the Church (1895); N. Y. Tribune, Jan. 28, 1883.]

J. C. A.

SCHECHTER, SOLOMON (Dec. 7, 1850–Nov. 15, 1915), Hebraist and author, son of Isaac and Chaya Rachel Schechter, was born in Fokshan (Focsani), Roumania. He received his early education, which was confined exclusively to Hebrew literature, from his father; at ten he went to a Hebrew school at the neighboring town of Piatra and at fourteen to Lemberg, where he studied under a great Talmudist, Rabbi Joseph Saul Nathanson. In 1875 he went to Vienna; there, under the guidance of Isaac Hirsch Weiss and Lector Meir Friedmann, the knowledge he had acquired in the Roumanian schools became methodized. He received the rabbinical diploma in 1879 but never exercised the functions of that office. After studying in Berlin, at the Hochschule für die Wissenchaft des Judenthums and attending lectures at the University of Berlin, he went in 1882 to England, where he began an active scholarly and literary career. Here in 1887 he married Mathilda Roth, a native of Breslau who was then teaching in England; by her he had a son and two daughters. He was a lecturer in Talmud at Jews' College in London when in March 1890 the readership in Talmud and rabbinical literature at Cambridge University fell vacant and he was appointed to the post. Though he probably did not know more than a few words of English until he was thirty-five years of age, he rapidly acquired an amazing knowledge of the language and a style attained by few.

Among his first scholarly publications were a number of Hebrew ethical wills (1885), which he found in the British Museum; Saadya's explanation of the rules of interpretation; and a critical edition of the *Aboth de Rabbi Nathan* (1887), one of the minor tractates of the Babylonian Talmud. He received a traveling scholarship to Italian libraries in 1893 and two years later he was invited to Philadelphia to deliver a course of lectures at the newly inaugurated Gratz College. In 1896 he made a discovery that gave him a world-wide reputation. He identified a fragment of a manuscript as a part of the lost original Hebrew of the oldest book of the Apocrypha, the Wisdom of Ben Sira or Ecclesiasticus. Shortly thereafter he undertook a visit to Cairo to investigate the so-called Genizah, a sort of literary burial place, which it was known existed in Jewish synagogues. For months he worked underground with great hardship, which was detrimental to his health, but he finally brought back to Cambridge some fifty thousand manuscripts and fragments, mostly in Hebrew and Arabic, probably the largest collection of manuscript material ever found by one man. In it he discovered many of the remaining chapters of Ecclesiasticus, published in 1899 as *The Wisdom of Ben Sira, Portions of the Book Ecclesiasticus from Hebrew Manuscripts in the Cairo Genizah Collection.* He gave a series of lectures based upon this on the social life of the Jews in the age of Jesus, the Son of Sira (*Stud-*

ies in Judaism, 2 ser., 1908), which tended to disprove many theories that had been advanced concerning the dates of various books in the Biblical canon.

Besides being reader at Cambridge, he had been appointed a curator of the university library, Goldsmith professor of Hebrew at the University of London, and an examiner at the University of Manchester. Still he was not happy in England. As a lover of freedom he had long been attracted by America; moreover, he wished for a more Jewish atmosphere and field of activity. When in 1901 he was invited to become president of the Jewish Theological Seminary in New York, he accepted, breathed new life into the seminary, collected a new faculty, and within a very short time became the acknowledged leader of Jewish scholarship in America. He founded the United Synagogue of America, was one of the editors of the Bible Translation of the Jewish Publication Society, of the *Jewish Quarterly Review,* and of the first edition (1901) of *The Jewish Encyclopaedia.* After arranging his administrative work he issued a number of publications, some of them based upon the Cairo manuscripts. The first of these (1903) was entitled *Saadyana Geniza Fragments of R. Saadya Gaon,* mostly, though not exclusively, unpublished documents of Saadia Gaon, the great scholar of the ninth century; in 1912 he published a document relating to the conversion of the King of Khazars to Judaism (*Jewish Quarterly Review,* n.s., vol. III, p. 485 ff.). But his most important publication after *The Wisdom of Ben Sira* was a two-volume work, *Documents of Jewish Sectaries* (1910). He stimulated other scholars to search among the manuscripts he had collected, and many chapters of Jewish history and works of Jewish literature are gradually being recovered through this great mass of material, so extensive that it will take many generations to explore. Under the modest title of *Some Aspects of Rabbinic Theology,* he published in 1909 the first approach to a methodical presentation of Jewish theology. He wrote many charming essays, collected under the title *Studies in Judaism,* in three series (1896, 1908, 1924), and *Seminary Addresses and Other Papers* (1915). He also edited the *Midrash Hag-gadol to Genesis* (1902), a collection of ancient homiletic interpretations of the Bible. His papers and articles in journals run into the hundreds. He was very imposing-looking, with a massive leonine head. He had great interest in general affairs, and at the time of the Boer War, to which he was opposed, he did not hesitate to speak his mind even in England. When the

World War broke out, his sympathies were with the Allies, and he was impatient because America did not at once support what he considered a righteous cause. Besides a distinguished reputation for knowledge, he had great charm of presentation that earned for him real celebrity.

[*Who's Who in America,* 1914–15; Schechter's Application and Testimonials for the post of Lecturer in Talmudic in the University of Cambridge, 1890, printed but not published; Samuel Schulman, in *Yearbook: Central Conference Am. Rabbis,* vol. XXVI (1916); G. F. Moore, in *Menorah Jour.,* Feb. 1916; F. I. Schechter, *Ibid.,* June 1922; Cyrus Adler, in *Am. Jewish Year Book,* 1916; *Students' Ann.,* vol. III (1916), Jewish Theological Sem.; Alexander Marx, "Solomon Schechter," *Pubs. Am. Jewish Hist. Soc.,* no. 25 (1917), pp. 177–92; Alexander Marx and S. M. Stroock, *Memorial Addresses . . . on . . . the Death of Dr. Solomon Schechter* (1917); Joshua Bloch, *Prof. Solomon Schechter, M.A., Litt.D.* (1915); Louis Ginzberg, in *Students, Scholars, and Saints* (1928); Norman Bentwich, *Solomon Schechter* (1931). C. A.

SCHEEL, FRITZ (Nov. 7, 1852–Mar. 13, 1907), violinist, conductor, was born in Lübeck, Germany, the son and grandson of musical conductors. His mother was a talented amateur musician. Scheel had his first musical training in his native town, piano lessons from F. Burjani, and violin instruction from Gottfried Herrmann. Before he was ten years of age Scheel was able to occupy one of the first violin desks in his father's orchestra and on occasion filled vacancies by playing the horn, trumpet, trombone, and tuba. He also organized and conducted a juvenile orchestra of his own. From 1864 to 1867 he studied the violin under Ferdinand David in Leipzig and in 1869 went to Bremerhaven, first as concert-master at the opera, and then as conductor of concerts. In 1873 he went to Schwerin as solo violinist and director of the court orchestra. After a term at Bremen, he went to Chemnitz in 1882 to succeed Hans Sitt as *Kapellmeister.* Here he directed an orchestra of seventy-two players, as well as the *Sitt Chor Gesangverein,* a chorus of several hundred voices. The orchestra became well known and was invited to travel to various cities in Saxony. In 1890 Scheel moved to Hamburg, where he alternated with Hans von Bülow as conductor of the Abonnement Concerts.

At the time he came to America, in 1893, Scheel was a musician with thorough experience in all branches of the profession. He made his first appearances in New York City, and then organized an orchestra which gave concerts at the Trocadero of the World's Columbian Exposition in Chicago. This enterprise was not successful, however, and Scheel later took an orchestra to San Francisco to play at the concerts of the Midwinter Fair. He was induced to remain in San Francisco, and became the first con-

ductor of the San Francisco Symphony Society. In 1899 Scheel went to Philadelphia, where he conducted an orchestra at Woodside Park, a summer resort. His concerts attracted the attention of the managers of the Philadelphia Symphony Society, an amateur organization, and he was elected conductor the same year. In 1901 the Philadelphia Orchestra Association was organized, and Scheel made conductor—a post which he held until his death. From the very beginning he insisted upon highly artistic and classical performances, sturdily resisting the demands of the managers for more "popular" programs. This policy, pursued with the rare skill, courage, and unflagging energy which characterized Scheel, laid the solid foundations upon which his successors have built (see the tribute by Leopold Stokowski, Wister, *post,* p. 85). In addition to his work with the orchestra, Scheel directed two choral organizations, the Orpheus and the Eurydice clubs. These labors proved too great a burden for his strength, and he began to suffer a gradual breakdown about a year before his death. He was survived by his widow, three daughters, and a son.

[F. A. Wister, *Twenty-five Years of the Philadelphia Orchestra* (1925); *Grove's Dict. of Music and Musicians, Am. Supp.* (1930); *Baker's Biog. Dict. of Musicians* (3rd ed., 1919); *Music World,* Jan. 1907; *Musician,* Sept. 1904; *Musical Record and Rev.,* Nov. 1903; *Public Ledger* (Philadelphia), Mar. 14, 1907.] J. T. H.

SCHELE DE VERE, MAXIMILIAN (Nov. 1, 1820–May 12, 1898), philologist, was the son of a Swedish *freiherr,* von Schele, officer in the Prussian army, and a French mother named De Vere. He was born in Wexiö, Sweden, but followed his father in allegiance to Prussia; in appearance and disposition he was characteristically French. As a child he evinced great aptitude for languages, early mastering Slavic, French, and German, and so augmenting his knowledge by study and travel that he had won reputation as a linguist before he reached his majority. His formal education was obtained at the Universities of Bonn, Berlin (Ph.D., 1841), and Greifswald (*Juris Utriusque Doctor,* 1842).

After a year or more in the Prussian diplomatic and military services, in 1843 he emigrated to Boston, where he gave private instruction in languages and studied modern Greek at Harvard. His refined and amiable nature combined with his attainments to win him many distinguished friends, and when, Sept. 23, 1844, he was elected professor of modern languages at the University of Virginia, he was recommended for the chair by Longfellow, Josiah Quincy, and Abbott Lawrence (Bruce, *post,* III, 83). In this capacity, he served the state with distinction and ability until advancing age compelled his resignation, fifty-one years later.

In addition to teaching the French, Spanish, Italian, and German languages and literatures and also the literary and political history of these nations, he deserves remembrance for having inaugurated the systematic study of Anglo-Saxon. Likewise, he offered successful courses in comparative philology, at a period when few American colleges had recognized the value of the comparative method. His classes were extremely popular, the students, under the prevailing elective system, seeking out Professor Schele as well for the courtesy and character of the man as for the interest and enthusiasm with which he presented his subject. His published studies of the genesis and development of the English language were original and in advance of similar effort elsewhere: among his more valuable works were his *Outlines of Comparative Philology* (1853), *Studies in English* (1867), *Americanisms; The English of the New World* (1871). He performed an enormous amount of scholarly labor, his other publications including, besides his work for the *Standard Dictionary* (1893–95) and some graceful addresses, articles for magazines and encyclopedias, historical romances, several volumes of popular science, translations from contemporary European authors (especially Friedrich Spielhagen and Emile Gaboriau), a Spanish and a French grammar and other language texts, and his valuable compilation, *Students of the University of Virginia, a Semi-Centennial Catalogue* (copyright 1878). All that he wrote was characterized by vivacity and smoothness of style, by studious accuracy and catholic culture.

Schele was twice married, each time to a daughter of Judge Alexander Rives of Albemarle County, Va.; first, on July 25, 1849, to Eliza Wydown Rives and, nine years after her death in 1851, on Mar. 21, 1860, to Lucy Brown Rives. A daughter by his first wife died in 1864. His own death occurred in Washington, D. C., whither he had removed after his retirement.

[J. S. Patton, in *Lib. of Southern Lit.*, vol. XI (copr. 1909), ed. by E. A. Alderman and J. C. Harris; D. M. R. Culbreth, *The Univ. of Va.* (1908); W. M. Thornton, in *Alumni Bull. of the Univ. of Va.*, July, Nov. 1894; P. A. Bruce, *Hist. of the Univ. of Va.*, vol. III (1921); J. R. Childs, *Reliques of the Rives* (1929), p. 606; *Washington Post,* May 13, 1898.]   A. C. G., Jr.

SCHELL, AUGUSTUS (Aug. 1, 1812–Mar. 27, 1884), lawyer, politician, business man, was the most prominent of four brothers who became well known in the financial circles of New York City. An elder brother, Richard, a brilliant talker, jovial, open-handed, everywhere welcome, was from 1840 to 1873 one of the most daring operators in Wall Street and also served a term in the state legislature and in the House of Representatives. Two younger brothers, Robert and Edward, became presidents of leading banks. All were born at Rhinebeck, N. Y., the sons of Christian and Elizabeth (Hughes) Schell, and the grandsons of Richard Schell, one of a group from the Rhenish Palatinate that settled in the vicinity of Rhinebeck shortly before the Revolution. Augustus graduated from Union College in 1830, studied a year at the celebrated law school at Litchfield, Conn., and read law under John Armstrong at Rhinebeck and John Slosson in New York City. Shortly after his admission to the bar (1833) he was admitted to the Slosson firm. His father having died early, his mother moved to the city and until her death in 1866 provided her sons with a home. It was late in life (March 1873) that Augustus married Anna, daughter of George S. Fox of New York City, who survived him. No children were born to them.

Schell became an expert in the expanding field of corporation law and gave his legal services more and more to firms in which he and Richard were financially interested. Close friends of "Commodore" Cornelius Vanderbilt, 1794–1877 [*q.v.*], they backed him in all his interests, particularly in building up the New York Central railroad system and in his fight with Daniel Drew [*q.v.*] over the Erie. Schell became a director of the New York and Harlem Railroad, 1862; of the Hudson River Railroad, 1864; of the New York Central, 1867; of the Lake Shore and Michigan Southern, 1869; and later of the Chicago and Northwestern, the Union Pacific, and a score of others. He was also a director of several banks and insurance companies and was long vice-president of the Union Trust Company. He was heavily interested in the Western Union Telegraph Company, served many years as chairman of its legal committee, and was senior vice-president at his death. His market operations were heavy. Together with Horace F. Clark and Jay Gould [*qq.v.*] he engineered the corner in Chicago and Northwestern stock, one of Wall Street's notable post–Civil War episodes. Though Richard's house failed in 1873, Augustus managed to weather the panic and at his death was worth several millions, eventually divided among his nieces and nephews.

As a ward leader and then district leader he rose in the Tammany organization until in 1852 he became chairman of the Tammany general committee. The same year he was Tammany's candidate for governor but at the state convention lost the nomination to Horatio Seymour [*q.v.*]. He was chairman of the Democratic state committee, 1853–55, and an efficient worker for Buchanan in 1856, his efforts being rewarded by appointment to the important post of collector of the port of New York, 1857–61. His political career was halted by the war and reconstruction periods, but he was drawn into a second period of political activity when he was persuaded to head a reorganization of Tammany Hall after the Tweed downfall. Accordingly, he succeeded William Marcy Tweed [*q.v.*] as Grand Sachem in 1872 and held the position until his death. He helped name the Committee of Twenty-one to reconstruct Tammany and again became chairman of the Tammany general committee. In 1872 a second attempt to nominate him for governor was prevented by the clever strategy of Samuel Jones Tilden [*q.v.*]. As chairman of the National Democratic Committee, 1872–76, Schell managed Greeley's presidential campaign and, according to John Kelly [*q.v.*], gave enough toward the campaign chest to make an ordinary man rich for life. He opened the National Democratic Convention at St. Louis in 1876, and though he joined with Kelly in opposing Tilden's nomination, he afterwards supported him liberally. Schell was an unsuccessful candidate for state senator, 1877, and for mayor of New York, 1878, having consented to run for these local offices for the sake of Tammany in crucial elections. He lacked appeal for the average Tammany voter, being something of "an old pump that the boys could never cotton to in a thousand years" (*New York Herald,* Nov. 1, 1877). In his later political activities he was closely allied with Kelly, of whose honesty and good intentions he was firmly convinced. He was interested in many clubs, societies, and institutions of the city. He served nineteen years as chairman of the executive committee of the New York Historical Society and was twice president. His favorite charity was the New York Institution for the Blind, of which he was president from 1866 until his death.

[The chief authority is the *Memoir of the Hon. Augustus Schell* (1885) by Francis Schell, a nephew, which contains in its appendix the memorial notice by Dr. George H. Moore of the N. Y. Hist. Soc. and John Kelly's intimate tribute. See also *U. S. Democratic Rev.,* Dec. 1857; *Encyc. of Contemporary Biog. of N. Y.* (6 vols., 1878–90); D. S. Alexander, *A Pol. Hist. of the State of N. Y.* (3 vols., 1906–09); J. F. McLaughlin, *The Life and Times of John Kelly* (1885); obituaries in *N. Y. Tribune, N. Y. Times,* Mar. 28, 1884.]

O. W. H.

SCHEM, ALEXANDER JACOB (Mar. 16, 1826–May 21, 1881), encyclopedist, editor, statistician, was born at Wiedenbrück, Westphalia, Germany, and was baptized Jacob Balthasar Alexander. He was the son of a vinegar manufacturer, Friedrich Schem, and his wife, Adolphine von Felgenhauer. He attended the Gymnasium at Paderborn (1839–43) and then studied Catholic theology at Bonn (1843–45) and at Tübingen (1845–46). Ordained a priest on Apr. 18, 1849, he officiated for two years as "Kaplan" in Bielefeld.

Finding himself less and less in accord with dogma, he gave up his allegiance to the Roman Catholic Church and emigrated to the United States in 1851. His first position was that of tutor in the home of the publisher, Friedrich Gerhard, whose oldest daughter Schem married in 1853. In the same year he accepted a position as teacher of ancient and modern languages at the Collegiate Institute, Mount Holly, N. J. From 1854 to 1860 he was professor of Hebrew and modern languages at Dickinson College and in 1858 published, in collaboration with George R. Crooks [*q.v.*], *A New Latin-English School-Lexicon.* He resigned his professorship in order to devote himself entirely to literary and journalistic work in New York.

In the pursuance of this work he wrote numerous articles for *The New American Cyclopædia* (1858–63), edited by C. S. Dana and George Ripley. He also published a work on church statistics, *The American Ecclesiastical Year-Book* (1860), which was followed by *The American Ecclesiastical Almanac* (1868) and *The American Ecclesiastical and Educational Almanac* (1869). From 1860 to 1869 he was foreign news editor of the *New York Tribune,* as well as a collaborator in preparing the *Tribune Almanac,* the *National Almanac,* and *The American Year-Book and National Register.* On leaving the *Tribune* in 1869, he became editor-in-chief of the *Deutsch-amerikanisches Conversations-lexikon* (11 vols., 1869–74). He was a contributor to *Johnson's New Universal Cyclopædia,* and in 1877 published, with Henry Kiddle, *The Cyclopædia of Education.* In addition to the above, he wrote a book on the Russo-Turkish war, *The War in the East* (1878), as well as numerous magazine articles. From 1874 until his death he was assistant superintendent of the public schools of New York and for some time an editorial contributor to *The Methodist* and *The Methodist Quarterly Review.*

Schem was a man of extraordinarily wide reading in twelve languages and his home in Hoboken was the resort of many scholars. He believed that the development of learning in nineteenth-century Germany was second only to that of

Athens in the fifth century, and he worked consistently for a better understanding among Americans of German scholarship. All his writings are characterized by deep seriousness, thorough scholarship, broad background. His one larger non-encyclopedic work, *The War in the East,* begins with a long discussion of the events that preceded the war, gives detailed descriptions of all the battles, and sketches the repercussions of the war in various diplomatic chancelleries of Europe. It is written in a readable style remarkable for a man who was not writing in his native tongue. Unlike many other German-Americans, Schem identified himself fully with the intellectual currents in the English language, without, however, turning his back entirely on undertakings in his own language, as his editorship of an encyclopedia in German shows. He is described as of stocky build, sociable in his habits, extremely tolerant in his views, and indefatigable in his labors—the last-named characteristic probably being responsible for his death, which occurred in Hoboken, since the death certificate reads as follows: "Primary Disease: Cerebral Hyperasthesia. Secondary Disease: Acute Diabetes. Remarks: The foundation of the whole disease was exhaustive mental labor."

[The most comprehensive sketch of Schem's life is in *Der Deutsche Pionier,* Dec. 1882; a short biog., probably written by himself, is found in *Deutsch-amerikanisches Conversations-lexikon,* IX (1873), 743–44; brief estimates of his lifework are given in Rudolf Cronau, *Drei Jahrhunderte deutschen Lebens in Amerika* (Berlin, 1909), and Georg von Bosse, *Das deutsche Element in den Vereinigten Staaten* (1908), pp. 440–41; the names of Schem's parents are from the record of his baptism, at Wiedenbrück; see also, *Appletons' Ann. Cyc. . . . 1882* (1883); *N. Y. Tribune,* May 24, 1881.]   A. E. Z.

SCHENANDOA [See SKENANDO, *c.* 1706–1816].

SCHENCK, FERDINAND SCHUREMAN (Aug. 6, 1845–Apr. 6, 1925), clergyman of the Reformed Church in America, was born at Plattekill, Ulster County, N. Y., the son of the Rev. Martin Luther Schenck and Abigail Van der Veer. His grandfather, Ferdinand S. Schenck, was a distinguished physician of Somerset County, N. J. Ferdinand was graduated from the College of New Jersey in 1865, and then entered the Albany Law School. Receiving the degree of LL.B. in 1867, he practised for two years, and then, convinced of a call to the ministry, gave up the law and became a student in the New Brunswick Theological Seminary. After his graduation and ordination, by the classis of Paramus, in 1872, he served successively four Reformed churches, all in the state of New York—in Clarkstown, 1872–77, Montgomery, 1877–90, Hudson, 1890–97, and University Heights, New York City, 1897–99.

In 1899 he was appointed by the General Synod of the denomination professor of practical theology in the New Brunswick Seminary. In this office he served for twenty-five years, becoming emeritus professor in 1924. His department of instruction included homiletics, liturgics, pastoral practice, and, in a comprehensive way, sociology, to which he gave enthusiastic attention when it first became an academic subject. Other fields of thought and instruction were also familiar to him and he was lecturer on the literary study of the Bible at New York University (1898–1900), acting professor of philosophy (1904–05), and acting professor of ethics (1907–08) at Rutgers College, and acting professor of homiletics at Princeton Theological Seminary (1909–10). In 1892 he was president of the General Synod of the Reformed Church in America.

Schenck's intellectual interests were wide and varied, as his services of instruction suggest; even science was not outside their range, astronomy being one of his favorite studies. His excellence as a preacher lay in the clearness and directness of his thought, the simplicity and aptness of his language, and in his somewhat informal yet dignified and fluent address. He had a warmth of sympathy and a graciousness of personal contact that made him helpful and beloved as a pastor and left a lasting impression upon his students. He wrote much and was the author of books on various subjects. Among them are *The Ten Commandments in the Nineteenth Century* (1889); *The Bible Reader's Guide* (1896); *The Ten Commandments and the Lord's Prayer* (1902); *Modern Practical Theology* (1903); *The Sociology of the Bible* (1909); *Christian Evidences and Ethics* (1910); *Young People's History of the Christian Church* (1911); *The Oratory and Poetry of the Bible* (1915); *The Apostles' Creed in the Twentieth Century* (1918); *Expository Sermons on the Heidelberg Catechism* (1920); and *A Guide to the Stars* (1922). On Aug. 26, 1874, he married Ellie S. Haring of Nyack, N. Y., by whom he had three daughters and two sons. He died at White Plains, N. Y.

[*Acts and Proc. of the . . . Gen. Synod of the Reformed Church in America,* 1925; E. T. Corwin, *A Manual of the Reformed Church in America* (1922); J. H. Raven, *Biog. Record: New Brunswick Theological Sem.* (1934); *Who's Who in America,* 1924–25; *Christian Intelligencer,* Apr. 15, 1925.]   W. H. S. D.

SCHENCK, JAMES FINDLAY (June 11, 1807–Dec. 21, 1882), naval officer, son of Gen.

William Cortenus Schenck and Elizabeth (Rogers) Schenck and brother of Robert Cumming Schenck [q.v.], was born in Franklin, Ohio. On July 1, 1823, he was appointed to West Point but, becoming deficient in his studies, was turned back and resigned. On Mar. 1, 1825, he was appointed midshipman in the navy, promoted to passed midshipman in 1831, to lieutenant in 1835, and to commander in 1855. He first saw service with the Mosquito Fleet in the West Indies against the pirates and in 1828 commanded the sloop *Surprise,* after which his naval career for several years was uneventful. But in 1845 he was assigned to the frigate *Congress* under Commodore Robert Field Stockton [q.v.] and served with that officer during the occupation and conquest of California. He was present at the capture of Santa Barbara and on Aug. 6, 1846, landed in a launch with twenty men at San Pedro and captured that port. At the head of a company of seamen he marched with Stockton's command on Los Angeles, entering the town on Aug. 13, 1846. As second lieutenant of the *Congress* he participated in the bombardment and capture of Guaymas, and the taking of Mazatlán. From May 1849 until 1852 he was in command of the United States mail steamer *Ohio*; in 1858 he was given command of the receiving ship *North Carolina* at the New York navy yard; and on Mar. 8, 1860, he sailed from San Francisco in command of the *Saginaw* for the East India station. His cruise in far eastern waters was uneventful but for one occurrence; on June 30, 1861, while anchored just outside Quin Hon Harbor, Cochin China, he was fired upon by a fort and returned the fire, silencing the guns. The *Saginaw* was de-commissioned at Hong Kong Jan. 3, 1862, as she proved unseaworthy, and Schenck returned to the United States on the merchantman *Swordfish* with his crew. In April 1862 he was given command of the frigate *St. Lawrence,* East Gulf Blockading Squadron, and on her did blockading duty for one year, when he was relieved. He was listed on the navy register from 1862 to 1864 as commander "Not recommended for promotion by the Advisory Board," but in 1864 he was commissioned commodore, dating from Jan. 2, 1863, skipping the grade of captain. On Oct. 14, 1864, he took command of the steamer *Powhatan* and later of the third division of the North Atlantic Blockading Squadron. In this dual rôle he participated in the two attacks on Fort Fisher. He was commended by Admiral David Dixon Porter [q.v.] for gallant conduct. During the next two years he commanded the naval station at Mound City, Ill. Commissioned rear admiral Sept. 21, 1868, he was retired by law, June 11, 1869.

His earlier years in the service were spent at a time when the navy was in an inactive stage that afforded little opportunity for advancement or active duty, but his Mexican War service showed that he had the qualities of a leader. The outbreak of the Civil War found him well past his youth, and it is probable that the advisory board held up his promotion for that reason. During both attacks on Fort Fisher, in a difficult and responsible position, he handled his division with efficiency and precision, his reports to Admiral Porter showing keen observation and judgment. He married Dorothea Ann Smith on July 27, 1829, and had two sons and two daughters. His life following his retirement was spent at Dayton, Ohio.

[A. D. Schenck, *The Rev. William Schenck, His Ancestry and His Descendants* (1883); L. R. Hamersly, *Records Living Officers U. S. Navy* (4th ed., 1890); *War of the Rebellion: Official Records (Navy),* 1 Ser., vols. I, VII, XI, XII, XVII; *Navy Reg.,* 1825–70; *U. S. Mil. Acad. Reg.,* 1824; unpublished archives, Office of Naval Records; log of U.S.S. *Saginaw,* MS., Navy Dept.; H. H. Bancroft, *Hist. of Cal.,* vol. V (1886); D. D. Porter, *The Naval Hist. of the Civil War* (1886); *Diary of Gideon Welles,* vol. II (1911); S. J. Bayard, *A Sketch of the Life of Com. Robert F. Stockton* (1856); *Cincinnati Commercial, Dayton Daily Democrat, Dayton Daily Jour.,* Dec. 22, 1882.]

L. H. B.

SCHENCK, ROBERT CUMMING (Oct. 4, 1809–Mar. 23, 1890), congressman, soldier, diplomat, was a son of Gen. William Cortenus Schenck and his wife, Elizabeth Rogers. The father, a descendant of Roelof Martense Schenck who came to New Amsterdam probably about 1650, had migrated from New Jersey to Ohio, where he served in the legislature and is said to have founded the town of Franklin. Here Robert was born. His father died in 1821, leaving the boy under the guardianship of Gen. James Findlay [q.v.] of Cincinnati. Robert graduated from Miami University in 1827, remained there three years longer studying and teaching, was subsequently admitted to the bar, and commenced practising law in Dayton. On Aug. 21, 1834, he married Rennelche W. Smith, whose sister was the wife of his brother James Findlay Schenck [q.v.].

Robert Schenck's political career began in 1838 with a fruitless campaign for election to the legislature on the Whig ticket. More successful later, he assumed the leadership of his party in the Ohio House during the terms of 1841–43. In the national House of Representatives, 1843–51, he proved himself a vigorous Whig partisan, and upon the expiration of his fourth term in 1851 he was named by President Fillmore as minister to Brazil. Here he served until October 1853, acting with John S. Pendleton [q.v.], chargé d'affaires of the United States to the Argentine Confederation, in negotiating commercial treaties with Uruguay (1852) and Paraguay (1853), which were never proclaimed, and two treaties with the Argentine Confederation, signed July 10 and 27, 1853. He failed, however, to secure from Brazil a treaty providing for the free navigation of the Amazon.

A strong anti-slavery man, Schenck was one of the first to urge Lincoln's nomination and was an active Republican campaigner in 1860. Appointed brigadier-general of volunteers May 17, 1861, he took part in the first battle of Bull Run, served under Rosecrans and Frémont in West Virginia, and was wounded at Second Bull Run in August 1862, his right wrist being permanently injured. On Aug. 30 he was promoted major-general of volunteers. Eliminated from active fighting, he was assigned in December 1862 to the command in Baltimore, where his measures were not always popular (Richard H. Jackson, *To Robert E.* [sic] *Schenck*, pamphlet, 1867, p. 3). In December of the following year he resigned his commission in order to sit once more in Congress.

In the House he disapproved strongly of Lincoln's moderation as shown in the Hampton Roads Conference (J. F. Rhodes, *History of the United States*, vol. V, 1904, pp. 51–52, note). A master of invective and vituperation, he distinguished himself for the violence of his attack on such "Copperheads" as Fernando Wood, whom he called "a specimen of the snake family" (*No Compromise with Treason; Remarks of Mr. Schenck . . . Apr. 11, 1864,* 1864) and for his opposition to President Johnson. He was chairman of the House committee on military affairs and later of the Ways and Means committee. He was an advocate of the contraction of the currency at the end of the war (*Public Credit-Gold Contracts: Speech . . . Feb. 22, 1869,* 1869).

Failing of reëlection to Congress in 1870, Schenck turned again to diplomacy. He was appointed, Feb. 10, 1871, a member of the Joint High Commission between the United States and Great Britain and in that capacity signed the Treaty of Washington, May 8, 1871. On Dec. 22 preceding he had been designated to succeed the discredited John Lothrop Motley [*q.v.*] as minister to Great Britain, and he traveled to his post in May 1871. Here he was called upon to conduct much of the routine business arising out of the Treaty of Washington and the arbitration of the *Alabama* claims. In spite of his failure to conclude a consular convention with Great Britain and to persuade Derby to support the United States in its demands on Spain for concessions in its Cuban policy (S. F. Bemis, *The*

American Secretaries of State, vol. VII, 1928, pp. 194–200), his record in London seems creditable, but in February 1876 he resigned under a cloud. He had allowed himself to be made a director of the "Emma" silver mine in Utah which in 1871 used his name in the sale of stock in Great Britain. He was reproved by the Secretary of State at that time, and the failure of the Emma Mine brought his resignation, which Grant reluctantly accepted. The committee on foreign affairs of the House, which investigated the incident, found no cause to impugn Schenck's integrity, but condemned such transactions by American diplomats (*House Report No. 579,* 44 Cong., 1 Sess., 1876). After Schenck's resignation he returned to Washington to practise law, achieved a reputation as an authority on draw poker (he published *Draw Poker* in 1880), and died in that city in 1890. He was survived by three of his six daughters.

[A. D. Schenck, *The Rev. Wm. Schenck, His Ancestry and His Descendants* (1883); Robt. C. Schenck, *U. S. A.* (n.d.), pub. by order of Union Central Com., 3rd Cong. District, Ohio; *In Memoriam, Gen. Robt. C. Schenck* (n.d.), proceedings at memorial service in Dayton; *Biog. Dir. Am. Cong.* (1928); Beckles Wilson, *America's Ambassadors to England* (1928); W. A. Taylor, *Hundred-Year Book and Official Reg. of the State of Ohio* (1891); *Papers Relating to the Foreign Relations of the U. S., 1871–76;* L. E. Chittenden, *The Emma Mine* (1876); War Dept. records; instructions and dispatches to and from Brazil and Great Britain, in Dept. of State; *Washington Post,* Mar. 24, 1890.]

E. W. S.

SCHERESCHEWSKY, SAMUEL ISAAC JOSEPH (May 6, 1831–Oct. 15, 1906), missionary to China, translator of the Bible into Chinese, bishop of the Protestant Episcopal Church, was born in Tauroggen, Russian Lithuania, the son of Samuel and Rosa (Salvatha) Schereschewsky. His father was of the Ashkenazim and his mother of the Sephardim Jews. Both parents died when he was young and he was reared by a half-brother and his wife, who hoped to see him become a rabbi. He was given a careful Jewish training at home, in his native town, and at the rabbinical schools in Krazi and Zitomir. He then spent some time in the University of Breslau. Becoming convinced by his study of the New and Old Testaments that he should become a Christian, in 1854 he went to the United States, where, in a Baptist church, he was immersed. From 1855 to 1858 he studied in the Western Theological Seminary, a Presbyterian institution at Allegheny, Pa., and then, having joined the Protestant Episcopal Church, he was a student from 1858 to 1859 in the General Theological Seminary, New York City.

Some time before completing his education he had formed the purpose of becoming a missionary and translating the Bible into Chinese. He was ordained deacon in New York in July 1859, and that same year arrived in Shanghai as an appointee of the missionary society of his church. Here, Oct. 28, 1860, he was ordained priest. He had begun the study of Chinese on his way out and continued it in Shanghai, making rapid progress, for he had a natural gift for languages. From 1863 to 1875 he spent most of his time in Peking. While there he joined with another missionary in translating the (Anglican) Book of Common Prayer into Mandarin, the vernacular used by the majority of the Chinese, and with four other missionaries in translating the New Testament into that dialect; the latter translation was published in 1872. He himself translated the entire Old Testament into Mandarin (1865–73), and it was published in 1874. In the meantime, 1868, he had married in Shanghai Susan M. Waring, and in 1875, with his wife and two children, he returned to the United States for an extended furlough. While there he was elected to the Protestant Episcopal bishopric of Shanghai. After much hesitation and once declining, he accepted and on Oct. 3, 1877, was consecrated.

In 1878 he returned to Shanghai and there with funds which he had raised while in the United States bought the Jessfield site and erected the first buildings of a college, St. John's (later St. John's University), which he organized and which became one of the leading institutions of higher education in China. In 1879 he translated the entire Prayer Book into classical Chinese. That year he moved to Wuchang, where, in 1881, weakened by overwork in the attempt to carry the duties of bishop, to conduct the local mission, and to continue his translating, he was suddenly smitten with an illness which left him almost completely paralyzed and with impaired speech, but with quite unimpaired mind. From 1882 to 1886 he was in Geneva, Switzerland, for medical care, and from 1886 to 1895 in the United States. In 1883 he resigned his bishopric and seemed destined to spend the rest of his life in idle invalidism. In 1886, however, he resumed once more his work of translation. He could write painfully by pressing the keys of a typewriter with one finger of one hand. Laboring in this fashion and aided by the devoted care of his wife, in the next few years he wrote out in romanized form a revision of his Mandarin version of the Old Testament and a translation of the entire Bible into what is known as "easy Wenli," a form of the Chinese classical style. In 1895 he returned to Shanghai to have this translation put into Chinese characters and published. Because of its better facilities for printing, he went to

Japan in 1897 and there, in Tokyo, spent the remainder of his days. He was able to see through the press his revision of the Mandarin version—which he had once more revised—and his Wenli version of the Bible, also revised. Both were of excellent quality and were widely used. He also completed a reference Bible in both Mandarin and Wenli, and at the time of his death was at work on a translation of the Apocrypha. In collaboration with another missionary he had also translated the Gospel of Matthew into Mongolian and he had prepared, but never published, a handbook of Mandarin, a grammar and chrestomathy, and a dictionary of the Mongolian tongue. He was humble-minded, large-hearted, of marked intellectual as well as linguistic gifts, and an indefatigable and persistent worker.

[*Spirit of Missions,* June 1877, Apr. 1903, Nov. 1906; *Chinese Recorder,* Mar. 1903, Nov. 1906; annual reports of the American Bible Society, 1897–98, and especially 1907, pp. 152–54; annual reports of the board of managers of the Domestic and Foreign Missionary Society of the Protestant Episcopal Church in the U. S. A.; *Who's Who in America,* 1906–07; *Churchman,* Oct. 20, 1906; *Japan Weekly Mail* (Tokyo), Oct. 20, 1906; information from friends and from a daughter, Miss Caroline Schereschewsky.]   K. S. L.

SCHEVE, EDWARD BENJAMIN (Feb. 13, 1865–June 18, 1924), musician, was born in Herford, Westphalia, Germany, the eldest of six children of Edward and Adelaide (Schöneborn) Scheve. Both parents came from Bonn on the Rhine. The father, a Baptist minister, was for many years director of the Kammerung Mission of West Africa. The mother possessed some poetic ability, and was also musical. At the age of eight, Edward began the study of piano and organ under a local teacher, continued at the Cologne Gymnasium and the Geisenheim Institut, and then went to Berlin, where he entered Theodor Kullak's academy in 1885, and for three years studied piano with A. König, organ with F. Grunicke, and composition with Albert Becker. He also taught in the Academy from 1886 until 1888, when he came to the United States. He settled in Rochester, N. Y., as music teacher and organist at the First Baptist Church, and remained until 1892. In the year 1890 he made a trip to Berlin where he was married on Oct. 9 to Lina Amelia Grosch, a singer. In 1892 he became organist of the First German Baptist Church and director of the German-American Conservatory in Chicago. He remained in Chicago for fourteen years, and gave many organ recitals and concerts of his own compositions. In 1906 he was called to the Grinnell College School of Music, Grinnell, Iowa, as professor of theory and composition and instructor in organ. He remained there until his death, which occurred at Longmont, Colo., while on an extended vacation.

Scheve was deeply religious and his devotion to his religious convictions was completely intertwined with his music. At Rochester, N. Y., where for several months he was organist of the Lake Avenue Baptist Church, he was officially known as the Minister of Music, so earnest was his effort to make the position a real spiritual ministry to those who came to worship. Among his most important compositions are the following: "Symphony in D minor, *Opus* 38"; a piano concerto, *Opus* 20; a violin concerto in E flat, *Opus* 35; an oratorio, 'The Death and Resurrection of Christ, *Opus* 11"; "Festival March" for orchestra, organ and chorus; and an organ sonata in E flat. He also wrote many songs, anthems, and piano pieces.

[Information secured from his widow; *Who's Who in America*, 1924–25; *Who's Who in Music and Drama* (1914); *Am. Supp. to Grove's Dict. of Music and Musicians* (1930); obit. notice in *Grinnell Register*, June 23, 1924.]   F. L. G. C.

SCHICKILLEMY [See Shikellamy, d. 1748].

SCHIEREN, CHARLES ADOLPH (Feb. 28, 1842–Mar. 10, 1915), inventor, manufacturer, was the eldest child of John Nikolaus and Wilhelmina (Langenbach) Schieren and was born in Neuss, near Düsseldorf, Germany. His father was a business man and a moving spirit in the political revolution of 1848, the failure of which necessitated his fleeing from Germany with his family. In 1856 he brought them to the United States. Young Schieren was then fourteen years old, but he had received a good common school education in Germany and upon his arrival in the United States engaged with his father in conducting a tobacco store in Brooklyn. In 1864, however, he obtained a position in the leather-belting establishment of Philip F. Passquay, New York City, and by his diligence and industry soon mastered the details of this business, particularly the manufacture of leather belting, so that when his employer died in 1865 he was able to conduct the business alone. When this was sold he continued with the successor until 1868; then with the savings he had accumulated he founded his own leather-belting manufactory in New York. For the succeeding fourteen years he conducted his ever growing business alone; in 1882 he took in a partner and the firm name was changed to Charles A. Schieren & Company but, while there were changes in partnership at various times thereafter, Schieren himself directed the affairs of the business to the day of his death. With the coming of high-speed electric

dynamos and motors in the late 1880's the existing types of leather belting proved unsatisfactory, and Schieren devoted much time and experiment to developing suitable belting. During 1887 and 1888 he secured eight patents for the newer forms of belting and for machines to manufacture them. One of these, a so-called "electric belt," perforated and coated with a composition, was the only belt in its day to withstand the terrific strain of high-speed electrical machinery. Another was a leather link belt composed of small leather links strung on steel pins and ingeniously joined together. These inventions, with one or two minor ones, brought him to the forefront of the leather trade as an authority on belting, a position he held throughout his life.

Schieren was a very public-spirited man and identified himself with several important reform movements in New York. Because of his qualities as a business man he was elected mayor of Brooklyn in 1893 and during his term of two years succeeded in bringing the city out of bankruptcy. The construction of the Williamsburg Bridge was planned during his administration and many parks were laid out, including the Narrows Shore Drive along the harbor. In 1898 he was appointed by President McKinley chairman of the Cuban relief committee and treasurer of the national Red Cross; he was a member of the commerce commission appointed by Governor Black to consider the enlargement of the Erie Canal; he served on the Ambrose Channel commission; and he was a member of the greater New York charter commission appointed by Governor Theodore Roosevelt. He was a founder of the Brooklyn Institute of Arts and Sciences, president of the Brooklyn Academy of Music, founder and vice-president of the Hide & Leather National Bank, and a trustee in a number of banks and insurance companies. In 1865 he married Mary Louise Bramm of Brooklyn and at the time of his death was survived by his widow, who lived but twenty-four hours longer, and four children.

[*Who's Who in America*, 1914–15; *Hide and Leather*, Mar. 13, 1915; *Shoe and Leather Reporter*, Mar. 18, 1915; obituary notices in *Brooklyn Daily Eagle*, Mar. 10, 1915, *N. Y. Times* and *N. Y. Tribune*, Mar. 11, 1915; Patent Office records; correspondence with Charles A. Schieren & Co.]   C. W. M.

SCHIFF, JACOB HENRY (Jan. 10, 1847–Sept. 25, 1920), financier, philanthropist, was born in Frankfurt-am-Main and died in New York City. He was the son of Moses and Clara (Niederhofheim) Schiff, and a member of a family that could trace its line back to 1370, through scholars of distinction and men of affairs. He was educated in the local schools and, in addition to secular and Jewish knowledge, gained a fair acquaintance with French and English. At fourteen he was apprenticed to a business firm. Four years later, with some difficulty, he secured his father's permission to come to America, arriving in New York Aug. 6, 1865. For a short time he was engaged with a brokerage firm in New York, and on Nov. 21, 1866, was licensed as a broker. In 1867 he joined the firm of Budge, Schiff & Company, which was dissolved in 1872.

Schiff meanwhile had become a citizen of the United States, being naturalized in September 1870. Upon the dissolution of his firm, he decided to go back to Germany and in the following year was offered a position as manager of the Hamburg Branch of the London & Hanseatic Bank. This connection did not last long, because Schiff returned to Frankfurt upon the death of his father in that same year, but in 1874 he was invited by Abraham Kuhn, senior partner of Kuhn, Loeb & Company, to return to New York and enter that firm. He accepted this proposal in January 1875, bringing to his new association not only his energy and foresight, but also his connections with Sir Ernest Cassel of London, with Edouard Noetzlin, president of the Banque de Paris et des Pays Bas, and with Robert Fleming, then of Dundee and later of London. Through these connections he was able to place large quantities of American securities on the European market. In 1885, at the age of thirty-eight, he became head of the firm.

Schiff was concerned with the financing of nearly all the important railroads in the East, which were not personally owned by families, especially the Pennsylvania Railroad and the Louisville & Nashville. Probably the most sensational episode in his financial career was the struggle between the Union Pacific Railroad and the Great Northern company for control of the Northern Pacific, in which Schiff was allied with Edward H. Harriman [q.v.] against James J. Hill [q.v.] and J. P. Morgan & Company. This contest, because of the importance of the interest, brought about a panic on the stock market, May 9, 1901, and resulted in the formation later that year of the Northern Securities Company. The legality of this organization was challenged, however, by President Theodore Roosevelt, under the anti-trust laws, and his view was sustained by the Supreme Court of the United States.

Schiff also took a hand in the reorganization of the Baltimore & Ohio Railroad (1896–99) and at various times aided the American Smelting & Refining Company, the Westinghouse Electric Company, and the Western Union Tele-

graph Company. One of his less fortunate ventures was his share, under the persuasion of Thomas Fortune Ryan and William C. Whitney [qq.v.], in financing a reorganization (1902) of the Metropolitan Street Railway Company of New York. As soon as the Federal Reserve Act was passed he resigned his connection with the National City Bank and other banks. He was largely concerned in the great insurance companies, particularly the Equitable Life Assurance Society, of which he was a director. This connection brought him under investigation by a joint committee of the New York legislature in 1905, but he was acquitted of all knowledge of the alleged unscrupulous practices of some of his associates (*Testimony Taken before the Joint Committee of the Senate and Assembly of the State of New York to Investigate . . . Life Insurance Companies*, 1905, II, 1297–1364; *State of New York, Assembly Document No. 41*, 1906, pp. 120 ff.). He was interested in the development of railroads and other enterprises in Mexico. In 1904, at the time of the Russo-Japanese War, he secured for Japan some $200,000,000, and in recognition of this service was awarded the Order of the Sacred Treasure and later the more distinguished Order of the Rising Sun. In 1911 he supported a Chinese loan, partly as a result of the influence of a young diplomat, Willard Straight, who thought that American capital invested in the Manchurian railways might serve to prevent future wars in the Far East.

Schiff was a strong opponent of the Silver Purchase Act of 1890 and actively supported the gold standard on all occasions. As early as 1902 he recognized that the inelasticity of the currency was a potential danger. He early accepted the right of laborers to combine for their own protection, favored arbitration in labor disputes, earnestly befriended the Henry Street Settlement and municipal charities, and supported the National Child Labor Committee. He was a Republican throughout his career, although he voted for Woodrow Wilson in both his campaigns for the presidency. He had a strong sympathy for the colored people and by his voice, his means, and his personal interest, helped to promote Tuskegee Institute and other negro schools in the South. His civic interests were so well known that in 1904 he was suggested as a Republican candidate for mayor of New York, but declined to be considered. He was a member of the board of education, however, and his advice was sought by reform mayors like William R. Grace and Seth Low. In 1908 he seriously put before the Chamber of Commerce the question of a proper budget for New York City.

Schiff recognized his special obligation to the Jewish people in the matter of charities or, as he preferred to call them, philanthropies. He was always glad to help establish loan funds and, with Robert W. De Forest, was instrumental in the establishment of a National Employment Exchange. He was greatly interested in the work of the Red Cross, in 1910 was appointed by the President as a member of the International Relief Board of the American Red Cross, and served as treasurer of the New York chapter for many years. He was president and a great benefactor of the Montefiore Hospital, to which he probably gave more personal attention than to any other single charitable institution. Out of his interest in the Henry Street Settlement there grew a further interest in district nursing to which he contributed much by his influence and his means. He was greatly interested in the establishment of free libraries in New York. He aided Columbia University, established the Semitic Museum at Harvard, built a students' hall for Barnard College in 1915 in celebration of the fiftieth anniversary of his arrival in New York, created an establishment at Cornell University for the promotion of studies in German culture, and furnished the funds for the establishment of the department of Semitic literature at the New York Public Library and a similar department at the Library of Congress in Washington. In 1909 he created a fund which rendered possible a new translation of the Bible, under Jewish auspices, published in 1917 by the Jewish Publication Society of America, and in 1914 he created another fund which resulted in the publication of the Schiff Library of Jewish Classics, some twenty volumes in number. He was one of the major supporters of the Jewish Theological Seminary of New York, gave very considerable funds to the Hebrew Union College in Cincinnati, and was one of the founders of the American Jewish Committee, organized in 1906 to meet emergencies arising among Jews in other countries. He was active in the work of the American Jewish Joint Distribution Committee to relieve suffering in Europe during the World War, and in the Jewish Welfare Board, which ministered to Jewish soldiers and sailors during the same period. His resentment toward Czaristic Russia because of Russia's treatment of the Jews was so strong that he declined to participate in the Anglo-French Dollar Loan, although it would have brought profit to his firm. He was very active in the various Liberty Loan Committees.

Jacob Schiff was a reader, fond of walking and bicycling, most punctilious in all his affairs, deeply religious in his outlook and habit of mind.

On May 6, 1875, he married Therese Loeb, by whom he had a son and a daughter. The former, Mortimer Leo Schiff (June 5, 1877–June 4, 1931), became a valued member of the firm and its head after the death of his father. He devoted a great part of his time to public philanthropic work and particularly interested himself in the Boy Scouts of America, of which organization he was elected president in May 1931.

[Cyrus Adler, *Jacob H. Schiff: His Life and Letters* (2 vols., 1928); B. J. Hendrick, "Great American Fortunes and Their Making: Street Railway Financiers," *McClure's Magazine*, Nov.–Dec. 1907; *Who's Who in America*, 1920–21; *N. Y. Times*, Sept. 26, 1920.]

C. A.

SCHILLING, HUGO KARL (Mar. 28, 1861–July 1931), philologist, Germanist, was born at Saalfeld in Thuringia, Germany, the son of Ferdinand and Henrietta Schilling. Descended from a family in which liberal culture was a tradition, he enjoyed the advantages of a thorough education. After graduating from the Gymnasium in his native city, at seventeen he entered the University of Leipzig where he devoted himself to Germanistic studies, acquired a thorough knowledge of the older Germanic dialects, and specialized particularly in the field of Old English. Two years in France and Ireland, while they delayed the completion of his university course, laid the foundation for a thorough practical command of French and English. In 1885 he received the degrees of M.A. and Ph.D. at Leipzig. In February 1886 he came to the United States and five years later became an American citizen. After a short period at the Johns Hopkins University he was professor of modern languages at Wittenberg College, Springfield, Ohio, until 1891. On July 14, 1887, he was married to Theresa T. Stitt of Carlisle, Ky., by whom he had two sons and two daughters. In 1891 he went to Harvard University as assistant professor of German, and in 1901 to the University of California as professor of the German language and literature and head of the department of German, a position he held for twenty-eight years.

As one of a group of leaders assembled at California by Benjamin Ide Wheeler [*q.v.*] to assist him in building up a great university, he had to do the work of a pioneer, to surround himself with competent assistants, to organize the work of his department, to build up library facilities adequate to the needs of graduate students, to establish and maintain worthy standards of scholarship. In addition he found time to give counsel and leadership to the teachers of German in the state and to assist them in establishing secondary instruction on a high level. His broad and accurate knowledge of history and literature, together with an unusual talent for lucid, simple, and direct presentation, made him especially effective in aiding students to an orientation in the whole field of German literature, while his semasiological insight and knowledge of the anthropological sciences made him an unusually stimulating teacher of linguistics. He was editor of *Modern Language Notes,* 1899–1901; a member of the editorial board of Publications in Modern Philology of the University of California, 1909–31; president of the Pacific coast division of the American Philological Association, 1907–08; president of the Modern Language Association of America, 1928, and a member of the Gesellschaft für deutsche Philologie in Berlin and the Goethe-Gesellschaft in Weimar. Among his published writings are: *König Ælfred's Angelsächsische Bearbeitung der Weltgeschichte des Orosius* (Halle, 1886); "Notes on the Finnsaga" (*Modern Language Notes,* June, Nov. 1886); "Das wort sie sollen lassen stahn und kein danck dazu haben" (*Ibid.,* Jan. 1901); "Die Fundationsgüter und Zehnten des Stiftes Gandersheim im elften Jahrhundert" (*Zeitschrift des Harzvereins für Geschichte und Altertumskunde,* vol. XXXIII, pt. 2, 1900, pp. 486–93); "Die vermeintliche Urkunde im Gandersheimer Plenar" (*Historische Vierteljahrschrift,* Jan. 2, 1901); "Altsächsische Namen im Gandersheimer Plenar" (*Beiträge zur Geschichte der deutschen Sprache und Literatur,* vol. XXVI, 1901, pp. 558–60); "The Semasiology of *Schenken* 'Skink'" (*Journal of Germanic Philology,* vol. IV, 1902, no. 4). After he became professor emeritus in 1929 he devoted himself to the preparation of a Goethe dictionary, a work to which he brought the fruits of a lifetime of study and upon which he was engaged at the time of his death. He died as the result of a cerebral hemorrhage that occurred while he was alone in the house.

[*Who's Who in America,* 1930–31; *Univ. of Cal.: In Memoriam* (1931); obituary in *N. Y. Times,* July 26, 1931; death notice in *San Francisco Examiner,* July 28, 1931; personal acquaintance.]   C. P.

SCHINDLER, SOLOMON (Apr. 24, 1842– May 5, 1915), Jewish rabbi, was born at Neisse, Germany, the son of Rabbi Julius L. and Bertha (Algasi) Schindler. At thirteen he entered the Breslau Rabbinical School and also attended the Gymnasium there, graduating in 1862. A tutor in private families until 1868, he then took charge of a small congregation in Westphalia but had to resign from it because of his liberal tendencies. At this he entered the Royal Teachers' Seminary at Büren and graduated in 1870. On June 24, 1868, he had married Henrietta Schutz of Holz-

hausen, who was his life-long companion; of the six children she bore him, three sons and one daughter survived. For a time he and his wife conducted a boarding-school but, the venture proving unsuccessful, in 1871 they set out for America, arriving with three infants and no resources. Although Schindler's radical views on the Bible made him hesitate to enter the rabbinate, he yielded to economic necessity after a few months and became rabbi of Congregation Adath Emuno at Hoboken, N. J., where he remained until called to Boston in 1874 to Temple Adath Israel. Once in the rabbinate, true to his convictions, he expounded his views freely and openly. Though personally modest, he was a vigorous and fearless preacher of intellectual radicalism, whose sermons were not hortative but analytical and didactic. In introducing reform Judaism into New England, he made innovations in the synagogue ritual which led to the resignation of fifteen of his forty Boston congregants, but he soon gained so much popularity that in ten years his congregation gave up its chapel and built an imposing structure to accommodate its increased membership and the growing number of Jewish and Christian auditors who came to hear him. In later life he preached a famous sermon, "Mistakes I Have Made," in which he recanted some of his more radical views on Judaism. From 1888 to 1894 he served as a member of the Boston School Board, having been nominated by all the political parties. After twenty years with his congregation he resigned from the rabbinate, though he maintained an active interest in his congregation, which elected him rabbi emeritus in 1908.

On his retirement he took up social work, in which he showed marked ability both as organizer and as administrator. In 1894 he organized the Federation of Jewish Charities of Boston, the first of its kind in American Jewish charity, and served as its superintendent from 1895 to 1899. From 1899 to 1909, when he retired from active work, he was superintendent of the Leopold Morse Home for Infirm Hebrews at Mattapan, Mass. His publications include *Messianic Expectations and Modern Judaism* (1886), in which he maintained that Jewish hopes had lost their national character; *Dissolving Views in the History of Judaism* (1888); *Israelites in Boston* (copyright 1889); a German translation, *Ein Rückblick* (1889), of Edward Bellamy's *Looking Backward,* and a sequel to it called *Young West* (1894). He tried prematurely to establish a Jewish newspaper in Boston in 1879, 1880, and 1893. A child of the age of evolution and the glorification of science, he applied the theory of evolution to his religion more logically than psychologically. Though intellectually a pessimist, he was emotionally an optimist with the heart of a poet, and the cynical iconoclastic philosophy he preached was tempered by a broad tolerance. A brilliant conversationalist, with a deep sense of humor and great *joie de vivre,* he had a fine capacity for making and retaining friends.

[*Who's Who in America,* 1914–15; *Jewish Encyc.* (ed. 1925), vol. XI, p. 102; *Jewish Year Book,* 1905–06; J. C. Rand, *One of a Thousand* (1890); Ephraim Deinard, *Hakundes* (1890); *Hist. of the Jews of Boston* (1892); *Jewish Advocate* (Boston), Apr. 3, 1908, Apr. 19, 1912, May 7, 1915; *N. Y. Times,* May 6, 1915; *Boston Transcript,* May 6, 1915.]   D. deS. P.

SCHIRMER, GUSTAV (Sept. 19, 1829–Aug. 6, 1893), music publisher, was born at Königsee, Saxony, the son of Ernst Rudolph Schirmer, and his second wife, Wilhelmine (Dünkler) Schirmer, daughter of the burgomaster of Saalfeld. He came from a family of Thuringian piano manufacturers. The musical lexicographer, Ernst Ludwig Gerber (1746–1819, Sondershausen), who knew the family, praised its products, and François Joseph Fétis in his *Biographie Universelle des Musiciens* (edition of 1878, vol. VII, p. 465) mentions a Johann Georg Schirmer, "piano manufacturer" (d. 1790), whose pianos were esteemed in Saxony. With one son by the husband's first marriage and five children by the second, of whom Gustav was the eldest, Schirmer's parents emigrated to New York in 1840 on board the bark *Autoleon,* landing in New York on October 8 after a voyage of forty-six days from Hamburg. Until he was fourteen Gustav attended school, occasionally earning a little money by selling matches. At fifteen he was apprenticed for a short time to a cabinetmaker. After several years of employment in the music business of Scharfenberg & Luis, he entered the employ of Kerksieg & Breusing, music dealers, where his ability and energy gained him rapid advancement to the position of manager of the store, which until 1880 was at 701 Broadway. In 1861 with a fellow employee, Bernard Beer, he acquired the business, the firm being changed to Beer & Schirmer. Five years later he bought out Beer's interest and established the house of "G. Schirmer, music publishers, importers and dealers." He married an American, Mary Fairchild, who survived him with their five daughters and two sons, one of them Rudolph Edward Schirmer [*q.v.*].

Equally strong were his ambition to succeed in business and his devotion to his family. When in 1873 he sent his wife and children abroad to spend two years in Weimar, he religiously wrote each of them one letter every week in his own hand, no matter how burdened with work he was. Being himself an indefatigable worker, he demanded untiring effort from his associates and employees. His ideal was German thoroughness and he patterned his organization after German models. He early developed intensive business relations not only with the large music concerns of Germany but with the leading houses of Paris, Brussels, London, Vienna, and Milan. Furthermore, he entered into personal relations with prominent European composers. Mrs. Schirmer's stay in Weimar led to closer acquaintance with Liszt and the illustrious coterie at the "Altenburg"; a photograph inscribed to her by Richard Wagner with "thanks and friendship" still hangs with many similar tokens in the executive office of the firm; and Schirmer was among the original patrons of Bayreuth, who helped to make possible the realization of Wagner's "Festspielhaus." When the composer Tchaikovsky visited New York in April 1891, on the occasion of the inauguration of Carnegie Hall, he repeatedly made mention in his diary of Schirmer and his family.

Certainly, Schirmer was not a mere plodding tradesman; he had vision and a real love and understanding of music. He played the piano as a relaxation, and in a letter he once cautioned his son Rudolph, who was taking violin lessons, to "play nicely in tune, and always with love and inner fire." But his principles in music as in business were strict, Teutonic, uncompromising. When his children took music lessons in Weimar, he frowned, despite his admiration for Wagner, upon a pot-pourri of *The Flying Dutchman* played by one of them, since no one had ever learned anything by playing musical medleys instead of Czerny's scales, Köhler's exercises, and Heller's études. This sound objection, however, did not prevent the company from selling medleys to anyone who asked for them. When the continuous growth of the business required larger quarters, a four-story building, occupied in 1880, was erected for it at 35 Union Square, and there the business remained until in 1910 it was moved to a seven-story building at 3 East Forty-third St. In 1891 Schirmer housed in a six-story building in West Sixteenth Street his own engraving and printing plant, which developed later into a model factory at Woodside, L. I. Although during the early years of music publishing in America the lack of any copyright convention between the United States and Europe enabled American publishers to engage in a flourishing and profitable business with "reprint editions" of the best European sellers, Schirmer was not content with such easy exploits but gave wholesome encouragement to native talent, in the discovery of which he showed great shrewdness. Self-made, he had in him the fine qualities of an old European tradition to the unfolding of which America gave new and rich opportunity. Thus he had succeeded, by the time of his death at Eisenach, Germany, at the age of only sixty-three, in creating a business and a cultural factor of national importance and international renown.

[Letters and family accounts; *N. Y. American,* Oct. 9, 1840; N. Y. directories; Modeste Tchaikovsky, *The Life and Letters of Peter Ilich Tchaikovsky* (1906), ed. and translated by Rosa Newmarch; obituaries in *Signale für die Musikalische Welt,* Sept. 1893, no. 42; *Metronome,* Sept. 1893; *N. Y. Tribune,* Aug. 8, 1893; identical articles on centenary of Schirmer's birth in *Musical America,* Sept. 1929, and *Musical Courier,* Sept. 14, 1929.]   C. E.

SCHIRMER, RUDOLPH EDWARD (July 22, 1859–Aug. 20, 1919), music publisher, was born in New York City, the son of Mary (Fairchild) and Gustav Schirmer [*q.v.*]. Educated in the New York public schools until 1873, he went with his mother, his younger brother Gustave (1864–1907), and four of his sisters to Weimar, Germany, where he spent two years in private schools and had lessons in violin and piano playing from Helene Stahr, pupil and protégée of Liszt, and daughter of Adolf Stahr (1805–1876), the friend of Liszt and early champion of Wagner. Thus the Schirmer family at Weimar came into contact with the circle of celebrities, literary and musical, that gathered around Liszt; on one occasion the two Schirmer boys took part in a children's concert that was given in honor of Liszt. In 1876 Rudolph entered the College of New Jersey (later Princeton) where he was active in the musical life of the college and was one of the presidents of the glee club. After his graduation in 1880 he attended the law school of Columbia College, was graduated in June 1884, and was admitted to the bar in the same year. For a short time he was affiliated with the law firm of Olcott, Mestre & Gonzalez in New York, but when his brother Gustave in 1885 left their father's music business to marry Grace Tilton of Boston and to found there the Boston Music Company (eminently successful later through the publication of compositions by Ethelbert Nevin and others), he abandoned the law in order to replace his brother in his father's business. In 1886 he married Martha Young Barnes of New York, who bore him one child that died in infancy. When bad health required the father to spend more time in Europe, a reconciliation between him and his son Gustave brought the latter back to the business to join with Rudolph in the management. After the father's death in 1893, when the business had been reorganized and incorporated, Rudolph became president and his brother Gustave (though retaining the independent control of his Boston business) secretary of G. Schirmer, Inc. After the untimely death of his brilliant brother Gustave in 1907, Rudolph assumed the sole direction of the New York business. With a keen appreciation of high artistic ideals and a relish for musical advance, he fostered many young and promising composers. In 1910 he moved the business to 3 East 43rd St. In 1912 he established a branch in London, which was maintained for a short time only. In 1915 he founded the *Musical Quarterly.* On Mar. 28, 1916, a week after a Nevada divorce from his first wife, he married Ann Swinburne, a talented concert singer and comic opera star, by whom he had a son. His health during the last years of his life having grown extremely precarious, he moved to Santa Barbara, Cal., where he died. He was a director of the New York Oratorio Society and of the New York Symphony Society, and a trustee of the Institute of Musical Art in New York.

[Letters and family accounts; obituaries in *New Music Rev.* and *Musical Quart.,* Oct. 1919; *Musical America,* Aug. 30, 1919; *N. Y. Times,* Aug. 21, Sept. 13, 1919.]   C. E.

SCHLATTER, MICHAEL (July 14, 1716–Oct. 31, 1790), German Reformed clergyman and educator, was born in St. Gall, Switzerland, the son of Paulus Schlatter, a bookkeeper, and of Magdalena (Zollikofer) Schlatter. After attending the gymnasium of his native city, he received theological training under the private tuition of Prof. Casper Wegelin of St. Gall and at the universities of Leyden in Holland and Helmstedt in Germany. On Apr. 10, 1739, he was examined for the ministry and ordained. For a while he was a private tutor in Holland, but in 1744 he became vicar to John Jacob Beyel, *Dekan* of Wigoldingen, Thurgau, Switzerland, and, a year later, Sunday evening preacher in Linsebühl, a suburb of St. Gall. In January 1746 he left St. Gall for Heidelberg, where he met Prof. Johan Caspar Cruciger, one of the leading men of the Reformed church of the Palatinate, who directed his attention to the needs of the Reformed churches of Pennsylvania. As a result, Schlatter offered his services to the Synods of Holland, under whose auspices the missionary work was carried on.

He was commissioned for service in Pennsylvania on May 23, 1746, and arrived at his post in September 1746, beginning at once a strenuous and many-sided missionary activity. His first efforts were directed towards organizing the Reformed churches of Pennsylvania into a synod under the supervision of the Reformed Church of Holland. This task was accomplished in September 1747, when the Coetus of the Reformed congregations of Pennsylvania was called into existence, with four ministers and twenty-eight elders. His next task was to organize the widely-scattered Reformed congregations into regular pastoral charges. He made a series of extensive missionary tours throughout Pennsylvania, Maryland, Virginia, and New Jersey, and found forty-six congregations which he organized into sixteen pastoral charges. There were, however, only four ordained Reformed ministers in the province, so he returned to Holland, in February 1751, in order to secure more pastors. His appeal, printed in Dutch in 1751 and in German in 1752, was so successful that he not only gained the consent of the Holland synods for a larger number of missionaries in Pennsylvania, but was also able to interest the states of Holland and West Friesland in his work, so that they voted a subsidy of fl. 2,000 annually for a period of five years for his work. With this financial backing Schlatter went to Germany where he secured six young men, who accompanied him to Pennsylvania.

After his return, when a growing dissension between the church leaders made congregational work very difficult, he turned his attention to the education of the children of the new settlers. He found few church schools, poorly equipped, and very unsatisfactory teachers. In the interests of this cause he returned once more to Holland in November 1753. In June 1754 the Synods of Holland released him from their employ so that he might accept the position of superintendent of schools in Pennsylvania under an appointment by an English society, which had been formed to carry on this educational work. The project was conducted in Pennsylvania by a body of general trustees, of whom William Smith, 1727–1803 [q.v.], was the secretary. In the fall of 1754, six so-called "charity schools" were opened, the number later being increased to nine. But this undertaking failed because the local Germans were antagonized by the political motives of the English society, and Schlatter retired in 1756. He then entered the British army as chaplain. On Mar. 25, 1757, John Campbell Loudoun [q.v.] appointed him as one of the chaplains of the Royal American Regiment and he took part in the siege of Halifax, the capture of Louisbourg, and in the expedition to capture Fort Duquesne.

Schlatter returned to Philadelphia in October 1759 and assumed the pastorate of several independent Reformed churches, notably Barren Hill, near Philadelphia. When Henry Bouquet [q.v.] organized an expedition to destroy the Indian forts on the banks of the Muskingum in 1764, Schlatter was commissioned as chaplain of the 2nd Pennsylvania Battalion and thus held a chaplain's commission both under the British and the provincial authorities. During the Revolution he was an ardent patriot, and suffered imprisonment and the loss of his property for his sentiments. He died in Philadelphia and was buried on Nov. 4, 1790, in the Reformed Cemetery, which is now part of Franklin Square, in Philadelphia. He was married to Maria Henrica Schleidorn, daughter of Henry Schleidorn of New York City. They had nine children, one son and five daughters surviving their parents.

[Biographia omnium ministrorum Sangallensium, No. 180, manuscript in the city library, St. Gall; Jacob Scherer, Stemmatologia Sangallensis, Vol. P, Geschlecht 109, also manuscript at St. Gall; Bürger Buch der Stadt St. Gallen, 1867; letters and documents in the city archives at St. Gall; letters and documents in the archives of the General Synod of the Reformed Church of Holland, at The Hague; Henry Harbaugh, The Life of Rev. Michael Schlatter (1857); J. I. Good, Hist. of the Reformed Ch. in the U. S. 1725–1792 (1899); J. H. Dubbs, The Reformed Church in Pennsylvania, part X of Proc. of the Pa.-German Soc., vol. XI (1902); W. J. Hinke, "Famous Pennsylvania-Germans, Michael Schlatter," Pa.-German, Oct. 1900; W. J. Hinke, ed., Minutes and Letters of the Coetus of the German Reformed Congregations of Pennsylvania (1903), and "Diary of the Rev. Michael Schlatter," in Jour. of the Presbyt. Hist. Soc., Sept., Dec. 1905.]   W. J. H.

SCHLESINGER, BENJAMIN (Dec. 25, 1876–June 6, 1932), labor leader, was a native of Krakai, province of Kovno, Lithuania, and the son of Nechemiah and Judith Schlesinger. His father's family name is not known to his descendants, since at some time in his life Nechemiah adopted his wife's maiden name, Schlesinger, as his surname. Born into a rabbinical family, he enjoyed a superior intellectual environment and evidently inherited a superior mental equipment. When transplanted from Krakai to Chicago in 1891, however, like most Jewish immigrant youths irrespective of their background, he was forced to resort to manual labor for a living. Accordingly, in common with large numbers of Russian Jews, he became a needle-trades worker, taking up the occupation of sewing-machine operator on cloaks and suits. Many of these superior immigrant youngsters pursued courses of study while plying their trade, thereby attaining a profession; but Schlesinger, from the outset, was caught in the vortex of official responsibilities connected with the labor movement, and his time and energy were absorbed in its service. From the age of seventeen, two years after he landed in America, he was a guiding spirit in the Jewish labor movement, either as a union official in the ladies' garment trades, or as manager of the *Jewish Daily Forward,* the outstanding Jewish socialist and labor organ. Through these positions he played a dominant rôle in shaping the destinies of both the union and the publication in their rise from poverty to affluence and power.

His first office was that of secretary of the Chicago Cloak Makers' Union, and he had not held this a year when he was elected treasurer of the newly formed International Cloak Makers' Union of America. In 1903 he was made president of the International Ladies' Garment Workers' Union, which was founded in 1900, one of its chief objects being to eliminate sweatshops from the needlework trades. Because of factional differences he was defeated in 1904, but was selected as general manager of the New York Cloak Makers' Union. Three years later he became business manager of the *Jewish Daily Forward,* which was then experiencing a serious struggle for existence. In this capacity he served from 1907 to 1912. In the meantime, controversies within the Ladies' Garment Workers' Union created a critical situation and Schlesinger was again chosen, in 1914, to guide its fortunes, remaining its president until he resigned in 1923. Returning to the *Forward* as business manager of its Chicago affairs, he continued with the paper until 1931, when for the third time he was called to head the International Ladies' Garment Workers' Union. He died in a sanitarium in Colorado Springs a few weeks after having been reëlected, almost unanimously, at the 1932 convention. He was survived by his wife, Rae (Schanhouse), two sons, and a daughter.

Schlesinger, like most Jewish labor leaders, was more the intellectual than the histrionic type. In public speeches his style was conversational rather than oratorical. He spoke fluently, directly, and informatively. Because of his ill health, which he attributed to working in sweatshops in his early youth, he displayed an irascibility which accentuated his domineering characteristics. His strength as a labor leader lay in his extraordinary ability as an organizer and administrator. He was also fearless and independent, as was demonstrated when the union under his presidency applied for an injunction against an employers' association that attempted to break a trade agreement in 1921—one of the first instances wherein a union turned the tables on employers. In this action he was opposed by both the conservatives and radicals in the labor movement, since he went counter to a cherished tra-

dition that unions must not resort to the use of injunctions in labor disputes. Since that time, however, many unions have followed the course laid down by the International Ladies' Garment Workers' under Schlesinger's leadership.

[L. L. Lorwin, *The Women's Garment Workers; a Hist. of the International Ladies' Garment Workers' Union* (1924); files of *Justice,* the official organ of the International Ladies' Garment Workers' Union; files of *Convention Proceedings* of the same organization; *N. Y. Times,* June 7–10, 1932; information regarding parents, wife, and place of birth from a son, Emil Schlesinger, Esq., New York City.]   D. J. S.

SCHLEY, WINFIELD SCOTT (Oct. 9, 1839–Oct. 2, 1909), naval officer, was born on his father's farm, "Richfields," Frederick County, Md., the son of John Thomas and Georgianna Virginia (McClure) Schley, descendant of John Thomas Schley of Bavaria, who settled in Frederick County in 1739, and of Scotch-Irish ancestors who came to Baltimore before the Revolution. In his ninth year the family moved to Frederick, where he attended local schools until his appointment to the United States Naval Academy in 1856. His first cruise after graduation was in the *Niagara* which was detailed to bear back to Japan the first representatives of that nation to visit the United States. Returning at the outbreak of the Civil War, the *Niagara* joined the Charleston blockade, and Schley's earliest command was the prize square-rigger *General Parkhill,* which he brought safely into Philadelphia. Subsequently in the *Potomac,* he twice volunteered for hazardous service off Mobile, first with a cutting-out expedition under Fort Morgan, and again, in January 1862, with a boat party to rescue the U.S.S. *Cuyler,* aground and under fire, both incidents showing courage and characteristic eagerness for distinction. He was made lieutenant in July 1862, and was executive of the gunboat *Winona* off Mobile and later on the Mississippi. In March 1863, he temporarily commanded the *Monongahela* in bombardments of Port Hudson, and was then navigator of the *Richmond.*

On Sept. 10, 1863, during leave, he was married to Annie Rebecca Franklin of Annapolis, Md., who bore him three children. He was executive of the *Wateree* in the Pacific from 1864 to 1866, then taught at the Naval Academy, and from 1869 to 1873 was executive of the *Benicia* of the Asiatic Squadron, showing gallantry as adjutant of land forces in a punitive expedition in Korea in June 1871. After another assignment to the Naval Academy as head of the modern languages department, he commanded the *Essex* in the South Atlantic from 1876 to 1879, and was lighthouse inspector at Boston, 1879–83.

Early in 1884 came hazardous duty as commander of an expedition sent into the Arctic to rescue the party under Lieut. A. W. Greely which had set out in 1881. In the *Thetis* and *Bear* Schley pushed vigorously northward, and on June 22 near Cape Sabine saved the seven survivors of Greely's party at the very brink of death, and returned safely after 1300 miles of perilous ice navigation. In recognition of his achievement he was made chief of the bureau of equipment and recruiting, where he remained until July 1889. The romantic story of the rescue is told in detail in Schley's and J. R. Soley's book, *The Rescue of Greely* (1885). His national prominence after this expedition was increased by the Valparaiso affair of Oct. 16, 1891, when two sailors from his ship, the *Baltimore,* were killed by a Chilean mob. Schley handled the matter firmly and tactfully, and won much acclaim on his return. He was inspector of the Third Lighthouse District, 1892–95; commander of the *New York* on the Atlantic coast, 1895–97; and then head of the lighthouse board. He was promoted to the rank of commodore in February 1898.

At the opening of the Spanish-American War he was selected to command the Flying Squadron at Hampton Roads, but with the arrangement—always troublesome in military undertakings—that, should his force operate with the Atlantic Squadron in the West Indies, the commander of the latter, William Thomas Sampson [*q.v.*], though two numbers his junior, should have chief command. When Cervera's ships reached Martinique, the Flying Squadron hastened to Key West, and under Sampson's orders was sent on to blockade Cienfuegos, the chief southern port of Cuba. In the Sampson-Schley controversy, into which the navy and the nation were plunged after the war, Schley's conduct during the crucial moments of the ensuing fortnight came under severe criticism. He was scored for delaying at Cienfuegos from May 22 till nightfall of the 24th, despite urgent advices to proceed immediately eastward to the harbor of Santiago, which the Spanish had entered on the 19th; for his slow movement thither; and for his failure thereafter to establish a close blockade. Instead of remaining at Santiago he temporarily turned back, and cabled on May 27, "Department's orders cannot be obeyed . . . am obliged to return to Key West . . . for coal" (Parker, *post,* pp. 129–130). Fortunately, when Sampson reached Santiago on June 1, Schley was still hanging on. His problems were undoubtedly trying, his information less than the navy department's, his every decision suscepti-

ble of defense; yet the final judgment must be that of the Court of Inquiry of 1901, reviewed and approved by President Roosevelt, that his "conduct . . . prior to June 1, 1898, was characterized by vacillation, dilatoriness, and lack of enterprise" (*Record of Proceedings, post,* II, 1830).

A worthy officer, of outstanding record, he wavered under responsibilities of high command. Much of this might have been erased by his creditable work in the battle at Santiago, had it not been for the new issues raised there. During the month-long blockade preceding the battle Sampson's and Schley's forces were joined, with slightly strained relations between first and second in command. At 9:00 on the morning of the action, July 3, Sampson in the *New York* had steamed about seven miles eastward for a conference with General Shafter. At 9:35 the Spanish ships emerged from the harbor and turned westward. Schley's flagship, the *Brooklyn,* westernmost of the blockading line, at first closed eastward toward the enemy, then made her much-debated semicircle outward and away from them—a maneuver defensible tactically, though it forced the *Texas* to back water to avoid collision—and continued the fight on parallel courses westward at greater range, still leading the American column and effectively engaging the Spanish ships until the last survivor, the *Cristobal Colon,* surrendered at 1:15 P.M. Sampson, never beyond sight of his forces, had meanwhile approached rapidly from the rear, and his ship was third to reach the *Colon* about 2:00 P.M. Nevertheless, Schley assumed, then and afterward, that he was in chief command during the battle. Influenced doubtless by his genial approachability and repelled by Sampson's coldness, the press and nation supported him and made him the hero, but the navy department and most of the officers as strongly opposed his claims. The provisional promotions of Aug. 10, advancing Schley six numbers and Sampson eight, thus reversing seniority, were not confirmed by the Senate, though both officers became rear admirals in 1899.

After the return of the fleet to New York on Aug. 20, Schley served on the Puerto Rico Evacuation Commission from September to October 1898; was president of the retirement board in 1899; and commander of the South Atlantic Squadron until shortly before his retirement on Oct. 9, 1901. Meanwhile, the controversy had continued, and an account of Santiago, bitterly hostile to him, published in E. S. Maclay's *History of the Navy* (1901), vol. III, led Schley to request a court of inquiry. Presided over by

Admiral Dewey, with Rear Admirals Benham and Ramsay as associates, the court gathered voluminous testimony from Sept. 12 to Dec. 12, 1901. It reached a judgment in general adverse to Schley, though on certain minor points, notably on the question of chief command during the battle (which was not properly before the court), Dewey rendered a minority opinion in his favor. Despite this blow, Schley retained much of his popularity, which he frankly enjoyed, and which he stimulated by his affability, humor, and the bluff, hearty manner of an old-time sailor. After retirement he made his home in Washington, D. C. His death from apoplexy occurred in New York City, and he was buried at Arlington.

[*Who's Who in America,* 1908–09; autobiography, *Forty-five Years Under the Flag* (1904); Park Benjamin, biog. sketch in *Rev. of Revs.* (N. Y.), Sept. 1901; James Parker, *Rear-Admirals Schley, Sampson, and Cervera* (1910); J. D. Long, *The New Am. Navy* (2 vols., 1903); *Record of Proc. of a Court of Inquiry in the Case of Rear-Admiral W. S. Schley* (2 vols., 1902), *House Document No. 485,* 57 Cong., 1 Sess.; "Nauticus," *The Truth About the Schley Case* (n.d.); *Army and Navy Jour.,* Oct. 7, 1911. A few of Schley's personal letters are preserved in the manuscripts division of the Lib. of Cong. See also the bibliog. for the Sampson article.]   A. W—t.

SCHMAUK, THEODORE EMANUEL (May 30, 1860–Mar. 23, 1920), Lutheran clergyman, the son of the Rev. Benjamin William and Wilhelmina Catherine (Hingel) Schmauk, was born at Lancaster, Pa. He was the grandson of Benjamin Friedrich Schmauk, who came from Württemberg, Germany, to the United States with his brother in 1819. He was graduated from the University of Pennsylvania in 1880, and from the Philadelphia Lutheran Theological Seminary in 1883, entering the same year upon a pastorate at Lebanon, Pa., where he served until his death. For the first fifteen years he was assistant to his father, who died in 1898. A man of towering physique, commanding presence, and marked ability as an organizer, Schmauk exerted an influence upon the General Council of the Evangelical Church in America which was perhaps surpassed by no one. He was editor of the three leading periodicals of the Council: the *Lutheran Sunday School Lessons and General Council Graded Series,* from 1896; the *Lutheran Church Review,* from 1895 and the *Lutheran,* the Council's official organ, from 1889. He wrote many practical booklets for Sunday school work, but was less fortunate in his book, *The Negative Criticism and the Old Testament* (1894), which was a more zealous than thorough work. He wrote against T. K. Cheyne and others of the negative critical school, also against James Hastings, the editor of *A Dictionary of the Bible* (5 vols., 1898–

1904), for their choice of liberal scholars to deal with vital subjects.

He was elected president of the General Council in 1903 and as such became the moderator and curator of its fundamental principle—an uncompromising confessionalism. He held many other positions of trust, being president of the trustees of the General Council, since 1907; trustee of Muhlenberg College; member of the church book committee; president of the board of directors of the Philadelphia seminary from 1908, and special lecturer from 1911; chairman of the committee on ways and means which planned the merging of the General Synod, General Council, and Synod of the South into the United Lutheran Church in America in 1918. He claimed that the General Council was the one conservative body in America accepting unreservedly both the "Confessions" and the "history of the church"; and, as such, was ecumenical in outlook and best adapted to weld together the various Lutheran synods—a claim, however, which failed to prevent the Augustana Synod, one-third of the communicants of the General Council, from seceding in 1918. He had but a faint understanding of the liberal cultural and deeply religious background of the people of Scandinavian antecedents. In his discussion about "confessional subscription" with James William Richard [*q.v.*] he showed little appreciation for the superior scholarship of his opponent, regarding his own book, *The Confessional Principle and The Confessions of the Lutheran Church* (1911), as a thorough refutation of Richard's patiently and carefully written volume, *The Confessional History of the Church* (1909).

His attitude toward the Bible was not legalistic; yet he could say that the Bible was inerrant. He opposed ecclesiastical "Unionism," yet assigned the Missouri Synod and the Joint Synod of Ohio to the realm of the closed mind. He maintained that extra-ecclesiastical agencies and organizations have no lawful power. Out of sympathy with the more advanced teaching of J. T. Beck, Karl Heim, and Paul Althaus, the philosophy of his attitude towards contemporary political events was rooted in the *Ständeordnungen* of passive Lutheranism. Schmauk's *magnum opus* is *A History of the Lutheran Church in Pennsylvania,* published in the *Proceedings and Addresses of the Pennsylvania-German Society* (vols. XI, XII, 1902–03) a comprehensive, though not critical, work, following his book *The Early Churches of Lebanon County* (1902). He was a member of the Lebanon County Historical Society and the Pennsylvania German

Society, being president of the latter in 1896. Schmauk died in Philadelphia and was survived by his sister. He was never married.

[Manuscript diary, archives of Philadelphia Luth. Theol. Seminary, Mt. Airy; G. W. Sandt, *Theodore Emanuel Schmauk* (1921); *Who's Who in America*, 1920–21; J. L. Chamberlain, ed., *Univ. of Pa.*, vol. II (1902); *Lutheran*, Apr. 1, 8, 1920; *Allg. Evangel.-Luth. Kirchenzeitung*, July 8, 1910; *Public Ledger* (Philadelphia), Mar. 24, 1920.]   J. O. E.

SCHMIDT, ARTHUR PAUL (Apr. 1, 1846– May 5, 1921), music publisher, was born at Altona, Germany. He was married on Dec. 24, 1868, to Helene Philippine Suck, many of whose family were musicians; his wife survived him but their one child, a daughter, died before him. After working for ten years as a clerk in the music store of G. D. Russell & Company in Boston, in October 1876 he began a prosperous and valuable career as a publisher and importer of music (chiefly at first as agent of the well-known Litolff edition), with branches later at Leipzig and New York. The publications listed in the catalogue in 1932 reached the number of nearly fifteen thousand. In January 1916 he transferred the business to Henry R. Austin, Harry B. Crosby, and Florence J. Emery as partners in the Arthur P. Schmidt Company.

A chief interest with him from the first was the encouragement of American composers. He often gave new writers their first opportunity and brought to better notice others who were already somewhat known. Most important, he was a pioneer in the publication of works in larger forms (orchestral scores and parts, for example) that had no possibility of being commercially successful. The first score of an important composition of the kind in the United States was the second symphony, "Im Frühling," of John Knowles Paine [*q.v.*], published in 1880 by subscription. For the large number of such works that followed in the form of orchestral and chamber music Schmidt himself was financially responsible, a remarkable undertaking when the cost of publishing such works is considered. Generous in all ways and not satisfied to restrict himself to the commercial and profitable side of the business, he was quite willing to spend money for an ideal. Furthermore, as a German who had come to the United States and found success, he wished (as he sometimes said) to repay the country in some way for his good fortune. This was his practical way of doing it, and his plan was to let no year pass without at least one such publication. In the forty years from 1880 to 1920 he published among others the larger works of such composers as Mrs. H. H. A. Beach, Arthur Bird [*q.v.*], George W. Chadwick, Ar-

thur Foote, Henry Hadley, Edward MacDowell [*q.v.*], and Sigismond Stojowski. The encouragement he thus gave to composers cannot be overestimated; in a period of remarkable development in American music he made a noteworthy contribution.

[*Grove's Dict. of Music and Musicians, Am. Supp.* (ed. 1930); obituaries in *Musical America*, May 14, 1921, and *Boston Transcript*, May 6, 1921; private information.]   A. F.

SCHMIDT, FRIEDRICH AUGUST (Jan. 3, 1837–May 15, 1928), Lutheran theologian, the son of Martin and Helena (Wirth) Schmidt, was born at Leutenberg, Thuringia, Germany, and came at the age of four with his parents to St. Louis, Mo., where he attended parochial school and Concordia Theological Seminary. He was graduated from the preparatory department of the seminary in 1853 and from the theological in 1857. He was pastor at Eden, N. Y., from 1857 to 1859, and at Baltimore, Md., from 1859 to 1861. For the following eleven years he was professor at Luther College, Decorah, Iowa, and from 1872 to 1876 professor of theology at his alma mater. When the Norwegian Synod established its own school of theology at Madison, Wis., in 1878, Schmidt was transferred to this institution, where he taught till 1886. Due to the acrid controversy about predestination, one-third of the Norwegian Synod started their own theological seminary in 1886 at the St. Olaf school in Northfield, Minn., and, on receiving synodical censure, organized themselves as the Anti-Missourian Brotherhood. Schmidt forthwith became a professor in this school. When the Brotherhood, in 1890, merged to form the United Norwegian Lutheran Church, Schmidt suffered another transfer to Augsburg Seminary in Minneapolis, Minn., where he taught until 1893. Because of friction in the new faculty and new church body, Augsburg Seminary was abandoned and the United Norwegian Lutheran Church founded the Luther Theological Seminary at St. Anthony Park, St. Paul, Minn., where Schmidt was professor of systematic theology from 1893 to 1912, when he resigned.

Schmidt's name figured extensively in the predestination controversy, there being few doctrinal controversies among the Lutherans of German or Norwegian antecedents in the West in which he did not participate. Up to 1878 he was an ardent admirer of the Missouri Synod and its leader, C. F. W. Walther, but when the latter began to press the claim that God elected man to salvation prior to the foundation of the world, independent of any fore-knowledge of faith, Schmidt changed his allegiance. To combat the new "Calvinism" he edited *Altes und Neues,*

1880–85, and *Lutherske Vidnesbyrd,* 1882–90. For these and similar efforts the Evangelical Lutheran Inter-Synodical Conference in 1882 refused to receive him as delegate from the Norwegian Synod. Schmidt knew his Latin tomes and seventeenth-century Lutheranism. In the controversy which engaged him for thirty-five years, his method of attack and defense was, like that of his opponents, scholastic—and antiquated, as if a Kant had never existed. Like them, he failed to recognize the limits of human knowledge about the will-problem and its distribution on various levels of discussion. His opponents regarded him as liberalistic and synergistic, but he was neither. Indeed he was liberal enough to stand for "open questions" in eschatology, to doubt the wisdom of subscribing to the Book of Concord as too theological for the laity, and to distinguish between fundamental and non-fundamental doctrines. But he believed in verbal inspiration and *jure divino* ministry, and regarded ecclesiastical "unionism" as sinful. He was happy that his one-time plan to study in Germany had been shattered because he considered it to be the land of rationalism. Besides the publications already mentioned, he edited the *Lutheran Watchman,* 1866–67, was joint editor of the *Luthersk Kirkeblad,* 1890–95, and *Der Sprechsaal,* 1901–03. He was author of *Naadevalgsstriden,* 1881, *Intuitu fidei,* 1895, and *Sandhed og Frihed,* 1914. Schmidt was a small-statured man, kind, sociable, honest to the core, and versatile. His wife was Caroline Sophia Allwardt, to whom he was married on Dec. 8, 1858. They had eight children, six of whom survived their father.

[*Who's Who in America,* 1920–21; *Who's Who Among Pastors in All the Norwegian Luth. Synods of America* (1928); O. M. Norlie, O. A. Tingelstad, K. T. Jacobson, *Luther Coll. Through Sixty Years* (1922); J. A. Bergh, *Den Norsk Lutherske Kirkes Historie i Amerika* (1914); Luth. Pub. Soc., *The Distinctive Doctrines and Usages . . . of the Evang. Luth. Ch.* (4th ed., 1914); *Luth. Quart.,* Jan. 1906.]   J.O.E.

SCHMUCKER, BEALE MELANCHTHON (Aug. 26, 1827–Oct. 15, 1888), Lutheran clergyman, was born at Gettysburg, Pa., the second of the twelve children of Samuel Simon Schmucker [*q.v.*] by his second wife, Mary Catherine Steenbergen. He graduated from Pennsylvania (later Gettysburg) College in 1844 and from the Gettysburg Theological Seminary in 1847, was licensed by the West Pennsylvania Synod in 1847, and was ordained by the Virginia Synod in 1849. On Mar. 6, 1860, he married Christiana M. Pretz of Allentown, by whom he had two sons. His first charge was Martinsburg and Shepherdstown, Va. (now W. Va.), where he succeeded his friend Charles Porterfield Krauth [*q.v.*] from 1848 to 1851. The winter of 1851–52 he spent in his father's house at Gettysburg, recovering from an affection of the throat. Subsequently he was pastor of St. John's English Lutheran Church, Allentown, 1852–62; of St. John's, Easton, with Philip Pfatteicher as his German colleague, 1862–67; of St. James', Reading, 1867–81; and of the Church of the Transfiguration, Pottstown, from 1881 till his death seven years later. Though exemplary in the fulfillment of his parochial duties, he exercised his greatest influence as a parliamentarian and scholar.

From his father he had inherited his dignity and self-control, his profound piety, his logical habits of thought, and his capacity for severe, sustained intellectual toil, but in their religious temper father and son differed radically. The elder Schmucker was the most gifted and most influential evangelical among the Lutherans of America; the younger, intellectually in closer sympathy with Charles Porterfield Krauth, became one of the leaders of the extreme churchly party which discredited Samuel Simon Schmucker and remoulded almost completely the doctrine and life of the Lutheran Church in America. The breach between father and son never became personal; amid the theological strife of that generation Beale could write of his father with a serenity, tenderness, and understanding profoundly moving; but there was tragedy, however concealed, in their intellectual estrangement.

He was English secretary of the board of directors of the Philadelphia Theological Seminary from 1864 to 1888, secretary of the board of foreign missions of the Ministerium of Pennsylvania and of the General Council of the Evangelical Lutheran Church in America. As a liturgical scholar he had no equal in the United States and few in Europe. His knowledge of the early Lutheran liturgies and of those of the undivided church was profound; he had an intuitive sense for the proprieties of worship; and his literary taste was impeccable. The first-fruit of his work in this field was *A Liturgy for the Use of the Evangelical Lutheran Church* (1860; 1868; 1871), in which he collaborated with A. T. Geissenhainer; it was nominally a translation of the second edition (1855) of the *Liturgie und Kirchenagende* edited by Charles Rudolph Demme [*q.v.*], but was really based on older, more conservative principles and was a finer achievement. With Frederic Mayer Bird [*q.v.*] he edited the *Hymns for the Use of the Evangelical Lutheran Church* (1865; 1868), which was the best American hymnbook that had yet appeared.

His drastic criticism, from the floor of the Min- isterium, of the provisional edition (1871) of the *Kirchenbuch* resulted in his addition to the committee engaged on it, and the completed *Kirchenbuch* (1877), like the English liturgies and hymnbooks of the Ministerium and the Gen- eral Council, bears the stamp of his taste and scholarship. When a joint committee of the Gen- eral Council, the General Synod, and the United Synod of the South was formed to prepare a Common Service for the use of the three bod- ies, Schmucker, Edward Traill Horn [*q.v.*], and George U. Wenner constituted the sub-commit- tee that did most of the work. He wrote the preface to the first edition of *The Common Serv- ice* (1888) published by the United Synod of the South, and he continued to work on the forms for ministerial acts until the end. His editorial work is incorporated in *The Church Book* (1891) and *The Common Service Book* (1919). No other one man has so influenced the liturgical development of the Lutheran Church in America.

Schmucker was averse to publishing anything under his own name, but late in life he produced a number of historical and biographical studies of importance, and he collaborated with William Julius Mann and Wilhelm Germann on an an- notated edition of the *Hallesche Nachrichten* (1886–95). He collected what was probably the best liturgical library in the United States (now at the Philadelphia Theological Seminary). On Oct. 15, 1888, he left his home in Pottstown to take the completed manuscript of *The Church Book* to the publishing house in Philadelphia. He ran to catch his train and died of a heart attack near Phoenixville. The burial service that he had completed two weeks before was used for the first time at his grave.

[Published material on Schmucker includes Adolph Spaeth, *Charles Porterfield Krauth* (2 vols., 1898– 1909) and "Memorial of Beale Melanchthon Schmuck- er," *Luth. Ch. Rev.*, Apr. 1889; H. E. Jacobs, "The Making of the Church Book," *Ibid.*, Oct. 1912; L. D. Reed, "Hist. Sketch of the Common Service," *Ibid.*, Oct. 1917; G. W. Sandt, "Luth. Leaders as I Knew Them: Rev. Beale M. Schmucker, D.D.," *Ibid.*, Jan. 1918; A. R. Wentz, *Hist. of the Gettysburg Theol. Sem.* (1926). The C. P. Krauth and B. M. Schmucker papers are in the library of the Lutheran Theological Seminary, Mount Airy, Phila.]   G. H. G.

SCHMUCKER, JOHN GEORGE (Aug. 18, 1771–Oct. 7, 1854), Lutheran clergyman, was born in Germany at Michelstadt in the Odenwald, the second of the six children of John Chris- topher Schmucker, and came to Pennsylvania with his parents in 1785. After tarrying a year in Lehigh and another year in Lancaster County, the family settled in the Shenandoah Valley just west of Woodstock, Va. There, in his nineteenth year, Schmucker began his preparation for the

ministry under Paul Henkel [*q.v.*], whom he ac- companied on one or more trips to the back coun- try. In later years he had tales to tell his chil- dren of encounters with Indians and border ruffians and of a narrow escape from drowning in a spring freshet. In 1790 he tramped north to Philadelphia to study for two years under J. H. C. Helmuth [*q.v.*] and J. F. Schmidt. He then became a catechist at Quickel's Church, York County, Pa., under the supervision of the cele- brated Jacob Goering, with whom he read He- brew.

He was licensed in 1793 and ordained in 1800 by the Ministerium of Pennsylvania. From 1794 to 1809 he was pastor of the Lutheran Church at Hagerstown, Md., and its affiliated congrega- tions; he came to Hagerstown a pale, emaciated, diffident youth, whom his parishioners regarded half with wonder and half with pity, but he de- veloped steadily into one of the ablest, most in- fluential ministers of his denomination. After Goering's death he was called to take charge of the congregations in and about York, Pa., and held this post from 1809 to 1836. On May 1, 1814, the York congregation dedicated a new church building, Christ Church, the act of con- secration being performed by Friedrich Valentin Melsheimer [*q.v.*]. Schmucker began about 1820 to conduct some of the services at Christ Church in the English language, and in 1829 he received a congenial assistant in the Rev. Jonathan Os- wald. A few years later he precipitated a local tempest by advocating temperance; for a while he was so unpopular that he could collect only half his salary. He was president (1820–21) of the Ministerium of Pennsylvania and one of the founders of the General Synod, the Gettysburg Theological Seminary, Pennsylvania (now Get- tysburg) College, and the West Pennsylvania Synod, and his services to all these organizations and institutions were important and continued over many years.

Schmucker's published works include *The Prophetic History of the Christian Religion, or Explanation of the Revelation of St. John* (2 vols., 1817–21); *Vornehmste Weissagungen der Heiligen Schrift* (1807); *Die Wächterstimme an Zion's Kinder* (1838); *Reformations-Geschichte zur Jubelfeier der Reformation* (1817); *Schwär- mergeist unserer Tage entlarvt zur Warnung erweckter Seelen* (1827); *Lieder-Anhang zum Evangelischen Gesangbuch der General Synode* (1833); and *Erklärung der Offenbarung Johan- nis* (n.d.). He left in manuscript a huge com- mentary on the Epistle to the Hebrews and an explanation of Luther's Shorter Catechism, which B. M. Schmucker described as "among the most excellent of its whole class, simple, clear, precise, thoroughly evangelical and distinctly Lutheran in doctrine" ("Luther's Small Catechism: Explanations Prepared for Use in America," *Lutheran Church Review,* July 1886, p. 173).

Schmucker resigned his pastorate at York in 1836 and was succeeded by Augustus Hoffman Lochman. He continued to act as pastor of Quickel's Church, which he served in his youth, until 1852. He was married twice; to Elizabeth Gross of Quickel's, who bore him twelve children and died in 1819; and in 1821 to Anna Hoffman, sister-in-law of John George Lochman [*q.v.*], who bore him seven children and outlived him. The last few years of his life were spent at Williamsburg, Blair County, Pa., where he died. He was buried in front of Christ Church at York. Great as were his services to the Lutheran Church of his generation, his most enduring claim on remembrance is that he was the father of Samuel Simon Schmucker [*q.v.*].

[*Evangelical Rev.,* Jan. 1855; W. B. Sprague, *Annals Am. Pulpit,* vol. IX (1869); J. G. Morris, *Fifty Years in the Luth. Ministry* (1878); Peter Anstadt, *Life and Times of Rev. S. S. Schmucker, D.D.* (1896); *Doc. Hist. Ev. Luth. Min. of Pa. . . . 1748–1821* (1898); B. M. Schmucker, "The Luth. Ch. in York, Pa.," *Luth. Quart.,* Oct. 1888; A. R. Wentz, *Hist. of the Gettysburg Theol. Sem.* (1926).]   G. H. G.

SCHMUCKER, SAMUEL SIMON (Feb. 28, 1799–July 26, 1873), Lutheran clergyman, theologian, educator, was born at Hagerstown, Md., where his mother, Elizabeth (Gross), and his father, the Rev. John George Schmucker [*q.v.*], were shepherding a small Lutheran flock. The atmosphere of the parental home was that of a warm pietism after the pattern of the German school of Spener and Francke, mixed with the rigorous Puritanism which then dominated American Protestantism. The home had contacts, however, with broad interests through the father's active participation in the affairs of organized Lutheranism. While still a youth it was given to the son to help carry forward to success the efforts of his father and a few others in the organization of the General Synod, the first united Lutheran Church in America.

Samuel's formal education consisted of discipleship under his father's theological preceptor, Dr. Justus H. C. Helmuth [*q.v.*], a veteran of the days of the patriarch Henry M. Mühlenberg [*q.v.*], who carried over the confessional strain from that earlier time. In 1819 Schmucker was graduated *gratiae causa* from the University of Pennsylvania, and in 1820, from the Princeton Theological Seminary, where he learned anew to respect puritanical notions and

practices (evidenced in his legalistic view of the Christian Sabbath, in strict observation of certain religious customs, and in a rather rigid sense of decorum), and where he came into a close fellowship with other denominational leaders which gave him a characteristic catholic outlook. All through the years he remained a student, and in his day he was the best-trained man in his church. Licensed in 1820 and ordained a year later, he served his only parish, consisting of five congregations with New Market, Va., as center, for nearly six years. He was three times married: first, Feb. 28, 1821, to Elenora Geiger of Hagerstown, Md., who died July 3, 1823, having borne him one son; second, Oct. 12, 1825, to Mary Catherine Steenbergen of the Shenandoah Valley, Va., who died Feb. 11, 1848, the mother of twelve children; third, Apr. 28, 1849, to Esther M. Wagner of Germantown, Pa. Of his four gifted sons, one, Beale Melanchthon [*q.v.*], became a conspicuous leader in the conservative camp opposing his father's liberal outlook.

Three *pia desideria* (as he called them) gripped him upon leaving Princeton: the translation of some one important work on Lutheran dogmatics, the establishment of a Lutheran theological seminary, and the founding of a college. All three were early realized: his *Biblical Theology of Storr and Flatt, Translated from the German* appeared in two volumes in 1826; in 1825, he was elected first professor in the theological seminary at Gettysburg, opened in 1826, which he helped to found; and the classical school, which he initiated in 1827, became, under a charter granted five years later, Pennsylvania College (now Gettysburg). From 1832 to 1834 Schmucker served as president of the college. His *desideria,* however, were more than realized. He framed model constitutions for congregations and synods; he published in 1834 the first English Lutheran work on systematic theology appearing in this country, *Elements of Popular Theology*; he helped to prepare hymnbooks, liturgical forms, new editions of Luther's catechism containing free interpretations; he took active part in the efforts toward church unity, particularly by his publication in 1838 of the widely discussed *Appeal to the American Churches* (a document antedating the fellowship plan of the present Federal Council of Churches) and by active participation in the organization of the Evangelical Alliance in 1846.

For many years he held the reins of theological leadership in the General Synod. In the 1840's, however, forces began to gather strength which ultimately took the reins from his hands. A huge tide of German immigration swept in and with it was transplanted to American soil a conservative Lutheran theology chained by a full allegiance to the symbolical books and treatises of the sixteenth and seventeenth century German theologians. Cognizant of the rising tide of conservatism, he launched, from about 1845 on, a quiet campaign defending in carefully prepared discourses the type of Lutheranism which he had come to know as consonant with "that liberty of thought which all Protestants must retain." From apologetics he turned to vigorous polemics, dividing the issue squarely between an "American" and an "Old" Lutheranism. The impending explosion came with the publication of the anonymous document called the *Definite Platform, Doctrinal and Disciplinarian, for Evangelical Lutheran District Synods* (1855), prepared by Schmucker, in which the advocates of an American Lutheranism sought to have adopted their confessional position in a recension of the Augsburg Confession as a minimum platform of agreement. The controversy was only aggravated; one by one his followers turned away to follow the new stream. The issuance of the manifesto, he came to believe, was a blunder, and he tried in vain to atone for it, but the time and tide were against him. Heresy charges instituted by the man who came to be his successor were opposed by those who had not in the heat of the controversy lost the perspective of gratitude. When he left his chair in 1864 he could truthfully say to his church and particularly to his some four hundred students that he had not in the main departed from the doctrines taught in the classroom nor from the liberal professorial oath formulated by himself thirty-eight years before.

His some forty-four published works reveal a systematic mind. He generally presented the argument of a theme only after he had carefully marshaled and set forth facts; he sought for intelligent judgment and not for emotional assent. By nature he was even-tempered and irenic; though graciously tolerant of the views of others, he steadfastly and openly defended convictions of his own. He excelled greatly in the virtue of integrity. The paradox of his professional life is a curious one: a savior of his church in the third decade of the nineteenth century, he was looked upon as its betrayer in the fifth and afterward; he set out to make his Church more Lutheran, and that same Church later waved him aside because he was not Lutheran enough.

[A list of the published works and discourses of Schmucker, together with much valuable source material, is given in Vergilius Ferm, *The Crisis in Am. Lutheran Theology* (1927). See also, B. M. Schmucker, "Samuel S. Schmucker," in *The Pa. Coll. Book,*

1832–1882 (1882) ; Peter Anstadt, *Life and Times of Rev. S. S. Schmucker, D.D.* (1896) ; A. R. Wentz, *Hist. of the Gettysburg Theological Sem.* (1926), and "The Work of S. S. Schmucker," in *Lutheran Quart.,* Jan. 1927 ; J. L. Chamberlain, *Universities and Their Sons: Univ. of Pa.,* vol. II (1902) ; Adolph Spaeth, *Charles Porterfield Krauth* (2 vols., 1898–1909).]

V. F.

SCHNAUFFER, CARL HEINRICH (July 4, 1823–Sept. 4, 1854), poet, soldier, editor, was a German political refugee in America after the Revolution of 1848. He was born in Heimsheim, near Stuttgart, Germany, the son of a dyer, Johann Heinrich Schnauffer, and Karoline (Hasenmaier) Schnauffer. Owing to the early death of his father Schnauffer's schooling was cut short and, after serving an apprenticeship in Grossbottwar, he entered the employ of a Mannheim merchant. His employer recognized his literary ability and gave him the necessary time for study. At this time Schnauffer met two men whose ideals influenced the whole course of his life, Gustav Struve and Friedrich Karl Franz Hecker [*qq.v.*], revolutionary leaders in Baden and emigrants to America after 1848. In 1846 he entered the university at Heidelberg, where he associated with the liberal student groups, and published his first volume of verse, strongly influenced by Pierre-Jean de Béranger and Ferdinand Freiligrath. In the next year he joined the staff of the liberal *Mannheimer Abendzeitung,* and in 1848 followed Hecker into the field and fought in a number of engagements of the ill-starred uprising of the South-German liberals. He fled to Switzerland, but in 1849 he joined in the renewed fighting, and on June 22 he was taken prisoner at Mannheim and transported to Prussia. He escaped from prison disguised as a locksmith, and once more took refuge in Switzerland where he wrote his *Todtenkränze,* inspired probably by a work of the same title by Christian von Zedlitz. But instead of the Austrian poet's resignation, Schnauffer sounds a ringing call to battle for freedom in the name of those executed by the reactionaries. In April 1850 he was seized by the Swiss government and forced to leave for London along with other revolutionary leaders. In London he met Struve and together they went to the estate of Thomas Fothergill, a friend from Heidelberg days who offered them asylum. He performed manual labor for his keep, among other things training race horses, and also began a five-act drama in the style of Schiller, *Koenig Karl I oder Cromwell und die englische Revolution,* which was privately printed in Baltimore in 1854. Characteristically the play ends with the death of the tyrant and the establishment of the British republic.

In Mannheim he had become engaged to Elise Wilhelmine Moos who had, however, emigrated to Baltimore, Md., with her family in 1847. For several years Schnauffer had no news of her but, in 1850, correspondence was renewed and in May of the following year he joined her in Baltimore where they were married. He identified himself enthusiastically with the "Turner" movement and founded, in October 1851, a German daily, *Baltimore Wecker,* which stood for popular education, freedom, and enlightenment, and opposed the current "Know-Nothingism." Unlike some other "Forty-eighters" Schnauffer never preached economic revolution, but in his lyrics he continually elaborated on the theme that the noble man should at all times be ready to fight and die for freedom. The best works by Schnauffer are poems in the style of Arndt or Herwegh, which expressed the ideals of the "Turner" so well that they became their favorite songs. His collected poems were published in 1879 under the title, *Lieder und Gedichte aus dem Nachlass von Carl Heinrich Schnauffer.* He died at the age of thirty-one from typhoid fever, just before news reached him that one of his lyrics had won the first prize at the "Turner" convention in Philadelphia. His widow continued the *Wecker* in his memory and in his spirit. No English-language paper in Maryland was anti-slavery and on the outburst of the Civil War a mob stormed the *Wecker* office, smashing its windows. At this moment Mrs. Schnauffer, with the smaller of her two children in her arms, stepped out of the building to face the mob and successfully appealed to them to abandon further destruction. Schnauffer was quite short in stature but military in bearing, and he had a personality that inspired enthusiastic devotion in his friends.

[*Jahrbücher der Deutsch-Amerikanischen Turnerei,* Apr. 1891; L. P. Henninghausen, "Reminiscences of the Political Life of the German-Americans in Baltimore during 1850–1860," *Seventh Ann. Report of the Soc. for the Hist. of the Germans in Md.,* 1892–93; J. T. Scharf, *Hist. of Baltimore City* (1881); *Baltimore Sun,* Sept. 5, 1854; reminiscences and unpublished letters furnished by his grandson, John Dickinson.]

A. E. Z.

SCHNEIDER, ALBERT (Apr. 13, 1863–Oct. 27, 1928), bacteriologist, was born in Granville, Ill., the son of John and Elizabeth (Burcky) Schneider. He married Marie Louise Harrington of Minneapolis, Minn., on June 28, 1892; they had one daughter. After taking the degree of M.D. at the College of Physicians and Surgeons, Chicago, Ill., in 1887, he became instructor in botany at the University of Minnesota. In 1894 he took the degree of M.S. at Minnesota; in 1897 he received the degree of Ph.D. at Columbia University and returned to teaching. He was professor of pharmacology and bacteriology at Northwestern University, 1897–1903; of pharmacognosy and bacteriology at the University of California, 1903–19; of pharmacology at the University of Nebraska, 1919–22; and dean of pharmacy at North Pacific College of Oregon, Portland, 1922–28. In addition, he was director of the experiment station of the Spreckels Sugar Company, 1906–07; pharmacognosist, United States Department of Agriculture, 1909–15; and editor of the *Pacific Pharmacist,* 1910–15, through which he attempted to raise the standards of pharmacy as a profession and to secure pure foods and drugs. Apart from his strictly professional work, he was a man of some inventive genius. Apparatus and instruments of his design were to be seen in his laboratory, and he invented a ventilating system for Pullman cars. He was interested in the scientific detection of criminals, wrote several papers on the subject, re-introduced the "lie detector" in 1927, and lectured at the police schools in Berkeley, Cal., and Portland, Ore., at various times.

His writings include books and articles on a wide range of subjects: bacteriology, botany, microscopy, food analysis, lichenology, toxicology, pharmacology, glandular therapy, and criminology. One of his early books was *The Limitations of Learning and Other Science Papers* (1900); later he wrote such technical books as *Pharmaceutical Bacteriology* (1912; 2nd ed. 1920), *Bacteriological Methods in Food and Drugs Laboratories* (1915), *The Microbiology and Microanalysis of Foods* (1920), and *The Microanalysis of Powdered Vegetable Drugs* (2nd ed., 1921). In 1896 he produced *A Compendium of General Botany,* translated from the German of Maximilian Westermaier. The papers he contributed with frequency to scientific journals exhibit great care in preparation. It was his habit to repeat experiments many times in a methodical way in order to satisfy himself that the results were worth publication; he strongly discouraged the type of research work that, as he expressed it, "clutters up" the journals. He was a member of the international jury of awards at the Panama Pacific International Exposition in 1915, one of a committee for the tenth revision of the United States Pharmacopoeia, a member of the American Pharmaceutical Association and of the American Association for the Advancement of Science. He died in Portland, Ore.

[*Who's Who in America,* 1928–29; J. McK. and Jaques Cattell, *Am. Men of Sci.* (ed. 1927); *Jour. Am. Pharmaceutical Assoc.,* Nov. 1928; *Morning Oregonian* (Portland), Oct. 28, 1928.]

F. G.

SCHNEIDER, BENJAMIN (Jan. 18, 1807–Sept. 14, 1877), missionary in Turkey, was born at New Hanover, Montgomery County, Pa., the son of Henry and Mary (Noyce) Schneider. After preparatory education at academies in Norristown and Reading, Pa., in 1826 he entered Hamilton College, but at the end of his second year transferred to Amherst, where he was graduated in 1830. He then attended Andover Theological Seminary, completing his course there in 1833. On Sept. 15 of the same year he married Eliza Cheyney, daughter of Josiah Abbott of Framingham, Mass., and on Oct. 2 was ordained to the ministry of the Presbyterian Church, at Nottingham, Md. Having been appointed a missionary to Turkey by the American Board of Commissioners for Foreign Missions, he sailed from Boston three months later and reached Smyrna on Jan. 14, 1834. Commissioned to establish a station at Brusa, he proceeded at once to his post and commenced the study of modern Greek and Turkish. For the next fifteen years that city was his headquarters for evangelical work, principally among Greeks and Armenians. Frequent tours on horseback spread his influence through the surrounding provinces. So great was the opposition from local Ottoman officials and priests of the Oriental Christian Churches, however, that in 1848 the sole tangible fruit of his labors in preaching and in distributing tracts and Bibles was a Protestant Church of seven members in Brusa.

In 1849 he was transferred to Aintab in South-Central Anatolia, and found among the Armenians there a more fertile field for his activities. The one small Protestant Church in the place developed during his seventeen years of work into two entirely self-supporting congregations with several hundred members, Sunday Schools, day schools, and a high school. Meanwhile, Aintab had become one of the largest centers of missionary work in Turkey, with several missionaries in residence. In Marash, Urfa, Diarbekir, Adana, and many other towns out-stations had been established and were flourishing under the care of missionaries or of native pastors who were given their theological training by Schneider. In 1856 his wife died at Aintab, and while on a furlough in the United States two years later he married her sister, Susan Maria. He returned in 1868 to his former post at Brusa and spent there four more years under conditions vastly more favorable to missionary work than had obtained during his former residence. Ill health forced him in 1872 to take another furlough of two years at home, and when he went back to the mission field it was to the less strenu-

ous task of teaching in the theological seminary at Marsovan (now Merzifon). His strength was unequal to the work, however, and after one more year of service he retired. He spent the last two years of his life in New Britain, Conn., and in Boston, where he died.

Among the pioneer missionaries to Turkey Schneider was preëminently the preacher rather than the translator or explorer. Though he wrote or translated books and tracts into modern Greek and Turkish, his strength was in the spoken rather than in the written word, and his sermons were renowned for an almost faultless mastery of these languages as well as for eloquence and persuasiveness. Strongly Calvinistic in his theology and preaching, he was nevertheless a man of great tolerance and simple sincerity.

[*Amherst Coll. Biog. Record* (1927); J. K. Greene, *Leavening the Levant* (1916); *Missionary Herald*, Dec. 1877.]   W. L. W., Jr.

SCHNEIDER, GEORGE (Dec. 13, 1823–Sept. 16, 1905), journalist and banker, was born in Pirmasens, Rhenish Bavaria, the son of Ludwig and Josephine (Schlick) Schneider. He obtained his early education at the Latin school of his native town. Upon reaching his majority he became engaged in journalism. Keenly interested in public affairs, he denounced the arbitrary government of his native state and in 1848 joined an insurrection against it. Having eventually to leave the country because of his political views, he went first to France and thence to the United States. Arriving in New York in July 1849, he was attracted by the glamorous stories of the new West. Within a few months he had reached St. Louis and founded the *Neue Zeit,* a paper which soon became conspicuous for its opposition to the extension of slavery. In 1851 the home of the *Neue Zeit* was destroyed by fire, and in August of the same year Schneider became managing editor of the *Illinois Staats-Zeitung,* a conservative weekly paper which he soon transformed into a thriving daily with a Sunday edition, the first in Chicago. Although more conservative than the *Neue Zeit,* the *Staats-Zeitung* bitterly opposed the Douglas program and the repeal of the Missouri Compromise. On Jan. 29, 1854, Schneider convoked a public meeting, perhaps the first of its kind in the United States, to draft resolutions against the Nebraska Bill, and on Mar. 16 at a mass meeting of German citizens in which Schneider was an active participant, Douglas was branded as "an ambitious and dangerous demagogue." On Feb. 22, 1856, Schneider was one of a group of anti-Nebraska editors who assembled at Decatur, Ill., and issued a call for the first Republican state convention in Illinois, to be held at Bloomington in the following May. At the Bloomington convention, with Lincoln's assistance, he managed to get a plank adopted which was a clear-cut pronouncement against Know-Nothing policies hostile to naturalized citizens, especially Germans, who were anti-slavery men. He also was chiefly responsible for the adoption of the tenth plank of the Philadelphia platform of 1856 which invited the "affiliation and coöperation of the men of all parties." He actively espoused Lincoln's candidacy for the presidency after his nomination in 1860, and the nation-wide circulation of the *Staats-Zeitung,* one of the most influential German papers in the Northwest, did much to consolidate the great foreign-born vote without which Lincoln would have failed of election (D. V. Smith, *Mississippi Valley Historical Review,* September 1932).

In 1861 he was appointed consul at Elsinore, Denmark, primarily to influence the public opinion of northern Europe in favor of the Union cause. Resigning from this office in 1862, he returned to the United States and in 1863 became collector of internal revenue for the Chicago district, having in the meantime (1862) disposed of his interest in the *Staats-Zeitung.* After four years in the internal revenue service, he became chief executive of the State Savings Institution at Chicago, and in 1871 he was chosen the first president of the newly organized National Bank of Illinois, a position that he held until 1897. Although he was now primarily interested in banking, he continued to be active in public life in Illinois. Declining to accept a diplomatic appointment to Switzerland in 1877, he became the treasurer of the Chicago South Park Board in the following year, serving in this capacity until 1882. As a director of the Chicago Festival Association, he was instrumental in 1885 in bringing excellent musical talent to Chicago. He was intensely interested in the formation of relief societies for German immigrants, and he served for many years as a director of the Illinois Humane Society, which through his efforts in 1879 established a separate department for helpless children. On June 6, 1853, he married Matilda Schloetzer, by whom he had seven children, all daughters. He died in Colorado Springs, Colo.

[*Who's Who in America,* 1903–05; *Trans. Ill. State Hist. Soc.,* no. 35 (1928); *Encyc. of Biog. of Ill.,* vol. I (1892); John Moses and Joseph Kirkland, eds., *Hist. of Chicago* (1895), vols. I, II; Newton Bateman and Paul Selby, eds., *Hist. Encyc. of Ill.* (1900); A. C. Cole, *The Era of the Civil War, 1848–1870* (1919); "Meeting . . . Commemorative of the Convention of May 29, 1856," *Trans. McLean County Hist. Soc.,* vol. III (Bloomington, Ill., 1900); *Chicago Daily Tribune,* Sept. 18, 1905; information from Chicago Pub. Lib.]

A. L. P.

SCHNEIDER, THEODORE (Apr. 7, 1703–July 10, 1764), Roman Catholic missionary, was born at Geinsheim in the diocese of Speyer in the Rhenish Palatinate. On the completion of his preparatory schooling at Speyer, he joined the Society of Jesus (Sept. 25, 1721) and made a brilliant record in philosophy and theology. Hoping to be sent to India as a missionary, he studied medicine. Fate and his provincial decreed a quite different future and he became professor of philosophy and polemics at the Jesuit College of Liège and later rector of the Jesuit House of Studies at the University of Heidelberg, the philosophy courses of the University then being in the charge of the Jesuits. In 1738 he was elected Rector Magnificus of the University. Two years later he was ordered by the General of the Society to go to the Pennsylvania missions, where the English Jesuits were finding difficulty in ministering to the Germans and it was feared they were being lost to the Church. After a brief sojourn in London, where he probably joined the English province, Schneider arrived in Philadelphia in 1741 and was assigned temporarily to St. Joseph's Church before going to Goshenhoppen in Berks County on the Philadelphia-Pottstown Road.

After living for a time with a German carpenter, Schneider built a house and chapel with the assistance of his Catholic fellow countrymen and friendly Mennonites. A powerful man, he was fitted for the rough life and arduous travel. A physician in a land where there were few healers of repute, he was welcomed on his journeys by the people regardless of creed. As a former rector of Heidelberg, he was glorified by the Germans, among whom there were some scholarly ministers. His character overcame much prejudice and gained him considerable favor. In his quest for Catholics and in his efforts to revive their faith, he traveled by horse and afoot to Philadelphia, and aided Robert Harding [*q.v.*] in the eastern counties of Pennsylvania and in a large portion of New Jersey, saying Mass in small chapels and in private homes. No man did more for the early Germans. Bishop Carroll described him as "a person of great dexterity in business, consummate prudence and undaunted magnanimity" (quoted in J. G. Shea, *post,* p. 387). He founded a number of chapels, built a large church at Goshenhoppen, established schools, and even taught little children himself. A diligent man, he kept records and, as an economy and a penance, he copied two complete missals of several hundred pages each (one of which is preserved in the archives of Georgetown University). Broken in health by labors and hardships, Father Schneider was awaiting a recall to Germany to recuperate, when he died after a brief illness.

[Lambert Schrott, *Pioneer German Catholics in the Am. Colonies* (1933); *Cath. Univ. Bull.*, Oct. 1907; J. G. Shea, *The Catholic Church in Colonial Days* (1886); Bernhard Duhr, *Deutsche Auslandsehnsucht im Achtzehnten Jahrhundert* (1928).]　　　R. J. P.

SCHNELLER, GEORGE OTTO (Jan. 14, 1843–Oct. 20, 1895), inventor, manufacturer, was the son of Henry and Elizabeth (Ruckert) Schneller and was born in Nürnberg, Germany. The father was a civil engineer and architect for the German government and directed his son's education, through private schooling and the local technical schools, toward engineering. At the age of seventeen, however, Schneller left his home and emigrated to the United States, landing in New York City. Being an excellent penman and having some knowledge of accountancy, he soon found employment in New York with a commission merchant dealing in brass goods. He became interested in brass manufacture and within a short time, giving up his position in New York, he went to Ansonia, Conn., then the center of the brass industry. There as cashier and accountant he entered the employ of Osborne and Cheesman Company, an influential and notably successful brass manufactory, and in the course of the succeeding eight years advanced rapidly. In 1870, however, he returned to Germany, primarily to visit his home, and there began the study of electrical engineering, as well as other subjects likely to fit him for a manufacturing career. When in 1872 he returned to the United States, he engaged in surveying in Ansonia, made a detailed map of Derby and Ansonia, and as a result of his earlier experience with brass manufacture tried his hand at invention. Between February 1872 and July 1873 he obtained four patents on corset springs. About 1874 he spent two years in a variety of mining ventures in the west but returned to Ansonia and bought a spectacle factory at Shelton, Conn., which he sold within six months. He then turned his attention to the manufacture of brass corset eyelets. In an effort to improve the slow and wasteful methods of insertion then in use, he devoted three or four years to experimentation. In the next few years he secured patents on a die for making eyelets (November 1880), an eyelet machine, and a punch and die for eyelet machines (May 1884), the latter two inventions being designed primarily for insert-

ing eyelets in corsets. Meanwhile in 1882 he bought the Osborne and Cheesman business, reorganized it as the Ansonia O. & C. Company, and began the manufacture of brass goods under his patent rights. Since by his process the amount of waste brass was greatly reduced and the rate of inserting eyelets greatly increased—three hundred dozen corsets could be completed in ten hours—the corset industry of the world was completely revolutionized. Until his death Schneller continued as manager, secretary, and treasurer of his company; he also founded and was treasurer of the Union Fabric Company in Ansonia. With all these activities he found time to continue his inventions, patenting among other things a hook and eye, a bustle, a machine for covering dress stays, a button press, and a button-fastening device. He was active in the building of the electric street railway system between Derby, Ansonia, and Shelton; he also served for a number of years on the board of education of Ansonia and represented that city in the lower house of the state legislature from 1891 to 1893. On May 1, 1873, in Ansonia, he married Clarissa Alling, who with their three children survived him.

[*Commemorative Biog. Record of New Haven County, Conn.* (1902), vol. I; *Leading Business Men of New Haven County* (1881); Patent Office records; *New Haven Evening Reg.*, Oct. 21, 1895.]　　　C. W. M.

SCHNERR, LEANDER (Sept. 27, 1836–Sept. 3, 1920), Roman Catholic cleric, third archabbot of St. Vincent, Latrobe, Pa., was born at Gommersdorf, Baden, Germany, the son of Ernst Schnerr, a Lutheran in faith and a brewmaster by trade, and Barbara Melly, a native of Bamberg, Bavaria, and a Catholic. The day after his birth the child was baptized in the local Catholic church, receiving the names Karl Otto August. A few years later the family emigrated to America and settled in Pittsburgh, Pa., where the father continued to follow his trade. Just before his fourteenth birthday, Karl entered the college at Latrobe, Pa., conducted by the Benedictines of St. Vincent Abbey, and after six years decided to become a member of that Order. He made his solemn vows on Jan. 6, 1857, taking the name Leander in religion. Two years later, Sept. 20, 1859, he was ordained priest by the Rt. Rev. George A. Carrell at Covington, Ky.

Appointed for the missionary field of St. Vincent Abbey, he began as pastor of Stony Hill, N. J., but was soon transferred to the congregations of Augusta and Mullin's Station, Ky. In 1861 Abbot Boniface Wimmer promoted him to priorship and the pastorate of St. Joseph

Church, Chicago, Ill. Here he worked faithfully for ten years, only to see the whole parish plant destroyed in the great fire of 1871. He began to rebuild at once, but before he could finish this task he was sent to St. Mary's, Erie, Pa. Five years later he became pastor of St. Joseph's Church, Johnstown, Pa., and in 1877, after a short administration of St. Bernard Church, Indiana, Pa., assumed charge of St. Mary's Church and priory at Pittsburgh. During the next fifteen years he was prominent in Catholic affairs in that city, especially among the Germans. He practically built a new St. Mary's and in 1884 founded St. Boniface parish. In 1892, after the resignation of the Rt. Rev. Andrew Hintenach, the second archabbot of St. Vincent, Father Leander was elected as his successor.

At his installation on Oct. 5, 1892, the cornerstone of a new abbey church was blessed and during the next twenty-eight years building operations rarely ceased at the archabbey; besides the church, a library, gymnasium, dormitory, various shops, and farm buildings were constructed. At the same time, the Archabbot sought to improve the course of studies. The classical and scientific departments were remodeled to conform to the requirements of the Association of Colleges of the Middle States and Maryland and the philosophical and theological courses were improved to obtain from the Roman authorities the power of granting doctors' degrees in both these branches of learning. Twice he went to Rome in the interest of the whole Order. In 1903 Pius X conferred on him the privilege of the Cappa Magna in church functions and in 1910 he was chosen as a member of the Roman Arcadia. He celebrated the golden jubilees of his profession and ordination in 1907 and 1909. In 1918 he asked the Roman authorities for a coadjutor and the capitulars of the archabbey chose his long-time secretary, Aurelius Stehle, as his successor in office.

Externally, with his stately figure and long flowing beard, Archabbot Leander seemed more a prophet of old than a churchman of the twentieth century. He was not a learned man, but eminently practical and very methodical in his ways. He contributed to the expansion of the Catholic Church and of the Order of St. Benedict in the United States by having St. Bede College, Peru, Ill., raised to an Abbey by Rome in 1910, and by fostering in a special manner the institute of lay-oblates of the Order, an association of men who follow their avocations in life but attach themselves in spiritual matters to a Benedictine monastery.

[Official documents, diary, and letters of the Archabbot, in St. Vincent Archives; *St. Vincent College Journal*, 1892–1920; *Pittsburgh Post*, Sept. 4, 1920.]

F. F.

SCHODDE, GEORGE HENRY (Apr. 15, 1854–Sept. 15, 1917), Lutheran clergyman and educator, the son of George F. and Mary Louise (Tücke) Schodde, was born in Allegheny, Pa. He was graduated in 1872 from the college and in 1874 from the theological department of Capital University, Columbus, Ohio. He pursued his studies further in the universities of Tübingen and Leipzig, receiving in 1877 the degree of Ph.D. from the latter. After returning from Europe he was pastor for one year in Canal Winchester, and for two years in Martins Ferry, both in Ohio. In 1880 he joined the faculty of Capital University as professor of Greek and in 1894 he taught, in addition, New Testament exegesis in the theological seminary of the same institution. His strength as a theologian lay in Biblical text criticism, a field in which he was unusually well informed, though not creative. He abided by the conservative findings of others and, as much as possible, by traditional interpretation without closing the door entirely upon the historical treatment of the text. He regarded the positions of Wellhausen as wholly indefensible; he admired the brilliancy of Harnack, but sought shelter under the rafters of Theodor Zahn. In evaluating creeds, doctrines, and denominations his criterion was orthodox. To him Chemnitz, Hollaz, and Johann Gerhard were "giants of theological thought and research" (Schodde, *The Protestant Church in Germany*, p. 20). He placed the Union Church of Germany, a church that is at least nine-tenths Lutheran, outside the pale of Lutheranism, and assigned the same fate to the Hohenzollerns. He could tolerate a state church, but his ideal was a free church of the Missouri Synod type.

Schodde's attitude was due to a confusion of archaic with historic Lutheranism and to the failure to utilize the research of the Luther-renaissance, well under way in Sweden and Germany at his death. It also caused him to judge the non-Lutheran branches of Protestantism unfairly. They constituted for him, following German theological classification, the Reformed. He called the Lutheran Church a "Bible Church," a distinction which he withheld from the "Reformed," claiming that in the latter it is held that the Spirit in His operations is not bound by certain mediums or instruments, but may and does operate in any way whatsoever (*Ibid.*, p. 14). Schodde was, no doubt, Christocentric in his religion, but his theology was Bibliocentric, historically a loan from some of the

Reformed rather than a heritage from Luther. He was a stranger to the real problems of the new century's theology which were precipitated upon the orthodox by German and Swedish scholars. He admired German theological scholarship, which he found to be "to a great extent evangelical and positive" but not distinctively Lutheran (*Ibid.*, p. 56 ff.).

His booklet, *The Protestant Church in Germany* (1901), is written in a kindly spirit; one other theological book, *Outlines of Biblical Hermeneutics,* was published shortly after his death. He wrote numerous articles and book reviews for church papers and theological magazines, and translated from Ethiopic, *The Book of Enoch* (1882), *The Book of Jubilees* (1888); from German, F. J. Delitzsch, *A Day in Capernaum* (1887), Bernhard Weiss, *The Religion of the New Testament* (1905), and, together with Epiphanius Wilson, *A Commentary on the New Testament* (4 vols., 1906). He was news-editor of the *Lutheran Standard* since 1889; and editor of the *Theological Magazine* since 1897. He also contributed articles to the *Independent, Sunday School Times,* the *Nation, Bible Student and Teacher* and the *Biblical Review.* He was married, on Dec. 22, 1881, to Mary Dorsch, who with one daughter, survived him. At the time of his death no other name on the clerical roll of the Joint Synod of Ohio was better known among the clergy of other Protestant denominations in the United States than that of Schodde.

[*Who's Who in America,* 1916–17; *The New Schaff-Herzog Encyc. of Religious Knowledge,* vol. X (1911); obituary article by Edward Pfeiffer, and an "Appreciation" by the editor, *Luth. Standard,* Sept. 29, 1917; *Ohio State Jour.,* Sept. 17, 1917.]   J.O.E.

SCHOENHOF, JACOB (1839–Mar. 14, 1903), economist, was born in Oppenheim, Germany, where his father was a school teacher. In 1861 Jacob emigrated to the United States and engaged in the wholesale lace business until 1884, when he retired. In 1867 he married Henrietta Werner.

Schoenhof's business career commenced with the development of large-scale factory industry in the United States, and with his German background he was able to describe the industry of the country as it stood in contrast, in all of its important implications, to the production methods employed in Europe. He was as much struck as had been John Rae, Mathew and Henry C. Carey, Daniel Raymond, and Friedrich List with the desirability of economic capacity as compared with the older objective of wealth in the form of mere physical output. A prosperous country, in his estimation, was one

which has as its principal productive equipment a high standard of living for the working classes, with resulting mental alertness, ingenuity in mechanical invention and business organization, and a high degree of adaptability to changing economic circumstances. His predecessors in this economic school, writing during an earlier stage of American industrial development, had been advocates of a protective tariff, but Schoenhof, seeing the country on the threshold of industrial maturity, was convinced that free trade was essential to her continued advance. The others had written when protection was reluctantly granted, he wrote when protection, ensconced by the Civil War, had begun to work a harmful limitation upon American foreign markets.

President Cleveland's first administration afforded special opportunity for the development and application of Schoenhof's characteristic ideas. Cleveland, at first uninformed on the tariff issue, advocated reduction of duties as the means of breaking up government favoritism and dispelling the surplus which high customs were piling up in the treasury. On Nov. 23, 1885, Schoenhof was appointed United States consul at Tunstall, England, and later, as the confidential agent of Thomas F. Bayard [*q.v.*], Cleveland's secretary of state, he studied industrial conditions in Great Britain, France, and Germany. Bayard was an orthodox Democrat, a believer in economic as well as in political individualism, and a persuasive, if implacable, foe of protection. Schoenhof interpreted his mission broadly, and studied the entire economy of Europe as it bore upon production methods. In most of his works, but particularly in *The Industrial Situation and the Question of Wages* (1885) and in *The Economy of High Wages* (1892) he sought to refute the argument, universally advanced by the protectionists, that killing competition would be offered to American industry by the low-paid labor of Europe were the tariff reduced. He showed, with lavish citation of instances, that high money wages were generally the accompaniment of low unit cost of production, thus forecasting the doctrine later associated with the name of Henry Ford. His wide first-hand observation as traveler and student was supplemented by his own experience as a manufacturer and merchant. The business depressions of 1884 and 1893, coupled with America's industrial proficiency, awoke in him many of the fears which have since been realized by "technological unemployment," and he urged the removal of impediments to trade as the condition of continually mounting output and the only means of insuring economic stability within the country.

While others of the active free trade school of writers dealt principally in theoretical contention, Schoenhof brought to his argument a vast amount of practical documentation, and with boldness and skill made the most of the apparent paradox in his reasoning to the effect that high indirect costs were low direct costs. His *History of Money and Prices* (1896), which owed something to the lesson of the return to specie payments in 1879, was a refutation of the quantity theory of prices that had influenced his earlier work; he concluded that "prices of commodities move in obedience to natural and inherent causes, independent of circulating money quantities," and result from the interplay of a wide variety of economic forces. Besides the works cited above, he wrote *The Destructive Influence of the Tariff Upon Manufacture and Commerce* (1883); *Wages and Trade in Manufacturing Industries in America and in Europe* (1884); *Technical Education in Europe, First Part: Industrial Education in France* (1888); *Influences Bearing on Production* (1888). In 1893 he was appointed assistant appraiser at the port of New York and served as such throughout Cleveland's second administration. He died in New York City.

[*Publishers' Weekly*, Mar. 21, 1903; *N. Y. Times* and *N. Y. Tribune*, Mar. 15, 1903.]   B. M.

SCHOFF, STEPHEN ALONZO (Jan. 16, 1818–May 6, 1904), engraver, was the great-grandson of Jacob Schoff, a German, who settled in New England in 1752. Born in Danville, Vt., third of the eight children of John Chase and Eunice (Nye) Schoff, Stephen removed with his parents, when he was about eight years old, to Bradford on the Merrimack, and subsequently to Newburyport, Mass., the latter place being chosen because of its superior schools. At sixteen he was indentured for five years to Oliver Pelton, a Boston engraver, but after three years, dissatisfied with his progress, he went to Joseph Andrews [*q.v.*] to study. To him, said Schoff, "I owe more than can ever be repaid" (Stauffer, *post*, p. 240). He and Andrews, going to Paris in 1839 or 1840, worked for a while in the studio of Paul Delaroche. On returning to the United States in 1842, Schoff found employment in banknote work, and at the same time, with the aid of A. B. Durand [*q.v.*], who did some work on the plate, he executed his "Caius Marius on the Ruins of Carthage," after the painting by Vanderlyn, for publication by the Apollo Association. This plate, which he seems to have considered his best, was engraved in the regular

linear manner of the line-engraver on copper or steel, a manner progressively developed and hardened since the days of Dürer and Goltzius. An interesting and illuminating contrast is offered by Schoff's much later engraving after the "Bathers" of William Morris Hunt [*q.v.*], in which the line is freely and spiritedly varied, broken and twisted to translate the tones, color-values, even brush-marks, of the painting. In this departure from conventions one may find an aim akin to that of the "new school" of American wood engraving of the last quarter of the nineteenth century. Next to this interpretation of Hunt, almost a *tour de force,* there may be set the same engraver's "Bay of New York," after G. L. Brown, of a delicacy that reminds one of the plates by British engravers after Turner for Samuel Rogers' *Italy.*

Throughout much of his long professional life Schoff was kept busy with banknote work, a specialty which gave occupation to many engravers and which had much influence on steel engraving in the United States. Like many engravers of his time, he, too, had to turn his hands to minor jobs in the day's work, jobs which did not bring out the best in a man, weak and conventional conceptions which resulted in inconsequential engraving. But plates such as those of his mentioned above are outstanding, as are his engravings of portraits such as those of William Penn and R. W. Emerson (after S. W. Rowse). He also engraved some of F. O. C. Darley's illustrations, and during the etching vogue of the eighties he reproduced paintings in etching, to which process he brought rich experience.

Schoff was married on Nov. 7, 1843, in Williamsburg, L. I., to Maria Josephine Rosalina Hastings (1824–82), by whom he had five children. He lived at different times in Boston, Washington, New York, Newtonville, Mass., and Brandon, Vt., and died in Norfolk, Conn.

[D. M. Stauffer, *Am. Engravers upon Copper and Steel* (1907), I, 240–41; W. H. Schoff, *The Descendants of Jacob Schoff* (1910); Frank Weitenkampf, *Am. Graphic Art* (2nd ed., 1924); S. R. Koehler's chapter on American etching in *Die Vervielfältigende Kunst der Gegenwart* (Vienna, 1892), pp. 218–19; *Who's Who in America*, 1903–05; *Hartford Courant,* May 7, 1904.]   F. W.

SCHOFIELD, HENRY (Aug. 7, 1866–Aug. 15, 1918), law teacher and legal writer, was born in Dudley, Mass., the son of John and Margaret (Thompson) Schofield. He was educated at Nichols Academy in Dudley and at Harvard College and Law School (A.B. 1887, A.M. and LL.B. 1890). Admitted to the Illinois bar in 1890, he practised for a year in Chicago and then spent a year in Washington as assistant to

Charles H. Aldrich, solicitor general of the United States. Returning to Chicago in 1892, he became associated in practice with Henry M. Bacon. From 1900 to 1902 he was assistant corporation counsel of Chicago. At this time the relations of the city to the local traction systems were giving rise to important questions relating to corporate franchises and the city's powers under its charter. "Constitutional provisions and successive statutory measures raised complex issues calling for great accuracy of research and large understanding of fundamental principles. His [Schofield's] absolute mastery of the whole intricate subject was soon acknowledged" (J. H. Wigmore, Foreword to Schofield's *Essays, post,* p. vi).

On Oct. 23, 1902, he married Marie Therese Stehlin of Chicago, by whom he had four children. Shortly before his marriage he had given up active practice and become professor of law in Northwestern University, lecturing on equity and constitutional law. Regarding his ability to make legal problems interesting, a former student, Prof. Albert Kocourek, writes: "He seemed to make small use of notes or memoranda, but spoke informally, and with the most remarkable ease, clearness, and attraction. He did not make the mistake of taking too much for granted either in the direct or collateral information of his auditors. . . . He never sought in the classroom or elsewhere to make an impression. His object was to make himself understood, and in this he undoubtedly succeeded" (Schofield's *Essays,* p. xii).

By contrast his written style was involved and overcrowded with ideas, but enthusiastically logical. In his investigations of legal problems he sought to reach the right views primarily for his own satisfaction and for his classes, and not at all for publication. Once he had come to what seemed to him a final conclusion about a problem, he lost all interest in its written exposition. If prior to that point his fellow teachers had not succeeded in getting him to put his views in writing, it would then be too late for them to do so. He never wrote a book, but produced a large number of articles and comments on important decisions in legal periodicals. These were collected after his death as *Essays on Constitutional Law and Equity and Other Subjects* (2 vols., 1921).

Because of their difficult style and the absence of systematic treatment, these essays have not had a wide influence, but are valued by legal scholars. Schofield's analysis of significant cases is acute, and his original thinking often demonstrates the fallacy of traditional views. His at-

tention was much directed to constitutional problems which have not been thoroughly discussed by other writers, such as the relations between federal and state courts, and the full faith and credit clause. His essay on "Freedom of the Press in the United States" (*Papers and Proceedings . . . American Sociological Society,* 1914) is a pioneer article of great value and the only satisfactory discussion of the constitutional right of free speech as it existed before the World War.

Many of Schofield's habits conformed to the laymen's notion of a typical professor. He was frequently absent-minded and would become so absorbed in reading that he had to be summoned to a waiting class of students. When interested in an important legal decision he would delve for months into everything bearing upon it in the remotest way, and meanwhile "it would be difficult to get him to talk of anything else because he felt that other things could wait until the matter then on his mind should be settled to his own satisfaction" (Costigan, in *American Law School Review, post,* p. 407). Despite this concentration he had a very real awareness of life and was well informed about many practical affairs. The charm and learning of his conversation were vividly remembered. He invariably selected the topic, often a difficult legal question, and carried on the dialogue on his own terms, delivering with occasional interjections from the listener a luminous essay. Always quiet and unobtrusive, he made no mention of the prolonged illness which cut short his career, but carried on his teaching and writing to the last possible day.

[Albert Kocourek, "Death of Professor Schofield," in *Ill. Law Rev.,* Oct.–Nov 1918, reprinted in large part in Schofield's *Essays;* G. P. Costigan, Jr., "Henry Schofield," in *Northwestern Alumni Jour.,* Nov. 30, 1918, reprinted in *Am. Law School Rev.,* Feb. 1919; *Class of 1887, Harvard Coll., Twenty-fifth Anniversary, 1887–1912* (n.d.); *Harvard Alumni Bull.,* Nov. 28, 1918; *Who's Who in America,* 1916–17; *Chicago Daily Tribune,* Aug. 17, 1918.]   Z. C., Jr.

SCHOFIELD, JOHN McALLISTER (Sept. 29, 1831–Mar. 4, 1906), soldier, was born in Gerry, Chautauqua County, N. Y., the son of James and Caroline (McAllister) Schofield. His father, a Baptist clergyman, was then pastor of a church at Sinclairville, N. Y., but in 1843 he moved to Freeport, Ill., and became a home missionary in Illinois, Iowa, and Missouri. Educated in the local public schools, John spent one summer as a surveyor on public lands in northern Wisconsin and one winter as teacher in a district school. In 1849 he was offered an appointment as cadet at West Point. He graduated in 1853 as No. 7 in his class and, having abandoned his original intention of studying law, accepted his commission as brevet second lieutenant, 2nd Artillery, with station at Fort Moultrie, S. C. Receiving in December his commission as second lieutenant in the 1st Artillery, he joined his battery in Florida, where it was serving in connection with Seminole Indian troubles. Promoted first lieutenant in 1855, he was ordered to West Point as assistant professor of natural and experimental philosophy. In June 1857 he was married to Harriet, daughter of Prof. W. H. C. Bartlett, his chief in the department of philosophy; she died in Washington about 1889, leaving two sons and a daughter. In 1860, without resigning his commission, he left West Point on a year's leave of absence and became professor of physics at Washington University, St. Louis, Mo.

Relinquishing his leave at the opening of the Civil War, he was detailed as mustering officer for the state of Missouri; a few days later he was commissioned major in the 1st Missouri Volunteer Infantry and assisted in organizing that regiment. In June he became chief of staff to Gen. Nathaniel Lyon [q.v.] in his operations in Missouri and served until Lyon's death at the battle of Wilson's Creek, Aug. 10, 1861, when he assumed command of his volunteer regiment and reorganized it as artillery. He was offered a captaincy in the new 11th Infantry of the regular army but declined it and soon afterward was promoted to that grade in his own regiment. In November 1861 he became brigadier-general of volunteers and until the autumn of 1862 held various territorial commands. From October 1862 to April 1863 he commanded the "Army of the Frontier" engaged in field operations in Missouri. He was nominated as major-general of volunteers in November 1863 but, because of the tense political situation in Missouri and the opposition of certain factions, his nomination was not confirmed, and in March he reverted to his rank as brigadier-general. Since this brought him under the command of former juniors, he avoided embarrassments by applying for a new assignment and for a short time commanded a division of the XIV Army Corps in Tennessee. In May, having been appointed major-general, he returned to St. Louis as commander of the Department of the Missouri.

In February 1864 he assumed command of the XXIII Corps and of the Department and Army of the Ohio, with which he took part in Sherman's Atlanta campaign as one of the three army commanders. When Sherman started on his march to the sea, Gen. George Henry Thomas [q.v.] was given command of all troops left in the west and began his concentration at Nash-

ville, Tenn. Schofield, with his own XXIII Corps and part of the IV Corps, covered this concentration against Hood's renewed attempt to invade Tennessee. Gradually retiring upon Nashville, Schofield's force fought the fierce battle of Franklin, which badly shattered Hood's army, and then rejoined Thomas to take part in the battle of Nashville, which definitely put an end to all danger from Hood. For his services in this campaign he was made brigadier-general in the regular army in November 1864 and brevet major-general in March 1865. The XXIII Corps was then moved by rail to Washington and by sea to the mouth of the Cape Fear River, where Schofield assumed command of the newly formed Department of North Carolina, his troops consisting of his own corps and the two divisions of Gen. Albert Howe Terry [q.v.] from Fort Fisher. With this force he first occupied Wilmington, N. C., and then effected a junction with Sherman at Goldsboro, N. C., Mar. 23, his command becoming the center grand division of Sherman's army in the operations against Johnston. He accompanied Sherman at the final meeting with Johnston on Apr. 26, when the terms of surrender were agreed upon, and was designated as commissioner for execution of the details. He remained in command of the Department until the formation of a provisional state government in June.

At the close of the war he was offered command of a force, to be organized under the Mexican republican flag, replacing the fifty thousand men who had been concentrated on the Mexican border with a view to their possible use in connection with the Maximilian affair. Before anything had been done, however, the secretary of state proposed that he go to France, ostensibly on leave but actually as a confidential agent of the State Department to deal with Mexican affairs. He went to France, 1865–66, remaining until it had been decided that the French forces should be recalled from Mexico. Upon his return he was assigned to duty in Virginia, where his command was known as the Department of the Potomac, and later as the First Military District. In the spring of 1868, during the confusion incident to the impeachment of President Johnson, he was made secretary of war, but resigned upon Grant's inauguration. His duties, which had to do both with problems of reconstruction and of army reorganization, were most heavy and perplexing. While he was secretary he took steps toward the organization of a light artillery school at Fort Riley, Kan., later the Mounted Service School and finally the United States Cavalry School. Leaving the War Department, he was promoted major-general and assumed command first of the Department of the Missouri and later of the Division of the Pacific. In 1872 he spent three months in Hawaii, accompanied by a navy officer and by an army engineer, to report upon the military value of the islands to the United States and made recommendations that led to the acquisition of Pearl Harbor as a naval base. From 1876 to 1881 he was superintendent of the United States Military Academy. While he was there he served as president of the board to review the case of Gen. Fitz-John Porter [q.v.], dismissed from the service by sentence of a court martial for misconduct at the battle of Manassas. After a year's leave spent in Europe, he commanded successively the Divisions of the Pacific, of the Missouri, and of the Atlantic. In 1888, upon the death of Sheridan, he became commanding general of the army; promoted to the grade of lieutenant-general in February 1895, he was retired because of age in September. In 1891 he was married for a second time to Georgia Kilbourne of Keokuk, Iowa. His autobiography, *Forty-Six Years in the Army,* was published in 1897. He died in St. Augustine, Fla.

[See G. W. Cullum, *Biog. Reg. Officers and Grads. U. S. Mil. Acad.* (3 ed., 1891), vol. II ; *War of the Rebellion: Official Records (Army)* ; *Battles and Leaders of the Civil War* (4 vols., 1887–88) ; J. D. Cox, *The March to the Sea* (1906) and *Atlanta* (1909) ; obituary in *N. Y. Tribune,* Mar. 5, 1906. For the period after the war, the best source of information is Schofield's autobiography, *Forty-Six Years in the Army* (1897). information has also been supplied by Col. R. M. Schofield of Honolulu, his son.]   O. L. S., Jr.

SCHOFIELD, WILLIAM HENRY (Apr. 6, 1870–June 24, 1920), scholar and author, was born at Brockville, Ontario, son of the Rev. William Henry Schofield and Anna (Parker) Schofield. His father died when the boy was young, and it was left to his mother to guide his early development and form his character and mental habits. She was fortunately admirably fitted for this task. A gifted and precocious student, Schofield received his first academic degree (A.B.) in 1889 from Victoria College, then located at Cobourg. After three years of teaching as master of modern languages at the Collegiate Institute, Hamilton, Ont., he entered the graduate school of Harvard University and received the degree of Ph.D. in 1895.

For the following two years he was in Europe as traveling fellow, studying medieval literature with Gaston Paris at the Collège de France and Old Norse with Sophus Bugge at Christiania. These two great scholars made a deep impression on him, and all the rest of his life he gratefully referred to them as his masters.

In Norway he was something of a phenomenon. He soon acquired a fluent command of the spoken language ; young, with an attractive and ingratiating personality, abounding in energy and enthusiasm, he was universally popular in the society of the Norwegian capital, and might have become a social lion, had not conscientious application to his studies held him to his books. His visit to Norway fell in the flowering time of Norwegian literature, the age of Ibsen and Björnson, Lie and Kielland. In later years he was accustomed to enliven his lectures at Harvard with anecdotes of his personal associations with the great men themselves. He made it his mission to correct misconceptions of American civilization current in Scandinavia, particularly after the appearance of Knut Hamsun's witty, temperamental, and one-sided book, *Fra det moderne Amerikas Aandsliv* (1889). A fruit of these efforts was an article on "Amerikas Universiteter" published in the Danish periodical *Tilskueren* (September 1897), which attracted much favorable comment. Interesting testimony of the impression which he made on cultivated Scandinavians is to be found in Georg Brandes's "Dansk og Norsk" (*Samlede Skrifter,* 1905, vol. XV).

In 1897 Schofield returned to America to resume his academic career as instructor in English at Harvard. From 1902 till 1906 he served as assistant professor in the same department, being appointed in the latter year professor of comparative literature, a post he held until his death. In connection with his new department he founded the series of *Harvard Studies in Comparative Literature,* of which he was himself editor. He continued to develop his interest in Scandinavian culture, giving the course in Old Norse instituted some years before by Prof. G. L. Kittredge and adding courses in the Dano-Norwegian language and Dano-Norwegian dramatists considered in their relations to European literature. As president of the American-Scandinavian Foundation for three and one-half years he labored energetically and successfully to promote intellectual cooperation between the United States and the Northern European countries.

Besides numerous articles contributed to American, Danish, French, and German periodicals, he published a series of books in widely various fields of scholarship: *Studies in the Libeaus Desconus* (1895) ; *The Home of the Eddic Poems* (1899), from the Norwegian of Sophus Bugge; *English Literature, from the Norman Conquest to Chaucer* (1906) ; *Chivalry in English Literature* (1912) ; *Mythical Bards and The*

Life of William Wallace (1920), issued in the year of his death. His scholarly contributions are distinguished by originality and independence of thought, careful organization, and an individual charm of style. He set the example corresponding to his precepts, demanding from his students attention to form no less than to substance.

On Sept. 4, 1907, he married Mrs. Mary Lyon Cheney of Boston, who accompanied him on a journey to Iceland and its saga-steads. In 1907–08 he was exchange professor at Berlin; in 1911, lecturer at the Sorbonne and the University of Copenhagen; in 1918, exchange professor at five Western colleges, posts which he filled with great distinction. During the World War he was active as a speaker for the National Security League and chairman of the Committee on International Relations in Education, with headquarters at Washington. He died at Peterboro, N. H., where a beautiful stone church, the gift of his wife, is inseparably associated with his memory.

[*Harvard Univ. Gazette,* May 7, 1921; *Who's Who in America,* 1920–21; D. R. Keys, in *Canadian Mag.,* Aug. 1906; *N. Y. Times,* June 25, 1920; personal acquaintance.]   F. S. C.

SCHOLTE, HENDRIK PETER (Sept. 25, 1805–Aug. 25, 1868), clergyman, pioneer, colonist, was born at Amsterdam, in the Netherlands, the son of Jan Hendrik Scholte, a box manufacturer, and Johanna Dorothea Roelofsz, daughter of an Amsterdam broker. He had excellent schooling, but at sixteen was compelled by his father's death to leave school and take charge of the factory. Left the sole survivor of the family by the death of his mother and brother, he sold the business and resumed his studies in Oct. 1827, at the Amsterdam Athenæum Illustre. Impressed by the atheistic tendencies of the time, especially among students, he decided to prepare for the Christian ministry, and entered the University of Leyden in May 1829. The next year his studies were interrupted by the bloodless "ten days' campaign" against Belgium's claim to independence from the Netherlands, for which service each of the student volunteers received a huge gold medal from a rich and patriotic Dutch lady. In May 1832 he received the degree of doctor of theology; in November he married Sara Maria Brand, daughter of a sugar refiner who had bought packing cases of his father.

Scholte soon became the leading spirit in a group of young clergymen who protested against the secularism of the State Church, seceded from it in 1834 in the name of a purer Christianity, were persecuted, fined, and imprisoned, and saw their congregations dispersed by police and troops. He edited a periodical, *De Reformatie,* devoted to the dissenting movement, and in this and a series of pamphlets urged emigration as an escape from intolerable ecclesiastical conditions in Holland. An emigration association was formed at Utrecht in 1846, with Scholte as president. In October a preliminary group of thirty sailed to the United States and reported favorably from St. Louis. The main body of emigrants, counting some eight hundred souls, left Holland in April 1847 in four sailing vessels. Scholte's wife having died in 1842, he had later married M. H. E. Krantz. Three daughters of the first marriage and two sons of the second grew to maturity. Scholte and his family traveled by steamer to Boston, whence he proceeded to Albany and Washington to secure information about lands open to settlement. In June 1847 the reunited colonists traveled by rail, canal, and wagon from Baltimore to St. Louis. Scholte and four others then proceeded by boat to Keokuk and by wagon on into Iowa to spy out the land, choosing a location in the newly formed Marion County, near the Des Moines River.

On the day of his arrival at the chosen site (which he named Pella after the place of refuge of the early Christians in Palestine, persecuted by Rome), Scholte immediately contracted with the few settlers in this frontier region for the purchase of all their claims, and entered new lands with the government to a total of 18,000 acres. Upon the arrival of the colonists he promptly had them all declare their intention to become citizens of the United States. Similarly, he insisted on the teaching of English in the school established and encouraged the adoption of American methods and standards. He had the town of Pella platted in September 1847 and was largely instrumental in the location there in 1853 of Central University (later Central College); he gave the grounds, contributed to the funds, and was president of the board of trustees.

The Dominie was personally active in every aspect of the development of the new community. He was gentleman farmer, owner of saw mills and brick and lime kilns, land agent, notary, printer, editor and publisher, broker, banker, express agent, dealer in farm implements, attorney, as well as clergyman; and through all these activities in a rapidly developing community he contrived not to amass a fortune. He built a church at his own expense and preached in it without salary. He took an active interest in politics; he was delegate at large from Iowa to the Chicago convention that nominated Abraham Lincoln, and was recognized as the outstanding representative of the new foreign vote which the supporters of Lincoln had the foresight to cultivate. He died at Pella, Iowa, shortly before his sixty-third birthday.

Scholte's publications after coming to America include *Eene Stem Uit Pella* (Amsterdam, 1848) and *Tweede Stem uit Pella* ('s Bosch, 1848). For some time he was editor of the *Pella Gazette*.

[Anthony Brummelkamp and A. C. van Raalte, *Landverhuizing, of waarom bevorderen wij de Volksverhuizing en wel naar Noord-Amerika en niet naar Java* (1846); John Nollen, *De Afscheiding: Een Gedenkschrift* (1897); Kommer van Stigt, *Geschiedenis van Pella, Iowa, en Omgeving* (Pella, 1897); Cyrenus Cole, "A Bit of Holland in America," *Midland Monthly*, Feb. 1895, and "Pella—A Bit of Holland in America," *Annals of Iowa*, Jan. 1898; Jacob Van der Zee, *The Hollanders of Iowa* (1912); *The Hist. of Marion County, Iowa* (1881), p. 670; W. M. Donnel, *Pioneers of Marion County* (1872).]   J. S. N.

SCHOMER, NAHUM MEIR (Dec. 18, 1849–Nov. 24, 1905), Yiddish novelist and playwright, was born in Nesvizh (Government of Minsk), Russia, a son of Isaac and Hodie Goldberg Shaikewitz. The name Schomer, his *nom de plume*, he afterwards adopted also as a family name, under which his surviving children in the United States are known. He was educated at home and at the famous Talmudic seminary of Volozhin. His orthodox parents intended him for the rabbinate, but his own inclinations led him into other fields. As a youngster he was known as a clever story-teller, with a fertile and inexhaustible imagination which he was to draw on later in his chosen vocation. Marrying at the age of twenty Dinah Bercinsky in Pinsk, he attempted to establish himself there as a merchant. Here he made his literary début in Hebrew journals with stories, historical sketches, and popular scientific articles, but soon relinquished Hebrew in favor of the common vernacular of the Jewish masses, the Yiddish. Shortly after his marriage he became manager of his uncle's business in Wilna, which necessitated some traveling. When he visited Roumania and in Bucharest came in contact with the Yiddish theatre, he resolved to become a dramatic author. Moving to Odessa, he became a theatrical manager and playwright, writing *Lebensbilder*, dramas of current life, the first in this genre to be produced in the Yiddish language. After the Yiddish theatre was closed in Russia by government decree he emigrated in 1889 to New York.

Schomer was an extremely prolific writer. In addition to fifteen novels in Hebrew he was the author of over two hundred in Yiddish, some of which are of bulky proportions; many others appeared in the Yiddish dailies. Over thirty of his plays were produced in Russia and later in the United States. He also experimented in New York as editor and publisher of several magazines. His place in Yiddish literature is that of a pioneer who sensed the need of the masses for a new kind of reading matter to replace the older folk-tales and morality chapbooks. At the time when he began to write, the Jews of the great ghettos in Russia, Lithuania, and Poland were shut up in their communities. Educated Jews, if interested in Jewish culture at all, confined themselves exclusively to Hebrew, while the uneducated masses, if able to read, were restricted solely to Yiddish, in those days considered a mere colloquial jargon. It was to the latter that Schomer addressed himself when he began writing. His novels were partly historical, partly reflections of the Jewish life of his immediate surroundings and of small towns and villages, and to a large extent imitations of French and German "Schundroman." As his language was simple, near to that spoken by the common people, his novels became so popular that in the span of little more than a decade his readers numbered hundreds of thousands and his name was a household word. With the development of the Yiddish literature and the springing up of more gifted talents, Schomer was the subject of violent attacks by his contemporaries, who accused him of serious literary deficiencies and of a deleterious effect upon the popular taste. But in spite of this harsh criticism he is to be credited with valuable services to Jewish life and literature. He helped to develop the habit of reading among the Yiddish-speaking masses, to mitigate the fanaticism that prevailed in small rural and urban communities, and to introduce to them entirely new conceptions of life.

[Zalmen Reisen, *Lexicon fun der Yiddisher Literatur*, vol. IV (Wilna, 1929), containing a long but admittedly incomplete list of Schomer's works; M. Pines, *Die Geschichte der jüdischdeutschen Literatur* (Leipzig, 1913); Leo Wiener, *The Hist. of Yiddish Lit. in the Nineteenth Century* (1899); Hutchins Hapgood, *The Spirit of the Ghetto* (1902); Leon Kobrin, *Erinerungen fun a Yiddishen Dramaturg* (1925), vol. I; *Am. Hebrew*, Dec. 1, 1905; *N. Y. Times*, Nov. 25, 1905.]   I. S.

SCHOOLCRAFT, HENRY ROWE (Mar. 28, 1793–Dec. 10, 1864), explorer, ethnologist, was born in Albany County, N. Y., the son of Lawrence and Margaret Anne Barbara (Rowe) Schoolcraft and the great-grandson of James Calcraft, as the name was then spelled, who emigrated from England to Albany County, N. Y., in 1727. Henry enjoyed the opportunities of the common school in Hamilton, N. Y., and was able to matriculate in Union College at fifteen. Later he attended Middlebury College. He favored language and natural science, especially geology and mineralogy. His father was a glass maker, and the boy studied this industry and in 1817 started at Utica, N. Y., a book on glass making. He began his explorations with a visit to the mineral regions of southern Missouri and Arkansas in 1817–18, then Indian country. His report, *A View of the Lead Mines of Missouri,* was published in New York in 1819. By this time he was considered a competent geologist, and he was sent on the Cass exploring expedition in 1820 to the upper Mississippi and the Lake Superior copper region. His *Narrative Journal of Travels through the Northwestern Regions of the United States . . . to the Sources of the Mississippi River* appeared in 1821. Later, in 1832, he made another expedition to the sources of the Mississippi, which he described in *Narrative of an Expedition through the Upper Mississippi to Itasca Lake, the Actual Source of the Mississippi* (1834), reissued as *Summary Narrative* in 1855 with an account of the earlier expedition of 1820 and an appendix of official reports and scientific papers. His wide acquaintance with the Indians led to his appointment in 1822 as Indian agent for the tribes of Lake Superior. Thereafter his predilections were for those Algonquian tribes inhabiting the vast forests around the great lake. In 1823 he married a quarter-blood Chippewa girl, who, though educated in Europe, understood and shared much of the primitive Indian culture. She died in 1842.

The importance of the Indian subject was firmly fixed in his mind, and for the remainder of his life he pursued his chosen work in season and out of season. Encouraged by the government, whose need was data on the Indian problem, he was given official promotion as superintendent of Indian affairs for Michigan in 1836 and served in the department until 1841. During this period he negotiated several treaties with the Chippewa, probably most important of which was the treaty of Mar. 28, 1836, whereby the United States obtained title to the northern third of the lower peninsula and the eastern half of the upper peninsula of Michigan. Always active in forwarding the study of Indians, he helped to found the Historical Society of Michigan in 1828 and the Algic Society of Detroit in 1832. In many ways he promoted the study of the ethnology of the Indian, both at home and abroad. His

literary remains are of impressive bulk. They consist of descriptions of his explorations, writings on the manners and customs of the Indians, and tales and legends. Of these perhaps the most important are *Algic Researches* (2 vols., 1839) concerning Indian mental characteristics, *Oneota,* originally issued in eight paper covers (1844–45) describing the Indian history and prospects, *Notes on the Iroquois* (1847), a popular account, and *Personal Memories of . . . Thirty Years with the Indian Tribes* (1851). Most of these works were literary rather than scientific, as is characteristic of the unspecialized anthropological science of the period. Realizing that the scientific material he had collected should be set in order, he projected an Indian encyclopaedia; but this was set aside for the great work on which his reputation as an ethnologist must rest. Subvented by the government, he began in 1851 *Historical and Statistical Information Respecting the History, Condition, and Prospects of the Indian Tribes of the United States* (6 pts., 1851–57). This work, six folio volumes, excellently illustrated with steel engravings from paintings by Seth Eastman, was a collaboration dominated by Schoolcraft. In spite of shortcomings, it contains valuable and indispensable material on the Indians and is a monument to a great American explorer and ethnologist.

Schoolcraft was fluent, interesting, convincing, and made a good public appearance. He traveled much and received many honors. He published nothing after 1857, and it is said that rheumatism and paralysis put an end to his work. He was survived by his wife, Mary (Howard) Schoolcraft of Beaufort District, N. C., to whom he was married in 1847.

[“Sketches of the Life of Henry R. Schoolcraft,” in *Personal Memories, ante*; G. W. Samson, *Henry R. Schoolcraft* (1864?); J. V. Brower, “The Mississippi River and its Sources,” *Minn. Hist. Soc. Colls.,* vol. VII (1893); J. H. Baker, “The Sources of the Mississippi,” *Ibid.,* vol. VI (1894); information from the files of the Office of Indian Affairs through the courtesy of Brent Morgan.]   W. H.

SCHÖPF, JOHANN DAVID (Mar. 8, 1752– Sept. 10, 1800), physician, scientist, traveler, was born in Germany at Wunsiedel in the principality of Bayreuth. The son of a well-to-do merchant, he began his education under private tutors, attended the Gymnasium at Hof 1767–70, and studied medicine and the natural sciences at the University of Erlangen 1770–73. Living in the Fichtelgebirge, he had studied mineralogy and metallurgy from his early years, and under Prof. J. C. D. von Schreber he became a serious student of zoölogy and botany. After hearing lectures on forestry at Berlin, he made a trip through Bohemia and Austria to the cities of northern Italy, took his medical degree at Erlangen in 1776, and began practice at Ansbach. The next year, giving up his plans for a voyage to India, he accepted a surgeon's commission in an Ansbach regiment destined for service with the British army in North America and arrived at New York June 4, 1777. His hope of seeing with his own eyes the flora, fauna, and geology of the New World was deferred, however, for six years, while his regiment did duty at New York and on the eastern tip of Long Island, in Rhode Island, and at Philadelphia. Schöpf, meanwhile, learned English well and read everything obtainable about America. At the close of the war he got permission to travel and on July 22, 1783, set out from New York. Accompanying him on the first half of his itinerary was an Englishman, Robert Hare, father of the chemist Robert Hare [q.v.].

They crossed New Jersey to Philadelphia and, after inspecting the Moravian towns of Bethlehem and Nazareth, journeyed through Reading, Lebanon, Carlisle, and Shippensburg to Fort Pitt. They returned through Maryland to Baltimore, Alexandria, Va., and Annapolis, reaching Philadelphia early in November. Schöpf then started south by the so-called "back road," which enabled him to pay a visit, rich for them both in friendship and mutual helpfulness, to G. H. E. Mühlenberg [q.v.] at Lancaster. At Leesburg, Va., the oncoming winter compelled him to change his route; he turned eastward to Fredericksburg and Richmond, continued on to Williamsburg and Yorktown, and then proceeded south through the Carolinas to Charleston, where he took sail for Florida. On Mar. 29, 1784, he embarked at St. Augustine for the Bahamas, and in October of that year he was once more with his friends in Bayreuth.

The fifteen years remaining to him, varied by travel in Italy and Holland, were peaceful, happy, and honorable. In 1795 he was created a Prussian Geheimer Hofrat and made president of the Ansbach Medicinal-collegium, which he continued to preside over when it was united in 1797 with that of Bayreuth. More than any other German of his time he made America his study. Among his articles and monographs are the first systematic work on American geology, *Beyträge zur Mineralogischen Kenntniss des Östlichen Theils von Nordamerika und seiner Gebürge* (Erlangen, 1787); the first paper on American ichthyology; the first on American frogs and turtles; one on the American climate and diseases; and a full American materia medica, *Materia Medica Americana, Potissimum Regni Vegetabilis* (Erlangen, 1787; reprinted in the Lloyd

Library Reproduction Series, Cincinnati, 1903). His last work was an admirable *Historia Testitudinum, Iconibus Illustrata* (Fasc. I–VI, Erlangen, 1792–1801). In all these works he shows himself an able descriptive scientist, but the whole man is seen only in his masterpiece, his *Reise durch einige der mittlern und südlichen vereinigten nordamerikanischen Staaten nach Ost-Florida und den Bahama-Inseln* (2 vols., Erlangen, 1788; American translation by A. J. Morrison, *Travels in the Confederation*, 2 vols., 1911). No aspect of man or nature escaped his eye and pencil. Among travelers in America it would be difficult to find his equal in combined breadth of interests, accuracy of observation and judgment, wit, and serene good temper. Among lesser figures he is one of the best examplars of the culture of the Enlightenment. His early death resulted from a malady of the throat.

[J. G. Meusel, *Lexikon der vom Jahr 1750 bis 1800 verstorbenen Teutschen Schriftsteller*, vol. XII (Leipzig, 1812), pp. 364–71, with full bibliographical direction; Friedrich Ratzel, article in *Allgemeine Deutsche Biographie*, vol. XXXII (Leipzig, 1891); Hermann Peters, "Johann David Schöpf, Ein deutscher Naturforscher des vorigen Jahrhunderts in Nordamerika," *Pharmaceutische Rundschau* (Milwaukee), July 1895, the best biography; Fred. Hoffman, "Fragmentary Notes from the Reports of Two Early Naturalists on North America," *Pharmaceutical Rev.*, Aug. 1898; A. J. Morrison, "Doctor Johann David Schoepf," *Ger.-Am. Annals*, Sept.-Dec. 1910; J. G. Rosengarten, *The German Soldier in the Wars of the U. S.* (2nd ed., 1890).]
G. H. G.

SCHOTT, CHARLES ANTHONY (Aug. 7, 1826–July 31, 1901), geodesist, magnetician, originally called Carl Anton, was born in the south German city of Mannheim, Baden, the eldest of four children of Anton Carl and Anna Maria (Hoffman) Schott. The family belonged to the middle class, the father being a merchant, and was in comfortable circumstances. Schott attended the public schools and lyceum of his native city until he was fourteen and then was sent to the Technische Hochschule at Karlsruhe, where he graduated in 1847 as a civil engineer. He had looked forward to entering the engineering service of the state, but the disturbed political conditions of the time prevented this. In the revolution of 1848 he served for a short time in the liberal ranks but found military life uncongenial. At this time, too, his father met with reverses in business and, being thrown on his own resources, Schott set out for the United States, arriving at New York in August 1848. In December 1848 he became a computer in the Washington office of the United States Coast Survey; the following spring he was assigned to field duty as hydrographic draftsman aboard a survey vessel but a year later was ordered back to the computing division in Washington. In 1853 he became a citizen of the United States, and on Jan. 1, 1854, he married Teresa Gildermeister in Washington.

To a sound training and natural ability, Schott added the qualities of industry and thoroughness. He won early recognition in the coast survey; in 1855 he was made chief of the computing division, and for nearly forty-five years he directed the work of that important division, playing no small part during these formative years in setting and maintaining high scientific standards. Into the computing division came the field data of the survey, which were tabulated, adjusted, correlated, and interpreted. The work involved various technical and scientific aspects of astronomy, geodesy, magnetism, map projections, and tides; to each of these subjects Schott contributed a number of papers that dealt primarily with the correlation and interpretation of observations. His principal contributions were in the fields of geodesy and terrestrial magnetism, both of which were in a relatively early stage of development. In 1898 the French Academy of Sciences awarded him its Wilde Prize with the citation that "the whole of this work furnishes one of the most important contributions in the history of terrestrial magnetism." He also wrote a number of memoirs dealing with meteorology and climatology, especially that of the Arctic regions, which appeared principally in the *Smithsonian Contributions to Knowledge* between 1859 and 1876. In 1869 he was a member of the government party sent to Springfield, Ill., to observe a solar eclipse, and in 1870 he was sent to Catania, Sicily, to observe the solar eclipse of December of that year. His work and attainments received wide recognition and brought him membership in numerous scientific societies, both at home and abroad; in 1872 he was elected to the National Academy of Sciences.

At the beginning of 1900, he was relieved of the administrative duties of chief of the computing division. He now devoted himself to the discussion of the arc measurements in the United States that resulted from the extension triangulation executed up to that time. This necessitated the adjustment of all the triangulation into a single net, a work that involved an enormous amount of computation. In the spring of the following year he fell ill, and in July he died in Washington. His first wife had died in 1862, leaving an only son. On Sept. 28, 1863, at Prairie Home, Ill., he married Bertha Gildermeister, a sister of his deceased wife, by whom he had four children.

[*Science*, Jan. 12, 1900, Aug. 9, 1901; *Bull. Philosophical Soc. of Washington*, Aug. 1905; *Nat. Acad.*

Sci. Biog. Memoirs, vol. VIII (1919); *Evening Star* (Washington, D. C.), Aug. 1901.]   H.A.M.

SCHOULER, JAMES (Mar. 20, 1839–Apr. 16, 1920), lawyer and historian, was born in West Cambridge (now Arlington), Mass. He was the son of William Schouler [*q.v.*], a native of Kilbarchan, Scotland, who was brought to America in early life, and Frances Eliza Warren, who came of colonial Massachusetts stock. In Scotland the name is often spelled Scouler; this conforms to the pronunciation still used by the American family. From Cincinnati, where the family were living at the time, James went to Harvard in 1855. His father's journalistic ventures were never financially successful, and while the son was at Harvard William Schouler returned to Boston in greatly straitened circumstances. Notwithstanding the family misfortunes young Schouler took an active part in college life, became editor of the *Harvard Magazine,* and won prizes in public speaking. He received his bachelor's degree in 1859. After teaching for a year in St. Paul's School, Concord, N. H., he began the study of law in the office of George D. Guild in Boston. At this time, also, he served as private secretary to his father, who had just been appointed adjutant-general of Massachusetts. He was admitted to the bar in 1862, but soon responded to Lincoln's call for volunteers and was commissioned second lieutenant of the 43rd Regiment, Massachusetts Volunteers. He went with his regiment to the coast of North Carolina, where he was detailed on signal service and saw little fighting. A fever which he contracted on his way home from this expedition greatly aggravated a physical defect which had already developed to some extent and which was to influence profoundly the whole future course of his life, that of deafness.

On his return to Boston in 1863 he took up the practice of law. A few years later he won an important case in the Supreme Court of the United States involving war claims against the government (*Hosmer* vs. *The United States, 9 Wall,* 432); this was the beginning of a fairly lucrative practice, much of which was concerned with war claims. In 1869 he opened a branch office in Washington, but as his deafness increased he turned more and more to legal writing. He had begun to contribute articles to the *American Law Review* (July 1867–October 1869), and for a time (1871–73) he published in Washington a legal quarterly, *The United States Jurist.* Treatises on the laws of domestic relations (1870), personal property (2 vols., 1873–76), bailments (1880), executors and administrators (1883), and wills (1887) established his reputation as a legal writer and brought him large royalties. For a number of years he gave annual courses of lectures in the law schools of Boston University (1883–1902) and the National University at Washington (1888–1908). In 1891 he was invited by Herbert B. Adams to give a course of lectures on American history to graduate students at the Johns Hopkins University and this connection continued until 1908; he then retired but established there, and later by his will endowed, a lectureship in history and political science which bears his name.

Schouler had published an article, "Our Diplomacy during the Rebellion," in the *North American Review* in April 1866, and about that time began to think of writing a history of the United States supplementing Bancroft. In 1873 he began serious work, but he was delayed in completing the first volumes by difficulties in finding a publisher. Five of the seven volumes of his *History of the United States of America under the Constitution* (covering altogether the period 1783–1877) appeared between 1880 and 1891, the sixth in 1899, and the seventh in 1913. On this work his reputation as a historian rests. This was the first attempt to cover in a scholarly way the period from the Revolution to the Civil War, although John Bach McMaster [*q.v.*] soon entered the same field. The latter's *History of the People of the United States* (8 vols., 1883–1913) appeared almost contemporaneously. The two works were written from quite different points of view and from different sources. To a large extent they supplement each other. Although Schouler's interpretation was primarily political and constitutional, he did not neglect social and economic forces. Yet such topics as population, agriculture, industry, commerce, education, literature, and religion are dealt with in separate chapters and not closely integrated with political events. He recognized, though to a lesser extent than McMaster, the importance of economic matters, but attempted no economic interpretation of history. As to his methods, Schouler says: "Original records and information are preferable to all others; but secondary sources of knowledge I have largely accepted as a labor-saving means, where I could bring my own accumulated knowledge and habits of verification to bear upon them, so as to judge fairly of their comparative worth" (*Historical Briefs,* p. 42). He was an industrious worker and explored some sources that had not been used before, in particular the manuscript papers of James Monroe and Andrew Johnson, and the recently published *Diary of Gideon Welles.* The first volumes of his *History* made the greatest impression. As he approached the Civil War, his narrative was colored by his own convictions of the righteousness of the Northern cause. In his last volume he presented an able vindication of Andrew Johnson. His style had certain eccentricities, which were duly criticised by his reviewers, but it had the merit of being cogent and readable. His other historical writings of importance were: *Thomas Jefferson* (1893); *Historical Briefs, with a Biography* (1896); *Constitutional Studies, State and Federal* (1897); *Alexander Hamilton* (1901); *Eighty Years of Union, Being a Short History of the United States, 1783–1865* (1903); *Americans of 1776* (1906); and *Ideals of the Republic* (1908).

Schouler was a man of striking appearance, cordial and kindly in manner, and not lacking in humor. He was always glad to confer with his students, although it was frequently necessary for them to write out the questions or topics on which they sought his advice. Music was his main recreation and he was a constant attendant at symphony concerts, using a mechanical device which enabled him to derive some pleasure from them. On Dec. 14, 1870, he married Emily Fuller Cochran of Boston; the union proved a happy one, although there were no children. She died in 1904 and Schouler spent the remaining years of his life at what had been for many years their summer home at Intervale, N. H.

[Edward Stanwood, "Memoir of James Schouler," *Mass. Hist. Soc. Proceedings,* LIV (1922), 283–88; "Biography," in his own *Historical Briefs* (1896), pp. 169–310; L. E. Ellis, "James Schouler," in *Miss. Valley Hist. Rev.,* Sept. 1929; critical reviews by W. A. Dunning, *Am. Hist. Rev.,* July 1900, and by H. B. Learned, *Ibid.,* April 1917; obituary in *Boston Evening Transcript,* Apr. 17, 1920; notes prepared for the writer by the historian's brother, Rev. William Schouler, of Baltimore.]   J.H.L.

SCHOULER, WILLIAM (Dec. 31, 1814–Oct. 24, 1872), editor and historian, was born at Kilbarchan, near Glasgow, Scotland, his parents being James and Margaret (Clark) Schouler. The family name was often spelled Scouler in Scotland and was pronounced "Skooler." The senior Schouler, a calico printer, came to the United States in 1816 and after brief residence on Staten Island, N. Y., went to Taunton and Lynn, Mass., and in 1832 engaged in textile manufacture at West Cambridge, Mass., a district later set off as part of the town of Arlington. After a common school education, the son learned his father's trade, but his primary interest was in politics, not calico. As a youth he sent readable contributions on political topics to the *Yeoman's Gazette,* Concord, Mass. He had meantime become a practical cloth printer, and he had married, Oct. 6, 1835, Frances Eliza Warren, daughter of Isaac Warren, by whom he had a daughter and a son, James [*q.v.*].

In 1841, with William Stevens Robinson [*q.v.*] as assistant editor a year later, he undertook to publish and edit the *Lowell Courier,* which had undergone vicissitudes but in their hands became an influential daily newspaper, later known as the *Lowell Courier-Citizen.* In the 1840's it supported the Whig party. After serving in the Massachusetts House of Representatives in 1844, 1845, and 1847, Schouler in 1847 sold his interest at Lowell and became editor-in-chief of the *Boston Daily Atlas.* He again served in the Massachusetts legislature as representative from Boston, 1849–53. Although he had been a stanch supporter of Daniel Webster, he indignantly repudiated his political leadership after the famous speech of Mar. 7, 1850. This change of policy caused so many New England Whigs to brand Schouler as a traitor that he gave up his Boston editorship and in 1853 bought a part ownership in the *Cincinnati Gazette.* This he sold three years later and soon became editor of the *Ohio State Journal* at Columbus. He was a delegate in 1856 to the first Republican National Convention. His political contacts presently brought him an appointment as adjutant-general of Ohio, but in 1858 an offer of the editorship of the *Boston Atlas and Daily Bee* led him to return to Massachusetts. In 1860 he was appointed adjutant-general of the commonwealth, an office he held until at the end of 1866 Gov. Alexander Bullock removed him, apparently on grounds of his hostility to his former Lowell fellow citizen, Gen. Benjamin Franklin Butler (*Boston Morning Journal, post*). This position at the Massachusetts state house gave Schouler an opportunity before and during the Civil War to reveal both his remarkable executive ability and his accurate, painstaking historianship. His *A History of Massachusetts in the Civil War* (2 vols., 1868–71) contains enough that is autobiographical to place its author among the dynamic figures of his era. His annual report of Dec. 31, 1860, included a warning of impending war that stirred Massachusetts toward preparation. In 1862 as adjutant-general, he made a notable inspection of Massachusetts troops beyond the Potomac, and later, through his skilful handling of the situation, a repetition in Boston of the New York draft riots of 1863 was prevented. He won the lasting admiration of Gov. John Albion Andrew [*q.v.*], whose correspondence, much of it unpublished, at the Massachusetts Historical Society contains many references to Schouler's activities and achievements; Andrew's last official act was to express his gratitude to Schouler.

Schouler's home in his last years was at West Roxbury. There he gratified the tastes of a scholarly man, fond of historical studies and the British classics. In 1868 he once more served in the Massachusetts legislature, and during 1870 he contributed to the *Boston Morning Journal* his "Political and Personal Recollections," a valuable source book for students of Massachusetts and American political and military history. In 1872 he was of the Republicans who bolted Grant, and at his death was a candidate for presidential elector on the Greeley ticket.

[See Benjamin and W. R. Cutter, *Hist. of the Town of Arlington, Mass.* (1880) for notes on the Schouler family; F. W. Coburn, *Hist. of Lowell and Its People* (1920), vol. I, for Schouler's editorship of the *Lowell Courier;* complete file of *Lowell Courier* from 1841, believed to be the only one in existence, in Concord, Mass. Pub. Lib.; archives of Adjutant-General's office, Mass. State House, for Civil War activities; James Schouler, *Hist. Briefs* (1896); William Schouler, *A Hist. of Mass. in the Civil War* (2 vols., 1868–71), which contains autobiog. material; obituary in *Boston Morning Jour.,* Oct. 25, 1872.]   F. W. C.

SCHRADIECK, HENRY (Apr. 29, 1846– Mar. 25, 1918), violinist, teacher, conductor, was born in Hamburg, Germany, the son of Heinrich Friedrich Schradieck, and Elizabeth Catharina Johanna (Rutting) Schradieck. He received his first violin lessons from his father, starting on his fourth birthday, and in his sixth year made his first public appearance, playing Beethoven's Sonata in F, *Opus* 17. The distinguished violinist, Teresa Milanollo, heard him play when he was eight years of age, and arranged for his instruction at the Brussels Conservatory, where he studied with Hubert Léonard for four years, winning the second prize in 1857, and the first in 1858. He then studied for two years with Ferdinand David at Leipzig and in 1863 became concert-master of the Bremen Orchestra and violin soloist at Reinthaler's *Privatkonzerte.* He taught violin at the Moscow Conservatory from 1864 to 1868, and lived during this period at Nicholas Rubinstein's home, being closely associated also with Anton Rubinstein, and with Tschaikowsky. He was concert-master of the philharmonic concerts at Hamburg for the following four years and then went to Leipzig, where he became concert-master of the *Gewandhaus* orchestra, leader of the violins at the opera, and professor of violin at the Conservatory succeeding David. In 1882 he was married to J. Alice Bechtel, an American studying in Germany.

The Leipzig years were the most brilliant of Schradieck's career. He was associated with Edvard Grieg, Pablo Sarasate, Joseph Joachim, Carl Reinecke, Salomon Jadassohn, E. F. Richter, Leopold Auer, and Joseph and Henri

Wieniawski, just as he had enjoyed frequent contacts with Brahms in Hamburg. In 1883 he accepted an invitation to become teacher of violin at the Cincinnati College of Music, Cincinnati, Ohio, where he stayed for six years. He also conducted the Cincinnati Symphony Orchestra during the seasons of 1886–87 and 1887–88. In 1889 he returned to Hamburg, where he taught at the Conservatory and played as concert-master in the Philharmonic Society, but he returned to America in 1894 and made his permanent home in Brooklyn, N. Y., where he lived until his death. From 1894 to 1898 he was the principal violin teacher at the National Conservatory of Music in New York. From 1899 he taught at the Combs Broad Street Conservatory in Philadelphia, and from 1912 at the American Institute of Applied Music in New York.

Schradieck's most lasting influence was as a teacher. Among his pupils, abroad and in America, were Maud Powell, Theodore Spiering [qq.v.], Nikolai Sokoloff, Maximilian Pilzer, Felix Weingartner, and Karl Muck. In spite of his international reputation as a performer and as a teacher, Schradieck went into comparative obscurity in his later years. Spiering, his pupil, commented on this after Schradieck's death : "I cannot but feel that Schradieck should never have given up the congenial atmosphere of Leipzig. . . . That a personality like Schradieck's could be brutally forced into semi-obscurity—as was the case during the last ten or more years of his life—demonstrates, to our shame be it said, to what extent the commercializing of art has progressed" (*Canadian Journal of Music, post,* p. 5). Schradieck's writings were almost entirely of an educational character and made an important contribution to the field of technical training in violin. Besides editing many of the standard works for violin, he was the author of *Die Schule der Violintechnik* (3 vols., 1899), *Tonleiter Studien, or Scale Studies for Violin* (1887), *Masterpieces for the Violin* (8 vols., 1895), and *Masterpieces for the Violin and Piano* (3 vols., 1895–96).

[*Who's Who in America,* 1908–09 ; *Internatl. Who's Who in Music* (1918) ; *Grove's Dict. of Music and Musicians, Am. Supp.* (1930) ; *Baker's Biog. Dict. of Musicians* (3rd ed., 1919) ; W. W. Todd, "Henry Schradieck—An Appreciation," *Violinist,* Aug. 1916 ; Theodore Spiering, "Henry Schradieck—A Personal Tribute," *Canadian Jour. of Music,* May 1918 ; *N. Y. Times,* Mar. 27, 1918.]
J. T. H.

SCHRIECK, SISTER LOUISE VAN DER (Nov. 14, 1813–Dec. 3, 1886), American foundress of the Sisters of Notre Dame de Namur, was born at Bergen-op-Zoom, Holland, the tenth of the thirteen children of Joseph and Clara Maria

(Weenan) Van der Schrieck, who though ardent Catholics suffered little in person or in fortune during the Napoleonic wars. Baptized Josephine, the child was reared in her native village and in Antwerp where the family moved about 1817, seeking both freedom from the politico-religious system, and enlarged opportunities in the exporting business in which the father and elder sons grew prosperous. She was schooled in a private academy and in the newly established institute of the Sisters of Notre Dame at Namur, a French foundation established at Amiens by Blessed Julie Billiart. Thereafter she continued her educaton under private tutors at home, assisted in the household, and devoted her spare time to religious missionary and social work among the oppressed poor of Antwerp and especially among the apprentice girls in the lace factories. Deeply religious and charitable, she could find little outlet for a life of service and hence with parental consent went to Namur, where in 1837 she entered the novitiate of the Notre Dame nuns. As discipline in her crowded home had been strict, she easily accepted the severe rule of privation, work, and prayer, and was professed as Sister Louise, May 17, 1839.

In the meantime Bishop John Baptist Purcell [q.v.], who had become acquainted with the community while seeking missionaries in Belgium for his frontier diocese, was petitioning the superior of the convent and the bishop of Namur for a colony of teaching nuns for Cincinnati, Ohio. His request was finally granted and on Sept. 3, 1840, eight volunteers, of whom Sister Louise was the youngest, started for America under Sister Louise de Gonzague (d. 1866) as superior and Father Louis Amadeus Rappe, a missionary who later became first bishop of Cleveland, as a protector. Arriving at the wharves of Cincinnati on Oct. 31, the sisters were established in a house on Sycamore Street, the first permanent foundation of the community outside of Belgium. The French Ladies met with favor not only among Catholics who attended their poor school and Sunday schools and boarding academy but among the socially aspiring women of the little packing and commercial town who would learn lace-making and a smattering of French. When in 1845 Sister Louise was named superior the Notre Dame convent had become an accepted institution in the community, and its numbers were increasing through local vocations and enlistments from Belgium. In 1846 Sister Louise assigned some of her German-speaking nuns to the first of the community's growing list of parochial schools, which for a generation could not be adequately staffed by

German religious communities. In 1848 she was appointed superior-provincial with a jurisdiction over all future foundations east of the Rocky Mountains, in which capacity she continued until her death. As a superior, she exacted strict obedience under a firm, benevolent rule; she clung steadfastly to the connection with Namur and to the original rule and purpose of the foundress even at the expense of rigidity and stiffness; and she tactfully managed bishops who vainly sought to make the community in their dioceses independent or diocesan. A capable administrator, she founded twenty-six convents in Washington, D. C., Philadelphia, Pa., and in cities of Ohio and Massachusetts. Her eight hundred nuns engaged in teaching in academies and parochial schools, including an occasional free school for negroes. Only during the Civil War, when she furnished nursing nuns for Fort Denison near Cincinnati, did she turn her full energies from Catholic education. At her death in Cincinnati her pioneer work was generally acclaimed, Archbishop William Henry Elder [*q.v.*] saying the requiem mass.

[Sister Helen Louise Nugent, *Sister Louise* (1931), an excellent biog. based on community archives in Namur and Cincinnati and on reminiscences of older nuns who served under the first superior, and *Sister Julia* (1928); *Extracts from the Memoirs of Sister Superior Louise* (Cincinnati, n.d.); M. E. Mannix, *Memoirs of Sister Louise . . . with Reminiscences of the Early Days of the Order in the U. S.* (1907); *Cincinnati Enquirer,* Dec. 4, 1886.]   R. J. P.

SCHRIVER, EDMUND (Sept. 16, 1812–Feb. 10, 1899), soldier, son of Daniel and Rebecca (Zinn) Schriver, was born in York, Pa., where he received his early schooling. He entered the United States Military Academy at seventeen; was graduated July 1, 1833, seventeenth in a class of forty-three; performed garrison duty in Tennessee and Alabama during 1833 and part of 1834 as brevet second lieutenant of the 2nd Artillery; and served as assistant instructor in infantry tactics at West Point from March 1834 to November 1835, receiving his regular second lieutenant's commission in July 1834. Excluding a brief interim in 1839 in the Florida War, he served in the office of the adjutant-general from November 1835 until September 1841. He was promoted first lieutenant, November 1836; was brevetted captain, July 1838, serving as assistant adjutant-general; and received his regular captaincy in August 1842. He served in the headquarters of the Department of the East from September 1841 to July 1846, when he resigned from the army to engage in private business. He was treasurer of the Saratoga and Washington railroad, N. Y. (1847–52), of the Saratoga and Schenectady railroad, and of the

Rensselaer and Saratoga railroad (1847–61); he also served for ten years as president of the latter road. He served Gov. Edwin Denison Morgan [*q.v.*] of New York as aide with the rank of colonel from April to July 1861.

Upon the outbreak of the Civil War, he was commissioned lieutenant-colonel, 11th U. S. Infantry. From July to October 1861 he served at Fort Independence, Mass., and from October 1861 to March 1862 at Perryville, Md.; he was then appointed chief of staff, 1st Corps, Army of the Potomac, and served in that capacity until January 1863 throughout the entire Fredericksburg campaign. In May 1862 he was promoted to the grade of colonel. He participated in the Shenandoah and in the northern Virginia campaigns, fighting at Cedar Mountain, the crossing of the Rappahannock, at Chantilly, and at Manassas in August 1862. He was acting inspector, Army of the Potomac, from January to March 1863 and inspector from then until March 1865. He participated in the battles at Chancellorsville and at Gettysburg, and the subsequent engagements which culminated in the Mine Run expedition of November–December 1863. He was in the Richmond campaign of 1865 from the Rapidan to Petersburg. For conspicuous service in the field, he was brevetted brigadier-general in August 1864 and major-general in March 1865. From March to June 1865 he was on special duty in the office of the secretary of war; he then made an inspection tour of all quartermaster depots and a general inspection of all army posts. Upon returning to Washington in November 1865, he had charge of the inspector's bureau for two periods, 1865–69 and 1871–76. In the intervening period, he was inspector of the United States Military Academy. During 1872–73 he inspected posts in Texas, New Mexico, and Kansas, and from 1876 to 1881 he was inspector-general of the Division of the Pacific. He had a great interest in and devoted considerable time to the affairs of the Freedmen's Bureau. He was retired, Jan. 4, 1881, and then made his home in Washington, D. C. He was buried in Oakwood Cemetery, Troy, N. Y.

[*War of the Rebellion: Official Records (Army),* esp. 1 ser., XII, pts. 1, 3, XXVII, pt. 3, XXX, pt. 1, XXXVI, pt. 3; G. W. Cullum, *Biog. Reg. Officers and Grads. U. S. Mil. Acad.* (3rd ed., 1891), vol. I; T. H. S. Hamersly, *Complete Regular Army Reg. of U. S.* (1880); records of York County Hist. Soc., York, Pa., and of health departments, Troy, N. Y., and Washington, D. C.; *Army and Navy Reg.,* Feb. 25, 1899; *Evening Star* (Washington), Feb. 11, 1899.]
                C. C. B.

SCHROEDER, JOHN FREDERICK (Apr. 8, 1800–Feb. 26, 1857), Episcopal clergyman, author, was born in Baltimore, Md., the son of Henry Schroeder, an immigrant from Hamburg, Germany, and his wife, Mary (Schley) of Frederick, Md. A quiet, precocious child, John had developed a special interest in ancient languages by the time he was eleven. He graduated with highest honors from the College of New Jersey (Princeton) in 1819, then spent a year studying oriental languages under a Philadelphia clergyman. After attending General Theological Seminary for a short time in 1821, he completed his preparation privately, and was ordained deacon by Bishop Kemp of Maryland in 1823 and priest a year later.

He served as rector of St. Michael's parish, Maryland, for a short time, and then (1823) was called as temporary assistant at Trinity Church, New York. His skill as a preacher won him a large following and he was given a permanent appointment within a year. He seems to have inclined toward the Evangelical party of his Church, and this fact probably lessened his favor with the parish authorities, but he retained his position for fifteen years, part of the time having immediate charge of St. Paul's Chapel. In 1829 he was rebuked by Bishop John Henry Hobart [q.v.] for his participation in a short-lived Protestant Episcopal Clerical Association which Hobart suspected of Evangelical tendencies, but Schroeder's relations with his Bishop were generally cordial. When Hobart died in 1830, Schroeder pronounced a eulogy upon him (*The Great Man in Israel,* 1830) and also wrote a sketch of his life, which was published in a *Memorial of Bishop Hobart* (1831). He was one of the clergymen who remained at their posts during the cholera epidemics of the early 1830's. In 1838 his wife's health required a visit to Europe, and shortly after his return he became involved in a dispute with the vestry over a question of precedence which led to his resignation in 1839 and, indirectly, to an unsuccessful attempt to separate St. Paul's Chapel from Trinity Parish. He then moved to Flushing, L. I., where he founded a girl's school (St. Ann's Hall), which he continued until his death. In 1846 he moved it to New York, where he became rector of the Church of the Crucifixion, and in 1852 to Brooklyn, where he served as rector of St. Thomas' Church until shortly before his death.

He was a frequent contributor to religious and secular periodicals, edited a collection of Maxims of Washington (1855), and wrote a biography of Washington which was published posthumously (*Life and Times of Washington,* 2 vols., n.d., 1857–61). He also delivered a number of public lectures, notably a series before the New York Athenæum on oriental literature, one before the New York Horticultural Society, *The Intellectual and Moral Resources of Horticulture* (1828), and another, *A Plea for the Industrious Poor and Strangers in Sickness* (1830), at the opening of the New York Dispensary. On May 22, 1825, he married Caroline Maria Boardman, a daughter of Senator Elijah Boardman and Mary Anna (Whiting) Boardman. By her he had eight children, four of whom survived him. In 1849 he published *Memoir of the Life and Character of Mrs. Mary Anna Boardman,* a rather sentimental biography of his mother-in-law for family distribution. Under different circumstances, Schroeder might have become a distinguished scholar, but his intellectual gifts never seem to have received the discipline necessary to fit them for the fullest usefulness.

[J. G. White, "John Frederick Schroeder," in *Memorial Biogs. of the New Eng. Hist. Geneal. Soc.,* vol. III (1883); Morgan Dix, *A Hist. of the Parish of Trinity Church in the City of N. Y.,* III (1905), 403–05, IV (1906), 197–211; S. H. Turner, *Autobiog.* (1863), pp. 135–65; J. H. Hobart, *A Pastoral Letter . . . on the Subject of the Protestant Episcopal Clerical Asso.* (1829); *Gen. Cat. of Princeton Univ.* (1908); *Church Journal* (N. Y.), Mar. 4, 1857; *Church Review,* Apr. 1857; *N. Y. Tribune,* Feb. 27, 1857.]

W. W. M.

SCHROEDER, SEATON (Aug. 17, 1849–Oct. 19, 1922), naval officer, was born in Washington, D. C., the son of Francis and Caroline (Seaton) Schroeder. Since his father was American chargé d'affaires and then minister to Sweden and Norway from 1849 to 1857, he acquired most of his elementary education abroad. He entered the United States Naval Academy in September 1864 and graduated in 1868. By 1872 he had become a lieutenant, but because of the stagnation in the naval service during this period he was retained in this grade for twenty-one years. He first served in the Pacific Fleet in the *Saginaw* and *Pensacola,* and from 1869–72 in the *Benicia* on the Asiatic station. In June 1871 he participated in the expedition of John Rodgers (1812–1882) [q.v.] against the Korean forts on the Salée River. In 1874–75 he served in the *Swatara* in her voyage round the world with the Transit of Venus expedition. After spending the next three years in hydrographic work in the Mediterranean, in 1879 he secured leave of absence to assist Henry Honeychurch Gorringe [q.v.] in transporting the obelisk in Central Park, New York City, from Egypt to New York, returning to his naval duties the following year. He served for three years as navigator of the Fish Commission steamer *Albatross,* was transferred to the office of naval intelligence, and in 1888 was assigned to duty in connection with the construction and equipment of the dynamite cruiser *Vesuvius,* which he subsequently commanded until 1893. In 1896 he was made executive officer of the battleship *Massachusetts,* holding the post during the operations off Santiago during the Spanish-American War. For his services during the war he was advanced three numbers in rank "for eminent and conspicuous conduct," and in 1899 he was promoted to the rank of commander. Appointed naval governor of Guam in 1900, he rendered most efficient service on the island, endearing himself to the native population. In 1903, when he was commissioned captain, he was transferred to Washington as chief intelligence officer. During the voyage of the Atlantic Fleet around the world he commanded the *Virginia* from Hampton Roads to San Francisco, where he was commissioned rear admiral in July 1908; during the remainder of the voyage he commanded successively the Fourth and Third Divisions of the fleet. From 1909 to 1911, when he was retired by age, he was commander-in-chief of the Atlantic Fleet. During the World War he was recalled to active duty as hydrographer to the Navy Department. He married Maria C. B. Wainwright, Jan. 16, 1879, and had two sons and three daughters.

An efficient, conscientious officer and a thorough seaman, imbued with a deep love of his profession, he expected scrupulous accuracy and strict attention to duty on the part of his subordinates. Keenly interested in naval development, he collaborated with Lieut. William H. Driggs in perfecting the Driggs-Schroeder gun, 1888–89, and wrote four separate treatises on torpedoes and torpedo boats: *The Development of Modern Torpedo Boats* (1886), *Development of Modern Torpedoes* (1887), *Modern Torpedoes* (1887), and *Modern Torpedo Boats* (1887). He also wrote *The Fall of Maximilian's Empire* (1887) and his autobiography, *A Half Century of Naval Service* (1922), as well as numerous professional articles in American and English naval journals. He collaborated with George M. Totten in writing *Coasts and Ports of the Bay of Biscay* (1876) and with Richard Wainwright in compiling *Arctic Azimuth Tables* (1881).

[See Navy Reg., 1868–1922; L. R. Hamersly, *Records of Living Officers U. S. Navy and Marine Corps* (6th ed., 1898) ; *Ann. Reports Navy Dept. . . . App. to Report of Chief of Bureau of Navigation* (1898); Lucien Young, *Cat. of Works by Am. Naval Officers* (1888); H. H. Gorringe, *Egyptian Obelisks* (1882); *Army and Navy Jour.,* Oct. 28, 1922; *Army and Navy Reg.,* Oct. 21, 1922; *Who's Who in America,* 1920–21; *Evening Star* (Washington, D. C.), Oct. 20, 1922. For

family material see O. A. Seaton, *The Seaton Family* (1906).]
　　　　　　　　　　　　　　　　　　　L. H. B.

SCHUESSELE, CHRISTIAN [See SCHUSSELE, CHRISTIAN, 1826–1879].

SCHULTZE, AUGUSTUS (Feb. 3, 1840–Nov. 12, 1918), Moravian clergyman, educator, author, editor, was the son of J. C. Louis and D. Frederica (Haessler) Schultze and was born at Nowawes, Prussia, a suburb of Potsdam. He received his academic training at Niesky in Silesia and his theological training at Gnadenfeld, where he took his bachelor's degree in divinity in 1861. For one year he taught Latin and Greek at the French Academy, Lausanne, Switzerland, and for eight years he occupied the chair of classics at Niesky, where on Sept. 16, 1869, he was ordained deacon in the Moravian church. In 1870 he was sent to Bethlehem, Pa., to fill the chair of classics in the Moravian College and Theological Seminary. In 1885 he became president of the institution, having meanwhile, Jan. 20, 1882, been ordained presbyter, at Bethlehem, by Bishop Edmund de Schweinitz [*q.v.*]. He served as president until July 1, 1918, and, as president emeritus, he continued his devotion to the classics as professor of Hebrew until his death.

From 1881 to 1893 he was secretary and member of the governing board of the northern diocese of the Moravian Church in America. He was a prolific writer both in German and in English. Many pages of the official papers of the Moravian Church attest the carefulness and clarity of his thinking during thirty years of editorial writing. In 1886 he published "A Brief History of the Widows' Society of Bethlehem" (*Transactions of the Moravian Historical Society,* vol. II, 1886, pp. 51–124) ; the following year he prepared the annual textbook of devotional readings in the Danish language (*Aarlig Dagbog,* 1888) ; and in 1890 he brought out *Die Missionsfelde der Erneuerten Brüderkirche.* Meanwhile he had published *A Brief Grammar and Vocabulary of the Eskimo Language of North-Western Alaska* (1889; 2nd ed., 1894), the result of long study and comparison of material submitted by oral evidence, since the language had, up to that time, no written expression. His next work was "The Old Moravian Cemetery of Bethlehem, Pa., 1742–1897" (*Transactions of the Moravian Historical Society,* vol. V, 1899), which, besides carefully locating all burials, gave concise sketches of every life, a truly gigantic task of research. Most of his theological works were published late in his life, the fruit of careful thought. They were *The Books of the Bible Briefly Analyzed* (1889), *The The-*

ology of Peter and Paul (1894), and *Christian Doctrine and Systematic Theology* (1909), the last being the flowering of lectures in dogmatics he had delivered and revised for many years. At the time of his sudden death in Bethlehem, from the effects of a fall, he was engaged in the revision of his Eskimo grammar, enlarged to include a translation of passages from the Bible into that tongue.

Schultze was married twice. His first wife, Julia Reck of Bethlehem, Pa., whom he married Dec. 26, 1871, died in 1874 leaving one son. His second wife, Adelaide E. Peter of Gnadenhutten, Ohio, whom he married July 5, 1876, died Feb. 3, 1918, leaving a son and three daughters.

[Obituary (MS.) in Archives of the Moravian Church, Bethlehem, Pa.; *Who's Who in America,* 1918–19; *Moravian,* Nov. 20, 1918; *Bethlehem Daily Times,* Nov. 13, 1918.]   A. G. R.

SCHURZ, CARL (Mar. 2, 1829–May 14, 1906), minister to Spain, Union soldier, senator from Missouri, and secretary of the interior, was born in the little town of Liblar on the Rhine, near Cologne. He attended the gymnasium at Cologne (1839–46) and became a candidate for the doctorate at the University of Bonn in 1847. His father, Christian Schurz, was first a village schoolmaster and then embarked in business; his mother, Marianne Jüssen, the daughter of a tenant farmer, was a woman of unusual force of character. Both made every sacrifice to help their son to the career of which he dreamed—a professorship of history. Fate in the form of the German revolutionary movement of 1848–49 intervened and altered Schurz's life as it marred or made the lives of many thousands of young Germans who beheld in the United States their ideal of popular government. Of these none was more ardent or more eloquent, and certainly none was more daring, than Schurz. At nineteen he was a leader of the student movement in his university, and was preaching its gospel to the peasants in his neighborhood through the columns of a democratic newspaper, and by word of mouth. His rare gift of oratory he discovered when he suddenly addressed, to great applause, a meeting in the university hall at Bonn to which he came without the slightest intention of speaking.

Profoundly influenced by Prof. Gottfried Kinkel of Bonn, one of the intellectual leaders of the struggle for democratic institutions, Schurz followed him in the abortive revolutionary movement upon Siegburg, on May 11, 1849. Thereafter he became a lieutenant and staff officer of the revolutionary army taking part in the final battles of the united rebel forces of Baden and the Palatinate at Ubstadt and Bruchsal, and those on the line of the Murg River in Baden on June 28–30, 1849. Sent by order into the fortress of Rastatt, just before it was surrendered, he was one of its defenders until the surrender more than three weeks later. Rightly expecting to be shot if captured, Schurz declined to deliver himself up to the conquering Prussians. With two companions he concealed himself for four days, finally escaping through an unused sewer which was their first place of refuge. (See Schurz's account, "The Surrender of Rastatt," *Wisconsin Magazine of History,* Mar. 1929.) They crossed the Rhine and entered French territory, Schurz finally joining the large colony of German refugees in Switzerland.

There he might have stayed indefinitely had it not been for the plight of his beloved teacher, Kinkel, who had been captured, put on trial for his life, and sentenced to life imprisonment. After being treated as a common felon, Kinkel was at length transferred to the prison at Spandau, a fortified town near Berlin. In response to Frau Kinkel's appeals, Schurz undertook the liberation of her husband. Twice, with the aid of a false passport, he reëntered Germany, where he was himself on the proscribed list. The necessary funds were furnished by friends of the Professor. After nine months of preparation and plotting with the complicity of a turnkey, Kinkel was lowered to the street from an unbarred attic window of the prison in the night of Nov. 6–7, 1850. In a waiting carriage Kinkel and Schurz left the city by the Hamburg road, only to alter their course and drive straight to Mecklenburg. They were successfully concealed in Rostock until a tiny schooner conveyed them to England. To this day no single incident of the Revolution is better known in Germany; no other has in it more elements of romantic daring and unselfish personal heroism. Schurz went to Paris in December 1850, but in the summer of 1851 was expelled from France by the police as a dangerous foreigner. He resided in England until after his marriage there to Margarethe (or Margaretha) Meyer, of Hamburg, July 6, 1852. During this period he won the friendship of Mazzini and Kossuth and other great leaders of the democratic movement in Europe. America beckoned him, however. In August he set sail for the United States, following in the footsteps of many of his associates-in-arms of the brief campaign of 1849. He and his wife lived in Philadelphia until 1855.

Before definitely settling, Schurz spent months in traveling through the Eastern and Middle-

Western portion of the United States, and set about acquiring that remarkable mastery of the English language which made it possible for him to make campaign speeches in English within five years after his arrival. In 1856 he purchased a small farm in Watertown, Wis., where an uncle's family had settled. Having espoused the anti-slavery cause with all the ardor and enthusiasm he gave to the revolution of 1849, Schurz was immediately drawn into Republican politics. Speaking in German, he campaigned for Frémont. The next year he was sent as a delegate to the Republican state convention which promptly nominated him for lieutenant-governor although he was not yet a citizen of the United States, a point that did not become pressing because he was defeated by 107 votes despite wide campaigning in both English and German. A year later, the campaign of 1858 found him speaking in Illinois for Abraham Lincoln and against Stephen A. Douglas. From that time on he was in demand for one campaign after another; in April 1859 he aided, by request, Senator Henry Wilson of Massachusetts in his fight against the Know-Nothing movement in that state, delivering one of his most famous speeches, "True Americanism" (*Speeches*, 1865, pp. 51–76), which helped to defeat a proposal to deny the ballot to foreign-born voters in Massachusetts for two years after federal naturalization.

Schurz was next put forward for the governorship of Wisconsin; the prize went, however, to another. He was then admitted to the bar and entered into a law partnership, but the anti-slavery cause and politics absorbed most of his time. Chairman of the Wisconsin delegation to the Chicago Republican convention of 1860 which nominated Abraham Lincoln, he and his fellow-delegates voted for Seward until the end. One of the committee which notified Lincoln of his nomination, Schurz spoke for him in Wisconsin, Illinois, Indiana, Ohio, Pennsylvania, and New York with great effectiveness among both natives and foreign-born. His greatest forensic effort—he considered it the greatest success of his oratorical career—was his speech in Cooper Union, Sept. 13, 1860 (*Ibid.*, pp. 162–221), which was devoted to a merciless critique of Stephen A. Douglas and was marked by sarcasm, humor, and his unusual power of clear exposition. It lasted for three hours and was received with the greatest enthusiasm. For all of these services, Lincoln, who had written to him on June 18, 1860, that "to the extent of our limited acquaintance, no man stands nearer my heart than yourself" (*Speeches, Correspondence,* I, 119), appointed Schurz minister to Spain,

although he was in the midst of raising the 1st New York ("Lincoln") Cavalry of which he expected to be colonel.

Arriving at Madrid in July 1861, Schurz devoted himself, like Charles Francis Adams and other American representatives in Europe, to advancing and safeguarding the Union cause abroad, and gave all his leisure time to military campaigns and tactics which he had studied ever since his brief military experience in Germany. Finding, however, that the Northern cause was greatly weakened by the failure of the government to become clearly anti-slavery, and receiving no encouragement in this matter from Secretary Seward, Schurz returned to the United States in January 1862, to put his views before Lincoln. The latter received him kindly, but persisted in his policy of awaiting a more favorable public opinion at home. Schurz then sought to rouse the public for immediate emancipation and to that end delivered an address, previously read and approved by Lincoln, at Cooper Union in March 1862 (*Speeches,* 1865, pp. 240–68), which coincided with the President's request to Congress for authority to cooperate with any state which might adopt gradual emancipation. Schurz resigned as minister in April, was appointed brigadier-general of volunteers, and was given not a brigade, but a division, in Frémont's army on June 10, 1862, thus being placed in command of troops some of whom were veterans of a year's standing.

That Schurz took his military duties seriously, and soon won the respect of his officers and men for his ability and personal courage is beyond question. He was frequently complimented in dispatches, and on one occasion after his troops passed in review with the Army of the Potomac, Lincoln confirmed the press reports that "the division commanded by General Schurz impressed the Presidential party as the best drilled and most soldierly of the troops that passed before them" (Schurz, *Reminiscences,* II, 407). At the second battle of Bull Run, Aug. 30, 1862, the new brigadier of two months' service and his division won high praise in one of the bloodiest and bitterest defeats of the Army of the Potomac, whose final withdrawal they covered. It was, however, the misfortune of this division and the corps to bear the brunt of Jackson's sudden attack at Chancellorsville. Badly placed by the corps commander, Gen. O. O. Howard—despite repeated protests and warnings by Schurz—the division broke and retired in disorder before the overwhelming Confederate onrush, but was finally rallied in part to aid in preventing what threatened to be a complete disaster. For this the XI Corps, and especially its German regiments, was violently abused and charged with cowardice in the press of the entire country. There resulted a long controversy between Schurz and Howard, but the former's efforts to obtain a court of inquiry and justice for his troops failed. Again at Gettysburg, where, because of the killing of General Reynolds and the consequent advancement of General Howard, Schurz took command of the XI Corps, his troops bore the brunt of the Confederate attack upon the right wing. After heavy losses they retired in some disorder through the town to Cemetery Ridge, again in obedience to orders from Howard. Once more there were unwarranted charges that the Germans had failed to stand their ground.

That Schurz was himself not held responsible for the Chancellorsville disaster appears from the fact that on Mar. 14, 1863, he was promoted to major-general. After Gettysburg, the corps was transferred to the western field. Here Schurz again became involved in a controversy, this time with General Hooker. A court of inquiry subsequently found that his conduct had been entirely correct and proper. After Chattanooga the depleted XI and XII Corps were merged into a new XX Corps, and Schurz was appointed to command a corps of instruction at Nashville. Unable to brook the prospect of inaction, Schurz, after some months, asked to be relieved of his command, conferred with Lincoln, and then made many speeches on behalf of the President's reëlection. The end of the war found him chief of staff to Major-General Slocum in Sherman's army. He resigned immediately after the surrender of Lee. Throughout his military service Schurz corresponded irregularly with Lincoln, a most unwise procedure but one welcomed by the President except on one occasion when he found it necessary to rebuke the General, which event, however, did not interrupt their warm friendship (Schurz, *Speeches, Correspondence*, I, 211–13, 219–21). At best it was an anomalous situation; a political campaigner and intimate of the President had been put into a most responsible military command and was known to be in direct relations with the Commander-in-Chief. Had not Schurz displayed real soldierly capacity, and much discretion, the situation might easily have become an impossible one. Instead, he won the regard of Sherman, Hancock, and many others who ranked among the best of the Northern generals.

Before Schurz could decide upon his next course of action, President Johnson asked him to visit the Southern states and to report at length to him upon conditions there. Schurz traveled from July to September 1865, and wrote a lengthy report that has extraordinary historical value to this day, because of its detailed analysis of the situation, its clarity of statement, and its vision (*Speeches, Correspondence*, I, 279–374). Since, however, Schurz thought the extension of the franchise to the colored people should be a condition precedent to the readmission of the Confederate states, his report was unwelcome to Johnson, who neither acknowledged its receipt nor allowed it to be published until Congress demanded it (*Senate Executive Document No. 2*, 39 Cong., 1 Sess.).

With this task accomplished, Schurz accepted an invitation from Horace Greeley to represent the *New York Tribune* as its Washington correspondent, in which capacity he observed the beginning of the struggle between Congress and the President over reconstruction. Resigning in the spring of 1866, Schurz next became editor-in-chief of the Detroit *Post,* then just established by leading Michigan Republicans. Here he remained only a year, when he became joint editor, with Emil Preetorius [*q.v.*], of the St. Louis *Westliche Post,* and one of the proprietors of this German-language daily. This third chapter in his journalistic career was also destined to be a short one. A delegate to the Republican National Convention which met to nominate Grant for the presidency in 1868, Schurz was at once chosen temporary chairman of the convention, and made the keynote address. He drew up the resolution in the platform calling for the removal of disqualifications upon "the late rebels" (*Reminiscences,* III, 284–85). As usual, he made many speeches in the campaign which followed. After a bitter contest between the Radicals and Liberals in the party, he was himself nominated for the United States Senate from Missouri, and duly elected by the legislature (Ross, *post*, p. 29). On Mar. 4, 1869, two days after his fortieth birthday, he took his seat in Washington.

He speedily found himself in the group of anti-Grant senators, joining Sumner in the defeat of Grant's plan to annex Santo Domingo, and opposing at many points the "spoils-loving and domineering partisans" of the President. On Dec. 20, 1869, years before the policy it outlined was adopted, Schurz introduced a bill to create a permanent civil-service merit system (*Congressional Globe,* 41 Cong., 2 Sess., pp. 236–38). William A. Dunning and Frederic Bancroft have written in their addenda to Schurz's unfinished memoirs that his "whole conception of public policy was far above the play of merely personal and party interests"; and that his senatorial career was accordingly one of "exceptional seriousness and dignity" (*Reminiscences,* III, 317–18). He was at his best in his incessant attacks upon public corruption. The news that he would speak at a given hour usually crowded the public galleries. But the high rank he took and held in the Senate, and his national reputation as an orator and a leader, did not assure him reëlection in 1875, for, because of the Republican split, the Democrats had gained control of the Missouri legislature. He was again compelled to turn to journalism and the lecture platform for support.

Schurz, who was disgusted with Grant and distrustful of the Democrats, had probably done more than any other leader to promote the Liberal Republican movement (Ross, pp. 44–50; Schurz, *Speeches, Correspondence,* II, 59–69, 254–60). He was the permanent president of the Cincinnati convention of 1872 that organized the new party and, although profoundly disappointed by the nomination of Horace Greeley and without hope of success, was active in the campaign. His speeches "were naturally against Grant rather than for Greeley" (*Reminiscences,* III, 352). In 1876, to the dismay and anger of many of his Liberal Republican associates, he supported Hayes, being assured that the latter was sound on the money question, would restore the South, and would promote civil-service reform (*Speeches, Correspondence,* III, 249–59; *Reminiscences,* III, 368). On Mar. 4, 1877, Schurz entered the cabinet of Hayes as secretary of the interior. His secretaryship is still remembered because of his enlightened treatment of the Indians (much misunderstood at the time), his installing a merit promotion system in his department, his preservation of the public domain, and the beginning of the development of national parks.

On leaving the cabinet Schurz began his fourth venture into journalism. At the invitation of Henry Villard [*q.v.*], who had just purchased the New York *Evening Post* and the *Nation,* he became head of a triumvirate of remarkable editors comprising besides himself, Edwin L. Godkin and Horace White [*qq.v.*]. The brilliant chapter in journalism which they thus began ended in two and a quarter years, in the fall of 1883, because of differences as to editorial methods and policies between Schurz and Godkin (Nevins, *post,* pp. 455–56). The friendship of the three men remained unbroken; until his death Schurz was a valued counselor of the *Evening Post.* As an editorial writer it was

plain that his style was often more oratorical than journalistic, and lacking in terseness. To both the *Evening Post* and to Schurz, because of his rousing speeches, was attributed to a considerable degree Blaine's loss of New York state in 1884, and the election of Cleveland to the presidency.

Schurz's final venture into journalism began in 1892, when in succession to George William Curtis he for six years contributed the leading editorials to *Harper's Weekly.* Their authorship was at first kept secret, as had been his contribution of many articles to the *Nation,* prior to its amalgamation with the *Evening Post* in 1881, notably some regular letters from Washington in 1872 and 1873. In 1898 his connection with *Harper's Weekly* was ended by his refusal to support the drift toward the war with Spain. When the war came Schurz warmly opposed it, as he did the annexation of the Philippines, declaring that fatal violence was being done the anti-imperialistic, peace-loving ideal of America, free from all entangling foreign alliances. He once wrote that foreign-born citizens were "more jealously patriotic Americans than many natives are," since they watch the progress of the Republic "with triumphant joy at every success of our democratic institutions, and with the keenest sensitiveness to every failure, having the standing of this country before the world constantly in mind" (*Reminiscences,* I, 120). This describes his own attitude toward his adopted country.

The latter years of his life Schurz gave to literary labor, to letters upon public questions, and to occasional public speeches. The latter were as always carefully memorized, were marked by a lofty tone, and, like those delivered in the Senate, were "emphasized by graceful diction, and impressive delivery" (*Reminiscences,* III, 318). An ardent admirer and supporter of Grover Cleveland, except occasionally, as in the matter of the Venezuelan episode of 1895, Schurz championed William J. Bryan in 1900 on the anti-imperialist issue, as he had opposed him on the free-silver question four years earlier. He was for years (1892–1900) president of the National Civil-Service Reform League, and of the Civil Service Reform Association of New York (1893–1906). In every mayoralty election in New York, in which he resided from 1881 on, he made his influence felt in the struggle for good government. Indeed, he held in his last years the unique position of a veteran statesman, a public-spirited citizen, and political philosopher, representing particularly a great group of his fellow-citizens, and battling uninterruptedly for his conception of an America minding its own business, and keeping aloof from foreign aggression and foreign involvements.

Carl Schurz was a man of great personal charm, of commanding presence, despite a very tall and rather lanky figure, of a gay, vivacious, and unusually happy spirit, which was never daunted by his bitter disappointments in the trend of domestic and foreign policy from 1898 on. Devoted to his family, an amateur pianist of talent, blessed with a great sense of humor, together with much playful irony, he took cheerfully those periods of his life when he went counter to public opinion, and willingly paid the price therefor. He remained until his death extraordinarily rich in friends and admirers. His wife died in 1876. Of two sons and two daughters, three survived him; all died without issue. Besides his speeches and unfinished reminiscences (see below), mention should be made of his admirable *Life of Henry Clay* (2 vols., 1887), a notable essay on Lincoln in the *Atlantic Monthly,* June 1891 (also printed separately, 1891 and later), and a pamphlet, *The New South* (1885).

[There are Schurz papers in the Lib. of Cong., and there is a collection of private letters in the Wis. Hist. Soc. Various editions of speeches and writings are: *Speeches of Carl Schurz* (1865); Frederic Bancroft, ed., *Speeches, Correspondence and Pol. Papers of Carl Schurz* (6 vols., 1913); *The Reminiscences of Carl Schurz* (3 vols., 1907–08), containing, in vol. III, "A Sketch of Carl Schurz's Political Career, 1869–1906," by Frederic Bancroft and W. A. Dunning; a German edition, containing letters not in the American, *Lebenserinnerungen* (3 vols., 1906–12); Joseph Schafer, ed. and transl., *Intimate Letters of Carl Schurz, 1841–1869 (Pubs. of the State Hist. Soc. of Wis., Collections,* Vol. XXX, 1928). Among works about Schurz are: Anton Erkelenz and Fritz Mittelmann, eds., *Carl Schurz, der Deutsche und der Amerikaner* (1929); Otto Dannehl, *Carl Schurz* (1929); C. V. Easum, *The Americanization of Carl Schurz* (1929); Joseph Schafer, *Carl Schurz, Militant Liberal* (1930); C. M. Fuess, *Carl Schurz, Reformer* (1932). See also T. A. Dodge, *The Campaign of Chancellorsville* (1881); E. D. Ross, *The Liberal Republican Movement* (1919); T. S. Barclay, *The Liberal Republican Movement in Mo., 1865–1871* (1926); Allan Nevins, *The Evening Post* (1922); F. M. Stewart, *The National Civil Service Reform League* (1929); obituaries and comment, *Evening Post* (N. Y.), May 14, 1906; *N. Y. Times,* May 15, 1906; *Nation* (N. Y.), May 17, 1906; *Harper's Weekly,* May 26, 1906.]   O. G. V.

SCHUSSELE, CHRISTIAN (Apr. 16, 1826– Aug. 21, 1879), painter, teacher, the son of a baker of good standing, was born in Guebviller, Haut Rhin, Alsace, while that province was French. As a child he spent much time drawing and painting, adorning the walls and doors of his attic at home with copies of pictures seen in the churches of his native village. At the age of fifteen, although entirely self-taught, he was painting portraits of his neighbors. In 1841 he was sent to Strasbourg to enter the art academy,

where he studied the practice of lithography. Two years later he went to Paris, where he worked at first under Paul Delaroche and then with Englemann and Graf. Subsequently he entered the studio of Yvon, painter of battle scenes at Versailles, and was commissioned to make drawings from the pictures at the Versailles gallery for elaborate chromolithographic reproductions. The revolution of 1848, however, put an end to his contract, and turned the young painter's thoughts toward the United States.

While in Paris he had met Cecilia Muringer, the young daughter of an Alsatian lithographer who resided in Philadelphia, and it was to that city Schussele directed his steps upon his arrival in America. He soon married the youthful Cecilia, by whom he had two daughters. In Philadelphia he first worked at chromolithography, supplementing such employment with designing for wood engravers, but his real interest lay in painting. In the spring of 1851 he completed a picture entitled "The Artist's Recreation" which was exhibited at the Pennsylvania Academy of the Fine Arts. A year later came "Clear the Track," a coasting scene, purchased by the president of the Academy. In 1854 this picture was engraved by John Sartain [q.v.] for the Art Union of Philadelphia, thus establishing Schussele's reputation and popularizing his work. Much encouraged, he devoted himself henceforth entirely to his brush. Among his best-known paintings are "Franklin before the Lords in Council" (1856); "Men of Progress" (1857), now in Cooper Institute, N. Y.; "Zeisberger Preaching to the Indians" (c. 1859), painted for the Moravian Society of Bethlehem; "King Solomon and the Iron Worker" (1860), painted for James Harrison, and "Washington at Valley Forge" (1862). Many of Schussele's works were further popularized through Sartain's engravings.

Schussele and his friend Schmolze, who decorated the ceiling of the Philadelphia Academy of Music, were among the first painters to bring to America talent trained in Paris art schools. Schussele was active in local art affairs, a member of the Philadelphia Sketch Club, and for several years president of the Artists' Fund Society. In 1863 he was attacked by scrivener's palsy in the right hand; he completed "Home on Furlough" and "McClellan at Antietam" during that year, but with difficulty. Two years later the disease had so progressed that he found painting painful and sought a cure in Europe. He visited his native place and at Paris underwent an unsuccessful operation. In 1868 he returned to Philadelphia, courageously facing his limitations. Nothing daunted by his physical handicap, he continued to paint, and was unanimously elected to fill the newly established chair of drawing and painting at the Pennsylvania Academy of the Fine Arts, a post which he held until his death. His physical condition made it impossible for him to execute many canvases, but he completed "Queen Esther Denouncing Haman to Ahasuerus" in 1869 and "The Alsatian Fair" in 1870. Despite the palsy that gradually affected his entire body, he continued his teaching almost to the end. He died in the country home of his son-in-law, John Crump, at Merchantville, N. J.

[Sources include: "Philadelphia Art Schools," editorial, in *Public Ledger* (Phila.), Aug. 20, 1879; obituary, *Ibid.*, Aug. 22, 1879; letter (1932) from Schussele's grandniece, Eva Clad; information from Harriet Sartain, Dean, School of Design for Women, Phila.; *Cat. of Loan Exhibition of Hist. Portraits, Pa. Acad. of the Fine Arts, Dec. 1, 1877 to Jan. 15, 1878* (1877); *Descriptive Cat. of the Permanent Colls. of Works of Art* (Pa. Acad. of the Fine Arts, 1897; 1902); *Am. Art Rev.*, Nov. 1879; Frank Weitenkampf, *Am. Graphic Art* (1912). Schussele's name is spelled variously in secondary accounts but according to Miss Harriet Sartain, whose family knew his intimately, he himself used the spelling here given.]   D. G—y.

SCHUTTLER, PETER (Dec. 22, 1812–Jan. 16, 1865), wagon maker, was born in the village of Wachenheim, Grand Duchy of Hesse Darmstadt, Germany. He came to the United States in 1834 and worked first in a wagon shop in Buffalo, N. Y., where he was paid seven dollars a month and his board, and then in Cleveland, Ohio. His inventive skill showed itself in a minor way in his use of a saw instead of an axe for cutting out wagon gearing. Having gathered together a little capital, he went into business for himself but he did not succeed, and after a year or two he moved to Sandusky, Ohio, where he worked at his own bench as a wagon maker for six years. There he married Dorothy Gauch, a native of Prussia, by whom he had three children, a son and a daughter born during the sojourn in Sandusky and another son born in Chicago. Through careful saving he had accumulated from three to four hundred dollars, and with his mind bent on opening a wagon shop he left in 1843 by boat for Chicago. He found no less than thirteen wagon shops already established in the city. Nevertheless, he went to work and made by hand the frames of several wagons, which were ironed on shares by P. W. Gates. He built his own shop and lived in a board shanty behind it. A brief interlude in the brewery business with his father-in-law was marked by failure and left him firmly decided to continue with the wagon business.

With the settlement of the western states, the demand for wagons increased. He hired a blacksmith and helper and ironed his own wagons; later he installed an eight horse-power engine, all work having previously been done by hand; in 1849, with the Gold Rush well under way, he built a new shop of brick, forty feet by seventy and four stories high, and began to manufacture buggies, carriages, and harness, as well as wagons. Though the shop burnt to the ground in 1850, it was immediately rebuilt and he returned to the manufacture of wagons alone. The Schuttler wagon helped to displace the old prairie schooner, prevailingly in use until 1850; it had a capacity of thirty-five hundred pounds and was very strongly made, though it was of comparatively light weight and easy running, and commanded a premium of fifty dollars over other makes. The Mormons were among Schuttler's best customers. During the Civil War he refused to modify the design of his wagon in order to secure army contracts. By 1856 he had forty men at work and was turning out a hundred and thirty-five wagons a week. Up to this time, he himself worked in the plant, directed the work of his men, kept the books, and made the sales. In 1855 he traveled with his elder son, Peter, to Germany and returned to build the finest mansion in Chicago. He died a rich man, leaving the wagon business to Peter. His wife and the three children all survived him. The name of the company remained in the list of Chicago firms for many years; in 1934 it appeared in the Chicago telephone directory as "Peter Schuttler Co., Wagons," but no wagons were manufactured after 1925.

[*Biog. Sketches of the Leading Men of Chicago* (1868); *Chicago and Its Makers* (1929), edited by Paul Gilbert and C. L. Bryson; *Chicago Tribune*, Jan. 17, 1865.]   E. A. D.

SCHUYLER, EUGENE (Feb. 26, 1840–July 16, 1890), diplomat, scholar, was born at Ithaca, N. Y., the son of George Washington Schuyler [*q.v.*] and Matilda (Scribner). Allied by blood or marriage with some of the first families of his state and the son of a man prominent in public affairs, he enjoyed every social, political, and cultural advantage. Graduating from Yale College in 1859, he remained there two years longer doing graduate work in languages and philosophy, and receiving the degree of Ph.D. in 1861. He then studied law at the Columbia Law School, from which he was graduated in 1863, was admitted to the bar, and began practice in New York.

His interest in language study, however, led him in 1865 to apply for a diplomatic post and on July 15, 1867, he was appointed consul at

Moscow, serving in this capacity until the latter part of 1869. During the next nine years he was successively consul at Revel, secretary of legation at Saint Petersburg, and secretary of legation and consul general at Constantinople. In the fall of 1876, while holding the last-named post, he published, before submitting it to the Department of State, a report on Turkish atrocities in Bulgaria which was widely circulated throughout Europe and, later, in America (in J. A. MacGahan, *The Turkish Atrocities in Bulgaria,* London, 1876). It was said that "His report did more to influence England than any other document of the [Russo-Turkish] war" (Memorandum of Jan. 4, 1878, in Notes from Turkish Legation, Department of State), but it invited the criticism that he was subject to Russian influence. His cooperation with the Russian secretary of legation at Constantinople in drafting a plan for an autonomous Bulgaria did not improve his relations with the Porte (Department of State, Notes from Turkish Legation, memorandum of Jan. 4, 1878). The Turkish envoy at Washington protested unofficially in January 1877 and again a year later. Consequently, Schuyler was ordered to report at Washington and was in July 1878 appointed to Birmingham, where he remained only a few months before going to Rome as consul general. He had been married at Paris, in July 1877, to Gertrude Wallace King, daughter of Charles King [*q.v.*], a president of Columbia College.

In June 1880 he became the first American diplomatic representative to Rumania, then a principality, and in July 1882, minister resident and consul general to Greece, Rumania, and Serbia. When Rumania became a kingdom he was instructed to follow the lead of the European powers in recognizing the new government, with which instructions he complied on Apr. 6, 1881. He played a similar rôle in the recognition of the new Serbian government to which he was accredited. Empowered to negotiate treaties with Rumania and Serbia, he conducted negotiations to the satisfaction of the Department, and his commercial treaty with Rumania signed Apr. 11, 1881, and his commercial treaty and consular convention with Serbia, both signed Oct. 14, 1881, were duly ratified by the United States government. The Rumanian treaty, however, did not go into force. After two pleasurable years at Athens, the legation there being abolished in 1884, he returned to the United States to lecture at the Johns Hopkins and Cornell universities and to write. In 1886, however, he went back to Europe and settled at Alassio, where he remained until 1889.

In March of that year he accepted the offer of Secretary of State, Blaine to be assistant secretary of state, but the nomination was withdrawn because of opposition in the Senate committee on foreign relations. He accepted an appointment to Cairo a few weeks later, was taken ill at that post, and died in Italy. In an era of mediocrity in the American foreign service, Schuyler was an outstanding figure.

His literary work was considerable. He edited John A. Porter's *Selections from the Kalevala* (1868) and published *Fathers and Sons* (1867), a translation of Turgeniev's work, and *The Cossacks* (1878), from the Russian of Tolstoi. His *Turkistan: Notes of a Journey in Russian Turkistan, Khokand, Bukhara, and Kuldja* (2 vols., 1876) was critical of Russian administration in the East. His most extensive work was *Peter the Great* (2 vols., 1884), first published in *Scribner's Monthly,* and it was perhaps the frankness of his *American Diplomacy and the Furtherance of Commerce* (1886) which lost him the appointment as assistant secretary of state. He also wrote for the *North American Review, Scribner's Magazine, The Nation,* and other periodicals. From several foreign governments he received decorations.

[*Eugene Schuyler: Selected Essays, with a Memoir by Evelyn Schuyler Schaeffer* (1901); report on conditions in Bulgaria enclosed with dispatch No. 106, Nov. 21, 1876, from the Minister at Constantinople to the Secretary of State (MS., Dept. of State); *Papers Relating to the Foreign Relations of the U. S.,* 1881, 1883; letters, instructions, and dispatches in archives of Dept. of State; *Obit. Record Grads. Yale Univ., 1890–1900* (1900); G. W. Schuyler, *Colonial N. Y.* (2 vols., 1885); *N. Y. Tribune,* July 19, 1890.]   E. W. S.

SCHUYLER, GEORGE WASHINGTON (Feb. 2, 1810–Feb. 1, 1888), state official, author, was born at Stillwater, N. Y., the son of John H. and Annatje (Fort) Schuyler and a descendant of Philip, a younger son of Philip Pieterse Schuyler, founder of the family in America. In 1811 his father left Saratoga County and purchased a farm several miles west of Ithaca, where George spent his boyhood. Having chosen the ministry for his life's work, he prepared for college and received the bachelor's degree from the University of the City of New York in 1837, but his theological studies, at Union Seminary, were interrupted by his decision to engage in business in order to "extricate a brother from difficulties" (*Colonial New York,* II, 377). He married, on Apr. 18, 1839, Matilda Scribner, daughter of Uriah and Martha Scribner of New York City, a half-sister of Charles Scribner [*q.v.*], and they established a home in Ithaca, where two sons and three daughters were born. Schuyler was highly successful in his mercantile and banking enterprises in Tompkins County. Always active in religious work, he transferred his membership in 1842 from the Presbyterian Church to the Reformed Dutch Church (later Congregational), which he served for many years either as deacon or elder.

In politics Schuyler was a Whig with pronounced anti-slavery sentiments which prompted him to follow William H. Seward into the Republican party. His first political recognition came from the Union Republican convention of 1863 which nominated him for state treasurer. Running on a ticket headed by Chauncey M. Depew [q.v.] as candidate for secretary of state, and pledged to support the Lincoln administration, he was elected and served two years. The convention of 1865 denied him a renomination, but Gov. Reuben E. Fenton [q.v.] appointed him superintendent of the banking department (1866–70) with full responsibility for the banking institutions operating under state charter. Incensed by the reconstruction policies and the political corruption of the Grant régime, Schuyler joined the "reformers" who organized the Liberal Republican movement in 1872. With the support of Democrats and Liberal Republicans he was elected to the state assembly, where he served (1875) as chairman of the committee on banking and participated in the framing of a general savings-bank law. He enthusiastically applauded Gov. Samuel J. Tilden [q.v.] for his exposure of the corrupt "canal ring," and in January 1876 the governor named him auditor of the Canal Department. Here he served until 1880, correcting many of the most notorious abuses and waging a vigorous campaign for the abolition of tolls and the creation of a system of free commercial waterways. He gave generously of his time to the work of Cornell University, serving for twenty years on the board of trustees and acting as treasurer, without compensation, from 1868 to 1874.

Schuyler's interest in the genealogy of his own family drew him into extensive researches in the colonial history of New York, and in 1885 he published *Colonial New York: Philip Schuyler and His Family,* in two volumes. Although the work was not a comprehensive history of the province, the sketches of the Schuylers were set against the background of seventeenth and eighteenth century New York, which had been carefully, at times brilliantly, reconstructed from manuscript and printed sources. Completed only three years before his death, these volumes stand today as their author's most enduring monument.

[There is a very brief autobiographical sketch in G. W. Schuyler, *Colonial New York* (1885), II, 377. See also D. S. Alexander, *A Pol. Hist. of the State of N. Y.,*

vol. III (1909); *First Half-Century Book . . . of the First Church of Christ, Congregational, of Ithaca, N. Y.* (1881); *Cornell Era,* Feb. 4, 1888; *N. Y. Times,* Feb. 2, 1888.]   J. A. K—t.

SCHUYLER, JAMES DIX (May 11, 1848–Sept. 13, 1912), hydraulic and railroad engineer, was born at Ithaca, N. Y., the youngest of nine children of Philip Church and Lucy M. (Dix) Schuyler, and a descendant of Philip, younger brother of Peter Schuyler [q.v.]. His early education was received at Friends College, but for the most part his professional attainments and achievements were the result of his own constant study and reading and of his long and varied experience. He began his engineering career in 1869 as assistant on the location and construction of the Kansas Pacific Railway in Western Kansas and Colorado, and thereafter the West became his home. For six years he continued in railroad work, serving the Denver & Rio Grande Railroad, the North Pacific Coast Railroad in California, and the Stockton & Ione Railroad, of which he was chief engineer.

In 1877 he was made chief assistant state engineer of California and placed in charge of irrigation investigations in Great Central Valley. Resigning this position in 1882, he became chief engineer and general superintendent of the Sinaloa & Durango Railroad in Mexico. Returning to California, he undertook contract work in San Francisco. He built a section of the sea wall on the water front of the city (1884–85); raised the Sweetwater dam (1887–88); and constructed the Hemet dam, at that time the highest masonry dam in western America. In these and other enterprises he showed such skill and ability that thereafter he was a prominent figure in his profession and enjoyed a wide and successful business as consultant, his field of activity including Mexico, British Columbia, Japan, Brazil, and Hawaii. Among the projects with which he was connected were water supply systems for Denver; Ogden, Utah; and Los Angeles. As one of three consulting engineers appointed to report on plans for the Los Angeles aqueduct, fed by the Owens River some 250 miles distant, he made suggestions that ultimately resulted in the avoidance of twenty-five miles of heavy construction, and a saving of several million dollars. He was one of the commission of consulting engineers appointed by President Theodore Roosevelt in 1909 to judge the feasibility of the Gatun Dam and the other structures for the Panama Canal. His paper upon "Recent Practice in Hydraulic-Fill Dam Construction," presented in 1907 before the American Society of Civil Engineers (*Transactions,* LVIII, 1907), received the Thomas Fitch Rowland Prize for the best paper of the year and did much to stimulate the use of this important method of earth dam construction. It is noteworthy that he was twice winner of this prize, his first success having occurred in 1889, when he presented a paper on "The Construction of the Sweetwater Dam" (*Ibid.*, XIX, 1888). He contributed extensively to technical and scientific journals, but his best-known work is his book entitled *Reservoirs for Irrigation, Water-Power, and Domestic Water Supply,* published in 1901, with a second edition in 1908.

Schuyler's most notable work was in connection with dam designing and construction and especially in the development of the use of hydraulic fill dams, in which field he was a pioneer and leading authority. He was a prominent member of the American Society of Civil Engineers, serving as vice-president and director. In July 1889 he was married to Mrs. Mary Ingalls Tuliper of San Diego, Cal., who survived him. He died at Ocean Park, Cal.

[*Engineering News*, Apr. 17, 1913; *Trans. Am. Soc. Civil Engineers*, vol. LXXVI (1913); *Press Reference Lib.: Notables of the Southwest* (1912); *Who's Who in America*, 1912-13.]　　　　　　　　H. K. B.

SCHUYLER, LOUISA LEE (Oct. 26, 1837–Oct. 10, 1926), leader in welfare work, was a daughter of George Lee and Eliza (Hamilton) Schuyler of New York, and a great-granddaughter of Gen. Philip John Schuyler and of Alexander Hamilton [*qq.v.*]. Her father, a grandson of General Schuyler, married a cousin who was a grand-daughter of Hamilton and his wife, Elizabeth Schuyler, thus continuing the union of two families distinguished in Revolutionary history. Louisa, her younger sister Georgina, and her brother Philip were reared in a home of unpretentious wealth, described sixty years later in J. H. Choate's autobiography, *The Boyhood and Youth of Joseph Hodges Choate* (1917). The sisters passed many of their girlhood days at the country seat of their grandfather, James Alexander Hamilton [*q.v.*], near Dobbs Ferry, twenty miles up the Hudson. One of the earliest indications of Louisa Schuyler's interest in what has since become known generally as "welfare" work was her appearance at twenty-three as a volunteer teacher for the Children's Aid Society. Within a year the outbreak of the Civil War opened to her, as to thousands of other young Americans, new channels of service and grave responsibilities. She was active from the first in the women's war-relief work organized by Dr. Henry Whitney Bellows [*q.v.*] out of which grew the United States Sanitary Commission, the organization that anticipated

the Red Cross of a later date. In the four years of war she developed marked executive ability and organized information as well as express services but spent her strength so prodigally that almost seven years of rest, largely passed in Europe and Egypt, were required to achieve recuperation.

On her return to New York in 1871 with improved health, she became interested in the care and treatment of dependents committed to poorhouses and other local institutions. A project of her own, the State Charities Aid Association, was formed in 1872 at her father's house with the purpose of promoting visitation and inspection of public institutions by private citizens. In the beginning she had little help but in the course of time the association became an important factor in reforming abuses and in rallying the friends of constructive welfare effort, and similar societies were founded in other states. Within two years, impelled by conditions revealed to the State Charities visitors at Bellevue Hospital in New York City, she appealed successfully for the opening of a nurses' training school at Bellevue, the first in America. In their investigations the association's visitors found nothing more impressive than the plight of dependent insane confined in county poorhouses. The wrongs endured by these unfortunates had been eloquently set forth by Dorothea Lynde Dix [*q.v.*], and some of the extreme abuses had been abolished, but scientific methods of care and treatment could not be had in the average local almshouse of the time. Consequently, Miss Schuyler led a campaign for state care of the insane; in 1890, after many rebuffs, she was at last completely successful and all insane inmates of county poorhouses were by law transferred to commodious, well-administered state hospitals. As a trustee of the Russell Sage Foundation from its formation she became especially interested in work for the prevention of blindness. She was president of the foundation's committee out of which grew in 1915 the National Committee (later Society) for the Prevention of Blindness, an agency which has been the means of recovering vision for countless thousands of American children. The woman whose associates declared that she had "the mind of a lawyer and the will-power of a captain of industry," succeeded as completely in this as in her other humanitarian efforts. Illness overtook her old age, and even while she was engrossed in the task of preserving to others the priceless gift of vision she was herself deprived of its enjoyment. At almost eighty-nine she rounded out a lifetime of distinctively fruitful service.

[See G. W. Schuyler, *Colonial New York: Philip Schuyler and His Family* (2 vols., 1885); L. P. Brockett and Mary C. Vaughan, *Woman's Work in the Civil War* (1867); F. G. Peabody, *Reminiscences of Present-Day Saints* (1927); *Louisa Lee Schuyler, 1837–1926* (n.d.), published by Nat. Committee for the Prevention of Blindness; scattered references in W. R. Stewart, *The Philanthropic Work of Josephine Shaw Lowell* (1911); obituary and editorial, *N. Y. Times,* Oct. 11, 1926. For the story of the renovation of Bellevue Hospital, see Elizabeth C. Hobson, *Recollections of a Happy Life* (1916).]

W. B. S.

SCHUYLER, MARGARITA (1701–August 1782), colonial hostess, was the daughter of Johannes (1668–1747) and Elizabeth (Staats) Schuyler and was baptized Jan. 12, 1701. Her father, the youngest son of Philip Pieterse Schuyler, founder of the family in America, had participated in two expeditions against the French, had been a trusted emissary of Governor Bellomont in his diplomatic contest with the French authorities (1697–1701), and had labored to hold the Iroquois faithful to the English alliance despite French intrigues. As mayor of Albany (1703–06) and member of the board of commissioners of Indian affairs, he realized that New York's evolving policy of neutrality, dictated by the Albany merchants, placed an additional burden of frontier defense on New England, and he strove to assist the New England villages in warding off raids from disaffected eastern tribes. Thus Margarita's childhood was filled with the talk of her elders concerning military expeditions, Indian raids, conferences with the Mohawks and the Onondagas, and strife with the French Canadians. Her knowledge of such subjects was greatly enlarged as a result of her marriage, Dec. 29, 1720, to her cousin, Philip, son of Col. Peter Schuyler [*q.v.*].

The young couple established their home in a large brick house at "The Flatts," on the Hudson just north of Albany. The household routine moved so smoothly under Margarita's expert guidance that she had ample time to make her home the social center of the northern frontier. The Schuylers entertained not only the provincial aristocracy but also British officers and a host of merchants and officials interested in the fur-trade and in Indian relations. Mrs. Schuyler was as well informed as her husband, and many an English official was indebted to her for valuable advice on the traits of neighboring Indian tribes, the difficulties of transportation and the current state of relations with the French. Even after her husband's death in 1758, she continued to make "The Flatts" a sort of military and political headquarters. Having no children of her own, she found pleasure in adopting and educating many of her nephews and nieces and for half a century there was always some representative of the younger generation of Schuylers under her tutelage. By these beneficiaries of her generous affection she was greatly beloved. After 1765 she leased a house in Albany where she continued to hold court, but by this time the grace and beauty of her youth were gone. Her guests saw an excessively large woman who "filled a great chair from which she seldom moved. Her aspect was composed, and her manner such as was, at first, more calculated to inspire respect, than conciliate affection" (*Memoirs of an American Lady,* II, 145). Her last years were darkened by the shadows of the American Revolution, for she remained a firm and respected Loyalist to the end. In her will, however, which divided her considerable estate among ten nephews and nieces, she did not discriminate against those members of her family who had supported the colonial cause. She died at Albany in August 1782.

[A. M. Grant, *Memoirs of an American Lady* (2 vols., London, 1808), repr. in 1876 with notes by Joel Munsell, corrected in G. W. Schuyler, *Colonial N. Y.* (2 vols., 1885) and K. S. Baxter, *A Godchild of Washington* (1897); Peter Wraxall, *An Abridgement of the Indian Affairs . . . in the Colony of N. Y.* (1915), ed. by C. H. McIlwaine; E. B. O'Callaghan, *Docs. Rel. to the Col. Hist. of the State of N. Y.,* vols. IV (1854), V, IX (1855).]

J. A. K—t.

SCHUYLER, MONTGOMERY (Aug. 19, 1843–July 16, 1914), journalist, author, was born in Ithaca, N. Y., the son of the Rev. Anthony and Eleanor (Johnson) Schuyler. He was a descendant of Arent Schuyler, fourth son of Philip Pieterse Schuyler, American founder of the family, who came from Holland in 1650, settling at Beverwyck (Albany). Montgomery Schuyler entered Hobart College in 1858, but left without graduating. In 1865 he went to New York City and was soon a member of the brilliant group of young writers gathered about Manton Marble [*q.v.*], then editor of the *World*. He remained on the staff of the *World* until 1883 and then went to the *New York Times,* where he continued until his retirement from active journalism in 1907. Meanwhile, he had been managing editor of *Harper's Weekly* (1885–87) and reader for Harper & Brothers (1887–94). After 1912 he regularly contributed book reviews and articles on literary subjects to the New York *Sun.*

An omnivorous reader and student, Schuyler was able not only to give his editorial and feature writing both dignity and literary grace, but also to illuminate it with an inexhaustible supply of apt quotation and allusion. One series of sketches done for the *Times,* descriptive of an Easterner's impression of the West as seen on the first trip of the "Los Angeles Limited," was enlarged and published in book form as *West-*

ward the Course of Empire (1906). Schuyler also wrote much for the magazines, largely on literature and architecture. Although not a trained architect, he became, after the death of Russell Sturgis [*q.v.*], probably the foremost critic and historian of American architecture. With W. C. Conant, he published *The Brooklyn Bridge* (1883), some of his architectural essays appeared as *American Architecture: Studies* (1892), and a slender volume on *The Woolworth Building* was privately printed in 1913; but most of the material is scattered through the files of periodicals, in particular the *Architectural Record,* of which he was one of the founders (1891). He threw his influence on the side of the Gothic as against the classic tradition; later, he was interested in the skyscraper as an expression of modern American culture.

In the days when the Century Club was a focal center of social and intellectual life in New York, Schuyler was one of the wittiest conversationalists at the Saturday night reunions, where he counted among his intimate friends Homer Martin, John La Farge, Henry Holt, William C. Brownell, F. Hopkinson Smith, and Austin Flint [*qq.v.*]. On his retirement from the *Times* in 1907, he went to live at New Rochelle, where both he and his wife took an active interest in every plan for civic improvement. He had been married, on Sept. 16, 1876, to Katherine Beeckman Livingston, daughter of Robert Dwight and Mary (Armour) Livingston, of New York City, thus becoming allied with two other famous old New York families, the Beeckmans and the Livingstons. His wife was a woman of wit, energy, and talent, who is said to have given up an operatic career to marry him. When she died the shock of the loss seems to have hastened her husband's death, which took place at New Rochelle scarcely more than a week later. They were survived by two sons; a third son died in infancy.

[*Who's Who in America,* 1914–15; *N. Y. Times,* July 8, 17, 1914; *N. Y. Tribune,* July 8, 17, 1914; *Sun* (N. Y.), July 17, 1914; E. R. Smith, "Montgomery Schuyler and the History of American Architecture" (with a bibliog. listing fifty-eight books and articles by Schuyler on architecture), *Architectural Record,* Sept. 1914; G. W. Schuyler, *Colonial N. Y.: Philip Schuyler and His Family* (1885), vol. II; personal recollections of Schuyler's son, Robert Livingston Schuyler.] E. M. S.

SCHUYLER, PETER (Sept. 17, 1657–Feb. 19, 1724), soldier and official of colonial New York, was born at Albany (then Beverwyck), the second son of Philip Pieterse Schuyler, an emigrant from Amsterdam, and his wife, Margarita (Van Slichtenhorst), daughter of the resident director of Rensselaerwyck. Philip Pieterse, whose name first appears in the Albany

records on the occasion of his marriage in 1650, was engaged in trade and held the offices of magistrate and captain under both Dutch and English governments. Peter Schuyler may have attended a school founded at Albany in 1650, but his education was derived chiefly from early and prolonged application to public affairs in periods of incessant border warfare. At twenty-seven he was a lieutenant of cavalry in the Albany militia, later he was advanced to the rank of colonel, and when in 1686 Albany received its charter from Gov. Thomas Dongan [*q.v.*], Schuyler became its first mayor, and thus head of the board of Indian commissioners.

Three years later, Jacob Leisler [*q.v.*], who had seized control of New York, ordered the election of new aldermen and a new mayor of Albany, but the citizens refused to recognize his authority and Schuyler continued in office. After the massacre at Schenectady and the destruction of that town by French and Indians, Feb. 9, 1690, he wrote to the governor of Massachusetts appealing for help and asking cooperation in a spring campaign against the French, expressing the conviction that only the conquest of New France would arrest the scourge from which the newer settlements were suffering. In the face of danger and upon the advice of Massachusetts and Connecticut, the men of Albany in March yielded to Leisler's demands, but his commissioners promptly reinstated Schuyler and the other officers. In the following summer Schuyler took part in the unsuccessful cooperative campaign led by Fitz-John Winthrop of Connecticut against Quebec. In October, he was removed as mayor of Albany by order of Leisler, but after the arrival of Governor Sloughter in March 1691 and Leisler's imprisonment Schuyler resumed his duties as if they had never been interrupted.

Schuyler seemed to hold himself responsible for the safety of the pioneer front and always maintained a remarkable influence over the New York Iroquois (by whom he was affectionately called Quidor—their version of Peter), attending numerous conferences with them and visiting their villages to curb the operations of Canadian emissaries as well as to cement the old treaty between the Five Nations and the colony. In 1691 he led a company to Canada, proving in several engagements his superior soldierly qualities, and two years later he routed a party of French near Schenectady. Governor Sloughter made him a judge of common pleas in 1691 and recommended him for the council, and in March 1692, under Governor Fletcher, he was appointed.

Having enjoyed the favor of Fletcher, Schuyler could not win the graces of his successor, Richard Coote [*q.v.*], Earl of Bellomont, who adopted all the quarrels of the preceding ten years in the colony and was jealous, furthermore, of Schuyler's influence in Indian affairs. Nevertheless, in 1698 Bellomont sent him to Frontenac to announce the terms of the Treaty of Ryswick and provide for the return of prisoners of war, and employed him in provisioning the troops. In preparing for the abortive expeditions of 1709 and 1711 against Canada, Schuyler displayed characteristic energy. Between those undertakings he visited the court of Queen Anne, taking with him several Mohawk chiefs, including the famous Hendrick [*q.v.*]. On this occasion, it is said, he declined the dignity of knighthood (G. W. Schuyler, *post*, II, 37; for a disparaging view see E. B. O'Callaghan, *The Documentary History of the State of New York*, 4th ed., vol. III, 1850, pp. 541–42). Schuyler commanded the esteem of Gov. Robert Hunter [*q.v.*]; and, on Hunter's return to England, Schuyler as president of the council was acting governor from July 13, 1719, to Sept. 17, 1720. Some of his appointments alarmed Hunter as indications of a policy of change, and the new governor, William Burnet [*q.v.*], fearing Schuyler as a dangerous leader of opposition, brought about his removal from the council, after nearly fifty years of public service.

Schuyler was married twice: in 1681 or 1682 to Engeltie Van Schaick, by whom he had four children, three of whom died young, and in 1691 to Maria Van Rensselaer, daughter of Jeremiah Van Rensselaer, who also became the mother of four. Margarita, daughter of his first wife, married the nephew of the first Robert Livingston [*q.v.*]; Philip, one of three sons of the second wife, married his cousin Margarita Schuyler [*q.v.*]. Peter Schuyler owned numerous land grants, of which the most extensive was in the Saratoga patent.

[E. B. O'Callaghan, *Docs. Rel. to the Col. Hist. of the State of N. Y.*, vols. III–VII (1853–56), vol. IX (1855); *Calendar of N. Y. Colonial MSS. Indorsed Land Papers* (1864); *Calendar of Council Minutes, 1668–1783* (1902), being *N. Y. State Lib. Bull. 58*; G. W. Schuyler, *Colonial New York* (2 vols., 1885); Wm. Smith, *The Hist. of the Late Province of N. Y.* (1830), vol. I; Peter Wraxall, *An Abridgement of the Indian Affairs . . . in the Colony of N. Y.* (1915), ed. by C. H. McIlwain; H. L. Osgood, *The Am. Colonies in the Eighteenth Century*, vols. I, II (1924).]
R. E. D.

SCHUYLER, PHILIP JOHN (Nov. 11, 1733–Nov. 18, 1804), soldier and statesman, eldest son of Johannes and Cornelia (Van Cortlandt) Schuyler, belonged to the fourth genera-

tion of the family which was established in America by Philip Pieterse and Margarita (Van Slichtenhorst) Schuyler. Born at Albany, N. Y., where his father—merchant, alderman and Indian commissioner—died in 1741, Philip was reared in the Dutch tradition by his mother and his aunt, Margarita Schuyler [*q.v.*]. At the age of fifteen he was sent to New Rochelle to complete his formal education under Rev. Peter Stouppe, zealous and eccentric pastor of the French Protestant Church. There he learned to speak French and became so proficient in mathematics that in later years he delighted to solve surveying and engineering problems and to correspond with David Rittenhouse [*q.v.*] on the mathematics of astronomy. The two years at New Rochelle were marred by attacks of rheumatic gout, a hereditary malady which he had occasion to dread throughout his entire life. His study of books was soon supplemented by practical experience drawn from commercial and social contacts. In Albany he moved easily in the circles of the Dutch aristocracy. On his visits to New York he was welcomed by the De Lanceys and the Livingstons, talked politics with William Smith the younger and John Morin Scott [*qq.v.*], attended gay balls and receptions, and enjoyed the acting of the Hallams at the Nassau Street Theatre. However carefree he may have seemed to his associates, he was a purposeful and ambitious young man when he came of age in 1754 and waived his right of primogeniture that his sister and two brothers might share in their father's estate.

He played a minor but not unimportant rôle in the last phase of the struggle between Great Britain and France for North America. In 1755 Gov. James De Lancey [*q.v.*] commissioned him to raise and command a company in Gen. William Johnson's expedition against Crown Point. He participated in the skirmish at Lake George on Sept. 8, 1755, was designated to escort the French prisoners to Albany, took advantage of the brief furlough to marry, Sept. 17, Catherine, talented daughter of John Van Rensselaer of Claverack, and within a few weeks was back at Fort Edward, striving to create a depot of military stores. In the spring of 1756 he was a member of the force under Col. John Bradstreet [*q.v.*] which carried provisions to Oswego and cleared the Oneida portage of enemy raiders, and he became a devoted friend of his superior officer. The following year he resigned his commission, but continued to be interested in the provisioning of the armies, from which he derived a substantial income. He returned to the service in 1758 as a deputy commissary with the rank of major, served under Lord Howe [q.v.] in Abercromby's ill-fated expedition against Ticonderoga, and was with Bradstreet at the capture of Fort Frontenac on Lake Ontario. During the campaigns of 1759–60 he was stationed at Albany, where he collected and forwarded provisions to Amherst's forces. It was valuable experience, for it taught the future general how essential to the success of any army is an efficient service of supply.

In February 1761, Schuyler sailed for England to settle with the War Office the accounts of his friend, Colonel Bradstreet. While there he studied reports of British imports, hoping that his own estates might in the future supply some of the mother country's needs. He was particularly interested in new means of transportation and concluded that English canals could be duplicated in America. He returned to his native province eager for the life of a country gentleman. The final settlement in 1763 of his father's estate, which included one-third of his grandfather's lands, brought him thousands of acres in the Mohawk Valley and along the Hudson, while from his uncle Philip's estate he received additional land in the Saratoga patent and the old Schuyler homestead near West Troy. Saratoga was the favored portion of his heritage. There he cut choice timber from forests of pine and hard woods, developed water-power for his sawmills and gristmills, built the first water-driven flaxmill in the province, maintained a fleet of one schooner and three sloops on the Hudson, and started the products of his plantations and mills on trade routes which terminated in the West Indies or Great Britain. Elected to the Assembly in 1768, he was frankly hostile to ministerial or parliamentary interference with provincial commerce and industry. Although he constantly fought the De Lancey-Colden coalition of royalists, he never sympathized with the radicals among the "Sons of Liberty" or condoned mob violence. Nevertheless, Lieutenant-governor Cadwallader Colden [q.v.] regarded him as a great trouble maker and wrote in 1775 that Schuyler "wish'd to bring this Colony into all the dangerous & extravagant Schemes which Disgrace too many of the Sister Colonies" ("Colden Letter Books," post, II, 399).

Schuyler heartily approved the acts of the First Continental Congress, attended the convention (Apr. 20, 1775) which named New York's delegates to the Second Continental Congress, and accepted membership in the provincial delegation. On June 15 he was appointed one of the four major-generals under Washington and assigned to command the Northern Department, consisting of New York, in order "to sweeten and to keep up the spirit of that province" (Burnett, post, I, 137). With the half-hearted support of New England he recruited and provisioned an army, strengthened the garrisons at Ticonderoga and Crown Point, enlarged Fort Stanwix, checked the intrigues of Sir John Johnson [q.v.] with restless leaders of the Six Nations, and organized the expedition of 1775–76 against Canada. Ill health compelled him to turn over immediate command of the Canadian forces to Gen. Richard Montgomery [q.v.]. Although his skilful handling of the commissariat was an important factor in Montgomery's success at Montreal, the ultimate failure of the Canadian offensive discredited Schuyler with the New Englanders, many of whom disliked him as a severe disciplinarian and resented his support of New York's claims to the "New Hampshire Grants" (later Vermont).

This mutual antagonism between "Yorker and Yankee," aggravated in 1776 by Schuyler's quarrel with Gen. David Wooster [q.v.] and his controversy with Gen. Horatio Gates [q.v.], partly explains his serious difficulties during the Burgoyne campaign. In March 1777 he was reprimanded by Congress on a flimsy pretext put forward by the New Englanders, and Gates was given an independent command in the Northern Department. Two months later the legislators reversed themselves and recalled Gates (Journals of the Continental Congress, V, 526, VII, 180, 202, 364; Burnett II, 3, 11, 48). Returning to his post, Schuyler found an army "weak in numbers, dispirited, naked, in a manner, destitute of provisions . . . with little ammunition, and not a single piece of cannon" (Jared Sparks, Correspondence of the American Revolution, 1853, I, 394). He was not dismayed, however, and with the exception of his indecision concerning the defense of Ticonderoga, which was terminated by St. Clair's abandonment of the fort, July 6, 1777, he played a difficult game well. His retreat was cleverly designed to impede the British advance and to permit new levies of militia to harass Burgoyne, while his dispatch of Gen. Benedict Arnold [q.v.] to relieve Fort Stanwix wrecked St. Leger's plans. Schuyler did not reap the fruits of his labors, however, for Congress, alarmed by the loss of Ticonderoga, ordered Gates to supersede him, Aug. 4, 1777 (Journals, VIII, 604). There were ugly rumors that the New York general had been both incompetent and disloyal. That Schuyler ever responded to British efforts to win him over is doubtful, but data recently discovered in the

British headquarters papers in the William L. Clements Library may ultimately throw new light on the whole question.

At Schuyler's insistence, and after months of wrangling, Congress preferred charges of incompetence against him. He was acquitted with honor by a court martial in October 1778, and the following spring his resignation from the service was accepted. He remained, however, on the Board of Commissioners for Indian Affairs, advising Washington concerning the Sullivan-Clinton expedition against the Six Nations in 1779 and using his influence in Congress to emphasize the Indian menace along the New York frontier. He participated in the congressional sessions of November-December 1779 and February-April 1780, devoting himself to a report on depreciated currency and the issuance of new bills of credit, which Congress adopted with slight modification (*Journals,* Mar. 13–18, 1780; Burnett, V, 66–67, 71). From Apr. 13 to Aug. 11, 1780, he served as chairman of the committee at Headquarters authorized to assist Washington in reorganizing the staff departments of the army and in devising a scheme of effective cooperation with the French forces.

Schuyler held public office continuously from 1780 to 1798. In the state Senate, which he entered in September 1780, he advocated greater governmental power for both state and nation. He complained that New York had not treated its creditors fairly, suggested the funding of the state debt, urged the legislature to surrender all western land claims to the federal government, and insisted that the states confer upon congressional control of interstate and foreign commerce. His position on the Council of Appointment enabled him to rally the Federalists against the "junto" of George Clinton [*q.v.*], whose principles were "a state impost, no direct taxation, keep all power in the hands of the legislature, give none to Congress" (H. C. Van Schaack, *Memoirs of the Life of Henry Van Schaack,* 1892, p. 151). Like most of the great landlords in New York, Schuyler supported the movement which culminated in the Philadelphia Convention of 1787. Intimately associated with the career of his son-in-law, Alexander Hamilton [*q.v.*], he counseled the Federalists in their successful campaign to secure ratification of the Constitution by the Poughkeepsie convention. With Rufus King [*q.v.*] he represented New York in the first Senate of the United States, and became an aggressive champion of Hamilton's financial program. His holdings of government securities in 1791 probably exceeded $60,000, and Senator William Maclay

[*q.v.*] noted that opposition to the funding of the national debt caused Schuyler's hair to stand "on end as if the Indians had fired at him" (*The Journal of William Maclay,* 1927, p. 228). After the short term he was defeated for reëlection in 1791 by Aaron Burr [*q.v.*]; his own victory over Burr six years later was an empty honor, for ill health sent him into permanent retirement in January 1798.

From his various estates—in the Saratoga patent, at Cortlandt Manor, along the Mohawk, and in Dutchess County—he received large revenues. If his Saratoga lands may be regarded as typical, he usually rented farms for cash, two pounds per hundred acres annually, on the basis of a twenty-one year lease (Ledger of Rents at Saratoga, 1760–1805, New York Public Library). Although he scorned the unscrupulous land speculator, his own real-estate deals were considerable. Always a stalwart champion of the aristocratic landlords, he also joined the financiers who were becoming interested in banking, manufacturing, and transportation. His own investments included state and federal securities, stock in the Bank of the United States and the Bank of Albany, and shares in the Northern Inland Lock Navigation Company, and the Western Inland Lock Navigation Company. The last two ventures were incorporated under an act of 1792 which he guided through the state legislature. He regarded them as forerunners of a comprehensive canal policy in which he could render service to the state. In the same spirit of benefaction, while a member of the Board of Regents, he promoted a plan for the establishment of Union College at Schenectady and subscribed one hundred pounds toward its endowment.

Physically, Schuyler was a powerful man: tall, erect, and of commanding presence. His portrait by John Trumbull shows a strong countenance dominated by piercing eyes. He was always fashionably dressed, and his conduct seems to have been as conventionally correct as his clothes. His austere manner impressed many as arrogance and added to the list of his enemies, but those who knew him well were his devoted friends and fully appreciated his great service to the American cause in the dark days before Saratoga. Despite his long record in public office, he was seldom happy away from his family, which included three sons and five daughters who survived infancy. The loss of his wife in 1803 hastened his own death a year later. He was buried in the Albany Rural Cemetery, where a tall granite shaft now marks his grave.

[Schuyler Papers in the N. Y. Pub. Lib.; letters in N. Y. State Lib. and Lib. of Cong.; Gates Papers and James Duane Papers in N. Y. Hist. Soc.; B. J. Lossing, *The Life and Times of Philip Schuyler* (2 vols., 1860–73); Bayard Tuckerman, *Life of Gen. Philip Schuyler* (1903); G. W. Schuyler, *Colonial N. Y.* (2 vols., 1885); E. C. Burnett, *Letters of Members of the Continental Cong.* (vols. I–VII, 1921–34); Peter Force, *Am. Archives* (9 vols., 1837–53); *Journals of the Continental Cong.* (1904–); H. P. Johnston, *The Correspondence and Public Papers of John Jay* (4 vols., 1890–93); "The Colden Letter Books," vol. II, being *N. Y. Hist. Soc. Colls.*, vol. X (1878); *Proc. of a Gen. Court Martial . . for the Trial of Maj. Gen. Schuyler, Oct. 1, 1778* (1778); *Public Papers of George Clinton* (10 vols., 1899–1914); E. W. Spaulding, *N. Y. in the Critical Period* (1932).]   J. A. K—t.

SCHWAB, JOHN CHRISTOPHER (Apr. 1, 1865–Jan. 12, 1916), economist and librarian, was born in New York City, the son of Gustav Schwab, a merchant, head of Oelrichs & Company, and Eliza Catherine (von Post) Schwab. On both sides he was descended from German stock; on his mother's, from Henry Melchior Mühlenberg [*q.v.*]. After preparation in private schools he attended Yale College, from which he was graduated with the degree of A.B. in 1886, and continued there as a graduate student for a year, working under William Graham Sumner and Arthur Twining Hadley [*qq.v.*]. He then spent a year in Berlin and a year in Göttingen, studying economics and finance, and received the degree of Ph.D. from the latter institution in 1889. After a year devoted to research in New York, he was made lecturer in political economy at Yale and remained in that institution until his death, being appointed professor of political economy in 1898. His special interest was in public finance. His doctoral thesis, published in German at Göttingen in 1889 and at Jena in 1890, appeared in expanded form under the title *History of the New York Property Tax* (1890) as a publication of the American Economic Association. His most important publication was *The Confederate States of America, 1861–1865: a Financial and Industrial History of the South During the Civil War* (1901). He aimed to base this work on all accessible material, published and unpublished; he examined the archives of the Confederacy and of the Southern states for documents, and utilized files of newspapers of a number of different cities. Thoroughly prepared to interpret the facts he had collected and scrupulously fair in his judgments, he made an important contribution both to national history and to the knowledge of economic behavior under conditions of disordered finance and currency.

Beyond the ordinary services of a professor he was a leader in the reform of the college curriculum by the introduction of new subjects and greater freedom of choice, and showed his practical ability by planning and organizing the elaborate ceremonies, extending over several days and prepared for more than a year in advance, which marked the bicentennial celebration of the college. In recognition of the unusual combination in him of executive ability and scholarship, he was appointed librarian of Yale University, July 1, 1905. Most of his predecessors, distinguished scholars who showed rare judgment in enriching the collection, had not been especially interested in systematizing it and in facilitating its use. Following a much more liberal policy, Schwab extended the hours of use, opened the stacks to qualified students, and devised more effective arrangements for the purchase and distribution of books. In the eleven years during which he served as librarian, the total number of books was greatly increased. He married, Oct. 5, 1893, Edith Aurelia Fisher, daughter of Samuel Sparks Fisher of Cincinnati, by whom he had two children, a daughter and a son. He died in New Haven.

[*Who's Who in America*, 1914–15; Lucy S. White, *Fort Number Eight: The Home of Gustav and Eliza Schwab* (1925); *Obit. Record Grads. Yale Univ.* (1916); *Reports of Librarian of Yale Univ.*, 1905–15; *Yale Alumni Weekly*, Jan. 21, 1916; obituary in *New Haven Evening Reg.*, Jan. 12, 1916; personal acquaintance.]   C. D.

SCHWARZ, EUGENE AMANDUS (Apr. 21, 1844–Oct. 15, 1928), entomologist, was born in Liegnitz, Silesia, the son of Luise (Harnwolf) and Amandus Schwarz, cloth merchant and member of the Common Council of Liegnitz. As a boy, he became acquainted with the elder Gerhardt, a highly skilled entomologist, who taught him the fundamentals of entomology and of the natural sciences. After gymnasium days, he was sent by his parents to the University of Breslau. His main studies were supposed to be philological, but he retained a strong interest in entomology. His first entomological publication appeared in 1869. In 1870 he was with the German army before Paris, in the distributing hospital of the medical corps. After the Franco-Prussian War he returned to the University of Breslau, and in 1872 was a student at the University of Leipzig. During these years he devoted almost his entire attention to entomological studies; finally, fearing to tell his parents that he had neglected to prepare himself for the career they had planned for him, he left Europe without notifying his family and arrived in the United States in December 1872. Bringing with him a letter of recommendation from a famous German entomologist, he was employed by Dr. Hermann August Hagen [*q.v.*] in the Museum of Comparative Zoology at Cambridge. At Cambridge he met Henry Guernsey Hubbard, and the acquaintance ripened into a lifelong friendship. When Hubbard graduated from Harvard, Schwarz went with him to Detroit, Mich., where they founded the Detroit Scientific Association and began the building up of collections. During the winter of 1874–75 they went to Florida together and began a study of the entomological fauna there; in the following year Schwarz repeated the journey. In the summer of 1877 he went with Hubbard on an expedition to the Lake Superior region, where they made a collection of an enormous number of beetles, the basis of their study entitled *The Coleoptera of Michigan* (1879). In 1878 Schwarz went to Colorado to collect *Coleoptera* for John Lawrence LeConte [*q.v.*], but the season had hardly started when he was offered a position in the Department of Agriculture by Charles Valentine Riley [*q.v.*]. This he accepted and spent the following winter investigating the cotton worm from Texas to the Bahamas.

For more than fifty years he remained in the service of the United States government, holding a position with the Bureau of Entomology after March 1881. He was considered to be the most learned coleopterist in America, possibly the most learned in the world. He was, in addition, a general entomologist, whose knowledge of the literature of entomology was stupendous, and one of the best field men in the government service. He was connected with many important investigations, many of which he conducted, and he was the guide and mentor of the younger men who joined the force. In 1898 he was made custodian of the *Coleoptera* in the United States National Museum, and toward the close of his active life in August 1926, when he retired, he was almost completely immersed in museum work. He shunned publicity and would not allow the editors of *Who's Who in America* or of the *American Men of Science* to mention his name. His published bibliography contains almost four hundred titles, mainly relating to *Coleoptera,* but a large field of biological observation. He was one of the founders of the Entomological Society of Washington and in 1916 was made its honorary president for life. He never married.

[*Proc. Entomological Soc. of Washington,* vol. XXX (1928), with portrait, bibliog., and map of Schwarz's expeditions; *Annals Entomological Soc. of America,* Mar. 1929; *Entomological News,* Jan. 1929; *Science,* Nov. 9, 1928; *Evening Star* (Washington, D. C.), Oct. 16, 1928.]   L. O. H.

SCHWATKA, FREDERICK (Sept. 29, 1849–Nov. 2, 1892), explorer, was born at Ga-

lena, Ill., the son of Frederick Schwatka. At the age of ten he was taken by his family to Salem, Ore., where he worked as a printer and attended Willamette University. In 1867 he received an appointment to West Point, from which he graduated in June 1871. Commissioned as second lieutenant in the 3rd Cavalry, he served at various army posts throughout the United States and at the same time studied both medicine and law. He was admitted to the Nebraska bar in 1875 and the following year received a medical degree from the Bellevue Hospital Medical College in New York City.

But it was neither as a lawyer nor as a doctor that he established his reputation. He became interested in exploration, and his adventurous imagination was seized by reports brought from the Arctic regions by Capt. Thomas F. Barry concerning the fate of the famous expedition of Sir John Franklin (see *Dictionary of National Biography*). For thirty years following the loss of this expedition British and American explorers had sought the bodies or the papers of the Franklin party. Schwatka persuaded the American Geographical Society to organize a new search in the Arctic. This expedition, commanded by Schwatka and William Henry Gilder [*q.v.*] of the *New York Herald,* sailed from New York on June 19, 1878, in the *Eothen.* The explorers did not return for more than two years. During their search in King William Land in 1879–1880 they performed the longest sledge journey then on record, being absent from their base of supplies for eleven months and twenty days and traversing 2,819 geographical or 3,251 statute miles. Schwatka's search resolved the last doubts about the fate of the Franklin expedition. He discovered the wreckage of the one untraced ship, located many of the graves of members of the party, gave other mortal remains decent burial, brought back various relics, and established beyond doubt that Franklin's records were lost. "Schwatka's search," described by Gilder in articles in the *Herald,* became a popular phrase, and his discoveries were hailed as a triumph of Arctic exploration. In 1885 he resigned from the army and thereafter devoted himself to expeditions and to writing and lecturing. He explored the course of the Yukon River, described in his *Along Alaska's Great River* (1885) and *Nimrod in the North* (1885); he commanded the Alaskan expedition launched by the *New York Times* in 1886 and published his *The Children of the Cold* (1886); and he later visited northern Mexico and described the Tarahumari Indians of Chihuahua in a volume published posthumously, *In the Land of Cave and Cliff Dweller*

(1893). His amazing and spectacular journeys, much as they appealed to the popular imagination, resulted in no great contributions to scientific knowledge; he did establish the fact, however, that white men could exist and carry on useful scientific work in the Arctic if they conformed to native habits. During the last years of his life he suffered intensely from a stomach complaint which necessitated the use of laudanum. He died in Portland, Ore., of an overdose of this drug.

[G. W. Cullum, *Biog. Reg. . . . Officers and Grads. U. S. Mil. Acad.*, vol. III (1891); *Twenty-Fourth Ann. Reunion . . . Grads. U. S. Mil. Acad.* (1893); Newton Bateman and Paul Selby, *Hist. Encyc. of Ill.* (1900); W. H. Gilder, *Schwatka's Search* (1881); obituaries in *N. Y. Times, N. Y. Tribune*, Nov. 3, 1892; information from Charles Montague of N. Y. City.]　F. M.

SCHWEINITZ, EDMUND ALEXANDER de (Mar. 20, 1825–Dec. 18, 1887), Moravian bishop and historian, the son of Lewis David von Schweinitz [*q.v.*], and Louisa Amelia (Ledoux) de Schweinitz, was born in Bethlehem, Pa. Reared in a vibrating religious atmosphere, all of his education was directed to the end of preparing him for the Moravian ministry. He was enrolled in the parochial school for three years, studied at the preparatory school at Nazareth Hall, Nazareth, Pa., for five years, and then entered the theological seminary at Bethlehem. At the age of nineteen he sailed for Europe, visited a number of Moravian centers, and matriculated at the University of Berlin, where he sat under August Neander and other eminent scholars. In 1846 he returned to America and accepted a teaching post at Nazareth Hall, offering also, during this four-year period, instruction in the theological seminary.

After a brief pastorate at Dover, Ohio, he returned to Europe and at Herrnhut, Saxony, was married in 1850 to Lydia J. de Tschirschky, of a noble Silesian family. Once more in America he was placed in charge of the Moravian Church at Lebanon, Pa., and later was called to Philadelphia to preside over the First Church in that city. In 1855 he added to his duties the professorship of theology in the seminary, the theological students, few in number, taking up their residence in his Philadelphia parsonage. He also became the editor of the *Moravian,* a weekly church paper, which appeared first on Jan. 1, 1856. Up to this period the entire Unitas Fratrum or Moravian Church membership had been under the full control of the General Synod, meeting from time to time at Herrnhut, Saxony. Elected as a delegate from the United States to the Synod in 1851, de Schweinitz exerted himself successfully in bringing about certain fundamental alterations in the principles of church government. As a result, the Synod granted local autonomy to the American province.

During the period of the Civil War de Schweinitz was in charge of the Lititz Church in Pennsylvania, and in 1864 was transferred to Bethlehem, where he remained for sixteen years. In 1867, resigning the editorship of the *Moravian,* he accepted the presidency of the theological seminary—which, after having been shifted from Bethlehem to Nazareth, and from Nazareth to Philadelphia, now was permanently established at Bethlehem—and succeeded in enlisting the financial support of the local churches in its behalf. His elevation to the Episcopate followed three years later, and in 1879 he was elected to the highest office within the Moravian Church when he became president of the General Synod. As a result of this accumulation of executive duties, he was compelled to resign his pastorate of the Bethlehem Church, and in 1885 he also gave up the presidency of the theological seminary to concentrate his attention on the work of the Moravian missionary society.

In 1859 he had published *The Moravian Manual*; in 1861, a work entitled *Systemic Benevolence*; in 1865, *The Moravian Episcopate*; in 1870, the two volumes of *The Life and Times of David Zeisberger,* a work of excellent scholarship and historical value; in 1881, *Some of the Fathers of the Moravian Church*; and in 1885, the first volume of a projected monumental history of the Moravian Church entitled *The History of the Church Known as the Unitas Fratrum.* In 1877 he published *The Financial History of the American Province of the Unitas Fratrum and of its Sustentation Fund,* and in 1887, *The Centennial Anniversary of the Society of the United Brethren for Propagating the Gospel Among the Heathen.* His unceasing labors undermined his health, but he continued his activities as a bishop and author up to the time of his death. He left behind him his unfinished volume on the history of the renewed Unitas Fratrum. His first wife died in 1866, leaving two sons and two daughters. He was married a second time in 1868 to Isabel Allison Boggs and had one child.

[Manuscript records of the Moravian Church in the Bethlehem, Pa., archives; *In Memoriam, Edmund Alexander de Schweinitz, S.T.D. Episcopus Fratrum* (n.d.); J. T. Hamilton, *A Hist. of the Ch Known as the Moravian Ch.* (1900); W. N. Schwarze, *Hist. of the Moravian Coll. and Theol. Seminary, Trans. Moravian Hist. Soc.,* vol. VIII (1909); Augustus Schultze, *Guide to the Old Moravian Cemetery of Bethlehem, Pa., 1742–1910* (1912), also in *Proc. and Addresses, Pa.-German Soc.,* vol. XXI (1912); *Press* (Philadelphia, Pa.), Dec. 19, 1887.]　L. H. G.

SCHWEINITZ, EMIL ALEXANDER de
(Jan. 18, 1866–Feb. 15, 1904), biochemist, was
born at Salem, N. C., the son of Bishop Emil
Adolphus de Schweinitz and the grandson of
Lewis David von Schweinitz [q.v.]. His mother
was Sophia A. Herman of Salem, N. C. He was
christened Emil Adolphus, but in his maturity
changed his middle name to Alexander. His father was the administrator of the affairs of the
southern province of the Moravian Church and
the head of the Salem Academy. The boy's early
education was acquired at Nazareth Hall, and
the Moravian college at Bethlehem, Pa. Subsequently he entered the University of North Carolina where he received the A.B. degree in 1882
and the Ph.D. in 1885. He then studied at the
Universities of Berlin and Göttingen in Germany, receiving from the latter the degree of
Ph.D. in chemistry in 1886. He was made assistant in the division of chemistry in the Department of Agriculture in 1888. On Jan. 1,
1890, he was transferred to the Bureau of Animal Industry and placed in charge of the research in biochemistry. A separate division was
created for this work in 1894 and de Schweinitz
remained its head until his death.

His work was confined to research concerning
the metabolic products of disease-producing bacteria, the chemical composition of these bacteria,
and the production of means of immunity from
them. He took particular interest in devising
methods of protection from animal scourges such
as hog cholera, tuberculosis, and glanders, and
he was the first to record the use of attenuated
human tubercle bacilli for the creation of immunity in animals, his scheme being thus in contrast to the bovine *Bacillus-Calmette-Guerin.*
His published works consist of a large number
of monographs and reports, several of which
were prepared in collaboration with Dr. Marion
Dorset, and published by his department between 1894 and 1900. *The War with the Mi-
crobes* was published in the *Smithsonian Institution Annual Report,* 1896 (1898), but had
previously been printed in *Science,* Apr. 9, 1897.
His last work done in conjunction with Dr.
Dorset appeared in 1905, *The Comparative
Virulence of Human and Bovine Tubercle Bacilli.* He represented the United States at the
international congress on medicine and hygiene
which met in Paris in 1900. In addition to his
labors for the government he was dean and professor of chemistry in the medical school of Columbian (now George Washington) University,
Washington, D. C. The new buildings and hospital of that institution are, in a real sense, a
monument to his arduous labors. His death was

caused by uremic poisoning induced by an attack of typhoid fever which he had suffered the
preceding summer. He was unmarried and was
survived by three sisters.

[*Who's Who in America,* 1903–05 ; Marion Dorset,
"Emil Alexander de Schweinitz," *Proc. of the Wash-
ington Acad. of Sciences,* vol. X (1908) ; *Washington*
(D. C.) *Post,* Feb. 16, 1904.]   A. G. R.

SCHWEINITZ, LEWIS DAVID von (Feb.
13, 1780–Feb. 8, 1834), clergyman of the Mora-
vian Church, botanist, and pioneer mycologist
of America, was born at Bethlehem, Pa., the eldest son of Baron Hans Christian Alexander von
Schweinitz of Leubla, Saxony, who came to
America in 1770. He changed the German form
of his name, Ludwig David von Schweinitz, to
Lewis, and sometimes used Louis von or de
Schweinitz. His sons adopted the form de
Schweinitz. His mother was Anna Dorothea
Elizabeth, daughter of Baron Johannes de Watte-
ville and Henrietta Benigna Justina, daughter of
Nicholaus Lewis, Count Zinzendorf [q.v.]. At
seven years of age he was sent to Nazareth Hall,
where, during eleven years he was distinguished
for his linguistic abilities, his satiric humor, and
for his awakening interest in botany. He accompanied his family to Germany in 1798 and
entered the Moravian theological seminary at
Niesky, in Silesia, where he distinguished himself in theological studies. He also continued
most ardently his investigations in plant life under the inspiring direction of J. B. de Albertini,
with whose assistance he published in 1805 his
first work, *The Fungi of Lusatia,* a volume of
four hundred pages in Latin, containing twelve
plates showing seventy-three new species, drawn
and engraved by von Schweinitz. He taught at
Niesky until 1807 when he began a pastorate of
seven years at Gnadenberg. He then served at
Gnadau in Saxony until March 1812 when he
was appointed general agent of the Moravian
Church at Salem, N. C.

In the midst of the troublous days of the Napoleonic breakdown and the War of 1812, he
started with his bride Louisa Amelia Ledoux,
daughter of a Huguenot family of Stettin, via
Denmark for Sweden in order to embark from a
neutral country. The travelers were detained
for some months at Kiel where his attainments
so impressed the authorities that they conferred
upon him the degree of Ph.D., *causa honoris.*
After thrilling adventures on the privateer-in-
fested Atlantic they reached New York late in
the year and at once set out for Salem. In spite
of arduous official duties as administrator of the
province and as head of the Salem Academy, he
nevertheless found time to explore that unchart-

ed botanical area and to keep up a constant correspondence with experts in England, Germany, and France. His next work, *The Fungi of North Carolina,* also in Latin, was published in 1818 at Leipzig, under the editorial care of Dr. D. F. Schwaegrichen. It described over 1,000 species of which 300 were new to science. In 1821 he published, at Raleigh, N. C., a pamphlet describing seventy-six *Hepaticae,* of which nine had been discovered by him, and in the same year submitted to the *American Journal of Science* (published in volume V, 1822), a monograph on the genus *Viola,* naming five new species. He was offered the presidency of the University of North Carolina which he declined because of the pressure of his work (*Popular Science Monthly,* Apr. 1894, p. 837).

In 1821 he became administrator of the northern province of the Moravian Church and removed to Bethlehem, Pa., where he continued his botanical researches and diligently advanced his herbarium. When Thomas Nuttall [*q.v.*] was called to England and unable to continue the description of the plants collected by Thomas Say on the expedition of Stephen Harriman Long [*q.v.*] to the Northwest, von Schweinitz completed the task. The catalogue was published in the second volume of W. H. Keating, *Narrative of An Expedition to the Source of St. Peter's River* (1824). In 1823 he made an analytical table of the genus *Carex* which he presented to the New York Lyceum of Natural History, and which, having been edited by John Torrey, was published under both names in the *Annals* of the society, June and October 1825. The *American Journal of Science* published his "List of the Rarer Plants found near Easton, Penn." in August 1824. During his absence at a meeting of the General Synod in Germany, the *Journal of the Academy of Natural Sciences* of Philadelphia published, volume V, part 1 (1825), his description of a new American species of *Sphaeriae.* When he returned to America early in 1826 he devoted his attention to his greatest work, *A Synopsis of North American Fungi,* which he presented, in 1831, to the American Philosophical Society of Philadelphia. It classifies over 3,000 species of 246 genera of which 1,200 species and seven genera were of his own discovery (see *Transactions,* volume IV, new series, 1834).

An unusual pressure of official duties at this time cut off his out of door exercise, and sedentary work undermined his health. A trip to Indiana in the summer of 1831 to establish a church at Hope was temporarily beneficial, but the cold winter of 1833–34 and certain unfortunate exposures cancelled this gain. He died in Beth-

lehem and was buried in the Moravian Cemetery, his widow and four sons surviving him. Edmund Alexander de Schweinitz [*q.v.*] was his son, and Emil Alexander de Schweinitz [*q.v.*], his grandson. Von Schweinitz' collection of plants from all parts of the world, containing 23,000 phanerogams and many thousand cryptogams, was bequeathed to the Academy of Natural Sciences in Philadelphia and is there preserved.

[E. A. de Schweinitz, Hist. of the de Schweinitz Family, manuscript in the archives of the Moravian Church, Bethlehem, Pa.; manuscript journal in the archives at Herrnhut, Saxony; "The Corresp. of Schweinitz and Torrey," edited by C. L. Shear and N. E. Stevens, in *Memoirs of the Torrey Botanical Club,* vol. XVI, no. 3, July 1921; W. R. Johnson, *A Memoir of the Late Lewis David von Schweinitz* (1835); "The Journey of Lewis David von Schweinitz to Goshen . . . in 1831," translated by Adolf Gerber (1927), also published in *Ind. Hist. Soc. Pubs.,* vol. VIII (1930); "Memoirs of Brother Louis David De Schweinitz," *United Brethren's Missionary Intelligencer,* 3rd quart., 1834; *Popular Sci. Monthly,* Apr. 1894; J. H. Martin, *Hist. Sketch of Bethlehem in Pa.* (1872); *Poulson's Am. Daily Advertiser,* Feb. 13, 1834.]

A. G. R.

SCIDMORE, ELIZA RUHAMAH (Oct. 14, 1856–Nov. 3, 1928), author and traveler, was born in Madison, Wis., the daughter of George Bolles and Eliza Catherine (Sweeney) Scidmore. She was a descendant of Thomas Skidmore (Scudamore), who came to America from Gloucester, England, in 1635 with the company of Gov. John Winthrop, Jr. She was educated in private schools and spent a year, 1873–74, at Oberlin College. She then began writing society letters from Washington to such newspapers as the *New York Times* and the *St. Louis Globe-Democrat.* Graduating from this apprenticeship, she went to Alaska, where she obtained material for newspaper articles which were later incorporated in her first book, *Alaska, Its Southern Coast and the Sitkan Archipelago* (1885). From that time on, she was an inveterate traveler, not only visiting Europe, but also living for many years in the Orient, where she made prolonged stays in Japan, India, China, Java, and the Philippines at a time when "around the world" cruises and guidebooks to the East were still unborn.

She joined the National Geographic Society in 1890, three years after its organization, and during the earlier part of her long membership served as corresponding secretary, associate editor, foreign secretary, and member of the board of managers, the only woman upon whom this honor had ever been bestowed. In 1891 she published *Jinrikisha Days in Japan,* and in 1893, *Appletons' Guide-Book to Alaska and the Northwest Coast.* She served as one of the secretaries to the Oriental Congress held in Rome in 1897 and published her *Java, the Garden of the East* the same year. In 1900 her *China, the Long-Lived Empire* appeared. She was a delegate to the Oriental Congress held in Hamburg in 1902, and the following year brought out her *Winter India*. In 1907 she published *As the Hague Ordains,* for which she was decorated by the Japanese Emperor. In addition to writing she appeared frequently as a lecturer. She was a regular contributor to such publications as the *National Geographic Magazine, Outlook, Century, Asia, World Today,* and *Harper's Weekly.* Her work for the *Geographic* was especially noteworthy because of its illustrations, for she was an accomplished photographer. In an article in the *Century* (Mar. 10, 1910) she relates her long-continued efforts to have Japanese cherry trees planted in Washington, a project which was later carried out by others.

Her writings are noteworthy not only for the material chosen for treatment, but also for their vividness of style. She wrote with the conviction that international friendliness could be promoted by an understanding of the underlying psychology of the customs of peoples alien to her own countrymen. This conviction prevented her books from having the ephemeral quality frequently found in books of travel. Her political articles give evidence of her knowledge of existing conditions and of her penetrating ability to foresee coming political difficulties. Her imaginative faculty enabled her to see the awakening inhabitants of Madura "yawning like alligators." Written in praise of the Japanese treatment of prisoners during the Russo-Japanese War, *As the Hague Ordains* is a delightful book in the memoir style that found favor with readers of belles-lettres. Although known chiefly as a writer, she also merits recognition as an ambassador of good will between America and Japan. In 1925 she settled in Geneva, where she was an ardent advocate of the League of Nations. The Japanese Government requested that her ashes be interred in Yokohama, and the urn containing them was taken there by the Japanese minister to Switzerland.

[E. C. Hawley, *A Geneal. and Biog. Record of the Pioneer Thomas Skidmore* (1911); M. W. Cameron, *The Biog. Encyc. of Am. Women,* vol. I (1924); Oliver Martin, "How the Japanese Cherry Trees Came to Washington," in *Transmitter* (Chesapeake and Potomac Telephone Company), Apr. 1934; *Who's Who in America,* 1920–21; *Woman's Who's Who of America,* 1914–15; *Evening Star* (Washington), Nov. 3, 1928; *N. Y. Times,* Nov. 4, 1928.]   E. W. H.

SCOLLARD, CLINTON (Sept. 18, 1860–Nov. 19, 1932), poet, was born in Clinton, N. Y.,

the son of James Isaac and Elizabeth (Stephens) Scollard. He received his early education at Clinton Liberal Institute, and graduated from Hamilton College in 1881. He then taught at the Brooklyn Polytechnic Institute until February 1883, when, for his health, he visited Florida, Arizona, and California. A year later he received the degree of A.M. from Hamilton, and in subsequent years he continued his graduate studies at Harvard—where he met Bliss Carman and Frank Dempster Sherman—and at Cambridge, England. While abroad he made the acquaintance of Edmund Gosse, Austin Dobson, and Andrew Lang; and a trip to the Near East left a marked impression on his mind. In 1888 he joined the faculty of Hamilton College as professor of English, continuing as such until 1896; during the year 1911–12 he acted in the same capacity.

Scollard's devotion to literature is marked both by his work as a college professor and by the forty-odd books he published in his lifetime. His first volume, *Pictures in Song* (1884), following a popular trend in American poetry, contained verse chiefly in the miniature forms, those of the French occupying a conspicuous place. A few years later he abandoned this style for the more vigorous "Vagabondia" note made popular by Bliss Carman and Richard Hovey [q.v.], but, as with Carman, the spirit of the open road finally yielded to a more mystical view of Nature, which Scollard sought to interpret in its manifold relations to human life. A great admirer of Poe, he found much that was best in life in dreams and visions, but he felt wistfully, too, the Platonic impermanence of our hopes and ideals. If Scollard caught some of Poe's dream-like quality, he retained, however, nothing of his gloom, for his poetry is significant for its courageous optimism.

Scollard's work displays a painstaking care in versification, which he inherited from the late nineteenth century. Seldom carried out of himself by the stress of passion, he seems at times too conscious of the form in which he is working; yet a charming lyricism frequently pervades his work, suggesting a remoteness from the concerns of every-day life. This feeling of escape sought expression in a varied subject matter, often connected with his travels; *Songs of Sunrise Lands* (1892) and *Italy in Arms and Other Poems* (1915) illustrate his absorbing interest in the Orient and in Italy. His return to contemporary American life, however, is evinced in several volumes of lyrics inspired by the World War. Scollard's prose works include a number of romances of Renaissance Italy, a book of nature essays, and a volume of foreign travel sketches.

Scollard was twice married: first, in 1890, to Georgia Brown of Jackson, Mich., by whom he had a daughter; they were divorced in 1924 and that same year he married Jessie B. Rittenhouse, the poet. One of his most intimate friends was Frank Dempster Sherman [q.v.], to whom he was drawn by a community of poetic and academic interests; *A Southern Flight* (1905), a volume of verse done in collaboration, was the chief literary product of this friendship. On Sherman's death in 1916, Scollard wrote *Elegy in Autumn* (1917), in which his friend is addressed as "brother in song," and edited *The Poems of Frank Dempster Sherman* (copr. 1917), for which he composed an excellent critical introduction. Scollard was a member of a number of literary associations, including the National Institute of Arts and Letters. He died of heart disease at his home in Kent, Conn.

[The most important source is *The Singing Heart: Selected Lyrics and Other Poems of Clinton Scollard* (1934), ed., with a memoir by Jessie B. Rittenhouse; others are: *Who's Who in America*, 1932–33; *Who's Who in N. Y.*, 1929; *N. Y. Times*, Nov. 20, 1932; *New York Herald Tribune*, Nov. 20, 1932; *Hamilton Coll. Bull.*, Apr. 1933; *Lit. Digest*, Mar. 11, 1933; *Class of '81, Hamilton Coll.: The Record of Forty Years, 1881–1921* (n.d.); J. B. Rittenhouse, *The Younger Am. Poets* (1904); H. W. Cook, *Our Poets of Today* (1923); *Publishers' Weekly*, Nov. 26, 1932; *Clinton Scollard* (n.d.), a pamphlet, with a memorial address by W. P. Shepard and a bibliog. by J. D. Ibbotson; letters from Miss Jessie B. Rittenhouse and J. D. Ibbotson, librarian of Hamilton College. Scollard's papers and MSS. are in the Hamilton College library.]

N. F. A.

SCOTT, AUSTIN (Aug. 10, 1848–Aug. 15, 1922), educator, president of Rutgers College, was born at Maumee, near Toledo, Ohio, the son of Jeremiah Austin and Sarah (Ranney) Scott. He was named Frank Austin, but dropped the first name soon after reaching maturity. Graduated from Yale College with the degree of A.B. in 1869, he spent a year at the University of Michigan, where in 1870 he received the degree of A.M.; and then went abroad and studied at the University of Berlin and the University of Leipzig, receiving the degree of Ph.D. from Leipzig in 1873. His chief interest was history, especially political history, and his ability and learning brought him into important connections even in student days. In Germany, he assisted George Bancroft, at that time minister of the United States to Germany, in preparing his history of the United States. He was also charged with the responsibility of bearing important dispatches from Berlin to Washington.

On his return to the United States he was instructor in German at the University of Michi-

gan from 1873 to 1875, and then, for seven years, an associate in history at Johns Hopkins University, organizing there a seminar of American history. During this period he continued as assistant to Bancroft, assembling and arranging historical material for him. In 1883 he was called to be professor of history, political economy, and constitutional law at Rutgers College. He remained with the college until his death forty years later, becoming at once an important influence in its life. He was an unusual teacher, with abundant learning in his field, fluency of speech, vivacity of manner, and a quick turn of wit. The passing generations of students found him an effectual master of the classroom and acknowledged great indebtedness to his courses and his personality. The subject to which he gave most attention was constitutional law and to his work in this field was due his chief distinction. In time his title became professor of political science.

Austin Scott's eminence and influence as a teacher, his vigorous participation in all faculty activities, and his familiarity with certain administrative questions led to his election as president of Rutgers College in November 1890, and he was inaugurated Feb. 1891. He served with great devotion for fifteen years, during which time the college property and endowment were increased and the educational program enlarged. A gymnasium and a library were erected and the teaching staff was kept at a high level of efficiency. A friendly suit with the state resulted in a clarification of the relations between the state and Rutgers College, the scientific school of which had been made in 1864 the state college for the benefit of agriculture and the mechanic arts. During the entire time of his service as president he continued to some extent the teaching which was always the work most agreeable to him, and in 1906 he resigned the presidency in order to confine himself again to his professorial duties. For sixteen years more he gave valued teaching service to the students and generous administrative support to the succeeding president.

He took an active interest in the civic affairs of New Brunswick. For many years he was president and chief contributor to the Historical Club. In 1912 he was elected mayor of the city on the Democratic ticket and served in that office for three years with advantage to the material and moral welfare of the community. He was an elder in the Second Reformed Church and took an important part in its enterprises; he was also one of the board of superintendents of the New Brunswick Theological Seminary. On Feb.

21, 1882, he married Anna Prentiss Stearns, daughter of Jonathan French Stearns of Newark, N. J. He died at his summer home, Granville Centre, Mass., and was buried there.

[*Memorial Meeting for Austin Scott, Ph.D., LL.D.* (1923); W. H. S. Demarest, *Hist. of Rutgers Coll.* (1924); *Proc. N. J. Hist. Soc.,* vol. VII (1922); *Yale Univ. Obit. Record,* 1923; *Who's Who in America,* 1920–21; *N. Y. Times,* Aug. 17, 1922.]   W. H. S. D.

SCOTT, CHARLES (c. 1739–Oct. 22, 1813), soldier, governor of Kentucky, was born in that part of Goochland County, Va., which later became Powhatan County. Scottsville, formerly the county seat of Powhatan, was named in his honor. In his seventeenth year he served as a non-commissioned officer under Washington in the Braddock campaign. At the commencement of the Revolution, he raised the first companies of volunteers from south of James River to enter actual service, and commanded them at Williamsburg, Va., in July 1775. He was appointed lieutenant-colonel of the 2nd Virginia Regiment, Feb. 13, 1776, became colonel of the 5th in May, was transferred to the 3rd in August, and on Apr. 2, 1777, was commissioned brigadier-general in the Continental Army. A great part of the winter of 1777–78 he spent at Valley Forge. He rendered gallant service at Trenton, Germantown, Monmouth, and Stony Point, and in 1780 was captured at Charleston, S. C., remaining on parole thereafter until his exchange near the close of the war. He was brevetted major-general Sept. 30, 1783, and was one of the original members of the Society of the Cincinnati.

By an act of the Virginia legislature in October 1783, Scott was designated one of a deputation of officers of the Continental line to appoint superintendents and surveyors to locate and survey the western lands given by law to the officers and soldiers on the Continental establishment. He removed to Kentucky two years later and settled in that part of Fayette afterwards taken to form the county of Woodford. In 1789 and 1790 he represented Woodford County in the Virginia Assembly. In April 1790 he took part in the fruitless expedition of Gen. Josiah Harmar [q.v.] against the Indians on the Scioto, and in 1791 was a member of the local board of war and commandant of the Kentucky district, with the rank of brigadier-general. Between May 23 and June 4, 1791, with Col. James Wilkinson [q.v.] as second in command, he conducted an expedition against the Indians on the Wabash River, and in the fall, advancing from Cincinnati with a force of Kentuckians, he was with Gen. Arthur St. Clair [q.v.] at the disastrous defeat of Nov. 4, 1791. In 1792 Scott County, created out of Woodford County, was named for him. On Oct. 24, 1793, with 1,000 mounted Kentuckians, he joined Gen. Anthony Wayne [q.v.] for another projected campaign against the Indians, but the operation was abandoned. In the following summer, however, at the head of about 1,500 mounted Kentucky volunteers, Scott took part with Wayne's army in the battle of the Fallen Timbers (Aug. 20, 1794), which resulted in a decisive victory over the Indians.

Scott had only an elementary English schooling, but in the rugged life of the frontier he gained a fund of practical wisdom which richly reinforced his naturally sound judgment and good sense. He was frank and direct in speech, simple and unaffected in social intercourse. A type of the strong man of the frontier whose military leadership led to leadership in politics, he was chosen presidential elector from Kentucky in 1793, 1801, 1805, and 1809, and in August 1808 was elected governor of the state. He served in that capacity four years. In his public utterances before the War of 1812 he boldly declared the duty of his fellow countrymen in the emergency, and one of his last official acts was to commission Gen. William Henry Harrison [q.v.] of the United States Army a major-general of the Kentucky militia in order to give him unquestioned authority over Kentucky troops participating in the northwestern campaign.

Scott married, Feb. 25, 1762, Frances Sweeney of Cumberland County, Va., by whom he had several children. She died in October 1804, and on July 25, 1807, he married Judith Cary (Bell) Gist, widow of Col. Nathaniel Gist and daughter of Capt. David Bell, formerly of Buckingham County, Va. She survived him, dying in 1833. Scott died at her home, "Canewood," in Clark County, Ky., and on Nov. 8, 1854, his body was reinterred in the State Cemetery, Frankfort.

[F. B. Heitman, *Hist. Reg. and Dict. U. S. Army* (1903); Henry Howe, *Hist. Colls. of Va.* (1846); T. L. Crittenden, in *Obituary Addresses Delivered upon the Occasion of the Re-interment of the Remains of Gen. Charles Scott* (1855); William Littell, *The Statute Law of Ky.* (5 vols., 1809–19), esp. I, 442, 629, II, 140, III, 582; Lewis and R. H. Collins, *Hist. of Ky.* (2 vols., 1874); Thomas Boyd, *Mad Anthony Wayne* (1929); *Ky. Gazette,* Feb. 5, 1791, Jan. 23, 1800, Oct. 26, 1813; *Ky. Reporter,* Nov. 6, 1813; *Va. Mag. of Hist. and Biog.,* Jan. 1925; *Ind. Mag. of Hist.,* Mar. 1925; "Governors Messages and Letters . . . Wm. Henry Harrison," *Ind. Hist. Colls.,* vols. VII, IX (1922); *Reg. Ky. State Hist. Soc.,* Sept. 1903, inaccurate in certain details; court records; acquaintance with members of the family.]   S. M. W.

SCOTT, COLIN ALEXANDER (Feb. 11, 1861–Apr. 5, 1925), psychologist, educational reformer, was born in Ottawa, Canada, the son of Isabel Laird (Scott) and the Rev. Robert

Scott. The family later moved to New York City, where the father's work brought them into happy association with Henry Ward Beecher. The son attended the preparatory department of the College of the City of New York in 1876–77 and later Queen's University, Kingston, Ont., where he took the degree of B.A. in 1885. Meanwhile, in 1881, while he was still an undergraduate, he married Helen McColl of Kingston, daughter of the noted Gaelic scholar, by whom he had two daughters and three sons. Although he won honors in chemistry at Queen's University, he was much interested in philosophy and psychology; his graduate study at Clark University (Ph.D., 1896) was in psychology, his doctoral thesis, "Old Age and Death," being published in the *American Journal of Psychology* for October 1896. He taught psychology at the Chicago Normal School, 1897–1901; at Miami University, Oxford, Ohio, 1901–02; at Tufts College, 1910–11; at the Boston Normal School, 1902–10, 1911–15. From 1915 to 1925 he was professor of education at Mount Holyoke College.

His teaching, which was of a radically new kind, found expression in his *Social Education* (1908). He endeavored to foster his conception of socialized teaching in primary and secondary schools as well as in collegiate work, and he had opportunities to carry out his theories in Brookline and in Springfield, Mass., where he was head of the department of records and results in the public schools. But his distaste for the political means necessary to effect important changes in American institutions militated against the practical success of his ideas. His purpose was not only to link the classroom with spontaneous outside interests, with the homes of the pupils, with arts and industries, but also to establish conditions in the classroom that should freely elicit leadership, cooperative undertakings, means of self-government, and sympathetic understanding. The means he employed were various. Perhaps the central one was that later elaborated by others into the "project-method," the "Dalton Plan," and similar widely advertised plans by which self-organized groups voluntarily pursue their own interests during a portion of the school day. Objective tests of progress were employed, such as machines (in some cases of Scott's invention) by which pupils could themselves measure their progress from week to week. His ideas gained impetus through a social education club organized by faculty members of Harvard University, of Massachusetts Institute of Technology, and of Tufts College, together with numerous secondary school teachers,

and by the publication (March 1907–January 1908) of the *Social Education Quarterly*.

Early in his career he found it difficult to decide between painting and teaching as a profession. For a time, 1885–87, he studied in the Ontario Art School, and all his life he painted for pleasure. He exhibited widely in the East, winning high praise for the dramatic vitality, vivid intuition, and joyous quality of his work. At the time of his death he was working on a book on sex and art. As a cultivated scholar rich in kindling ideas he would have graced the presidency of a university, but his detestation of power as such, his self-effacing generosity, and his disinterested liberality led him to choose a life in which his ideas and his art might exert their own influence. He died in Boston.

[*Who's Who in America,* 1924–25; full obituary in *Springfield Daily Republican,* Apr. 7, 1925; brief obituaries in *Boston Transcript,* Apr. 6, 1925, and *Jour. of Education,* Apr. 9, 1925; personal acquaintance.]

J. M. W.

SCOTT, DRED (*c.* 1795–Sept. 17, 1858), slave, was born of slave parents in Southampton County, Va. His early years were spent on the plantation of his master, Capt. Peter Blow, who, in 1827, removed with his family and slaves to St. Louis, Mo. Upon his death in 1831, Scott was assigned to Elizabeth Blow, a daughter. He was purchased two years later by John Emerson, a surgeon in the United States Army, with whom, as a servant, he spent three years in Illinois and two in Wisconsin Territory. He married Harriet, a slave woman purchased by his owner in 1836. Left by Emerson at St. Louis in 1838, he became the body servant of Col. Henry Bainbridge at Jefferson Barracks, and upon Emerson's death, passed to his widow, Irene (Sanford) Emerson. She hired Scott to various families in the city. He was shiftless and unreliable, and therefore frequently unemployed and without means to support his family. He often became a charge upon the bounty of Taylor and H. T. Blow [*q.v.*], the wealthy sons of his former owner, who seemed to feel partially responsible for him. Mrs. Emerson could have emancipated him but did not do so, and left him in St. Louis when she removed to Massachusetts in the middle forties. It seems probable that Scott attempted unsuccessfully to arrange for the purchase of himself and his family (*New York Tribune,* Apr. 10, 1857).

In April 1846, Henry T. Blow instituted and financed suits in the state courts to secure the freedom of Scott and of his family. The contention was that a slave, after sojourning in free territory, was free upon his return to Missouri. The ignorant and illiterate negro comprehended little of its significance, but signed his mark to the petition in the suit. While the case was before the state courts, 1846–52, he remained under the nominal control of the sheriff, being hired out for $5.00 per month until the termination of the suit. After an adverse decision had been delivered by Judge William Scott [*q.v.*] in 1852 (*Scott, a Man of Color,* vs. *Emerson,* 15 *Mo.* 576), it was arranged to take the case to the federal courts, and, for jurisdictional purposes, Dred Scott was transferred by a fictitious sale to his owner's brother, John F. A. Sanford of New York. During the interval when the case was in the federal courts, 1854–57, Scott remained in St. Louis, under practically no restraint, a mere pawn in the game, with no regular employment, running errands and performing janitor service. As a local celebrity, he enjoyed greatly his new and unexpected prominence. The United States Supreme Court in 1857 held that Scott was not free by reason of his removal either to Illinois or to Wisconsin Territory. His status was determined by the courts of Missouri which had decided that he was not free. Not being a citizen of Missouri, within the meaning of the Constitution, he was not entitled, as such, to sue in the federal courts (*Dred Scott* vs. *Sandford,* 19 *Howard,* 393). In May 1857 he was transferred, no doubt by another fictitious sale, to Taylor Blow, who very obviously intended to emancipate him and his family. This action was taken on May 26 of that year (*Missouri Republican,* May 27, 1857). The fact that Mrs. Emerson had meanwhile become the wife of Calvin Clifford Chaffee of Massachusetts, a radical anti-slavery congressman, was the source of much ironical comment and hastened the manumission. Physically unfitted for steady and hard labor, Scott spent the remainder of his life as the good-natured and lazy porter at Barnum's Hotel, St. Louis, where he was an object of interest and curiosity to the guests. He died of tuberculosis, and Henry T. Blow paid his funeral expenses.

[Sources include Blow MSS., in Mo. Hist. Soc., St. Louis; E. W. P. Ewing, *Legal and Historical Status of the Dred Scott Decision* (1909); J. D. Lawson, *Am. State Trials,* vol. XIII (1921); *Proc. . . . Mo. Bar Asso. . . . 1907* (1908), p. 233; E. S. Corwin, "The Dred Scott Decision in the Light of Contemporary Legal Doctrines," *Am. Hist. Rev.,* Oct. 1911, repr., with some verbal changes, in his *The Doctrine of Judicial Review* (1914); Helen T. Catterall, "Some Antecedents of the Dred Scott Case," *Am. Hist. Rev.,* Oct. 1924; F. H. Hodder, "Some Phases of the Dred Scott Case," *Miss. Valley Hist. Rev.,* June 1929; J. M. Turner, "Dred Scott" (manuscript copy, 1882, Mo. Hist. Soc., St. Louis); *Providence Daily Post,* Mar. 17, 1857; *N. Y. Tribune,* Apr. 10, 1857; *Mo. Republican,* May 27, 1857; *Washington Union,* June 2, 1857; *New Hampshire Patriot and State Gazette* (Concord), June 3, 1857; *St. Louis News,* Sept. 20, 1858. In the official printed reports of the Dred Scott case the name of the owner, correctly Sanford, is persistently misspelled.]   T. S. B.

SCOTT, FRED NEWTON (Aug. 20, 1860–May 29, 1931), rhetorician, was born in Terre Haute, Ind., the son of Mary (Bannister) and Harvey D. Scott, a lawyer who was a congressman from Indiana in 1855 and for some years a county judge. After taking the degrees of A.B., 1884, A.M., 1888, and Ph.D., 1889, at the University of Michigan, meanwhile serving as library assistant and later as assistant librarian, Scott became an instructor in English and for almost forty years was a member of the university faculty. As head of the department of rhetoric, 1903–21, and of rhetoric and journalism, 1921–27, he exerted a wide influence. He encouraged the establishment of schools of journalism in state colleges, modified the teaching of English composition in colleges through his treatment of the paragraph as the unit of discourse (in *Paragraph-Writing,* 1891, with J. V. Denny), and was a stimulating teacher of graduate students, with the power of suggesting lines of thought often very original. He was president of the Modern Language Association of America, 1907; one of the founders and the first president of the National Council of Teachers of English, 1911–13; president of the North Central Association of Colleges and Secondary Schools, 1913, and of the American Association of Teachers of Journalism, 1917. A member of several British learned societies as well, he had a wide acquaintance and a high reputation among foreign scholars. In 1887 he married Isadore Thompson, daughter of Prof. Bradley M. Thompson of the law school of the University of Michigan, by whom he had a daughter and two sons. A year after her death in 1922, he married Georgia Jackson of New York City, who with his three children survived him. Upon his retirement in 1927 as professor emeritus, he and his wife lived in Tucson, Ariz.; he died in San Diego, Cal.

Although Scott's distinction rests particularly upon his influence as a teacher, his list of more than a hundred publications contains convincing evidence of his scholarly interests and attainments. He edited among other things De Quincey's *Essay on Style, Rhetoric, and Language* (1891) and Herbert Spencer's *The Philosophy of Style* (1892); with C. L. Meader, he translated three plays from the Russian of Leonid Andreyeff, *Plays* (1915), and he wrote numerous essays and technical articles that appeared in magazines ranging from the *Classical Journal* to the *Atlantic Monthly* on subjects that varied from the prosody of Walt Whitman to the psychology of speech. His chief concern was always with matters of style and with the fundamentals of literary effect and appreciation. His most ambitious work, done in collaboration with C. M. Gayley, was *An Introduction to the Methods and Materials of Literary Criticism* (1899), which at the time broke relatively new ground. But his richly suggestive essays on prose rhythms and on his theory of the fundamental distinction between poetry and prose (reprinted in *The Standard of American Speech and Other Papers,* 1926) were perhaps more important. His writing was smooth, polished, urbane, packed with implication. In general he seemed content with indicating fresh approaches to problems of speech and writing, and seldom worked out in fullness even the most promising of his ideas; *The Standard of American Speech* contains ideas enough in brief essay form for many scholarly volumes. Modest and extremely reticent, with a grave courtesy, he was to many of his students an enigmatic figure, whose preference was always for questioning rather than for arriving at fixed conclusions. He was keenly sensitive and easily wounded, but he had a delicate wit and took great pleasure in good talk. He had some reputation as an after-dinner speaker. He was perhaps half the scholar, half the old-style journalist who could write excellent editorials in a style not so far from Addison and sometimes much better for the purpose in hand.

[See Blackford Condit, *The Hist. of Early Terre Haute from 1816 to 1840* (1900) for information on Scott's father; *Univ. of Mich. Cat. of Grads. . . . 1837–1921* (1923); *The Fred Newton Scott Anniversary Papers* (1929), with portrait and bibliog., ed. by C. D. Thorpe and C. E. Whitmore; *Who's Who in America,* 1930–31; J. L. Brumm, in *Mich. Alumnus,* June 27, 1931; brief obituary in *Language,* Sept. 1931; *N. Y. Times,* May 31, 1931; information from Scott's family and friends.]   D. G—d.

SCOTT, GUSTAVUS (1753–Dec. 25, 1800), lawyer and patriot, was the son of James Scott and Sarah (Brown) Scott. His father had emigrated to America before the middle of the eighteenth century, and was rector of Dettingen Parish, Prince William County, Va., from 1745 until his death in 1782. Gustavus, with his elder brother, John, went to Scotland in 1765, and is said to have studied at King's College, Aberdeen. Two years later he entered Essex Court, Middle Temple, London, where he was engaged in the study of law until 1771, being called to the English bar in November 1772. On his return to America he began to practise law with marked success in Somerset County on the Eastern Shore of Maryland. He became a leader of the liberal

party, was elected a delegate to the Maryland Convention, and took his seat in that body on Aug. 7, 1775. He joined the Association of the Freemen of Maryland for resistance to attempts to enforce acts of Parliament by military power, and served as spokesman for the committee of observation relative to military affairs in his county. He served as a member of the constitutional convention of 1776 which drafted the first state constitution of Maryland, and soon after the adoption moved to Dorchester County. In January 1781 he joined in an appeal to the governor of the state for such arms, ammunition, and supplies as would afford more adequate military protection for his county and the entire Eastern Shore.

Dorchester County elected him a member of the Maryland House of Delegates in 1780. He took his seat on Nov. 20, for a term of one year, and served again from December 1783 until January 1785. There is no evidence of active or important service during his first term, but in the second he became one of the more prominent leaders, serving on the committees which drafted the most important bills. He represented Maryland on a joint commission of Maryland and Virginia which submitted a report in response to which Virginia, in 1784, and Maryland, in 1785, chartered the Potomac Navigation Company for the improvement of the Potomac River; this ultimately resulted in the construction of the Chesapeake and Ohio Canal. He participated in the drafting of a bill for the establishment of a state university, and was in favor of granting James Rumsey [*q.v.*] a monopoly for making and selling steamboats "on a model by him invented" (*Votes and Proceedings, post,* First Session, November 1784, p. 13). The Maryland Assembly, on Dec. 4, 1784, elected Scott a delegate to the Continental Congress for a term of one year, but his health was impaired at this time, and, although his credentials were presented, there is no record of his service in that body. He retired to private life and resumed the practice of law until 1793, when he was appointed chairman of a committee to combat the yellow fever in Baltimore. The following year President Washington appointed Scott to a vacancy in the board of commissioners for the city of Washington and characterized him as "a gentleman eminent in the profession of the Law—a man of character & fortune . . ." (letter to Tobias Lear, Aug. 28, 1794, Washington Papers, Library of Congress). He died at his home "Rock Hill," Washington, D. C., and was buried on his farm in Virginia nine miles distant. He was married to Margaret Hall Caile on Feb. 16.

1777, and they had five sons and four daughters. William Lawrence Scott [*q.v.*] was his grandson.

[*Votes and Proc. of the House of Delegates of the State of Md.*, 1780–85; E. A. Jones, *Am. Members of the Inns of Court* (1924); J. A. Ames, "Genealogies of Four Families of Dorchester County," *Md. Hist. Mag.*, Mar. 1916; Corra Bacon-Foster, "The Story of Kalorama," *Records of the Columbia Hist. Soc.*, vol. XIII (1910), vol. XVII (1914); H. E. Hayden, *Va. Genealogies* (1931); W. B. Bryan, *A Hist. of the Natl. Capitol*, vol. I (1914); *Federal Gazette* (Baltimore, Md.), Dec. 31, 1800.]   N. D. M.

SCOTT, HARVEY WHITEFIELD (Feb. 1, 1838–Aug. 7, 1910), editor, was born on a farm near Groveland, Tazewell County, Ill., the son of Ann (Roelofson) and John Tucker Scott and brother of Abigail Jane Scott Duniway [*q.v.*]. He was a descendant of John Scott who settled in North Carolina shortly before the Revolutionary War. In 1852 he went with his family overland to Oregon. After two years in the lower Willamette Valley he moved with his father to a farm near Shelton in the newly formed territory of Washington, but in September 1856 he returned to Oregon to work on a farm near Oregon City. In December he entered Tualatin Academy, but for lack of funds he was forced to leave school the next April and was unable to continue his education except irregularly until 1859, when he entered Pacific University, Forest Grove, Ore. He graduated in 1863, supporting himself meanwhile by working as a teamster, a woodcutter, and a teacher. After another year of school-teaching he became librarian of the Portland library and studied law in a private office. Though he passed his bar examinations, he never actively practised law. He married Elizabeth Nicklin of Salem, Ore., Oct. 31, 1865, and after her death Margaret McChesney of Latrobe, Pa., June 28, 1876.

In April 1865 he began to write editorials for the Portland *Morning Oregonian*, recognized as the chief spokesman in the state for the Republican party, and a year later Henry Lewis Pittock [*q.v.*], the owner of the paper, made him its editor. He also served as collector of the port of Portland from October 1870 to May 1876, when Senator John Hipple Mitchell [*q.v.*] of Oregon had him removed. According to Scott (*Morning Oregonian*, July 5, 1898), this was because of his refusal longer to contribute financial support to the *Portland Bulletin*, the newspaper organ of Mitchell and Ben Holladay [*q.v.*]. He had left the *Oregonian* in 1872, but in April 1877 he returned as editor and part owner, a connection that lasted until his death. He was never an avowed candidate for an elective office, although in 1903 he made overtures to Republican party leaders for support in the legislative

ballot for United States senator. (For a telegram from Scott to George C. Brownell, see *Oregon Journal*, Feb. 28, 1903, and Lincoln Steffens, "U'Ren, the Lawgiver," *American Magazine*, March 1908, p. 539). He declined a diplomatic appointment to Belgium in 1905 and one to Mexico in 1909. He was president of the Oregon Historical Society, 1898–1901, of the Lewis and Clark Exposition, 1903–04, and a director of the Associated Press 1900–10. He died in Baltimore, Md., of heart failure following a surgical operation; he was survived by his wife, three sons, and a daughter.

He was well equipped for the work of an editor. Persistent reading had given him so thorough an acquaintance with great literary masterpieces that he could quote at will from many, and he read widely in history, economics, religion, theology, and metaphysics as well. He made the *Oregonian* the strongest journal in the Pacific Northwest and brought it national recognition, and he himself came to be numbered among the great editors of the nation, with a style that was, although somewhat dogmatic, forceful and convincing. A thorough-going individualist and conservative, he stood out against all the social and reform movements of his day. He opposed free high schools, state supported schools of higher education, prohibition, woman's suffrage, and the "Oregon System" of direct primary, initiative, referendum, and recall. He was unsympathetic towards the demands of labor and hostile to the socializing tendencies of his time. He conducted a vigorous campaign for "sound money" and fought in turn the Greenback movement and Free Silver. He was a lifelong advocate of "tariff for revenue only" and insisted that his party's policy of protection created monopolies and enriched the few at the expense of the many. On other issues, however, he stood with the conservative wing of his party. After his death his writings were collected by his son and published as *Religion, Theology and Morals* (2 vols., 1917); *History of the Oregon Country* (6 vols., 1924); and *Shakespeare* (1928).

[*Who's Who in America*, 1908–09; articles by Alfred Holman, L. M. Scott, and C. H. Chapman, in *Quart. Ore. Hist. Soc.*, June 1913, the first two being reprinted in H. W. Scott, *Hist. of the Ore. Country* (1924), vol. I; O. C. Leiter, in *Journalism Quart.*, Jan. 1929, an excellent appreciation; obituary and editorial in *Morning Oregonian* (Portland), Aug. 8, 1910.]   R. C. C.

SCOTT, IRVING MURRAY (Dec. 25, 1837–Apr. 28, 1903), ship-builder, was the son of Quaker parents, John and Elizabeth (Leittig) Scott, and was born on his father's farm at Hebron Mills, Baltimore County, Md. Through the grist mill his father ran in connection with his farm, Scott early developed an interest in mechanics. Accordingly, after attending the district school near his home, he took a three-year course at Milton Academy in Baltimore and at the same time began an apprenticeship as machinist. Upon completing this he worked for a time in the shop of Obed Hussey, manufacturer of reaping machinery, and then in 1857, at the age of twenty, entered the steam-engine manufactory of Murray and Hazlehurst in Baltimore. By studying at night in the Baltimore Mechanics' Institute he became proficient in drafting and soon was transferred to the designing department and placed in charge of the construction of stationary engines and fire engines. In 1860 he went to San Francisco to erect an engine purchased from his employers by Peter Donahue; upon completing this he continued to work in Donahue's iron works for two years. After a few months as chief draftsman in the Miners' Foundry and Machine Works in San Francisco, he went back to Donahue as superintendent. In 1865, when Donahue retired, he was taken into the business as a partner, and from that time until his death he was associated with it. During the succeeding ten years he conducted a foundry and iron works, in which the mining machinery for the Comstock mines in Nevada was designed and manufactured. He also designed improved steam engines with a cut-off of his own invention.

In 1880, in a trip around the world, he made an exhaustive study of manufacturing industries, particularly of ship-building in France and England. Soon after his return to the United States in 1882 he and his partners incorporated their business under the name of the Union Iron Works and in 1883 began a ship-building plant covering approximately twenty acres of land; and in 1884 the construction of ships was begun. Two years later Scott secured a contract from the federal government for the construction of the warship *Charleston*, completed in 1889, the first battleship built on the Pacific Coast. In quick succession between 1892 and 1901 followed the *Olympia*, the *San Francisco*, the *Oregon*, the *Wisconsin*, and the *Ohio*, which established Scott's worldwide reputation as a shipbuilder. In 1898 he went to St. Petersburg (later Leningrad) to advise the Russian government in the building of warships. He was intensely interested in all civic affairs of San Francisco and served as president of the Mechanics' Institute of San Francisco, regent of the University of California, and trustee of Stanford University. He was married in 1863 to Laura Harde of Cov-

ington, Ky. (*San Francisco Call, post*); at the time of his death in San Francisco he was survived by his widow and two children.

[*Who's Who in America*, 1901–02; *Trans. Amer. Soc. Mech. Engineers*, vol. XXIV (1903); Alonzo Phelps, *Contemporary Biog. of California's Representative Men* (1881); *San Francisco Call, San Francisco Chronicle*, Apr. 29, 1903.]   C. W. M.

SCOTT, JAMES WILMOT (June 26, 1849– Apr. 14, 1895), journalist, was born in Walworth County, Wis. Both his grandfather and father were newspaper men. His father, David Wilmot Scott, removed to Galena, Ill., shortly after the birth of his son, where he became associated with Charles H. Ray in publishing the *Jeffersonian*. There it was that James Scott became the prize declaimer of the Galena schools and at the age of eleven, upon the outbreak of the Civil War, became a drummer boy engaged in recruiting duty in Illinois. After graduating from the Galena High School, he attended Beloit College two years. Having learned the printer's trade in his father's office, he went to New York soon after his return from college. There he became intensely interested in floriculture, and he contributed short articles to horticultural periodicals. However, his early training asserted itself. He returned to Galena, Ill., and with his father founded the *Industrial Press*.

In 1875, he went to Chicago, where for the remainder of his life he was associated with journalism. In Chicago he first purchased an interest in the *National Hotel Reporter* but at the end of six years withdrew to found a paper of his own. In May 1881 he organized the Chicago Herald Company, in which he later obtained the controlling interest. The growth of the *Chicago Herald* was remarkable, as it was one of the youngest dailies in the western metropolis and a pioneer among two-cent morning papers. Within ten years it had increased from four to twelve pages, and the Herald Company boasted of a fine building equipped with twenty modern presses. The Sunday edition reached a size of forty-eight pages by 1887, featuring new departures in the newspaper field. Although at first supporting the Republican party, in its first year it became independent Democrat, and it supported Cleveland and hard money. The policy of the paper was distinctly conservative, but it consistently advocated a reduction in tariff duties and civil service reform. So successful was the *Chicago Herald* under his management, that he was chosen president of the American Newspaper Publishers' Association, president of the Chicago Press Club for three years, and president of the United Press, an organization for the collection and distribution of news. In connection with the World's Columbian Exposition, he rendered important service in bringing the fair to Chicago. As a member of the committee on arrangements and chairman of the press committee, his was an important voice in the fair. In 1890 plans for the establishment of an evening paper resulted in the appearance of the *Chicago Evening Post.* In 1895 the *Chicago Times* was purchased in order to consolidate it with the *Herald,* but before the plans were completely realized he died suddenly in New York City (see sketch of Herman H. Kohlsaat). Scott was a bluff, big, hearty individual and the soul of fellowship. He was typical of the West in his time and a man of liberal ideas. Through the years he stood firm for civil service reform and was never a violent partisan in politics. In Chicago and the Middle West, he was a power for reform in government and for clean politics. He was married to Carrie Green in 1873. Their one child died in infancy.

[Joseph Kirkland, *The Story of Chicago,* vol. II (1894) ; John J. Flinn, *The Handbook of Chicago Biog.* (copr. 1893) ; *Historical Encyc. of Ill.,* ed. by Newton Bateman and Paul Selby (1920) ; A. T. Andreas, *History of Chicago,* vol. III, 1886 ; John Moses and Joseph Kirkland, *History of Chicago* (1895), vol. II ; *A History of the City of Chicago* (1900) ; F. W. Scott, "Newspaper Periodicals in Ill.," revised ed. *Ill. State Hist. Lib. Colls.,* vol. VI (1910) ; *Chicago Daily Tribune, Chicago Record, New York Herald,* Apr. 15, 1895.]   T. E. S.

SCOTT, JOB (Oct. 18, 1751–Nov. 22, 1793), Quaker preacher, was born in Providence, R. I., the son of John and Lydia (Comstock) Scott. He was received as a member of the Society of Friends by his request, apparently about 1771. On June 1, 1780, he married Eunice Anthony, daughter of Daniel and Mary Anthony, who died in 1791 having borne him six children. As early as 1774 he was conducting a school in Providence for Friends' children, and in 1778 he took charge of a school at Smithfield, R. I., established by the local Monthly Meeting of Friends. In 1783 he removed with his family to Glocester, R. I., where he apparently practised medicine for a time in a non-professional way. He had a small library of medical books and was occasionally referred to by contemporaries as a "doctor of physic." Little is known of his activities after his removal to Glocester, however, save those connected with his religious work.

He was one of the outstanding Quaker preachers of his day and traveled widely "in the ministry." In 1784 he went on a preaching pilgrimage to Quaker settlements in Vermont and New York, and in 1786 he spent six months in Pennsylvania and New Jersey. Three years later he started on a visitation of Friends' meetings that led him along the Atlantic seaboard as far south as Georgia. Of this journey he wrote in his journal : "I was out on this exercising journey a year and about fifteen days, and travelled, by computation, about five thousand three hundred miles" (*Works, post,* I, 353). His last religious journey began when he set sail from Boston in December 1792 for England. Arrived at his destination, he began his usual work of visiting Quaker centers and also of holding meetings among those who were not Friends. He spent some time in Wales and in Bristol and vicinity, returning to London in time for the Friends' Yearly Meeting. Thence he went to Liverpool and took ship to Ireland, where he visited the various Friends' centers and attended the national Half-Year's Meeting at Dublin. Soon after, at Ballitore, he was stricken with smallpox and died at the age of forty-two years.

Historically, the most important thing about Job Scott is his place in the field of religious thought. He was a thoroughgoing mystic and has been called the most outstanding example of quietism in the history of American Quakerism (Jones, *post,* I, 78). His ideal was the utter abasement and death of all his natural powers so that the divine spirit could work through him without hindrance. Even when on special religious journeys he often sat through the meetings "in awful silence," not being sure of the divine promptings to speak. While visiting Friends' meetings in Pennsylvania in 1786 he wrote in his journal: "For twenty days past, I have not dared to open my mouth in one of the public meetings for worship that I have attended; I have been at fifteen" (*Works,* I, 223). Little schooled, he developed various advanced ideas of religion and of Biblical interpretation that anticipated some of the views of Christian modernism. The Scriptures to him were a "very good means of information" but not so important as the inward promptings of the divine spirit (*Ibid.,* I, 44). Christ, in his view, was the eternal spirit of God, once clothed in human flesh, but always, before and since that time, striving to enter into and regenerate human hearts. Thus there is no righteousness imputed nor forgiveness secured to men because of the death of Jesus on the cross. There was precedent for Scott's modernistic views in specific statements of some of the earliest Quaker leaders especially in the doctrine of the Light Within; yet Scott seemed to see with peculiar clarity the ultimate import of the earlier teachings.

During his lifetime his undoubted piety and uprightness apparently shielded him from criticism. After his death, however, doubts of his soundness grew. His own Yearly Meeting (New England) became afraid to publish his works in full. A few years later came the issue between liberalism and orthodoxy that led, among Friends, to the great separation of 1827–28 into the Hicksite and Orthodox branches. Scott's views then became thoroughly suspect among Orthodox Friends, while his writings were published in full under Hicksite auspices—*The Works of that Eminent Minister of the Gospel, Job Scott* (2 vols., 1831), edited by John Comly, the first volume of which contains the most complete printing of Scott's journal. If Friends generally had accepted his emphasis on the spiritual nature of religion they might have escaped the Great Separation, and met the later findings of science and of literary criticism unafraid. Therefore, some students of Quaker history are now looking upon Job Scott not as a heretic but as a prophet.

[H. W. Wilbur, *Job Scott, an Eighteenth Century Friend* (1911); R. M. Jones, *The Later Periods of Quakerism* (2 vols., 1921); *Friends' Miscellany*, Aug. 1834–Mar. 1835; Joseph Smith, *A Descriptive Cat. of Friends' Books* (1867), II, 546–50; manuscript material by and about Scott at Moses Brown School, Providence, R. I.]   R. W. K.

SCOTT, JOHN (*c.* 1630–1696), adventurer, was born, probably at Ashford in Kent, England, and, according to the most probable story, brought to America as a boy by Emmanuel Downing, the father of Sir George Downing, and bound out to Lawrence Southwick of Massachusetts Bay, the husband of Cassandra Southwick, the Quakeress. Thence he went to Long Island, made himself obnoxious to the Dutch, and was imprisoned by them in 1654. On his release he returned to Southampton on Long Island as a blacksmith, "keeping cowes" and trading with the Indians in land, became a freeman, was tax commissioner, married a Deborah Rayner, and visited Narragansett Bay, Boston, and, possibly, Newfoundland. In 1660 he went to England, gained the notice of Thomas Chiffinch, brother of William Chiffinch, and came to the attention of Joseph Williamson, afterward secretary to Sir Henry Bennet who was later Earl of Arlington. He became associated with a group of claimants to the Narragansett lands between Rhode Island and Connecticut known as the Atherton Company, made the acquaintance of one Daniel Gotherson and his wife Dorothea, Quakers, and, through his fancied resemblance to the portraits of her family, the Scotts of Scots Hall in Kent, he gained their confidence. They intrusted to him some £2,000 to invest for them in Long Island land, and their son, whom, upon reaching America, he sold to a New Haven inn-

keeper in 1663. He failed to obtain the grant to large tracts in Long Island which he sought, and the claims of the Atherton Company were thrown out by the Privy Council; but it seems he helped to suggest the seizure of New Amsterdam, and when he returned to Long Island he posed as a representative of the government, on the strength of a document purporting to be a royal grant, though it bore no signature. He was appointed one of three commissioners to negotiate with the Dutch, became "president" of the English settlements on Long Island, declared their independence of Connecticut, and led a futile expedition against Breuckelen. The Dutch recognized his title. Connecticut made him a magistrate but presently arrested him, put him in prison in Hartford, annulled his title, fined him, and put him under bond. Thence he escaped to take some small part in the surrender of New Amsterdam to the English expedition under Richard Nicolls [*q.v.*], whence he returned to his old mode of life at Southampton. It seems that he avenged himself for his failure to gain any advantage from the capture of New Amsterdam by advising that the boundaries of the new province of New York should not include New Jersey.

Accused of dishonest land transactions, of theft, fomenting sedition, and using the pretended royal patent to defraud, he escaped arrest by flight to the West Indies, where he obtained a commission under Lord Willoughby in Sir Tobias Bridge's regiment and saw some service against the French at St. Kitt's in 1665–66. Court-martialed and dismissed for cowardice, he went to England in 1667, renewed his connection with Williamson and Arlington, and, apparently on the strength of a volume he purported to be writing on the coasts and islands of America, which included a description of Guiana, he was made royal geographer. That post he lost, with the favor of Arlington and Williamson, upon Nicoll's return with his story of Scott's behavior and a petition of Mrs. Gotherson to the King. He fled to Holland, where he seems to have had a commission in the Dutch service, and, dismissed for dishonesty, went to Bruges, whence he was driven out for sketching the fortification. Thence he seems to have taken service under the Prince de Condé, going later to Paris, where he set up as a map-maker and geographer. He was throughout, apparently, a spy in the service of various governments. About 1677 he seems to have come into touch with the Duke of Buckingham and presently appeared as a witness in the Popish Plot and against Samuel Pepys, whom he accused of being a Roman Catholic and selling naval secrets to the French. Pepys was arrested but, brought before the Commons, not merely cleared himself but brought such a mass of testimony against Scott as to ruin him. Shortly thereafter Scott killed a man in a drunken quarrel. He was compelled to flee the country, apparently to Norway, and Pepys seized his papers. With the Revolution of 1688 Scott returned to England, was pardoned, and died.

Two hundred years later, as part of the testimony offered in the Venezuelan boundary dispute in 1895, his "Description of Guiana" and his "Relation" brought his name into some prominence. It seems probable from various incidents in his career that he did not write the important parts of these documents but obtained them from their real authors and passed them off as his own, and that conclusion is borne out by examination of the manuscripts.

[The material for this sketch is in "Colonel John Scott" by the present author, published with notes in the *Society of Colonial Wars Publications*, no. 30 (1918), as a separate volume (1918) and is reprinted with additions in his *Conflicts with Oblivion* (1923); its sources are the documents in the Pepys Coll., in Bodleian Lib., Oxford, England, in the Connecticut archives, the records of Southampton, N. Y., and like materials; see also J. C. Pilling, *Bibliog. of the Algonquin Languages* (1891), pp. 397–400; G. D. Scull, *Dorothea Scott* (1883).]   W. C. A.

SCOTT, JOHN MORIN (c. 1730–Sept. 14, 1784), lawyer, Revolutionary leader, was born in New York City, the only child of John Scott, a New York merchant, and a great-grandson of Sir John Scott, baronet, of Ancrum, Roxburghshire, Scotland. His mother was Marian, youngest daughter of Pierre and Marie (Jamain) Morin, Huguenots from La Rochelle. After graduating at Yale College in 1746, Scott studied law in the office of the elder William Smith [q.v.], and was admitted to the New York bar in 1752. In law, letters, and politics, early in his career, he definitely aligned himself with the Whig cause. In the celebrated case of *Cunningham* vs. *Forsey* (1764), as counsel for the respondent, he successfully maintained that no appeal in questions of fact lay from the provincial supreme court to the governor in council. In this position he was actively supported by Chief Justice Daniel Horsmanden [q.v.], and his stand, an eminently popular one, was subsequently affirmed on appeal (*Acts of the Privy Council . . . Colonial Series, 1745–1766,* 1911, p. 749). He was one of the most active practitioners of the law in the American colonies; his docket for the April term, 1767, of the New York Supreme court of judicature contained 114 cases. At the height of his career he lived in sumptuous style in a handsome rural residence in what is now West Forty-third Street,

between Eighth and Ninth Avenues. John Adams described it in 1774 as "an elegant seat" and the proprietor as "a sensible man, but not very polite," who was reputed to be "one of the readiest speakers upon the continent" (*The Works of John Adams,* 1850, II, 346, 349). Scott also had extensive holdings in the Schoharie Valley and Dutchess County.

He was actively associated with William Livingston and the younger William Smith [qq.v.] in literary contributions in behalf of the Whig Presbyterian cause in New York. These appeared in the *Independent Reflector* (1752–53) and in the "Watch Tower" column of the *New York Mercury* (1754–55). His bill for the establishment of King's College upon non-sectarian principles was printed and circulated in 1754 throughout the province. Other contributions of these collaborators include the publication in 1757 of *A Review of the Military Operations in North America . . . 1753–1756,* in defense of Governor Shirley of Massachusetts (reprinted in *Collections of the Massachusetts Historical Society,* 1 ser. VII, 1801), and the series known as the "American Whig" which appeared in the columns of James Parker's *New York Gazette* (1768–69). Scott is known to have been the sole author of the significant essay against the Stamp Act, signed "Freeman," contained in three numbers of John Holt's *New York Gazette* in June 1765, and he was one of the organizers of the New York Sons of Liberty.

He served as alderman of New York City, 1756–61. As a candidate for the Assembly in 1769, indorsed by the Liberty party, he was decisively defeated in a contest marred by charges of bribery and intimidation (I. N. P. Stokes, *The Iconography of Manhattan Island,* vol. IV, 1922, p. 791). On the eve of the Revolution, Scott was listed among the more extreme agitators and was not sent as a delegate to the Continental Congress in 1774. He was a leader of the radical party in the provincial congresses of New York in 1775–77 and of the democratic forces in the constitutional convention of the latter year. The day of the adoption of the constitution he was appointed a member of the committee to prepare a plan for establishing the new government (*Journals of the Provincial Congress . . . of New York,* 1842, I, 892–98), and on its adoption, May 8, he was made a member of the Council of Safety. The week before, he had been elected to the new supreme court but, defeated by John Jay for the chief justiceship, declined to serve (*Ibid.,* I, 910). In the gubernatorial election of the same year Scott ran against George Clinton and Philip Schuyler [*qq.v.*] and polled a number of votes from the middle districts of the state, although the ballots of the southern counties gave the election to Clinton (E. A. Werner, *Civil List of the Colony and State of New York,* 1888, p. 164). In 1778 he was appointed secretary of state, in which office he was succeeded upon his death in 1784 by his son, Lewis Allaire.

Despite the pressure of his political activities, Scott was drawn into the military conflict, participating in the battle of Long Island as a brigadier-general. He later served with General Heath in the lower part of West Chester, but resigned in the spring of 1777 to become state senator, in which position he continued until 1782. He served also as a member of the Continental Congress from 1779 to 1783. As one of the delegates from New York to settle the boundary dispute with Vermont, he opposed the appointment by Congress of a court of commissioners to act in the matter and favored quick action to check the claims of the smaller states (Hiland Hall, *The History of Vermont,* 1868, p. 317; E. C. Burnett, *Letters of Members of the Continental Congress,* vol. V, 1931, pp. 390, 391).

About 1752 Scott married Helena, daughter of Capt. Petrus and Helena (Hoogland) Rutgers, of New York City. A son and a daughter survived him, two sons having died young. Exposure in military service is said to have greatly aggravated a predisposition to acute rheumatism which resulted in his death in early middle age shortly after his return to his native city upon its evacuation by the British.

[Biog. notices appear in F. B. Dexter, *Biog. Sketches Grads. Yale Coll.,* vol. II (1896); Maria S. B. Chance and Mary A. E. Smith, *Scott Family Letters* (1930); *Biog. Dir. Am. Cong.* (1928); B. J. Lossing, *Pictorial Field-Book of the Revolution* (1852), I, 805 n. See also E. B. O'Callaghan, *Docs. Rel. to the Col. Hist of the State of N. Y.,* vol. VII (1856); Thomas Jones, *Hist. of N. Y. during the Rev. War* (2 vols., 1879), ed. by E. F. De Lancey; *Memoirs of the L. I. Hist. Soc.,* vol. III (1878). Many of Scott's law papers are available in the office of the Commissioner of Records, New York City, and, in abundance, in the following boxes: "Supreme Court Pleadings," 1–66; "Supreme Court, Miscellaneous, 1771–1789," 320–631.]

R. B. M.

SCOTT, JOHN PRINDLE (Aug. 16, 1877–Dec. 2, 1932), composer, was born at Norwich, N. Y., the son of Warren L. Scott and Delia (Prindle) Scott. Possessed of a beautiful, clear, baritone voice, he spent four years, from 1896 to 1900, studying in the undergraduate school and conservatory of music at Oberlin College, Oberlin, Ohio. He had the opportunity of singing in the Second Congregational Church choir at Oberlin under the direction of Prof. A. S.

Kimball, teacher of singing at the college, and G. W. Andrews, organist and professor of composition in the conservatory, and was also soloist in the college glee club. In 1914 he furnished a dozen contributions to the book of Oberlin songs, writing for some of them both words and music. After leaving Oberlin he spent two years at Saginaw, Mich., teaching singing and then entered upon a season of public concerts. In his native town he led the church choir and organized the DeKoven male quartet. During the war he was leader of singing in community houses in New York.

Increasing deafness made it necessary for Scott to give up his concerts, and he turned to composition. Among his sacred works were numerous vocal solos and anthems for Christmas and Easter, and also "The Lord is my Shepherd," "Consider the lilies," and "Come ye blessed." He composed the music for the words of A. A. Toms, "O haste the day when wars shall cease." Perhaps the best-known and loved of his secular songs is "The Old Road." Prizes were awarded him for songs written for the state of Nebraska and for Ohio University, Athens, Ohio, and he was presented a very handsome loving-cup by his neighbors in McDonough, N. Y., in appreciation for the "musical sings" which he conducted for a number of years, bringing to them many artists seldom heard in so small a town. Scott was never married. He maintained a summer home at McDonough, called "The Scottage," and during his later years divided his winters between New York City and Washington, D. C. The last concert given in his honor was in Barker Hall, Y. W. C. A., Washington, on the evening of Apr. 11, 1932, when "The Old Road" was rendered by the Chesapeake and Potomac Male Choir. Other pieces of his composition included "Old Bill," "Revelation," "The Dearest Place," "Good Luck, Mr. Fisherman," "Even Song," and "The Trumpet shall sound"—a program which illustrates the versatility of his musical work. With his love for music Scott combined a remarkable sense of humor which made him a delightful companion. He had a magnetic personality, charming social graces, and a deeply spiritual nature which found adequate expression in his sacred compositions.

[Information from the family; *Who's Who in America,* 1932–33; *Internatl. Who's Who in Music* (1918); *Etude,* July 1928; *Evening Star* (Washington, D. C.), Apr. 12, Dec. 3, 1932; *N. Y. Times,* Dec. 3, 1932.]

F. J. M.

SCOTT, LEROY (May 11, 1875–July 21, 1929), author, was born in Fairmount, Ind., the son of Eli J. and Eleanor (Reader) Scott. After graduating from Indiana University in 1897, he worked for a few months on a Louisiana newspaper owned by his brother and then went to Chicago, where he was a reporter for the *Chicago Journal*. In 1900 and 1901 he was assistant editor of the *Woman's Home Companion*. He had developed an interest in settlement work as a result of living at Hull House in Chicago, and in 1902 he became assistant headworker of the University Settlement, New York City. Here he met Miriam Finn, whom he married on June 24, 1904; they had two daughters and a son.

When in 1904 he gave up settlement work to devote himself to writing, he did not give up his interest in social reform. His first novel, *The Walking Delegate* (1905), showed not merely his confidence in organized labor but also his hope for far-reaching social reorganization. In *To Him That Hath* (1907) he revealed the difficulties of a man who has been in prison, and in *Counsel for the Defense* (1912) he described a woman's struggle for economic independence. *The Shears of Destiny* (1910) was concerned with the Russian revolutionary movement and was based on Scott's observations, made during a visit to Russia with his wife in 1905–06. From 1904 to 1912 he wrote frequently for the magazines on such topics as unemployment, life insurance, and strike-breaking. After his return from Russia he contributed several articles to the *Outlook* and to *Everybody's* on conditions in that country, and especially on the activities of the revolutionaries. In short, he is to be numbered among the muck-rakers. He was always moderate in his methods, but a strong social purpose informed what he wrote and is to be observed in his novels as well as his articles. It also found expression in other activities, for he was interested in organizing the Women's Trade Union League, an active worker for child-labor laws, and one of the founders and an executive of the Intercollegiate Socialist Society. When the muck-raking movement declined, he took advantage of another form of popular fiction. In *Partners of the Night* (1916) he dealt with crime and its detection, and the success of the book encouraged him to write a series of stories about the activities of criminals and policemen. These novels were based on an exact knowledge of criminal methods, derived from careful investigation, and all of them indicated the need for changes in the social structure and in the handling of offenders against the law; although the social moral may not have been plain to most of Scott's readers, it was constantly in his mind. His last novel, *The Trail of Glory* (1926), dealt with some of the problems of an amateur tennis

champion. He was drowned at Chateaugay Lake, N. Y. At his best he was a skilful story-teller, but he commonly employed romantic and improbable plots, showed no great insight into character, and had no stylistic distinction. He frankly and successfully competed with writers whose sole aim was to divert their readers; his work is on a higher level than theirs only because of the sincerity and firmness of his social purpose.

[*Who's Who in America*, 1928–29; "Our Own Times," *Reader Mag.*, Sept. 1905; Griffin Mace, "Nine Books of the Month," *Bookman*, May 1912; brief obit. in *Publishers' Weekly*, Aug. 3, 1929; *N. Y. Times*, July 22 and 28, 1929; information from Mrs. Scott.]

G. H.

SCOTT, ORANGE (Feb. 13, 1800–July 31, 1847), anti-slavery leader, was born in Brookfield, Vt., the eldest of the eight children of Lucy (Whitney) and Samuel Scott, a laboring man. The family lived at various places in Vermont and spent six years in Stanstead in Lower Canada. The boy's total schooling was about thirteen months. Beginning to feel religious concern in his twenty-first year, he experienced conversion at a camp-meeting held near Barre, Vt., late in 1820. At this time he was working as a farm laborer, but he was soon giving his Sundays to religious work, assisting the Methodist preacher in charge of the local circuit. His success was such that in November 1821 he gave up farming entirely and began the work of a circuit preacher. In 1822 he was received into the New England Conference on trial and by 1825 was a fully ordained minister in the Methodist Episcopal Church. His advancement was rapid, and within a few years he became, through reading and private study, a most effective speaker. His first important church was in Charlestown, Mass., where he achieved considerable distinction through a public discussion with a Universalist minister. On May 7, 1826, he was married to Amy Fletcher of Lyndon, Vt., who died in April 1835 leaving five children. In 1829, after serving a number of smaller circuits, he was sent to Springfield, Mass., the next year was made presiding elder of that district, and in 1831 was delegate to the General Conference. In 1833 he came in contact for the first time with the anti-slavery movement and was soon an ardent abolitionist. Appointed presiding elder of the Providence district in 1834 he took the leadership in a movement to open the columns of *Zion's Herald,* the Methodist paper in Boston, to a discussion of the slavery issue. This was accomplished, and he became the most active contributor. He also began to deliver public lectures on slavery in the larger New England cities.

When the slavery question came before the General Conference of 1836 at Cincinnati, he made an *Address* (1836) on the subject and was a recognized abolition leader. As a consequence of this abolition activity the bishop refused to reappoint him to the Providence district. After a year's pastorate at Lowell, Mass., he accepted an agency for the American Anti-Slavery Society and spoke throughout New England and New York. In 1838 he published "An Appeal to the Methodist Episcopal Church" in the only number published of the *Wesleyan Anti-Slavery Review*. At the session of the New England Conference in 1838 Bishop Elijah Hedding [*q.v.*] charged Scott with using coarse and disrespectful language, but the charges were not sustained. In 1839 Scott with Jotham Horton undertook the publication of the *American Wesleyan Observer* to plead the abolition cause among Methodists in preparation for the General Conference of 1840. He was a member of that Conference and again led the abolition forces. The radicals however were unable to stem the tide of conservative opinion. He became again the pastor of St. Paul's Church in Lowell, Mass., chosen regardless of episcopal authority. This action led to a bitter fight with the appointing authorities, which was one of the reasons that made Scott consider withdrawal from the Methodist Episcopal Church.

The secession movement rapidly developed under Scott's leadership, ably assisted by Jotham Horton and LaRoy Sunderland. These three leaders withdrew from the Methodist Episcopal Church on Nov. 8, 1841. They began the publication of the *True Wesleyan* on Jan. 7, 1843, to agitate withdrawal of all abolition Methodists to form a new ecclesiastical body, with opposition to slavery as its chief cornerstone. A preliminary convention at Andover, Mass., on Feb. 1, 1843, provided for a general convention at Utica, N. Y., on May 31. Scott was the president of the Utica convention, and there the Wesleyan Methodist Connection of America was formed. In the interests of this new Wesleyan Methodist Church he became the publishing agent in charge of the *True Wesleyan*, and when this business was moved to New York City he took up his residence at Newark, N. J., though his family remained in Newbury, Vt. In 1845 he made an extended tour of the western states that proved disastrous to his health, which had been failing for some time. In 1846 he published his reasons for his withdrawal in a book, *The Grounds of Secession from the M. E. Church: Being an Examination of her Connection with Slavery, and Also of her Form of Government*. A revised and

corrected edition was published in 1848. In 1846 he took his family to Newark and attempted to continue his work; but his condition grew rapidly worse, and he died at his home in Newark. He was survived by his widow, Eliza (Dearborn) Scott, whom he had married on Oct. 6, 1835. They had two children.

[The chief sources are his writings, *ante,* and autobiog. in L. C. Matlack, *The Life of Rev. Orange Scott* (1847), which is paged continuously and bound in same vol. with his *Memoir of Rev. Orange Scott* (1848); see also J. N. Norwood, *The Schism in the Methodist Episcopal Church* (1923); L. C. Matlack, *The Hist. of Amer. Slavery and Methodism from 1780 to 1849* (1849).]   W. W. S.

SCOTT, ROBERT KINGSTON (July 8, 1826–Aug. 12, 1900), Union soldier and governor of South Carolina, was born in Armstrong County, Pa., the son of Jane (Hamilton) and John Scott, a farmer. In 1842 the boy went to Stark County, Ohio, to seek educational advantages. In 1850 he went to California, where, for brief periods, he engaged in mining and the practice of his profession. After visiting Mexico and South America he settled in Florida, Henry County, Ohio, probably in 1851, to practise medicine. There he was married to Rebecca J. Lowry and had two children. Aid in the suppression of a cholera epidemic soon gave him considerable local prestige. Profitable investments in real estate enabled him to withdraw gradually from medicine and to engage in merchandising. On the outbreak of the Civil War, Governor Dennison appointed him a major with instructions to organize the 68th Ohio Infantry. In July 1862 he was promoted to the rank of colonel. He received honorable mention for gallantry in action and commanded a brigade in Sherman's march to the sea. On Jan. 12, 1865, he was promoted to the rank of brigadier-general and at the end of the war was brevetted a major-general.

Returning to Ohio after the war, he was recalled into active service almost immediately and made chief of the South Carolina branch of the Freedmen's Bureau with the title of assistant commissioner. He served in that capacity until July 1868. The conservative press of South Carolina praised him for the wise and moderate manner in which he administered the affairs of the bureau. Popularity engendered by his services as the chief dispenser of the charity of the federal government led to his nomination, in March 1868, for governor by the newly formed Union Republican party of South Carolina. He was easily elected. In 1870 he was reëlected by a large majority over Robert B. Carpenter, the candidate of an attempted coalition between Democrats and Republican reformers. As governor from July 1868 to November 1872 Scott was largely responsible for the scandals and disorders that characterized the introduction of Republican rule in South Carolina. His policies led to the increase of the public debt to thrice the amount it had been when he assumed office, and he concealed this fact from responsible investigators. When an attempt was made to impeach him, he stopped the proceedings by bribing the legislature with public funds. He was a leader in conspiracies to defraud the state of money by manipulating printing contracts and the stocks of the Blue Ridge Railroad. Provoking the formation of bands of the Ku-Klux Klan by the unscrupulous tactics through which he obtained reëlection, he professed inability to suppress these organizations and called in the aid of Federal troops. It is probable that Scott would have made a competent governor under normal conditions. His previous record had been creditable and his inaugural address bespoke a desire for conciliation and constructive achievement. That he was not callous to the better interests of the state is attested by his endeavor at times to stem the tide of corruption by the use of the veto. But it would have been impossible for him to make his administration satisfactory to the whites in whose hands ultimately lay the control of the state's destiny. After a half-hearted resistance to the corrupt officials who surrounded him, he conveniently succumbed to their suggestions and personally profited from their acts. He was "subject alike to alcoholic and female allurements," and on one occasion the state officials paid an actress to induce the drunken governor to sign an issue of bonds (E. P. Mitchell, *Memoirs of an Editor*, 1924, p. 326).

On the expiration of his term of office he retired from politics and settled in Columbia as a real estate agent. He declared the experiment of negro suffrage a mistake and in 1876 supported the state Democratic ticket; but on the return of the Democrats to power in 1877 he prudently left South Carolina in the face of possible prosecution and returned to Henry County, Ohio. There he engaged in the real estate development for the rest of his life. On Christmas Day 1880 he killed Walter G. Drury, a young drug clerk, whom he believed responsible for making his young son drunk. On a plea of accidental homicide he was acquitted of the charges that grew out of this act. He died in Henry County.

[*Men of Northwestern Ohio* (1898); L. C. Aldrich, *Hist. of Henry and Fulton Counties, Ohio* (1888); F. B. Heitman, *Hist. Register and Dictionary of the U. S. Army* (1903), vol. I; F. B. Simkins and R. H. Woody, *S. C. during Reconstruction* (1932); *Report of the*

Joint Investigating Committee on Public Frauds . . . Made to the General Assembly of S. C. . . . 1877–78 (1878), esp. pp. 215–21, 271–76, 563, 587–92; *Special Message of . . . Robert K. Scott, Governor . . . in Reply to Charges Made Against Him* (1872); *Charleston Daily News*, Mar. 9, 1868, Aug. 22, 1872; *News and Courier* (Charleston), Dec. 29, 30, 1880; *State* (Columbia, S. C.), Aug. 15, 1900.]   F. B. S—s.

SCOTT, SAMUEL PARSONS (July 8, 1846–May 30, 1929), lawyer, author, Hispanic scholar, was born at Hillsboro, Ohio, the son of William Scott, a lawyer and banker, and his wife, Elizabeth Jane Parsons. He attended the public schools and Miami University, where he graduated B.A. in 1866, studied law, was admitted to the bar in 1868, and practised at Leavenworth, Kan., and later at San Francisco. In 1875, because of his father's failing health, he left his practice and returned to Hillsboro to attend to the extensive property interests which he later inherited. Thenceforth he devoted himself to intellectual pursuits, with business as an avocation. A long sojourn in Spain resulted in a series of articles contributed to *Lippincott's, The Continent,* and *Potter's American Monthly.* In 1886 these papers, collected and revised, with some additional material, were published in book form under the title *Through Spain.* Meanwhile, Scott had begun work on his most ambitious original production, *History of the Moorish Empire in Europe* (3 vols., 1904), in the preface of which he stated that the work "engaged the attention of the author for more than twenty years." His bibliography was extensive, but he neglected to cite authorities for specific points. He was evidently indebted to *A History of the Intellectual Development of Europe* (1863) by John W. Draper [*q.v.*], and was even more favorable in his estimate of Arab culture and influence (Cf. his chap. xiii with Draper's chap. xvi). He held that the Moorish invasion was a deliverance from Visigothic oppression and depicted the Arab régime as the most brilliant period of peninsular history, the Christian hero, *El Cid,* as a cruel and treacherous outlaw, and the Spanish church as a perpetual instrument of enslavement and corruption.

For the remaining quarter century of his life, Scott's chosen task was the translation into English of the chief monuments of the Spanish and the Civil law. He was one of the founders of the Comparative Law Bureau of the American Bar Association and under its auspices published in 1910, with the title of *The Visigothic Code,* his translation from the Latin of the *Forum Judicum* (*Fuero Juzgo*). He had failed, however, to familiarize himself with the Continental literature of the subject, especially with the later texts; the accuracy of his translation was questioned; and his preface and notes drew adverse criticism from the reviewers; nevertheless, the fact remains that his was the first attempt to put the work into English and it stimulated an interest in the subject. His rendering of *Las Siete Partidas,* the famous medieval code of Spain, appeared posthumously under the same auspices in 1931; but in this instance the Bureau officers had edited the text, the translation had been carefully checked, and an introduction, index, table of contents, and copious bibliography had been prepared by others. Unfortunately, his translations of the Roman legal landmarks, including the *Corpus Juris,* were printed just as he had left them, unedited and unchecked, under the misleading title of *The Civil Law* (17 vols., 1932).

On Oct. 10, 1895, when he was nearly fifty, Scott married Elizabeth Woodbridge Smart of Paint, Ohio. He was by that time deep in his literary labors and the union proved uncongenial. No formal separation took place; but in his will he directed that his wife should receive only a relatively small portion of his estate, allowing a considerable sum for the publication of his remaining manuscripts. This provision was disregarded by his executor, and the works remain unpublished. These include translations of *El Fuero Viejo de Castilla, El Fuero Real, Las Leyes del Estilo, El Ordenamiento de Alcala, Las Leyes Nuevas, El Ordenamiento de las Tafurerias, Las Leyes de Toro, Leyes para los Adelantados Mayores,* and *El Código Penal de España.* In connection with his labors Scott accumulated a large and select library. He died at his home in Hillsboro.

[Scott's *Moorish Empire* was reviewed by F. W. Williams, in *Am. Hist. Rev.,* Jan. 1905; his *Visigothic Code,* by Paul Vinagradoff, in *Law Quart. Rev.,* July 1911, and by Munroe Smith, in *Columbia Law Rev.,* Nov. 1911; *Las Siete Partidas* by A. S. de Bustamante y Sirvén, in *Tulane Law Rev.,* Feb. 1932, by D. E. Grant, in *Columbia Law Rev.,* Apr. 1932, and by A. S. Aiton, in *Am. Bar Asso. Jour.,* May 1932. For biography see C. S. Lobinger, *Ibid.,* Sept. 1929; *Who's Who in America,* 1928–29; *Gen. Cat. Miami Univ., 1809–1909* (n.d.); *Cincinnati Enquirer,* May 31, 1929.]

C. S. L.

SCOTT, THOMAS ALEXANDER (Dec. 28, 1823–May 21, 1881), railroad executive, was born at Fort Loudon, Franklin County, Pa., the seventh in a family of eleven children. His father, Thomas Scott, kept a tavern at which the passengers on the stagecoaches stopped for refreshments. His mother, Thomas Scott's second wife, was Rebecca Douglas. The boy attended a country school in the winter months, until at the age of ten he lost his father, and then he worked as a handy man in a general supply store until he was about seventeen, when he went to Columbia, Pa., as a clerk in the office of Maj. James Patton, his brother-in-law, who was collector of tolls on the state system of public roads and canals.

He remained in the employ of the state until 1845, then engaged in private business ventures at Columbia, with an interval in 1847–49 when he was chief clerk in the office of the collector of tolls at Philadelphia. In 1850 he became station agent for the railroad at Duncansville, the point of transfer between the Pennsylvania Railroad and the state canals on the one hand and the Allegheny Portage Railroad over the mountains on the other. In December 1852, when the Pennsylvania Railroad was completed to Pittsburgh, his abilities had so far developed that he was appointed third assistant superintendent in charge of the division starting westward from Altoona, with his office at Pittsburgh. On Jan. 1, 1858, he became general superintendent, and on Mar. 21, 1860, first vice-president of the Pennsylvania Railroad.

In this capacity, as the war clouds thickened early in 1861, Scott advised the President-Elect, who was in Harrisburg as the guest of Governor Curtin, not to go directly to Washington as he had intended, but to return secretly to Philadelphia and proceed thence, with the same secrecy, to the Capital. This plan was adopted, the telegraph wires were disconnected, and Lincoln reached Washington ahead of the time published in the newspapers and by another route. Upon the outbreak of hostilities, Simon Cameron [*q.v.*] of Pennsylvania, then secretary of war, summoned Scott to Washington (Apr. 21, 1861) to operate the Northern Central railroad from Harrisburg to Baltimore for the purpose of transporting men and munitions. Taking with him from the Pennsylvania Railroad service a young telegraph operator named Andrew Carnegie, Scott reported to Cameron. On May 3, 1861, he was commissioned colonel of United States Volunteers; and by an act of Congress of Aug. 3, 1861, he was appointed assistant secretary of war to supervise all government railways and transportation lines. Although he had only advisory power, in the months before his resignation, June 1, 1862, he laid the foundation of a working system. In September 1863 he was called back into the government service and given the temporary appointment of colonel and assistant quartermaster-general on the staff of Major-General Joseph Hooker for the special task of transporting some 13,000 men, with their artillery, wagons, and horses, from Virginia through Nashville to Chattanooga. From time to time throughout the war, Scott was called upon for advice and suggestions regarding the government's use of railroads.

Meanwhile, under the presidency of J. Edgar Thomson [q.v.], with Scott as vice-president, the Pennsylvania Railroad was beginning its period of greatest expansion. In 1862 the company leased the Philadelphia & Erie, which provided a connection between the Atlantic seaboard and the Great Lakes; in 1868–69 control was secured, through lease or stock ownership, of the newly built lines reaching consecutively from Pittsburgh to Cincinnati, Indianapolis, St. Louis, and Chicago; while in 1871 the United Canal and Railroad Companies of New Jersey were leased, extending the line from Philadelphia into New York City. Other leases and purchases opened the railroad's entrance into Baltimore and Washington. The Pennsylvania Company was organized in 1870, with Scott as president, for the purpose of operating and managing all the lines leased and controlled by the Pennsylvania Railroad west of Pittsburgh. In 1871 Scott was instrumental in having the Pennsylvania take a financial interest in the Southern Railway Security Company, which controlled a number of railroad systems built or being constructed south of Richmond, Va. He believed that these roads would prove valuable traffic feeders to the Pennsylvania, but his expectations were not fulfilled and about ten years later the Pennsylvania sold what was left of its investment in the Southern company. In the meantime, the Union Pacific Railroad, which was then the only transcontinental line, had fallen into financial difficulties, and it occurred to Scott that it might be brought into the Pennsylvania's control. On Mar. 8, 1871, he was elected president of that company, succeeding Oliver Ames, 1807–1877 [q.v.], but retained office only until Mar. 6, 1872, eventually selling his holdings to Jay Gould [q.v.]. On June 3, 1874, upon the death of Thomson, Scott succeeded him as president of the Pennsylvania Railroad Company. His task thenceforth was chiefly to consolidate and strengthen the system which had been so greatly expanded. From 1872 to 1880 he was also president of the Texas & Pacific Railway Company.

Scott was a man of striking appearance. He had a keen and quick apprehension, an even temper, inexhaustible patience, and great charm of manner. In spite of his limited schooling he had acquired the habit of wide reading which gave his speech the mark of an educated man. He was married in the fall of 1847 to Anna Margaret Mullison, daughter of Reuben Mullison, of Columbia, Pa. She died in 1855, leaving a son and a daughter, a second daughter having died in infancy. Ten years later Scott married Anna Dike Riddle, of Pittsburgh. A daughter and two sons, one of whom died in boyhood, were born of this marriage. In 1878 Scott suffered a paralytic stroke, but recovered sufficiently to continue his executive work until June 1, 1880, when he resigned the presidency of the Pennsylvania. He died at his home, "Woodburn," near Darby, Pa., less than a year later.

[The date of birth here given is that appearing in "Thomas A. Scott," biog. address by John P. Green, vice-president of the Pa. RR., formerly Scott's private secretary, and in other memoranda in Pa. RR. archives. Other sources for Scott's career include *Encyc. of Contemporary Biog. of Pa.* (1889), vol. I; J. W. Jordan, *Encyc. of Pa. Biog.*, vol. VII (1916); *Mag. of Western History*, June 1889; W. B. Wilson, *Hist. of the Pa. RR. Company* (1899), vol. II; H. W. Schotter, *The Growth and Development of the Pa. RR. Company* (1927); R. E. Riegel, *The Story of the Western Railroads* (1926); *Am. Hist. Rev.*, July 1917; *N. Y. Tribune*, May 22, 1881; *Phila. Press*, May 21, 25, 1881; *Public Ledger* (Phila.), May 23, 1881.]   S. H. C.

SCOTT, THOMAS FIELDING (Mar. 12, 1807–July 14, 1867), Protestant Episcopal clergyman, first missionary bishop of Oregon and Washington Territory, was born in Iredell County, N. C. He was educated at Chapel Hill School, N. C., and at Franklin College (University of Georgia), Athens, graduating from the latter with honors in 1829. Licensed to preach in the Presbyterian Church, he served as a missionary in Hall and Franklin counties and at Columbus, Ga. Subsequently he had more important charges at La Grange and Savannah, Ga., and at Columbia, Tenn. The turning point in his career came about 1842 when he met Bishop James Hervey Otey and Bishop Leonidas Polk. Under the inspiration of these friends he "made thorough study of the Scriptural and historical claims of Episcopacy," came to "the firm and unalterable conclusion that the doctrine was true," and regretfully abandoned Presbyterianism (manuscript biographical sketch, *post*). He was ordained deacon by Bishop Stephen Elliott at St. Paul's Church, Augusta, Ga., Mar. 12, 1843, and priest by Bishop Elliott at Christ Church, Macon, Ga., Feb. 24, 1844. He served successively as rector of St. James' Church, Marietta, Ga., and Trinity Church, Columbus, Ga.

In 1853 he was appointed missionary bishop of the new diocese in the remote Northwest, was consecrated at Christ Church, Savannah, Ga., Jan. 8, 1854, and commenced his work in Oregon in the following April. The district placed in his charge was extensive, conditions of travel were painfully arduous, means of communication were inconstant, money was scarce, and competent assistants almost impossible to secure. For thirteen years, however, in spite of pathetic handicaps, he struggled on, laying the foundations necessary for the achievements of his successor. Several times he was called upon to administer the diocese of California as well. In 1860 he returned East for a few months on business of the church. The unremitting strain of his labors influenced his health, and he fell ill of Panama fever on his way to the General Convention of 1868. He died in New York, and was buried in Trinity Cemetery. In 1830 he had married Evelyn Appleby of Jackson, Ga., by whom he was survived.

Bishop Scott was a man of great energy of mind and wide information. He was gentle in manner and spontaneously generous of spirit, but was capable of forceful and apt expression of his views. As a preacher he was popular in both the South and West. His vision was greater than his opportunity, but he is gratefully remembered for his pioneer endeavors and considered by many an authentic martyr of the American Church.

[W. S. Perry, *The Episcopate in America* (1895); *N. Y. Tribune,* July 16, 1867; sermons, letters, and biog. sketch by Mrs. Scott in Colburn Collection of autographic and bibliographic material regarding American bishops, archives of Washington Cathedral, Washington, D. C.]   J. W. F.

SCOTT, WALTER (Oct. 31, 1796–Apr. 23, 1861), preacher and religious reformer, was born at Moffat, Dumfriesshire, Scotland, the sixth child of John Scott, a music teacher, and Mary (Innes) Scott. He received a good musical education, became a skilled flutist, and was graduated from the University of Edinburgh in 1818. That same year, on invitation of his uncle, George Innes, who had a position in the New York custom house, he emigrated to the United States. For a time he served as tutor in an academy on Long Island. Traveling to Pittsburgh on foot, he arrived there May 7, 1819, and became assistant to George Forrester, who was conducting a private school. Forrester was an immersed Haldanean preacher who had come from Scotland not long before and had organized a church in Pittsburgh. Scott, a Presbyterian, was converted to Forrester's views, was immersed, and joined his church. On Forrester's death by drowning, Scott took over his duties both in connection with the church and with the school. Having read a pamphlet put forth by a Scotch Baptist Church in New York, he resigned his position and went there to learn more about the institution, but was not greatly pleased with what he found. Invited back to Pittsburgh by Nathaniel Richardson as tutor for his son

Robert, he returned to establish a small school and care for the church.

In the winter of 1821–22 he first met Alexander Campbell [*q.v.*] in Pittsburgh and was deeply impressed by his teaching. Scott suggested the name *The Christian Baptist* for the magazine which Campbell began to publish in August 1823, and contributed to the second number an article entitled "On Teaching Christianity," which an editorial note announced as stating "a Divinely authorized plan of teaching the Christian religion." This was followed by three others on the same theme. He became one of the most regular and copious contributors to the periodicals and made Campbell's cause his own. While Campbell thought chiefly of reforming the church, Scott's primary interest was in the conversion of individuals. He continued to conduct his academy in Pittsburgh until 1826, but early in that year moved to Steubenville, Ohio. In August he visited the annual meeting of the Mahoning Baptist Association (of which Campbell was then a member) and preached before it; in 1827, he visited it again and was invited to preach. Although he was neither a member of the Association nor a Baptist, he was chosen as its evangelist. Applying to the process of conversion the principles on which Campbell had based his proposed reformation of the church, Scott developed a remarkably effective technique of evangelism, stressing three points: faith (the belief of testimony regarding the sonship and messiahship of Jesus); repentance (of past sins); baptism (by immersion for remission of sins). Under this preaching over a thousand new members were added in a year to the churches of the Mahoning Association. It was largely through Scott's urgency that the Association was dissolved and the "Reformers" ceased to consider themselves Baptists.

Scott, who had already moved to Canfield, Ohio, soon moved to Cincinnati, where he began the publication of a monthly magazine, the *Evangelist,* and then to Carthage, Ohio, where he lived for thirteen years, traveling and preaching in Ohio, Kentucky, Virginia, and Missouri. For a very short time he was president of Bacon College. In 1844 he returned to Pittsburgh, preached for a church in that city and for one in Allegheny, and published a weekly paper, the *Protestant Unionist.* From 1850 to 1854 he was principal of a female academy at Covington, Ky. From the latter date until his death in 1861 he lived in Mason County, Ky. He was the author of two books: *The Gospel Restored* (1836), and *The Messiahship, or the Great Demonstration* (1859). He was thrice married: on Jan. 3, 1823, to Sarah Whitsett, who died in 1849, having borne him four sons and a daughter; in 1850, to Annie B. Allen, who died in 1854, by whom he had a daughter; and in 1855, to Mrs. Eliza Sandige, who survived him. Scott's significance in the history of the Disciples of Christ is that he established the evangelistic pattern and the form and method of propaganda to which the rapid growth of this group of Christians was largely due.

[William Baxter, *Life of Elder Walter Scott, with Sketches of his Fellow-laborers, William Hayden, Adamson Bentley, John Henry, and Others* (1874); Robert Richardson, *Memoirs of Alexander Campbell* (2 vols., 1868–70); W. E. Garrison, *Religion Follows the Frontier* (1931); the *Christian Baptist*, 1823–29; files of the *Millennial Harbinger*, 1830–61, with obituary notice, May 1861.]   W. E. G.

SCOTT, WILLIAM (June 7, 1804–May 18, 1862), jurist, was born at Warrenton, Fauquier County, Va., of a family resident in the state and province since early colonial days. After his graduation from Fauquier Academy, he studied law with a local attorney and was admitted to the bar in 1825. The next year he removed to Missouri and settled at the then flourishing town of Old Franklin. The choice was not a wise one, for there were many leading lawyers in the locality and, as Scott was hot-tempered and excitable, his experienced opponents found it easy to confuse and irritate him during trials. His industry and knowledge of the law, however, won the respect of the profession and led to his appointment in 1835 as judge of the ninth circuit. The same year he married Elizabeth Dixon, of Jefferson City, by whom he had six children. Living at Union, he traveled on circuit through the large district. As a judge he won immediate recognition. He decided cases soon after hearing the arguments, since there was no opportunity in the pioneer community to examine carefully reports and opinions difficult of access, and he frequently deferred to local conditions and discarded common law doctrines to meet the immediate situation. This frontier judicial pragmatism suited admirably both lawyers and litigants; he was highly regarded for his sense of justice and kind heart.

In August 1841 he was appointed to the supreme bench, an action that was widely indorsed by Democrats and by Whigs alike (*Jeffersonian Republican*, Aug. 28, 1841). He served eighteen years. His opinions, necessarily dealing with a great variety of subjects, were marked by brevity and by conservatism. His legal ability did not equal that of his colleagues, Hamilton Rowan Gamble and William Barclay Napton [qq.v.], but he was industrious, just, and com-

petent. He wrote many opinions in cases involving master and slave, including *Emerson* vs. *Harriet* and *Emerson* vs. *Dred Scott* (1848, 11 *Mo.*, 413), and he spoke for the majority in *Scott, a Man of Color* vs. *Emerson* (1852, 15 *Mo.*, 576). In the latter case, he overruled eight Missouri precedents in holding that the laws of other states and territories had no extra-territorial effect in Missouri except as Missouri recognized them, and that a slave who is taken by his master into territory where slavery is prohibited could not, after returning with his master to Missouri, maintain a suit for freedom. He also charged that the free states, in obstructing the return of fugitive slaves, refused to recognize the law of the slave states. The decision assumed, therefore, a political significance. He was an ardent Democrat and during the middle forties became active in the group of radical, pro-slavery opponents of Thomas Hart Benton. He approved the disunionist Jackson Resolutions of 1849 and supported the anti-Benton faction during the bitter party warfare of the fifties. On two occasions, in 1855 and in 1861, he received a significant legislative vote for United States senator. In 1849 Gov. Austin Augustus King [q.v.], a Benton Democrat, did not reappoint Scott, but two years later, when the judiciary became elective, he was chosen for a term of six years; in 1857 he was reëlected. He was large and awkward, weighing two hundred and fifty pounds, an ineffective speaker who rarely attempted a public address. Although not an active disunionist, he strongly indorsed the southern attitude in 1860–61 and was in sympathy with the pro-confederate state administration. When he refused to subscribe to the oath of loyalty promulgated by the state convention, his office was declared vacant (*Journal of the Missouri State Convention*, 1861, pp. 10, 16). After his appointment to the supreme court in 1841 he moved to a farm near Jefferson City, where he lived until his death in 1862; in the excitement of the war his passing was scarcely noticed by the bar.

[W. V. N. Bay, *Reminiscences of the Bench and Bar of Mo.* (1878); *The Hist. of the Bench and Bar of Mo.* (1898), ed. by A. J. D. Stewart; H. L. Conard, *Encyc. of the Hist. of Mo.* (1901), vol. V; Helen T. Catterall, "Some Antecedents of the Dred Scott Case," *Am. Hist. Rev.*, Oct. 1924; *Jeffersonian Republican*, Aug. 1841; *Mo. Republican, Daily Mo. Democrat*, May 19, 1862; 7–31 *Mo. Reports*.]   T. S. B.

SCOTT, WILLIAM ANDERSON (Jan. 31, 1813–Jan. 14, 1885), Presbyterian clergyman, educator, and author, was born of Scotch-Irish ancestry in Bedford County, Tenn., the son of Eli and Martha (Anderson) Scott. At the age of fifteen he united with the Cumberland Presbyterian Church. His determination to gain an education led him to employ numerous expedients. Needing books where books were few, on one occasion he entered into an agreement with a neighbor who owned a Greek New Testament to buy the volume for three days' plowing. While toiling among stumps, rocks, and dampness in fulfilling his part of the agreement, he contracted a severe cold which resulted in life-long lameness. Licensed to preach when seventeen, he did missionary work for about a year, then entered Cumberland College at Princeton, Ky., from which he was graduated in 1833. After nine months at Princeton (N. J.) Theological Seminary, he was ordained, May 17, 1835, by the Presbytery of Louisiana and then served as a missionary in Louisiana and Arkansas (1835–36) and as principal of the Female Academy at Winchester, Tenn. (1836–38). For the next two years he had charge of the Hermitage Church, on the Tennessee estate of Andrew Jackson, also serving as president of Nashville Female Seminary; from 1840 to 1842 he supplied a church at Tuscaloosa, Ala.

His pastoral eminence began in 1842 when he commenced a ministry of twelve years at the First Presbyterian Church, New Orleans. While here he became one of the leading clergymen of the city and influential throughout the South and the Southwest. Early in 1854 a group of San Francisco men invited him to that city to organize a church. Arriving there in May, he was instrumental in forming Calvary Church for which a building was erected in the heart of the then semi-lawless city. While pastor here Scott founded and edited the *Pacific Expositor,* a religious publication. With the outbreak of the Civil War in 1861, although his aggressive labors had made Calvary Church "the greatest force for righteousness on the Pacific coast" (Wicher, *post,* p. 129), he found his outspoken Southern sympathies so unacceptable that in October he departed for England. After his return he served the Forty-second Street Church, New York, a congregation of Southern sympathizers, from 1863 to 1870, and then went back to San Francisco, where he organized St. John's Church, which had as a nucleus numerous old Southern families. For many years it was one of the city's strong churches.

Scott's educational work in the West had commenced when in 1856 he helped found City College, San Francisco, an institution which survived for twenty years. The educational center which still (1935) lives to honor his name, however, is San Francisco Theological Seminary, now at San Anselmo. Established in 1871, it at

first occupied two rooms of City College. Scott was a director until his death, the first president of the directors, the first elected professor—to the chair of logic and systematic theology—and the first faculty president. Much of the later high standing of the institution is attributed to his early initiative, faithful work, and influence with persons of wealth. The site of the San Anselmo buildings was donated by A. W. Foster, his parishioner and son-in-law. Scott remained actively connected with the seminary, as well as with the St. John's pastorate, until his death, at San Francisco.

He was the author of ten or more religious books which had a considerable circulation throughout the United States. Among the best known were *The Wedge of Gold; or, Achan in El Dorado* (1855), *Trade and Letters* (1856), *The Bible and Politics* (1859), and *The Christ of the Apostles' Creed* (1867). In 1858 he was elected moderator of the Presbyterian General Assembly (Old School). On Jan. 19, 1836, he married Ann Nicholson of Kilkeel, Ireland.

[E. A. Wicher, *The Presbyterian Church in Cal.* (1927); Alfred Nevin, *Encyc. of the Presbyterian Church in the U. S. A.* (1884); *Princeton Theological Sem. Biog. Cat.* (1909); *N. Y. Observer,* Jan. 29, 1885; *Presbyterian Banner,* Jan. 21, 1885; *Herald and Presbyter,* Jan. 28, 1885; *Daily Alta California* (San Francisco), Jan. 15, 1885; information as to certain facts from Scott's grand-daughter, Miss Lou Foster, San Rafael, Cal.]   P.P.F.

SCOTT, WILLIAM LAWRENCE (July 2, 1828–Sept. 19, 1891), railroad and coal magnate, was born in Washington, D. C., the son of Robert James and Mary Ann (Lewis) Scott, and a grandson of Gustavus Scott [*q.v.*]. His father died about 1835; with three other children William was brought up by his mother at Fortress Monroe and attended the academy at Hampden, Va. From 1840 to 1846 he was a page in the House of Representatives, continuing his schooling when Congress was not in session. After learning the coal-forwarding business as a shipping clerk under Charles M. Reed of Erie, Pa., in 1850 he formed a partnership in the same trade with Morrow B. Lowry and a year later became a partner in the coal firm of John Hearn and Company. This marked the beginning of his prosperity. His holdings in coal and iron came to be extensive and important; he manufactured iron in Pennsylvania and Missouri and controlled coal lands in Pennsylvania, Illinois, Iowa, and Missouri, and coal distributing companies in Pennsylvania and the Middle West. The W. L. Scott Company, formed after Hearn's death in 1871, became one of the largest producing and shipping coal firms in the United States.

Well before this time he had reached out to

the allied field of railways. By his marriage, Sept. 19, 1853, to Mary Matilda Tracy of Erie. he had joined himself with a wealthy family prominent in railroading. In 1861 he began operations with the Erie and Pittsburgh Railroad, then not completed; by 1866 he and his associates had completed the road and linked it with the Pittsburgh, Fort Wayne, and Chicago Railway, and shortly afterward he became president of the Erie and Pittsburgh, which bought and closed a canal that competed with it by tapping the Pennsylvania bituminous coal fields. With John F. Tracy, his brother-in-law, president of the Chicago, Rock Island, and Pacific, he promoted the extension of that road from central Iowa to the Missouri River, a work completed in 1869, and he was one of the builders of the first elevated railroad in New York City. He was interested financially in the development of the Canada Southern, Union Pacific, and Canadian Pacific railways, was one of the promoters of the New York, Philadelphia, and Norfolk, and was a stockholder and director of many other roads. His other business interests included banking and real estate. He also acquired farm lands in Erie County and in Virginia, where he bred shorthorn cattle and race horses, but he is said to have been unable to bear defeat and sold out his racing stable a number of times.

Politics, though a side issue with him, was a subject in which he was intensely interested. He was mayor of Erie in 1866 and again in 1871, and his business talent secured for the city the best "waterworks" system known to the times. Three times a delegate to the National Democratic Convention, in 1884 and 1886 he was elected to Congress from a normally Republican district. As a conservative Democrat he supported a low tariff and the gold standard and sponsored the Chinese exclusion bill. He was a warm admirer of Samuel Jones Tilden [q.v.] and a friend of Cleveland. His funeral at Erie was attended by notables in finance and politics, including the governor of the state and President Cleveland. Leaving an estate estimated to be between twenty and thirty millions, he was survived by his wife and two daughters. He was typical of the public-spirited but highly individualistic capitalists of the second half of the nineteenth century: a heavy investor in United States bonds during the darkest days of the Civil War, a citizen charitable and humane to the poor of Erie, but an alleged exploiter of the miners who worked for him and an object of bitter enmity on the part of labor unionists. Coming on the scene at a time when the coal and railroad industries offered great opportunities, he exhibited the ten-

acity of purpose and the talent for administration that could make effective use of them.

[H. E. Hayden, *Va. Genealogies* (1891); *Pittsburgh Commercial Gazette*, Sept. 21, 1891; *Nelson's Biog. Dict. and Hist. Reference Book of Erie County, Pa.* (1896); *Biog. Directory Am. Cong.* (1928); long biog. sketch in *N. Y. Tribune*, Sept. 21, 1891.]   S. J. B.

SCOTT, WINFIELD (June 13, 1786–May 29, 1866), soldier, pacificator, and presidential nominee, was born on the family estate, "Laurel Branch," fourteen miles from Petersburg, Va. His grandfather, James Scott of the clan Buccleuch, having supported the Pretender, escaped to the colonies after the battle of Culloden in 1746. His father, William Scott, a successful farmer who had been a captain in the American Revolution, died when Winfield was in his sixth year, leaving four children, two boys, James and Winfield, and two girls. His mother, Ann Mason, was the daughter of Daniel Mason and the grand-daughter of John Winfield, one of the wealthiest men in the colony (*Memoirs*, I, 3). To her inspiration her son later attributed the continued successes of his long career. Unfortunately she died when he was seventeen. He was already six feet two and of bulky proportions. Two years later he stood six feet five, weighed about 230 pounds, and was physically the strongest man in the neighborhood. He did good scholastic work under the able instruction of James Hargrave and James Ogilvie. It was doubtless fortunate for him that because of legal hindrances he did not inherit the fortune of his grandfather but had to content himself with his modest patrimony. In 1805 he entered the College of William and Mary, but, because of his age and the contention between the student atheists and faculty churchmen, did not remain long. The same year he voluntarily left the institution to study law in the office of David Robinson in Petersburg.

In 1807 he witnessed in Richmond the trial of Aaron Burr. Though impressed by John Marshall, he regretted the outcome (*Ibid.*, I, 16). Following the outrage committed by the *Leopard* on the *Chesapeake*, and immediately after Jefferson's proclamation, he enlisted in the Petersburg troop of cavalry, galloping off with it on July 3. A few weeks later as a lance corporal he was instrumental in capturing a small boat containing two British officers and six men. Later in the year he went to Charleston, S. C., where he hoped to be more quickly admitted to the bar. At the prospect of hostilities, he personally approached President Jefferson in Washington and was tentatively promised a captaincy, but found himself, in March 1808, in Petersburg on the same law circuit as before.

On May 3, the coveted commission of captain of light or flying artillery arrived. Straightway he recruited a company in Petersburg and Richmond and was ordered to Norfolk to be embarked for New Orleans, where he arrived Apr. 1, 1809. The narrowness, unprogressiveness, and inefficiency of many of the army officers of that time decided him to return to the law. But on his way home, when he learned that charges had been preferred against him, he immediately quashed his resignation and went back to face them. It seems that he had stated candidly to another officer that Gen. James Wilkinson [q.v.], his department commander, had been as great a traitor as Burr in the testimony given at the trial. Gossip had carried the news to Wilkinson, who set Scott before a court for ungentlemanly conduct and trumped up specifications of fraud. The court suspended Scott from the army for a year because of unofficerlike conduct in making adverse statements against a superior, exonerated him from all suspicion of dishonesty, and recommended a nine-month remittance of the sentence (Mansfield, post, p. 28). However, the full year was approved, and Scott began in 1810 his enforced absence at home. Becoming "domesticated" with Benjamin Watkins Leigh [q.v.], he improved his liberal education by conversation and reading and his professional education by the study of foreign military works. In the fall of 1811, he set out to join his command with a party of five, traveling by wagons, learning the customs of the Creeks and Choctaws en route, and cutting the first roads through to Baton Rouge. During the winter of 1811–12 he served on Brig.-Gen. Wade Hampton's staff in New Orleans. In the intervals of his peacetime duties he continued to pursue the law, but in February 1812, when he learned that Congress had provided for the addition of 25,000 to the army in prospect of war with Great Britain, he left for Washington with Hampton, to be apprised there that he had been promoted to the rank of lieutenant-colonel. He was immediately ordered to Philadelphia to recruit a regiment, but in September he obtained permission to proceed to Niagara.

He reported to Brig.-Gen. Alexander Smyth at Buffalo Oct. 4, 1812, and came first under fire Oct. 8, at a naval engagement in which some of his troops participated. At the battle of Queenstown Scott begged to accompany the detachment that crossed into Canada, but did not do so on account of his superior rank. However, after Van Rensselaer was wounded, he crossed and was consequently with the heroic group which an overwhelming number of volunteers

on the American shore refused to assist. While an unarmed prisoner he was set upon by two stalwart Indians brandishing knives and tomahawks, but was saved by his presence of mind and massive strength, and the timely entrance of a British officer. On Nov. 20, he was paroled and taken to Boston; and in March he was sent to Philadelphia as an adjutant-general with the rank of colonel. Detailed for duty on the northern front, he planned and executed, as Dearborn's adjutant-general, the successful attack on Fort George, where he was wounded when one of the British magazines exploded. In the fall he was placed in command of Fort George, which had carelessly been left defenseless before an aggressive enemy. By supreme efforts, working sometimes twenty out of twenty-four hours, he restored it to strength. Leaving there Oct. 13, he joined Wilkinson's army on the St. Lawrence, commanding a battalion of infantry in Brown's advance guard, defeating the British, and capturing prisoners at the engagement on Uphold's (given by him as Hooppole) Creek. Through the uninterrupted succession of ignominious land defeats of the war, Scott chafed. Almost alone he realized that an exacting apprenticeship of training and knowledge was essential for the prevention of useless sacrifice and the attainment of victory, all the more necessary since soldierly schooling had been held in contempt since the Revolution. President Madison and Secretary Monroe, impressed by his apparent efficiency, sent him to Albany to supervise the preparations for another offensive on the Niagara, promising him a brigadier's commission. However, since affairs temporarily subsided in that quarter, Scott found himself in Albany supervising munitions at the arsenal.

On Mar. 9, 1814, he was made a regular brigadier-general. On Mar. 24 he went to Buffalo, where he played the chief part in training the only American troops who gave a wholly good account of themselves on land during the War of 1812. In the stifling heat of July 4 and 5, it was his brigade that drove the enemy in a running fight for sixteen miles to the Chippewa. Without the aid of Brown, Porter, and Ripley, his 1100 men defeated Riall, who had 1700. It was also his brigade that bore the brunt of the fighting on July 25 at Lundy's Lane, probably as stubbornly and bravely fought a contest as took place on American soil. He had two horses killed under him and was so severely wounded late in the battle that he had to be carried from the field. In this period of military ineffectiveness, it is not difficult to understand how Scott became overnight the idol of the country and a hero abroad. Honors were heaped upon him. He was at once brevetted a major-general. On his journey east and south, invalided, he was stopped by ovations in every town. Congress voted him a medal, as did Virginia, though neither was actually presented until 1825. Gov. Daniel D. Tompkins personally presented him, in 1816, with a sword awarded by New York State. He was elected an honorary member of the Society of the Cincinnati.

Since his wounds prevented him from joining Jackson in New Orleans, Scott made his headquarters in Baltimore, where he became head of a board of inquiry on General Winder in the fiasco of Bladensburg and of another board to write the first standard set of American drill regulations, *Rules and Regulations for the Field Exercise and Manœuvres of Infantry* (1815). In the reduction of the army after peace was declared, when Congress caused the discharge of five officers out of every six, Scott, through the absence or tardiness of his seniors, became virtually the head of a board to make the selections. The difficult task was carried out with sympathy and efficiency. On July 9, 1815, he sailed to Europe, where he met many distinguished personages and studied French military methods. Returning home in 1816, he took up his headquarters in New York City. On Mar. 11, 1817, he married Maria D. Mayo, daughter of John Mayo of Richmond, Va.

During the routine work of a department commander in peace, Scott's vitality vented itself in constructive writing. His "Scheme for Restricting the Use of Ardent Spirits in the United States" (Philadelphia *National Gazette*, Dec. 14, 17, 19, 20, 1821), a plea for light wines and beer to the exclusion of hard liquors, preceded and, according to Scott, led to the formation of the first temperance societies in the country (*Memoirs*, I, 205; Mansfield, *post*, pp. 182–84, 189). In 1818 he began an elaborate set of Military Institutes, which were duly provided for by Congress. He served as the president of boards of tactics in 1815, 1821, 1824, and 1826. In order to gain more knowledge of this subject he traveled again in Europe during 1829. In 1834–35, he alone revised and enlarged the *Infantry-Tactics* (3 vols., 1835) for the army; this work remained the sole standard down to the Civil War, though widely plagiarized before and during that conflict.

In 1828 Scott, who was the logical successor to Jacob Brown as commanding general of the army, was passed over in favor of Alexander Macomb [*q.v.*]. Scott tendered his resignation, which was not accepted, and then protested in vain against being placed under the command of a former junior. For some time there was lack of harmony between the two generals. His chance for active duty came when he set out on July 8, 1832, with about 950 troops to end the Black Hawk War, but on Lake Huron his command was struck by Asiatic cholera. Against the warnings of the doctors he untiringly went among the afflicted. At this time he issued his famous order that any man found intoxicated must dig a grave of his own size and contemplate it with the understanding that he would soon fill it if he persisted in wanton drinking (Ganoe, *post*, pp. 171–72). Because of the cholera, he could not bring up his troops in time for the battle of the Bad Axe. Scarcely recovered from what was felt to be a taint of the plague, he arrived at West Point to find a summons from the Secretary of War. In Washington he was personally commissioned by President Jackson to watch the Nullifiers in South Carolina. Proceeding thence, by his tact, his sagacity in withholding the appearance of military threat, and his kindly dealings with the leaders, he did much to preserve peace in a time of crisis. He was again personally commissioned in 1835 by Jackson to prosecute the war against the Seminoles and Creeks in Florida and the adjacent states. Deprived of everything needful for a campaign, he was unable to make headway beyond the making of vigorous preparations. Jackson had apparently not recovered from the animosity engendered in 1817, when Scott had criticized an order of his as mutinous and had in turn been called a "hectoring bully" (J. S. Bassett, *Correspondence of Andrew Jackson*, II, 1927, pp. 291–92, 325, 338–39, 344; James Parton, *Life of Andrew Jackson*, 1860, II, 371–82). Impatient of Scott's delay, Jackson relieved him later during the Creek campaign, superseded him by Jesup, and placed him before a court of inquiry for not prosecuting the war with vigor. The court not only exonerated him, but praised his "energy, steadiness and ability" (*Proceedings of the Military Court of Inquiry in the Case of Major General Scott . . .*, 1837, being *Senate Document No. 224*, 24 Cong., 2 Sess.). When he returned to the command of the Eastern Division in New York, he was tendered a public dinner and his conduct was applauded.

A great task of pacification came to Scott when, on Jan. 5, 1838, he was commissioned to restore tranquillity on the Canadian border (*Army and Navy Chronicle*, Jan. 18, 1838). The entire military force of the country was then engaged in the South and West. Appearing alone at various points along the northern frontier with unabating rapidity through the long winter, Scott made friends of the leaders on both sides, wrote letters, made speeches, and by the sheer force of his dominant personality was able to prevent another major conflict (*Ibid.,* Feb. 15, 22; Mar. 8, 29, 1838). Scarcely had he finished this exacting commission, when in the spring of 1838 he was entrusted by Van Buren with probably the most difficult ordeal of pacification ever to confront a single individual in the United States. Some 16,000 Cherokees of South Carolina and Tennessee, already enraged at the encroachments and thievery of the whites, were to be dispossessed of their lands and taken beyond the Mississippi. Scott was ordered to conduct them. Changing his psychological approach to satisfy the Indian mood and equation, he ceaselessly went among them, showing them the disaster and fruitlessness of war, mingled with the chiefs, convinced them of his honesty, and finally turned their hatred into complaisance (*Ibid.,* Apr. 12, June 14, Nov. 15, 1838; *Senate Document No. 1,* 25 Cong., 3 Sess., pp. 440 ff.). In addition to leading them westward he had them submit to vaccination without a casualty or a sign of disturbance. He was unable to accompany them all the way because he was called to Washington again by the President to enter upon another great enterprise of pacification. The activities of the "Canadian Patriots" had redoubled, and the Maine boundary disputes were seriously threatening war with Great Britain. Blood had been spilt. Scott hastened east, holding conferences with the governors of Kentucky and Ohio on the way, to find that the country was agog over the brewing strife. Without having lain down during the preceding eighty hours, he presented himself to the Secretary of War. He was immediately turned over to President Van Buren, who gave him full powers to avert the war that then seemed unavoidable. After being instrumental in the passage through Congress of several bills that would aid him in his undertaking, he traveled northward, stopping in Boston long enough to gain the assistance of Gov. Edward Everett. On arriving in Maine, he set out to know personally the members of the legislature and to understand their views. At the same time he initiated correspondence with Lieutenant-Governor Harvey of New Brunswick. Acting energetically and diplomatically through the next weeks, he was able to win over various prominent legislators, to bring about concessions from the British, and finally to induce a meeting of minds that threw the contentions into arbitration between Great Britain and the United States. (For his movements,

see *Army and Navy Chronicle,* Nov. 29, 1838; Dec. 13, 20, 1838; Jan. 3, 10, 1839; Feb. 28, 1839; Mar. 21, 1839; see also H. S. Burrage, *Maine in the Northeastern Boundary Controversy,* 1919, pp. 272–73. Channing wrote: "His exploits in the field, which placed him in the first rank of our soldiers, have been obscured by the purer and more lasting glory of a Pacificator and of a Friend to Mankind" (*The Works of William E. Channing,* 1841, vol. V, 113).

In 1839 Scott's name was mentioned by the Whigs for the presidency, and he felt he was being honestly supported. But his main supporters were merely using him as a mask for their determination to beat Clay, as they did at the Harrisburg convention by nominating Harrison. In June 1841 Scott, on the death of Macomb, was made general-in-chief of the army with headquarters in Washington. His influence upon the service was salutary and profound. During the next five years he was particularly zealous in eradicating cruel punishments and unnecessarily harsh discipline. Although strict in his requirements and rigid as to the niceties of dress and deportment, he was harder on no one than on himself; and he coupled with his apparent inflexibility a personal kindness and sympathy for the individual that made men love and respect him as a leader. He urged and aided officers not only to become well-schooled in their profession, but also to build up their personalities by proper contacts and broad culture. Although he was not a graduate of the United States Military Academy, he manifested an outspoken pride in that institution. It was in this interval of upbuilding in the army that, in connection with a retrenchment bill, an amendment was introduced in Congress to abolish Scott's office, but after John Quincy Adams and C. J. Ingersoll had flayed the proposal with ridicule, it was voted down by a large majority (Mar. 29, 1844, *Congressional Globe,* 28 Cong., 1 Sess., p. 461). In 1842 he was proposed by the Pennsylvania state convention for the presidency. He publicly proclaimed his support of Clay, but there is reason to suppose that he was greatly disappointed at the latter's nomination in 1844.

When war with Mexico approached, Scott, who had seemingly accomplished enough for his country to satisfy the healthiest ambitions, was nearing sixty, but his most hazardous and signal achievement lay before him. As hostilities became evident in 1845, he indorsed Zachary Taylor [*q.v.*] to command the army of occupation at Corpus Christi. Realizing Taylor's limitations, as well as strength, he supplied him with one of the ablest officers in the service, Capt.

W. W. S. Bliss, as his adjutant-general. Despite tactical victories, the fruitlessness of the northern campaign was shortly demonstrated, and Scott desired to take command in person, but he refused to supplant a junior without substantial augmentation of troops. He had, however, worked out a practical strategic plan that would, as he put it, "conquer a peace" (*Congressional Globe,* 29 Cong., 1 Sess., Appendix, pp. 650–51). President Polk, inimical to anything that might advance Scott's political prestige, termed him "visionary" (*Diary,* May 14, 1846). It was at this time that Secretary of War Marcy sent a very peremptory letter to Scott, who was at the time in a restaurant near the War Department. Scott in his reply stated that he had stepped out to take "a hasty plate of soup" (*Memoirs,* II, 385). The Democratic organs, ignoring Scott's labors, later made capital of the phrase to his disparagement. His reputation was at a low ebb, but meanwhile Taylor's successes were bringing the war no nearer a finish. Scott had to be looked to as the only one with a feasible solution. Secretary Marcy, Senator Thomas H. Benton, and others forced Polk to acquiesce. Between the President and Scott there took place a brotherly reconciliation, sincere on Scott's part but formal on Polk's.

On Nov. 23, 1846, Scott was ordered to set out, with full powers, for the scene of hostilities (Smith, *post,* I, 355). He arrived at Camargo to find that Taylor in defiance of his and the President's instructions was not at hand. To this delay were added lack of boats and sailors, and frustrations because of rains and northers. By Mar. 9, 1847, through ceaseless effort, he landed 10,000 men opposite Sacrificios Island below Vera Cruz. It was then that smallpox threatened his command. Against the advice of his senior officers to take the city by assault, he chose to invest it from the rear; the mortalities connected with the capture, Mar. 26, proved to be less than twenty. Immediately fresh obstacles arose. No reënforcements and less than a fourth of his transportation arrived. Yellow fever would be rampant in the city the next month, and the administration was hedging on the fulfillment of his plan. It was felt that Xenophon had been faced with fewer difficulties. Nevertheless, on Apr. 8, Scott pushed forward with a small, poorly equipped force to climb the 8,000-foot mountains toward the distant capital. His advance guard was held up at the stronghold of Cerro Gordo and the command awed into a state of uncertainty; by his arrival morale was restored, an attack organized, and victory secured in the face of inefficiency on the part of some of his senior officers. At once he moved onward to Jalapa where halfway to his goal he was met by sterner obstacles than the enemy. Two companies and seven regiments left him in a body because of the expiration of their enlistments, and the administration had sent neither money nor reënforcements. Although his urgent notes brought ineffective response from the home government and collapse seemed inevitable, he again moved forward, May 6, toward Puebla with not over 4000 privates. Fortunately he did not encounter the expected resistance of 20,000 Mexicans and entered the city with little opposition, but his soldiers had been paid for only two months out of eight and the inhabitants were actively hostile. He secured friendly intercourse with the natives and by vigorous training of the soldiers and incoming recruits increased the efficiency of his command. Then money came and his force was raised to 10,900 effectives. He set off once more on Aug. 5, brushing past barricades until he arrived in the Valley of Mexico. Although Gideon J. Pillow [*q.v.*] by exceeding his instructions brought on the battle of Contreras, Scott's tenacity brought victory. Then promptly he won Churubusco. He has been criticized for not at once assaulting the capital which lay open before him, but analysis shows that he again forsook personal glory in the hope that an armistice would save life and treasure. In this he proved to be mistaken and the bloody battles of Molino del Rey and Chapultepec followed. Although Molino del Rey was perhaps a tactical error, the masterly handling of the assault on Chapultepec and the capture of the city of Mexico fully compensated for it. Scott marched into the capitulated capital Sept. 14, little more than five months after his start from Vera Cruz.

After a miraculous campaign, he entered upon the more difficult task of adjusting a tattered, victorious army to the sane government of occupied territory. So long as his experienced soldiers remained, he had little trouble. His control was so humane and firm that a deputation of Mexicans asked him to be their dictator. Rarely if ever in history was a conquered nation so restored to contentment and order (Smith, II, 323–24). The influx of undisciplined recruits disturbed him, but he managed by redoubled exertions to maintain tranquillity. During this period he sent home, from local revenues, $118,000 to be applied to an army asylum, which afterwards became the Soldiers' Home. The opportunity for the administration to undercut Scott politically came when Pillow sent his own version of Scott's later battles to newspapers in the United States. The account was flattering to Pillow and adverse to the Commander-in-Chief. William Jenkins Worth and Col. James Duncan did much the same thing. When Scott called the officers to account, he was met with defiance and insubordination. He at length preferred charges which he sent to the President, but Polk without further inquiry released the three offenders from arrest, restored one of them to his highest brevet rank, superseded Scott by Butler, and placed the victorious commander before a hand-picked court of inquiry. Justin H. Smith observes that Scott "was a large man, had done a large work and merited large treatment. But there was nothing large about the administration. The confines of mediocrity hemmed it in" (*Ibid.*, II, 188). On Mar. 21, 1848, the court convened in Mexico, but soon adjourned to meet May 29 in Frederick, Md. On Apr. 22, Scott took leave of an army that on the whole loved and trusted him. Robert E. Lee, an engineer on his staff, stated that after performing a task of supreme magnitude he "was turned out as an old horse to die" (Fitzhugh Lee, *General Lee*, 1894, p. 46). Avoiding public honors, Scott stealthily made his way to Elizabeth, N. J., but he was unable to escape the clamor altogether. New York City tendered him a reception and an unprecedented ovation. Congress voted him its second thanks and another gold medal. The charges against him were withdrawn. A resolution to tender him the pay, rank, and emoluments of a lieutenant-general was introduced in Congress, but through political opposition it did not pass until 1855, when he became the first since Washington to hold that office.

In 1852 the Whigs gave him the nomination for the presidency. The campaign was essentially without issues but was marked by exceptionally scurrilous attacks on Scott by newspapers and stump-speakers. Clay and Webster died during the campaign. Other Whig leaders badly advised Scott, whose straight-forwardness was an easy target for the Democrats. He was overwhelmingly defeated by Franklin Pierce [*q.v.*]. It was the last of his entries into the lists for the presidency, although as late as 1860 he retained some hope of being sent to the White House (Coleman, *Crittenden, post,* II, 184–85). After the inauguration of Pierce, on account of differences of opinion on policy with the Secretary of War, Scott again removed his headquarters to New York City. In 1857 he opposed the war against the Mormons as unnecessary and undertaken for profit, but he was overruled. In 1859 he was again called upon to perform the functions of pacificator. Though seventy-three years of age and crippled from a recent fall, he set out Sept. 20 for the extreme Northwest, where controversy over the possession of San Juan Island in Puget Sound had again brought the relations between Great Britain and the United States to the breaking point. After he had mingled with both sides and conducted a judicious correspondence, serious complications were averted.

In October 1860, foreseeing the eventual Civil War, he pleaded with the President to reënforce the southern forts and armories against seizure, but to Buchanan and John B. Floyd his was a voice crying in the wilderness. On Oct. 31, and Dec. 12 he renewed his urgings, but with no better success. In January 1861, he brought back the headquarters of the army to Washington, where at his advanced age he actively oversaw the recruiting and training of the defenders of the capital. He personally commanded Lincoln's bodyguard at the inauguration and put the city in a state of defense. Being a Virginian, he was doggedly besought to join the South, but in spite of natural leanings he stuck to his beliefs and remained with the Union. To Lincoln he accorded all aid in his power. Though he did not approve of George B. McClellan as first choice for command of the Army of the Potomac, he supported him even when the younger man's methods were at least discourteous. Had much of his general plan for the conduct of the Federal forces been heeded, the war would have been curtailed; but since he was too old to mount a horse, he was thought to be too old to give advice. On Oct. 31, 1861, he requested retirement on account of infirmities. The next day Lincoln and the whole cabinet left their offices in a body, repaired to Scott's home, and there the President read an affecting eulogy to the old man. Scott was retired with full pay and allowances the same day. In his first message to Congress Lincoln wrote of Scott: "During his long life the nation has not been unmindful of his merit; yet, in calling to mind how faithfully, ably, and brilliantly he has served his country, from a time far back in our history when few of the now living had been born, and thenceforward continually, I cannot but think we are still his debtors" (Nicolay and Hay, *Abraham Lincoln. Complete Works*, 1894, vol. II, 104). On his journey to New York, Scott was accompanied by the secretaries of war and the treasury. On Nov. 9, 1861, he went abroad, but in Paris upon hearing of the *Trent* affair he immediately returned to America, should his counsel be needed. At West Point he received the Prince of Wales and in 1865 presented to General Grant, one of his subalterns in the Mexican War, a gift with the inscription, "from the oldest to the greatest general" (Wright, *post*, p. 322). When his end was near he was conveyed from New York City to West Point where he died within fifteen days of his eightieth birthday. He was buried in the national cemetery there, some of the most illustrious men of the country attending the funeral. His wife, who died in Rome in 1862, is buried beside him. Of his seven children, two sons and two daughters died early, to his great grief; three married daughters survived him.

Scott had been the associate of every president from Jefferson to Lincoln and the emissary in critical undertakings of most of them. In his public career of nearly half a century he had been a main factor in ending two wars, saving the country from several others, and acquiring a large portion of its territory. Supreme political preferment was doubtless denied him because of conditions and his idiosyncrasies. Called "Fuss and Feathers" because of his punctiliousness in dress and decorum, he often gave the impression of irritability. He possessed a whimsical egotism, was inclined to flourishes of rhetoric, often unfortunate, and was too outspoken in his beliefs for his own advancement. On the other hand, the openness of his generous character led him into acts incomprehensible to calculating natures. He was a scholar, but knew when to discard rules, so that the letter of directions did not shackle him. His initiative and self-reliance never deserted him. He made use of his many talents unsparingly, and the only one of his hazardous undertakings he failed to carry out beyond the most sanguine expectations was that of his own ambition to reach the presidency.

[*Memoirs of Lieut.-General Scott, LL.D. Written by Himself* (2 vols., 1864), rhetorical but still valuable; E. D. Mansfield, *Life and Services of General Winfield Scott* (1852), the best of the campaign biographies; M. J. Wright, *General Scott* (1894); A. M. B. Coleman, *The Life of John J. Crittenden* (2 vols., 1871), containing letters of Scott; Dunbar Rowland, ed., *Jefferson Davis, Constitutionalist*, vols. II, III (1923), containing Scott-Davis correspondence; James Wilkinson, *Memoirs of My Own Times* (3 vols., 1816); M. M. Quaife, ed., *The Diary of James K. Polk* (4 vols., 1910); G. T. Curtis, *Life of James Buchanan* (2 vols., 1883); Harrison Ellery, ed., *The Memoirs of Gen. Joseph Gardner Swift* (1890); W. A. Croffut, ed., *Fifty Years in Camp and Field. Diary of Major-General Ethan Allen Hitchcock, U. S. A.* (1909); correspondence, papers, and documents in Old Files Section, Adjutant-General's Dept., Washington, D. C.; E. A. Cruikshank, *The Documentary Hist. of the Campaign upon the Niagara Frontier* (9 vols., 1896–1908); C. J. Ingersoll, *Hist. Sketch of the Second War between the U. S. . . . and Great Britain*, vols. I, II (1845–49); 2 ser., vols. I, II (1852); B. L. Lossing, *The Pictorial Field-Book of the War of 1812* (1868); J. H. Smith, *The War with Mexico* (2 vols., 1919); L. D. Ingersoll, *A Hist. of the War Dept. of the U. S.* (1879); Emory Upton, *The Military Policy of the U. S.* (1904); W.

A. Ganoe, *The Hist. of the U. S. Army* (1924); obituary in *N. Y. Tribune*, May 30–June 2, 1866; suggestions from Maj. C. W. Elliott, who is preparing a biography of Scott.]   W. A. G.

SCOVEL, HENRY SYLVESTER (July 29, 1869–Feb. 11, 1905), journalist and engineer, better known simply as Sylvester Scovel, was born at Denny Station, Allegheny County, Pa., the son of the Rev. Sylvester Fithian and Caroline (Woodruff) Scovel, and a descendant of Arthur Scovell, who came to Boston about 1660 and settled in Middletown, Conn., in 1670. His father was a Presbyterian minister, son of a president of Hanover College in Indiana, who also became a college president, serving at the University of Wooster, in Wooster, Ohio, from 1883 to 1899. Scovel was educated in the public schools of Pittsburgh and the Michigan Military Academy, from which he was graduated in 1887. For a few months he attended the University of Wooster and spent portions of four years at the University of Michigan, working his way between times as timekeeper in various blast-furnace construction plants. He later worked as an engineer in Tennessee, Kentucky, and Pennsylvania.

Although there is no record of his previous newspaper experience, his aggressiveness as a promoter of several enterprises in Chicago and Cleveland apparently led to his appointment in 1895 as correspondent for the *Pittsburgh Dispatch* and the *New York Herald* to cover the increasingly serious disturbances in Cuba. Here his activities proved so unwelcome to the Spanish authorities that they arrested him in Havana in 1896. By this time he had become a rather conspicuous figure, and after his escape from confinement he was engaged by the New York *World*. During the next two years he made his reputation as one of the most brilliant actors in the drama of the Spanish-American conflict. According to the *World* he did more than any other man to proclaim the wrongs of the Cubans and to arouse the American people against the Spanish régime of oppression. For eleven months he lived with the insurgents, sharing all the hardships and dangers of their guerrilla warfare. With characteristic daring and resourcefulness he ran the Spanish military and police lines twenty times. Finally on Feb. 7, 1897, he was again captured by the Spaniards. This incident created considerable excitement throughout the country; many state legislatures passed resolutions demanding his release, and at the insistence of the Senate the United States government made such strong representations to Spain that he was given his freedom.

After accomplishing his particular mission in Cuba, he was sent by the *World* in 1897 to cover the Turco-Greek conflict, but when the tension between the United States and Spain increased he was recalled and arrived in Cuba just before the *Maine* disaster. When war was declared he was assigned to duty as correspondent for his paper, and he remained with the American forces until the evacuation by Spain in 1899. In this service he was apparently almost as troublesome to his own military authorities as he had been to the Spanish. His zeal for the news led him constantly to disobey army regulations. Official dispatches show that he greatly irritated the American command and that he was summarily threatened with court martial. Boyish in appearance and manner, daring and determined to the point of recklessness, he could not be diplomatic. But, as the files of the *World* show, he "got the story." From 1899 to 1902 he served as consulting engineer to the Cuban customs service of the United States military government of the island. This post he resigned to engage in various commercial promotion projects in Havana, where he died. He was married on Apr. 5, 1897, to Frances Cabanné of St. Louis, Mo.

[*Who's Who in America*, 1903–05, and the obit. article in the N. Y. *World*, Feb. 13, 1905, are the best available general sources. See also F. E. Chadwick, *The Relations of the U. S. and Spain: the Spanish-Am. War* (2 vols., 1911), and *Correspondence Relating to the War with Spain . . . Between the Adjutant-Gen. of the Army and Mil. Commanders* (2 vols., 1902), the latter containing the text of official dispatches concerning Scovel; Walter Millis, *The Martial Spirit* (1931); *Commemorative Biog. Record of Wayne County, Ohio* (1889); H. W. Brainard, *A Survey of the Scovils or Scovills in England and America* (1915); *Pittsburgh Dispatch*, Feb. 13, 1905.]   P. K.

SCOVEL, SYLVESTER [See SCOVEL, HENRY SYLVESTER, 1869–1905].

SCOVELL, MELVILLE AMASA (Feb. 26, 1855–Aug. 15, 1912), agricultural chemist and educator, the son of Nathan and Hannah (Aller) Scovell, was born at Belvidere, N. J. He was a descendant of John Scovell, who emigrated from England to Connecticut in the seventeenth century. Shortly after his birth, the family moved to Chicago and later to a farm in Champaign County, Ill. After graduation from the local high school in 1871, he entered the Illinois Industrial University (later the University of Illinois), where he specialized in chemistry, becoming student-assistant in his second year, and took three degrees, B.S., 1875; M.S., 1877; Ph.D., 1908. As secretary to John Milton Gregory [*q.v.*] he was influenced by the intellectual atmosphere created by the president of the university. Becoming instructor in chemistry at

Illinois in 1875, he was advanced to a professorship in 1880, a position he held until 1884. On Sept. 8, 1880, he married Nannie D. Davis of Monticello, Ill.

With Henry Adams Weber [*q.v.*] he patented processes for clarifying the juice of sugar-producing plants and for manufacturing glucose, sugar, and syrup from sorghum. He served as secretary of the Illinois Cane Growers' Association in 1880–81, and of the Mississippi Valley Cane Growers' Association during 1881–84. He was superintendent of the Kansas Sugar Works at Sterling, Kan., in 1884, and the following year, as special agent for the United States Department of Agriculture, he managed the diffusion batteries for extracting sugar from sorghum and sugar-cane in Kansas and Louisiana. In 1885 he became the first director of the Kentucky Agricultural Experiment Station. During his twenty-seven years at Lexington he made notable contributions as chemist, agronomist, pure-food exponent, educator, and administrator. As author or joint author he prepared over seventy publications. His first years at Lexington were largely devoted to analyzing and testing fertilizers, the state fertilizer control having been placed with the station; among the accomplishments of Scovell and his associates in this field was a modification of the Kjeldahl method for the determination of nitrogen in nitrates. Later, as a member of the United States Food Standards Commission, he devoted himself to the investigations and educational work that resulted in the enactment of national and state pure-food legislation. He aided in the development of the state department of agriculture at Frankfort, Ky., and his ardent and efficient support of the state fair aroused popular interest in improved agricultural methods and products. His interest in dairying was stimulated by his study of the accuracy and reliability of the Babcock test while he was chairman of the committee on the comparative tests of dairy breeds at the Columbian Exposition in Chicago. In connection with this work he invented a milk-sampling tube. He judged dairy cattle at many fairs and expositions, becoming perhaps the best-known and best-liked judge in America, and the model dairy at his station farm contributed greatly to the public health of the city of Lexington and to the development of dairying in Kentucky. In 1910, in addition to directing the experiment station, he became dean of the agricultural college at the University of Kentucky. In 1911 he visited the Channel Islands as representative of James Ben Ali Haggin [*q.v.*] to purchase cattle for the Elmendorf farm. He was an active member of many professional organizations, including the Association of Official Agricultural Chemists, under whose auspices much of his most effective work was done. Probably his greatest contribution lay in his work as an able administrative officer and as a builder of public sentiment for agricultural education.

[H. W. Brainard, *A Survey of the Scovils or Scovills* (1915); *Who's Who in America*, 1912–13; J. M. and Jaques Cattell, *Am. Men of Sci.* (1910); *Twenty-Fifth Ann. Report . . . Ky. Agricultural Experiment Station*, 1912; *Proc. . . . Soc. for the Promotion of Agricultural Sci.*, vol. XXXIII (1913); U. S. Dept. Agriculture, *Experiment Station Record*, Oct. 1912; *Mech. Engineering and Electrical Engineering Record*, Nov. 1908; *Breeder's Gazette*, Aug. 21, 1912; *Jersey Bull. and Dairy World*, Aug. 21, 1912; *Louisville Times*, Aug. 16, *Courier-Journal* (Louisville), Aug. 16, 18, 1912.]
E. E. E.

SCOVILLE, JOSEPH ALFRED (Jan. 30, 1815–June 25, 1864), journalist and novelist, was born in Woodbury, Conn., the son of Joseph and Caroline (Preston) Scovill and a descendant of John Scovell, who was born in England and died about 1700 at Haddam, Conn. At about twenty-two, Scoville became employed as a merchant in New York; a year later he entered into a short-lived partnership with Lloyd L. Britton. Gradually he now drifted into journalism and politics. In October 1842 we find him writing to his friend John Caldwell Calhoun [*q.v.*] of a "matter of vital importance"—none other than "the control of Tammany Hall" (*American Historical Association Annual Report, 1899, post,* p. 856). Unsuccessful in this ambition, he was nevertheless instrumental in finding a publisher in the North for the *Life of John C. Calhoun* (1843), a campaign biography presumably written by Calhoun himself; and in April 1843 he was made editor of the *Spectator,* a newspaper published in Washington in the interests of Calhoun. Although he failed to please Calhoun's friends, and for this reason remained editor of the paper for only a short time, he continued in the good graces of Calhoun himself, who, probably in the middle or late forties, appointed Scoville his private secretary.

Returning to New York after Calhoun's death in 1850, he became editor of the *New York Picayune,* in part a humorous paper, but about 1852 he resigned to start the *Pick,* a humorous sheet of his own, which he continued to bring out until 1855. Two years later he edited for a brief period the *Evening State Gazette.* It was probably during the fifties that he came under the influence of James Gordon Bennett [*q.v.*], editor of the *New York Herald,* whose sensational journalistic methods profoundly affected him. Scoville's fearless indulgence in personalities and other forms of scandal, together with

his marked Southern sympathies, made him an object of extreme dislike in the North during the war. His novel *Vigor* (1864), republished in England as *Marion* (3 vols., 1864), dealt broadly with the theme of seduction in American bourgeois society. The dedication to Bennett and the introduction of Calhoun as a character suggest the truth of common report that the novel had a significant autobiographical basis. The general antipathy to the story, which by most was called "indecent," although by a few of Scoville's friends "unfortunate," was heightened at this time by the publication in the London *Morning Herald* and *Evening Standard* of Scoville's articles denouncing the Lincoln administration and the prosecution of the war by the North. For the publication of these articles Scoville was brought before Gen. John Adams Dix and warned against any further criticism of the North and its war policies. Another novel, *The Adventures of Clarence Bolton,* has been ascribed to him, but no copy of the work seems to have survived. Of his literary work, *The Old Merchants of New York City* (5 ser., 1863–66?), giving in a rambling, gossipy form the history of the city's commercial life, is perhaps the most important. His customary style was simple and vigorous but, owing to his love of short, detached sentences, his work frequently makes difficult reading. He usually wrote under the pseudonym either of Manhattan or of Walter Barrett. It was during a visit to South Carolina that he met Caroline Schaub, whom he afterwards married. He is said to have acquired financial independence by his literary labors and to have left his wife and daughter well provided for. He died in New York.

[See H. W. Brainard, *A Survey of the Scovils or Scovills in England and America* (1915); William Cothren, *Hist. of Ancient Woodbury, Conn.* (1854–79), vol. I, p. 665, vol. III, p. 80; N. Y. city directories, 1837–64; *N.Y. Leader*, July 2, 1864; *N.Y. Commercial Advertiser,* June 22, 1864; *World* (N. Y.), June 27, 1864; T. L. Nichols, *Forty Years of Am. Life* (1864), vol. II, pp. 221–26; J. A. Scoville, *The Old Merchants of N. Y. City* (1863–66), ser. 2–4, *passim*; Gaillard Hunt, *John C. Calhoun* (1908); W. M. Meigs, *The Life of John Caldwell Calhoun* (1917), vol. II; "Correspondence of John C. Calhoun," in *Am. Hist. Assoc. Ann. Report, 1899* (1900), vol. II; F. L. Mott, *A Hist. of Am. Magazines, 1741–1850* (1930); Goldwin Smith, in *Atlantic Monthly*, Dec. 1864; S. A. Allibone, *A Crit. Dict. of Eng. Lit.* (3 vols., 1858–71). Critical discussions of *Vigor* (*Marion*) may be found in the *Reader* (London), May 21, July 16, Aug. 27, Oct. 22, 1864.]
N. F. A.

SCRANTON, GEORGE WHITFIELD (May 23, 1811–Mar. 24, 1861), iron manufacturer, was born in Madison, Conn., the son of Theophilus and Elizabeth (Warner) Scranton and a descendant of John Scranton who settled in Guilford, Conn., in 1639. His father was the owner of a stage line running from New Haven to Saybrook. He was educated in the common school and at Lee's Academy in his native town. In 1828 he went to live with an uncle at Belvidere, N. J., and obtained work as a teamster; soon afterward he was employed as a clerk in a store there and in a short time was admitted as a partner. In 1835 he married Jane Hiles of Belvidere, sold his interest in the store, and engaged in farming. Four years later, in partnership with his brother Selden, he purchased the lease and stock of an iron furnace at Oxford, N. J., where he met with considerable success. In May 1840 he and his brother, with William Henry, Sanford Grant, P. H. Mattes, and Joseph C. Platt, formed the Lackawanna Iron and Coal Company to acquire an extensive tract of coal-bearing land in the Lackawanna Valley, including the present site of the city of Scranton, Pa., which he founded in the same year. He and his associates conducted experiments in smelting iron with anthracite coal and by January 1842 had developed a successful process. Although they began the manufacture of bar-iron to be converted into nails, they soon planned to build a rolling-mill for the manufacture of railroad iron. Lacking the necessary capital, they contracted to furnish rails to the Buffalo, New York & Erie Railroad at a rate lower than the current one upon the condition that the road advance funds to enable them to proceed with manufacturing. After this start Scranton saw the company develop rapidly into a firmly established and highly lucrative business. In 1846 his first cousin, Joseph Hand Scranton (1813–1872), son of Jonathan Scranton, became general manager of the iron works and in 1858 its president; he also organized the First National Bank of Scranton and was the chief organizer of the Scranton Gas and Water Company.

From 1859 until his death George Scranton served in Congress in the House of Representatives as a Republican. He was not a politician in the ordinary sense, but the nature of his business made him a firm believer in protection for home industries. He was actively interested in the development of transportation facilities in the Lackawanna Valley and projected and constructed the Northumberland division of the Delaware, Lackawanna & Western railroad, of which he was president for several years, as he was of the Cayuga & Susquehanna railroad. He died in Scranton, survived by his wife, two sons, and a daughter. He is described as a man of inexhaustible energy and great moral integrity and is said to have had the faculty of impressing his ideas upon the minds of other men, qualities that had much to do with his rise from poverty and obscurity to wealth and prominence.

[Erastus Scranton, *A Geneal. Reg. of the Descendants of John Scranton of Guilford, Conn.* (1855); F. L. Hitchcock, *Hist. of Scranton and Its People* (1914), vol. I, with portrait; David Craft, *Hist. of Scranton, Penn.* (1891); *Biog. Directory of the Am. Congress, 1774–1927* (1928); Horace Hollister, *Hist. of the Lackawanna Valley* (2nd ed., 1869); obituary in *Daily Nat. Intelligencer,* Mar. 27, 1861.]   J.H.F.

SCREWS, WILLIAM WALLACE (Feb. 25, 1839–Aug. 7, 1913), editor, was born at Jernigan in Barbour (now Russell) County, Ala., the son of Benjamin and Mourning (Drake) Screws, both of English ancestry. The father, a merchant and a leader of the Whigs in his section of the state, came originally from North Carolina, where the family had lived for several generations; the mother's people came from Massachusetts to North Carolina. William Wallace is said to have been named for the hero of Jane Porter's popular story, *The Scottish Chiefs* (1810). Although he was prepared for college in the schools of Glenville, Ala., and made an excellent record in Latin, Greek, and English literature, he never entered college, for in the panic of 1857 his father failed in business and he had to earn his own living. After working for two years at odd jobs, he went to Montgomery to read law in the office of Thomas H. Watts; though he was not yet of age he was admitted to the bar June 15, 1859. He cast his first vote in 1860 for the Bell-Everett ticket. Although he opposed secession, he enlisted in the army immediately after the secession of Alabama. He saw service with the Montgomery True Blues in Florida and with Hilliard's Legion in Kentucky and in Tennessee, where he took part in the battle of Chickamauga. When Hilliard's Legion was reorganized into the 59th and 60th Regiments, he became first lieutenant of the 59th and took part in the siege of Knoxville. With Gracie's brigade he saw service in the Virginia campaigns of 1864 about Petersburg until he was wounded in the battle of Drewry's Bluff. In 1865, during the evacuation of Richmond, he was captured at Sailor's Creek, taken to Johnson's Island in Lake Erie, and held in prison until June 1865.

He returned to Montgomery to take up the practice of law; during the war, however, he had done some work as a correspondent for the *Montgomery Advertiser,* and he was offered a place on the editorial staff. In a few weeks he was offered a half interest in the paper, with his own time to pay for it; in less than a year he was editor, and presently he was sole owner as well. As editor of the most important Democratic paper in the state, he directed the policies of the party for half a century. Like Henry Watterson and Edwin Lawrence Godkin [*qq.v.*] he was one of the school of personal journalists; he himself shaped the policy of his paper and made the editorial page the center of interest. He was master of a vigorous, simple, and direct style; it is said that he never used a metaphor. Through the *Advertiser* he led the opposition to the reconstruction government in the state. He was relentless in exposing its corruption and tireless in his efforts to destroy it. When the attempt was made to issue bonds for the Alabama and Chattanooga Railroad he opposed it, although his paper was seriously embarrassed at the time and he was offered over fifty thousand dollars to permit the use of its columns for bond issue propaganda. He fought the Farmers' Alliance on the ground that it would inevitably become a political party and divide the white vote of the state. The Alliance boycotted the *Advertiser* and Screws lost heavily, but he never changed his position in the matter. In spite of the fact that he possessed great political influence, he refused political offices throughout his career. During his long life he held only three, and those were insignificant: he was secretary of state in Alabama from 1878 to 1882, he held a position in the Library of Congress during the first Cleveland administration, and he was postmaster of Montgomery, 1893–97. He died suddenly at his summer home at Coosada, Elmore County, Ala., survived by his wife, Emily Frances Holt of Augusta, Ga., whom he had married Apr. 25, 1867, and three sons. Although he was a prolific writer he never published a book; aside from his editorials and newspaper articles he left only an article on the history of Alabama journalism, written for *The Memorial Record of Alabama* (1893, vol. II).

[See esp. *Montgomery Advertiser*, Aug. 8–11, 1913. The Dept. of Hist. and Archives at Montgomery contains some unpublished materials; brief accounts of Screws are to be found in *The Memorial Record of Ala.* (1893), vol. II; B. F. Riley, *Makers and Romance of Ala. Hist.* (n.d.); T. M. Owen, *Hist. of Ala. and Dict. of Ala. Biog.* (1921), vol. IV; *Who's Who in America*, 1912–13.]   H. F—r.

SCRIBNER, CHARLES (Feb. 21, 1821–Aug. 26, 1871), publisher, was born in New York City, the son of Uriah Rogers Scribner and the latter's second wife, Betsey Hawley. He was descended from Benjamin Scrivener, who was in Norwalk, Conn., in 1680; the family name was changed to its present form after 1742. Uriah Scribner was a prosperous merchant and gave his son every educational advantage. Charles Scribner was graduated from the College of New Jersey (Princeton) in 1840 and studied law but because of bad health gave up practice. In 1846, with Isaac D. Baker as partner, he turned to publishing. The firm of Baker & Scribner made its bow in modest quarters, which formed part of the chapel of the old Brick Meeting House at Park Row and Nassau Street. Baker died and Scribner proceeded to carry on alone, under his own name, in 1850. In 1857 he took in another partner, Charles Welford, organizing the firm of Scribner & Welford to import books, though the publishing continued under his own name. Andrew C. Armstrong was admitted to partnership in 1864, and Edward Seymour in 1869, but the name of the publishing firm remained the same until the death of the founder in 1871, when it became Scribner, Armstrong & Co., the importing firm being Scribner, Welford & Armstrong. It was in 1878 that the final form of Charles Scribner's Sons was established.

The Scribner list, from the outset, was strong in theological and philosophical publications, written by leading authorities, especially those of the Presbyterian Church, such as the Alexanders, Archibald [*q.v.*] and James W., and Presidents Theodore Dwight Woolsey and Noah Porter [*qq.v.*] of Yale. The firm also published the English edition of Johann Peter Lange, *A Commentary on the Holy Scriptures* (25 vols., 1865–80), edited by Philip Schaff [*q.v.*]. Much attention was also given to secular literature. The once widely popular works of Joel T. Headley [*q.v.*], *Napoleon and his Marshals* (1847) and *Washington and His Generals* (1847), bore the Scribner imprint. This also aided the circulation of the works of the internationally known geographer, Arnold Henry Guyot [*q.v.*]. Publications of a more general character included *People I Have Met* (1850), by Nathaniel P. Willis [*q.v.*], a book which greatly heightened the reputation of the house. Mention may be made also of the writings of Donald Grant Mitchell [*q.v.*], better known as "Ik Marvel," *Reveries of a Bachelor* (1850) and *Dream Life* (1851). It was during the last decade of Scribner's life that the firm began to publish reprints and translations of English and European works, of the solid character exemplified by such names as Froude, Mommsen, Ernst Curtius, Friedrich Max Mueller, and Rawlinson. Dean Stanley, Gladstone, and Jowett were later added to the list. The foundations for a liberal tradition were well and truly laid, signifying a quick response to the demands of a more and more exacting reading public. The house grew up while Washington Irving and James Fenimore Cooper were still upon the scene. It reckoned with a generation that appreciated the rising New England group and that welcomed the visits of Dickens and Thackeray. It was committed to a standard of good taste. The elder Scribner established an educational publishing business, but in 1883 the firm sold its school textbook business, maintaining only higher textbooks.

Charles Scribner sponsored a periodical entitled *Hours at Home,* a miscellany edited by the Rev. J. M. Sherwood. It lasted for nearly five years (1865–70) but the fastidious publisher was not quite satisfied. "I want to issue a magazine," he said, "that is handsomely illustrated, beautifully printed, and that shall have as contributors the best authors of the day. I should like to make it different from any now published and to reach also other classes of readers" (Unpublished Papers). He fulfilled his ambition when in November 1870, he brought out the first number of *Scribner's Monthly.* It was launched auspiciously under the editorship of Dr. J. G. Holland, assisted by Richard Watson Gilder [qq.v.], but in 1881 was sold to the Century Company and became *The Century Illustrated Monthly Magazine. Scribner's Magazine* was founded in 1887 by the younger Charles Scribner.

Scribner was married, June 13, 1848, to Emma Elizabeth Blair, the daughter of John Insley Blair [q.v.] of Blairstown, N. J., a capitalist who was active in railroading and other large business affairs. He died at Luzerne, Switzerland. His sons, John Blair, Charles [q.v.], and Arthur Hawley, carried on his work.

[G. W. Schuyler, *Colonial New York* (1885), II, 439–55, for the Scribner genealogy; "Charles Scribner's Sons. The Hist. of a Publishing House, 1846–1894," *Scribner's Mag.,* Dec. 1894; J. C. Derby, *Fifty Years Among Authors, Books and Publishers* (1884); obituaries in *N. Y. Times,* Aug. 28, 1871; *The Trade Circular and Publishers' Bulletin,* Sept. 25, 1871; *Scribner's Monthly,* Oct. 1871.]   R. C.

SCRIBNER, CHARLES (Oct. 18, 1854–Apr. 19, 1930), publisher, was born in New York City, the second son of Charles Scribner [q.v.] and his wife, Emma Elizabeth Blair. He began his education in a private school, entered the College of New Jersey (Princeton) in 1871, and was graduated four years later. He went immediately into the publishing house and on the death of his brother, John Blair Scribner, in 1879, became head of the firm, known since 1878 as Charles Scribner's Sons; it was incorporated in 1904. He was succeeded as president in 1928 by his brother, Arthur H. Scribner, but was chairman of the board from that date until his death. During the period of more than fifty years that he remained with the house, he expanded its scope until it became probably the most comprehensive publishing business in the country, and enhanced its prestige.

Inheriting a sound tradition, he brought to its maintenance the acumen of a business man and the discrimination of a man of letters. A portrait of him would, indeed, be incomplete that failed to recognize his peculiarly warm and enlightened literary sympathies. Among the many publications that are significant of his love of books, mention may be made of the beautiful edition of Thomas Shelton's translation, *The History of . . . Don Quixote* (4 vols., 1906–07), illustrated by Daniel Vierge. He cherished a good book and delighted to give it beautiful form. The history of his long administration of the house of Scribner is studded with incidents illustrating his enthusiasm and taste. These were indicative partly of his initiative and partly of the remarkable teamwork developed amongst the men who surrounded him—his younger brother Arthur, his literary adviser, William Crary Brownell [q.v.], and the successive editors of *Scribner's Magazine,* Edward L. Burlingame [q.v.] and Robert Bridges. Through their concerted efforts the Scribner imprint became a kind of blue ribbon which a host of distinguished authors, native and foreign, were glad to wear.

Charles Scribner took immense pride in his list and was constantly bent upon strengthening it, not being hidebound in his fidelity to tradition but remaining accessible always to the appeal of "new blood." Among American writers of fiction, he published books by Edith Wharton, Thomas Nelson Page, Henry James, Robert Grant, George W. Cable, Richard Harding Davis, John Fox, F. Hopkinson Smith, and, in later days, such new men as Ernest Hemingway and Ring Lardner. In letters at large there may be cited Eugene Field, Henry van Dyke, H. C. Bunner, Brander Matthews, James Huneker, Barrett Wendell, George Santayana, and Theodore Roosevelt. He was the publisher of these authors and he was their friend. As durable ties existed between him and British writers like Robert Louis Stevenson, George Meredith, Rudyard Kipling, J. M. Barrie, and John Galsworthy. His collected editions of them were not simply commercial ventures but labors of love. He was notable, also, for the encouragement he gave young artists and illustrators, many of whom later achieved distinction. The house had its educational books, its subscription department, and that which embraces religious books. In 1881, as a result of his first great decision, *Scribner's Monthly* was sold, to become *The Century Illustrated Monthly Magazine,* under an agreement which restrained the house from entering the periodical field again for five years. *St. Nicholas,* which the firm had published since November 1873, was also sold to the Century Company in 1881. In 1887 was brought out *Scribner's Magazine,* which he had probably anticipated from the beginning. In July 1917 Scribner took over from Forbes & Company the magazine *Architecture.* The subject was close to his sympathies for the house had long been largely interested in the issuance of architectural books. To facilitate and enhance the functioning of all these activities he built in 1908 the Scribner Press, a plant from which much fine printing has flowed. He also developed a notable bookstore that made a specialty of rare books.

From the inception of the plans for the *Dictionary of American Biography,* Charles Scribner was deeply interested in the enterprise. His advice was sought on many occasions. On the choice of the firm as publishers of the *Dictionary,* he and his brother gave themselves whole-heartedly to promotion of the work. There were numerous experiments to secure a format which would be not only attractive in appearance but also of proper dignity and quality for a work which promised to be so distinguished and permanent. As one expression of confidence in the enterprise, they made a generous contribution to assist in the preparation of the manuscript for press.

It is as a wise, generous, and eclectic publisher that Scribner will be remembered, but there were other phases of his activity that demand consideration. His business acumen fitted him to be for years a useful director of the National Park Bank, where he was elected a vice-president in 1926 and served through the period which witnessed the merging of the institution with the Chase National Bank. His judgment served him well, too, as a worker in the interests of his alma mater. When Princeton gave him an honorary degree of Doctor of Letters in 1925, the citation ran: "He stands today as a symbol for whatever is most courteous, honorable and fruitful of good in American endeavor. In his half century since graduation, the head of the house has given every year to labor and love for Princeton. Intimate in her councils, alert in stimulating her literary life, old in wisdom and young in spirit, constant in helping her needs, his unobtrusive, bright and kindly influence is part of all the best we have." The Princeton University Press, an institution organized "not for pecuniary profit," was beautifully housed and thoroughly equipped through his generosity. He had also an ardent enthusiasm for Skidmore College for young women, founded at Saratoga Springs,

N. Y., by the wife of his elder brother. During the last years of his life he was a member of the board of trustees and gave unstintingly of his time and money for the welfare of the college. He was one of the leaders in the fight for international copyright and was present with William Appleton and Robert Underwood Johnson when President Harrison signed the bill of 1891. When the American Publishers' Association was formed in 1900, he was among those who most effectively put their shoulders to the wheel.

His was a rich life and a happy one. He was married to Louise Flagg, the daughter of the Rev. Dr. Jared B. Flagg [*q.v.*], and had two children, a daughter and a son and namesake who, in 1932, became the head of the house. Scribner died at his home in New York.

[*Princeton Alumni Weekly,* May 2, 1930, containing tributes; *Publishers' Weekly,* Apr. 26, 1930; editorials in *N. Y. Times,* Apr. 21, 1930, and *American Mercury,* Aug. 1930; information in regard to the firm from Charles Scribner's Sons; personal acquaintance.]

R. C.

SCRIPPS, EDWARD WYLLIS (June 18, 1854–Mar. 12, 1926), newspaper publisher, was born on a farm near Rushville, Ill., the youngest of the five children of James Mogg Scripps and his third wife, Julia (Osborn) Scripps. He was a half-brother of James Edmund Scripps and Ellen Browning Scripps [*qq.v.*]. He attended a district school near his home and a private school conducted by his half-sister Ellen. At eighteen he began his newspaper work as an office boy on the *Detroit Tribune,* of which his half-brother James was manager. When James in 1873 started the Detroit *Evening News,* the first cheap, popular evening paper in the United States, Edward helped to build up the circulation of the new paper, and became first a member of the news staff and then city editor. In the fall of 1877 he gave up his position to accompany another half-brother, George H. Scripps, on a year's tour of Europe. During his travels he conceived the idea of establishing a paper of his own, and he succeeded in obtaining a promise of about $10,000 from his two half-brothers and his cousin, John Scripps Sweeney, in support of a one-cent evening paper in Cleveland, Ohio. On Nov. 2, 1878, he brought out the first issue of the Cleveland *Penny Press,* its business, editorial and printing offices housed in a four-room shack in an alley. Thus at twenty-four he laid the foundation for an impressive career as owner of a chain of daily papers extending from the Middle West to the Pacific.

Pioneers in establishing cheap evening papers in the Mississippi Valley, in 1880 Edward and his brothers bought the two-cent *Evening Chron-*

icle of St. Louis, and a year or two later a struggling paper in Cincinnati that they named the *Penny Post,* later the *Cincinnati Post.* These two papers with the Detroit *Evening News* and the Cleveland *Penny Press,* constituted the first chain of daily newspapers in the United States. Disagreements with James over the management of the papers led Edward to relinquish control of all the papers except the *Cincinnati Post.* He took Milton Alexander McRae [*q.v.*] into partnership in 1889, and formed the Scripps-McRae League of Newspapers with McRae and George H. Scripps in 1895. Following the decline of the old United Press in the nineties and the rise of the new Associated Press, organized in Chicago in 1892, as the dominant news-disseminating agency in the United States, Scripps felt the need of an independent means of obtaining telegraph news, and in 1897 he organized the Scripps-McRae Press Association to cover the field west of Pittsburgh. In 1904 this organization purchased the Publishers' Press, a similar independent organization that covered the territory east of Pittsburgh. In 1907 the two agencies were combined into the United Press Associations generally known simply as the United Press, the first press association operated in connection with a chain of daily papers. Out of a column of miscellany, which Ellen Scripps prepared for the *Cleveland Press* while she was on the staff of the Detroit *Evening News,* grew the Newspaper Enterprise Association, organized in 1902 by Edward Scripps to supply his papers and others with cartoons, illustrations, and feature articles; this, known as the "NEA," became the first newspaper syndicate connected with a chain of daily papers.

In 1891 Scripps moved to San Diego, Cal., near which he built a villa called "Miramar." Two years later he acquired an interest in the *San Diego Sun,* the first of the Scripps Coast League of newspapers, a chain that later included papers in Seattle, Tacoma, Spokane, Portland, Denver, San Francisco, Los Angeles, Fresno, and Sacramento. To serve these papers with telegraph news, he organized the Scripps Coast Press Association. In 1908 he and McRae retired in favor of Scripps' eldest son, James. The newspapers built up by Scripps were designed, as he used to say, for the "95 per cent.," the common people. Editorially they were independent in politics, sympathetic with union labor, and liberal in their general attitude; in 1912 they supported Theodore Roosevelt for the presidency and in 1924 Robert Marion LaFollette [*qq.v.*]. While retaining a controlling interest in all his papers, Scripps sold stock to members of the edi-

torial and business staffs, and at the time of his death approximately two-fifths of the stock of his papers was in the hands of his employees. With his sister Ellen he endowed the Scripps Institution for Biological Research at La Jolla, Cal. (later the Scripps Institution of Oceanography). In 1920 he established the Science Service, an organization designed to furnish the press with the results of research presented in popular form. He also provided for the Scripps Foundation for population research at Miami University, Oxford, Ohio. He had married on Oct. 5, 1885, Nackie Benson Holtsinger of Westchester, Ohio, by whom he had six children. He died on his yacht in Monrovia Bay, off the coast of Liberia; he was survived by his wife, two daughters, and a son.

[J. E. Scripps, *A Geneal. Hist. of the Scripps Family* (1903); *Who's Who in America,* 1924–25; N. D. Cochran, *E. W. Scripps* (1933); Gilson Gardner, *Lusty Scripps: the Life of E. W. Scripps* (1932); M. A. McRae, *Forty Years in Newspaperdom* (1924); W. E. Ritter, "The Marine Biological Station of San Diego," *Univ. of Cal. Pubs. in Zoology,* Mar. 9, 1912; obit. in *Detroit News,* Mar. 14, 1926.]   W. G. B.

SCRIPPS, ELLEN BROWNING (Oct. 18, 1836–Aug. 3, 1932), newspaper woman and philanthropist, was born in London, England, the daughter of James Mogg Scripps and his second wife, Ellen Mary (Saunders) Scripps. When she was seven or eight, the family came to the United States and settled near Rushville, Ill. She was graduated from Knox College in 1859. For a time she taught school, but after the death of her father in 1873 she turned to newspaper work, in which her brother, James Edmund Scripps, and her half-brother, Edward Wyllis Scripps [*qq.v.*], were already engaged. She went to Detroit, invested her savings in the *Detroit Advertiser and Tribune,* owned by her brother James, and worked as a proof-reader and reporter. When the paper was destroyed by fire, she assisted in launching the Detroit *Evening News.* Her energy and industry, especially in editing for many years a special feature section of miscellany, contributed to the paper's success. In 1878, when her half-brother Edward founded the Cleveland *Penny Press,* she became a stockholder and a regular contributor. Later she invested in the *Cincinnati Post* and other journals in the Scripps-McRae League of Newspapers, which afterwards became the Scripps-Howard chain. More than once she came to Edward Scripps's assistance financially and saved the newspaper chain from failure. She has been called one of the pioneers in modern American journalism.

About 1891 she settled in California, where

she made her home with her brother Edward and his family at their ranch, "Miramar," near San Diego. She invested heavily and profitably in San Diego real estate, and from the fortune she accumulated she gave generously to various enterprises and institutions. She converted the family farm at Rushville, Ill., into the Scripps Memorial Park and later erected a community house upon the site of the farmhouse. She gave liberally to Knox College and to the Bishop School for Girls at La Jolla, Cal., and founded Scripps College at Claremont, Cal. To the city of San Diego she gave a community house and playground, and buildings and equipment for a zoological garden. She provided a lodge and caretakers for the Torrey Pines Park in San Diego and bequeathed to the city as an addition to the park her land holdings of several hundred acres. She and her brother Edward were among the incorporators and were the chief financial supporters of the Marine Biological Association of San Diego, which afterwards, under the name of the Scripps Institution for Biological Research, was moved to La Jolla and transferred to the University of California, becoming in 1925 the Scripps Institution of Oceanography. With her brother she also established at La Jolla the Scripps Memorial Hospital. In 1917 she became a member of the board of directors of the National Recreation Association. In her will she listed bequests and established trust funds totaling more than two million dollars. In spite of her many public benefactions, she succeeded in avoiding publicity and led a very quiet life.

[J. E. Scripps, *A Geneal. Hist. of the Scripps Family* (1903); N. D. Cochran, *E. W. Scripps* (1933); M. A. McRae, *Forty Years in Newspaperdom* (1924); W. E. Ritter, "The Marine Biological Station of San Diego," *Univ. of Cal. Pubs. in Zoology,* Mar. 9, 1912; *Berkeley Daily Gazette,* Aug. 3, 11, 1932; obituary and portrait in *Recreation,* Oct. 1932; *San Diego Union,* Aug. 4, 1932; *N. Y. Times,* Aug. 4, 1932.]   P. O. R.

SCRIPPS, JAMES EDMUND (Mar. 19, 1835–May 29, 1906), newspaper publisher, son of James Mogg Scripps and his second wife, Ellen Mary (Saunders) Scripps, was born in London, England. His grandfather had been the publisher in London of the *Sun* and of the *Literary Gazette,* and editor and publisher of the *True Briton* (Cochran, *post,* p. 3). His father, a bookbinder, emigrated to the United States in 1844 and settled on a farm near Rushville, Ill. There James grew up and went to a district school. After attending a Chicago business college, he worked in the city for a time as a bookkeeper. In 1857 he began his newspaper career as a reporter on the *Democratic Press,* published by his cousin, John Locke Scripps, which was

merged in 1858 with the *Chicago Daily Tribune.* In 1859 he became commercial editor of the *Detroit Daily Advertiser;* two years later he was part owner of the paper, and in 1862, when it was merged with the *Detroit Tribune,* he retained his interest and was made first business manager and then editor of the combined papers. On Sept. 16, 1862, he was married to Harriet Josephine Messinger of Peru, Vt. His newspaper experience led him to believe that there was an opportunity in Detroit for a small, cheap, but well-written evening paper in which both news and editorial comment should be condensed for busy readers. Accordingly on Aug. 23, 1873, he launched the *Evening News,* a two-cent, four-page daily paper, independent in politics, printed for a time on the press of the *Detroit Free Press.* When, despite the panic of 1873, he decided to set up a printing plant of his own, he obtained additional capital from his brother, George H. Scripps, and his sister, Ellen Browning Scripps [q.v.], who also joined the editorial staff. Within a year the little two-cent *Evening News* had secured twice as large a circulation as any of its five-cent rivals. Although Scripps's original intention seems to have been to publish a paper modeled on the *Springfield Republican* and the New York *Evening Post,* the news staff that he employed actually produced a much livelier and more popular little news sheet that appealed to working men and their wives. It was the pioneer among the small, cheap evening papers that developed in the Middle West during the seventies and eighties.

In 1878, with his brother George H. Scripps and their cousin, John Scripps Sweeney, he lent about $10,000 to his half-brother Edward Wyllis Scripps [q.v.], who had helped to build up the circulation of the *Evening News* and was now about to start a one-cent evening paper in Cleveland, Ohio. This was the *Penny Press,* later the *Cleveland Press.* Later he joined Edward in establishing two more papers: in 1880 the *Evening Chronicle* in St. Louis, a two-cent paper, which in 1887 became the first penny paper west of the Mississippi River; and a year or two later the Cincinnati *Penny Post,* later the *Cincinnati Post,* in which he had previously invested. These papers in Detroit, Cleveland, St. Louis, and Cincinnati, owned jointly by the three Scripps brothers, with their sister Ellen and their cousin, formed the first chain of daily newspapers in the United States. In 1887 he entered into an agreement with his two brothers concerning the control and management of the papers, and spent two years abroad for his health. After his return his conservatism led to differences, and he ceased to take an active part in the combination. In 1903 he relinquished his holdings in all but the *Evening News,* later called the *Detroit News.* In 1891 he entered the morning newspaper field in Detroit by purchasing the *Detroit Tribune,* which he continued as a morning paper. When the agitation for Free Silver began in the nineties, he espoused the cause of William Jennings Bryan in both his Detroit papers, although personally he had always been a stanch Republican. His advocacy of Free Silver and Bryan in 1896 cost both papers heavily in patronage, and after McKinley's election he returned to the Republican party. In 1902 he was elected to the Michigan state Senate as an advocate of home rule for municipalities.

He was interested in art, architecture, and early printed books, of which he had a large collection. From its inception he served on the commission of the Detroit Museum of Art (later the Detroit Institute of Arts) and contributed to it both money and paintings that he collected on his trips abroad. To the city of Detroit he gave a park that bears his name. He wrote *Five Months Abroad* (1882), *Memorials of the Scripps Family* (1891), *A Genealogical History of the Scripps Family* (1903), and numerous pamphlets. He died in Detroit, survived by his wife, three daughters, and one son.

[J. E. Scripps, *A Geneal. Hist. of the Scripps Family* (1903); *Who's Who in America,* 1906–07; N. D. Cochran, *E. W. Scripps* (1933); Gilson Gardner, *Lusty Scripps: the Life of E. W. Scripps* (1932); L. A. White, *The Detroit News: 1873–1917* (1918); M. A. McRae, *Forty Years in Newspaperdom* (1924); C. M. and M. A. Burton, *Hist. of Wayne County and the City of Detroit, Mich.* (1930), vol. II; obituary in *Detroit News,* May 29, 1906.]   W. G. B.

SCRUGGS, WILLIAM LINDSAY (Sept. 14, 1836–July 18, 1912), diplomat, author, descended from Richard Scruggs who was in Virginia as early as 1665, was the eldest of seven children born to Frederick and Margaret (Kimbrough) Scruggs. His birthplace was his father's plantation, twenty miles above Knoxville, Tenn., on the French Broad River. He attended the grammar school near his home, was further instructed by a private tutor, and finished at Strawberry Plains College in East Tennessee. In 1858 he was principal of the Hamilton Male Academy and on Aug. 3 of that year he married Judith Ann Potts of Stafford County, Va. Removing to Georgia in 1861, he was admitted to the bar, but instead of practising law edited the Columbus *Daily Sun,* 1862–65. He subsequently moved to Atlanta, where from 1870 to 1872 he edited the *Atlanta Daily New Era.*

Politically Scruggs was a Unionist, reflecting the influence of his early environment, and he labored editorially for an intelligent reconstruction of the seceded states. His services were rewarded when he was appointed minister to Colombia, in April 1873. He was arbitrator in a claims case between the British and Colombian governments, settling it satisfactorily to both; he also negotiated a successful settlement of a long-standing maritime case, that of the *Montijo.* Recalled Aug. 16, 1876, when further appropriations for the legation were withheld by Congress, he served as consul at Chin-Kiang, and then at Canton, China, and in 1882 returned to Colombia as minister resident, becoming minister plenipotentiary two years later. Before retiring to private life under Cleveland's administration in December 1885, he succeeded in dissuading the Colombian government from enforcing an increase in customs duties at Panama and Colon.

After Harrison's inauguration, Scruggs returned to the diplomatic service as minister to Venezuela, Mar. 30, 1889, and became deeply interested in the dispute with Great Britain over the British Guiana boundary. After the election of Cleveland, he left his post, Dec. 15, 1892, although he was not formally recalled until Feb. 3, 1893. His espousal of Venezuela's cause won him appointment by that government as its legal adviser and special agent in August 1894. Almost immediately he published an able polemic pamphlet, *British Aggressions in Venezuela; or the Monroe Doctrine on Trial* (1894), and persuaded L. F. Livingston, the congressman from his district in Georgia, to introduce a resolution (Jan. 10, 1895) recommending that both parties to the dispute refer their differences to arbitration. Scruggs pressed his views upon the secretary of state, W. Q. Gresham [*q.v.*], but without complete success, and when the latter fell ill he carried his case directly to President Cleveland. The administration's course was clearly plotted in a dispatch from the new secretary, Richard Olney [*q.v.*], to Ambassador Bayard, July 20, 1895, and confirmed by the President's message to Congress the following December. Scruggs could hardly have asked for more, although it does not appear from the writings of either Olney or Cleveland whether they were moved by his personal pleas or by the considerations of the case itself which he had been instrumental in making an issue. As special agent of Venezuela Scruggs appeared before the Boundary Commission established in 1895, on whose findings the final arbitration (1897–99) was based. His *Brief Concerning the Question of Boundary between Venezuela and British Guiana* was published in 1898.

Scruggs had now finished his public career. Thereafter he wrote extensively, publishing *The Colombian and Venezuelan Republics* (1900; 1905); *Evolution of American Citizenship* (1901); "The Monroe Doctrine; Whence It Came, What It Is, and What It Is Not" (*Southern Law Review,* May 1902), and numerous other articles for historical, economic, and legal reviews. He was a well-read man and a good linguist, especially in Spanish. He bore a striking facial resemblance to Roscoe Conkling, but was tall and slender. His wife, by whom he had one son and four daughters, died in 1897. He survived her fifteen years, dying of apoplexy at his home in Atlanta.

[E. H. S. Dunklin, *Scruggs Geneal.* (1912); *Who's Who in America,* 1910–11; T. D. Jervey, "William Lindsay Scruggs—A Forgotten Diplomat," *South Atlantic Quart.,* July 1928; *Papers Relating to the Foreign Relations of the U. S.,* 1874–76, 1883–85, 1890; *Atlanta Constitution,* July 19, 1912; W. L. Scruggs, *The Colombian and Venezuelan Republics,* mentioned above; Instructions and Dispatches in archives of the Dept. of State.]   G. V. B.

SCRYMSER, JAMES ALEXANDER (July 18, 1839–Apr. 21, 1918), cable and telegraph promoter, capitalist, was a son of James Scrymgeour Scrymser and his wife, Ann Thompson. He was born and grew up in New York City, attending College Hill Academy at Poughkeepsie, N. Y., where he was graduated in 1856. At the outbreak of the Civil War in 1861 he was in his twenty-second year and had made no choice of a profession or calling. With Francis Channing Barlow [*q.v.*], he enlisted as a private in the 12th New York Infantry, one of the units that went to the defense of Washington in the spring of 1861. He was soon commissioned a second lieutenant in the 43rd New York and later received a staff appointment in the division commanded by Gen. William Farrar Smith [*q.v.*]. He served with the VI Corps, winning a captaincy, and later in the XVIII Army Corps, and is said to have been in all the battles of the Army of the Potomac for three years.

Returning to New York after his discharge from military service at the end of the war, he had his attention directed to the need of telegraphic communication between the United States and Cuba. Cyrus Field's final and successful attempt to lay the Atlantic cable was well under way, and submarine cable systems had been projected in many parts of the world. For the International Ocean Telegraph Company, incorporated in 1865, Scrymser undertook almost single-handed to see that 235 miles of cable were laid from Florida to Cuba and secured sufficient capital to complete the task in 1867. He had from the first been the motive power of the enterprise, and within a few years he became its titular head as well. When, in 1878, Jay Gould acquired the property and annexed it to the Western Union system, Scrymser resigned the presidency and at once turned his attention to the development of telegraph lines in Mexico and Central America. He raised the capital for laying a cable from Galveston, Tex., to Vera Cruz, Mexico, and was the chief executive of the Mexican Cable (later Telegraph) Company after it began to operate in 1881. Within a year new construction enabled the extension of the service to Central and South America, the Central and South American Cable (later Telegraph) Company having been organized in 1879. The company held a fifty-year exclusive concession granted by Porfirio Diaz, president of Mexico, and controlled Mexico's land wires. Its business increased rapidly; by 1893 more than 5,000 miles of cables and land lines had been added to the original "via Galveston" system of 4,600 miles. This addition included a cable from Chorillos, Peru, to Valparaiso, Chile, by way of Iquique, Chile. Land lines connected it with Buenos Aires and Scrymser's company had an exchange agreement with the West Coast of America Telegraph Company (British). The rate, which in 1882 had been seven dollars and a half a word from the United States to Buenos Aires, was reduced to sixty-five cents in 1915. A "via Colon" route from New York to the west coast of South America was completed in 1907, and in 1917 a New York to Brazil line was completed. Scrymser's methods were unobtrusive, direct, and wholly without flourish. Although he was interested in social-welfare efforts and gave much of his time and money to their promotion, his name rarely got into print. In the movement for vacation schools he was active for years. In 1892, When Dr. Charles Henry Parkhurst [*q.v.*] was beginning his crusade in New York against the alliance of the police with protected vice, it was Scrymser who planned the great Cooper Union meeting that brought to the lone clergyman the open and substantial aid of influential elements in the city's population (C. H. Parkhurst, *My Forty Years in New York,* 1923). In 1869 Scrymser was married to Mary C. Prime of New York, who survived him. He died in New York City.

[*Who's Who in America,* 1916–17; obit., *N. Y. Times,* Apr. 22, 1918; *Personal Reminiscences of James A. Scrymser in Times of Peace and War* (priv. printed, 1915); *A Half Century of Cable Service to the Three Americas* (1928).]   W. B. S.

SCUDDER, HORACE ELISHA (Oct. 16, 1838–Jan. 11, 1902), editor and writer, born in Boston, was the youngest boy in a family of six sons and one daughter, children of Charles Scudder, merchant, a deacon of the Union Church of that city, and Sarah Lathrop (Coit) Scudder. The fifth son, Samuel Hubbard Scudder [q.v.], became a distinguished entomologist. The Scudders had lived for generations on Cape Cod; the Coit progenitors included Gov. John Winthrop of Massachusetts. In one of Horace E. Scudder's earliest and best books, *Life and Letters of David Coit Scudder, Missionary in Southern India* (1864), a biography of an older brother, the pious and happy influences of his own youth in a household of strict orthodoxy are clearly suggested. After preparatory studies in the Roxbury and Boston Latin schools, he entered Williams College, where he was editor of the *Williams Quarterly* and graduated in 1858. Here he acquired a love for Greek which led to a lifelong habit of reading Homer and other classics—always including the Greek Testament—daily before breakfast. Soon after his graduation he went to New York as a teacher of private pupils and a writer of stories for children—collected under the titles *Seven Little People and Their Friends* (copr. 1862) and *Dream Children* (1864), both published anonymously. The sympathetic understanding of children and the strain of imagination that marked these stories seemed to foreshadow a career in creative writing; instead, he soon found himself, as he put it in later years, "at the desk of a literary workman."

Under the "honorable name" of "Literary Workman," he has been commemorated by T. W. Higginson [q.v.]. As a single designation the term applies to the larger portion of Scudder's activities more accurately than any other that could be chosen. His chief work, relating more to books than to magazines, was that of an editor. It began through an early association with Henry O. Houghton [q.v.], who in 1864 was combining his established business of printing at the Riverside Press, Cambridge, Mass., with that of publishing, under the firm name of Hurd & Houghton. In this organization Scudder, having returned from New York to Boston, became a reader of manuscripts and general editorial assistant. With an unswerving loyalty to the Riverside Press and to the succession of firms out of which Houghton, Mifflin & Company emerged in 1880, he held this post for the rest of his busy life.

In 1867 the young firm and the young editor launched a juvenile monthly, the *Riverside Magazine for Young People*. Scudder's interest in children here found full expression, not only through his own writings, but in the pains he devoted to the excellent woodcut illustrations and to the securing of such contributors as Hans Christian Andersen, Jacob Abbott, Frank R. Stockton, and Sarah Orne Jewett. Four volumes (1867–70) completed this undertaking. In 1872 he became a member of the firm of Hurd & Houghton, but after three years retired from the partnership in order to apply himself exclusively to editorial duties. In *Henry Oscar Houghton; a Biographical Outline* (1897) he referred (p. 92) to the sentiment for the word "Riverside" entertained by the head of the firm: "'Riverside,' he once said to me, 'is like a diamond which I can hold up before my eye, and turn it this way and that, and let the light fall on it, and see it sparkle.'" For the quality of the light thus described Scudder was largely responsible. The motto, *Tout bien ou rien,* appearing, first in 1885, on the title-pages of innumerable volumes that received his editorial oversight might well have been his own rule. From the planning of books, singly or in series, such as the American Commonwealths and the Riverside Literature series, from the critical reading of manuscripts to preface-writing and index-making, no task was too large or too small to call for the best he had to give.

These labors were largely unseen. While pursuing them he accomplished also the writing of a number of books of his own. Of these the most popular were the eight juvenile "Bodley Books" of travel produced between 1876 and 1884. Among his other books not already mentioned were *The Dwellers in Five-Sisters Court* (1876), a novel; *Stories and Romances* (1880); *Noah Webster* (1882), in the American Men of Letters Series; *Life and Letters of Bayard Taylor* (2 vols., 1884), with Marie Hansen-Taylor; *A History of the United States* (1884), for schools; *Men and Letters* (1887); *George Washington; an Historical Biography* (1890); *Childhood in Literature and Art* (1894); and *James Russell Lowell, a Biography* (2 vols., 1901). His fugitive writing, which was considerable, dealt chiefly with historical, critical, and biographical topics. From 1890 to 1898 he served "the house" of his devotion as editor of the *Atlantic Monthly.*

On Oct. 30, 1873, he married Grace Owen, of Cambridge, who, with one of their twin daughters, survived him. He served the cause of education as a trustee of Williams and Wellesley colleges and of the Episcopal Theological School in Cambridge. In the cause of letters, he rendered notable service as a pioneer in the provision of the best reading for the young, and also through the infinite patience and kindness of his dealings with a host of aspirants to authorship. Of average height and inclined to rotundity, he was noticeable in his later years chiefly for his large bushy beard, which once drew from him the characteristic, whimsical confession to a great curiosity to see what he was like underneath it, if only he dared to cut it off. He died at Cambridge, in the house he had occupied for many years.

[Beyond autobiog. passages in books mentioned, sources include A. V. G. Allen, "Memoir of Horace E. Scudder, Litt. D.," in *Proc. Mass. Hist. Soc.,* 2 ser. XVII (1903), reprinted with slight changes as "Horace E. Scudder; An Appreciation," in *Atlantic Mo.,* Apr. 1903; T. W. Higginson, in *Proc. Am. Acad. of Arts and Sciences,* vol. XXXVII (1902); *Atlantic Mo.,* Mar. 1902; *Who's Who in America,* 1901–02; *Boston Transcript,* Jan. 13, 1902; personal recollections, and information from Scudder's daughter, Mrs. Ingersoll Bowditch.]   M. A. DeW. H.

SCUDDER, JOHN (Sept. 3, 1793–Jan. 13, 1855), missionary to India, a descendant of Thomas Scudder who settled in Salem, Mass., in 1635, and a grandson of Nathaniel Scudder [*q.v.*], was born in Freehold, N. J. His father, Joseph Scudder, was a lawyer, and his mother, Maria Johnston, was a daughter of Col. Philip Johnston of the 1st New Jersey Regiment, who was killed at the battle of Long Island. At the College of New Jersey, where he graduated in 1811, John was known as a young man of integrity and eminent Christian character. The ministry was the profession of his choice but he was deterred from entering it by the stubborn opposition of his father. Graduating from the College of Physicians and Surgeons, New York, in 1813, he began practice in that city, his home with a family named Waterbury daughter Harriet he married. His succ his profession was immediate and he s to be on the way to an extensive and luc practice when the chance reading of a tra titled *The Conversion of the World; or, Claims of Six Hundred Millions* turned hir resistibly toward the mission field. Accordir he accepted an appointment from the Ameri Board of Commissioners for Foreign Missions and sailed from Boston for India, June 8, 1819, as its first medical missionary to that country; his wife, who was in warm sympathy with his purpose, accompanied him. They were stationed at Jaffna, the northern province of Ceylon, where they soon acquired the Tamil language and Mrs. Scudder engaged in school work, while her husband began his life employment of preaching and healing. A member of the Reformed Dutch Church, he was ordained by a council of missionaries, May 15, 1821. A hospital was opened,

boarding and day schools were established, and Scudder began the training of native medical students. With him, however, medical work was always subordinate to the great end of evangelization.

In 1836 he was transferred to Madras, where a mission station with a printing press was established. From here as a center he began making extensive tours, often being absent for several months, and once crossing the entire peninsula of India, preaching, healing, and distributing literature. Worn by hardships and the fierce opposition which he encountered, reduced by jungle fever and with one arm paralyzed, he was ordered to America in 1842. His health being greatly benefitted by the voyage, he spent three active years in promoting the cause of missions. Through his influence missionary societies were everywhere organized, and he developed an especial facility in addressing children. While in the United States he attended the ordination of his son, Henry Martyn Scudder, who immediately embarked as a missionary to India. Returning to India in 1846, Scudder resumed work in Madura but in 1849 removed to Madras, where in connection with his son he began an extensive work which he continued till 1854, when because of declining health he made a voyage to South Africa. Being somewhat recovered, he resumed preaching, but died suddenly at Wynberg early in 1855. His son Joseph, who had accompanied him, took his body back to Madras, where it was buried beside that of his wife who had died in November 1849.

Scudder wrote many tracts in the Tamil language, and, after his return from his sojourn in America, many tracts and booklets in English which were issued by the American Tract Society. He had a refined and pleasing address and an intellect of high order. In person he was tall and strong, with an iron will and indomitable courage. On one occasion he lanced a cancer from his own foot without assistance of any ind. He always preached twice a day and often stood in the burning sun for eleven consecutive hours, preaching, and distributing literature. Of his fourteen children, eight sons and two daughters lived to maturity. Seven of the sons became missionaries and one died while in preparation for the work.

[J. B. Waterbury, *Memoir of the Rev. John Scudder, M.D.* (1870); H. H. Holcomb, *Men of Might in India Missions* (1901); pp. 167–89; C. C. Creegan, *Pioneer Missionaries of the Church* (1903), pp. 150–62; Rufus Anderson, *Hist. of the Missions of the A.B.C.F.M. in India* (1874); A. M. Scudder, *A Brief Sketch of the Life and Work of Rev. John Scudder, M.D., His Wife and Descendants* (pamphlet, 1912); P. E. Faure and W. Robertson, *Funeral Addresses . . . on the Occasion of the Interment of the Rev. John Scudder, M.D.*

(1855); letters and extracts from Scudder's journals in the *Panoplist* and its successor, the *Missionary Herald* (1819–1855).]   F. T. P.

SCUDDER, JOHN MILTON (Sept. 8, 1829–Feb. 17, 1894), eclectic physician, was born in Harrison, Hamilton County, Ohio, the son of John Scudder. His father, a cabinet maker by trade, died while his children were still young, and John, to assist his mother, began work in a button factory in the neighboring town of Reading. Later, he returned to Harrison, taking up his father's trade and adding that of painting; still later, he opened a general store. He had the advantages of the village schools and received some further instruction. On Sept. 8, 1849, he married Jane Hannah, of Harrison.

Becoming interested in medicine through Dr. Milton L. Thomas, a local eclectic practitioner, he studied with him and subsequently entered the Eclectic Medical Institute in Cincinnati, graduating in 1856 as valedictorian of his class. In the session following his graduation he was appointed professor of general, special, and pathological anatomy. He began practice in the old section of Cincinnati known as Fulton, and in a short time became one of the busiest and most prosperous physicians of the city. Meanwhile, the fortunes of the Eclectic Medical Institute were at a low ebb, and in 1861 he practically gave up practice to become dean and devote his time and energies to building up the school. In 1858 he had been appointed professor of diseases of women and children; in 1860 he changed to the chair of pathology and principles and practice of medicine; in 1887 he transferred to the chair of hygiene and physical diagnosis, which he occupied for the rest of his life. With the management of the school, he took over the editorship of the moribund *Eclectic Medical Journal,* which he revived and conducted for over thirty years (1861–94). For a short time he edited the *Journal of Health,* a periodical of popular medicine, and also, for a year (1870–71), *The Eclectic,* a literary journal. Immediately upon his taking charge of the school and the *Journal,* they prospered, and from that time to the day of his death, Scudder was the foremost eclectic physician of the country. Aggressive, yet tactful, he was by nature well fitted for leadership; in addition, he was a shrewd business man.

Through the editorial pages of the *Journal* he exercised a continuing influence upon the whole profession of eclectic medicine, and through his writings and his lectures he introduced and established the eclectic doctrine and practice of "specific medication." From the beginning of his teaching career, he continued to produce books which collectively comprised for years the standard textbooks of eclectic medicine. Like his editorials, these books are well written and well arranged. The more important are *Practical Treatise on the Diseases of Women* (1857); *Materia Medica and Therapeutics* (1860); *Eclectic Practice of Medicine* (1864); *Domestic Medicine; or Home Book of Health* (1865), which, under different titles, went through more than twenty editions; *Principles of Medicine* (1867); *Eclectic Practice in Diseases of Children* (1869); *Familiar Treatise on Medicine* (1869); *Specific Medication and Specific Medicines* (1870); *Specific Diagnosis* (1874). An illness in 1891 necessitated the curtailment of much of his activities. He died in his sleep at his winter home in Daytona, Fla. His first wife having died, on Feb. 4, 1861, he married her sister, Mary Hannah. Four sons of this second marriage entered the practice of medicine or dentistry.

[*Bull. of the Lloyd Lib. of Botany, Pharmacy, and Materia Medica* (1912), no. 19; *Eclectic Medic. Jour.* (Cincinnati), Jan. 1895; H. W. Felter, *Hist. of the Eclectic Medic. Inst., Cincinnati, Ohio* (1902); H. A. Kelly and W. L. Burrage, *Am. Medic. Biogs.* (1920); *Cincinnati Times-Star,* Feb. 19, 1894.]   J. M. P—n.

SCUDDER, NATHANIEL (May 10?, 1733–Oct. 16, 1781), soldier, member of the Continental Congress, was descended from Thomas Scudder who emigrated from Wiltshire, England, to Salem, Mass., about 1635. The descendants of Thomas were millers at Huntington, Long Island. Authorities disagree as to whether Nathaniel was born there on Oct. 16, 1733, or near Freehold, N. J., on May 10. At any rate, he was the eldest of the six children of Jacob and Abia (Rowe) Scudder who removed from Huntington and finally settled just southeast of Princeton, N. J., at a place later called Scudder's Mills. He was graduated from the College of New Jersey, now Princeton University, with its fourth class in 1751. He then studied medicine and after a whirlwind romance married, on Mar. 23, 1752, Isabella, the daughter of the wealthy Kenneth Anderson of Monmouth County. They had three sons and two daughters. Nathaniel had a large and apparently lucrative practice at Freehold, Manalapan, and other parts of Monmouth County, and he seems to have endeared himself to all. He took a strong interest in religion, was an elder in the Tennent Church near Freehold, and is said to have worsted Thomas Paine in a religious controversy. He was a trustee of Princeton from 1778 until his death.

As the Revolution approached, he played an active part in public affairs. He was a leader at the Freehold meeting on June 6, 1774, where he drafted resolutions of sympathy for Boston, and soon became a member of the local committee of public safety. He was a delegate to New Jersey's first provincial congress at New Brunswick that year and was speaker of the legislature in 1776. A lieutenant-colonel of the 1st Monmouth County Regiment of militia, he succeeded George Taylor as colonel on Nov. 28, 1776. Some of his property was destroyed during the British occupation at that time, the chief item in his bill of damages being a new colonel's uniform. In 1777 he was elected a delegate to the Continental Congress, where he first appeared on Feb. 9, 1778, and served until just before his second term expired on Dec. 1, 1779. He was frequently absent from the sessions of the Congress, as he was appointed on committees dealing with the quartermaster service, which required personal attention. He was present at the battle of Monmouth, near his own home, during a recess of the Congress. His most important service was writing a letter from Freehold on July 13, 1778, two weeks after that battle, to John Hart, speaker of the New Jersey legislature, urging strongly that the state's delegates to Congress be empowered to ratify and sign the Articles of Confederation (Burnett, *post*, III, p. 326). Some say that he appeared before the hesitant legislature in person. At any rate, his efforts were successful, for the necessary authorization was made on Nov. 20, and the Articles were signed by Scudder and his colleagues on Nov. 26.

After retiring from Congress, he resumed his military duties, assisting David Forman in repelling Loyalist raids. Three days before the Yorktown surrender, when some Loyalist refugees from Sandy Hook tried to land at Black Point, near Shrewsbury, N. J., he was killed. He was buried in the Tennent churchyard on the Monmouth battlefield.

[Sec. of State's Office, Trenton, Manuscript Book 12, p. 479; Book 24, p. 135; records in files for General Alumni Catalogue, Princeton University; Stephen Wickes, *Hist. of Medicine in N. J.* (1879); H. L. Cooley, *Genealogy of Early Settlers of Trenton and Ewing* (1883); *Letters of Members of the Continental Cong.*, vols. II–IV (1923–28), ed. by E. C. Burnett; *N. J. Archives*, 2 ser. vol. I (1901); *Pa. Mag. of Hist. & Biography*, no. III (1879); *A Brief Narrative of the Ravages of the British and Hessians at Princeton* (1906), ed. by V. L. Collins; F. B. Heitman, *Hist. Register of Officers of the Continental Army* (1893); W. S. Stryker, *Official Register of the Officers and Men of N. J. in the Rev. War* (1872), pp. 344, 355.]
R. G. A.

SCUDDER, SAMUEL HUBBARD (Apr. 13, 1837–May 17, 1911), entomologist, was born in Boston and died in Cambridge, Mass. Son of Charles and Sarah Lathrop (Coit) Scudder and

brother of Horace Elisha Scudder [*q.v.*], he was of Puritan origin on both sides. His father was a well-to-do hardware and commission merchant. At the age of sixteen Samuel was sent to Williams College. His interest in entomology was aroused during his freshman year by a case of butterflies in the room of a friend, and before the end of his junior year he had decided to devote his life as far as possible to that science. After taking his bachelor's degree at Williams in 1857, he studied in the Lawrence Scientific School under Agassiz, gaining the degree of B.S. in 1862 and the faculty of attention to minute detail that characterized all his later work. He was an assistant to Agassiz until 1864, and then served as custodian of the Boston Society of Natural History until 1870. On June 25, 1867, he married Ethelinda Jane Blatchford. From 1870 to 1879 he held no salaried position, but in the latter year became assistant librarian of Harvard University, resigning in 1882. In 1886 he was appointed a paleontologist in the United States Geological Survey, being charged with the study of fossil insects. Resigning this position in 1892, he thenceforth worked at his home in Cambridge until he was paralyzed, a number of years before his death.

Outside the field of entomology, he published two large and important works: *Catalogue of Scientific Serials of All Countries . . . 1633–1876* (1879) and *Nomenclator Zoologicus* (2 parts, 1882–84), the latter still of enormous value to zoologists a generation later. He was for a long time a member of the Appalachian Club, and wrote many articles for its journal, *Appalachia.* For the Boston Society of Natural History he edited *Entomological Correspondence of Thaddeus William Harris, M.D.* (1869). His true life work, however, dealt with three general topics—American diurnal *Lepidoptera,* the *Orthoptera,* and fossil insects—and here he made striking advances and established himself as one of the great leaders in American entomology. His monumental treatise on butterflies, *The Butterflies of the Eastern United States and Canada, with Special Reference to New England* (3 vols., 1888–89), was the result of thirty years of research in the life histories and affinities of these interesting creatures. While technical in the main, it is filled with popular excursuses treating of a number of extremely interesting subjects relating to New England and its butterflies. His essays on migration, geographical distribution, protective coloration, dimorphism, and other evolutionary aspects attractively opened broad fields of research. He also wrote several smaller and more popular books on butterflies, including

Butterflies: Their Structure, Changes, and Life Histories (1881); *The Life of a Butterfly: A Chapter in Natural History for the General Reader* (1893); *A Brief Guide to the Commoner Butterflies of the Northern United States and Canada* (1893); *Frail Children of the Air: Excursions into the World of Butterflies* (1895); *Every-Day Butterflies* (1899).

He was the greatest American orthopterist of his time, and his work on fossil insects was profound, very extensive and of a pioneer character. The closing years of his productive life were largely devoted to fossil insects and *Orthoptera*. Among his major publications in these fields were: *A Classed and Annotated Bibliography of Fossil Insects* (1890), *The Tertiary Insects of North America* (1891), *Index to the Known Fossil Insects of the World* (1891), *Tertiary Rhynchophorous Coleoptera of the United States* (1894), and *Revision of the American Fossil Cockroaches* (1895), all issued as Bulletins, Monographs, or Reports of the United States Geological Survey; *Revision of the Orthopteran Group Melanopli* (United States National Museum, 1897); and *Alphabetical Index to North American Orthoptera Described in the Eighteenth and Nineteenth Centuries* (Boston Society of Natural History, 1901). Scudder's bibliography comprised 791 scientific titles. His papers were mainly of a descriptive character, but he wrote many popular articles. In the course of his life he named and described 1,884 species, of which 1,144 species and 233 genera are fossil insects, 630 species and 106 genera are recent *Orthoptera*, and the remainder are fossil insects and recent butterflies. He received the Walker prize of the Boston Society of Natural History in 1898. He became a member of the National Academy of Sciences in 1877 and of the American Philosophical Society in 1878. He was an honorary fellow of the Royal Society of Canada and the Entomological Society of London, and foreign associate of the national entomological or zoological societies of The Hague, St. Petersburg, Vienna, Moscow, Madrid, Buenos Aires, and Brussels. He was probably the broadest and most highly cultured American worker in his field in his generation and has been called "the greatest scholar and most charming writer among American entomologists." Personally he was a man of great charm, tall, slender, kindly, and possessed of a keen sense of humor. His final illness, which took the form of creeping paralysis, began in 1896, shortly after the death of his only son.

[A. G. Mayor, in *Memoirs Nat. Acad. Sci.*, vol. XVII (1924); *Science*, Sept. 15, 1911; *Psyche*, Dec. 1911; *Entomological News*, July 1911; *Appalachia*, July 1911; *Canadian Entomologist*, July 1911; *Entomologist's Record* (London), Sept. 15, 1911; *Boston Transcript*, May 17, 1911.]   L. O. H.

SCULL, JOHN (1765–Feb. 8, 1828), pioneer newspaper editor, was born in Reading, Pa., the son of Jasper Scull, of well-to-do Quaker stock. His great-grandfather, Nicholas Scull, emigrated to Philadelphia with his brother John in 1685; his grandfather, Nicholas Scull, II, was the first surveyor-general of the province of Pennsylvania; and his father held offices in Northampton and Berks counties, Pa. His father's sister, Mary Scull, was the mother of Nicholas Biddle, 1750–1778 [q.v.]. Opportunities for the son's formal education were doubtless limited, but he evidently acquired a command of good forthright English. In the summer of 1786, young John Scull journeyed over the mountains with his partner, Joseph Hall, to establish in Pittsburgh the first newspaper west of the Alleghenies. Apparently he had been induced to go partly through the persuasions of Hugh Henry Brackenridge [q.v.]. Press, types, ink, and paper were brought over the mountains by pack-horse, and the first issue of the Pittsburgh *Gazette* appeared on July 29, 1786. There was no mail-route, and at first the young editor delivered his papers by hand within the village and relied on chance travelers to serve his outlying subscribers. The paper had apparently two chief objects—to attract immigrants to the region, and to support the Federalist party. In the former purpose Scull was aided by Brackenridge's articles praising the western region; but over the latter he and Brackenridge had by 1800 developed bitter antagonism. Before this, however, Scull had published the third volume of Brackenridge's *Modern Chivalry* (1793), the first book, aside from hymn books, almanacs, and the like, to be printed west of the Alleghenies.

Scull's public service to Pittsburgh was considerable aside from his printing. He helped secure a post-route to Pittsburgh and was postmaster from 1789 to 1796; he was president, from 1814 to 1819, of the second bank established in Pittsburgh; he was one of the incorporators of the Western University of Pennsylvania, now the University of Pittsburgh, in 1819; and he was a member of the first council of the borough of Pittsburgh in 1804. During the Whiskey Rebellion, under threat of personal violence, he opened his columns to communications denouncing the excise, but he refrained from editorial indorsement of the insurgents. In 1789 he was married to Mary, the daughter of Col. John Irwin of Westmoreland County, and he had two sons and one daughter. In 1816 he retired from the publication of the *Gazette*, and in 1826 he moved to his farm near the present town of Irwin, Pa., where he died (*Pittsburgh Mercury*, Feb. 19, 1828). His descendants have been prominent in western Pennsylvania, at the bar, in newspaper publication, and in banking.

[Materials on Scull are scattered, fragmentary, and contradictory. The most detailed accounts for family data are in L. B. Thomas, *The Thomas Book* (1896), *Hist. of Bedford and Somerset Counties, Pa.* (1906), vol. III, pp. 16–25, and J. N. Boucher, ed., *Hist. of Westmoreland County, Pa.* (1906), vol. III, pp. 504–508. For the *Gazette*, see R. G. Thwaites, "The Ohio Valley Press before the War of 1812–15," *Proc. of the Am. Antiq. Soc.*, Apr. 1909, n. s., vol. XIX (1909), and the works cited therein. The most complete file of the *Gazette* is in the Carnegie Library of Pittsburgh. Consult also N. B. Craig, *The Hist. of Pittsburgh* (1851), pp. 188–206 (2nd ed. 1917), C. W. Dahlinger, *Pittsburgh, a Sketch of Its Early Social Life* (1916), and J. N. Boucher, ed., *A Century and a Half of Pittsburg and Her People* (1908), vol. II, pp. 79–80, 297, 419, 420.]   S. J. B.

SCULLIN, JOHN (Aug. 17, 1836–May 28, 1920), railroad builder, street-railway operator, manufacturer, was born on a farm near Helena, N. Y., the third of seven children of Nicholas and Mary (Kenney) Scullin, natives of Ireland. He was educated in the country schools and the academy at Potsdam, N. Y. Accustomed to hard work from boyhood, he crossed into Canada at nineteen to serve the Grand Trunk Railway as water-carrier, brakeman, ballast-train conductor, and construction contractor. On Aug. 18, 1863, he married Hannah Perry of Montreal, and that year he went to Minnesota, where he became a construction contractor for the Minneapolis & Cedar Valley Railroad, later part of the Chicago, Milwaukee & St. Paul system. Attracted by reports of gold in Idaho territory, he joined an ox-team party of prospectors, seven of whom were killed by Indians. Leaving the Northwest after several months, he was back in New York by 1865, ready to resume railroad building. Opportunities being more numerous in the West, he settled in Leavenworth, Kan., in 1866 and soon acquired contracts to lay forty miles of the Union Pacific Railroad. In 1868 he built the Missouri Valley railway between Maryville and Savannah, Mo., and the Chicago, Rock Island & Pacific from Leavenworth to Cameron, Mo. In 1869 he undertook his most important railroad construction, that of the major portion of the Missouri-Kansas-Texas system, which began with the section from Emporia, Kan., to Texas and ended with the Missouri division terminating at Moberly in 1874. He also built parts of the Galveston, Harrisburg & San Antonio and the Denison & Southeastern railroads. It was as construction contractor for the Missouri-Kansas-

Texas system that he won one of railroad building's most famous races, the prize being the privilege to build in Indian territory. To defeat his competitors, he laid twenty-six and a half miles of tracks in eleven days, reaching the boundary near Chetopa, Kan., June 6, 1870. A rugged man, he reveled in the railroad camp's rough life.

In 1875 he brought his family from Sedalia, Mo., to St. Louis, where he invested in street railways. In 1883 as president of the Mexican National Construction Company he built the Mexican National railroad from Mexico City to San Luis Potosí and from Acambaro to Morelia. Though he was urged to stay in Mexico, he returned to St. Louis in 1885 to become a street-railway operator. He unified several lines, instituted a system of transfers, and went directly from horse power to electricity while his competitors experimented with cable cars. Selling his interests in 1899, he formed the next year the Scullin-Gallagher Iron and Steel Company, later the Scullin Steel Company, which manufactured large railroad castings and rolling mills and prospered greatly during the World War. He was important in St. Louis banking circles as well as in various railway and transportation companies. In his later life he spent much time on the farm where he had grown up, to which he felt a great attachment. Active in business to the last, he died of uremic poisoning in St. Louis, leaving a son and two daughters, his wife and three sons having predeceased him. He was buried in Calvary Cemetery. Generous in his benefactions, he always stipulated that nothing be said about them. His personal property, not including real estate, was appraised at approximately two and a half million.

[See *The Book of St. Louisans* (1906), ed. by J. W. Leonard; William Hyde and H. L. Conard, *Encyc. of the Hist. of St. Louis* (1899), vol. IV; W. B. Stevens, *Eleven Roads to Success, Charted by St. Louisans Who Have Traveled Them* (1914); Edward King, "The Great South: the New Route to the Gulf," *Scribner's*, July 1873, for an account of the race to Indian territory; *St. Louis Post-Dispatch*, Aug. 22, 1897, and May 29 (obituary), June 3, Aug. 11, 1920. Family information has been supplied by Harry Scullin, a son, of St. Louis.]   I. D.

SEABURY, GEORGE JOHN (Nov. 10, 1844–Feb. 13, 1909), chemist and pharmacist, the son of Michael J. Seabury and Agnes Z. (Calender) Seabury, was born in New York City. His family had been represented in America prior to the Revolution. He received his early education in the public schools of New York City, and then turned to higher studies in chemistry, pharmacy, and medicine. During the Civil War he served in the 12th New York Volunteer Regiment, and was wounded at Gaines's

Mill and Malvern Hill during the Peninsular campaign in 1862. At the close of the war he resumed his professional studies and spent some time in Europe, especially at the Universities of Göttingen and Heidelberg, where he became interested in the discoveries of Sir Joseph Lister in antiseptics and the applications of the germ theory. On his return to the United States, he founded the firm of Seabury and Johnson, pioneers in the manufacture of plasters and surgical dressings, of which he became president and sole owner in 1885.

In 1876 he became a member of the American Pharmaceutical Association and was chairman of the section on commercial interests from 1894 to 1896 and for five terms held a similar relation to the committee on the status of pharmacists in the army, the navy, and the public health and marine hospital service of the United States. He was one of the founders of the New York State Pharmaceutical Association and was president in 1895. He was also a member of the New York College of Pharmacy and a large contributor to its building fund. Always an ardent champion of the cause of the retail druggist in maintaining fair retail prices, he wrote voluminously on that subject, and on many public questions as well. Many of his articles were published collectively in his book *Shall Pharmacists Become Tradesmen* (1899). The most significant of his other literary efforts was *The Constructive and Reconstructive Forces . . . Essential to Maintain American International Supremacy* (1902).

His interest in military affairs continued throughout his life and he was long a member of the famous "Old Guard" of New York City. He did much towards promoting rifle practice in the National Guard and served as honorary secretary and director of the National Rifle Association. He was an active Republican and though importuned to accept office, preferred to remain politically independent. In 1909 he served as a presidential elector for Taft and Sherman. Among the active interests of a very busy life, Seabury included a great enthusiasm for art and music. He died at his home in New York City and was survived by two of his four children. His wife, Ella Green Bensen, to whom he had been married in 1866, preceded him in death.

[Information from the family; *Oil, Paint, and Drug Reporter*, Feb. 22, 1909; *Natl. Druggist*, Mar. 1909; *N. Y. Times*, Feb. 15, 1909.]   M.B.

SEABURY, SAMUEL (Nov. 30, 1729–Feb. 25, 1796), first bishop of the Episcopal Church in America, was born at Groton, Conn., son of the Rev. Samuel Seabury, minister of the Con-

gregational church in North Groton, by his first wife, Abigail (Mumford) Seabury. He was a descendant of John Seabury who emigrated from England to Boston in Massachusetts Bay in 1639, and whose grandson John, married the grand-daughter of John Alden and moved from Duxbury, where his father had settled, to Stonington, Conn., and later, to Groton. Early in 1730 Samuel's father entered the priesthood of the Church of England. He was sent by the Society for the Propagation of the Gospel as a missionary to New London, Conn., and in 1742 was transferred to Hempstead, L. I., to spend the remainder of his life as missionary, physician, and schoolmaster.

Young Samuel entered Yale College in 1744 and received the degree of B.A. in 1748. While studying physic and awaiting the required age for ordination, he served as catechist at Huntington, L. I. He spent the year 1752–53 at the University of Edinburgh, completing his medical training. On Dec. 21, 1753, at Fulham Palace, he was ordained deacon, and two days later, priest. Licensed by the Bishop of London to preach in New Jersey, he was sent by the Society for the Propagation of the Gospel as a missionary to New Brunswick, where he arrived on May 25, 1754. Soon after his return from abroad, he espoused the cause of the Anglicans who were then fighting for control of the proposed King's College, New York, and wrote some of the newspaper articles that appeared in their behalf, thus beginning his career as a controversialist and a pamphleteer, in which he ranked second only to Rev. Thomas B. Chandler [*q.v.*] as a champion of the English Church and government in America. On Oct. 12, 1756, Seabury married Mary Hicks, daughter of Edward Hicks of Staten Island, and the following year, Jan. 12, he was transferred to Jamaica, L. I. When the rector at Westchester, N. Y., resigned, early in 1765, Seabury asked for a transfer to that parish and his request was granted, his induction taking place on Mar. 1, 1767. In addition to his parish duties, he practised medicine and conducted a school. In 1767 the New York City clergy recommended him to Sir William Johnson as the man best fitted to begin a mission at Johnstown, N. Y. They described him as "a Man of great good Sense, of a cheerful Disposition, . . . a good Divine, and an agreeable Preacher, his skill in Medicines also much esteemed" (Vance, *post*, pp. 12-13 note). After much persuasion, he visited Johnstown in 1769, but declined to undertake the work. He served in 1766–67 as secretary of the Convention of New York, composed of Anglican clergy, took an active part in its campaign to secure bishops for America, and in the resulting literary struggle between the Anglicans and the Dissenters. In reply to a series of articles styled "The American Whig," opposing an episcopate, written by William Livingston [*q.v.*] and others and appearing in James Parker's *New York Gazette* (1768), Seabury, Charles Inglis [*q.v.*], and others replied with "A Whip for the American Whig," published in Gaine's *New York Gazette and Weekly Mercury* (Apr. 4, 1768–July 10, 1769).

With the beginning of the acts of the British Parliament that finally set off the revolutionary conflagration, Seabury and his colleagues began their major literary struggle to keep the colonies loyal to the Crown. His most important pamphlets were signed A. W. Farmer. With clear, homely, and forceful language and arguments, he endeavored to convince the liberty-seeking Americans that their greatest freedom and good lay in their submitting to, and remaining under, the British government, and in securing the changes they desired through peaceful and orderly appeals to that government. These pamphlets were ably answered by the seventeen-year-old Alexander Hamilton [*q.v.*], then a student in King's College. Early in 1775, Seabury entered actively into the Loyalists' campaign to prevent the election of committees and delegates to Provincial and Continental congresses and to nullify the measures enacted by those bodies. He and all his colleagues went into hiding, Apr. 29, 1775, to shield themselves from the wrath of the patriots, aroused by the news of Lexington and Concord. He did not remain hidden long; and, on Nov. 22, a troop of Connecticut horsemen, led by Isaac Sears [*q.v.*], took him prisoner and sent him to New Haven for confinement; on Dec. 23, he was released. The following year, Sept. 1, he entered the British lines on Long Island, and later served as a guide to the army both on the Island and in Westchester County. When the British took possession of New York City, he removed his family thither, and resided there during the war. Myles Cooper and T. B. Chandler [*qq.v.*], fellow Loyalists who had fled to England, secured for him a gift of fifty pounds, a chaplaincy of a man-of-war, and the degree of D.D. from Oxford. In 1777 he was appointed chaplain of the provincial hospital in New York, and was transferred by the Society for the Propagation of the Gospel as missionary to Staten Island. The year following, he was made chaplain of the King's American Regiment raised by Col. Edmund Fanning [*q.v.*]. His wife died Oct. 12, 1780.

The Episcopal clergy of Connecticut, on Mar. 25, 1783, chose Jeremiah Leaming [*q.v.*] and Seabury as suitable candidates for Episcopal consecration to serve the Church in the now independent colonies. Leaming declined the honor and Seabury sailed for England on June 7, to obtain consecration. Since the Anglican authorities believed themselves debarred on legal grounds from performing the rite, he proceeded to Scotland, where on Nov. 14, 1784, he was consecrated by the non-juring Scottish prelates. Embarking for America, Mar. 15, 1785, he reached Newport, R. I., on June 20 and soon sailed for New London, Conn., where he resided as rector of St. James' Church and bishop of Connecticut and Rhode Island until his death. He began at once the revival and reorganization of the churches in his diocese. By Dec. 15, 1785, he had ordained twelve priests from six states, and on July 13, 1792, he reported having traveled more than 6,000 miles, confirmed more than 10,000, and ordained thirty priests and eight deacons. His greatest desires were to see a "valid Episcopacy," free from interference by the laity; and a "strong, complete," and "cordial . . . union in all the churches from uniformity in our worship" (Seabury to William White, Aug. 19, 1785, Nov. 1, 1789, White MSS., New York Historical Society). He stood for unity in essentials and liberty in non-essentials, but had little sympathy for the prevailing liberalizing ideas of his American brethren. His persistent, kindly efforts were eventually successful in uniting the English and Scottish branches into one American Church. As his troubled and fruitful life drew to a close, he felt the cares of his diocese bearing heavily upon him. "To do good to God's Church, and be an humble instrument in His hand to support it, when its destruction seemed near & its enemies rejoiced in the prospect, was what first determined me to do as I have done," he wrote, Oct. 9, 1793 (Hawks MSS., New York Historical Society). During his episcopate, he took no part in politics, and withdrew himself from every study, pursuit, and meditation, "but the sole one of building up the Church of Christ in this country" (letter of Nov. 5, 1794, Hawks MSS.). His labors continued until his death came upon him suddenly, while making parish calls, in his sixty-eighth year. He was survived by three daughters and three sons. His remains were interred in the public burying ground in New London, but now repose beneath the altar of St. James' Church in that city. Two collections of his sermons, *Discourses on Several Subjects* (2 vols., 1793), and *Discourses on Several Important Subjects* (1798), were published.

[Manuscript and transcript colls. of Judge Samuel Seabury, Easthampton, L. I., of the N. Y. Hist. Soc., of the Lib. of Cong., of the Soc. for the Propagation of the Gospel, and of the Public Record Office of Great Britain; W. J. Seabury, *Memoir of Bishop Seabury* (1908); E. E. Beardsley, *Life and Correspondence of the Right Reverend Samuel Seabury* (1881); C. H. Vance, *Letters of a Westchester Farmer by the Rev. Samuel Seabury* (1930), with an introductory essay; F. B. Dexter, *Biog. Sketches Grads. Yale Coll.*, vol. II (1896); W. S. Perry, *The Hist. of the Am. Episcopal Church* (1885), vol. II; *Hist. Mag. of the Protestant Episcopal Church*, Sept. 1934.]   C. H. V.

SEABURY, SAMUEL (June 9, 1801–Oct. 10, 1872), Protestant Episcopal clergyman, was born in New London, Conn., the eldest son of Charles Seabury, then rector of St. James' Church, and the grandson of Bishop Samuel Seabury [*q.v.*]; his mother, Anne (Saltonstall), was a descendant of Richard Saltonstall [*q.v.*]. In 1814 Charles Seabury moved to Setauket, Long Island, as rector of Caroline Church. Because of his poverty he was unable to afford his children a formal higher education. Samuel, however, pursued classical and theological studies while working in New York, and, later, while teaching school in Brooklyn. The influence of Henry U. Onderdonk [*q.v.*], then rector of St. Ann's Brooklyn, confirmed him in the high churchmanship traditional in his family. On Apr. 12, 1826, he was ordained deacon by Bishop John Henry Hobart [*q.v.*] in All Saints' Chuch, New York. After several short engagements he took charge of St. George's, Hallet's Cove (now Astoria), which under him became an organized parish. Here Hobart ordained him to the priesthood on July 7, 1828. Shortly afterwards, he became classical instructor at Muhlenberg's famous school in Flushing. While here he projected a series of textbooks announced in *The Study of the Classics on Christian Principles* (1831).

On Sept. 1, 1833, he became editor of *The Churchman*. Although specially concerned with the diocese of New York, this was the principal weekly of the Episcopal Church. Seabury continued its high-church tradition and maintained an excellent standard of scholarly as well as popular articles. The opening years of his editorship were marked by controversies on minor points of doctrine with his predecessor, William R. Whittingham [*q.v.*], and with the faculty of the General Theological Seminary. From 1835 to 1838 he taught Evidences at the General Seminary. In the latter year the Church of the Annunciation was founded for him.

Loyally supporting Bishop Benjamin T. Onderdonk [*q.v.*], Seabury welcomed the Oxford movement. In 1843 he recommended as examining chaplain and defended as editor the ordination of Arthur Carey, who was attacked for his adherence to Newman's principles. In the fall Carey became his assistant at the Church of the Annunciation, and after the young man's death in April 1844, Seabury delivered a generous tribute to his devotion and pastoral zeal in *The Joy of the Saints* (1844). Seabury continued to support tractarianism and stood by Onderdonk when he was attacked, his policy leading to the foundation of the *Protestant Churchman* in 1846. He was one of the leaders of the high-church party which retained control of the diocesan convention, and in 1848 became a member of the standing committee, to which fell the administration of the headless diocese. In 1850 he barely missed election as provisional bishop.

With the growth of the Church of the Annunciation, he had resigned his editorship in February 1849. In 1853, after the consecration of Bishop Jonathan M. Wainwright [*q.v.*], he refused reëlection to the standing committee. During the next decade his parish enjoyed considerable prosperity. It was conducted on conservative tractarian principles, with daily services. His teachings are illustrated in several sermons preserved from this period and in *The Continuity of the Church of England* (1853). His *American Slavery ... Justified* (1861) was a not very happy excursion into politics. In 1862 he was elected professor of Biblical Learning at the General Seminary, which, until 1866, being in financial difficulties, gave him a residence, but no salary; he retained his rectorship until 1868, when he surrendered it to his son, William J. Seabury. His work as professor is said to have been conscientious and successful, although he was not primarily a Biblical scholar nor greatly interested in detailed exegesis. His publications of this period include *Mary the Virgin as Commemorated in the Church of Christ* (1868), a defense of the doctrine of her perpetual virginity, and *The Theory and Use of the Church Calendar* (1872).

While Seabury had welcomed and defended the tractarians, his own views remained those of the old high churchmanship of his youth. In the eucharist he stressed the commemorative sacrifice rather than the real presence and devotional habits deduced from that doctrine. Never concerned about ceremonial, he took little part in the "ritualistic" controversy of the later sixties; but in the seminary disputes of 1869–71 he sided with the majority of the faculty against Prof. George F. Seymour [*q.v.*]. Increasing ill health gradually obliged him to give up all but the most essential duties of his position. He died shortly after his return from the summer vacation of 1872. His son, William, edited and published in 1874 some of his father's writings under the title *Discourses Illustrative of the Nature and Work of the Holy Spirit, and Other Papers*. Seabury was married three times: first, May 17, 1829, to Lydia Huntington Bill, by whom he had two daughters; she died on Apr. 16, 1834, and on Nov. 17, 1835, he married Hannah Amelia Jones, by whom he had a son and three daughters; after her death, Sept. 18, 1852, he was married, Oct. 17, 1854, to Mary Anna, daughter of Samuel and Catharine (Schuyler) Jones.

[S. R. Johnson, *A Discourse . . . in Memory of Samuel Seabury* (1873), a brief memoir somewhat inaccurate as to dates; W. S. Perry, *The Hist. of the Am. Episcopal Church* (1885), vol. II; *Hist. Mag. of the Protestant Episcopal Church,* Sept. 1934; *Churchman,* Oct. 19, 26, 1872; *Church Rev.,* July 1885.]

E. R. H., Jr.

SEAGER, HENRY ROGERS (July 21, 1870–Aug. 23, 1930), economist, was born in Lansing, Mich., the son of Schuyler Fiske Seager, a lawyer, and Alice (Berry) Seager. Graduating at the University of Michigan in 1890, he did further work during the succeeding years at the Johns Hopkins University, at the Universities of Halle, Berlin, and Vienna, and at the University of Pennsylvania, where he received the Ph.D. degree in 1894. That year he was appointed instructor in economics in the Wharton School of Finance and Commerce, and in 1896 he was made an assistant professor; in 1902 he became adjunct professor, and in 1905, professor, in Columbia University, where he served till death. On June 5, 1899, he was married to Harriet Henderson of Philadelphia, who died in 1928; their son survived him.

Seager's training as an economist was in English classicism, in the German historical method, and in the peculiar Austrian approach. His published work shows clearly the influence of each. His greatest admiration was for Simon N. Patten [*q.v.*], with whom he served at the University of Pennsylvania but whose influence on his thought was slight. Seager's mind was orderly and compressive rather than brilliant and generalizing; conservatism was perhaps its distinguishing characteristic. He was solid and patient, slow to conclude, and even slower to write his conclusions. One result of this was that he was less a writing scholar than one who worked with students. Literally hundreds of dissertations passed through his careful hands at Columbia and many generations of students heard his lectures on labor and on corporation problems. Always active in meliorative activities, he assisted materially in the establishment of a system of workmen's compensation in New York; he was a supporter of the *Survey* (formerly *Charities and the Commons*) and for many years a member of its board of directors. During the war he served as secretary of the Shipbuilding Labor Adjustment Board, and, in 1919–20, he was executive secretary of the President's Second Industrial Conference. He was one of the founders and three times president of the American Association for Labor Legislation. He was frequently consulted by philanthropists, legislators, and publicists; he was a member of the editorial board of *The Political Science Quarterly,* and in 1922 was president of the American Economic Association. In all these varied activities he had one purpose: to better social conditions within the framework of *laissez-faire*. He possessed a determined faith that this could be done and worked constantly to show the way. Melioration consisted in making changes here and there, which while not disturbing fundamental arrangements, reduced their burden on less favored individuals. Improvement consisted in legal change, and a large part of his effort was always directed toward reform by legislation.

His most considerable work is *Principles of Economics,* first published under this title in 1913, which grew out of his *Introduction to Economics* (1904 and later editions) and appeared in its final form in 1923. The most important of his other writings are *Trust and Corporation Problems* (1929), with C. A. Gulick, Jr., and the posthumous volume, *Labor and Other Economic Essays* (1931), to which is attached his complete bibliography. Somewhat more than the final half of the *Principles of Economics* is devoted to essays on important problems: banking, the tariff, railroads, trusts, taxation, labor, and social insurance. The theoretical section begins with a consideration of consumption, progresses through value and production, and ends with distribution. There were many books published during this period with much the same outline; but Seager's was characterized by emphasis on all that pertained to human welfare. This led to stress on consumption and on the demand side of the value equilibrium, as well as to extra consideration of monopoly gains. The discussion of distribution was carried out within the framework of the "specific productivity" analysis but with more than usual weight given to such subjective influences as the balancing, in consumers' and producers' minds, of marginal disutilities over against marginal utilities. The conclusions were usually optimistic. Seager believed in progress and believed that, under the going system, it was being achieved. He felt, for instance, that capital goods were multiplying more rapidly than population and that this would tend to raise standards of living. He did not believe, however, that the possibilities of progress which inhere in the system insure automatic betterment. Groups of interested people, with journals and propaganda, need to be vigilant in the public interest. This duty of the good citizen, as Seager saw it, was best exemplified in his own career. He never became aware of a duty that he did not forthwith perform. In his posthumous *Labor and Other Economic Essays* his program is outlined: "The two great objects to be aimed at are: I. To protect wage-earners in the continued enjoyment of standards of living to which they are already accustomed. II. To assist them to attain to higher standards of living" (p. 131). The contingencies which were the principal threats to existing standards were "(1) industrial accidents, (2) illness, (3) invalidity and old age, (4) premature death, (5) unemployment" (*Ibid.*). All these, Seager felt, were legitimate objects of collective action. As for raising standards, this was largely dependent on industrial advance and on better education.

To all persons of Seager's generation the rather sudden rise of a complete alternative system in Russia offered a shock to which adjustment was necessarily slow. Because everything there was so antithetical to the system to which so many theoretical hostages had been given, the immediate impulse was to belittle Soviet accomplishments. Seager was exposed to the full force of the new ideas. Gradually they gained weight in his mind until at last his essential honesty compelled, not acceptance, but exploration. In 1930, with a group of companions, he undertook a journey to the scene of these new economic adventures, in the midst of which he was taken ill. He died in Kiev of pneumonia, Aug. 23, 1930. He was thus lost to the world at the close of an old period and the beginning of a new one. His identification with the economy of the opening decades of the nineteenth century was a fortuitous one, but his progress into the new years cannot be said to have fairly started. He remains an economist of *laissez-faire,* of more than usual significance in foreshadowing the ameliorative program which so soon became a center of interest.

[S. M. Lindsay, in *Columbia Univ. Quart.*, Feb. 1930, pp. 228–431; *Am. Economic Rev.*, Dec. 1930, pp. 794–97; *Pol. Science Quart.*, Mar. 1931, pp. 107–08; "Introduction" by W. C. Mitchell to *Labor and Other Economic Essays* (1931); *Who's Who in Am.*, 1930–31; obituary in *N. Y. Times*, Aug. 24, 1930.]

R. G. T.

SEALSFIELD, CHARLES (Mar. 3, 1793– May 26, 1864), novelist, wrote under this name consistently after 1845. His real name was Karl Anton Postl, and he was born in Poppitz, Moravia, the eldest child of Anton and Juliane (Rabel) Postl. His father was the justice of the village. Destined for service in the church, Karl attended the *Untergymnasium* at Znaim from 1802 to 1807, and in 1808, entered the college of the *Kreuzherrenstift* in Prague, five years later becoming a novice in the monastery. After a few years of monastic life the impetuous and somewhat eccentric young monk, chafing under the Metternich system, sought freedom in flight. All efforts to find him on the part of the police of Prague and Vienna were ineffectual; the fugitive monk, Karl Postl, had vanished forever. In the fall of 1823, however, one Charles Sealsfield appeared in New Orleans. He traveled through the Southern states, through the Mexican province of Texas, and probably also in Mexico, observing with the eye of the artist, the historian, and the ethnographer. In 1824 he came to Kittanning on the Alleghany, near Pittsburgh, where he remained until late in 1825. He returned once more to New Orleans in 1826 and in August sailed thence for Havre.

In 1827 the well-known firm of J. G. Cotta of Stuttgart published the two volumes of *Die Vereinigten Staaten von Nordamerika, nach ihrem Politischen, Religiösen, und Gesellschaftlichen Verhältnisse Betrachtet, by Charles Sidons,* a pseudonym which Sealsfield never used again. In 1828 this work appeared anonymously in English translation in two parts: *The United States as They Are,* and *The Americans as They Are; Described in a Tour through the Valley of the Mississippi. By the Author of Austria as it is.* Before the second part appeared, Sealsfield had already published his vitriolic denouncement of the Metternich régime in *Austria as it is; or Sketches of Continental Courts, By an Eye Witness.* The sale of this book was forbidden in Germany and Austria. In June 1827 Sealsfield returned to America and resided for a time in Philadelphia as correspondent for Cotta's German journals, but he soon returned to his former home at Kittanning, Pa., where he wrote the first of his novels, *Tokeah; or the White Rose,* published in 1828 in two volumes. This novel, which championed the cause of the American Indian, was later rewritten and appeared in German as *Der Legitime und die Republikaner* (3 vols., 1833). In 1828 Sealsfield returned once more to the Southwest and to Mexico, and apparently entered upon various business enterprises. He was active as a journalist from 1829 until 1832, but retired in the latter year to Switzerland where he continued to reside save for return visits to the land of his adoption in 1837, 1850, and 1853.

It was during his sojourn in America that Sealsfield first conceived those plans by which he created a new type of fiction, the ethnographical novel. Instead of concentrating on a single character, he desired to operate with a whole people as his hero. Its social, political and religious life, the clash and conflict of the various cultures and nationalities represented, were all to be depicted. "To transfuse the freshly pulsating blood of the transatlantic Republic into the senile veins of the Old World, to acquaint his countrymen with the spirit of true liberty he considered his sacred duty, a duty which he felt obliged to take upon himself as a mission entrusted to him by a higher power" (see Smolle, *post*, p. 18). The period of Sealsfield's greatest literary activity falls between the years 1834 and 1843. *Der Virey und die Aristokraten; oder Mexiko im Jahre 1812,* in three volumes, appeared in 1834; *Lebensbilder aus der Westlichen Hemisphäre,* five volumes, in 1846; *Morton oder die Grosse Tour,* in 1835; *Die Deutschamerikanischen Wahlverwandtschaften,* four volumes, 1839–40; *Das Cajütenbuch, oder Nationale Charakteristiken,* two volumes, 1841; and *Süden und Norden,* three volumes, 1842–43. All of these novels dealt with the people of the United States and of Mexico. They were widely read and brought fame and fortune to their author, who came to be called the "Great Unknown." Sealsfield continued his anonymity until 1845, when, upon the insistence of his publishers, his complete works were published in fifteen volumes, 1845–47, under the name of Charles Sealsfield. In 1858 he bought a small estate near Solothurn, Switzerland, and spent his remaining years there in great seclusion. He had become a citizen of the United States and insisted upon remaining so during the years of his residence in Europe. Only upon the death of the bachelor recluse of Solothurn, through a provision in his will, was it finally revealed to the world that Charles Sealsfield and the fugitive monk, Karl Postl, were one and the same.

[Franz Brümmer, article in *Allgemeine Deutsche Biog.,* vol. XXXIII (1891); Leo Smolle, *Charles Sealsfield* (Vienna, 1875); A. B. Faust, *Charles Sealsfield* (dissertation, Johns Hopkins University, 1892), and *Charles Sealsfield . . . Der Dichter Beider Hemisphären* (1897); B. A. Uhlendorf, *Charles Sealsfield–Ethnic Elements and National Problems in his Works* (1922); Emil Soffé, *Charles Sealsfield* (Brünn, 1922); Milosch Djordjewitsch, *Charles Sealsfields Auffassung des Amerikanertums und seine literarhistorische Stellung* (Weimar, 1931); *Times* (London), June 6, 1864.]

P. A. B.

SEAMAN, ELIZABETH COCHRANE (May 5, 1867–Jan. 27, 1922), journalist, known as Nellie Bly, was born at Cochran Mills, Armstrong County, Pa. She was educated at home until 1880 when she was sent to school at Indiana, Pa. About 1881 she moved with her family to Pittsburgh, where she began her journalistic career. Having read in the *Pittsburg Dispatch* an article on "What Girls Are Good For," she wrote an angry letter to the editor, who, though he declined to print it, was fascinated by her power of vehement expression. She joined the staff of the *Dispatch,* wrote a series of articles on the conditions of working girls in Pittsburgh, and later became society editor with charge of the drama and art departments. Her pseudonym of Nellie Bly was given her by the managing editor, George A. Madden, who took the name from a popular song of Stephen Collins Foster [*q.v.*]. In 1887, accompanied by her mother, she spent several months in Mexico and produced a series of articles that were published in the *Dispatch*; they were later collected under the title of *Six Months in Mexico* (1888), where she reports that Joaquin Miller [*q.v.*], having met her in Mexico City and learned her story, said, "Little Nell, you are a second Columbus." Returning from Mexico, she found Pittsburgh too limited a field for her abilities and went to New York, where she joined the staff of the *World.* On Sept. 22, 1888, she was asked by the *World* to have herself committed to the insane ward at Blackwell's Island to investigate conditions there. She gained admittance and was declared insane by six doctors; after ten days her release was secured, and her reports resulted in an investigation by the grand jury, though hers was a less successful exposure than that of the Bloomingdale (N. Y.) Asylum made by James Julius Chambers [*q.v.*] in 1872 for the *New York Tribune.* She recounted her experiences in *Ten Days in a Mad-House* (copyright 1887). In 1889 she published *The Mystery of Central Park,* an ephemeral story of little merit that had appeared in the *World.* In the fall of 1889 G. W. Turner conceived the idea of sending her around the world in less than the eighty days of Jules Verne's Phileas Fogg, the exploit for which she is best known. She began her famous tour from New York on Nov. 14 and completed it the following Jan. 25, having circled the world in seventy-two days, six hours, and eleven minutes, with a stop at Amiens, France, to interview Jules Verne. The publication of *Nelly Bly's Book: Around the World in Seventy-two Days* (1890) marked the height of her journalistic career. In 1895 she married Robert

L. Seaman, an aged and wealthy Brooklyn man-ufacturer. When he died in 1904 she took over the management of his properties, which in-cluded the Ironclad Manufacturing Co., makers of enamelled iron ware, and the American Steel Barrel Co. The dishonesty and insubordination of employees, however, brought about protracted litigation from which she emerged successful but impoverished. Once more she turned to news-paper work but her later career was uneventful. She was on the staff of the *New York Journal* when she died in New York City in 1922.

[Nellie Bly's best known exploits are described in her *Ten Days in a Mad-House* (copr. 1887) and *Nelly Bly's Book: Around the World in Seventy-two Days* (1890). See also *A Woman of the Century* (1893), ed. by Frances E. Willard and Mary A. Livermore; *World* (N. Y.), *N. Y. Times, N. Y. Evening Jour., Pittsburg Dispatch,* Jan. 28, 1922.]   F. M.

SEARING, LAURA CATHERINE RED-DEN (Feb. 9, 1840–Aug. 10, 1923), poet and journalist, was born in Somerset County, Md., daughter of Wilhelmine (Waller) and Littleton James D. Redden. In her early life, her parents moved to St. Louis, Mo. Until she was about eleven she was unusually healthy; then, after a serious illness, she suddenly became completely deaf and was unable to speak except with great effort and in a sepulchral tone. Her sensitive-ness soon led to the development of an impedi-ment in her speech, so that she depended entirely upon writing for conversation except with those who understood the manual alphabet, which she learned while attending the Missouri Institution for Deaf Mutes at St. Louis. She began her literary career in 1859 with editorial work on a religious paper published in St. Louis and with miscellaneous articles and poems contributed to the *St. Louis Republican.* Writing under the pseudonym Howard Glyndon, she expressed such intense patriotism and devotion to the Union cause that her articles were widely copied, and she was sent to Washington as correspondent for the *Republican* during the Civil War. Her first two books were published while she was in the capital: *Notable Men in "the House"* (1862), a series of informal sketches, some by other writers, and *Idyls of Battle* (1864), a volume of war poems. One of the poems, "Belle Missouri," was adopted as the war song of the loyalists of Missouri.

From February 1865 to the close of 1868 she was in Europe, writing articles for the *St. Louis Republican,* the *New York Times,* and the *New York Sun,* and studying languages. Upon her return to New York, she severed her connection with the *Times* but wrote for the *New York Eve-ning Mail* as a staff member and for the *New*

York Tribune. Her poems continued to appear in *Harper's Monthly* and *Harper's Weekly,* the *Atlantic Monthly, Putnam's Magazine, Galaxy, Arena,* and the *Alaska-Yukon Magazine.* Her most successful volume of verse, *Sounds from Secret Chambers,* was published in 1873. About 1871 she learned of the new Clarke school for articulation at Northampton, Mass. There, af-ter long patient effort under the guidance of Alexander Graham Bell [*q.v.*], she learned the control of pitch, tone, and enunciation through feeling, so that she could speak freely and natu-rally. Lip-reading she never mastered, being forced to discontinue study of it under Zerah C. Whipple in Mystic, Conn., where she had gone for her health, seriously impaired now by the double strain of all her study and her literary engagements. In 1876 she was married at Mys-tic, Conn., to Edward W. Searing, a New York attorney who was a native of Sherwood, N. Y., where they made their home. After 1886 she made her permanent home in Santa Cruz, Cal. For some years before her death she was a semi-invalid, living at the San Mateo home of her only child, writing nothing after 1908, talking little, and seeing but few of her friends. She was buried in Holy Cross Cemetery, San Mateo.

As a poet she retained her memory of sounds and her sense of rhythm, and experimented with many rhymes and meters; contemporary critics commented upon her almost invariable accuracy in both. Of "The Hills of Santa Cruz" in the volume *El Dorado* (1897) her friend Whittier said, "It is fine in conception and felicitous in execution." Religious faith, courage in spite of disillusionment and difficulties, and devotion to a cause, she expressed with a simple sincerity. She had a close familiarity with the Bible and with the great English and American poets. Her newspaper articles dealt in an easy, informal style with people, politics, places, books, and art. In 1921 her daughter published a complete edi-tion of her poems, *Echoes of Other Days.*

[Laura C. R. Searing, *Echoes of Other Days* (1921), with preface by Elsa S. McGinn, contains the best per-sonal information; see also *Who's Who in America,* 1914–15; G. C. Perine, *Poets and Verse Writers of Md.* (n.d.); *Volta Rev.,* Feb. 1923; obituaries in *News* (San Mateo), Aug. 10, 1923; *Bulletin* and *Times* (San Fran-cisco), *San Francisco Chronicle,* Aug. 11, 1923.]
                                                    R. W. B.
                                                    J. F. M.

SEARLE, ARTHUR (Oct. 21, 1837–Oct. 23, 1920), astronomer, was born in London, England, the eldest son of Thomas and Anne (Noble) Searle. His mother, who came from Derby, England, was of English birth and ancestry, but his father, although a partner in a firm of London bankers, was a citizen of the

United States and a descendant of Thomas Dudley, second governor of the colony of Massachusetts Bay. In 1840 Thomas Searle returned to America with his wife and two sons. Within the next two years the parents died, leaving the children to the care of relatives in Brookline, Mass. Searle received his early education in private schools in Brookline and Roxbury and in the Brookline high school; he graduated from Harvard College in 1856, the second scholar in his class. Ancient and modern languages, philosophy, music, mathematics, and the sciences all interested him; his first article, published in the *Harvard Magazine* of April 1855, was on "The Plurality of Worlds," though at that time he had no thought of making astronomy a profession. After his graduation he tried teaching, farming, statistical work, and work in a broker's office; he once joined a project to raise sheep in California, and later he taught English and logic for a term at the University of the Pacific, Santa Clara, Cal.

In 1868 he took a position resigned by his brother as computer and observer at the Harvard Observatory, looking upon it merely as a temporary occupation. To his surprise he found that the work suited him very well, for to his clear, active mind accuracy and precision were second nature. He was appointed assistant in 1869, assistant professor in 1883, Phillips Professor of Astronomy in 1887, and professor emeritus in 1912. After the death of Prof. Joseph Winlock [*q.v.*] in 1875, Searle was acting director of the observatory until Edward Charles Pickering [*q.v.*] became director in 1877. Besides his observatory work he taught astronomy at Radcliffe from 1891 to 1912. He was married Jan. 1, 1873, to Emma Wesselhoeft (d. Dec. 19, 1914), daughter of Dr. Robert Wesselhoeft of Boston and Brattleboro, Vt., by whom he had two daughters. His astronomical work included micrometric and photometric observations of stars, planets, asteroids, and comets, a careful investigation of the zodiacal light and the gegenschein, and the laborious observations and reductions necessary for the Astronomische Gesellschaft catalogue of 8337 stars between 9° 50′ and 14° 10′ south declination. He collected and published the meteorological observations made at the Harvard Observatory from 1840 to 1888 (*Annals of the Astronomical Observatory of Harvard College,* vol. XIX, pt. 1, 1889), and he wrote a history of the observatory from 1855 to 1876 (*Ibid.,* vol. VIII, 1876). A skilful mathematician, for over forty years he was the chief consultant in the mathematical discussions of all investigations of the observatory. Besides

various articles in periodicals, he published *Outlines of Astronomy* (1874).

Although he had a brilliant career as an astronomer he would probably have made an equal success in almost any other field. As a diversion he wrote verse both in Latin and English. He also wrote on mathematical and philosophical subjects; his *Essays I–XXX* (1910) contains a discussion of space and time that is particularly interesting in the light of the theory of relativity. His extremely retiring disposition probably accounts for his not accepting the invitation of Benjamin Apthorp Gould [*q.v.*] in 1869 to go to Córdoba, Argentina, as his assistant. From youth he had not cared for even the ordinary pleasures of society; yet he had warm friends and many acquaintances, and all who knew him well were delighted with his conversational powers and his keen sense of humor. He died in Cambridge, Mass., survived by his daughters.

[See *Who's Who in America,* 1920–21; *Memorial of the Harvard Coll. Class of 1856* (1906); Jeremiah Smith, in *Harvard Grads. Mag.,* Mar. 1921; Margaret Harwood, in *Popular Astronomy,* Aug.–Sept. 1921; E. S. King, in *Proc. Am. Acad. Arts and Sci.,* vol. LVII (1922); S. I. Bailey, *Hist. and Work of Harvard Observatory, 1839 to 1927* (1931); *Boston Transcript,* Oct. 25, 1920. Many of Searle's articles are listed in *Cat. of Sci. Papers, Fourth Ser., 1884–1900,* vol. XVIII (1923), compiled by the Royal Soc. of London.]

M. H.

SEARLE, JAMES (1733–Aug. 7, 1797), merchant and member of the Continental Congress, was born probably in New York City, the youngest child of John and Catherine (Pintard) Searle. His fluent literary style and frequent use of Latin phrases in correspondence suggest that he had received considerable schooling before he went to join his brother John in Madeira, where first as employee and later as a member of John Searle & Company he remained sixteen years. Married in 1762 to Ann (or Nancy) Smith of Waterford, England, he removed soon afterward to Philadelphia, where he acted as agent for his brother while engaging in commercial ventures of his own which brought him prosperity and standing among the merchants of that city. From the beginning of the difficulties with Great Britain, he was actively patriotic, signing the Philadelphia non-importation agreement of 1765 and participating in all later mercantile protests. Returning in November 1775 from a visit to England, he took part in the war preparations, becoming a lieutenant-colonel of Pennsylvania militia, one of the managers of the United States lottery, and, in 1778, a member of the Naval Board. He was constantly a supporter of the attempts of the Continental Congress to raise funds and his wife was a leader among the patriotic ladies of Philadelphia.

In November 1778, Searle was elected to the Continental Congress. He was an active member, serving on many committees, including those on the marine and on commerce and the special committee to investigate foreign affairs and the conduct of the American commissioners abroad. In the faction-ridden Congress he allied himself with the radical Lee-Adams group, seconding James Lovell and Richard Henry Lee [qq.v.] in their hostility to Silas Deane [q.v.] and Beaumarchais. The radicals, trusting him, nominated him for secretary to the embassy to Spain, September 1779, but his name was withdrawn. When Pennsylvania voted to send a special envoy abroad, Searle was appointed, July 1780, as its agent "to such countries or states as you shall Judge most likely to favour your views" to "negotiate with any publick bodies, private companies, or Individuals" (*Pennsylvania Archives*, 4 ser. III, 1900, p. 770), for a loan of £200,000, to be expended largely in Europe for military supplies. Departing immediately for Paris, Searle satisfied himself that Franklin, being the "declared Enemy of private state loans" (Searle to Reed, Feb. 14, 1781, Joseph Reed Papers, *post*) would do nothing to aid him, and, armed with a letter from Reed to John Adams and with introductions to business houses, he proceeded to Amsterdam, where he soon realized that Adams' pessimism about securing money for America was justified. He returned to France, consulted with the Farmers General and the Company of Lyons, but could secure aid only on terms he was unable to meet. Discouraged, he wrote to Joseph Reed that the possibility of borrowing money for a state was even less than for the Continental Congress and that certain men, primarily Deane and Edward Bancroft [q.v.], were doing everything possible to prevent European aid to America. After one more futile journey into Holland, he gladly accepted notice that Pennsylvania had ordered his recall, no discredit for his failure being attached.

Receiving also news that his wife had died (1781) and that much of his fortune had been dissipated through unwise moves made by his partners during the war, he returned to the United States in considerable despondency to face several unprosperous years in New York and New Jersey. John Searle & Company, with thousands of pounds in uncollectable American debts, was badly crippled and Searle's difficulties were increased through his inability to secure full payment from Pennsylvania for his services abroad. In 1787 he expected bankruptcy, but he received in 1788 an appointment as agent for a Madeira firm with a fixed salary and additional

commissions, reëstablished himself in Philadelphia, and spent his remaining years in comfort, if not in the wealth of his pre-Revolutionary days. He was married a second time, in 1785, to Isabella West of Monmouth County, N. J., and by this marriage had several children.

[Joseph Reed Papers in N. Y. Hist. Soc.; manuscript collections of the Pa. Hist. Soc.; W. B. Reed, *Life and Correspondence of Joseph Reed* (2 vols., 1847); E. C. Burnett, *Letters of Members of the Continental Cong.*, vols. I–VII (1921–34); *Pa. Archives*, vols. VIII–IX (1853–54); "The Deane Papers," *N. Y. Hist. Soc. Colls.*, Pub. Fund Ser., vols. XXII–XXIII (1890–91); *Pa. Mag. of Hist. and Biog.*, July 1915; Henry Simpson, *The Lives of Eminent Philadelphians* (1859); *Claypoole's Am. Daily Advertiser* (Phila.), Aug. 8, 1797.]   M. E. L.

SEARLE, JOHN PRESTON (Sept. 12, 1854–July 26, 1922), clergyman of the Reformed Church in America, professor of theology, was born at Schuylerville, N. Y., the son of Rev. Samuel Tomb and Cornelia Fonda (Southworth) Searle. He was of a family that furnished the ministry with at least one member in every generation from the coming of Rev. William Searle of Branford, England, to America in 1692. His grandfather, Jeremiah Searle, his grandmother's father, Jacob Tomb, and two of his father's brothers were clergymen. The family tradition and his home life naturally turned John Preston Searle toward the same calling. He was graduated from Rutgers College in 1875 with honors and from the New Brunswick Theological Seminary in 1878. Entering the service of the Reformed (Dutch) Church in America, to which, in New York State, his grandfather had transferred the family connection from the Congregational Church of New England, he was licensed by the Classis of Passaic and ordained by the Classis of New Brunswick. That same year, 1878, he became pastor of the church in Griggstown, N. J., remaining as such for three years. His intellectual gifts and preaching ability were early recognized, and in 1881 he was called to the large and influential First Church of Raritan, Somerville, N. J., where he became greatly honored as a preacher and greatly beloved as a pastor.

His ability and practical interest in affairs soon brought him to the general knowledge of the denomination and its institutions. In 1893 the General Synod chose him professor of didactic and polemic theology, later systematic theology, in the New Brunswick Theological Seminary. He filled this office until his death nearly thirty years later. He was insistent on a sound theology and was well furnished with the learning related to it. As a teacher and as a man he won the confidence and affection of the students and continued to be their helper and adviser after their graduation. Bringing into the life and management of the Seminary his aptness for affairs, he became president of the faculty in 1902, and chairman of the official committee on grounds and buildings, holding these positions with his professorship to the end. He was also an influential member of allied institutions and boards. From 1898 he was one of the trustees of Rutgers College and from 1906 he was secretary of the board. He was a member of the Board of Foreign Missions of the Reformed Church from 1894 and vice-president of it from 1896. In 1917 he was chosen president of the General Synod of the Church. He was one of the founders of the Council of Reformed and Presbyterian Churches and at one time its president.

His publications were chiefly sermons, addresses on special occasions, and contributions to papers and periodicals. He prepared for his students an "Outline Sketch of Theological Encyclopedia" (1907) and was incessantly useful in the drawing up of thorough and important reports for the committees of official bodies to which he belonged. In addition to intellectual clearness he exhibited a singularly spiritual quality in his preaching and conduct of worship, which was made the more appealing by his unusually rich and sympathetic voice. On Dec. 12, 1882, he was married to Susan Bovey, of Cherokee, Iowa, by whom he had four children.

[C. E. E. Corwin, *A Manual of the Reformed Church in America* (1922); *The Acts and Proceedings . . . of the General Synod of the Reformed Church in America, June 1923*; *Biog. Record, Theological Sem. New Brunswick, 1784–1934* (1934); *Who's Who in America, 1922–23*; *N. Y. Times,* July 28, 1922.]   W. H. S. D.

SEARS, BARNAS (Nov. 19, 1802–July 6, 1880), Baptist clergyman, educator, was a descendant of Richard Sears who emigrated from England to Plymouth, Mass., sometime before 1633, later moving to Marblehead, and from there to Yarmouth. The son of Paul and Rachel (Granger) Sears, Barnas was born and grew up on his father's farm at Sandisfield, Berkshire County, Mass., one of ten children. By building stone walls in the summer and teaching in the winter he secured funds for his education, and was able, after a period in the University Grammar School, Providence, to enter the class of 1825 at Brown University. After graduation he spent two years at Newton (Mass.) Theological Institution, and on July 11, 1827, was ordained pastor of the First Baptist Church, Hartford, Conn. A bronchial affection led him to resign in the spring of 1829, and in the fall he became professor of languages in Hamilton (N. Y.)

Literary and Theological Institution (now Colgate University). On July 6, 1830, he married Elizabeth Griggs Corey of Brookline, Mass.; five children were born to them. From 1833 to 1835 he studied in Germany and France, returning to Hamilton to occupy the chair of Biblical theology. In less than a year, however, he was called to Newton Theological Institution to be professor of Christian theology.

He was now fully launched on an educational career, which, marked by considerable variety, was to continue until his death. He taught at Newton from 1836 to 1848, and from 1839 was president of the institution. During this period he was for a time, 1838–41, editor of the *Christian Review,* to which, as well as to the *Bibliotheca Sacra,* he contributed important articles. He also published *A Grammar of the German Language* (1842), based upon C. H. F. Bialloblotzky's eighth English edition of Georg Heinrich Noehden's work; *The Ciceronian: or the Prussian Method of Teaching the Elements of the Latin Language* (1844); and was the principal author of *Classical Studies: Essays on Ancient Literature and Art* (1843), his collaborators being Bela B. Edwards and Cornelius C. Felton [*qq.v.*]. In 1848 he entered the field of public-school education, succeeding Horace Mann [*q.v.*] as secretary of the Massachusetts Board of Education. This position he held for seven years, during which time, not only by his administrative ability but also by his imperturbable temper and genial personality, he won favor for the reforms Mann had initiated and gave them permanence. Called to the presidency of Brown University in 1855, he again succeeded a notable educator, Francis Wayland [*q.v.*]. The administration of President Sears, covering a period of twelve years, though disturbed by conditions incident to the Civil War, was one of peace and quiet, if not notable progress. He brought about modifications in the educational system introduced by Wayland, which in some respects was not working well; the funds of the University were augmented; salaries and scholarships were increased; and a chemical laboratory was built. To his administrative duties were joined those of the professorship of moral philosophy. His personal characteristics made him extremely popular with the students.

In 1867 George Peabody [*q.v.*] established the Peabody Education Fund for the promotion of education in the South. The chairman of the trustees, Robert C. Winthrop [*q.v.*], asked Sears to draw up a statement of his views as to how the Fund should be administered. The outline which he presented so impressed the trustees that they invited him to become general agent. The possibilities of the work appealed to him, and though he was happy in his position at Brown, his old bronchial trouble had returned and he welcomed the chance to live in the South. Accordingly, he accepted the invitation and in September 1867 moved to Staunton, Va. His inauguration of the work for which the Fund was devised was perhaps the most important achievement of his career. The specific recommendations regarding the ends to be sought and the methods to be employed contained in his first report became the stereotyped policy of the trustees. In carrying it out Sears met a difficult and delicate situation with a patience, tact, and wisdom that won confidence and support in the South and ensured success. To the heavy demands of his office he devoted himself vigorously almost up to the time of his death, which occurred at Saratoga, N. Y.; he was buried in Walnut Street Cemetery, Brookline, Mass.

In addition to the publications already mentioned, Sears was the author of *The Life of Luther* (1850) and *Objections to Public Schools Considered* (1875). He also edited (1873) P. M. Roget's *Thesaurus of English Words and Phrases.* He was not an original thinker but his learning was varied and sound; although he was not one to blaze new trails, his dignity and courtesy, his emotional stability, his sagacity and determination, gave him favor with men, and made him an effective administrator.

[S. P. May, *The Descendants of Richard Sares (Sears) of Yarmouth* (1890); Alvah Hovey, *Barnas Sears* (copr. 1902); W. C. Bronson, *The Hist. of Brown Univ.* (1914); J. L. M. Curry, *A Brief Sketch of George Peabody and a Hist. of the Peabody Education Fund Through Thirty Years* (1898); reports of the Mass. Board of Education, 1848–55; *Proceedings of the Trustees of the Peabody Education Fund,* vol. I (1875), vol. II (1881); *Boston Transcript,* July 7, 1880].
H. E. S.

SEARS, EDMUND HAMILTON (Apr. 6, 1810–Jan. 16, 1876), Unitarian clergyman, author, was born in Sandisfield, Berkshire County, Mass., a descendant of Richard Sears who came to Plymouth about 1630, and the son of Joseph and Lucy (Smith) Sears. His father, a landholder and farmer, without education himself, had a marked fondness for books and an instinctive liking for poetry. "My earliest recollections," says the son, "are associated with his reading or rather chanting of poetry. . . . He was a great admirer of Pope's Iliad and would read it by the hour" (Robbins, *post,* pp. 224–25). Hard work and long hours on the farm together with the scarcity of money made education for Edmund a casual and limited affair. He was abnormally shy and timid and all his life shrank

from possibility of criticism. When he was ten he made his first venture in poetry and was only twelve when he wrote and delivered a full-sized discourse "to a full assembly of alder-bushes." At this early age he produced sermons "and lyrics without number." When he was sixteen opportunity came for him to enter Westfield Academy, which he attended for about nine months. In 1831 he entered Union College, Schenectady, N. Y., and by the exercise of rigid economy was able to complete the course, graduating in 1834. His marked literary ability won him an editorial position on the college paper, the *Parthenon,* and a prize for poetry he had written.

After graduating he read law but soon accepted an opportunity to teach in the academy at Brattleboro, Vt. While here he studied theology under the direction of the Rev. Addison Brown and later entered the Harvard Divinity School. Graduating therefrom in 1837, he received an appointment as missionary of the American Unitarian Association and served for the most part at Toledo, Ohio. On his return East he was invited to become minister of the Unitarian Church in Wayland, Mass., where he was ordained on Feb. 20, 1839. On Nov. 7 of that year he married Ellen Bacon of Barnstable, Mass., by whom he had three sons and a daughter. Called to the Unitarian Church in Lancaster, he was installed there Dec. 23, 1840. He was frail in body and seven years later was obliged to relinquish his pastorate, and retire to a small farm in the town of Wayland. Having recovered much of his strength, he yielded to the importunities of his friends in the Wayland Church and again (1848) became their minister, serving in that capacity for seventeen years. In 1866 the church at Weston, Mass., invited him to its pulpit and he accepted. A fall from a tree in 1874 shattered his strength beyond recovery, and he died at his home in Weston some two years later.

Sears was much sought after by larger churches than those he served, but the narrow limits of his physical strength, the exceeding frailty of his voice, and his instinctive bashfulness made him prefer the quieter and more secluded places. Through his writings, however, he reached a large circle. From 1859 to 1871 he served as one of the editors of the *Monthly Religious Magazine.* His writings were marked by a rare mysticism and devotional spirit particularly satisfying to many at that time. Most notable of his books was *The Fourth Gospel, the Heart of Christ* (1872). Though largely forgotten now, it was forceful and important enough in its day to be referred to as "the most unique and precious contribution to Christian literature" (Peabody, *post,* p. 203). His *Regeneration* (1853) and *Athanasia; or Foregleams of Immortality* (1858) were widely read. His interest in family history and genealogy led him to publish in 1857 *Pictures of the Olden Time as Shown in the Fortunes of a Family of Pilgrims,* dealing with his ancestors, and *Genealogies and Biographical Sketches of the Ancestry and Descendants of Richard Sears* (1857). Though his sermons and other prose writings are now quite forgotten, his hymns remain a living force in Christian worship. Two of them at least, "Calm on the listening ear of night" and "It came upon a midnight clear," are among the best known and most beloved in Protestant hymnals.

[*In Memoriam: Edmund Hamilton Sears . . . Ellen Bacon Sears . . . Katharine Sears* (1898); S. A. Eliot, *Heralds of a Liberal Faith* (1910), vol. III; R. C. Winthrop and A. P. Peabody in *Proc. Mass. Hist. Soc.,* vol. XIV (1876); Chandler Robbins, "Memoir of Rev. Edmund Hamilton Sears," *Ibid.,* vol. XVIII (1881); *Unitarian Rev.,* Feb. 1876; *Christian Reg.,* Jan. 22, 29, 1876; *The Hist. of the Church in Weston* (1900); *Boston Daily Advertiser,* Jan. 18, 1876.]   C.G.

SEARS, ISAAC (*c.* July 1, 1730–Oct. 28, 1786), Revolutionary leader, was born at West Brewster, Mass., and christened at Harwich, July 12, 1730. He was a son of Joshua and Mary (Thacher) Sears, and a descendant of Richard Sears who emigrated from England to Plymouth, Mass., about 1630. His father moved to Norwich, Conn., about 1734. At twenty-two Isaac was commanding a sloop trading between New York and Canada; and from then until his death he was nearly always either commander or part owner of a merchantman or a privateer. He married Sarah Drake, and had eleven children.

While commanding privateers during the French and Indian War he won a reputation for bravery which made him a recognized leader among the sailors and petty artisans of the New York waterfront. When the Stamp Act was passed, he became a leader of the resistance in New York City and with John Lamb [*q.v.*] and Joseph Allicocke projected a continental military union of the Sons of Liberty. During the next decade, Sears was at the head of nearly every demonstration of mob violence in New York City, his success as a leader of the populace winning him the appellation "King," and membership on most of the important patriotic committees as well as a seat in the first Provincial Congress. In 1774 he led the Sons of Liberty in returning the first tea ship and dumping the cargo of the second into the river. With Alexander McDougall [*q.v.*], another radical

member of the Committee of Fifty-one, he wrote a letter to the Boston Committee of Correspondence, May 15, 1774 (printed in Stokes, *post,* IV, 852–53), proposing a meeting of delegates from the principal towns. While this action was disclaimed by the New York Committee, it was practically ratified by the Committee's letter of May 23, recommending the holding of a general congress.

When arrested for his anti-British activities, Apr. 15, 1775, Sears was rescued at the prison door by his admirers and paraded through the streets like a great hero. Upon the arrival in New York, Apr. 23, 1775, of the news of Lexington and Concord, he and 360 followers put to flight the Loyalist leaders and officials, seized a supply of arms from the arsenal and the keys of the Custom House, and began regular military exercises. Thereafter, although nominally governed by various committees and congresses, until Washington's army arrived the city was virtually under the dictatorship of Sears and his comrades. Late in 1775 he removed to New Haven, but in November led a raid into New York, burning a naval supply ship, threatening to seize the provincial records (removed at once by order of Governor Tryon to the warship in which he had taken refuge), imprisoning the Rev. Samuel Seabury [*q.v.*] and other Westchester Loyalists, and destroying the New York shop of the Loyalist printer James Rivington [*q.v.*]. This raid was condemned by the Revolutionary Committee of New York City, the Provincial Congress, and the New York delegation to the Continental Congress, but public opinion was elated by the raiders' display of patriotic spirit. In January 1776 General Lee commissioned Sears to administer the oath of allegiance to Loyalists on Long Island, to recruit volunteers in Connecticut, and to capture British supplies for the colonial forces.

During 1777–83, Sears resided in Boston, promoting privateering and otherwise endeavoring to aid the American cause. After the war, he resumed his general merchandise business in New York. With Alexander McDougall and Marinus Willett [*q.v.*], he waited upon Rivington, Dec. 31, 1783, and silenced his paper forever. In 1784 and 1786 he was elected to the state Assembly. He was made a trustee and a vestryman (1784–86) of Trinity Church, and in 1784 vice-president of the reorganized Chamber of Commerce of the State of New York. On Feb. 4, 1786, with Samuel Shaw [*q.v.*] and Thomas Randall, he sailed for China to promote a business venture but died of fever at Canton in October, and was buried on French Island, in Canton Harbor.

[Material on Sears is found in the Horatio Gates, Benedict Arnold, William Alexander (Lord Stirling), John Lamb, Alexander McDougall, and F. L. Hawks MSS., in the N. Y. Hist. Soc.; William Smith Papers, N. Y. Pub. Lib.; papers of the Earl of Dartmouth and the Public Record Office, in England. Published authorities include: S. P. May, *The Descendants of Richard Sares (Sears)* (1890); *The Journals of Major Samuel Shaw, with a Life of the Author by Josiah Quincy* (1847); I. N. P. Stokes, *The Iconography of Manhattan Island* (6 vols., 1922–28); I. Q. Leake, *Memoir of the Life and Times of Gen. John Lamb* (1850); C. L. Becker, *Hist. of Pol. Parties in the Province of N. Y. 1760–76* (1909); H. B. Dawson, *The Sons of Liberty in N. Y.* (1859) and *Westchester County, N. Y., during the Am. Rev.* (1886), which appears also in J. T. Scharf, *Hist. of Westchester County, N. Y.* (1886), vol. I; Peter Force, *Am. Archives*, 4 ser. (6 vols., 1837–46); J. A. Stevens, *Biog. Records of the N. Y. Chamber of Commerce* (1867); Thomas Jones, *Hist. of N. Y. during the Revolutionary War* (2 vols., 1879), ed. by E. F. De Lancey. Certain information has been supplied by M. J. Weig, Esq., who is preparing a dissertation (Univ. of Chicago), N. Y. and Mass. Mobs and Mob Leaders in the Prelude to the American Revolution.]　　　C. H. V.

SEARS, RICHARD WARREN (Dec. 7, 1863–Sept. 28, 1914), merchant, was born in Stewartville, Minn., the son of James Warren and Eliza A. (Benton) Sears, both of English ancestry. His father was a wagon maker who had built up a substantial fortune that he lost in a stock-farm venture when Richard was about fifteen. Two years later, after his father's death, the boy was working in the general offices of the Minneapolis and St. Louis Railway at Minneapolis and supporting his mother and sisters. Believing that he might earn more in a small town, he succeeded in having himself moved to Redwood Falls, Minn., where as station agent he did chores for his board and slept in the loft of the railroad station. He made profits for himself on the side by selling coal and lumber as well as by shipping venison, blueberries, and other commodities purchased from the Indians, and he was started on his way to fortune in 1886 when the town jeweler refused to accept a shipment of watches sent him by the wholesaler. No freight had been paid, and the watches remained in the railway station. Obtaining permission to dispose of them, Sears wrote letters describing his merchandise and offering it for sale at what must have seemed bargain prices. When the supply of watches was exhausted, he had a gratifying profit and a new idea for making money. Buying more watches, he began to advertise in a small way in the St. Paul newspapers; in a few months he abandoned railroading and late in 1886 established himself in the mail-order business in Minneapolis under the name of the R. W. Sears Watch Company.

By the end of a year he was advertising in periodicals of national circulation and had made enough money to move to Chicago, where he did business under the same name. As watches began to come back for adjustment and repair he hired as a watchmaker A. C. Roebuck. In 1889, feeling that he had made enough money to retire, he sold his business for $100,000 and went to Iowa to become a country banker. But banking was not exciting enough for his volatile temper. He was by nature a promoter, forever beset by new ideas (some of them far from practical), always dynamic, the "Barnum of merchandising" in his day. When he sold out in Chicago he had agreed not to go into the same business there for a period of three years; this did not prevent him, however, from returning to Minneapolis, summoning Roebuck, and establishing a mail-order business for the sale of watches and jewelry under the name of A. C. Roebuck & Company, which later became Sears, Roebuck & Company. In 1893 the company was moved to Chicago, where the business increased at a prodigious rate. The catalogue, originally a book of watches that listed some twenty-five items, grew in a few years to a thousand pages. In 1895 when Julius Rosenwald [*q.v.*], a Chicago clothing manufacturer, bought Roebuck's interest in the firm, sales were $500,000; by 1900 they were $11,000,000.

In addition to his duties as president, a position he held until 1909, Sears planned and actually wrote all the advertising, which amounted in 1896 to between fifty and sixty thousand dollars' worth of newspaper space a month. He experimented endlessly in other ways. He sold automobiles by mail, manufacturing a "horseless carriage" for the purpose, and in the early years of the company he started a chain of four or five food stores but this enterprise, like that of the automobile project, took valuable time from the more successful and rapidly growing mail-order business and was dropped. Although Rosenwald supplied the capital demanded by a rapidly growing business and provided the still more valuable administrative ability that could organize the enterprise and keep it functioning smoothly, it was "Dick" Sears's personality that permeated the organization in these early days and his generous spirit for the most part that created the good will which became the most valuable possession of the firm. On June 20, 1895, he had married Anna Lydia Meckstroth of Minneapolis; there were two sons and two daughters, all of whom survived him. After his retirement in 1909 he lived on his farm north of Chicago; he died in Waukesha, Wis.

[*Who's Who in America*, 1914–15; *The Book of Chicagoans* (2nd ed., 1911), vol. II; Robert Littell, "The Great Am. Salesman," *Fortune*, Feb. 1932; obituary in *Chicago Daily Tribune,* Sept. 29, 1914; unpublished material at Sears, Roebuck & Co., Chicago.]

E. A. D.

SEARS, ROBERT (June 28, 1810–Feb. 17, 1892), publisher and compiler, was born at St. John, New Brunswick, a son of Thatcher Sears and his second wife, Abigail (Spurr) Sears, and a descendant of Richard Sares or Sears who was in Plymouth, Mass., in 1633. His father, a furrier and hatter, was a Connecticut Loyalist who had emigrated from the United States to New Brunswick at the close of the Revolution with a group of his compatriots (Lorenzo Sabine, *Biographical Sketches of Loyalists of the American Revolution,* 1864, vol. II, pp. 272–73). The elder Sears died when Robert was nine years old, leaving several other minor children, and Robert's formal schooling was not long continued; he seems to have acquired a fair mastery of English after he entered on an apprenticeship in the printing trade. As soon as he reached his majority he found his way to New York City as a journeyman printer and there succeeded in maintaining himself by his trade, although seriously hampered by the recurring cholera epidemics of that period. In 1832 he married Harriet Howard Martin (d. 1881), by whom he had eight children, and set up a printing and publishing business of his own, but this first attempt was short-lived. However, he had formed an ambition to compile, publish, and market reference books bearing his own imprint, and in due time it came to fruitage. In his thirtieth year he brought out a three-volume work entitled *Pictorial Illustrations of the Bible* (1840–41), which he advertised throughout the United States and of which 25,000 sets were sold, a notable achievement for that date in America. Encouraged by this success the young publisher three years later announced *The Wonders of the World, in Nature, Art, and Mind* (1843), a popular illustrated treatise that was hailed by the *Southern Quarterly Review* of January, 1843, as neither strikingly original nor profound but as sound in structure and tendency. For this, as for his other publications, he employed the best available wood-engravers of the day to supply illustrations. He required so much of this work that he came to have distinction among the publishers of his time as a patron of the engraving art, a distinction possibly due less to the artistic value than to the relatively large number of the cuts that embellished the Sears books.

Sears was credited with at least one merit not generally conceded to the publishers of his day: he could write simple and graceful English.

This is especially to be noted in his *A New and Complete History of the Holy Bible* (1844), the text of which he composed himself (*Southern Quarterly Review,* October 1843). He was also one of the earliest of the New York publishers to make a serious effort to serve the nation as a whole, without regard to sectional differences. He built up a selling organization that seems to have been as efficient in the South and West as in the East. Between 1844 and 1849 he edited and published under various titles a magazine, finally known as the *New Pictorial Family Magazine,* that carried gazetteer material covering every state in the Union, with statistics kept up to date; this appealed with peculiar force to a shifting population eager to learn about new lands opening for settlement in the forties. In 1848 he condensed the gazetteer data and published it separately as *A New and Popular Pictorial Description of the United States.* He published several other digests of knowledge and *The Pictorial History of the American Revolution* (1845). His last important venture was a *Pictorial Bible* (1858) containing more than a thousand engravings. On the outbreak of the Civil War he retired and went to Canada, where he passed the rest of his life, dying at Toronto.

[S. P. May, *The Descendants of Richard Sares (Sears) of Yarmouth, Mass.* (1890); William Hunt, *Am. Biog. Panorama* (1849), with portrait; S. A. Allibone, *A Crit. Dict. of Eng. Lit.,* vol. II (1870); *N. Y. Daily Tribune,* Feb. 19, 21, 1892.]

W. B. S.

SEATON, WILLIAM WINSTON (Jan. 11, 1785–June 16, 1866), journalist, was born at the stately homestead "Chelsea" in King William County, Va., the son of Augustine and Mary (Winston) Seaton. The Seatons, whose forefather, Henry, settled in Gloucester County, Va., in 1690, were of Scottish, and the Winstons of English, ancestry; both were of the Virginia gentry. First trained by tutors, William entered Ogilvie's academy in Richmond, where he acquired a taste for drama, literature, art, and journalism. At eighteen, having already gained a practical knowledge of printing in a Richmond newspaper office, he entered on his journalistic career. After brief service as an assistant editor of the Richmond *Virginia Patriot,* he edited successively the Petersburg *Republican* and the *North Carolina Journal* of Halifax, N. C. In 1809 he moved to Raleigh, N. C., and became associated with the elder Joseph Gales [q.v.] of the *Raleigh Register,* a Jeffersonian newspaper; on Mar. 30 of the same year he married Gales's daughter, Sarah Weston Gales. In 1812 he joined his brother-in-law, the younger Joseph Gales [q.v.], as associate editor of the *National Intelligencer* of Washington, D. C.

Seaton's policy as an editor of the "Court Paper" for fourteen years became conservative, nationalistic, and free from partisanship. His characteristically short and dignified editorials can hardly be distinguished from those of Gales. His ablest work, however, was done as a reporter of the debates in the Senate while Gales reported the debates of the House. Masters of shorthand, the brothers-in-law were the exclusive reporters of Congress from 1812 to 1829. Upon the authorization of Congress their shorthand reports, with those of the earlier reporters, covering the years from 1789 to 1824, were published by Gales & Seaton (42 vols., 1834–56), as *The Debates and Proceedings in the Congress of the United States,* better known by the half-title, *Annals of Congress.* They also issued the *Register of Debates in Congress,* covering the years 1824–37 (14 vols. in 29, 1825–37), and the monumental series, *American State Papers* (38 vols., 1832–61).

Seaton was sanguine in nature and amused by the bitter attacks made upon him by editors and congressmen of opposite views. He preferred Crawford to Adams for president in 1824, and never accepted the leadership of Jackson, whom he respected as an honest, patriotic citizen but considered a rough frontiersman and an advocate of a low type of democracy. Seaton's personal tastes were aristocratic, although he sympathized with the laboring class, gave freely to the unfortunate, and died a poor man. He was genial, generous, captivatingly courteous, and a good conversationalist; in appearance he was tall, vigorous and handsome. He traveled in America and Europe. Among his friends he counted the leading Southern politicians and planters, and also Daniel Webster. He maintained a farm and a shooting-box in Prince George County to which he could retreat with friends of like tastes and his fine dogs to relax after a strenuous season in Washington. He was skilled in the use of the rod and gun. His witty and charming wife, who translated Spanish documents for him to use in the *National Intelligencer,* was a capable and attractive hostess, maintaining an elegant house to which came men and women of the higher circles of society.

Seaton was a Whig, a Free Mason, and a Unitarian. Much of his time was given to public service. He was an alderman of Washington from 1819 to 1831 and mayor from 1840 to 1850. He served on many committees, made numerous addresses, gave the city a progressive administration, developed the local educational system, led the movement for the Washington Monument, was active in the organization of the

Smithsonian Institution and acted as its treasurer from 1846 until his death. He served in the state militia in Virginia, enrolled as a private in the War of 1812, and saw service at Bladensburg. For many years he was an official in the American Colonization Society; he favored gradual emancipation and freed his own slaves, but opposed the Garrison abolitionists and maintained that the national government should not interfere with slavery. Though he was at all times a compromiser on slavery, he was stanchly Unionist. He retired from his editorial work in 1864. His two sons died in 1827 and 1835, respectively; his wife died in 1863, leaving only his daughter, Josephine, to survive him.

[Josephine Seaton, *William Winston Seaton of the "National Intelligencer"* (1871); *Atlantic Monthly,* Oct. 1860, July 1871; Frederic Hudson, *Journalism in the U. S. from 1690 to 1872* (1873); A. C. Clark, "Col. William Winston Seaton and His Mayoralty," *Records of the Columbia Hist. Soc.,* vols. XXIX–XXX (1928); Joseph Henry, "A Sketch of the Services of the Late Hon. W. W. Seaton in Connection with the Smithsonian Institution," *Ann. Report . . . Smithsonian Inst. . . . 1866* (1867), repr. in W. J. Rhees, *The Smithsonian Inst.* (1879); O. A. Seaton, *The Seaton Family* (1906); *Daily Nat. Intelligencer,* June 18, 19, 20, 1866.]

W. E. S.

SEATTLE (c. 1786–June 7, 1866), chief of the Dwamish, Suquamish, and allied Indian tribes, was the son of Schweabe, a chief of the Suquamish Indians, and Scholitza, the daughter of a Dwamish chief. It is sometimes, though probably erroneously, said that his baptismal name was Noah Sealth. Born in the neighborhood of the city that now bears his name, he was living there when the first settlers went to the region. He befriended them, signed the treaty of Point Elliott on Jan. 22, 1855, to provide for land cession and agency administration, and remained loyal to the whites during the uprising led by Kamaiakan and Leschi [qq.v.]. He became a Roman Catholic and instituted the custom of holding morning and evening services in the tribe, a custom continued after his death. He was unwilling that the rising village of Seattle, Wash., should be named for him, since local Indian belief held that after his death his spirit would be troubled each time human lips spoke the syllables of his name, and in his old age he formed the habit of seeking gifts from the citizens as a kind of tax to recompense himself in advance for this oft-broken sleep of eternity.

[C. B. Bagley, "Chief Seattle and Angeline," *Wash. Hist. Quart.,* Oct. 1931; T. W. Prosch, "Seattle and the Indians of Puget Sound," *Ibid.,* July 1908; Frank Carlson, *Chief Sealth* (1903); L. D. Buchanan, *Souvenir of Chief Seattle and Princess Angeline* (copr. 1909); C. M. Scammon, "Old Seattle, and his Tribe," *Overland Monthly,* Apr. 1870; A. A. Denny, *Pioneer Days on Puget Sound* (1908), ed. by Alice Harriman; Hazard Stevens, *The Life of Isaac Ingalls Stevens*

(1900), vol. I; H. H. Bancroft, *Hist. of Wash.* (1890); *Report of Commissioner of Indian Affairs*, 1854, p. 245; *Ibid.*, 1858, pp. 228, 230; *Ibid.*, 1867, p. 38; *Ibid.*, 1872, p. 295.]   K. E. C.

SEAWELL, MOLLY ELLIOT (Oct. 23, 1860–Nov. 15, 1916), author, daughter of John Tyler and Frances (Jackson) Seawell, was born on a plantation in Gloucester County, Va., in a house, "The Shelter," which had been a Revolutionary hospital. Her mother was a native of Baltimore; her father, a nephew of President Tyler, was a lawyer and a student of the classics. Her childhood in the tidewater region of Chesapeake Bay influenced the settings of the novels she was later to write, and an uncle, Joseph Seawell, who lived with the family, contributed to her future literary material by his stories of his seafaring experiences. With occasional intervals at school for instruction in the standard subjects, she was educated in an informal fashion at home, where riding, dancing, and the conduct of a household were given much consideration. At her father's death, she and her mother removed first to Norfolk, Va., then to Washington, D. C., where she spent the remainder of her life.

At Norfolk about 1886 she began to write sketches and stories. After a trip to Europe, which added to her experience and to her material, she became a contributor to several magazines, using pen-names at first but finally overcoming her reticence sufficiently to write under her own name. In Washington she contributed correspondence about politics to New York papers. Her first novel, *Hale-Weston* (1889), written for *Lippincott's Magazine,* was very successful and was translated into German. Her first juvenile story, *Little Jarvis* (1890), a navy tale, won a *Youth's Companion* prize and fixed her prepossession for naval subjects. Later she took *New York Herald* prizes of $3000 and $1000 with *The Sprightly Romance of Marsac* (1896), a novelette, and *John Mainwaring, Financier* (1908), a short story. As she became experienced she developed a number of types of fiction: stories of the American navy, of Virginia before and after the Civil War, of French life in Paris and the provinces, of English historical periods, of Washington society. Some of her best volumes of fiction are *Throckmorton* (1890), *Midshipman Paulding* (1891), *A Virginia Cavalier* (copyright 1896), *The History of the Lady Betty Stair* (1897), *The Lively Adventures of Gavin Hamilton* (1899), *The House of Egremont* (1900), *Papa Bouchard* (1901), *Francezka* (1902), *The Fortunes of Fifi* (1903), *The Château of Montplaisir* (1906), *The Victory* (1906), *The Secret of Toni* (1907), *The*

Last Duchess of Belgarde (1908), *The Imprisoned Midshipmen* (1908), *The Whirl; a Romance of Washington Society* (1909), *Betty's Virginia Christmas* (1914), *The Diary of a Beauty* (1915). Her *Twelve Naval Captains* (1897) is said to have been used as a textbook in the United States Naval Academy. Certain public questions of her day interested her, and some of them supplied her with subjects for her writing. *Despotism and Democracy* (1903) is a discussion of Washington society and politics; "On the Absence of the Creative Faculty in Women," published in the *Critic*, Nov. 29, 1891, and *The Ladies' Battle* (1911) present her view of woman's suffrage, to which she was opposed. As a writer of fiction she had the ability to create both character and atmosphere. Though sometimes slight, her plots are usually adequate and often full of amusing incidents; her style is sprightly and humorous and, though her popularity has waned, her books are still very readable. For many years her home in Washington was a meeting-place for writers and artists, but after the deaths of her mother and sister and the failure of her own health she led a retired life. She died at her Washington home and was buried in Baltimore, Md.

[Gaillard Hunt, in *Lib. of Southern Lit.*, vol. XI (1909), ed. by E. A. Alderman, J. C. Harris, and C. W. Kent; *Who's Who in America*, 1908–09, 1916–17; Frances E. Willard and Mary A. Livermore, *Am. Women* (1897), vol. II; obituaries in *Evening Star* (Washington), *N. Y. Herald*, Nov. 16, 1916.]   S. G. B.

SEBASTIAN, BENJAMIN (*c.* 1745–March 1834), jurist, Spanish agent, was possibly connected with the Sebastians of Fairfax County, Va., and the vicinity. After serving some years as a clergyman (*Virginia Magazine of History and Biography,* October 1933, p. 299), he removed to Kentucky, where a warrant, recorded on Mar. 27, 1784, granted him land as a three-year soldier of the Virginia line, and another warrant, dated Feb. 10, 1785, listed him among those obtaining land in Jefferson County, Ky. He was admitted to the practice of law at Louisville in 1784 and was licensed as attorney on Mar. 6, 1786, by the supreme court of the Kentucky district (*Filson Club Historical Quarterly,* July 1932, p. 262; First Order Book, Filson Club Library). At once he became prominent in law and in politics. A member of the famous "Political Club" at Danville he, like others of its leading members, was suspected of Spanish leanings. In the series of conventions leading up to statehood for Kentucky he espoused prompt separation from Virginia as a step toward obtaining the free navigation of the Mississippi. His attitude, especially in the convention of 1788, led James

Wilkinson [*q.v.*] to recommend him, the following year, for a Spanish pension—a recommendation that drew from the Spanish governor of Louisiana, Esteban Miró [*q.v.*], an offer to bestow substantial land grants upon Sebastian and his companions, should they choose to settle in Louisiana. Nothing came of this colonization project but for other services less openly professed and undertaken in conjunction with Wilkinson, Sebastian hoped to obtain from the Spanish government a substantial pension.

On June 28, 1792, he was appointed one of the judges for the appellate court of the state. This appointment, however, did not prevent him from continuing his correspondence with the Spaniards. Three years afterward both he and George Muter were subjected to a hostile address in both houses of the state legislature because of a decision regarding land titles, but the resolution did not receive a two-thirds majority. In this same year, 1795, the new Spanish governor of Louisiana, Francisco Luis Hector de Carondelet [*q.v.*], renewed overtures to the Kentuckians through Sebastian, now evidently more approachable than General Wilkinson. Through the Spanish intermediary, Thomas Power, Sebastian was induced to confer with Manuel Gayoso de Lemos [*q.v.*], commandant at Natchez, at New Madrid. When some differences arose over the proposed duties on river trade, Sebastian accompanied the Spaniard to New Orleans, in order to settle the question with Carondelet in person. The treaty with Spain providing for the navigation of the Mississippi and a port of deposit rendered unnecessary any private arrangement, and Sebastian thereupon returned to Kentucky. He bore a letter from Carondelet completely justifying his conduct, but this did not forestall considerable speculation among his neighbors concerning this visit. Two years later Power suggested an immediate separation of the western country from the eastern states and the establishment of its independence with Spanish aid. A hundred thousand dollars would be available for the initial expenses and an equal sum, together with warlike equipment, when independence was declared. Those who should lose office because of this service were to receive from the Spanish government a pension equal to the forfeited salary. These proposals, although intended more particularly for Wilkinson, were brought by Sebastian to the attention of his friends, Harry Innes and George Nicholas [*qq.v.*], both of whom seem to have promptly repudiated them. Nevertheless Sebastian went to New Orleans, in 1798, for further conference with Gayoso, who was then governor

of Louisiana, and continued to receive his Spanish pension.

In 1804 the payment of this pension proved his undoing. Already suspected by his fellow citizens, the death of the merchant in Natchez through whom one of his vouchers was cashed gave his enemies definite proof of his dealings. At the same time the much discussed visit of Aaron Burr [*q.v.*] caused a revival of the scandals connected with the earlier Spanish conspiracy. The Federalist faction in Kentucky found in Sebastian an easy mark for their virulent attacks, and in November they obtained a petition asking the legislature to investigate his conduct (see sketch of Joseph M. Street). Fearful of the consequences Sebastian resigned at the end of 1806, but the committee continued its work and procured, especially from his associate Innes, testimony that made his guilt certain. The exposure meant elimination from public life. About 1810 he removed to Grayson County and there and in Livingston County purchased extensive tracts of land, built a saw-and-grist-mill, and engaged in general merchandise. In 1821 he gave his son Charles power of attorney to represent him. His will was recorded Mar. 17, 1834 (Durrett MSS., *post*). A man of striking presence and of considerable ability, his moral principles were not sufficient to withstand his monetary needs. In a period of uncertain allegiance he followed a course of intrigue that promised to protect personal interest at the expense of state and nation. Thus far he was guilty but, of the dubious group with which he associated, he was the only one to pay full penalty for his guilt.

[Photo-film enlargements from the Papeles de Cuba esp. legajo 2374; Harry Innes Papers, esp. vols. XVIII, XIX, XXIII, in Lib. of Cong.; manuscript material in Filson Club Lib., Louisville, Ky.; Wayne Papers in possession of Pa. Hist. Soc.; Durrett MSS., Univ. of Chicago; Sebastian report, in *Annals of Cong.*, 1 Sess., cols. 2760–90 and *Am. State Papers: Miscellaneous Docs.*, vol. I (1834), pp. 933–35; T. M. Green, *The Spanish Conspiracy* (1891); J. M. Brown, *The Political Beginnings of Kentucky* (1889); Charles Gayarré, *Hist. of La.*, vol. III (1854) with material from the Spanish archives; *Reprints of Littell's Political Transactions*, ed. by Temple Bodley in the *Filson Club Pubs.*, vol. XXXI (1926), esp. introduction; S. F. Bemis, *Pinckney's Treaty* (1926); I. J. Cox, *The West Florida Controversy* (1918); J. A. James, *The Life of George Rogers Clark* (1928); A. P. Whitaker, *The Spanish-American Frontier* (1927) and *The Mississippi Question* (1934); W. R. Jillson, "Old Kentucky Entries and Deeds," *Filson Club Publications*, no. 34 (1926), p. 360, and "Kentucky Land Grants," *Ibid.*, no. 33 (1925), p. 116.]   I. J. C.

SECCOMB, JOHN (Apr. 25, 1708–Oct. 27, 1792), Congregational clergyman, was born at Medford, Mass., son of Peter and Hannah (Willis) Seccomb, and grandson of Richard Seccomb, who settled at Lynn about 1660. He graduated

Seccomb

Seddon

from Harvard in 1728. While at the college he had written poems for the amusement of his friends, and in 1730 when Matthew Abdy, college bedmaker and sweeper, died, Seccomb was inspired to write "Father Abbey's Will," a humorous poem in fifteen six-line stanzas cataloguing the objects which Abdy might have bequeathed to his wife. It was printed in December of that year. He afterwards added "A Letter of Courtship to his virtuous and amiable Widow," twelve stanzas supposed to be written by the sweeper at Yale. These verses had no merit as poetry, but their rhymes and phrasing were neat and amusing. They were published together in Boston in 1731, were dispatched to England by Governor Belcher and printed in 1732 in both the *London Magazine* and the *Gentleman's Magazine,* and were popular among several generations of New Englanders. They were reprinted in the *Massachusetts Magazine* in November 1794, and privately in Cambridge by John L. Sibley in 1854.

Seccomb was ordained minister in the town of Harvard, Mass., on Oct. 10, 1733. In 1739 there was a revival of religion in his congregation, which, stimulated by the Great Awakening which began in New England in 1740, continued for four years. Writing to *The Christian History* (Mar. 17, 1743/44), Seccomb reported that nearly one hundred had been converted, chiefly among the young people; some, he added, had been "so sensibly affected with their Danger that they dare not close their Eyes to sleep lest they should awake in Hell; and would sometimes *arise in the Night* and go to the Windows . . . expecting to hear the Sounding of the Trumpet to summon all Nations to appear before him." Seccomb had been married on Mar. 10, 1737, to Mercy, daughter of the Rev. William Williams of Weston and had had four children. In 1757 she accused him of misconduct; a church council acquitted him of all charges, but, feeling that he could no longer usefully serve as pastor, he asked for a dismission. In 1763 he went as minister to the Congregational church at Chester, Nova Scotia, probably on the invitation of Jonathan Belcher, Jr., lieutenant-governor of the province, whom he had known at college. His income was only twenty pounds a year, and he was compelled to appeal for help in Boston; his difficulties were finally ended by an inheritance, and he stayed at Chester until his death. While there he published three sermons, somewhat pompous in tone and quite undistinguished. Doctrinally, he was an old-fashioned Calvinist.

[H. S. Nourse, *Hist. of the Town of Harvard* (1894); Charles Brooks, *Hist. of Medford* (1855); E. A. and

G. L. Duyckinck, *Cyc. of Am. Literature* (1875), vol. I; *Proc. Mass. Hist. Soc.,* 2 ser. vol. IV (1889).]
H. B. P.

SEDDON, JAMES ALEXANDER (July 13, 1815–Aug. 19, 1880), congressman and Confederate secretary of war, was descended from Thomas Seddon who emigrated from England to Virginia early in the eighteenth century, settled on a large tract of land in Stafford County, near Fredericksburg, and built "Snowden," which was burned during the Civil War by Federal troops. James Alexander Seddon, his great-grandson and the son of Susan Pearson (Alexander) and Thomas Seddon, a banker, was born in Fredericksburg. He graduated from the law school of the University of Virginia in 1835 and began to practise in Richmond, where he was successful and popular. He served in the federal House of Representatives from 1845 to 1847 and again from 1849 to 1851. Peremptorily declining another nomination, he retired to "Sabot Hill," his estate in Goochland County to enjoy the quiet life of a country gentleman and to manage his large property. Though lacking in humor, he was courtly, widely read, and a clever conversationalist. He was known as an ardent follower of Calhoun. In 1845 he was married to Sarah Bruce, the daughter of James Bruce of Halifax, a member of a distinguished Virginia family. She was vivacious and charming, with musical propensities. "Sabot Hill" became a center of hospitality in the happy decade preceding the Civil War. In the peace convention of 1861 he was a member of the committee on resolutions and introduced a minority report (Chittenden, *post,* pp. 47–48) recognizing the right of peaceful secession, and, together with the majority of his delegation, he voted against the compromise proposal of the convention. He was the leader on the floor of the secessionists members and sought assurance from the convention and the delegates of the Republican states that there should, in no event, be war. He was elected to the first Confederate Congress. In November 1862, when George Wythe Randolph [*q.v.*] resigned his position as secretary of war, Jefferson Davis prevailed upon Seddon to assume the important and difficult post. This appointment marked a return to the civilian control so criticized in the case of Judah P. Benjamin. It would have been difficult to obtain for this post a military officer with the requisite ability and energy, combined with deference to Davis. On the whole the choice of Seddon, though much criticized, was a good selection. A politician and man of the world, he brought to his task not only devotion and intellectual capacity but the needed tact

545

and administrative ability. Physically, he was described as gaunt and emaciated, with a sallow and cadaverous look, resembling "an exhumed corpse after a month's interment" (Jones, *post,* I, 380).

He assumed his position in the lull following Antietam and Perryville, when Lee was busy reorganizing his army. A study of the records during this period indicates that Davis largely controlled the conduct of the armies. Yet Seddon had large influence over the president, especially until the summer of 1863, and he continued to hold his confidence. The Confederate military policy was in general too defensive and did not require sufficient coordination of the scattered armies. At times, however, Seddon made decisions that showed sound judgment. Early in 1863 he urged that Joseph E. Johnston take direct command of the western army, and he strove, tactfully but persistently, to make Johnston assume the offensive before Vicksburg. The month before Gettysburg, he wrote Lee a letter heartily concurring in his desire for offensive action. None of the Confederate secretaries of war were more considerate of Lee or worked in closer harmony with him. One of Seddon's blunders was his suggestion that Longstreet be detached for the attack on Suffolk. His chief defect, however, seems to have been his inclination to defer deciding troublesome administrative questions, especially those relating to the commissary and its chief. As a result of his consenting to the removal of Johnston before the fall of Atlanta, Seddon incurred much unpopularity. Early in 1865, when the Confederate situation had become desperate, the Virginia delegation to Congress requested the reorganization of the cabinet. As a consequence, he resigned. Jefferson Davis denounced Congress for what he deemed an unconstitutional interference with his cabinet and wrote a cordial letter to Seddon (Rowland, *post,* VI, 458–61).

Seddon "was completely crushed by the collapse of the Southern Confederacy and considered his life to have been a complete failure" (letter to the writer from his son, Judge James A. Seddon, Jr. of St. Louis). He was imprisoned by the Northern government but was soon released. Retiring to "Sabot Hill," he engaged in agricultural pursuits as far as his health would permit. For many years before his death he was an invalid and suffered from neuralgic pains. He died at "Sabot Hill."

[After Seddon's death it was found that most of his papers had disappeared, presumably destroyed by him; see Edward Pollard, *Life of Jefferson Davis, with a Secret Hist. of the Southern Confederacy* (1869), a critical appraisal; H. J. Eckenrode, *Jefferson Davis*

(1923), a more sympathetic view; L. G. Tyler, *Encyc. of Va. Biog.* (1915), vol. III; W. C. Bruce (a nephew), *Recollections* (copr. 1931); J. B. Jones, *A Rebel War Clerk's Diary* (2 vols., 1866); *Jefferson Davis . . . Letters, Papers, and Speeches* (1923), ed. by Dunbar Rowland, vols. V–X; L. E. Chittenden, *A Report of the Debates and Proceedings in the Secret Sessions of the Conference . . . 1861* (1864); G. S. Boutwell, *Reminiscences* (1902), vol. I; *War of the Rebellion: Official Records (Army)*; *Daily Dispatch* (Richmond), Aug. 20, 1880; *Va. Mag. of Hist.*, Apr. 1904, p. 442; *Wm. and Mary Coll. Quart.*, Oct. 1901, p. 138; suggestions from Douglas S. Freeman, Richmond.]   R. D. M.

SEDELLA, ANTOINE [See ANTOINE, PÈRE, 1748–1829].

SEDGWICK, ARTHUR GEORGE (Oct. 6, 1844–July 14, 1915), lawyer and journalist, son of Theodore Sedgwick, 1811–1859 [*q.v.*], and Sarah (Ashburner), was born in New York City. He was educated at Harvard, receiving the degree of A.B. in 1864. On completing his undergraduate course he was commissioned as first lieutenant of the 20th Massachusetts Infantry and began a brief and unfortunate military career. He was captured by the Confederates at Deep Bottom, Va., in July 1864 and confined in Libby Prison. While there he suffered a serious illness. He was paroled in September and the following February was discharged from the army on account of physical disability. In March he entered the Harvard Law School, from which he received the degree of LL.B. in 1866. In November 1868 he was admitted to the bar and began practising in the office of Chandler, Shattuck & Thayer in Boston.

On the advice of his brother-in-law, Charles Eliot Norton [*q.v.*], he gave considerable time to writing. Some of his articles were published in the *Nation* before he was twenty-one. In 1868 or 1869 he sent an article every week to that journal. He was also engaged with Oliver Wendell Holmes, Jr., in editing (1870–73) the *American Law Review*. In 1872 he returned to New York to become managing editor of the *Evening Post,* but after a few weeks he resigned because of interference by the business office with his editorial policies. He then became assistant editor of the *Nation,* with which he remained in more or less close association until 1905. From 1881 to 1885 he was also assistant editor of the *Evening Post.* From his first contribution his style impressed the reader as the *Nation's* own. It had much clarity, energy, and personal savor, combined with economy of words. He was at his best in writing short essays on modes and manners, some of which were of more than local and temporary importance.

In 1875 he was admitted to the New York bar and practised for six years. With F. S. Wait he wrote *A Treatise on the Principles and Practice*

Governing the Trial of Title to Land (1882). He edited the fifth, and was co-editor of the seventh, eighth, and ninth, editions of his father's *A Treatise on the Measure of Damages.* In 1896 he published *Elements of Damages,* which, with revisions and additions, was republished in 1909 as *Elements of the Law of Damages.* He delivered a course of legal lectures in 1885–86 at the Lowell Institute in Boston and in 1909 he was Godkin lecturer at Harvard University, speaking in criticism of the working of some traditional principles of democracy in the United States. His lectures were published in 1912 under the title, *The Democratic Mistake.* In his opinion the people of the United States had erred in expecting to obtain responsible government through the election of a great number of officers who served only short terms; the ballot alone would not insure good government. His book was not very favorably received.

Sedgwick married Lucy Tuckerman, Nov. 16, 1882, and had two daughters. After his wife's death in 1904 he spent most of his time at Stockbridge, Mass., keeping an office in New York solely to receive mail. In the summer of 1914 he was injured in an automobile accident from which he never fully recovered. The next spring he had a severe attack of pneumonia. Despondent over his ill health, he took his own life.

[The anniversary number of the *Nation,* July 8, 1915, contains autobiog. material; see also Allan Nevins, *The Evening Post, A Century of Journalism* (copr. 1922); Gustav Pollak, *Fifty Years of Am. Idealism: The N. Y. Nation, 1865–1915* (1915); *Harvard Coll. Class of 1864, Secretary's Report,* no. 6 (1889), no. 8 (1914); *Who's Who in America,* 1914–15; *N. Y. Tribune,* July 15, 1915; *Nation,* July 22, 29, 1915.]   E. C. S.

SEDGWICK, CATHARINE MARIA (Dec. 28, 1789–July 31, 1867), author, was the daughter of Pamela (Dwight) and Theodore Sedgwick, 1746–1813 [*q.v.*], both descendants of seventeenth-century settlers in New England. She was born in Stockbridge, Mass. Throughout her life she was closely identified with this region; her novels dealing with the natural beauty and local customs of the Berkshires are among the first attempts to use American material in fiction. Born into a family of distinction and of modest wealth, she was accustomed to the companionship of books and of cultivated people. She listened to intelligent talk, read widely, and like other girls of her time and class learned to perform all household duties. The district school, with brief periods in boarding schools in Boston and Albany, provided what formal education she had, but she was given private instruction in several languages. When she was in her eighteenth year her mother died, and the following

year her father remarried. During the next six years she spent her time largely in Albany with her brother Theodore, 1780–1839 [*q.v.*], or in New York with her sister Mrs. Watson. After her father's death in 1813 she presided over the house in Stockbridge. Later she lived with a much-loved brother in Lenox in the summers and spent her winters in New York with other relatives, who were all deeply devoted to her.

Her literary work grew out of her belief in the importance of the American home. In 1822 she published anonymously her first novel, *A New-England Tale,* frankly designed to "lend a helping hand to some of the humbler and unnoticed virtues" and to set forth humble rustic scenes; two years later came *Redwood,* conventionally romantic in plot but with a background of simple home life. In these pioneer works the American domestic novel had its beginning. A series of novels—*The Travelers* (1825), designed for the entertainment and instruction of young readers, *Hope Leslie* (1827), a story of domestic life among the early settlers in New England, *Clarence; or a Tale of Our Own Times* (1830), and *The Linwoods; or "Sixty Years Since" in America* (1835)—established her as the most popular authoress in the country. Although marked by extravagant and imitative romanticism, they contain realistic presentations of domestic scenes. Harriet Martineau recommended them, with some reservations, in the *Westminster Review* of October 1837 as true pictures of American life, and several were translated into foreign languages. Her *Letters from Abroad to Kindred at Home* (1841) records the pleasant experiences of a sojourn of fifteen months abroad in 1839–40. Besides her longer works, she published two biographical sketches (an account of Lucretia M. Davidson in Sparks's *The Library of American Biography,* 1 ser., vol. VII, 1837, and a *Memoir of John Curtis, a Model Man,* 1858), many short tales, and a number of books designed to be helpful to persons of the less favored classes. Believing that the safety of the republic depended upon the domestic virtues of the people, she tried to render wholesome living and unaffected goodness attractive. Her moral purpose dominates *Home* (1835), *The Poor Rich Man, and the Rich Poor Man* (copyright 1836), *Live and Let Live; or Domestic Service Illustrated* (1837), *Means and Ends; or Self-Training* (1839), *Wilton Harvey* (1845), *Morals of Manners* (1846), *Facts and Fancies for School-Day Reading* (1848), and her last novel, *Married or Single?* (1857), written when she was sixty-eight to contradict the idea that unmarried women were useless.

Her life was outwardly an uneventful one.

She took a quietly helpful part in the philanthropic movements of the day but did not ally herself with any radical reform. She was active in the work of the Unitarian Church, to which she turned in 1821 for greater religious freedom, and for many years she gave efficient help to the Women's Prison Association of New York. Her adventures consisted of her good works, her books, and, outstandingly, her friends. Both in New York and in Lenox she attracted the admiration of gifted men and women. Bryant praised her "perfection of high breeding," Hawthorne called her "our most truthful novelist," and Fanny Kemble Butler, the actress, her friend for over thirty years, described her as "one of the most charming, most amiable, and most excellent persons" she had ever known. Foreign visitors sought her out in Lenox, where her home was a center of hospitality, and where as the years passed she devoted herself more and more to her wide correspondence and her gardening. A journey westward as far as the Mississippi gave her great pleasure in 1854, but for the most part during her later life she seldom left New England. She died after a period of invalidism in the West Roxbury home of a niece who had always been to her as a daughter.

[R. De W. Mallary, *Lenox and the Berkshire Highlands* (1902); H. D. Sedgwick, "The Sedgwicks of Berkshire," *Berkshire Hist. and Sci. Soc. Colls.*, vol. III (1900); *Life and Letters of Catharine M. Sedgwick*, ed. by Mary E. Dewey (1871); S. A. Allibone, *A Crit. Dict. of Eng. Lit.*, vol. II (1870); *A Woman of the Century* (1893), ed. by Frances E. Willard and Mary A. Livermore; obituary in *Boston Daily Advertiser*, Aug. 1, 2, 1867; death notice in *Boston Transcript*, July 31, 1867; information from the family.]   B. M. S.

SEDGWICK, JOHN (Sept. 13, 1813–May 9, 1864), soldier, was born at Cornwall Hollow, Conn., the son of Benjamin Sedgwick, farmer and ardent churchman, and Olive (Collins) Sedgwick. The American progenitor of the family was Robert Sedgwick [*q.v.*]. His grandfather, Major John Sedgwick, was an officer in the American War of the Revolution. John Sedgwick, II, was a manly, robust boy, strong-willed, and a leader among his associates. He received his early education in the common schools of Cornwall, with a few months at an academy at Sharon, Conn., and some special instruction at the parsonage of the Rev. William Andrews. For two winters he taught school. Soon afterward he entered the United States Military Academy and was graduated with the class of 1837. He was commissioned in the artillery, and for a decade saw service in the Seminole War, assisted in moving the Cherokee Indians west of the Mississippi, served on the northern frontier during the Canadian border disturbances, and

on various garrison assignments. In 1846 he joined General Taylor's army on the Rio Grande, and saw arduous service until transferred to Scott's army at Vera Cruz, Mexico. He took an active part in all the battles of the Mexican War leading up to the final assault upon the city of Mexico, and for his services at the battles of Churubusco and Chapultepec was brevetted captain and major, respectively. After about eight years of garrison duty, during which he was promoted to the rank of captain, he was honored by appointment as major of the newly organized 1st Regiment of Cavalry. He participated in the Utah Expedition of 1857–58, and in the warfare with the Kiowa and Comanche Indians, 1858–60.

At the outbreak of the Civil War Sedgwick was engaged in constructing the frontier post of Fort Wise, Colo. Quick promotion to the ranks of lieutenant-colonel, colonel, and brigadier-general of United States Volunteers followed, and he received the important assignments of a brigade and a division in the Army of the Potomac. He participated in most of the battles of McClellan's campaign on the Peninsula, including Glendale where he was severely wounded on June 30, 1862. He was promoted major-general of volunteers on July 4, 1862. He took a prominent part in the battle of Antietam, where he was again wounded, in the battle of Chancellorsville, and in the Rappahannock campaign, during which he commanded the V and the VI Corps. Soon afterwards he led his corps in the storming of Marye's Heights at Fredericksburg, Va., and in the battle of Salem Heights on May 3 and 4, 1863. Although not reaching Gettysburg until the second day of the great battle, he entered that contest also and took part in the pursuit of Lee's retiring army. In the subsequent Rapidan campaign he commanded the right wing of the Army of the Potomac with the V and VI Corps, and did brilliant service at the Rappahannock Station in the operations at Mine Run. In the Richmond campaign, still commanding the VI Corps, he was actively engaged in the battle of the Wilderness early in May 1864. A few days later at Spotsylvania, while personally directing the location of artillery, he was shot and killed by a Confederate sharpshooter. A painting of Sedgwick's death, by Julian Scott, hangs in the public library of Plainfield, N. J. He was buried in his native town in Connecticut, where an impressive monument was dedicated to him on May 30, 1892. In 1868, a bronze statue at West Point, and in 1913 an equestrian statue at Gettysburg, were unveiled with appropriate ceremonies. Sedgwick never married. Generous and affable, but withal a strict disciplinarian, this brilliant leader was affectionately known to his soldiers as "Uncle John."

[E. S. Welch, *John Sedgwick, Major-General* (1899); *Corresp. of John Sedgwick* (2 vols., 1902–03); G. W. Cullum, *Biog. Reg. . . . U. S. Mil. Acad.* (1891); *The Centennial of the U. S. Mil. Acad.* (1904), vol. II; E. C. Starr, *A Hist. of Cornwall, Conn.* (1926); T. S. Gold, *Hist. Records of the Town of Cornwall* (1904); M. T. McMahon, *Gen. John Sedgwick, Address before the Vt. Officers' Reunion Soc., Nov. 11, 1880* (1880); *Hartford* (Conn.) *Daily Courant*, May 11, 12, 13, 17, 18, 1864.]   C. D. R.

SEDGWICK, ROBERT (*c.* 1613–May 24, 1656), colonist, soldier, son of William Sedgwick and Elizabeth Howe, was baptized at Woburn, Bedfordshire, England, May 6, 1613. "Nurst up in Londons Artillery garden" as a member of the city train bands, he settled in Charlestown in New England in 1636. Because he was "stout and active in all feats of war," he was chosen captain for Charlestown in 1637. To increase the efficiency of the colonial militia by creating a "school of soldiery" for its officers, he helped organize the Military Company of the Massachusetts, and was its captain in 1640, 1645, and 1648. In 1637 he established a "very commodious" brewery, and in 1644 with six others was granted a monopoly of the Indian trade of the colony for twenty-one years. The success of these and other commercial activities enabled him in 1647 to endow Harvard College with a substantial shop in Boston. He served as deputy from Charlestown to the General Court from 1637 to 1644 and again in 1648, and occasionally as assessor of rates, boundary surveyor, arbitrator of petty disputes, and keeper of the peace. The General Court in 1652 recognized his achievements, especially in fortifying Charlestown harbor, by electing him major-general of the colony. Late in 1653 he returned to England and received from Cromwell a commission to lead an expedition against the Dutch of Manhattan Island, who had been troubling the New Haven and Connecticut settlers. He reached Boston with four ships and 200 men in June 1654, raised an additional 700, and would have proceeded against the Dutch even after news came of peace with the Netherlands, had not the New Englanders abandoned the enterprise. Though France and England were nominally friendly, he decided to turn his fleet against the French engaged in trading and fishing on the New England coast, easily captured the Acadian forts of St. John, Port Royal, and Pentagoet on the Penobscot, and garrisoned them. Cromwell showed his approval by giving him charge of twelve ships and 800 men sent to reinforce the joint naval and military expedition of Penn and Venables, operating against the Spanish West Indies. Sedgwick

found the English precariously occupying Jamaica, which they had seized after an ignominious reverse at Hispaniola (Santo Domingo). There had been dissensions between Penn and Venables, who had already gone to England to present their respective cases, leaving their starving and shelterless men dying of dysentery. Sedgwick's efforts to ameliorate the condition of the army were frustrated by its insubordination and general worthlessness. Convinced at length that God did not favor the Western Design, and worried over his inability to carry out his share of the Protector's extensive anti-Spanish program, he died in Jamaica, broken-hearted, on May 24, 1656. His secretary in Jamaica described him as "generally beloved and esteemed by al sorts of people . . . a truly religious man, and of the most innocent conversation I ever accompanied" (Birch, *post*, V, 154–55). Though Sedgwick's widow, Joanna Blake, returned to England and remarried, many of their descendants have been prominent in New England life.

[*Trans. and Colls. Am. Antiq. Soc.*, vol. III (1857); Thomas Birch, *A Coll. of the State Papers of John Thurloe* (1742), vols. II, IV, V; *Calendar of State Papers, Colonial, 1574–1660* (1860); *Calendar of State Papers, Domestic, 1655, 1655–6, 1656–7* (1881–83); *Colls. Mass. Hist. Soc.*, 3 ser. VII (1838), 4 ser. II (1854), 5 ser. I (1871); Edward Johnson, *Wonder Working Providence of Sions Saviour in New England* (1654; ed. by W. F. Poole, 1867); *New-Eng. Hist. and Geneal. Reg.*, Apr. 1888, Oct. 1916; *Col. Soc. of Mass. Pubs.*, vols. III (1900), XV (1925); O. A. Roberts, *Hist. of the Military Company of the Massachusetts Now Called The Ancient and Honorable Artillery Company*, vol. I (1895); N. B. Shurtleff, *Records of the Governor and Company of the Mass. Bay*, vols. I, II (1853), III (1854).]   R. L. J.

SEDGWICK, THEODORE (May 9, 1746–Jan. 24, 1813), legislator and jurist, was born in West Hartford, Conn. His father, Benjamin Sedgwick, who kept a small store, was a great-grandson of Gen. Robert Sedgwick [*q.v.*]. His mother, Ann (Thompson) Sedgwick, came from Wallingford, Conn. In 1748 Benjamin Sedgwick moved to the new township of Cornwall where, when Theodore was ten, he died, leaving little property. Through the sacrifices of his older brother, Theodore entered Yale in 1761, intending to prepare for the ministry. He left before graduating because of infractions of college discipline, but in 1772 received his degree as of 1765. From divinity he soon turned to law, studying under his second cousin, Col. Mark Hopkins, in Great Barrington, Mass. Here he began practice after his admission to the Berkshire County bar in April 1766. Shortly afterward he moved to Sheffield, the next town southward. In 1768 (Mason, *post*, p. 21) he married Eliza, daughter of Jeremiah Mason of Franklin,

Conn., and aunt of Senator Jeremiah Mason [q.v.]. She died childless in 1771, of smallpox thought to have been caught from her husband when combing out his hair after he had been discharged from quarantine for the disease. On Apr. 17, 1774, he married Pamela, daughter of Gen. Joseph Dwight of Great Barrington by his second wife, Abigail Williams, who was half-sister of Col. Ephraim Williams [q.v.], founder of Williams College, and had been previously married to John Sergeant [q.v.], missionary to the Indians. To Sedgwick's second marriage ten children were born, eight of whom attained maturity. Among these were Theodore, 1780–1839, and Catharine Maria [qq.v.], while later generations of Judge Sedgwick's descendants included many other persons of distinction in law and literature.

Sedgwick soon became active in the struggle against Great Britain, although as late as May 1776, he was opposed to independence. He was clerk of the county convention called in 1774 to consider resistance to British taxation. Early in 1776 he became military secretary to Gen. John Thomas, whom he accompanied on his invasion of Canada. After Thomas' death on May 30, Sedgwick gave up soldiering—except possibly as a volunteer aid in the Burgoyne campaign—but he performed valuable service in 1776–77 in getting supplies on moderate terms for the northern department of the Continental Army. He served in the legislature as representative in 1780, 1782, 1783, 1787, 1788, and as senator in 1784 and 1785. He was speaker of the House in 1788. Meanwhile he continued practising law and was the leading Massachusetts lawyer west of the Connecticut in 1785, when he established his home in Stockbridge. In his most famous case (1783) he defended a negro slave, Elizabeth Freeman (Mumbet), against the master from whom she had fled. Sedgwick successfully argued that slavery had been abolished in Massachusetts by the Bill of Rights of 1780, which declared all men to be "born free and equal." The liberated negress became nurse of Sedgwick's children and died in his house.

After the recognition of independence Sedgwick became a Federalist and his career was for a time national. He was a member of the Continental Congress, 1785–88. His strenuous activity in suppressing Shays's Rebellion led the insurgents to threaten his life and an unsuccessful attempt was made to attack his house. In the Massachusetts convention of 1788 he was a prominent advocate of ratification of the Federal Constitution. Soon afterward, he was elected to the First Congress by a majority of only seven votes. He continued as representative in the Second, Third, and Fourth congresses. He was a vigorous debater and was chairman of important committees, reported the first fugitive slave law, all bills admitting new states, and some of the first ten constitutional amendments. He led the opposition to Livingston's motion requiring the papers leading up to the Jay treaty (*Annals of Congress,* 4 Cong., 1 sess., p. 514), and thus helped establish the inability of the House to participate in treaty-making. On Hamilton's resignation, Sedgwick declined an offer of the secretaryship of the Treasury. On the resignation of Senator Caleb Strong in June 1796, Sedgwick was elected to the Senate, of which he was president *pro tempore* for a few weeks in 1798. When his term expired in 1799, he returned to the House and was speaker during the Sixth Congress, retiring in March 1801. He was a Federalist of the Adams wing but was an intimate correspondent of all the party leaders.

In 1802 he was appointed for life to the supreme judicial court of Massachusetts, which at once began to show the effect of his personality and ability. Although his decisions did not permanently influence the law, they "were famous in their day for clearness and beauty" (Dexter, *post,* III, 149), and he won the high regard of the bar by introducing a new standard of courteous and cordial treatment from the bench. His hopes of succeeding Chief Justice Dana in 1806 were disappointed by the selection of Theophilus Parsons [q.v.].

In 1807 Mrs. Sedgwick died after several attacks of insanity, attributed to her cares and trials during her husband's absence on public duty. In November 1808, much to his children's distaste, he married his third wife, Penelope, daughter of Dr. Charles Russell of Boston and Elizabeth (Vassall) Russell. She survived Sedgwick, having had no children. He died while visiting Boston in 1813, and was buried in the family cemetery at Stockbridge.

Sedgwick was of large size, "with a prepossessing face and a dignified, almost showy manner" (Dexter, p. 149). Aristocratic despite his humble origin, he was rather overbearing to common people and habitually spoke of them as Jacobins and *sans-culottes,* but he kept open house in Stockbridge for rich and poor alike and his relations with his children were delightful. He was a trustee of Williams College from its foundation until his death, and a corporate member of the American Academy of Arts and Sciences.

[The fullest accounts are by H. D. Sedgwick, "The Sedgwicks of Berkshire" (1900), *Berkshire Hist. and Sci. Soc. Colls.*, vol. III; F. B. Dexter, *Biog. Sketches Grads. Yale Coll.*, vol. III (1903), with bibliog.; B. W. Dwight, *The Hist. of the Descendants of John Dwight of Dedham, Mass.* (1874), vol. II; M. E. Dewey, *Life and Letters of Catharine M. Sedgwick* (1871). See also L. H. von Sahler, "Two Distinguished Members of the Sedgwick Family—Robert and Theodore," *N. Y. Geneal. and Biog. Record*, Apr. 1901; T. W. Mason, *Family Record . . . Descent from Maj. John Mason* (1909); *Biog. Dir. Am. Cong.* (1928), which is authority for day of birth; *Proc. Mass. Hist. Soc.*, 2 ser. I (1885), and *U. S. Mag. and Democratic Rev.*, Feb. 1840, pp. 129–34, giving information about the negress Mumbet; Theophilus Parsons, *Memoir of Theophilus Parsons* (1859), p. 194; A. B. Hart, *Commonwealth Hist. of Mass.*, vols. III (1929), IV (1930); *Letters from Charles Sedgwick to His Family and Friends* (privately printed, 1870), ed. by C. M. Sedgwick; T. S. Gold, *Hist. Records of the Town of Cornwall* (1904); *Columbian Centinel* (Boston), Jan. 27, 1813. Sedgwick's judicial opinions are in 1–9 *Mass. Reports*.]
Z. C., Jr.

SEDGWICK, THEODORE (December 1780–Nov. 7, 1839), lawyer and writer, was the second child and first son among the ten children born to Judge Theodore Sedgwick [q.v.] and his second wife, Pamela (Dwight)...

ist principles of his father...

[H. D. Sedgwick, "The Sedgwicks of Berkshire" (1900)... J. H. B—h.]

SEDGWICK, THEODORE (Jan. 27, 1811–Dec. 8, 1859), author, lawyer, and diplomat, was born at Albany, N. Y., the son of Theodore

Sedgwick [q.v.], the second of that name, and of Susan Anne Livingston (Ridley) Sedgwick. Catharine Maria Sedgwick [q.v.] was his aunt. Prepared for college in the public schools of New York City and at Stockbridge, Mass., the family seat, he graduated at Columbia in 1829. He studied law, was admitted to the bar in 1833, and in the same year was appointed attaché at the United States legation in Paris under Edward Livingston [q.v.]. Here he enjoyed a number of stimulating personal contacts, notably with De Tocqueville, the historian, who became his friend and correspondent.

Returning to New York in 1834, Sedgwick began a law practice which in the next sixteen years grew to be very extensive. Ill health, however, made it impossible for him to continue in his profession after 1850, and during 1851–52 he traveled in Italy, Switzerland, France, and England. Upon his return to New York he became president of the newly incorporated Association for the Exhibition of the Industry of all Nations ("Crystal Palace Association"), in which capacity he carried on a voluminous correspondence with eminent men all over the world. After a year, however, the delicate state of his health forced him into retirement, first in New York and then at Stockbridge, where he partially recuperated. In 1857 President Buchanan offered him the post of minister to the Netherlands and later that of assistant secretary of state, both of which offices he declined. In 1858 he was persuaded to accept the position of United States district attorney of the southern district of New York, in which capacity he served until his death in December 1859, at Stockbridge.

Sedgwick was a keen student of legal, judicial, and political problems, and wrote extensively on these subjects. In politics he was, like his father, an advocate of Jeffersonian principles, but some later democratic developments, such as the popular election of judges, "filled him with disgust, and he labored . . . energetically to have the system altered" (Harper's Weekly, Dec. 31, 1859). He contributed largely to Harper's Monthly and Harper's Weekly, and under the pseudonym Veto, to the New York Evening Post, then edited by William Cullen Bryant. In the year he was admitted to the bar he published a biography of his great-grandfather, A Memoir of the Life of William Livingston (1833), and thereafter books and articles from his pen appeared at frequent intervals: What is a Monopoly? (1835); A Statement of Facts in Relation to the Delays and Arrears of Business in the Court of Chancery of the State of New York (1838); Review of the Memoirs of the Life of

Sir Samuel Romilly (1841); Constitutional Reform (1843); Thoughts on the Proposed Annexation of Texas (1844); The American Citizen (1847), an address at Union College; Address . . . Delivered before the Columbia College Alumni Association . . . Oct. 27, 1858 (1858). In 1840 he edited A Collection of the Political Writings of William Leggett, in two volumes. His most important publication was A Treatise on the Measure of Damages, or, an Inquiry into the Principles Which Govern the Amount of Compensation Recovered in Suits at Law (1847; 9th edition, ed. by Arthur George Sedgwick and J. H. Beale, 4 vols., 1912). For some years the only work in English on the subject, this study, in the opinion of a contemporary, was "characterized by a philosophic spirit . . . and by accuracy of detail," and "may well take its place by the side of the more famous works of Chancellor Kent and Mr. Justice Story" (Solicitors' Journal, Jan. 14, 1860, p. 183). In 1857 he published another considerable volume, A Treatise on the Rules Which Govern the Interpretation and Application of Statutory and Constitutional Law, of which a second edition was issued in 1874, with additional notes by J. N. Pomeroy.

Sedgwick was a man of methodical habits, preserving and carefully labeling all his private correspondence and official documents. He married, Sept. 28, 1835, Sarah Morgan Ashburner, of a Stockbridge family, and was the father of seven children, three of whom died in infancy. His son Arthur George Sedgwick [q.v.] followed his father's profession and a daughter, Susan, married Charles Eliot Norton [q.v.].

[H. D. Sedgwick, "The Sedgwicks of Berkshire" (1900), Berkshire Hist. and Sci. Soc. Colls., vol. III; B. W. Dwight, The Hist. of the Descendants of John Dwight of Dedham, Mass. (1874), II, 744–45; Sedgwick's correspondence as president of the Crystal Palace Company, in N. Y. Hist. Soc.; MSS. in the possession of E. L. W. Heck; Horace Greeley, Art and Industry as Represented in the Exhibition at the Crystal Palace, New York, 1853–4 (1853); Harper's Weekly, Dec. 31, 1859; Solicitors' Journal and Reporter (London), Jan. 14, 1860; N. Y. Daily Tribune, Dec. 10, 1859; Evening Post (N. Y.), Dec. 9, 1859.]

E. L. W. H.

SEDGWICK, WILLIAM THOMPSON (Dec. 29, 1855–Jan. 21, 1921), biologist, teacher, and foremost American epidemiologist, was born at West Hartford, Conn. He was the son of William and Anne Louise (Thompson) Barbour Sedgwick and a descendant of Robert Sedgwick [q.v.]. Despite the death of his father when he was eight years of age, Sedgwick attended the Hartford High School and later the Sheffield Scientific School at New Haven, from which he was graduated in 1877. He then entered the Yale Medical School, but the many deficiencies in the teaching of medicine in those days turned him toward pure science. In 1879 he secured a fellowship in biology at the newly established Johns Hopkins University, Baltimore, Md., already distinguished by a faculty of very capable men. Here he came under the influence of a student of Huxley, Henry Newell Martin [*q.v.*], with whom he served for two years as associate in biology after taking his Ph.D. in 1881. On Dec. 29 of that year, he was married to Mary Katrine Rice of New Haven.

In 1883 Francis Amasa Walker, president of the Massachusetts Institute of Technology, called Sedgwick, whom he remembered as one of his brilliant students at Yale, to be assistant professor of biology. A year later he became associate professor, and in 1891 was appointed professor. For the next thirty years he was head of the department of biology, or biology and public health as it became in 1911, of the Institute. During his career as a teacher, Sedgwick trained hundreds of public-health workers, many of whom are numbered among the leading sanitarians in the United States and abroad. He was also active in public service. In 1888 he was named as consulting biologist to the Massachusetts State Board of Health, a connection which he maintained in some form until his death. When the board was reorganized in 1914 as the State Department of Health he became a member of its Public Health Council. As consulting biologist he conducted many notable investigations on sewage disposal, using the facilities of the Lawrence Experiment Station, which had been established in 1886. In the midst of these studies a severe epidemic of typhoid fever swept down the Merrimac Valley in 1890. Sedgwick and Hiram Francis Mills [*q.v.*] traced this epidemic to a polluted brook in Chelmsford above the Lowell water supply. Two years later he investigated another epidemic of typhoid fever at Springfield, Mass., and ascertained the cause to be a contaminated milk supply. He was an early advocate of the pasteurization of milk, and he also made a most important contribution to sanitary science by demonstrating how water and sewage could be disinfected by the use of chlorine (Jordan, etc., *post*, p. 43).

For many years Sedgwick was the foremost American interpreter of sanitary science. In 1902 he published his noteworthy *Principles of Sanitary Science and the Public Health,* a classic work on this subject. He was also author with E. B. Wilson of *General Biology* (1886), with Theodore Hough [*q.v.*] of *The Human Mechanism* (1906), with H. W. Tyler of *A Short History of Science* (1917), and he edited

the two volumes of the *Life and Letters of William Barton Rogers* (1896). He served as chairman of the administrative board of the school for health officers maintained jointly by the Massachusetts Institute of Technology and Harvard University from 1913 to 1922. He was president of numerous scientific societies, including the Society of American Bacteriologists in 1900, the American Society of Naturalists in 1901, and the American Public Health Association in 1914–15. He was a member of the Advisory Board of the Hygienic Laboratory of the United States Public Health Service and of the International Health Board of the Rockefeller Foundation. In 1920 he was exchange professor at the Universities of Leeds and Cambridge in England, where he represented his country as well as his professional interests so admirably that he was called the United States "ambassador of health" (Tobey, *post*, p. 244). He died suddenly of heart disease in Boston and was buried at West Hartford, Conn.

[*Who's Who in America,* 1920–21; E. O. Jordan, G. C. Whipple, and C.-E. A. Winslow, *A Pioneer of Public Health, William Thompson Sedgwick* (1924); *Yale Univ., Obit. Record, 1921* (1921); J. A. Tobey, *Riders of the Plagues* (1930); G. C. Whipple, "The Public Health Work of Professor Sedgwick," *Science,* Feb. 25, 1921; S. C. Prescott, "Life and Work of William Thompson Sedgwick," *Tech. Rev.,* Apr. 1921.]

J.A.T.

SEDLEY, WILLIAM HENRY [See SMITH, WILLIAM HENRY, 1806–1872].

SEE, HORACE (July 17, 1835–Dec. 14, 1909), naval architect, inventor, was born in Philadelphia, Pa., the son of Richard Colhoun See and Margarita (Hilyard) Sellers See. After receiving an early education in private schools, he entered the shops of I. P. Morris & Company in Philadelphia and learned the trade of machinist. A particular interest in ship-building led him to Chester, Pa., where he obtained employment with the firm of Neadie & Levy, shipbuilders. He then worked for the National Armor and Shipbuilding Company at Camden, N. J., and after a number of years in this establishment became superintendent of the George W. Snyder Machine Works in Pottsville, Pa. He returned to the ship-building industry about 1870 when he entered the employment of William Cramp & Sons in Philadelphia. He was promoted to be designer and superintending engineer for that company in 1879, and for ten years continued to design vessels and machinery of greatly improved construction and performance, introducing new methods of work and higher standards, and developing a ship-building plant which could bear comparison with those of Great Britain. During his régime the government contracts for the first vessels of the "New Navy," let under an expansionist program, were received, and he designed the triple expansion engines for six of the cruisers that were built, including the *Yorktown, Bennington, Philadelphia,* and *Vesuvius.*

In 1889 he resigned from William Cramp & Sons to engage in private practice as a marine engineer and architect. He established his office in New York City and at once became consulting engineer for the Newport News Shipbuilding and Dry Dock Company, Newport News, Va. He was also retained by the Southern Pacific Company and by the Pacific Mail Steamship Company as superintending engineer. He served as superintendent for the Cromwell Steamship Company, and was consultant for the Morgan Line. In the course of this work he designed five private yachts, among which were the *Corsair* and *Atalanta*; the steamships *Mariposa, Queen of the Pacific, Caracas* and *Olivette*; the machinery for a number of liners in South American trade; the United States cruisers *Yankee* and *Dixie*; the hospital ship *Solace*; several wrecking launches, and a number of New York police launches. In all of these vessels he introduced many of his inventions, such as a hydro-pneumatic ash ejector and a folding hatch cover. He also invented an automatic siphon fire hydrant, a double furnace water-tube boiler, and introduced a method for producing true crankshafts for multiple-cylinder engines by using his patented cylindrical mandrel for face bearings. In the early part of the Civil War he served as a private in the "Gray Reserves," and in 1862 was a corporal, 7th Regiment, Philadelphia Militia. He was adjutant of the 20th Regiment of the National Guard of Pennsylvania during the riots of 1877, and was later captain of the 1st Pennsylvania Regiment. He was a member of the American Society of Naval Architects and Marine Engineers, of the British Institute of Naval Architects, and of the American Society of Mechanical Engineers, of which he was president in 1888. His wife, Ruth Ross Maffet, of Wilkes-Barre, Pa., to whom he had been married on Feb. 20, 1879, survived him at the time of his sudden death in New York City. He was buried in Philadelphia.

[*Who's Who in America,* 1910–11; *Trans. Am. Soc. Mechanical Engineers,* vol. XXXII (1911); *Jour. Am. Soc. Naval Engineers,* Feb. 1910; *Public Ledger* (Philadelphia), Dec. 16, 1909; Patent Office records.]
C. W. M.

SEED, MILES AINSCOUGH (Feb. 24, 1843–Dec. 4, 1913), manufacturer, was born in Preston, England, the son of Richard and Ann (Ainscough) Seed. He received a public school education in England, and became vitally interested in photography, then in its infancy. He studied the sciences and continued to do research in physics, astronomy, and chemistry, and to experiment particularly with different processes for making and developing photographic plates. Believing that better opportunities were to be found in America for applying the results of his experiments, he emigrated to the United States in 1865 and settled in St. Louis, Mo., where he obtained a position in the photographic gallery of John Scholton. He soon became chief operator and manager and continued in this work for a number of years, devoting his spare time to further experiments at his home in an effort to simplify the process that he had developed for producing photographic negatives. After several years of persistent effort he perfected a process for the manufacture of a photographic dry plate which appeared so promising a contribution to photography that, with the financial help of friends, he formed the M. A. Seed Dry Plate Company in St. Louis in 1882 and began to manufacture his new product. While the dry plate was a vast improvement over the earlier wet plate, it was so revolutionary a step that for a number of years after he began to manufacture the product Seed found it necessary to travel all over the United States to demonstrate its possibilities and methods of use in order to build up a market.

The introduction of the dry plate fixed the use of chemicals, revolutionized photographic apparatus, and compelled the opticians who manufactured lenses to improve and enlarge the field of their products. By reason of his tenacity he succeeded in overcoming the prejudice of photographers against this new product simply by capitalizing on his personal contacts throughout the country. He remained in close touch with his plant and personally superintended the processing of the plates. In the course of ten years not only did he manufacture dry plates but he also produced celluloid films for negatives, and introduced positive celluloid films, lantern slides, and double-coated non-inhalation plates. His dry plate was the first one sensitive enough to be used for X-ray purposes and for astronomical pictures. As a result, a larger market was opened up to the product of Seed's manufactory and the M. A. Seed Dry Plate Company expanded at a rapid rate. In 1902 he sold the business as well as his formulae to the Eastman Kodak Company, Rochester, N. Y., for the succeeding five years being employed as special advisor to that company. In 1907 he retired and a few years later settled in Pelham, N. Y., where he lived until his death. He was very fond of flowers and gardening, and his homes both in St. Louis and Pelham possessed beautiful gardens in which he cultivated extensive varieties of flowers, ferns, palms, cacti, and water plants. He was also a learned student of the Bible. He was married in 1872 to Martha Krause of St. Louis, and after her death he was married in 1881 to her sister, Lydia. He was survived by his widow and nine children, two being children of his first wife.

[*Willson's Photographic Mag.,* Jan. 1914; *Snap Shots,* published by George Murphy, Inc., Dec. 1913, Jan. 1914; *Bull. of Photography,* Dec. 10, 1913; *N. Y. Times,* Dec. 6, 1913; Natl. Museum correspondence with associates and family.]   C. W. M.

SEEGER, ALAN (June 22, 1888–July 4, 1916), soldier and poet, was born in New York City, the son of Charles Louis and Elsie Simmons (Adams) Seeger, both of New England ancestry. During his early years the family lived on Staten Island, and Alan attended the Staten Island Academy and later the Horace Mann School, New York. In 1900 his father's business took him to Mexico, whither he was accompanied by his family. Returning to the United States when he was fourteen, Alan studied at the Hackley School, Tarrytown, N. Y., and in 1906 entered Harvard College.

Self-centered, extremely individualistic both in garb and in behavior, inviting no intimacy, he at first took little part in the life of the University, finding happiness in solitude and perusing books with the delight of a voyager discovering new countries. He contributed poems to the *Harvard Monthly,* was editor in his senior year, and during the last part of his course mingled more with his fellows. He was turning from intellectual satisfactions to the keener pleasures to be had through the senses, the attainment of which thereafter became his ruling passion (see *Letters and Diary of Alan Seeger,* 1917, pp. 184 ff.). He courted beauty with abandon, not the beauty of form and appearance merely, but the beauty of love and of that which lies in experiencing all that is in the nature of things. After graduating he spent two years in New York, doing little, restless and unhappy; he could not find what he craved, and of American standards and conventions he was contemptuous. In the autumn of 1912 he went to Paris. Here he found congenial surroundings, the beauty that he sought, and the inspiration for his poetry. At the beginning of the World War he enlisted in the Foreign Legion.

His passionate affection for France and especially for Paris was one of the motives which led him to enlist, but it was not the principal one; neither was he much moved by any

theory as to the possible moral effect of the war. A fatalist, he believed that war is a law of nature and force the "ultimate arbitrament among humanity, no less than in the rest of the universe." A man fights on the side destiny determines, and "playing a part in the life of nations he is taking part in the largest movement his planet allows him. He thrills with the sense of filling an appointed necessary place in the conflict of hosts . . . and feels . . . a kind of companionship with the stars" (*ante,* p. 38). Eager to experience life in its intense and violent, as well as in its rare and refined forms, Seeger entered the war. "How could I let millions of men know an emotion that I remained ignorant of?" he wrote to a friend (*Ibid.,* p. 186). For almost two years he was in active service, much of the time subjected to the rigorous ordeal of the trenches, individualistic as ever, keeping much to himself, contemptuous of the opinions of others, but full of zest and always a good soldier. After serving on the Aisne he went with his regiment to Champagne, where he took part in the offensive of September 1915. The inactivity of the trenches irked him: he ventured out between the lines by himself on dangerous expeditions; he was eager for the fierce exhilaration of the assault and the glory of victory, or, if fate so decided, the experience of wounds and death. In the battle of the Somme, on July 4, 1916, his great moment came. Going over with the first wave of attack on the village of Belloy-en-Santerre, he was cut down by machine gun fire. He was seen to crawl into a shell hole and the next morning he was found dead. The Croix de Guerre was conferred upon him posthumously and also the Médaille Militaire. Surrounded by the grime and confusion of trench life he produced poems self-revealing and of no little merit, including his widely known "I have a rendezvous with Death," and his "Ode in Memory of the American Volunteers Fallen for France." With his earlier works, these were published in *Poems of Alan Seeger* (1916), with an introduction by William Archer.

[In addition to works cited above, see *Harvard Graduates' Mag.,* Dec. 1916; M. A. De Wolfe Howe, *Memoirs of the Harvard Dead in the War Against Germany,* vol. I (1920); P. A. Rockwell, *Am. Fighters in the Foreign Legion* (1930); *Scribner's,* Jan. 1917; *Outlook,* Mar. 18, 1925; *Century,* Dec. 1926.]   H. E. S.

SEELYE, JULIUS HAWLEY (Sept. 14, 1824–May 12, 1895), clergyman, educator, and publicist, was born at Bethel, Conn., the son of Seth and Abigail (Taylor) Seelye and the brother of L. Clark Seelye [*q.v.*]. He was graduated from Amherst College in 1849 and from the Auburn Theological Seminary in 1852. He then went for a year of philosophical study at the University of Halle. On his return in 1853 he was installed as pastor of the First Dutch Reformed Church in Schenectady, where for five years he discharged his duties with signal success and at the same time pursued his philosophical studies under the direction of Laurens P. Hickok [*q.v.*]. On Oct. 23, 1854, he was married to Elizabeth Tillman James of Albany. They had four children. In 1858 he accepted the chair of philosophy at Amherst College and began a term of service that was to last, with the exception of one short interval, till his death, thirty-seven years later. On his thirty-fourth birthday he began the work that was to bring him great renown as a philosopher of the intuitive school. A distinguished colleague who knew him well throughout his adult life thus described his philosophic teaching: "Believing the transcendental philosophy as represented by Dr. Hickok to be the truth, the whole truth and nothing but the truth, he carries it with him as a personal presence . . . and breathes it as an element of life and power into all of his classes. At the same time accepting the religion of Christ as a revelation from God for men . . . he holds up that religion as truth without any mixture of error, that life as perfection without any mixture of frailty, and makes his pupils feel that to become Christian philosophers, Christian scholars, Christian ministers, Christian men, is the highest aspiration of which their nature is capable" (Tyler, *post,* p. 435). To him religion and philosophy were inseparable. As a leader of youth he was dignified, well poised, resourceful, strong and benignant. Charles H. Parkhurst [*q.v.*] said of him: "He quickened us, not his words but he; not his explanations and exposition and demonstrations but he" (*Congregationalist,* May 16, 1895).

He became the acknowledged leader of an able faculty, and when President William Augustus Stearns [*q.v.*] died in 1876 he became president. The exigencies of the office soon led him to give up most of his class work, but the power of his personality became even more effective throughout the college. His faith in youth, and his understanding, led him to devise the "Amherst plan," a system of student self government, which under his administration proved highly successful at Amherst and profoundly affected the practices in other institutions throughout the country. In other respects also his administration was notable. The pecuniary resources of the college were more than doubled, the physical plant enlarged and im-

proved, and the standard for admission and graduation substantially raised. He was widely recognized as a persuasive and powerful preacher. His tall, broad and stalwart figure, his massive but finely shaped head, and his melodious and resonant voice all contributed no doubt to his success in the pulpit. But more effective yet was his very apparent spiritual quality—the rare but essential union of intellect and emotion —which was set forth not only in his sermons but in his life. That his teaching and example were powerful indeed is clearly evidenced by the large number of leaders in religious circles who acknowledge him as the chief human force in their lives. Further evidence of his persuasiveness is to be found in the record of his visit to India in 1872, where he delivered a series of "Lectures to Educated Hindus," *The Way, the Truth, and the Life* (1873), which aroused much interest among the high-caste natives and were printed and widely circulated at the expense of one of them. In 1887, as chairman of the board of visitors of the Theological Seminary at Andover, he voted for a sentence of "admonition" for all five of the leaders accused of heresy but was outvoted by the other two visitors in the case of Egbert Coffin Smyth [*q.v.*], who was dismissed. In this trial controversies arose which are still undetermined, but Seelye emerged with a greatly enhanced reputation for magnanimity and liberality.

Throughout his life he was a close student of public affairs. His work as a member of the Massachusetts commission for the revision of the tax laws of the state, combined with local dissatisfaction over party management as well as country-wide criticism of the Republican party, led to his election to Congress on an independent ticket without his conducting any campaign. In Congress, from 1875 to 1877, he generally preferred to act with the Republicans, but he was uniformly opposed to the many proposals whose purpose was to keep alive the animosities of the Civil War. He also acted independently in 1877 by voting against accepting the action of the electoral commission in counting the vote of Louisiana for Hayes. He published many articles on religious and political subjects. He translated Albert Schwegler's *History of Philosophy* (1856), edited and revised L. P. Hickok's *Empirical Psychology* (1882) and also Hickok's *System of Moral Science* (1880), and wrote *Christian Missions* (1875), *Duty* (1891), and *Citizenship* (1894).

[*Amherst Literary Monthly,* June 1895; W. S. Tyler, *Hist. of Amherst College* (1873); *The Andover Defence* (1887); personal acquaintance.]   F. L. T.

SEELYE, LAURENUS CLARK (Sept. 20, 1837–Oct. 12, 1924), college president, was born in Bethel, Conn., the descendant of Robert Seely who was captain of one of the vessels of John Winthrop's fleet, which sailed from England to Salem, Mass., in 1630. His parents, Seth and Abigail (Taylor) Seelye, were both descended from Puritan families that had for some seven generations been thrifty farmers and merchants, and pillars of the Congregational Church. He was the youngest son of a large family and, partly on account of his delicate health, was surrounded in youth by more tenderness and affection than was usual among his undemonstrative kinsfolk. His second brother, Samuel, then minister in Wolcottville (now Torrington), Conn., prepared him for college, and in 1853 he entered Union College at Schenectady, N. Y., graduating in 1857, shortly before he was twenty. While there he lived in the house of his maternal uncle, Laurens P. Hickok [q.v.]. His theological training was begun in the Theological Seminary at Andover, but in his second winter his health was such that he was sent to Europe. He traveled widely through Great Britain, France, Italy, Germany, Switzerland, Spain, Egypt, and Palestine, spending in all nearly three years, and in 1861–62 completing his theological studies in Berlin and Heidelberg. His first and only charge was the North Congregational Church of Springfield, Mass., to which he was inducted in January 1863. Here he ministered for two and a half years with great acceptance. On Nov. 17, 1863, he married Henrietta Chapin of Albany, descended from a Puritan stock similar to his own. In 1865, influenced partly by a return of the bronchial affection that had been the cause of his leaving Andover, he gave up his church to accept the Williston professorship of rhetoric, oratory, and English literature at Amherst College, where his brother Julius Seelye [q.v.] was then professor of philosophy. This position he filled with marked success for eight years, when he resigned to accept, after much hesitation, the presidency of Smith College, which it was proposed to open in the neighboring town of Northampton. Here he found his life work. In 1870 Sophia Smith of Hatfield had left somewhat less than $400,000 to found a college for women, and in the following year it had been chartered by the Massachusetts legislature. But the endowment seemed so inadequate that at first Seelye refused to undertake the responsibility. In 1873, however, he accepted, and from this date his whole energies were devoted to the interests of Smith College. During the two years of deliberation he had matured his ideas of what

such a college should be, and he was ready with a program. The new institution, according to the will of the founder was to "furnish for her own sex means and facilities for education equal to those which are afforded now in our Colleges to young men."

The new president began by insisting on entrance requirements of equal difficulty with those of the New England colleges for men and an equal level of achievement for the degree. There was to be no preparatory school attached, where unprepared candidates might find a haven, for he feared the effect on collegiate standards of such an appendage. The students were to live in small homelike groups, not in one large dormitory such as had been built at Vassar College. Special attention was to be given to art and music. The funds at his disposal for the carrying out of these aims were miserably small; public opinion was far from being unanimous as to their desirability; the local community showed little enthusiasm. But from the time the first class of fourteen entered in September 1875, the institution went forward, carried by Seelye's faith, energy, and practical capacity. After a quarter of a century the number of students was 1133, and the assets had been multiplied by five. Ten years later, when he retired, there were 1635 students, so that it was the largest institution of its kind. The history of Seelye's life from 1873 to 1910 is the history of his college. He did his share as citizen and as church member and was in all ways a leader in his community, but he lived for Smith College. To a remarkable extent he succeeded in realizing his ideals. All the main characteristics he aimed at he built into it, standing always for sound scholarship but putting character and good breeding first. Though in appearance and manner he displayed some of the austerity of his Puritan forebears, his fundamental warmth earned him the affectionate devotion of both students and faculty. The growth of the college in equipment and endowment were due more to the care and skill of his management than to the generosity of outsiders. After his retirement in 1910 till his death, he continued to live in Northampton, taking an interest in church and state, and serving for three years on a commission on the Massachusetts Agricultural College at Amherst. In 1923 he published *The Early History of Smith College,* and in 1925 *Prayers of a College Year* was published posthumously. He was survived by his widow and five children.

[*The Early Hist. of Smith College, ante*; H. C. S. Rhees, *Laurenus Clark Seelye* (1929); Vida Scudder, "Seelye of Smith," *New Republic,* Jan. 14, 1925; *Smith*

College Alumnae Quart., Nov. 1924, May 1925; personal acquaintance.]   W. A. N.

SEEVERS, WILLIAM HENRY (Apr. 8, 1822–Mar. 24, 1895), legislator, jurist, was born on a plantation in Shenandoah County, Va., of pioneering stock. His father, James Seevers, was a soldier in the War of 1812; his mother was Rebecca (Wilkins). William had no more than come of age when he was elected sheriff. At the end of his term he followed his parents, in June 1844, to Mahaska County, Iowa, where he continued the study of law he had begun in Virginia. On Mar. 28, 1846, he was admitted to the bar and opened an office in Oskaloosa, Iowa. He married Caroline M. Lee, Feb. 20, 1849, and made his home in Oskaloosa all the rest of his life.

It was not long before he entered politics. In 1848 he was elected prosecuting attorney of Mahaska County, and served two terms in that capacity. The Whigs nominated him for the office of state auditor in 1850, but he was defeated. Meanwhile, he had developed a reputation for being a capable attorney. In 1852 he was elected judge of the third judicial district of Iowa and occupied that office nearly four years, though he resigned before the end of his term to resume active law practice. Seevers had several able partners at various times, among them his brother-in-law Micajah T. Williams, his cousin George W. Seevers, and Marcellus E. Cutts. His reputation attracted many clients with important cases commanding large fees.

His first conspicuous public achievement was in the state legislature. As a representative in the seventh General Assembly, the first under the constitution of 1857, he served as chairman of the committee to which all bills were referred so that the statutes might be brought into conformity with the organic law. It was an arduous position, involving tremendous responsibility, and the fact that much of the legislation of that session has survived three-quarters of a century is eloquent testimony to his ability. Fourteen years later he was appointed chairman of the commission to codify the statutes of Iowa, and *The Code . . . of the State of Iowa* published in 1873 bears further evidence of his legislative competence. Again in 1876 he was a member of the Iowa House of Representatives.

Before this session of the legislature had ended, Seevers was appointed to fill a vacancy in the Iowa supreme court caused by the resignation of the chief justice. For nearly thirteen years he was a member of that tribunal, in 1876, 1882, and 1887–1888 serving as chief justice. He possessed the rare quality of judicial-mind-edness and was a careful legalist. Indeed, he was so legalistic in his attitude that he lost popular favor, particularly by his decision that a constitutional amendment prohibiting the manufacture and sale of intoxicating liquor had not been legally adopted (*Koehler and Lange* vs. *Hill,* 60 *Iowa,* 543). The resolution adopted by the Eighteenth General Assembly had contained a meaningless phrase which was omitted in the enrolled amendment; the Nineteenth General Assembly had approved the amendment as enrolled and in that form it had been ratified by the people. In the opinion of the supreme court, written by Justice Seevers, the amendment was invalid because it had not passed two successive General Assemblies in the same form, though the meaning was identical. One of the five justices dissented. Chiefly as a result of this decision, Seevers failed to be renominated by the Republicans and retired from the bench at the end of his term in December 1888. Thereafter, until a few weeks before his death, he was active in the legal profession, being engaged in a trial two days before he was stricken with paralysis. Five children survived him.

[*Iowa State Register* (weekly ed.), Mar. 29, 1895; E. H. Stiles, *Recollections and Sketches of Notable Lawyers and Public Men of Early Iowa* (1916); Johnson Brigham, *Iowa: Its Hist. and Its Foremost Citizens* (1915), vols. I, II; *Portr. and Biog. Album of Mahaska County, Iowa* (1887); *Annals of Iowa,* 3 ser. II (1895); C. C. Cole and E. C. Ebersole, *The Courts and Legal Profession of Iowa* (1907), vol. I; information as to certain facts from Seevers' daughter; his opinions, in 43–74 *Iowa Reports.*]   J. E. B.

SEGHERS, CHARLES JEAN (Dec. 26, 1839–Nov. 28, 1886), Roman Catholic prelate and missionary, was born in Ghent, Belgium, the son of Charles Francis and Pauline Seghers, and as an orphan was reared by uncles who were apparently comfortably situated. Trained at the College of Ste. Barbe at Ghent, at the diocesan seminary, and at the American College at Louvain, he was ordained a priest at Mechlin, May 31, 1863, and enlisted for the Canadian missions at Vancouver under Bishop Modeste Demers of Victoria. From the time of his arrival on Nov. 17, 1863, he entered into his arduous work with marked zeal despite his delicate health, learning the native dialects, living with the Indians, and serving the scattered tribesmen, hunters, and settlers. In 1869 he accompanied Demers to the Vatican Council. When Demers died two years later, he became administrator of the diocese, and in 1873 he was appointed bishop. Consecrated in June 1873 by Archbishop François Norbert Blanchet [*q.v.*], he visited Europe and more especially his native Belgium in quest of missionaries and financial assistance, for he was intent on bringing Catholicity to Alaska, which knew only a single priest, an Oblate Father.

On his return he busied himself with building chapels, establishing an occasional school, opening mission stations for the Indians (who were acquainted with Christian doctrines through the use of Blanchet's guide or "Catholic Ladder"), and founding St. Joseph's Hospital at Victoria. Not until July 1877 was he able to make his preliminary survey of Alaska. At that time, with Father Mandart, he spent several desperate months of privation at St. Michael, Ulukuk, Nulato, Kaltag, and in various native villages of the Yukon region which knew civilization only through half-breeds and hunter-traders. In 1878 he assigned Father Althoff to establish a mission at Wrangell but could do no more, for he was suddenly named coadjutor to the aged Archbishop Blanchet of Oregon City (Portland), whom he succeeded two years later. His régime was marked only by normal progress and extensive visitations in 1879 and 1882 into the outlying regions of Idaho and of Montana, which at his request was made a vicariate under Bishop John Baptist Brondel [q.v.], who was transferred from Victoria in 1884. While he was in Rome, where he was called in 1883, he made clear his desire to return to British Columbia and to Alaska, on which he had published a widely read account, "The Cross in the North" (*New York Freeman's Journal*, Sept. 21–Nov. 2, 1878, *passim*). On his return, he took part in the Third Plenary Council of Baltimore, in which he spoke on Indian missions, and resigned his archepiscopal see for the episcopal seat at Victoria, to take up his duties in British Columbia and Alaska in 1884, a quite unusual sacrifice. In 1885 he established missions at Juneau and Sitka, Alaska, under Fathers Althoff and Heymen, erected a school and hospital at Juneau, founded two academies for girls, and invited the Jesuits to enter this forbidding mission field. A year later, accompanied by two Jesuits, Paschal Tosti (later prefect-apostolic of Alaska) and Aloysius Robaut, and Frank Fuller, a white attendant, he journeyed over the Chilkoot Pass for the headwaters of the Yukon, where he hoped to establish a mission at Nulato in fulfillment of an earlier promise to the Ten'a tribesmen. Leaving the Jesuits at the mouth of the Stewart River to found a mission among the Stickeen Indians, he continued on with Fuller, who was apparently so affected by fatigue and privation that he developed symptoms of insanity. At Yessetlatoh where they found shelter in an abandoned fishing cabin, Seghers was awakened early in the morning and shot dead by Fuller, who was brought by the Indian guides to Trader Frederickson and later convicted and sentenced at Sitka to ten years of imprisonment. The remains of the unfortunate missionary were taken to St. Michael and two years later buried in the crypt of his cathedral at Victoria.

[Henry Van Rensselaer, "The Apostle of Alaska," *Am. Cath. Quart. Rev.*, Jan. 1888; R. H. Clarke, *Lives of the Deceased Bishops of the Cath. Ch. in the U. S.*, vol. III (1888), pp. 509–32; Maurice De Baets, *Mgr. Seghers, l'Apôtre de l'Alaska* (Paris, 1896); A. G. Morice, *Hist. of the Cath. Ch. in Western Canada* (1910), vol. II; files of *Cath. Sentinel* (Portland), 1870–86; *N. Y. Freeman's Jour.*, Aug. 6, Sept. 24, 1887; *Cath. Ency.*, vol. I (1907), p. 250, vol. XIII (1912), p. 682; index of *Am. Cath. Hist. Researches*; Sadliers' ann. Cath. directories, esp. that for 1888, p. 35.]

R. J. P.

SEGUIN, EDOUARD (Jan. 20, 1812–Oct. 28, 1880), psychiatrist, was born at Clamecy, France, the son of T. O. Seguin (Kelly and Burrage, *post*) of a family of distinguished physicians. Educated at the College of Auxerre and at the Lycée St. Louis in Paris, he studied medicine and surgery in the medical schools of France and came especially under the influence of Jean Marc Itard and Jean Étienne Esquirol, a famous alienist and one of the pioneers of modern psychiatry. While he was interested in general medicine, he applied himself especially to the study of mental diseases and, at a very early day, to the study of idiots, for whom no scientific treatment had been devised. In 1839 he opened a school for idiots in France that met with the approval of authoritative medical bodies and academies, and was the forerunner of many similar institutions throughout the world. Insisting again and again that the idiot's brain was neither diseased nor abnormal but arrested in its growth, he developed a theory of training that has been universally accepted and a method of physiologic education that has been the foundation of the more successful handling of the imbecile and the idiot. In 1846 he published his chief work, *Traitement Moral, Hygiène et Éducation des Idiots,* which was indorsed by the French Academy and was used as a textbook throughout the world.

Having developed very decided social and political views, he felt uneasy in the revolutionary atmosphere of 1848, and about 1850 he emigrated to the United States. He first lived for some years in Ohio, but he was interested in the work in psychiatry that was going on in a number of different places, among them Syracuse, Mt. Vernon, and New York, where he took an active part in organizing the school for defectives on Randall's Island. In 1861 he received the degree of M.D. from the University of the City of New York (later New York University). In 1866 he published a second book, *Idiocy and Its Treat-*

ment by the Physiological Method, in which he was aided by his son, Edward Constant Seguin [*q.v.*]. This supplied to English and American neurologists and psychiatrists much of the material upon which modern methods of treating mental defectives have been based. There is some doubt as to the relative importance of the kindergarten, the Montessori, and the Seguin methods of training; Seguin himself makes very liberal allusion to the kindergarten methods and acknowledges his indebtedness to all such early masters in his field as Horace Mann, Samuel Gridley Howe, and Hervey Backus Wilbur [*qq.v.*]. In his later years he became much interested in medical thermometry and wrote a number of articles that helped to popularize the use of the clinical thermometer, among them *Family Thermometry* (1873), *The Clinical Thermoscope and Uniformity of Means of Observations* (1875), and *Medical Thermometry and Human Temperature* (1876). He had something of a roving spirit and for that reason failed to establish a great practice anywhere, although he might easily have done so. In 1880 he was married for a second time to Elsie Mead, who for many years after his death conducted a school for the training of defective children. He was a man of many amiable qualities and of remarkable unselfishness. Possessed of a wide general culture, he enjoyed painting and poetry, and is said to have written very good verse.

[Seguin's name appears in the records of New York University as O. Edouard Seguin; on the title-pages of his English books it is usually Edward Seguin. See *Am. Medic. Biogs.* (1920), ed. by H. A. Kelly and W. L. Burrage; Henry Holman, *Seguin and His Physiological Method of Education* (1914); C. L. Dana, in *Annals of Medic. Hist.*, Dec. 1924; obituary in *N. Y. Tribune,* Oct. 29, 1880.]   B. S.

SEGUIN, EDWARD CONSTANT (1843– Feb. 19, 1898), neurologist, was born in Paris, the son of Edouard Seguin [*q.v.*]. At the age of seven he was brought by his father to the United States. In 1864 he was graduated from the College of Physicians and Surgeons in New York. Two years before his graduation he was appointed a medical cadet in the regular army. While the training was irregular, the experiences he gained in those stirring times made amends for the lack of classroom instruction, and they also made of him a thorough American patriot. Shortly after his graduation he was appointed acting assistant surgeon at Little Rock, Ark.; in the spring of 1865 he showed signs of incipient tuberculosis and had himself transferred to New Mexico, where he acted as post surgeon. Returning to New York in 1869, he came under the influence of Dr. William Henry Draper at

the New York Hospital. His earliest interests were in general medicine. In 1866 he published a short paper on the use of the thermometer in clinical medicine, which contained what was probably the first temperature chart on record in the United States (Kelly and Burrage, *post*), and in 1867 two short papers on subcutaneous injections of quinine in malarial fevers, a special form of treatment suggested by Draper. It is of especial interest, inasmuch as this was before the era of asepsis, that he made much of the fact that the hypodermatic needle must be kept clean.

As the son of the elder Seguin, it seems natural that he should have become interested in nervous diseases. He had always insisted upon the importance of a broad general medical training; now, in order to acquire special knowledge of mental and nervous diseases, he went to Paris in 1869 and studied under the great masters of the day, Charles Édouard Brown-Sequard, Jean Martin Charcot, and Louis Antoine Ranvier. Interested in the question of cerebral localization, he contributed much to the recognition of functional and organic nervous diseases, which at that time was making great strides under the influence of Charcot in France, of Leyden and Carl Wilhelm Nothnagel in Germany, and of Hughlings Jackson in England.

On his return to America he became one of the triad of early American neurologists, the other two being Silas Weir Mitchell and William Alexander Hammond [*qq.v.*], both older men of world-wide reputation. From 1868–73 he was lecturer on diseases of the nervous system at the College of Physicians and Surgeons in New York and from 1873–87 clinical professor. He was one of the founders of the American Neurological Association and of the New York Neurological Society and served as president of both. From 1876–78 he was editor of *American Clinical Lectures* and from 1879–84 of *Archives of Medicine.* In 1882 his wife, Margaret Amidon, killed herself and her three small children (*New-York Tribune,* Nov. 1, 1882). Seguin later married again and was in active practice until 1894, when there appeared the first symptoms of the illness that led to his death four years later. Feeling that some of the procedures he had recorded would be of use to medical science, he collected his scientific papers and published them in 1884 as *Opera Minora.* In addition to his excellent contributions to the knowledge of mental and spinal diseases, he may be remembered for his faith in the efficacy of drugs properly administered; he was responsible for a treatment that was often successful when others had failed in which iodides were given in large doses. He was an inspiring teacher and a very careful diagnostician, who took unusual pains to get at all the underlying factors of a case and kept wonderfully accurate and detailed clinical records. Through both his teachings and his practice he had great influence upon the development of neurology in the United States.

[Am. Medic. Biogs. (1920), ed. by H. A. Kelly and W. L. Burrage; Bernard Sachs, in Medic. News, May 7, 1898; C. L. Dana, in Annals of Medic. Hist., Dec. 1924; Phila. Medic. Jour., Feb. 26, 1898; N. Y. Tribune, Feb. 21, 1898; personal association.]   B. S.

SEIDENSTICKER, OSWALD (May 3, 1825–Jan. 10, 1894), philologist, historian, was born in Göttingen, Hanover, the eldest of the five children of Georg Friedrich Seidensticker. His father (Feb. 16, 1797–Dec. 24, 1862) was an influential and highly respected lawyer, a veteran of the Napoleonic wars, in which he had fought on both the French and the Austrian side. As the most prominent of the leaders of the liberal political movement in Hanover, he was arrested for his part in the so-called uprising at Göttingen on Jan. 8, 1831, and after legal proceedings had dragged on for seven years, was finally sentenced to life-imprisonment and remanded to prison at Celle. This family calamity left a deep mark on the character of the son, depriving him of a normally carefree youth and making him reserved, serious, and resolute. While his mother maintained the family by conducting a private school, he attended the Gymnasium and matriculated in 1843 at the University of Göttingen as a student of classical philology. In 1845 his father was released on condition that he emigrate at once, without seeing friends or family, to the United States. He landed at New York, where various German societies welcomed him with banquets, gifts, and speeches. He lived the rest of his life in Philadelphia as a journalist, accountant, and, finally, an official of the customs house. In 1846, as soon as he had taken his doctor's degree at Göttingen with a dissertation *De Oenopida Chio* (1846), Oswald and the other members of the family joined the father in Philadelphia.

Seidensticker studied medicine for two years in Philadelphia but found the work distasteful and turned instead to teaching. He was employed in a private school at Jamaica Plain, Mass., 1849–52, and then conducted schools of his own at Bayridge, near Boston, 1852–55, in Brooklyn, 1855–58, and in Philadelphia, 1858–68. On Dec. 30, 1858, he married Emma Logo of Philadelphia. In 1867 he was appointed instructor in German in the University of Pennsylvania and was advanced next year to the rank of professor. During his tenure of twenty-five years he never asked for leave and was never absent until five days before his death. To the German work of the University he gave a prestige that it has maintained to the present day.

His interest in the history of the Germans in Pennsylvania was first stimulated by Abraham H. Cassell, the Dunker antiquary and book-collector of Harleysville, Pa. Seidensticker was quick to perceive the significance and wealth of the field and made it the work of his leisure hours. He was the first student of Pennsylvania German history to bring to the subject broad culture, literary power, and a mind thoroughly trained in modern methods of historical investigation. To Heinrich Armin Rattermann's paper, *Der Deutsche Pionier,* he contributed a remarkable series of monographs on various phases of the subject, and in his later years he wrote with equal charm in English for the *Pennsylvania Magazine.* His separate publications consist of: *Geschichte der Deutschen Gesellschaft von Pennsylvanien* (1876); *Die Erste Deutsche Einwanderung in Amerika und die Gründung von Germantown in 1683* (1883); *Bilder aus der Deutsch-pennsylvanischen Geschichte* (1885)— a popularization of his monographs in the *Pionier;* and *The First Century of German Printing in America, 1728–1830* (1893). He also did much writing for newspapers. He was one of the chief supporters of the German Society of Pennsylvania and of the Pennsylvania Historical Society, and was the founder of the Deutsche Pionier-Gesellschaft of Philadelphia. He visited Germany in 1874 and again in 1891. In his latter years he enjoyed to the full the admiration and affection felt for him by many colleagues and friends throughout the United States. He died at his home in Philadelphia after an illness of a few days. His wife and daughter survived him.

[E. R. Schmidt and others, *Dr. Oswald Seidensticker, . . . Ein Lebensbild* (1894); C. F. Huch, "Georg Friedrich Seidensticker," *Ger.-Am. Annals,* Oct. 1904; H. A. Rattermann, "Dr. Oswald Seidensticker und die deutsch-amerikanische Geschichtsforschung," *Deutsch-Amerikanische Geschichtsblätter,* July 1911; *Public Ledger* (Phila.), Jan. 11, 12, 15, 1894.]   G. H. G.

SEIDL, ANTON (May 7, 1850–Mar. 28, 1898), musician, conductor, was born at Pest, Hungary. None of the printed accounts of his life gives the names of his parents, and by some it was supposed that he was the natural son of Franz Liszt (Finck, *My Adventures, post,* p. 200). In 1870 he entered the Leipzig Conservatorium, where he studied music under Ernst Ferdinand Wenzel, Oscar Paul, and Ernst Friedrich Richter; he also matriculated as a student at the university and attended lectures on logic and philosophy. In the same year he returned to Pest, principally for the purpose of studying with Hans Richter, a musician who had been assisting Wagner in preparing the score of *Die Meistersinger*. Upon Richter's recommendation Seidl was engaged by Wagner in 1872 to help him in his work at Bayreuth. He was employed in making the first copy of the *Nibelungen* score, and during the six years he was with Wagner he helped to complete the scores of *Die Götterdämmerung* and *Parsifal*. Wagner came to lean heavily on his assistant, and he entrusted to him many of the details of the first Bayreuth festival in 1876. In 1879 Seidl was appointed conductor at the Leipzig Opera House, where in the season of 1881–82 he conducted the first performances of the *Nibelungen* cycle ever heard in Berlin. The following season he was appointed conductor of the Travelling Wagner Theatre, with which he toured through England and most of Europe. In 1883 he became conductor of the Bremen Opera House. On Feb. 29, 1884, he married Auguste Kraus, a singer who had been associated with the Travelling Wagner Theatre.

A year later he was invited by Edmund C. Stanton, director of the Metropolitan Opera House, to come to New York as conductor of German opera to fill the vacancy caused by the death of Leopold Damrosch [*q.v.*]. He made his début at the Metropolitan conducting a performance of *Lohengrin*, Nov. 23, 1885, and achieved an immediate success. From this time until his death he made his home in New York and in 1891 became a naturalized American citizen. When German opera was temporarily dropped at the Metropolitan in 1891, he became conductor of the Philharmonic Society of New York, succeeding Theodore Thomas [*q.v.*], who had been called to Chicago. He held this position for the seven remaining years of his life, but in 1895–97 he again conducted German opera at the Metropolitan, and in 1897 he visited London and Bayreuth to conduct special performances. During this period of his life he received many invitations from abroad to leave America; he refused them all when a movement was inaugurated in New York to form a permanent Seidl orchestra and to guarantee its expenses. While these plans were materializing he died suddenly of ptomaine poisoning. He was survived by his wife; there were no children. His influence on American musical life was tremendous. He conducted many American premières of Wagner operas (see *Grove's Dictionary, post,* for a complete list), and with his traditions and the years he had spent with Wagner he was able to produce absolutely authentic performances and interpre-

tations. In 1893 he also conducted the American première of the "New World" symphony by Anton Dvořák, who was his intimate friend. Though he had little time for literary work, he acted as editor-in-chief of *The Music of the Modern World* (2 vols., 1895–97), which contained his valuable article "On Conducting," and contributed an important article on "The Development of Music in America" to the *Forum* of May 1892.

[*Anton Seidl, A Memorial by His Friends* (1899), ed. by H. T. Finck, contains the fullest account of Seidl's life. See also *Grove's Dict. of Music and Musicians* (3rd ed., 1928), vol. IV, and *Am. Supp.* (rev. ed., 1930) ; H. T. Finck, *My Adventures in the Golden Age of Music* (1926) ; obituary in *N. Y. Tribune,* Mar. 29, 1898.]   J. T. H.

SEILER, CARL (Apr. 14, 1849–Oct. 11, 1905), laryngologist, was born in Switzerland. Educated abroad, chiefly in Berlin, he studied medicine in Vienna and Heidelberg and then came to the United States with his mother, Emma Seiler, a teacher of singing and a student of voice production. They settled in Philadelphia, where Seiler continued his medical studies at the University of Pennsylvania and received the degree of M.D. in 1871. His thesis, "The Physiology of the Voice," shows the influence of his mother, who in 1858 had studied the action of the larynx in voice production by means of a laryngeal mirror and had written several books on the subject. Immediately after his graduation he devoted himself to laryngology, beginning his work with Dr. Jacob da Silva Solis Cohen [*q.v.*], a distinguished laryngologist, first as a special pupil and later as assistant. In 1876 he married Carrie G. Linn, daughter of Claudius B. Linn of Philadelphia; they had two daughters and a son. From 1877–95 he was instructor and lecturer in laryngology in the University of Pennsylvania and chief of the throat dispensary of the University hospital. He became a fellow of the American Laryngological Association in 1879 and vice-president in 1882. A few years after his resignation from the faculty of the University of Pennsylvania in 1895 he left Philadelphia and lived first in Scranton, later in Reading, Pa., where he died.

He was greatly interested in the microscope and in his earlier years was recorder of the biological and microscopical section of the Academy of Natural Sciences of Philadelphia. In 1881 he published a *Compendium of Microscopical Technology*; the following year he had privately printed a slender quarto volume of photographic reproductions of microscopic histologic preparations. He made a number of contributions to current medical literature, but his only outstanding work was his *Handbook of Diagnosis and*

Treatment of Diseases of the Throat and Nasal Cavities (1879), of which there were several editions under the title *Handbook of the Diagnosis and Treatment of the Throat, Nose, and Naso-Pharynx*. In the fourth and last, published in 1893, he gave the formula of an alkaline, antiseptic wash or spray for the nose that continues to hold its place in the esteem of laryngologists. As this was a great improvement on the previously used Dobell's solution and as Seiler also suggested a method by which the formula could be made up in compressed tablets to be dissolved in water for use, it won immediate popularity, and "Seiler's tablets" for years continued to be sold in great numbers. He was an able surgeon and had great skill in devising special instruments. A man of wide culture and an excellent musician, he was a delightful teacher and a pleasant companion.

[*Am. Medic. Biogs.* (1920), ed. by H. A. Kelly and W. L. Burrage; *Physicians and Surgeons of the U. S.* (1878), ed. by W. B. Atkinson; obituaries in *Jour. Am. Medic. Assoc.,* Oct. 21, 1905, and *Pub. Ledger* (Phila.), Oct. 11, 1905, which give date of death as Oct. 10; personal acquaintance.]   F. R. P.

SEIP, THEODORE LORENZO (June 25, 1842–Nov. 28, 1903), Lutheran clergyman, college president, was born at Easton, Pa., the son of Reuben L. and Sarah A. (Hemsing) Seip. He attended Weaversville Academy, catching from its principal, H. F. Savage, a graduate of Amherst College, a love of Latin and Greek that never left him, and in 1860 he entered Pennsylvania (later Gettysburg) College. During June and July 1863 he was a soldier in the 26th Pennsylvania Volunteers, and for some months of 1864 he was a delegate of the United States Christian Commission in Tennessee and Georgia. Graduating from college in 1864, he became a member of the first class in the Lutheran Theological Seminary in Philadelphia. In the summer of 1865 he was an inspector of the United States Sanitary Commission in Virginia. Toward the close of his seminary course in 1867 he was appointed assistant in the Allentown Collegiate Institute, which was reorganized that summer as Muhlenberg College with Frederick Augustus Muhlenberg [*q.v.*] as its president. Seip was ordained June 16, 1867, by the Ministerium of Pennsylvania but, declining a call to St. John's, Quakertown, he stayed on at the college as principal of its preparatory department. Muhlenberg College became the work of his life. Besides conducting the academy he acted as assistant professor of Greek, 1867–72, and also gave instruction, when necessary, in other subjects. He was professor of Latin, 1872–76, though still giving some instruction in Greek also; was financial

agent of the college from February 1876 till June 1877, collecting some $33,000 sorely needed to pay the debts and current expenses; was professor of Greek and Latin, 1877–80, and Mosser-Keck professor of Greek, 1880–85. During all these years he acted also as secretary of the faculty. On the retirement of John Philip Benjamin Sadtler [*q.v.*] as president at the close of 1885, Seip was elected to his place immediately and unanimously. He had worked loyally and indefatigably under its first two presidents in the long, chill spring of its early growth; his own administration of eighteen years was a period of increasing usefulness and efficiency. The chief problems were still financial, but they were no longer so pressing, and the college was able to assume an honorable place among institutions of its class. Seip's personal qualities made him an almost ideal president of a small college; there was no phase of the work with which he was not familiar, and his urbane, dignified, friendly bearing made friends for him and for Muhlenberg College wherever he was known. He was one of the founders in 1887 of the College Association of Pennsylvania and was president of the Ministerium of Pennsylvania, 1895–98. He was twice married: in 1866 to Emma Elizabeth Shimer of Bath, who died in 1873, leaving him with two sons and a daughter; and in 1877 to Rebecca Keck of Allentown. Music was his favorite recreation. He died at Allentown after a short illness. John August William Haas succeeded him as president of Muhlenberg College.

[*Who's Who in America,* 1903–05; biog. sketch by S. A. Ziegenfuss in S. E. Ochsenford, *Muhlenberg Coll.* (1892); E. S. Breidenbaugh, *The Pa. Coll. Book, 1832–82* (1882); L. D. Reed, *The Phila. Sem. Biog. Record, 1864–1923* (1923); *Pub. Ledger* (Phila.), Nov. 30, 1903.]   G. H. G.

SEISS, JOSEPH AUGUSTUS (Mar. 18, 1823–June 20, 1904), Lutheran clergyman, author, was born on his father's farm near Graceham, Frederick County, Md., of German stock, the eldest of the four sons of John and Eliza (Schuler) Seiss. The family name had originally been Süss. He attended the parochial school; received additional instruction in Latin, history, and the Bible from the pastor, Ambrose Rondthaler; and was confirmed at the age of sixteen in the Moravian Church. Neither his father nor his bishop, however, would allow the boy to study for the ministry. In later life Seiss was never known to take orders from anybody, and his ambition was not to be thwarted now. He left home and, with some assistance from a Lutheran clergyman, Reuben Weiser, betook himself to Gettysburg, Pa., where, for the next two years, he pursued a special course of study in Pennsylvania

College and its affiliated academy. He mastered the Greek Testament and evinced literary ability, but he was compelled to interrupt his studies and teach school for a living. At this juncture the Lutheran Synod of Virginia offered to license him if he would enter upon the work at once, and Seiss, not without misgivings, consented; he was licensed to preach when only nineteen years of age and was ordained two years later.

No other Lutheran clergyman in America has risen to prominence so early. After a year of missionary activity at Mount Sidney and Harrisonburg, Va., he was pastor from 1843 to 1847 at Martinsburg and Shepherdstown, Va. (now W. Va.), from 1847 to 1852 at Cumberland, Md., and from 1852 to 1858 at the Lombard Street Church in Baltimore. In 1843 he married Elizabeth Barnitz, who bore him two sons and three daughters, dying in 1900. His first book, *Popular Lectures on the Epistle to the Hebrews* (1846), was written while his coevals were still theological students, and his reputation as an eloquent preacher was already growing. While in Baltimore he published several other books, carried on a lively, urbane controversy with the Baptist clergyman, Richard Fuller [*q.v.*], and was elected president of the Lutheran Synod of Maryland. In 1858, when St. John's, Philadelphia, the largest English Lutheran congregation in America, sought a worthy successor to Philip Frederick Mayer [*q.v.*], Seiss was its unanimous choice. During his pastorate of sixteen years St. John's prospered despite its location in a decaying neighborhood. In 1864–65, during a period of ill health, he visited Europe and the Near East. Dissatisfied with the location of St. John's, he founded the Church of the Holy Communion at Broad and Arch Streets and was its pastor from 1874 until his death thirty years later.

He was dowered with an astounding capacity for work. One of the founders of the General Council of the Evangelical Lutheran Church in North America, he was its president in 1888 and one of its most active and influential leaders. He was the most admired preacher of his denomination and its most prolific author, his publications extending to more than one hundred separate titles, besides numerous contributions to periodicals. From 1867 to 1879 he was editor of the *Lutheran*. He was president of the board of directors of the Philadelphia Lutheran Theological Seminary from 1865 until his death, managing its affairs with great business acumen and unremitting attention to detail. Henry Eyster Jacobs considered him the chief instrument in establishing the Seminary. He was a close student of liturgics and hymnology. His various

publications in these fields are still useful, and the English *Church Book* of the General Council owes much to him both in substance and form. The same purity of language that made him a master of liturgical form is in evidence in his sermons. He considered the writing of each a work of art and labored to make it perfect. No one else has so influenced the style and content of English Lutheran preaching. His principal volumes of sermons are: *Lectures on the Gospels for the Sundays and Chief Festivals of the Church Year* (2 vols., 1868–72); *Lectures on the Epistles* (2 vols., 1885); *Lectures on the Gospels and Epistles for the Minor Festivals of the Church Year* (1893); *Beacon Lights* (1900); *The Christ and His Church* (1902); and *Recent Sermons* (1904). He was in his day a noted student of eschatology, and his *The Apocalypse: A Series of Special Lectures* (1865) went through many editions and was translated into German and Dutch.

Seiss had the great advantage that he not only worked, but looked, like a great man. He was tall and majestic in his carriage, with a leonine head, a magnificent voice, and equally magnificent manners. A certain arbitrariness in the exercise of his power and a reserve that amounted at times to coldness prevented him from becoming a popular leader. He was more admired and feared than loved, but he was loved. For several months before his death he was confined to his bed; a few weeks before the end he rose to affix his signature, still firm and bold, to the diplomas of the graduating class at the Philadelphia Seminary.

[G. W. Sandt, "Dr. Seiss Has Passed Away," *Lutheran*, June 23, 1904, and "Lutheran Leaders as I Knew Them: J. A. Seiss," *Lutheran Ch. Rev.*, Jan. 1918; G. F. Krotel, "Joseph Augustus Seiss, D.D., LL.D., L.H.D.," *Lutheran*, June 30, 1904; H. E. Jacobs, "Joseph Augustus Seiss," *Ibid.*, July 14, 21, 28, 1904, and "The Making of the Church Book," *Lutheran Ch. Rev.*, Oct. 1912; T. E. Schmauk, "The Death of Dr. Seiss," *Ibid.*, July 1904; J. C. Jensson (Roseland) *Am. Lutheran Biogs.* (1890); L. W. Johnston and F. A. Johnston, *Descendants of My Great-Grandparents* (1924); Adolph Spaeth, *Charles Porterfield Krauth* (1898–1909); E. E. Sibole, *Centennial . . . of Saint John's Church, Phila., 1806–1906* (copr. 1906); J. A. Seiss, *Bibliographica* (privately printed, 1887); *The Alumni Record of Gettysburg Coll., 1832–1932* (1932); L. D. Reed, ed., *The Phila. Sem. Biog. Record, 1864–1923* (1923); *Public Ledger* (Phila.), June 21, 1904.]
G. H. G.

SEIXAS, GERSHOM MENDES (Jan. 15, 1746–July 2, 1816), rabbi, was born in New York City, the son of Isaac Mendez Seixas and Rachel Levy. His father, a native of Lisbon, emigrated to New York in 1730 and established himself in a mercantile business; about 1765 he moved to Newport, R. I., where he resided until his death in 1780. On July 3, 1768, Gershom was chosen as rabbi of Shearith Israel, the Spanish and Portuguese synagogue of New York. His salary was fixed at eighty pounds annually plus a house, firewood, and perquisites. In 1775 he asked for £140 annually and offered to resign if his request were not granted. As a result his salary was raised to that amount, and in 1784 was increased to £200. He contrived on this income to raise two considerable families: by his first wife, Elkaly Cohen, whom he married on Sept. 6, 1775, and who died in 1785, he had four children; by his second, Hannah Manuel, whom he married Nov. 1, 1789, he had eleven.

As rabbi Seixas performed for the Jewish community of New York (and occasionally, somewhat in the manner of a circuit rider, for coreligionists in nearby regions) all the important religious ceremonies. He was for many years the community's chief professor of Hebrew language, literature, and laws. In addition, through a great portion of his fifty-year ministry he was one of the chief spokesmen of American Jewry and recognized as its representative by American society as a whole. His life in New York was interrupted in August 1776, when he quit the city in company with a considerable number of his congregation prior to its investment by the British forces. Most of the evacuating Jews went to Philadelphia, where Seixas joined them after four years in Stratford, Conn., bringing with him the congregation's sacred Scrolls of the Law. In Philadelphia he helped found a new synagogue, Mickve Israel, and served as its rabbi for two years, returning to New York in 1784.

Seixas was, apparently, strictly orthodox in religious principle. The first rabbi to preach sermons in English in an American synagogue, he constantly advocated the new democratic doctrine of full participation by Jews in the life of the state. His Revolutionary patriotism, his appeals (e.g., on the occasion of British-Indian raids on the Northwest Territory in 1813) to his flock to "support the country in its position at all hazards, because . . . it is sufficient for us to know that our rulers are chosen to be Judges on all affairs . . ." (quoted in *Jewish Comment*, Jan. 10, 1902), and the tone of his public prayer for the safety of the state and its rulers illustrate his views of the duty of the Jews in the new democratic régime. On the other hand, he made it plain that the obligation was reciprocal; when the council of censors of Pennsylvania made eligibility to an Assembly seat dependent on recognition of divine origin of the New Testament, Seixas and two other Jews protested formally against an unconstitutional religious test

which was "unjust to the members of a persuasion that had always been attached to the American cause" (Westcott, *post*, p. xxxii). At least two of his sermons were published: *Religious Discourse, Delivered in the Synagogue . . . the 26th November 1789, Agreeable to the Proclamation of the President . . . to be Observed as a Day of Public Thanksgiving* (1789), said to have been one of the first national Thanksgiving sermons preached; and *A Discourse Delivered . . . on the Ninth of May 1798, Observed as a Day of Humiliation* (1798).

Seixas was in fairly frequent communication with Jewish communities and individuals in other parts of the Americas and in Europe. He consulted with the *Beth Din* (Court of Judgment) of the London synagogue on religious problems, helped raise building funds for synagogues in other cities, and supplied David Ottensoser with Americana for his *Geschichte der Jehudim* (Fuerth, 1821). He founded the still extant Hebra Hased Va-Amet, one of New York's earliest charitable organizations and, from 1784 to 1815, when he resigned, served as regent and trustee of Columbia College. Seixas seems to have exchanged pulpits on occasion with other New York clergymen, as, for example, in August 1800, when he addressed the congregation of St. Paul's. He also participated in public "exegetical disquisitions" with prominent Gentile Hebraists. He was buried in the New Bowery cemetery of Shearith Israel Congregation.

[The chief sources for the life of Seixas are manuscript documents in the archives of the Congregation Shearith Israel, N. Y. City, and of the Am. Jewish Hist. Soc.; a considerable number of the latter are printed in its *Publications* of 1896, 1913, 1914, 1920, 1926; see also L. Hühner, "The Patriot Jewish Minister of the Am. Revolution," in *Jewish Comment* (Baltimore), Jan. 10, 1902; Thompson Westcott, *Names of Persons Who Took the Oath of Allegiance to the State of Pa. . . . with a Hist. of the "Test Laws" of Pa.* (1865); *Jewish Encyc.*, vol. XI; Jacob La Motta, *Funeral Address . . . Previous to the Interment . . . of the Rev. Gershom M. Seixas* (1816); Naphtali Phillips, *An Eulogium to the Memory of the Rev. Gershom M. Seixas* (1816); H. S. Morais, *The Jews of Phila.* (1894); *N. Y. Evening Post*, July 2, 1816.]   H. S.

SÉJOUR, VICTOR (June 2, 1817–Sept. 21, 1874), dramatist, was born in New Orleans, La. He was christened Juan Victor Séjour Marcou et Ferrand and was the illegitimate son of François Marcou, a free man of color from Santo Domingo, and Eloisa Phillipe Ferrand, a quadroon of New Orleans. His parents were married afterwards in 1825. François owned and ran a dry-cleaning establishment on Chartres Street in New Orleans and was sufficiently well-off to send his son to the Ste. Barbe Academy conducted by Michel Seligny, an intelligent and well-educated colored man. Victor showed an early interest in literature and when only seventeen read one of his poems in French before a meeting of La Société des Artisans, a social and benevolent association of the Creole mulattoes. Soon after this his family sent him to a college in Paris. When he left it he continued to live in France and made his début as an author with an heroic poem, *Le Retour de Napoléon,* published in 1841. It was so well received that he was welcomed in literary circles and came to know both Alexandre Dumas and Émile Augier, the distinguished French playwright.

His association with Augier turned his attention to the stage, and his first play, *Diégarias* was produced in the Théâtre Français in 1844. It was followed in 1849 by *La Chute de Séjan,* probably an adaptation of Ben Jonson's *Sejanus.* These early dramas of Séjour's were in heroic grandiose verse bristling with pompous, sonorous phrases. Those which followed were more frankly melodramatic. In all, there were twenty-one of his plays produced in Paris; two of them were written in collaboration with Théodore Barrière, and one each with Jules Brésil and Adolphe Jaime, the younger. His greatest successes were *Richard III,* 1852; *Les Noces Vénitiennes,* 1855; *Le Fils de la Nuit,* 1856; *Les Grands Vassaux,* 1859; *Les Fils de Charles Quint,* 1864, and *Les Volontaires de 1814,* 1862, the only work based upon an American theme, that of the brave defenders of New Orleans against the English. All of these were published within a year or two of their production. An insatiable reader of Shakespeare and Victor Hugo, he frankly acknowledged that the greatest source of his inspiration came from them. He had a thorough knowledge of stage direction and was so conscientious a craftsman that he tried to improve his plays until the very last minute, even going so far as to hand little memorandum slips with changes in lines to the actors on first nights as they went on the stage. During the initial performance of *Le Fils de la Nuit,* after the first four acts had been played, he rehearsed during the intermission an entirely new version of the last act. For some time all Paris flocked to his opening nights. The spectacular magnificence of his settings and the sumptuousness of the costumes struck the fancy of the populace which secretly regretted the pageantry and heroics of the first Napoleon, and Séjour's plays became successful in spite of the hollow ring of his pretentious dialogue. Unfortunately, however, popular taste changed, and the grandiose spectacles, which were all he knew how to produce, lost favor. He fell on evil days and was

forced to hawk about from manager to manager his two plays, *Cromwell* and *Le Vampire,* the latter a great fantastic drama. After a heartbreaking experience, for a man who had once had all Paris at his feet, *Le Vampire* was accepted by the Gaîté, but before the play could be produced he was taken to the charity ward of a hospital in Paris, where he died of galloping consumption, the result of the privations he had suffered during his penniless days. He was buried in the cemetery of Père-Lachaise.

[E. L. Tinker, *Les Écrits de Langue Française en Louisiane au XIXe Siècle* (Paris, 1932), with bibliog.; R. L. Desdunes, *Nos Hommes et Notre Histoire* (Montreal, 1911); Pierre Larousse, *Grand Dictionnaire Universel du XIXe Siècle* (17 vols., 1866–90); Gustave Vapereau, *Dictionnaire Universel des Contemporains* (1880); *Lib. of Southern Lit.,* vol. XV (copr. 1910), ed. by L. L. Knight; J. W. Davidson, *The Living Writers of the South* (1869); *Le Gaulois* (Paris), Sept. 22, and *Figaro* (Paris), Sept. 24, 25, 1874; death notice in *Le Soleil* (Paris), Sept. 23, 1874.]   E. L. T.

SELBY, WILLIAM (1739?–December 1798), musician and composer, was probably born in England. Little is known of his early life and the date of his birth must be conjectured from the death notice in the *Columbian Centinel* (Boston) Dec. 12, 1798, which gives his age as fifty-nine. His first appearance in Boston was recorded in a concert advertisement of Oct. 4, 1771, for it was undoubtedly he who was announced as "a gentleman lately arrived from London." O. G. Sonneck (see *Early Concert-Life, post,* p. 262) believed that he was also identical with the William Selby, who, as organist of St. Sepulchre's, played the organ at an anniversary of the Charity School, London, in 1767. By 1772 Selby was acting as organist of King's Chapel in Boston and participating in concerts as an organist and harpsichordist. For a short time in 1774 he played the organ at Trinity Church in Newport, R. I., and in the same city he announced his intention of opening a dancing school. The latter project may or may not have been responsible for his leaving Newport, but in any case he returned to Boston, and by 1777 was again organist at King's Chapel. During the Revolution Selby was forced to seek other fields than music for a livelihood, and in 1780 he kept a small shop, but by October 1782, he is again mentioned as organist at King's Chapel, and once more became active in the musical life of Boston.

Selby was chiefly interested in instrumental music before the war, but he now became engaged in what proved to be his most important contribution to the musical future of Boston, the development of choral singing. He was undoubtedly of great influence in the movement which led to the organization of the Handel and Haydn Society more than fifteen years after his death. While his predecessors had been content with the singing of hymns and anthems, Selby led his singers in the study of cantatas and oratorios as is evidenced particularly by three of the concerts organized and directed by him. The first of these, given on Apr. 30, 1782, advertised a program of "Musica Spiritualis" and contained works by Handel, Arne, and other composers of the period. On Jan. 10, 1786, the Musical Society of Boston (presumably founded by Selby in 1785) offered a concert for the benefit of the prisons. The program consisted of selections from Handel's *Messiah,* an overture by Bach, and works by Selby himself. The third concert, given on Jan. 16, 1887, presented works of Handel, Piccini, and more compositions by Selby. He composed "Ode in Honour of General Washington" which was performed at a concert given for his benefit by the Musical Society on Apr. 27, 1786, and when Washington visited Boston in 1789, the concerts arranged in his honor featured more of Selby's works.

Practically the only compositions by Selby that are extant today are a few songs, some of which are printed in the *Massachusetts Magazine:* "On Musick," April 1789; "The Rural Retreat," October 1789; "Ode for the New Year," January 1790; "The Lovely Lass," July 1790. These songs were later reprinted in the *American Musical Miscellany* (1798), and another, "Ptalæmon to Pastora," appeared in *The Gentlemen and Ladies Town and Country Magazine,* March 1789. Two major works were advertised for subscription in 1782 and 1790, but no record has been found of actual publication: "The New Minstrel," a collection of original compositions, one number to be issued every month, and "Apollo, and the Muse's Musical Compositions," a collection of sacred and secular songs and choruses, as well as instrumental pieces. In addition to these works, the organ and harpsichord concertos which Selby played on concert programs were presumably of his own composition. He was married in Boston on Jan. 7, 1792, to Susannah Parker, who survived him.

[O. G. Sonneck, *Early Concert-Life in America* (1907), and *Bibliog. of Early Secular Am. Music* (1905); J. T. Howard, *Our Am. Music* (1931); *Grove's Dict. of Music and Musicians, Am. Supp.* (1930); *A Vol. of Records . . . containing Boston Marriages* (1903); *Continental Jour.* (Boston), Jan. 13, 1780.]
                                                    J. T. H.

SELDEN, GEORGE BALDWIN (Sept. 14, 1846–Jan. 17, 1922), patent attorney, inventor, son of Henry Rogers and Laura Anne (Baldwin) Selden, was born in Clarkson, N. Y. He was of English ancestry, seventh in descent from Thomas Selden who was in Hartford, Conn., in 1639. His father was an able lawyer, lieutenant-governor of New York in 1856 and judge of the court of appeals for two terms in the sixties. After young Selden had attended the local schools and St. Albans (Vt.) Classical Preparatory School, he went to the University of Rochester, 1861–64, his parents having moved to Rochester in 1859, but he did not finish his course. He is said to have enlisted in the 6th New York Cavalry at the beginning of the Civil War. In 1865 he entered Yale College as a classical student. Since he was interested in engineering and technology he found classical studies irksome and therefore welcomed, in a way, a call to go to his father, who had become seriously ill while traveling in Europe. Returning to the United States in 1867, he entered the Sheffield Scientific School for a few months but once more went to Rochester, entered the law offices of his father and uncle, studied law for three years, and in 1871 was admitted to the bar.

Being particularly interested in mechanical subjects, he specialized in patent law, handling the occasional invention and patent litigation cases his father obtained. This was hardly enough, however, to satisfy his interest in technology, and as fast as he could afford it he equipped a shop of his own for experimental work. From his youth he had been interested in mechanical transport on roads, particularly in self-propelled vehicles; he now began a series of investigations on road traction and on the various power agencies. By 1873 he had abandoned steam as the power for a road locomotive, and he began the study of engines using liquid and gaseous fuels. Having a family to support and very little money, he progressed slowly, but in 1875 he had built an engine, which turned out to be unsuccessful, operated by the expanded products of combustion of a mixture of kerosene and laughing-gas. Meanwhile he had engaged in other inventive work, especially in the design of machinery to prepare barrel hoops, and in 1875 he obtained a patent for a machine for shaving half-round hoops; he secured three patents for improvements in 1876 and two more in 1877, all of which he sold at a meager profit. He continued his work on a self-propelled vehicle, especially after 1876, when he came to the conclusion that the type of internal combustion engine best suited to his purpose was one invented by George Brayton in 1872 and 1874 using hydrocarbon liquid fuels. The Brayton engine was a very heavy two-cycle stationary design with an open crankcase. Selden reduced its weight by inclosing the crankcase, increased its power by changing the manner of furnishing fuel to the cylinders, and by 1877 had made a light-weight, high-speed, three-cylinder gasoline compression engine of the Brayton type. He then designed a road-locomotive, virtually an automobile, which combined an engine, running gear, driving wheels, propeller-shaft and clutch, and a carriage body, and on May 8, 1879, applied for a patent. For years he tried without success to secure financial help so that he could build a machine in accordance with his design. Appreciating that he was ahead of his time and acting wholly within his rights, he delayed the issue of a patent to him until Nov. 5, 1895, sixteen years later, when he was granted patent No. 549,160 for a "road engine."

Meanwhile the automobile had made rapid strides, and on Nov. 4, 1899, Selden sold the rights to his patent on a royalty basis to W. C. Whitney of the Columbia Motor Company and Electric Vehicle Company of New Jersey. In 1900 the Electric Vehicle Company successfully brought suit for infringement of the Selden patent against the Winton Motor Carriage Company (104 *Federal Reporter*, 814). As a result nine other automobile makers banded together as the Association of Licensed Automobile Manufacturers and purchased the right to use the Selden patent at a royalty of 1¼ per cent. of the retail price of all automobiles sold. By 1906 Selden was receiving royalties from almost all of the automobile manufacturers in the United States and was able to organize his own company in Rochester, the Selden Motor Vehicle Company. In 1903 he and the Columbia Motor Company instituted an infringement suit against the New York agents of the Ford Motor Company, which had refused to pay royalties. In September 1909, after many delays, the case was argued before the United States circuit court of the southern district of New York, and again the Selden patent was sustained (*Electric Vehicle Company* vs. *C. A. Duerr & Company,* 172 *Federal Reporter,* 923). The Ford Motor Company took an appeal, and on Jan. 11, 1911, a written decision was handed down that Selden had a valid and true patent but that the defendants were not guilty of infringement because they were using the Otto four-cycle type of engine and not the Brayton two-cycle type designated in the patent (*Columbia Motor Car Company* vs. *C. A. Duerr & Company,* 184 *Federal Reporter,* 893). Inasmuch as all manufacturers were using the Otto type of engine this was a far-reaching victory for the automobile industry. Although the patent had but a few

months more to run, Selden's royalties stopped at once. He then turned to his own automobile business, but unfortunately he was a more successful lawyer and inventor than manufacturer and lost heavily in the venture. On Dec. 14, 1871, he had married Clara Drake Woodruff of Rochester, who died in 1903; in April 1909 he married Jean Shipley. At the time of his death in Rochester he was survived by his wife, two sons, and two daughters.

[S. S. Rogers, E. S. Lane, and E. V. D. Selden, *Selden Ancestry* (copr. 1931); *Hist. of the Class of 1868 of Yale Coll.* (1914); J. R. Doolittle, ed., *The Romance of the Automobile Industry* (1916), pp. 15–16, 55–71; L. H. Weeks, *Automobile Biogs.* (copr. 1904); Leroy Scott, "Selden's Explosion Buggy," *Tech. World Mag.,* Sept. 1906; *Motor Age,* Jan. 12, 1911, on the Ford-Selden case; T. F. MacManus and Norman Beasley, *Men, Money and Motors* (1929); U. S. Nat. Museum records; Patent Office records; obituary in *Democrat and Chronicle* (Rochester, N. Y.), Jan. 19, 1922; correspondence with family.]

C. W. M.

SELFRIDGE, THOMAS OLIVER (Feb. 6, 1836–Feb. 4, 1924), naval officer, the son of Rear Admiral Thomas Oliver Selfridge and Louisa Cary (Soley) Selfridge, was born in Charlestown, Mass. His great-great-grandfather, Edward A. Selfridge, had emigrated to Massachusetts from Scotland in the early part of the eighteenth century. He was appointed to the United States Naval Academy from Massachusetts on Oct. 3, 1851, as acting midshipman, and was graduated at the head of his class in 1854. He was promoted successively to the rank of passed midshipman in 1856, master in 1858, and lieutenant in 1860. His first sea duty was on the *Independence* in the South Pacific, from whence, after a short period spent in coast survey work, he was transferred to the *Vincennes* of the African Squadron, to assist in the suppression of the slave trade. He returned to the United States early in 1860, being assigned to the sloop-of-war *Cumberland* the following September. On this ship he was present at the destruction of the Norfolk navy yard in April 1861, and participated in the bombardment and capture of the forts at Hatteras Inlet. In the famous engagement between the *Cumberland* and the iron-clad *Merrimac,* Selfridge was in command of the forward gun-battery, and in this position bore the brunt of the *Merrimac's* raking fire, saving himself only as the *Cumberland* sank with her flag flying. A vivid account of this battle is given by Selfridge in his *Memoirs,* published in 1924. In June 1862 he was assigned to the torpedo boat *Alligator,* the first submarine to be tried out in the Civil War, but this craft proved to be a failure because of her lack of speed and insufficient ventilation. Promoted to the rank of lieutenant commander in July 1862, he was at once sent to the Mississippi Squadron and given command of the gunboat *Cairo,* operating against Vicksburg. This vessel was blown up by a torpedo in December, whereupon he was ordered to the *Conestoga.* During the siege of Vicksburg he commanded a shore battery of naval guns. After the surrender he commanded a flotilla of gunboats with the *Conestoga* as flagship, and succeeded in capturing the Confederate steamers *Louisville* and *Elmira.* When the *Conestoga* was sunk by collision in March 1864 he was ordered to command the *Osage,* and participated in the Red River expedition, supporting General Banks's command. He assisted in the construction of the famous Red River dam, and commanded the entire fleet in the passage of the dam.

When Admiral Porter was transferred to the East, he selected Selfridge to accompany him, giving him command of the gunboat *Huron,* in which he took part in both attacks on Fort Fisher. In the second attack he commanded a landing party of bluejackets and marines in an assault on the fort. He was recommended for a promotion of thirty numbers on the navy list for his conspicuous gallantry during the war, but the recommendation was never acted upon by Congress. In 1869 he was commissioned commander and ordered to conduct a survey of the Isthmus of Darien for an interoceanic canal. He explored all the country south of Panama to the headwaters of the Atrato River in South America and drew up a report which was published in 1874. Four years later he was selected to survey the Amazon and Madeira Rivers, and the following year was invited by Ferdinand de Lesseps to attend a congress on interoceanic canals, meeting in Paris. For his work on the Darien survey he was given the decoration of the Legion of Honor of France, and made an honorary member of the Royal Geographical Society of Belgium. In 1881 he was commissioned captain and given command of the Naval Torpedo Station at Newport, R. I., where he conducted numerous experiments with torpedoes and torpedo-nets. He was court-martialled in 1888 for conducting target practice in Japanese territorial waters, but was acquitted. In 1894 he was commissioned commodore and in 1896 rear admiral. As special representative of the United States he was present at the coronation of Tsar Nicholas II of Russia in 1896. He was married to Ellen F. Shepley in August 1865, and had four sons by this marriage. She died in 1905, and in 1907 he married Gertrude Wildes,

who survived him. After his retirement in 1898, he resided in Washington, D. C.

[*Who's Who in America,* 1922–23; *Memoirs of Thomas O. Selfridge, Jr.* (1924); L. R. Hamersly, *The Records of Living Officers of the U. S. Navy and Marine Corps* (6th ed., 1898); *Argument of Linden Kent . . . in behalf of Capt. T. O. Selfridge, . . . June 8, 1888* (n.d.); Cyril Field, *The Story of the Submarine* (1908); *Army and Navy Jour.,* Feb. 16, 1924; Lucien Young, *Cat. of Works by Am. Naval Authors* (1888); *Evening Star* (Washington, D. C.), Feb. 5, 1924.]

L: H. B.

SELIGMAN, ARTHUR (June 14, 1871–Sept. 25, 1933), merchant, banker, governor of New Mexico, was born at Sante Fé, N. Mex., the oldest of four children of Bernard and Frances (Nusbaum) Seligman. By both parents he was of German-Jewish stock. His father emigrated to Philadelphia from Frankfort-on-the-Main, where he had been employed in the Rothschild banking house. In 1856, however, he followed an older brother, Sigmund, to Santa Fé, and there in 1862 the mercantile house of Seligman & Clever became "Seligman Bros.," a trade name which was to endure for over sixty years. The mother was of a mercantile family in Harrisburg, Pa.

Arthur studied with private tutors, at Swarthmore College Preparatory School (1887), and at the Pierce business college, Philadelphia. Late in 1888 he began his career as a merchant in Santa Fé. On July 4, 1896, he married Frankie E. Harris of Cleveland, Ohio, by whom he had a son and a daughter. From the year of his father's death (1903) to 1926 he was president of Seligman Bros. He early acquired stock in the First National Bank of Santa Fé, and helped to make it the most important banking house between Denver and El Paso. He was long a director and its president from 1924. From boyhood he was keenly interested in the various forms of Indian and Spanish-American handicraft, and all his life he was a collector, especially of Navajo blankets, *santos,* and paintings by Southwestern artists.

He had his first taste of politics as a youth, campaigning with his father. His own political career was notable for the fact that of the many positions of honor and responsibility in which he served from 1888 to 1933 only two were salaried offices. As mayor of Santa Fé (1910–12) he was able and public spirited, and his long and distinguished service to the Democratic party in state and nation was crowned in 1930 by his election as governor of New Mexico, and his reëlection in 1932. Although he always voted the straight ticket, his closest advisers in legislative matters were both conservative and progressive Republicans. During periods of Republican dominance in the state, the healthful and constructive opposition was due in large measure to him. "To many . . . his reliance on men of opposite partisan opinion seemed inconsistent, but results proved it excellent generalship" (*New Mexico Historical Review, post,* p. 311). In an editorial of the *Santa Fe New Mexican,* Sept. 26, 1933, he was characterized as "an able business executive, with tremendous capacity for work; . . . a shrewd, resourceful political manager . . . a man of unruffled temper who took defeat or victory alike calmly; an inveterate politician, who loved the political battle of wits and strategy, and whose poker political face kept the opposition uneasy through many a campaign. . . . He ofttimes exasperated by Fabian tactics and indirection, and played his cards close to the chest." Becoming governor at a time when questions of taxation and revenue made the position a difficult one, he succeeded in keeping expenditures within the state income; he acknowledged to his intimates, however, that taxes would have to be increased to give the people what they wanted. On the other hand, he doubted the wisdom of the vast sums appropriated by the federal government, realizing that the money must eventually come out of the pockets of the tax payers.

Suave, fastidious in dress, aristocratic in taste but democratic in policy, always prominent in social life, he sought and attained a large measure of power through business and political channels. Intensely loyal to his numerous friends and an enemy to be feared, for more than a quarter of a century he had few peers in Democratic circles of the Southwest. The strong position of the Democratic party in New Mexico at the time of his death was largely due to his long, shrewd, and able leadership. He was connected with no church or synagogue; was a life member of the Historical Society of New Mexico; and, from 1920, a member of the Democratic national committee.

[R. E. Twitchell, *Old Santa Fe* (1925); P. A. F. Walter, "Arthur Seligman," in *N. Mex. Hist. Rev.,* Oct. 1933; *Who's Who in America,* 1932–33; *Santa Fe New Mexican,* Sept. 25–28, 1933; personal acquaintance.]   L. B. B.

SELIGMAN, ISAAC NEWTON (July 10, 1855–Sept. 30, 1917), banker and civic leader, born in Staten Island, N. Y., was a son of Joseph Seligman [*q.v.*] and Babette (Steinhardt) Seligman. As a small boy he was tutored by Horatio Alger, Jr.; later he attended Columbia Grammar School and Columbia College, where he was active in the college crew. He graduated with honor in 1876, and became a loyal member of the Alumni Association. His business career began in the New Orleans branch of the international banking house of J. & W. Seligman & Company, which his father had founded. He was transferred to the New York office in 1878, two years before his father died. On the death of his uncle, Jesse Seligman [*q.v.*], in 1894, he became the head of the house. During his membership the firm maintained United States government connections and was particularly interested in the flotation of loans for Venezuela and the financial rehabilitation of that country, and in loans for other countries of Central and South America and the Orient. Under Isaac Seligman's leadership the firm also had charge of the reorganization of several important American railroads, including the Pere Marquette, and of the American Steel & Wire Company and the Cramp Steamship Company. He was very active in municipal political reform movements, particularly in the Citizens' Union (of which he was treasurer for years), interested himself greatly in civil service reform, and was vice-president of the New York Chamber of Commerce and chairman of its committee on taxation. He was one of the founders of the Child Labor Association. For years he served as treasurer of the City and Suburban Homes Company, which became the principal model tenement-house enterprise of the city. He also served as a member of the Committee of Fourteen and later of the Committee of Seven, which sought to remedy the social evil, and was head of the Civic Forum and vice-president of the People's Institute. He was a vice-president of the United Hebrew Charities, an officer of St. John's Guild, and a trustee of Temple Emanu-El. The public became so accustomed to seeing him figure as treasurer of enterprises involving the raising of funds for important civic and charitable purposes that the absence of his name in such connection in any particular instance became a cause for comment. Governor Morton appointed him a trustee of the Manhattan Hospital for the Insane and Governor Theodore Roosevelt reappointed him. He was deeply interested in music, and was a trustee of the New York Symphony Society and of the New York Oratorio Society, and a founder of the Institute of Musical Art. On Nov. 18, 1883, he married Guta Loeb, a daughter of Solomon Loeb of the banking firm of Kuhn, Loeb & Company. Four children were born of this marriage: two daughters who died young and a son and a daughter who survived their father. His death, in New York, resulted from a fractured skull, sustained in a fall from his horse.

[H. S. Mott, in *N. Y. Geneal. and Biog. Record*, Oct. 1918; *Am. Jewish Hist. Soc. Pubs.*, no. 28 (1922); G. S. Hellman, *The Family Reg. of the Descendants of David Seligman* (1913); *Who's Who in America*, 1916-17; *N. Y. Times*, Oct. 1, 1917.]   M. J. K.

SELIGMAN, JESSE (Aug. 11, 1827–Apr. 23, 1894), banker and philanthropist, was born at Baiersdorf, Bavaria, a son of David and Fanny (Steinhardt) Seligman and a younger brother of Joseph Seligman [*q.v.*]. After graduating from the Gymnasium at Erlangen, he joined his brothers in the United States in 1841, spending some years in Alabama with several of them and in 1848, with his brother Henry, moving to Watertown, N. Y. Here they opened a dry-goods store and Jesse became intimate with U. S. Grant, a friendship which was later renewed in California. In 1850, a year after the beginning of the gold rush, Jesse and his brother Leopold went to San Francisco with a supply of merchandise and established what rapidly became a very lucrative business. Jesse Seligman showed his good judgment by selecting as his store the only brick building in the town, with the result that his business was the only one which escaped in the fire of May 1851. He was an active member of the San Francisco Vigilance Committee (see Mary F. Williams, *History of the San Francisco Committee of Vigilance of 1851*, 1921, p. 443) and became a member of the famous San Francisco Committee of Twenty-one, which in 1857 effected the election to both municipal and state offices of candidates pledged to clean and honest government.

In that same year he moved to New York City and became an active member of the importing and clothing firm of which his brother Joseph was the head. He brought a large sum accumulated in California as his contribution to this enterprise and to its successor, the banking firm organized in 1862 under the style of J. & W. Seligman & Company. From the beginning of the banking venture he was an important factor in the main office in New York City, and after the death of Joseph Seligman in 1880, he became head of the firm, continuing in that capacity until he died. During this period the firm became particularly active in flotations of railway securities in the South and Southwest; it also headed the American Syndicate that placed the Panama Canal shares and served as a fiscal agent for the United States government.

Jesse Seligman was a vice-president of the Union League Club of New York for many years, but resigned in 1893 when his son was blackballed because of his race. He was influential in the civic and philanthropic life of New York, and at the time of his death it was said in newspaper obituaries that he had twice declined the Republican nomination for mayor. He served for several decades before his death as president of the Hebrew Benevolent and Orphan Asylum of New York City, and was selected by Baron de Hirsch in 1891 as an original member of the Board of Trustees of the Baron de Hirsch Fund, but his philanthropies were not limited by race or creed. He enjoyed the confidence and esteem of President Grant and several of his successors and their advisers, and was for a generation one of the leading financiers of the country. Seligman married in Munich, Oct. 18, 1854, Henrietta Hellman, who with six of their seven children survived him. He died at Coronado, Cal.

[*In Memoriam: Jesse Seligman* (1894), which includes an autobiographical address giving an interesting account of the family's early experiences in America, delivered at a banquet tendered to him Oct. 1, 1891, to celebrate the fiftieth anniversary of his arrival in America; G. S. Hellman, *The Family Reg. of the Descendants of David Seligman* (1913); *The Jewish Encyc.* (1905), vol. XI; *World* (N. Y.), Apr. 24, 1894.]   M. J. K.

SELIGMAN, JOSEPH (Nov. 22, 1819–Apr. 25, 1880), financier and civic leader, a native of Baiersdorf, Bavaria, was the eldest in the family of eight sons and three daughters born to David and Fanny (Steinhardt) Seligman. He graduated from the Gymnasium of Erlangen and began the study of medicine but, dissatisfied with the lack of opportunities for Jews in Germany, emigrated to the United States in 1837. For some time he was secretary to the Pennsylvania financier Asa Packer [*q.v.*]. As his means permitted, he sent for all seven of his brothers, to whom he bore almost a paternal relationship. William and James arrived in 1839 and engaged in business with him at Lancaster, Pa. Jesse [*q.v.*] came over in 1841, and Henry, Leopold, Abraham, and Isaac soon followed. The elder brothers started a small dry-goods business in Alabama, but in 1848 they moved north, and Joseph, William, and James became clothing merchants in New York City. By 1857 all the brothers had united their capital under Joseph's leadership in a New York clothing and importing firm. They paid for their European purchases with gold bar exported from California under the supervision of Henry Seligman, who had gone to San Francisco during the gold rush and remained there. Joseph's standing in New York City within the next few years was marked by his choice as a vice-president of a huge Union mass meeting in New York City, Apr. 20, 1861, and his election as president of the German Hebrew Orphan Asylum. From a letter of his, Jan. 24, 1862 (MS., Treasury Department, Washington), it appears that the government then owed the Seligmans a million dollars for clothing supplied to the army.

Early in 1862 the clothing firm was transformed into the international banking house of J. & W. Seligman & Company, with its chief office in New York City. Branches were opened soon afterwards in Frankfurt-am-Main, London, Paris, San Francisco, and New Orleans, each in charge of one or more of the brothers, with Joseph as the head of the firm. The Frankfurt branch, Seligman & Stettheimer, organized by Joseph himself in 1862 and left in charge of his brothers Henry and Abraham as resident partners, was able to render particularly valuable service to the Union cause during the Civil War. United States bonds amounting to approximately $200,000,000 were sold in Frankfurt during this trying period, largely through its agency. These sales have been characterized as scarcely less important than the Union victory at Gettysburg (W. E. Dodd, *Robert J. Walker*, 1914), since at that time it was almost impossible to sell a United States bond in English or French markets (Hugh McCulloch, *Men and Measures of Half a Century*, 1888, pp. 183–84). Doubtless in appreciation of its services, on Feb. 28, 1871, the Frankfurt house was appointed fiscal agent of the United States government in connection with the conversion of the 5–20's to new 5% bonds. The New York and London houses were given similar status soon afterwards, and they also acted for years as fiscal agents for the State and Navy departments. The Frankfurt and London houses were members of the Jay Cooke syndicate which entered into the contract of Aug. 11, 1871, with Secretary Boutwell for the conversion of $130,000,000 in 5–20's from 6% to 5% after the effort in the preceding February had failed. Members of the Seligman firm had become intimate with U. S. Grant prior to 1850 and again in California in the decade before the Civil War ; after Grant became president, Joseph Seligman was one of his confidential financial advisers, notably at a memorable New York conference on Sept. 21, 1873, in the midst of the panic of that year. President Grant tendered him the post of Secretary of the Treasury, but he declined it for personal reasons.

While the refunding operations of the seventies were under consideration, after the failure of Jay Cooke & Company the Secretary of the Treasury summoned Seligman and other leading financiers to Washington to advise him as to the best method of reducing the government's interest payments and paving the way for the resumption of specie payments. Each financier was requested to prepare separately his proposed plan for immediate submission to the Secretary. The following day, the Secretary announced that he had selected the Seligman firm to execute the plan, and they induced the Rothschilds to join in the undertaking (information furnished by Prof. Edwin R. A. Seligman). The contract of July 28, 1874, with Secretary Bristow, covering a $55,000,000 conversion with an option for $122,-000,000 more confirms this story. The firm also figured prominently in five other conversion contracts, 1875–79, and during much of this period Joseph Seligman was recognized as practically the mouthpiece of the Treasury (*John Sherman's Recollections of Forty Years*, 1895, I, 570).

Seligman served for a number of years as a vice-president of the Union League Club of New York. He was an active member of the Committee of Seventy which ousted the "Tweed ring" from control of the city (*New York Times Supplement*, Sept. 5, 1871). He was appointed by Mayor Wickham as one of the five commissioners on rapid transit for New York City and was elected chairman by this commission, which laid out the New York elevated railroad system in its report of Sept. 2, 1875, and organized the Manhattan Railway Company (J. B. Walker, *Fifty Years of Rapid Transit*, 1918, pp. 107 ff.). In 1876 he became one of the chief organizers of the Society for Ethical Culture, with Prof. Felix Adler as its leader, interesting himself particularly in its industrial school. He had served previously, 1873–75, as an active member of the New York Board of Education. He was active in a large number of charitable and financial organizations, and for some years before his sudden death in New Orleans was regarded as the leading Jew in the United States. On Oct. 26, 1848, he had married Babette Steinhardt, who with all their children—four daughters and five sons—survived him.

[Joseph Jacobs in *The Jewish Encyc.* (1905), vol. XI ; *In Memoriam: Jesse Seligman* (1894) ; *Reminiscences of Isaac Seligman of London* (privately printed, 1926) ; family letters of Joseph Seligman in possession of G. S. Hellman ; Isaac Markens, *The Hebrews in America* (1888), pp. 141–42, 174 ; *N. Y. Times, N. Y. Herald, N. Y. Tribune*, Apr. 27, 1880 ; *The Family Reg. of the Descendants of David Seligman* (1913), ed. by G. S. Hellman ; Georg von Skal, *Hist. of German Immigration to the U. S.* (1908), pp. 61–62.] M.J.K.

SELIJNS, HENRICUS (1636–1701), Dutch Reformed clergyman, was the son of Jan Selijns Hendrickszoon and Janneken de Marees. He came from a good Amsterdam family which gave several ministers to the Church, received a brief, but apparently thorough, training for the ministry at the University of Leyden, and was the most cultured of all the Dutch preachers who came to New Netherland in the seventeenth century. When the *Deputati ad Res Indicas* of the Amsterdam Classis chose him from among three candidates for the ministry in New Netherland, his knowledge of English, rather uncommon at that time among the Dutch, was one of the qualifications that recommended him. He was ordained Feb. 16, 1660, and reached New Amsterdam on June 11 of that year. He had been promised a salary of 1,200 guilders, but found on arrival that no funds were available. The congregation at Breuckelen (Brooklyn) could not pay more than 300 guilders' worth in grain, to which Governor Stuyvesant offered to add 250 guilders on condition that Selijns preach every Sunday evening in the chapel on his Bouwerie. In a letter to the Amsterdam Classis, dated Oct. 4, 1660 (*Ecclesiastical Records, post*, I, 487–89), Selijns gave an account of his work and the conditions at Breuckelen. The settlement then consisted of thirty-one households, numbering 134 persons, twenty-five of whom were Church members. He started services in a barn, but next winter hoped to erect a church.

Selijns had signed a contract for four years, and in 1664 he returned to Holland and accepted a call to the parish of Waverveen, in the Province of Utrecht. Twice he refused a call to New Netherland, in 1670 after the death of Johannes Megapolensis [*q.v.*] and in 1677 after the death of Johannes Theodorus Polhemius; his salary troubles at Breuckelen had made him wary. In 1681, however, he was prevailed upon to accept a call to New York to fill the vacancy left by the passing of Willem van Nieuwenhuizen. He took the precaution this time of having the conditions drawn up and witnessed before an Amsterdam notary. These guaranteed him a salary of 1,000 guilders, free rent and fuel, a stipend for the Wednesday evening services, and free passage to America for himself and his family. He landed in New York on Aug. 6, 1682, and started preaching immediately. For the sake of the children, "who multiply more rapidly here than anywhere else in the world" (*Ecclesiastical Records*, II, 829), he held a catechetical class on Sunday evenings; three times a year he preached to the people at Bergen, and once a year at Harlem. Labadists from Holland proselytized among his congregation and he had to warn his flock against the "enthusiastic principles" of the Quakers. The rebellion of Jacob Leisler, who was a deacon in the Dutch Reformed Church, brought him further troubles. Since the majority of his elders and deacons

were magistrates and as such opposed to the champion of the common people, he took sides against Leisler, thus antagonizing the members of his congregation who saw in Leisler the leader of a just cause. He was a popular preacher, however, and, to quote from a testimonial signed by Governor Stuyvesant and his fellow elders and deacons in 1670, "left a deep impression among our members by the faithfulness of his ministry, the piety of his life, his peculiar zeal in instructing and catechizing, and his kind and affectionate intercourse" (*Ibid.*, I, 608). A tolerant man in ecclesiastical matters, he allowed the Rev. Mr. Daillé to preach to his French congregation in the Dutch church after Selijns' second service, the English chaplain having the use of it after his morning service. He was on terms of friendship also with the English ministers in Boston, and prefixed a long Latin poem to Cotton Mather's *Magnalia Christi Americana* (1702). Thanks to his persistent efforts, the Dutch Reformed Church, in 1696, obtained the first church charter granted in the colony. The Rev. Gualterus Du Bois was called as his colleague in 1700, and Selijns died in September of the following year (*Ecclesiastical Records*, III, 1484). He had been married twice: first, July 9, 1662, to Machtelt Specht of Utrecht, Holland, who died in 1686, and second, Jan. 10, 1694, to Margaretha de Riemer, widow of Cornelis van Steenwijck.

[*Ecclesiastical Records—State of N. Y.* (7 vols., 1901–16), ed. by E. T. Corwin; E. T. Corwin, *A Manual of the Reformed Church in America* (1902); A. Eekhof, *De Hervormde Kerk in Noord-Amerika* (2 vols., 1913) and article in *Nieuw Nederlandsch Biografisch Woordenboek*, III (1914), 1159–66; H. C. Murphy, *Anthology of New Netherland* (1865), which contains a memoir and a collection of Selijns' poetical effusions—chiefly occasional verse—in the original Dutch and in English translation.]   A. J. B.

SELIKOVITSCH, GOETZEL (May 23, 1863–Nov. 27, 1926), Egyptologist, author, journalist, was born in Rietavas, Russia (now Lithuania), the son of David and Rachel (Zundelewitz) Selikovitsch. As a youngster his brilliant record as a student in Hebrew and the Talmud won him the reputation of a boy prodigy. He attended several Talmudic schools and was tutored privately in the Russian and German languages and in secular subjects. In 1879 he went to Paris, where he studied at the École des Hautes Études, displaying a special aptitude for oriental languages, mastering Egyptian, Ethiopic, Arabic, and Sanskrit and their literatures. He was graduated in 1884 and was attached for a short while to the Bibliothèque Nationale in Paris. In 1885 he was engaged by the British war office as chief interpreter to Lord Wolseley for the Arabic and Nubian dialects during the British expedition to relieve General Gordon from the Sudanese at Khartum, but was released from his duties when it was suspected that he was sympathetic with the natives. Before his return to France he visited Abyssinia, Morocco, Algeria, and Asia Minor, familiarizing himself with the life and customs of the natives and their tongues. The results of his travels and researches published in French and Hebrew journals gained for him a wide reputation. He came to the United States in 1887 and lectured on hieroglyphics and Egyptology at the University of Pennsylvania and the Franklin Institute in Philadelphia. He had hoped to follow an academic career, but personal reasons compelled him to relinquish this idea, and he thereafter took up Yiddish journalism as a profession. A journalist of talent and a prolific writer, he found in the Yiddish press a medium for the exploitation of his versatile personality. For several years he edited Yiddish periodicals in Boston, Chicago, and New York City, and in 1901 he joined the staff of the *Jewish Daily News* in New York City, with which he was associated until his death.

Of a restless, adventurous disposition, a true Parisian Bohemian, Selikovitsch was unable to concentrate his real powers in any one field. He was fond of life and of living, possessed a keen sense of humor, and took a vivid interest in everything that went on about him. In addition to scholarly contributions in French and Hebrew, made possible by his extraordinary erudition and phenomenal linguistic knowledge, he also wrote, in Yiddish, feuilletons, poems and trivial novels under various pseudonyms. A collection of speeches in Yiddish, Hebrew, and English, and a series of editorials and articles and a method for the study of the Arabic language written in Yiddish appeared in book form. His Yiddish journalism gained for him no worthwhile recognition, with the exception, perhaps, of his weekly column conducted for a number of years in the *Jewish Daily News* entitled "Literatur un Lomdos" (literature and learning), in which he displayed, in the shape of book reviews unusual familiarity with every conceivable subject in several literatures. He wrote a lucid and arresting style. He was himself not at all proud of his work in Yiddish, and remarked in his autobiography that it was dictated purely by financial considerations. Towards his writings in Hebrew, however, he adopted a different attitude. These were for him a labor of love and are of lasting literary value. Of his Hebrew works which attracted commendation are *Ziure*

Massá (Warsaw, 1910), travel sketches of Africa, and *Torath Buddha* (New York, 1922), an excellent translation into Hebrew from the Sanskrit of the Tripitaka. His treatises in other languages include *Le Shéol des Hébreux* (1881), and *The Dawn of Egyptian Civilization* (1887), published also in the *Journal of the Franklin Institute,* May 1887.

[Autobiographical notes in *Ziure Massá*; *Who's Who in Am. Jewry*, 1926; Zalmen Reisen, *Lexicon fun der Yiddisher Literatur*, vol. I (Vilna, 1926); Salomon Wininger, *Grosse jüdische National-Biographie,* vol. V.]
                                                    I. S.

SELLERS, COLEMAN (Jan. 28, 1827–Dec. 28, 1907), engineer, inventor, was born in Philadelphia, Pa., the youngest son of Coleman and Sophonisba (Peale) Sellers and a descendant of Samuel Sellers who received a grant of land in Pennsylvania in 1682. His father and a number of paternal ancestors had been engineers; his maternal grandfather was Charles Willson Peale [*q.v.*], the portrait painter. During Coleman's childhood his father died, and after attending private schools in Philadelphia and completing the course at Bolmar's academy, West Chester, Pa., when he was about seventeen, the boy spent two years on the farm of a kinsman. He then went to work in the Globe Rolling Mill, Cincinnati, Ohio, operated by his two older brothers. Here his mechanical ingenuity quickly asserted itself and under his direction the wiremill belonging to the plant was rebuilt and improved.

From childhood Sellers had been greatly interested in natural philosophy and in the solution of physical problems, and he constantly devoted his spare time to studying and making apparatus in order to demonstrate to himself new theories as they were announced. Thus while making wire for the new telegraph lines in the West, he secured a few batteries and constructed apparatus with which he was able to repeat the unusual electrical experiments announced by Michael Faraday. Because of his prompt and thorough investigation of scientific discoveries he became the mentor of a group of intellectual men in Cincinnati and frequently gave lectures, illustrated by practical experiments, on chemistry, physics, and electricity. At the age of twenty-one he became superintendent of the Globe Rolling Mill. In 1850–51 he undertook the design and construction of locomotives for the Panama Railroad and upon the completion of this contract, took charge of the locomotive works of James and Jonathan Niles in Cincinnati. Five years later, in 1856, he was induced by William Sellers [*q.v.*], his second cousin, to accept the position of chief engineer of William Sellers & Company in Philadelphia. In this capacity he obtained patents for a variety of inventions, notably the Sellers coupling. He was also much interested in the development of new systems of power transmission. In 1873 he became a partner in the firm.

Failing health led him to resign his position as chief engineer of William Sellers & Company in 1886, but subsequently he was induced to engage in active practice as a consulting engineer. Probably his greatest work in this capacity was in connection with the hydro-electric power development of Niagara Falls. He was consulting engineer of the Cataract Construction Company, a corporation formed to execute this work, and served on the International Niagara Commission which determined the types of turbines and generators and the methods of power transmission finally adopted. Sellers designed the first large dynamos installed in this power plant. Throughout his busy life he continued his interest in physics and telegraphy. In addition he was a microscopist and an expert photographer, devising valuable improvements in both photographic processes and apparatus. From the time of his return to Philadelphia in 1856 he was identified with the Franklin Institute, which he served as vice-president for several years and as president for five consecutive terms. He contributed much to the interest of the Institute's meetings by his lectures, always drawing large audiences. For a number of years after 1886 he was a non-resident professor of engineering practice at Stevens Institute of Technology, Hoboken, N. J., where he delivered lectures at intervals during the school year. He was a member of engineering and scientific societies both in the United States and in Europe, and was a charter member and president of the American Society of Mechanical Engineers. For his scientific attainments he was decorated by King Oscar II of Sweden and Norway with the Order of St. Olaf. Sellers vigorously opposed the movement toward the legal establishment of the metric system (*Transactions of the American Society of Mechanical Engineers,* vol. I, 1880). He was the author of several papers, notably, perhaps, "Electricity as Applied to the Transmission of Energy" (*Proceedings of the American Philosophical Society,* vol. XXXVIII, 1899) and "The Utilization of Niagara's Power," in *The Niagara Book* (1893). He married, Oct. 8, 1851, Cornelia Wells of Cincinnati, who with two sons and a daughter survived him. He died in Philadelphia.

[*Trans. Am. Soc. Mech. Engrs.,* vol. XXIX (1907); *Jour. Franklin Inst.,* Mar. 1908; *Who's Who in America,* 1906–07; *Public Ledger* (Phila.), *Phila. Inquirer, Phila. Record,* Dec. 29, 1907; Patent Office records; *Cassiers Mag.,* Aug. 1903; J. W. Jordan, *Encyc. of Pa. Biog.,* vol. XII (1919); J. W. Roe, *Eng. and Am. Tool Builders* (1916).]

C. W. M.

SELLERS, ISAIAH (*c.* 1802–Mar. 6, 1864), pioneer steamboat pilot, was born in Iredell County, N. C., lived and died on the Mississippi, and was buried in St. Louis. Uncertainty clouds the time and circumstances of his removal to the Mississippi Valley. According to Mark Twain's *Life on the Mississippi* Sellers made his inaugural river trip in 1811, "the year the first steamboat disturbed the waters of the Mississippi," but it has also been said that he went west in 1825 "when he was quite a young man" (Darby, *post,* p. 213). His own diary (Gould, *post,* p. 600) shows that he engaged in the commerce of the lower river from 1825 to 1828, shipping first from Florence, Ala., on the *Rambler,* next on the *General Carroll,* and then on the *President.* While he was on the *Carroll* he introduced bell-tapping as the pilot's signal to take soundings, a decided improvement over the shouted commands theretofore employed. Joining the *Jubilee,* he piloted his first steamboat to the upper river, and in 1836 at Pittsburgh he took charge of the palatial *Prairie,* the first boat with a stateroom cabin to visit St. Louis. As pilot of the *J. M. White II,* he made perhaps the most noteworthy of all steamboat runs on the Mississippi. Leaving New Orleans on May 4, 1844, he brought the *White* to St. Louis in the record time of three days, twenty-three hours, nine minutes. This mark stood for a quarter century, and by that time cut-offs had shortened the river's course and refueling from barges in midstream had come into vogue. According to the diary, Sellers introduced in 1857 the signal for meeting steamboats, a distinction freely accorded him by river historians (Hyde and Conard, *post,* p. 1922); although the United States Bureau of Navigation has no records to verify this, it recognizes that rules and signals later approved by Congress "had their source in such men as Isaiah Sellers." While he frequently acted as steamboat master, he preferred the post of pilot, the ninth renewal of his pilot's certificate being issued in St. Louis, Feb. 25, 1862. River disasters were common occurrences, but not once did a Sellers vessel figure in an accident. This remarkable record won him the confidence of business men and caused women passengers to wait for the *Aleck Scott,* long his boat. His years on the Mississippi made him an authority on its habits and changes. No other riverman knew landmarks so well as he, and none could point out more curiosities of nature to admiring passengers. Under the *nom de plume* of Mark

Twain, which Samuel Langhorne Clemens [*q.v.*] later appropriated, he was a contributor to the New Orleans *Daily Picayune* before Clemens took to the pilot's wheel. Indicative of his rank on the river were the honors accorded him when he died of pneumonia at Memphis on a downstream run. When the *Henry von Phul* returned his body to St. Louis, flags on all steamboats along the levee were at halfmast, as they were again seven days later when he was buried in Bellefontaine Cemetery. His wife Amanda had died twenty-one years before. The marble monument he ordered for his grave—a pilot on watch at his wheel—testifies to his high regard for his calling. Tall, dignified, and ruggedly handsome, with hair that in his later years was still "black as an Indian's," he was, wrote the second, if better known, Mark Twain, "the patriarch of the craft."

[S. L. Clemens, *Life on the Mississippi* (1883); E. W. Gould, *Fifty Years on the Mississippi* (1889); J. F. Darby, *Personal Recollections* (1880); William Hyde and H. L. Conard, *Encyc. of the Hist. of St. Louis* (1899), vol. IV; J. T. Scharf, *Hist. of St. Louis City and County* (1883), vol. II; *Daily Evening Gazette* (St. Louis), May 9, 1844; *Daily Mo. Democrat* (St. Louis), Mar. 10, 11, 1864; *Mo. Republican* (St. Louis), Mar. 10, 18, 1864; records of Bellefontaine Cemetery; information from Iredell County, N. C., county court, U. S. Bureau of Navigation, and C. J. Armstrong, Hannibal, Mo.]   I. D.

SELLERS, MATTHEW BACON (Mar. 29, 1869–Apr. 5, 1932), pioneer in aerodynamics, was born in Baltimore, Md., the son of Matthew Bacon and Annie L. (Lewis) Sellers. He was educated under private tutors and at private schools. Just when his interest in the dynamics of the air had its inception is not known, but the studies he undertook at the University of Göttingen in Germany seem to indicate that his interest in the subject came early in life. He spent a year at Évreux, France, and returned to the United States to study at Harvard University where he received the degree of LL.B. in 1892. He later took special courses at the Lawrence Scientific School (Harvard), and the Drexel Institute, Philadelphia. He began his active research work in aerodynamics in 1900, and continued to pursue it throughout his life, even while practising as a patent lawyer and aerodynamic consulting engineer in New York City. President Taft appointed him to the Aerodynamical Laboratory Commission, created in 1912, and in July 1915 President Wilson, on the recommendation of the secretary of the navy, Josephus Daniels, appointed him to serve as one of two representatives of the Aeronautical Society of America on the newly formed Naval Consulting Board. He resigned from the Board in 1918 to become its technical assistant, and re-

signed from that position in 1919 to resume his membership on it. Much of the work done by the Board in connection with aircraft investigation devolved upon him, his independence of thought and critical abilities rendering his assistance of high value. The problems of the helicopter particularly interested him since he felt that the basic idea was probably the oldest of all "heavier-than-air machines."

His theoretical research work led him to build an efficient quadroplane in 1911 for experimental purposes and he demonstrated its possibilities in actual flight. The invention and construction of the lightest aeroplane flying with the least power is attributed to him. He acted as his own pilot and thus was able fully to appreciate the technical difficulties to be encountered. He constructed a wind tunnel for testing propellers and airfoil shapes for discovering their aerodynamic possibilities. Five patents were issued to him: one for aerial apparatus in 1908, for an aeroplane in 1909, for his quadroplane in 1911, and two in 1914 were issued for improvements in steering and running gear on aeroplanes. While technical editor of *Aeronautics* from 1911 he aided others in presenting to the public the results of their work, reviewed books on aeronautics, and carried on a series of answers to questions involving the principles and experimental data of aerodynamics. His most prolific period of publication was from 1909 to 1916. The results of his experimental work appeared in aeronautical periodicals of the day and included his studies of arched surfaces, wings, propellers, wind tunnels, gyroscopic forces, lateral balance, the aerodynamic resistance of solid bodies, and all kindred subjects (see Brockett, *post*).

On June 18, 1918, he was married to Ethel Clark. She and their two sons survived him when he died of a heart attack while recovering from pneumonia at his home, Ardsley-on-Hudson, N. Y.

[Hist. records of the Navy Dept.; records of the Patent Office; *Who's Who in America*, 1930–31; Paul Brockett, *Bibliog. of Aeronautics, Smithsonian Miscellaneous Colls.*, vol. LV (1910), and *Bibliog. of Aeronautics, 1909–1916, Natl. Advisory Committee for Aeronautics* (1921); *N. Y. Times*, Apr. 6, 1932.]   P. B.

SELLERS, WILLIAM (Sept. 19, 1824–Jan. 24, 1905), machine tool builder, inventor, son of John and Elizabeth (Poole) Sellers, was born in Upper Darby, Pa., on the family estate held under the original patent taken up by Samuel Sellers of Derbyshire, England, in 1682. After being educated in a private school maintained by his father, William at fourteen was apprenticed to his uncle, John Morton Poole of Wilmington,

Del., to learn the machinist's trade. He remained there for seven years, and then took charge of the machine shop of Fairbanks, Bancroft & Company in Providence, R. I. Some three years later he established his own manufactory of machine tools and mill gearing in Philadelphia, where he was soon joined by Edward Bancroft of Providence, with whom he organized the firm of Bancroft & Sellers. In 1853 his younger brother, John Sellers, became a partner, and after Bancroft's death in 1855 the firm name was changed to William Sellers & Company. For fifty years thereafter, until his death, Sellers served as president of this enterprise. From the beginning of his business venture, he departed from the accepted designs of mill machinery and tools. He was among the first to realize that architectural embellishments were a false feature of machine design and was one of the first to make the form of a machine follow the function to be performed. He made his products heavier too, although not unnecessarily so, and from the beginning adhered so closely to the standards he had adopted that fifty years after their original manufacture repair parts could be supplied for his machines.

Beginning in 1857, after Bancroft's death, he brought out a series of inventions, in a variety of fields, for which he was granted some ninety United States patents and many others in foreign countries. These inventions included machine tools of all kinds, steam injectors (which he introduced in the United States when in 1860 he secured the American rights to the patent of Henry Giffard of France), rifling machines, riveters, hydraulic machinery, steam hammers, and turntables. Probably the most original of his machines was the spiral geared planer, patented in 1862. In addition to his original manufacturing enterprises, Sellers in 1868 organized the Edge Moor Iron Company and became its president. This company furnished the iron work for the principal buildings of the Centennial Exhibition in Philadelphia in 1876, and all the structural iron work, except the cables, for the Brooklyn Bridge. He reorganized the William Butcher Steel Works in 1873, renaming it the Midvale Steel Company, and under his management it developed rapidly and became a leader in the production of heavy ordnance.

Sellers was elected a member of the Franklin Institute in 1847 and served as a member of the board of managers from 1857 to 1861 and again from 1864 to 1892, being president of the Institute, 1864–67. While holding this office, he made one of his most significant contributions to industry when he read a paper on "A System of Screw Threads and Nuts" (*Journal of the Franklin Institute,* May 1864), in which he proposed a system of screw threads to supply the need for a generally accepted standard. This paper had a great influence in the United States, and Sellers' system was adopted by the United States government in 1868 and by the Pennsylvania Railroad in 1869, soon thereafter becoming practically universal. It is known today as "the Sellers or United States standard." In 1868 Sellers was elected a member of the board of trustees of the University of Pennsylvania, in which capacity he served continuously thereafter throughout his life. He was a member of the National Academy of Sciences and of the foremost engineering societies of the United States, Great Britain, and France, and at the close of the Paris Exposition in 1889 was made a chevalier of the Legion of Honor. He was the author of "Memoir of James Eads" (*Biographical Memoirs of the National Academy of Sciences,* vol. III, 1895) ; and of "Machinery Manufacturing Interests" in *One Hundred Years of American Commerce* (1895, vol. II), edited by Chauncey M. Depew. Sellers was twice married: first, Apr. 19, 1849, to Mary Ferris of Wilmington, Del., by whom he had a daughter and two sons, one of whom died in infancy; second, Aug. 21, 1873, to Amelia Haasz of Philadelphia, who bore him two sons and a daughter who died young (Jordan, *post,* p. 221). He died in his eighty-first year, survived by his wife and four children.

[*Trans. Am. Soc. Mech. Engrs.,* vol. XXVI (1905) ; *Jour. Franklin Inst.,* May 1905 ; J. W. Roe, *English and Am. Tool Builders* (1916) ; J. W. Jordan, *Encyc. of Pa. Biog.,* vol. XII (1919) ; *Who's Who in America,* 1903–05 ; *Public Ledger* (Phila.), Jan. 25, 1905 ; Patent Office records.]   C.W.M.

SELLSTEDT, LARS GUSTAF (Apr. 30, 1819–June 4, 1911), painter, was born at Sundsvall, Sweden, a son of Erick and Eva Sellstedt. His paternal grandfather was a prosperous fuller and dyer (Sellstedt, *post,* p. 18) ; his maternal grandfather, a clergyman. Lars was educated at Sundsvall and at Hernösand but, when his father died of consumption in 1828 and his mother remarried, his stepfather treated him with such cruelty as to drive him to seek service at sea. In 1831 he became cabin-boy on a small Swedish trading vessel. Although he spent another winter at school in Sweden, for the most part his life after this was one of hardships and adventures, graphically described in his autobiography, *From Forecastle to Academy: Sailor and Artist* (1904). During a long voyage he learned English from Putnam Coffin, of Salem, Mass. Trying his hand, while voyaging on the South

American west coast, at making some drawings on whales' teeth, he found to his delight that he had artistic ability. He had learned, meantime, by experience that sailors were best treated on American ships, and he had heard that the most agreeable marine service in the world was that on the American Great Lakes. That information brought him in 1842 to Buffalo, which was at first only the headquarters of a young Swedish mariner taking various jobs on lake ships but later became his permanent home. His talent for drawing and painting, remarkable in an untaught sailor, attracted attention. His first commission, to do a lady's portrait, brought him two dollars and, more important, valuable criticism from a local artist. He had useful training as a draftsman while employed one summer on a United States topographical survey of the Lakes, and he finally ventured to take a studio at a hundred dollars a year, then a very high rent. Living on bread and milk, he managed to make his way until sitters began to come at fair prices. In 1849 he spent some months in the West Indies but without much success. On Jan. 19, 1850, he married Louise Lovejoy, with whom he moved to New York, believing Buffalo too small a place for his career. After a short time, however, he was forced to return to Buffalo, and there the young wife succumbed to Asiatic cholera. Sellstedt visited Stockholm in 1853 but once more came back to Buffalo and on June 11, 1856, married Caroline Scott, daughter of William K. Scott of Buffalo, a successful physician. Their home soon became a center of artistic activities.

Sellstedt had grown to be a cultivated, well-read man, deeply religious, active in many good causes. He painted well. His self-portrait, sent to the National Academy of Design in 1872, won commendation from Daniel Huntington [*q.v.*] and led to his election as an associate; in 1875 he became an Academician. He painted at Buffalo two presidents of the United States: Millard Fillmore, with whom he was intimately acquainted, and Grover Cleveland, whom he first knew as a young lawyer and an enthusiastic angler. Among his other portraits were those of several mayors, hung in the Buffalo city hall. The success of an art exhibition opened at Buffalo in December 1861, which he had helped to arrange, led to the establishment of the Buffalo Fine Arts Academy. Of this he was the principal organizer, and, in 1876–77, the president. In 1875, with his wife, he studied old masters in Europe and made many acquaintances among contemporary painters at Paris and Rome. One of his closest friends in America was the poet

David Gray, under whose encouragement he wrote creditable verse. In 1910 he published *Art in Buffalo*. He was active in the Saturn and Liberal clubs of Buffalo. His long life was saddened by the death of an only son, but it was otherwise in his later years one of notable happiness and of a philosophic calm.

[See esp. L. G. Sellstedt, *From Forecastle to Academy: Sailor and Artist* (1904). See also *Who's Who in America*, 1910–11; H. W. Sprague, in *Pubs. Buffalo Hist. Soc.*, vol. XVII (1913); *Buffalo Express*, June 5, 6, 1911. Information about Sellstedt's family has been supplied by his daughter, Mrs. Eva Sellstedt Potter of Buffalo.]   F. W. C.

SELYNS, HENRICUS [See SELIJNS, HENRICUS, 1636–1701].

SEMMES, ALEXANDER JENKINS (Dec. 17, 1828–Sept. 20, 1898), physician and Roman Catholic priest, was born in Georgetown, D. C., the son of Raphael Semmes of Nanjemoy, Charles County, Md., and Matilda (Jenkins), and a first cousin of Raphael Semmes [*q.v.*]. Both his grandfathers were officers of Maryland troops in the Revolutionary War. They were descendants of English Catholic gentry who came to Maryland in the following of the Calverts. Alexander received the degree of A.B. in 1850 from Georgetown College. He began the study of medicine in Paris and was given his medical degree in 1851 by the medical department of Columbian College, District of Columbia, after a year's course. For a short time he practised in Washington, and then joined an elder brother, Thomas Jenkins Semmes [*q.v.*], in New Orleans, where he became resident physician of Charity Hospital.

At the outbreak of the Civil War he was appointed surgeon of the 8th Louisiana Infantry and shortly thereafter was commissioned as surgeon in the Confederate army. He served for two years as brigade surgeon of Hay's Louisiana brigade in Jackson's corps of the Army of Northern Virginia and later was placed in charge of a section of the Jackson Military Hospital in Richmond. In addition to these duties, he was at various times medical inspector of the Department of Northern Virginia, inspector of hospitals, and member of the board for the examination of medical officers. With the close of the war he returned to New Orleans and renewed his connection with Charity Hospital as attending physician; subsequently, he moved to Savannah, Ga., where he became a highly successful practitioner and from 1870 to 1876 was professor of physiology at the Savannah Medical College. He had been married on Oct. 4, 1864, at Savannah, to Sarah Lowndes Berrien, daughter of John MacPherson Berrien [*q.v.*], attorney general in the cabinet of President Jackson and for many years United States senator from Georgia. She died within a year after their marriage.

At the height of his medical career Semmes applied to the bishop of Savannah for permission to enter the Catholic priesthood. After periods of study at Pio Nono College, near Macon, Ga., and at the Benedictine monastery of St. Vincent at Latrobe, Pa., he was ordained at Macon in 1878. For a short time he was engaged in parish duties and then, 1886, returned to Pio Nono College as its president and lecturer on English and American literature and history. He served thus for five years and was thereafter chaplain of the school and asylum of the Sisters of St. Joseph at Sharon, Ga., with mission duty throughout the state. He continued in this congenial work until a paralytic stroke in 1895 incapacitated him from further active service and he took up his abode with his brother in New Orleans. During his last months he was under the care of the Sisters of Charity at the Hôtel Dieu, where he died.

Father Semmes was a man of uncommon scholarship and his writings for medical and literary periodicals cover a wide range of topics. One of his earliest and most noteworthy articles is *Report on the Medico-Legal Duties of Coroners,* a pamphlet published in Philadelphia in 1857. Other publications include "Poisoning by Strychnia—The Gardiner Case," which appeared in *Stethoscope* (March 1855) and "Reports of Cases of Gunshot Wounds," in the London *Lancet* (June 23, Mar. 5, 1864). Deeply religious from early training, he is described as having been gentle and courteous and yet forceful, a man of ready sympathy and broad charity, qualities which well fitted him for his dual rôle of physician and priest.

[R. T. Semmes, *The Semmes and Allied Families* (1918); *Daily Picayune* (New Orleans), Sept. 21, 1898; W. B. Atkinson, *The Physicians and Surgeons of the U. S.* (1878); R. F. Stone, *Biogs. of Eminent Am. Physicians and Surgeons* (1894); H. A. Kelly and W. L. Burrage, *Am. Medic. Biogs.* (1920).]

J. M. P—n.

SEMMES, RAPHAEL (Sept. 27, 1809–Aug. 30, 1877), naval officer and author, the elder son of Richard Thompson Semmes and his wife Catherine (Middleton), was born in Charles County, Md., of French Catholic ancestry. His grandfather, Benedict Joseph Semmes, was born in Charles County in 1753. Raphael had one brother, Samuel Middleton, a lawyer, named for his maternal grandfather, and a sister who died in infancy. Both parents dying during his early childhood, the boy was brought up in George-

town, D. C., apparently in moderate circumstances by his uncle Raphael, father of Thomas Jenkins and Alexander Jenkins Semmes [*qq.v.*]. Probably owing to the influence of another uncle, Benedict J. Semmes, a Maryland planter prominent in politics, he was appointed by President Adams a midshipman in the United States Navy, Apr. 1, 1826.

His active naval career began on Sept. 8, 1826, when he reported for duty on a sloop-of-war of the Mediterranean Squadron. On Apr. 28, 1832, he completed the three-month course at the Naval School, Norfolk navy yard, and was passed for promotion; but though he stood second in his class it was five years before a vacancy occurred in the commissioned ranks and he was made a lieutenant (Feb. 9, 1837). During this long probationary period he served successively on the sloops *Lexington* and *Erie,* the frigate *Brandywine,* the schooner *Porpoise,* and the frigate *Constellation,* on the Mediterranean, West Indian, South American, and (during the Seminole War) Florida stations. He spent some time on hydrographic surveys and in charge of chronometers. During his considerable leaves of absence he studied and practised law in Maryland and Ohio. In Ohio he fell in love with the daughter of Oliver Marlborough Spencer and Electra (Ogden), Anne Elizabeth Spencer, to whom he was married on May 5, 1837. She and their six children survived him.

From 1837 to the outbreak of the Mexican War Semmes spent most of his time on survey duty on the southern coast and in the Gulf of Mexico on board the brig *Consort* and steamer *Poinsett* (his first command), interspersed with tours of shore duty at the Norfolk and Pensacola navy yards and sea duty on the sloop-of-war *Warren* and the brig *Porpoise.* After a short assignment to the frigate *Cumberland,* he took command (Oct. 23, 1846) of the brig *Somers* on the blockade of the eastern coast of Mexico. On Dec. 8, 1846, while chasing a blockade runner, this unlucky brig (on which the famous mutiny of 1842 had occurred) encountered a sudden tropical squall which knocked her on her beam ends. She sank in ten minutes with the loss of more than half her crew; but a court of inquiry not only exonerated Semmes of blame but also commended him for his seamanship. After the disaster he was detailed as flag-lieutenant to Commodore Conner; he was on shore with the naval artillery at the bombardment of Vera Cruz (March 1847), took part in the expedition against Tuxpan, and accompanied Scott's army to Mexico city on special duty. In addition, he served as a volunteer aide to Major-General

Worth, a divisional commander, who several times cited him for gallantry. In November 1847 he returned to his home at Prospect Hill on the Perdido River, Baldwin County, Ala., near Pensacola, Fla., where he had established his family in 1845.

During the period of peace, until 1861, he was on awaiting-orders status more than half the time, during which he wrote and published his memoirs and practised law. In October 1849 he moved his residence to a point near Mobile in order the better to educate his children. He served as commander of the storeship *Electra* and the schooner *Flirt,* as inspector of clothing and provisions at Pensacola, on sundry court-martial duty, as inspector of the 8th Light House District, and as secretary and as a member of the Light House Board. He became a commander on Sept. 14, 1855, and resigned from the United States service on Feb. 15, 1861.

He proceeded at once to the Confederate capital, where he gave to Congress his views on national defense. He was then dispatched to the North to purchase munitions, ordnance machinery, and ships. He made numerous contracts and succeeded in getting large quantities of percussion caps and powder shipped south before the commencement of hostilities. During his absence he was appointed a commander from Alabama, in the Confederate States Navy, on the first list of nominations confirmed by Congress (Mar. 16). Upon his return to Montgomery (Apr. 4), he was made chief of the Light House Bureau (Treasury Department); but on Apr. 18, 1861, he was relieved and given the first high-seas command in the new navy, the C.S.S. *Sumter,* under orders to "do the enemy's commerce the greatest injury in the shortest time" (quoted by him in *Official Records, Navy,* 1 ser., vol. I, 615). However, the *Sumter* was still only the packet steamer *Havana* lying in her berth at New Orleans, and Semmes had to turn naval constructor and ordnance expert in order to get her rebuilt, equipped, and armed as a man-of-war. With a battery of one eight-inch pivot gun and four thirty-two pounders in broadside, and a crew of 114 officers and men, the *Sumter* put to sea on June 30, 1861, entering upon a game which was to require of Semmes all the courage and audacity, skill and brilliancy, that his varied naval and legal training had developed in him. In every respect he measured up to the requirements, becoming the *beau ideal* of a commerce destroyer, ever outwitting the hostile cruisers sent after him, sensing the lanes and schedules of the enemy's merchantmen, and outarguing those foreign authorities who were disposed to refuse to

him the hospitalities of their ports. The third day at sea, July 3, 1861, off the Isle of Pines, West Indies, Semmes took and burned his first prize, the *Golden Rocket,* of Bangor, Me. After capturing nine other vessels in Caribbean waters, he cruised to Brazil and back to the West Indies, speaking nineteen vessels but finding only two of them to be American; the latter he burned. From this scarcity of Union flags he concluded that, in consequence of the alarm from his operations, the carrying trade of the United States was being rapidly broken up in this quarter; and so he turned across the Atlantic to Gibraltar, making six prizes on the way. Here he was quickly blockaded by the enemy; and, as the *Sumter* was in grave need of extensive repairs to hull and boilers for which no facilities were available, he laid her up (Apr. 13, 1862), discharging her crew and ordering the officers to the Confederacy. The *Sumter* was sold later to a British firm, which returned her to the commercial trade under the name *Gibraltar.* For "gallant and meritorious conduct in capturing and destroying the enemy's commerce on the high seas," Semmes was promoted captain (Aug. 21, 1862) and was voted the thanks of Congress (Sept. 9, 1862); but it was many months before word of these honors reached him.

Semmes's passage homeward was interrupted at Nassau (June 8, 1862) by the receipt of orders to take command of the *Alabama,* or *Enrica* as she had been christened, then nearing completion at Liverpool. In order to observe British neutrality regulations, the *Enrica* took on no warlike equipment in England; but proceeded under the British papers to the Azores, where just outside the maritime jurisdiction of Portugal she received her arms and stores from two consorts, and (Aug. 24, 1862) was transferred to the Confederate government and commissioned as a man-of-war with full ceremony to the tune of "Dixie" and salute guns. The *Alabama* was now officered and armed but had no crew. Semmes addressed the assembled crews, inviting enlistments in the Confederate service, and eighty-two men signed the muster roll. After a short shakedown cruise he set about his old business of destroying the enemy's commerce, commencing at the mid-Atlantic whaling grounds, where he burned ten prizes. Transferring his operations to the American coast, he sailed from Newfoundland Banks to the Caribbean Sea and thence into the Gulf of Mexico. Here he decoyed the U.S.S. *Hatteras* from the blockading squadron off Galveston (Jan. 11, 1863), and sank her in a thirteen-minute running fight. The antagonists were about equally matched. Though the engagement was fought at night, every man of the enemy was rescued by the Confederates and shortly paroled at Jamaica. The *Alabama* remained in the West Indies for a month and then drifted down the shipping lanes to the Brazil coast, where she operated for four months at the great cross roads of trade from the Pacific and Indian Oceans to America and Europe. In all on the American coast forty-four merchantmen had been captured. The bark *Conrad* of Philadelphia, next to the last prize made on this leg of the cruise, was converted into a tender as the bark-of-war *Tuscaloosa,* which in turn captured two merchantmen valued at $310,000. Semmes next sailed for the coast of Africa, arriving at Capetown on Aug. 5, 1863; and then proceeded on an extended cruise across the Indian Ocean through the Straits of Sunda to Singapore (Dec. 21, 1863), thence through the Straits of Malacca into the Bay of Bengal, the Arabian Sea, the Indian Ocean, up the Atlantic Ocean to Cherbourg, France, on June 11, 1864. Since the beginning of the war Semmes had captured a total of eighty-two merchantmen, valued at more than $6,-000,000, defeated and sunk a man-of-war, and had been the star actor in the dramatic and virtual extermination of the United States carrying trade. These successes brought him the epithet of pirate in the North, the admiration of the naval world abroad, and promotion to rear-admiral in the Confederacy (Feb. 10, 1865).

His smart man-of-war, now worn out by twenty-two months continuously at sea, needed general overhauling. While the *Alabama* was awaiting the permission of the Emperor to go into the imperial dockyard, the U.S.S. *Kearsarge* appeared off Cherbourg. By a strange coincidence this vessel happened to have been one of the blockaders of the *Sumter* at Gibraltar, and Semmes determined to fight her despite the disparity in the condition of the two ships. The enemy was lately out of a Holland dockyard, and hull and machinery were in perfect condition. The batteries and crews were about equal. On Sunday, June 19, 1864, with all of Cherbourg and half of Paris gathered on the cliffs to witness mortal combat, the *Alabama* steamed forth to meet the *Kearsarge,* which was in waiting beyond the three-mile line. At 10:57 A.M., the *Alabama* opened fire with her starboard broadside and the *Kearsarge* promptly replied with hers. Each combatant attempted to gain a raking position with the result that they fought in a circle of about one-quarter to one-half mile in diameter. At the beginning of the eighth rotation Semmes perceived that his ship was in a sinking condition and turned out of the circle, setting all sail

available in hope of making the French shore. He now opened with his port battery; but the ship filled so rapidly that the fires were soon extinguished, and he hauled down his colors and gave orders to abandon ship. She sank in about fifteen minutes stern first, at 12:24 noon. The *Kearsarge* made tardy efforts to rescue the Confederates, who were picked up mostly by neutral spectators, principally by the English yacht *Deerhound*. Semmes was in the water half an hour before being picked up by a boat from this yacht, which took him to England; there he was kindly received.

After a rest in Switzerland he returned to the Confederacy by way of Mexico. He arrived at Richmond in January 1865, and was assigned as a rear admiral to the command of the James River Squadron, which consisted of three ironclad rams and seven wooden steamers. As his anchorage was flanked by powerful shore batteries, Richmond was amply safe from the enemy's fleet; but when the capital was evacuated by the army Semmes was obliged to burn his own ships and turned his men into a naval brigade, which was surrendered at Greensboro, N. C., as a part of Johnston's army. Upon being paroled (May 1, 1865), he went to his home in Mobile, where he was arrested (Dec. 15, 1865) by order of the Secretary of the Navy, despite the protection which his parole should have afforded him. He was taken prisoner to Washington and held about three months on the absurd charge of having violated the usages of war in escaping from the *Alabama* after her colors had been struck. He was held for trial before a military commission, but after the Supreme Court denied the jurisdiction of these commissions (*Ex parte Milligan, 71 U. S., 2*) he was released by presidential order. Upon his return home he was elected probate judge of Mobile County (May 7, 1866); but was shortly driven out of office by military force under orders from the Secretary of War. In the fall of 1866, he accepted the chair of moral philosophy and English literature at the Louisiana State Seminary, then near Alexandria (now Louisiana State University, Baton Rouge); but was forced out of the professorship by political pressure before the end of the school year. He became editor of the *Memphis Daily Bulletin* and was soon hounded out of this employment. After making some profitable lecture tours, he returned to Mobile and engaged in the practice of law until his death at his home on Point Clear, Mobile Bay. He was buried the next day in the Catholic graveyard, Mobile, with full public honors and mourning.

His chief writings were *Service Afloat and*

Ashore during the Mexican War (1851), of which *The Campaign of General Scott, in the Valley of Mexico* (1852) is an abridgment; and *Memoirs of Service, Afloat, during the War between the States* (1869), later republished under a slightly different title. In addition he lent some of his papers to Saunders, Otley & Company, London, who published them as *The Cruise of the Alabama and the Sumter. From the Private Journals and Other Papers of Commander R. Semmes, C.S.N. and Other Officers* (2 vols., 1864). This work was reprinted in one volume in New York in 1864. It was translated: *Croisières de l'Alabama et du Sumter; livre de bord et journal particulier du Commandant R. Semmes et des autres officiers de son état-major* (Paris, 1864); and *Kruistogten van de Alabama en de Sumter* (Zwolle, 1865).

[Colyer Meriwether, *Raphael Semmes* (1913), with bibliography; R. T. Semmes, *The Semmes and Allied Families* (1918); Anonymous, *The Career of the Alabama (No. 290) from July 29, 1862, to June 19, 1863* (London, 1864), reprinted in *Magazine of History*, extra number, no. 2 (1908), pp. 103–35; Arthur Sinclair, *Two Years on the Alabama* (1895); W. M. Robinson, Jr., "The Alabama-Kearsarge Battle," *Essex Institute Hist. Collections*, Apr., July 1924; J. D. Bulloch, *The Secret Service of the Confederate States in Europe* (2 vols., 1884); *War of the Rebellion: Official Records (Navy)* and *(Army)*; unpublished records in the Naval library and records in the Old Records Division of the Adjutant General's Office, Washington, D. C.; *Mobile Daily Register*, Aug. 31, 1877; W. L. Fleming, "Raphael Semmes, Professor in Louisiana," in *Daily Picayune* (New Orleans), May 14, 1911.]
W. M. R., Jr.

SEMMES, THOMAS JENKINS (Dec. 16, 1824–June 23, 1899), lawyer, Confederate senator, was born in Georgetown, D. C., the son of Raphael Semmes, a merchant of that place, and Matilda (Jenkins) Semmes. He was a brother of Alexander Jenkins Semmes and a first cousin of Raphael Semmes [*qq.v.*]. He began his formal education at a primary school in Georgetown and was graduated from Georgetown College with high honors in 1842. After one year in the law office of Clement Cox at Georgetown, he entered the Harvard Law School, where he was graduated in January 1845. Admission to the bar in Washington the following March entitled him to begin legal practice, but his removal to New Orleans in December 1850 returned him to the ranks of a student for three months before he had mastered the civil law of Louisiana. Here a partnership with Matthew C. Edwards, a Harvard classmate, was terminated abruptly during the campaign of 1855 as a result of a violent speech by Semmes defending Roman Catholicism against the attacks of the Know-Nothings. Political recognition came to him almost at once and he was sent to the lower

house of the legislature in 1856. Appointed by President Buchanan in December 1857 as attorney for the eastern district of Louisiana, he prosecuted Gen. William Walker [*q.v.*] for breach of the United States neutrality laws in leading a filibustering expedition into Nicaragua. The jury disagreed, however, and the case was subsequently *nolle prossed* (*Daily Picayune*, New Orleans, June 3, 1858; W. O. Scroggs, *Filibusters and Financiers*, 1916, p. 369). Semmes resigned the district attorneyship within the year in order to enter and win the campaign for the post of attorney general of Louisiana, in which office he served from 1859 to 1861.

As a member of the Louisiana convention of 1861, he helped to draft the ordinance of secession. In February 1862 he took his seat at Richmond in the Confederate Senate, where he rendered able service until Lee's surrender. At the close of the war he made a hurried visit to Washington and secured a pardon from President Johnson so that upon his return to New Orleans he could resume at once the practice of his profession. His industry and resolution soon enabled him to replace his handsome residence and his law library, both of which had been confiscated.

The most notable part of his career followed the war years. He exerted a guiding influence in the constitutional convention of 1879, where his plea for the payment of the consolidated bonds in full was one of the best speeches made, and in the convention of 1898, as chairman of the judiciary committee; nevertheless it was as an attorney that he chiefly commanded attention. For years his name appeared as counsel in nearly every leading case before the civil courts of Louisiana. In 1873 he accepted appointment to the chair of Civil Law in the University of Louisiana (later Tulane University of Louisiana); pressure of work forced him to resign in 1879, but he subsequently resumed his connection and maintained it until his death. National recognition was accorded him in 1886 when he was elected president of the American Bar Association. Despite his many other responsibilities, he found time to serve for many years as president of the New Orleans School Board.

On Jan. 8, 1850, he married Myra Eulalia Knox, daughter of a Louisiana planter and banker. She, with three sons and two daughters, survived him.

[The accounts of Semmes in the following publications were apparently derived from family sources: E. L. Jewell, *Jewell's Crescent City Illustrated* (1873); *Report of the Twenty-second Ann. Meeting of the Am. Bar Asso.* (1899); R. T. Semmes, *The Semmes and Allied Families* (1918); articles in *Daily Picayune* and *Times-Democrat*, both of New Orleans, June 23, 24,

25, 1899. There are no manuscript materials in the possession of the family.]   E. L.

SEMPLE, ELLEN CHURCHILL (Jan. 8, 1863–May 8, 1932), anthropogeographer, was born at Louisville, Ky., the daughter of Andrew Bonner Semple and Emerin (Price) Semple. Her early training was in private schools in Louisville. She entered Vassar at the age of fifteen, and received the B.A. degree with highest honors in 1882, thereafter continuing graduate work in history, her major field of interest. In 1891 and 1892 she went to Germany to study at the University of Leipzig under Friedrich Ratzel, the greatest anthropogeographer of his time. She was Ratzel's first woman student, the only one in a group of about five hundred men. Although not allowed to matriculate, she was permitted to attend lectures by sitting in an adjoining room with the door ajar. She was considered one of Ratzel's most brilliant students and his influence turned her from history to geography as she began the many years of unrelenting study, investigation, and travel that made her a master in her field. Her first publication, "The Influence of the Appalachian Barrier upon Colonial History," appeared in the *Journal of School Geography,* February 1897. This was followed throughout her life by many others in both geographical and historical journals. From 1906 to 1923 she was special lecturer in anthropogeography at the University of Chicago. When the School of Geography was founded at Clark University in 1921, she was the first to be called to the staff and she remained a member until her death. During these times she lectured widely both in the United States and Europe. In 1914 she was awarded the Cullum Geographical Medal by the American Geographical Society in recognition of her work, and in 1921 she was president of the Association of American Geographers, the only woman ever to hold that position.

Her three works, ranking high as to subject matter and presentation, have become indispensable to the students of the field. *American History and Its Geographic Conditions* (1903) at once claimed and held wide attention, but *Influences of Geographic Environment,* published in 1911, with a second edition in 1927, was her *magnum opus.* Originally planned to be a simplified paraphrase or restatement of the principles embodied in Friedrich Ratzel's *Anthropo-Geographie* (see the preface), the author finally resolved her work into a formulation of principles based upon those of Ratzel and interpreted it for the Anglo-American mind. This book is said to "have shaped the whole trend and content of geographic thought in America, and laid the

foundation for the science which has since made such rapid progress" (Atwood, *post,* p. 267). Her last book, *The Geography of the Mediterranean Region* (1931), was heroically completed after she had seen the "end of the Long Trail" (*Vassar Quarterly, post*). It was the result of twenty years of research and field work in the Mediterranean and an exhaustive study of the older literature of the Mediterranean lands. Its historical content is even greater than that of her two earlier works. Her place of leadership among the geographers of her generation will go undisputed. She had indefatigable capacities for research. In the classroom she seemed somewhat hampered, but her contacts with individual students were extraordinarily fruitful. Her travels, always from a scientific interest, took her through most of the northern hemisphere. She died at West Palm Beach, Fla.

[*Who's Who in America,* 1930–31; W. W. Atwood, memorial in *Jour. of Geography,* Sept. 1932; M. T. Bingham, memorial in *Vassar Quart.,* July 1932; "Report on Research Work with Selected Bibliographies of the Faculty of Clark University," July 1, 1932; Clark University *Bull.,* no. 86; *N. Y. Times,* May 9, 1932.]   H. S. G.

SENEY, GEORGE INGRAHAM (May 12, 1826–Apr. 7, 1893), banker and philanthropist, was born at Astoria, N. Y. (later part of the borough of Queens, New York City), the only son of Robert and Jane A. (Ingraham) Seney. His grandfather was Joshua Seney, member of the Continental Congress and of the first Congress under the Constitution, and his grandmother was a daughter of James Nicholson [*q.v.*] of the Revolutionary navy. Robert Seney, a graduate of Columbia College, was a Methodist preacher whose patrimony sufficed to educate George at Wesleyan and New York universities. Graduating at the latter (then the University of the City of New York) in 1846, he was first employed in a Brooklyn bank and later in the Gallatin Bank and the Bank of North America in New York. Becoming paying teller in the Metropolitan Bank in 1853 and within four years cashier, he thereafter retained a place of prominence in New York financial circles for more than a quarter of a century. In the late seventies, at the time of his promotion to the presidency of the bank, he began to take an important part in railroad financing, at first in the construction of the New York, Chicago & St. Louis Railway and later in a project for connecting the Ohio Central Railroad with Kentucky, Tennessee, and Virginia roads in a system to be known as the East Tennessee, Virginia, and Georgia Railroad. In furthering this enterprise Seney, who had built up a reputation as a conservative banker, resorted to "stock-watering" and other reckless methods common in the railroad financiering of that day and thereby incurred the hostile criticism of so astute an observer as Henry Clews (*Twenty-Eight Years in Wall Street*, 1877, pp. 162–67). His rashness brought his own fortunes and those of some of his associates to the brink of ruin. By 1884 several of the affiliated roads were bankrupt, and in May of that year, the month of the Grant-Ward episode in Wall Street, the Metropolitan Bank, seriously involved in the railroad failures through loans, was forced to close its doors. Seney at once resigned the presidency and transferred to the bank property valued at $1,500,000, including his art collection and a costly residence in Brooklyn. The Metropolitan reopened for business but only for a few months. Seney, however, retrieved a large part of his personal estate. The depositors were paid in full.

As a man of wealth he had become known for generous giving, but his philanthropic activities antedated his acquirement of riches. Dr. J. M. Buckley (*Christian Advocate, post*) is authority for the statement that when Seney's yearly income was under $5,000 he gave away one-fifth of it, and this at a period when a growing family must have made heavy demands on his purse. For many years he was a trustee of Wesleyan University, to which he gave more than $500,-000. He gave about $100,000 to Emory University, where he erected the building known by his name and added to the endowment. During the four years prior to the closing of the bank he gave $410,000 for the Methodist Hospital in Brooklyn. The total of his benevolences was estimated at $2,000,000. He was an assiduous collector of paintings and made several gifts to the Metropolitan Museum of Art in New York. After the bank failure his collection was sold for over $200,000, and he later acquired many pictures that brought still higher prices at auction sales. He was aided in his selection of purchases by Samuel Putnam Avery [*q.v.*]. In 1890 he headed the subscription list for the erection of the Washington Memorial Arch. In 1849 he had married Phoebe Moser, of a well-known Brooklyn family; with three sons and six daughters, she survived him at his death from angina pectoris in New York City.

[Comment on the failure of the Metropolitan Bank in *Commercial and Financial Chronicle*, May 17, 1884, and in *Blackwood's Edinburgh Mag.*, July 1884; *Ann. Reports M. E. Hospital in Brooklyn, N. Y.*, 1887–97, with portrait; obituaries in *Christian Advocate* (N. Y.), Apr. 13, 1893; *N. Y. Herald, N. Y. Times, N. Y. Tribune*, Apr. 8, 1893.]   W. B. S.

SENN, NICHOLAS (Oct. 31, 1844–Jan. 2, 1908), surgeon, was born in Buchs, Canton of St. Gall, Switzerland, to John and Magdelena Senn, who emigrated to America about 1852 and settled in the village of Ashford, Wis. After graduating from high school in Fond du Lac in 1864, he taught school and read medicine until 1866, when he entered the Chicago Medical College, from which he was graduated two years later. In 1869 he was married to Amelia S. Muehlhauser of La Crosse, Wis., who with two sons survived him. Following an internship of eighteen months in the Cook County Hospital he settled for practice in Elmore, Wis., but in 1874 he moved to Milwaukee, where he was appointed attending physician to the Milwaukee Hospital. During 1877–78 he studied at the University of Munich, which conferred upon him the degree of M.D. Returning to practice in Milwaukee he was in 1884 appointed professor of surgery at the College of Physicians and Surgeons in Chicago; in 1890 he became professor of surgery and surgical pathology in Rush Medical College, and in the following year he succeeded Charles Theodore Parkes as head of the department of surgery there. Later he became professor of surgery at the Chicago Polyclinic and lecturer on military surgery at the University of Chicago. For nine years he traveled between Milwaukee and Chicago to fill his lecture and clinic engagements, until in 1893 he removed his residence to Chicago. A pioneer in antiseptic surgery, with an unusual knowledge of surgical pathology, he quickly attracted the attention of the profession of the Middle West through his clinics. He was one of the first in this section to systematically pursue experimental surgery upon animals, and he devised one of the earliest mechanical aids for intestinal anastomosis. His experimental work upon abdominal surgery, including gunshot wounds of the intestines, gave him a local preeminence in this field. Though a skilful and daring operator, with a thorough knowledge of anatomy and pathology, he was never able fully to master the technique of surgical asepsis. Furthermore, though he commanded a vast surgical service and a large professional following, he left no group of Senn disciples to perpetuate his traditions. His practice was lucrative, and he was a liberal contributor toward the advancement of medical education. He gave a clinical building to Rush Medical College at a cost of about one hundred thousand dollars; and upon the death of Professor William Baum of the University of Göttingen, he purchased his library of old and rare medical books, the collections of fifty years, and presented it to the Newberry Library of Chicago.

He was a rapid and voluminous writer upon

surgical subjects, military medicine, and travel. His books include *Experimental Surgery* (1889), *Intestinal Surgery* (1889), *Surgical Bacteriology* (1889), *Principles of Surgery* (1890), *Pathology and Surgical Treatment of Tumors* (1895), *War Correspondence* (1899), and *Medico-Surgical Aspects of the Spanish-American War* (1900). His observations upon first aid on the battlefield and the conservative surgery of gunshot wounds are noteworthy. From the beginning of his professional career he had been interested in military medicine. Surgeon general of Wisconsin for a time and later a brigadier-general in the National Guard of Illinois, in 1891 he founded the Association of Military Surgeons of the United States and served as president for the first two years. During the Spanish-American War he saw service in Cuba as chief-surgeon of the VI Army Corps, with the grade of lieutenant-colonel. His pride in his uniform caused considerable amusement to his friends, but his teaching and example had a large influence in stimulating interest throughout the profession in medico-military knowledge. In his later years he traveled much throughout the world. From South America he sent a series of letters to the *Journal of the American Medical Association,* and in 1902 he published the well-illustrated *Around the World via Liberia.* Many of his journal articles were apparently written hurriedly and from memory, and are without lasting value. Physically he was short and heavy set, and quick and impulsive in speech and action. Though kindly and sympathetic by nature, he had a temper easily aroused, and at such times he was a formidable fighter. He was an indefatigable student and worker; even his holidays were filled with exacting activities. In 1907 in South America he suffered an acute dilation of the heart, the result of a mountain ascent of 16,000 feet; he was brought back to Chicago, where he died in St. Joseph's Hospital in a room he had endowed.

[*Who's Who in America*, 1906–07; *Am. Medic. Biogs.* (1920), ed, by H. A. Kelly and W. L. Burrage; F. M. Sperry, *A Group of Distinguished Physicians and Surgeons of Chicago* (1904); I. A. Watson, *Physicians and Surgeons of America* (1896); *Surgery, Gynecology, and Obstetrics,* Feb. 1908; *Mil. Surgeon,* Feb. 1908; *Chicago Daily Tribune,* Jan. 3, 1908; personal information.]   J. M. P.–n.

SENNETT, GEORGE BURRITT (July 28, 1840–Mar. 18, 1900), ornithologist, was born in Sinclairville, Chautauqua County, N. Y., the only child of Mary (Burritt) and Pardon Sennett, a prosperous blast-furnace operator. His interest in ornithology apparently did not reveal itself until he was fully grown and well estab-

lished in business. He graduated from Erie Academy, intending to enter Yale, but his eyesight was such that he had to abandon further academic study and he spent the next four years in Europe. In 1865 he began his industrial career as a manufacturer of oil-well machinery at Meadville, Pa.; nearly thirty years later he moved his large works to Youngstown, Ohio, where he died. He served two terms, 1877–81, as mayor of Meadville and did much to make it a sanitary, well-planned city. He married Sarah Essex, by whom he had a daughter.

He did his ornithological work wholly in his spare time. Although he made extensive collections in western Minnesota, where he went in the spring of 1876 on his first ornithological expedition, he never published his results. His most prolonged and important studies dealt with the bird life of the lower Rio Grande region of southern Texas, then virtually a new field for the naturalist. In 1877, having arranged his business affairs so as to have more leisure time, he made a stay of two months along the Rio Grande; in 1878 he made a second trip there, covering a slightly longer period, and in 1882 a third. He published the results of only the first two Texas trips. Although he never went there again, he kept up his interest in the region and dispatched collectors there to gather material for him. It was his intention to study each season's work and publish the results as soon as possible, but his business interests encroached more and more on his time and interfered with his scientific work. His proposed monographic work on the avifauna of the lower Rio Grande he did not live to write; the materials he had gathered over a period of many years, however, were utilized by others (among them Ludlow Griscom and M. S. Crosby, "Birds of the Brownsville Region, Southern Texas," *Auk,* July, October 1925, and January 1926). In 1883 he deposited his splendid collections of birds and mammals in the American Museum of Natural History in New York, where he often worked during the winters from 1883 to 1896. The twenty-nine scientific papers he published are both accurate and reflective. The most important of them are "Notes on the Ornithology of the Lower Rio Grande, Texas, from Observations Made During the Season 1877" (*Bulletin of the United States Geological and Geographical Survey of the Territories,* vol. IV, 1878), "Further Notes on the Ornithology of the Lower Rio Grande of Texas from Observations made During the Spring of 1878" (*Ibid.,* vol. V, 1879), and "Descriptions of a New Species and Two New Subspecies of Birds from Texas" (*Auk,*

January 1888). He described ten forms of birds new to science, and four birds were named in his honor.

[See *Auk,* Jan. 1901; *Ohio State Jour.* (Columbus), Mar. 19, 1900. Many of Sennett's publications are listed in *Cat. of Sci. Papers, Fourth Ser., 1884–1900,* vol. XVIII (1923) of the Royal Society of London.]
H. Fr—n.

SEQUOYAH (1770?–Aug., 1843), inventor of the Cherokee syllabary, was born in the Indian town of Taskigi, Tenn. His father was possibly Nathaniel Gist, a trader who abandoned the mother, a woman of mixed Indian blood, before the birth of the child. During infancy and youth Sequoyah seems to have borne only his Indian name, later taking that of his father, which he understood to be Guess. He grew to manhood wholly ignorant of the English language and but meagerly acquainted with any of the arts and usages of civilization. He was for some years a hunter and fur-trader, but an accident suffered on a hunting trip crippled him for life. He had a natural bent for craftsmanship, which he turned to use in a number of ways, chiefly as a fashioner of the silver ornaments eagerly sought by his people. Increasing contact with the whites caused him to ponder deeply over their "talking leaves"—the written and printed pages by which they communicated ideas—and he resolved to master the secret and apply it to the benefit of his people. It was about 1809 when he began his study, and it was not until 1821, after enduring much ridicule and opposition, that he completed his table of characters for the eighty-five or eighty-six syllables in the Cherokee language. A council of the chief men of the tribe approved his work, with the result that in a short time thousands of his people had learned to read and write. In 1822 he visited the western Cherokees in Arkansas to introduce his syllabary and in the following years made his home with them, removing with them in 1828 to Oklahoma. There his invention of an alphabet continued to stimulate printing of books and a newspaper in Cherokee and to be important in contributing toward the development of the state. For some years he was active in the political life of his tribe, in which he was highly honored. In 1828, as an envoy, he visited Washington. The Cherokee National Council in 1841 voted him an allowance for his invention and two years later altered the gift to an annuity of $300, to be continued, in case of his death, to his widow. He had before this time retired from public affairs and had visited many tribes in a search for the elements of a common speech and grammar. Early in 1843 he set out to find a band of Cherokees who, according to tradition, had removed

west of the Mississippi before the Revolution. Somewhere in the southwest, possibly in the state of Tamaulipas, Mex., he fell ill and died.

He was married and had several children. It was with the aid of a six-year-old daughter that in 1821 he gave the first successful test of his invention. He was a man of mild and benignant countenance, with an engaging manner, and his character was upright and devotedly altruistic. He has been sometimes called the ablest intelligence produced among the American Indians. His fame is perpetuated in the name of the genus of California giant redwoods and in the statue of him placed by the state of Oklahoma in Statuary Hall of the National Capitol.

[J. B. Davis, "The Life and Work of Sequoyah," *Chronicles of Oklahoma,* June 1930; F. W. Hodge, *Handbook of Am. Indians,* pt. II (1910); G. E. Foster, *Sequoyah, the Am. Cadmus and Modern Moses* (1885); K. D. Sweetser, *Book of Indian Braves* (1913); Jas. Mooney, "Myths of the Cherokee," *U. S. Bureau of Am. Ethnology Nineteenth Ann. Report* (1900), pp. 108–27, 147–48; "Statue of Sequoyah," *House Doc. 240, 68 Cong., 1 Sess.* (1917); Emmet Starr, *Hist. of the Cherokee Indians* (1921); S. C. Williams, "Nathaniel Gist, Father of Sequoyah," *East Tenn. Hist. Soc. Pubs.,* no. 5 (1933); Wm. A. Phillips, "Sequoyah," *Harper's Mag.,* Sept. 1870.]
W. J. G.

SERGEANT, HENRY CLARK (Nov. 2, 1834–Jan. 30, 1907), inventor, was born in Rochester, N. Y., said to be the son of Isaac and Ruby (Clark) Sergeant. His parents moved to Ohio when he was young, and after a common school education he went to work in a machine shop. This stimulated his inventive faculties, especially in the direction of special machinery for systematic manufacture. Although he was only eighteen years old, he designed some special machines for the manufacture of wheel spokes, hubs, and felloes, and obtained contracts for his employer for making such wheel parts in quantity. Two years later he was made a partner in a wagon-wheel manufactory but, disliking factory routine, he soon resigned and spent the succeeding six years in a variety of commercial pursuits. He began serious inventive work as well and secured his first patent in 1854 for a steam boiler feed. This was followed by a number of others, among them a patent for the invention of a marine engine governor later adopted by the United States navy; four patents on steam boilers and pumps; one on a gas regulator in 1862; three for brick machines in 1867; and one for a fluting machine in 1869. During this sixteen-year period he lived in many places; in fact, over the forty-year period between 1854 and 1893 he lived in twenty-six different cities and towns. Gradually working eastward, he came to New York City in 1868 and there established a machine shop of his own, building a variety of machines and developing many crude ideas brought to him by other inventors. When the business grew he formed the partnership of Sergeant and Cullingworth and took new quarters in a shop owned by José F. de Navarro. To this shop came Simon Ingersoll [q.v.] about 1870 to develop his idea of a rock drill. The future of such a machine attracted Sergeant and, while it is not known just how much he contributed to the success of the original Ingersoll drill, at least one patent was issued jointly to the two men. At all events, he induced Navarro to buy out Ingersoll and organize the Ingersoll Rock Drill Company, through which the drill was introduced into rock excavating. Meanwhile he turned his attention to operating the drill by means of compressed air rather than steam and to improving the air compressor; in the course of a few years his improved drills had entirely supplanted the older steam drills. In 1883, however, he sold his interest in his shop and in the Ingersoll Drill Company and went to Colorado to engage in silver mining, but he came back east two years later with an entirely new rock drill, patented in 1884, that had a novel valve motion, and formed the Sergeant Drill Company, with a manufactory in Bridgeport, Conn. Two years later his company and the Ingersoll company joined as the Ingersoll-Sergeant Rock-Drill Company with Sergeant as president, but within a short time he disposed of the bulk of his interests and went abroad to live. After several years he returned, this time as a director in the Ingersoll-Sergeant company, to devote his whole time to invention, and in the succeeding years he perfected among many others his most notable inventions: the "auxiliary" and the "arc" valves; the "tappet" drill; the Sergeant release rotation for rock drills; and the piston inlet valve for air compressors. He had married Caroline Luckhaupt in Columbus, Ohio, on Mar. 19, 1860, and at the time of his death in Westfield, N. J., he was survived by four children.

[Compressed Air Mag., Mar. 1907, June 1910; Patent Office records; obituary in N. Y. Tribune, Feb. 1, 1907, N. Y. Times, Jan. 31, 1907; correspondence with the Ingersoll-Rand Co.]   C. W. M.

SERGEANT, JOHN (1710–July 27, 1749), missionary to the Housatonic Indians, was the son of Jonathan and Mary Sergeant. His grandfather, Jonathan, had settled in New Haven, Conn., in 1644, and the second Jonathan had been one of the Branford, Conn., congregation which removed to New Jersey some twenty-two years later and founded Newark, in which place John Sergeant was born. Unfitted for farm work or a trade as a result of a scythe-cut on his

left hand, he prepared for college and graduated from Yale in the class of 1729. Copies of his Commencement address, *A Valedictorian Oration, by John Sergeant, Delivered at Yale College in the Year 1729*, were printed in 1882 from the manuscript in the possession of Williams College. From 1731 to 1735 he was a tutor at Yale and was "one of the most successful holders of that office in the early history of the College" (Dexter, *post*, p. 395). In addition to his teaching he also pursued studies in theology.

Meanwhile, several clergymen united in an effort to provide Christian instruction for the Indians in what is now Berkshire County, Mass. These Indians were few in number, of good reputation, and occupied two tracts of land— one in the present town of Sheffield, and the other in Stockbridge. To this missionary project the Boston commissioners of the Society for the Propagation of the Gospel in New England gave their support, and the Indians themselves, their consent. Two of the clergymen, having heard that Sergeant had said "he had rather be employ'd as a Missionary to the Natives, if a Door should open for it, than accept a Call any English parish might give him" (Dexter, p. 395), visited him at New Haven in September 1734, and told him the door was open. He readily consented to accept the mission, and later wrote that he would have been ashamed to own himself a Christian had he not been willing to do so, both because of the need of the Indians, and also because the "pains taken by those of the Romish Church, not only in other parts but also in America . . . should methinks excite us to emulation, who at least think we profess Christianity in much greater purity" (Hopkins, *post*, in *Magazine of History*, p. 20). Sergeant spent October and November with the Indians, got them to erect a building between their two settlements to serve as school and church, and returned to New Haven, with two Indian boys, to complete his year at the college, having left Timothy Woodbridge, who was to be his assistant, in charge.

In July 1735 he entered permanently upon his missionary work, and on Aug. 31, was ordained to the Congregational ministry at Deerfield, Mass. Until his death in his thirty-ninth year he lived and worked among the Indians, beloved by them and regarded as their father and best friend. He mastered their language, becoming able to speak it, they said, better than they could themselves, and translated into it some prayers, portions of the Bible, and Watts's shorter catechism. He enjoyed the high regard and cordial support of Gov. Jonathan Belcher [q.v.]. In

1736 the General Court secured a tract of land six miles square in what is now Stockbridge that the two settlements of Indians might be united. Later it ordered a meeting house and a school house built there. Sergeant interested himself particularly in the education of the boys and girls, placing some of the former in English homes, and one of his chief ambitions was the establishment of a boarding school in which industrial training should be given to both sexes, a project which was achieved shortly before his death. One of his sermons, *The Causes and Danger of Delusions in the Affairs of Religion Consider'd and Caution'd Against, with Particular Reference to the Temper of the Present Times,* was published in 1743, and the same year, *A Letter from the Rev^d. Mr. Sergeant of Stockbridge to Dr. Colman of Boston; Containing Mr. Sergeant's Proposal of a More Effectual Method for the Education of Indian Children.* On Aug. 16, 1739, he married Abigail, daughter of Col. Ephraim Williams of Stockbridge and half-sister of the founder of Williams College. A son, John, was also a missionary to the Indians, another son was a prominent physician and officer in the Revolution, and a daughter was the grandmother of Mark Hopkins [*q.v.*]. Jonathan Dickinson Sergeant [*q.v.*] was a nephew.

[Samuel Hopkins, *Hist. Memoir Relating to the Housatunnuk Indians* (1753), reprinted in *Mag. of Hist.* (New York, 1911), Extra No. 17; W. B. Sprague, *Annals Am. Pulpit,* vol. I (1857); F. B. Dexter, *Biog. Sketches, Grads. Yale Coll.,* vol. I (1885); E. F. Jones, *Stockbridge, Past and Present* (1854).]   H.E.S.

SERGEANT, JOHN (Dec. 5, 1779–Nov. 23, 1852), lawyer, congressman, was born in Philadelphia, the third child of Jonathan Dickinson Sergeant [*q.v.*] and Margaret (Spencer) Sergeant, and elder brother of Thomas Sergeant [*q.v.*]. He was orphaned at fourteen, and at sixteen, in 1795, was graduated from the College of New Jersey. He then began an apprenticeship in the house of Ellison & Perot, where he learned the rudiments of finance. In March 1797 he entered the law office of Jared Ingersoll [*q.v.*] and on July 17, 1799, was admitted, in Philadelphia, to the practice of law. Within six years, aided by a comfortable fortune, he had established himself, and for the next half-century he was an acknowledged leader of a famous bar.

In 1800 he was appointed by Gov. Thomas McKean [*q.v.*] to be deputy attorney general for Chester County and Philadelphia. Two years later Thomas Jefferson made him commissioner of bankruptcy for Pennsylvania (*Luzerne Federalist,* July 12, 1802). He was elected to the legislature in 1805, and in 1806 declined reëlection as well as an offer of the recordership of

Philadelphia (Meredith, *post,* p. 9). Elected to the legislature again in 1807, he served as chairman of the committee on roads and inland navigation, and, though he did not (as claimed, *Ibid.,* p. 9) report the first bill giving direct aid to internal improvements in Pennsylvania, he did demonstrate a deep and lasting interest in transportation and also in banking. At this time, furthermore, he revealed one of his fundamental traits of character as a public man by introducing a bill prohibiting masquerades as dangerous to public morals. Probably his growing law practice among a wealthy clientele and his identification with the vested interests brought about his temporary retirement from politics and, with it, his transition from a McKean-Jefferson Republican to a firm Federalist. Having scholarly tastes, he naturally fell in with the circle of intellectuals led by Joseph Dennie, Nicholas Biddle, and Joseph Hopkinson [*qq.v.*]. His resulting friendship with Biddle lasted until the latter's death and in consequence Sergeant had an influence in the banking affairs of the nation that has never been fully recognized.

He was elected to the Fourteenth Congress to fill the vacancy caused by the death of Jonathan Williams, and served in that body from 1815 to 1823, from 1827 to 1829, and, again, from 1837 to Sept. 15, 1841. He gave entire support to the "American system," despite bitter opposition to a high tariff by the Philadelphia Chamber of Commerce and the mercantile interests of his constituency. The woollen manufacturers of the Middle States, however, wrote him that "the Manufacturing Part of Society . . . observe your zealous regard for their interest" (Sergeant MSS., Historical Society of Pennsylvania, *post,* Jan. 20, 1816). He opposed the Missouri Compromise, favored uniform bankruptcy laws, championed internal improvements, and throughout his terms in Congress was the chief legal and political adviser to the Second Bank of the United States. In 1816, armed with plenary powers and letters of introduction, he was sent by the Bank on a mission to Europe to obtain specie to bolster the banking structure of the country. The skilful diplomacy which this thirty-seven-year-old lawyer used in wresting a signal victory from such lords of the world's financial capital as Baring Brothers and Reid, Irving & Company is a significant index to his abilities. A historian of the Bank, R. H. C. Catterall, criticizes the "pitiably inadequate" amount of specie kept on hand, but does not mention the strategic victory won by Sergeant in the face of great difficulties (*The Second Bank of the United States,* 1903, p. 29); yet Sergeant's successful mission undoubtedly had an ameliorating effect upon the depression of 1819. Besides serving as a director of the Bank and as its adviser, Sergeant fought some of its most notable legal battles before the Supreme Court (Charles Warren, *The Supreme Court in United States History*, 1922, II, 90, 108, and *passim*). He is credited with having had more influence than anyone else in inducing Biddle to apply for a renewal of the Bank's charter (Catterall, pp. 217–18; but *cf.* R. C. McGrane, *The Correspondence of Nicholas Biddle Dealing with National Affairs*, 1919, p. 147). His position on public questions made him an ideal, but unsuccessful, National Republican candidate for vice-president in 1832 (E. M. Carroll, *Origins of the Whig Party*, 1925). In 1834 the Bank sought Sergeant's election to the United States Senate, and, though the attempt failed, it did prevent the election of Richard Rush [*q.v.*], an unfriendly candidate (*Memoirs of John Quincy Adams*, vol. IX, 1876, p. 40).

He was president of the board of canal commissioners of Pennsylvania in 1825–26, and was named a member of the Panama Congress of 1826, though he never proceeded farther than Mexico city on his way to Tacubaya. He was president of the constitutional convention of Pennsylvania in 1837–38 and took the lead in the fight over the judiciary. His stature can be measured by the offices that he declined: these included a seat on the bench of the United States Supreme Court, a cabinet position under Harrison, and the embassy to England under Tyler (H. A. Wise, *Seven Decades of the Union*, 1872, p. 219; H. L. Carson, *The Supreme Court of the United States*, 1891, p. 343; Meredith, *post*, p. 27). His great strength was as a forensic legalist, less eloquent than intellectual, but powerful enough to win such battles as the Girard Will Case (2 *Howard*, 127) over such opponents as Webster. In the famous cases he conducted before the Supreme Court—*Osborn* vs. *United States Bank* (9 *Wheaton*, 738), *Worcester* vs. *Georgia* (6 *Peters*, 515), etc.—he was the advocate of national powers as opposed to state rights, and though he usually defended the strongholds of vested interests, he also fought legal battles for purely humanitarian ends, as in the Cherokee cases (5 *Peters*, 1). He headed several humanitarian and scholarly enterprises in Philadelphia, and his printed lectures were so extensive and well received that his admirers in 1832, possibly as an aid to his campaign of that year, gathered a number of them into a volume, *Select Speeches of John Sergeant of Pennsylvania*, in an effort "to rescue from the precarious tenure of ephemeral publications the reputa-

tion of an eminent man." He was married June 23, 1813, to Margaretta Watmough, by whom he had ten children.

[Sergeant MSS., 5 vols., Conarroe MSS., Etting Papers, and Poinsett Papers in Hist. Soc. of Pa.; Hopkinson MSS. in hands of Hopkinson family, Phila.; Biddle, Sergeant, Clay, and Webster MSS. in Lib. of Cong.; Sergeant MSS. and Canal Board Papers, in Pa. State Lib.; Biog. Dir. Am. Cong. (1928); W. M. Meredith, *Eulogium on the Character and Services of the Late John Sergeant* (1853); Horace Binney, *Remarks to the Bar of Phila. on the Occasion of the Deaths of Charles Chauncey and John Sergeant* (1853); S. R. Gammon, *The Presidential Campaign of 1832* (1922); Edward Stanwood, *A Hist. of Presidential Elections* (1884); *Proc. and Debates of the Convention of . . . Pa., to Propose Amendments to the Constitution . . . 1837* (vols. I–XIII, 1837–39); *Pa. Mag. of Hist. and Biog.*, Oct. 1924; *Public Ledger* (Phila.), Nov. 25, 1852.]   J. P. B.

SERGEANT, JONATHAN DICKINSON (1746–Oct. 8, 1793), lawyer, congressman, was born in Newark, N. J., the eldest son of Jonathan and Abigail (Dickinson) Sergeant, and a descendant of Jonathan Sergeant who came to New Haven, Conn., in 1644, and soon moved to Branford. His father was a brother of John Sergeant [*q.v.*], missionary to the Indians; his maternal grandfather was the Rev. Jonathan Dickinson [*q.v.*], first president of the College of New Jersey. His father was treasurer of that institution from 1750 to 1777 and the man under whom he studied law, Richard Stockton, 1764–1828 [*q.v.*], was a trustee. Sergeant was graduated there in 1762, and the following year from the University of Pennsylvania. Like most other young Princetonians, he fell in with the Sons of Liberty and took a prominent part in the Stamp Act controversy.

Six short years, 1774 to 1780, cover the entire official life of Sergeant, yet they were momentous enough to prove that John Adams was correct in speaking of the sociable young lawyer in 1774 as a "cordial friend to American liberty" (*The Works of John Adams*, vol. II, 1850, p. 356). He was clerk of the first Provincial Congress of New Jersey in July 1774; served on the Somerset and Princeton committees of correspondence in 1774 and 1775; was secretary of the second Provincial Congress, and at the meeting in August 1775 was made provincial treasurer, receiving in October the thanks of that body for his services (*Minutes of the Provincial Congress . . . of New Jersey*, 1879, p. 253). In February 1776 he was chosen to represent New Jersey in the Continental Congress, but in June he resigned to accept a seat in the New Jersey Provincial Congress, in which he took the lead in forming a state constitution (C. R. Erdman, *The New Jersey Constitution of 1776*, 1929). Here he learned his first lessons in the art of protecting liberty with laws, directed against the Loyalists, such as he later became expert in enforcing. On Nov. 30, 1776, he was again chosen member of the Continental Congress, serving until September 1777. When Hessians burned his Princeton home on Dec. 25, 1776, he definitely moved his residence to Philadelphia, identifying himself with Pennsylvania politics. He was active in committee work, but as early as February 1777, he wrote that his zeal in the cause had reduced his private affairs to a "melancholy complexion" and offered to resign (Emmet MSS., no. 795, in New York Public Library; *Selections from the Correspondence of the Executive of New Jersey from 1776 to 1786,* 1848, pp. 24–25, 27). He was appointed attorney general of Pennsylvania on July 28, 1777, but not commissioned until Nov. 1, and apparently he engaged in private practice in the interim. His extraordinary procedure in the typical trial of Samuel Rowland Fisher, a Quaker and suspected Loyalist, shows that Sergeant, like most Revolutionary public prosecutors, took rather literally the ancient maxim *inter arma leges silent.* As one of the McKean-Bryan "Constitutionalists," he was made a member of the council of safety because Thomas Wharton thought him a "worthy young man." Here his "honest zeal in noting irregularities of Continental officers" brought him two physical beatings at the hands of army contractors who took advantage of his small person. Arduous labor and small pay did not deter him from conducting a "great . . . number of capital trials" before his resignation, Nov. 20, 1780. He assisted the state in several notable trials, chief of which was the Connecticut-Pennsylvania dispute arbitrated at Trenton in November and December 1782. He declined public office after the Revolution, devoting his attention to law. In June 1787, his twenty-eight-year-old wife, Margaret Spencer, whom he had married Mar. 14, 1775, died, leaving him eight children, two of whom were John and Thomas [*qq.v.*], and on Dec. 20, 1788, he married Elizabeth, daughter of David Rittenhouse [*q.v.*], by whom he had two daughters and a son. His defense in 1788 of the Anti-Federalist editor, Eleazar Oswald, indicates that he was still in alignment with the Bryan faction.

Zeal for Republican principles led him to espouse the French Revolution, and during the excitement of the Genet episode, he took a leading part. Years later John Adams said he was informed that "nothing but the yellow fever, which removed Dr. Hutchinson and Jonathan Dickinson Sergeant from this world, could have saved the United States from a fatal revolution of Government" (*Works,* vol. X, 1856, p. 47). Later John Sergeant sought to clear his father's name of the stigma which he considered Adams thus put upon it. It is true, however, that Sergeant's courageous efforts in behalf of the yellow fever victims brought on his own early death.

[Numerous Sergeant MSS. are in the Revolutionary Papers, XXI to LIX and Post-Revolutionary Papers, I to LIV in the Pa. State Lib.; some MSS. are in the Gratz Coll., Conarroe MSS., IX, 66, 67, 68, and Etting Papers, in the Hist. Soc. of Pa. The only adequate biog. sketch is E. F. Hatfield, "Jonathan Dickinson Sergeant," *Pa. Mag. of Hist. and Biog.,* II (1878), pp. 438–42; see, also, E. C. Burnett, *Letters of Members of the Continental Congress,* vols. I, II (1921–23); and W. C. Ford, *Jours. of the Continental Cong.,* vols. IV–VIII (1906–07); "Jour. of Samuel Rowland Fisher," *Pa. Mag. of Hist. and Biog.,* Apr. 1917; *Pa. Colonial Records; Pa. Archives;* T. J. Rogers, *A New Am. Biog. Dictionary* (2nd ed., 1824); *Memorial Biogs. of the New Eng. Hist. Geneal. Soc.,* IV (1885), 69–75.]
J. P. B.

SERGEANT, THOMAS (Jan. 14, 1782–May 5, 1860), jurist, author of legal works, the son of Jonathan Dickinson Sergeant [*q.v.*] and Margaret (Spencer), was born in Philadelphia. He graduated second in his class at the College of New Jersey in 1798; then entered the law office of Jared Ingersoll [*q.v.*]; and was admitted to the Philadelphia bar on June 8, 1802. Shortly afterwards, Thomas McKean [*q.v.*] appointed him clerk of the mayor's court, indicating that Thomas Sergeant, like his brother John [*q.v.*], was allied with the McKean-Jefferson Republicans. In 1812 and again in 1813 he was elected to the legislature, but political life attracted him less strongly than the bench, and on Oct. 20, 1814, he accepted a commission as associate judge of the district court of Philadelphia and held this post until 1817.

In the latter year he was appointed secretary of the commonwealth by Gov. William Findlay. During his incumbency he sponsored legislation for, and directed the establishment of, the state law library at Harrisburg. He did not escape the general investigation that was made of Findlay's administration by the legislature. On Dec. 17, 1818, a dissatisfied office seeker in a petition to the legislature charged Sergeant with nepotism and favoritism in the disposal of minor offices. A committee of inquiry was appointed, but reported that the complaints had not been substantiated and asked that the charges be dropped. On July 6, 1819, Sergeant resigned as secretary and the same day was appointed attorney general, which office he held until the administration of Gov. Joseph Hiester [*q.v.*] began in 1820. Subsequently, he devoted himself to his legal practice and scholarly pursuits until April 1825, when he was appointed solicitor of the district for Philadelphia County. In April 1828 he became postmaster of Philadelphia and served as such throughout Jackson's first administration. His next appointment, Feb. 3, 1834, was that of associate justice of the Pennsylvania supreme court. During the twelve years he occupied this position his decisions, chiefly limited to expounding the equity decisions of the court, were noted for their brevity, clarity, and accuracy: one of his successors stated that he was never reversed in a single instance. Like his brother, he strongly opposed the amendment in the constitutional convention of 1837–38 proposing popular election of judges, and so bitter was his resentment at its inclusion in the state constitution that he resigned his judgeship, Oct. 1, 1846, largely on that account. He was provost of the Law Academy of Philadelphia from 1844 to 1855, trustee of the University of Pennsylvania from 1842 to 1854, president of the Historical Society of Pennsylvania, and a member of the American Philosophical Society.

His greatest achievements were in the field of legal writing. As a young lawyer he contributed articles and poems to periodicals and newspapers; he soon, however, confined himself to legal researches and writings. His first important work was *A Treatise upon the Law of Pennsylvania Relative to the Proceeding by Foreign Attachment* (1811). There followed at various intervals: *Constitutional Law: Being a Collection of Points Arising upon the Constitution and Jurisprudence of the United States, Which Have Been Settled by Judicial Decision and Practice* (1822), of which a second edition under a somewhat different title appeared in 1830; *Reports of Cases Adjudged in the Supreme Court of Pennsylvania, 1814–1829* (17 vols., 1818–29), in collaboration with William Rawle [q.v.]; *Sketch of the National Judiciary Powers Exercised in the United States Prior to the Adoption of the Present Federal Constitution* (1824); and *View of the Land Laws of Pennsylvania* (1838). He was one of the editors of *Reports of Cases Argued and Determined in the English Courts of Common Law* (1822–25) and also of *The Law Library* (104 vols., 1833–60). He was married on Sept. 14, 1812, to Sarah Bache, grand-daughter of Benjamin Franklin, by whom he had three sons and a daughter.

[A few of Sergeant's MSS. are in the Gratz Coll., the Coryell Papers, and the McKean Papers, in the possession of the Hist. Soc. of Pa.; there is also in the same repository a volume of newspaper clippings, chiefly obituary notices of Thomas Sergeant. Published sources include *Memorial Biogs. of the New England Hist. Geneal. Soc.*, vol. IV (1885); J. H. Martin, *Martin's Bench and Bar of Phila.* (1883); *Report of the Committee Appointed to Investigate the Official Conduct of Thomas Sergeant, Secretary of the Commonwealth* (1819); *Pennsylvanian* (Phila.), May 7, 1860.]
J. P. B.

SERRA, JUNÍPERO (Nov. 24, 1713–Aug. 28, 1784), Franciscan missionary, was born in Petra, Mallorca, the son of Margarita Ferrer and Antonio Serra. He was baptized Miguel José but took the name Junípero when he finished his probation and made his religious profession in 1731. He entered the Franciscan Order at Palma on Sept. 14, 1730. In St. Francis Friary at Palma he studied philosophy and theology and was ordained priest. Previously honored by the Lullian University of Palma with the degree of Doctor of Theology, he soon gained distinction as professor of philosophy and pulpit orator. A brilliant career in the Church and in the Franciscan Order was awaiting him when in 1749 he obtained permission to join a band of Franciscans destined for the Apostolic College of San Fernando in Mexico city. Here, with Francisco Palóu [q.v.] as one of his companions, he arrived on Jan. 1, 1750. His first missionary field was among the Indians of Sierra Gorda, northeast of Querétaro. Nine years later he was recalled and appointed for the San Sabá mission in Texas. When this project failed to materialize, he spent the next years in Mexico city as preacher and confessor. In 1767, when the Franciscans of the College of San Fernando replaced the banished Jesuits in Lower California, he was sent as *presidente* to this new field.

At the instance of the visitor general, José de Gálvez, the authorities of San Fernando agreed to cooperate with the government by founding missions in Upper California, those of the peninsula being entrusted to the Dominican friars. Accordingly five Franciscans with Serra as *presidente* accompanied the military expedition of Gaspar de Portolá [q.v.] northward. On July 16, 1769, the San Diego mission was founded, the first of the twenty-one eventually erected on the California coast. During the next fifteen years Serra was the guiding force that resulted in the successful occupation of what is today the state of California. During his presidency nine missions were founded: San Diego, San Carlos, San Antonio, San Gabriel, San Luis Obispo, San Francisco de Assisi, San Juan Capistrano, Santa Clara, and San Buenaventura. In 1773 he went to Mexico but late in the next year returned to California. At the close of 1783, seven months before his death, more than six thousand Indians were recorded as baptized, while more than five thousand had been confirmed. Equally astounding was the material progress under the missions. The live stock totaled nearly 30,000 heads; the annual harvest amounted to about 30,-000 bushels of grain and vegetables; the work-shops furnished the necessaries of civilized living. Although Serra suffered from an injury to his leg that had occurred when he first came to Mexico, at regular intervals he held official visitations, traveling on foot from mission to mission and aiding the missionaries by his counsel and encouragement. He died suddenly at the mission of San Carlos, near Monterey. His diary and some letters remain.

He was a man of deep faith and boundless trust in God. Of a keen mind and indomitable will, he mastered the situations that repeatedly threatened Spain's California project, and under his guidance and inspiration Spain's hold on California became secure. In his differences with the military authorities, none could honestly question either his patriotism as a Spaniard or his sincerity and sense of justice as head in spiritual matters and as protector of the rights of the Indians. The missionary friars found in him a sympathetic and congenial confrère, and a solicitous and appreciative superior, while the Indians revered him as a loyal and affectionate friend. Thin and frail in appearance and grave in demeanor, he was wholly absorbed in his missionary labors. Among other memorials are a bronze statue of him in Golden Gate Park, San Francisco, and a granite monument at Monterey. Of the tributes paid to his memory in recent years, the most significant is the statue in the Capitol at Washington, D. C., unveiled on Mar. 1, 1931, as a token of homage to a pioneer missionary who ranks among the foremost in American history.

[Two important works are those of Francisco Palóu, *Noticias de la Nueva California* (4 vols., 1874, ed. by J. T. Doyle), translated and ed. by H. E. Bolton as *Hist. Memoirs of New Cal.* (4 vols., 1926), and *Relación Historica de la Vida y Apostólicas Tareas del Venerable Padre Fray Junipero Serra* (Mexico, 1787), ed. by G. W. James as *Francisco Palóu's Life and Apostolic Labors of the Venerable Father Junipero Serra* (1913). See also Zephyrin Engelhardt, *The Missions and Missionaries of Cal.*, vols. I, II (1908–12), and *Mission San Carlos Borromeo* (1934); H. H. Bancroft, *Hist. of Cal.*, vol. I (1884); Helen Hunt Jackson, *Father Junipero Serra and the Mission Indians of Cal.* (1902); H. I. Priestley, *José de Gálvez* (1916), *Univ. of Cal. Pubs. in Hist.*, vol. V; C. E. Chapman, *The Founding of Spanish Cal.* (1916); D. S. Watson, *The Founding of the First Cal. Missions* (1934), with some hitherto unpublished letters; Agnes Repplier, *Junipero Serra, Pioneer Colonist of Cal.* (1933), a popular biography; material in the archives of the Santa Barbara and San Carlos missions.]   F. B. S—k.

SERRELL, EDWARD WELLMAN (Nov. 5, 1826–Apr. 25, 1906), civil and military engineer, was born in London, England, but was a United States citizen by birthright. His parents were William and Anne (Boorn) Serrell, and he

was the tenth of their eleven children. Brought to the United States when he was four and a half years old, he received his early education in the schools of New York City, then took up civil engineering under the direction of his father and elder brother.

From 1845 up to the time of the Civil War, Serrell was engaged in railroad and bridge design and construction. He was successively assistant engineer to the commissioners of the Erie Railroad, and assistant to the chief of the topographical engineers, United States Army. As assistant engineer of the Panama Survey (1848), he accompanied the expedition that located the route between Aspinwall and Panama. Later he had charge of the surveys for the Northern Railroad of New Hampshire, and for a time was engineer of the Central Railroad of New Jersey. He prepared plans and supervised the construction of the suspension bridge across the Niagara River at Lewiston (1850); superintended the construction of the bridge at St. John, N. B.; and planned the bridge over the St. Lawrence at Quebec. Subsequently, he was concerned with the building of the Hoosac Tunnel, the Bristol Bridge over the Avon River in England, which had one of the largest spans of any bridge in that country at the time, and the Union Pacific Railroad.

At the outbreak of the Civil War, he organized and commanded the 1st New York Engineers, with the rank of lieutenant-colonel, but was soon made its colonel. Later he became chief engineer of the X Corps, United States Army, and afterward, chief engineer and chief of staff of the Army of the James. During the siege of Charleston, S. C., he devised and, under fire from the Confederate forces, personally supervised the construction of a battery in a swamp where, it is said, an iron rod would bury itself by its own weight. This battery, dubbed the "Swamp Angel," threw shells into the streets of Charleston, five miles away, and was hailed as a triumph of engineering skill. When he was mustered out, Feb. 13, 1865, he had served in 126 actions, and on Mar. 13, was brevetted brigadier-general. During the war he made many useful inventions, including practical improvements in armor plate, impromptu gun carriages, and the development of electric coast defenses.

Serrell prepared many reports on railroads and canals and served as consulting engineer for numerous corporations, including the American Isthmus Ship Canal Company. He projected an interoceanic canal from San Blas to Pearl Island Harbor, which he claimed could be built at sea level, with no locks, on a straight line less than

thirty miles from ocean to ocean, and at comparatively small expense. In 1868 he reported
on the location of a suspension bridge to cross
the Hudson River from Anthony's Nose, just
above Peekskill, on the east, to Fort Clinton, on
the west side. His last important engineering
work, in the early nineties, was in promoting the
construction of a bridge at this location in connection with a railroad from the Pennsylvania
coalfields to New England. The enterprise, however, was never carried to completion. Serrell
died in New York City. He was married on Apr.
6, 1848, to Jane, daughter of the Rev. Jesse
Pound. She died in September 1896 and on Sept.
6, 1900, he married Marion Seaton, daughter of
Orville A. Roorbach.

[*Who's Who in America,* 1906–07; P. F. Mottelay
and T. Campbell-Copeland, *The Soldier in Our Civil
War,* vol. II (1885); report of adjutant general's office,
Albany, 1898; F. B. Heitman, *Hist. Reg. and Dict. U.
S. Army* (1903); *Engineering News,* May 3, 1906;
Who's Who in N. Y., 1905; *N. Y. Times,* Apr. 26,
1906.]   B. A. R.

SERVOSS, THOMAS LOWERY (Oct. 14,
1786–Nov. 30, 1866), merchant, ship-owner, was
representative of the Northerners who made
threefold profits in the cotton belt by selling
Northern goods, sending back cotton in return
and also transporting those goods in both directions. He was born in Philadelphia, the son of
Jacob and Isabella Servoss. His father was a
merchant, trading between Philadelphia and Albany, N. Y. The yellow fever left Thomas an
orphan in 1798 and four years later he entered
the great Philadelphia counting-house of Daniel
W. Coxe who, with forty vessels, carried on a
brisk trade with the lower Mississippi. Servoss
was married to Elizabeth Courtney at Philadelphia on Oct. 31, 1807. Three years later he started by way of Pittsburgh and the Ohio River to
settle at Natchez, Miss., promising his reluctant
young wife that as soon as he made money
enough, he would return to settle down as a merchant in Philadelphia or New York City. At
Natchez, he entered into partnership with one
Henry Turner of that place, became one of the
most popular residents of the town, and developed a very profitable trade. His particular
correspondent in the East was Peter H. Schwenk
of New York, a brother-in-law, who sent his
manufactures and received cotton in return. Servoss is credited with having sent the shipments of
rifles needed for the defense of New Orleans in
1815, but the accounts of that transaction, without naming him particularly, throw little credit
on the contractor (See A. S. Colyar, *Life and
Times of Andrew Jackson,* 1904, I, 262). Servoss kept his promise to his wife and went to

New York in 1816, but it was too late and she
died there on Mar. 3, 1817.

After the death of his wife, Servoss returned
to the Mississippi, settled at New Orleans, and
engaged in business on a larger scale. He was
married in New Orleans to Louisa H., daughter
of the prominent John Pintard [*q.v.*] of New
York, on Apr. 4, 1824. His business prospered
until the "cotton panic" of 1825, when he lost,
among other things, 500 bales through the failure of the firm of Jeremiah Thompson [*q.v.*].
He then returned to New York City where he
lived until his death. By 1827 he was living on
Broome Street, and he later moved to Harlem.
His New Orleans friends sent him goods on
consignment, and in 1827 he established a regular and very profitable line of sailing packets between New York and New Orleans. He ran this
"Louisiana Line" until about 1831, when he sold
it to Edward Knight Collins [*q.v.*]. This was
one of the most successful of the coastal packet
lines, for New Orleans shipped a considerable
amount of its cotton, even for ultimate foreign
export, to New York. This venture seems to
have restored the Servoss fortune. Servoss was
a director of the North American Trust & Banking Company, and a trustee of the Chambers
Street Bank for Savings. He was active in the
American Bible Society, probably through the
influence of John Pintard, and he built St. Clements Episcopal Church on Amity Street for his
friend, the Rev. Louis Pintard Bayard, who became rector. His appearance in his last years
was described as "grand, noble and venerable,"
with a "towering form, very much resembling
that of General Scott" (Scoville, *post,* p. 179).
In addition to an infant son who died at Natchez,
he had one son by his first marriage and a son
and two daughters by his second.

[J. A. Scoville (Walter Barrett, pseud.), *The Old
Merchants of N. Y.,* ser. 4 (1866); family papers;
Longworth's N. Y. Directory, various editions; *Am.
Ann. Cyc., 1866* (1867), p. 583; *N. Y. Herald,* Dec. 2,
1866.]   R. G. A.

SESSIONS, HENRY HOWARD (June 21,
1847–Mar. 14, 1915), railroad car builder, inventor, was born in Madrid, St. Lawrence County,
N. Y., the son of Milton and Rosanna (Beals)
Sessions. He was of English ancestry, a descendant of John Sessions, who emigrated to
Connecticut in 1768. Henry attended school in
his native town until he was fifteen years old,
and then, being mechanically inclined, began an
apprenticeship in the railroad car and machine
shop of the Central Vermont Railroad at Northfield, Vt., of which shop his father was master
car builder. Upon completing his apprenticeship
he continued as a journeyman car builder under

his father until 1870, when he became master car builder of the Rome, Watertown & Ogdensburgh Railroad at Rome, N. Y. After serving in this capacity for eight years, in the hope of bettering himself he went West and at Sioux City, Iowa, became master car builder for the Sioux City & St. Paul Railroad. Early in 1880 he was made master car builder of the International and Great Northern Railroad at St. Paul, Minn., but the following year he went to Texas and during the years 1881–85 held similar positions with the Texas & Pacific Railroad and the St. Louis, Iron Mountain, and Southern railroads, respectively.

Because of his long and varied experience in car construction, in 1885 he was appointed superintendent of the Pullman Company, Pullman, Ill. Two years later he devised several improvements on the railroad car which brought him world-wide recognition. One of these was the bellows projection on the ends of passenger cars which permitted close connection of the cars in a train and provided safe passage from one to another. The original patent for this invention was granted Nov. 15, 1887 (No. 373,098). The following year he improved the "vestibule," as it came to be called, by devising spring equalizers to permit cars to take curves readily (patented May 15, 1888), and on May 14, 1889, he patented the design and manufacture of the fabric bellows coupling that came into common use. A number of other inventions were completed by him in 1891–92, among them a railroad car brake and a car heater. He also designed the standard steel platform for passenger cars. This last contrivance led to his becoming associated with the Standard Coupler Company of New York in 1896 as vice-president and director. In this capacity he continued his work of inventing improvements for railway rolling stock, in the course of which he perfected a street railway air brake, a metallic buffer beam, the friction draft rigging, and the radial buffing and draft rigging for railway cars, the last named being patented Feb. 3, 1903 (No. 719,519) and assigned to the Standard Coupler Company. During this work Sessions maintained his residence in Chicago, where he died. In 1872 he married Nellie L. Maxham of Rome, N. Y.

[F. C. Sessions, *Materials for a Hist. of the Sessions Family* (1890); *Railway Age Gazette*, Mar. 19, 1915; Jos. Husband, *The Story of the Pullman Car* (1917); T. C. Clarke and others, *The Am. Railway* (1889); *N. Y. Times*, Mar. 16, 1915; Patent Office records.]

C.W.M.

SESTINI, BENEDICT (Mar. 20, 1816–Jan. 17, 1890), Roman Catholic priest, mathematician, astronomer, was born at Florence, Italy. He received his earlier education at the Scuola Pia, near his native town, and so early evinced a mastery of mathematical computation that at the age of eighteen he was appointed assistant to Fr. Inghirami, then the director of the Osservatorio Ximeniano, at Florence. On Oct. 30, 1836, he entered the Society of Jesus at Rome. Three years later he began his philosophical and theological studies at the Roman College and here was privileged to have as professor Fr. Andrea Caraffa, one of the leading mathematicians of his time, who materially encouraged him in the prosecution of the researches of his choice. On the advice of Caraffa he was assigned as assistant astronomer of the Roman Observatory, then under the directorship of Fr. M. DeVico, whose name is identified with one of the periodic comets. During his incumbency at this observatory, which lasted till 1848, Sestini made a special study of star colors and his results were published under the titles *Memoria Sopra i Colori delle Stelle del Catalogo di Baily Osservati* (1845) and *Memoria Seconda Intorno ai Colori delle Stelle . . .* (1847). He was ordained to the priesthood in 1844.

Following the outbreak of the Revolution in Rome in 1848, he emigrated to the United States and became connected with Georgetown University, Washington, D. C., where, at the observatory of the University, he resumed his researches. During the year 1850 he made studies of the sun's surface. Availing himself of a cloudless sky, persisting from Sept. 20 to Nov. 6 of that year, he was able to follow the sun spots, then very pronounced, noting the rate of travel over the surface and the changes in their appearances and, being a skilled draftsman, to commit them to paper. Engravings of the sketches were published in an appendix to *Astronomical Observations Made During the Year 1847 at the National Observatory, Washington,* vol. III (1853). These are rated as among the best studies of the sun's maculae antedating the application of photography to investigations of the skies. In addition to his researches in astronomy, Sestini taught mathematics and natural sciences to the Jesuit seminarians then resident at Georgetown College. In 1852 he published *A Treatise of Analytical Geometry*. This was followed by *A Treatise on Algebra* (1855, 1857). In 1856 there appeared his *Elements of Geometry and Trigonometry* and in 1871, *Manual of Geometrical and Infinitesimal Analysis*. He also wrote *Theoretical Mechanics* (1873), *Principles of Cosmography* (1878), and *Animal Physics* (1874), all of which were privately printed for the use of his scholars. In 1878 he organized an expedition to Denver, Colo., for the observation of the total eclipse of the sun, an account of which was published in the *American Catholic Quarterly Review* (October 1878).

Possessed of no little architectural skill, Sestini is accredited with the planning and the supervision of the construction of Holy Trinity and Saint Aloysius churches, Washington, D. C., and of the Jesuit Seminary at Woodstock, Md. At the last-named institution he frescoed on the ceiling of the college library the solar system of Copernicus. In 1866 he began the publication of the *Messenger of the Sacred Heart,* a periodical which came to have the widest circulation of any Catholic magazine in the United States and possibly in the world. He remained at Georgetown till 1869, except for a year spent at Frederick devoted to studies in ascetic theology, three years at Boston College, and two years at Gonzaga College, Washington, D. C., in which institution he taught higher mathematics. From 1869 to 1885 he gave instruction in astronomy and geology at Woodstock. In the latter year his health became impaired and he was forced to resign the editorship of the *Messenger of the Sacred Heart.* He thereupon entered into retirement at the Jesuit novitiate at Frederick, Md., where, having suffered a severe stroke of paralysis, he died.

[*Woodstock Letters,* XIX, 259, XXX, 99 ; *Messenger of the Sacred Heart,* Mar., May, June, July 1890 ; Carlos Sommervogel, *Bibliothèque de la Compagnie de Jésus,* vol. VII (1896) ; *Washington Post,* Jan. 18, 1890.]
F. A. T.

SETH, JAMES (May 6, 1860–July 24, 1924), philosopher, was born at Edinburgh, Scotland. Both his father, Smith Kinmont Seth, and his mother, Margaret (Little), came of well-to-do country stock. James attended schools in Edinburgh, where his father held a position with the Commercial Bank, and in 1876 entered the University. In 1881 he received the degree of master of arts with first-class honors and the following year he won a Ferguson Scholarship, open to all graduates of the four Scottish Universities. Intending to become a minister, he was for four years a student in the Theological College of the Free Church of Scotland, and was then duly licensed by the Free Church Presbytery of Edinburgh. During his theological course, he spent two semesters at German universities.

His philosophical studies, which he had continued to pursue, determined his career. In 1886 he was called to succeed Dr. Jacob G. Schurman as professor of metaphysics and ethics in Dalhousie College, Halifax, Nova Scotia. After six years there he came to the United States to fill a professorship of philosophy in Brown University, Providence, R. I. In 1891 he had published

Freedom As Ethical Postulate, and during four years spent at Brown he completed *A Study of Ethical Principles,* his most important work, which was published in 1894. In his ethical theory he sought to mediate between Utilitarianism and the Kantian and other rationalistic systems, finding in Personality a conception that unites the truth of both. Not the least merit of the book is its felicitous style, a quality found in all his writings. In 1896 Seth accepted a call from his old friend Dr. Schurman, then president of Cornell University, to the Sage Professorship of Moral Philosophy in that institution. In January of the following year he became co-editor of the *Philosophical Review,* serving in that capacity until November 1902. After the death of his former teacher, Prof. Henry Calderwood, he became the successful candidate for the chair of moral philosophy in the University of Edinburgh, a position which he held from 1898 till the year of his death. At Edinburgh he held the satisfaction of working side by side with his brother, Andrew Seth Pringle-Pattison, who held the chair of logic and metaphysics, once occupied by Sir William Hamilton.

In his *Study of Ethical Principles* Seth had emphasized the ethical meaning of the state. Keenly alive to the moral obligations of citizenship, he devoted increasing thought and effort to social problems. He became interested in methods for the control of the liquor traffic, and was one of four Scottish citizens invited by the Temperance Legislation Board to visit Norway to study the Samlag system, long tested in that country. The results of his observation were given in an article in the *Contemporary Review* (December 1906). He was also keenly interested in the effort of a minority of the Poor Law Commission to secure the repeal of the Poor Law, and gave active support to Sidney and Beatrice Webb in their campaign against this antiquated measure. The deplorable conditions of poverty and degradation which he found existing in quarters of his native city spurred him to promote the foundation of the Edinburgh School of Social Study and Training in connection with the University. The aim of the new school was, in his own words, "by opening the mind of the student to the inter-connections of the several social problems and the subtle action and reaction of causes and effects, to develop in him a scientific understanding of social facts. For," he adds, "we cannot doubt that, here as elsewhere, knowledge is power" (memoir by A. Seth Pringle-Pattison, in *Essays,* p. xxix). His contributions to periodicals were numerous and in 1912 he published *English Philosophers and*

Schools of Philosophy. After his death, his brother Andrew edited *Essays in Ethics and Religion with Other Papers by James Seth* (1926), with memoir and bibliography.

Sensitive and somewhat shy, Seth had a most winning personality, which attracted and held a wide circle of devoted friends. Not the least of his charms was a quaint humor which could, on occasion, assume an ironic edge against all pretense and vulgar self-seeking. It was doubtless as a teacher that he exercised his most important influence. Many hundreds of students both in America and in Scotland will long remember with gratitude his kindly presence and his persuasive initiation into those ethical problems which touch all that is deepest in life and character. He never married.

[In addition to memoir mentioned above, see *Who's Who*, 1924; J. H. Muirhead, "Prof. James Seth," *Nature*, Aug. 23, 1924; *Times* (London), July 26, 1924; *Morning Chronicle* (Halifax), July 26, 1924.]

W. G. E.

SETON, ELIZABETH ANN BAYLEY (Aug. 28, 1774–Jan. 4, 1821), foundress of the American Sisters of Charity, was born in New York City. Her father, Dr. Richard Bayley [*q.v.*], was the first professor of anatomy at King's College and staff surgeon to General Sir Guy Carleton; her mother was Catharine Charlton, daughter of Rev. Richard Charlton, rector of St. Andrew's Episcopal Church, Richmond, Staten Island. She died when her daughter was only three years old, and the entire education of Elizabeth devolved upon the father. Realizing that his child possessed rare moral and intellectual qualities, Dr. Bayley employed unusual methods, which taught her to be unselfish and to think clearly and independently. These traits were further developed by her personal experiences during the days of the American Revolution. Those stirring times schooled the child to alertness and endurance, and fostered that patriotism which all her life was the faithful companion of her religious inspiration.

When not quite twenty, Jan. 25, 1794, she married a wealthy young merchant, William Magee Seton, whose ancestors had figured prominently in Scottish literature and history, and whose father, William, had settled in New York in 1763. To this union were born two sons and three daughters. Domestic cares, however, did not prevent her from being so devoted to the poor that she came to be called "The Protestant Sister of Charity." In 1797, with Isabella Marshall Graham [*q.v.*] and other leading women, she founded the first charitable organization in New York, and probably the first in the United States, the Society for the Relief of Poor Widows

with Small Children. In 1803 she accompanied her husband to Italy in the hope that his health, which had been shattered by worry over the loss of his fortune, would be restored. This hope proved vain, however, for he died at Pisa in December of that year. In Italy she made her first contact with Catholicism, and when she returned to New York she joined the Church of Rome, making her profession of faith in old St. Peter's, Barclay Street, on Mar. 14, 1805. This step estranged her family and friends at a time when she most needed their assistance. After several vain attempts to support herself in New York, in June 1808 she accepted an invitation to open a school for girls in Baltimore. Guided by the Sulpician Fathers at St. Mary's Seminary, she conducted classes in a house on Paca Street, and there, in the spring of 1809, with four companions, formed the community which adopted the name "Sisters of St. Joseph." In the summer they moved to Emmitsburg. They adopted, with some modifications, the rules of the Daughters of Charity of St. Vincent de Paul, and after 1812 were known as the Sisters of Charity of St. Joseph. This first native religious community was destined to number more than ten thousand women and to conduct a nation-wide system of charitable and educational institutions, among them the country's first Catholic orphanage, its first Catholic hospital, and its first maternity hospital. Because Mother Seton had her sisters open in Philadelphia the earliest American parish school, and sent them virtually everywhere to help the bishops in their work of education, she is considered the patroness of the parochial school system in America. Her community may be said to be the index of her character. It ministers to practically every type of educational and social need of the American people, for the glory of God and the good of the country.

As the first superior of the community, Mother Seton braved the hardships of its early days. In spite of the poverty that continually threatened its existence, she somehow formed her sisters into effective teachers and model religious. She herself taught French and music many hours daily, mothered the children of the school and the poor of the neighborhood, wrote thousands of letters, translated French biographies, prepared original meditations, composed exquisite hymns, among them a version of "Jerusalem, My Happy Home," for which she also wrote the music; yet all the while she led a life of recollection. Many of her writings were edited by her grandson, Robert Seton [*q.v.*], and published under the title, *Memoirs, Letters, and Journal of Elizabeth Seton* (2 vols., 1869).

Her extraordinary spiritual discernment made her a power for good when the Church in America was still in its infancy. With the spread of her influence after her death, her reputation for sanctity increased and about 1907 her Cause for canonization was introduced by James Cardinal Gibbons, successor in the see of Baltimore of her nephew, James Roosevelt Bayley [*q.v.*].

[Archives of St. Joseph Mother House, Emmitsburg, Md.; archives of the Cathedral, Baltimore, Md.; *Memoirs, Letters, and Journal* mentioned above; C. I. White, *Life of Mrs. Eliza A. Seton* (3rd ed., 1879); Hélène Bailly de Barberey, *Elizabeth Seton* (1927), translated and adapted by J. B. Code; J. B. Code, *Great Am. Foundresses* (1929) and *Mother Seton and Her Sisters of Charity* (1930); Robert Seton, *An Old Family, or the Setons of Scotland and America* (1899).]

J. B. C.

SETON, ROBERT (Aug. 28, 1839–Mar. 22, 1927), Roman Catholic prelate, was born in Pisa, Italy. His father was William Seton, a naval officer, son of Mother Elizabeth Ann Seton [*q.v.*]; his mother, Emily Prime, daughter of Nathaniel Prime, of the historic banking house of Prime, Ward & King. Of noble Scottish and English lineage on his father's side, and connected on his mother's with some of the foremost American families of wealth and social prominence, he possessed a family pride so extravagant at times that it led to eccentricities which made him an enigma even to his coreligionists in America. His childhood was spent at the Seton home, "Cragdon," in Westchester County, N. Y., and at eleven he followed his brother William Seton [*q.v.*] as a student at Mount St. Mary's College, Emmitsburg, Md., close to the convent of St. Joseph, where his grandmother had founded the American Sisters of Charity. Two years later, he accompanied his parents to southern France, where his mother died at Pau, in 1854. For the next three years he traveled on the Continent, studied at several European institutions, and finally made a short visit to America.

Although the life of a soldier appealed to his romantic nature, he finally decided to become a priest. With this end in view he went to Rome in 1857, where he became a student at the Urban College of the Propaganda until the opening of the North American College in 1859 when he enrolled as its first student. He aroused the interest of Pius IX who in November 1861 had him transferred to the Accademia Ecclesiastica dei Nobili, an institution for the education of nobles studying for the priesthood. Even here, among the scions of the greatest European houses, Seton remained stanchly American, his militant patriotism often getting him into serious difficulties. Once, refusing to attend a reception given by the Roman patriciate for Maxi-

milian and Carlotta, who were about to embark for Mexico on their anti-American Napoleonic venture, he would have been expelled, but for the Pope's intervention. After a brilliant course of studies, first at the Roman College and afterwards at the Roman University, commonly called the Sapienza, he was ordained priest, Apr. 16, 1865. The following year the Pope made him a private chamberlain and one year later named him a prothonotary apostolic, the first American so honored. The same year he received the degree of bachelor of laws and doctor of divinity. In his early twenties he had become the accepted American representative in the ecclesiastical world of Rome.

For some unknown reason, however, he decided against a career that would have led possibly to the cardinalate, and elected to return to America. Here for more than a quarter of a century he led a quietly busy life, first as chaplain to the Sisters of Charity, at St. Elizabeth's Convent, near Madison, N. J., then as pastor of St. Joseph's Church, Jersey City, giving occasional lectures on his great hobby, Christian archeology, at various American colleges and universities. Suddenly in 1902 he returned to Rome, where for twelve years he served as the unofficial link between the Vatican and things and people American. The Rome of the Temporal Sovereignty had disappeared, but he found four of his old classmates cardinals, one a patriarch, two archbishops, two canons of the Vatican, and three others high in ecclesiastical circles. In 1903 he refused the then vacant archbishopric of Chicago, but four months later accepted the mitre in another form when Pius X appointed him titular archbishop of Heliopolis *in partibus infidelium.* The years that followed, the most beautiful of Robert Seton's life, were the years of which Shane Leslie speaks, when the aged archbishop "had become perfect, almost exquisite, in Roman etiquette as well as in pontifical ceremonies" (Introduction to Seton's *Memories of Many Years,* p. 22).

Meanwhile, across the Atlantic he had become almost legendary. In 1914, however, financial reverses had so reduced his patrimony that he reappeared among his countrymen as an impoverished old aristocrat, seeking a home on the eve of a great international conflict. He took up his residence at Emmitsburg, near the tomb of Mother Seton, but a longing for Europe drew him back once more, and he spent three years in France, Spain, and England. When he returned to America he lived at the Convent of St. Elizabeth, cared for by the same sisterhood to which he had given his services as a priest shortly after his ordination. A faithful priest, a distinguished scholar, and a unique personality, he had a career, which in length and strangeness of fortune was without parallel among his countrymen. In 1862 he published *Essays on Various Subjects Chiefly Roman,* and in 1869 he edited many of Mother Seton's writings—*Memoirs, Letters, and Journal of Elizabeth Seton.* Another of his works was a scholarly genealogical study, *An Old Family, or the Setons of Scotland and America* (1899). His own memoirs, *Memories of Many Years,* appeared in 1923. He was also correspondent for the *New York Times,* under the name Fyvie.

[In addition to Seton's own publications, sources of information are archives of St. Joseph Coll., Emmitsburg, Md., of the Coll. of St. Elizabeth, Convent Station, N. J., and of the North Am. Coll., and the Acad. of Noble Ecclesiastics, Rome, Italy; *Catholic News* (N. Y.), Mar. 26, Apr. 2, 1927; *N. Y. Times,* Mar. 23, 1927.]   J. B. C.

SETON, WILLIAM (Jan. 28, 1835–Mar. 15, 1905), author, was born in New York City, the son of William Seton, a lieutenant in the United States navy, and Emily (Prime) Seton. A descendant of William Seton who came to New York in 1763, he was the grandson of Elizabeth Ann Bayley Seton and brother to Monsignor Robert Seton [*qq.v.*], the distinguished Roman Catholic divine. Tracing his ancestry back to the Setons of Parbroath, an ancient Scottish family, he was recognized in Burke's *A Genealogical and Heraldic Dictionary of the Peerage and Baronetage* (1901) as the head of the Parbroath branch of the family. After a brief stay at St. John's College, Fordham, he continued his studies at Mount St. Mary's College, Emmitsburg, Md. Leaving this institution in the early fifties before taking a degree, he studied for a time at the University of Bonn. Upon his return to New York, he entered the law office of T. J. Glover and was admitted to the bar just before the outbreak of the Civil War. He answered the first call for troops, and as captain in the 4th New York Infantry was twice wounded in the battle of Antietam (George Seton, *post,* p. 311). With the advent of peace he devoted himself to literature, giving special attention for some years to the writing of fiction. About 1886, however, while in Europe, he became so absorbed in the study of science that he thereafter gave most of his time to scientific pursuits. He now made annual visits to Paris, where he became acquainted with such authorities as Albert Gaudry and Albert de Lapparent.

Seton began his literary career with the novel *Nat Gregory, or the Old Maid's Secret* (1867). This was succeeded by two historical novels, *Ro-*

mance of the Charter Oak (1871), "a Picture of Colonial Times" in Connecticut, and *The Pride of Lexington* (1873), a story of the American Revolution; later followed by *Rachel's Fate, and Other Tales* (1882) and several other novels. *The Pioneer* (1874), Seton's single excursion into the realm of poetry, which was dedicated to Bryant, deals in a somewhat Wordsworthian manner with a young New Hampshire couple who seek a new home in the wilderness. It is probably, however, as a popularizer of the theory of evolution that Seton did his most effective literary work. Avoiding the ultra-technical, he sought to present clearly to the average man the discoveries of natural science. The simplicity of his handling of scientific subjects is well exemplified in *A Glimpse of Organic Life* (copyright 1897), a work in dialogue form designed primarily for young people but effectively written. Somewhat more technical is his defense of the theory of evolution contributed to the *Catholic World,* November 1897, called "The Hypothesis of Evolution." His interest in science is further reflected in a biographical sketch of Michel-Guillaume Jean de Crèvecœur [*q.v.*] written for the *Magazine of American History,* September 1889. He was also a contributor to a pamphlet entitled *Hear the Other Side* (188–), a plea for freedom of worship among the children committed to the "House of Refuge" on Randall's Island. On Jan. 3, 1884, he married Sarah Redwood Parrish of Philadelphia, a Catholic convert from the Society of Friends, who died in 1895; their only child died in infancy. Toward the close of his life he became well known as a philanthropist. He died in New York and is buried with other members of the family at Mount St. Mary's.

[Monsignor (Robert) Seton, *An Old Family, or the Setons of Scotland and America* (1889), with portrait; George Seton, *A Hist. of the Family of Seton* (1896), vol. I; *Cath. Encyc.* (1912), vol. XIII; *N. Y. Daily Tribune,* Mar. 16, 17, 1905; "Living Cath. Men of Science," *Cath. World,* with portrait, Mar. 1898; *A Supp. to Allibone's Critical Dict. of Eng. Lit. and British and Am. Authors* (1891), ed. by J. F. Kirk; letter from the Rev. B. J. Bradley, president of Mount St. Mary's College.]   N. F. A.

SETTLE, THOMAS (Jan. 23, 1831–Dec. 1, 1888), politician, jurist, was born in Rockingham County, N. C., the fourth child of Thomas and Henrietta (Graves) Settle, and a descendant of Josiah Settle who emigrated from England to North Carolina in the middle of the eighteenth century. His father, a member and speaker of the House of Commons, congressman, and judge of long service, was prominent in state affairs. The younger Thomas graduated from the University of North Carolina in 1850, was private secretary to his brother-in-law, Gov. David S

Reid [*q.v.*], studied law under Judge Richmond M. Pearson [*q.v.*], with whom he was later on the North Carolina supreme bench, was licensed in 1854, and began practice in Rockingham County. About this time, he married Mary, the daughter of Tyre Glenn of Surry County, by whom he had six daughters and three sons.

His father was a Whig, but Settle, in 1852, became a Democrat, and in 1854 began his political career as a member of the House of Commons; he was twice reëlected and during his last term served as speaker. In 1856 he was a Buchanan elector, and in 1860 he supported Douglas. When the cotton states seceded, he opposed similar action by North Carolina. In February 1861 he was chosen a delegate to the convention which the people rejected and about the same time was elected solicitor of the fourth judicial circuit. When the call for troops came, he eagerly volunteered and became a captain in the 3rd North Carolina Regiment. At the close of the year's term of enlistment, however, he did not again volunteer, but resumed the office of solicitor. In 1865 he was a delegate to the "Johnson" convention where, as chairman of the committee on the abolition of slavery and of that on the state debt, he wrote and offered the ordinances abolishing slavery and repudiating the war debt; he also took a prominent part in every question before the convention. In November he was elected to the state Senate and was chosen speaker. In the campaign he had supported William W. Holden [*q.v.*] for governor, and he was, at this period, in hearty accord with President Johnson's policy. At the second session of the convention, however, he gradually identified himself with the group in opposition and favored the ratification of the Fourteenth Amendment. When it was rejected, he championed the congressional policy of reconstruction, participated in the political meeting which organized the radical party in the state, and introduced the resolution which identified it with the Republican party; yet at no time was he possessed by the bitter radicalism which characterized the majority of his party associates.

In April 1868 he was elected associate justice of the supreme court of North Carolina and served until February 1871, when President Grant appointed him minister to Peru. Disliking the position and the climate, early in 1872 he resigned. He was president of the Republican National Convention of 1872 and in the autumn was an unsuccessful candidate for Congress. In December he was reappointed to the supreme court and served until 1876 when he resigned

to accept the Republican nomination for governor. The brilliant campaign carried on by him and his opponent Zebulon B. Vance [*q.v.*] was one which in character and spirit brought honor to both. Settle gave an excellent account of himself but went down in defeat. On Jan. 30, 1877, President Grant appointed him district judge for Florida, and he filled that office until his death.

Settle was a superbly handsome man with a magnetic personality. He was genial, witty, and affectionate in personal intercourse, and courageous and tolerant in his public relationships. His mind was quick and acute, and he was a well-informed and persuasive debater. He was best fitted for the political arena, but made an excellent though in no sense a great judge. He was impartial, humane, and just, and his judicial opinions were terse, concise, and clear.

[W. P. Bynum, Address, in 139 *N. C. Reports*, 649; *Jour. of the Convention of the State of N. C.*, 1865, 1866; 63–65 and 68–75 *N. C. Reports*; Sidney Andrews, *The South Since the War* (1866); J. H. Wheeler, *Reminiscences and Memoirs of N. C. and Eminent North Carolinians* (1884); *Appletons' Ann. Cyc., 1888* (1889); *Morning Star* (Wilmington, N. C.), Dec. 2, 4, 1888.]   J. G. deR. H.

SEVERANCE, CAROLINE MARIA SEYMOUR (Jan. 12, 1820–Nov. 10, 1914), founder of woman's clubs, was born in Canandaigua, N. Y., the daughter of Orson and Caroline M. (Clarke) Seymour. Her father was a banker and her home a comfortable one. His death, when she was a child, brought her under the guardianship of an uncle, a strict Presbyterian, whose influence overshadowed that of her Episcopalian mother. She described herself as a serious and supersensitive child, whose life was darkened by her mother's constant grief for her father and tortured by a sense of sin and the threat of eternal punishment which she heard described in the Presbyterian pulpit. When she was fifteen she graduated from the Female Seminary at Geneva, N. Y., valedictorian of her class. On Aug. 27, 1840, she was married, in Auburn, N. Y., to Theodoric C. Severance of Cleveland, a banker; they were the parents of five children. Louis Henry Severance [*q.v.*] was their nephew.

The first years of her married life were spent in Cleveland where she soon became active in public affairs. Having attained some prominence at Woman's Rights conventions, she was invited in 1853 to read a paper before the Mercantile Library Association of Cleveland—the first, according to her own statement, ever presented by a woman before such a society. Her subject was "Humanity; a Definition and a Plea," and she was requested to repeat the reading on several occasions. The Ohio Woman's Rights Association then asked her to prepare a tract on woman's rights for circulation, and she later presented a memorial to the state legislature on behalf of civil equality for women. In 1855 the family moved to Boston and here she soon began to plan what she had long desired, an organization of women associated for mutual benefit and social work. Then came the Civil War when, in the work for the Sanitary Commission and the Freedman's Bureau, women took an important part in great enterprises. When the war was over she took the lead in furthering the desire of some of the women in Boston for a continued association and was instrumental in founding the New England Women's Club. On Feb. 10, 1868, the society was formed and on Mar. 10, 1868, a constitution was adopted. The object of the club was to organize the social force of the women then working alone or in small circles. Men were eligible to membership but the club was to be officered and controlled by women. Mrs. Severance was elected president and held that office until 1871 when she was succeeded by Julia Ward Howe [q.v.]. In 1875 the Severance family moved to Los Angeles, Cal. Her interest in women's organizations did not cease, however, and three years later she founded the Woman's Club of Los Angeles, which existed until 1887. She was also the founder of the Los Angeles Free Kindergarten Association, reorganized in 1891 as the Friday Morning Club, of which she became the first president. Later, the Los Angeles Fellowship Club was formed in her home, as was the Severance Club, an organization of both men and women. She was also instrumental in founding the Ebell Club of Los Angeles. Because of her activity she became known as "the mother of clubs." She wrote papers on a wide variety of topics of public interest, and was a trustee of the public library and of the Unitarian church.

[*Who's Who in America*, 1914–15; J. A. Sprague, *Hist. of the New England Women's Club* (1894); E. G. Ruddy, ed., *The Mother of Clubs* (1906); *Los Angeles Daily Times*, Nov. 11, 1914.]   B. R.

SEVERANCE, FRANK HAYWARD (Nov. 28, 1856–Jan. 26, 1931), author, historian, was born in Manchester, Mass., the son of Lucius Warren and Maria Lucretia (Hayward) Severance. He was directly descended from Richard Warren who came to Plymouth in the Mayflower. The family later was among the earliest settlers in the Champlain Valley but returned to Manchester; when the Civil War ruined Lucius Severance's business, he moved to White-

water, Wis. Severance entered Knox College in 1874 but in 1875 he went to Cornell University, where he partly earned his way by working as a printer during the first two years. During the last two years he was an assistant in microscopic botany and editor of the *Cornell Review* and of the *Cornell Era,* where he published some articles on Cayuga legendry. After receiving the bachelor's degree in 1879, he became a reporter on the *Gazette* at Erie, Pa.; a year later he went to Buffalo as marine editor on the *Buffalo Express*. On Aug. 19, 1885, he married Lena Lillian Hill of Isle Lamotte, Vt., who had been a classmate of his at Cornell. He soon became city editor and in 1886 managing editor of the *Illustrated Sunday Express,* a position he held until 1901, when he was called upon to become secretary of the Buffalo Historical Society. While on the *Express* he reported the funeral of President Garfield and the Johnstown flood of 1889.

It was between 1881 and 1886 that he began assembling information on the Niagara frontier and while he was managing editor of the *Illustrated Sunday Express* that he began to write on the subject. In appreciation of a series of stories on behalf of the Indians of western New York the Seneca Indians adopted him into their tribe, giving him the name of Da-deh'-o-gwat-hah, the carrier of news. He was invited to many of their festivals and to ceremonies of which few whites were permitted to be observers. His writings include *Old Trails on the Niagara Frontier* (1899), *The Story of Joncaire* (1906), *Studies of the Niagara Frontier* (1911), *The Picture Book of Earlier Buffalo* (1912), *Peace Episodes on the Niagara* (1914), and *An Old Frontier of France* (2 vols., 1917). He edited the publications of the Buffalo Historical Society from 1896 to 1930, and in 1904 William Walton's *The Captivity and Sufferings of Benjamin Gilbert and his Family* (1784). He also contributed to historical magazines and encyclopedias. He helped to arouse interest in the early history of western New York and the Great Lakes region not only by writing but by lecturing before historical and learned societies. A trained historian and an editor of marked ability, he served the Buffalo Historical Society as an able guide in its research in regional history, and his work as director of the museum gave the society a position of importance.

His travels included a number of trips to Europe and a tour of the world. Having had a keen interest in natural science from boyhood, he studied the trees of India and Burmah during a winter he spent in those countries; on three occasions he visited Japan, where he found much to interest him in the strangeness and variety of plant growths. He was president of the New York State Historical Association, 1923–25, and served as a member of the fine arts commission of New York state. He was an attendant of Westminster Presbyterian Church in Buffalo. At the time of his death he was survived by his wife, two daughters, and a son.

[*Who's Who in America*, 1930–31; biog. sketch in *Proc. N. Y. State Hist. Assoc.*, vol. XXIII (1925); *N. Y. State Hist. Assoc. Quart. Jour.*, Jan. 1931; *Buffalo Courier Express, Buffalo Evening News*, Jan. 27, 1931; *N. Y. Times*, Jan. 28, 1931; additional information from the Severance family.]   A. H. S.

SEVERANCE, LOUIS HENRY (Aug. 1, 1838–June 25, 1913), capitalist and philanthropist, was the younger of the two sons of Solomon Lewis Severance and Mary (Long) Severance. His paternal ancestor, John Severans, who is known to have been living in Ipswich, England, in 1635 and in Boston, Mass., in 1637, was one of the original proprietors of Salisbury, Mass. One of his descendants, Robert Severance, studied medicine with Dr. John Long in Shelburne, Mass., and married the daughter of his patron. Both doctors lived out their time in Shelburne, notable physicians of western Massachusetts. A grandson of Dr. John Long, Dr. David Long, Jr., settled in Cleveland in 1810. Thither, too, the six sons of Dr. Robert Severance, Solomon, Lewis, Theodoric, Cordenio, Erasmus, and John, were attracted a few years later. Solomon Lewis Severance opened a dry goods store, and in 1833 married Mary Long, the only child of Dr. David Long, Jr. Solomon died in 1838, about a month before his son Louis Henry was born. The widowed mother returned with her small family to her father's home, where the boys grew to manhood. Louis Henry Severance attended Cleveland public schools and in his eighteenth year found employment in the Commercial National Bank. Except for 100 days' service with the Union army in 1863, he remained in the banking business until near the end of the Civil War. The oil industry in western Pennsylvania then offered him the opportunity he had been awaiting. In 1864 he went to Titusville, Pa., to engage in the production of oil. Ten years later he returned to Cleveland, drawn into the Standard Oil Company of Ohio. From 1876 until his death, he was a stockholder of that company, and from 1876 until his retirement from active duties in 1894, served as its treasurer. He spent most of the remaining years of his life in New York City, although he died in Cleveland.

Severance's interests and industrial influence were extended through investments in oil, salt,

sulphur, and steel. In the nineties, in association with Herman Frasch [*q.v.*], F. B. Squire, and Frank Rockefeller, he formed the Union Sulphur Company, which employed a revolutionary process, invented by Frasch, of dissolving and pumping sulphur from its sources and thereby made the United States a great world producer of sulphur. His chief interest outside of business was in the Presbyterian Church and especially its missions. Hospitals and churches in Japan, Korea, and India stand as monuments to his philanthropy. Severance Hospital and the Severance Medical College at Seoul, Korea, are his benefactions. In 1907–08 he traveled around the world, inspecting missions generally. He was a trustee and generous supporter of Oberlin College, Western Reserve University, and the College of Wooster. After Wooster had been destroyed by fire in 1901, Severance, almost alone, rebuilt the institution on a larger and more attractive scale. He also gave liberally to the Young Men's Christian Association.

Severance was a gentleman of the old school, urbane, conservative in his tastes, critical in his judgments, but always kindly. He was married twice: on Aug. 13, 1862, to Fannie Buckingham Benedict, who died twelve years later, and in 1894 to Florence, daughter of Stephen D. Harkness, a member of the Standard Oil group; she died in 1895. To the first marriage two sons and two daughters were born; a son and two daughters survived their father.

[J. F. Severance, *The Severans Geneal. Hist.* (1893); G. V. Wickham, *The Pioneer Families of Cleveland* (1914), vol. II; E. M. Avery, *A Hist. of Cleveland and Its Environs* (1918), vol. II; *Cleveland Plain Dealer*, June 26, 1913.]   E. J. B.

SEVIER, AMBROSE HUNDLEY (Nov. 4, 1801–Dec. 31, 1848), representative and senator from Arkansas, was born in Greene County, Tenn., the son of John Sevier, the great-grandson of Valentine Sevier who emigrated from England to Baltimore in the middle of the 18th century, and the grand-nephew of John Sevier [*q.v.*]. His mother was probably Susannah (Conway) Sevier, also called Susan and Ann, the sister of James Sevier Conway and Elias Nelson Conway [*qq.v.*]. She divorced her husband, married again in 1812, and died about 1815. The boy received such education as the frontier afforded and studied law with his father. At the age of nineteen he removed to Missouri, and to Arkansas in 1821. There he was soon elected clerk of the territorial House of Representatives, served as a member from 1823 to 1827, and became speaker in 1827. On Aug. 26 of that year he was married to Juliette Johnson, the niece of James and Richard Mentor

Johnson and the sister of Robert Ward Johnson [*qq.v.*], and thereby became a member of the politically powerful Johnson family. They had five children.

Next year Henry W. Conway, the territorial delegate to Congress, was killed in a duel with Robert Crittenden, and Ambrose was elected to succeed him. He had himself already fought a duel, and in Congress he opposed a bill to prohibit dueling in the District of Columbia on the ground that it was a bill to protect members of Congress who had slandered their masters, the people. He kept his seat as delegate from Feb. 13, 1828, to June 15, 1836, when Arkansas was admitted as a state, having taken a prominent part in bringing about that result. As a Democrat he was elected senator and served in that capacity until March 1848. He was tall and handsome, with an irresistible laugh that won him many friends. He was *un bon vivant* and played his part in a banquet in his honor where fifty-eight toasts were drunk (Little Rock *Arkansas Gazette*, Nov. 30, 1830, Nov. 31, 1833; Little Rock *Arkansas Advocate*, Nov. 14, 1832). He worked constantly for his territory and state and obtained numerous favors from Congress, particularly donations of land (Little Rock *Arkansas Gazette*, Jan. 27, Feb. 10, Mar. 14, 1829, Oct. 31, 1832). He was made a member of the committee on Indian affairs and favored the organization of an Indian territory out of the region west of Missouri and Arkansas. He supported Linn's Oregon Bill and declared that the United States should occupy and govern that territory to carry out the Monroe Doctrine. Naturally he supported Polk's Oregon policy, championing even in bellicose language the resolution to give notice of the termination of the treaty of joint occupation (*Congressional Globe,* 27 Cong., 3 Sess., p. 154; 29 Cong., 1 Sess., app. p. 389). He voted to recognize the independence of Texas in 1837, for the treaty of annexation in 1844, and for the second joint resolution, which gave the president the choice of proceeding by treaty or direct annexation; but he took little part in the discussion. He took an active interest in the Mexican War. As chairman of the committee on foreign relations he introduced and pushed through the "3 million dollar bill" appropriating money for peace negotiations (*Congressional Globe,* 29 Cong., 2 Sess., p. 305). When the Trist treaty of peace was amended by the Senate, President Polk, his personal friend, asked Sevier to serve as minister to Mexico to conclude the negotiations. He hesitated but finally resigned, on Mar. 15, 1848, to accept. He was accompanied by Nathan Clifford [*q.v.*].

When the state legislature met in November 1848, Sevier was a candidate for reëlection, but after the legislature had balloted for three days he withdrew. He had been taken ill after his appointment to go to Mexico, had recovered, but was attacked again while in Mexico. From this he never fully recovered, and he died at his home, a large cotton plantation near Little Rock, Ark.

[*The Diary of James E. Polk,* 4 vols. (1910), ed. by M. M. Quaife; John Hallum, *Biog. and Pictorial Hist. of Ark.,* vol. I (1887); Fay Hempstead, *Hist. Rev. of Ark.* (1911); D. T. Herndon, *Centennial Hist. of Ark.* (1922), vol. I; Zella Armstrong, "The Sevier Family," *Notable Southern Families,* vol. IV (1926); *Ark. and its People,* 4 vols. (1930), ed. by D. Y. Thomas; *Biog. Dir. of Am. Cong.* (1928); *Ark. State Democrat* (Little Rock), Jan. 12, 1849; date of birth from inscription on grave in Mt. Holly Cemetery, Little Rock, Ark., quoted in *Ark. Hist. Asso. Pubs.,* vol. II (1908), p. 279.]   D. Y. T.

SEVIER, JOHN (Sept. 23, 1745–Sept. 24, 1815), pioneer, soldier, first governor of the state of Tennessee, was born near the present New Market, Va. When he emigrated from the Shenandoah Valley to the remote frontier region that is now East Tennessee, he was already, at the age of twenty-eight, the father of six or seven children. That was perhaps a sufficient reason for his moving to a country where land was cheap. Given the circumstances of his ancestry and early life, it is no surprise that he turned pioneer. His grandfather had emigrated from France to England, his father, Valentine, from London to Baltimore and thence to the Shenandoah Valley. There Valentine had married Joanna Goade, acquired a farm and a tavern, built up a large trade in furs and rum with Indians and white settlers, and speculated in land. John, the eldest of seven children, soon began to repeat the pattern of his father's life. After receiving a rather haphazard education he married in 1761 a girl of the neighborhood, Sarah Hawkins, moved from place to place, engaged in farming and trading, and laid off town lots at New Market, where he established a tavern and gave the Baptists a site for a church. With this varied training, great courage and personal magnetism, and probably a captain's commission in the militia, he was ready for leadership on a new frontier. The Appalachian Valley system pointed the way southwestward to the Holston River, where he would find in the process of formation a community similar to the one in which he had grown up.

He arrived in the Holston settlements with his family and belongings in December 1773. For the next seventeen years he continued to move down the valley with the advancing frontier. From 1783 to 1790 his home was on the Nolachucky River and after 1790 in or near

Knoxville. From the outset he was one of the acknowledged leaders of the backwoodsmen. It is said that he visited the region in 1771 and 1772 and was made a commissioner of the Watauga Association. He was certainly a member of the local Committee of Safety in 1776, when he signed a petition in that capacity requesting North Carolina to extend its jurisdiction over the Watauga and Holston settlements. When the request was granted, he was elected a representative to the Provincial Congress, which then appointed him lieutenant-colonel of militia. Though an active supporter of the revolutionary cause, he took little part in the fighting until 1780 and seems to have been occupied chiefly with various minor civil offices. It was in 1780, just after the migration of James Robertson to Middle Tennessee had cleared the field of his chief rival, that he rose to preëminence in the Watauga country. In this year he won undying fame among his people by leading two hundred and forty men across the Smokies to the victory of the southern frontiersmen over the British at King's Mountain. Immediately upon his return he set out upon an expedition against the Cherokee that marked the beginning of his career as harrier of the Indians. These events occurred shortly after his marriage on Aug. 14, 1780, to Catherine Sherrill, about seven months after the death of his first wife. In 1781 and 1782 he made three raids against the Indians and in the former year again crossed the mountains with two hundred men to aid Francis Marion against the British.

The "critical period" in American history was certainly a critical period in the life of John Sevier. With the British expelled and the Indians humbled, expansive forces were released along the whole western frontier, and nowhere was the tendency to dispersion more marked than in the settlements on the Holston and Watauga rivers. In most of the symptomatic developments Sevier was deeply concerned. At the close of the Revolution he joined with William Blount [q.v.] and others in a project for the establishment of a colony at Muscle Shoals. While he was thus engaged, a movement for a separate state was set on foot by his neighbors. At first he opposed it, since it might interfere with his Muscle Shoals venture, and he was satisfied with his brigadier-general's commission and other concessions hurriedly offered by North Carolina. Finding the movement irresistible, he put himself at the head of it, was elected governor of the state of Franklin, and tried to convert the new state into an instrument for promoting his Muscle Shoals enterprise. For that

and other purposes a military expedition against the Indians was concerted with the state of Georgia. His conduct alienated many of the pioneers, among them doctrinaire liberals who had had quite different plans for the new state. The failure of the Georgians to furnish the expected aid injured his prestige, and the opposition crystallised when a feud broke out between the Sevier and Tipton families. After some skirmishing over the county court records, which may be related to subsequent scandals over land titles, the Sevier faction was defeated in a "battle" in February 1788 which, though there were few casualties, resulted in the virtual extinction of the state of Franklin.

Because he had expressed the spirit of his times with too much vigor, he found himself at the age of forty-three a man with a blasted career. If he had played with land speculation, so had almost every other man in public life in the South and West. If he had scourged the Indians, it was an article of the frontier creed that Indian-baiting was a public service. If he had espoused the Franklin movement, it was only because public opinion had forced him to do so. Yet these things had proved his undoing. In the East, in North Carolina, in his own home country, he was denounced as a reckless disturber of the public peace, and his very life was in danger. In his desperation he took refuge on the extreme frontier with "a lawless banditti," as the governor of North Carolina called his followers. There he sank to the level of a bushwhacker, defied the efforts of Congress to control Indian affairs, and entered into a dubious correspondence with Spanish agents who were seeking to disrupt the Union. Arrested after a brawl in October 1788, he fled to the mountains, when released on bail, and wrote the North Carolina authorities demanding justice and hinting broadly at secession.

A fortunate turn of events in national affairs made possible his rehabilitation, and he was adroit enough to take full advantage of the opportunity. In 1788 North Carolina had failed to ratify the federal constitution, but the successful establishment of the new government made early ratification a certainty. Identifying himself with the rising cause, Sevier came forth as a stanch "federalist,"—indeed, he had always been a friend to the Union when he thought the Union could help the West. Fortunately for him, he had influential friends in the East, among them William Blount, who had long been associated with him in land speculation. There was moreover a general feeling that the recent disturbances on the frontier had been due in part to the blunders of the Confederation and that the new era should begin with a clean slate. The result was that, when Sevier was elected to the North Carolina Senate in 1789, he was fully pardoned, seated, and restored to his position as brigadier-general. As a member of the state convention that met simultaneously, he voted with the majority for the ratification of the federal constitution. When North Carolina completed the cession of its western territory to Congress, Blount was appointed governor, and Sevier was commissioned brigadier-general of militia in 1791. In the meanwhile he had served a brief term in Congress, 1789 to 1791, as the representative of North Carolina's western district before the act' of cession was accepted.

The next twenty years of his life, which he spent in Tennessee, were comparatively uneventful. The sharp contrast between their sobriety and the romantic exploits of his earlier years suggests that the Franklin fiasco had cured him of his love of adventure. He took no part in the Genet affair or in the conspiracies of William Blount and Aaron Burr. His last fling in land speculation in the grand manner was a brief connection with the South Carolina Yazoo Company in 1790; and, though while governor of Tennessee he gave some encouragement to the Muscle Shoals enterprise of Zachariah Cox in 1798, he seems to have taken no part in it personally. His last campaign against the Indians was fought in 1793. In 1798–99 he was ready to fight again, but this time under federal authority as brigadier-general in the provisional army. Even politics occupied but little of his time during the territorial period. He was a member of the legislative council in 1794, but he did not sit in the convention that drew up the first constitution of the state of Tennessee in 1796. If his diary is to be trusted, he gave little thought to anything but his plantation, his iron works, his store, his slaves, and his wife and eighteen children. Land speculation he had by no means forgotten, for in 1795 he patented 66,000 acres of land lying on the Cumberland River; but now it was a purely business transaction. He and his wife moved in polite society, drinking tea at the governor's house, dining out, playing whist, and attending balls. He was a trustee of two colleges, Washington College in Tennessee and Blount College (University of Tennessee), and though not a churchmember, employed a Presbyterian minister to tutor his children and was frequently seen at church with his wife. The leader of "a lawless banditti" had been transformed into a pillar of society.

Most of the remaining years of this Indian fighter were spent in civil employment. Elected the first governor of Tennessee, he served three successive terms, as many as the constitution permitted, from 1796 until 1801, and three more terms from 1803 to 1809. The choice was a natural one, for he was a military hero, still a dashing figure, unaffectedly cordial in his manner, neither cultured nor illiterate, an experienced public officer, and bound by ties of blood and intimate friendship to many families throughout the state. A quarrel with Andrew Jackson, which began about 1796, embittered the rest of his life. Jackson complicated the issue by preferring charges of land frauds that may or may not have been true, but the real source of the difficulty lay in conflicting military ambitions. It was a sign of the changing times that in 1801 the young politician and judge, Jackson, who had never fought a campaign since early youth, was elected major-general of militia over Sevier, the hero of some thirty-five battles and skirmishes. Though the encounter of 1803, in which the affair culminated, was farcical, it left a deep impression upon Sevier, who dreamed that his father appeared to him to assure him that Jackson was "a very wicked base man, and a very improper person for a judge" (Diary, *post,* Dec. 10, 1803).

After his retirement from the governorship, he was elected to the state Senate for one term 1809–11, was then sent to Congress again, and served from 1811 until his death. In the latter body he apparently never took part in debate, though he attended regularly, voted on many important questions, and served on several committees. He usually supported the administration and voted for the declaration of war in 1812, urging that "fire and sword" be carried into the Creek Indian country, where "British emissaries" were no doubt lurking, and that the Floridas be annexed. In 1815 he was appointed a member of the commission to survey the boundary of the Creek cession obtained by Jackson in 1814. He died in Alabama while on this service, and was buried at Fort Decatur on the Tallapoosa River. His remains were later removed to Knoxville, Tenn.

[Sevier Collection in Lib. of State of Tenn., Nashville, some of which already pub. in *East Tenn. Hist. Soc. Pubs.,* no. 1–5 (1929–33); "The Diary of John Sevier," *Tenn. Hist. Mag.,* Oct. 19–April 1920, and in S. G. Heiskell, *Andrew Jackson and Early Tenn. Hist.,* 2nd ed. (2 vols. 1920); C. S. Driver, *John Sevier* (1932); F. M. Turner, *Life of Gen. John Sevier* (1910); S. C. Williams, *Hist. of the Lost State of Franklin* (1924); Zella Armstrong, "The Sevier Family," *Notable Southern Families,* vol. IV (1926); A. P. Whitaker in *Miss. Valley Hist. Rev.,* Sept. 1925, Dec. 1926; A. V. Goodpasture, "Genesis of the Jackson-Sevier Feud," *Am. Hist. Mag.* (Nashville), Apr. 1900.]
A. P. W.

SEWALL, ARTHUR (Nov. 25, 1835–Sept. 5, 1900), shipbuilder, son of William Dunning and Rachel (Trufant) Sewall and brother of Frank Sewall [*q.v.*], was born at Bath, Me. He was descended from Henry Sewall, who had come from Coventry, England, in 1634 and settled in Newbury, Mass.; his great-grandfather, Dummer Sewall, had moved in 1760 from York, Me., to Georgetown (later Bath), which partly through Sewall influence was to become "the great American shipyard." His father dabbled in railroads and politics and built twenty-nine vessels between 1823 and 1854. After a common school education in Bath, Arthur was sent to Prince Edward Island to become familiar with the cutting of ship timber. He began his active shipbuilding career in 1854 as the American merchant marine reached its zenith. With his elder brother, Edward, he formed the firm of E. & A. Sewall and commenced work in the family yard on the Kennebec. The *Holyhead,* of some 1100 tons, launched in 1855, was the first of his eighty vessels. Upon Edward's death he took a son and a nephew as partners, and the firm in 1879 became A. Sewall & Company. Though English vessels, utilizing iron, steel, and steam, were driving the wooden American sailing vessels out of competition, the Sewalls specialized in the latter type, doing much to keep it alive in the period of decline. They generally retained ownership of the ships they built and at one time owned a fleet of more than twenty-five. Their shipwrights and captains were usually natives of the Kennebec valley. Sewall was given much of the credit for the excellent *esprit de corps* of both groups and for the absence of labor problems; it was said that there was not a single job in his shipyard that he could not perform ably with his own hands. During the Civil War he refused to have his ships take advantage of British registry, and his *Vigilant* was captured on her maiden voyage by the Confederate raider, *Sumter*. In the decade following the war, the Sewalls turned out a number of celebrated ships, including the *Undaunted, Eric the Red, El Capitan, Occidental, Oriental, Continental, Harvester, Reaper, Thrasher,* and *Granger*. Then came a depression without even the usual "ship a year," but in the early nineties they built their "Big Four," the *Rappahannock, Shenandoah, Susquehanna,* and *Roanoke*. Averaging more than 3000 tons, these were the largest and the last of the great American wooden full-rigged ships. The next step was iron. Sewall was interested in Gen. Thomas W. Hyde's Bath Iron Works, organized in 1889, which built the *Machias, Castine,* and *Katahdin*

for the new navy. After visiting England to study the latest methods he began to build steel sailing vessels, and in 1894 the steel *Dirigo* was launched. His last ship, launched a month after his death, was the *William P. Frye,* sunk Jan. 28, 1915, the first American vessel sunk by the Germans in the World War. Unlike Donald McKay [*q.v.*] and other clipper constructors, Sewall introduced relatively few innovations into naval architecture. His importance comes rather from his large-scale construction of sailing vessels far into the era of steam; during the latter half of the nineteenth century he built, owned, and operated more sailing vessels than anyone else in America.

He was drawn into other fields of business activity more because of his sound common sense and executive ability than because of his wealth. He was at various times president of the Eastern Railroad and of the Central Railroad, and a director of the Boston and Maine Railroad. From 1871 until his death he was president of the Bath National Bank. He was the most prominent of the Maine Democrats, those constant supporters of forlorn hopes in that Republican stronghold, but the only elective offices he ever received were as councilman and alderman in Bath. Since he was an ardent imperialist and a believer in the tariff as a weapon in international trade, his position as a Democrat might have seemed anomalous except for his opposition to the gold standard. He was a delegate to the national conventions in 1876, 1880, and 1888; in the next two campaigns he served on the executive committee of the Democratic national committee, and in 1896 he was nominated for vice-president on the fifth ballot and took an active part in the campaign. In 1859 he had married Emma Duncan Crooker, daughter of a Bath shipbuilder; of their three sons two survived him, one of them Harold Marsh Sewall [*q.v.*]. His portrait, showing a firm chin and straightforward expression indicates why he could be called "a gentleman who was without fear and without offense" and "the epitome of gallant gentility" (*Lewiston Evening Journal,* Nov. 15, 1924). In 1900 he was stricken with apoplexy at his summer home at Small Point, just below Bath, where he died.

[G. T. Little, ed., *Geneal. and Family Hist. of the State of Me.* (1909), vol. II, pp. 522–24; P. M. Reed, *Hist. of Bath and Environs* (1894); L. C. Hatch, ed., *Maine, A Hist.* (1919), vol. V, with portrait; *Ill. Hist. Souvenir of the City of Bath, Me.* (1899), pp. 311–12, with list of Sewall ships; F. C. Matthews, *Am. Merchant Ships,* 1 ser. (1930); H. V. Poor, *Manual of the Railroads of the U. S.,* esp. for 1885 and 1894; Henry Hall, "Ship-Building Industry in the U. S.," *Reports of Tenth Census* (1884), vol. VIII, p. 71, with list of Sewall ships; obituaries in *Evening Express* (Port-

land, Me.), *Bath Times*, Sept. 5, and *Daily Eastern Argus* (Portland, Me.), Sept. 6, 1900.]
R. G. A.

SEWALL, FRANK (Sept. 24, 1837–Dec. 7, 1915), Swedenborgian clergyman, was born in Bath, Me., the son of William Dunning and Rachel (Trufant) Sewall, and the brother of Arthur Sewall [*q.v.*]. After graduating from Bowdoin College in 1858, he spent two years in travel in Italy and study at Tübingen in Germany under the great Swedenborg scholar, Johann Friedrich Immanuel Tafel. In 1862 he took the degree of A.M. at Bowdoin. In 1869 he married Thedia Redelia Gilchrist, a sister of William Wallace Gilchrist [*q.v.*]; his wife, with their five daughters, survived him at the time of his death in Washington, D. C. Significant for his later development were his upbringing in a family connected with the New Church in Bath from its earliest days, his early appreciation of nature, music, and art, and his years abroad. Ordained on Aug. 23, 1863, into the ministry of the General Convention of the New Jerusalem in the United States of America (Swedenborgian), he held pastorates in Glendale, Ohio, 1863–70; Urbana, Ohio, 1870–86; Glasgow, Scotland, 1886–87; and Washington, D. C., 1889–1915. To these pastorates he brought not only a keen mind but also a warm human sympathy and insight that endeared him to many who could not appreciate his intellectual gifts. Active in the larger concerns of the Church, he served as president (later called general pastor) of the Ohio Association in 1871 and 1872, and as general pastor of the Maryland Association from 1893 to 1915.

The range of his interests and activities was unusual, but his chief contribution to the life of the New Church was to the development of its forms of worship. The subject had interested him from college days, and his earliest published books were *The Christian Hymnal* (1867) and *A Prayerbook and Hymnal for the Use of the New Church* (1867). He was the chairman and the guiding spirit of the two committees that produced the *Magnificat* (1910), a hymnal, and the *Book of Worship* (1912), authorized by the General Convention in 1912. To them he contributed not only his knowledge but many of his own compositions, both musical and literary. He was also devoted to the cause of New Church education and worked for it throughout his life, especially during his years as president of Urbana (Ohio) University, 1870–86. He looked forward to the day when human society would be so organized as to give expression to Swedenborg's doctrine of love as the ultimate reality of the universe, and he saw that to bring about

such a result and to live in such a world made demands on education which traditional forms were not prepared to meet. In 1896 he published *The Angel of the State; or the Kindergarten in the Education of the Citizen*. Another major interest was philosophy, particularly that of Swedenborg. Products of this interest were *The New Metaphysics* (1888), *Swedenborg and Modern Idealism* (1902), a translation of Swedenborg's *De Anima* under the title of *The Soul, or Rational Psychology* (1887), and the introduction and notes to Emanual F. Goerwitz's translation of Immanuel Kant's *Dreams of a Spirit-Seer* (London, 1900). He was the author of several volumes of sermons, including *The Pillow of Stones* (1876) and *The Hem of His Garment* (1876), and of *The Ethics of Service* (1888), *Reason in Belief* (1906), and *The Pulpit and Modern Thought* (1905). In the field of literature he published *Dante and Swedenborg, with Other Essays on the New Renaissance* (1893), a translation of the *Poems of Giosuè Carducci* (1892), and *The Trophies: Sonnets* (1893), translations from José Maria Heredia.

[Three chapters of a biography by Sewall's daughter, Alice A. S. James, appeared in the *New-Church Rev.*, Jan., July, Apr. 1921. See also G. T. Little, ed., *Geneal. and Family Hist. of the State of Me.* (1909), vol. II; *Who's Who in America*, 1914–15; *Jour. . . . of the Gen. Convention of the New Jerusalem in the U. S. A.*, 1916; *New-Church Messenger*, Jan. 5, 19, May 17, 1916; *New-Church Rev.*, Apr. 1916; *Evening Star* (Washington, D. C.), Dec. 7, 1915.]
F. R. C.

SEWALL, HAROLD MARSH (Jan. 3, 1860–Oct. 28, 1924), diplomat, descended from Henry Sewall who first came to New England in 1634, was born in Bath, Me., the son of Arthur [*q.v.*] and Emma Duncan (Crooker) Sewall and a member of a wealthy shipbuilding family. He graduated A.B. (1882) and LL.B. (1885) at Harvard and through his father's influence as a Democrat, was appointed vice-consul at Liverpool. In 1887, he was appointed consul general at Apia, Samoa. The position was a highly responsible one, for the rivalry of the German, British, and American consuls, frequently supported by cruisers, more than once threatened war. Important decisions had to be made on the spot, for the nearest cable station was at Auckland, New Zealand. On Aug. 24, 1887, shortly after Sewall's arrival, the aggressive German consul Becker, backed by four warships, made a *coup d'état* which nearly gave Germany control of the islands. Becker declared war on the native "king," Malietoa, and set up his rival, Tamatese, with a German as prime minister. Robert Louis Stevenson, who witnessed the events, declared that Sewall was for a while the only one to resist this measure—"standing forth in bold, consistent and sometimes rather captious opposition, stirring up his government at home with clear and forcible dispatches and on the spot grasping at every opportunity to thrust a stick into the German wheels" (Stevenson, *post*, p. 89). Sewall announced his support of Malietoa, steadily protested against Becker's actions, and even released a prisoner personally. His British colleagues, Wilson and then de Coëtlegen, were less active. President Cleveland and Secretary Bayard were less imperialistic than the young consul, however, and enjoined neutrality upon him. To present his views at Washington, Sewall returned on leave late in August 1888, but at a hearing before a Senate sub-committee in January 1889 offended Bayard, who requested his resignation. Sewall was thus absent from Samoa during the naval crisis ended by the hurricane of Mar. 15, 1889. This episode marks his shift to the Republicans, who attached him, as special disbursing agent, to the commission which participated in the Berlin agreement of June 14, 1889, by which the independence of Samoa was recognized. Sewall's firm opposition to Becker had helped to make this solution possible. Under congenial Republican auspices, in 1890, Sewall returned as consul general to Apia, remaining until 1892 and securing the site of the naval station at Pago Pago. With the return of the Republicans to power in 1897 he was appointed minister to Hawaii, and in that capacity received the transfer of the sovereignty of the islands from President Samuel B. Dole [*q.v.*] on Aug. 12, 1898. He remained in Hawaii as special agent of the United States until the establishment of regular territorial government in 1900.

During the remainder of his life he made his home at Bath, Me. One of the wealthiest men in the state, he was noted for his hospitality. On Sept. 14, 1893, he had married Camilla Loyall Ashe of San Francisco, and they had two sons and two daughters. He sat in the Maine House of Representatives in 1897–98 and 1903–07 and in the state Senate 1907–09, was a delegate to his party's national conventions in 1896 and 1916 and in 1900 was the first member of the Republican national committee from Hawaii. He was an unsuccessful candidate for Congress in 1914. He headed the state Committee of Public Safety in 1917 and was on the advisory committee of the Washington Arms Conference. He died in New York, to which place he had gone for a slight operation.

[*Papers Relating to the Foreign Relations of the U. S.*, 1887–92, 1897–98; *Sen. Ex. Doc. 31*, 50 Cong.,

2 Sess., pp. 162–63; R. L. Stevenson, *A Foot-note to History* (1892); G. H. Ryden, *The Foreign Policy of the U. S. in Relation to Samoa* (1933); *Class of 1882, Harvard Coll., Sixth Report* (1907); E. J. Carpenter, *America in Hawaii* (1899); *Who's Who in America*, 1924–25; G. T. Little, *Geneal. and Family Hist. of the State of Me.* (1909), II, 524; *Lewiston Evening Journal*, Oct. 29, 1924; *N. Y. Times*, Oct. 29, 1924.]
R. G. A.

SEWALL, JONATHAN (Aug. 17, 1728– Sept. 26, 1796), lawyer, writer, Loyalist, was the son of Jonathan and Mary (Payne) Sewall, of Boston. The first of his ancestors to come to America was his great-grandfather, Henry Sewall, who emigrated in 1634 and the following year settled in Newbury, Mass., but later returned to England. By 1681 the family was permanently established in Salem, where Jonathan's grandfather, Stephen, died in 1725. Left destitute at an early age by the death of his father, the boy was educated through the charity of friends who had been impressed by his unusual promise. After his graduation from Harvard in 1748, he maintained for a number of years a small Latin school in Salem. This he abandoned in 1756 to read law with Judge Chambers Russell of Lincoln, Mass., and later, with a minimum of legal training, he set up an office in Charlestown. In the pursuit of his profession he frequently came into contact with John Adams and then began the intimacy between the two men which caused Adams to refer to him as the best friend he had in the world (*Works*, II, 302–03). His associates during this period were ardent patriots, with whose sentiments he seems for a time to have been in complete accord. On Jan. 21, 1764 (*Boston Marriages, 1752–1809*, 1903, p. 422), he married Esther Quincy.

On the death in 1760 of his uncle, Stephen Sewall, chief justice of the superior court, the young lawyer undertook the administration of the estate. Finding his uncle's affairs badly involved, he appealed to the General Court for a grant of money with which to satisfy the creditors. The refusal of the Court to grant this petition apparently alienated him from the cause of the patriots. According to Adams, he was especially indignant with James Otis, who had opposed the grant. Friends of the Crown were quick to take advantage of his resentment. By appointing him to a succession of offices they bound him to the royal cause. He was first made solicitor general, then, in 1767, attorney general, and in 1768 judge of the vice-admiralty court of Halifax. On Governor Hutchinson's departure from Massachusetts, Sewall was one of the signers of the barristers' address to him. Close upon this open display of his allegiance to the royal government came a conversation between Sewall and Adams which marked the irreparable rift between the friends. On a Portland hill they discussed the future of America and their own fortunes. Sewall, convinced of the speedy defeat of the colonists, urged Adams to abandon his intention of attending the Philadelphia congress. In reply to his arguments Adams used the memorable words: to "swim or sink, live or die, survive or perish with my country [is] my unalterable determination" (*Works*, IV, 8).

In September 1774 Sewall left his Cambridge home for Boston, from which place he sailed for England early in 1775. His name was included in the act of banishment of 1778 and his property was declared forfeited the next year. For a time he remained in London, one of the group of Loyalists who dined together weekly while they waited for word that the Revolution was crushed and that they might return from their exile. While in London he changed the spelling of his name to Sewell, the form in which he found it recorded at the Herald's office (letter, Mar. 11, 1782, in Massachusetts Historical Society). In 1777 he removed to Bristol where, save for brief excursions, he resided until 1788. In that year he embarked for Halifax, with the hope, as he told John Adams in a brief reunion with him in London, of making provision for his children. This hope he was able to fulfil. His elder son, Jonathan, became chief justice of Lower Canada; the younger, Stephen, became solicitor general. Sewall himself died in St. John, New Brunswick, never having revisited his native land.

Of Sewall's abilities John Adams thought highly: "He possessed a lively wit," Adams wrote, "a pleasing humor, a brilliant imagination, great subtlety of reasoning, and an insinuating eloquence" (*Works*, II, 78). Little record of his legal practice or of the conduct of his offices is available, but in the famous case of *James* vs. *Lechmere,* he gained a decision in favor of the freedom of a slave two years before Lord Mansfield's famous decision in the Somerset case (*Collections of the Massachusetts Historical Society,* 4 ser. IV, 1858, pp. 334–35). Under the names Philanthropos and Long J., he was a frequent and able contributor to the press, though he was not the author of the letters by Massachusettensis, as Adams supposed when he answered those letters in 1774 and 1775. To him was attributed the writing of Gage's proclamations (B. J. Lossing's notes in John Trumbull, *M'Fingal*, edition of 1860, at p. 202). Mercy Otis Warren satirized him in her political drama *The Group* (1775) and John Trumbull

paid his respects to him in *M'Fingal* (1775) with these words:

> "Did not our grave Judge Sewall hit
>   The Summit of news-paper wit?
> Fill'd ev'ry leaf of ev'ry paper
>   Of Mills and Hicks and mother Draper;
> Drew proclamations, works of toil,
>   In true sublime of scarecrow style;
> Wrote farces too, gainst Sons of Freedom
>   All for your good and none would read 'em."

[The Mass. Hist. Soc. possesses a manuscript volume of Sewall's letters, parts of which were published in its *Proceedings,* 2 ser. X (1896); for sources, see *The Works of John Adams* (1850–56), especially vols. II, IV; Lorenzo Sabine, *Biog. Sketches of Loyalists of the Am. Revolution* (1864), vol. II; *Jour. and Letters of the Late Samuel Curwen* (1842), ed. by G. A. Ward; J. H. Stark, *The Loyalists of Mass.* (1910); E. A. Jones, *The Loyalists of Mass.* (1930); E. E. Salisbury, *Family Memorials,* vol. I (1885).]   E. D.

SEWALL, JONATHAN MITCHELL (1748–Mar. 29, 1808), lawyer and occasional poet, a grand-nephew of Samuel Sewall [*q.v.*], the diarist, was born in Salem, Mass., where he was baptized on Mar. 27, but spent all his mature life in Portsmouth, N. H. His father, Mitchell Sewall, a graduate of Harvard in 1718 and clerk of the inferior court at Salem, died in October following Jonathan Mitchell's birth. Shortly thereafter the boy was adopted by his bachelor uncle, Stephen Sewall, chief justice of Massachusetts from 1752 until his death in 1760. His mother, Elizabeth (Prince) Sewall, died in 1758. Thus doubly orphaned by the deaths of his parents and guardian, Jonathan Mitchell was left at the age of twelve to make his own way. He is said to have entered Harvard College, but he did not graduate and no trace of him can now be found in the college archives. For a short time he was employed as a clerk in a store; then he studied law in the office of Judge John Pickering, *c.* 1738–1805 [*q.v.*], of Portsmouth and was duly admitted to the bar. In 1773 he was made register of probate for Grafton County, N. H., presumably to induce him to settle in a thinly populated region which at that time was unprovided with lawyers, but there is no indication that he ever assumed the office. Though his career was interrupted by periods of illness, he rose to be a respected lawyer of Portsmouth with a local reputation for patriotic oratory and occasional poetry. Without ever becoming a candidate for office he took part in politics as a vehement Federalist. After gracing countless public occasions by the display of his talents, he died a bachelor, eminently public-spirited, lettered, and bibulous.

As a poet he first attracted attention by a patriotic ballad called "War and Washington," written at the outbreak of the Revolution and sung by the army in all parts of the country. Thereafter he lost no occasion to act as volunteer laureate of Washington's virtues. When the President visited Portsmouth in 1789, Sewall composed three adulatory odes to be sung at the ceremony of welcome. His *Versification of President Washington's Excellent Farewell-Address* appeared in 1798, and at the commemorative service held in Portsmouth after Washington's death Sewall was chosen to pronounce a eulogy, published in 1800 as *Eulogy on the Late General Washington.* He had previously delivered the first Fourth of July oration at Portsmouth, 1788, and his speeches and odes were in frequent demand at Federalist banquets. His *Miscellaneous Poems,* published at Portsmouth in 1801, consist of patriotic effusions, verse paraphrases of Ossian, epilogues, occasional lyrics, and a few epigrams. They are ephemeral productions. A single couplet from his "Epilogue to Cato" gained wide currency by its use with a slight change as the motto of the *New World* of Park Benjamin, 1809–1864 [*q.v.*], but the most lasting of his compositions are the epitaphs still decipherable on Portsmouth gravestones.

[*Vital Records of Salem, Mass., . . . to 1849,* vols. II (1918), VI (1925); Hamilton Child, *Gazetteer of Grafton County, N. H.* (1886), p. 39; C. W. Brewster, *Rambles about Portsmouth,* vols. I (1859), II (1869); Nathaniel Adams, *Annals of Portsmouth* (1825), p. 318; A. H. Locke, *Portsmouth and Newcastle, N. H., Cemetery Inscriptions* (1907); E. A. and G. L. Duyckinck, *Cyc. of Am. Lit.* (2 vols., 1855); A. M. Payson and Albert Laighton, *The Poets of Portsmouth* (1865), containing reprints of Sewall's poetry; Samuel Kettell, *Specimens of Am. Poetry* (1829), vol. I, pp. 198–200; "Mortuary" from the *Lit. Mirror* (Portsmouth), in the *Port Folio,* June 25, 1808, pp. 415–16.]

G. F. W.

SEWALL, JOSEPH ADDISON (Apr. 20, 1830–Jan. 17, 1917), first president of the University of Colorado, was born in Scarboro, Me., the son of Stephen and Mary Milliken Sewall. His father was a country doctor with a large practice and a small store of worldly goods. The boy was educated in the public schools of Portland and Biddeford, and studied medicine in Boston. He began the practice of medicine in Bangor, Me., but, unable to endure the rigors of the New England climate, in 1854 he moved to Illinois. There he continued his practice and also taught school. The academic year 1859–60 he spent at the Lawrence Scientific School of Harvard University. From 1860 to 1877 he was professor of natural science in the Illinois State Normal University at Normal.

In 1877, on the recommendation of Gov. John L. Routt, he was appointed the first president of the infant University of Colorado. When admitted to the Union in 1876, Colorado was still a frontier state with a population of barely 135,-

000; only one high school class had been graduated within its borders. The prospective university possessed but one building, located on a treeless, boulder-strewn hillside overlooking the town of Boulder. Its support was to come from a mill levy which, on the basis of the property valuation in the new state, was expected to bring in $9,000 a year. The institution was opened in September 1877, with two teachers, including the president, two departments (normal and preparatory), and forty-four students; the following year a college department was added. From such humble beginnings Sewall guided the course of the university for the next decade, developing the physical resources, assembling a faculty, and determining the spirit and ideals of the establishment. While fully appreciating the value of the standard classical curriculum of the time, the new president was anxious to give the youth of his frontier state a practical education, hence he stressed also science and the study of history and government as a basis for citizenship. In the midst of great discouragement the foundations were well laid. Although the growth of the University was substantial in the early years, it was not as rapid as some of its supporters desired; the president was blamed, and in 1887 he resigned to become professor of chemistry at the University of Denver, where he also served as dean of the school of pharmacy.

After he retired from teaching in 1899 he acted as chemist for the city of Denver. In addition to proficiency in chemistry, he was a botanist and the author of *A Condensed Botany* (copr. 1872). He was tall and dignified in manner, and a forceful and entertaining public speaker. In his work as teacher and administrator he was assisted by his wife, Ann Edwards (Foss), to whom he was married in Tonica, Ill., on Feb. 11, 1858, and who with four of their six children survived him. In the closing words of his inaugural address, 1877, he declared: "When the University of Colorado shall have an honorable place and name among the institutions of learning of the land, and I shall be sleeping in the shadow of these mountains, or elsewhere, I would ask no prouder eulogy than that some good and true friend should say of me, 'He was in at the birth, he directed its infant steps, and now behold the full grown man.'" In 1914 the University of Colorado recognized his pioneer service in its behalf by conferring on him the degree of doctor of laws.

[*Boulder County News,* for 1877; *Denver Times,* Jan. 18, 1917; *Rocky Mountain News,* Jan. 19, 1917; information from a daughter, Miss Jane Sewall, Boston, Mass., and from Miss Mary Rippon, Boulder, Col.; J. R. Brackett, "Little Journeys in the Year One," in

The Coloradoan, vol. IV (1902), pub. by the class of 1903, and "The Univ. of Colorado; Its Origin and Development," *Civic Quart.,* Jan. 1912.]   C. B. G—z.

SEWALL, MAY ELIZA WRIGHT (May 27, 1844–July 22, 1920), feminist, was born in Milwaukee, Wis., the daughter of Philander Montague and Mary Weeks (Brackett) Wright. A precocious child, she was reading Milton at the age of seven. After studying in the public schools and with her father she taught in Waukesha, Wis., to earn money for a college education. Graduated from Northwestern University in 1866, she taught in Corinth, Miss., Plainville, Mich., and Frankfort, Ind. In Frankfort she married Edwin Thompson, the principal of the school, and with him removed to Indianapolis, where both of them taught in the high school until Mr. Thompson's death, about 1876. On Oct. 30, 1880, she married Theodore Lovett Sewall, a graduate of Harvard who had established a classical school for boys in Indianapolis. Not long after, she established with him the Girls' Classical School; after his death, she was principal for many years.

A feminist from the beginning of her life, she began as soon as she went to Indianapolis to gather groups together to work for public purposes. She was a charter member of many Indianapolis clubs and a founder of the Indiana Association for Promoting Woman's Suffrage. Following the visit of Pundita Ramabai to America, she formed the Ramabai Circle to assist in freeing the women of India from their ancient bondage. One of the first members of the Association of Collegiate Alumnae when it was organized in 1882, she helped in 1883 to organize the Western Association of Collegiate Alumnae, which later joined with the older association. From the outset of her association with these university women she had a vision of a world federation which in 1919 came to completion. From 1883 to 1912 she assisted in suffrage campaigns from Nebraska to Wisconsin and was for many years chairman of the executive committee of the National Suffrage Association. In 1888 she was chairman of the committee which arranged and carried through the first meeting of the National Council of Women in Washington, where she presented a plan for forming an International Council as well; from 1888 to 1899 she held various offices in the National Council. In 1891–92 she traveled abroad to awaken an interest in the World's Congress of Representative Women, at which she presided, held in Chicago in 1893 as a part of the program for the Columbian Exposition. From that time she was a prominent figure in the In-

ternational Council of Women. She had been a delegate to its meetings in 1889 and in 1899 she became its president, succeeding Lady Aberdeen. She assisted in the formation of fifty women's clubs of various sorts; in 1889, when the Federation of Women's Clubs was formed, she rightly became its first president. In 1894 she edited *The World's Congress of Representative Women,* and in 1915 she published *Women, World War, and Permanent Peace.* Soon after her husband's death in 1895 she became profoundly interested in psychical research. In 1920 she published *Neither Dead nor Sleeping,* an account of her personal experiences.

[H. I. Brackett, *Brackett Geneal.* (1907); *Who's Who in America,* 1916–17; *The Hist. of Woman Suffrage* (6 vols., 1881–1922); Marion Talbot and Lois K. M. Rosenberry, *Hist. of the Am. Assoc. of Univ. Women* (1931); *Proc. Gen. Federation of Women's Clubs, Proc. Nat. Council of Women, Proc. Internat. Council of Women,* 1889–1915, *passim; Jour. Assoc. of Collegiate Alumnae,* July, Aug., 1920; obituaries in *Indianapolis News,* July 23, 1920, and *N. Y. Times,* July 24, 1920.]   L. K. M. R.

SEWALL, SAMUEL (Mar. 28, 1652–Jan. 1, 1730), merchant, colonial magistrate, diarist, was the grandson of Henry Sewall, a linen draper of Coventry, England, who acquired a considerable fortune and was several times mayor. In 1634 Samuel's father, Henry, emigrated to New England, where he married Jane, daughter of Stephen and Alice (Archer) Dummer. They soon returned to England, where Samuel, the second of eight children, was born at Bishopstoke. Some months afterward the family moved to Baddesley. There Samuel received his first schooling, going later to the grammar school at Rumsey.

When he was nine years old the family returned to New England and settled in Boston. After further preparation, Samuel entered Harvard College, from which he graduated in 1671. At this time he seems to have been undecided whether he would enter the ministry or embark on a mercantile career. On Nov. 5, 1673, he was chosen resident fellow, or tutor, at Harvard, and was installed on Nov. 26. On Feb. 28, 1675/6 he married the first of his three wives, Hannah, daughter of John Hull [*q.v.*], by whom he had fourteen children.

Made a freeman Apr. 29, 1679 ("Records of the Suffolk County Court," *Publications of the Colonial Society of Massachusetts,* vol. XXX, 1933, p. 1015), he began a long political career. From Oct. 12, 1681, to Sept. 12, 1684, he managed the colony's printing press. He was present at the General Court on Nov. 7, 1683, as deputy from Westfield, Hampden County, and from 1684 to 1686 he was a member of the Council. The twelve months from November 1688 were devoted to a trip to England, during which he spent some time in London and traveled through the provinces, visiting both Cambridge and Oxford. The trip was primarily on private business connected with his mercantile enterprises, but he appeared before the King and Council and gave some assistance to Increase Mather [*q.v.*] in his efforts to recover the Massachusetts charter. Upon his return to Massachusetts, he resumed his position on the Council as one of the officers elected in 1686, and in 1691 he was named a councilor in the new charter which the colony was forced to receive. This post he continued to hold until he declined reelection in 1725.

On June 13, 1692, the governor, Sir William Phips [*q.v.*], appointed him one of the special commissioners of oyer and terminer to try the cases of witchcraft at Salem. The court met during July and August and sentenced nineteen persons to death, the executions taking place Sept. 22, 1692. Sewall was the only one of the judges who ever publicly admitted that he had been in error in this matter. The part he played long preyed on his mind, and for some reason he considered himself as more guilty than any of the other judges. The legislature appointed Jan. 14, 1697, to be a fast day for whatever might have been done amiss in the tragedy, and on that day Sewall stood up in the Old South Church, Boston, while the clergyman, the Rev. Samuel Willard, read a confession of error and guilt which Sewall wished to make for himself thus publicly. On Dec. 6, 1692, he had been appointed a justice of the superior court. He was made a commissioner of the Society for the Propagation of the Gospel in New England in 1699, and shortly afterward became its local secretary and treasurer. He always showed much interest in the Indians and also in the negro slaves, publishing in 1700 a tract entitled *The Selling of Joseph*, one of the earliest appeals in the antislavery cause. He believed that the Indians should be set apart on permanent reservations and taught the English language and habits.

Sewall continued to hold various offices until almost the close of his life. In 1701 he was made captain of the Ancient and Honorable Artillery Company. He became judge of probate for Suffolk County in 1715, and chief justice of the superior court of judicature in 1718, which office he held for ten years. He was typical of the provincial judge of his time, without preliminary training in the law and with an unsystematic reading acquaintance with the legal classics ("Diary," *post*, I, 419). Yet he was a competent jurist and of more than average liberality, as evidenced by his modification of the rigorous miscegenation act of 1705 (*Ibid.*, II, 143), his opposition to high-handed interpretations of the treason laws (*Ibid.*, p. 149), and his stand against capital punishment for counterfeiting (*Ibid.*, III, 277).

In the field of authorship he is credited with *Proposals Touching the Accomplishment of Prophesies Humbly Offered* (1713); *A Memorial Relating to the Kennebeck Indians* (1721); and *Phaenomena Quaedam Apocalyptica ad Aspectum Novi Orbis Configurata, or, Some Few Lines Towards a Description of the New Heaven as It Makes to Those Who Stand upon the New Earth* (1697). With Edward Rawson, he wrote *The Revolution in New England Justified* (1691). He also composed many verses which circulated in manuscript form. Chiefly, however, he is remembered for his diary, which was published in three volumes by the Massachusetts Historical Society a century and a half after his death. It covers the period from 1674 to 1729, with a gap of about eight years, 1677–85. There are other American diaries of higher importance from a political point of view, but none in which the journalist's entire world is so vividly reproduced. In it is given an incomparable picture of the mind and life of a Puritan of the transition period. Sewall, as unwittingly portrayed by himself, emerges as mercenary, mercantile, of average mentality, conventional, Puritanically introspective, morbidly fond of dwelling on death, yet playful, affectionate, honorable, strong, and fearless. The rich merchant who could plead for slaves and publicly abase himself for wrongdoing on the bench in the Boston of 1690–1700 was no ordinary man.

Sewall's first wife died Oct. 19, 1717, and on Oct. 29, 1719, he married Abigail, daughter of Jacob Melyen and widow of James Woodmansey and William Tilley. She died on May 26, 1720. Subsequently he courted Madam Katherine Winthrop, with gifts of sermons, gingerbread, and sugar almonds at three shillings a pound (he gave her half a pound); but the lady insisted on his keeping a coach and wearing a wig, which, with a disagreement over a marriage settlement, cooled her suitor's ardor ("Diary," III, 262–75). On Mar. 29, 1722, however, he married Mary Gibbs, daughter of Henry Shrimpton. By his last two wives he had no children. At his death he was buried in the Granary Burying Ground, Boston.

[The "Diary of Samuel Sewall," in 3 vols., was pub. as *Mass. Hist. Soc. Colls.*, 5 ser. V–VII (1878–82); an abridged edition, *Samuel Sewall's Diary*, ed. by Mark Van Doren, was pub. in 1927; Sewall's letter-book, containing mercantile matters chiefly, is printed in *Mass. Hist. Soc. Colls.*, 6 ser., I. II (1886–88) ; "Letters of Samuel Lee and Samuel Sewall Relating to New England and the Indians," ed. by G. L. Kittredge, appears in *Colonial Soc. of Mass. Pubs.*, vol. XIV (1913). The Judge's son, Joseph Sewall, preached and published a funeral sermon, *The Orphan's Best Legacy* (1730). Other sources include J. L. Sibley, *Biog. Sketches of Grads. of Harvard Univ.*, vol. II (1881) ; G. E. Ellis, *An Address on the Life and Character of Chief-Justice Samuel Sewell* (1885) ; Emory Washburn, *Sketches of the Judicial Hist. of Mass. from 1630 to . . . 1775* (1840) ; N. B. Shurtleff, *Records of the Governor and Company of the Mass. Bay* (1854), vol. V ; John Noble, *Records of the Court of Assistants of the Colony of the Mass. Bay*, vol. I (1901) ; minutes and files of the superior court of judicature, Suffolk County Court House, Boston ; R. C. Winthrop, *A Difference of Opinion Concerning the Reasons Why Katherine Winthrop Refused to Marry Chief Justice Sewall* (1885) ; V. L. Parrington, *Main Currents in Am. Thought*, vol. I (1927).]   J.T.A.

SEWALL, STEPHEN (Apr. 4, 1734–July 23, 1804), Hebraist and classicist, was born in York, Me., the youngest of ten children of Nicholas and Mehitable (Storer) Sewall, and a descendant of Henry Sewall of Newbury, Mass., who arrived at Boston in 1634. The extreme poverty of his father, a tanner, forced him to leave school and to learn the carpenter's trade at which he worked until he acquired the means to prepare himself for Harvard. At college he supported himself by teaching grammar school in Cambridge. Upon his graduation in 1761, he succeeded Judah Monis [*q.v.*] as the instructor in Hebrew at Harvard. During 1762–63 he was also librarian of the college library. On Oct. 2, 1764, he was made the first incumbent of the newly established Hancock professorship of Hebrew and other Oriental languages, and on June 19, 1765, he was publicly installed in this new office, which he held for twenty years. Like other Harvard teachers at that time, he received occasional grants from the General Court of Massachusetts to supplement his insufficient salary.

Trained both in Hebrew and in the classics, he retained his interest in both throughout his active life. Early in his academic career, on Sept. 12, 1763, he submitted to the corporation of Harvard College a plan for the promotion of classical learning in which the most interesting feature is a recommendation to relieve students from compulsory composition of verse and to encourage this sort of exercise only among those who have "a genius and fondness" for it. He himself wrote four odes in Latin, two in Greek, and one in English (numbers 3, 5, 12, 14, 15, 16, 23 in *Pietas et Gratulatio Collegii Cantabrigiensis apud Novanglos*, 1761). His interests included politics and science as well. An early supporter of the Revolution, he represented Cambridge in the General Court as a

Whig in 1777. He was one of the sixty-two original members of the American Academy of Arts and Sciences, and his "Magnetical Observations, Made at Cambridge" appeared in the first volume of *Memoirs of the American Academy of Arts and Sciences* (1785). He is said to have been married twice. On Aug. 9, 1763, he married Rebecca, daughter of Edward Wigglesworth, the first Hollis Professor of Divinity at Harvard; she died in December 1783. Their only child had died in infancy. In September 1785, after having been for nearly three years incapable of performing his duties on account of physical and mental debility, from which there seemed to be no likelihood of his recovery, he was removed from his professorship by the concurring vote of the two governing boards of the college, but, "in consideration of his long and faithful services," he was allowed by them thirty pounds. After about nineteen years of retired life and gradual decay, he died in Cambridge. His published writings include *An Hebrew Grammar Collected Chiefly from Those of Mr. Israel Lyons and the Rev. Richard Grey* (1763), *Nocte Cogitata auctore, anglice scripta, Young, D.D., quae lingua Latii donavit America* (1786), *Carmina Sacra, quae latine graeceque condidit America* (1789), *The Scripture Account of the Schechinah* (1794), and *The Scripture History Relating to the Overthrow of Sodom and Gomorrah* (1796). Lectures on Hebrew and Oriental literature, a lexicon of the Chaldee language in the Old Testament, a Greek and English lexicon, and a discussion of the quantity of Greek vowels exist in manuscript in the library of Harvard College. According to T. M. Harris (*post*), he was considered by his contemporaries the "finest classical scholar and the most learned in Hebrew and oriental languages" that Harvard had produced.

[T. M. Harris, memoir written in 1728, MS. in Harvard Coll. Lib. ; Benjamin Peirce, *A Hist. of Harvard Univ.* (1833) ; Josiah Quincy, *The Hist. of Harvard Univ.* (1840), vol. II ; S. A. Eliot, *A Sketch of the Hist. of Harvard Coll.* (1848), pp. 155–57, 173 ; E. E. Salisbury, *Family-Memorials* (1885) ; *Essex Inst., Hist. Colls.*, vol. XXV (1888) ; A. C. Potter and C. K. Bolton, *The Librarians of Harvard Coll.* (1897) ; S. A. Allibone, *A Crit. Dict. of Eng. Lit.*, vol. II (1870).]
                                                    H.A.W.

SEWARD, FREDERICK WILLIAM (July 8, 1830–Apr. 25, 1915), journalist and diplomat, was born at Auburn, N. Y., the son of William Henry [*q.v.*] and Francis (Miller) Seward. In 1849 he graduated from Union College, and then became secretary to his father who had just been elected to the United States Senate. After admisson to the bar, through the influence of his father he became, in 1851, a member of the staff of the Albany *Evening Journal,* conducted by Thurlow Weed [*q.v.*], and served on this paper continuously, most of the time as associate editor, for the next ten years.

With his father's entry into the State Department, Frederick became assistant secretary of state. He had special charge of the consular service, but played a part in the preparation of many diplomatic dispatches. He was present at the signing of the Emancipation Proclamation. In the spring of 1865, when the Secretary was incapacitated by a carriage accident, Frederick became acting secretary of state. In this connection he sent out the notices for the last of Lincoln's cabinet meetings (Apr. 14, 1865), attended the meeting itself, and left an interesting account of what occurred on that day (*Reminiscences,* pp. 254–57). On the same night on which the President was assassinated, one of the conspirators forced his way into William Seward's house. Frederick met him in the hall, and there a tussle ensued in which the younger Seward was seriously hurt, without, however, being able to prevent the would-be murderer reaching his father's bedside and inflicting painful wounds upon him. In 1866 Frederick was sent with Vice-Admiral David D. Porter [*q.v.*] on a diplomatic mission which had in view the leasing or purchasing of the Bay of Samana, in the island of Santo Domingo. The negotiations broke down, temporarily, but some months later a treaty was negotiated in Washington, which, however, was never ratified by the Senate.

With the change of administration in 1869 the two Sewards retired to private life, and Frederick accompanied his father to Mexico. In 1874, two years after his father's death, he was elected to the New York Assembly, and in the subsequent session he introduced two constitutional amendments, providing for a superintendent of public works and a superintendent of prisons; a bill for the construction of an elevated railway (the first of its kind); and a measure for the reduction of canal tolls. He was nominated for secretary of state of New York in the fall, but was defeated in the election. With the advent of the Hayes administration, Seward again went to Washington as assistant secretary of state (Mar. 21, 1877–Oct. 31, 1879). In this capacity he laid down the policy pursued by the administration with regard to the recognition of Porfirio Diaz in Mexico, negotiated for the lease of the harbor of Pago-Pago in Samoa, and prepared the presidential proclamation which resulted in the sending of troops to Pittsburgh in connection with the riots of 1877. After retiring from office he took little part in public

life. In 1877 he published *Autobiography of William H. Seward from 1801 to 1834, with a Memoir of His Life and Selections from His Letters, from 1831 to 1846,* reprinted in 1891 as *William H. Seward: An Autobiography,* which he supplemented by *Seward at Washington* (2 vols., 1891), and "Seward's West Indian Cruise" (*Godey's Magazine,* April–November 1894). His *Reminiscences of a War-Time Statesman and Diplomat* (1916) was published after his death. On Nov. 9, 1854, he married Anna M. Wharton of Albany.

[In addition to Seward's own writings, see *Encyc. of Contemporary Biog. of N. Y.* (4 vols., 1878–85); *Outlook,* May 5, 1915; *Who's Who in America,* 1914–15; *Who's Who in New York City and State,* 1907; *N. Y. Times,* Apr. 26, 1915.]   D. P.

SEWARD, GEORGE FREDERICK (Nov. 8, 1840–Nov. 28, 1910), diplomat, was the son of George W. and Tempe (Leddell) Seward of Florida, N. Y. He was educated at Seward Academy, Florida, and at Union College, which he entered in 1857 but from which he withdrew before graduating. On Oct. 24, 1861, his uncle, William H. Seward [*q.v.*], being then secretary of state, he was appointed United States consul at Shanghai, China, an important post, and on Sept. 2, 1863, he became consul general there. During his service at Shanghai he was sent to investigate conditions at the consulate at Bangkok (1868), and on June 27, 1868, was commissioned special diplomatic agent to Korea and empowered to negotiate a commercial and claims convention (*Senate Document 40,* 54 Cong., 2 Sess., p. 8). Feeling, however, that circumstances were not favorable, he never undertook the mission. He was married, Aug. 4, 1870, to Kate Sherman of Marysville, Cal.

After nearly fifteen years of the consular service, he was appointed on Jan. 7, 1876, minister to China to succeed Benjamin P. Avery [*q.v.*]. His services in these positions seem to have met with considerable approval, for he received praise from "Chinese" Gordon and the former American minister, Anson Burlingame, as well as from representatives of the British, French, and Danish governments. Denmark in return for his friendly services in obtaining security for a Danish telegraph system from the Chinese government bestowed on him the Order of the Knights of Danebrog, and France honored him with the Order of the Commander of the Dragon of Annam. In 1866 and 1869 he was president of the North China branch of the Royal Asiatic Society. As minister he supported the American vice consul at Shanghai, O. B. Bradford, who, with considerable British capital, succeeded in building China's pioneer steam railroad at Woosung. In spite of Seward's efforts, the Chinese bought the line soon after its opening in 1876 and destroyed it. Aside from his interest in modernizing China, he worked in harmony with the Chinese government, showing sympathy for its position during the Lew Chew dispute with Japan and urging his own government not to press the Chinese with regard to the question of immigration. California was in arms against the Oriental invaders and Seward was instructed in April 1879 to work towards a new immigration treaty with China. On Mar. 3, 1879, however, a committee of the House of Representatives had recommended that Seward be impeached of "high crimes and misdemeanors while in office." The alleged offenses included irregularities in his accounts as consul general, arbitrary administration, and fraudulent dealings with the Chinese in the Woosung railroad matter. Although steps toward impeachment were taken by the hostile Democratic House in both the Forty-fifth and Forty-sixth congresses (*Congressional Record,* Mar. 3, and June 4, 1879), the prosecution was uncertain of its position and the impeachment was never tried. Nevertheless Seward's usefulness to the State Department was ended and his resignation was requested Dec. 27, 1879. The immigration treaty of 1880 with China toward which he had worked was negotiated by a commission of which his successor, James B. Angell [*q.v.*], was a member.

Seward left Peking on Aug. 16, 1880, and the next year published his best-known volume, *Chinese Immigration in Its Social and Economical Aspects.* He was also the author of *The United States Consulates in China* (1867); *The Treaty With Spain* (1898); *The Russian-Japanese War* (1904); *Insurance is Commerce* (1910); and a series of reports on taxation which he made as chairman of a committee of the Chamber of Commerce of the State of New York. He was connected with numerous business ventures, and in 1887 became vice-president, and, in 1893, president, of the Fidelity and Casualty Company, which office he held at the time of his death. His wife and four children survived him.

[*N. Y. Herald,* Nov. 29, 1910; *Who's Who in America,* 1910–11; Tyler Dennett, *Americans in Eastern Asia* (1922); *Papers Relating to the Foreign Relations of the U. S.,* 1868–1881; *Congressional Record*; *House Report, No. 134* and *No. 141,* 45 Cong., 3 Sess. and manuscript material in the Department of State.]

E. W. S.

SEWARD, THEODORE FRELINGHUYSEN (Jan. 25, 1835–Aug. 30, 1902), musician, humanitarian, author, was born in Florida, N. Y., the son of Israel and Mary (Johnson)

Seward. He was a great-grandson of Col. John Seward of the American Revolution. He spent his early boyhood in Florida, N. Y., and received his first education at Seward Institute, founded by his great-uncle, Samuel S. Seward, the father of William Henry Seward [*q.v.*]. Later he went to Boston, where he studied music with Lowell Mason, George Frederick Root, and Thomas Hastings, 1784–1872 [*qq.v.*]. This association and training started him on his career as hymnologist and teacher. He was organist and teacher at New London, Conn., from 1857 to 1859, and in this city was married to Mary Holden Coggeshall on June 12, 1860. He was in Rochester, N. Y., until 1862, when he went to New York City and established headquarters for his editorial and literary work. He taught for a time at Teachers College (later merged with Columbia University), was editor of the *Musical Pioneer* from 1864, of the *Musical Gazette* from 1867, and of the *Tonic Sol-Fa Advocate* from 1881 to 1886 when it was superseded by the *Musical Reform* of which he was editor until 1888. He moved to Orange, N. J., in 1868 and later to his permanent residence in East Orange. From 1870 he was music director of the public schools of East Orange and organist at the North Orange Baptist Church and the Brick Presbyterian Church of East Orange. About 1869 he became interested in the singing of negroes, and was musical director of the second European tour of the Fisk University Jubilee Singers, editing and arranging a collection of *Jubilee Songs* (1872). In helping to preserve the negro spirituals he made his most distinctive contribution.

During his European trip Seward was much impressed with the English Tonic Sol-Fa system, and he became its principal advocate in the United States. He published two treaties on the subject— *The Tonic Sol-Fa Music Reader* (1880), and *A Revolution in Music Teaching* (1888). He edited a number of song and hymn collections, among them *The Temple Choir* (1867), *The Coronation* (1872), and *The Vineyard of Song* (1874). With Lowell Mason he was the author of *The Pestalozzian Music Teacher* (1871). His association with sacred music broadened into a larger concern with religious matters, and the later years of his life were occupied largely with religious writings and the organization of religious societies. In 1891 he instituted the Brotherhood of Christian Unity, in 1897 the Don't Worry Club, and in 1901 the Golden Rule Brotherhood. His published writings in this field include *The School of Life* (1894), *Heaven Every Day* (1896),

Don't Worry (1897), and *How to Get Acquainted with God* (1902). He died at the home of his
daughter in East Orange, N. J.

[Material for this article has been obtained largely
from members of the Seward family, notably from Dr.
F. W. Seward, of Goshen, N. Y.; see also *Grove's Dict.
of Music and Musicians, Am. Supp.* (1930); *Who's
Who in America,* 1901–02; and *N. Y. Times,* Sept. 1,
1902.]   J. T. H.

SEWARD, WILLIAM HENRY (May 16,
1801–Oct. 10, 1872), statesman, was born in
Florida, Orange County, N. Y., the son of Dr.
Samuel S. and Mary (Jennings) Seward. After
preparatory studies in Florida and the neighboring village of Goshen, he was sent at the age of
fifteen to Union College. Graduating in 1820,
he began to read law and was admitted to the
bar in 1822, establishing himself the next year
in Auburn, N. Y., which was to be his home for
the rest of his life. Seward's convivial temperament as well as his profession fitted him for politics; the question was with what political group
he would affiliate himself. His family had been
Democratic-Republicans of the strictest persuasion, but with praiseworthy independence the
rising young lawyer chose to ally himself with
the opposing elements. In this decision the principal factors, according to his *Autobiography*
(p. 54) written nearly fifty years later, were his
distrust of the Southern Jeffersonians, and his
great interest in internal improvements. At any
rate, Seward voted for DeWitt Clinton for governor, and John Quincy Adams for president in
1824, and wrote a good "Address" in support of
the former (*Works,* III, 335). The enthusiasm
which he then felt for Adams was never dimmed,
and undoubtedly had its part in forming his own
political ideals as time went on.

The closing years of the 1820's saw the rise
of the Anti-Masonic movement in western New
York. To this Seward found himself drawn,
both by expediency and by conviction. In the
deliberations of the new organization, as indeed
in previous political discussions, the rising young
politician was drawn close to Thurlow Weed
[*q.v.*], whose casual acquaintance he had first
made in 1824 and with whom he was to maintain one of the most intimate and long-standing
friendships in American political annals. It was
due to Weed's influence that Seward stood for
and was elected in the fall of 1830 to the state
Senate. In this body he served for the next four
years, as a distinguished member of the minority and later as its leader. He played a prominent part in the debates on Andrew Jackson's
bank policy; he sustained the President in his
opposition to Nullification; he continued to advocate internal improvements; he supported abolition of imprisonment for debt. Defeated for
reëlection in 1833, he was unanimously nominated for governor in 1834. By this time the
Whig party had supplanted the Anti-Masons,
and it was under the Whig banner that Seward
was to fight for the next twenty years. In this
first Whig candidacy, however, he was defeated,
by William L. Marcy [*q.v.*]. The next few years
Seward devoted to the practice of law, and he
acquired a modest competence through his success as agent for the Holland Company, in settling disputes with settlers in Chautauqua County (*Autobiography,* p. 328; *Works,* III, 461).

The Whigs carried the New York legislature
in the election of 1837 and Seward's political
ambitions, which he professed were dead in 1834,
rapidly came to life again, with the governorship as their objective. The contest for the nomination lay between him and the dignified Francis
Granger [*q.v.*], nearly nine years his senior.
Seward professed to be willing to let the convention decide, but an active organization was
set on foot, the young voters being particularly
active in his favor. Weed, after some hesitation,
decided that his protégé should have the nomination, and in a closely contested convention
battle Seward was chosen. In the electoral campaign itself, he was compelled for the first time
to face the issue of slavery. His attitude in 1838
can hardly be called an advanced one. By the
abolitionists he was asked three questions,
whether he was in favor of (1) a law granting
trial by jury to all fugitives, (2) of abolishing
the special qualifications for negro voters, and
(3) of repealing a law permitting the importation and detention of slaves in the state of New
York for a period of nine months. He answered
the first question in the affirmative, but the other
two in the negative, declaring that the subjects
with which they dealt did not enter "into the
political creed" of his party (*Works,* III, 426–
32).

The election of 1838 resulted in a victory for
Seward, as did that of 1840, though by a reduced
plurality. His four years in the governorship
reveal the natural ardor and optimism of his
temperament, his strong humanitarian sympathies, and also his impulsiveness and tendency to
challenge majority opinion. Always warmly convinced of the desirability of internal improvements, Seward courageously urged them upon
successive legislatures (see his message of 1840,
Works, II, 212–55). In the midst of the depression, he refused to acquiesce in the suspension
of activities already undertaken, and from first
to last boldly defended large expenditures. In
this particular case the policy cannot be said to

have succeeded. The state's credit was adversely affected, its bonds selling at a discount of twenty per cent. in 1841. When the Democrats regained control of both houses of the legislature in the fall elections, they proceeded to suspend virtually all but the most necessary expenditures, and to levy additional taxes. Seward, however, stoutly insisted that his policy had been wise, and that the obstacles to its accomplishment were merely a blind distrust of the future, on the part of foreign investors and of the American people. His natural impulsiveness, as well as his generosity of feeling, was illustrated also by his attitude on the question of public education in New York City. The schools there, conducted by a private corporation, the Public School Society, had been unacceptable to the rapidly growing Catholic population, and, furthermore, did not attract the children of the immigrant classes. In his message of 1840, after consulting with his old friend, Dr. Eliphalet Nott of Union College, Seward recommended "the establishment of schools in which they (the children of New York) may be instructed by teachers speaking the same language with themselves and professing the same faith" (*Works,* II, 215). This recommendation caused a storm of criticism from the nativist elements in the state, stronger in the Whig than in the Democratic party. Seward was compelled to retreat from the position which he had assumed, though he succeeded in securing the establishment of public schools free from sectarian influence in the city.

On the slavery question Seward took advanced ground during his term of office. He refused to surrender three sailors, who had instigated the flight of a fugitive slave to New York, when the extradition of these men was demanded by the state of Virginia. His act provoked so much irritation in Virginia as to bring about reprisals against New York shipping. But it was typical of his humanitarian spirit, and it won him the ardent support of the growing abolitionist element (for the controversy, 1839–41, see *Works,* II, 449 ff.). No one would maintain, however, that Seward was an uncompromising idealist in the governorship. He dispensed offices on the strict spoils basis, as was the custom of the time; he signed a law requiring registration of voters in New York City under party pressure and very much against his personal convictions; and it may be that other motives than humanitarian interest were operating in the evolution of the policies above described. But he declined to be a candidate for reëlection in 1842, and his letters show that he felt himself at this time to be too far in advance of public opinion to prosper politically.

The years in the governorship depleted Seward's financial resources. During the next seven years he worked assiduously to restore them, at first in his old field, the court of chancery, but, after a little, more and more in patent cases. From time to time he took criminal cases, involving trial before a jury. One of the most striking involved the death sentence on a poor imbecile negro, Freeman, in whose defense Seward made in 1846 one of the most eloquent of his speeches (*Works,* I, 391–475); this he afterwards declared he would have repeated without the alteration of a word. A case which won him still more fame was that in which in a suit for damages he unsuccessfully defended in 1846–47 Van Zandt, an Ohio farmer, who had assisted in the flight of fugitive slaves (*Ibid.,* I, 476 ff.). In these years of private practice Seward was very far from abandoning his interest in politics. He took part in almost every campaign, often outside the borders of the state. He also ardently championed the cause of Irish freedom, gaining the support of the Irish-American voters as a result. The tide was running more and more his way, also, with regard to the question of slavery. By 1848 anti-slavery sentiment had become so strong that it was possible for him to be elected to the United States Senate, many Democrats, as well as all the Whig members of the legislature, voting for him.

When Seward entered the Senate the slavery question had become acute, and the question of its relation to the disposition of the territories just acquired from Mexico was assuming portentous proportions. In the celebrated debate growing out of Henry Clay's famous resolutions of 1850, Seward took his stand firmly against all compromise, and in favor of the unconditional admission of California as a free state. In his well-known speech of Mar. 11 he declared that there was no reason to jumble together a variety of important questions in a single measure, as Clay had wished to do; he boldly asserted that the fugitive-slave law was impossible of enforcement in the North; he wished to abolish, not only the slave trade, as proposed by Clay, but also slavery in the District of Columbia; he was opposed to leaving the territories to organize themselves with or without slavery. In a prescient sentence he declared that the slave system would either be removed "by gradual voluntary effort, and with compensation," within the framework of the Union, or the Union would be dissolved, and civil wars ensue, bringing on violent but complete and immediate emancipation

(*Works*, I, 86 ff.). While thus boldly expressing his views, he disavowed any desire to act by unconstitutional or unlawful means. It was in the speech of Mar. 11, 1850, that he used the famous phrase, "a higher law than the Constitution" (*Ibid.*, II, 74). Partisanship immediately caught up the expression, and sought to make it appear that he advocated action outside of and beyond the great American charter. The context of the speech itself clearly indicates that he was merely declaring that in the discharge of its duties the Senate must take account of moral principle as well as constitutional prescriptions. None the less, when taxed with the phrase, Seward resorted to rather shuffling and unconvincing explanations.

In the years immediately following the compromise measures, the politician in Seward dominated. It may be that he was beginning to nourish presidential ambitions, but it is not necessary to make this assumption to understand his course. He was, after all, still an intense Whig partisan, and he had, in common with Weed, a great interest in party manipulation and party victory. He had favored the candidacy of Zachary Taylor in 1848, precisely because it served to raise so few perplexing questions of principle; and now he worked zealously to secure the nomination of General Winfield Scott in 1852, on much the same grounds. Though he disliked the compromise measures and was by no means convinced of their finality, he nevertheless made no serious effort to prevent the Whigs from indorsing them in the national nominating convention of 1852, and he avoided a vote on the question of repeal of the fugitive-slave law when Sumner brought the matter before the Senate in the session of 1852. In the meantime his place in the Senate gave opportunity for the expression of that ardent nationalism and republicanism which Seward doubtless felt sincerely, and which was highly expedient politically, but which he voiced with such recklessness as to lay him open to the charge of demagogy. He played a leading rôle in the welcome to Kossuth, introducing a resolution of protest against the Russian intervention in Hungary; and he again championed the cause of the Irish.

The elections of 1852 left the Whig party completely routed. The future appeared hardly bright to a rising anti-slavery leader; but soon came the Kansas-Nebraska bill, reopening the whole controversy with regard to slave and free territory. In the debates on this measure, Seward showed greater caution and less forthright courage than in the discussions of 1850. His double rôle of

party leader and opponent of slavery, in a measure imposed such a course. However, though he did not take the lead in opposition to the measure, he spoke vigorously and frankly against it, warning the South of the conflict to which he felt it would inevitably give rise. The year 1854 saw not only the rise of the Republican party in the West, but of the Know-Nothing party, principally in the East and South. For Weed and Seward these new organizations created natural embarrassment. Reluctant to abandon the old partisan vessel, they propitiated the anti-Nebraska men by committing the Whigs to a strong anti-slavery platform; by shrewd subterranean work they managed to inter-penetrate the Know-Nothing party and secure Seward's reëlection to the Senate. This latter success was the more remarkable since Know-Nothingism was contrary to the very essence of Seward's political philosophy, and was known to be so. As the Kansas question continued to hold the stage in national politics, the necessity of abandoning the old Whig party, or of merging it in the rising Republican organization, became more and more obvious. The merger was effected in the fall of 1855, and in the campaign of that year Seward signalized the change by speeches of the most forthright character on slavery.

From 1855 to 1860 Seward embodied the growing anti-slavery sentiment of the North as much as any man. That sentiment was grounded on genuine moral convictions; but it was often blindly partisan, and reckless of the crisis which it was rapidly promoting. In the struggle over Kansas in 1856 he took the extreme view, advocating its admission as a free state under the Topeka Constitution (though a fairer solution, perhaps, lay in the Toombs bill, calling for a new election in the territory); in common with other Republicans he denounced the Dred Scott decision as the product of a conspiracy; and on Oct. 25, 1858, he made at Rochester, N. Y., the famous speech in which he declared that the slavery struggle was "an irrepressible conflict" between opposing and enduring forces (*Works*, IV, 292). Yet Seward was not always a firebrand; in 1858, partly perhaps for tactical reasons, he supported the Douglas idea of a decision by popular sovereignty in the territory of Kansas, of course opposing the Lecompton Constitution; and the "irrepressible conflict" speech itself was followed by one in which, perhaps under the influence of the storm of comment which he had aroused, he praised the moderation of the slave-holders, and sought to blame the free Democracy of the North for the events of the last few years. On grounds of political expediency he had been passed over in 1856 in the Republican National Convention for Frémont; and some of his shifts of attitude may be attributed to the fact that he had his eye on the presidential nomination of 1860.

In 1859 Seward went abroad, meeting many celebrities in England and France, and returning to a great reception in New York. In February 1860, he again advocated the admission of Kansas as a free state, and made a speech which may be regarded as an expression of the platform on which he would stand for the Republican nomination (Feb. 29, 1860, *Ibid.*, IV, 619–43). Its general tenor was extremely conciliatory and moderate; with rare exceptions, Seward optimistically believed that Republicanism involved no threat to the unity of the American people. When the Republican National Convention met in Chicago in June 1860, he was undoubtedly the leading candidate, but the hostility of Horace Greeley, the opposition of the Know-Nothings, and Seward's own too widely known radical utterances, conspired to deprive him of the nomination. It was a severe blow, but he bore it with his usual outward equanimity and with very real generosity. He campaigned for the Republican ticket throughout the North, minimizing the Southern threats of secession, and urging the election of Lincoln. In the crisis which followed the election Seward showed characteristic elements of strength and weakness. His invincible optimism inclined him to minimize the dangers that lay ahead; yet, in the face of secession, he employed the language and the method of conciliation. He was also one of the Senate committee of thirteen constituted to consider means of composing the situation; as the spokesman of the section, and at the suggestion of Weed, he proposed on Dec. 24 that Congress guarantee slavery in the slave states, and request the repeal of the personal liberty laws in exchange for the grant of jury trial to fugitive slaves (*Senate Report No. 288,* 36 Cong., 2 Sess., pp. 10, 11, 13). His speech of Jan. 12, 1861, made after three more states had seceded, was admirable in its spirit (*Works,* IV, 651–69). Clearly avowing his loyalty to the Union, he again spoke in the most conciliatory vein, advocating a constitutional convention to settle outstanding difficulties, and even suggesting, in departure from the Republican platform, the admission of the remaining territories as two states without regard to slavery. It is entirely possible that he personally favored the Crittenden Compromise; but the influence of the President-elect was thrown on the other side, and Seward voted against this proposal when it came before the Senate on Mar. 2.

As early as Dec. 8, Seward had been offered the office of secretary of state by Lincoln. He accepted on Dec. 28; and although he was deeply displeased at the selection of Chase and Blair as cabinet colleagues, and even sought to reverse his decision as late as Mar. 2, he yielded to the entreaties of the President. He took office on Mar. 4, no doubt believing that he would be, and deserved to be, the dominant figure in the administration, and the man who could best avert the perils of civil war. In the critical period from Mar. 4 to Apr. 12, 1861 (the date of the firing on Sumter), Seward appears at very far from his best. He still retained the delusion that he might determine the course of the administration; and his famous memorandum, "Some Thoughts for the President's Consideration, Apr. 1, 1861," admits of no apology. In this reckless document he advocated embroiling the United States with most of Europe and waging actual war on Spain and France, as a means of solidifying the Union (Nicolay and Hay, *post,* II, 29). The only concrete grievance on the horizon was the Spanish re-annexation of Santo Domingo, and this had not been officially consummated. A madder or wilder project than Seward's could hardly have been devised. Nor is it possible to imagine anything more arrogant than the last sentence of his memorandum, in which he virtually suggested that the President abdicate his power to the Secretary of State. Seward's course with regard to secession itself is not easy to justify. It is understandable that he entered into negotiations with the Confederate commissioners sent to Washington to demand the surrender of the forts still held by the Union government in the South; but it is not so easy to justify machinations behind the back of the President, by which the reënforcement of Fort Pickens was delayed, and the expedition to Sumter, when it sailed, weakened by the absence of the *Powhatan.* Seward was not even resolutely pacifist; on one occasion he spoke of using force to collect the revenue, and in general he was in favor of holding the Gulf forts, perhaps with a view to a possible war with Spain, though not of holding Sumter. No doubt much to his discomfiture, and with many a wound to his pride, he saw himself overruled and the decisive events which culminated in the opening of the Civil War directed by the chief whose real measure he had not yet taken.

Seward's conduct of the office of secretary of state during the four years of the war deserves high praise. More than any preceding secretary he conducted his diplomatic correspondence with an eye to public opinion at home. It is no chance that the publication of diplomatic dispatches in one or more annual volumes put out by the State Department begins with him (*Papers Relating to the Foreign Relations of the United States,* 2 vols., 1861). He no doubt wrote almost too much for the American public, as compared with those to whom his dispatches were actually directed. But in so doing he did much both to inspirit and to restrain public opinion as occasion demanded. His early dispatches were too blustering in tone, and might have gotten him into serious trouble sometimes had it not been for the wisdom of Lincoln. As time went on, he dropped the truculent tone and expressed the views of the United States with dignity and force. On the occasion of the seizure of Mason and Slidell on board the *Trent,* an act received with something like ecstasy by Northern opinion, he behaved with great coolness in the midst of popular excitement. When the protest of the British government against such action arrived, it was the Secretary, this time somewhat against the opinion of the President, who decided that the protest must be heeded. The dispatch in which he conceded the surrender of the Southern commissioners is a masterpiece (*Works,* V, 295–309). Written with an eye to making palatable an act sure to be violently condemned by the hotheads in the United States, it flattered Northern opinion by its specious reasoning, and made the action appear as in accord with fundamental American traditions.

The possibility of European intervention in the Civil War Seward met, on the whole, with similar adroitness. The optimism of his dispatches, their profound self-confidence, and their array of facts, could hardly fail to make an impression. This tone, maintained through good fortune and bad, and coupled with warning after warning of the dangerous consequences of intervention, was, in general, just what the situation demanded. At times Seward was still a little bumptious, and his habit of publishing many of his dispatches was often irritating, but the general principle was sound. He could depend, too, on the tact and high diplomatic skill of Charles Francis Adams in interpreting his instructions. Seward made skilful use abroad of the question of slavery to check the anti-Northern agitation in France and England. On the Emancipation Proclamation he was at first conservative, because of his fear of its domestic consequences. When it was first discussed in July 1862, he urged Lincoln to postpone action, at least until a Federal victory (Nicolay and Hay, II, 479). But when the preliminary proclamation was issued after Antietam, he used it with great effect in his dispatches to Adams and W. L. Dayton.

The danger of intervention seemed greatest in the fall of 1862 and the winter of 1863. At the end of October, the French government sought to secure joint action with Great Britain and Russia looking to an armistice. The proposal was rejected, and Seward wisely made no protest. But when the French directly proffered mediation early in 1863, Seward responded in one of his most effective dispatches (Feb. 6, 1863, *Senate Executive Document No. 38, 37* Cong., 3 Sess., p. 11–16).

In his correspondence Seward adroitly defended the broad interpretation of continuous voyage in dispatches that suggest Sir Edward Grey's half a century later, and he protested vigorously against the outfitting of Confederate privateers in British ports. His steady pressure, combined with the skill of Adams, finally led the British government to take due precautions, in the case of the Laird rams, while his protests in the case of the *Alabama* laid the basis for solid pecuniary claims later. Nowhere was Seward more adroit than in his treatment of the French intervention in Mexico, and the establishment of Maximilian on a Mexican throne. From an early period he made the distaste of the United States for the whole project obvious; yet he suavely assumed the rumors of monarchy to be ill-founded as long as he could do so, and until the end of the war never let anything like menace enter into his tone. When the House of Representatives on Apr. 4, 1864, condemned the schemes of Louis Napoleon (*Congressional Globe,* 38 Cong., 1 Sess., p. 1408), Seward penned a masterly dispatch in which he soothed French susceptibilities, explaining that the opinion of the legislative branch of the government did not alter executive policy (Apr. 7, 1864, *Diplomatic Correspondence of the United States,* 1865, vol. III, 356–57). When the Civil War was over, there was much sentiment for vigorous action against the French. Seward handled this delicate situation magnificently. He temporized while he could; the situation of the French grew more and more difficult; and then in dispatches gradually mounting in tone he edged his adversary, Drouyn de L'huys, from one position to another, until he finally secured the promise of the evacuation of Mexico in a fixed period of time. In the latter part of the correspondence Seward fell into his old habit of writing for domestic consumption; and the same may be said of his correspondence with Austria on the same subject; but the total effect of his activity is admirable.

Seward was, in temperament and conviction, an expansionist. During the 1850's this sentiment came in conflict with his anti-slavery views, and led him to oppose such projects as the purchase of Cuba. But when the war was over the strong instinct revived. In 1867 he negotiated the cession of Alaska, and with the aid of Sumner secured the prompt ratification of the treaty by the Senate. He sought to acquire the two most important islands of the Danish West Indies; but this agreement was never ratified. He encouraged overtures from the Dominican Republic looking to incorporation in the United States, again unsuccessfully. In his instructions to the American minister at Honolulu he advocated the annexation of Hawaii. Seward's views were those which a later generation was to accept.

In domestic affairs Seward exercised a constant influence both on the Lincoln and the Johnson administrations. He had a large, indeed it may be said the chief, responsibility for the treatment of political prisoners at the beginning of the war, and contrary to his general temperament he here showed much rigor. He exercised, as has been seen, a positive influence on the policy of the administration with regard to the border states and emancipation. He performed heavy labors as a sort of political liaison officer, and his interest in problems of patronage, while not always wisely exerted, was continuous. In the Johnson administration he was a central figure. He advocated a conciliatory policy towards the South, wrote some of Johnson's most important veto messages, and supported the President in many speeches, making "the swing around the circle" with him in 1866. By doing so he lost both popularity and influence, and he valued both dearly; but whatever the reaction of the moment, the judgment of time has been that he was wiser than his opponents.

The burdens of his last four years at Washington Seward sustained in circumstances that would have daunted a man less tenacious and industrious. He had suffered serious injury in a carriage accident in the spring of 1865, and this had been followed by the brutal attack upon him in his house which was contemporaneous with the assassination of Lincoln; yet he was soon transacting the public business with as much skill and coolness as ever. At the end of his term of office, despite the fact that he was partially crippled, he went around the world, the first important American political figure to do so, and much enjoyed the enthusiasm which his visit evoked. He returned to Auburn in the autumn of 1871, and there increasing paralysis overtook him. He died on Oct. 10, 1872. On Oct. 20, 1824, he had married Frances Miller, the daughter of his law partner. A woman of liberal sympathies and humanitarian views, she undoubtedly influenced his later career, and especially his attitude toward slavery. They had three sons and two daughters, one of whom died in infancy. Frederick William Seward [q.v.] was closely associated with his father. A nephew, Clarence Armstrong Seward (Oct. 27, 1828–July 24, 1897), who became an orphan in childhood and was brought up in his uncle's family, served for a brief time in 1865 as assistant secretary of state and attained prominence as a corporation lawyer. His cousin, George Frederick Seward [q.v.], another nephew of William H. Seward, was launched upon his diplomatic career under the latter's influence.

In Seward the politician and the statesman are interestingly, and on the whole happily, commingled. It is easy to discover occasions on which he equivocated, as politicians do; it is easy to discover occasions on which he sought the applause of the multitude, not always careful of the consequences. Even in his diplomacy, and strikingly in his early utterances on questions of foreign affairs, this is true. Yet Seward chose his early political creed, it would appear, from conviction; he associated himself with definite policies, and loved to do so; much earlier than most anti-slavery leaders of the political stripe, he adopted that important cause; he often showed real courage in advocating it. He made serious blunders, and might have made more, in estimating the true value of the conflicting forces at the end of 1860 and the beginning of 1861 but his years at the State Department are years of steady growth, and of very creditable achievement, while his rôle in maintaining national morale must not be underestimated. He was the partisan of a wise policy of reconciliation when the war was over. The unswervingly independent mind has its uses in the world; but its possessor is not apt to succeed in politics. It may be fairly argued that Seward combined devotion to principle, and flexibility as to means, in such proportions as to make him most effective.

As a human being, few could have been more lovable. Cheerful, generous, loathing personal controversy, he had a wide range of interests and of sympathies. He read much and widely; he traveled extensively, going to Europe several times, and seeing a great deal of his own country. He was a little vain, and he had his political enemies; he is dwarfed by the master-spirit of his great chief; but, compared with the irascible Stanton, the pompous Sumner, the intriguing Chase, and many others, he looms up as one of the most attractive, as well as most important, figures in a critical period of American history.

[*Autobiography of William H. Seward, from 1801 to 1834, with a Memoir of His Life, and Selections from His Letters, from 1831 to 1846* (1877), ed. by F. W. Seward, the continuation of this by F. W. Seward, *Seward at Washington* (2 vols., 1891) ; G. E. Baker, ed., *The Works of William H. Seward* (5 vols., 1884) ; *Life of Thurlow Weed* (2 vols., 1883–84), including his autobiography, ed. by Harriet A. Weed, and a memoir by T. W. Barnes ; J. D. Hammond, *The Hist. of Pol. Parties in the State of N. Y.* (3 vols., 1842–48) ; D. S. Alexander, *A Political Hist. of the State of N. Y.*, vol. II (1906) ; *Papers Relating to the Foreign Relations of the U. S.* (2 vols., 1861), and *Papers Relating to Foreign Affairs* (14 vols., 1862–66), bound and usually cited as *Diplomatic Correspondence of the U.S.* ; Gideon Welles, *Lincoln and Seward* (1874) ; F. W. Seward, *Reminiscences of a War-Time Statesman and Diplomat* (1916) ; Olive R. Seward, ed., *William H. Seward's Travels Around the World* (1873) ; J. G. Nicolay and John Hay, *Abraham Lincoln, Complete Works* (2 vols., 1894) ; Frederic Bancroft, *The Life of William H. Sew-* ard (2 vols., 1900), which is sympathetic yet critical, and is exceedingly well proportioned ; T. K. Lothrop, *William Henry Seward* (1896) and E. E. Hale, Jr., *William H. Seward* (1910), of less importance ; an interesting sketch in Gamaliel Bradford, *Union Portraits* (1916) ; C. F. Adams, *Seward and the Declaration of Paris* (1912) ; Tyler Dennett, "Seward's Far Eastern Policy," in *Am. Hist. Rev.*, Oct. 1922 ; studies of Seward's Mexican policy in J. M. Callahan, *Am. Foreign Policy in Mexican Relations* (1932), and Dexter Perkins, *The Monroe Doctrine, 1826–1867* (1933) ; detailed study of his policy toward Great Britain in E. D. Adams, *Great Britain and the Am. Civil War* (2 vols., 1925) ; general treatment by H. W. Temple in S. F. Bemis, ed., *The Am. Secretaries of State and Their Diplomacy*, vol. VII (1928) ; unpublished materials in the possession of Mrs. Thomas G. Spencer, Rochester, N. Y., and W. H. Seward, Auburn, N. Y. ; unpublished correspondence in Dept. of State, Washington, D. C.]
                                   D. P.